ISBN 978-0-332-67365-3
PIBN 10983688

COMPLIMENTS OF . .

BOARD OF RAILROAD COMMISSIONERS.

JAMES F. JACKSON, CHAIRMAN,
GEORGE W. BISHOP,
CLINTON WHITE.

No. 20 BEACON STREET,
BOSTON.

CHARLES E. MANN, CLERK.

BLIC DOCUMENT . . . . No. 14.

Commonwealth of Massachusetts.

THIRTY-SIXTH ANNUAL REPORT

OF THE

BOARD OF RAILROAD COMMISSIONERS.

JANUARY, 1905.

BOSTON:
WRIGHT & POTTER PRINTING CO., STATE PRINTERS,
18 POST OFFICE SQUARE.
1905.

APPROVED BY

THE STATE BOARD OF PUBLICATION.

Commonwealth of Massachusetts.

RAILROAD COMMISSIONERS.

JAMES F. JACKSON, Fall River, *Chairman*, .	Term expires July 1, 1906.
GEORGE W. BISHOP, Newtonville, . .	Term expires July 1, 1907.
CLINTON WHITE, Melrose, ...	Term expires July 1, 1905.

CHARLES E. MANN, Malden, *Clerk.*
ALLAN BROOKS, Ayer, *Assistant Clerk.*
FRED E. JONES, Brookline, *Accountant.*
GEORGE F. SWAIN, Boston, *Bridge Engineer.*

RAILROAD INSPECTORS.

DANIEL M. WHEELER, Worcester, . .	Term expires October 1, 1906.
GRAFTON UPTON, Everett, ...	Term expires October 1, 1905.
JOHN Q. HENNIGAN, East Milton, . . .	Term expires October 1, 1907.
LEWELLYN H. McLAIN, Melrose, . . .	Term expires October 1, 1906.

OFFICE, No. 20 BEACON STREET, BOSTON.

INDEX.

Commissioners' Report.

Part I.

Railroad Corporations and Street Railway Companies.

Commonwealth of Massachusetts.

To the Honorable Senate and House of Representatives of the Commonwealth of Massachusetts in General Court assembled.

We respectfully submit the thirty-sixth annual report of the Board of Railroad Commissioners : —

RAILROAD CORPORATIONS.

Returns for the year ending June 30, 1904, have been received from forty-seven railroad corporations. Eleven only of these corporations have been engaged in actual railroad operation. Three of them, the Boston and Albany (New York Central and Hudson River, lessee), the Boston and Maine, and the New York, New Haven and Hartford, have operated over 96 per cent of the railroad mileage and conducted nearly 98 per cent of the entire passenger and freight business covered by the statistics hereinafter given.

Changes in the number of corporations making return to the Board have been few in the last ten years. As new companies there were added to the list in 1895 the Cape Ann Granite and the Providence and Springfield, and in 1897 the Chester and Becket. The New York Central and Hudson River, lessee of the Boston and Albany, has made return since 1901. In 1895 the Brookline and Pepperell was consolidated with the Fitchburg. In 1897 the Worcester and Shrewsbury, a narrow gauge road, was made a part of the Worcester Consolidated street railway. In 1898 the Fall River was consolidated with the Old Colony, and in 1901 the Central Massachusetts was merged with the Boston and Maine. The merger of the New England with the New York, New Haven and Hartford, anticipated in the report of the Board for 1899, has not yet been completed. Within the period named several roads, the New York and Boston Inland, in 1896, the Martha's Vineyard, in 1897, and the Southbridge, Sturbridge and Brookfield, in 1898, have been abandoned.

During the past year there has been a net decrease (owing to changes in location and remeasurements) of 2.540 miles in the length of railroad line located in this state, an increase of 2.010 miles of second main track and an increase of 20.720 miles of side track.

There are now in Massachusetts 2,108.420 miles of main and branch railroad line. The total length of railroad track within the state, including second, third and fourth main track and side track, is 4,490.304 miles.

Railroad Interest in Street Railways.

A prominent feature in the recent history of steam railroads has been the growth of a policy favoring the purchase of street railway properties. Whatever may be urged against this policy, it may be said in its favor that it brings into the conduct of street railway affairs the judgment and knowledge which come from long experience in dealing with transportation problems and as well greater financial strength and larger resources.

The usefulness of the street railway in bringing people to the steam railroad from the different sections of the cities and towns which it serves and in distributing them again at the end of the railroad journey will be generally recognized. Even where these railways have been interurban in character and to some extent competitors of the railroads, we doubt if the passing of control into the hands of their rivals need be attended by detriment to the public interests. The competition between the steam railroad and the street railway must eventually end in each system giving to the public the service which it is best capable of performing, and it is by no means clear that in order to bring this about in the wisest way it is at all essential that the competitive conflict between these companies be prolonged. The two systems ought to work together advantageously under one administration, subject, as they would be, to the supervision enforced under our statutes, changes in service upon one or the other being made only in furtherance of a greater comfort and convenience in travel.

The laws of neighboring states encourage this evolution in transportation enterprise. A review by the Legislature of the reasons for the present character of our laws upon this subject would seem to be timely.

STATISTICS.

BOSTON, January 2, 1905.

Board of Railroad Commissioners, Hon. JAMES F. JACKSON, *Chairman.*

GENTLEMEN: — I submit the following compilations of statistics from the returns of the several railroad companies to the Board for the year ending June 30, 1904.

The following table gives the length of railroad line and track in this state June 30, 1904, as compared with the previous year: —

In the following tables the 4.200 miles of road owned by the Hartford & Connecticut Western are not included.

Railroad Mileage in Massachusetts, 1903 and 1904.

RAILROAD MILEAGE.	1903.	1904.	Increase.
	Miles.	Miles.	Miles.
Length of main and branch line,	2,110.960	2,108.420	2.540*
Length of second track,	867.697	867.697	-
Length of third track,	40.130	41.080	.950
Length of fourth track,	34.110	35.170	1.060
Length of side track,	1,416.687	1,437.937	21.250
Total, reckoned as single track,	4,469.584	4,490.304	20.720

* Decrease.

Mileage Owned.

The total length of railroad line *owned* by the Massachusetts companies *in* and *out* of the state is 3,791.320[1] miles; and the total length of railroad track so owned is 7,633.374[3] miles. The miles of main and branch line, of second, third and fourth main track, and of side track, owned June 30, 1904, and the increase over the previous year, are stated in the following table: —

Mileage Owned by Massachusetts Companies 1903 and 1904.

MILEAGE OWNED.	1903.	1904.	Increase.
	Miles.	Miles.	
Length of main and branch line,	3,793.860	3,791.320[1]	2.540*
Length of second track,	1,323.197	1,323.197	-
Length of third track,	99.750	100.700	.950
Length of fourth track,	93.730	94.790	1.060
Length of side track,	2,290.797	2,323.367[2]	32.570
Total, reckoned as single track,	7,601.334	7,633.374[3]	32.040

* Decrease.

1 Includes 18.340 miles electric street railway.

2 Includes .950 of a mile of electric street railway.

3 Includes 19.290 miles electric street railway track.

Mileage Operated.

The length of railroad line *operated* by the Massachusetts companies, *within* and *without* the state, including roads operated under lease or contract as well as roads owned, is 4,935.670[1] miles; and the total length of track so operated is 9,390.834[3] miles, — as shown in detail, with the increase for the year, in the next table: —

Mileage Operated by Massachusetts Companies, 1903 and 1904.

MILEAGE OPERATED.	1903.	1904.	Increase.
	Miles.	Miles.	Miles.
Length of main and branch line, .	4,906.730	4,935.670[1]	28.940
Length of second track, . . .	1,410.037	1,428.207	18.170
Length of third track, . . .	114.800	115.750	.950
Length of fourth track, . . .	107.430	108.490	1.060
Length of side track, ...	2,765.527	2,802.717[2]	37.190
Total, reckoned as single track, .	9,304.524	9,390.834[3]	86.310

1 Includes 46.220 miles electric street railway. 2 Includes 3.400 miles electric street railway.
3 Includes 49.620 miles electric street railway, operated by the Boston & Maine.

Assets and Liabilities.

The gross assets of the companies, June 30, 1904, were $456,996,-116.00. The several classes of assets, and the increase or decrease in each class as compared with 1903, appear in the following table: —

Gross Assets, June 30, 1903 and 1904.

ASSETS.	1903.	1904.	Increase.
Construction, ...	$293,236,332	$287,892,759	$5,343,573*
Equipment, ...	32,957,122	41,205,887	8,248,765
Land and buildings, ...	1,497,218	1,517,412	20,194
Stocks in other companies, . .	34,815,527	46,797,636	11,982,109
Bonds in other companies, . .	7,329,727	13,017,088	5,687,361
Other permanent property, . .	2,445,520	2,582,634	137,114
Cash and current assets, . . .	40,880,067	36,191,443	4,688,624*
Miscellaneous assets, ...	19,619,336	27,791,257	8,171,921
Gross Assets, ...	$432,780,849	$456,996,116	$24,215,267

* Decrease.

The gross liabilities at the same date, including capital stock but excluding sinking and other special funds, were $416,593,865.28. The several kinds of liabilities, and the amount of each as compared with 1903, are shown in the next table: —

Gross Liabilities, June 30, 1903 and 1904.

LIABILITIES.	1903.	1904.	Increase.
Capital stock,	$235,834,466	$237,423,886	$1,589,420
Funded debt,	133,435,355	152,841,358	19,406,003
Real estate mortgages,	858,300	683,300	175,000*
Current liabilities,	20,218,457	21,513,406	1,294,949
Accrued liabilities,	3,930,561	4,131,915	201,354
Gross liabilities, †	$394,277,139	$416,593,865	$22,316,726
Surplus,	38,503,710	40,402,251	1,898,541
Sinking and special funds, ‡	9,090,302	9,342,453	252,151

* Decrease. † Exclusive of sinking and other special funds. ‡ Included in surplus above.

A comparison of the foregoing tables shows that there was an increase over the previous year of $24,215,267 in gross assets, and an increase of $22,316,726 in gross liabilities, — a balance of $1,898,541 in favor of assets, enlarging by that amount the aggregate surplus of the companies.

Gross Assets, Liabilities and Surplus for Ten Years, 1895–1904.

YEARS.	Gross Assets.	Gross Liabilities.	Surplus.	Per Cent. Surplus to Capital.
1895,	$360,639,658	$346,739,520	$13,900,138	7.18
1896,	380,502,835	363,623,710	16,879,124	8.23
1897,	385,439,818	367,353,742	18,086,076	8.78
1898,	390,322,164	367,679,526	22,642,638	11.01
1899,	400,265,132	375,363,693	24,901,439	11.68
1900,	405,188,330	377,008,891	28,179,439	13.03
1901,	419,743,521	385,417,287	34,326,234	16.32
1902,	418,298,274	383,106,669	35,191,605	16.70
1903,	432,780,849	394,277,139	38,503,710	16.33
1904,	456,996,116	416,593,865	40,402,251	17.02

The gross assets, the gross liabilities including capital stock, and the surplus of the companies, with the percentage of surplus to capital stock, at the end of each of the last ten years, are given in the preceding table.

Funded and Floating Debt.

The aggregate funded debt of the companies, June 30, 1904, was $152,841,358.41 — an increase of $19,406,003.40 from the previous year, resulting from additions and deductions in the case of the following companies: —

Additions: —	
Boston & Lowell,	$250,000 00
Boston & Maine,	905,053 40
New England,	1,500,000 00
New York, New Haven & Hartford,	19,941,700 00
Total additions to funded debt,	$22,596,753 40
Deductions: —	
Chatham,	$1,000 00
Connecticut River,	6,750 00
Fitchburg,	2,405,000 00
Old Colony,	742,000 00
Vermont & Massachusetts,	36,000 00
Total deductions from funded debt,	$3,190,750 00
Net increase of funded debt,	$19,406,003 40

Unfunded Debt.

The amount of real estate mortgages outstanding June 30, 1904, was $683,300.00 — a decrease of $175,000.00 from the previous four years.

The total unfunded debt, including the above mortgages, was $26,328,621.15 — an increase of $1,321,302.72 over the previous year.

The gross debt, funded and unfunded, was $179,169,979.56 — an increase of $20,727,306.12.

The net debt (the gross debt less $36,191,442.93 of cash and current assets) was $142,978,536.63 — an increase of $25,415,930.61.

In computing the net debt, the sum of $27,791,257.21 returned as "miscellaneous assets," covering materials and supplies on hand, etc., is not included with cash and current assets in the deduction from gross debt.

The funded debt, unfunded debt, gross debt and net debt, for each of the last ten years, are shown in the following table: —

Funded, Unfunded, Gross and Net Debt, 1895–1904.

YEARS.	Funded Debt.	Unfunded Debt.*	Gross Debt.	Net Debt.†
1895,	$128,991,353	$24,241,320	$153,232,673	$132,723,454
1896,	132,202,380	26,315,353	158,517,733	138,270,496
1897,	135,816,380	25,865,710	161,682,090	141,054,983
1898,	140,554,407	21,358,612	161,913,019	141,997,181
1899,	138,001,534	24,106,877	162,108,411	138,565,122
1900,	136,024,534	24,771,094	160,795,628	135,577,061
1901,	148,479,015	26,632,386	175,111,401	137,698,384
1902,	149,777,542	22,602,341	172,379,883	136,471,224
1903,	133,435,355	25,007,318	158,442,673	117,562,606
1904,	152,841,358	26,328,621	179,169,979	142,978,537

* Including real estate mortgages. † Gross debt less cash and current assets.

Capital Stock and Dividends.

The aggregate capital stock of the forty-four Massachusetts corporations, June 30, 1904, was $237,423,885.72 — a net increase of $1,589,420.00 over the previous year, resulting from additions in the case of the following companies: —

Additions: —	
New York, New Haven & Hartford,	$776,920 00
Old Colony,	812,500 00
Total increase of capital stock,	$1,589,420 00

The total amount of dividends declared the last year was $14,985,-815.50 — an increase of $1,490,627.00 over the previous year. Thirty-one of the forty-four corporations declared dividends varying in rate from 1 to 12 per cent, and thirteen paid no dividends.

Two companies paid 12 per cent; three paid 10 per cent; three paid 9 per cent; one paid 8¾ per cent; four paid 8 per cent; one paid 7 per cent on common and 6 per cent on preferred; three paid 7 per cent; three paid 6 per cent; one paid 5¾ per cent; two paid 5 per cent; two paid 4 per cent; one paid 3 per cent; one paid 2½ per cent; two paid 2 per cent; one paid 1½ per cent; and one paid 1 per cent.

The amount of the capital stock of the thirty-one dividend paying companies was $235,848,245.70* on which the average rate of dividend was 6.35 per cent.

The following table gives the total capital stock outstanding at the end of the year; the net income available for dividends (after paying all expenses, interest, taxes, rentals and other charges); the amount of dividends declared; and the average percentage of dividends to total capital stock, for each of the last ten years: —

Capital Stock, Net Income and Dividends, 1895–1904.

YEARS.	Capital Stock.	Net Divisible Income.	Dividends Declared.	Percentage to Total Capital Stock.
1895, ...	$193,506,847	$11,326,019	$11,364,565	5.87
1896, ...	205,105,977	11,625,746	11,260,994	5.49
1897, ...	205,671,652	11,467,847	11,522,998	5.60
1898, ...	205,766,507	11,823,827	11,599,462	5.64
1899, ...	213,255,282	12,798,630	12,143,749	5.69
1900, ...	216,213,263	13,665,720	12,498,947	5.78
1901, ...	210,305,886	13,529,627	13,049,306	6.20
1902, ...	210,726,786	13,818,341	13,201,264	6.26
1903, ...	235,834,466*	13,778,968	13,495,189	5.97
1904, ...	237,423,886	14,821,360	14,985,816	6.35

* Including common stock on which, in the case of two of these companies, no dividend was paid.

Income and Expenditures.

The total income of the companies from all sources, for the year ending June 30, 1904, was $108,091,599.50, and the total expenditures, including dividends paid, were $108,256,055.03 — showing a deficit for the year of $164,455.53 to be deducted from surplus account.

The sources of total income, and the amount derived from each source as compared with the previous year, were as follows: —

Total Income, 1903 and 1904.

INCOME.	1903.	1904.	Increase.
Gross earnings from operation, . .	$93,325,932	$95,280,348[1]	$1,954,416
Rentals from lease of road, . .	10,673,455	11,056,595	383,140
Income from other sources, . .	1,641,616	1,754,657	113,041
Total income, ...	$105,641,003	$108,091,600	$2,450,597

[1] Includes $170,334 from electric street railways.

The items of the total expenditures, with the surplus for the year, and the increase or decrease in each item as compared with the previous year, are shown in the following table: —

Total Expenditures, 1903 and 1904.

EXPENDITURES.	1903.	1904.	Increase.
Expenses of operation,	$67,774,864	$69,145,285[2]	$1,370,421
Interest on debt and loans,	6,533,985	6,526,803	7,182*
Taxes,	5,017,971	5,102,355	84,384
Rentals of leased roads,	12,287,658	12,237,054	50,604*
Other charges on income,	247,556	258,743	11,187
Dividends paid,	13,495,189	14,985,816	1,490,627
Total expenditures,	$105,357,223	$108,256,056	$2,898,833
Surplus for the year,	283,780	164,456[d]	448,236*

[2] Includes $179,362 for operating electric street railways. * Decrease. [d] Deficit.

Earnings and Expenses of Operation.

The gross earnings and expenses of operation the last year are classified, and compared with those of the previous year, in the following table: —

Gross Earnings and Expenses of Operation, 1903–1904.

EARNINGS AND EXPENSES.	1903.	1904.	Increase.
Revenue from passengers,	$36,513,615	$36,944,760[1]	$431,145
from mails, express, etc.,	6,010,467	6,303,573	293,106
Revenue from freight,	48,490,675	49,917,831	1,427,156
from elevators, etc.,	1,227,080	1,082,979	144,101*
Other earnings from operation,	1,084,095	1,031,205	52,890*
Gross earnings from operation,	$93,325,932	$95,280,348[2]	1,954,416
Operating expenses,	67,774,864	69,145,285[3]	1,370,421
Net earnings from operation,	$25,551,068	$26,135,063	$583,995

* Decrease.
[1] Includes $169,836 from electric street railways.
[2] Includes $170,334 from electric street railways.
[3] Includes $179,362 for electric street railways.

The next two tables show the revenue from passenger service and freight service respectively, the other earnings from operation, and the gross earnings from operation, on each of the three leading roads for the last year, and on all of the roads for each of the past ten years: —

Gross Earnings from Operation (Three Roads) in 1904.

RAILROAD COMPANIES.	Revenue from Passenger Service.	Revenue from Freight Service.	Other Earnings from Operation.	Gross Earnings from Operation.
Boston & Albany,	$4,963,495	$4,969,102	$321,895	$10,254,492
Boston & Maine,	13,971,273*	20,658,269	265,066	34,894,608
N. Y., N. H. & Hartford,	23,425,173	24,413,541	444,195	48,282,909

* Inc udes $170,334 from electric street railways.

Gross Earnings from Operation for Ten Years, 1895–1904.

YEARS.	Revenue from Passenger Service.	Revenue from Freight Service.	Other Earnings from Operation.	Gross Earnings from Operation.
1895,	$33,396,319	$33,682,562	$1,076,025	$68,154,906
1896,	36,395,024	37,885,071	606,385	74,886,480
1897,	34,745,628	36,514,714	674,431	71,934,773
1898,	34,680,057	38,204,984	714,493	73,599,534
1899,	35,325,236	39,310,129	794,697	75,430,062
1900,	37,732,243	43,625,099	833,951	82,191,293
1901,	37,788,899	43,883,434	713,253	82,385,586
1902,	39,959,789	45,984,272	976,504	86,920,565
1903,	42,524,082	49,717,755	1,084,095	93,325,932
1904,	43,248,333	51,000,810	1,031,205	95,280,348

Ratio of Operating Expenses to Gross Earnings.

The following tables give in like manner the gross earnings from operation, the operating expenses, the ratio of operating expenses to gross earnings, and the net earnings from operation of the three leading companies for the last year, and of all the companies for ten years: —

Ratio of Operating Expenses to Gross Earnings (Three Roads) in 1904.

RAILROAD COMPANIES.	Gross Earnings from Operation.	Operating Expenses.	Percentage of Expenses to Earnings.	Net Earnings from Operation.
Boston & Albany,	$10,254,492	$7,139,476	69.62	$3,115,016
Boston & Maine,	34,894,608[1]	25,271,908[2]	72.42	9,622,700
N. Y., N. H. & Hartford,	48,282,909	35,159,211	72.82	13,123,698

1 Includes $170,334 from electric street railways.
2 Includes $179,362 for electric street railways.

Ratio of Operating Expenses to Gross Earnings, 1895–1904.

YEARS.	Gross Earnings from Operation.	Operating Expenses.	Percentage of Expenses to Earnings.	Net Earnings from Operation.
1895, ...	$68,154,906	$46,446,304	68.15	$21,708,602
1896, ...	74,886,480	52,362,382	69.92	22,524,098
1897, ...	71,934,773	49,413,299	68.69	22,521,474
1898, ...	73,599,534	50,890,883	69.28	22,708,651
1899, ...	75,430,061	51,490,351	68.26	23,939,710
1900, ...	82,191,293	56,900,642	69.23	25,290,651
1901, ...	82,385,586	57,293,591	69.54	25,091,995
1902, ...	86,920,565	61,355,821	70.59	25,564,744
1903, ...	93,325,932	67,774,864	72.62	25,551,068
1904, ...	95,280,348	69,145,285	72.57	26,135,063

Earnings and Expenses per Mile of Road Operated.

The average gross earnings and expenses of operation, and the net earnings from operation, per total mile of road operated by the three leading companies for the last year, and by all of the companies for each of the past ten years, are shown in the following tables: —

Earnings and Expenses per Mile of Road Operated (Three Roads) in 1904.

RAILROAD COMPANIES.	Gross Earnings.	Operating Expenses.	Net Earnings.
Boston & Albany, ...	$26,127	$18,190	$7,937
Boston & Maine, ...	15,507*	11,206*	4,301*
N. Y., N. H. & Hartford, ...	23,461	17,084	6,377

* Not including electric street railways.

Earnings and Expenses per Mile of Road Operated, 1895–1904.

YEARS.	Gross Earnings.	Operating Expenses.	Net Earnings.	YEARS.	Gross Earnings.	Operating Expenses.	Net Earnings.
1895, .	$15,660	$10,672	$4,988	1900, .	$16,894	$11,696	$5,198
1896, .	15,845	11,079	4,766	1901, .	16,864	11,728	5,136
1897, .	15,229	10,461	4,768	1902, .	17,785	12,554	5,231
1898, .	15,571	10,766	4,805	1903, .	19,020	13,813	5,207
1899, .	15,773	10,767	5,006	1904, .	19,304	14,009	5,295

Earnings and Expenses per Revenue-Train Mile.

The average gross earnings and expenses of operation, and the net earnings from operation, per total mile run by trains earning revenue, on all of the roads, for each of the last ten years, have been as follows: —

Earnings and Expenses per Total Revenue-Train Mile, 1895–1904.

YEARS.	Gross Earnings.	Operating Expenses.	Net Earnings.	YEARS.	Gross Earnings.	Operating Expenses.	Net Earnings.
1895, .	$1.637	$1.115	$0.522	1900, .	$1.791	$1.240	$0.551
1896, .	1.664	1.163	.501	1901, .	1.825	1.269	.556
1897, .	1.638	1.125	.513	1902, .	1.853	1.308	.545
1898, .	1.637	1.132	.505	1903, .	1.887	1.370	.517
1899, .	1.653	1.128	.525	1904, .	1.864	1.352	.512

Earnings and Expenses per Revenue-Train Mile (Three Roads) in 1904.

RAILROAD COMPANIES.	Gross Earnings per Passenger-Train Mile.	Gross Earnings per Freight-Train Mile	PER TOTAL REVENUE-TRAIN MILE.		
			Gross Earnings.	Operating Expenses.	Net Earnings.
Boston & Albany, . .	$1.402	$2.095	$1.735	$1.208	$0.527
Boston & Maine, . . .	1.229*	2.438	1.762*	1.273*	.489
N. Y., N. H. & Hartford, .	1.482	3.078	2.034	1.481	.553

* Does not include electric street railways.

The average gross earnings from operation per passenger-train mile and per freight-train mile, and the gross and net earnings and operating expenses per total revenue-train mile, on the three leading railroads of the state, are given for the last year in the preceding table.

The *expenses* of operation per passenger-train mile and per freight-train mile, respectively, cannot be stated, because the operating expenses of the passenger department are not kept by the companies separately from those of the freight department.

Earnings and Expenses per Total Train Mile.

The average gross earnings and operating expenses per train mile of *all* trains, including switching, construction and other trains not earning revenue, on all of the roads for the last ten years, and on each of the three leading roads for the last two years, are stated in the following tables: —

Earnings and Expenses per Total Train Mile, 1895–1904.

YEARS.	Gross Earnings.	Operating Expenses.	Net Earnings.	YEARS.	Gross Earnings.	Operating Expenses.	Net Earnings.
1895, .	$1.313	$0.895	$0.418	1900, .	$1.392	$0.964	$0.428
1896, .	1.303	.913	.390	1901, .	1.350	.939	.411
1897, .	1.296	.890	.406	1902, .	1.359	.959	.400
1898, .	1.304	.902	.402	1903, .	1.383	1.004	.379
1899, .	1.335	.911	.424	1904, .	1.381	1.002	.379

Earnings and Expenses per Total Train Mile (Three Roads) in 1903 and 1904.

RAILROAD COMPANIES.	Gross Earnings.		Operating Expenses.		Net Earnings.	
	1903.	1904.	1903.	1904.	1903.	1904.
Boston & Albany, . . .	$1.440	$1.364	$0.956	$0.949	$0.484	$0.415
Boston & Maine, . . .	1.183	1.207*	.850	.872*	.333	.335
N. Y., N. H. & Hartford, .	1.589	1.572	1.175	1.144	.414	.428

* Does not include electric street railways.

Volume of Traffic.

Train Mileage.

The total number of miles run by passenger trains (including in the passenger train mileage one-quarter of the mixed train mileage) the last year, on the roads of all the companies, was 31,876,672 — an increase of 951,263 miles over the previous year; by freight trains (including three-quarters of the mixed train mileage), 19,250,202 — an increase of 727,115 miles; and by all other trains 17,874,984 — a decrease of 156,821 miles, making the total number of miles run by trains of all kinds 69,001,858 — an increase of 1,521,557 miles over the previous year.

The mileage of passenger, freight and other trains, for each of the last ten years, is stated in the following table : —

Train Mileage for Ten Years, 1895–1904.

YEARS.	Miles Run by			Total Train Mileage.
	Passenger Trains.	Freight Trains.	Other Trains.	
1895,	24,302,800	17,019,851	10,582,973	51,905,624
1896,	26,392,246	18,354,625	12,610,907	57,357,778
1897,	26,236,109	17,452,890	11,834,184	55,523,183
1898,	27,046,501	17,721,128	11,666,838	56,434,467
1899,	27,749,110	17,691,524	11,067,915	56,508,549
1900,	28,220,270	17,680,269	13,151,881	59,052,420
1901,	28,528,070	16,624,823	15,888,988	61,041,881
1902,	29,651,287	17,261,795	17,032,739	63,945,821
1903,	30,925,409	18,523,087	18,031,805	67,480,301
1904,	31,876,672	19,250,202	17,874,984	69,001,858

The next table shows the train mileage on each of the three leading railroads of the state for the last year : —

Train Mileage (Three Roads) in 1904.

RAILROAD COMPANIES.	Miles Run by			Total Train Mileage.
	Passenger Trains.	Freight Trains.	Other Trains.	
Boston & Albany,	3,539,638	2,371,489	1,608,631	7,519,758
Boston & Maine,	11,232,987	8,471,880	9,071,870	28,776,737
N. Y., N. H. & Hartford,	15,807,929	7,932,862	6,981,419	30,722,210

Passenger Traffic.

The total number of passengers carried the last year was 124,483,-665,* — an increase of 1,320,872 passengers over the previous year. Each passenger on the steam roads travelled on the average a distance of 17.49 miles, making the total passenger mileage 2,133,524,-260.†

* Includes 2,567,868 on electric street railways.

† Not including electric street railways.

The total volume of passenger traffic for each of the last ten years is shown in the following table: —

Passenger Mileage for Ten Years, 1895–1904.

YEARS.	Passengers Carried.	Average Journey. (Miles.)	Total Passenger Mileage.	Average Passengers per Train Mile.
1895, ...	107,856,348	15.17	1,636,197,381	67
1896, ...	111,629,051	15.89	1,773,733,208	67
1897, ...	102,743,890	16.29	1,674,175,174	64
1898, ...	101,940,722	16.47	1,678,640,940	63
1899, ...	102,043,980	16.82	1,716,081,605	62
1900, ...	108,768,303	17.08	1,858,253,279	66
1901, ...	108,758,528	17.09	1,859,200,923	65
1902, ...	115,645,897	17.14	1,982,170,406	67
1903, ...	123,162,793	17.16	2,112,874,995	68
1904, ...	124,483,665*	17.49†	2,133,524,260†	67†

The passenger mileage on the three leading railroads during the last year was as follows: —

Passenger Mileage (Three Roads) in 1904.

RAILROAD COMPANIES.	Passengers Carried.	Average Journey. (Miles)	Total Passenger Mileage.	Average Passengers per Train Mile.
Boston & Albany, . . .	10,350,181	23.93	247,709,954	70
Boston & Maine, . . .	40,257,301*	18.09†	681,938,257†	61†
N. Y., N. H. & Hartford, .	63,130,459	17.99	1,135,702,328	71

* Includes 2,567,868 on electric street railways.
† Not including electric street railways.

Freight Traffic.

The total number of tons of freight hauled on all the roads the last year was 43,727,514 — a decrease of 265,464 tons from the previous year. Each ton of freight was hauled on the average a distance of 90.22 miles, making the total freight mileage 3,945,026,293 — an increase of 16,032,374 miles, or tons hauled one mile, over the previous year.

Freight Mileage for Ten Years, 1895–1904.

YEARS.	Tons of Freight Hauled.	Average Haul. (Miles.)	Total Freight Mileage.	Average Tons per Train Mile.
1895, ...	30,858,173	83.01	2,561,598,881	148
1896, ...	34,605,838	83.18	2,878,369,521	155
1897, ...	33,276,416	84.80	2,821,770,240	160
1898, ...	35,338,724	85.54	3,022,770,499	172
1899, ...	36,228,084	88.65	3,211,643,434	182
1900, ...	40,316,711	85.81	3,459,439,263	195
1901, ...	39,463,814	89.07	3,515,066,493	211
1902, ...	41,440,170	86.70	3,592,963,862	208
1903, ...	43,992,978	89.31	3,928,993,919	212
1904, ...	43,727,514	90.22	3,945,026,293	205

The preceding table gives the total volume of freight traffic for each of the last ten years.

The next table gives the freight mileage on the three leading roads for the last year: —

Freight Mileage (Three Roads) in 1904.

RAILROAD COMPANIES.	Tons of Freight Hauled.	Average Haul. (Miles.)	Total Freight Mileage.	Average Tons per Train Mile.
Boston & Albany, . .	4,699,465	106.86	502,207,880	212
Boston & Maine, . .	19,395,452	89.11	1,728,422,684	204
N. Y., N. H. & Hartford, .	17,560,485	94.61	1,661,382,186	209

Fares and Freights.

Passenger Fares.

The average passenger fare per mile on the Massachusetts railroads for each of the last thirty years, as ascertained from the annual returns to the Board, is given in the following table: —

Average Passenger Fare per Mile (All Massachusetts Roads) for 30 Years, 1875 to 1904.

YEARS.	Fares.	YEARS.	Fares.	YEARS.	Fares.
	Cents.		Cents.		Cents.
1875, . . .	2.30	1885, . . .	1.88	1895, . . .	1.78
1876, . . .	2.23	1886, . . .	1.88	1896, . . .	1.79
1877, . . .	2.22	1887, . . .	1.85	1897, . . .	1.80
1878, . . .	2.18	1888, . . .	1.90	1898, . . .	1.78
1879, . . .	2.11	1889, . . .	1.87	1899, . . .	1.77
1880, . . .	2.05	1890, . . .	1.82	1900, . . .	1.75
1881, . . .	2.02	1891, . . .	1.83	1901, . . .	1.75
1882, . . .	2.00	1892, . . .	1.83	1902, . . .	1.73
1883, . . .	2.00	1893, . . .	1.83	1903, . . .	1.73
1884, . . .	1.92	1894, . . .	1.80	1904, . . .	1.72*

The following table gives the average passenger fares per mile on the *five* leading Massachusetts railroads, taken singly and as a group, for the years 1870, 1880 and 1890, and for each of the last three years, 1902 to 1904 inclusive: —

Average Passenger Fare per Mile (Five Roads) in 1870, 1880, 1890 and 1902–1904.

RAILROAD COMPANIES.	1870.	1880.	1890.	1902.	1903.	1904.
	Cents.	Cents.	Cents.	Cents.	Cents.	Cents.
Boston & Albany, ...	2.78	2.09	1.86	1.72	1.73	1.68
Boston & Maine, ...	2.14	2.14	1.83	1.76	1.77	1.78*
Fitchburg, ...	2.56	1.88	1.91	–	–	–
New England, ...	–	2.12	1.96	–	–	–
N. Y., N. H. & Hartford, .	2.38	1.92	1.73	1.74	1.73	1.73
All five companies, . .	2.40	2.01	1.81	1.75	1.74	1.74

* Does not include electric street railways.

Freight Rates.

In the tables which follow, the average rates per ton mile for the transportation of merchandise on the railroads of this state are shown for the same years and intervals of years, for all of the roads and for the same groups of roads, as in the preceding tables of passenger fares.

The first table gives the average freight rate per ton mile on all of the roads for each of the last thirty years: —

Average Freight Rate per Ton Mile (All Massachusetts Roads) for 30 Years, 1875 to 1904.

YEARS.	Rates.	YEARS.	Rates.	YEARS.	Rates.
	Cents.		Cents.		Cents.
1875, . . .	2.45	1885, . . .	1.59	1895, . . .	1.28
1876, . . .	2.17	1886, . . .	1.64	1896, . . .	1.28
1877, . . .	2.07	1887, . . .	1.62	1897, . . .	1.25
1878, . . .	1.92	1888, . . .	1.55	1898, . . .	1.22
1879, . . .	1.82	1889, . . .	1.50	1899, . . .	1.18
1880, . . .	1.84	1890, . . .	1.45	1900, . . .	1.22
1881, . . .	1.71	1891, . . .	1.42	1901, . . .	1.20
1882, . . .	1.71	1892, . . .	1.36	1902, . . .	1.24
1883, . . .	1.72	1893, . . .	1.39	1903, . . .	1.23
1884, . . .	1.64	1894, . . .	1.33	1904, . . .	1.27

The following table shows the average rate per ton mile on the *five* leading railroads of the state, taken singly and as a group, in 1870, 1880 and 1890, and for each of the last three years, 1902 to 1904: —

Average Freight Rate per Ton Mile (Five Roads) in 1870, 1880, 1890 and 1902-1904.

RAILROAD COMPANIES.	1870.	1880.	1890.	1902.	1903.	1904.
	Cents.	Cents.	Cents.	Cents.	Cents.	Cents.
Boston & Albany, ...	2.19	1.21	1.11	.97	.97	.99
Boston & Maine, ...	4.45	2.56	1.76	1.12	1.13	1.18
Fitchburg, ...	4.81	1.37	.99	-	-	-
New England, ...	-	2.86	1.22	-	-	-
N. Y., N. H. & Hartford, .	4.09	2.41	2.07	1.46	1.41	1.42
All five companies, . .	2.95	1.65	1.44	1.24	1.23	1.26

Cost of Repairs, Wages and Fuel.

The average cost of certain specified items of repairs and renewals, and also of wages and fuel, per total train mile, on all of the roads for the past six years, and on each of the three leading roads for the last year, appears in the following tables: —

Cost of Repairs, etc., per Total Train Mile, 1899–1904.

REPAIRS, WAGES, ETC.	1899.	1900.	1901.	1902.	1903.	1904.
Repair of roadbed,* . . .	$0.120	$0.109	$0.101	$0.105	$0.098	$0.100
Renewal of rails, . . .	.009	.006	.005	.005	.004	.007
Repair of bridges, . . .	.013	.018	.014	.016	.016	.016
Repair of locomotives, . .	.051	.069	.055	.053	.049	.056
Repair of passenger cars, . .	.034	.036	.039	.041†	.070†	.059†
Repair of freight cars, . .	.041	.039	.040	.166‡	.096‡	.116‡
Wages, ...	.315	.328	.324	.329	.343	.356
Fuel, ...	.096	.109	.119	.130	.174	.157
Totals, ...	$0.679	$0.714	$0.697	$0.875	$0.850	$0.867

* Including renewal of ties. † Per total passenger-train mile.
‡ Per total freight-train mile.

Cost of Repairs, etc., per Total Train Mile (Three Roads) in 1904.

REPAIRS, WAGES, ETC.	Boston & Albany.	Boston & Maine.	N. Y., N. H. & Hartford.
Repair of roadbed,*	$0.094	$0.098	$0.104
Renewal of rails, ...	.002	.004	.011
Repair of bridges, ...	.011	.009	.024
Repair of locomotives, ...	.074	.048	.061
Repair of passenger cars,† . . .	.066	.070	.052
Repair of freight cars,‡	.096	.128	.114
Wages, ...	.298	.312	.417
Fuel, ...	.148	.154	.165
Totals, ...	$0.789	$0.823	$0.948

* Including renewal of ties. † Per total passenger-train mile.
‡ Per total freight-train mile.

The next table gives the cost of repairs per locomotive and per car on each of the same three roads the last year: —

Cost of Repairs per Locomotive and per Car (Three Roads) in 1904.

RAILROAD COMPANIES.	Per Locomotive.	Per Passenger Car.*	Per Freight Car.
Boston & Albany, ...	$1,984 52	$590 57	$62 96
Boston & Maine, ...	1,364 58	492 00	63 91
N. Y., N. H. & Hartford, . . .	1,765 01	400 00	52 87

* Including baggage, express and mail cars.

Rolling Stock.

The following table shows the amount of rolling stock (owned and leased) of all the companies, as returned at the end of each of the last seven years: —

Schedule of Rolling Stock, 1898–1904.

ROLLING STOCK.	1898.	1899.	1900.	1901.	1902.	1903.	1904.
Locomotives, . .	2,072	2,091	2,102	2,169	2,202	2,277	2,390
Passenger cars, . .	3,174	3,144	3,161	3,255	3,263	3,338	3,508
Baggage, express and mail cars, . .	577	582	610	566	627	650	654
Freight cars, . .	35,491	33,935	34,292	33,801	33,452	34,825	37,938
Gravel cars, etc., .	1,890	1,937	1,980	1,850	1,801	1,865	1,887

Number of Employees.

The average number of persons employed during the last year by all the railroad corporations making returns to the Board was 60,156, an increase of 1,268 over the previous year. The following table gives the average number of employees for each of the last ten years: —

Average Number of Employees, 1895–1904.

YEARS.	Number of Employees.	YEARS.	Number of Employees.
1895, ...	46,533	1900, ...	53,045
1896, ...	52,127	1901, ...	53,564
1897, ...	50,924	1902, ...	56,388
1898, ...	51,602	1903, ...	58,888
1899, ...	51,881	1904, ...	60,156

Respectfully submitted,

FRED E. JONES,
Statistician.

Summary of Railroad Accidents.

The number of casualties on railroads reported by the several companies during the year ending June 30, 1904, is shown by the following table:—

	Killed.	Injured.	Total.
Passengers,	4	70	74
Employees,	87	417	504
Travellers on highway at grade crossings,	31	29	60
Trespassers,	139	75	214
Unclassified,	3	7	10
Total,	264	598	862

In addition to the above, there were reported during the year 36 accidents from which no personal injury resulted.

The total number of casualties, namely, 862, shows an increase of 21 over the number reported for the year ending June 30, 1903, and a decrease of 85 from the average number reported annually for the preceding ten years. Of the whole number of casualties, 264 were fatal, as against 263 reported for the year ending June 30, 1903, and as compared with an average of 234 for the preceding ten years, while 598 were not fatal, as compared with 578 for the preceding year and as against an average of 713 for the preceding ten-year period.

Of the total number of persons injured, 26 were children,— 9 fatally.

Passengers.

Of the total number of passengers killed, 2 were killed from causes beyond their own control and 2 were killed through their own fault or imprudence. Of the total number injured, namely, 70, 32 were injured from causes beyond their own control, while 38 were injured through their own fault. The total number of passengers killed and injured during the preceding year was 7 and 49 respectively. The average number of passengers killed and injured annually during the ten years 1894–1903, was 8 and 92 respectively.

The following table shows the ratio of passengers killed and injured to total number of passengers carried in Massachusetts: —

PASSENGERS CARRIED, ETC.	1903.	1904.
Total number of passengers carried in Massachusetts,[1]	98,530,234	97,532,638
Total miles travelled in Massachusetts,	1,690,299,996	1,706,819,408
Passengers *killed* by causes beyond their control,	1	2
Ratio to total passengers carried,	1 to 98,530,234	1 to 48,766,319
Ratio to total miles travelled,	1 to 1,690,299,996	1 to 853,409,704
Passengers *injured* by causes beyond their control,	31	32
Ratio to total passengers carried,	1 to 3,178,394	1 to 3,047,895
Ratio to total miles travelled,	1 to 54,525,806	1 to 53,338,107
Passengers *killed* by their own fault or want of care,	6	2
Ratio to passengers carried,	1 to 16,421,705	1 to 48,766,319
Passengers *injured* by their own fault or want of care,	18	38
Ratio to passengers carried,	1 to 5,473,901	1 to 2,566,648

[1] The total number of passengers carried in Massachusetts is estimated to be about 80 per cent of the total number carried on the several roads both in and out of the state.

Employees.

During the year, 87 employees were killed and 417 were injured, as compared with 95 killed and 466 injured during the preceding year. The following table shows the character of accidents to employees: —

	Killed.	Injured.		Killed.	Injured.
Coupling and uncoupling,	10	90	Derailments,	1	11
Overhead obstructions,	1	18	All other,	46	143
Falling and jumping,	22	132	Total,	87	417
Collisions,	7	23			

The average number of employees killed and injured annually during the preceding ten years was 65 and 487 respectively..

Grade Crossings.

The number of travellers on highways killed at grade crossings during the year was 31 and the number injured was 29, as against 26 killed and 12 injured for the preceding twelve months.

Of the total number killed, 17 were killed at grade crossings protected by gates or flagmen, 10 at unprotected crossings, while 4 were killed at private crossings. Of the total number injured, 20 were injured at protected, 7 at unprotected and 2 at private crossings.

The following table shows, for the year ending June 30, 1904, the number and character of casualties at grade crossings on the different railroads: —

Casualties at Grade Crossings during the Year ending June 30, 1904.

RAILROADS.	At Protected Crossings.		At Unprotected Crossings.		Total.		Total Grade Crossings.	Total Persons Killed or Injured.	Ratio of Accidents to Crossings.
	Killed.	Injured.	Killed.	Injured.	Killed.	Injured.			
Attleboro Branch,	–	–	–	–	–	–	14	–	–
Boston & Albany,	–	5	–	–	–	5	203	5	1 to 41
Boston & Maine,	12	–	2	–	14	–	768	14	1 to 55
Boston, Revere Beach & Lynn,[2]	1	–	–	–	1	–	11	1	1 to 11
Cape Ann Granite,	–	–	–	–	–	–	2	–	–
Grafton & Upton,	–	–	–	–	–	–	29	–	–
Hoosac Tunnel & Wilmington,[2]	–	–	–	–	–	–	–	–	–
Nantucket Central,[2]	–	–	–	–	–	–	5	–	–
New London Northern,	–	–	–	–	–	–	44	–	–
New York, New Haven & Hartford,	4	15	12[3]	9[4]	16[3]	24[4]	846	40	1 to 21
Totals for year,	17	20	14[3]	9[4]	31[3]	29[4]	1,922	60	1 to 32
Totals for year ending June 30, 1903,	16	5	10	7	26	12	1,927	38	1 to 51

[1] The ratio at protected crossings was 1 to 30; at unprotected crossings, 1 to 36.
[2] A narrow-gauge railroad.
[3] Includes 4 killed at private crossings.
[4] Includes 2 injured at private crossings.

Trespassers.

The total number of trespassers killed during the year was 139, of whom 134 were unlawfully on the track and 5 were unlawfully on cars. Trespassers injured numbered 75, 51 being unlawfully on the track and 24 unlawfully on cars. There were 4 probable suicides.

The number of trespassers killed and injured during the year ending June 30, 1903, was 128 and 44 respectively, while the average number for the ten preceding years was 130 and 96 respectively.

There were 3 persons killed and 7 injured whose proper classification in the reports of accidents was undeterminable.

A change in the form of reports of accidents to the Board has been made which we think will lead to some improvement in their classification and analysis.

Railroad Bridges.

Massachusetts Board of Railroad Commissioners, Hon. James F. Jackson, *Chairman.*

Gentlemen: — I beg leave to make the following report with reference to the bridges on the steam railroads of the Commonwealth: —

The following tables, which are similar to those published in previous reports, give statistics regarding the number and kind of bridges. Table I gives the number of bridges of each type, while Table II gives the total length of bridges of stone, wood, and metal.

TABLE I. — *Number and Description of Railroad Bridges in Massachusetts, June 30, 1904.*

RAILROADS.	Pile Bridges.	Wooden Trestles.	Wooden Stringers.	Braced or Trussed Stringers.	Wooden or Combination Trusses.	Stone or Brick Arches.	I-Beams.	Plate Girders.	Metal Riveted Trusses.	Metal Pin-connected Trusses.	Rails.	Pin-connected Metal Swing Bridges.	Metal Folding, Rolling Lift or Jack-knife Draws.	Pratt, Howe or other Wooden Jack-knife Draws.	Plate Girder Swing Bridges.	Trussed Beam Swing Draws.	Total Spans Stone Bridges.	Total Wooden and Combination Bridges (Fixed Spans).	Total Metal Bridges (Fixed Spans).	Total Movable Bridges.	Grand Totals.	Total Length of Pile and Trestle Bridging (Approximate).
Boston & Albany,	7	4	–	–	2	50	55	93	66	–	–	–	2	2	–	–	50	13	214	4	281	3,497
Boston & Maine,	61	19	68	7	20	88	78	279	56	48	–	1	1	10	2	1	88	173	473	15	749	21,924
Boston, Revere Beach & Lynn,	5	–	–	–	–	–	–	–	–	–	–	–	1	–	1	–	–	5	–	2	7	5,055
Grafton & Upton,	1	–	3	–	1	1	–	1	–	–	–	–	–	–	–	–	1	5	1	–	7	48
New London Northern,	5	3	8	1	6	1	2	17	12	–	–	–	–	–	–	–	1	23	31	–	55	558
New York, New Haven & Hartford,	78	9	86	4	12	124	46	407[1]	15	28	11	2	1	3	1	–	124	189	507	7	827	15,179
Totals,	157	35	165	12	41	264	181	797	159	76	11	3	5	15	4	1	264	408	1,226	28	1,926	46,261
Deduct as counted twice,	–	–	–	–	–	–	–	4	–	–	–	–	–	–	–	–	–	–	4	–	4	–
Net totals,	157	35	165	12	41	264	181	793	159	76	11	3	5	15	4	1	264	408	1,222	28	1,922	46,261

[1] Including 2 steel arches.

TABLE II. — *Length of Bridging of Wood, Stone, and Metal, June 30, 1904.*

RAILROADS.	WOODEN BRIDGES.		STONE BRIDGES.		METAL BRIDGES.	
	Number.	Total Length (Feet).	Number.	Total Length (Feet).	Number.	Total Length (Feet).
Boston & Albany, . . .	15	3,794	50	1,260	216	11,443
Boston & Maine, . . .	184	24,503	88	1,766	477	26,079
Boston, Revere B. & Lynn, .	5	5,055	–	–	2	130
Grafton & Upton, . . .	5	130	1	15	1	46
New London Northern, . .	23	1,513	1	19	31	1,977
N. Y., N. H. & Hartford, .	192	17,646	124	3,196	507	22,111
Totals, ...	424	52,641	264	6,256	1,234	61,786

The following work has been done by the railroad companies during the past year: —

On the Boston & Albany railroad one new plate girder bridge of two spans has been built on the Saxonville branch, two plate girder spans and one riveted lattice bridge have been rebuilt as plate girders, and one wooden truss span has been replaced by I-beams.

On the Boston, Revere Beach & Lynn railroad the pile bridge over the Saugus River has been repaired and somewhat strengthened.

On the Boston & Maine railroad the following work has been done on the different divisions: On the Eastern division, one wooden stringer span has been strengthened by placing a pile bent beneath it, and one pile bridge has been partly rebuilt; on the Western division, three new plate girder bridges have been built in the abolition of grade crossings at Malden, and one wooden stringer span has been rebuilt; on the Southern division, two pile bridges have been rebuilt and repairs made to several other structures; on the Massachusetts Central branch, four wooden stringer spans have been rebuilt; on the Worcester and Nashua division, one plate girder bridge has been filled, and one stone arch has had the wing walls buttressed; on the Nashua, Acton & Boston branch, one pile bridge has been strengthened; on the Connecticut River division, one plate girder bridge has been rebuilt; on the Fitchburg division, the Charles River draw has been rebuilt, two riveted truss spans have been replaced by plate girders, and the masonry of a wooden stringer span has been rebuilt. On this division some new bridges have been reported this year which were previously supposed to be less than ten feet in span.

On the New London Northern railroad one wooden stringer span has been rebuilt.

On the New York, New Haven & Hartford railroad the following work has been done on the different divisions: On the Midland division, one wooden stringer span has been filled, two plate girder spans have been rebuilt, one wooden truss bridge has been replaced by plate girders, one wooden stringer span has been replaced by plate girders, and one pile bridge has been strengthened; on the Shore Line division, one wooden stringer span and one braced I-beam span have been replaced by plate girders, and one wooden trestle has been partly replaced by I-beams; on the Northampton division, two new plate girder bridges have been built, and one plate girder bridge replaced by I-beams; on the Berkshire division, four pile bridges have been rebuilt and six strengthened; two wooden trestles and two I-beams have been strengthened, one plate girder span has been replaced by I-beams, and five plate girder spans have been strengthened, two wooden stringer spans have been replaced by I-beams, one by plate girders, and one span rebuilt as a wooden stringer; on the Worcester division, five plate girder spans have been rebuilt, a trussed wooden stringer span on a siding replaced by a plate girder, and one Howe truss span replaced by plate girders; on the Providence division, one wooden stringer span has been replaced by I-beams; on the Old Colony system, seven new plate girder bridges have been built (five of them at Fall River), one plate girder span has been filled, one new I-beam bridge has been built, one new riveted truss has been built, one new brick arch has been built, six plate girder, one I-beam and seventeen wooden stringer spans have been rebuilt (one of the latter only partially), one new jack-knife draw span built on the Boston Y, three wooden stringer spans, two pile bridges and one wooden trestle have been strengthened, one pile bridge and one wooden truss bridge have been rebuilt, and nine pile bridges have been repaired.

TABLE III. — *Bridge Work Done in the Year ending June 30, 1904.*

RAILROADS.	NEW BRIDGES BUILT.			BRIDGES REBUILT OR REPLACED.			BRIDGES STRENGTHENED.		
	Wood.	Stone.	Metal.	Wood.	Stone.	Metal.	Wood.	Stone.	Metal.
Boston & Albany,	–	–	2	1[1]	–	3	–	–	–
Boston & Maine,	–	–	3	9[2]	–	3	2	1	–
Boston, Revere Beach & Lynn,	–	–	–	–	–	–	1	–	–
New London Northern,	–	–	–	1	–	–	–	–	–
N. Y., N. H. & Hartford,	1	1	11	34[3]	–	17	15	–	7
Totals,	1	1	16	45	–	23	18	1	7

[1] 1 as steel. [2] 1 only partly. [3] 21 as wood, 12 as metal, 1 as stone.

The strengthening and rebuilding of bridges is still continuing on some of the roads with undiminishing rapidity, necessitated by the still increasing weight of rolling stock and heavier train loads.

Respectfully submitted,

GEO. F. SWAIN,
Bridge Engineer.

ISSUES OF STOCK AND BONDS.

The following tables show the issues of railroad stock and bonds authorized and approved during the year ending December 31, 1904: —

Issue of Capital Stock.

RAILROAD COMPANY.	Date when Authorized.	Amount Authorized.
Old Colony,	May 25,	$462,500

Issues of Bonds.

RAILROAD COMPANIES.	Date when Authorized.	Amount Authorized.
Boston & Maine,	December 8,	$500,000
Old Colony,	February 25,	498,000

STREET RAILWAY COMPANIES.

Massachusetts Street Railway Companies.

Annual reports for the year ending September 30, 1904, have been received from one hundred and two street railway companies.

Reports of the operations of the Amesbury and Hampton (Exeter, Hampton and Amesbury, of New Hampshire, lessee) and of the Haverhill and Plaistow (Exeter, Hampton and Amesbury, of New Hampshire, lessee), and of the Webster and Dudley and the Worcester and Webster (Consolidated — formerly Worcester and Connecticut Eastern — of Connecticut, lessee), were also received.

Companies added to the List.

Two new companies were organized during the year under the general law and added to the list, namely, the Horse Neck Beach and the Plymouth, Carver and Wareham.

The Lowell, Acton and Maynard, organized under special law, having built and operated its railway, has been added to the list.

Companies dropped from the List.

During the last fiscal year ten companies have been dropped from the list, as follows: The Gloucester and Rockport, the Greenfield and Deerfield, the Haverhill and Andover, the Lawrence and Reading, the Middleton and Danvers, the Milton, the Phillipston, and the Reading, Wakefield and Lynnfield having been consolidated with other companies; the Cape Cod, the construction of its railway having been abandoned; and the Marlborough, its property having been sold under foreclosure.

Consolidation of Companies.

During the year the Commonwealth Avenue (December 31, 1903) and the Wellesley and Boston (December 31, 1903) were consolidated with the Newton; the Framingham Union (December 21, 1903) with the Framingham, Southborough and Marlborough; the Framingham, Southborough and Marlborough (February 1, 1904) with the Boston and Worcester; and the Marlborough and Framingham (December 21, 1903) with the Boston and Worcester.

The individual companies have made reports to these several dates.

Operation of Companies.

Owing to consolidations there were at the end of the year ninety-seven existing companies. Of this number sixty-six operated their railways; five railways were operated by receivers; nineteen were operated under lease or contract by other companies, in four instances foreign companies; one was being constructed; one was not in operation; and five companies had organized and paid in a portion of their capital stock but had not commenced the construction of their railways.

Railway Mileage.

New Mileage.

There have been added during the last year to the mileage of the Massachusetts companies 32.839 miles of street railway line and 18.903 miles of second track, making 51.742 miles of additional main track. There have also been added 1.838 miles of side track, making a total addition of 53.580 miles of track reckoned as single track.

Mileage Owned.

The Massachusetts companies now own 2,191.812 miles of street railway lines, 382.840 miles of second main track and 149.660 miles of side track, making a total length of track owned 2,724.312 miles. This statement excludes the track in the subway.

All of the street railway mileage owned is located in this state except 18.766 miles of main track and .760 of a mile of side track belonging to the Woonsocket, — in all 19.526 miles of track, — which is located in Rhode Island. All the track owned is surface street railway track, with the exception of 6.644 miles of elevated railway line and 6.468 miles of elevated second track. Of the sidings, all are surface track with the exception of 2.903 miles of elevated track. All of the elevated track is confined to Boston.

The Old Colony leases and operates the Newport and Fall River, having a mileage of 18.926 miles, located in Rhode Island; and the Boston and Northern leases and operates the Nashua, having a mileage of 14.899 miles located in New Hampshire. Accordingly 52.591 miles of main track were operated outside the state.

Mileage Operated.

The total miles of main track (including trackage rights) operated is 2,654.479, — an increase of 33.517 over the previous year.

Street Railway Conditions.

The street railway returns of the year are suggestive. Of seventy-four operating companies, thirty failed to earn expenses and fixed charges; twenty-five paid dividends; of the twenty-five which paid dividends fourteen earned them during the year. Five companies, as stated above, have been in the hands of receivers.

Very few companies beside keeping their railways in good repair reserved for depreciation what prudent management would require. Generally present necessities only have been met, the future with its inevitable expense of replacement and reconstruction being allowed to look out for itself.

Under chapter 483 of the Acts of 1902 the Board prepares a yearly list of companies which appear from their returns to have properly earned and paid a dividend of at least five per cent for the five years immediately preceding. Thirteen companies were found to be entitled to a place upon the list submitted in January, 1903; the list of January, 1904, contained the names of twelve companies; that submitted this year contains the names of ten companies.

Our attention has been repeatedly called to the unusual expenses consequent upon the severity of last winter's weather and to the loss of receipts in the summer owing to the coolness of the season. But it is not safe to count upon mild winters and warm summers in this part of the country, and while it is agreed that the past year was an extraordinary one it is plain that the weather did not drive five companies into insolvency and others perilously near it. The evil is more radical. In the early days of the change from horse to electric railway, promotion ran wild with the idea that immense profits were to be realized in the extension of the old and in the construction of new railways as electric roads in any and every direction; that where no business was in sight, it would appear under the creative magic of the electric car. The test of this opinion, necessarily a test of years in which novelty disappears, is now practically complete. Experience has shown that with the more expensive roadbed and equipment, the heavier rail and larger cars, there has not been the corresponding and expected development of permanent business. Operating cost, too, in heating cars and in repair and renewal of plant, has proved larger than was expected. With the new accommodation and the nearer approach to railroad conditions has come the increased demand of the public for expenditures in the interest of safety and comfort which had not been counted upon, as for example, in construction of double track, installment of signal systems and establishment of waiting rooms. Hurried along by the natural enthusiasm for the new type of railway with its many most attractive features, capital, sometimes deliberately misled, has been invested in undertakings for which there was no sufficient demand and which are now represented by roads run, not only without return upon the investment, but at an actual loss of capital. In such cases the future promises as possible events: the acceptance of an unsatisfactory service as better than nothing; an increase in fares; or the abandonment of the railway. It is a source of gratification that under our restrictive laws, while capital has taken its own risk as to the earning capacity of these enterprises, in no case has there been an issue of stock or bonds in excess of the fair cost of the railway property, to act as a contributing factor to the existing troubles.

Upon some railways fares have been raised, and with encouraging results, but this action is usually unpopular and is often taken at the risk of lessening the volume of business. It is, moreover, at times complicated by agreements made between companies and town officials when locations and privileges in the streets were granted. If, however, this is the remedy, it is better that it be applied than that the public lose the benefits which the railways bring.

Another incident of the present situation has been the enforcement upon certain systems of a seemingly arbitrary distinction between the long and the short distance ride, to the provocation of the through traveller, who is loth to admit that there is any justification for it. The zone system has never been favored in this state. Instead there has been adopted the five-cent fare within city and town limits, in some cases between centers of adjoining towns. As new grants of location have been sought the five-cent fare has been made good for greater and greater distances, frequently through the use of transfer checks. This low fare promotes a better distribution of population in large communities and is conveniently paid and collected, while the company has been enabled to reap a profit in the frequency with which cars have been filled and refilled with persons taking short rides. In one notable and exceptional instance this fare covers five cities which were deemed to be so closely connected as to make practically one continuous community and so to give the company the advantage of continually changing patronage from point to point. The attempt, however, upon interurban lines to maintain these local concessions and at the same time to establish a sort of mileage basis for through travel, with arbitrary fare limits, has naturally led to frequent complaints from those who think they are unjustly denied privileges which are given to others. The companies as well as the travelling public would be benefited by the establishment of a more satisfactory system of fares upon these railways. Much study has been and is being given to the matter, but as yet the problem remains unsolved.

Changes in Laws.

Confusion exists in some of the street railway laws in consequence of legislation at different times to accomplish specific purposes under new conditions without regard to harmony in the whole body of law. An illustration is found in the following sections of chapter 112 of the Revised Laws:

Section 40. The board of aldermen or the selectmen shall from time to time establish such regulations as to the rate of speed and as to the mode of use of the tracks within their city or town as the interest and convenience of the public may require, subject to the approval, revision or alteration of the board of railroad commissioners; and a street railway company whose servants or agents wilfully or negligently violate any such regulation shall forfeit not more than five hundred dollars for each offence.

Section 42. The board of aldermen or the selectmen may from time to time make such regulations as to the manner and extent of use of tracks, and the number and routes of cars of any and all companies which run over such tracks within their city or town, as the interest of public travel may require, and, subject thereto, the directors of a street railway company may from time to time establish regulations for the use of its road and cars, subject to the approval, revision or alteration of the board of railroad commissioners.

We believe it would make for a more effective administration of the laws governing street railways if such statutes were revised upon some simple principle which shall preserve original jurisdiction in local boards and give supervisory power to this Board as the public good may require.

In organizing street railway companies the amount of capital stock which must be named in the agreement of association is now fixed at ten thousand dollars for each mile of proposed railway unless the railway is to be wholly outside of any city, in which case it may be not less than twenty-five hundred dollars. It was the evident purpose of the Legislature to require as a preliminary step in these proceedings a subscription of capital which would be fairly commensurate with the undertaking. The difference between the character, and so the cost, of roadbed and equipment now demanded in building street railways and that demanded in the days of horse railways, at which time the present laws were enacted, is very marked. If the policy named, which we believe is a good one, is not to be abandoned the amount of capital required to be stated in the agreement of association should be increased.

We also renew the recommendation of last year that street railway companies be given a larger right to construct their roads upon private lands in cases where the public interests would be thereby promoted. It is surely better that such authority be given by general laws under suitable restriction than that it should be obtained by way of special acts which change an existing policy under circumstances that often forbid close scrutiny of purposes and careful consideration of reasons.

During the year 343 docketed cases and 185 formal complaints in addition to the docketed cases have been presented and considered, in connection with which 357 public hearings have been given.

Statistics.

Boston, January 2, 1905.

Board of Railroad Commissioners, Hon. James F. Jackson, *Chairman*.

Gentlemen: — I submit the following compilations of statistics from the reports of the several street railway companies to the Board for the year ending September 30, 1904.

The following table gives the length of railway line and track, and total reckoned as single track reported by the companies for the year ending September 30, 1904, as compared with the previous year: —

Street Railway Mileage Owned, 1903 and 1904.

MILEAGE OWNED.	1903.	1904.	Increase.
	Miles.	Miles.	Miles.
Length of railway line, ...	2,158.973	2,191.812	32.839
Length of second track, ...	363.937	382.840	18.903
Total length of main track, .	2,522.910	2,574.652	51.742
Length of side track, ...	147.822	149.660	1.838
Total, reckoned as single track, .	2,670.732	2,724.312	53.580

Mileage Operated.

The total miles of main track operated (including trackage rights) September 30, 1904, is 2,654.479, — an increase of 33.517 miles over the previous year. All of the track operated is in this state except 52.591 miles located in Rhode Island and New Hampshire.

Assets and Liabilities.

The gross assets of the companies September 30, 1904, were $140,843,739.79. The several classes of assets, and the increase in each class as compared with 1903, are shown in detail in the following table: —

Gross Assets, September 30, 1903 and 1904.

ASSETS.	1903.	1904.	Increase.
Construction, ...	$65,632,216	$69,581,366	$3,949,150
Equipment, ...	25,214,728	26,201,913	987,185
Land and buildings, ...	30,415,216	32,296,112	1,880,896
Other permanent property, . .	1,237,951	1,446,944	208,993
Cash and current assets, . . .	10,455,046	6,554,738	3,900,308*
Miscellaneous assets, ...	5,909,058	4,762,667	1,146,391*
Gross assets, ...	$138,864,215	$140,843,740	$1,979,525

* Decrease.

The gross liabilities at the same date, including capital stock, were $136,049,485.24. The several kinds of liabilities, and the amount of each as compared with 1903, were as follows : —

Gross Liabilities, September 30, 1903 and 1904.

LIABILITIES.	1903.	1904.	Increase.
Capital stock,	$68,404,480	$68,542,038	$137,558
Funded debt,	41,411,500	46,674,884	5,263,384
Real estate mortgages,	72,000	62,000	10,000*
Current liabilities,	19,981,491	17,434,432	2,547,059*
Accrued liabilities,	3,251,940	3,336,132	84,192
Gross liabilities,†	$133,121,411	$136,049,486	$2,928,075
Sinking and other special funds,	1,612,984	1,641,386	28,402
Surplus,‡	4,129,820	3,152,868	976,952*
Totals,	$138,864,215	$140,843,740	$1,979,525

* Decrease. † Exclusive of sinking and other special funds.
‡ Includes premium on sales of stock and bonds.

It will be seen by comparing the last two tables that while there was an increase in gross liabilities of $2,928,075, there was an increase in gross assets of only $1,979,525, thus reducing the aggregate surplus of the companies by the amount of $948,550.

The gross assets, the gross liabilities including capital stock, and the surplus of the companies, with the percentage of surplus to capital stock, at the end of each of the last ten years, are shown in the following table : —

Gross Assets, Liabilities and Surplus for Ten Years, 1895–1904.

YEARS.	Gross Assets.	Gross Liabilities.	Surplus.	Percentage of Surplus to Capital.
1895,	$56,212,671	$55,357,081	$855,590	3.06
1896,	62,187,775	61,117,714	1,070,061	3.48
1897,	67,509,916	66,483,414	1,026,502	3.14
1898,	77,607,326	75,889,625	1,717,701	4.41
1899,	85,764,845	83,279,891	2,484,954	6.01
1900,	98,700,075	95,062,946	3,637,129	7.43
1901,	107,250,656	103,598,042	3,652,614	6.76
1902,	123,200,558	119,441,792	3,758,766	6.26
1903,	138,864,215	133,121,411	5,742,804	8.40
1904,	140,843,740	136,049,486	4,794,254	6.99

Capital Stock and Dividends.

The aggregate capital stock of the ninety-seven companies, September 30, 1904, was $68,542,037.50, — a net increase of $137,558.00 over the preceding year.

Dividends.

The total amount of dividends declared the last year was $3,214,496.24, — a decrease of $371,752 over the preceding year. Thirty-eight out of the one hundred and two companies paid dividends ranging from 1 to 11 per cent, and sixty-four companies declared or paid no dividends.

One company paid 11 per cent; one paid 10 per cent; five paid 8 per cent; one paid 8 per cent on preferred and 7 per cent on common; one paid 7.22 per cent; one paid 7.20 per cent; one paid 7 per cent; ten paid 6 per cent; one paid 5.5 per cent; six paid 5 per cent; two paid 4 per cent; one paid 3.75 per cent; two paid 3 per cent; one paid 2.5 per cent; one paid 2 per cent; one paid 1.5 per cent; and two paid 1 per cent.

Capital Stock, Net Income and Dividends, 1895–1904.

YEARS.	Capital Stock.	Net Divisible Income.	Dividends Declared.	Percentage on Total Capital Stock.
1895, ...	$27,906,685	$2,257,355	$1,606,196	5.76
1896, ...	30,727,818	2,280,776	1,802,847	5.87
1897, ...	32,670,273	2,593,147	1,965,243	6.02
1898, ...	38,933,917	2,534,002	2,076,233	5.33
1899, ...	41,380,143	2,502,942	2,318,398	5.60
1900, ...	48,971,168	3,037,502	2,409,874	4.92
1901, ...	54,069,933	3,398,183	3,417,117	6.32
1902, ...	60,036,328	3,388,851	3,138,711	5.23
1903, ...	68,404,480	3,602,917	3,586,248	5.24
1904, ...	68,542,038	2,998,114	3,214,496	4.69

Funded and Floating Debt.

The aggregate funded debt of the companies, September 30, 1904, was $46,674,884, — an increase of $5,263,384 over the preceding year.

Floating Debt.

The amount of real estate mortgages outstanding September 30, 1904, was $62,000, — a decrease of $10,000 from the preceding year.

The total unfunded debt, including the above mortgages, was $20,832,564, — a decrease of $2,472,867.

The gross debt, funded and unfunded, was $67,507,448, — an increase of $2,790,517.

The net debt (the gross debt less $6,554,738 of cash and current assets) was $60,952,710, — an increase of $6,690,825. In computing the net debt, the sum of $4,762,667 returned as "miscellaneous assets," covering materials and supplies on hand, etc., is not included with cash and current assets in the deduction from gross debt.

The funded debt, unfunded debt, gross debt, cash and current assets, and net debt, for each of the last ten years, are shown in the following table: —

Funded, Unfunded, Gross and Net Debt, 1895–1904.

YEARS.	Funded Debt.	Unfunded Debt.*	Gross Debt.	Cash and Current Assets.	Net Debt.†
1895, ...	$22,284,500	$5,165,896	$27,450,396	$2,428,150	$25,022,246
1896, ...	24,236,000	6,153,896	30,389,896	1,911,651	28,478,245
1897, ...	28,007,600	5,805,541	33,813,141	3,370,650	30,442,491
1898, ...	29,132,700	7,823,008	36,955,708	7,130,861	29,824,847
1899, ...	29,928,500	11,971,248	41,899,748	6,053,677	35,846,071
1900, ...	34,373,000	11,718,778	46,091,778	10,347,849	35,743,929
1901, ...	34,312,500	15,215,609	49,528,109	3,986,857	45,541,252
1902, ...	37,751,000	21,654,464	59,405,464	6,370,679	53,034,785
1903, ...	41,411,500	23,305,431	64,716,931	10,455,046	54,261,885
1904, ...	46,674,884	20,832,564	67,507,448	6,554,738	60,952,710

* Including real estate mortgages. † Gross debt less cash and current assets.

Capital Investment.

The total capital investment (capital stock and net debt) of the street railway companies of the state advanced the last year from $122,666,365 to $129,494,748, — an increase of $6,828,383.

Cost and Capital Investment per Mile.

The average cost of the street railways of the state, per mile of main track (including the cost but not the length of side track), as it stood on the books of the companies September 30, 1904, was $27,025.14 for construction; $10,176.73 for equipment; and $13,105.68 for lands, buildings (including power plants) and other permanent property, — making a total average cost of $50,307.55 per mile of main track.

The following table gives the average cost, classified as above, and also the average capital investment (amount of outstanding capital stock and net debt), per mile of main track, as reported by all of the companies at the end of each of the last ten years: —

Cost and Capital Investment per Mile of Main Track, 1895–1904.

YEARS.	Construction.	Equipment.	Other Permanent Property.*	Total Cost per Mile.	Capital Investment per Mile.†
1895, ...	$23,984	$10,479	$14,266	$48,729	$49,120
1896, ...	23,396	9,805	12,840	46,041	46,373
1897, ...	22,755	9,374	12,329	44,458	44,683
1898, ...	22,537	8,957	11,735	43,229	44,958
1899, ...	22,863	8,518	11,598	42,979	45,040
1900, ...	23,443	8,510	11,684	43,637	44,273
1901, ...	23,953	8,678	11,666	44,297	45,757
1902, ...	24,495	9,026	11,889	45,410	46,261
1903, ...	26,015	9,994	12,546	48,555	48,621
1904, ...	27,025	10,177	13,106	50,308	50,295

* Chiefly lands, buildings and power plants. † Outstanding capital stock and net debt.

Income and Expenditures.

The total income of the companies from all sources, for the year ending September 30, 1904, was $27,759,334.51, and the total expenditures (including dividends) were $27,975,717.19, — making a net loss of $216,382.68 to be deducted from the surplus of previous years.

The sources of total income, and the amount derived from each source as compared with 1903, were as follows: —

Total Income, 1903 and 1904.

INCOME.	1903.	1904.	Increase.
Gross earnings from operation, . .	$25,540,811	$26,207,246	$666,435
Rentals from lease of railway, . .	1,284,274	1,318,838	34,564
Income from other sources, . .	202,566	233,250	30,684
Total income, ...	$27,027,651	$27,759,334	$731,683

The items of total expenditure, with the increase in each item over the previous year, are shown in the following table: —

Total Expenditures, 1903 and 1904.

EXPENDITURES.	1903.	1904.	Increase.
Expenses of operation,	$17,519,367	$18,397,291	$877,924
Interest on debt and loans,	2,350,391	2,670,989	320,598
Taxes,	1,725,312	1,761,083	35,771
Rentals of leased railways,	1,394,283	1,486,385	92,102
Other charges on income,	435,382	445,473	10,091
Dividends paid,	3,586,248	3,214,496	371,752*
Total expenditures,	$27,010,983	$27,975,717	$964,734
Surplus for the year,	16,668	216,383d	233,051*

* Decrease. *d* Deficit.

Earnings and Expenses of Operation.

The gross earnings and expenses of operation the last year are classified and compared with those of the previous year, in the following table: —

Gross Earnings and Expenses of Operation, 1903 and 1904.

EARNINGS AND EXPENSES.	1903.	1904.	Increase.
Revenue from passengers,	$24,921,452	$25,619,597	$698,145
from mails and merchandise,	82,837	93,344	10,507
from tolls, advertising, etc.,	536,522	494,306	42,216*
Gross earnings from operation,	$25,540,811	$26,207,247	$666,436
Operating expenses,	17,519,367	18,397,291	877,924
Net earnings from operation,	$8,021,444	$7,809,956	$211,488*

* Decrease.

Volume of Traffic.

The total number of passengers carried during the last year on the railways of the one hundred and two companies making returns to the Board was 520,056,511, — an increase of 15,394,268 passengers over the previous year.

The total number of miles run by street cars was 107,897,456, — an increase of 390,644 miles over the previous year.

The following table gives the total volume of traffic, itemized as above, for each of the last ten years: —

Volume of Traffic for Ten Years, 1895–1904.

YEARS.	Total Passengers Carried.	Average Number per Mile of Main Track Operated.	Total Car Miles Run.
1895,	259,794,308	238,963	43,655,560
1896,	292,358,943	226,452	53,613,685
1897,	308,684,224	212,403	61,577,917
1898,	330,889,629	207,982	68,206,418
1899,	356,724,213	205,098	73,367,235
1900,	395,027,198	200,262	81,750,768
1901,	433,526,935	195,683	93,005,225
1902,	465,474,382	188,787	100,280,687
1903,	504,662,243	192,548	107,506,812
1904,	520,056,511	195,917	107,897,456

Earnings and Expenses of Operation.

The following table gives the gross earnings from operation, the operating expenses, the ratio of operating expenses to gross earnings, and the net earnings for each of the last ten years: —

Percentage of Operating Expenses to Gross Earnings, 1895–1904.

YEARS.	Gross Earnings from Operation.	Operating Expenses.	Percentage of Expenses to Earnings.	Net Earnings.
1895,	$13,184,342	$9,088,086	68.93	$4,096,256
1896,	14,844,262	10,563,371	71.16	4,280,891
1897,	15,815,267	10,904,040	68.95	4,911,227
1898,	16,915,405	11,672,731	69.01	5,242,674
1899,	18,151,550	12,378,488	68.20	5,773,062
1900,	19,999,640	13,159,947	65.80	6,839,693
1901,	21,766,340	14,565,141	66.92	7,201,199
1902,	23,486,474	15,912,852	67.75	7,573,622
1903,	25,540,811	17,519,367	68.59	8,021,444
1904,	26,207,247	18,397,291	70.20	7,809,956

The following tables give for each of the last ten years the average gross earnings, operating expenses, and net earnings from operation, (1) per total mile of main track owned, (2) per car mile run and per passenger carried, — thus showing more in detail the changes from year to year in the earnings, cost, and net results of operation.

Gross and Net Earnings from Operation per Mile of Main Track Owned, 1895–1904.

YEARS.	Average per Mile of Track Owned.		
	Gross Earnings.	Expenses of Operation.	Net Earnings.
1895,	$12,127	$8,359	$3,768
1896,	11,627	8,274	3,353
1897,	11,187	7,713	3,474
1898,	10,998	7,589	3,409
1899,	10,459	7,132	3,327
1900,	10,452	6,878	3,574
1901,	9,998	6,690	3,308
1902,	9,609	6,510	3,099
1903,	10,124	6,944	3,180
1904,	10,178	7,145	3,033

Gross and Net Earnings from Operation per Car Mile Run and per Passenger Carried, 1895–1904.

YEARS.	Average per Car Mile.			Average per Passenger.		
	Gross Earnings.	Expenses of Operation.	Net Earnings.	Gross Earnings.	Expenses of Operation.	Net Earnings.
	Cents.	Cents.	Cents.	Cents.	Cents.	Cents.
1895,	30.20	20.82	9.38	5.07	3.50	1.57
1896,	27.69	19.70	7.99	5.08	3.61	1.47
1897,	25.68	17.71	7.97	5.12	3.53	1.59
1898,	24.80	17.11	7.69	5.11	3.52	1.59
1899,	24.74	16.87	7.87	5.09	3.47	1.62
1900,	24.46	16.10	8.36	5.06	3.33	1.73
1901,	23.40	15.66	7.74	5.02	3.36	1.66
1902,	23.42	15.87	7.55	5.05	3.42	1.63
1903,	23.76	16.30	7.46	5.06	3.47	1.59
1904,	24.29	17.05	7.24	5.04	3.54	1.50

Employees and Equipment.

The number of persons employed by the street railway companies, and also the number of cars, vehicles and electric motors owned, are given in the following table for each of the last ten years : —

Employees and Equipment, 1895–1904.

YEARS.	Employees.	Cars.	Other Vehicles.	Electric Motors.
1895, ...	8,048	4,426	1,755	4,704
1896, ...	9,130	4,913	1,876	5,958
1897, ...	9,716	5,344	1,953	6,908
1898, ...	10,416	5,734	1,997	7,643
1899, ...	11,944	6,042	2,076	8,530
1900, ...	12,766	6,531	2,371	9,545
1901, ...	14,749	6,997	2,488	11,284
1902, ...	15,292	7,144	2,577	12,504
1903, ...	15,823	7,403	2,644	13,611
1904, ...	16,519	7,383	2,728	13,870

Street Railway Accidents.

The whole number of persons injured in connection with street railway operation, as reported by the companies for the year ending September 30, 1904, was 5,078, of whom 92 received fatal injuries, and 4,986 injuries not fatal.

The number of passengers injured was 3,372, of whom 21 were injured fatally.

The injuries to employees were 161 in all, 5 of which were fatal.

The number of injuries to travellers and others on the street was 1,545, of which 66 were fatal.

In the following table the accidents of the last year are classified as above, and are compared with those of the previous year: —

Summary of Accidents Reported in 1903 and 1904.

KILLED AND INJURED.	Killed.		Injured.		Totals.	
	1903.	1904.	1903.	1904.	1903.	1904.
Passengers, ...	16	21	2,552	3,351	2,568	3,372
Employees, ...	9	5	152	156	161	161
Other persons, ...	59	66	1,186	1,479	1,245	1,545
Totals, ...	84	92	3,890	4,986	3,974	5,078

From the above table it appears that 5 more passengers, 4 less employees, and 7 more travellers and other persons on the street, received fatal injuries than in 1903.

Of those receiving injuries not fatal, there were reported 799 more passengers, 4 more employees, and 293 more travellers and other persons on the street, than in 1903.

Altogether, there appear to have been injured, fatally and otherwise, 804 more passengers, and 300 more travellers and other persons, — in all 1,104 more, — the last than the preceding year.

Respectfully submitted,

FRED E. JONES,
Statistician.

STREET RAILWAY BRIDGES.

To the Board of Railroad Commissioners, HON. JAMES F. JACKSON, *Chairman.*

GENTLEMEN : — I beg leave to submit the following statement with reference to the street railway bridges in this Commonwealth for the year 1904 : —

There are now 415 bridge spans classified upon our list as street railway bridges, including all bridges which either have been built or are maintained, in whole or in part, by street railway companies and for which they are therefore in some degree responsible. These may be classified as follows : 42 pile bridges, 28 wooden trestles, 10 steel trestles, 40 wooden stringers, 4 braced or trussed wooden stringers, 4 wooden trusses, 6 stone or brick arches, 106 I-beams, 83 plate girders, 76 riveted trusses, 12 pin connected trusses, and 4 movable bridges.

Since last year several bridges hitherto classified as street railway bridges have been removed from the list, either because they have been abandoned or because they have been found to be not properly street railway bridges. On the other hand a number of new bridges have been constructed.

The following table gives a comparison of the bridge work for which plans have been finally approved and the structures completed, as compared with the work done during 1903 : —

Comparison of Bridge Work Done during the Years 1903 and 1904.

YEAR.	NEW SPANS ON THE LIST.			SPANS REBUILT.			SPANS STRENGTHENED.		
	Wood.	Stone.	Metal.	Wood.	Stone.	Metal.	Wood.	Stone.	Metal.
1903, ...	6	1[1]	15[2]	7[3]	–	4	–	–	1
1904, ...	4	–	21[4]	–	–	1	–	–	7[5]

[1] Old highway bridge replaced. [2] Including 1 old highway bridge replaced.

[3] 1 as an arch, 6 replaced by 12 metal.

[4] Including 9 highway bridge spans strengthened for the first time, and therefore new on the list.

[5] Including 6 highway bridge spans.

It was observed last year that the construction of new bridges had proceeded less rapidly than during 1902, the number of new bridges built in 1902 being less than in 1901. A further reduction in number is apparent this year, there having been 16 new bridges built in 1904 as against 20 in 1903, excluding in each case highway bridges which have been strengthened, and thus appear on our list for the first time, though not new structures. The new bridges built have generally been built strictly according to the specifications recently approved by the Board, although in a few instances some variation has been allowed, either because of local conditions or because the street railway company desired to have the structure approved for lighter cars than those adopted in the specifications of the Board.

The following table gives the length of bridges of different materials at the present time as compared with corresponding figures of a year ago: —

	1903.	1904.
	Feet.	Feet.
Length of wooden bridges,	24,105	23,393
Length of stone bridges,	244	244
Length of metal bridges,	16,584	17,826

It will be noted that the length of wooden bridges has slightly decreased, the length of stone bridges has remained the same, while the length of metal bridges has somewhat increased, owing to the replacing of several wooden bridges with metal and to the building of a number of new metal bridges, as noted in the previous table.

The following is a summary of the work done during the past year on each of the different street railways in the state: —

On the Boston & Northern street railway one new riveted truss has been built, carrying a highway as well as the street railway, two plate girder spans have been rebuilt, two plate girder spans and one I-beam have been strengthened, and one old plate girder has been rebuilt as two plate girder spans. All of these bridges which have been rebuilt or strengthened carry a highway as well as the street railway.

On the Boston & Worcester street railway a new track has been laid over one of the plate girder spans, requiring the construction of a new structure for this track.

On the Greenfield, Deerfield & Northampton street railway one new plate girder span has been built.

On the Hoosac Valley street railway one plate girder span has been rebuilt and three new I-beam spans have been built.

On the Lexington & Boston street railway two I-beam bridges have been omitted from the list of last year, having been considered to be state highway bridges.

On the Leominster, Shirley & Ayer street railway four new plate girder spans, one new steel trestle and one new I-beam span have been built, and one I-beam span carrying a highway has been strengthened.

On the Pittsfield street railway one new plate girder bridge has been built and one existing highway bridge strengthened.

On the Springfield street railway one plate girder span has been repaired and the long bridge across the Connecticut river, known as the North End bridge, has been materially strengthened in the floor.

On the Worcester & Holden street railway four spans of wooden stringers on concrete piers have been built.

The work of inspecting all the street railways of the state, with the object of making a list and gaining necessary information regarding every bridge, whether classified as a street railway bridge or not, has been continued but is not yet completed. In the course of this work several city, town or county bridges have been found to be seriously defective, either from lack of strength or through poor condition. This calls attention to the fact that while the Board has power to make recommendations regarding any structure over which a street railway passes, or to prohibit running over such a structure if it is dangerous, provided its condition becomes known, the law does not provide specific means for ascertaining the condition of such structures or for ensuring their being maintained in good condition. Requests have, in a number of cases, been made of towns or steam railroad companies for plans of such structures which are under their jurisdiction but over which street railways run. It is hoped in time to collect this information regarding every such bridge.

Respectfully submitted,

GEO. F. SWAIN,
Bridge Engineer.

Issues of Stock and Bonds.

The following tables show the issues of street railway stock and bonds authorized and approved during the year ending December 31, 1904: —

Issues of Capital Stock.

RAILWAY COMPANIES.	Date when Authorized.	Amount Authorized.
Berkshire,	April 20,	$200,000
Boston & Worcester,	April 21,	100,000
Boston & Worcester,	November 2,	160,000
Conway Electric,	September 6,	64,000
Dedham & Franklin,	October 28,	75,000
Hampshire,*	July 29,	60,000
Hoosac Valley,	July 13,	100,000
Lawrence & Methuen,	February 25,	25,000
Leominster, Shirley & Ayer,	November 9,	100,000
Martha's Vineyard,†	October 1,	8,000
Pittsfield Electric,	September 16,	100,000
Templeton,	June 20,	50,000
Waltham,	July 19,	40,000
West End,	July 27,	150,000
Worcester & Holden,	December 14,	25,000

* On the petition of this company, its capital stock as fixed in its agreement of association was reduced from $100,000 to $60,000.

† On the petition of this company, its capital stock as fixed in its agreement of association was reduced from $12,000 to $8,000.

NOTE. — Issues of capital stock for the purposes of consolidation will be found in the Appendix.

Issues of Bonds.

RAILWAY COMPANIES.	Date when Authorized	Amount Authorized.
Amherst & Sunderland,	January 1,	$117,000
Berkshire,	November 22,	200,000
Blue Hill,	May 4,	50,000
Boston & Northern,	June 21,	9,660,000
Boston & Worcester,	April 21,	200,000
Boston & Worcester,	November 21,	160,000
Conway Electric,	July 13,	35,000
Haverhill & Southern New Hampshire,	February 25,	80,000
Hoosac Valley,	July 13,	400,000

Issues of Bonds — Concluded.

RAILWAY COMPANIES.	Date when Authorized.	Amount Authorized.
Lawrence & Methuen,	February 25,	$125,000
Leominster, Shirley & Ayer,	December 23,	100,000
Lowell & Pelham,	February 25,	40,000
Newton,	June 9,	250,000
Old Colony,	June 21,	6,812,000
West End,	September 1,	750,000
Worcester & Holden,	March 29,	25,000
Worcester & Shrewsbury Railroad,	December 21,	22,000

JAMES F. JACKSON,
GEORGE W. BISHOP,
CLINTON WHITE,
Commissioners.

APPENDIX.

APPENDIX.

ORDERS RELATING TO RAILROADS AND STREET RAILWAYS.

FARES AND SERVICE.

Complaint of John J. Fox and others concerning the service on the Abington, Rockland and Whitman line of the Old Colony street railway.

J. J. Fox for petitioners.

B. W. Warren for company.

Two charges are brought against the company, one of overcrowding cars, the other of irregularity in the running of cars.

Although it is shown that frequently, if not generally, some of the passengers who take cars late in the afternoon have to stand in the aisle, yet it would appear that there is sufficient room for them to stand apart and to permit the conductor to pass through the car without embarrassment. We do not consider that these facts make out a case of overcrowding.

The evidence proves that during January and February delays of from ten to fifteen minutes were common, and that there have been occasional delays for thirty minutes and even longer. This is so largely attributable to the unprecedented weather conditions that we cannot hold the company accountable for the discomfort experienced by its patrons. It is notorious that from the conditions which have followed the storms of this winter and have continued while streets have been filled upon the sides of the railway with snow and ice, the regular running of cars has been seriously interrupted. The drifting of the snow and the alternate melting and freezing of the snow and ice, the natural use of the railway in heavy teaming as the cleared part of the highway, have made it impossible to operate railways with the usual regularity. The extent and effect of these interruptions is not always understood by those who are feeling the annoyance of the delays in the failure to reach their destination upon schedule time.

The complaint is supported by a written communication numerously signed, while on the other hand the company presents a written endorsement of its position signed by selectmen and other representative citizens.

The complainants admit that during the last ten days the service has been satisfactory. We shall expect it to continue so.

JAMES F. JACKSON,
GEORGE W. BISHOP,
CLINTON WHITE,
Commissioners.

MARCH 25, 1904. [5445]

Complaint of the selectmen of Amesbury concerning operation of the Citizens' Electric and other street railways.

The recent collision between public officials of Amesbury and the street railway companies, owing to differences of opinion in regard to the removal of snow, the use of salt and a discontinuance of one of the tracks in Main street, presents questions which we consider in the order in which they have been named.

(1) Section 41, chapter 112, Revised Laws, requires companies to remove snow from their tracks "in such manner as may be approved by the superintendent of streets." This means something more than running a plow over the railway and throwing the snow upon the sides of the street. It contemplates an arrangement between the company and the town under which the two can work together and promptly make the public ways convenient for all classes of travel. An arrangement providing a method for doing the work with a fair distribution of the cost ought to be readily made.

(2) The indiscriminate use of salt upon street railways to relieve tracks from snow and ice is a public nuisance, producing results which are not only an annoyance, but a menace to health. On the other hand, a moderate use of salt upon frogs and switches and upon heavy grades or sharp curves is justified as a measure for the protection of those who travel upon railways. This restricted use we approve; any larger use we condemn.

(3) The selectmen insist that during the winter months only one of the tracks in Main street should be open to use; an understanding to this effect was in force for several years.

Main street is a much used thoroughfare and not very wide. While it is true that the accumulation of snow and ice upon the sides of this street may become the occasion of accident, this danger can be largely averted, if not wholly eliminated, by co-operation between the town and the company in clearing away the snow after a storm. On the other hand, the use of double tracks instead of a single track where cars are run in opposite directions is always to be encouraged, for the reason that in preventing collisions it promotes safety and in preventing delays it promotes regularity in the operation of the railway.

Under the circumstances we are unwilling to establish a precedent for the discontinuance of a double track service.

JAMES F. JACKSON,
GEORGE W. BISHOP,
CLINTON WHITE,
Commissioners.

FEBRUARY 15, 1904. [5425]

Complaint of the selectmen of Bedford and citizens of Billerica and Woburn concerning fares on the Lexington and Boston street railway.

E. G. LOOMIS for town of Bedford.

F. A. FISHER for town of Billerica.

C. A. HIGHT for company.

The Lexington and Boston street railway was opened to use in 1900. The arrangement as to fares between the company and the several towns through which it passes provided for five-cent fares both within town boundaries and between town centres.

The consequent overlapping of fare limits has led to confused ideas among passengers as to their rights and has made it extremely difficult, and in fact often impossible, to collect the fares to which the company was entitled. The public has thus been annoyed and the company unable to obtain a fair return for the service rendered. As a remedy for this condition of things, the company recently re-arranged its fare limits, preserving the five-cent rate within towns and disregarding that between town centres. Those who in consequence of this change now have to pay ten cents, where they formerly paid five cents, complain that the new rate is unreasonable.

In view of all the circumstances, including the assurances given the selectmen upon the strength of which locations were granted, we believe the complaint well grounded. Holding this opinion, the Board suggested at the first hearing that some system of fares by tickets, or otherwise, be adopted, which would practically secure the concessions promised for local travel and yet enable the company to collect its regular and proper charges from those who used its lines.

A plan for accomplishing this end has now been presented which we think ought to be given a trial. It involves the issue of tickets, irredeemable but good until used, which will give to rightful holders the benefit of the old five-cent fare between centres. Experience will test the merit of the new arrangement.

JAMES F. JACKSON,
GEORGE W. BISHOP,
CLINTON WHITE,
Commissioners.

July 12, 1904. [5521]

Complaint of the mayor and other citizens of Beverly concerning service and fares upon the Boston and Northern street railway.

Albert Boyden for city.

B. W. Warren for company.

The far reaching consequences of the winter's storms and cold in their effect upon street railways have not been always understood. During and immediately after a storm the difficulties in operating a railway are apparent. It has not been so plain why delays in the service and the use of old and worn out cars should follow these storms for days and weeks. The truth is that the attempt to maintain a service during the intense cold, and while streets were banked with snow and ice, has been accompanied by extraordinary strain and wear and tear upon the car equipment. In Beverly and in other places the damage done to the equipment has continually thrown cars out of commission and made it necessary to draw not only upon the usual reserve supply, but to bring into use cars which were not in fit condition for satisfactory service. The company has wisely felt that it was better to bring out everything that could be employed in maintaining a service of some sort, rather than to give up altogether the attempt to operate its lines.

Obviously, the annoyances recently experienced in Beverly are attributable in large degree to unexpected conditions for which the company was not prepared.

But apart from all that relates to the past winter, it is evident that the railway track should be reconstructed in certain places and that there should be a substantial improvement in respect to supply of power. We have reason to believe that these changes will be carried into effect at a reasonably near day.

We understand that an arrangement for the running of a through car to Salem Willows has already been made.

JAMES F. JACKSON,
GEORGE W. BISHOP,
CLINTON WHITE,
Commissioners.

April 22, 1904. [5456]

Complaint of residents of West Roxbury relative to half fares for school children upon the Boston Elevated railway.

J. P. Nickerson for petitioners.

Section 72, chapter 112, Revised Laws, originally chapter 197, Acts of 1900, provides that "the rates of fare charged by street or elevated railway companies for the transportation of pupils of the public schools between a given point, from or to which it is necessary for them to ride in travelling to or from the school houses in which they attend school and their homes, whether such school houses are located in the city or town in which the pupils reside or in another city or town, shall not exceed one-half the regular fare charged by such street or elevated railway company for the transportation of other passengers between said points."

The complainants contend that this statute applies to the Boston Elevated Railway Company in operating that part of the Old Colony street railway which it leased under the authority of chapter 388, Acts of 1902.

Their contention is that section 10, chapter 500, Acts of 1897, which exempts the Boston Elevated Railway Company from any reduction in its five-cent fare for a period of twenty-five years upon any of the lines "owned, leased or operated by it", does not relieve it from the general law above quoted, for the reason that this general law had imposed upon the railway leased a "burden, duty or obligation" within the later language of the same section, which is as follows: —

During said period of twenty-five years no taxes or excises not at present in fact imposed upon street railways shall be imposed in respect of the lines owned, leased or operated by said corporation, other than such as may have been in fact imposed upon the lines hereafter leased or operated by it at the date of such operating contract or of such lease or agreement hereafter made therefor, nor any other burden, duty or obligation which is not at the same time imposed by general law on all street railway companies.

To our minds, however, the Legislature intended to deal exhaustively with the question of fares in the earlier part of the section, and in the later provision as to "other burden, duty or obligation" had in contemplation matters other than fares.

The original act relative to pupils attending public schools expressly excepted the Boston Elevated Railway Company. It is true that the words "roads now owned, leased or operated" were added, but these words are to be treated as a further amplification of the field covered by the exemption rather than as a limitation of the privilege expressly given in the preceding phrase.

If this view of the law is wrong, the error can be readily remedied through a criminal prosecution of the company for violation of the statute.

By the Board,

JAMES F. JACKSON.
Chairman.

MAY 4, 1904. [5436]

Complaint of James L. Bowlby, president, and Luke Hillard, secretary of the Master Teamsters' Association, concerning methods in force in receiving and delivering freight at railroad terminals.

The complainants ask that the following changes be inaugurated in connection with the receipt and delivery of freight at Boston railroad terminals:

"That freight on any one load going to any one house shall all be promptly and properly received at any one designated door of said freight house.

"That all freight delivered by the corporation to us from any freight house shall be promptly and properly brought to any one designated door of said house.

"That notifications of arrival of freight shall not be issued until the proper bills and checks for getting same have been placed in the hands of the cashier, correctly marked as to location of goods; and if house freight, the house and door shall be specified, if track delivery freight, the specific track shall be shown.

"That all receipts for goods delivered to said corporations shall be signed as soon as proper delivery of same has been effected."

We cannot recommend the adoption of the first two suggestions. Companies ought to have the right, within reasonable bounds, to designate the different doors at which goods to be carried to different points shall be delivered. This is in the interest of a prompt and efficient service, enabling a company to properly prepare and station its cars in readiness to receive freight. The rule, however, should be given some elasticity, and not be strictly enforced in instances where some variation from it will save shippers annoyance and loss of time without appreciably inconveniencing the companies.

Companies can fairly be asked, when unloading cars, to so separate from other freight that which belongs to the particular consignee as to make it possible for him to find and take his goods without unreasonable delay or inconvenience. Teamsters ought not to be required to sort freight in the effort to pick out that which belongs to those whom they represent. On the other hand, companies ought not to be required to sort freight arriving from different points for the same consignee and to place it ready for delivery at a particular door. Co-operation on the part of employees is of the utmost importance for the saving of time and labor and is something which it is in the interest of all parties to promote.

We are of the opinion that the last two requests ought to be granted. Notice of the arrival of freight should be given seasonably; but undue haste in giving it is unnecessary loss to somebody when, as the result, a consignee in promptly responding to it finds the company unprepared to deliver the goods.

Delivery checks should contain a designation of door if house freight, and of track if bulk freight.

In all ordinary cases receipts for goods delivered should be promptly given, and not delayed to meet the convenience of the companies or their employees.

The methods heretofore pursued upon different roads are not the same and have not been made the subject of equal criticism. It is also true that since the hearing measures have been taken to remedy, to some extent, conditions which were the ground of complaint.

JAMES F. JACKSON,
GEORGE W. BISHOP,
CLINTON WHITE,
Commissioners.

JULY 12, 1904. [5455]

Complaint of the mayor and aldermen of Haverhill concerning fares upon the Haverhill and Southern New Hampshire street railway.

E. S. ABBOTT for city.

E. B. FULLER for company.

The Haverhill and Southern New Hampshire street railway has been in operation about two years. The company secured from the board of aldermen of Haverhill a location in that city, offering as an inducement therefor a five-cent fare within the city limits. This arrangement as to fare was made one of the conditions of the grant of location.

In the recent case of Keefe against the Lexington and Boston Street Railway Company it is decided that a condition in a street railway location which purports to establish fares is not legally binding upon the company, as boards of aldermen and selectmen under existing statutes have no authority to regulate fares upon street railways.

The Haverhill and Southern New Hampshire company has now raised its fares and among other changes has increased the charge between Haverhill square and Ayer's Village from five to ten cents. It is contended that under the old rates the company has been unable to operate its railway at a profit.

In establishing the new fare limits the company has carried out a sort of mileage basis for rates, claiming that between three and four miles is as far as it ought to carry a passenger for five cents. This theory overthrows the commonly recognized rule of fixing fare limits with reference to points where patrons regularly take or leave the cars in large numbers. We doubt the wisdom of the change, as we believe that the interests of the public, and in the end those of the company, will be better served by adherence to the theory that fare limits should be governed by the location of communities rather than by exact distances.

The Haverhill and Southern New Hampshire street railway is part of a system controlled by companies having a separate corporate existence but a common ownership of stock and a common management. An examination of conditions of traffic upon all parts of this system is therefore pertinent to the decision of the question presented here. If we assume that these companies may rightfully undertake to increase their receipts in some way we are not satisfied that the ten-cent fare between Haverhill square and Ayer's Village is justifiable. Haverhill square is about five miles from Ayer's Village, and both places are in the city of Haverhill. The new fare of ten cents between these two points makes the rate about two cents per mile, which is higher than suburban rates upon steam railroads.

Nor is a ten-cent fare between these two points a reasonable charge when compared with other fares in force upon street railways under conditions which permit some measure of comparison.

Boards of aldermen and selectmen in granting street railway locations naturally inquire into the purposes of those who seek to obtain them. If at such a time, instead of relying upon its right to leave fares to future determination as to what may prove to be reasonable charges, a company chooses to pledge itself to specific rates, its failure to realize at once the expected profit from the undertaking would hardly justify the establishment of a higher rate in violation of the assurances given. Relying upon these assurances, not only may the public authorities have been induced to grant rights in the streets in the expectation of relieving congested city and town centres by a better distribution of homes, but individuals, in many instances in considerable numbers, may have been led to change their places of residence and mode of life.

We are of the opinion that the increase in fare between Haverhill square and Ayer's Village imposes a disproportionate burden upon that part of the travelling public which is required to pay it, and for that reason a lower charge must be recommended.

JAMES F. JACKSON,
GEORGE W. BISHOP,
CLINTON WHITE,
Commissioners.

June 27, 1904. [5529]

Complaint of the selectmen of Hull concerning fares and service upon the Old Colony street railway.

J. O. Burdett for town.

B. W. Warren for company.

Three complaints are made, one alleging insufficiency of power, another annoying delays and the third unreasonable charges.

As to the power plant of the company, it is enough to say that the need of changes is admitted, and that the necessary improvements are now under way.

The annoyance at certain times from delays upon sidings can be largely, if not wholly, eliminated by the action of the public authorities in enabling the company to establish different division lines.

The company in its statement at the hearing has now agreed to restore the five-cent fare enjoyed before the recent change in rates.

We find no ground for any further action at the present time.

JAMES F. JACKSON,
GEORGE W. BISHOP,
CLINTON WHITE,
Commissioners.

July 12, 1904. [5550]

Complaint of the selectmen of Marion, Mattapoisett and Wareham concerning fares on the New Bedford and Onset street railway.

Henry H. Crapo for company.

When the New Bedford and Onset Street Railway Company was seeking locations in Marion, Mattapoisett and Wareham, the management was very sanguine in regard to the prospective business of the company and assured the selectmen that certain low fares would undoubtedly be established. The selectmen made these fares a part of the grants of location, and they were afterward duly put in force by the company and were maintained until last June, when a general increase in charges went into effect. The selectmen and patrons of the railway now complain that this increase in fares is unwarranted.

Our Supreme Court has decided that selectmen have no authority over fares upon street railways, and that the acceptance of a location which purports to fix them does not create any contract between the company and the town.

There are two ways in which to deal with a company which fails to render to the public a proper service in respect to either accommodations or fares: one through the exercise of the power to revoke locations, a power to be used in the first instance by local boards; the other through the exercise of the authority of this Board in such matters. The first is a drastic remedy, but the right remedy when promoters of a railway have been guilty of bad faith in securing a location or in attempting to hold one in defiance of the obligations which attach to it.

Usually the arrangement between a town board and a company in respect to fares has been only an incident of the location, and if the fares agreed upon have proved too low to permit the payment of dividends it has demonstrated lack of foresight rather than the practice of fraud on the part of the company. In such cases it is clearly better for all concerned that some equitable rearrangement of fares take place than that a company lose its property and the people their facilities for travel.

The jurisdiction of this Board is clearly defined. The question can only be whether or not an existing fare is reasonable, but the promise of a company to maintain certain fares has more or less bearing upon the reasonableness of a subsequent charge. Full dividends are not ordinarily expected in the first days of any enterprise. There is a period of experiment which precedes that of the "going concern". When a company before opening its railway pledges itself to specific fares it may rightly be asked to experiment with such fares a reasonable length of time, even though stockholders must meanwhile go without dividends for a longer period than would have been necessary had no pledges been given. It is a risk which the stockholders fairly take in authorizing these pledges.

The selectmen of Marion, Mattapoisett and Wareham, who were promised certain fares which have recently been withdrawn, properly request that a careful examination of the affairs of the company be made, and rightfully claim that the public ought not to bear the burden of the increase in rates unless it is made to appear that such increase is just.

The New Bedford and Onset street railway was opened in August, 1901. An examination of the receipts and expenditures of the company shows that its earnings for the first fourteen months were $2357.10 less than its expenses; that its net earnings for the year ending September 30, 1903, with no charge for depreciation of property, were $8182.82; and that the net earnings for the year ending September 30, 1904, with no charge for depreciation of property, were $3358.57. No dividends have been paid to shareholders.

The capital stock of the company is $500,000 and its bonded indebtedness is $280,000. When this stock and bond issue was under consideration, the Board made a minute inquiry into the cost of the railway. It was found that the work of construction had been of a high standard and that in consequence the company had an excellent roadbed and overhead equipment, with rolling stock of most modern type. A complete signal system has since been installed. The power plant was larger than necessary to supply this railway with power, and had been erected with a view to selling power to what was then and is still a connecting railway. We do not hesitate to say that if the recent increase in fares was made in order to secure a return upon any unnecessary investment in power plant, or to make good a loss in rental of surplus power, or to recoup unnecessary expense in operating this power plant, we should deem the increase in fares unreasonable. After careful examination, however, we do not find that this change in fares was made in order to meet any such loss or expense or to pay dividends upon such investment.

An unusual item of expense in construction was the large outlay for street improvements, particularly in one of the towns in which locations were obtained. To the extent that changes in or additions to highways are made necessary in order to accommodate a street railway, it is clearly right that the company should pay the cost. To compel a company, however, to meet the whole expense of a new highway which is to be built for the use of the general public as well as that of the railway is a questionable policy. To say nothing of the consequent unequal distribution of advantages and disadvantages between different towns, it is to be borne in mind that the travelling public must contribute in fares to dividends on the capital invested in this added cost of the railway.

In June last, when fares were advanced, this railway, at the end of substantially three years of continuous operation, had earned, when proper charges for depreciation are taken into account, practically nothing for stockholders, who were then facing a probable loss of capital in a deficit for the year now closed. Under all the circumstances we believe it would be unfair to recommend that the company at this time return to the old fares.

Independent of the assurances given before the railway was built, there can be no question but that the existing fares are within the bounds of what are reasonable charges. In fact the experience thus far had with them points to a yet distant day for the payment of dividends. The problem of the near future would still seem to be one of maintenance of property. Should it prove otherwise, and the business of the company in the future warrant a return to lower fares, the result of the present inquiry will in no way prejudice the complainants in renewing their petition.

In the meantime such concessions as may be made by way of excursion rates should be given without discrimination against communities and all reasonable accommodation should be furnished in respect to the number and running time of cars. We understand that since the hearing some changes have been made in the car service to meet the suggestions of selectmen.

JAMES F. JACKSON,
GEORGE W. BISHOP,
CLINTON WHITE,
Commissioners.

NOVEMBER 11, 1904. [5624]

Complaints of residents of Nantucket and of Dukes County concerning the rates charged and the service rendered by the New Bedford, Martha's Vineyard and Nantucket Steamboat Company.

A. H. GARDNER for Town of Nantucket.

H. N. HINCKLEY for Town of Tisbury.

G. W. ELDREDGE for Vineyard Haven.

C. W. CLIFFORD for company.

These complaints were brought under chapter 173, Acts of 1903, which read as follows:

The board of railroad commissioners is hereby empowered and directed to perform the same duties in respect to regulating the rates for transporting freight or passengers charged by steamship companies that serve as common carriers throughout the year between two or more ports in this commonwealth, which the said board is now or may hereafter be empowered to perform in the case of railroads and railways.

Section 2, chapter 1, Revised Laws, reads in part:

The sovereignty and jurisdiction of the commonwealth extend to all places within the boundaries thereof, subject to the concurrent jurisdiction granted over places ceded to the United States.

Section 3 reads:

The territorial limits of this commonwealth extend one marine league from its sea shore at extreme low water mark. If an inlet or arm of the sea does not exceed two marine leagues in width between its headlands, a straight line from one headland to the other is equivalent to the shore line.

As the distance between headlands on the mainland and on Nantucket considerably exceeds two marine leagues, the statute above quoted excludes from the domain upon the seacoast over which the state exercises sovereignty a portion of the waters which lie between Nantucket and the mainland, such waters belonging to the high or open sea.

Trade between New Bedford and Nantucket may suggest domestic rather than foreign commerce, even though the voyage be for a part of the way upon waters outside the territory of Massachusetts. But the decisions of the Supreme Court of the United States establish the principle that state jurisdiction over commerce is confined to cases where not only the termini but the entire route covered by the shipment is within the state territory. The railroad commission of Arkansas attempted to regulate a rate for the shipment of goods between two towns in that state. The line of railroad over which these goods were carried ran from Arkansas into the Indian Territory and thence back into Arkansas to the point of destination. It was held that although the places of shipment and delivery were both in Arkansas, the state railroad commission had no power to regulate the rate.

Hanley v. Kansas City Southern Ry. Co., 187 U. S. 617.

Mr. Justice Holmes, in the opinion, referring to transportation by water, says:

> It is decided that navigation on the high seas between ports of the same state is subject to regulation by Congress and is not subject to regulation by the state.

Mr. Justice Field, in an earlier case, says:

> To bring the transportation within the control of the state as part of its domestic commerce the subject transported must be within the entire voyage under the exclusive jurisdiction of the state.

Pacific Coast S. S. Co. v. Railroad Commissioners, 9 Sawyer, 255.

The law therefore is definitely settled with regard both to land and water transportation.

The direct steamship route to Nantucket and that ordinarily, if not necessarily, adopted lies for a part of the way upon the high sea, beyond the jurisdiction of Massachusetts as defined by the legislature, and where the national authority is exclusive. It is clear therefore that the Board cannot supervise steamship rates or service between New Bedford or Woods Hole and Nantucket.

This construction of chapter 173, Acts of 1903, assumes it to be valid and applies its provisions according to the rule established by legislative act and judicial decision. The conclusions reached do not in any way touch upon the power of the legislature to amend or repeal the charter of a company incorporated in this state.

The authority of the Board over the running of steamboats on the Lord's day, to which reference has been made, rests upon the police power of the state over waters within its territorial limits, and any conditions in such licenses which attempt to govern the service outside the state limits are significant only as the basis of an understanding upon the violation of which the license may be revoked.

The steamship company further contends that Massachusetts has no power to regulate commerce upon Buzzards Bay or Vineyard Sound, even though it be carried on wholly within the state boundaries.

We do not understand this to be the law, and rule that although Buzzards Bay and Vineyard Sound do connect with and form a part of the highways used in commerce between the states and with foreign countries, and are therefore subject to all acts of Congress which regulate such commerce and protect navigation, these waters are nevertheless a part of the state domain, and subject to the laws of Massachusetts in so far as such laws do not interfere with the actual exercise of the national authority.

The regulation of rates and fares charged upon steamships plying between ports within these waters in the conduct of a purely domestic trade we assume to be within the power of the legislature, and chapter 173, Acts of 1903, is an exercise of this power.

The Board will therefore upon request consider any question of charges made by this company in transporting passengers or freight between New Bedford, Woods Hole and Martha's Vineyard.

JAMES F. JACKSON,
GEORGE W. BISHOP,
CLINTON WHITE,
Commissioners.

MARCH 30, 1904. [5386-5440]

Petition of the Newton and Boston Street Railway Company for consent to withdrawal of transfers.

Petition of D. Frank Lord and others for restoration of service upon the Newton and Boston street railway.

W. H. COOLIDGE, C. A. HIGHT for company.

W. S. SLOCUM for City of Newton.

C. E. STEARNS for City of Waltham.

D. E. DOW for Needham citizens.

Two petitions are before us, one by the company for authority to withdraw transfers, the other by patrons for the restoration of service.

The first is a proceeding under section 74, chapter 112, Revised Laws, which provides that "no corporation which operates a street railway shall withdraw or discontinue the use of transfers from one car or line of cars to another without the approval of the Board." It is doubtful whether this statute applies to the transfers in question here, and there are, besides, other possible complications connected with their proposed withdrawal; but, as this seems to have been the wish of parties, we have treated the situation as one in which our decision might have a practical value.

That the public can only be well served when the company which serves it is able to realize a reasonable return upon the capital honestly invested, is too plain a truth to need discussion.

A voluntary association, the Boston and Suburban Electric Company, holds as a stockholder the controlling interest in the Newton and Boston and the Newton companies and in other properties. What those who are thus associated do with the dividends which they receive from their shares in railway stocks or what value they place upon such shares is of no more importance to those who use these railways and pay the fares which support them than if the controlling stockholder were an individual. The Board deals only with the capitalization of the railway companies, their methods of constructing, maintaining and operating their railways, and the corporate receipts and expenditures. That a common ownership and management makes the several Newton railways to all intents and purposes parts of one local system, is a fact to be given due weight.

The Newton and Boston company was incorporated under the general law in 1892. The original location, granted in December, 1891, extended from Newtonville to Newton Centre. In May, 1892, the company was given an extension of location to Newton Highlands and Newton Upper Falls. A location in Needham was secured later. In November, 1897, the company leased the Newtonville and Watertown railway, thus increasing the mileage of track operated to about twelve miles.

The number of passengers carried upon the Newton and Boston railway in 1898 was 1,163,232. Of these nineteen per cent were carried upon transfers. In 1903, the number of passengers carried was 1,689,292. Of these more than one half used transfers, thus paying half fare. This half fare covered a possible ride of four and a half miles in one direction and six and a half miles in the other.

The company has paid dividends in four years only, viz., in 1896 to 1899 inclusive, the total amount thus distributed being $16,812.50. No one of these dividends should have been paid, as the money ought to have been applied to the maintenance of the property.

If we were to fix the exact amount of the yearly losses which the company appears to have sustained, it would be necessary to rearrange the figures given at the hearing and to criticise the fact that the cost of power charged against itself has been greater than that charged by it against the companies which it has supplied with power. But it is enough for present purposes that, making all allowances for overcharges or changes in accounts, the company since 1899 has unquestionably met with a heavy annual loss in operation which has impaired its assets to the extent of one hundred twenty-five thousand dollars. Such a state of affairs cannot continue. Were every debt wiped out no one would take the property as a gift, provided the railway is to be run in the future under like conditions with those of the past.

An appraisal shows that the railway has a replacement value of between $450,000 and $500,000. The outstanding capital stock of the company amounts to $200,000 and the outstanding bonds to $200,000. The floating indebtedness is $285,000. This indebtedness includes the operating losses and certain expenses of construction which cannot now be properly capitalized, the two constituting the impairment of the property.

We have determined to approve a withdrawal of transfers upon this railway for a limited period as an experimental measure, with the understanding that during such period no dividends shall be paid, and that net earnings, should there be any, shall be devoted to the reduction of the floating indebtedness of the company.

As the withdrawal of these transfers will not only benefit the Newton and Boston but as well the Newton company, with which they are exchanged, we have considered the extent to which that company will be benefited thereby, and are convinced that, taking the most sanguine view of any resulting increase in earnings, there need be no fear that such increase will bring to the stockholders of the Newton company any more than a reasonable return upon its proper capitalization.

The period for which the Board consents to a withdrawal of transfers upon the Newton and Boston street railway, other than those between its own cars and lines, is that ending September 30, 1905. The Board will then review the questions now presented in the light of the experience thus gained, with the purpose of recommending such action as will give to the company an opportunity to operate the railway under reasonable conditions and secure to the public full protection of rights and privileges.

The second of the two petitions relates to the action of the company in changing its schedule from twenty to thirty-minute time. This change was made as another measure of retrenchment.

During a part of the day the light travel justifies this arrangement, but at other times we think that a better service should be given. Accommodation in car service is paramount to the question of fares, and we recommend that the company provide a more frequent service through the busy hours of travel in the morning and in the evening. Something more than a mere restoration of the former service might well be given during this part of the day.

JAMES F. JACKSON,
GEORGE W. BISHOP,
CLINTON WHITE,
Commissioners.

MAY 25, 1904. [5424—5427]

Complaint of the selectmen of North Brookfield concerning service upon the Warren, Brookfield and Spencer street railway.

The Warren, Brookfield and Spencer street railway was opened to the public June 26, 1896. The largest dividend that the company has paid in any year is four per cent. In 1897, 1898, 1902 and 1903 it paid no dividend.

Were the question one of fares, the Board would agree that the financial condition of the company prohibited any reduction in revenue. So too if the question were one of providing any kind of convenience which prosperous companies might well be asked to supply but which is not absolutely necessary to comfort in travel.

That a company is entitled to a fair return upon actual investment is a rule so often announced as to have become somewhat stale in the statement. It is a pertinent query, however, to what extent a company can inaugurate a public service and then because it proves to have weak earning capacity for that reason impose upon the public an inefficient conduct of the business. It is clear that everything absolutely essential to safety and ordinary comfort in travel should be provided, even though the entire earnings are exhausted in the effort. To this extent the investor and not the public must take the chances of the enterprise. But there are cases where the proper carrying out of the undertaking not only fails to return dividends, but risks the principal which has been invested. In such instances, the uninviting suggestion of a receivership promises nothing but a second receivership a little later on. Practically one of three things must happen. The service must be abandoned altogether, or the public must accept something less than satisfactory only because it is better than nothing, or fares must be raised to provide the income necessary to furnish proper accommodations.

The case in hand comes near presenting a situation of this kind. Two cars are run between North Brookfield and Spencer in the morning and at night. These cars are overcrowded, and this means the daily discomfort and inconvenience of patrons. The only remedy is an additional car or the substitution of a larger car for that now in use. The number of people who find the railway a convenience, notwithstanding the overcrowding, makes it undesirable from every standpoint that the service be abandoned. Can the company reasonably be asked to provide either an additional car or a larger car without increasing its fares? While it may not be clear that the necessary outlay would be immediately offset by additional revenue, we seriously doubt whether in the end it would work any invasion of the earnings of the company. We therefore recommend that relief be furnished to the petitioners in one of these two ways. Should the result be an operating loss, the matter can be heard again in the light of the suggestions above named.

JAMES F. JACKSON,
GEORGE W. BISHOP,
CLINTON WHITE,
Commissioners.

JANUARY 14, 1904. [5371]

Petition of the selectmen of Southampton relative to service on the Northampton division of the New York, New Haven and Hartford railroad.

H. P. MOSELEY for petitioners.

J. H. BENTON, JR., for company.

Under a recent order the New York, New Haven and Hartford Railroad Company discontinued, among other trains, that which had been leaving Northampton at 6.44 A.M., arriving at Westfield at 7.12 A.M., and returning had left Westfield at 7.25 A.M., arriving at Northampton at 7.45 A. M.

The record of this train shows that owing to the small number of passengers carried it had been run for a long time at a daily loss. This was undoubtedly the reason of its discontinuance.

But the train cannot be treated as independent of the rest of the system with which it forms a connecting link. The fact, too, that its patrons, among whom are quite a number of pupils in regular attendance upon schools at a distance from their homes, are necessarily dependent upon it for transportation, has a material bearing upon the case.

Clearly, without reference to any question under the lease, the train is to be considered as a part of the general service of the company which ought not to be withdrawn, and we are therefore gratified to learn that following the hearing it has been restored.

JAMES F. JACKSON,
GEO. W. BISHOP,
CLINTON WHITE,
Commissioners.

APRIL 11, 1904. [5472]

Complaint of the selectmen of Swampscott concerning fares upon the Boston and Northern street railway.

W. H. NILES for town.

I. M. GARFIELD for company.

The people of Swampscott now have the benefit of the Lynn transfer system, together with a five-cent fare between any part of Swampscott and the town house in Salem over the direct or upper line. This meets the convenience of by far the greater number of those who are regular patrons of the railway.

The changes suggested by the petitioners, generally extending the five-cent fare from Swampscott into all parts of Salem, would reduce receipts at a time when, with the approval and at the suggestion of the Board, the company is making large expenditures in the improvement of its property, and when its receipts do not warrant a lessening of revenue.

While, however, the present fares are not as a whole excessive, there is one charge to which we think exception is well taken even under present circumstances. It is that paid by passengers who travel between Swampscott and Salem over what is known as the lower route, which passes for a short distance through Marblehead. The people of Swampscott who ride to certain points in Salem over this line pay fifteen cents, while other residents of the town who reach these points by the upper line pay only ten cents. We think this is an unjust discrimination, and recommend that it be removed.

JAMES F. JACKSON,
GEORGE W. BISHOP,
CLINTON WHITE,
Commissioners.

JUNE 23, 1904. [5431]

Complaint of the mayor of Taunton concerning service upon the Norton and Taunton street railway.

The Norton and Taunton street railway very early in its history passed into the hands of creditors who have since made a commendable effort to improve the property and to give as good service as the limited receipts of the company would permit.

It would appear that the motor equipment of the cars is not at all times sufficient for a satisfactory performance of the work to be done. All parties interested have expressed their willingness to leave to the Board the determination of the question whether the company should devote funds which properly become available for the improvement of the property to the strengthening of the motor equipment, in order to increase the efficiency of the cars.

In our opinion such an outlay is desirable, and we would recommend that the company provide for it as soon as its earnings will permit.

JAMES F. JACKSON,
GEORGE W. BISHOP,
CLINTON WHITE,
Commissioners.

APRIL 21, 1904. [5463]

Complaint of Citizens of Taunton, New Bedford and Fall River concerning train service on the New York, New Haven and Hartford railroad.

It is apparent that during the last two months the methods pursued upon the New York, New Haven and Hartford railroad in the conduct of its train service between the city of Boston and the cities of Taunton, New Bedford and Fall River have been very annoying to patrons. Not only have certain trains been discontinued and the running time of other trains lengthened, but express trains have been burdened by consolidation at Mansfield with trains between Providence and Boston, to the demoralization of the published schedule.

While the company has an unquestioned right to introduce measures of economy in its business management, it does not appear to be in such financial stress as would explain the present order of things upon this part of its system. On the contrary, the company has recently adopted a policy involving large expenditures in the development of its interstate traffic. Although this enterprise is in itself most commendable, we cannot agree that increased accommodation shall be furnished upon interstate lines at the expense of proper accommodation for communities within the state. The important place which the cities of Fall River, New Bedford and Taunton occupy in connection with state traffic and the amount of patronage which they bestow upon this railroad entitle them to an express service of a high order, one at least as good as that which was given before the recent changes went into effect.

We recommend therefore that this service be restored to its former efficiency.

JAMES F. JACKSON,
GEORGE W. BISHOP,
CLINTON WHITE,
Commissioners.

SEPTEMBER 15, 1904. [5598]

Complaint of the selectmen of Wakefield concerning street railway fares.

M. E. S. CLEMONS for town.

I. M. GARFIELD for company.

The question is whether certain fares upon the Boston and Northern street railway are excessive or unjust to any class of passengers.

The five-cent fare was established on street railways when in the main these were local enterprises. It was a fare convenient for collection, one which tended to promote the general welfare by encouraging a wider distribution of homes in thickly settled communities, and one which served the public on the whole acceptably.

With the same fare for everybody, companies found in the multitude of short rides compensation for the low rate for the long ride, so the average result furnished a reasonable return.

As a consequence of the consolidation of railways, of concessions made by the companies, and of action taken by the Board, the limits of the five-cent fare have been from time to time largely extended. The Board has recommended this fare generally within town boundaries, and in some cases between the centres of the larger municipalities and the centres of adjoining towns, an arrangement which happily works to the advantages of those who travel daily to and from their work. In brief, for one reason and another, the five-cent fare has been made to apply to travel for widely differing distances, in order to meet a great variety of local conditions.

With the taking on of an interurban service, companies have introduced a so-called through fare, subdivided into five-cent fares collected at fixed points. These fare limits are not always co-extensive with the local fare limits, a fact which has given rise to the suggestion of discrimination against through passengers. But it is to be borne in mind that the interurban business is often the development of the long distance patronage, without a corresponding development of the more profitable short distance riding, and that if comparison of fares is to be made, it should be between the through fare and the average local fare.

As to the particular fares to which our attention has been called in this case, we are satisfied after an examination of the receipts and expenditures of the company that no one of them is more than a reasonable charge for the accommodation furnished. Such inequalities as exist are the result of differences in the conditions under which the service has been extended, and in the concessions which have been made from time to time in the public interest, without reference to the adoption of any perfected general system of charges. We find no actual injustice in any instance, and do not believe that at this time there is any call for a more scientific nicety in the adjustment of rates which are in themselves not excessive.

What is needed is not change in fares, but improvement in service. From more than one community which this railway serves we are receiving complaints that cars are insufficient in number and not properly heated, and that long delays are frequent. These complaints are in part due, it is true, to the extraordinary severity of the winter, which has found transportation companies generally unprepared for the unexpected demands upon their resources. Making due allowance, however, for all that is unusual, it is plainly evident that there is imperative need of more cars and large additions to power plants upon parts of this system.

For the last four years the company has been at great expense in improving many lines which were in lamentable condition when acquired by it. Other lines need similar attention. It is our duty to insist upon the vigorous prosecution of this work of improvement. We cannot at the same time ask the company to lessen its revenue and to weaken its ability to furnish the remedy for real evils.

JAMES F. JACKSON,
GEORGE W. BISHOP,
CLINTON WHITE,
Commissioners.

MARCH 3, 1904. [5326]

Complaint of the selectmen of Wakefield and of citizens of Reading and Winchester concerning fares on the Boston and Northern street railway.

M. E. S. CLEMONS for petitioners.

B. W. WARREN for company.

These complaints present instances where the two systems of fare in effect upon street railways, one for local and the other for through travel, necessarily enforced under arbitrary rules, naturally provoke adverse criticism from patrons. We are not convinced, however, that the complainants suffer from any unjust discrimination. Applying the principle that a reasonable compensation is to be allowed a company for a service rendered, and having in mind the interest of the travelling public in preserving the rule of a five-cent fare within thickly settled communities, we cannot recommend that the company either reduce fares or extend transfer privileges.

The situation here is very similar to that which was more fully discussed in the decision of the Wakefield case published March 3, 1904.

JAMES F. JACKSON,
GEORGE W. BISHOP,
CLINTON WHITE,
Commissioners.

NOVEMBER 11, 1904. [5602]

Complaint of citizens of Wayland and Natick concerning service upon the Natick and Cochituate street railway.

C. B. WILLIAMS }
E. L. MCMANUS } for petitioners.

A. D. CLAFLIN for company.

It is claimed that the patrons of this road have been and are seriously discommoded by irregularity and delays in the running of cars and that the methods used in operating the railway are unsafe.

There is no doubt that the unusual severity of the winter has made it more than ordinarily difficult to operate this road, but it is clear, and the company admits, that the supply of electric power has been insufficient for a proper conduct of the business. The company has no power plant of its own, but has relied upon power furnished from an electric plant in Natick. The street railway company, having endeavored without success to obtain an adequate supply of power from this source, has already taken steps to secure it elsewhere. We expect, therefore, that this, the principal source of trouble to patrons, will be removed at a reasonably near day.

Some statements were made at the hearing which would tend to show uncertainty in the enforcement of the rule that a car must not leave a turnout until the arrival of the car which is expected to meet it there. This rule is necessary for safety. No exception to it should be permitted unless under unusual circumstances, in which case the car in proceeding should be so safeguarded as to prevent the possibility of accident.

The suggestion was also made that at times cars were "coasted" or run upon down grades while the power was off the line. This should be prohibited, as it jeopardizes the safety of passengers for whose protection every device for stopping the car should always be ready for instant application, and jeopardizes travel upon the highway through the possible approach of an unlighted car after dark.

JAMES F. JACKSON,
GEORGE W. BISHOP,
CLINTON WHITE,
Commissioners.

MARCH 15, 1904. [5446]

Petition of residents of Hingham and other towns relative to service on the South Shore branch of the New York, New Haven and Hartford railroad.

R. L. ROBBINS, LINCOLN BRYANT } for Hingham petitioners.

F. A. FARNHAM for company.

The number of persons who live the year round in suburban towns and transact business daily in Boston is a growing one. This class of travel has peculiar need of the morning and evening trains and furnishes a regular patronage which entitles it to favorable consideration.

To Hingham and places beyond excellent accommodation has been given in the past, in winter as well as in summer, upon the New York, New Haven and Hartford railroad, and coincident with this, if not in consequence of it, a considerable number of people have taken up their residence in these towns. Recently the railroad company has consolidated the train formerly leaving Boston at 6.10 P.M., and running express to Hingham, with the short distance accommodation train which had closely followed it.

It is true that the company is warranted in closely scrutinizing its expenditures from time to time and in attempting all reasonable economy; and it is true that the accommodation train which has been united with the express is a necessary service which, taken alone, nets a decided daily loss to the company.

There is evidently a large demand for accommodation by people desiring to leave Boston at the same time every day for different points upon this line. Is the consolidation of the two trains which formerly served them a necessary requirement of prudent management? This question should be answered, we think, through a study of the returns of both trains taken together and not from a consideration of the business done by either train independent of that done by the other. So viewed, the service as a whole warrants us in believing that the former schedule can be restored without the imposition of any unjust burden upon the company or upon any other portion of the travelling public. We recommend that this be done.

JAMES F. JACKSON,
GEORGE W. BISHOP,
CLINTON WHITE,
Commissioners.

DECEMBER 19, 1904. [5648]

LEASES AND CONSOLIDATIONS.

Petition of the Boston and Worcester and the Framingham, Southborough and Marlborough street railway companies for approval of the terms of the proposed purchase by the Boston and Worcester Street Railway Company of the property and franchises of the Framingham, Southborough and Marlborough Street Railway Company with a view to the consolidation of the two companies.

It appearing, after due notice and hearing, that the railways of the contracting companies are connecting railways; that the terms of purchase and sale provide that the property and franchises of the Framingham, Southborough and Marlborough Street Railway Company shall be duly conveyed to the Boston and Worcester Street Railway Company and that the Boston and Worcester Street Railway Company shall assume and pay all outstanding debts and obligations of the Framingham, Southborough and Marlborough Street Railway Company; that the terms of purchase and sale have been duly agreed to by the directors and stockholders of each of the contracting companies, and involve no decrease in the facilities for travel and no increase in the rates of fare; that such purchase and sale is lawful and consistent with the public interests, — it is

Ordered, That the approval of the Board be hereby given to the terms of this contract of purchase and sale, a copy of which contract is upon file in this office.

And it appearing that an increase in the capital stock of the Boston and Worcester Street Railway Company is contemplated in the terms of said purchase and sale for the purpose of effecting an exchange of stock, share for share, that such increase is reasonably requisite therefor, and that an issue of such additional stock involves no increase in the aggregate amount of the capital stock and the indebtedness of these companies, — it is

Ordered, That the approval of the Board be hereby given to an increase in the capital stock of the Boston and Worcester Street Railway Company by the issue of shares not exceeding one thousand eight hundred fifty (1850) in number, amounting at par value to one hundred eighty-five thousand dollars ($185,000), in addition to the amount of its capital stock now issued and outstanding, the said additional shares to be issued only in accordance with and for the purpose of carrying out the terms of the said contract and in exchange, share for share, for the outstanding shares of the Framingham, Southborough and Marlborough Street Railway Company, the certificates of the last named shares to be upon exchange surrendered and cancelled.

Attest: CHARLES E. MANN,
FEBRUARY 1, 1904. [5413] Clerk.

Petition of the Haverhill and Southern New Hampshire Street Railway Company for approval of a lease of its railway and properties to the Hudson, Pelham and Salem Electric Railway Company.

It appearing, after due notice and hearing, that the Haverhill and Southern New Hampshire Street Railway Company, a corporation duly organized under the laws of the Commonwealth of Massachusetts, acting under authority granted to it in chapter 355, Acts of 1901, has duly authorized a lease of its railway and properties to the Hudson, Pelham and Salem Electric Railway Company, a corporation duly organized under the laws of the State of New Hampshire; that the public convenience will be promoted by the operation of the railways under one management, and that the provisions of such lease are lawful and consistent with the public interests, — it is

Ordered, That the terms of the lease above named, a copy of which is on file in this office, be hereby approved.

Attest: CHARLES E. MANN,
FEBRUARY 25, 1904. [5419] Clerk.

Petition of the Lawrence and Methuen Street Railway Company for approval of a lease of its railway and properties to the Hudson, Pelham and Salem Electric Railway Company.

It appearing, after due notice and hearing, that the Lawrence and Methuen Street Railway Company, a corporation duly organized under the laws of the Commonwealth of Massachusetts, acting under authority granted to it in chapter 356, Acts of 1901, has duly authorized a lease of its railway and properties to the Hudson, Pelham and Salem Electric Railway Company, a corporation duly organized under the laws of the State of New Hampshire; that the public convenience will be promoted by the operation of the railways under one management, and that the provisions of such lease are lawful and consistent with the public interests, — it is

Ordered, That the terms of the lease above named, a copy of which is on file in this office, be hereby approved.

Attest: CHARLES E. MANN,
FEBRUARY 25, 1904. [5419] Clerk.

Petition of the Lowell and Pelham Street Railway Company for approval of a lease of its railway and properties to the Hudson, Pelham and Salem Electric Railway Company.

It appearing, after due notice and hearing, that the Lowell and Pelham Street Railway Company, a corporation duly organized under the laws of the Commonwealth of Massachusetts, acting under authority granted to it in chapter 309, Acts of 1903, has duly authorized a lease of its railway and properties to the Hudson, Pelham and Salem Electric Railway Company, a corporation duly organized under the laws of the State of New Hampshire; that the public convenience will be promoted by the operation of the railways under one management, and that the provisions of such lease are lawful and consistent with the public interests, — it is

Ordered, That the terms of the lease above named, a copy of which is on file in this office, be hereby approved.

Attest: CHARLES E. MANN,
Clerk.

FEBRUARY 25, 1904. [5419]

Petition of the New England and the Milford, Franklin and Providence railroad companies for approval of the terms of a lease.

It appearing, after due notice and hearing, that the railroads of these companies connect with each other, and that the terms of the proposed lease of the railroad, franchise and property of the Milford, Franklin and Providence Railroad Company to the New England Railroad Company are lawful and consistent with the public interests, — it is

Ordered, That the terms of the lease above named, a copy of which is on file in this office, be hereby approved.

Attest: CHARLES E. MANN,
Clerk.

JANUARY 15, 1904. [5385]

Petition of the New England and of the Milford and Woonsocket railroad companies for approval of the terms of a lease.

It appearing, after due notice and hearing, that the railroads of these companies connect with each other, and that the terms of the proposed lease of the railroad, franchise and property of the Milford and Woonsocket Railroad Company to the New England Railroad Company are lawful and consistent with the public interests, — it is

Ordered, That the terms of the lease above named, a copy of which is on file in this office, be hereby approved.

Attest: CHARLES E. MANN,
Clerk.

JANUARY 15, 1904. [5385]

EXTENSION OF FRANCHISE.

Exigency for Building Railroad.

Petition of the New England Railroad Company for a certificate of exigency for the building of an extension of its railroad.

The proposed extension of this railroad to provide for an entrance into Boston independent of the Boston and Albany railroad follows the recent suggestion of this Board that something be done for an improvement of the service upon this line.

We hereby certify that the public necessity and convenience require the construction by the New England Railroad Company of an extension of its railroad in the towns of Needham and Dedham and in the city of Boston, from a point near the Needham station to a point on the Boston and Providence railroad near West Roxbury station, as shown upon a plan submitted herewith.

JAMES F. JACKSON,
GEORGE W. BISHOP,
CLINTON WHITE,
Commissioners.

February 29, 1904. [5439]

Petition of the New England Railroad Company that the Board fix a route for a proposed extension of its railroad.

J. H. Benton, Jr., for petitioner.
T. M. Babson for City of Boston.
R. M. Morse for Town of Brookline.
W. S. Slocum for City of Newton.

The New England Railroad Company proposes to extend its road in this state from a point near the Needham station to a point on the Boston and Providence railroad near the West Roxbury station, and so obtain a direct entrance into Boston.

This enterprise, besides promoting the public interests in other important ways, will relieve passengers upon the Woonsocket division of the New York, New Haven and Hartford system from the annoying delays incident to the taking of the cars from that division into Boston over the Boston and Albany railroad.

The Board, after full consideration, on February 29, 1904, decreed that public necessity and convenience demanded this extension.

Since that time a route for the railroad has been fixed by the selectmen in the towns of Needham and Dedham.

Upon the petition of the New England Railroad Company the board of aldermen of Boston, in July, passed an order fixing a route in that city, but the order provided that it should become operative only upon the surrender by the Old Colony Railroad Company of a large claim which it holds against the City of Boston and which is now the subject of litigation. The petitioner declined to accept this condition, claiming that it related to a matter foreign to the extension of its railroad, and one which concerned a different corporation. The board of aldermen refused to recede from its position, and the railroad company, in accordance with the provisions of section 43, chapter 111 of the Revised Laws now asks this Board to fix a route in Boston, presenting the same plan for a location that was before the board of aldermen and received its approval, as far as any objections to the route itself are concerned.

The Town of Brookline remonstrates against the adoption of the proposed route for the reason that it passes through certain lands in Boston which the Town holds as a part of its system of water works. Through its counsel it contends that as a matter of law a railroad cannot be located through these premises without special act of the Legislature.

There can be little if any doubt that the facts bring this case within the rule that lands already devoted to a public use cannot be taken under general laws for another inconsistent use.

On the other hand, a careful study of the territory through which the proposed extension must be built, if the railroad is to reach Boston, shows that there is no other reasonably practicable route which can be substituted for that which crosses this property. While the importance of protecting systems of water supply is fully appreciated, the large public interests to be secured through the development of these transportation facilities for commercial purposes and for the convenience of travel are entitled to great consideration.

Believing that the construction of the railroad through the lands of the Town would occasion injuries which could be measured by money damages, the Board is of the opinion that the route for the railroad should be fixed in accordance with the plan presented, but believes that it is without authority to so fix the route under the general law.

JAMES F. JACKSON,
GEORGE W. BISHOP,
CLINTON WHITE,
Commissioners.

NOVEMBER 11, 1904. [5553]

GRADE CROSSINGS AND BRIDGES.

Railroad and Railway Crossings.

Petition of the Amherst and Sunderland Street Railway Company for extension of time for maintaining grade crossing of the New London Northern railroad in the town of Amherst.

It appearing, after due notice and hearing, that the conditions existing in the locality where Main street crosses the New London Northern railroad in the town of Amherst have not changed since the issue of the order of the Board sanctioning the temporary grade crossing of the railroad by the railway at this place at the same level therewith, and that under the circumstances consent should be given to a continuance of the right to maintain this crossing, — it is

Ordered, That the period during which the petitioner was authorized to maintain a crossing of its railway and the railroad at the same level at this place, under the order of the Board dated July 22, 1897, be extended to July 22, 1907.

Attest: CHARLES E. MANN,

January 9, 1904. [5408] *Clerk.*

Petition of the Berkshire Street Railway Company for extension of time for maintaining grade crossing of railway and railroad in the city of Pittsfield.

It appearing, after due notice and hearing, that the conditions existing in the locality where Dalton road crosses the Boston and Albany railroad (New York Central and Hudson River Railroad Company, lessee), justify an extension of the time for maintaining the temporary crossing of railroad and railway at this place at the same level, — it is

Ordered, That the period during which the petitioner was authorized to maintain a crossing of its railway and the railroad at the same level at this place, under the order of the Board dated May 22, 1902, be extended to October 1, 1906.

Attest: CHARLES E. MANN,

May 11, 1904. [5499] *Clerk.*

Petition of the Berkshire Street Railway Company for extension of time for maintaining grade crossing of railway and railroad in the city of Pittsfield.

It appearing, after due notice and hearing, that the work of eliminating the existing grade crossing of highway and the New York, New Haven and Hartford Railroad at Holmes road in Pittsfield is being prosecuted but is not yet completed, — it is

Ordered, That the period during which the petitioner was authorized to maintain a crossing of its railway and the railroad at the same level at this place, under the order of the Board dated June 3, 1902, be extended to January 1, 1905.

Attest: CHARLES E. MANN,
Clerk.

MAY 11, 1904. [5499]

Petition of the Berkshire Street Railway Company for extension of time for maintaining grade crossing of railway and railroad in the town of Lee.

It appearing, after due notice and hearing, that the work of eliminating the existing grade crossing of highway and the New York, New Haven and Hartford railroad at Pleasant street in the town of Lee is being prosecuted but is not yet completed, — it is

Ordered, That the period during which the petitioner was authorized to maintain a crossing of its railway and the railroad at the same level at this place, under the order of the Board dated June 3, 1902, be extended to January 1, 1905.

Attest: CHARLES E. MANN,
Clerk.

MAY 11, 1904. [5499]

Petition of the Hoosac Valley Street Railway Company for extension of time for maintaining grade crossing of railway and railroad in the town of Adams.

It appearing, after due notice and hearing, that proceedings for the elimination of the existing grade crossing of highway and the Pittsfield and North Adams railroad (New York Central and Hudson River Railroad Company, lessee), at Maple Grove in the town of Adams are pending, — it is

Ordered, That the period during which the petitioner was authorized to maintain a crossing of its railway and the railroad at the same level at this place, under the order of the Board dated March 28, 1902, be further extended to October 1, 1905, the authority granted hereunder to be exercised upon the conditions and subject to the restrictions and regulations named in said order.

Attest: CHARLES E. MANN, *Clerk.*

JUNE 4, 1904. [5513]

Petition of the Boston Elevated Railway Company for modification of order relative to the crossing of its railway and the New York, New Haven and Hartford railroad in Neponset.

In view of the conditions existing at the place of the grade crossing sanctioned under the order of this Board dated November 5, 1903, and for other reasons which in the opinion of the Board justify an exception to its general rule, it is

Ordered, That in place of the second paragraph of the regulations which are made a part of the above named order, there be substituted the following language:

Every street car on approaching the railroad shall be operated in accordance with Rules numbered 50, 61 and 112 of the code of regulations published by the company, with supplement, under date of July, 1903, a copy of which code is on file in this office.

Attest: CHARLES E. MANN, *Clerk.*

JULY 7, 1904. [5317]

PRIVATE RAILROADS.

Petition of the American Smokeless Powder Company for consent to the construction of a private freight track across a highway in the town of Acton.

It appearing that the selectmen of Acton have consented to the construction and maintenance of the proposed track for private use, and that the county commissioners of Middlesex County, by their decree dated May 9, 1904, have adjudged that public necessity requires the crossing of the proposed railroad at the same level with the highway; and that such construction and operation is consistent with the public interests, — it is

Ordered, That the consent of the Board be hereby given to the construction and maintenance of a railroad to be operated by steam power upon and across the old Stow road in said Acton, for private use in the transportation of freight.

This consent is given upon the condition that a flagman display a flag by day and a lantern by night whenever an engine, car or train approaches, and while it is passing over said crossing, and that no engine, car or train shall cross at a greater speed than four miles an hour.

Attest: CHARLES E. MANN, *Clerk.*

MAY 16, 1904. [5490]

Petition of Lovejoy's Wharf Trust for consent to maintenance of a freight track for private use across Beverly street in Boston.

It appearing that a railroad track for private use has been constructed across Beverly street in Boston in accordance with authority granted therefor to the Dennis and Lovejoy Wharf and Warehouse Company, and that all parties in interest have consented to the transfer of the right to maintain this railroad to the petitioner; and that the further maintenance of this railroad across the public way by the petitioner under suitable restrictions and safeguards is consistent with the public interests, — it is

Ordered, That the consent of the Board which was given to the maintenance of the above named railroad by the Dennis and Lovejoy Wharf and Warehouse Company be extended and given to the maintenance of the same by the petitioner, subject to the conditions named in the former order of the Board issued under date of December 19, 1902.

Attest: CHARLES E. MANN,
Clerk.

MAY 10, 1904. [5507]

Petition of Farnam Brothers Lime Company for consent to the construction of a railroad for private use in transportation of freight across a highway in Cheshire.

It appearing that the selectmen of Cheshire have consented to the construction and maintenance of the proposed railroad across the highway; that the county commissioners of Berkshire County have adjudged that public necessity requires that the railroad cross the highway at a level therewith; and that the same is consistent with the public interests, — it is

Ordered, That the consent of the Board be hereby given to the construction and maintenance by the petitioner of a railroad to be operated by steam power upon and across the town way near the Cheshire reservoir, so-called, in said Cheshire, for private use in the transportation of freight, as shown upon a plan filed with this petition.

This consent is given upon the condition that a flagman shall display a flag by day and a lantern by night whenever an engine, car or train is approaching, and while it is passing over said crossing, and that no engine, car or train shall cross at a greater speed than four miles an hour.

Attest: CHARLES E. MANN,
Clerk.

OCTOBER 5, 1904. [5618]

Petition of Joseph B. Howland, superintendent of the State Colony for the Insane, for consent to the construction of a temporary freight track across a highway in Gardner.

It appearing that the selectmen of Gardner have consented to the construction and maintenance of the proposed temporary track for private use; that the county commissioners of Worcester County have adjudged that public necessity requires the crossing of the proposed railroad at the same level with the highway; and that such construction and operation is consistent with the public interests, — it is

Ordered, That the consent of the Board be hereby given to the construction by the petitioner of a temporary railroad to be operated by steam power upon and across Beech street in said Gardner, for private use in the transportation of gravel.

This consent is given upon condition that a flagman shall display a flag by day and a lantern by night whenever an engine, car or train approaches and passes over said crossing, and that no engine, car or train shall cross at a greater speed than four miles an hour.

Attest: ALLAN BROOKS,
AUGUST 15, 1904. [5576] *Assistant Clerk.*

Petition of William H. Dewhirst for consent to the construction of a railroad for private use in transportation of freight across a highway in Groveland.

It appearing that the selectmen of Groveland have consented to the construction and maintenance of the proposed railroad across the highway; that the county commissioners of Essex county have adjudged that public necessity requires that the railroad cross the highway at a level therewith; and that the same is consistent with the public interests, — it is

Ordered, That the consent of the Board be hereby given to the construction and maintenance by the petitioner of a railroad for private use in the transportation of freight, to be operated by steam power upon and across the highway leading from Groveland to South Groveland, as shown upon a plan filed with this petition.

This consent is given upon the condition that a flagman shall display a flag by day and a lantern by night whenever an engine, car or train is approaching and while it is passing over said crossing, and that no engine, car or train shall cross at a greater speed than four miles an hour.

Attest: CHARLES E. MANN,
NOVEMBER 4, 1904. [5615] *Clerk.*

Petition of the American Tube Works for consent to the construction of a freight track across a highway in Somerville.

It appearing that the aldermen of Somerville have consented to the construction and maintenance of the proposed track for private use, and that the county commissioners of Middlesex County, by their decree dated January 6, 1904, have adjudged that public necessity requires the crossing of the proposed railroad at the same level with the highway, and that such construction and operation is consistent with the public interests, — it is

Ordered, That the consent of the Board be hereby given to the construction by the petitioners of a railroad to be operated by steam power upon and across Dane street in said Somerville for private use in the transportation of freight.

This consent is given upon condition that a flagman shall display a flag by day and a lantern by night whenever an engine, car or train approaches and passes over said crossing, and that no engine, car or train shall cross at a greater speed than four miles an hour.

Attest: CHARLES E. MANN,
Clerk.

JANUARY 14, 1904. [5373]

SAFEGUARDS AT CROSSINGS.

Petition of citizens of North Andover for the establishment of safeguard at the Essex street crossing of the Boston and Maine railroad in that town.

This matter having been called to the attention of the railroad company, and a conference between the representative of the company and the selectmen having resulted in an agreement that an electric bell be installed at the crossing in question, there would seem to be no need of further formal action by the Board.

By the Board,

JAMES F. JACKSON,
Chairman.

MAY 5, 1904. [5464]

Petition of the selectmen of Sheffield for the establishment of safeguard at the crossing of highway and railroad.

It appearing that the public safety and convenience so require, — it is

Ordered, That the New York, New Haven and Hartford Railroad Company shall, between the hours of eight o'clock in the morning and eight o'clock in the evening of every day, maintain a flagman at the crossing of the railroad and the highway in the village of Ashley Falls in the town of Sheffield, who shall display a flag by day and a lantern by night to give suitable warning of any approaching engine, car or train.

Attest: CHARLES E. MANN,
Clerk.

MAY 5, 1904. [5470]

Petition of the selectmen of Westport for additional safeguard at railroad crossing.

The branch railroad operated by the New York, New Haven and Hartford Railroad Company between Fall River and New Bedford crosses the main highway between these cities in the town of Westport. Two passenger and two freight trains pass over this road daily each way, the passenger trains ordinarily running at a speed of thirty or forty miles an hour. While those who use the highway have a clear view of trains approaching from the west, their view of trains approaching from the east is partially obstructed.

Not long ago an electric bell was installed at this place, for the protection of travellers. We are satisfied that some additional precaution should be taken, and therefore recommend that the speed of trains in approaching and in crossing the highway be restricted to a rate not exceeding fifteen miles an hour. The enforcement of this rule will increase the efficiency of the warning given by the electric signal and in case of emergency will both enable an engineer to bring his train quickly to a stop and give the traveller greater opportunity to avoid peril.

By the Board,

JAMES F. JACKSON,
Chairman.

FEBRUARY 26, 1904. [5428]

Petition of the New York, New Haven and Hartford Railroad Company for approval of gates at drawbridge over Fort Point channel in the city of Boston.

After consideration, it appearing that the New York, New Haven and Hartford Railroad Company has a connecting track which crosses Fort Point channel in South Boston by a drawbridge, that the distance between this drawbridge and the main track on each side is less than five hundred (500) feet, and that therefore it is not possible to erect the gates prescribed in section 174, chapter 111, Revised Laws, at a distance of five hundred (500) feet, — it is

Ordered, That the approval of the Board be hereby given to the placing of a gate on the west side of said drawbridge at a distance of not less than two hundred and fifty (250) feet, and on the east side of said drawbridge at a distance of not less than two hundred and twenty (220) feet, as shown on a plan on file with the petition.

Attest: CHARLES E. MANN,
JULY 13, 1904. [5549] *Clerk.*

BRIDGES AT HEIGHT LESS THAN EIGHTEEN FEET.

Application of the City of Boston for consent to the construction of highway bridges at a height less than eighteen feet above the tracks of the Boston and Albany railroad.

The special commission appointed by the Superior Court to consider the abolition of certain grade crossings of highway and railroad in East Boston having adopted a plan for separating these grades which calls for the construction of several highway bridges at a height less than eighteen feet in the clear above the railroad tracks; and all parties having agreed to the changes suggested by the Board to secure a height of not less than fifteen and one-half feet for the two lowest of these bridges, instead of a height of fifteen feet as proposed, if said plan shall be hereafter carried out, — it is

Ordered, That the consent of the Board be hereby given to the construction of bridges over the tracks of the Boston and Albany railroad in East Boston at a clear height of not less than sixteen (16) and fifteen and one-half ($15\frac{1}{2}$) feet, respectively, above the tracks of the railroad, as shown upon the plan and set forth in the report to be filed in the Superior Court by the special commission above named.

Attest: CHARLES E. MANN,
FEBRUARY 11, 1904. [5434] *Clerk.*

Petition of the Boston and Maine Railroad relative to height of Forbes bridge in Chelsea.

After consideration, it is

Ordered, That the consent of the Board be hereby given to the maintenance of the Forbes bridge over the tracks of the Boston and Maine railroad in the city of Chelsea, at a clear height of not less than seventeen and one-half ($17\frac{1}{2}$) feet above the tracks of the railroad.

Attest: CHARLES E. MANN,
JULY 12, 1904. [5552] *Clerk.*

Application of the mayor and aldermen of Newton relative to construction of bridges at less than eighteen feet above the tracks of the Boston and Albany railroad.

After consideration, it is

Ordered, That the consent of the Board be hereby given to construction of bridges over the tracks of the Boston and Albany railroad in the city of Newton, at Langley road, Centre, Rogers, Hyde, Walnut and Boylston streets, in connection with the abolition of grade crossings in said city, at a clear height of not less than sixteen (16) feet above the tracks of the railroad.

Attest: CHARLES E. MANN,
JANUARY 14, 1904. [5411] *Clerk.*

CHANGE OF GRADE OF RAILROADS.

Petition of Samuel K. Hamilton, Theodore C. Hurd and Edmund K. Turner, special commissioners, for change in grade of the Fitchburg railroad in the town of Ayer.

It appearing that certain changes in the grade of the Fitchburg railroad are necessary for the convenience and safety of the public, if the plan adopted by the petitioners for the abolition of a grade crossing of highway and railroad in the town of Ayer is to be carried out, — it is

Ordered, That the consent of the Board be hereby given to the proposed changes in the grade of the Fitchburg railroad as properly incidental to the decision made by the petitioners in connection with the abolition of the above named crossing.

Attest: CHARLES E. MANN,
OCTOBER 13, 1904. [5631] *Clerk.*

Application of the City of Boston for consent to changes in the grade of the Boston and Albany railroad in connection with the abolition of certain grade crossings in East Boston.

The special commission appointed by the Superior Court to consider the abolition of certain grade crossings of highway and railroad in East Boston have adopted a plan for separating these grades which calls for changes in the grade of the Boston and Albany railroad, and said changes appearing to be necessary if said plan shall be hereafter carried out, — it is

Ordered, That the consent of the Board be hereby given to the changes in the grade of the Boston and Albany railroad in East

Boston in the manner and to the extent shown upon the plan and set forth in the report to be filed in the Superior Court by the special commission above named, as the same have been changed to meet the suggestion of the Board for securing the construction of certain bridges at a height not less than fifteen and one-half (15½) feet in the clear above the railroad tracks.

Attest: CHARLES E. MANN,
Clerk.

FEBRUARY 11, 1904. [5434]

Petition of the selectmen of Hingham for consent to a change in the grade of a railroad as a part of the plan adopted by the special commission appointed by the Superior Court to consider the abolition of a certain grade crossing in that town.

After due notice and hearing and full consideration, — it is

Ordered, That the consent of the Board be hereby given to the following change in the grade of the Old Colony railroad (New York, New Haven and Hartford Railroad Company, lessee), in the town of Hingham, proposed by the special commission above named in connection with its plan for the abolition of said crossing:

The grade of the tracks of the railroad shall be raised at the crossing ten and seventy-three one-hundredths (10.73) feet and from the middle of the crossing northerly the grade of the railroad shall be level for about one hundred feet, then connected by a proper vertical curve with a grade which shall descend at the rate of one foot in one hundred feet until it intersects the present grade of the railroad.

The grade of the railroad southerly from the middle of the crossing shall be level for about one hundred feet, then connected by a proper vertical curve with a grade which shall descend at the rate of three-tenths (0.3) of a foot in one hundred feet until it intersects the present grade of the railroad.

Attest: CHARLES E. MANN,
Clerk.

JANUARY 14, 1904. [5402]

Petition of the mayor and aldermen of Newton for approval of change of grade of Boston and Albany and New England railroads in Newton.

It appearing that the special commissioners appointed by the Superior Court to consider the abolition of certain grade crossings of highways and railroads in the city of Newton have determined that changes in the grades of the Boston and Albany and the New England railroads are necessary in connection with the plan adopted for the abolition of said grade crossings, and that such changes in the grades of said railroads are necessary for the convenience and security of the public, — it is

Ordered, That the consent of the Board be hereby given to changes in the grades of the Boston and Albany and the New England railroads in the city of Newton in the manner and to the extent set forth in the report of said special commissioners, and described upon the plan accompanying the same.

Attest: CHARLES E. MANN, *Clerk.*

JANUARY 4, 1904. [5389]

Petition of Edmund K. Turner, William W. McClench and James P. Magenis, commissioners, for change in grade of the Fitchburg railroad in the city of North Adams.

It appearing that a certain change in the grade of the Fitchburg railroad is necessary for the convenience and safety of the public if the plan adopted by the petitioners for the abolition of the grade crossing of Main street and the railroad in the city of North Adams is to be carried out, — it is

Ordered, That the consent of the Board be hereby given to said change in the grade of the Fitchburg railroad, as properly incidental to the decision made by the petitioners in connection with the abolition of the above named crossing as proposed by them.

Attest: CHARLES E. MANN, *Clerk.*

JULY 13, 1904. [5560]

Petition of Dana Malone, Edmund K. Turner and Henry A. Wyman, special commissioners, for change of grade of the New England railroad, in the town of Walpole.

It appearing that certain changes in the grade of the New England railroad (New York, New Haven and Hartford Railroad Company, lessee), are necessary for the convenience and safety of the public, if the plan adopted by the petitioners for the abolition of a certain grade crossing of a highway known as Kendall street and the railroad in the town of Walpole is to be carried out, — it is

Ordered, That the consent of the Board be hereby given to the changes in the grade of the New England railroad (New York, New Haven and Hartford Railroad Company, lessee), as properly incidental to the decision made by the petitioners in connection with the abolition of the above named crossing as proposed by them.

Attest: CHARLES E. MANN, *Clerk.*

MAY 11, 1904. [5505]

Certificates relative to Abolition of Grade Crossings.

Petition of the selectmen of Acton relative to abolition of grade crossings in that town.

R. E. Joslin for town.

W. H. Coolidge for Boston and Maine railroad.

A. W. DeGoosh for Commonwealth.

The railroad company opposes the issue of a certificate in this case on the ground that such action would not be consistent with the public interests in view of the amount of other work of this kind which is now under way upon the Boston and Maine railroad.

Aside from this suggestion every known reason for the abolition of a grade crossing of highway and railroad is found to justify the prosecution of the work in this instance. The crossings in question are upon the main line of the railroad where trains pass frequently; the highways are important and much used; the plan proposes the merging of three grade crossings into one under pass at a reasonable expense; and in view of the present cost of maintaining existing safeguards, the improvement is a measure of economy for the railroad company.

While we agree that the public interests are directly connected with the prosperity of the railroad company and appreciate the fact that the burden of expenditures incurred in connection with the abolition of grade crossings might be under certain conditions a matter for grave consideration, we have no reason to believe that the financial resources of the company will be unduly taxed by the requirement that these crossings be abolished.

In regard to certain technical questions affecting the relation of a certain street railway company to this improvement the Board has no jurisdiction.

In accordance with these views:

The Board hereby certifies that in its opinion the adoption of the plan set forth in the report of the special commission duly appointed by the Superior Court to consider the abolition of the grade crossings of Maynard and Stow streets and County road and the Fitchburg railroad (Boston and Maine Railroad, lessee), in the town of Acton, and the incurring of the expenditure therein authorized, are consistent with the public interests, and are reasonably required to secure a fair distribution between the different cities, towns and railroads of the Commonwealth of the public money appropriated for the abolition of grade crossings, and that such expenditure will not in its judgment exceed the amount to be paid by the Commonwealth under the provisions of law relating thereto.

JAMES F. JACKSON,
GEORGE W. BISHOP,
CLINTON WHITE,
Commissioners.

MAY 31, 1904. [5494]

Petition of the Selectmen of Attleborough, for abolition of certain grade crossings in that town.

After due notice and hearing, an examination of the proposed plan for the abolition of certain grade crossings of highways and railroads in the town of Attleborough, as set forth in the report of the special commissioners, and a consideration of the expenditure therein authorized,

The Board hereby certifies that in its opinion the adoption of said plan and the incurring of such expenditure are consistent with the public interests, and are reasonably required to secure a fair distribution between the different cities and towns and railroads of the Commonwealth of the public money appropriated for the abolition of grade crossings, and that such expenditure will not in its judgment exceed the amount to be paid by the Commonwealth under the provisions of law relating thereto.

Attest: CHARLES E. MANN,
Clerk.

JANUARY 1, 1904. [5390]

Petition of the Selectmen of Attleborough for certificate relative to the abolition of grade crossings in that town.

J. M. HALLOWELL for town.

J. H. BENTON, JR., for railroad companies.

A. W. DEGOOSH for Commonwealth.

When the plan for abolishing grade crossings of highway and railroad in Attleborough was first presented we were informed that all parties were in accord. The case, however, has been reopened before the special commissioners, and now comes again before us upon their report, which, after a re-hearing, is unchanged.

The Commonwealth now contends that the plan calls for an improper expenditure in station improvements and is further objectionable in providing for a double in place of a single track, and in creating a public way where a private way has heretofore existed.

The changes contemplated in Attleborough are upon the main line of the system operated by the New York, New Haven and Hartford Railroad Company and are obviously very important. As might be expected, they can only be made at a large cost, the estimated outlay being about eight hundred thousand dollars.

The Commonwealth claims that a saving in expense would be made by raising the old station instead of building a new one. Were the building of the new station shown to be merely an improvement in station accommodations and not fairly incident to the work of eliminating the grade crossings, we should be compelled to withhold our certificate.

The special commissioners, however, have found that it is impracticable to raise and use the old station. This conclusion rests upon the suggestion of three out of four engineers of high standing, and we take it to mean that the raising and use of the old station would create conditions which would deprive the public of suitable accommodation and of conveniences which they now enjoy. In a review of the facts we find so much ground for this opinion that we do not think we are called upon in the public interests to disturb it.

The other questions which have been raised by the Commonwealth are such as will be fully presented upon the record to the Supreme Judicial Court and the rights of the Commonwealth protected.

We therefore certify that in our opinion the adoption of the plan and the incurring of the expenditure proposed in the report of the special commissioners appointed by the Superior Court in connection with the proceedings to abolish certain grade crossings of highway and railroad in the town of Attleborough, are consistent with the public interests, and are reasonably required to secure a fair distribution between the different cities, towns and railroads of the Commonwealth of the public money appropriated for the abolition of grade crossings, and that such expenditure will not in our judgment exceed the amount to be paid by the Commonwealth under the provisions of law relating thereto.

JAMES F. JACKSON,
GEORGE W. BISHOP,
CLINTON WHITE,
Commissioners.

JUNE 30, 1904. [5532]

Petition of the board of aldermen of the city of Boston for certificate relative to abolition of grade crossings in East Boston.

A. J. BAILEY for city,

SAMUEL HOAR for Boston and Albany railroad,

A. W. DEGOOSH for Commonwealth,

J. H. BENTON, JR., for New York, New Haven and Hartford railroad,

NATHAN MATTHEWS, JR., for East Boston Land Company,

W. S. SLOCUM for City of Newton.

Every reason which would ordinarily be named for approving the separation of highway and railroad crossings is to be found in the circumstances which exist here. The amount and character of the business done upon the railroad, although it is exclusively a freight traffic, the importance of the uses of the highways, the length of time which the preliminary proceedings have covered, and the general public interest expressed in the improvement, all speak to favorable action upon the petition.

Moreover, the Legislature, in approving the lease of the Boston and Albany railroad to the New York Central and Hudson River Railroad Company required an express agreement looking to the abolition of grade crossings upon the Grand Junction railroad, of which this is a part, thus placing beyond all question the propriety of the work.

The plan for the changes is the result of the best engineering skill and of careful consideration by public boards. There is no question as to the condition of the fund appropriated to meet the contribution of the Commonwealth, and no suggestion that the expenditure from any standpoint would be improper or undesirable. Therefore

The Board hereby certifies that in its opinion the adoption of the plan and the incurring of the expenditure proposed in the report of the special commission appointed by the Superior Court to consider the abolition of certain grade crossings of highway and railroad in East Boston are consistent with the public interests and are reasonably required to secure a fair distribution between the different cities, towns and railroads of the Commonwealth, of the public money appropriated for the abolition of grade crossings, and that such expenditure will not in its judgment exceed the amount to be paid by the Commonwealth under the provisions of law relating thereto.

JAMES F. JACKSON,
GEORGE W. BISHOP,
CLINTON WHITE,
Commissioners.

APRIL 6, 1904. [5544]

Petition of the selectmen of Chelmsford for approval of plan for the abolition of a grade crossing of highway and railroad in that town.

F. A. FISHER for town.

W. H. COOLIDGE for railroad company.

The Legislature of 1902, after a thorough review of what had thus far been accomplished toward the abolition of grade crossings of highways and railroads, to the cost of which the Commonwealth had contributed five million dollars, made a second state appropriation of five million dollars toward the further prosecution of the work. At the same time section 159, chapter 111, Revised Laws was changed by chapter 440, Acts of 1902, so as to read as follows:

> No final decree shall be made by said superior court upon any report of commissioners setting forth a plan for the abolition, discontinuance or alteration of a grade crossing, adopting or confirming such plan or authorizing any expense to be charged against the commonwealth, until the board of railroad commissioners, after a hearing, shall have certified in writing that in their opinion the adoption of such plan and the expenditure to be incurred thereunder are consistent with the public interests, and are reasonably requisite to secure a fair distribution between the different cities, towns and railroads of the commonwealth, of the public money appropriated in the preceding section for the abolition of grade crossings.

A special commission appointed by the Superior Court has adopted a plan for separating grades at the place where the highway known as Princeton street crosses the Stony Brook railroad (Boston and Maine railroad, lessee), in Chelmsford.

The railroad company contends that in view of the amount and character of the work of this kind in which it is actually engaged in other places, and of the comparatively light traffic upon this branch line, the proposed separation of grades in Chelmsford is not called for at the present time.

The duty of the Board, under the change in the statute, to secure as far as it may a "fair distribution" of the public money appropriated for the purpose of abolishing grade crossings, affords no reason for delaying the general progress of this most important improvement. Nor do we understand that the object of the change was to secure a geographical division of the work, or exact proportions in the expenditures made by the different companies. The end to be attained is rather an order of procedure which will authorize expenditures where most needed in the general public interests, with due regard to the amount of financial burden imposed at any one time upon a particular city, town or corporation. The statute looks to the future, not to the past.

It is impossible to accurately measure and apportion the amount of peril that exists at different grade crossings. In selecting one crossing rather than another for abolition, the first factor to be considered is the relative importance of the travel at these places, and in determining this the travel upon both the railroad and the highway is to be considered, since a grade crossing is a menace to both.

In this instance we have a public way which has been selected as an important thoroughfare by the State highway commission, and upon which large expenditures have been made, in constructing it as a state road for long distances on both sides of the railroad. The present and future uses of this highway make it an important avenue of travel. A considerable number of trains pass over the crossing daily. No objection is made to the plan for separating the grades, and the cost, estimated at forty thousand dollars ($40,000), does not seem disproportionate to the advantages to be gained.

While the Board recognizes the amount and character of the work already under way in other places upon the Boston and Maine railroad system, we are nevertheless persuaded that this particular improvement should be promptly prosecuted, and accordingly

The Board hereby certifies that in its opinion the adoption of the plan and the incurring of the expenditure proposed in the report of the special commission appointed by the Superior Court to consider the abolition of the grade crossing of Princeton street and the Stony Brook railroad in the town of Chelmsford are consistent with the public interests, and are reasonably required to secure a fair distribution between the different cities, towns and railroads of the Commonwealth, of the public money appropriated for the abolition of grade crossings, and that such expenditure will not in its judgment exceed the amount to be paid by the Commonwealth under the provisions of law relating thereto.

JAMES F. JACKSON,
GEORGE W. BISHOP,
CLINTON WHITE,
Commissioners.

FEBRUARY 9, 1904. [5199]

Petition of the Selectmen of Greenfield for certificate relative to abolition of grade crossing in that town.

After due notice and hearing, an examination of the proposed plan for the abolition of the grade crossing of Russell street and the Vermont and Massachusetts and the Connecticut River railroads, both operated by the Boston and Maine Railroad, in the town of Greenfield, as set forth in the report of the special commissioners duly appointed by the Superior Court to consider the same, and an inquiry into the expenditures therein authorized,

The Board hereby certifies that in its opinion the adoption of said plan and the incurring of such expenditure are consistent with the public interests, and are reasonably required to secure a fair distribution between the different cities, towns and railroads of the Commonwealth, of the public money appropriated for the abolition of grade crossings, and that such expenditure will not in its judgment exceed the amount to be paid by the Commonwealth under the provisions of law relating thereto.

Attest: CHARLES E. MANN,
Clerk.

MAY 4, 1904. [5486]

Petition of the Town of Hingham for certificate relative to abolition of grade crossing of highway and railroad.

J. O. Burdett for town.

J. H. Benton, Jr., for railroad company.

A. W. DeGoosh for Commonwealth.

It is agreed that the character of the crossing in question warrants the expense to be incurred in abolishing it, and that the plan adopted by the special commission is a suitable one.

The New York, New Haven and Hartford Railroad Company, however, seeks to have this petition, which was brought under the old law, disapproved, in order that a new petition may be brought under the recent statute providing for contribution by street railway companies to the cost of abolishing grade crossings of highway and railroad.

The Commonwealth, however, which would alone benefit by street railway contribution, does not appear to join in this view of the case, but endorses the argument of the petitioners, that the public interests in this instance will be best served by avoiding delays and forwarding the contemplated improvement under this petition. As we are of this mind,

We hereby certify that in our opinion the adoption of the plan and the incurring of the expenditure proposed in the report of the special commission appointed by the Superior Court to consider the abolition of the grade crossing of Rockland street and the New York, New Haven and Hartford railroad in the town of Hingham, are consistent with the public interests, and are reasonably required to secure a fair distribution between the different cities, towns and railroads of the Commonwealth, of the public money appropriated for the abolition of grade crossings, and that such expenditure will not in our judgment exceed the amount to be paid by the Commonwealth under the provisions of law relating thereto.

JAMES F. JACKSON,
GEORGE W. BISHOP,
CLINTON WHITE,
Commissioners.

September 22, 1904. [5597]

Petition of the Selectmen of Lee for certificate relative to abolition of grade crossing in that town.

After due notice and hearing, an examination of the proposed plan for the abolition of the grade crossing of Pleasant street and the railroad operated by the New York, New Haven and Hartford Railroad Company in the town of Lee, as set forth in the report of the special commissioners duly appointed by the Superior Court to consider the same, and an inquiry into the expenditure therein authorized,

The Board hereby certifies that in its opinion the adoption of said plan and the incurring of such expenditure are consistent with the public interests, and are reasonably required to secure a fair distribution between the different cities, towns and railroads of the Commonwealth, of the public money appropriated for the abolition of grade crossings, and that such expenditure will not in its judgment exceed the amount to be paid by the Commonwealth under the provisions of law relating thereto.

Attest: CHARLES E. MANN,
APRIL 14, 1904. [5466] *Clerk.*

Petition of the New York, New Haven and Hartford Railroad Company for certificate relative to abolition of grade crossing at Lenoxdale in the town of Lenox.

After due notice and hearing, an examination of the proposed plan for the abolition of the grade crossing of the highway and the railroad operated by the New York, New Haven and Hartford Railroad Company at Lenoxdale in the town of Lenox, as set forth in the report of the special commission duly appointed by the Superior Court to consider the same, and an inquiry into the expenditure therein authorized,

The Board hereby certifies that in its opinion the adoption of said plan and the incurring of such expenditure are consistent with the public interests, and are reasonably required to secure a fair distribution between the different cities, towns and railroads of the Commonwealth, of the public money appropriated for the abolition of grade crossings, and that such expenditure will not in its judgment exceed the amount to be paid by the Commonwealth under the provisions of law relating thereto.

Attest: CHARLES E. MANN,
JUNE 2, 1904. [5510] *Clerk.*

Petition of the selectmen of Lexington for certificate relative to abolition of grade crossing in that town.

After due notice and hearing, an examination of the proposed plan for the abolition of the grade crossing known as Grant street and the Boston and Lowell railroad (Boston and Maine Railroad, lessee), in the town of Lexington, as set forth in the report of the special commissioners duly appointed by the Superior Court to consider the same, and an inquiry into the expenditure therein authorized,

The Board hereby certifies that in its opinion the adoption of said plan and the incurring of such expenditure are consistent with the public interests, and are reasonably required to secure a fair distribution between the different cities, towns and railroads of the Commonwealth, of the public money appropriated for the abolition of grade crossings, and that such expenditure will not in its judgment exceed the amount to be paid by the Commonwealth under the provisions of law relating thereto.

Attest: CHARLES E. MANN,

FEBRUARY 25, 1904. [5322] *Clerk.*

Petition of the mayor and aldermen of Newton for certificate relative to abolition of grade crossings in that city.

W. S. SLOCUM for City of Newton.

SAMUEL HOAR for Boston and Albany railroad.

A. W. DEGOOSH for Commonwealth.

A. J. BAILEY for City of Boston.

J. H. BENTON, Jr., for New York, New Haven and Hartford railroad.

C. W. WITTERS for Central Vermont railway.

NATHAN MATTHEWS, Jr., for East Boston Land company.

A special commission appointed by the Superior Court has adopted a plan for separating grades where Glenn avenue, Langley road, Institution avenue and Cypress, Centre, Rogers, Hyde, Walnut, Boylston and Cook streets cross the Boston and Albany railroad in Newton.

The New York Central and Hudson River Railroad Company, lessee of the Boston and Albany railroad, contends that the work of separating these grades should be postponed.

The Legislature of 1902, after reviewing what had been accomplished in abolishing grade crossings of highways and railroads, appropriated an additional five million dollars in furtherance of the work. At the same time the law was changed to read as follows:

> No final decree shall be made by said superior court upon any report of commissioners setting forth a plan for the abolition, discontinuance or alteration of a grade crossing, adopting or confirming such plan or authorizing any expense to be charged against the commonwealth, until the board of railroad commissioners, after a hearing, shall have certified in writing that in their opinion the adoption of such plan and the expenditure to be incurred thereunder are consistent with the public interests, and are reasonably requisite to secure a fair distribution between the different cities, towns and railroads of the commonwealth, of the public money appropriated in the preceding section for the abolition of grade crossings.

The railroad company contends that it ought not to be required to carry on at the same time the work of separating grades in both East Boston and Newton. In favoring the East Boston and opposing the Newton project, the company urges that the improvement contemplated in East Boston is of great public importance and should be given precedence over that proposed in Newton, which, it argues, affects a smaller public and is of much less general interest. The further claim is made that Boston is entitled at this time to receive the benefit of the public fund, while Newton is not, having already enjoyed great advantages from the large expenditures made in abolishing grade crossings upon the main line of the Boston and Albany railroad.

The main purpose of the legislation of 1902 was to provide for carrying on the work of eliminating perils and annoyances which still threatened the public safety and convenience from the existence of grade crossings. Just what or exactly where expenditures had already been made in eliminating similar perils was of lesser moment. The statute does not contemplate that a corporation shall necessarily be relieved from future outlay on account of the work done in preceding years. For economic reasons, in other words to obtain greater security and convenience in the running of trains and larger freedom from expense in maintaining safeguards, a company with ample resources might well have expended large sums of money in doing away with these crossings.

We assume it to be our duty under the law now in force to secure an order of procedure which will be for the general welfare, with a view at the same time to a fair distribution of the public money among the different cities, towns and corporations, and with due regard to the amount of financial burden imposed upon any one of them. In the application of this rule there must always be indirectly felt to a greater or less extent the effect of expenditures already made in different communities.

As said in the Chelmsford case, it is impossible to accurately measure and apportion the amount of peril that exists at different crossings. In selecting one rather than another for abolition, the first factor to be considered is the relative importance of the traffic and travel which is affected, in determining which the uses made of both railroad and highway are to be considered.

The significance of the comparison between conditions in East Boston and in Newton would be greater if these two cases arose in an ordinary way under the general law. In each of these instances the Legislature has itself taken action looking to an early separation of grades. Chapter 468, Acts of 1900, in approving the lease of the Boston and Albany railroad to the New York Central and Hudson River Railroad Company, provides for grade crossing changes upon the Grand Junction railroad. Chapter 163, Acts of 1903, authorized the construction of a trestle in Newton, clearly in the contemplation that it would be a temporary affair, warranted by the prospect of early action in abolishing the crossings which rendered the structure necessary.

But aside from these considerations, a large public interest and importance attaches to the changes proposed in Newton. Not far from seventy trains are run daily excepting Sunday over this circuit, serving a large travelling public. Many of the streets which cross the railroad at grade are important thoroughfares. The number of passengers carried over this line and the large travel upon the ten highways which cross it, fairly warrant the prompt prosecution of the work. Nor do we find any reason for the belief that it is impracticable to carry forward both enterprises at the same time.

For these reasons

The Board hereby certifies that in its opinion the adoption of the plan and the incurring of the expenditure proposed in the report of the special commission appointed by the Superior Court to consider the abolition of certain grade crossings of highway and railroad in Newton are consistent with the public interests, and are reasonably required to secure a fair distribution between the different cities, towns and railroads of the Commonwealth, of the public money appropriated for the abolition of grade crossings, and that such expenditure will not in its judgment exceed the amount to be paid by the Commonwealth under the provisions of law relating thereto.

JAMES F. JACKSON,
GEORGE W. BISHOP,
CLINTON WHITE,
Commissioners.

APRIL 5, 1904. [5422]

Petition of the Hoosac Valley Street Railway Company for certificate relative to abolition of grade crossing in the city of North Adams.

Upon inquiry we find that the special commission appointed by the Superior Court to consider the proper method of abolishing the grade crossing of the highway and the Fitchburg railroad in North Adams, known as the Braytonville crossing, gave much study to the problem of drainage and careful attention to all suggestions of the city bearing upon the solution of that problem.

After a careful review of the facts and a personal inspection of the premises we believe that the plan adopted by that commission, which included in its membership an engineer of large experience and high standing, best meets the difficulties encountered in the surrounding conditions, and therefore

We hereby certify that in our opinion the adoption of the plan of the special commission above named and the incurring of the expenditure necessary to carry the same into effect are consistent with the public interests, and are reasonably required to secure a fair distribution between the different cities, towns and railroads of the Commonwealth, of the public money appropriated for the abolition of grade crossings, and that such expenditure will not in our judgment exceed the amount to be paid by the Commonwealth under the provisions of law relating thereto.

By the Board,

JAMES F. JACKSON,
Chairman.

NOVEMBER 9, 1904. [5601]

Petition of the selectmen of Walpole for certificate relative to abolition of certain grade crossings in that town.

After due notice and hearing, an examination of the proposed plan for the abolition of the grade crossings of Main, Oak, Elm, Spring, West, Kendall and Plympton streets and the railroad operated by the New York, New Haven and Hartford Railroad Company in the town of Walpole, as set forth in the report of the special commission duly appointed by the Superior Court to consider the same, and an inquiry into the expenditure therein authorized,

The Board hereby certifies that in its opinion the adoption of said plan and the incurring of such expenditure are consistent with the public interests, and are reasonably required to secure a fair distribution between the different cities, towns and railroads of the Commonwealth, of the public money appropriated for the abolition of grade crossings, and that such expenditure will not in its judgment exceed the amount to be paid by the Commonwealth under the provisions of law relating thereto.

Attest: CHARLES E. MANN,
Clerk.

JUNE 30, 1904. [5520]

ALTERATION OF CROSSINGS.

Designation of member of the Board for appointment on special commission.

In the matter of the alteration of the crossing of Maple street, Danvers, over the tracks of the Boston and Maine railroad, under section 137, chapter 111, Revised Laws, the Board has designated George W. Bishop, one of its members, for appointment by the Superior Court on a special commission to determine the questions named in said section.

For the Board,

CHARLES E. MANN,
Clerk.

JANUARY 7, 1904. [5405]

Designation of member of the Board for appointment on special commission.

In the matter of the alteration of the crossing of Ashland street and the tracks of the Boston and Maine railroad in the city of North Adams, the Board, acting under the provisions of section 137, chapter 111, Revised Laws, designates Clinton White, one of its members, for appointment by the Superior Court on a special commission to determine the questions named in said section.

For the Board,

CHARLES E. MANN,
Clerk.

JANUARY 25, 1904. [5418]

Designation of member of the Board for appointment on special commission.

In the matter of the alteration of the crossing of Hancock street and the tracks of the New York, New Haven and Hartford railroad in the city of Quincy, the Board, acting under the provisions of section 137, chapter 111, Revised Laws, designates George W. Bishop, one of its members, for appointment by the Superior Court on a special commission to determine the questions named in said section.

For the Board,

CHARLES E. MANN,
Clerk.

JANUARY 29, 1904. [5435]

METHOD OF CROSSING.

Second report to the Superior Court, of the Board, sitting as special masters in the case of the New York, New Haven and Hartford Railroad Company v. Hingham Street Railway Company.

We, the special masters appointed by order of the court in this cause, having been requested by the Old Colony Street Railway Company, as the successor of the Hingham Street Railway Company and of the Nantasket Electric Street Railway Company, to modify our former report, do hereby, after hearing the parties, and with their consent and approval, present the following substitute therefor:

First. The Old Colony Street Railway Company, the successor as aforesaid, ought to maintain and operate the trolley wires of its railway at Broad Bridge crossing, so called, and at Weir River crossing, so called, both in the town of Hingham in said Commonwealth, by a device like that shown on Plan A, on file in the office of the Board of Railroad Commissioners in the city of Boston in said Commonwealth; and at Wade's crossing, so called, in the town of Hull in said Commonwealth, by a device like that shown on Plan B, on file in said office.

Second. Such further decree as may be entered in said cause upon this our second and substituted report, should contain a paragraph similar to paragraph ninth in the interlocutory decree of the eighth day of June, 1896, to the end that this report may hereafter be modified as may be found desirable.

JAMES F. JACKSON,
GEORGE W. BISHOP,
CLINTON WHITE,
Commissioners.

MAY 9, 1904. [5268]

Petition of Elwyn H. Bemis for establishment of private crossing over the New York, New Haven and Hartford railroad in Northborough.

H. E. COTTLE for petitioner.

H. W. BEAL for company.

This petition is brought under section 144, chapter 111 of the Revised Laws. The argument of the petitioner is that he has been deprived of a way across the railroad, which had been gained by prescription, by the taking of the land for railroad purposes in connection with the abolition of certain grade crossings in Northborough; and that although he has brought suit in the courts for compensation on account of the injury, money damages will not make good the loss suffered through the closing of this way from one part of his premises to the other. He therefore urges that a private right of crossing be re-created for his benefit.

It is admitted that the statute does not create any new right of crossing; and no claim is made of a right of way by necessity, as known at common law, since there is communication between the different parts of the petitioner's estate by a route over the highway. The case rests wholly upon the claim that a more convenient right of crossing existed which had been acquired by prescription and which has been destroyed. Assuming this to be so, we are met point blank by the difficulty that there is nothing in the wording of the statute or of the decisions interpreting it, which indicates that it was intended to afford the relief sought.

Further, if the petition be treated as a request for an equivalent of what has been taken away, it would mean the re-establishment of a private grade crossing as an incident of the abolition of public grade crossings over a railroad. As a matter of sound public policy the

Board must decline to grant such a request unless the circumstances presented show a situation of extreme hardship.

Both as a matter of law and upon the merits, therefore, we are of the opinion that the petition must be dismissed.

By the Board,

JAMES F. JACKSON,
Chairman.

DECEMBER 19, 1904. [5548]

Petition of the Hoosac Valley Street Railway Company for consent to the construction of a railroad for private use in the transportation of freight across a highway in Adams.

It appearing that the selectmen of Adams have consented to the construction and maintenance of the proposed railroad across the highway; that the county commissioners of Berkshire county have adjudged that public necessity requires that the railroad cross the highway at a level therewith; and that the same is consistent with the public interests, — it is

Ordered, That the consent of the Board be hereby given to the construction and maintenance by the petitioner of a railroad, for private use in the transportation of freight, upon and across the highway leading from the west line of the Pittsfield and North Adams branch of the Boston and Albany railroad westerly to Howland avenue, as shown on a plan filed with this petition.

This consent is given upon the condition that a flagman shall display a flag by day and a lantern by night whenever an engine, car or train is approaching, and while it is passing over said crossing, and that no engine, car or train shall cross at a greater speed than four miles an hour.

Attest: CHARLES E. MANN,
Clerk.

DECEMBER 16, 1904. [5694]

LOCATIONS IN HIGHWAYS.

Petitions of the Maplewood and Danvers and the Haverhill and Boxford street railway companies for approval of locations in the cities of Malden and Melrose and the towns of Boxford, Middleton, Danvers, Peabody, Lynnfield and Saugus.

E. B. FULLER
M. E. S. CLEMONS } for petitioners.

B. W. WARREN for Boston and Northern street railway.

JOSEPH WIGGIN for City of Malden.

STARR PARSONS for Town of Lynnfield.

S. J. ELDER
E. J. POWERS } for abuttors.

We consider both petitions at the same time, as they have in view a single undertaking, the establishment of a street railway service between Haverhill and Boston.

The Boston and Maine Railroad, the Boston and Northern Street Railway Company, and the owners of certain real estate abutting upon highways in which grants of location have been made, remonstrate against the granting of these petitions, while the residents generally of the cities and towns through which the railway would pass actively favor the enterprise.

Chapter 399 of the Acts of 1902 reads in part as follows: "No location . . . granted by a board of aldermen or a board of selectmen . . . of the tracks of a street railway company . . . shall be valid until the Board of Railroad Commissioners has certified after public notice and a hearing that such location is consistent with the public interests."

Although counsel have contended for a different construction of this statute, we believe that it means that no certificate should be issued under it in any case where it appears that the construction of a proposed railway is detrimental to the general welfare for any reason. Under this rule the character, the usefulness and the effect of an enterprise are subjects of inquiry.

If it were clear that a contemplated railway would never pay operating expenses, or that the parties interested in it were unfit to exercise the franchise, or that the capital necessary to carry it out could not be secured, it would be our duty to refuse a certificate, and so prevent the encumbering of streets with useless tracks or the exploiting of a mere paper scheme for idle or illegitimate ends.

So, too, if an enterprise had for its object merely the introduction of a new competitor into a field that is already occupied, we would refuse our certificate upon the ground that the usual fruit of such competition is at best only a transitory gain, which is outweighed by the permanent disadvantages that follow. On the other hand, we are not called upon to prevent private capital from taking the risks involved in an enterprise which from the standpoint of the public promises a new and substantial service.

The proposed railway, if built, would open a new avenue of travel and afford many people a convenience not now enjoyed. The character of the highways upon which locations have been obtained, and the fact that the railway will run for quite a distance upon private land, makes possible a quicker and more direct service than that furnished upon any existing street railway, and of a character essentially different from that provided upon the steam railroad. It would bring street car accommodation to several communities now without it, and tend to exert an active influence in building up a section with natural advantages as yet unimproved.

Although the contemplated road would compete to some extent with the Boston and Maine railroad and the Boston and Northern street railway, we cannot believe that the competition would be so serious as to warrant us in accepting the suggestion of these companies that the undertaking should be prohibited. Admitting that it would be detrimental to the public interests to cripple or seriously hamper an existing service, we do not believe that the building of the proposed railway would inflict such radical injury upon either of these remonstrants.

The local travel upon this line would at first be small, and the financial success of the undertaking rest largely upon through traffic, but it is not clear that the patronage as a whole would be inadequate to meet expenses. In other words, it is a case where private capital should be left to make its own study of the risks; and abundant warning as to what the risks are is to be found in the recent experience of street railway companies.

The Legislature has so far favored the project as to have conferred upon one of the companies unusual powers with reference to construction over private land and the bridging of the Merrimac river. No one will contend in the light of recent accidents that it is not wise to avoid heavy grades and sharp curves by constructing such railways in part at least upon private land.

Residents upon Pleasant street in Haverhill are naturally concerned in the preservation of the trees which adorn that highway, but the reasons for locating the railway in this street seem controlling; and it does not necessarily follow that the building of the railway should mean the destruction of the trees.

The remonstrants have presented a large number of requests for rulings upon what are claimed to be matters of law. While it is extremely doubtful whether these requests have any standing under section 98, chapter 112, of the Revised Laws, we make in reply a general statement in addition to what has already been said, giving the views of the Board and sustaining the contention of the remonstrants upon some points and the contention of the petitioners upon others.

1. A condition which requires that a company keep any part of the street in repair is in direct conflict with the general law.

2. A condition which predetermines the schedule time of cars, the character of accommodations, or rates of fare, is objectionable for the reason that the general law provides other methods to protect the public interests as they arise from time to time.

3. A condition which fixes for all time the location of a structure such as a car barn or power plant, is against a sound public policy for the reason that such structures should be maintained where, in connection with the development of a system, experience may show that they will best contribute to the efficiency of the service.

4. A condition which may work the forfeiture of a location after the railway has been built upon it, without a hearing of parties interested or in a manner contrary to the general law providing for revocation of rights, is plainly improper.

On the other hand

1. Street railway termini named in an agreement of association are subject to greater uncertainty than the termini of a steam railroad. The variation between the northerly terminus of the Maplewood and Danvers railway, described in the agreement of association, and the terminus afterward established is unimportant.

2. The attempt to enforce as a contract a condition by which the company ought to be bound does not make the location objectionable. As an effort to alter the legal status of the parties it is probably ineffective.

3. A company may well be asked in some instances to make good the encroachment of a railway upon the other uses of an existing highway, and so to bear the expense of widening and improving it. In other instances it would be unjust to those who support the railway by fares to require an investment of railway capital in street improvements.

4. A requirement that the poles of a company shall support wires used in other public works under conditions which prevent impair-

ment of the street railway service, and which do not impose an unreasonable burden upon a company, is unobjectionable.

As these locations stand we cannot issue a certificate. To properly bring them again before us a petition must be filed upon which a public hearing will be given. Changes in the conditions attached to locations should be made upon petition of the company and by proper action at meetings of the local boards. The advisability of giving a public hearing upon such petition is left, as far as our subsequent action is concerned, to their discretion.

By the Board,

JAMES F. JACKSON,
Chairman.

DECEMBER 7, 1904. [5465-5595]

Petition of the Pittsfield Electric Street Railway Company for approval of locations in the city of Pittsfield.

B. W. WARREN } for petitioner.
WM. TURTLE }

JOHN C. CROSBY for City of Pittsfield.

The board of aldermen of Pittsfield for the year 1903, at its last meeting, granted several locations to the Pittsfield Electric Street Railway Company. The succeeding board of aldermen at its first meeting voted to rescind that action. In the meantime the company had filed its petition with this Board under the provisions of chapter 399, Acts of 1902.

The remonstrants ask for a ruling that there are no locations properly before us. We cannot take that view of the situation, but rule that the powers of boards of aldermen in granting street railway locations are expressly defined by statute; that when a grant has once been formally made, and the company has filed with this Board its petition for a certificate, it is too late for the aldermen to rescind their action without the consent of the company. There would seem to be still less authority for one board to revoke the action of its predecessor, even though it be admitted that such boards are for certain purposes continuing bodies.

However, the public interests of Pittsfield are now in charge of the government of 1904, and its members are entitled to have their reasons why we should not approve these locations fully considered.

Some of these questions are purely technical. It is claimed that three of the petitions for location were filed in 1902, and that no action upon them could be taken in the following year. Again, it is claimed that the company having neglected to present plans at the public hearing, and the committee to which the petitions were referred having failed to report upon them, the aldermen had no authority to pass the order granting the locations. We rule, to the contrary, that the aldermen of 1903 had the right to treat the petitions filed in 1902 as properly before them; that while it is desirable that plans be presented at public hearings of this character, there is no law requiring it; and that a board may lawfully dispense with the services of its own committee; indeed, in this case it could not well do otherwise, as the committee consisted of two who would not agree.

We come to the suggestion that the aldermen of 1903 did not fully protect the public interests. We find, however, that the orders of location have been carefully drawn, that the company is required to properly build and drain its roadbed and to hereafter maintain its railway in conformity with the rest of the highway, making all changes necessary to secure a proper travelled road and sidewalk; and to fulfil these obligations in a manner satisfactory to the board of public works. Provision is made for the reimbursement of the city for all cost or expense incurred in consequence of the construction and maintenance of the railway.

Some criticism has been made as to the position of the track for short distances in certain localities. If this criticism is well grounded, it is a matter of minor detail which can be readily remedied at a later time.

The orders provide that as to any part of the locations which shall not have been constructed and put in use on or before December 1, 1904, the grant shall have become void. This is essentially unlike the objectionable forfeiture clause in the Springfield grant, as it conflicts with no statutory process better adapted to secure the public interests.

Although the grants were made at the last meeting of the outgoing board of aldermen, these locations had been before the board for more than a year, public hearings had been given at which no one had appeared in opposition, an official view of the premises had been taken and the whole subject had been deliberately considered.

Upon the whole, the Board is satisfied that these locations are consistent with the public interests, and will issue its certificate to that effect as soon as the position of poles shall have been approved by the board of aldermen. It has been our practice to request that pole locations in city streets be determined by local boards before the issue of a certificate, even though it be claimed that they are incidental to the track locations.

JAMES F. JACKSON,
GEORGE W. BISHOP,
CLINTON WHITE,
Commissioners.

MARCH 1, 1904. [5404]

Petition of the Western Massachusetts Street Railway Company for approval of locations in Lee and Chester.

After due notice and hearing and full consideration, we hereby certify that the location for the tracks of the Western Massachusetts street railway in the highway which leads from West Becket post office to East Lee, near Green Water pond in the town of Lee, granted in an order of the selectmen of said town dated April 5, 1902, and the location for the tracks of said railway in the Huntington and Chester road, Maple and Main streets and Becket road, in the town of Chester, granted in an order of the selectmen of that town dated March 17, 1902, copies of which orders, with accompanying plans, are on file in this office, are consistent with the public interests.

This certificate is issued upon the understanding that wherever in the several towns through which this railway passes the location of its tracks leaves the travelled road too narrow for the proper accommodation of those using it, the company at its own expense shall provide a road of the width and character previously enjoyed; and upon the further understanding that nothing contained in the conditions attached to the foregoing locations shall be construed as intended to limit the authority of any public board.

JAMES F. JACKSON,
GEORGE W. BISHOP,
CLINTON WHITE,
Commissioners.

NOVEMBER 22, 1904. [5114]

Petition of the Worcester and Webster Street Railway Company for certificate relative to location in Oxford.

The location recently given the petitioner in the town of Oxford connects its railway with the Worcester and Southbridge railway and thus secures a safer and more convenient route into Worcester. This is desirable.

The selectmen of Auburn, fearing a diversion of travel from the existing line of the Worcester and Webster railway and a consequent loss of accommodation for their townspeople, undertook when granting locations to prevent this by attaching to these locations conditions intended to defeat any attempt at building such a connecting link as the location now before us. We doubt the right of selectmen to stop the development of transportation facilities both within and without their borders in this way, but we recognize at the same time the right of the selectmen and of the townspeople to ask that their interests in the existing line of railway be properly protected.

If the building of the line in which the remonstrants are interested were now under consideration, we would hesitate to approve its present route, for the reason that it would seem practicable to build upon some other route equally serviceable and less objectionable in grade. However, the location was granted and the railway built before this Board was given any authority over street railway locations, and it is only fair that those who are now served by it, some of whom have established their homes in reliance upon it, should receive proper protection. Therefore we have called upon the company to declare its purposes in connection with the new location, and approve it only upon the understanding that the company will continue to give the remonstrants an adequate service between Oxford Heights and Worcester, meaning by adequate service, for the present at least, one which is equivalent to that now enjoyed.

In accordance with these views,

The Board hereby certifies that the location for the tracks of the Worcester and Webster street railway in Old Main street and the road from Charlton to Auburn in the town of Oxford, granted in an order of the selectmen of said town dated September 29, 1904, a copy of which order, with accompanying plan, is on file in this office, is consistent with the public interests.

JAMES F. JACKSON,
GEORGE W. BISHOP,
CLINTON WHITE,
Commissioners.

NOVEMBER 19, 1904. [5623]

Under the provisions of chapter 399 of the Acts of 1902, the Board has during the period covered by this report issued certificates that the locations or alterations of locations for the tracks of various street railway companies granted by local authorities were consistent with the public interests. Under prior legislation it has also approved locations granted street railway companies in the city of Boston, the city of Cambridge and the town of Brookline.

Appended is a list of highway locations granted to various street railway companies and approved by the Board: —

Blue Hill Street Railway Company.

September 29, 1904, Milton — Location in Blue Hill and Canton avenues, established under an order of the selectmen dated September 9, 1904. [5614]

Boston and Northern Street Railway Company.

January 15, 1904, North Reading — Location and alteration of location granted to the Lawrence and Reading Street Railway Company in orders of the selectmen dated April 14, 1903 and May 6, 1903, and established in part under decree of the Massachusetts Highway Commission dated August 27, 1903. [5378]

June 9, 1904, Andover — Location in Main street, established under an order of the selectmen dated April 25, 1904. [5508]

June 24, 1904, Stoneham — Location in Main and Franklin streets, established under an order of the selectmen dated May 12, 1904. [5536]

July 19, 1904, Beverly — Location in Bridge, River, West Federal and Federal streets, established under an order of the board of aldermen dated April 18, 1904. [5541]

September 22, 1904, Danvers — Alteration of location in Maple street at Whipple's bridge, established under an order of the selectmen dated September 10, 1904. [5609]

September 23, 1904, Medford — Location and alteration of location in Winthrop and High streets, established under an order of the board of aldermen dated September 13, 1904. [5611]

October 27, 1904, Stoneham — Location and relocation in Montvale avenue, established under an order of the selectmen dated October 10, 1904. [5638]

November 16, 1904, Haverhill — Location and relocation in Main street in the Bradford district, established under an order of the board of aldermen dated September 10, 1904. [5654]

December 9, 1904, Woburn — Location and relocation in Montvale avenue and Elm street, established under an order of the city council dated October 24, 1904. [5662]

Boston and Worcester Street Railway Company.

May 25, 1904, Marlborough — Location in Mill street, established under an order of the board of aldermen dated May 16, 1904. [5519]

May 25, 1904, Westborough — Location in Lyman and East Main streets, established under an order of the selectmen dated May 18, 1904. [5518]

Dartmouth and Westport Street Railway Company.

September 19, 1904, Dartmouth — Location and alteration of location in Kempton street, established under an order of the selectmen dated July 23, 1904, and acted upon favorably by the Massachusetts Highway Commission in its vote of August 25, 1904. [5590]

October 17, 1904, Dartmouth — Location and alteration of location in Kempton street, established under an order of the selectmen dated August 27, 1904. [5625]

Hampshire Street Railway Company.

December 21, 1904, South Hadley — Location in highway near the residence of Mr. Dexter Burnett, established under an order of the selectmen dated November 7, 1904. [5676]

Hartford and Worcester Street Railway Company.

March 31, 1904, Leicester — Location in Main, Forest, Brook, Stafford, Wilson and Henshaw streets, established under an order of the selectmen dated February 12, 1904. [5458]

Hoosac Valley Street Railway Company.

January 13, 1904, North Adams — Location in Hodges road, established under an order of the city council dated July 7, 1903. [5289]

March 29, 1904, Williamstown — Location in North Hoosac, Bridges, Sand Springs and Simonds roads, established under an order of the selectmen dated March 2, 1904. [5467]

April 27, 1904, Williamstown — Location in Southworth, Main and Water streets, River and New Ashford roads, established under an order of the selectmen dated March 10, 1904. [5484]

July 20, 1904, Adams — Location in Columbia street and Howland avenue, established under an order of the selectmen dated March 21, 1904. [5556]

September 7, 1904, Williamstown — Location in Sand Springs and Simonds roads, established under an order of the selectmen dated August 10, 1904. [5599]

Newton Street Railway Company.

January 25, 1904, Waltham — Location in Moody and Pine streets, established under an order of the board of aldermen dated December 21, 1903. [5403]

December 30, 1904, Waltham — Pole relocation in Moody street, established under an order of the board of aldermen dated November 21, 1904. [5697]

Old Colony Street Railway Company.

March 10, 1904, Fall River — Alteration of location in Stafford road, established under an order of the board of aldermen dated February 1, 1904. [5448]

March 14, 1904, Braintree — Permission to erect and maintain certain poles for the support of feed and stay wires and other devices for conducting electricity over and across Commercial, Elm, Adams, Union, Middle, Pearl, Plain, Grove and Liberty streets and Hillside road, established under an order of the selectmen dated January 25, 1904. [5437]

April 12, 1904, Fall River — Permission to construct and maintain manholes and connecting conduit in Ferry street, established under an order of the board of aldermen dated December 21, 1903. [5483]

June 24, 1904, Taunton — Location in Somerset and Railroad avenues and South street, established under an order of the board of aldermen dated June 1, 1904. [5535]

July 5, 1904, Fall River — Location in President avenue, Davol and Brownell streets and Remington avenue, established under an order of the board of aldermen dated July 6, 1903, as amended June 6, 1904. [5546]

July 5, 1904, Milton — Location in Brook road, established under an order of the selectmen dated June 10, 1904. [5547]

November 16, 1904, Abington — Location and alteration of location in Washington street, established under an order of the selectmen dated October 5, 1904. [5656]

November 16, 1904, Whitman — Location and alteration of location in Washington street, established under orders of the selectmen dated June 21, 1904 and July 28, 1904. [5655]

Pittsfield Electric Street Railway Company.

July 13, 1904, Pittsfield — Location in North, Tyler, Melville, First, Adam, Second, Lincoln, Fourth, Curtis, Brown and Kellogg streets; in Wahconah and North streets; in Peck's road and Lake avenue; in New West, West, Onota and Linden streets, established under orders of the board of aldermen dated January 1, 1904, as amended June 6, 1904. [5404]

September 16, 1904, Pittsfield — Location in Linden street, Dewey and Columbus avenues, South John and West streets, established under an order of the board of aldermen dated July 18, 1904, as amended September 13, 1904. [5578]

South Middlesex Street Railway Company.

April 6, 1904, Framingham — Location and alteration of location in Waverley street, established under an order of the selectmen dated February 18, 1904. [5461]

April 12, 1904, Sherborn — Location and alteration of location in Waverley street, established under an order of the selectmen dated March 16, 1904. [5475]

October 26, 1904, Hopkinton — Relocation in Main street, established under an order of the selectmen dated September 30, 1904. [5634]

Union Street Railway Company.

March 10, 1904, Dartmouth — Alteration of location in Elm street, established under an order of the selectmen dated January 16, 1904. [5457]

December 8, 1904, New Bedford — Location for spur track in William street, established under an order of the board of aldermen dated November 10, 1904. [5658]

Uxbridge and Blackstone Street Railway Company.

October 6, 1904, Northbridge — Location in North Main and Main streets, established under an order of the selectmen dated August 3, 1904. [5588]

West End Street Railway Company.

January 12, 1904, Somerville — Location and rights, established under orders of the board of aldermen dated October 22, 1903. [5374]

May 16, 1904, Boston, Everett, Brookline, Belmont — Locations and rights, established under orders of the authorities of Boston (233rd location), Everett (104–3 ; 105–4), Brookline (106–4 ; 103–3 ; 44–9), and Belmont (17–8). [5497]

July 27, 1904, Boston, Everett, Medford, Somerville, Brookline — Location and rights, established under orders of the authorities of Boston (permission to attach wires to pole on Main street, Ward 4), Everett (36–5), Medford (19–6), Somerville (52–4) and Brookline (45–9). [5559]

August 15, 1904, Cambridge — Location and rights, established under an order of the board of aldermen dated August 2, 1904 (55–2). [5585]

August 30, 1904, Boston — Locations and rights, established under orders of the board of aldermen (234th, 235th, 236th, 237th locations). [5591]

October 13, 1904, Boston, Somerville — Location and rights, established under orders of the authorities of Boston (238th location; permission to attach wires to poles on Summer street extension) and Somerville (53–4 ; 54–4). [5629]

October 24, 1904, Watertown — Location and rights, established under orders of the selectmen dated October 7, 1904 (25–10). [5636]

Worcester Consolidated Street Railway Company.

September 20, 1904, Worcester — Location in Pleasant street, established under an order of the board of aldermen dated July 18, 1904. [5586]

Worcester and Holden Street Railway Company.

October 19, 1904, Holden — Location in Princeton road and Depot street, established under an order of the selectmen dated August 25, 1904. [5622]

Worcester and Northern Street Railway Company.

August 18, 1904, Holden, Princeton, Westminster — Locations, established under orders of the selectmen of Holden and Princeton dated March 18, 1904 and February 28, 1903 respectively, as amended by orders dated August 17, 1904 and August 16, 1904, respectively, and under an order of the selectmen of Westminster dated April 6, 1904. [5534]

LOCATIONS ON PRIVATE LAND.

Under the provisions of general laws the Board has during the year granted authority to various street railway companies to construct their railways in part upon private land for the purpose of avoiding undesirable grades and curves in the public highway and for other purposes incidental to the use of these highways, or avoiding the crossing of the railway with a steam railroad, these orders being based in each case upon evidence that public necessity and convenience demanded such action. A summary of these orders follows: —

Hampshire Street Railway Company.

December 21, 1904, South Hadley — To avoid grades and curves in highway. [5678]

Hoosac Valley Street Railway Company.

January 15, 1904, North Adams — To avoid grades and curves in highway. [5290]

September 7, 1904, Williamstown — To avoid grades and curves in highway. [5557]

Uxbridge and Blackstone Street Railway Company.

October 6, 1904, Northbridge — To avoid grades and curves in highway. [5588]

Worcester and Holden Street Railway Company.

December 8, 1904, Holden — To obtain convenient access to the Central Massachusetts railroad. [5665]

Worcester and Northern Street Railway Company.

August 18, 1904, Holden, Princeton, Westminster — To avoid grades and curves in highway. [5534]

Worcester and Webster Street Railway Company.

November 19, 1904, Oxford — To avoid grades and curves in highway. [5623]

CERTIFICATE PRELIMINARY TO OPERATION — RAILROAD.

Petition of the Boston and Maine Railroad for certificate in connection with the relocation of tracks of the Central Massachusetts Branch and the Worcester, Nashua and Rochester railroad at Oakdale station in West Boylston.

The Board, having made an examination of the relocated portion of the Worcester, Nashua and Rochester railroad, the relocated portion of the Central Massachusetts Branch of the Boston and Maine railroad near the Oakdale station in West Boylston, and the single track "Y" railroad connecting the two before named roads, each described on a plan on file with the petition, hereby certifies that all laws relating to construction have been complied with, and that they appear to be in a safe condition for operation.

Attest: CHARLES E. MANN,
Clerk.

MAY 3, 1904. [5452]

CERTIFICATES PRELIMINARY TO OPERATION — STREET RAILWAYS.

During the year the Board, having made examinations of a part or the whole of the railways of various street railway companies, issued its certificates that all laws relating to construction had been complied with, and that they appeared to be in a safe condition for operation. A detailed list of these certificates follows: —

Blue Hill Street Railway Company.

September 30, 1904, Milton — Thirteen thousand nine hundred seven feet second main track in Blue Hill avenue. [5621]

Boston Elevated Railway Company.

December 6, 1904, Boston — In East Boston tunnel, from Maverick square to Court street. [5669]

Boston and Northern Street Railway Company.

August 15, 1904, Andover — One thousand feet in Main street. [5583]

August 31, 1904, Saugus — Four thousand eight hundred forty-five feet single track in Lincoln avenue and Central street. [5580.]

Boston and Worcester Street Railway Company.

June 15, 1904, Shrewsbury, Northborough — About four thousand six hundred fifty feet second main track across Fruit street and over private land in Shrewsbury, about three thousand two hundred seventy-five feet second main track over private land in Northborough. [5540]

June 22, 1904, Westborough — One mile second main track over private land. [5543]

July 1, 1904, Westborough — Eighty-five one-hundredths of a mile second main track over private land and across East Main and Lyman streets. [5551]

August 5, 1904, Westborough, Southborough — One thousand feet second main track over private land in Westborough, ten thousand six hundred feet second main track over private land and across Parkerville, Central and Cemetery roads in Southborough. [5581]

Greenfield, Deerfield and Northampton Street Railway Company.

June 23, 1904, Deerfield — Fourteen hundred feet over bridge at Sprout's crossing. [5482]

Hoosac Valley Street Railway Company.

January 19, 1904, North Adams — Over bridge crossing the Hoosic river at Braytonville. [5392]

July 7, 1904, Adams, North Adams — Over private land in Adams, over private land and through East road, Ashland and Main streets in North Adams, about four and thirty-three one-hundredths miles; connecting track in Ashland, Main and Eagle streets in North Adams, about ninety feet; side track on private land near line between Adams and North Adams, about 700 feet; total distance over private land about two and twenty-two one-hundredths miles, in highways about two and eleven one-hundredths miles. [5555]

December 31, 1904, Williamstown — About one and twenty-five one-hundredths miles in North Hoosac and Sand Springs roads and over private land. [5709]

Leominster, Shirley and Ayer Street Railway Company.

July 25, 1904, Leominster, Lunenburg, Shirley — In Prospect street and over private land in Leominster, in Tophet and Reservoir roads and over private land in Lunenburg, over private land and in Main street in Shirley, total distance of about twenty-seven thousand twenty-five feet. [5567]

August 31, 1904, Shirley, Harvard, Ayer — In Front street and over private land in Shirley, over private land in Harvard, in Main street, over private land, across Fitchburg division of the Boston and Maine railroad and in West Main street in Ayer, total distance of about three and five-tenths miles. [5592]

Old Colony Street Railway Company.

February 26, 1904, Boston (West Roxbury, Dorchester) — Second main track in Washington, South and Brandon streets, Belgrade avenue, Beech, Centre, Spring, Ashland, Oakland and River streets. [5372]

August 15, 1904, Norwood — Five hundred five feet in Washington street. [5587]

August 31, 1904, Fall River — Six thousand four hundred fifty feet in Bay street. [5566]

September 27, 1904, Fall River — Two thousand nine hundred sixty-two feet double track in President avenue, Davol and Brownell streets and Remington avenue. [5608]

October 25, 1904, Milton — One thousand five hundred eighteen feet double track in Blue Hills Parkway and Brook road. [5635]

December 14, 1904, Boston (West Roxbury) — About five thousand six hundred eighty-five feet double track in Hyde Park avenue. [5668]

Pittsfield Electric Street Railway Company.

August 20, 1904, Hinsdale — Two thousand fifty feet in state highway, over east branch of Housatonic river, and in Plunkett and Main streets. [5584]

November 7, 1904, Hinsdale — Five hundred feet in Main street and over Housatonic river. [5647]

South Middlesex Street Railway Company.

October 12, 1904, Natick, Sherborn, Framingham — Five thousand one hundred feet second main track in West Central street in Natick, fifty feet second main track in Waverley street in Sherborn, four thousand feet second main track in Waverley street in Framingham. [5633]

December 5, 1904, Natick, Sherborn, Framingham — Reconstructed main track, five thousand two hundred feet in West Central street in Natick, forty feet in Waverley street in Sherborn, four thousand two hundred fifty feet in Waverley street in Framingham. [5641]

December 5, 1904, Framingham — About seven hundred seventy-one feet in Waverley street. [5660]

Waltham Street Railway Company.

January 1, 1904, Waltham — Four hundred three feet in South street. [5391]

West End Street Railway Company.

August 15, 1904, Boston — Double track in Summer street. [5582]

September 26, 1904, Medford — Seven thousand three hundred sixty-three feet double track in Medford square, High street and Playstead road. [5619]

Worcester Consolidated Street Railway Company.

October 26, 1904, Worcester — Six hundred ninety-one feet in Pleasant street. [5640]

Worcester and Holden Street Railway Company.

December 10, 1904, Holden — About two thousand seventy-three feet single track in Princeton road and Depot street and over private land. [5650]

REGULATION OF SPEED OF STREET RAILWAY CARS.

Approval of regulations for speed of cars upon street railways in the town of Brookline.

It is *Ordered*, That the regulations relative to speed of cars upon street railways in the town of Brookline, established by the selectmen of said town, as revised and approved, be as follows:

1. Except in spaces reserved for street railways no street car shall be operated at a rate of speed greater than fifteen (15) miles an hour. This exception shall not apply to Boylston street between Heath and Lee streets.

2. No street railway car shall be operated at a rate of speed greater than eight (8) miles an hour at any of the following points: —

On Harvard street at School street and Aspinwall avenue;

On Boylston street at Cypress street, at Warren street and Sumner road, and at Dunster road;

On Cypress street at Walnut street.

Inward bound cars approaching Harvard square and approaching the junction of Washington and Boylston streets shall not be operated at a rate of speed greater than eight miles an hour. Cars must be run with the utmost caution at all the points specified.

3. Unless authority is specially given no single truck car shall be operated at a rate of speed exceeding fifteen (15) miles an hour.

4. Before taking any heavy descending grade the speed of every car must be so reduced as to test the working of the brake.

5. Wherever the railway occupies a portion of, or is close to, the travelled road the speed of every car must be, from time to time, so reduced as to permit the safe use of the road by others.

6. Every car shall come to a full stop before crossing another street railway at grade.

7. In approaching any public or private way crossed by the railway the speed of every car must be so reduced that the car may be stopped in season to avoid collision with any person or vehicle rightfully using such way.

8. In rounding curves and in all cases where the view of the motorman is obstructed, the speed of every car must be reduced to meet this condition of limited vision of railway and highway.

9. A car must always be under such control as to enable the motorman to stop it in season to avoid collision or injury in every emergency which it is reasonable to expect may arise.

Attest: CHARLES E. MANN,
JULY 7, 1904. [5539] *Clerk.*

Approval of regulations for speed of cars upon street railways in the town of Natick.

The so-called reservation upon which the Boston and Worcester street railway is located in Natick is so meagre in extent and in many places so ineffectually separated from the travelled road, that we cannot consent to a rate of speed for street cars in excess of twenty-five miles an hour.

That the selectmen have authorized a higher rate, that at the public hearing the expression of views on the part of representative citizens was unanimous in favor of a higher rate, are facts which have been duly considered, but which do not convince us that the safety and convenience of those who travel upon the highway would be properly protected if we should consent to a rate of speed, under present conditions, higher than that above named.

It is therefore *Ordered*, That the regulations relative to speed of cars upon street railways in the town of Natick, established by the selectmen of said town, as revised and approved, be as follows:

1. On Pond street between Cemetery street and South Main street, South Main street between Pond street and East Central street, East Central street between South Main street and McGrath's lane, North Main street between the Wayland town line and a point opposite the North Natick school house, North Main street between Worcester street and Main street, Main street between North Main street and South avenue, South avenue, Hanchett avenue, Union street between Morse lane and Eliot street, Eliot street between Union street and Water street, Water street between Eliot street and the Charles River bridge, the speed of cars shall not exceed fifteen (15) miles an hour.

On East Central street between McGrath's lane and the Wellesley town line, Union street between Union square and Morse lane, Water street between the Charles River bridge and Dover street, Dover street between Water street and the Dover town line, West Central street between the Sherborn town line and Mill street, Mill street between West Central street and Pond street, Pond street between Mill street and Cemetery street, North Main street between Worcester street and a point opposite the North Natick school house, and on Worcester street, the speed of cars shall not exceed twenty-five (25) miles an hour.

2. Unless authority is specially given no single truck car shall be operated at a rate of speed exceeding fifteen (15) miles an hour.

3. Before taking any heavy descending grade the speed of every car must be so reduced as to test the working of the brake.

4. Wherever the railway occupies a portion of, or is close to, the travelled road, the speed of every car must be, from time to time, so reduced as to permit the safe use of the road by others.

5. Every car shall come to a full stop before crossing another street railway at grade.

6. In approaching any public or private way crossed by the railway the speed of every car must be so reduced that the car may be stopped in season to avoid collision with any person or vehicle rightfully using such way.

7. In rounding curves and in all cases where the view of the motorman is obstructed the speed of every car must be reduced to meet this condition of limited vision of railway and highway.

8. A car must always be under such control as to enable the motorman to stop it in season to avoid collison or injury in every emergency which it is reasonable to expect may arise.

By the Board,

JAMES F. JACKSON,
Chairman.

JULY 6, 1904. [5339]

Approval of regulations for speed of cars upon street railways in the town of Southborough.

It appears that, as stated in the communication received April 8, 1904, the selectmen of Southborough have established the following regulations as to speed of cars upon street railways in that town: —

Pursuant to the provisions of section 40 of chapter 112 of the Revised Laws and chapter 143 of the Acts of 1903 the selectmen of Southborough hereby establish the following regulations as to the rate of speed and the mode of use of tracks within the town of Southborough, such regulations being required in the interest and for the convenience of the public:

Between the boundary line between Southborough and Framingham and the highway at the foot of Slawson's Hill not exceeding twenty (20) miles an hour.

Between the highway at the foot of Slawson's Hill and the Baptist church in Fayville not exceeding six (6) miles an hour.

Between the Baptist church and White's corner not exceeding twenty-five (25) miles an hour.

Between White's corner and the station of the New York, New Haven and Hartford Railroad Company in Southborough Centre not exceeding twenty (20) miles an hour.

Between the station of the New York, New Haven and Hartford Railroad

Company in Southborough Centre and Andrews' saw mill not exceeding six (6) miles an hour.

Between Andrews' saw mill and the line between Southborough and Marlborough not exceeding twenty (20) miles an hour.

Between the boundary line between Westborough and Southborough and the line between Marlborough and Westborough not exceeding twenty (20) miles an hour; except that at the crossing of the main road from Southborough to Westborough, at O'Leary's corner, at the crossing of the old road to Northborough and at the highways which meet near the overhead bridge over the tracks of the New York, New Haven and Hartford Railroad Company the cars shall be slowed to a speed not exceeding four (4) miles an hour.

It is *Ordered*, That the foregoing regulations be revised by the addition of the following rules, and that as so revised they be hereby approved: —

1. Unless authority is specially given no single truck car shall be operated at a rate of speed exceeding fifteen (15) miles an hour.

2. Before taking any heavy descending grade the speed of every car must be so reduced as to test the working of the brake.

3. Wherever the railway occupies a portion of, or is close to, the travelled road, the speed of every car must be from time to time so reduced as to permit the safe use of the road by others.

4. Every car shall come to a full stop before crossing another street railway at grade.

5. In approaching any public or private way crossed by the railway the speed of every car must be so reduced that the car may be stopped in season to avoid collision with any person or vehicle rightfully using such way.

6. In rounding curves and in all places where the view of the motorman is obstructed, the speed of every car must be reduced to meet this condition of limited vision of railway and highway.

7. A car must always be under such control as to enable the motorman to stop it in season to avoid collision or injury in every emergency which it is reasonable to expect may arise.

Attest: CHARLES E. MANN,
JULY 7, 1904. [5432] *Clerk.*

Petition of the selectmen of Winchester for approval of regulations for speed of cars upon street railways in the town of Winchester.

While in substantial agreement with the views of the selectmen of Winchester, we believe it better that the phraseology used in other cases should be used in this, and that the rate fixed here be that established elsewhere under similar conditions, namely, fifteen miles per hour.

It is therefore

Ordered, That the regulations fixing the rate of speed upon street railways in the town of Winchester, as revised and approved, be established as follows:

The speed of cars upon street railways located in the public streets in the town of Winchester shall not exceed the rate of fifteen (15) miles per hour.

This rate of speed is subject to the following *limiting rules*, which are made an essential part of this regulation:

1. Unless authority is specially given, no single truck car shall be operated at a rate of speed exceeding fifteen (15) miles an hour.

2. Before taking any heavy descending grade, the speed of every car must be so reduced as to test the working of the brake.

3. Wherever the railway occupies a portion of, or is close to, the travelled road, the speed of every car must be from time to time so reduced as to permit the safe use of the road by others.

4. Every car shall come to a full stop before crossing another street railway at grade.

5. In approaching any public or private way crossed by the railway, the speed of every car must be so reduced that the car may be stopped in season to avoid collision with any person rightfully using such way.

6. In rounding curves and in all cases where the view of the motorman is obstructed, the speed of every car must be reduced to meet this condition of limited vision of railway or highway.

7. A car must always be under such control as to enable the motorman to stop it in season to avoid collision or injury in every emergency which it is reasonable to expect may arise.

JAMES F. JACKSON,
GEORGE W. BISHOP,
CLINTON WHITE,
Commissioners.

JANUARY 12, 1904. [5381]

In addition to the above, the Board has issued orders approving regulations for speed of cars in the town of Framingham, at rates of 15, 20 and 25 miles an hour; in the town of Gardner, the rates being 10 and 15 miles an hour; in the city of Lowell, the rates being 10 and 15 miles an hour; and in the town of Seekonk, the rates being 15 and 20 miles an hour, these rates in each case being subject to the limiting rules which appear in each of the orders printed in full.

STATIONS AND STATION ACCOMMODATIONS.

Petition of the Boston Elevated Railway Company for approval of platform extensions at stations in Boston.

On the petition of the Boston Elevated Railway Company, the consent of the Board is hereby given to the proposed extension of elevated station platforms for the accommodation of five car trains in accordance with the plans hereinafter mentioned, said proposed extensions being modifications or changes of the structure heretofore erected in accordance with plans approved by the Board, and the following plans showing such proposed extensions are hereby approved by the Board, to wit: — plans numbered 26653, 26655, 26656, 26659, 26676, 26678, 26680, 26681, 26683, 26684, 26665, 26668, 26669, 26673, and dated July 7, 1904.

The above mentioned plans are modifications of plans numbered 25022, 25024, 25026, 25027, 25030, 25031, 25032, 25033, 25034, 25035, 25036, 25038 and 25041, approved by the Board July 11, 1898; and of plans 20007, 20008, 20112, 20113, 20151, 20192, 20163, 20190, 20168, 20189, 20170, 20186, 20187, 20188, 20204, 20205, 20051, 20052, 20053, 20054, 20055, approved by the Board July 26, 1898; and of plans numbered 25022, 25038, 20013, 20014, approved by the Board January 20, 1899; and of plan numbered 20224, approved by the Board July 17, 1900; and of plans numbered 20023, 20126, 20127, 20226, 20227, 20228, 20465, 20466, 26318, approved by the Board July 18, 1900; and of plans numbered 20471, 20469, 20470, 27550, 27555, approved by the Board November 9, 1900; and of plan numbered 20232, approved by the Board May 31, 1901.

JAMES F. JACKSON,
CLINTON WHITE,
Commissioners.

JULY 27, 1904. [5564]

Petition of the Boston Elevated Railway Company for approval of plan for temporary footbridge connecting the Boston Elevated railway and the Boston and Maine railroad at the North Union Station.

The annexed plan is approved as showing a proposed temporary structure for connecting the Boston Elevated railway and the North Union Station.

JAMES F. JACKSON,
GEORGE W. BISHOP,
CLINTON WHITE,
Commissioners.

APRIL 1, 1904. [5481]

Footwalk at Dudley street station, Boston.

Upon the petition of the Boston Elevated Railway Company dated March 25, 1904, the plan annexed thereto, numbered 10,723, showing a footwalk thirty-five (35) feet in length added to the elevated structure in Dudley street, Roxbury, the same being a modification of plan numbered 25,451, approved by the Board under date of April 18, 1899, is hereby approved and consent given to the changes shown.

JAMES F. JACKSON,
GEORGE W. BISHOP,
CLINTON WHITE,
Commissioners.

APRIL 22, 1904. [5477]

Petition of the Mount Hope Citizens' Association and others for transfer station at Forest Hills and for extension of transfer privileges.

J. P. NICKERSON for petitioners.

J. T. BURNETT for company.

Residents of that part of Boston which has recently received the benefit of a five-cent fare through the lease of a portion of the Old Colony street railway to the Boston Elevated Railway Company, regularly take elevated trains to and from Dudley street or use the Jamaica Plain line of surface cars.

The petitioners ask that transfer checks be issued in connection with other lines of surface cars and that a transfer station be established at Forest Hills. The first request we endorse, and recommend that the company extend to the surface lines running to Forest Hills, and known as the Columbus avenue and the Forest Hills and North Station lines, the check system now in force in connection with the Jamaica Plain line.

We believe, however, that the change between elevated trains and particular lines of surface cars should continue for the present under cover at Dudley street.

The contemplated extension of the elevated system to Forest Hills will afford a substantial remedy for the congestion which now exists at Dudley street during certain hours of the day, but in our opinion the establishment of a transfer station under present conditions at Forest Hills would bring but little relief in the way of a better distribution of travel, and would call for an expenditure in maintenance of station and the consequent provision for shelter disproportionate to the benefits to be realized.

JAMES F. JACKSON,
GEORGE W. BISHOP,
CLINTON WHITE,
Commissioners.

DECEMBER 12, 1904. [5604]

Petition of the Boston Elevated Railway Company for approval of plan showing proposed relocation of stairways at the State street elevated station.

Upon the petition of the Boston Elevated Railway Company, dated August 10, 1904, the plan annexed thereto, numbered 11807, showing proposed modifications of the easterly stairways and connecting passageways at its State street elevated station, the same being a modification of plans numbered 25032 and 25033, approved by the Board July 11, 1898; plan numbered 20189, approved by the Board July 26, 1898; plan numbered 20469, approved by the Board November 9, 1900, and of plan numbered 26681, approved by the Board July 27, 1904, is hereby approved and consent given to the changes shown.

JAMES F. JACKSON,
GEORGE W. BISHOP,
CLINTON WHITE,
Commissioners.

SEPTEMBER 20, 1904. [5589]

Petition of the John L. Whiting and Son Company and others for an elevated station on Washington street between Dover and Northampton streets, Boston.

C. H. INNES for petitioners.

F. E. SNOW for company.

Many patrons of the Boston Elevated railway who have occasion to ride regularly between Franklin square and other parts of Boston, and owners of real estate in that locality, urge the need of an additional station upon the Elevated railway for their accommodation.

The question is one of conflicting public interests which it is difficult to weigh with any exact nicety of result. A new station here would undoubtedly be a convenience to those who now have to change between elevated trains and surface cars in order to complete their journey, at a loss sometimes of several minutes; while the delay which an additional stop would necessitate would mean a lesser individual inconvenience, but to a greater number of patrons interested in quick conveyance to other points upon this system.

The distance between stations upon the Elevated railway must vary, stations in the principal business centers being properly more frequent than in districts immediately adjoining.

The construction of the subway in Washington street and the future extension of the elevated system will make it necessary in the near future to study anew the problems connected with the distribution of travel. Pending these changes, and in the light of what seems to be the paramount importance of rapid transit, we do not believe that we ought at this time to recommend the construction of an additional station as requested at or near Franklin square.

JAMES F. JACKSON,
GEORGE W. BISHOP,
CLINTON WHITE,
Commissioners.

DECEMBER 12, 1904. [5473]

Complaint of Charles S. Rackemann and others concerning station accommodations at Readville, on the New York, New Haven and Hartford railroad.

H. E. BOLLES for petitioners.

J. H. BENTON, JR., for company.

In carrying out the recent work of abolishing grade crossings of railroad and highway at Readville a subway was constructed for the use of those who desire to cross the Providence Division of the New York, New Haven and Hartford railroad. In adopting the plan for this improvement the question whether the crossing should be over or under the railroad was fully and carefully considered and it was decided that a subway was preferable even at a greater cost. Nothing which has since happened inclines us to doubt the wisdom of this conclusion, or to ask the company to construct both a subway and an over pass at this point. If trouble exists in reference to drainage it can be and should be readily removed.

The complaint, however, that under the present methods of operating the different divisions of the railroad, passengers who have occasion to take trains upon the New England Division are unreasonably subjected to exposure to storm and inclement weather is well founded. We are of the opinion that the company is under obligation to provide a suitable shelter for these patrons, and we recommend the adoption of such measures as will afford the public proper accommodation while awaiting the arrival of trains at this place.

JAMES F. JACKSON,
GEORGE W. BISHOP,
CLINTON WHITE,
Commissioners.

JUNE 20, 1904. [5485]

Petition of the Roslindale Citizens' Association for recommendation favoring a subway instead of overhead crossing at Clarendon Hills station.

J. A. COULTHURST for petitioner.

F. A. FARNHAM for company.

The New York, New Haven and Hartford Railroad Company has proposed to construct a footbridge at Clarendon Hills station in order to provide a way across its premises for those who use its trains less perilous than that by crossing the tracks at grade. It has already expended several thousand dollars in carrying out this project.

Assuming that subways are often preferable to overhead crossings, there are at this place conditions from an engineering standpoint, as well as reasons from the character of the traffic, which make it desirable that the way across the railroad premises should be overhead rather than underneath.

It is plain that the petitioners are interested in something other than a mere way for the exclusive use of patrons of the railroad. They claim that there was formerly a highway crossing here for the use of the general public, and urge a present necessity for such a crossing. This raises questions over which the Board has no jurisdiction, a fact which seems to have been fully recognized in the steps taken, though as yet unsuccessfully, to secure special legislation to meet the case.

Dealing with the crossing as one for exclusive use of passengers, to which point of view we are confined by law, we cannot ask the company to abandon its plan for overhead crossing at this point.

JAMES F. JACKSON,
GEORGE W. BISHOP,
CLINTON WHITE,
Commissioners.

OCTOBER 11, 1904. [5526]

Petition of the Boston and Maine Railroad for approval of a relocation of passenger station in the city of Waltham.

It appearing, after due notice and hearing, that the board of aldermen of Waltham has approved the proposed relocation of passenger station and that the public interests will be promoted by such change, — it is

Ordered, That the approval of the Board be hereby given to the relocation of the Clematis Brook station on the Southern Division of the Boston and Maine railroad in the city of Waltham, by the removal of the same a distance of about two thousand feet to a point near the junction of Waverley Oaks road and a new street to be known as Marianne road, as shown upon a plan on file with this petition.

Attest: CHARLES E. MANN,

JUNE 2, 1904. [5515] *Clerk.*

Petition of the selectmen of Wilmington for recommendation that Silver Lake station in that town be relocated.

Under the provisions of section 15, chapter 111, Revised Laws, the Board has full authority to recommend that the station at Silver Lake in the town of Wilmington be relocated.

This station is now especially convenient for a large number of patrons. In the location to which the petitioners wish that it be moved, it would be especially convenient for other patrons. The change would withdraw a particular advantage from one part of the travelling public and bestow it upon another.

Weighing the convenience of all classes of patrons we find no such general public demand as would warrant us in recommending that the present location of the station be changed.

JAMES F. JACKSON,
GEORGE W. BISHOP,
CLINTON WHITE,

OCTOBER 1, 1904. [5565] *Commissioners.*

ISSUES OF STOCK AND BONDS.

Petition of the Amherst and Sunderland Street Railway Company for approval of an issue of bonds.

It appearing, after due notice and hearing, and further inquiry, including an examination of the assets and liabilities of the petitioner and an appraisal of its property, that the proposed issue of bonds is for lawful purposes and is consistent with the public interests, — it is

Ordered, That the approval of the Board be hereby given to an issue by the Amherst and Sunderland Street Railway Company of coupon or registered bonds to an amount not exceeding at par value one hundred seventeen thousand dollars ($117,000), said bonds to be payable in twenty years from the date thereof and to bear interest at the rate of five per cent per annum, as an issue of bonds reasonably necessary and of the amount required for the purposes to which the proceeds of such bonds are to be applied as hereinafter provided:

1. The proceeds of bonds amounting at par value to fifty-one thousand five hundred dollars ($51,500) are to be applied toward the payment and refunding of certain outstanding bonds amounting at par value to fifty-one thousand five hundred dollars ($51,500), the issue of which bonds was duly approved in the order of this Board dated January 28, 1902.

2. The proceeds of bonds amounting at par value to sixty-five thousand five hundred dollars ($65,500), are to be applied toward the payment of certain floating indebtedness properly incurred in the construction and equipment of the railway and in the purchase of property necessary for its operation.

Attest: CHARLES E. MANN,
Clerk.

JANUARY 1, 1904. [5380]

Petition of the Berkshire Street Railway Company for approval of an issue of additional capital stock.

It appearing, after due notice and hearing, and further inquiry, including an examination of the assets and liabilities of the petitioner and an appraisal of its property, that the proposed issue of stock has been duly authorized for a lawful purpose and is consistent with the public interests, — it is

Ordered, That the approval of the Board be hereby given to the issue by the Berkshire Street Railway Company of additional shares of capital stock not exceeding two thousand (2000) in number, amounting at par value to two hundred thousand dollars ($200,000), as an issue of stock reasonably necessary and of the amount required for paying certain floating indebtedness properly incurred in the construction and equipment of its railway and in the purchase of property necessary for its operation.

And it is *Determined*, That the value at which the new shares of stock shall be offered to stockholders pursuant to law is one hundred dollars ($100) per share.

Attest: CHARLES E. MANN, *Clerk.*

APRIL 20, 1904. [5449]

Petition of the Berkshire Street Railway Company for approval of an issue of bonds.

It appearing, after due notice and hearing and further inquiry, including an examination of the assets and liabilities of the petitioner and an appraisal of its property, that the proposed issue of bonds is for a lawful purpose and consistent with the public interests, — it is

Ordered, That the approval of the Board be hereby given to an issue by the Berkshire Street Railway Company of coupon or registered bonds to an amount not exceeding at par value two hundred thousand dollars ($200,000), said bonds to be payable in twenty years from date thereof and to bear interest at the rate of five per cent per annum, as an issue of bonds reasonably necessary and of the amount required for the purpose of paying certain floating indebtedness properly incurred in the construction and equipment of the railway and in the purchase of property necessary for its operation.

Any excess in the proceeds of this issue of bonds over the amount above named which may be realized from premiums shall be held for application to the cost of other permanent additions to and improvements in the railway property whenever such application shall be approved by the Board.

Attest: CHARLES E. MANN, *Clerk.*

NOVEMBER 22, 1904. [5616]

Petition of the Blue Hill Street Railway Company for approval of an issue of bonds.

It appearing, after due notice and hearing, and further inquiry, including an examination of the assets and liabilities of the petitioner and an appraisal of its property, that the proposed issue of bonds is for a lawful purpose and is consistent with the public interests, — it is

Ordered, That the approval of the Board be hereby given to the issue by the Blue Hill Street Railway Company of coupon or registered bonds to an amount not exceeding at par value fifty thousand dollars ($50,000), said bonds to be payable in twenty years from the date thereof and to bear interest at the rate of five per cent per annum, as an issue of bonds reasonably necessary and of the amount required for the purpose of paying floating indebtedness properly incurred in the construction and equipment of the railway and in the purchase of property necessary for its operation.

Attest: CHARLES E. MANN, *Clerk.*

MAY 4, 1904. [5493]

Petition of the Boston and Maine Railroad for approval of an issue of bonds.

It appearing, after due notice and hearing, and upon such further investigation as was deemed requisite, that the proposed issue of bonds is for a lawful purpose and consistent with the public interests, — it is

Ordered, That the approval of the Board be hereby given to an issue by the Boston and Maine Railroad of coupon or registered bonds to an amount not exceeding at par value five hundred thousand dollars ($500,000), said bonds to be payable on February 2, 1925, and to bear interest at the rate of three and one-half per cent per annum, as an issue of bonds reasonably necessary and of the amount required for the purpose of paying and refunding at maturity bonds of the company maturing February 2, 1905.

Attest: CHARLES E. MANN, *Clerk.*

DECEMBER 8, 1904. [5670]

Petition of the Boston and Northern Street Railway Company for approval of an issue of mortgage bonds.

B. W. WARREN for company.

It appearing, after due notice and hearing and such further investigation as was deemed requisite, that said company has been authorized under chapter 256 of the Acts of 1904 to issue bonds for the purpose of retiring outstanding bonds and funded indebtedness and for other lawful purposes; that the funded indebtedness of the petitioner now outstanding, including funded indebtedness created by other companies which the petitioner has assumed and agreed to pay, as particularly described in a schedule on file with the petition, amounts in the aggregate to eight million four hundred thirty-two thousand five hundred dollars ($8,432,500); that there are beside certain mortgage bonds amounting to one million four hundred ninety-five thousand dollars ($1,495,000) executed by the Lynn and Boston Railroad Company and now held in trust by the Old Colony Trust Company of Boston, duly authorized for the purpose of retiring certain prior issues of bonds of said company, of the Naumkeag Street Railway Company, of the Lynn Belt Line Street Railway Company and of the Essex Electric Street Railway Company, all a part of the funded indebtedness, described in the above named schedule; and certain mortgage bonds amounting to two hundred thirty-six thousand dollars ($236,000) executed by the Naumkeag Street Railway Company and now held in trust by the Manhattan Trust Company of New York, duly authorized for the purpose of retiring certain prior issues of bonds of the last-named company, a part of the funded indebtedness described in said schedule; and certain mortgage bonds amounting to three hundred forty-two thousand dollars ($342,000) executed by the Lowell, Lawrence and Haverhill Street Railway Company, and now held in trust by the American Loan and Trust Company of Boston, duly authorized for the purpose of retiring the prior issue of bonds of the Merrimack Valley Street Railway Company, a part of the funded indebtedness, described in said schedule; that for the purpose of retiring all of the said bonds and funded indebtedness aforesaid the issue of mortgage bonds to the amount of eight million four hundred thirty-two thousand five hundred dollars ($8,432,500), and for the purpose of funding floating indebtedness the issue of mortgage bonds to the amount of one million two hundred twenty-seven thousand five hundred dollars ($1,227,500) has been duly authorized by the stockholders of the petitioning company, and that such issues are for lawful purposes and consistent with the public interests, — it is

Ordered, That the approval of the Board be hereby given to the issue by the Boston and Northern Street Railway Company of coupon or registered bonds to an amount not exceeding nine million six hundred sixty thousand dollars ($9,660,000), payable in fifty years from the date thereof and bearing interest at the rate of four per cent per annum, as an issue of bonds reasonably necessary and of the amount required for the purposes hereinafter named; — said bonds to be secured by a mortgage of the railway, franchises, rights and property of the company in form and substance as shall be approved by this Board; this issue to be without prejudice to any right which the company has to make further issue of bonds to be secured by said mortgage under the provisions of the statute above named and as contemplated by the vote of stockholders.

1. Of the issue herein approved bonds to the amount of eight million four hundred thirty-two thousand five hundred dollars

($8,432,500) at face value or the proceeds thereof shall be applied solely to the retirement of an equal amount of the outstanding funded indebtedness described in said schedule and numbered therein one (1) to twenty-one (21) inclusive, and of the bonds held in trust for their retirement, as hereinbefore stated, by the Old Colony Trust Company, the Manhattan Trust Company and the American Loan and Trust Company.

The approval of the issue of the foregoing bonds is upon condition that the trustee to be named in the indenture of mortgage to be executed to secure them shall be the Adams Trust Company of Boston or some other trust company to be named by this Board; that all of these bonds shall upon execution be delivered to such trustee and issued from time to time only by such trustee; that each bond shall in terms expressly require authentication by the trustee before it is issued or becomes a valid obligation of the company; that said indenture of mortgage shall provide that no bond to be used for the retirement of the funded indebtedness now outstanding shall be issued until an outstanding bond or evidence of funded indebtedness of equal face value has been surrendered to and cancelled by the trustee, and that no such bond shall be issued for the retirement of bonds now outstanding for the retirement of which the Old Colony Trust Company, the Manhattan Trust Company and the American Loan and Trust Company now hold bonds in trust as hereinbefore stated until an equal amount not only of such outstanding bonds but of the bonds so held in trust for retirement of the same (to the amount so held in trust) has been surrendered and cancelled by the trustee; so that when the full amount of bonds hereunder approved for the purpose of retiring outstanding funded indebtedness shall have been issued all of the now outstanding funded indebtedness, amounting as above stated at face value to eight million four hundred thirty-two thousand five hundred dollars ($8,432,500) together with the bonds held in trust amounting at face value to two million seventy-three thousand dollars ($2,073,000) shall have been surrendered and cancelled.

2. Of the issue hereunder approved bonds amounting at face value to one million two hundred twenty-seven thousand five hundred dollars ($1,227,500) or the proceeds thereof shall be applied solely to the payment and funding of floating indebtedness found to have been properly incurred in making certain permanent additions to and improvements in the railway of the petitioner as particularly described in the schedule on file with the petition.

Attest: CHARLES E. MANN,
Clerk.

JUNE 21, 1904. [5511]

Trustee and terms approved.

Upon the application of the Boston and Northern Street Railway Company, it is

Ordered, That the indenture of mortgage from the Boston and Northern Street Railway Company to the Adams Trust Company dated July 1, 1904, a copy of which is on file in this office, is hereby approved as to the trustee named therein, and as to the terms thereof relative to the deposit and withdrawal of the bonds secured thereby which are authorized for the purpose of paying or retiring the existing funded indebtedness of said company in accordance with the provisions of chapter 256 of the Acts of the General Court for the year 1904 and as contemplated in the order of the Board dated June 21, 1904.

Attest: CHARLES E. MANN, *Clerk.*

JUNE 21, 1904. [5511]

Petition of the Boston and Worcester Street Railway Company for approval of an issue of additional capital stock.

It appearing, after due notice and hearing, and further inquiry, including an examination of the assets and liabilities of the petitioner and an appraisal of its property, that the proposed issue of stock has been duly authorized for a lawful purpose and is consistent with the public interests, — it is

Ordered, That the approval of the Board be hereby given to the issue by the Boston and Worcester Street Railway Company of additional shares of capital stock not exceeding one thousand (1000) in number, amounting at par value to one hundred thousand dollars ($100,000), as an issue of stock reasonably necessary and of the amount required for paying certain floating indebtedness properly incurred in the construction and equipment of its railway and in the purchase of property necessary for its operation.

And it is *Determined*, That the value at which the new shares of stock shall be offered to stockholders pursuant to law is one hundred dollars ($100) per share.

Attest: CHARLES E. MANN, *Clerk.*

APRIL 21, 1904. [5474]

Petition of the Boston and Worcester Street Railway Company for approval of an issue of bonds.

It appearing, after due notice and hearing, and further inquiry, including an examination of the assets and liabilities of the petitioner and an appraisal of its property, that the proposed issue of bonds is for a lawful purpose and is consistent with the public interests, — it is

Ordered, That the approval of the Board be hereby given to the issue by the Boston and Worcester Street Railway Company of coupon or registered bonds to an amount not exceeding at par value two hundred thousand dollars ($200,000), said bonds to be payable in twenty years from the date thereof and to bear interest at the rate of four and one-half per cent per annum, as an issue of bonds reasonably necessary and of the amount required for the purpose of paying certain floating indebtedness properly incurred in the construction and equipment of the railway and in the purchase of property necessary for its operation.

Attest: CHARLES E. MANN,
APRIL 21, 1904. [5474] *Clerk.*

Petition of the Boston and Worcester Street Railway Company for approval of an issue of additional capital stock.

It appearing, after due notice and hearing and such further investigation as was deemed necessary, that the proposed issue of additional capital stock is for a lawful purpose and consistent with the public interests, — it is

Ordered, That the approval of the Board be hereby given to the issue by the Boston and Worcester Street Railway Company of additional shares of capital stock not exceeding one thousand six hundred (1,600) in number, amounting at par value to one hundred sixty thousand dollars ($160,000), as an issue of stock reasonably necessary for paying certain floating indebtedness properly incurred in the construction and equipment of the railway of the company and in the purchase of property necessary for its operation.

And it is

Determined, That the value at which the new shares of stock shall be offered to stockholders according to law is one hundred dollars ($100) per share.

Attest: CHARLES E. MANN,
NOVEMBER 2, 1904. [5642] *Clerk.*

Petition of the Boston and Worcester Street Railway Company for approval of an issue of bonds.

It appearing, after due notice and hearing, and further inquiry, including an examination of the assets and liabilities of the petitioner and an appraisal of its property, that the proposed issue of bonds is for a lawful purpose and consistent with the public interests, — it is

Ordered, That the approval of the Board be hereby given to an issue by the Boston and Worcester Street Railway Company of coupon or registered bonds to an amount not exceeding at par value one hundred sixty thousand dollars ($160,000), said bonds to be payable in twenty years from date thereof and to bear interest at a rate not to exceed four and one-half per cent per annum, as an issue of bonds reasonably necessary and of the amount required for the purpose of paying certain floating indebtedness properly incurred in the construction and equipment of the railway and in the purchase of property necessary for its operation.

Any excess in the proceeds of this issue of bonds over the amount above named which may be realized from premiums shall be held for application to the cost of other permanent additions and improvements to and in said railway property whenever such application shall be approved by the Board.

Attest: CHARLES E. MANN,
NOVEMBER 21, 1904. [5643] *Clerk.*

Petition of the Conway Electric Street Railway Company for approval of an issue of bonds.

It appearing, after due notice and hearing, and further inquiry, including an examination of the assets and liabilities of the petitioner and an appraisal of its property, that the proposed issue of bonds is for a lawful purpose and is consistent with the public interests, — it is

Ordered, That the approval of the Board be hereby given to an issue by the Conway Electric Street Railway Company of coupon or registered bonds to an amount not exceeding thirty-five thousand dollars ($35,000) at par value, said bonds to be payable in twenty years from date thereof and to bear interest at a rate not to exceed five per cent per annum, as an issue of bonds reasonably necessary and of the amount required for the purpose of paying certain floating indebtedness properly incurred in the construction and equipment of the railway and in the purchase of property necessary for its operation, but on condition that no bonds shall be issued under the authority herein given unless at the same time there shall be surrendered to the company and cancelled by it an equal amount of the bonds which the company has deposited as collateral security for the floating indebtedness above described.

With the consent of the company, all authority to issue bonds under prior orders of the Board is hereby revoked.

Attest: CHARLES E. MANN,
JULY 13, 1904. [5528] *Clerk.*

Petition of the Conway Electric Street Railway Company for approval of an issue of additional capital stock.

It appearing, after due notice and hearing, and further inquiry, including an examination of the assets and liabilities of the petitioner and an appraisal of its property, that the proposed issue of stock is for a lawful purpose and consistent with the public interests, — it is

Ordered, That the approval of the Board be hereby given to the issue by the Conway Electric Street Railway Company of additional shares of capital stock not exceeding six hundred forty (640) in number, amounting at par value to sixty-four thousand (64,000) dollars, as an issue of stock reasonably necessary and of the amount required for the purpose of acquiring the property of the Conway Electric Light and Power Company, as described in the copy of indenture on file with the petition, under authority of chapter 284 of the Acts of 1903.

And it is *Determined*, That the value at which the new shares of stock shall be offered to stockholders according to law is one hundred (100) dollars per share.

Attest: CHARLES E. MANN,
SEPTEMBER 6, 1904. [5488] *Clerk.*

Petition of the Dedham and Franklin Street Railway Company for authority to issue capital stock.

It appearing, after due notice and hearing, that the petitioner has been duly incorporated under the provisions of section 13, chapter 112, Revised Laws, for the purpose of holding, owning and operating the street railway formerly belonging to the Norfolk Western Street Railway Company and purchased at a sale made by the receivers under a decree of the Circuit Court of the United States; that the fair cost of replacing the property so acquired is in excess of seventy-five thousand dollars ($75,000); that an issue of capital stock to the amount of seventy-five thousand dollars ($75,000) is lawful and consistent with the public interests, — it is

Ordered, That the approval of the Board be hereby given to an issue by the Dedham and Franklin Street Railway Company of shares of capital stock not exceeding seven hundred fifty (750) in number, amounting at par value to seventy-five thousand dollars ($75,000), as an issue of stock reasonably necessary and of the amount required for the purposes contemplated in the statute above named.

Said shares are to be issued to the subscribers to the capital stock of the company, or their assigns, upon the full payment of the par value thereof in cash; and no shares are to be issued until the whole amount of the capital stock as above fixed has been actually paid in cash.

Attest: CHARLES E. MANN,
Clerk.

OCTOBER 28, 1904. [5617]

Petition of the Hampshire Street Railway Company for authority to reduce its capital stock.

It appearing, after due notice and hearing, and such examination of the financial condition of the company as was deemed requisite, that this petition is presented in accordance with a vote of stockholders at a meeting called for the purpose, and that the proposed reduction of capital stock from one hundred thousand dollars ($100,000), the amount named in the agreement of association, to sixty thousand dollars ($60,000), is consistent with the public interests and with the limitations imposed by all laws to which the company is subject, — it is

Ordered, That the reduction in the capital stock of the Hampshire Street Railway Company from one hundred thousand dollars ($100,-000), the amount named in the agreement of association, to sixty thousand dollars ($60,000), be hereby authorized, subscribers to said agreement being severally entitled to repayment of their proportionate part of the three thousand eight hundred dollars ($3,800) paid by them in excess of the amount of the capital stock as above fixed.

Attest: CHARLES E. MANN,
Clerk.

JULY 29, 1904. [5563]

Petition of the Hampshire Street Railway Company for approval of an issue of original capital stock.

It appearing, after due notice and hearing, and upon such investigation as was deemed requisite, that the petitioner has been duly incorporated under the general law, and that it has an authorized capital stock of sixty thousand dollars ($60,000) which has been duly subscribed; that the proposed issue of capital stock is for a lawful purpose and consistent with the public interests, — it is

Ordered, That the approval of the Board be hereby given to the issue by the Hampshire Street Railway Company of shares of capital stock not exceeding six hundred (600) in number, amounting to sixty thousand dollars ($60,000), at par value, the proceeds of such shares to be applied only toward the payment and capitalization of the necessary cost of building and equipping its railway upon locations duly granted to it.

Such shares are to be issued to the subscribers to the capital stock of the company, or their assigns, upon the full payment of the par value thereof in cash; and no shares are to be issued until the whole amount of the capital stock as above fixed has been actually paid in.

Attest: CHARLES E. MANN,
JULY 29, 1904. [5563] Clerk.

Petition of the Haverhill and Southern New Hampshire Street Railway Company for approval of an issue of bonds.

It appearing, after due notice and hearing, and further inquiry, including an examination of the assets and liabilities of the petitioner and an appraisal of its property, that the proposed issue of bonds is for a lawful purpose and is consistent with the public interests, — it is

Ordered, That the approval of the Board be hereby given to an issue by the Haverhill and Southern New Hampshire Street Railway Company of coupon or registered bonds to an amount not exceeding at par value eighty thousand dollars ($80,000), said bonds to be payable in twenty years from the date thereof and to bear interest at the rate of five per cent per annum, as an issue of bonds reasonably necessary and of the amount required for the purpose of paying certain floating indebtedness properly incurred in the construction and equipment of the railway and in the purchase of property necessary for its operation.

Attest: CHARLES E. MANN,
FEBRUARY 25, 1904. [5031] Clerk.

Petition of the Hoosac Valley Street Railway Company for approval of an issue of additional capital stock.

It appearing, after due notice and hearing, and further inquiry, including an examination of the assets and liabilities of the petitioner and an appraisal of its property, that the proposed issue of stock has been duly authorized for a lawful purpose and is consistent with the public interests, — it is

Ordered, That the approval of the Board be hereby given to the issue by the Hoosac Valley Street Railway Company of additional shares of capital stock not exceeding one thousand (1,000) in number, amounting at par value to one hundred thousand dollars ($100,000), as an issue of stock reasonably necessary and of the amount required for the purposes hereinafter named:

1. The proceeds of shares not exceeding two hundred and fifty (250) in number, amounting at par value to twenty-five thousand

dollars ($25,000), are to be applied exclusively to the payment of floating indebtedness properly incurred in the construction and equipment of its railway and in the purchase of property necessary for its operation.

2. The proceeds of shares not exceeding four hundred and twenty-eight (428) in number, amounting at par value to forty-two thousand eight hundred dollars ($42,800), are to be applied exclusively to the payment of the necessary cost of purchasing and installing the additional power plant particularly described in the schedule on file with this petition.

3. The proceeds of shares not exceeding two hundred and eighty-eight (288) in number, amounting at par value to twenty-eight thousand eight hundred dollars ($28,800), are to be applied exclusively to the payment of the necessary cost of building the extension of railway in Williamstown leading from the Boston and Maine railroad station through North Hoosac street to the Vermont state line, as particularly described in said schedule.

4. The proceeds of shares not exceeding thirty-four (34) in number, amounting at par value to three thousand four hundred dollars ($3,400), are to be applied exclusively to the payment of the necessary cost incurred in connection with the abolition of the grade crossings described in said schedule.

And it is *Determined*, That the value at which the new shares of stock shall be offered to stockholders according to law is one hundred five dollars ($105) per share.

Attest: CHARLES E. MANN, *Clerk.*

JULY 13, 1904. [5530]

Petition of the Hoosac Valley Street Railway Company for approval of an issue of bonds.

It appearing, after due notice and hearing, and further inquiry, including an examination of the assets and liabilities of the petitioner and an appraisal of its property, that the proposed issue of bonds is for a lawful purpose and is consistent with the public interests, — it is

Ordered, That the approval of the Board be hereby given to the issue by the Hoosac Valley Street Railway Company of coupon or registered bonds to an amount not exceeding at par value four hundred thousand dollars ($400,000), said bonds to be payable in twenty years after date thereof and to bear interest at a rate not exceeding five per cent per annum, as an issue of bonds reasonably necessary and of the amount required for the purposes to which the proceeds of such bonds are to be applied as hereinafter provided:

1. The proceeds of bonds amounting at par value to one hundred

thousand dollars ($100,000) are to be applied exclusively to the payment and refunding of certain outstanding bonds amounting at par value to one hundred thousand dollars ($100,000), the issue of which bonds was duly approved in the order of this Board dated June 3, 1895.

2. The proceeds of bonds amounting at par value to three hundred thousand dollars ($300,000) are to be applied exclusively toward the payment of certain floating indebtedness properly incurred in the construction and equipment of the railway and in the purchase of property necessary for its operation.

Any excess in the proceeds of these bonds over the amounts to be applied as above provided which may be realized from premiums shall be held for application to the necessary cost of other permanent additions to and improvements in the railway property whenever such application shall be approved by the Board.

Attest: CHARLES E. MANN,
JULY 13, 1904. [5530] *Clerk.*

Petition of the Lawrence and Methuen Street Railway Company for approval of an issue of additional capital stock.

It appearing, after due notice and hearing, and further inquiry, including an examination of the assets and liabilities of the petitioner and an appraisal of its property, that the proposed issue of capital stock has been duly authorized for a lawful purpose and is consistent with the public interests, — it is

Ordered, That the approval of the Board be hereby given to the issue by the Lawrence and Methuen Street Railway Company of additional shares of capital stock not exceeding two hundred and fifty (250) in number, amounting at par value to twenty-five thousand dollars ($25,000), as an issue of stock reasonably necessary and of the amount required for paying certain floating indebtedness properly incurred in the construction and equipment of the railway and in the purchase of property necessary for its operation.

And it is *Determined*, That the value at which the new shares of stock shall be offered to stockholders pursuant to law is one hundred dollars ($100) per share.

Attest: CHARLES E. MANN,
FEBRUARY 25, 1904. [5031] *Clerk.*

Petition of the Lawrence and Methuen Street Railway Company for approval of an issue of bonds.

It appearing, after due notice and hearing, and further inquiry, including an examination of the assets and liabilities of the petitioner and an appraisal of its property, that the proposed issue of bonds is for a lawful purpose and is consistent with the public interests, — it is

Ordered, That the approval of the Board be hereby given to the issue by the Lawrence and Methuen Street Railway Company of coupon or registered bonds to an amount not exceeding at par value one hundred twenty-five thousand dollars ($125,000); said bonds to be payable in twenty years from the date thereof and to bear interest at the rate of five per cent per annum, as an issue of bonds reasonably necessary and of the amount required for the purpose of paying certain floating indebtedness properly incurred in the construction and equipment of the railway and in the purchase of property necessary for its operation.

Attest: CHARLES E. MANN, *Clerk.*

FEBRUARY 25, 1904. [5031]

Petition of the Leominster, Shirley and Ayer Street Railway Company for authority to issue original capital stock.

It appearing, after due notice and hearing, and upon such investigation as was deemed requisite, that an issue of original capital stock to the amount and for the purpose hereinafter named is consistent with the public interests, — it is

Ordered, That the approval of the Board be hereby given to the issue by the Leominster, Shirley and Ayer Street Railway Company of original shares of capital stock not exceeding one thousand (1,000) in number, amounting at par value to one hundred thousand dollars ($100,000), the proceeds of such shares to be applied exclusively to the payment and capitalization of the necessary cost of building and equipping its railway upon locations duly granted to it.

Such shares are to be issued to the subscribers to the capital stock of the company, or their assigns, upon the full payment of the par value thereof in cash, and no shares are to be issued until the whole amount of capital stock as above fixed has been actually paid in.

Attest: CHARLES E. MANN, *Clerk.*

NOVEMBER 9, 1904. [5645]

Petition of the Leominster, Shirley and Ayer Street Railway Company for approval of an issue of bonds.

It appearing, after due notice and hearing, and further inquiry, including an examination of the assets and liabilities of the petitioner and an appraisal of its property, that the proposed issue of bonds is for a lawful purpose and consistent with the public interests, — it is

Ordered, That the approval of the Board be hereby given to an issue by the Leominster, Shirley and Ayer Street Railway Company of coupon or registered bonds to an amount not exceeding at par value one hundred thousand dollars ($100,000), said bonds to be payable on February 1, 1921, and to bear interest at the rate of five per cent per annum, as an issue of bonds reasonably necessary and of the amount required for the purpose of paying certain floating indebtedness properly incurred in the construction and equipment of the railway and in the purchase of property necessary for its operation.

Any excess in the proceeds of this issue of bonds over the amount above named which may be realized from premiums shall be held for application to the cost of other permanent additions to and improvements in the railway property whenever such application shall be approved by the Board.

Attest: CHARLES E. MANN, *Clerk.*

DECEMBER 23, 1904. [5671]

Petition of the Lowell and Pelham Street Railway Company for approval of an issue of bonds.

It appearing, after due notice and hearing, and further inquiry, including an examination of the assets and liabilities of the petitioner and an appraisal of its property, that the proposed issue of bonds is for a lawful purpose and is consistent with the public interests, — it is

Ordered, That the approval of the Board be hereby given to the issue by the Lowell and Pelham Street Railway Company of coupon or registered bonds to an amount not exceeding at par value forty thousand dollars ($40,000), said bonds to be payable in twenty years from the date thereof and to bear interest at the rate of five per cent per annum, as an issue of bonds reasonably necessary and of the amount required for the purpose of paying certain floating indebtedness properly incurred in the construction and equipment of the railway and in the purchase of property necessary for its operation.

Attest: CHARLES E. MANN, *Clerk.*

FEBRUARY 25, 1904. [5031]

Petition of the Martha's Vineyard Street Railway Company for authority to issue original capital stock in amount less than that named in agreement of association.

It appearing, after due notice and hearing, and an examination of the financial condition and property of the company, that an issue of original capital stock to the amount and for the purpose hereinafter named is consistent with the public interests, — it is

Ordered, That the approval of the Board be hereby given to a reduction in the capital stock of the Martha's Vineyard Street Railway Company from twelve thousand (12,000) dollars, the amount named in the agreement of association, to eight thousand (8000) dollars, and to the issue by said company of original shares of capital stock not exceeding eighty (80) in number, amounting at par value to eight thousand (8000) dollars, the proceeds of such shares to be applied only to the payment and capitalization of the necessary cost of building and equipping its railway upon locations duly granted to it.

Such shares are to be issued to the subscribers to the capital stock of the company, or their assigns, upon the full payment of the par value thereof in cash; and no shares are to be issued until the whole amount of capital stock as above fixed has been actually paid in.

Attest: CHARLES E. MANN,
Clerk.

OCTOBER 1, 1904. [5574]

Petition of the Newton Street Railway Company for approval of an issue of bonds.

It appearing, after due notice and hearing, and further inquiry, including an examination of the assets and liabilities of the petitioner and an appraisal of its property, that the proposed issue of bonds is for a lawful purpose and is consistent with the public interests, — it is

Ordered, That the approval of the Board be hereby given to the issue by the Newton Street Railway Company of additional coupon or registered bonds to an amount not exceeding at par value two hundred fifty thousand dollars ($250,000), said bonds to be payable on the first day of July, 1912, and to bear interest at the rate of five per cent per annum, as an issue of bonds reasonably necessary and of the amount required for the purpose of paying floating indebtedness properly incurred in the construction and equipment of the railway and in the purchase of property necessary for its operation.

Attest: CHARLES E. MANN,
Clerk.

JUNE 9, 1904. [5426]

Petition of the Old Colony Railroad Company for approval of an issue of bonds.

It appearing, after due notice and hearing, and such further investigation as was deemed requisite, that the petitioner proposes to issue bonds amounting at par value to four hundred ninety-eight thousand dollars ($498,000) for a lawful purpose, and that such issue is consistent with the public interests, — it is

Ordered, That the approval of the Board be hereby given to an issue by the Old Colony Railroad Company of coupon or registered bonds to an amount not exceeding at par value four hundred ninety-eight thousand dollars ($498,000), said bonds to be payable on December 1, 1925, and to bear interest at the rate of four per cent per annum, as an issue of bonds reasonably necessary and of the amount required for the purpose of refunding certain funded indebtedness of the company which will mature April 1, 1904.

Any excess in the proceeds of these bonds over the amount to be applied as above stated, realized from premiums, shall be applied to the cost of permanent additions to and improvements in the railroad property of the petitioner.

Attest: CHARLES E. MANN,

FEBRUARY 25, 1904. [5447] *Clerk.*

Petition of the Old Colony Railroad Company for approval of an issue of additional stock.

It appearing, after due notice and hearing, and such further investigation as was deemed necessary, that the proposed issue by the petitioner of additional shares of capital stock to the amount of four hundred sixty-two thousand five hundred dollars ($462,500) has been duly authorized for lawful purposes and is consistent with the public interests, — it is

Ordered, That the approval of the Board be hereby given to an issue by the Old Colony Railroad Company of additional shares of capital stock not exceeding four thousand six hundred and twenty-five (4625) in number, amounting at par value to four hundred sixty-two thousand five hundred dollars ($462,500), as an issue of stock reasonably necessary and of the amount required to provide for the payment of outstanding bonds amounting to seven hundred fifty thousand dollars ($750,000) to become due July 1, 1904, and for the payment of certain obligations of the company amounting to one hundred seventy-five thousand dollars, ($175,000) incurred as the necessary cost of certain permanent improvements in the railroad property.

It further appearing that the proposed increase in stock does not exceed four per cent of the existing capital stock of the company and that the directors desire to dispose of the same by public auction in manner provided by law, the Boston Daily Advertiser, Boston Transcript and Boston Herald are prescribed as the daily newspapers in which the notice of such sale shall be published by the petitioner.

Any excess in the proceeds of these shares over the amount to be applied as above stated, realized from premiums, shall be applied to the cost of permanent additions, alterations and improvements to and in the railroad property upon approval by the Board.

Attest: CHARLES E. MANN, *Clerk.*

MAY 25, 1904. [5516]

Petition of the Old Colony Railroad Company for approval of application of proceeds received from sale of capital stock.

After consideration, it is

Ordered, That the approval of the Board be hereby given to the application by the petitioner, to the cost of permanent improvements in and additions to its property in Fall River, of eight thousand five hundred seventy-one dollars and eighty-seven cents ($8,571.87), which is the amount of proceeds received from the sale of the four thousand six hundred and twenty-five (4,625) shares of capital stock contemplated under the order of the Board dated May 25, 1904, in excess of the amount required for payment of the outstanding bonds and the mortgage indebtedness named in said order.

Attest: CHARLES E. MANN, *Clerk.*

JULY 7, 1904. [5516]

Petition of the Old Colony Street Railway Company for approval of an issue of mortgage bonds.

B. W. WARREN for petitioner.

It appearing, after due notice and hearing, and such further investigation as was deemed requisite, that said company has been authorized under chapter 255 of the Acts of 1904 to issue bonds for the purpose of retiring outstanding bonds and funded indebtedness and for other lawful purposes; that the funded indebtedness of the petitioner now outstanding, including funded indebtedness created by other companies which the petitioner has assumed and agreed to pay, as particularly described in a schedule on file with the petition, amounts in the aggregate to four million six hundred sixty-seven thousand dollars ($4,667,000); that there are beside certain mortgage bonds amounting to sixty-four thousand dollars ($64,000) executed by the Brockton Street Railway Company and now held in trust by the State Street Trust Company, of Boston, duly authorized for the purpose of retiring certain prior issues of bonds of said company, a part of the funded indebtedness described in the above named schedule; and certain mortgage bonds amounting to two hundred sixty-five thousand dollars ($265,000) executed by the South Shore and Boston Street Railway Company and now held in trust by the American Loan and Trust Company, of Boston, duly authorized for the purpose of retiring certain prior issues of bonds of the Rockland and Abington Street Railway Company, the Braintree and Weymouth Street Railway Company, and the Bridgewater, Whitman and Rockland Street Railway Company, all a part of the funded indebtedness described in the above named schedule; that for the purpose of retiring all of the said bonds and funded indebtedness aforesaid the issue of mortgage bonds to the amount of four million six hundred sixty-seven thousand dollars ($4,667,000), and for the purpose of funding floating indebtedness, and for other purposes in the petition of the company set forth, the issue of mortgage bonds to the amount of two million, one hundred forty-five thousand six hundred dollars ($2,145,600) has been duly authorized by the stockholders of the petitioning company, and that such issues are for lawful purposes and consistent with the public interests, — it is

Ordered, That the approval of the Board be hereby given to the issue by the Old Colony Street Railway Company of coupon or registered bonds to an amount not exceeding six million eight hundred twelve thousand dollars ($6,812,000), payable in fifty years from the date thereof and bearing interest at the rate of four per cent per annum, as an issue of bonds reasonably necessary and of the amount required for the purposes hereinafter named; — said bonds to be secured by a mortgage of the railway, franchises, rights and property of the company in form and substance as shall be approved by this Board; this issue to be without prejudice to any right which the company has to make further issue of bonds to be secured by said mortgage under the provisions of the statute above named and as contemplated by the vote of stockholders.

1. Of the issue herein approved bonds to the amount of four million six hundred sixty-seven thousand dollars ($4,667,000) at face value or the proceeds thereof shall be applied solely to the retirement of an equal amount of the outstanding bonds described in said schedule and numbered therein one (1) to twenty-five (25) inclusive, and of the bonds held in trust for their retirement, as hereinbefore stated, by the State Street Trust Company and the American Loan and Trust Company; provided, however, that if, under the provisions of the mortgage securing the bonds held in trust by the State Street Trust Company, any of said bonds so held in trust shall hereafter be exchanged for any of the bonds to retire which the same were authorized, the bonds so issued in exchange shall be deemed to be outstanding bonds capable of retirement under this order in lieu of those included in the issues described in said schedule.

The approval of the issue of the foregoing bonds is upon condition that the trustee to be named in the indenture of mortgage to be executed to secure them shall be the Old Colony Trust Company, of Boston, or some other trust company to be named by this Board; that all of these bonds shall upon execution be delivered to such trustee and issued from time to time only by such trustee; that each bond shall in terms expressly require authentication by the trustee before it is issued or becomes a valid obligation of the company; that said indenture of mortgage shall provide that no bond to be used for the retirement of bonds now outstanding shall be issued until an outstanding bond of equal face value has been surrendered to and cancelled by the trustee, and that no such bond shall be issued for the retirement of bonds now outstanding for the retirement of which the State Street Trust Company and the American Loan and Trust Company now hold bonds in trust as hereinbefore stated until an equal amount not only of such outstanding bonds but of the bonds so held in trust for retirement of the same (to the amount so held in trust) has been surrendered and cancelled by the trustee; so that when the full amount of bonds hereunder approved for the purpose of retiring outstanding funded indebtedness shall have been issued all of the now outstanding bonds amounting as above stated at face value to four million six hundred sixty-seven thousand dollars ($4,667,000), together with the bonds held in trust amounting at face value to three hundred twenty-nine thousand dollars ($329,000) shall have been surrendered and cancelled.

2. Of the issue hereunder approved bonds amounting at face value to four hundred eighty-six thousand dollars ($486,000) or the proceeds thereof shall be applied solely to the payment and funding of floating indebtedness found to have been properly incurred in making certain permanent additions to and improvements in the railway of the petitioner as particularly described in the schedule on file with the petition.

3. Of the issue hereunder approved bonds amounting at face value to one million six hundred fifty-nine thousand dollars ($1,659,000) or the proceeds thereof shall be applied solely to the necessary cost of building, equipping and installing the alternating current system of electric power as described in the petition of said Old Colony Street Railway Company.

Attest: CHARLES E. MANN, *Clerk.*

JUNE 21, 1904. [5512]

Trustee and terms approved.

Upon the application of the Old Colony Street Railway Company, it is

Ordered, That the indenture of mortgage from the Old Colony Street Railway Company to the Old Colony Trust Company dated July 1, 1904, a copy of which is on file in this office, is hereby approved as to the trustee named therein, and as to the terms thereof relative to the deposit and withdrawal of the bonds secured thereby which are authorized for the purpose of paying or retiring the existing funded indebtedness of said company in accordance with the provisions of chapter 255 of the Acts of the General Court for the year 1904 and as contemplated in the order of the Board dated June 21, 1904.

Attest: CHARLES E. MANN, Clerk.

JUNE 29, 1904. [5512]

Petition of the Pittsfield Electric Street Railway Company for approval of an issue of additional capital stock.

It appearing, after due notice and hearing and further inquiry, including an examination of the assets and liabilities of the petitioner and an appraisal of its property, that the proposed issue of stock is for a lawful purpose and consistent with the public interests, — it is

Ordered, That the approval of the Board be hereby given to the issue by the Pittsfield Electric Street Railway Company of additional shares of capital stock not exceeding one thousand (1000) in number, amounting at par value to one hundred thousand (100,000) dollars, as an issue of stock reasonably necessary and of the amount required for the purposes hereinafter named:

1. The proceeds of shares not exceeding three hundred sixty-four (364) in number, amounting at par value to thirty-six thousand four hundred (36,400) dollars, are to be applied exclusively to the payment of floating indebtedness properly incurred in the construction and equipment of the railway of the company and in the purchase of property necessary for its operation.

2. The proceeds of shares not exceeding six hundred thirty-six (636) in number, amounting at par value to sixty-three thousand six hundred (63,600) dollars, are to be applied exclusively to the payment of the necessary cost of building certain extensions of the railway of the company in Pittsfield in Wahconah street, Peck's road and Lake avenue; in New West, West, Onota and Linden streets; and in Melville, First, Adam, Second, Lincoln, Fourth, Curtis, Brown and Kellogg streets, as described in the schedule on file with this petition.

And it is *Determined*, That the value at which the new shares of stock shall be offered to stockholders according to law is one hundred ten (110) dollars per share.

Attest: CHARLES E. MANN,
Clerk.

SEPTEMBER 16, 1904. [5577]

Petition of the Templeton Street Railway Company for approval of an issue of additional capital stock.

It appearing, after due notice and hearing, and further inquiry, including an examination of the assets and liabilities of the petitioner and an appraisal of its property, that the proposed issue of stock has been duly authorized for a lawful purpose and is consistent with the public interests, — it is

Ordered, That the approval of the Board be hereby given to the issue by the Templeton Street Railway Company of additional shares of capital stock not exceeding five hundred (500) in number, amounting at par value to fifty thousand dollars ($50,000), as an issue of stock reasonably necessary and of the amount required for paying certain floating indebtedness properly incurred in the construction and equipment of its railway and in the purchase of property necessary for its operation.

And it is *Determined*, That the value at which the new shares of stock shall be offered to stockholders according to law is one hundred dollars ($100) per share.

Attest: CHARLES E. MANN,
Clerk.

JUNE 20, 1904. [5517]

Petition of the Waltham Street Railway Company for approval of an issue of additional capital stock.

It appearing, after due notice and hearing, and further inquiry, including an examination of the assets and liabilities of the petitioner and an appraisal of its property, that the proposed issue of stock has been duly authorized for a lawful purpose and is consistent with the public interests, — it is

Ordered, That the approval of the Board be hereby given to the issue by the Waltham Street Railway Company of additional shares of capital stock not exceeding four hundred (400) in number, amounting at par value to forty thousand dollars ($40,000), as an issue of stock reasonably necessary and of the amount required for paying certain floating indebtedness properly incurred in the construction and equipment of its railway and in the purchase of property necessary for its operation.

And it is *Determined*, That the value at which the new shares of stock shall be offered to stockholders according to law is one hundred dollars ($100) per share.

Attest: CHARLES E. MANN,
JULY 19, 1904. [5558] *Clerk.*

Petition of the West End Street Railway Company for a modification in the form of the order of the Board approving an issue of bonds.

It appearing that the change in the order of the Board which is desired by the petitioners is a reasonable one and in no way inconsistent with the public interests, — it is

Decreed, That the order of the Board dated January 10, 1896 approving an issue of bonds by the petitioner not exceeding $2,275,-000 for the purpose of funding certain mortgage indebtedness and certain outstanding bonded debt, be hereby amended so as to read in part as follows:

Provided, however, that no bonds shall be issued to fund the mortgage indebtedness aforesaid unless a mortgage note of an amount at least equal to the amount of bonds so issued is paid and cancelled and the mortgage securing the same duly discharged, and that no bonds shall be issued to refund the outstanding bonds aforesaid unless bonds of an amount at least equal to the amount of bonds so issued are paid and cancelled, and that no bonds shall be issued in excess of the actual amount necessary to pay the mortgage notes and bonds aforesaid; but nothing in this order shall be construed to prohibit the issue and sale of bonds for the retirement of bonds of the Charles River Street Railway Company amounting to $150,000, to become due April 1, 1904, in advance of the actual payment and cancellation of said Charles River Street Railway bonds and the mortgage securing the same.

Attest: CHARLES E. MANN,
FEBRUARY 25, 1904. [5442] *Clerk.*

Petition of the West End Street Railway Company for approval of an issue of additional capital stock and application of proceeds of former issues of stock and bonds.

It appearing, after due notice and hearing, and upon such investigation as was deemed requisite, that the petitioner proposes to make an issue of additional stock to the amount hereinafter approved and that such issue is for a lawful purpose and consistent with the public interests, — it is

Ordered, That the approval of the Board be hereby given to an issue by the West End Street Railway Company of additional common shares of capital stock not exceeding three thousand

(3,000) in number, amounting at par value to one hundred fifty thousand dollars ($150,000), as an issue of stock reasonably necessary and of the amount required for the purpose of paying in part the necessary cost of permanent additions and improvements to and in the railway property of the petitioner made by the Boston Elevated Railway Company in accordance with the terms of the lease between said companies and described in the schedule on file with this petition.

It further appearing that the proposed increase in stock does not exceed four per cent of the existing capital stock of the company and that the directors desire to sell such stock by public auction in Boston, the Boston Daily Advertiser, the Boston Evening Transcript and the Boston Herald are prescribed as the daily newspapers in which the notice of the time and place of such sale shall be published by the petitioner.

And it is further

Ordered, That the approval of the Board be hereby given to the application of forty-two thousand three hundred sixty-one dollars and thirty-one cents ($42,361.31), realized as a part of the proceeds of bonds and stock issued under orders of the Board dated respectively January 10, 1896, March 19, 1903, and December 1, 1903, and being the amount received by the company in excess of that required for the purposes named in said orders, toward the cost of permanent additions and improvements to and in the property of the company made under the terms of the above named lease and described in the above named schedule.

Attest: CHARLES E. MANN,
JULY 27, 1904. [5561] *Clerk.*

Petition of the West End Street Railway Company for approval of an issue of bonds.

It appearing, after due notice and hearing, and upon such investigation as was deemed necessary, that the petitioner proposes to make an issue of bonds to the amount of seven hundred fifty thousand dollars ($750,000), that the proposed issue is for a lawful purpose and is consistent with the public interests, — it is

Ordered, That the approval of the Board be hereby given to an issue by the West End Street Railway Company of bonds not exceeding at par value seven hundred fifty thousand dollars ($750,000), payable thirty years from date thereof and bearing interest at the rate of four per cent per annum, as an issue of bonds reasonably necessary and of the amount required for the payment of the cost of permanent additions and improvements to and in the railway property of the petitioner made by the Boston Elevated Railway Company in accordance with the terms of the lease between said companies and described in the schedule on file in this office.

Any excess in the proceeds of this issue of bonds over the amount to be applied as above stated, which may be realized from premiums, shall be held for application to the cost of other permanent additions and improvements to and in said railway made under the terms of the above named lease, whenever such application shall be approved by the Board.

Attest: ALLAN BROOKS,
Assistant Clerk.

SEPTEMBER 1, 1904. [5562]

Petition of the Worcester and Holden Street Railway Company for approval of an issue of bonds.

It appearing, after due notice and hearing, and further inquiry, including an examination of the assets and liabilities of the petitioner and an appraisal of its property, that the proposed issue of bonds is for a lawful purpose and is consistent with the public interests, — it is

Ordered, That the approval of the Board be hereby given to the issue by the Worcester and Holden Street Railway Company of coupon or registered bonds to an amount not exceeding at par value twenty-five thousand dollars ($25,000), said bonds to be payable in twenty years from the date thereof and to bear interest at the rate of five per cent per annum, as an issue of bonds reasonably necessary and of the amount required for the purpose of paying certain floating indebtedness properly incurred in the construction and equipment of the railway and in the purchase of property necessary for its operation.

Attest: CHARLES E. MANN,
Clerk.

MARCH 29, 1904. [5468]

Petition of the Worcester and Holden Street Railway Company for approval of an issue of additional capital stock.

It appearing, after due notice and hearing, and upon further inquiry, including an examination of the assets and liabilities of the petitioner and an appraisal of its property, that the proposed issue of additional capital stock is for a lawful purpose and consistent with the public interests, — it is

Ordered, That the approval of the Board be hereby given to the issue by the Worcester and Holden Street Railway Company of additional shares of capital stock not exceeding two hundred fifty (250) in number, amounting at par value to twenty-five thousand dollars ($25,000), as an issue of stock reasonably necessary for paying certain floating indebtedness properly incurred in the construction and equipment of the railway and in the purchase of property necessary for its operation.

And it is

Determined, That the value at which the new shares of stock shall be offered to stockholders according to law is one hundred dollars ($100) per share.

Attest: CHARLES E. MANN,
DECEMBER 14, 1904. [5661] *Clerk.*

Petition of the Worcester and Shrewsbury Railroad Company for approval of an issue of bonds.

It appearing, after due notice and hearing, and upon such further investigation as was deemed requisite, that the proposed issue of bonds is for a lawful purpose and consistent with the public interests, — it is

Ordered, That the approval of the Board be hereby given to an issue by the Worcester and Shrewsbury Railroad Company of coupon or registered bonds to an amount not exceeding at par value twenty-two thousand dollars ($22,000), said bonds to be payable in twenty years from date thereof and to bear interest at the rate of five per cent per annum, as an issue of bonds reasonably necessary and of the amount required for the purpose of refunding bonds of the company maturing January 1, 1905.

Any excess in the proceeds of this issue of bonds over the amount above named which may be realized from premiums shall be held for application to the cost of permanent additions to and improvements in the railway property whenever such application shall be approved by the Board.

Attest: CHARLES E. MANN,
DECEMBER 21, 1904. [5679] *Clerk.*

Petitions of the Worcester and Southbridge, the Southbridge and Sturbridge and the Worcester, Rochdale and Charlton Depot street railway companies for approval of terms of purchase and sale, and for approval of an increase in capital stock by the Worcester and Southbridge Street Railway Company.

The issue here is whether from a practical point of view the consolidation of these railways is consistent with the public interests. We are of the opinion that it is; that they can be operated better as one system than as three; that one administration of affairs in such cases is always better than three.

The proposed consolidation involves no increase in rates of fare or decrease in facilities for travel, while a distinct gain to the public is realized from the understanding that incident to this union of properties the aggregate indebtedness of the companies is to be very largely reduced by the cancellation of outstanding claims and the railway capitalized upon a conservative basis.

It appearing, therefore, that the proper steps have been taken looking to the conveyance of the property and franchises of the Southbridge and Sturbridge and the Worcester, Rochdale and Charlton Depot street railway companies to the purchasing company, and that the terms of purchase and sale have been duly determined by the directors and stockholders of each of the contracting companies, — it is

Ordered, That the approval of the Board be hereby given to the terms of the contracts of purchase and sale, copies of which contracts are upon file in this office.

And it appearing that an increase in the capital stock of the Worcester and Southbridge Street Railway Company is contemplated in the terms of said purchase and sale for the purpose of effecting an exchange of stock, share for share, and that such increase is reasonably requisite therefor, and that an issue of such additional stock involves no increase in the aggregate amount of the capital stock and the indebtedness of these companies, — it is

Ordered, That the approval of the Board be hereby given to an increase in the capital stock of the Worcester and Southbridge Street Railway Company by the issue, in addition to the amount of its capital stock now outstanding, of shares not exceeding six hundred (600) in number, amounting at par value to sixty thousand dollars ($60,000), for the purpose of an exchange, share for share, for the outstanding shares of the capital stock of the Southbridge and Sturbridge Street Railway Company; and of shares not exceeding four hundred (400) in number, amounting at par value to forty thousand dollars ($40,000), for the purpose of an exchange, share for share, for the outstanding shares of the capital stock of the Worcester, Rochdale and Charlton Depot Street Railway Company, the certificates of shares in the last named company and in the Southbridge and Sturbridge Street Railway Company to be upon such exchange surrendered and cancelled.

JAMES F. JACKSON,
GEORGE W. BISHOP,
CLINTON WHITE,
Commissioners.

DECEMBER 27, 1904. [5626-5627]

SUNDAY TRAINS AND BOATS.

Petition of the superintendent of the Boston and Albany railroad (New York Central and Hudson River Railroad Company, lessee) for authority to operate Sunday trains.

Ordered, That the Boston and Albany Railroad (New York Central and Hudson River Railroad Company, lessee) be hereby authorized to run on the Lord's day during the period ending November 1, 1904, the trains specified in the schedule dated June 30, 1904, on file with the petition, subject to the following conditions: —

1. No train shall be run in whole or in part as a special or excursion train.

2. The rates of fare on the passenger trains shall in no case be less than those on regular week-day trains between the same stations or points upon said railroad.

All orders heretofore passed authorizing the running of trains on the Lord's day on the Boston and Albany railroad (New York Central and Hudson River Railroad Company, lessee) are hereby revoked, such revocation to take effect at the same time that the above named schedule is put in force.

Attest: CHARLES E. MANN,

JULY 5, 1904. [5554] *Clerk.*

By similar orders, schedules of regular Sunday trains, deemed to be necessary for the public accommodation, have been authorized by the Board on the New York, New Haven and Hartford railroad, the Boston and Maine railroad and the Boston, Revere Beach and Lynn railroad.

Petition of the Providence, Fall River and Newport Steamboat Company for authority to run steamboats on the Lord's day.

It appearing, upon due consideration, that the public necessity, convenience and welfare so require, — it is

Ordered, That authority be hereby given to the Providence, Fall River and Newport Steamboat Company to run, during the year 1904, within the waters of this Commonwealth upon its route from Fall River to Newport and thence to Block Island, one steamboat in the forenoon of every Lord's day, and upon the return trip therefrom one steamboat in the afternoon of every Lord's day, upon the following conditions:

1. Such boats shall not touch nor receive or discharge passengers at any intermediate point between Fall River and Block Island, excepting Newport and Narragansett Pier, either going or returning, and shall be run during such portion of the year only as regular week-day boats are run on the route aforesaid.

2. The fares and ticket rates charged or collected for transportation on said boats shall in no case be less than the regular week-day fares and rates charged or collected by said company for transportation between the same points on said route.

3. No spirituous or malt or other intoxicating liquor shall be sold or furnished by said company, or shall be allowed to be sold or furnished by any person, on said boats or on any grounds or premises owned or controlled by said company, at which said boats land or touch; and no gaming or other unlawful sport shall be permitted thereon.

4. No person who is under the influence of liquor, or who is noisy, disorderly, profane or indecent in language or behavior, shall be allowed to ride on said boats; and no offensive conduct of any kind shall be permitted thereon.

5. The authority hereby given may be revoked at any time, in the discretion of the Board, without previous notice to said company.

Attest: CHARLES E. MANN,
MARCH 18, 1904. [5471] *Clerk.*

Petition of committee of Catholic organizations of Taunton for permission for Sunday train from Taunton to Fall River and return.

Ordered, That the New York, New Haven and Hartford Railroad Company be hereby authorized to run a special train from Taunton to Fall River and return on Sunday, May 8, 1904, for the exclusive use of the Catholic organizations of Taunton; *provided, however*, that said train shall not be run as a public excursion train, and that the rates of fare shall not be less than those charged on regular week-day trains.

Attest: CHARLES E. MANN,
MAY 2, 1904. [5459] *Clerk.*

Petition of the Swedish Campmeeting Committee of Worcester for permission for a Sunday train from Worcester to Sterling Junction and return.

Ordered, That the Boston and Maine Railroad be hereby authorized to run a special train from Worcester to Sterling Junction and return on Sunday, July 24, 1904, for the exclusive use of the Swedish Methodists of Worcester who desire to attend a campmeeting at Sterling Junction; *provided, however*, that said train shall not be run as a public excursion train, and that the rates of fare shall not be less than those charged on regular week-day trains.

Attest: CHARLES E. MANN, *Clerk.*

JUNE 9, 1904. [5409]

Petition of the Boston and Maine Railroad for permission for Sunday trains from Boston to Concord, New Hampshire, and return.

Ordered, That the Boston and Maine Railroad be hereby authorized to run special trains on its lines in Massachusetts from Boston to Concord, New Hampshire, and return on Sunday, July 17, 1904, for the exclusive use of those desiring to attend the dedication of the Christian Science Church at Concord, New Hampshire; *provided, however*, that said trains shall not be run as public excursion trains, and that the rates of fare shall not be less than those charged on regular week-day trains.

Attest: ALLAN BROOKS, *Assistant Clerk.*

JULY 14, 1904. [5409]

A number of other special Sunday trains have been authorized by the Board in the course of the year, for what were deemed to be good and exceptional reasons.

MISCELLANEOUS.

Action of the Board under section 8, chapter 111, Revised Laws, relating to the duties of the assistant clerk.

Ordered, That in the absence of Mr. Charles E. Mann, clerk of the Board, Mr. Allan Brooks, assistant clerk, exercise the authority and perform the duties of clerk.

Attest: CHARLES E. MANN, *Clerk.*

APRIL 8, 1904. [5487]

Appointment of railroad inspector.

Ordered, That John Q. Hennigan, of East Milton, be hereby appointed a railroad inspector under the provisions of chapter 111, Revised Laws, for the term of three years, beginning with the first day of October, 1904.

Attest: CHARLES E. MANN, *Clerk.*

SEPTEMBER 12, 1904. [5606]

STREET RAILWAY CAR HEATING.

Circular.

It is hereby *Ordered*, That the requirement of the Board in respect to the heating of cars by street railway companies, made under date of August 1, 1895, pursuant to chapter 136, Acts of 1895, now section 53, chapter 112, Revised Laws, be modified and changed so as to read as follows:

1. All electric box cars used by street railway companies for the transportation of passengers in the months of October, November, December, January, February, March and April in each year shall be equipped with suitable apparatus for heating by electricity, unless other than electric heaters are specially authorized by the Board.

2. Every street railway company shall, during the months above named, whenever the outside temperature is less than fifty degrees above zero (Fahrenheit), maintain, in all box cars in use for transporting passengers, an inside temperature (as nearly as may be) of not less than fifty nor more than sixty degrees above zero, except at

times when the company is temporarily prevented from so doing by storms, accident or other controlling emergency.

3. This order shall take effect immediately.

Attest: CHARLES E. MANN,
MARCH 30, 1904. [5479] Clerk.

Petition of the Boston and Northern Street Railway Company for authority to install hot water heater for experimental purposes.

Upon the statement made by Mr. P. F. Sullivan, President of the Boston and Northern Street Railway Company, — it is

Ordered, That the Boston and Northern Street Railway Company be hereby authorized to install in one of the cars operated by it a hot water heater for the purpose of experimenting with this method of heating cars, this authority to continue until revoked.

Attest: CHARLES E. MANN,
APRIL 4, 1904. [5480] Clerk.

EXEMPTION FROM STEAM HEATING.

Petition of the Central New England Railway Company for exemption from the law as to steam heating.

Ordered, That the Central New England Railway Company be until the first day of October, 1904, hereby exempted from the law requiring passenger cars to be heated by steam from the locomotive in respect to a combination baggage and passenger car running on a mixed train which leaves Springfield at about 11.25 A.M. and returning reaches Springfield at about 3.36 P.M., said car to be heated by either the Baker or the Johnson heater heretofore approved by the Board.

Attest: CHARLES E. MANN,
FEBRUARY 9, 1904. [5430] Clerk.

Petition of the New York, New Haven and Hartford Railroad Company for exemption from the law as to steam heating.

Ordered, That the New York, New Haven and Hartford Railroad Company be, until the first day of October, 1905, hereby exempted from the law requiring passenger cars to be heated by steam from the locomotive in respect to passenger cars on mixed trains in which freight cars are placed between the locomotive and passenger cars, upon the Air Line-Northampton, Berkshire and Plymouth divisions of its road, said passenger cars to be heated by the Baker or the Johnson heater heretofore approved by the Board.

Attest: CHARLES E. MANN,
JULY 19, 1904. [5571] Clerk.

Whistling of Locomotives.

Complaint of citizens of East Boston relative to whistling at the crossing of Maverick street and the Boston, Revere Beach and Lynn railroad.

After due notice and hearing, and a view, — it is

Ordered, That the whistling of locomotives on the Boston, Revere Beach and Lynn railroad as a crossing signal for trains approaching Maverick street in East Boston be hereby prohibited; provided, however, that the whistle shall be sounded at this crossing if when the engineer comes in view of the same he finds special occasion for whistling to avoid accident.

Attest: CHARLES E. MANN,
June 20, 1904. [5522] *Clerk.*

Exemption from Fencing.

Petition of the Metropolitan Water and Sewerage Board for exemption from duty of erecting and maintaining fences on a portion of the Central Massachusetts railroad in Clinton near the Wachusett reservoir.

After consideration, — it is

Ordered, That the Boston and Maine Railroad be hereby exempted from erecting and maintaining fences upon the sides of that part of the Central Massachusetts railroad which is located in the town of Clinton and adjoins the Wachusett reservoir at the places marked A–B, B–C and D–E upon the plan accompanying the petition, a copy of which plan is on file in this office.

Attest: CHARLES E. MANN,
January 4, 1904. [5383] *Clerk.*

Approval of Ballasted Track.

Petition of the Boston Elevated Railway Company for approval of the installation of ballasted track for experimental purposes.

It is

Ordered, That the installation of certain ballasted track upon the elevated structure upon Atlantic avenue at the foot of Pearl street, and the proposed erection of a canvas fence about six hundred (600) feet on each side of the track, be hereby approved, all for experimental purposes in the effort to abate the noise arising from the operation of the railway.

Attest: CHARLES E. MANN,
April 4, 1904. [5501] *Clerk.*

TEMPORARY GRADE CROSSING.

Petition of the Westborough and Hopkinton Street Railway Company for extension of time for maintaining grade crossing of the New York, New Haven and Hartford railroad in Hopkinton.

It appearing, after due notice and hearing, that the conditions existing in the locality where Main street crosses the New York, New Haven and Hartford railroad in the town of Hopkinton have not changed since the issue of the order of the Board sanctioning the temporary grade crossing of the railroad by the railway at this place at the same level therewith, and that under the circumstances consent should be given to a continuance of the right to maintain this crossing, — it is

Ordered, That the period during which the petitioner was authorized to maintain crossing of its railway and the railroad at the same level at this place, under the order of the Board dated November 22, 1901, and amended under order of the Board dated July 5, 1902, be extended to the first day of January, 1908.

Attest: CHARLES E. MANN,
DECEMBER 27, 1904. [5698] *Clerk.*

NEW STREET RAILWAY COMPANIES.

Petition of the Western Massachusetts Street Railway Company for certificate of compliance with laws preliminary to obtaining a charter.

By order of the Board of Railroad Commissioners, I, the undersigned, Clerk of said Board, hereby certify that the requirements of law preliminary to the establishment of a Street Railway Corporation, as set forth in chapter 112 of the Revised Laws and acts in addition thereto, have been complied with by the subscribers to the annexed articles of Association for the formation of the Western Massachusetts Street Railway Company.

CHARLES E. MANN,
BOSTON, Dec. 10, 1904. *Clerk.*

Communication from the Secretary of the Commonwealth as to charters granted purchasers of certain roads.

CHARLES E. MANN, Esq., *Clerk, Board of Railroad Commissioners.*

DEAR SIR: — I beg to inform you that under the provisions of section 13 of chapter 112, Revised Laws, charters have been issued from this office to-day to the Taunton and Buzzards Bay Street Railway Company, representing the purchasers of the Middleborough, Wareham and Buzzards Bay

Street Railway Company, and the Taunton and Pawtucket Street Railway Company, representing the purchasers of the Bristol County Street Railway Company. Under date of September 17 last, a charter was also issued to the Dedham and Franklin Street Railway Company, representing the purchasers of the Norfolk Western Street Railway Company.

Very respectfully,

WM. M. OLIN,
Secretary.

BOSTON, December 22, 1904.

STREET RAILWAYS EARNING FIVE PER CENT DIVIDENDS.

Communication.

To the Honorable Board of Commissioners of Savings Banks of the Commonwealth of Massachusetts, Hon. WARREN E. LOCKE, *Chairman.*

GENTLEMEN: — Pursuant to the provisions of chapter 483, Acts of 1902, we transmit the following list of street railway companies incorporated in this Commonwealth which appear from the returns made by them to have annually earned and properly paid, without impairment of assets or capital stock, dividends of not less than five per cent (5%) upon their capital stock for the past five years, —

Athol & Orange,
Boston & Northern,
Dartmouth & Westport,
East Middlesex,
Fitchburg & Leominster,
Holyoke,
Hoosac Valley,
Northampton,
Pittsfield Electric,
Springfield,
Union,
West End.

Very truly yours,

JAMES F. JACKSON,
Chairman.

JANUARY 15, 1904. [5573]

RAILROAD AND STREET RAILWAY ACCIDENTS.

Circular.

The Board of Railroad Commissioners respectfully calls to your attention the provisions of section 263, chapter 111, Revised Laws, which, as amended by chapter 297, Acts of 1903, reads as follows:

Every railroad and street railway corporation shall give immediate notice of an accident on its road, which results in a loss of life, to the medical examiner of the county who resides nearest to the place of accident, and shall also, within twenty-four hours, give notice to the board of any such accident or of any accident of the description of accidents of which the board may require notice to be given. For each omission to give such notice the corporation shall forfeit not more than one hundred dollars.

Under the authority of the foregoing provision of law the Board requires that reports be made : —

1. Of all accidents resulting in serious personal injury, as well as in loss of life, whether of passengers, employees or others.

2. Of all accidents which do not result in personal injury, but which cause serious detention of passenger trains or electric cars.

When an accident occurs at a station, it should be so reported and the name of the station given; when it occurs elsewhere, the place should be described with reasonable accuracy.

The word "station" will be deemed to mean that part of the railroad premises within which trains are customarily stopped for the purpose of receiving or discharging passengers.

The word "road" will be deemed to mean all parts of premises the use of which is ordinarily necessary to the operation of the railroad or railway.

The accidents to be reported are those which are incident to the movement of any engine or car.

Each report should include a brief statement of the character of the accident and the nature of the injury and be in accordance with the accompanying form.

By order of the Board,

CHARLES E. MANN,
Clerk.

NOVEMBER 1, 1904. [5711]

SPECIAL REPORT TO THE GENERAL COURT.

Resolve relative to the operation of the ferry between the town of Fairhaven and the city of New Bedford.

To the Honorable, the Senate and the House of Representatives, in General Court assembled.

The Board of Railroad Commissioners respectfully submits its report of the investigation made pursuant to the following Resolve, duly approved February 27, 1904 : —

Resolved, That the board of railroad commissioners is hereby directed, after such notice and hearing as it may deem proper, to consider whether public necessity and convenience require the further operation of a ferry between the town of Fairhaven and the city of New Bedford under the provisions of chapter three hundred and ninety-two of the acts of the year eighteen hundred and ninety-four, and to report these facts and its conclusions in the matter, and such recommendations as it may deem proper, to the next general court.

Public hearings were given in New Bedford and in Boston, at which the City of New Bedford was represented by its mayor and city solicitor; business associations of New Bedford and of Fairhaven by committees; and the New York, New Haven and Hartford Railroad Company by its counsel.

In February, 1896, the ferry between Fairhaven and New Bedford, which had been operated in connection with the Fairhaven Branch railroad from 1854 to 1873 and had then been discontinued, was again opened to public use under chapter 392 of the Acts of 1894. It has since been in continuous operation.

The books of the company show that for the year 1896 the expense of operating the ferry was in round numbers $7,100 and receipts were $5,500; in 1897 the expense was $8,600 and receipts were $6,800; in 1898 the expense was $6,100 and receipts were $4,400; in 1899 the expense was $6,600 and receipts were $4,100; in 1900 the expense was $7,900 and receipts were $4,000; in 1901 the expense was $7,200 and receipts were $3,100; in 1902 the expense was $8,400 and receipts were $1,800; in 1903 the expense was $8,000 and receipts were $1,800. To June of the past year the expense was $3,031 and the receipts were $702. The aggregate gross earnings of the ferry during the eight years have been $32,282.86 and the aggregate operating expenses $63,052.15, with nothing charged to depreciation of ferry boat and plant.

Taking the year ending March 1, 1899, as showing the business of the ferry in the earlier and more prosperous part of this last period of operation, and the year ending June 30, 1904, as showing the business of the ferry under what are practically the present conditions, we find that during the first-named year the number of passengers using the ferry in travelling between New Bedford and Fairhaven was 50,241, and the revenue received from this source $2,512.05, and that for the year ending in June last the number of passengers was 27,600, the revenue $1,380; that the number of passengers using the ferry to and from New Bedford and points beyond Fairhaven was in the first-named year 35,428, and the revenue $1,771.40, while for the year ending in June last the passengers between New Bedford and points beyond Fairhaven were 8,296, and the revenue $414.80.

The average number of passengers a day over this ferry was 263 in 1899 and 108 in 1904; the average daily revenue in 1899, $13.37, in 1904, $5.47. In 1899 the number of trips a day was 38, in 1904 it was 37; the average number of passengers a trip in 1899 was 7, in 1904, 3; the average revenue a trip in 1899 was $0.35, in 1904, $0.15.

It may be assumed that the period beginning August 27 and ending November 19, 1904, fairly indicates the usual amount of baggage carried over the ferry, and we find that the total number of pieces carried during that time was 986, an average of 13 pieces a day. Another test of this business, the record for the three days November

26, November 28 and November 29 of this year, taken at random, shows 4 pieces carried from New Bedford and 9 pieces to New Bedford, an average of 4 pieces a day.

The figures above given were furnished by the company at the request of the Board, and were duly verified.

The New Bedford and Onset street railway was opened to the public in August, 1901, and the new bridge between Fairhaven and New Bedford was completed in August, 1902. The construction of this street railway and the opening of this bridge diverted travel from the ferry into other channels from which there is little or no prospect that it will ever return. As the result, therefore, the disadvantages under which the ferry had been operated were decidedly increased, and bad as the financial showing was ten years ago, it is worse now.

But it has been said that if the ferry had been properly equipped and maintained, and operated with charges that were not prohibitive, the volume of business would have been much larger. In the light of experience, some of the rates may well be thought to have been high, although when they were established in 1894 they were deemed reasonable by the company and apparently by the public. It is evident, too, that physical conditions at the ferry slips have been discouraging to those concerned in the transportation of loaded wagons. Still, the fact that no complaint has been made about either the tolls or the lack of facilities, strongly suggests an absence of interest in the ferry and a lack of desire to use it under any circumstances.

We have sought information from available sources to aid us in estimating the amount of business which might be done over the ferry in the future under the most favorable conditions. As the result, we reach the conclusion that were the plant equipped with every arrangement for the suitable accommodation of patrons and operated with reduced charges, and even with a train schedule upon the railroad especially adapted to the convenience of travel between New Bedford and towns on the Cape, it would still be impossible to develop sufficient traffic to make the receipts equal or even approach expenditures. The location of communities and the character of the business relations between them and other centres, and the existence of the abundant conveniences for travel by the street railways and by the new bridge, restrict the field for development of business by way of the ferry within very narrow limits.

To meet the query whether there might not be profit in operating the Fairhaven Branch railroad with which to offset the loss in operating the ferry, we have examined the record of both the passenger and freight traffic over that line. It would appear that the financial history of this branch has been discouraging from the outset, and that the paralleling of the railroad with the New Bedford and Onset street railway made further serious inroads upon a revenue already small. The larger part of what remains of the passenger traffic is with Boston or cities and towns north of Tremont, and the train schedule has been made to accommodate travel of this kind rather than that with towns south of Tremont. Assuming that the schedule could be changed to favor travel between New Bedford and places on the Cape, we are convinced that the existence of the competing street railway and the conditions of traffic, present and prospective, forbid any great increase in the business over this branch.

On the other hand, it is a matter of common knowledge that, however unprofitable the ferry or the branch railroad may be, the extensive and growing business interests of New Bedford bring to the company upon its other lines an increasingly large traffic, which it is fair to suppose is decidedly profitable.

But there is another point of view. In accordance with the provisions of chapter 124 of the Acts of 1854 the proprietors of the New Bedford and Fairhaven ferry transferred their property and charter rights to the Fairhaven Branch Railroad Company. The ferry thereby became a part of the railroad, constituting its connecting link with New Bedford. In 1894, the Legislature directed the Old Colony Railroad Company, which had acquired this line, to resume the operation of the ferry. In commenting upon this statute our supreme court said:

"A railroad company has by no means an absolute power to determine what parts of its lines it will operate. Its franchises are granted for the public good and in exercising them it is largely subject to the control and direction of the Legislature. Either by virtue of the police power or of the reserved power to alter charters many acts may be required which involve expense and which a railroad corporation would not if left to itself undertake."

Brownell v. *Old Colony Railroad, 164 Mass. 29.*

Treating the ferry as a constituent part of the railroad, the separate gain or loss in operating it is not of controlling importance. If the line between Tremont and New Bedford is to be continued, and we assume that it is, the ferry or some equivalent for it is indispensable to the proper performance of the service which has been undertaken.

The question is, then, whether a fair equivalent for the ferry can be provided through other methods of taking care of passengers and baggage at this end of the line. No such equivalent now exists. Street cars run at intervals of fifteen minutes between Fairhaven and New Bedford, but no attempt is made to connect with train service upon the railroad. An express service is available for the carriage of baggage, but at charges in excess of those for the carriage of baggage to and from the ferry slip in New Bedford.

But there would seem to be no reason why an arrangement could not be made which would establish a connection between the street cars and railroad trains at the Fairhaven station, and provide an express service for transportation of baggage at a cost no greater than that now incurred in using the ferry. Were this arrangement for street railway and express service carried out, and a cab service furnished at reasonable rates, passengers would receive full consideration, and would enjoy in the privilege of prompt transportation to different parts of New Bedford, without substantial loss of time and for a five-cent fare, advantages greater than those now possessed.

Naturally the proposal to discontinue the ferry would under any circumstances meet with disfavor from those, few in number, who now find it a peculiar personal convenience for which no exact substitute could be furnished. Beside this opposition from patrons of the ferry, there probably would be remonstrance from persons who hold to the sentiment that a railroad company should never be permitted to abandon or essentially change any service which it has undertaken, no matter how large a loss its continuance might entail upon the company and no matter what effect it might have upon the performance of other obligations to the public. Such a sentiment, however, rests upon a superficial view of the conduct of railroad business, for it is obvious that the losses which a company sustains at one point in response to a public demand, will be made good at some other point at the public expense. The real issue is ultimately between different public interests.

The ferry between New Bedford and Fairhaven is undoubtedly a convenience to some people, and might be more useful if every effort of the management were directed to that end; but the most sanguine view of the future must contemplate a large daily loss in operating it, a loss to be met by the public otherwise interested in the freight and passenger service of this railroad. If the operation of the ferry were an exceptional instance of unprofitable business, the effect upon other interests would be unappreciable. Demands, however, are continually made upon railroad companies to provide accommodation at less than cost. Some of these demands are reasonable. Unprofitable service must be performed in certain instances, and it is right that the burden of it should be borne by the general travelling and shipping public. In other instances, the accommodation of the few should give way to the larger interests of the greater number. It is plainly necessary, even if the general welfare alone is consulted, that the affairs of a company be prudently administered, and that a rule be applied in respect to demands of this kind which will require the performance of every rightful obligation to the public and at the same time secure the practice of a reasonable economy in the management of business.

In view of the facts disclosed by this investigation, and the conclusions drawn therefrom, we respectfully recommend that the Legislature decline to sanction the discontinuance of the ferry under existing conditions, but that it authorize such discontinuance upon the establishment of a substitute service of the kind described.

Various tables and statements, giving in detail the facts and figures upon which this report is based, are attached hereto as exhibits.

For the Board,

JAMES F. JACKSON,
Chairman.

JANUARY 16, 1905. [5570]

FALL RIVER BRIDGE.

Proceedings of the Railroad Commissioners, the Harbor and Land Commissioners and the Bristol County Commissioners, sitting as a joint board, in reference to new bridge between Fall River and Somerset.

January 12, 1904, the joint board, composed of the state boards of railroad and of harbor and land commissioners and the county commissioners of Bristol, acting under chapter 462, Acts of 1903, after having given several public hearings and made a careful inquiry through personal and expert investigation, unanimously decided that it was not desirable that the new bridge between Fall River and Somerset should accommodate steam railroad as well as other travel, but that the public interests would be best served by an independent highway bridge. This conclusion was based on the following findings:

1. Slade's Ferry bridge is safe for the uses now made of it, although in the near future the demands of traffic will probably call for the rebuilding of the existing structure.

2. It is altogether better that a railroad company have sole authority over the construction and maintenance of all important bridges upon its lines.

3. A union bridge would always permit conditions annoying to those using the highway underneath or at the side.

4. The cost of a suitable union bridge at this place would be far in excess of one million dollars, and in the distribution of this cost a very heavy tax would in all probability be imposed upon the county, city and towns.

A substantial independent highway bridge can probably be constructed well within one million dollars.

March 15, 1904, after further inquiry and consideration, the joint board decided that the new bridge should be located at the foot of Brightman street on the easterly side of the river, with a westerly terminus at the old ferry slip.

In accordance with the statute, a plan, showing the location and character of the new bridge, was presented to the board of harbor and land commissioners, who gave a public hearing for the benefit of all parties interested in navigation, and thereafter recommended a slight change in the width of the draw. The joint board, after adopting the suggested change in the draw, caused plans to be prepared and a petition to be presented to the War Department asking its approval of the proposed structure.

October 18, 1904, a hearing upon this petition was given at Fall River, before Lieutenant Colonel Joseph H. Willard, U. S. A., at which the following statement in explanation of the action of the joint board was presented by the chairman.

"The Legislature of Massachusetts, after an extended public discussion, decided that a new bridge was needed across Taunton river, between Fall River and Somerset, to meet the existing and growing demands of travel between the three cities of Fall River, Providence and Taunton, and the intervening and surrounding towns. Therefore, without a dissenting voice it enacted Chapter 462 of the Acts of 1903, making the state boards of railroad and of harbor and land commissioners and the county commissioners of Bristol county a joint board to locate and construct such a new bridge at a cost not to exceed one million dollars.

"The first question before the board was whether the bridge should accommodate steam railroad as well as other travel. After public hearings in both Fall River and Boston, an expert examination of Slade's Ferry bridge, and careful consideration of all arguments and suggestions, it was determined that the steam railroad should be excluded from the new bridge.

"It was also concluded that while at present there is no call to encumber the bridge with a street railway, it ought to be so constructed that if, in the future, the public interests should demand it, a street railway could be accommodated.

"Various locations were personally inspected; surveys, soundings and experiments were made, and estimates of cost obtained.

"As the result of its study of different types, the board selected what is known as the deck bridge, with a roadway on top, giving a clear view on all sides. The bascule draw was adopted, as it costs less to construct and less to operate; is opened more quickly and obstructs navigation less than the swinging draw. Again it was deemed important that the bridge should be erected at such height above the water as to allow the passage of tugs, mastless barges and small boats, without opening the draw.

"Having determined upon a bridge exclusively for highway uses and with the foregoing features, it was obviously out of the question to locate it within one or two hundred feet of the present railroad bridge, or to yoke it up with that structure. One of the prime objects to be attained in securing an additional highway was an opportunity to cross the river without exposure to the peril and discomfort of crossing in close proximity to a railroad. To build the new bridge beside the old Slade's Ferry bridge would defeat this purpose and authorize a needless expenditure of hundreds of thousands of dollars in accomplishing nothing better than could be secured by repairing the present bridge. Located at this point, a bridge would necessarily be at a low level, a bascule draw of little advantage, and the whole structure a piece of patchwork, a disfigurement of the surrounding landscape. The legislature commanded the construction of a new bridge, not repairs or changes in the old one.

"At the preliminary hearings a preference was expressed by many people for a location at President avenue or Brownell street; these two sites, though at best northerly locations, being somewhat nearer the business centers of Fall River.

"The two controlling reasons for rejecting the Brownell street and President avenue sites were, first, the great cost of construction at either place, and second, the fact that the selection of either would involve an invasion of harbor and wharf properties, the possession of which is a public wealth, of which there is no surplus to be thrown away or lightly surrendered.

"An estimate, based upon the best attainable figures, showed the probable cost of a bridge at President avenue to be about one million two hundred thousand dollars, an amount plainly prohibitive under the terms of the statute. The estimated cost of a similar bridge at Brownell street was about one million dollars, at or near Slade's Ferry bridge eight hundred and twenty thousand dollars, and at Brightman street seven hundred thousand dollars.

"While a bridge at Brownell street would be convenient for quite a number of people, who transact business in Fall River and reside for a part or all of the year in South Somerset, the board did not see its way clear to grant them this accommodation at the necessary sacrifice of harbor and wharf facilities, and at so large an extra cost of construction.

"At the location selected, known as the Brightman street site, the narrowness of the river, the nearness to the surface of the rock bottom upon which it is essential that the bridge should rest, and the high level of the lands on either side are all conditions which make it possible to secure the most desirable qualities both in construction and in appearance, together with the highest convenience in use, at a cost far less than that necessary to obtain the same advantages at any other site. This, too, is a natural crossing place, in line, as statistics show, with the main trend of travel and connecting directly with existing highways.

"The land damages will be trifling in amount, not exceeding, according to estimate of unprejudiced experts, five thousand dollars on the east and fifteen hundred dollars on the west side of the river. In brief, this choice of location offers the best conditions for building, protects harbor and wharf properties from invasion, injures no premises now devoted to commercial uses and saves a large amount of money which, if available, is needed for other public improvements."

Further proceedings are stayed, pending the action of the War Department.

JAMES F. JACKSON,
Chairman of Joint Board.

EXPENSES OF OFFICE.

Advertising,	$31 67
Carpenter work,	136 08
Carpets, etc ,	254 08
Electric lighting, etc.,	174 99
Expert services,	5,050 43
Expressage,	160 11
Furniture and repairs,	113 00
Janitor,	1,000 00
Maps, etc.,	28 00
Newspapers, publications, etc ,	98 84
Postage,	419 58
Printing annual report,	4,654 77
Printing and binding,	860 82
Railroad inspectors' expenses,	800 29
Rent of office,	4,500 00
Stationery and office supplies,	829 17
Stenographers and extra clerical services,	2,135 50
Sundries,	229 12
Telephone and telegrams,	336 06
Travelling expenses,	408 54
Total office expenses,*	$22,221 05

* Exclusive of salaries fixed by statute.

TABULATED STATEMENTS

COMPILED FROM THE

Returns of Railroad Corporations

FOR THE

Year ending June 30, 1904.

DESCRIPTION OF RAILROADS OWNED AND OPERATED.

RAILROADS AND BRANCHES. (LEASED ROADS IN ROMAN.) (BRANCHES IN ITALICS.)	1.—TERMINI. From	1.—TERMINI. To	2.—LENGTH OF LINE. Total.	2.—LENGTH OF LINE. In Massachusetts.	3.—SECOND TRACK. Total.	3.—SECOND TRACK. In Massachusetts.	4.—SIDE TRACK. Total.	4.—SIDE TRACK. In Massachusetts.	5.—Total Length computed as Single Track.
ATTLEBOROUGH BRANCH,[1]	Attleborough,	No. Attleborough,	3.570	3.570	–	–	1.570	1.570	5.140
BERKSHIRE. (See New York, New Haven & Hartford.)	–	–	–	–	–	–	–	–	–
BOSTON & ALBANY (*operated by the New York Central & Hudson River, Lessee*),	Boston,	Albany, N. Y.,	199.910	[illegible]	233.550[2]	194.990[2]	220.980	187.790	654.440
Athol,	Springfield,	Athol,	[illegible]	45.260	–	–	9.590	9.590	54.850
Grand Junction,	Cottage Farm,	East Boston,	9.450	9.450	5.110	5.110	23.450	23.450	38.010
Hudson,	Chatham, N. Y.,	Hudson, N. Y.,	17.330	–	1.000	–	6.750	–	25.080
Milford,	So. Framingham,	Milford,	12.000	12.000	–	–	6.390	6.390	18.390
Millbury,	Millbury Jct.,	Millbury Village,	3.280	3.280	–	–	.980	.980	4.260
Newton Highlands,	Beacon St., Boston,	Riverside Jct.,	9.890	9.890	9.890	9.890	7.040	7.040	26.820
Newton Lower Falls,	Riverside Jct.,	Newton L. Falls,	1.090	1.090	–	–	.830	.830	1.920
Saxonville,	Natick,	Saxonville,	3.700	3.700	–	–	2.380	2.380	6.080
Spencer,	Spencer,	South Spencer,	2.180	2.180	–	–	1.170	1.170	3.350
Chester & Becket,	Chester,	Chester [illegible],	5.270	5.270	–	–	2.110	2.110	7.380
North Brookfield,	East Brookfield,	North Brookfield,	4.000	4.000	–	–	1.310	1.310	5.310
Pittsfield & North Adams,	Pittsfield,	North Adams,	18.550	18.550	–	–	7.770	7.770	26.320
Prov., Webster & Springfield,	Webster Jct.,	[illegible],	11.230	11.230	–	–	3.240	3.240	14.470
Ware River,	Palmer,	Winchendon,	49.350	49.350	–	–	7.400	7.400	[illegible]
BOSTON & LOWELL. (See *Boston & Maine.*)	–	–	–	–	–	–	–	–	–
BOSTON & MAINE,	Boston,	Portland, Me.,	115.310	36.560	82.740[3]	38.090[3]	115.630	72.580	313.680
	Boston,	Portland, Me.,	108.290	41.450	58.110[4]	42.180[4]	[illegible]	52.860	243.300
	Conway Jct., Me.,	Intervale Jct., N.H.,	73.370	–	–	–	26.080	–	99.450
	Rochester, N. H.,	Portland, Me.,	53.860	–	–	–	23.870	–	77.730
	No. Cambridge,	Northampton,	95.690	95.690	–	–	[illegible]	24.990	120.680
Charlestown,	East Somerville,	Charlestown,	1.090	1.090	1.090	1.090	–	–	2.180
Chelsea Beach,	Revere Jct.,	Saugus River Jct.,	3.340	3.340	2.490	2.490	.220	.220	6.050

[1] Operated by electricity.

[2] Including 16.830 miles of third track and 16.810 miles of fourth track.

[3] Including 1.530 miles of third track.

[4] Including .730 mile of third track.

Description of Railroads Owned and Operated — Continued.

RAILROADS AND BRANCHES. (LEASED ROADS IN ROMAN.) (BRANCHES IN ITALICS.)	1. — TERMINI.		2. — LENGTH OF LINE.		3. — SECOND TRACK.		4. — SIDE TRACK.		5. — Total Length computed as Single Track.
	From	To	Total.	In Massachusetts.	Total.	In Massachusetts.	Total.	In Massachusetts.	
BOSTON & MAINE — Con.									
Dover & Winnepiseogee,	Dover, N. H.,	Alton Bay, N. H.,	29.000	–	–	–	7.120	–	36.120
East Boston,	[illegible]re,	East Boston,	3.470	3.470	1.560	1.560	10.970	10.970	16.000
Essex,	[illegible],	Essex,	6.000	6.000	–	–	1.970	1.970	7.970
Gloucester,	Beverly,	Rockport,	16.940	16.940	8.990	8.990	4.920	4.920	30.850
Lawrence,	Salem,	North Andover,	19.890	19.890	1.640	1.640	7.790	7.790	29.320
Marblehead,	S[illegible]n,	[illegible]d,	3.520	3.520	–	–	.880	.880	4.400
Medford,	[illegible]d Jct.,	Medford,	2.000	2.000	2.000	2.000	1.960	1.960	5.960
Methuen,	Lawrence,	State Line, N. H.,	3.750	3.750	1.000	1.000	14.350	14.350	19.100
Newburyport City,	N [illegible]buryport,	Newburyport,	1.970	1.970	–	–	1.270	1.270	3.240
Orchard Beach,	Old Orchard, Me.,	Saco [illegible]er, Me.,	3.270	–	–	–	.360	–	3.630
Portsmouth,[1]	Portsmouth, N. H.,	N. Hampton, N.H.,	18.340	–	–	–	950	–	19.290
Portsmouth & Dover,	Portsmouth, N. H.,	Dover, N. H.,	10.880	–	–	–	3.220	–	14.100
Salisbury,	Salisbury,	[illegible]y,	3.[illegible]90	3.790	–	–	2.430	2.430	6.220
[illegible]s,	[illegible]ett,	West Lynn,	9.550	9.550	9.550	9.550	5.940	5.940	25.040
Somersworth,	[illegible]l, N. H.,	Somersworth, N.H.,	2.750	–	–	–	1.810	–	4.560
South Reading,	Peabody,	Wakefield Jct.,	8.120	8.120	–	–	2.200	2.200	10.320
Swampscott,	Swampscott,	Marblehead,	3.960	3.960	.520	.520	1.300	1.300	5.780
[illegible]on,	Portland, Me.,	Portland, Me.,	1.120	–	–	–	–	–	1.120
[illegible]st Amesbury,	Merrimac,	Newton Jct., N.H.,	4.450	2.130	–	–	.620	.420	5.070
Wolfborough,	Sanbornville, N.H.,	Wolfboro', N. H.,	12.030	–	–	–	1.070	–	13.100
Connection Lowell & Law[illegible] [illegible] Lowell & Andover R.R.,	Lowell,	Lowell,	.250[2]	.250[2]	.370	.370	–	–	.620
Boston & Lowell,	Boston,	Lowell,	26.750	26.750	26.750	26.750	64.640	59.280	118.[illegible]40
Bedford & Billerica,	Bedford,	Billerica,	7.630	7.630	–	–	.800	.800	8.430
[illegible]e,	Wilmington,	Wilmington Jct.,	3.210	3.210	–	–	1.580	1.580	4.790
Lexington,	Somerville,	Lexington,	8.110	8.110	8.110	8.110	3.680	3.680	19.900
Lowell & Lawrence,	Lowell,	Lawrence,	12.420	12.420	–	–	6.730	6.730	19.150
Middlesex Cent[illegible]al,	Lexington,	Concord,	11.080	11.080	–	–	3.680	3.680	14.760
Mystic,	Somerville,	Mystic Wharves,	2.250	2.250	.850	.850	32.510	32.510	35.610

Salem & Lowell,	Peabody,	Tewksbury,	16.800	16.800	–	–	7.430	7.430	24.230
Stoneham,	[illegible]le Jct.,	Stoneham,	2.500	2.500	–	–	1.560	1.560	4.060
Woburn,	Winchester,	No. Woburn Jct.,	8.200	6.200	6.200	6.200	3.300	3.300	15.700
Concord & Montreal,	Nashua, N. H.,	Groveton, N. H.,	181.070	–	36.620[3]	–	115.320	–	333.010
Concord & Manchester,[1]	Concord, N. H.,	Manchester and Pennacook, N.H.,	27.880	–	–	–	2.450	–	30.330
Franklin & Tilton,	[illegible]in, N. H.,	[illegible]n, N. H.,	4.950	–	–	–	3.750	–	8.700
Hooksett,	Hooksett, N. H.,	Bow Jct., N. H.,	7.590	–	–	–	3.720	–	11.310
Lake Shore,	Lakeport, N. H.,	[illegible]ton Bay, N. H.,	17.280	–	–	–	1.930	–	19.210
Manchester & No. Weare,	Manchester, N. H.,	[illegible]er, N. H.,	24.500	–	–	–	8.720	–	33.220
Mount Washington,	[illegible]ng Road, N. H.,	Mt. Wash'ton, N.H.,	20.170	–	–	–	5.070	–	25.240
New Boston,	Parker's, N. H.,	New Boston, N. H.,	5.190	–	–	–	.820	–	8.010
Profile & Franconia,	Bethlehem J., N.H., Bethlehem J., N.H.,	Profile House, N.H., Bethlehem, N. H.,	12.[illegible]40	–	–	–	1.750	–	14.590
Suncook Valley,	Suncook, N. H.,	[illegible]ld, N. H.,	17.410	–	–	–	4.010	–	21.420
Suncook Valley Extension,	Pittsfield, N. H.,	Ctr. Barnst'd, N.H.,	4.460	–	–	–	1.210	–	5.670
Tilton & Belmont,	Belmont J., N. H.,	Belmont, N. H.,	4.170	–	–	–	.650	–	4.820
Whitefield & Jefferson,	Whitefield J., N.H., [illegible]ff. Mead's, N.H.,	Berlin, N. H., Jefferson, N. H.,	33.690	–	–	–	13.270	–	46.960
Concord & Portsmouth,	Portsmouth, N. H.,	Manchester, N. H.,	39.870	–	–	–	15.660	–	55.530
Connecticut River,	Springfield,	Keene, N. H.,	74.000	50.080	36.800[4]	36.800[4]	61.530	54.420	172.330
Chicopee Falls,	Chicopee Jct.,	[illegible]e Falls,	2.350	2.350	–	–	1.850	1.850	4.200
Easthampton,	Mt. Tom Jct.,	Easthampton,	3.500	3.500	–	–	1.360	1.360	4.860
Conn. & Pass. Rivers,	White Riv. Jct., Vt.,	[illegible]a Line,	110.300	–	–	–	41.620	–	151.920
Danvers,	Wakefield Jct.,	Danvers,	9.260	9.260	–	–	2.280	2.280	11.540
Delaware & Hudson,*	Mechanicville, N.Y.,	Crescent, N. Y.,	–	–	6.940	–	–	–	8.940
Fitchburg,	Boston,	Fitchburg,	49.650	49.650	55.570[5]	55.570[5]	86.700	86.700	191.920
	Greenfield,	Rotterdam J., N.Y.,	105.250	44.010	70.600	44.010	90.590	32.520	266.440
	[illegible]te Line, Vt.,	Troy, N. Y.,	40.300	–	–	–	10.450	–	50.750
	Ashburnham Jct.,	Bellows Falls, Vt.,	53.850	10.760	–	–	25.230	4.010	79.080
Ashburnham,	So. Ashburnham,	Ashburnham,	2.590	2.[illegible]90	–	–	.520	.520	3.110
Greenville,	Ayer,	[illegible]e, N. H.,	23.[illegible]40	14.060	–	–	4.340	2.370	27.980
Ice,	Charlestown,	Charlestown,	.660	.660	.490	.490	–	–	1.150
Marlborough,	South [illegible]n,	Marlborough,	12.350	12.350	–	–	[illegible]920	3.920	16.270
Milford,	Squannacook Jct.,	Milford, N. H.,	21.730	9.560	–	–	4.230	2.150	25.960

1 Electric street railway.

2 Total length, .370 mile double track, of which .120 mile of one track is owned by the Lowell & Andover.

3 Including 1.350 miles of third track.

4 Including .800 miles of third track.

5 Including 3.900 miles of third track and 2.020 miles of fourth track.

* Trackage rights.

Description of Railroads Owned and Operated — Continued.

RAILROADS AND BRANCHES. (LEASED ROADS IN ROMAN.) (BRANCHES IN ITALICS.)	1. — TERMINI. From	1. — TERMINI. To	2. — LENGTH OF LINE. Total.	2. — LENGTH OF LINE. In Massachusetts.	3. — SECOND TRACK. Total.	3. — SECOND TRACK. In Massachusetts.	4. — SIDE TRACK. Total.	4. — SIDE TRACK. In Massachusetts.	5. — Total Length computed as Single Track.
BOSTON & MAINE — Con.									
Fitchburg — Con.									
Peterborough,	Winchendon,	Peterboro', N. H.,	15.930	2.250	-	-	2.100	-	18.030
Saratoga,	Saratoga, N. Y.,	Schuylerville, N. Y.,	25.820	-	-	-	4.310	-	30.130
	Schuyler Jct., N. Y.,	Schuylerville, N. Y.,							
Watertown,	West Cambridge,	Waltham,	6.630	6.630	6.480	6.480	4.780	4.780	17.890
Worcester,	Worcester,	Winchendon,	35.740	35.740	-	-	14.170	14.170	49.910
Grand Trunk,*	Lenoxville, P. Q.,	Sherbrooke, P. Q.,	2.950	-	-	-	-	-	2.950
Horn Pond Branch,	Woburn Branch,	Horn Pond,	.663	.663	-	-	.076	.076	.739
Kennebunk & Kennebunkp't,	Kennebunk, Me.,	Kennebunkp't, Me.,	4.500	-	-	-	930	-	5.430
Lowell & Andover,	Lowell,	Lowell Jct.,	8.850	8.850	7.280	7.280	6.230	6.230	22.360
Manchester & Keene,	Greenfield, N. H.,	Keene, N. H.,	29.590	-	-	-	2.620	-	32.210
Manchester & Lawrence,	State Line, N. H.,	Manchester, N. H.,	22.390	-	-	-	10.790	-	33.180
Manchester & Milford,	Grasmere Jct., N. H.,	East Milford, N. H.,	18.540	-	-	-	1.100	-	19.640
Massawippi Valley,	Canada Line,	Lenoxville, P. Q.,	31.950	-	-	-	6.480	-	38.430
Stanstead,	Stanstead Jct., P. Q.,	Stanstead, P. Q.,	3.510	-	-	-	.960	-	4.470
Nashua, Acton & Boston,	North Acton,	Nashua, N. H.,	20.120	15.140	-	-	5.300	2.910	25.420
Nashua & Lowell,	Lowell,	Nashua, N. H.,	14.500	9.250	14.500	9.250	13.040	8.140	42.040
Newburyport,	Bradford,	Newburyport,	26.980	26.980	-	-	4.920	4.920	31.900
	Georgetown,	Danvers,							
N. Y., N. H. & Hartford,*	North Acton,	Concord Jct.,	4.210	4.210	-	-	-	-	4.210
Northern,	Concord, N. H.,	White River J., Vt.,	69.500	-	-	-	25.960	-	95.460
Bristol,	Franklin, N. H.,	Bristol, N. H.,	13.410	-	-	-	1.060	-	14.470
Concord & Claremont,	Concord, N. H.,	Claremont J., N. H.,	70.900	-	-	-	12.740	-	83.640
	Contoocook, N. H.,	Hillsboro' B'ge, N. H.,							
Peterboro' & Hillsboro',	Peterboro', N. H.,	Hillsboro' B'ge, N. H.,	18.510	-	-	-	2.450	-	20.960
Pemigewasset Valley,	Plymouth, N. H.,	Lincoln, N. H.,	22.930	-	-	-	13.410	-	36.340
	Campton, N. H.,	Campton Vil., N. H.,							
Peterborough,	Wilton, N. H.,	Greenfield, N. H.	10.500	-	-	-	1.580	-	12.080
Stony Brook,	No. Chelmsford,	Ayer Junction,	13.160	13.160	-	-	6.060	6.060	19.220
Troy & Bennington,	Hoosic Jct., N. Y.,	State Line, Vt.,	5.040	-	-	-	1.070	-	6.110

Troy Union,*	Troy, N. Y.,	Troy, N. Y.,	2.130	–	2.130	–	–	–	4.260
Vermont & Massachusetts,	Fitchburg,	Greenfield,	55.780	55.780	55.780	55.780	41.280	41.280	152.840
Turner's Falls,	Turner's Falls Jct.,	Turner's Falls,	2.800	2.800	–	–	.640	.640	3.440
Wilton,	Nashua, N. H.,	Wilton, N. H.,	15.500	–	–	–	5.010	–	20 510
Worc., Nashua & Rochester,	Worcester,	Rochester, N. H.,	94.480	39.460	18.130	18.130	50.130	31.590	162.740
BOSTON & PROVIDENCE. (See *N. Y., N. H. & Hartford.*)	–	–	–	–	–	–	–	–	–
BOSTON, REVERE BEACH & LYNN,[1]	East Boston,	Lynn,	8.800	8.800	8.800	8.800	3.100	3.100	20.700
Winthrop,	Orient Heights,	Winthrop,	4.400	4.400	4.400	4.400	1.000	1.000	9.800
CAPE ANN GRANITE,	Lanesville,	Pigeon Cove,	1.436	1.436	–	–	.781	.781	2.217
CHATHAM. (See *New York, New Haven & Hartford.*)	–	–	–	–	–	–	–	–	–
CHESTER & BECKET. (See *Boston & Albany — N. Y. Central & H. R., Lessee.*)	–	–	–	–	–	–	–	–	–
CONNECTICUT RIVER. (See *Boston & Maine.*)	–	–	–	–	–	–	–	–	–
DANVERS. (See *Boston & Maine.*)	–	–	–	–	–	–	–	–	–
FITCHBURG. (See *Boston & Maine.*)	–	–	–	–	–	–	–	–	–
GRAFTON & UPTON,	North Grafton,	Milford,	16.500	16.500	–	–	3.790	3.790	20.290
Electric Loop,	Brooks St., Upton,	West Upton,	2.620	2.620	–	–	–	–	2.620
HOLYOKE & WESTFIELD. (See *N. Y., N. H. & Hartford.*)	–	–	–	–	–	–	–	–	–
HOOSAC TUNNEL & WILMINGTON,[1]	Hoosac Tunnel,	Wilmington, Vt.,	25.000	8.220	–	–	3.000	1.000	28.000
HORN POND BRANCH. (See *Boston & Maine.*)	–	–	–	–	–	–	–	–	–
[illegible] & ANDOVER. (See *Boston & Maine.*)	–	–	–	–	–	–	–	–	–
MILFORD, FRANKLIN & PROV. (See *N.Y., N.H. & Hartf'd.*)	–	–	–	–	–	–	–	–	–
MILFORD & WOONSOCKET. (See *N.Y., N.H. & Hartf'd.*)	–	–	–	–	–	–	–	–	–
NANTUCKET CENTRAL,[1]	Nantucket,	Siasconset,	8.500	8.500	–	–	.200	.200	8.700

[1] A narrow-gauge railroad.

* Trackage rights.

Description of Railroads Owned and Operated — Continued.

RAILROADS AND BRANCHES. (LEASED ROADS IN ROMAN.) (BRANCHES IN ITALICS.)	1.—TERMINI.		2.—LENGTH OF LINE.		3.—SECOND TRACK.		4.—SIDE TRACK.		5.—Total Length computed as Single Track.
	From	To	Total.	In Massachusetts.	Total.	In Massachusetts.	Total.	In Massachusetts.	
NASHUA, ACTON & BOSTON. (See *Boston & Maine.*)	-	-	-	-	-	-	-	-	-
NASHUA & LOWELL. (See *Boston & Maine.*)	-	-	-	-	-	-	-	-	-
NEWBURYPORT. (See *Boston & Maine.*)	-	-	-	-	-	-	-	-	-
NEW ENGLAND. (See *N. Y., N. H. & Hartford.*)	-	-	-	-	-	-	-	-	-
NEW HAVEN & NORTHAMPTON. (See *N. Y., N. H. & Hartf'd.*)	-	-	-	-	-	-	-	-	-
NEW LONDON NORTHERN (operated by the *Central Vt. R.R. Co.*),	New London, Ct.,	Brattleboro', Vt.,	121.000	54.900	-	-	38.700	13.500	159.700
NEW YORK, NEW HAVEN & HARTFORD,	W'dlawn J., N.Y.,	Providence, R. I.,	173.770	-	284.410[1]	-	145.650	-	603.830
	New Haven, Ct.,	Springfield,	60.170	5.950	60.170	5.950	90.630	8.490	210.970
Henderson Street,	Auburn, R. I.,	Providence, R. I.,	3.580	-	1.660	-	.890	-	6.[illegible]30
Housatonic,	Bridgeport, Ct.,	State Line, Mass.,	74.[illegible]90	-	-	-	20.050	-	95.020
	Brookfield J., Ct.,	Danbury, Ct.,	5.360	-	-	-	1.160	-	6.520
	Botsford, Ct.,	Huntington, Ct.,	9.790	-	-	-	3.050	-	12.840
Litchfield,	Hawleyville, Ct.,	Litchfield, Ct.,	32.280	-	-	-	4.130	-	36.410
Loop,	Stonington, Ct.,	Stonington, Ct.,	.970	-	-	-	-	-	.970
Middletown,	Berlin, Ct.,	[illegible], Ct.,	9.700	-	-	-	5.700	-	15.400
New Britain,	Berlin, Ct.,	New Britain, Ct.,	3.180	-	3.180	-	9.190	-	15.550
New Canaan,	[illegible], Ct.,	New Canaan, Ct.,	7.660	-	-	-	1.020	-	8.680
Pontiac,	Auburn, R. I.,	Pontiac, R. I.,	4.890	-	-	-	.390	-	5.080
Suffield,	Windsor Locks, Ct.,	Suffield, Ct.,	4.320	-	-	-	[illegible]170	-	5.490
Valley,	Fenwick, Ct.,	Hartford, Ct.,	46.200	-	-	-	10.820	-	57.020
West River,	New Haven, Ct.,	New Haven, Ct.,	1.660	-	-	-	-	-	1.660
Berkshire,	West Stockbridge,	State Line, Ct.,	20.530	20.530	-	-	6.390	6.390	26.920
Boston & Albany,*	Ashland Jct.,	Ashland,	.220	.220	-	-	-	-	.220
Boston & Albany,*	Springfield Jct.,	Springfield,	.590	.590	-	-	-	-	.590

Boston & Albany,*	Worcester Jct.,	[illegible]r,	.150	.150	.150	.150	–	–	.300
Boston & Maine,*	Shelburne Jct.,	Shelburne Falls,	4.670	4.670	–	–	–	–	4.670
Boston & Maine,*	Lowell Jct.,	Lowell,	.570	.570	–	–	–	–	.570
Boston & Maine,*	Sterling Jct.,	Worcester,	11.940	11.940	11.940	11.940	–	–	23.[illegible]
Boston & New York Air Line,	New Haven, Ct.,	Willimantic, Ct.,	52.260	–	5.230	–	16.910	–	74.400
Colchester,	Turnerville, Ct.,	[illegible]er, Ct.,	3.590	–	–	–	1.030	–	4.620
Boston & Providence,	Boston,	Providence, R. I.,	41.890[2]	38.700	67.650[3]	60.160[4]	65.440[2]	48.640	174.980
Connection with New England R.R.,	Readville,	Readville,	1.200	1.200	1.200	1.200	–	–	2.400
Dedham,	Readville,	Dedham,	2.470	2.470	2.470	2.470	14.480	14.480	19.420
India Point,	East Junction,	India Point, R. I.,	8.050	3.490	–	–	8.450	.290	16.500
Stoughton,	Canton Jct.,	Stoughton,	4.050	4.050	4.050	4.050	2.920	2.920	11.020
West Roxbury,	Forest Hills Sta.,	Dedham,	5.370	5.370	5.370	5.370	3.580	3.580	14.320
Boston Terminal,*	Boston Station,	Fort Point Channel,	.420	.420	1.260[5]	1.260[5]	–	–	1.680
[illegible]m,	Chatham,	Harwich,	7.070	7.070	–	–	.770	.770	7.840
Central New England,*	Hopewell J., N.Y.,	Poughkeepsie, N.Y.,	13.570	–	1.170	–	–	–	14.740
Danbury & Norwalk,	Danbury, Ct.,	Wilson's Pt., Ct.,	26.280	–	–	–	20.130	–	46.410
Hawleyville,	Bethel, Ct.,	Hawleyville, Ct.,	5.950	–	–	–	.640	–	6.590
Ridgefield,	Branchville, Ct.,	Ridgefield, Ct.,	3.970	–	–	–	.420	–	4.390
Harlem River & Port Chester,	Harlem Riv., N.Y.,	New Rochelle, N.Y.,	11.500	–	14.000[6]	–	75.870	–	101.370
Holyoke & Westfield,	Westfield,	Holyoke,	10.320	10.320	–	–	14.280	14.280	24.600
Mid., Meriden & Waterbury,	Westfield, Ct.,	Waterbury, Ct.,	26.000	–	–	–	6.890	–	32.890
Milford, Franklin & Prov.,	Franklin,	Bellingham,	4.650	4.650	–	–	.440	.440	5. 90
Milford & Woonsocket,	Ashland,	Bellingham,	15.130	15.130	–	–	3.820	3.820	18.950
Nantasket Beach,	Nantasket Jct.,	Pemberton,	6.950	6.950	6.880	6.880	4.500	4.500	18.330
Naugatuck,	Naugatuck J., Ct.,	Winsted, Ct.,	56.550	–	10.460	–	28.720	–	95.730
Watertown,	Waterbury, Ct.,	Watertown, Ct.,	4.440	–	–	–	.710	–	5.150
Newburg, Dutch. & Conn.,*	Hopewell J., N.Y.,	Wicopee J., N.Y.,	10.950	–	–	–	–	–	10.950
New England,	Boston,	Hopewell J., N.Y.,	213.560	50.630	115.360	50.630	152.400	67.540	481.320
	Wicopee J., N. Y.,	Fishkill-on-Hudson, N. Y.,	1.710	–	–	–	9.330	–	11.040
Dedham,	Dedham Jct.,	Dedham,	1.530	1.530	–	–	.750	.750	2.280
Islington,	Islington,	Dedham,	2.000	2.000	–	–	.110	.110	2.110

1 Including 55.320 miles of third track and 55.320 miles of fourth track.

* Trackage rights.

2 Including only one-half the length of joint tracks between Providence station and Boston switch, so-called, viz.: 5.000 miles of first or single track; 5.000 miles of second track; 4.300 miles of third track; 4.300 miles of fourth track; and 10.120 miles of sidings; these distances being the total length.

3 Including 12.880 miles of third track and 12.880 miles of fourth track.

4 Including 10.730 miles of third track and 10.730 miles of fourth track.

5 Including .420 mile of third track and .420 mile of fourth track.

6 Including 1.250 miles of third track and 1.250 miles of fourth track.

Description of Railroads Owned and Operated — Continued.

RAILROADS AND BRANCHES. (LEASED ROADS IN ROMAN.) (BRANCHES IN ITALICS.)	1. — TERMINI.		2. — LENGTH OF LINE.		3. — SECOND TRACK.		4. — SIDE TRACK.		5. — Total Length computed as Single Track.
	From	To	Total.	In Massachusetts.	Total.	In Massachusetts.	Total.	In Massachusetts.	
NEW YORK, NEW HAVEN & HARTFORD — Con.									
New England — Con.									
Melrose,	Melrose, Ct.,	Rockville, Ct.,	7.220	–	–	–	.310	–	7.530
[illegible]e,	Providence, R. I.,	Willimantic, Ct.,	57.760	–	1.270	–	22.850	–	81.880
South [illegible]n Freight,	South Boston,	South Boston,	1.040	1.040	1.040	1.040	–	–	2.080
Southbridge,	E. Thompson, Ct.,	Southbridge,	17.360	12.010	–	–	3.290	2.780	20.650
Springfield,	E. Hartford, Ct.,	Springfield Jct.,	28.310	8.140	–	–	7.020	4.080	35.330
Woonsocket,	Cook St., Newton,	Woonsocket, R. I.,	28.670	27.600	–	–	7.750	5.380	36.420
New Haven & [illegible]by,	New Haven, Ct.,	Derby Jct., Ct.,	10.760	–	–	–	7.[illegible]0	–	18.340
Huntington,	Derby, Ct.,	Huntington, Ct.,	3.790	–	–	–	2.070	–	5.860
New Haven & Northampton,	New [illegible]en, Ct.,	[illegible]e Jct.,	94.840	43.380	–	–	47.180	23.880	141.820
New Hartford,	Farmington, Ct.,	No. Hartford, Ct.,	14.090	–	–	–	3.760	–	17.850
Turner's Falls,	South Deerfield,	[illegible]r's Falls,	10.070	10.070	–	–	2.690	2.690	12.760
Williamsburg,	Northampton,	Williamsburg,	7.510	7.510	–	–	2.210	2.210	9.720
New York & Harlem,*	Grand Central Depot, N. Y.,	Woodlawn J., N.Y.,	12.030	–	36.090[1]	–	–	–	48.120
Norwich & [illegible]r,	[illegible]r,	Groton Jct., Ct.,	70.970	17.830	–	–	36.450	11.530	107.420
Connection with New London Northern R.R.,	[illegible]h, Ct.,	Norwich, Ct.,	.630	–	–	–	.270	–	.900
Old Colony,	Boston,	Newport, R. I.,	67.600	51.410	52.610[2]	52.610[2]	55.820	49.000	176.030
	[illegible]er Park,	[illegible]et Jct.,	36.310	36.310	26.920[3]	26.920[3]	3[illegible]0	34.130	97.360
	Middleborough,	Provincetown,	85.660	85.660	19.720	19.720	17.030	17.030	122.410
	Raynham,	[illegible]on Jct.,	3.380	3.380	3.380	3.380	1.180	1.180	7.940
	Braintree,	Kingston,	32.340	32.340	8.410	8.410	6.730	6.730	47.480
	South [illegible]ree,	Plymouth,	26.040	26.040	4.280	4.280	12.740	12.740	43.060
	Framingham,	Lowell,	26.120	26.120	4.360	4.360	1[illegible]80	1[illegible]80	41.560
	New Bedford,	[illegible]g,	91.250	91.250	50.350[4]	.[illegible]0[4]	66.050	[illegible]50	207.650
Adamsdale,	No. Attleborough,	[illegible]e,	3.860	3.860	–	–	1.610	1.610	5.470
Attleborough,	[illegible]ro' Br. Jct.,	Attleborough,	8.600	8.600	–	–	2.650	2.650	11.250
Bridgewater,	[illegible]an,	Bridgewater,	6.120	6.120	–	–	1.780	1.780	7.900

Brockton,	Elmwood,	[illegible]e,	.750	.750	–	–	–	–	.750
Connection with New England R.R.,	Boston,	Boston,	.230	.230	.230	.230	–	–	.460
Connection with Prov. & Wor. R.R.,	Attleborough,	Attleborough,	.220	.220	–	–	–	–	.220
Dorchester & Milton,	Neponset,	Mattapan,	3.300	3.300	–	–	1.500	1.500	4.80[illegible]
Easton,	Matfield,	Easton,	7.560	7.[illegible]	–	–	.920	[illegible]920	8.480
Extension to Plymouth & Mid. R.R.,	Middleborough,	Middleborough,	.420	.420	–	–	–	–	.420
Fairhaven,	Fairhaven,	Tremont,	15.170	15.170	–	–	1.490	1.490	16.660
Fall River,	Fall River,	New Bedford,	12.250	12.250	–	–	4.260	4 [illegible]60	16.510
Granite,	Atlantic,	Braintree,	5.410	5.410	–	–	3.450	3.450	8.[illegible]60
Hanover,	No. Abington,	Hanover,	7.800	7.800	–	–	3.700	3.700	11.500
Hyannis,	Yarmouth,	Hyannis,	5.050	5.[illegible]	–	–	2.680	2.680	7.730
[illegible]r,	Lancaster Br. Jct.,	Lancaster Mills,	1.630	1.630	–	–	.380	.380	2.010
Marlborough,	Marlborough Jct.,	[illegible]h,	1.470	1.470	–	–	1.420	1.420	2.890
Middleboro' & Taunt on,	Middleborough,	Taunton Jct.,	8.040	8.040	–	–	1.540	1.540	9.[illegible]80
Prison,	So. Framingham,	Reformatory,	.620	.620	–	–	.540	.540	1.160
[illegible]t,	Harrison Square,	[illegible]ut Jct.,	2.390	2.390	–	–	1.170	1.170	3.560
Sterling,	Pratt's Jct.,	Sterling Jct.,	5.030	5.030	–	–	1.350	1.350	6.380
Stoughton,	Stoughton Jct.,	Stoughton,	1.650	1.650	1.650	1.650	.580	.580	3.[illegible]80
[illegible]le & [illegible]m,	Walpole Jct.,	Norwood Jct.,	5.760	5.760	–	–	3.210	3.210	8.970
Warren,	Fall River,	Warren,	7.950	5.820	–	–	1.220	.380	9.170
Whittenton Y.,	Taunton,	[illegible]n,	.980	.980	–	–	–	–	.[illegible]80
Wrentham,	[illegible]le Jct.,	No. Attleborough,	11.880	11.880	–	–	3.660	3.660	15.540
Wrentham,	N. Attleboro' Jct.,	No. Attleborough,	.970	.970	–	–	–	–	.970
Wood's Hole,	Buzzards Bay,	Wood's Hole,	17.540	17.540	–	–	2.830	2.830	20.370
Pawtuxet Valley,	[illegible]c, R. I.,	Hope, R. I.,	5.670	–	–	–	1.450	–	7.120
Plymouth & Middleborough,	Plymouth,	Middleborough,	15.030	15.030	–	–	1.020	1.020	16.050
Providence & Springfield,	Providence, R. I.,	Pascoag, R. I.,	20.890	–	–	–	4.350	–	25.240
	Pascoag, R. I.,	Douglas Jct.,	6.840	1.630	–	–	1.300	.700	8.140
Prov., Warren & Bristol,	India Point, R. I.,	Bristol, R. I.,	14.150	–	7.770	–	9.240	–	31.160
India Point,	India Point, R. I.,	India Point, R. I.,	.750	–	–	–	–	–	.750

[1] Including 12.030 miles of third track and 12.030 miles of fourth track.
[2] Including 2.910 miles of third track and 2.870 miles of fourth track.
[3] Including 2.740 miles of third track and 2.740 miles of fourth track.
[4] Including .910 mile of third track.
* Trackage rights.

Description of Railroads Owned and Operated — Concluded.

RAILROADS AND BRANCHES. (LEASED ROADS IN ROMAN.) (BRANCHES IN ITALICS.)	1. — TERMINI.		2. — LENGTH OF LINE.		3. — SECOND TRACK.		4. — SIDE TRACK.		5. — Total Length computed as Single Track.
	From	To	Total.	In Massachusetts.	Total.	In Massachusetts.	Total.	In Massachusetts.	
NEW YORK, NEW HAVEN & HARTFORD — Con.									
Providence & Worcester, .	Providence, R. I., .	Worcester, . .	40.900[1]	25.500	44.180[2]	24.480	63.270	23.330	148.350
East Providence, . .	Valley Falls, R. I.,	E. Providence, R.I.,	7.000	.500	6.600	.500	8.420	–	22.020
R. I. & Mass. in Mass., . .	Franklin, . .	State Line, R. I., .	6.520	6.520	–	–	.860	.860	7.380
R. I. & Mass. in R. I., . .	State Line, R. I., .	Valley Falls, R. I.,	7.070	–	–	–	.830	–	7.900
Rockville, ...	Vernon, Ct., . .	Rockville, Ct., .	4.430	–	–	–	1.020	–	5.450
Stockbridge & Pittsfield, .	Vandeusenville, .	Pittsfield, . .	22.020	22.020	–	–	14.340	14.340	36.360
West Stockbridge, . . .	W. Stockbridge, .	State Line, N. Y.,	2.640	2.640	–	–	.930	.930	3.570
Woonsocket & Pascoag, . .	Woonsocket, R. I.,	Harrisville, R. I., .	9.450	–	–	–	1.040	–	10.490
NORTH BROOKFIELD. (See *Boston & Albany — N. Y. Central & H. R., Lessee.*)	–	–	–	–	–	–	–	–	–
NORWICH & WORCESTER. (See *N. Y., N. H. & Hartford.*)	–	–	–	–	–	–	–	–	–
OLD COLONY. (See *New York, New Haven & Hartford.*)	–	–	–	–	–	–	–	–	–
PITTSFIELD & NORTH ADAMS. (See *Boston & Albany — N. Y. Central & H. R., Lessee.*)	–	–	–	–	–	–	–	–	–
PLYMOUTH & MIDDLEBOROUGH. (See *N. Y., N.H. & Hartf'd.*)	–	–	–	–	–	–	–	–	–
PROVIDENCE & SPRINGFIELD. (See *N. Y., N.H. & Hartf'd.*)	–	–	–	–	–	–	–	–	–
PROVIDENCE, WEBSTER & SPRINGFIELD. (See *Boston & Albany — N. Y. Central & H. R., Lessee.*)	–	–	–	–	–	–	–	–	–
PROVIDENCE & WORCESTER. (See *N. Y., N.H. & Hartf'd.*)	–	–	–	–	–	–	–	–	–

RHODE ISLAND & MASSACHUSETTS. (See *New York, New Haven & Hartford.*)	-	-	-	-	-	-	-	-	-
STOCKBRIDGE & PITTSFIELD. (See *N.Y., N.H. & Hartf'd.*)	-	-	-	-	-	-	-	-	-
STONY BROOK. (See *Boston & Maine.*)	-	-	-	-	-	-	-	-	-
UNION FREIGHT, ...	Boston, . .	Boston, . .	2.431	2.431	.937	.937	1.280	1.280	4.648
VERMONT & MASSACHUSETTS. (See *Boston & Maine.*)	-	-	-	-	-	-	-	-	-
WARE RIVER. (See *Boston & Albany—N. Y. Central & H. R., Lessee.*)	-	-	-	-	-	-	-	-	-
WEST STOCKBRIDGE. (See *N. Y., N. H. & Hartford.*)	-	-	-	-	-	-	-	-	-
WORCESTER, NASHUA & ROCHESTER. (See *Boston & Maine.*)	-	-	-	-	-	-	-	-	-
TOTALS, ...	. . . . . .	. . . . .	4,935.670	2,131.190	1,652.447	957.297	2,802.717	1,437.937	9,390.834

[1] Including only one-half the length of joint tracks between Providence station and Boston switch, so-called, viz.: 5.000 miles of first or single track; 5.000 miles of second track; 4.300 miles of third track; 4.300 miles of fourth track; and 10.120 miles of sidings; these distances being the total length.

[2] Including 2.150 miles of third track and 2.150 miles of fourth track.

NOTE.—The 1,652.447 miles of second track owned and operated, as given in the above totals, include 115.750 miles of third track and 108.490 miles of fourth track. The 957.297 miles of second track *in Massachusetts* include 41.500 miles of third track and 35.590 miles of fourth track.

TABULATED STATEMENTS FROM RETURNS OF RAILROAD CORPORATIONS.

OPERATING RAILROADS.	6.—ATTLEBOROUGH BRANCH.*	7.—BOSTON & ALBANY.†	8.—BOSTON & MAINE.	9.—BOSTON, REVERE BEACH & LYNN.‡
ASSETS.				
Construction,	$121,779 19	–	$42,979,441 32	$1,445,927 38
Equipment,	–[1]	–	7,223,320 26	258,434 89
Lands,	–	–	1,305,676 24	85,087 00
Stocks and bonds of other companies,	–	–	10,645,053 51	–
Other permanent property,	–	–	121,521 67	131,000 00
Total permanent investments,	121,779 19	–	62,275,013 00	1,920,449 27
Cash and current assets,	2,163 26	–	9,619,225 92	235,573 22
Miscellaneous assets,	–	–	3,713,624 21	21,641 64
GROSS ASSETS,	123,942 45	–	75,607,863 13	2,177,664 13
LIABILITIES.				
Capital stock, common,	$131,700 00	–	$23,838,070 70	$850,000 00
preferred,	–	–	3,149,800 00	–
Total capital stock,	131,700 00	–	26,987,870 70	850,000 00
Funded debt,	–	–	31,405,008 41	850,000 00
Real estate mortgages,	–	–	594,800 00	–
Current liabilities,	–	–	6,946,667 63	374,731 74
Accrued liabilities,	–	–	3,121,059 99[2]	8,500 00
Total indebtedness,	–	–	42,067,536 03	1,233,231 74
Sinking and other special funds,	–	–	2,742,162 55	35,000 00
GROSS LIABILITIES,	131,700 00	–	71,797,569 28	2,118,231 74
INCOME.				
Revenue from passengers,	$7,651 40	$4,169,392 11	$12,338,181 53[3]	$589,743 25
from mails,	–	369,374 58	457,551 43	–
from express,	--	345,831 33	1,027,086 51	--

from extra baggage and storage, . . .	–			–
from other passenger service, . . .	–	35,695 76	–	–
Total passenger revenue, ...	7,651 40	4,963,494 98	13,971,273 22[4]	589,743 25
Revenue from freight, ...	3,043 00	4,956,504 13	20,363,605 38	–
from other freight service, ...	–	12,597 60	294,663 48	–
Total freight revenue, ...	3,043 00	4,969,101 73	20,658,268 86	–
Total passenger and freight revenue, . . .	10,694 40	9,932,596 71	34,629,542 08	589,743 25
Other earnings from operation, ...	–	321,895 78	265,066 11	–
Gross earnings from operation, ...	10,694 40	10,254,492 49	34,894,608 19	589,743 25
Income from other sources, ...	410 08	–	576,884 17	16,613 81
GROSS INCOME, ...	11,104 48	10,254,492 49	35,471,492 36	606,357 06
EXPENDITURES.				
Operating expenses, ...	$8,722 52	$7,139,476 07	$25,271,907 63[5]	$525,224 92
Interest on funded and other debts, ...	–	–	1,482,295 64	52,970 06
Taxes, ...	2,183 00	944,214 21	1,633,269 90	10,713 46
Rentals paid, ...	–	2,410,623 11	5,083,277 96	–
Other charges upon income, ...	–	–	151,285 00	–
Dividends paid, ...	15,804 00	–	1,778,999 50	17,000 00
GROSS EXPENDITURES, ...	26,709 52	10,494,313 39	35,401,035 63	605,908 44
CONDENSED EXHIBIT FOR THE YEAR.				
Net income from operation, ...	$1,971 88	$3,115,016 42	$9,622,700 56	$64,518 33
Income from other sources, ...	410 08	–	576,884 17	16,613 81
Total income above operating expenses, . . .	2,381 96	3,115,016 42	10,199,584 73	81,132 14
Interest, taxes, rentals, and other charges, . . .	2,183 00	3,354,837 32	8,350,128 50	63,683 52
Net divisible income, ...	198 96	239,820 90*d*	1,849,456 23	17,448 62
Amount of dividends declared, ...	15,804 00	–	1,778,999 50	17,000 00
Percentage of dividends declared, ...	12.0	–	–[6]	2.0
SURPLUS FOR THE YEAR, ...	15,605 04*d*	239,820 90*d*	70,456 73	448 62

* Operated by electricity. ‡ A narrow-gauge railroad. *d* Deficit.
† Operations of the New York Central & Hudson River, lessee. For financial statement of the Boston & Albany R.R. Co. see column 18.
[1] Equipment leased.
[2] Including amounts which will be due leased roads on termination of leases, $1,823,079.10.
[3] Includes $169,835.70 from electric street railways.
[4] Includes $170,334.44 from electric street railways.
[5] Includes $179,362.36 for operating electric street railways.
[6] Seven per cent on common and six per cent on preferred capital stock.

Tabulated Statements from Returns of Railroad Corporations — Continued.

OPERATING RAILROADS.	6. — Attleborough Branch — Con.	7. — Boston & Albany — Con.	8. — Boston & Maine — Con.	9. — Boston, Revere Beach & Lynn — Con.
Surplus.				
Surplus June 30, 1903,	$8,097 49	–	$1,565,165 45	$58,983 77
for the year,	15,605 04*d*	–	70,456 73	448 62
Additions during the year,	–	–	–	–
Deductions during the year,	250 00	–	97,547 23	–
Total Surplus June 30, 1904,	7,757 55*d*	–	3,810,293 85[3]	59,432 39
Volume of Traffic, etc.				
Passengers carried,	154,833	[illegible]	40,257,301[4]	9,743,855
Average length of journey,	–	23.930 miles.	18.090 miles.[5]	5.866 miles.
Total passenger mileage,	–	247,709,954	681,938,257[5]	57,158,595
Average fare per mile for local tickets,	–	1.537 cents.	1.763 cents.[5]	1.030 cents.
for mileage tickets,	–	2.000 "	–[6]	–
for time and commutation tickets,	–	.888 "	–[7]	–
for interline tickets,	–	2.017 "	.771 cents.	–
Passengers carried to Boston,	–	[illegible]	9,922,117	4,009,940
from Boston,	–	3,648,589	10,245,650	4,009,940
Tons of freight hauled,	–	[illegible]	19,395,452	–
average length of haul,	–	106.860 miles.	89.110 miles.	–
Total freight mileage,	–	502,207,880	1,728,422,684	–
Average rate per ton mile, local freight,	–	2.362 cents.	2.124 cents.	–
interline freight,	–	.763 "	.771 "	–
Miles run by passenger trains,	45,389	3,532,848	11,188,201[5]	692,849
by freight trains,	1,281	[illegible]	8,337,524	–
by mixed trains,	–	27,158	179,142	–
Total mileage of trains earning revenue,	46,670	[illegible]	19,704,867[5]	692,849

Miles run by switching trains,	–	1,512,294	7,444,385	4,611
by construction and other trains,	–	96,337	1,627,485	–
Total train mileage,	46,670	7,519,758	28,776,737[5]	697,460
EQUIPMENT.				
Number of locomotives,	–[1]	279	1,0 1	15
of passenger and combination cars,	–	302	1,228	79
of dining, parlor and sleeping cars,	–	3[2]	9	–
of baggage, express and mail cars,	–	80	302	–
of other passenger service cars,	–	12	66	–
of freight cars (basis 8 wheels),	–	3,601	16,913	–
of officers' and pay cars,	–	5	7	–
of gravel and other cars,	–	461	733	18
MISCELLANEOUS.				
Whole number of stockholders,	6	–	7,543[8]	246
number in Massachusetts,	1	–	4,855[9]	221
Amount of stock held in Massachusetts,	$100 00	–	$16,235,500 00[10]	$824,700 00
Total miles of road operated,	3.570	392.490	2,290.300[11]	13.200
operated in Massachusetts,	3.570	336.600	789.500	13.200
Highway grade crossings* in Massachusetts,	14	203	768	11
Average number of employees,	12	5,439	22,999	413

1 Equipment leased.
2 Not including 19.39% of 4 buffet cars in "Boston & Chicago" line.
3 Including $2,272,218.90 for "premium on common stock sold."
4 On steam roads, 37,689,433; on electric street railways, 2,567,868.
5 Does not include electric street railways.
6 500 miles, 2¼ cents; 1,000 miles, 2 cents.
7 Within suburban circuit, 1 to 2 cents; outside suburban circuit, 2 to 2¼ cents.
8 Common, 6,818; preferred, 725.
9 Common, 4,283; preferred, 572.
10 Common, $13,685,700; preferred, $2,549,800.
11 Includes 46.220 miles of electric street railway.
* Including those on leased lines.

d Deficit.

Tabulated Statements from Returns of Railroad Corporations — Continued.

OPERATING RAILROADS.	10. — CAPE ANN GRANITE.	11. — CENTRAL VERMONT.*	12. — GRAFTON & UPTON.	13. — HOOSAC TUNNEL & WILMINGTON.†
ASSETS.				
Construction,	$22,381 63	–	$523,917 68	$436,566 29
Equipment,	10,500 00	–	68,082 32	77,853 74
Lands,	–	–	–	–
Stocks and bonds of other companies,	–	–	–	–
Other permanent property,	–	–	–	–
Total permanent investments,	32,881 63	–	592,000 00	514,420 03
Cash and current assets,	–	–	6,920 15	23,441 19
Miscellaneous assets,	–	–	–	9,886 93
GROSS ASSETS,	32,881 63	–	598,920 15	547,748 15
LIABILITIES.				
Capital stock, common,	$20,000 00	–	$250,000 00	$250,000 00
preferred,	–	–	–	–
Total capital stock,	20,000 00	–	250,000 00	250,000 00
Funded debt,	–	–	268,000 00	250,000 00
Real estate mortgages,	–	–	–	–
Current liabilities,	13,174 99	–	74,000 00	42,356 74
Accrued liabilities,	–	–	–	4,166 67
Total indebtedness,	13,174 99	–	592,000 00	296,523 41
Sinking and other special funds,	–	–	–	–
GROSS LIABILITIES,	33,174 99	–	592,000 00	546,523 41
INCOME.				
Revenue from passengers,	–	$196,013 16	$28,081 61	$14,807 01
from mails,	–	17,929 32	1,133 51	1,115 26
from express,	–	19,419 91	3,604 80	1,886 92

from extra baggage and storage,	–	2,239 19	–	–
from other passenger service,	–	–	–	–
Total passenger revenue,	–	235,601 58	32,819 92	17,809 19
Revenue from freight,	$4,788 21	774,929 81	42,217 44	49,612 71
from other freight service,	–	–	–	–
Total freight revenue,	4,788 21	774,929 81	42,217 44	49,612 71
Total passenger and freight revenue,	4,788 21	1,010,531 39	75,037 36	67,421 90
Other earnings from operation,	–	–	–	–
Gross earnings from operation,	4,788 21	1,010,531 39	75,037 36	67,421 90
Income from other sources,	–	25,096 71	53 96	756 72
GROSS INCOME,	4,788 21	1,035,628 10	75,091 32	68,178 62
EXPENDITURES.				
Operating expenses,	$4,714 38	$863,078 73	$60,891 30	$50,870 48
Interest on funded and other debts,	–	–	14,148 56	13,501 91
Taxes,	37 35	47,778 97	459 76	1,585 80
Rentals paid,	–	203,952 50	–	–
Other charges upon income,	–	–	–	–
Dividends paid,	–	–	–	5,000 00
GROSS EXPENDITURES,	4,751 73	1,114,810 20	75,499 62	70,958 19
CONDENSED EXHIBIT FOR THE YEAR.				
Net income from operation,	$73 83	$147,452 66	$14,146 06	$16,551 42
Income from other sources,	–	25,096 71	53 96	756 72
Total income above operating expenses,	73 83	172,549 37	14,200 02	17,308 14
Interest, taxes, rentals, and other charges,	37 35	251,731 47	14,608 32	15,087 71
Net divisible income,	36 48	79,182 10*d*	408 30*d*	2,220 43
Amount of dividends declared,	–	–	–	5,000 00
Percentage of dividends declared,	–	–	–	2.0
SURPLUS FOR THE YEAR,	36 48	79,182 10*d*	408 30*d*	2,779 57*d*

* Operating the New London Northern under lease. † A narrow-gauge railroad. *d* Deficit.

Tabulated Statements from Returns of Railroad Corporations — Continued.

OPERATING RAILROADS.	10. — CAPE ANN GRANITE — Con.	11. — CENTRAL VERMONT — Con.	12. — GRAFTON & UPTON — Con.	13. — HOOSAC TUNNEL & WILMINGTON — Con.
SURPLUS.				
Surplus June 30, 1903,	$329 84*d*	–	$7,328 45	$8,040 97
for the year,	36 48	–	408 30*d*	2,779 57*d*
Additions during the year,	–	–	5,000 00	–
Deductions during the year,	–	–	5,000 00	4,036 66
TOTAL SURPLUS JUNE 30, 1904,	293 36*d*	–	6,920 15	1,224 74
VOLUME OF TRAFFIC, ETC.				
Passengers carried,	–	495,984	305,193	32,524
average length of journey,	–	16.280 miles.	8.000 miles.	11.790 miles.
Total passenger mileage,	–	8,076,799	2,441,544	383,436
Average fare per mile for local tickets,	–	2.920 cents.	0.900 cent.	4.000 cents.
for mileage tickets,	–	2.000 "	–	3.000 "
for time and commutation tickets,	–	1.200 "	–	–
for interline tickets,	–	2.070 "	–	2.200 cents.
Passengers carried to Boston,	–	–	–	–
from Boston,	–	–	–	–
Tons of freight hauled,	22,801	1,627,018	80,809	50,215
average length of haul,	1.436 miles.	31.390 miles.	9.000 miles.	15.670 miles.
Total freight mileage,	32,742	51,066,363	727,281	786,663
Average rate per ton mile, local freight,	–	–	3.640 cents.	6.307 cents.
interline freight,	–	–	2.910 "	–

Miles run by passenger trains,	–	306,890	210,719	31,560
by freight trains,	1,782	414,982	17,640	7,820
by mixed trains,	–	–	–	6,846
Total mileage of trains earning revenue,	1,782	721,872	228,359	46,226
Miles run by switching trains,	–	196,591	10,908	–
by construction and other trains,	–	–	275	679
Total train mileage,	1,782	918,463	239,542	46,905
EQUIPMENT.				
Number of locomotives,	1	14	4	6
of passenger and combination cars,	–	13	–[1]	4
of dining, parlor and sleeping cars,	–	–	–	–
of baggage, express and mail cars,	–	2	–	–
of other passenger service cars,	–	6	–	2
of freight cars (basis 8 wheels),	15	162	–	115
of officers' and pay cars,	–	–	–	–
of gravel and other cars,	–	42	–	6
MISCELLANEOUS.				
Whole number of stockholders,	6	–	17	44
number in Massachusetts,	6	–	15	16
Amount of stock held in Massachusetts,	$20,000 00	–	$239,200 00	$168,600 00
Total miles of road operated,	1.436	121.000	19.120	25.000
operated in Massachusetts,	1.436	54.900	19.120	8.220
Highway grade crossings * in Massachusetts,	2	44	29	–
Average number of employees,	4	768	30	58

* Including those on leased lines. *d* Deficit.

[1] Passenger service performed with electric cars furnished by the Milford & Uxbridge Street Railway Company.

Tabulated Statements from Returns of Railroad Corporations — Continued.

OPERATING RAILROADS.	14. — NANTUCKET CENTRAL.*	15. — NEW YORK, NEW HAVEN & HARTFORD.	16. — UNION FREIGHT.
ASSETS.			
Construction,	$35,000 00 (Construction and Equipment)	$45,982,160 71	$401,069 67
Equipment,		15,380,976 22	12,000 00
Lands,	–	–	–
Stocks and bonds of other companies,	–	41,937,085 93	13,000 00
Other permanent property,	–	–	–
Total permanent investments,	35,000 00	103,300,222 86	426,069 67
Cash and current assets,	–	13,985,879 67	25,758 80
Miscellaneous assets,	–	19,150,791 30	1,402 85
GROSS ASSETS,	35,000 00	136,436,893 83	453,231 32
LIABILITIES.			
Capital stock, common,	$18,000 00	$80,000,000 00	$300,000 00
preferred,	–	–	–
Total capital stock,	18,000 00	80,000,000 00	300,000 00
Funded debt,	17,000 00	34,491,000 00	–
Real estate mortgages,	–	–	88,500 00
Current liabilities,	2,620 00	6,426,795 16	5,684 64
Accrued liabilities,	–	598,062 00	–
Total liabilities,	19,620 00	41,515,857 16	94,184 64
Sinking and other special funds,	–	272,000 00	7,862 50
GROSS LIABILITIES,	37,620 00	121,787,857 16	402,047 14
INCOME.			
Revenue from passengers,	$3,880 30	$19,597,010 00	–
from mails,	99 23	665,182 66	–
from express,	554 46	1,549,731 25	–

from extra baggage and storage,	232 67	188,498 24	–
from other passenger service,	–	1,424,750 82	–
Total passenger revenue,	4,766 66	23,425,172 97	–
Revenue from freight,	–	23,637,823 21	$85,306 94
from other freight service,	–	775,717 77	–
Total freight revenue,	–	24,413,540 98	85,306 94
Total passenger and freight revenue,	4,766 66	47,838,713 95	85,306 94
Other earnings from operation,	–	144,195 25	48 01
Gross earnings from operation,	4,766 66	48,282,909 20	[illegible]54 95
Income from other sources,	–	906,435 84	910 00
Gross Income,	4,766 66	49,189,345 04	[illegible]64 95
Expenditures.			
Operating expenses,	$4,725 89	$35,159,210 70	$56,461 98
Interest on funded and other debts,	1,020 00	1,059,661 35[1]	2,493 01
Taxes,	40 77	2,455,434 27	2,672 97
Rentals paid,	–	4,420,282 74	–
Other charges upon income,	–	–	5,000 00
Dividends paid,	–	6,006,448 00	21,000 00
Gross Expenditures,	5,786 66	49,101,037 06	87,627 96
Condensed Exhibit for the Year.			
Net income from operation,	$40 77	$13,123,698 50	$28,892 97
Income from other sources,	–	906,435 84	910 00
Total income above operating expenses,	40 77	14,030,134 34	29,802 97
Interest, taxes, rentals, and other charges,	1,060 77	7,935,378 36	10,165 98
Net divisible income,	1,020 00*d*	[illegible]4,755 98	19,636 99
Amount of dividends declared,	–	6,006,448 00	21,000 00
Percentage of dividends declared,	–	8.0	7.0
Surplus for the Year,	1,020 00*d*	88,307 98	1,363 01*d*

* A narrow-gauge railroad. [1] Includes $226,228.62 for interest on instalments on account of new capital stock. *d* Deficit.

Tabulated Statements from Returns of Railroad Corporations — Continued.

OPERATING RAILROADS.	14. — NANTUCKET CENTRAL — Con.	15. — NEW YORK, NEW HAVEN & HARTFORD — Con.	16. — UNION FREIGHT — Con.
SURPLUS.			
Surplus June 30, 1903,	$1,600 00*d*	$13,819,565 66	$50,409 69
for the year,	1,020 00*d*	88,307 98	1,363 01*d*
Additions during the year,	–	9,039,856 76	2,137 50
Deductions during the year,	–	8,298,693 73	–
TOTAL SURPLUS JUNE 30, 1904,	2,620 00*d*	14,649,036 67	51,184 18
VOLUME OF TRAFFIC, ETC.			
Passengers carried,	13,335	63,13[illegible]	–
average length of journey,	8.500 miles.	17.990 miles.	–
Total passenger mileage,	113,347	1,[illegible]5[illegible]8	–
Average fare per mile for local tickets,	3.423 cents.	[illegible] cts.	–
for mileage tickets,	–	2.000 "	–
for time and commutation tickets,	–	[illegible] "	–
for interline tickets,	–	1.994 "	–
Passengers carried to Boston,	–	10,482,[illegible]	–
from Boston,	–	10.466,087	–
Tons of freight hauled,	–	1[illegible]60,[illegible]5	291,269
average length of haul,	–	94.610 miles.	1.375 mls.
Total freight mileage,	–	1,661,382,186	400,494
Average rate per ton mile, local freight,	–	2.783 cents.	21.353 [illegible]
interline freight,	–	1.022 "	–

Miles run by passenger trains,	7,000	1 [illegible]5, [illegible]2	–
by freight trains,	–	[illegible]6, [illegible]1	25,331
by mixed trains,	–	[illegible]8, 68	–
Total mileage of trains running trains,	7,000	2 3[illegible]0,791	25,331
Miles run by switching trains,	–	[illegible]5, 10	–
by construction and other trains,	–	46, [illegible]9	–
Total train mileage,	7,000	3 [illegible]2, [illegible]0	25,331
EQUIPMENT.			
Number of locomotives,	1	1,055	4
of passenger and combination cars,	3	[illegible]8	–
of dining, parlor and sleeping cars,	–	[illegible]3	–
of baggage, express and mail cars,	1	[illegible]9	–
of other passenger service cars,	–	–	–
of freight cars (basis 8 wheels),	3	[illegible]8	–
of officers' and pay cars,	–	13	–
of gravel and other cars,	1	[illegible]9	–
MISCELLANEOUS.			
Whole number of stockholders,	5	11,622	3
number in Massachusetts,	5	[illegible]1	3
Amount of stock held in Massachusetts,	$ [illegible]0 00	$ [illegible]0 00	$300,000 00
Total miles of road operated,	8.500	2,057.960	2.431
operated in Massachusetts,	8.500	893.050	2.431
Highway grade crossings * in Massachusetts,	5	[illegible]6	–
Average number of employees,	16	[illegible]	42

* Including those on leased lines.

d Deficit.

Tabulated Statements from Returns of Railroad Corporations — Continued.

LEASED RAILROADS.*	17. — BERKSHIRE. 1	18. — BOSTON & ALBANY. 2	19. — BOSTON & LOWELL. 3	20. — BOSTON & PROVIDENCE. 1	21. — CHATHAM. 1
ASSETS.					
Construction,	$600,000 00	$28,015,484 61	$12,320,779 85	$5,046,088 30	$98,435 58
Equipment,	–	3,572,400 00	833,583 94	871,234 35	–
Other permanent property,	3,970 00	–	3,279,105 50	419,703 36	2,055 55
Cash and current assets,	11,640 42	8,256,398 48	700,169 13	164,051 31	2,210 42
Other assets and property,	–	1,000,000 00[4]	–	–	–
GROSS ASSETS,	615,610 42	40,844,283 09	17,133,638 42	6,501,077 32	102,701 55
LIABILITIES.					
Capital stock,	$600,000 00	$25,000,000 00	$6,599,400 00	$4,000,000 00	$68,200 00
Funded debt,	–	8,485,000 00	8,528,000 00	2,170,000 00	17,000 00
Current and accrued liabilities,	91 50	114,694 08	361,026 85	247,792 50	170 00
Sinking and other special funds,	–	5,700,721 31	209,147 66	–	–
GROSS LIABILITIES,	600,091 50	39,300,415 39	15,697,574 51	6,417,792 50	85,370 00
In[illegible]e, EXPENDITURES, ETC.					
Total i[illegible]e [illegible] all [illegible]s,	$36,646 00	$2, [illegible]6,844 03	$877,656 68	$495,933 86	$4,320 43
Total [illegible]s,	413 75	9, [illegible]8 68	7,000 00	6,561 62	119 48
[illegible]t on f[illegible]d and [illegible]r [illegible],	–	[illegible]5, [illegible]10 00	342,704 68	86,800 00	1,071 00
[illegible]s, [illegible], [illegible],	–	78, [illegible]00 00	–	–	263 91
N[illegible]t divisible [illegible]e,	36,232 25	2,193,755 35	527,952 00	402,572 24	2,866 04
[illegible]t of [illegible]s d[illegible]cl[illegible],	36,000 00	2,187, [illegible]00 00	527,952 00	400,000 00	–
Percentage of [illegible]s [illegible]d,	6.0	8.75	8.0	10.0	–
[illegible]r the [illegible]r,	232 25	6,255 [illegible][5]	–	2,572 24	2,866 04
[illegible]l [illegible]s, [illegible]e [illegible], 1904,	15,518 92	1,543,867 70	1,436,063 91	83,284 82	17,331 55[6]

* Leased to and operated by [1] New York, New Haven & Hartford, [2] New York Central & Hudson River, [3] Boston & Maine.
[4] Improvements at East Boston, $700,000; Cunard dock and wharf property, $300,000. [5] Charged off for future expenditures. [6] Crediting $10.

Tabulated Statements from Returns of Railroad Corporations — Continued.

LEASED RAILROADS.*	22. — CHESTER & BECKET. 1	23. — CONNECTICUT RIVER. 2	24. — DANVERS.†	25. — FITCHBURG. 2	26. — HOLYOKE & WESTFIELD. 3
ASSETS.					
Construction,	$136,893 98	$3,597,366 50	$239,678 15	$40,131,779 09	$460,000 00
Equipment,	–	455,977 66	–	3,828,354 47	–
Other permanent property,	–	642,457 50	–	3,022,040 36	–
Cash and current assets,	105 11	187,790 20	–	392,881 94	28,916 68
Other assets and property,	–	–	–	1,174,968 45	–
GROSS ASSETS,	136,999 09	4,883,591 86	239,678 15	48,550,024 31	488,916 68
LIABILITIES.					
Capital stock,	$50,000 00	$2,630,000 00	$67,500 00	$24,360,000 00[4]	$260,000 00
Funded debt,	50,000 00	2,263,150 00	125,000 00	19,010,000 00	200,000 00
Current and accrued liabilities,	62,356 30	183,767 89	25,000 00	4,448,868 82	–
Sinking and other special funds,	–	558 81	–	–	–
GROSS LIABILITIES,	162,356 30	5,077,476 70	217,500 00	47,818,868 82	460,000 00
[illegible]E, EXPENDITURES, ETC.					
T[illegible]al [illegible]ne [illegible]m all [illegible],	$662 67	$349,065 00	–	$1,878,070 61	$41,361 94
T[illegible]al [illegible]s,	8 00	2,000 00	–	8,744 11	32 55
I[illegible]t on [illegible]d [illegible]nd other debts,	4,312 58	84,065 00	–	977,496 54	8,000 00
Rentals, [illegible], [illegible]c.,	–	–	–	23,829 96	2,906 85
Net divisible [illegible]e,	3,657 91*d*	263,000 00	–	868,000 00	29,932 54
A[illegible]t of [illegible]s [illegible]d,	–	263,000 00	–	868,000 00	31,200 00
Percentage of [illegible]s [illegible],	–	10.0	–	5.0	12.0
[illegible]s for the [illegible]r,	3,657 91*d*	–	–	–	1,267 46*d*
[illegible]l [illegible]s, [illegible] [illegible], 1904,	25,357 21*d*	193,884 84*d*	$22,178 15	731,155 49[5]	28,916 68

* Leased to and operated by [1] Boston & Albany (New York Central & Hudson River, lessee), [2] Boston & Maine, [3] New York, New Haven & Hartford.
† This road is virtually owned by the Boston & Maine, and its earnings and expenses are included in the return of that company.
[4] Common, $7,000,000; preferred, $17,360,000. [5] Debiting $11,307.98. *d* Deficit.

Tabulated Statements from Returns of Railroad Corporations — Continued.

LEASED RAILROADS.*	27. — HORN POND BRANCH. 1.	28. — LOWELL & ANDOVER. 1	29. — MILFORD, FRANKLIN & PROVIDENCE. 2	30. — MILFORD & WOONSOCKET. 2	31. — NASHUA, ACTON & BOSTON. 1
ASSETS.					
Construction,	$15,238 46	$767,050 24	$101,308 23	$173,381 13	$1,057,031 20
Cash and current assets,	–	1,892 16	2,350 78	76 99	6,257 41
GROSS ASSETS,	15,238 46	768,942 40	103,659 01	173,458 12	1,063,288 61
LIABILITIES.					
Capital stock,	$2,000 00	$625,000 00	$100,000 00	$148,600 00	$500,000 00
Funded debt,	–	–	10,000 00	60,000 00	500,000 00
Current and accrued liabilities,	–	–	–	–	709,982 90
GROSS LIABILITIES,	2,000 00	625,000 00	110,000 00	208,600 00	1,709,982 90
INCOME, EXPENDITURES, ETC.					
Total income from all sources,	–[3]	$52,538 88	$2,300 00	$4,700 00	–
Total expenses,	–	192 50	–	179 25	–
Interest on funded and other debts,	–	–	600 00	3,000 00	–
Rentals, taxes, etc.,	–	16 34	2 50	–	–
Net divisible income,	–	52,330 04	1,697 50	1,520 75	–
Amount of dividends declared,	–	56,250 00	1,500 00	1,486 00	–
Percentage of dividends declared,	–	9.0	1.5	1.0	–
Surplus for the year,	–	3,919 96*d*	197 50	34 75	–
Total surplus, June 30, 1904,	$13,238 46	143,942 40	6,340 99*d*	35,141 88*d*	$646,694 29*d*

* Leased to and operated by [1] Boston & Maine, [2] New York, New Haven & Hartford.

[3] Used only for the transportation of ice; no income reported.

d Deficit.

Tabulated Statements from Returns of Railroad Corporations — Continued.

LEASED RAILROADS.*	32. — NASHUA & LOWELL. 1	33. — NEWBURYPORT.†	34. — NEW ENGLAND. 2	35. — NEW HAVEN & NORTHAMPTON. 2	36. — NEW LONDON NORTHERN 3
ASSETS.					
Construction,	$684,242 07	$597,386 32	$39,398,211 79[4]	$5,731,586 62	$3,064,629 47
Equipment,	218,242 95	–	2,416,608 87	850,430 62	248,420 44
Other permanent property,	–	–	–	33,081 50	155,000 00
Cash and current assets,	64,952 07	–	886,344 08	375,220 21	67,531 55
GROSS ASSETS,	967,437 09	597,386 32	42,701,164 74	6,990,318 95	3,535,581 46
LIABILITIES.					
Capital stock,	$800,000 00	$220,340 02	$25,000,000 00[5]	$2,460,000 00	$1,500,000 00
Funded debt,	–	300,000 00	18,000,000 00[4]	2,600,000 00	1,500,000 00
Current and accrued liabilities,	1,210 50	–	52,715 73	–	13,277 14
Sinking and other special funds,	–	–	–	375,000 00	–
GROSS LIABILITIES,	801,210 50	520,340 02	43,052,715 73	5,435,000 00	3,013,277 14
INCOME, EXPENDITURES, ETC.					
Total income from all sources,	$75,319 10	–	$1,120,241 00	$299,205 95	$213,552 50
Total expenses,	941 90	–	241 00	15,152 50[6]	4,874 66
Interest on funded and other debts,	–	–	970,000 00	142,000 00	68,522 20
Rentals, taxes, etc.,	–	–	–	40,917 28[7]	–
Net divisible income,	74,377 20	–	150,000 00	01,136 17	140,155 64
Amount of dividends declared,	72,000 00	–	150,000 00	98, 00 00	135,000 00
Percentage of dividends declared,	9.0	–	3.0	4.0	9.0
Surplus for the year,	2,377 20	–	–	2,736 17	5,155 64
Total surplus, June 30, 1904,	166,226 59	$77,046 30	351,550 99*d*	1,555,318 95	522,304 32[8]

* Leased to and operated by [1] Boston & Maine, [2] New York, New Haven & Hartford, [3] Central Vermont. *d* Deficit.
† This road is virtually owned by the Boston & Maine, and its earnings and expenses are included in the return of that company.
[4] Including $11,500,000, the amount of underlying first mortgage bonds issued by New York & New England, subject to which the New England holds its title.
[5] Common, $20,000,000; preferred, $5,000,000.
[6] Including $15,000 for payment to sinking fund.
[7] Rental paid Holyoke & Westfield Railroad.
[8] Crediting $963.70.

Tabulated Statements from Returns of Railroad Corporations — Continued.

LEASED RAILROADS.*	37. — NORTH BROOKFIELD. 1	38. — NORWICH & WORCESTER. 2	39. — OLD COLONY. 2	40. — PITTSFIELD & NORTH ADAMS. 1	41. — PLYMOUTH & MIDDLEBOROUGH. 2
ASSETS.					
Construction,	$100,000 00	$3,983,816 51	$29,956,723 97	$438,752 57	$305,000 00
Equipment,	–	179,750 67	3,161,518 83	11,247 43	–
Other permanent property,	–	503,107 08	1,611,166 72	–	–
Cash and current assets,	555 11	401,280 61	519,274 60	–	–
Other assets and property,	–	450,869 65	3,268,072 18	–	–
GROSS ASSETS,	100,555 11	5,518,824 52	38,516,756 30	450,000 00	305,000 00
LIABILITIES.					
Capital stock,	$100,000 00	$3,006,600 00	$17,880,125 00[3]	$450,000 00	$80,000 00
Funded debt,	–	1,200,000 00	15,519,200 00	–	225,000 00
Current and accrued liabilities,	–	79,848 00	1,253,485 07	–	–
GROSS LIABILITIES,	100,000 00	4,286,448 00	34,652,810 07	450,000 00	305,000 00
INCOME, EXPENDITURES, ETC.					
Total income from all sources,	$3,013 10	$290,806 05	$1,890,621 47	$22,500 00	–
Total expenses,	–	2,580 40	6,860 98	–	–
Interest on funded and other debts,	–	48,000 00	677,387 49	–	–
Rentals, taxes, etc.,	504 48	–	–	–	–
Net divisible income,	2,508 62	240,225 65	1,206,373 00	22,500 00	–
Amount of dividends declared,	2,500 00	240,000 00	1,206,373 00	22,500 00	–
Percentage of dividends declared,	2.5	8.0	7.0	5.0	–
Surplus for the year,	8 62	225 65	–	–	–
Total surplus, June 30, 1904,	555 11	1,232,376 52	3,863,946 23[4]	–	–

* Leased to and operated by [1] Boston & Albany (New York Central & Hudson River, lessee), [2] New York, New Haven & Hartford.

[3] Including "common stock liability" of $8,725.

[4] Crediting $120.47 and including $3,096,619.04 for premium on stock and bonds sold.

Tabulated Statements from Returns of Railroad Corporations — Continued.

LEASED RAILROADS.*	42. — PROVIDENCE & SPRINGFIELD. 1	43. — PROVIDENCE, WEBSTER & SPRINGFIELD. 2	44. — PROVIDENCE & WORCESTER. 1	45. — RHODE ISLAND & MASSACHUSETTS.†	46. — STOCKBRIDGE & PITTSFIELD. 1
ASSETS.					
Construction,	$1,267,450 00	$243,361 12	$4,276,250 00	$112,321 13	$448,700 00
Equipment,	–	–	828,887 40	–	–
Other permanent property,	–	–	–	–	2,550 00
Cash and current assets,	28 14	1,770 24	122,291 35	2,500 00	8,398 25
GROSS ASSETS,	1,267,478 14	245,131 36	5,227,428 75	114,821 13	459,648 25
LIABILITIES.					
Capital stock,	$517,450 00	$160,000 00	$3,500,000 00	$100,000 00	$448,700 00
Funded debt,	750,000 00	–	1,500,000 00	–	–
Current and accrued liabilities,	–	62,986 99	–	–	516 00
GROSS LIABILITIES,	1,267,450 00	222,986 99	5,000,000 00	100,000 00	449,216 00
INCOME, EXPENDITURES, ETC.					
Total income from all sources,	$58,203 23	$6,837 55	$417,583 84	–	$27,376 00
Total expenses,	–	3 45	6,071 79	–	352 60
Interest on funded and other debt,	37,500 00	3,102 89	60,000 00	–	–
[illegible], taxes, etc.,	–	452 70	–	–	–
Net divisible income,	20,703 23	3,278 51	351,512 05	–	27,023 40
Amount of dividends declared,	20,698 00	–	350,000 00	–	26,922 00
Percentage of dividends declared,	4.0	–	10.0	–	6.0
Surplus for the year,	5 23	3,278 51	1,512 05	–	101 40
Total surplus, June 30, 1904,	28 14[3]	22,144 37	227,428 75	$14,821 13	10,432 25

* Leased to and operated by [1] New York, New Haven & Hartford, [2] Boston & Albany (New York Central & Hudson River, lessee).

† This road is virtually owned by the New York, New Haven & Hartford Railroad Company, and its earnings and expenses are included in the return of that company.

[3] Debiting $250, reconveyance of land.

Tabulated Statements from Returns of Railroad Corporations — Concluded.

LEASED RAILROADS.*	47. — STONY BROOK. 1	48. — VERMONT & MASSACHUSETTS. 1	49. — WARE RIVER. 2	50. — WEST STOCKBRIDGE.†	51. — WORCESTER, NASHUA & ROCHESTER. 1
ASSETS.					
Construction,	$276,601 19	$6,005,618 42	$1,115,163 82	$39,600 00	$4,138,584 99
Equipment,	21,492 38	261,233 64	–	–	415,336 03
Other permanent property,	–	2,107 65	–	–	–
Cash and current assets,	648 81	12,687 50	–	–	74,257 17
GROSS ASSETS,	298,742 38	6,281,647 21	1,115,163 82	39,600 00	4,628,178 19
LIABILITIES.					
Capital stock,	$300,000 00	$3,193,000 00	$750,000 00	$39,600 00	$3,099,800 00
Funded debt,	–	772,000 00	–	–	1,776,000 00
Current and accrued liabilities,	–	12,687 50	365,163 82	–	31,860 00
GROSS LIABILITIES,	300,000 00	3,977,687 50	1,115,163 82	39,600 00	4,907,660 00
INCOME, EXPENDITURES, ETC.					
Total income from all sources,	$21,500 00	$194,580 00	$52,500 00	–	$250,150 32
Total expenses,	379 91	3,000 00	–	–	2,267 10
Interest on funded and other debts,	–	–	–	–	71,040 00
Rentals, taxes, etc.,	–	–	–	–	–
Net divisible income,	21,120 09	191,580 00	52,500 00	–	176,843 22
Amount of dividends declared,	24,000 00	191,580 00	52,500 00	–	176,203 00
Percentage of dividends declared,	8.0	6.0	7.0	–	5.75[6]
Surplus for the year,	2,879 91*d*	–	–	–	640 22
Total surplus, June 30, 1904,	1,257 62*d*[3]	2,303,959 71[4]	–	–[5]	279,481 81*d*

* Leased to and operated by [1] Boston & Maine, [2] Boston & Albany (New York Central & Hudson River, lessee).

† This road is virtually owned by the New York, New Haven & Hartford Railroad Company, and its earnings and expenses are included in the return of that company.

[3] Crediting $567.93.

[4] Crediting $36,005.86 and debiting $100.79.

[5] Debited with $450 for accounts receivable, thus cancelling surplus.

[6] On 30,644 shares capital stock.

d Deficit.

COMPARATIVE AND SUMMARY STATEMENTS

COMPILED FROM

Returns of Railroad Corporations.

COMPARISON OF RETURNS FOR THE YEARS 1903 AND 1904.

MILEAGE, ASSETS, ETC.	1903.	1904.	Increase.	Decrease.
Description of Road Owned.	Miles.	Miles.	Miles.	Miles.
Length of road and branches,	3,793.860	3,791.320[1]	-	2.540
in Massachusetts,	2,110.960	2,108.420	-	2.540
Length of second track,*	1,516.677	1,518.687	2.010	-
in Massachusetts,	941.937	943.947	2.010	-
Length of side track,	2,290.797	2,323.367[2]	32.570	-
in Massachusetts,	1,416.687	1,437.937	21.250	-
Total length as single track,	7,601.334	7,633.374[3]	32.040	-
in Massachusetts,	4,469.584	4,490.304	20.720	-
Assets.				
Construction,	$293,236,332 43	$287,892,759 18	-	$5,343,573 25
Equipment,	32,957,121 82	41,205,887 11	$8,248,765 29	-
Lands,	1,497,218 52	1,517,411 91	20,193 39	-
Stocks in other companies,	34,815,526 59	46,797,635 82	11,982,109 23	
Bonds of other companies,	7,329,726 78	13,017,087 48	5,687,360 70	
Other permanent property,	2,445,520 16	2,582,634 36	137,114 20	-
Total permanent investments,	372,281,446 80	393,013,415 86	20,731,969 56	-
Cash on hand,	10,699,956 09	7,657,771 42	-	3,042,184 67
Bills receivable,	1,726,785 90	4,502,616 23	2,775,830 33	-
Other current assets,	28,453,325 43	24,031,055 28	-	4,422,270 15
Total cash and current assets,	40,880,067 42	36,191,442 93	-	4,688,624 49
Materials and supplies,	6,790,444 79	7,043,221 16	252,776 37	-
All other assets,	12,828,890 76	20,748,036 05	7,919,145 29	-
Total miscellaneous assets,	19,619,335 55	27,791,257 21	8,171,921 66	-
Gross Assets,	$432,780,849 27	$456,996,116 00	$24,215,266 73	-
Profit and loss balance (deficit),	1,537,596 41	1,550,380 54	12,784 13	-
Total as per balance sheet,	$434,318,445 68	$458,546,496 54	$24,228,050 86	-
Liabilities.				
Capital stock, common,	$207,324,665 72	$208,914,085 72	$1,589,420 00	-
preferred,	28,509,800 00	28,509,800 00	-	
Total capital stock,	235,834,465 72	237,423,885 72	1,589,420 00	-
Funded debt,	133,435,355 01	152,841,358 41	19,406,003 40	-
Real estate mortgages,	858,300 00	683,300 00	-	$175,000 00
Current liabilities,	20,218,456 74	21,513,406 41	1,294,949 67	-
Accrued liabilities,	3,930,561 69	4,131,914 74	201,353 05	-
Total indebtedness,†	158,442,673 44	179,169,979 56	20,727,306 12	-
Gross Liabilities,	$394,277,139 16	$416,593,865 28	$22,316,726 12	-
Profit and loss balance (surplus),	40,041,306 52	41,952,631 26	1,911,324 74	-
Total as per balance sheet,	$434,318,445 68	$458,546,496 54	$24,228,050 86	-
Income.				
From passengers,	$36,513,615 08	$36,944,760 37[4]	$431,145 29	-
mails,	1,496,165 05	1,512,386 01	16,220 96	-
express,	2,835,642 24	2,948,115 18	112,472 94	-
extra baggage and storage,	387,103 66	382,625 03	-	$4,478 63
other passenger service,	1,291,556 12	1,460,446 58	168,890 46	-
Total passenger revenue,	42,524,082 15	43,248,333 17[5]	724,251 02	-
From freight,	48,490,674 64	49,917,830 83	1,427,156 19	-
other freight service,	1,227,079 93	1,082,978 85	-	144,101 08
Total freight revenue,	49,717,754 57	51,000,809 68	1,283,055 11	-
Other earnings from operation,	1,084,094 78	1,031,205 15	-	52,889 63
Total earnings from operation,	93,325,931 50	95,280,348 00[5]	1,954,416 50	-
Rentals from lease of road,	10,673,454 99	11,056,595 20	383,140 21	-
Income from other sources,	1,641,616 02	1,754,656 30	113,040 28	-
Gross Income,	$105,641,002 51	$108,091,599 50	$2,450,596 99	-

* Including third and fourth main track. † Exclusive of sinking and other special funds.
[1] Includes 18.340 miles electric street railway owned by the Boston & Maine.
[2] Includes .950 of a mile electric street railway owned by the Boston & Maine.
[3] Includes electric street railway owned by the Boston & Maine.
[4] Includes $169,835.70 earnings from passengers on electric street railways operated by the Boston & Maine.
[5] Includes $170,334.44 earnings on electric street railways operated by the Boston & Maine.

Comparison of Returns, etc., — Concluded.

EXPENDITURES, ETC.	1903.	1904.	Increase.	Decrease.
Expenditures.				
Operating expenses,	$67,774,863 74	$69,145,284 60[1]	$1,370,420 86	-
Interest on debt and loans,	6,533,984 59	6,526,802 91	-	$7,181 68
Taxes,	5,017,971 42	5,102,355 01	84,383 59	-
Rentals paid,	12,287,658 05	12,237,053 59	-	50,604 46
Other charges on income,	247,556 46	258,743 42	11,186 96	-
Total charges on income,	24,087,170 52	24,124,954 93	37,784 41	-
Dividends paid,	13,495,188 50	14,985,815 50	1,490,627 00	-
Gross Expenditures,	$105,357,222 76	$108,256,055 03	$2,898,832 27	-
Condensed Exhibit for the Year.				
Gross earnings from operation,	$93,325,931 50	$95,280,348 00[2]	$1,954,416 50	-
Operating expenses,	67,774,863 74	69,145,284 60[2]	1,370,420 86	-
Net earnings from operation,	25,551,067 76	26,135,063 40	583,995 64	
Income from all other sources,	12,315,071 01	12,811,251 50	496,180 49	-
Total income above operating expenses,	37,866,138 77	38,946,314 90	1,080,176 13	
Interest, taxes and other charges,	24,087,170 52	24,124,954 93	37,784 41	
Net divisible income,	13,778,968 25	14,821,359 97	1,042,391 72	-
Amount of dividends declared,	13,495,188 50	14,985,815 50	1,490,627 00	-
Surplus for the year,	$283,779 75	$164,455 53*d*	-	$448,235 28
Percentage of dividend earned,	5.97*	6.24	0.27	-
of dividend declared,	5.93*	6.31	0.38	-
Volume of Traffic.				
Miles run by passenger trains,	30,817,100	31,791,218	974,118	-
by freight trains,	18,198,160	18,993,842	795,682	-
by mixed trains,	433,236	341,814	-	91,422
by other trains,	18,031,805	17,874,984	-	156,821
Total train mileage,	67,480,301	69,001,858	1,521,557	-
Total passengers carried,	123,162,793	124,483,665[3]	1,320,872	-
passenger mileage,	2,112,874,995	2,133,524,260[4]	20,649,265	-
Total tons of freight hauled,	43,992,978	43,727,514	-	265,464
freight mileage,	3,928,993,919	3,945,026,293	16,032,374	-
Equipment, etc.				
Locomotives,	2,277	2,390	113	
Passenger cars,	3,338	3,508	170	-
Baggage and mail cars,	650	654	4	-
Freight cars (basis 8 wheels),	34,825	37,938	3,113	-
All other cars,	1,865	1,887	22	-
Stock held in Massachusetts,	$122,399,300 00	$128,102,900 00	$5,703,600 00	-
Total number of stockholders,	49,898	50,827	929	
in Massachusetts,	35,913	36,828	915	
Average number of employees,	58,888	60,156	1,268	
Total miles of road operated,	4,906.730	4,935.670[5]	28.940	
in Massachusetts,	2,121.790	2,131.190	9.400	
Total miles of track operated,	9,304.524	9,390.834[6]	86.310	-
in Massachusetts,	4,481.824	4,526.424	44.600	
Highway crossings at grade,†	1,927	1,922	-	5
protected,	1,103	1,103	-	-
unprotected,	824	819	-	5

* Not including instalments on common stock to be issued. † In Massachusetts. *d* Deficit.
[1] Includes $179,362.36 for electric street railways operated by the Boston & Maine.
[2] Includes earnings and expenses of electric street railways operated by the Boston & Maine.
[3] Includes 2,567,868 passengers carried on electric street railways operated by Boston & Maine.
[4] Does not include mileage of passengers carried on electric street railways operated by the Boston & Maine.
[5] Includes 46.220 miles electric street railway operated by the Boston & Maine.
[6] Includes 49.620 miles electric street railway operated by the Boston & Maine.

Summary of Returns for the Years 1898 to 1904, inclusive.

MILEAGE, ASSETS, LIABILITIES, ETC.	1898.	1899.	1900.	1901.	1902.	1903.	1904.
Railroad Mileage.							
Miles of main and branch line in Massachusetts,	2,107.630	2,108.510	2,108.900	2,107.510	2,106.450	2,110.960	2,108.420
of second track,*	923.167	926.627	937.407	935.197	939.237	941.937	943.947
of side track,	1,305.717	1,326.957	1,370.047	1,373.517	1,391.157	1,416.687	1,437.937
Total track in Massachusetts,	4,336.514	4,362.094	4,416.354	4,416.224	4,436.844	4,469.584	4,490.304
Assets.							
Cost of construction,	$284,317,836 34	$286,395,398 69	$290,000,635 68	$288,850,804 00	$289,699,626 69	$293,236,332 43	$287,892,759 18
of equipment,	28,867,842 63	28,662,842 63	28,952,561 26	29,024,463 27	29,057,279 12	32,957,121 82	41,205,887 11
of other permanent property,	37,824,088 51	43,126,668 59	42,055,897 73	45,177,895 27	44,789,943 19	46,087,992 05	63,914,769 57
Total permanent investments,	351,009,767 48	358,184,909 91	361,009,094 67	363,053,162 54	363,546,849 00	372,281,446 30	393,013,415 86
Cash and current assets,	19,915,838 04	23,543,288 48	25,218,566 43	37,413,016 83	35,908,659 11	40,880,067 42	36,191,442 93
Miscellaneous assets,	19,396,558 29	18,536,933 39	18,960,668 59	19,277,341 86	18,842,766 00	19,619,335 55	27,791,257 21
Gross Assets,	390,322,163 81	400,265,131 78	405,188,329 69	419,743,521 23	418,298,274 11	432,780,849 27	456,996,116 00
Liabilities.							
Capital stock,	$205,766,507 35	$213,255,282 35	$216,213,262 65	$210,305,885 72	$210,726,785 72	$235,834,465 72	$237,423,885 72
Funded debt,	140,554,406 91	138,001,533 61	136,024,533 61	148,479,014 96	149,777,541 66	133,435,355 01	152,841,358 41
Real estate mortgages,	1,261,300 00	858,300 00	858,300 00	858,300 00	858,300 00	858,300 00	683,300 00
Current and accrued liabilities,	20,097,311 95	23,248,576 97	23,912,793 91	25,774,086 24	21,744,041 12	24,149,018 43	25,645,321 15
Total indebtedness,	161,913,018 86	162,108,410 58	160,795,627 52	175,111,401 20	172,379,882 78	158,442,673 44	179,169,979 56
Gross Liabilities,†	367,679,526 21	375,363,692 93	377,008,890 17	385,417,286 92	383,106,668 50	394,277,139 16	416,593,865 28
Surplus,‡	22,642,637 60	24,901,438 85	28,179,439 52	34,326,234 31	35,191,605 61	38,503,710 11	41,952,631 26
Net debt,	$141,997,180 82	$138,565,122 10	$135,577,061 09	$137,698,384 37	$136,471,223 67	$117,562,606 02	$142,978,536 63
General Exhibit for the Year.							
Total earnings from operation,	$73,599,534 41	$75,430,061 42	$82,191,293 10	$82,385,586 45	$86,920,564 97	$93,325,931 50	$95,280,348 00[1]
Operating expenses,	50,890,883 11	51,490,350 93	5[illegible]0,642 04	57,293,590 83	61,355,821 10	67,774,863 74	69,145,284 60[1]
[illegible] earnings from operation,	22,708,651 30	23,939,710 49	25,290,651 06	2[illegible]5 62	25,564,743 87	25,551,067 76	26,135,063 40
[illegible]als from [illegible] lease of [illegible] road,	6,[illegible]56 07	6,902,718 14	6,895,520 93	10,557,324 47	10,674,846 80	10,673,454 99	11,056,595 20
[illegible] from all other [illegible] sources,	1,340,616 67	1,177,902 49	1,103,821 42	1,364,653 78	1,779,610 40	1,641,616 02	1,754.656 30
Total income [illegible] the operating expenses,	29,915,524 04	3[illegible]20,331 12	33,289,993 41	37,013,973 87	38,019,201 07	37,866,138 77	38,946,314 90
Interest on debt and [illegible],	6,398,333 62	6,321,272 91	6,196,653 06	6,410,410 63	6,654,454 24	6,533,984 59	6,526,802 91
Taxes,	4,014,266 51	4,389,403 07	5,005,730 17	4,884,370 18	5,056,901 77	5,017,971 42	5,102,355 01
Rentals paid,	7,523,913 93	8,366,943 68	8,270,958 18	11,967,615 91	12,265,186 84	12,287,658 05	12,237,053 59
Other charges upon [illegible],	155,183 06	144,081 34	150,932 08	221,950 25	224,317 12	247,556 46	258,743 42
Total charges [illegible] [illegible],	18,091,697 12	19,221,701 00	19,624,273 49	23,[illegible]846 97	24,200,859 97	24,087,170 52	24,124,954 93
Net divisible [illegible],	11,823,826 92	12,798,630 12	13,665,719 92	13,529,626 90	[illegible]1 10	13,778,968 25	14,821,359 97

Amount of dividends declared,	11,599,462 50	12,143,749 00	12,498,946 91	13,049,306 39	13,201,263 50	13,495,188 50	14,985,815 50
Gross income from all sources,	80,806,407 15	83,510,682 05	90,190,635 45	94,307,564 70	99,375,022 17	105,641,002 51	108,091,599 50
Gross expenditures,	80,582,042 73	82,855,800 93	89,023,862 44	93,827,244 19	98,757,944 57	105,357,222 76	108, [illegible] 03
Surplus for the year,	224,364 42	[illegible] 12	1,166,773 01	480,320 51	617,077 60	283,779 75	[illegible] 53*d*
Percentage of dividends earned,	5.75	6.00	6.32	6.40	6.56	5.97§	6.24
of dividends declared,	5.64	5.69	5.78	6.20	6.26	5.93§	6.31
Stock held in Massachusetts,	$122,411,900 00	$121,766,200 00	$124,170,600 00	$119,748,800 00	$119,816,300 00	$122,399,300 00	$128,102,900 00
Total number of stockholders,	48,513	48,834	49,672	48,431	48,544	49,898	50,827
in Massachusetts,	35,411	35,903	36,388	35,113	35,098	35,913	36,828
Volume of Traffic.							
Miles run by passenger trains,	27,046,501	27, [illegible]	28,121,038	28,415,913	29, [illegible]	30,817,100	31,791,218
by freight trains,	17,721,128	17, [illegible]	17,382,575	16,288,353	16, [illegible]	18,198,160	18,993,842
by mixed trains,	205,345	180,401	[illegible]	448,627	460,473	433,236	341,814
Total revenue-train mileage,	44,972,974	45,621,035	45, [illegible]	45,152,893	46,913,082	49,448,496	51,126,874
Miles run by other trains,	11,461,493	10,887,514	13,151,881	15, [illegible]	17,032,739	18,031,805	17,874,984
Total train mileage,	56,434,467	56, [illegible]	59,052,420	61,041,881	63,945,821	67,480,301	69,001,858[2]
Passengers carried,	101, [illegible]	102, [illegible]	108, [illegible]	108, [illegible]	115,645,897	123,162,793	[illegible][3]
Average length of journey (miles),	16.47	16.82	17.08	17.09	17.14	17.16	17.49[2]
Total passenger mileage,	1,678,640,940	1,716, [illegible]	1,858, [illegible]	1,859, [illegible]	1,982, [illegible]	2,112,874,995	2,133, [illegible][2]
Average fare per mile (cents),	1.78	1.77	1.75	1.75	1.73	1.73	1.72[2]
Passengers to and from Boston,	48, [illegible]	49,174,631	52,334,148	51, [illegible]	53,502,206	55, [illegible]	56,415,252
Tons of freight hauled,	35,338,724	36, [illegible]	40,316,711	39,463,814	41, [illegible]	43, [illegible]	43, [illegible]
Average length of haul (miles),	85.54	88.65	85.81	89.07	86.70	89.31	90.22
Total freight mileage,	3,022, [illegible]	3,211,643,434	3,459, [illegible]	3,515, [illegible]	3,592,963,862	3,928,998,919	3,945, [illegible]
Average rate per ton mile (cents),	1.22	1.18	1.22	1.20	1.24	1.23	1.27
Equipment.							
Number of employees,	51,602	51,881	53,045	53,564	56,388	58,888	60,156
of locomotives,	2,072	2,091	2,102	2,169	2,202	2,277	2,390
of passenger cars,	3,174	3,144	3,161	3,255	3,263	3,338	3,508
of baggage, express and mail cars,	577	582	610	566	627	650	654
of freight cars (basis 8 wheels),	35,491	33,935	34,292	33,801	33,452	34,825	37,938
of all other cars,	1,894	1,937	1,980	1,850	1,801	1,865	1,887

* Including third and fourth main track. † Exclusive of sinking and other special funds. ‡ Includes sinking and other special funds.

§ Not including instalments on common stock to be issued. *d* Deficit.

[1] Includes electric street railways operated by the Boston & Maine. [2] Does not include electric street railways operated by the Boston & Maine.

[3] Includes 2,567,868 passengers carried on electric street railways operated by the Boston & Maine.

TABULATED STATEMENTS

COMPILED FROM THE

Reports of Street Railway Companies

FOR THE

YEAR ENDING SEPTEMBER 30, 1904.

TABULATED STATEMENTS FROM REPORTS OF STREET RAILWAY COMPANIES.

	RAILWAY COMPANIES.	ASSETS SEPTEMBER 30, 1904.						
		1. — Construction.	2. — Equipment.	3. — Land and Buildings.	4. — Other Permanent Property.	5. — Cash and Current Assets.	6. — Miscellaneous Assets.	7. — Gross Assets.
1	{Amesbury & Hampton,	$156,815 73	$30,597 61	$53,060 12	-	$13,500 00	-	$253,973 46
	{Amesbury & Hampton (lessee),[1]	-	-	-	-	-	-	-
2	Amherst & Sunderland,	144,357 90	48,133 36	39,089 21	-	3,524 77	$3,462 83	238,568 07
3	Athol & Orange,	93,914 03	37,322 58	8,000 00	$17,000 00	1,087 70	750 00	158,074 31
4	Berkshire,	1,326,747 52	285,541 71	470,041 85	34,912 35	58,377 62	27,560 03	2,203,181 08
5	Blue Hill,	381,425 79	131,085 48	111,333 59	-	30,544 61	9,103 80	663,493 27
6	Boston & Chelsea,	121,000 00	-	-	-	-	-	121,000 00
7	Boston Elevated,	7,313,098 76	1,845,500 09	5,337,144 90	319,577 79	3,564,190 82	2,044,347 01	20,423,859 37
8	Boston & Northern,	12,370,760 73	4,726,762 63	3,768,836 14	183,573 52	621,362 15	428,219 80	22,099,514 97
9	Boston & Revere Electric,	73,815 23	9,919 79	4,901 80	-	-	-	88,636 82
10	Boston & Worcester,	2,294,898 62	496,985 25	683,727 73	-	179,780 06	49,594 07	3,704,985 73
11	{Bristol County,[2]	332,904 28	122,725 58	103,613 70	-	158,354 01	9,496 17	727,093 74
	{Bristol County (receivers),	-	-	-	-	6,223 75	21,117 49	27,341 24
12	Bristol & Norfolk,	150,307 51	16,588 85	5,100 00	-	1,255 86	-	173,252 22
13	Brockton & Plymouth,	379,112 15	102,289 68	225,667 35	26,000 00	36,204 72	9,662 39	778,936 29
14	Citizens' Electric,	322,711 40	96,853 47	95,685 62	-	25,055 78	13,918 77	554,225 04
15	Commonwealth Avenue,*[3]	200,996 68	233,443 39	105,280 50	-	5,724 26	-	545,444 83
16	Concord & Boston,[2]	87,625 06	-	306 00	-	39,333 73	-	127,264 79
17	Concord, Maynard & Hudson,	220,157 63	82,066 77	108,345 89	-	8,354 11	21,389 60	440,314 00
18	Conway Electric,	73,223 34	10,996 79	9,457 21	2,200 00	4,352 31	110 00	100,339 65
19	Cottage City & Edgartown Traction,	46,424 13	10,751 09	4,745 60	-	1,798 00	423 01	64,141 83
20	Dartmouth & Westport,	178,609 36	110,558 84	583 83	12,374 50	9,333 30	2,356 59	313,816 42

21	East Middlesex, ...	344,518 03	102,105 79	58,662 11	-	1,473 64	222 00	506,981 57
22	East Taunton, ...	148,299 57	18,029 86	6,251 02	-	1,912 12	-	174,492 57
23	Essex County,[4]	14,875 44	-	-	-	-	-	14,875 44
24	Fitchburg & Leominster, . . .	577,221 22	177,355 28	121,167 21	81,685 33	16,627 68	37,906 74	1,011,963 46
25	Fram., Southboro' & Marlboro',*[5] .	252,691 59	45,124 84	437 84	-	1,326 53	258 69	299,839 49
26	Framingham Union,*[6] . . .	114,713 42	42,152 19	8,831 02	-	2,298 78	324 10	168,319 51
27	Gardner, Westminster & Fitchburg,	236,900 01	59,830 01	74,064 02	22,662 94	7,125 47	7,163 41	407,745 86
28	Georgetown, Rowley & Ipswich, .	263,168 34	64,884 64	84,057 11	-	5,946 42	1,320 08	419,376 59
29	Greenfield, Deerfield & Northamp.,	283,629 82	55,843 16	19,236 49	-	884 15	1,445 89	361,039 51
30	Greenfield & Turner's Falls, . .	226,902 29	33,774 20	38,871 02	-	7,383 48	-	306,930 99
31	Hampshire, ...	60,058 38	-	-	-	6,010 92	-	66,069 30
32	Hampshire & Worcester, . . .	211,168 17	41,284 69	66,574 88	-	2,165 56	12,081 03	333,274 33
33	Hartford & Worcester,[4] . . .	-	-	-	-	30,000 00	-	30,000 00
34	Haverhill & Amesbury, . . .	658,691 12	141,239 92	56,547 16	-	13,762 70	7,016 81	877,257 71
35	Haverhill, Danvers & Ipswich,[4] .	5,378 86	-	-	-	-	-	5,378 86
36	Haverhill, Georgetown & Danvers,	100,429 13	21,076 24	5,525 00	-	4,290 27	4,096 69	135,417 33
37	Haverhill & Plaistow, . . .	61,421 41	8 65	6,489 66	-	5,025 00	-	72,944 72
	Haverhill & Plaistow (lessee),[1] .	-	-	-	-	-	-	-
38	Haverhill & Southern New Hamp.,	160,429 61	56,658 83	3,830 67	-	-	-	220,919 11
39	Holyoke, ...	773,821 66	314,442 94	376,804 20	34,000 00	32,324 60	37,222 92	1,568,616 32
40	Hoosac Valley, ...	581,552 64	148,548 96	139,773 18	22,158 40	1,780 12	398 93	894,212 23
41	Horse Neck Beach,[7]	31,111 28	287 65	1,200 00	100 00	222 03	-	32,920 96
42	Interstate Consolidated, . . .	246,781 08	1,218 92	27,000 00	-	32,708 92	-	307,708 92
43	Lawrence & Methuen, . . .	271,256 22	64,267 60	16,790 29	-	-	-	352,314 11
44	Leominster, Shirley & Ayer, . .	205,648 84	4,308 74	13,795 82	-	5,340 35	2,441 68	231,535 43
45	Lexington & Boston, ...	658,673 09	347,307 21	231,818 36	-	20,938 50	4,491 29	1,263,228 45

[1] Exeter, Hampton & Amesbury of New Hampshire.
[2] Railway in hands of receivers.
[3] Consolidated with the Newton December 31, 1903.
[4] Obtained a certificate of incorporation, but has not commenced the construction of its railway.
[5] Consolidated with the Boston & Worcester February 1, 1904.
[6] Consolidated with the Boston & Worcester December 31, 1903.
[7] Railway in process of construction.

Tabulated Statements from Reports of Street Railway Companies — Continued.

	RAILWAY COMPANIES.	Assets September 30, 1904 — Continued.						
		1. — Construction.	2. — Equipment.	3. — Land and Buildings.	4. — Other Permanent Property.	5. — Cash and Current Assets.	6. — Miscellaneous Assets.	7. — Gross Assets.
46	Linwood,	$6,013 10	$12,961 71	–	–	$391 42	$269 17	$19,635 40
47	Lowell, Acton & Maynard,	45,409 63	–	–	–	173 39	5,000 00	50,583 02
48	Lowell & Boston,[1]	242,450 52	67,008 26	$35,087 01	–	113,293 57	1,985 37	459,824 73
	Lowell & Boston (receivers),	–	–	–	–	3,844 08	3,603 98	7,448 06
49	Lowell & Fitchburg,[2]	22,998 30	–	1,001 70	–	–	–	24,000 00
50	Lowell & Pelham,	55,149 10	41,953 97	133 64	–	–	–	97,236 71
51	Marlborough & Framingham,*[3]	72,575 00	15,000 00	15,000 00	–	1,153 18	–	103,728 18
52	Marlborough & Westborough,	214,694 97	60,546 50	84,560 67	$15,648 71	811 90	3,038 56	379,301 31
53	Martha's Vineyard,	6,414 29	1,366 45	2,500 00	–	71 14	–	10,351 88
54	Medfield & Medway,	214,788 67	21,320 03	1,352 39	–	1,217 90	–	238,678 99
55	Middleboro', Wareham & Buz. Bay,[1]	474,129 57	120,386 35	16,346 12	–	7,180 82	–	618,042 86
	Middleboro', Wareham & Buz. Bay (receivers),	–	–	–	–	8,666 06	15,000 00	23,666 06
56	Milford, Attleboro' & Woonsocket,	387,659 75	82,493 47	87,337 81	31,414 86	27,562 66	–	616,468 55
57	Milford & Uxbridge,	489,564 30	183,077 08	219,414 26	28,355 24	8,107 80	15,102 41	943,621 09
58	Mount Tom,	58,216 46	4,900 00	36,883 54	–	735 98	–	100,735 98
59	Natick & Cochituate,	158,339 85	56,491 96	31,426 26	–	34,440 48	27 77	280,726 32
60	Natick & Needham,[1]	66,371 44	24,750 00	1,050 00	–	260 77	–	92,432 21
61	New Bedford & Onset,	570,482 42	95,991 87	195,900 26	–	7,922 41	3,643 50	873,940 46
62	Newton,	945,488 60	529,505 99	253,624 07	–	72,661 97	30,143 77	1,831,424 40
63	Newton & Boston,	205,354 68	124,457 45	193,964 90	–	13,693 25	1,698 75	539,169 03
64	Newtonville & Watertown,	108,564 94	–	–	–	2,684 69	–	111,249 63
65	Norfolk & Bristol,	265,746 04	39,338 65	79,168 69	–	19,740 28	8,593 45	412,587 11

66	Norfolk Western,[1]	175,981 59	28,895 63	49,262 31	–	1,323 33	1,639 27	257,102 13
	Norfolk Western (receiver),	–	–	–	–	6,584 75	160 36	6,745 11
67	Northampton,	386,554 95	166,812 03	158,319 55	2,010 76	13,565 58	9,222 64	736,485 51
68	Northampton & Amherst,	284,547 96	58,207 56	49,258 00	–	3,613 20	3,452 15	399,078 87
69	North End,	100,480 28	51,355 04	13,674 76	–	528 50	–	166,038 58
70	Norton & Taunton,	476,283 46	68,678 46	77,701 11	–	1,695 79	5,177 54	629,536 36
71	Norwood, Canton & Sharon,	128,741 16	12,856 61	7,815 37	–	3,463 39	2,435 55	155,312 08
72	Old Colony,	8,555,586 42	2,475,830 76	2,843,199 77	230,981 59	537,955 21	409,935 91	15,053,489 66
73	Pittsfield Electric,	334,678 75	101,634 56	58,905 67	–	2,008 94	–	497,227 92
74	Plymouth, Carver & Wareham,[2]	1,111 59	–	–	–	20,276 41	–	21,388 00
75	Plymouth & Sandwich,	51,989 82	9,227 17	3,374 64	–	1,520 16	–	66,111 79
76	Providence & Fall River,	249,837 60	93,970 25	31,187 58	–	6,747 70	4,714 72	386,457 85
77	Shelburne Falls & Colrain,	70,754 88	10,686 64	26,013 68	868 06	2,112 57	1,047 62	111,483 45
78	Somerville,	153,000 00	–	–	–	–	–	153,000 00
79	Southbridge & Sturbridge,	120,632 46	22,544 41	9,843 96	8,312 06	7,233 12	–	168,566 01
80	South Middlesex,[1]	202,118 38	80,241 03	133,039 87	500 00	26,692 83	2,412 29	445,004 40
81	Springfield,	1,973,754 37	662,264 19	1,127,253 71	–	117,331 18	46,994 18	3,927,597 63
82	Springfield & Eastern,	507,502 41	118,905 33	91,274 18	27,697 76	22,963 59	5,416 31	773,759 58
83	Templeton,	391,768 98	–	–	–	4,522 69	–	396,291 67
84	Union,	789,478 70	267,153 65	477,274 83	–	29,760 24	51,139 23	1,614,806 65
85	Uxbridge & Blackstone,	158,811 47	27,445 55	12,228 76	–	540 14	251 21	199,277 13
86	Waltham,	263,459 38	14,548 69	2,608 26	–	48,424 65	16,578 39	345,619 37
87	Warren, Brookfield & Spencer,	253,987 89	40,726 32	66,089 22	–	10,704 66	1,753 63	373,261 72
88	Webster & Dudley,	114,590 84	12,968 91	7,765 76	–	–	–	135,325 51
	Webster & Dudley and Worcester & Webster (lessee),[5]	–	–	–	–	–	–	–
89	Wellesley & Boston,*[6]	100,816 96	53,896 60	5,240 00	–	3,673 32	–	163,626 88
90	Westborough & Hopkinton,	84,915 45	5,200 00	200 00	–	641 67	317 78	91,274 90

[1] Railway in hands of receivers.
[2] Obtained a certificate of incorporation, but has not commenced the construction of its railway.
[3] Consolidated with the Framingham, Southborough & Marlborough December 21, 1903.
[4] Railway in hands of a receiver and not in operation.
[5] The Consolidated Railway of Connecticut, formerly the Worcester & Connecticut Eastern.
[6] Consolidated with the Newton December 31, 1903.

Tabulated Statements from Reports of Street Railway Companies — Continued.

	RAILWAY COMPANIES.	Assets September 30, 1904 — Concluded.						
		1. — Construction.	2. — Equipment.	3. — Land and Buildings.	4. — Other Permanent Property.	5. — Cash and Current Assets.	6. — Miscellaneous Assets.	7. — Gross Assets.
91	West End, ...	$11,384,616 62	$8,562,434 93	$11,429,471 57	$276,764 30	$62,740 96	$1,207,201 98	$32,923,230 36
92	Winnisimmet, ...	50,000 00	-	-	-	74 85	50 00	50,124 85
93	Woonsocket (of Rhode Island), .	409,672 10	132,458 52	15,596 95	-	10,680 08	-	568,407 65
94	Worcester & Blackstone Valley, .	268,433 02	68,018 69	130,077 78	8,628 24	1,671 19	-	476,828 92
95	Worcester Consolidated, . . .	3,400,554 26	1,387,107 31	1,250,429 46	44,052 89	279,600 49	137,196 08	6,498,940 49
96	Worcester & Holden, ...	221,825 00	47,962 14	58,466 44	-	4,636 39	5,615 23	338,505 20
97	Worcester, Roch. & Charl. Depot,[1]	109,917 22	-	-	-	-	-	109,917 22
98	Worcester & Shrewsbury R.R., .	70,803 58	52,710 86	-	-	3 07	-	123,517 51
99	Worcester & Shrewsbury St. R'y, .	11,700 00	8,300 00	-	-	22 05	-	20,022 05
00	Worcester & Southbridge,[1] . .	640,792 18	164,700 00	330,417 00	-	26,829 32	522 75	1,163,261 25
101	Worcester & Webster, . . .	245,595 87	89,026 63	144,891 77	-	12,000 00	-	491,514 27
102	Woronoco, ...	209,205 41	75,338 83	72,620 17	15,464 87	4,253 20	4,005 79	380,888 27
	Totals,[2]	$69,581,366 06	$26,201,913 30	$32,296,112 19	$1,446,944 17	$6,554,737 70	$4,762,666 37	$140,843,739 79

[1] This report is made from an appraisal of the property as assets, and capital stock and debts as liabilities. When the present management took charge of the company there were no books of account found.

[2] Not including the companies marked *, these companies having been consolidated during the year.

Tabulated Statements from Reports of Street Railway Companies — Continued.

	RAILWAY COMPANIES.	LIABILITIES SEPTEMBER 30, 1904.						
		8. — Capital Stock.	**9.** — Funded Debt.	**10.** — Real Estate Mortgages.	**11.** — Current Liabilities.	**12.** — Accrued Liabilities.	**13.** — Sinking and other Special Funds.	**14.** — Gross Liabilities.
1	Amesbury & Hampton,	$100,000 00	$100,000 00	–	$39,938 51	–	–	$239,938 51
	Amesbury & Hampton (lessee),[1]	–	–	–	–	–	–	–
2	Amherst & Sunderland,	120,000 00	–	–	124,468 21	$1,910 64	–	246,378 85
3	Athol & Orange,	74,500 00	60,000 00	–	–	750 00	–	135,250 00
4	Berkshire,	976,600 00	800,000 00	–	338,109 60	16,023 77	–	2,130,733 37
5	Blue Hill,	300,000 00	250,000 00	–	142,177 84	–	$418 26	692,596 10
6	Boston & Chelsea,	121,000 00	–	–	–	–	–	121,000 00
7	Boston Elevated,	13,300,000 00	–	–	811,622 64	2,373,020 16	1,579,755 92	18,064,398 72
8	Boston & Northern,	9,660,000 00	9,432,500 00	–	2,716,369 27	234,932 73	–	22,043,802 00
9	Boston & Revere Electric,	50,000 00	27,000 00	–	23,000 00	–	–	100,000 00
10	Boston & Worcester,	1,564,900 00	1,557,000 00	–	487,481 06	37,450 09	888 25	3,647,719 40
11	Bristol County,[2]	200,000 00	200,000 00	–	407,500 83	–	–	807,500 83
	Bristol County (receivers),	–	–	–	24,591 83	472 17	–	25,064 00
12	Bristol & Norfolk,	100,000 00	70,000 00	–	8,477 69	222 94	–	178,700 63
13	Brockton & Plymouth,	295,000 00	295,000 00	–	175,585 57	6,427 58	1,034 75	773,047 90
14	Citizens' Electric,	240,000 00	210,000 00	–	70,732 29	9,327 42	–	530,059 71
15	Commonwealth Avenue,*[3]	292,000 00	75,000 00	$2,500 00	187,563 87	1,811 03	–	558,874 90
16	Concord & Boston,[2]	50,000 00	–	–	87,060 00	–	–	137,060 00
17	Concord, Maynard & Hudson,	175,000 00	165,000 00	–	95,826 28	2,062 50	–	437,888 78
18	Conway Electric,	35,950 00	–	–	64,636 85	771 55	–	101,358 40
19	Cottage City & Edgartown Traction,	60,000 00	–	–	4,200 00	–	–	64,200 00
20	Dartmouth & Westport,	150,000 00	90,000 00	–	3,982 96	6,653 82	13,200 00	263,836 78

1 Exeter, Hampton & Amesbury of New Hampshire. 2 Railway in hands of receivers. 3 Consolidated with the Newton December 31, 1903.

Tabulated Statements from Reports of Street Railway Companies — Continued.

	RAILWAY COMPANIES.	Liabilities September 30, 1904 — Continued.						
		8. — Capital Stock.	**9.** — Funded Debt.	**10.** — Real Estate Mortgages.	**11.** — Current Liabilities.	**12.** — Accrued Liabilities.	**13.** — Sinking and other Special Funds.	**14.** — Gross Liabilities.
21	East Middlesex,	$297,700 00	$220,000 00	–	$20 00	–	–	$517,720 00
22	East Taunton,	110,000 00	45,000 00	–	1,181 63	$2,354 65	–	158,536 28
23	Essex County,[1]	12,500 00	–	–	2,375 44	–	–	14,875 44
24	Fitchburg & Leominster,	350,000 00	300,000 00	–	343,604 27	3,328 33	–	996,932 60
25	Fram., Southboro' & Marlboro',*[2]	185,000 00	60,000 00	–	52,874 06	522 19	–	298,396 25
26	Framingham Union,*[3]	30,000 00	47,000 00	–	59,310 90	421 76	$888 25	137,620 91
27	Gardner, Westminster & Fitch.,	185,000 00	150,000 00	–	78,557 65	–	–	413,557 65
28	Georgetown, Rowley & Ipswich,	180,000 00	180,000 00	–	59,984 07	3,529 34	–	423,513 41
29	Greenfield, Deerfield & Northamp.,	180,000 00	150,000 00	–	30,879 01	–	1,895 10	362,774 11
30	Greenfield & Turner's Falls,	130,000 00	130,000 00	–	33,077 99	–	–	293,077 99
31	Hampshire,	60,000 00	–	–	150 00	581 89	–	60,731 89
32	Hampshire & Worcester,	155,000 00	135,000 00	–	66,490 61	–	–	356,490 61
33	Hartford & Worcester,[1]	30,000 00	–	–	–	–	–	30,000 00
34	Haverhill & Amesbury,	150,000 00	490,000 00	–	260,380 51	10,032 59	–	910,413 10
35	Haverhill, Danvers & Ipswich,[1]	5,000 00	–	–	378 86	–	–	5,378 86
36	Haverhill, Georgetown & Danvers,	60,000 00	35,000 00	–	25,000 00	1,871 43	–	121,871 43
37	{Haverhill & Plaistow,	30,000 00	30,000 00	–	9,794 72	–	–	69,794 72
	{Haverhill & Plaistow (lessee),[4]	–	–	–	–	–	–	–
38	Haverhill & Southern New Hamp.,	80,000 00	80,000 00	–	68,687 09	–	–	228,687 09
39	Holyoke,	700,000 00	600,000 00	–	172,101 87	31,547 10	–	1,503,648 97
40	Hoosac Valley,	400,000 00	350,000 00	–	100,436 06	–	–	850,436 06

41	Horse Neck Beach,[5]	22,710 00	-	-	10,210 96	-	-	32,920 96
42	Interstate Consolidated, . . .	275,000 00	-	-	-	-	-	275,000 00
43	Lawrence & Methuen, . . .	150,000 00	125,000 00	-	82,873 43	-	-	357,873 43
44	Leominster, Shirley & Ayer, . .	56,247 00	-	-	171,700 64	1,003 12	-	228,950 76
45	Lexington & Boston, ...	525,000 00	350,000 00	-	385,933 00	190 67	-	1,261,123 67
46	Linwood, ...	12,000 00	-	-	5,156 16	-	-	17,156 16
47	Lowell, Acton & Maynard, . .	20,000 00	-	-	31,103 10	-	-	51,103 10
48	Lowell & Boston,[6]	90,000 00	90,000 00	-	331,318 26	-	-	511,318 26
	Lowell & Boston (receivers), . .	-	-	-	12,919 77	-	-	12,919 77
49	Lowell & Fitchburg,[1]	24,000 00	-	-	-	-	-	24,000 00
50	Lowell & Pelham, ...	40,000 00	40,000 00	-	19,473 60	-	-	99,473 60
51	Marlborough & Framingham,*[7] .	105,000 00	-	-	843 87	76 34	-	105,920 21
52	Marlborough & Westborough, . .	160,000 00	160,000 00	-	59,826 61	2,374 23	-	382,200 84
53	Martha's Vineyard, ...	9,167 50	-	-	652 35	-	-	9,819 85
54	Medfield & Medway, ...	100,000 00	100,000 00	-	43,341 79	2,542 55	-	245,884 34
55	Middleboro', Wareham & Buz. Bay,[6]	150,000 00	150,000 00	-	321,984 31	-	-	621,984 31
	Middleboro', Wareham & Buz. Bay (receivers), ...	-	-	-	16,623 48	272 23	-	16,895 71
56	Milford, Attleboro' & Woonsocket,	315,000 00	250,000 00	-	34,272 36	-	-	599,272 36
57	Milford & Uxbridge, ...	440,000 00	415,000 00	-	88,701 44	5,168 82	-	948,870 26
58	Mount Tom, ...	100,000 00	-	-	-	-	-	100,000 00
59	Natick & Cochituate, ...	100,000 00	-	-	167,192 65	62 50	-	267,255 15
60	Natick and Needham,[8] . . .	50,000 00	42,384 00	-	2,500 00	-	-	94,884 00
61	New Bedford & Onset, . . .	500,000 00	280,000 00	-	57,218 83	9,872 34	-	847,091 17
62	Newton, ...	722,000 00	575,000 00	$2,500 00	478,453 31	1,257 21	7,500 00	1,786,710 52
63	Newton & Boston, ...	200,000 00	200,000 00	-	302,396 56	-	-	702,396 56
64	Newtonville & Watertown, . .	50,000 00	-	-	59,650 00	-	-	109,650 00
65	Norfolk & Bristol, ...	200,000 00	-	-	214,679 01	28,070 48	-	442,749 49

1 Obtained a certificate of incorporation, but has not commenced the construction of its railway.
2 Consolidated with the Boston & Worcester February 1, 1904.
3 Consolidated with the Boston and Worcester December 31, 1903.
4 Exeter, Hampton & Amesbury of New Hampshire.
5 Railway in process of construction.
6 Railway in hands of receivers.
7 Consolidated with the Framingham, Southborough & Marlborough December 21, 1903.
8 Railway in hands of a receiver and not in operation.

Tabulated Statements from Reports of Street Railway Companies — Continued.

	RAILWAY COMPANIES.	LIABILITIES SEPTEMBER 30, 1904 — Concluded.						
		8. — Capital Stock.	**9.** — Funded Debt.	**10.** — Real Estate Mortgages.	**11.** — Current Liabilities.	**12.** — Accrued Liabilities.	**13.** — Sinking and other Special Funds.	**14.** — Gross Liabilities.
66	Norfolk Western,[1]	$100,000 00	$100,000 00	-	$85,479 78	$4,549 10	-	$290,028 88
	Norfolk Western (receiver), . .	-	-	-	15,332 01	3,808 10	-	19,140 11
67	Northampton, ...	300,000 00	225,000 00	-	193,000 00	-	-	718,000 00
68	Northampton & Amherst, . . .	180,000 00	180,000 00	-	42,431 44	-	-	402,431 44
69	North End, ...	110,000 00	75,000 00	-	-	-	-	185,000 00
70	Norton & Taunton, ...	297,000 00	296,000 00	-	79,537 05	-	-	672,537 05
71	Norwood, Canton & Sharon, . .	62,500 00	-	-	134,190 00	1,376 12	-	198,066 12
72	Old Colony, ...	6,812,600 00	5,667,000 00	-	2,458,425 63	106,327 50	-	15,044,353 13
73	Pittsfield Electric, ...	200,000 00	200,000 00	-	50,000 00	-	$5,916 53	455,916 53
74	Plymouth, Carver & Wareham,[2] .	21,388 00	-	-	-	-	-	21,388 00
75	Plymouth & Sandwich, ...	36,800 00	-	-	25,343 92	-	-	62,143 92
76	Providence & Fall River, . . .	165,000 00	165,000 00	-	62,591 69	4,341 74	-	396,933 43
77	Shelburne Falls & Colrain, . .	50,000 00	50,000 00	-	5,057 70	387 78	-	105,445 48
78	Somerville, ...	153,000 00	-	-	-	-	-	153,000 00
79	Southbridge & Sturbridge, . .	60,000 00	60,000 00	-	29,118 90	2,857 01	-	151,975 91
80	South Middlesex,[1]	100,000 00	100,000 00	-	251,042 69	2,562 04	8,351 50	461,956 23
81	Springfield, ...	1,958,400 00	1,500,000 00	-	301,172 44	21,814 10	-	3,781,386 54
82	Springfield & Eastern, . . .	370,000 00	330,000 00	-	52,564 01	4,430 86	-	756,994 87
83	Templeton, ...	75,000 00	-	-	364,063 69	-	-	439,063 69
84	Union, ...	900,000 00	400,000 00	-	126,112 38	7,625 28	-	1,433,737 66
85	Uxbridge & Blackstone, . . .	80,000 00	80,000 00	-	30,425 71	941 59	-	191,367 30

86	Waltham, ...	100,000 00	–	–	277,239 31	–	–	377,239 31
87	Warren, Brookfield & Spencer, .	150,000 00	125,000 00	–	56,645 08	5,100 45	10,426 11	347,171 64
	Webster & Dudley, ...	50,000 00	30,000 00	–	–	77,376 79	–	157,376 79
88	Webster & Dudley and Worcester & Webster (lessee),[3]	–	–	–	–	–	–	–
89	Wellesley & Boston,*[4]	115,000 00	–	–	34,136 59	–	7,500 00	156,636 59
90	Westborough & Hopkinton, . .	40,000 00	40,000 00	–	12,524 36	1,293 09	–	93,817 45
91	West End, ...	16,089,250 00	15,981,000 00	–	4,229 17	–	–	32,074,479 17
92	Winnisimmet, ...	50,000 00	–	–	–	–	–	50,000 00
93	Woonsocket (of Rhode Island), .	300,000 00	170,000 00	–	133,354 63	2,860 24	–	606,214 87
94	Worcester & Blackstone Valley, .	60,000 00	–	–	393,597 49	1,836 01	–	455,433 50
95	Worcester Consolidated, . . .	3,550,000 00	1,060,000 00	$59,500 00	1,468,696 68	23,728 79	–	6,161,925 47
96	Worcester & Holden, ...	125,000 00	125,000 00	–	80,056 68	–	–	330,056 68
97	Worcester, Roch. & Charl. Depot,[5]	40,000 00	40,000 00	–	86,000 00	–	–	166,000 00
98	Worcester & Shrewsbury R.R., .	36,825 00	22,000 00	–	–	–	–	58,825 00
99	Worcester & Shrewsbury St. R'y, .	20,000 00	–	–	–	–	–	20,000 00
100	Worcester & Southbridge,[5] . .	500,000 00	500,000 00	–	789,156 40	19,678 83	–	1,808,835 23
101	Worcester & Webster, . . .	150,000 00	150,000 00	–	–	249,151 80	12,000 00	561,151 80
102	Woronoco, ...	250,000 00	75,000 00	–	50,000 00	–	–	375,000 00
	Totals,[6]	$68,542,037 50	$46,674,884 00	$62,000 00	$17,434,431 67	$3,336,132 07	$1,641,386,42	$137,690,871 66

1 Railway in hands of receivers.

2 Obtained a certificate of incorporation, but has not commenced the construction of its railway.

3 The Consolidated Railway of Connecticut, formerly the Worcester & Connecticut Eastern.

4 Consolidated with the Newton December 31, 1903.

5 This report is made from an appraisal of the property as assets, and capital stock and debts as liabilities. When the present management took charge of the company there were no books of account found.

6 Not including the companies marked *, these companies having been consolidated during the year.

Tabulated Statements from Reports of Street Railway Companies — Continued.

	RAILWAY COMPANIES.	PROPERTY ACCOUNTS: ADDITIONS AND DEDUCTIONS DURING THE YEAR.						
		15. — Additions to Railway.	**16.** — To Equipment.	**17.** — To Land and Buildings.	**18.** — To other Permanent Property.	**19.** — Total Additions.	**20.** — Deductions.	**21.** — Net Additions.
1	{Amesbury & Hampton,	$7,210 52	$11 25	$2,212 34	–	$9,434 11	–	$9,434 11
	{Amesbury & Hampton (lessee),	–	–	–	–	–	–	–
2	Amherst & Sunderland,	3,214 67	848 89	4,133 80	–	8,197 36	–	8,197 36
3	Athol & Orange,	–	9,869 60	–	–	9,869 60	–	9,869 60
4	Berkshire,	33,940 29	22,736 47	60,980 37	$9,587 81	127,244 94	–	127,244 94
5	Blue Hill,	107,798 74	55,739 30	6,107 43	–	169,645 47	$6,130 00	163,515 47
6	Boston & Chelsea,	–	–	–	–	–	–	–
7	Boston Elevated,	2,179,739 41	231,167 19	232,246 38	159,234 41	2,802,387 39	–	2,802,387 39
8	Boston & Northern,	831,716 65	288,430 37	100,867 10	–	1,221,014 12	646,711 61	574,302 51
9	Boston & Revere Electric,	–	–	–	–	–	–	–
10	Boston & Worcester,	500,121 11	218,202 05	142,310 95	–	860,634 11	–	860,634 11
11	{Bristol County,	–	–	–	–	–	–	–
	{Bristol County (receivers),	–	–	–	–	–	–	–
12	Bristol & Norfolk,	154 95	5,788 85	–	–	5,943 80	9,000 00	3,056 20*d*
13	Brockton & Plymouth,	5,739 92	–	–	26,000 00	31,739 92	30 00	31,709 92
14	Citizens' Electric,	–	–	–	–	–	–	–
15	Commonwealth Avenue,	–	734 60	443 43	–	1,178 03	–	1,178 03
16	Concord & Boston,	–	–	–	–	–	–	–
17	Concord, Maynard & Hudson,	4,045 70	866 10	–	–	4,911 80	–	4,911 80
18	Conway Electric,	6,358 50	275 00	–	2,000 00	8,633 50	–	8,633 50
19	Cottage City & Edgartown Traction,	–	–	–	–	–	–	–
20	Dartmouth & Westport,	6,157 88	26,905 99	–	458 52	33,522 39	3,905 12	29,617 27

21	East Middlesex,	-	-	-	-	-	-	-
22	East Taunton,	-	-	6,000 00	-	6,000 00	20 00	5,980 00
23	Essex County,	2,446 31	-	-	-	2,446 31	-	2,446 31
24	Fitchburg & Leominster,	3,410 55	7,740 07	5,588 55	1,806 92	18,546 09	200 00	18,346 09
25	Fram., Southboro' & Marlboro',	105,728 91	-	-	-	105,728 91	-	105,728 91
26	Framingham Union,	-	-	-	-	-	-	-
27	Gardner, Westminster & Fitchburg,	3,126 45	-	-	-	3,126 45	-	3,126 45
28	Georgetown, Rowley & Ipswich,	10 00	172 00	-	-	182 00	-	182 00
29	Greenfield, Deerfield & Northamp.,	2,886 09	4,547 98	1,033 83	-	8,467 90	717 89	7,750 01
30	Greenfield & Turner's Falls,	12,068 29	3,546 00	4,446 01	-	20,060 30	1,326 72	18,733 58
31	Hampshire,	543 64	-	-	-	543 64	-	543 64
32	Hampshire & Worcester,	10,144 30	-	590 85	-	10,735 15	-	10,735 15
33	Hartford & Worcester,	-	-	-	-	-	-	-
34	Haverhill & Amesbury,	13,026 65	1,372 93	735 61	-	15,135 19	262 50	14,872 69
35	Haverhill, Danvers & Ipswich,	905 70	-	-	-	905 70	-	905 70
36	Haverhill, Georgetown & Danvers,	-	-	-	-	-	-	-
37	{Haverhill & Plaistow,	6,285 30	8 65	489 66	-	6,783 61	-	6,783 61
	{Haverhill & Plaistow (lessee),	-	-	-	-	-	-	-
38	Haverhill & Southern New Hamp.,	2,072 26	759 97	-	-	2,832 23	-	2,832 23
39	Holyoke,	7,852 47	5,434 21	1,900 46	-	15,187 14	3,400 00	11,787 14
40	Hoosac Valley,	91,124 51	25,879 00	26,057 21	5,811 26	148,871 98	-	148,871 98
41	Horse Neck Beach,	-	-	-	-	-	-	-
42	Interstate Consolidated,	-	-	-	-	-	-	-
43	Lawrence & Methuen,	2,221 40	774 93	45 00	-	3,041 33	188 80	2,852 53
44	Leominster, Shirley & Ayer,	199,837 66	4,308 74	13,795 82	-	217,942 22	-	217,942 22
45	Lexington & Boston,	3,516 68	1,863 17	2,423 05	-	7,802 90	20,193 60	12,390 70*d*

d Net deduction.

Tabulated Statements from Reports of Street Railway Companies — Continued.

	RAILWAY COMPANIES.	PROPERTY ACCOUNTS: ADDITIONS AND DEDUCTIONS DURING THE YEAR — Continued.						
		15. — Additions to Railway.	**16.** — To Equipment.	**17.** — To Land and Buildings.	**18.** — To other Permanent Property.	**19.** — Total Additions.	**20.** — Deductions.	**21.** — Net Additions.
46	Linwood,	-	$3,801 10	-	-	$3,801 10	-	$3,801 10
47	Lowell, Acton & Maynard,	-	-	-	-	-	-	-
48	{Lowell & Boston,	-	-	-	-	-	-	-
	{Lowell & Boston (receivers),	-	-	-	-	-	-	-
49	Lowell & Fitchburg,	-	-	-	-	-	-	-
50	Lowell & Pelham,	$318 13	464 96	$50 64	-	833 73	-	833 73
51	Marlborough & Framingham,	-	-	-	-	-	-	-
52	Marlborough & Westborough,	1,042 09	-	-	$200 00	1,242 09	-	1,242 09
53	Martha's Vineyard,	-	-	-	-	-	-	-
54	Medfield & Medway,	-	-	-	-	-	-	-
55	{Middleboro', Wareham & Buz. Bay,	-	-	-	-	-	-	-
	{Middleboro', Wareham & Buz. Bay (receivers),	-	-	-	-	-	-	-
56	Milford, Attleboro' & Woonsocket,	-	-	518 68	332 32	851 00	-	851 00
57	Milford & Uxbridge,	620 50	19,828 94	1,311 49	-	21,760 93	-	21,760 93
58	Mount Tom,	-	-	-	-	-	-	-
59	Natick & Cochituate,	10,525 77	5,315 04	21,473 65	-	37,314 46	$207 50	37,106 96
60	Natick & Needham,	-	-	-	-	-	-	-
61	New Bedford & Onset,	938 14	1,994 05	1,551 70	-	4,483 89	668 70	3,815 19
62	Newton,	305,257 55	294,069 16	139,432 30	-	738,759 01	82,007 97	656,751 04
63	Newton & Boston,	4,956 80	6,803 07	8,318 24	-	20,078 11	20,728 46	650 35*d*
64	Newtonville & Watertown,	-	-	-	-	-	-	-
65	Norfolk & Bristol,	-	-	-	-	-	14,987 48	14,987 48*d*

No.	Railroad							
66	Norfolk Western,	–	–	–	–	–	–	–
	Norfolk Western (receiver),	–	–	–	–	–	–	–
67	Northampton,	243 12	1,670 63	–	–	1,913 75	900 00	1,013 75
68	Northampton & Amherst,	2,582 61	–	1,378 16	–	3,960 77	–	3,960 77
69	North End,	–	–	–	–	–	–	–
70	Norton & Taunton,	1,155 38	3,964 83	1,521 87	–	6,642 08	–	6,642 08
71	Norwood, Canton & Sharon,	26 62	150 00	17 75	–	194 37	–	194 37
72	Old Colony,	583,698 09	116,155 87	753,711 92	–	1,453,565 88	347,941 89	1,105,623 99
73	Pittsfield Electric,	27,092 26	11,740 00	–	–	38,832 26	–	38,832 26
74	Plymouth, Carver & Wareham,	–	–	–	–	–	–	–
75	Plymouth & Sandwich,	150 00	–	–	–	150 00	–	150 00
76	Providence & Fall River,	1,247 90	4,020 30	–	–	5,268 20	–	5,268 20
77	Shelburne Falls & Colrain,	–	–	–	–	–	–	–
78	Somerville,	–	–	–	–	–	–	–
79	Southbridge & Sturbridge,	800 08	–	–	–	800 08	–	800 08
80	South Middlesex,	50,000 00	–	58,058 45	–	108,058 45	1,358 69	106,699 76
81	Springfield,	33,378 55	2,631 15	104,046 58	–	140,056 28	–	140,056 28
82	Springfield & Eastern,	576 27	130 65	545 77	114 47	1,367 16	–	1,367 16
83	Templeton,	–	–	–	–	–	17 27	17 27*d*
84	Union,	3,854 36	4,356 30	18,274 27	–	26,484 93	5,783 46	20,701 47
85	Uxbridge & Blackstone,	3,238 93	663 60	206 66	–	4,109 19	–	4,109 19
86	Waltham,	11,496 40	–	–	–	11,496 40	7,795 50	3,700 90
87	Warren, Brookfield & Spencer,	718 29	–	–	–	718 29	–	718 29
88	Webster & Dudley,	–	–	–	–	–	–	–
	Webster & Dudley and Worcester & Webster (lessee),	–	–	–	–	–	–	–
89	Wellesley & Boston,	–	2,200 00	–	–	2,200 00	100 00	2,100 00
90	Westborough & Hopkinton,	131 65	5,200 00	–	–	5,331 65	–	5,331 65

d Net deduction.

Tabulated Statements from Reports of Street Railway Companies — Continued.

	RAILWAY COMPANIES.	Property Accounts: Additions and Deductions during the Year — Concluded.						
		15. — Additions to Railway.	**16.** — To Equipment.	**17.** — To Land and Buildings.	**18.** — To other Permanent Property.	**19.** — Total Additions.	**20.** — Deductions.	**21.** — Net Additions.
91	West End,	$539,900 87	$325,464 74	$287,998 65	$3,358 84	$1,156,723 10	$75,743 98	$1,080,979 12
92	Winnisimmet,	–	–	–	–	–	–	–
93	Woonsocket (of Rhode Island),	8,514 49	–	–	–	8,514 49	–	8,514 49
94	Worcester & Blackstone Valley,	15,878 97	1,115 90	3,114 07	–	20,108 94	–	20,108 94
95	Worcester Consolidated,	4,634 76	3,840 49	63,382 68	–	71,857 93	9,997 59	61,860 34
96	Worcester & Holden,	37,624 39	18,506 86	16,790 70	–	72,921 95	–	72,921 95
97	Worcester, Roch. & Charl. Depot,	–	–	–	–	–	–	–
98	Worcester & Shrewsbury R.R.,	–	–	–	–	–	–	–
99	Worcester & Shrewsbury St. R'y,	–	–	–	–	–	–	–
100	Worcester & Southbridge,	–	–	–	–	–	–	–
101	Worcester & Webster,	–	–	–	–	–	–	–
102	Woronoco,	3,169 01	4,282 41	19,036 50	5,199 70	31,687 62	35 00	31,652 62

d Net deduction.

Tabulated Statements from Reports of Street Railway Companies — Continued.

	RAILWAY COMPANIES.	INCOME FOR THE YEAR ENDING SEPTEMBER 30, 1904.						
		22. — From Passengers.	**23.** — From Mails and Merchandise.	**24.** — From Tolls, Rents, Advertising, etc.	**25.** — Total Earnings from Operation.	**26.** — Rentals from Lease of Railway.	**27.** — Miscellaneous Income.	**28.** — Gross Income.
1	Amesbury & Hampton,[1]	-	-	-	-	$9,000 00	-	$9,000 00
1	Amesbury & Hampton (lessee),[2]	$24,729 62	$672 73	$82 71	$25,485 06	-	-	25,485 06
2	Amherst & Sunderland,	28,375 01	3,015 12	243 68	31,633 81	-	-	31,633 81
3	Athol & Orange,	39,388 80	-	125 00	39,513 80	-	-	39,513 80
4	Berkshire,	192,539 85	588 45	428 86	193,557 16	-	$6,737 77	200,294 93
5	Blue Hill,	72,450 30	200 00	213 80	72,864 10	-	-	72,864 10
6	Boston & Chelsea,[3]	-	-	-	-	7,260 00	-	7,260 00
7	Boston Elevated,	12,078,800 39	24,015 04	288,537 64	12,391,353 07	-	45,240 72	12,436,593 79
8	Boston & Northern,	3,717,364 36	1,094 12	32,510 00	3,750,968 48	-	15,444 94	3,766,413 42
9	Boston & Revere Electric,[4]	-	-	-	-	2,500 00	-	2,500 00
10	Boston & Worcester,	368,758 38	287 50	1,837 63	370,883 51	-	-	370,883 51
11	Bristol County,[5]	21,532 91	-	346 95	21,879 86	-	-	21,879 86
11	Bristol County (receivers),[6]	25,257 69	-	80 85	25,338 54	-	-	25,338 54
12	Bristol & Norfolk,	8,331 45	60 00	269 47	8,660 92	-	-	8,660 92
13	Brockton & Plymouth,	98,156 19	371 38	224 97	98,752 54	-	5,306 73	104,059 27
14	Citizens' Electric,	96,631 98	542 16	690 02	97,864 16	-	-	97,864 16
15	Commonwealth Avenue,[7]	13,948 20	-	1,243 69	15,191 89	-	-	15,191 89

[1] Leased to the Exeter, Hampton & Amesbury of New Hampshire.
[2] Exeter, Hampton & Amesbury of New Hampshire.
[3] Leased to the Boston Elevated and operated by the Boston & Northern.
[4] Leased to and operated by the Boston & Northern.
[5] Operations to May 3, 1904.
[6] Operations from May 3, 1904.
[7] Operations to December 31, 1903, when consolidated with the Newton.

Tabulated Statements from Reports of Street Railway Companies — Continued.

	RAILWAY COMPANIES.	Income for the Year ending September 30, 1904 — Continued.						
		22. — From Passengers.	**23.** — From Mails and Merchandise.	**24.** — From Tolls, Rents, Advertising, etc.	**25.** — Total Earnings from Operation.	**26.** — Rentals from Lease of Railway.	**27.** — Miscellaneous Income.	**28.** — Gross Income.
16	Concord & Boston,[1]	-	-	-	-	$1,742 54	$98 00	$1,840 54
17	Concord, Maynard & Hudson, .	$52,081 53	$471 14	$1,393 01	$53,945 68	-	-	53,945 68
18	Conway Electric, ...	2,917 46	6,776 92	-	9,694 38	-	-	9,694 38
19	Cottage City & Edgartown Traction,	5,272 30	-	-	5,272 30	-	-	5,272 30
20	Dartmouth & Westport, ...	133,679 65	12,919 88	1,363 03	147,962 56	-	-	147,962 56
21	East Middlesex,[2]	-	-	-	-	30,000 00	33 25	30,033 25
22	East Taunton, ...	34,115 26	-	529 01	34,644 27	-	-	34,644 27
23	Essex County, ...	-	-	-	-	-	-	-
24	Fitchburg & Leominster, . . .	202,176 70	-	613 32	202,790 02	-	23,612 98	226,403 00
25	Fram., Southboro' & Marlboro',[3] .	9,015 49	-	172 17	9,187 66	-	-	9,187 66
26	Framingham Union,[4]	7,286 65	162 50	337 65	7,786 80	-	-	7,786 80
27	Gardner, Westminster & Fitchburg,	59,542 99	23 67	1,610 97	61,177 63	-	326 36	61,503 99
28	Georgetown, Rowley & Ipswich, .	35,866 83	200 00	394 08	36,460 91	-	-	36,460 91
29	Greenfield, Deerfield & Northamp.,	49,126 73	127 01	1,499 24	50,752 98	-	-	50,752 98
30	Greenfield & Turner's Falls, . .	58,908 19	2,115 90	4,679 03	65,703 12	-	-	65,703 12
31	Hampshire, ...	8,413 12	2,115 40	174 40	10,702 92	-	-	10,702 92
32	Hampshire & Worcester, . . .	27,199 68	-	83 30	27,282 98	-	-	27,282 98
33	Hartford & Worcester, . . .	-	-	-	-	-	-	-
34	Haverhill & Amesbury, . . .	106,208 24	486 40	2,318 84	109,013 48	-	-	109,013 48
35	Haverhill, Danvers & Ipswich, .	-	-	-	-	-	-	-

36	Haverhill, Georgetown & Danvers,	29,150 57	–	259 59	29,410 16	–	–	29,410 16
37	Haverhill & Plaistow,[5] . . .	–	–	–	–	2,700 00	–	2,700 00
	Haverhill & Plaistow (lessee),[6] .	15,061 54	–	55 95	15,117 49	–	–	15,117 49
38	Haverhill & Southern New Hamp.,	39,837 17	–	140 80	39,977 97	–	–	39,977 97
39	Holyoke, ...	367,207 29	2,553 58	3,342 52	373,103 39	–	10,308 06	383,411 45
40	Hoosac Valley, ...	151,080 30	700 60	858 04	152,638 94	–	2,891 09	155,530 03
41	Horse Neck Beach, ...	–	–	–	–	–	–	–
42	Interstate Consolidated, . . .	150,664 67	–	–	150,664 67	–	–	150,664 67
43	Lawrence & Methuen, . . .	55,155 13	–	180 31	55,335 44	–	–	55,335 44
44	Leominster, Shirley & Ayer,[7] . .	3,918 80	–	–	3,918 80	–	–	3,918 80
45	Lexington & Boston, ...	152,818 17	–	9,177 71	161,995 88	–	–	161,995 88
46	Linwood, ...	12,348 45	–	–	12,348 45	–	–	12,348 45
47	Lowell, Acton & Maynard, . .	5,001 73	–	–	5,001 73	–	–	5,001 73
48	Lowell & Boston,[8]	3,218 55	–	611 26	3,829 81	–	–	3,829 81
	Lowell & Boston (receivers),[9] . .	3,802 80	–	69 89	3,872 69	–	–	3,872 69
49	Lowell & Fitchburg, ...	–	–	–	–	–	–	–
50	Lowell & Pelham, ...	16,153 92	–	38 33	16,192 25	–	–	16,192 25
51	Marlborough & Framingham,[10] .	7,634 40	–	147 62	7,782 02	–	–	7,782 02
52	Marlborough & Westborough, . .	31,976 77	–	726 31	32,703 08	–	1,000 00	33,703 08
53	Martha's Vineyard,[11]	–	–	–	–	–	–	–
54	Medfield & Medway, ...	19,400 00	–	152 98	19,552 98	–	–	19,552 98
55	Middleboro', Wareham & Buz. Bay,[12]	12,019 20	195 25	140 00	12,354 45	–	155 09	12,509 54
	Middleboro', Wareham & Buzzard's Bay (receivers),[13]	26,339 60	571 87	26 67	26,938 14	–	–	26,938 14

1 Railway in hands of receivers. Operated by the Lexington & Boston under a contract.

2 Leased to and operated by the Boston & Northern.

3 Operations to February 1, 1904, when consolidated with the Boston & Worcester.

4 Operations to December 21, 1903, when consolidated with the Boston & Worcester.

5 Leased to the Exeter, Hampton & Amesbury of New Hampshire.

6 Exeter, Hampton & Amesbury of New Hampshire.

7 Commenced operation July 3, 1904.

8 Operations to May 10, 1904.

9 Operations from May 10, 1904.

10 Operations to December 31, 1903, when consolidated with the Framingham, Southborough & Marlborough.

11 Operated by the Cottage City & Edgartown Traction. No income reported.

12 Operations to February 29, 1904.

13 Operations from February 29, 1904.

Tabulated Statements from Reports of Street Railway Companies — Continued.

	RAILWAY COMPANIES.	INCOME FOR THE YEAR ENDING SEPTEMBER 30, 1904 — Continued.						
		22. — From Passengers.	**23.** — From Mails and Merchandise.	**24.** — From Tolls, Rents, Advertising, etc.	**25.** — Total Earnings from Operation.	**26.** — Rentals from Lease of Railway.	**27.** — Miscellaneous Income.	**28.** — Gross Income.
56	Milford, Attleboro' & Woonsocket,	$77,702 61	-	$1,172 15	$78,874 76	-	-	$78,874 76
57	Milford & Uxbridge,	141,804 05	$364 26	576 37	142,744 68	-	-	142,744 68
58	Mount Tom,[1]	-	-	-	-	$6,000 00	$35 05	6,035 05
59	Natick & Cochituate,	86,156 73	272 79	3,008 80	89,438 32	-	-	89,438 32
60	Natick & Needham,[2]	-	-	-	-	-	48 21	48 21
61	New Bedford & Onset,	50,911 07	5,730 38	8,637 63	65,279 08	-	-	65,279 08
62	Newton,	272,344 26	-	11,197 98	283,542 24	-	-	283,542 24
63	Newton & Boston,	60,083 09	-	1,991 71	62,074 80	-	-	62,074 80
64	Newtonville & Watertown,[3]	-	-	-	-	8,136 50	-	8,136 50
65	Norfolk & Bristol,	47,981 21	188 15	1,841 97	50,011 33	-	-	50,011 33
66	Norfolk Western,[4]	5,581 29	-	22 85	5,604 14	-	-	5,604 14
	Norfolk Western (receiver),[5]	14,436 50	-	235 24	14,671 74	-	-	14,671 74
67	Northampton,	145,198 52	2,099 75	2,088 47	149,386 74	-	-	149,386 74
68	Northampton & Amherst,	56,361 63	1,105 13	200 00	57,666 76	-	-	57,666 76
69	North End,[6]	-	-	-	-	8,000 00	-	8,000 00
70	Norton & Taunton,	47,222 91	1,016 78	624 39	48,864 08	-	-	48,864 08
71	Norwood, Canton & Sharon,	7,837 15	-	425 09	8,262 24	-	-	8,262 24
72	Old Colony,	2,269,710 29	4,494 40	45,791 74	2,319,996 43	-	97,833 15	2,417,829 58
73	Pittsfield Electric,	153,957 91	-	110 00	154,067 91	-	100 00	154,167 91
74	Plymouth, Carver & Wareham,	-	-	-	-	-	-	-
75	Plymouth & Sandwich,	7,229 45	-	25 00	7,254 45	-	-	7,254 45

76	Providence & Fall River,	44,572 57	528 26	1,836 97	46,937 80	-	-	46,937 80
77	Shelburne Falls & Colrain,	8,264 59	6,847 74	1,019 80	16,132 13	-	-	16,132 13
78	Somerville,[7]	-	-	-	-	9,180 00	-	9,180 00
79	Southbridge & Sturbridge,	33,141 45	743 88	637 48	34,522 81	-	58 80	34,581 61
80	South Middlesex,[8]	69,137 30	200 00	253 96	69,591 26	-	-	69,591 26
81	Springfield,	939,881 85	1,504 09	6,476 97	947,862 91	-	-	947,862 91
82	Springfield & Eastern,	108,949 41	501 90	175 00	109,626 31	-	823 55	110,449 86
83	Templeton,	39,803 48	2,082 06	487 39	42,372 93	-	-	42,372 93
84	Union,	337,286 96	250 00	27,872 84	365,409 80	-	-	365,409 80
85	Uxbridge & Blackstone,	23,750 20	-	31 25	23,781 45	-	-	23,781 45
86	Waltham,[9]	11,802 66	-	8 47	11,811 13	-	-	11,811 13
87	Warren, Brookfield & Spencer,	63,202 15	-	309 96	63,512 11	-	-	63,512 11
88	Webster & Dudley,[10]	-	-	-	-	19,779 86	-	19,779 86
	Webster & Dudley and Worcester & Webster (lessee),[11]	78,696 05	317 29	1,054 56	80,067 90	-	2,179 16	82,247 06
89	Wellesley & Boston,[12]	12,055 20	-	774 72	12,829 92	-	-	12,829 92
90	Westborough & Hopkinton,	13,108 91	496 88	-	13,605 79	-	-	13,605 79
91	West End,[7]	-	-	-	-	1,192,497 50	56 49	1,192,553 99
92	Winnisimmet,[13]	-	-	-	-	3,000 00	-	3,000 00
93	Woonsocket (of Rhode Island),	118,910 60	267 83	210 00	119,388 43	-	-	119,388 43
94	Worcester & Blackstone Valley,	66,727 73	-	957 53	67,685 26	-	-	67,685 26
95	Worcester Consolidated,	1,320,561 83	2,002 28	13,876 75	1,336,440 86	-	-	1,336,440 86

1 Leased to and operated by the Holyoke.
2 Railway not in operation.
3 Tracks used by the Newton & Boston.
4 Operations to January 20, 1904.
5 Operations since January 20, 1904.
6 Leased to and operated by the Worcester Consolidated.
7 Leased to and operated by the Boston Elevated.
8 Operated by a receiver.
9 Operated by the Newton.
10 Leased to and operated by the Consolidated Railway of Connecticut.
11 The Consolidated Railway of Connecticut, formerly the Worcester and Connecticut Eastern.
12 Operations to December 31, 1903, when consolidated with the Newton.
13 Leased to and operated by the Boston & Northern.

Tabulated Statements from Reports of Street Railway Companies — Continued.

	RAILWAY COMPANIES.	INCOME FOR THE YEAR ENDING SEPTEMBER 30, 1904 — Concluded.						
		22. — From Passengers.	**23.** — From Mails and Merchandise.	**24.** — From Tolls, Rents, Advertising, etc.	**25.** — Total Earnings from Operation.	**26.** — Rentals from Lease of Railway.	**27.** — Miscellaneous Income.	**28.** — Gross Income.
96	Worcester & Holden, ...	$36,087 22	$47 77	$109 21	$36,244 20	-	-	$36,244 20
97	Worcester, Roch. & Charl. Depot,[1]	-	-	-	-	$900 00	-	900 00
98	Worcester & Shrewsbury R.R.,[2] .	-	-	-	-	2,650 00	$1,100 00	3,750 00
99	Worcester & Shrewsbury St. R'y,[2]	-	-	-	-	1,000 00	-	1,000 00
100	Worcester & Southbridge, . . .	87,097 23	2,015 94	2,031 99	91,145 16	-	18,610 96	109,756 12
101	Worcester & Webster,[3] . . .	-	-	-	-	14,491 51	-	14,491 51
102	Woronoco, ...	81,175 45	-	300 00	81,475 45	-	1,250 00	82,725 45
	Totals, ...	$25,619,596 52	$93,344 18	$494,305 54	$26,207,246 24	$1,318,837 91	$233,250 36	$27,759,334 51

1 Operated by the Worcester & Southbridge.
2 Leased to and operated by the Worcester Consolidated.
3 Leased to and operated by the Consolidated Railway of Connecticut.

Tabulated Statements from Reports of Street Railway Companies — Continued.

	RAILWAY COMPANIES.	Operating Expenses for the Year ending September 30, 1904.						
		29. — Salaries of Officers and Clerks.	**30.** — Office Expenses and Supplies.	**31.** — Legal Expenses.	**32.** — Insurance.	**33.** — Other General Expenses.	**34.** — Repair of Roadbed and Track.	**35.** — Repair of Electric Line System.
1	Amesbury & Hampton,	–	–	–	–	–	–	–
	Amesbury & Hampton (lessee),	$1,008 49	$240 32	–	$488 02	$279 03	$1,794 83	$615 17
2	Amherst & Sunderland,	1,917 18	162 50	$73 10	411 86	–	1,720 83	6 80
3	Athol & Orange,	1,596 00	185 04	–	2,057 65	2,837 41	1,231 66	429 46
4	Berkshire,	5,489 28	847 25	751 12	3,330 00	1,638 60	2,213 03	954 64
5	Blue Hill,	2,991 00	415 64	23 45	1,644 06	1,560 59	1,167 00	532 39
6	Boston & Chelsea,	–	–	–	–	–	–	–
7	Boston Elevated,	208,591 81	95,462 69	254,833 66	108,479 29	220,489 16	546,129 25	170,640 42
8	Boston & Northern,	83,731 59	20,013 55	22,229 53	234,581 33	55,633 39	91,909 75	40,601 14
9	Boston & Revere Electric,	–	–	–	–	–	–	–
10	Boston & Worcester,	11,292 00	2,256 70	–	6,000 00	5,566 83	10,898 01	3,959 22
11	Bristol County,	309 01	272 11	297 94	1,635 97	1,121 11	1,535 88	1,575 25
	Bristol County (receivers),	–	331 10	–	–	–	13 65	5 63
12	Bristol & Norfolk,	1,092 00	180 07	56 08	116 40	59 52	124 36	53 41
13	Brockton & Plymouth,	6,305 28	581 15	580 73	2,026 00	2,911 14	1,691 79	514 62
14	Citizens' Electric,	3,285 02	290 30	–	1,440 00	2,524 23	4,464 81	983 25
15	Commonwealth Avenue,	1,040 50	328 02	–	573 77	–	409 80	248 42
16	Concord & Boston,	–	–	–	–	–	–	–
17	Concord, Maynard & Hudson,	2,819 60	1,319 47	400 00	3,100 62	1,308 50	1,313 59	300 53
18	Conway Electric,	426 93	381 60	–	–	–	378 95	–
19	Cottage City & Edgartown Traction,	–	455 49	–	68 40	–	659 82	79 85
20	Dartmouth & Westport,	3,970 38	307 80	229 10	1,322 94	510 67	2,120 79	4,402 69

Tabulated Statements from Reports of Street Railway Companies — Continued.

	RAILWAY COMPANIES.	OPERATING EXPENSES FOR THE YEAR ENDING SEPTEMBER 30, 1904 — Continued.						
		29. — Salaries of Officers and Clerks.	**30.** — Office Expenses and Supplies.	**31.** — Legal Expenses.	**32.** — Insurance.	**33.** — Other General Expenses.	**34.** — Repair of Roadbed and Track.	**35.** — Repair of Electric Line System.
21	East Middlesex,	-	-	-	-	-	-	-
22	East Taunton,	$700 00	$30 08	$15 00	$216 30	$274 68	$2,146 92	$117 02
23	Essex County,	-	-	-	-	-	-	-
24	Fitchburg & Leominster,	8,032 93	2,519 63	30 47	1,968 71	30 25	5,431 50	1,338 60
25	Fram., Southboro' & Marlboro',	741 71	13 60	-	418 00	106 82	45 46	16 66
26	Framingham Union,	592 76	11 75	-	111 00	133 55	34 51	28 74
27	Gardner, Westminster & Fitchburg,	1,898 00	1,206 67	446 32	1,551 90	462 02	1,932 38	555 25
28	Georgetown, Rowley & Ipswich,	1,373 40	603 27	300 00	1,500 10	694 51	2,843 92	184 54
29	Greenfield, Deerfield & Northamp.,	3,499 79	987 66	-	1,536 74	747 85	1,299 43	-
30	Greenfield & Turner's Falls,	3,292 26	1,046 99	322 76	897 37	292 64	3,192 15	416 84
31	Hampshire,	-	22 80	-	-	8 69	629 97	-
32	Hampshire & Worcester,	1,500 00	858 72	-	404 50	1,850 97	1,579 54	-
33	Hartford & Worcester,	-	-	-	-	-	-	-
34	Haverhill & Amesbury,	2,323 44	135 82	-	1,620 00	1,622 70	3,152 24	595 68
35	Haverhill, Danvers & Ipswich,	-	-	-	-	-	-	-
36	Haverhill, Georgetown & Danvers,	590 60	68 21	300 00	359 60	441 63	1,363 40	374 14
37	{Haverhill & Plaistow,	-	-	-	-	-	-	-
	{Haverhill & Plaistow (lessee),	508 23	122 53	-	241 84	146 67	894 51	307 98
38	Haverhill & Southern New Hamp.,	1,616 50	413 78	37 28	439 00	454 94	2,132 03	625 18
39	Holyoke,	8,354 51	716 96	-	3,876 15	1,546 03	42,694 67	3,338 78
40	Hoosac Valley,	2,925 92	1,718 05	237 12	2,433 32	-	5,951 12	1,468 65

No.	Name							
41	Horse Neck Beach,	-	-	-	-	-	-	-
42	Interstate Consolidated,	2,925 00	100 00	-	-	-	23,000 00	-
43	Lawrence & Methuen,	2,300 22	578 52	78 73	616 55	582 59	2,947 01	868 50
44	Leominster, Shirley & Ayer,	72 07	22 59	-	-	-	-	-
45	Lexington & Boston,	8,073 09	4,430 65	2,750 50	4,274 35	301 98	4,865 13	2,783 91
46	Linwood,	1,443 75	515 48	-	-	-	83 24	-
47	Lowell, Acton & Maynard,	-	-	-	-	-	-	-
48	Lowell & Boston,	280 00	71 50	180 57	530 36	179 96	469 17	233 58
	Lowell & Boston (receivers),	348 54	50 00	5 00	679 80	-	2 31	-
49	Lowell & Fitchburg,	-	-	-	-	-	-	-
50	Lowell & Pelham,	469 23	119 44	32 63	137 67	140 62	668 80	195 03
51	Marlborough & Framingham,	676 94	-	-	110 11	107 01	202 13	16 43
52	Marlborough & Westborough,	1,581 46	341 54	85 35	1,228 79	821 97	745 82	114 03
53	Martha's Vineyard,	-	-	-	-	-	-	-
54	Medfield & Medway,	681 57	38 04	97 80	-	256 26	212 37	1,052 96
55	Middleboro', Wareham & Buz. Bay,	860 00	145 73	-	932 50	602 92	51 65	51 39
	Middleboro', Wareham & Buz. Bay (receivers),	305 92	-	22 60	1,085 01	-	291 76	-
56	Milford, Attleboro' & Woonsocket,	1,248 00	278 00	86 00	1,837 45	1,061 74	3,935 19	331 00
57	Milford & Uxbridge,	4,956 55	217 12	126 45	2,760 00	1,709 28	7,128 10	1,997 85
58	Mount Tom,	-	-	-	-	-	-	-
59	Natick & Cochituate,	6,832 61	1,741 71	647 50	843 87	241 75	5,785 08	46 37
60	Natick & Needham,	-	-	-	-	-	-	-
61	New Bedford & Onset,	1,323 46	106 98	10 00	1,127 50	234 58	676 47	778 09
62	Newton,	9,338 51	6,908 19	950 00	4,948 47	558 23	5,279 63	5,234 77
63	Newton & Boston,	2,207 52	1,579 06	2,650 00	2,370 46	125 60	3,420 76	2,253 93
64	Newtonville & Watertown,	-	-	-	-	-	-	-
65	Norfolk & Bristol,	5,239 18	150 05	1,611 59	1,280 24	459 56	1,299 66	959 91

Tabulated Statements from Reports of Street Railway Companies — Continued.

	RAILWAY COMPANIES.	OPERATING EXPENSES FOR THE YEAR ENDING SEPTEMBER 30, 1904 — Continued.						
		29. — Salaries of Officers and Clerks.	**30.** — Office Expenses and Supplies.	**31.** — Legal Expenses.	**32.** — Insurance.	**33.** — Other General Expenses.	**34.** — Repair of Roadbed and Track.	**35.** — Repair of Electric Line System.
66	Norfolk Western,	$982 00	$4 42	$150 00	$134 36	$88 23	$42 80	$47 50
	Norfolk Western (receiver),	492 95	62 61	26 33	220 62	1,000 12	1,174 15	2,476 12
67	Northampton,	5,400 00	1,841 83	564 11	2,083 77	177 91	9,765 91	3,510 63
68	Northampton & Amherst,	2,129 92	202 71	200 00	877 60	1,121 12	2,748 43	933 08
69	North End,	-	-	-	-	-	-	-
70	Norton & Taunton,	1,807 00	174 75	-	1,125 00	-	2,721 09	754 55
71	Norwood, Canton & Sharon,	1,000 00	67 27	-	-	171 36	77 12	85 74
72	Old Colony,	45,805 02	13,919 93	12,059 65	144,880 52	39,570 30	56,945 48	38,037 65
73	Pittsfield Electric,	3,800 00	573 72	3,268 40	998 70	646 67	8,882 42	1,691 28
74	Plymouth, Carver & Wareham,	-	-	-	-	-	-	-
75	Plymouth & Sandwich,	383 84	112 65	-	-	-	101 50	7 80
76	Providence & Fall River,	2,226 94	112 31	-	1,392 00	657 89	1,947 39	390 11
77	Shelburne Falls & Colrain,	880 97	79 34	-	514 99	-	1,832 58	131 82
78	Somerville,	-	-	-	-	-	-	-
79	Southbridge & Sturbridge,	609 99	99 01	53 00	-	683 61	1,179 59	63 69
80	South Middlesex,	2,338 85	1,743 82	-	1,728 00	-	1,473 13	1,039 86
81	Springfield,	25,500 00	1,384 96	4,811 77	10,771 76	5,126 82	42,368 20	14,195 20
82	Springfield & Eastern,	3,249 76	2,366 28	532 50	3,674 70	419 00	5,539 47	1,665 63
83	Templeton,	675 00	143 81	473 36	78 93	227 79	2,218 75	190 60
84	Union,	8,772 96	461 99	356 60	4,339 58	1,491 14	7,242 82	2,580 82
85	Uxbridge & Blackstone,	1,033 26	172 66	30 50	332 25	-	228 84	-

86	Waltham,	1,801 00	428 13	80 00	156 27	-	631 93	-
87	Warren, Brookfield & Spencer,	2,624 29	1,066 87	-	1,209 75	-	2,698 48	766 76
88	Webster & Dudley,	-	-	-	-	-	-	-
	Webster & Dudley and Worcester & Webster (lessee),	2,612 44	1,295 82	522 25	355 50	4,453 56	4,301 64	-1,372 77
89	Wellesley & Boston,	1,848 11	163 49	-	127 52	-	335 45	288 09
90	Westborough & Hopkinton,	1,293 00	541 48	269 62	139 10	-	284 42	40 54
91	West End,	-	-	-	-	-	-	-
92	Winnisimmet,	-	-	-	-	-	-	-
93	Woonsocket (of Rhode Island),	1,560 00	-	600 00	1,646 57	7,695 73	14,273 78	920 43
94	Worcester & Blackstone Valley,	2,422 00	372 48	-	1,528 30	431 17	3,220 53	314 05
95	Worcester Consolidated,	41,253 43	7,290 11	5,691 80	21,101 45	9,991 60	14,095 65	14,446 40
96	Worcester & Holden,	2,808 36	580 96	79 85	145 40	-	419 69	299 50
97	Worcester, Roch. & Charl. Depot,	-	-	-	-	-	-	-
98	Worcester & Shrewsbury R.R.,	-	-	-	-	-	-	-
99	Worcester & Shrewsbury St. R'y,	-	-	-	-	-	-	-
100	Worcester & Southbridge,	3,346 75	1,000 91	282 10	3,644 04	4,154 97	3,002 38	1,568 23
101	Worcester & Webster,	-	-	-	-	-	-	-
102	Woronoco,	4,579 00	564 79	756 00	1,457 83	314 24	2,059 83	1,142 24
	Totals,	$598,216 58	$188,731 03	$321,306 22	$614,278 48	$391,061 41	$997,979 28	$341,149 79

Tabulated Statements from Reports of Street Railway Companies — Continued.

	RAILWAY COMPANIES.	OPERATING EXPENSES FOR THE YEAR ENDING SEPTEMBER 30, 1904 — Continued.						
		36. — Repair of Buildings.	**37.** — Repair of Cars and Vehicles.	**38.** — Repair of Electric Car Equipment.	**39.** — Renewal of Horses, Harnesses, etc.	**40.** — Provender and Stabling for Horses.	**41.** — Cost of Electric Motive Power.	**42.** — Wages of Employees.
1	{Amesbury & Hampton,	-	-	-	-	-	-	-
	{Amesbury & Hampton (lessee),	$195 70	$1,665 63	$1,596 49	-	-	$7,467 43	$6,772 42
2	Amherst & Sunderland,	157 42	1,583 52	2,303 61	-	-	9,848 37	7,784 15
3	Athol & Orange,	-	829 20	1,429 48	-	-	6,074 84	7,481 39
4	Berkshire,	203 83	2,852 96	5,413 45	$29 48	$681 60	33,855 97	39,730 08
5	Blue Hill,	180 67	2,099 05	4,457 29	-	-	16,885 65	22,704 27
6	Boston & Chelsea,	-	-	-	-	-	-	-
7	Boston Elevated,	112,721 57	489,217 83	325,094 53	7,964 29	24,265 17	942,737 84	3,912,151 17
8	Boston & Northern,	20,306 62	141,202 70	169,160 50	1,172 42	8,907 17	419,388 10	1,025,214 62
9	Boston & Revere Electric,	-	-	-	-	-	-	-
10	Boston & Worcester,	115 47	18,920 71	16,467 46	-	-	58,335 07	58,182 80
11	{Bristol County,	33 87	4,507 31	5,397 78	-	-	12,687 78	8,334 24
	{Bristol County (receivers),	76 13	1,079 72	-	-	-	5,288 50	9,945 69
12	Bristol & Norfolk,	-	298 59	689 93	-	-	2,302 98	2,631 76
13	Brockton & Plymouth,	632 02	4,682 85	5,002 75	13 25	111 00	12,182 00	20,340 25
14	Citizens' Electric,	448 39	4,536 52	4,273 87	-	-	15,713 52	18,754 94
15	Commonwealth Avenue,	82 84	993 56	1,639 45	-	157 72	4,574 70	6,670 51
16	Concord & Boston,	-	-	-	-	-	-	-
17	Concord, Maynard & Hudson,	88 71	1,843 62	2,948 30	-	-	10,893 84	12,778 38
18	Conway Electric,	11 50	220 59	205 46	-	-	1,660 65	2,408 05
19	Cottage City & Edgartown Traction,	59 00	79 91	745 79	-	-	1,170 29	1,249 54
20	Dartmouth & Westport,	-	4,383 76	1,319 29	-	-	-	20,703 29

21	East Middlesex,	-	-	-	-	-	-	-
22	East Taunton,	39 79	799 45	633 40	-	-	5,994 19	7,900 15
23	Essex County,	-	-	-	-	-	-	-
24	Fitchburg & Leominster,	440 31	9,154 55	6,108 96	1,295 17	-	25,740 02	47,922 31
25	Fram., Southboro' & Marlboro',	-	150 02	3 12	-	-	2,966 11	3,157 23
26	Framingham Union,	2 01	96 50	177 61	-	-	1,360 25	2,286 69
27	Gardner, Westminster & Fitchburg,	84 17	1,790 97	1,654 49	-	-	9,495 37	13,450 72
28	Georgetown, Rowley & Ipswich,	22 60	5,696 56	14 55	-	-	2,597 18	11,562 71
29	Greenfield, Deerfield & Northamp.,	31 15	828 70	619 16	-	-	6,704 65	11,045 07
30	Greenfield & Turner's Falls,	33 44	2,495 28	2,590 15	-	-	7,240 91	17,004 07
31	Hampshire,	-	-	-	-	-	649 87	2,048 96
32	Hampshire & Worcester,	-	3,497 67	1,847 34	-	-	16,466 25	8,914 17
33	Hartford & Worcester,	-	-	-	-	-	-	-
34	Haverhill & Amesbury,	369 87	5,301 21	7,435 78	-	-	24,376 27	23,112 87
35	Haverhill, Danvers & Ipswich,	-	-	-	-	-	-	-
36	Haverhill, Georgetown & Danvers,	1 44	357 75	5 40	-	-	7,110 93	6,870 14
37	Haverhill & Plaistow,	-	-	-	-	-	-	-
	Haverhill & Plaistow (lessee),	95 74	827 26	803 52	-	-	3,793 47	3,421 13
38	Haverhill & Southern New Hamp.,	124 08	3,455 37	2,502 92	-	-	11,413 21	9,953 88
39	Holyoke,	1,392 07	20,403 88	17,207 75	-	-	42,078 50	94,579 29
40	Hoosac Valley,	67 96	7,962 58	6,067 43	-	-	40,461 68	33,345 02
41	Horse Neck Beach,	-	-	-	-	-	-	-
42	Interstate Consolidated,	-	-	-	-	-	36,024 18	44,567 96
43	Lawrence & Methuen,	167 57	4,996 87	3,678 81	-	-	16,170 21	13,874 76
44	Leominster, Shirley & Ayer,	3 94	-	-	-	13 73	478 30	308 75
45	Lexington & Boston,	563 57	7,561 17	5,496 02	-	835 71	24,006 96	42,499 85

Tabulated Statements from Reports of Street Railway Companies — Continued.

	RAILWAY COMPANIES.	OPERATING EXPENSES FOR THE YEAR ENDING SEPTEMBER 30, 1904 — Continued.						
		36. — Repair of Buildings.	**37.** — Repair of Cars and Vehicles.	**38.** — Repair of Electric Car Equipment.	**39.** — Renewal of Horses, Harnesses, etc.	**40.** — Provender and Stabling for Horses.	**41.** — Cost of Electric Motive Power.	**42.** — Wages of Employees.
46	Linwood, ...	–	$626 41	–	–	–	$1,841 28	$3,724 91
47	Lowell, Acton & Maynard, . .	–	–	–	–	–	2,002 39	2,829 10
48	Lowell & Boston, ...	$6 73	1,339 03	$2,357 77	–	–	4,985 52	2,964 49
	Lowell & Boston (receivers), . .	–	432 52	–	–	–	2,642 14	3,061 17
49	Lowell & Fitchburg, ...	–	–	–	–	–	–	–
50	Lowell & Pelham, ...	39 17	1,004 98	718 21	–	–	3,418 70	3,093 27
51	Marlborough & Framingham, .	1 60	158 47	116 64	–	–	2,833 08	3,412 26
52	Marlborough & Westborough, . .	162 54	927 40	2,677 96	–	–	4,773 46	8,109 78
53	Martha's Vineyard, ...	–	–	–	–	–	–	–
54	Medfield & Medway, ...	–	361 66	172 00	–	–	4,826 03	6,480 07
55	Middleboro', Wareham & Buz. Bay,	1 40	219 27	433 28	–	$69 47	4,205 71	4,877 48
	Middleboro', Wareham & Buz. Bay (receivers), ...	–	848 54	–	–	–	6,008 55	4,924 72
56	Milford, Attleboro' & Woonsocket,	116 00	4,913 71	3,548 30	–	–	13,734 11	23,349 99
57	Milford & Uxbridge, ...	1,455 54	4,112 57	3,707 78	–	–	21,761 34	39,766 60
58	Mount Tom, ...	–	–	–	–	–	–	–
59	Natick & Cochituate, ...	80 01	3,765 89	4,803 65	$296 63	–	18,709 30	26,627 87
60	Natick & Needham, ...	–	–	–	–	–	–	–
61	New Bedford & Onset, ...	206 22	3,969 03	1,306 92	–	–	11,222 83	10,553 70
62	Newton, ...	1,040 65	7,191 73	8,914 80	–	1,117 92	47,696 05	85,262 92
63	Newton & Boston, ...	815 75	5,130 04	4,007 46	–	552 27	1,652 58	23,288 08
64	Newtonville & Watertown, . .	–	–	–	–	–	–	–
65	Norfolk & Bristol, ...	56 08	2,535 11	6,317 89	–	–	16,042 30	16,453 03

66	Norfolk Western,	-	176 14	139 82	-	-	1,346 83	1,623 97
	Norfolk Western (receiver),	126 16	1,091 35	889 52	-	-	2,610 79	3,558 72
67	Northampton,	637 06	7,249 27	10,016 24	-	458 51	19,413 26	39,478 44
68	Northampton & Amherst,	209 48	2,099 72	4,699 05	-	-	18,178 30	9,323 22
69	North End,	-	-	-	-	-	-	-
70	Norton & Taunton,	12 54	3,060 24	3,670 96	-	-	10,941 53	15,076 35
71	Norwood, Canton & Sharon,	147 36	264 12	1,047 90	-	-	2,382 36	3,935 52
72	Old Colony,	5,450 79	75,890 06	85,629 37	391 61	3,389 13	384,103 66	608,418 15
73	Pittsfield Electric,	278 45	6,267 55	12,215 03	60 93	545 48	32,944 60	32,773 11
74	Plymouth, Carver & Wareham,	-	-	-	-	-	-	-
75	Plymouth & Sandwich,	-	167 43	-	-	-	1,920 33	2,036 00
76	Providence & Fall River,	105 56	4,817 81	4,812 24	-	-	11,012 18	8,329 49
77	Shelburne Falls & Colrain,	67 18	384 01	406 93	-	-	1,353 74	2,416 24
78	Somerville,	-	-	-	-	-	-	-
79	Southbridge & Sturbridge,	11 90	2,326 33	1,093 97	-	-	7,622 49	10,633 48
80	South Middlesex,	494 54	2,882 80	3,907 95	-	-	17,935 66	19,026 62
81	Springfield,	4,877 49	46,749 48	43,812 93	1,439 76	-	153,001 20	278,995 93
82	Springfield & Eastern,	462 31	3,026 94	2,911 38	-	-	25,164 99	24,087 13
83	Templeton,	-	2,188 29	2,241 92	-	-	10,669 07	12,980 73
84	Union,	2,686 97	13,033 98	7,676 63	163 84	339 09	44,759 60	111,120 50
85	Uxbridge & Blackstone,	11 00	506 91	315 90	-	-	4,292 96	5,880 41
86	Waltham,	-	-	-	-	-	-	-
87	Warren, Brookfield & Spencer,	1,120 54	1,582 70	1,928 18	-	-	10,302 55	15,772 68
88	Webster & Dudley,	-	-	-	-	-	-	-
	Webster & Dudley and Worcester & Webster (lessee),	184 62	4,434 65	3,238 75	-	-	13,755 65	15,325 97
89	Wellesley & Boston,	-	149 62	-	119 88	-	2,697 73	3,707 91
90	Westborough & Hopkinton,	-	845 32	176 55	-	-	5,110 52	2,761 00

Tabulated Statements from Reports of Street Railway Companies — Continued.

	RAILWAY COMPANIES.	OPERATING EXPENSES FOR THE YEAR ENDING SEPTEMBER 30, 1904 — Continued.						
		36. — Repair of Buildings.	**37.** — Repair of Cars and Vehicles.	**38.** — Repair of Electric Car Equipment.	**39.** — Renewal of Horses, Harnesses, etc.	**40.** — Provender and Stabling for Horses.	**41.** — Cost of Electric Motive Power.	**42.** — Wages of Employees.
91	West End,	-	-	-	-	-	-	-
92	Winnisimmet,	-	-	-	-	-	-	-
93	Woonsocket (of Rhode Island),	$728 27	$7,024 77	$4,872 02	$54 10	$608 62	$21,204 05	$34,251 45
94	Worcester & Blackstone Valley,	261 36	2,967 82	2,958 77	-	-	11,859 30	12,009 32
95	Worcester Consolidated,	6,318 10	49,145 65	48,821 67	615 78	4,546 30	201,585 37	288,523 88
96	Worcester & Holden,	79 43	741 85	18 86	-	-	9,886 25	8,052 96
97	Worcester, Roch. & Charl. Depot,	-	-	-	-	-	-	-
98	Worcester & Shrewsbury R.R.,	-	-	-	-	-	-	-
99	Worcester & Shrewsbury St. R'y,	-	-	-	-	-	-	-
100	Worcester & Southbridge,	334 30	5,699 47	6,203 29	-	-	12,060 78	16,958 00
101	Worcester & Webster,	-	-	-	-	-	-	-
102	Woronoco,	216 94	6,840 38	2,424 93	246 85	-	15,205 08	21,233 21
	Totals,	$167,557 49	$1,045,524 84	$900,205 26	$13,863 99	$46,598 89	$3,067,872 24	$7,458,733 11

Tabulated Statements from Reports of Street Railway Companies — Continued.

	RAILWAY COMPANIES.	OPERATING EXPENSES FOR THE YEAR ENDING SEPTEMBER 30, 1904 — Continued.						
		43. — Removing Snow and Ice.	**44.** — Damages for Injuries.	**45.** — Tolls for Trackage Rights.	**46.** — Rents of Buildings, etc.	**47.** — Other Transportation Expenses.	**48.** — Total Operating Expenses.	**49.** — Per Cent to Earnings from Operation.
1	Amesbury & Hampton,	-	-	-	-	-	-	-
	Amesbury & Hampton (lessee),	$1,257 70	$1,107 71	$696 66	$41 84	$1,806 02	$27,033 46	106.08
2	Amherst & Sunderland,	784 97	175 00	181 30	-	1,340 40	28,451 01	89.94
3	Athol & Orange,	479 00	-	-	-	676 77	25,307 90	64.05
4	Berkshire,	1,949 47	2,734 45	-	-	3,246 37	105,921 58	54.72
5	Blue Hill,	1,571 97	1,800 00	546 56	203 66	854 99	59,638 24	81.85
6	Boston & Chelsea,	-	-	-	-	-	-	-
7	Boston Elevated,	284,476 26	563,013 82	8,882 92	49,164 97	307,236 43	8,631,553 08	69.66
8	Boston & Northern,	137,055 52	16,055 42	49,034 72	18,672 39	86,709 07	2,641,579 53	70.42
9	Boston & Revere Electric,	-	-	-	-	-	-	-
10	Boston & Worcester,	2,074 83	934 27[1]	-	-	-	195,003 37	52.58
11	Bristol County,	454 92	-	703 60	-	3,194 05	42,060 82	-
	Bristol County (receivers),	-	50 00	641 51	-	24 75	17,456 68	-
12	Bristol & Norfolk,	156 19	-	268 22	100 00	98 09	8,227 60	95.00
13	Brockton & Plymouth,	896 81	1,134 85	-	-	985 66	60,592 15	61.36
14	Citizens' Electric,	2,425 93	705 38	-	-	-	59,846 16	61.15
15	Commonwealth Avenue,	329 29	677 61	50	50 04	15 60	17,792 33	-

[1] In addition to this amount $53,201.07 was paid on account of accidents and was charged against surplus account (see column 68), to which account $23,461.10 was credited as a contribution from stockholders (see column 67). Taking the similar action of 1903, $79,739.97 has been charged against surplus account for injuries to persons, and $50,000 credited to surplus account as a contribution from stockholders.

Tabulated Statements from Reports of Street Railway Companies — Continued.

	RAILWAY COMPANIES.	Operating Expenses for the Year ending September 30, 1904 — Continued.						
		43. — Removing Snow and Ice.	**44.** — Damages for Injuries.	**45.** — Tolls for Trackage Rights.	**46.** — Rents of Buildings, etc.	**47.** — Other Transportation Expenses.	**48.** — Total Operating Expenses.	**49.** — Per Cent to Earnings from Operation.
16	Concord & Boston,	-	-	-	-	-	-	-
17	Concord, Maynard & Hudson,	$1,393 24	$85 50	$750 00	-	$2,118 80	$43,462 70	80.57
18	Conway Electric,	-	-	-	$125 00	-	5,818 73	60.02
19	Cottage City & Edgartown Traction,	-	-	-	-	-	4,568 09	86.64
20	Dartmouth & Westport,	276 60	1,246 35	42,397 77	331 21	10,834 28	94,356 92	63.77
21	East Middlesex,	-	-	-	-	-	-	-
22	East Taunton,	305 94	85 41	423 80	1,723 73	801 99	22,207 85	64.10
23	Essex County,	-	-	-	-	-	-	-
24	Fitchburg & Leominster,	3,101 56	6,549 40	-	1,074 70	11,416 20	132,155 27	65.17
25	Fram., Southboro' & Marlboro',	278 64	63 80	-	-	18 48	7,979 65	-
26	Framingham Union,	3 74	-	-	-	-	4,839 11	-
27	Gardner, Westminster & Fitch.,	666 76	2,900 37	-	-	892 27	38,987 66	63.73
28	Georgetown, Rowley & Ipswich,	3,459 10	1,789 44	218 12	-	-	32,860 00	90.12
29	Greenfield, Deerfield & Northamp.,	2,098 16	24 75	-	-	1,378 64	30,801 75	60.69
30	Greenfield & Turner's Falls,	3,298 86	658 84	-	-	3,655 48	46,438 04	70.68
31	Hampshire,	265 62	-	-	-	489 25	4,115 16	38.45
32	Hampshire & Worcester,	575 61	1,468 66	-	-	690 69	39,654 12	145.34
33	Hartford & Worcester,	-	-	-	-	-	-	-
34	Haverhill & Amesbury,	3,250 46	123 73	152 09	-	-	73,572 16	67.49
3	Haverhill, Danvers & Ipswich,	-	-	-	-	-	-	-

36	Haverhill, Georgetown & Danvers,	1,163 27	2,889 07	485 81	–	–	22,381 39	76.10
37	Haverhill & Plaistow,	–	–	–	–	–	–	–
	Haverhill & Plaistow (lessee),	628 85	598 51	5 83	21 37	1,079 69	13,497 13	89.28
38	Haverhill & Southern New Hamp.,	762 69	1,645 85	67 61	71 24	2,474 41	38,189 97	95.53
39	Holyoke,	4,059 46	24,331 64	–	–	1,128 05	265,707 74	71.22
40	Hoosac Valley,	1,708 81	1,894 27	–	–	4,372 02	110,613 95	72.47
41	Horse Neck Beach,	–	–	–	–	–	–	–
42	Interstate Consolidated,	–	9,021 87	–	7,969 95	–	123,608 96	82.04
43	Lawrence & Methuen,	1,363 53	2,365 98	629 44	101 65	3,547 06	54,868 00	99.15
44	Leominster, Shirley & Ayer,	–	–	–	358 70	76 05	1,334 13	34.04
45	Lexington & Boston,	4,937 13	7,650 71	2,875 50	738 99	106 45	124,751 67	77.01
46	Linwood,	–	–	1,380 96	400 00	549 00	10,565 03	85.56
47	Lowell, Acton & Maynard,	25 63	–	–	654 99	9 70	5,521 81	109 84
48	Lowell & Boston,	1,376 40	175 20	–	–	317 01	15,467 29	–
	Lowell & Boston (receivers),	–	–	2 50	–	28 00	7,251 98	–
49	Lowell & Fitchburg,	–	–	–	–	–	–	–
50	Lowell & Pelham,	163 34	638 39	2,685 77	19 75	759 76	14,304 76	88.34
51	Marlborough & Framingham,	10 64	1 00	–	503 65	178 70	8,328 66	–
52	Marlborough & Westborough,	511 45	676 50	–	–	1,163 25	23,921 30	73.15
53	Martha's Vineyard,	–	–	–	–	–	–	–
54	Medfield & Medway,	449 14	38 00	–	453 67	487 61	15,607 18	79.82
55	Middleboro', Wareham & Buz. Bay,	492 26	–	–	1 00	356 81	13,300 87	–
	Middleboro', Wareham & Buz. Bay (receivers),	–	–	961 69	1,060 81	344 89	15,854 49	–
56	Milford, Attleboro' & Woonsocket,	819 55	1,826 47	366 46	267 92	186 00	57,905 89	73.45
57	Milford & Uxbridge,	2,704 47	13,594 29	–	–	2,012 62	108,010 56	75.67
58	Mount Tom,	–	–	–	–	–	–	–
59	Natick & Cochituate,	1,739 81	4,307 82	–	431 73	120 60	77,022 20	86.12
60	Natick and Needham,	–	–	–	–	–	–	–

Tabulated Statements from Reports of Street Railway Companies — Continued.

	RAILWAY COMPANIES.	OPERATING EXPENSES FOR THE YEAR ENDING SEPTEMBER 30, 1904 — Concluded.						
		43. — Removing Snow and Ice.	**44.** — Damages for Injuries.	**45.** — Tolls for Trackage Rights.	**46.** — Rents of Buildings, etc.	**47.** — Other Transportation Expenses.	**48.** — Total Operating Expenses.	**49.** — Per Cent to Earnings from Operation.
61	New Bedford & Onset,	$755 10	$830 53	-	$51 00	$4,807 54	$37,959 95	58.15
62	Newton,	6,403 33	13,606 95	$453 84	875 36	193 80	205,975 15	72.64
63	Newton & Boston,	2,623 62	3,004 10	3,330 27	595 82	67 96	59,675 28	96.13
64	Newtonville & Watertown,	-	-	-	-	-	-	-
65	Norfolk & Bristol,	1,639 64	771 46	57 92	41 55	-	54,915 17	109.81
66	Norfolk Western,	171 96	77 50	-	-	273 38	5,258 91	-
	Norfolk Western (receiver),	426 70	-	-	-	915 78	15,071 92	-
67	Northampton,	4,394 20	3,375 17	-	-	1,754 83	110,121 14	73.72
68	Northampton & Amherst,	1,602 25	497 25	-	75 00	4,762 75	49,659 88	86.12
69	North End,	-	-	-	-	-	-	-
70	Norton & Taunton,	5,079 10	268 93	864 12	440 00	3,730 27	49,726 43	101.76
71	Norwood, Canton & Sharon,	346 50	40	-	199 90	253 33	9,978 88	120.78
72	Old Colony,	36,029 29	8,942 52	905 32	11,612 95	60,488 03	1,632,469 43	70.37
73	Pittsfield Electric,	2,689 02	-	-	-	2,153 03	109,788 39	71.26
74	Plymouth, Carver & Wareham,	-	-	-	-	-	-	-
75	Plymouth & Sandwich,	244 19	-	-	-	-	4,973 74	68.56
76	Providence & Fall River,	232 18	670 06	-	-	-	36,706 16	78.20
77	Shelburne Falls & Colrain,	238 45	-	-	50 00	1,962 13	10,318 38	63.96
78	Somerville,	-	-	-	-	-	-	-
79	Southbridge & Sturbridge,	110 35	125 00	-	-	199 10	24,811 51	71.87
80	South Middlesex,	839 52	1,598 50	-	3,565 15	-	58,574 40	84.17

81	Springfield,	15,023 50	31,090 25	-	-	-	69,149 25	71.65
82	Springfield & Eastern,	2,528 50	449 44	-	334 00	966 21	77,378 24	70.58
83	Templeton,	1,028 62	289 45	-	-	210 72	33,617 04	79.34
84	Union,	3,218 78	16,136 24	-	8,629 38	5,439 84	28,450 76	65.26
85	Uxbridge & Blackstone,	77 48	-	-	-	464 82	13,346 99	56.12
86	Waltham,	467 78	-	337 67	878 75	20,542 51	25,324 04	214.41
87	Warren, Brookfield & Spencer,	1,300 41	796 13	-	-	266 57	41,435 91	65.24
88	Webster & Dudley,	-	-	-	-	-	-	-
	Webster & Dudley and Worcester & Webster (lessee),	618 81	2,206 50	-	126 21	1,370 19	56,175 33	70.16
89	Wellesley & Boston,	105 90	602 76	-	83 35	4 64	10,234 45	-
90	Westborough & Hopkinton,	350 58	150 00	-	-	686 69	12,648 82	92.97
91	West End,	-	-	-	-	-	-	-
92	Winnisimmet,	-	-	-	-	-	-	-
93	Woonsocket (of Rhode Island),	2,017 25	3,749 93	-	372 50	535 41	102,114 88	85.53
94	Worcester & Blackstone Valley,	538 12	3,682 64	554 15	-	-	43,120 01	63.71
95	Worcester Consolidated,	13,198 67	53,327 00	433 40	181 50	32,587 12	813,154 88	60.84
96	Worcester & Holden,	326 47	-	179 44	-	753 47	24,372 49	67.25
97	Worcester, Roch. & Charl. Depot,	-	-	-	-	-	-	-
98	Worcester & Shrewsbury R.R.,	-	-	-	-	-	-	-
99	Worcester & Shrewsbury St. R'y,	-	-	-	-	-	-	-
100	Worcester & Southbridge,	599 76	739 12	640 96	221 10	-	60,456 16	66.33
101	Worcester & Webster,	-	-	-	-	-	-	-
102	Woronoco,	1,962 19	293 75	-	485 43	248 29	60,030 98	73.68
	Totals,	$582,991 80	$822,321 91	$122,116 43	$113,361,91	$603,420 37	$18,397,291 03	70.20

Tabulated Statements from Reports of Street Railway Companies — Continued.

	RAILWAY COMPANIES.	Exhibit for the Year ending September 30, 1904.						
		50. — Net Earnings from Operation.	**51.** — All other Income.	**52.** — Total Income above Operating Expenses.	**53.** — Interest on Funded Debt.	**54.** — Interest and Discount on Unfunded Debt.	**55.** — Taxes.	**56.** — Rentals of Leased Railways.
1	Amesbury & Hampton,	-	$9,000 00	$9,000 00	$5,000 00	-	-	-
	Amesbury & Hampton (lessee),	$1,548 40*d*	-	1,548 40*d*	-	-	$564 87	$9,000 00
2	Amherst & Sunderland,	3,182 80	-	3,182 80	-	$4,756 50	1,980 84	-
3	Athol & Orange,	14,205 90	-	14,205 90	3,000 00	23 06	2,643 60	-
4	Berkshire,	87,635 58	6,737 77	94,373 35	40,000 00	12,500 00	9,729 11	-
5	Blue Hill,	13,225 86	-	13,225 86	7,864 58	8,469 42	3,250 64	-
6	Boston & Chelsea,	-	7,260 00	7,260 00	-	-	-	-
7	Boston Elevated,	3,759,799 99	45,240 72	3,805,040 71	629,599 90	-	925,418 67	1,223,043 17
8	Boston & Northern,	1,109,388 95	15,444 94	1,124,833 89	436,191 76	133,073 26	223,042 15	118,316 69
9	Boston & Revere Electric,	-	2,500 00	2,500 00	-	-	-	-
10	Boston & Worcester,	175,880 14	-	175,880 14	48,452 44	11,447 96	24,610 21	-
11	Bristol County,	20,180 96*d*	-	20,180 96*d*	6,000 00	3,253 57	3,308 18	-
	Bristol County (receivers),	7,881 86	-	7,881 86	5,017 61	-	587 01	-
12	Bristol & Norfolk,	433 32	-	433 32	3,500 00	1,397 56	136 58	-
13	Brockton & Plymouth,	38,160 39	5,306 73	43,467 12	13,159 37	9,802 75	5,162 14	-
14	Citizens' Electric,	38,018 00	-	38,018 00	10,500 00	2,999 50	5,766 91	-
15	Commonwealth Avenue,	2,600 44*d*	-	2,600 44*d*	937 50	2,671 46	1,505 21	-
16	Concord & Boston,	-	1,840 54	1,840 54	-	1,879 95	423 38	-
17	Concord, Maynard & Hudson,	10,482 98	-	10,482 98	8,250 00	6,323 25	3,190 03	-
18	Conway Electric,	3,875 65	-	3,875 65	-	3,550 39	178 70	-
19	Cottage City & Edgartown Traction,	704 21	-	704 21	-	169 50	188 28	-
20	Dartmouth & Westport,	53,605 64	-	53,605 64	4,500 00	643 47	6,448 20	-

21	East Middlesex, ...	-	30,033 25	30,033 25	-	-	-	-
22	East Taunton, ...	12,436 42	-	12,436 42	2,250 00	-	2,167 15	-
23	Essex County, ...	-	-	-	-	-	-	-
24	Fitchburg & Leominster, . . .	70,634 75	23,612 98	94,247 73	14,250 00	16,490 24	11,975 54	-
25	Fram., Southboro' & Marlboro', .	1,208 01	-	1,208 01	1,000 00	755 33	88 99	-
26	Framingham Union, ...	2,947 69	-	2,947 69	587 49	873 17	300 40	-
27	Gardner, Westminster & Fitchburg,	22,189 97	326 36	22,516 33	7,500 00	4,162 59	2,155 39	-
28	Georgetown, Rowley & Ipswich, .	3,600 91	-	3,600 91	9,000 00	3,448 36	995 07	-
29	Greenfield, Deerfield & Northamp.,	19,951 23	-	19,951 23	4,520 83	2,059 57	2,236 53	-
30	Greenfield & Turner's Falls, . .	19,265 08	-	19,265 08	6,445 00	1,101 20	2,086 80	-
31	Hampshire, ...	6,587 76	-	6,587 76	-	-	581 89	-
32	Hampshire & Worcester, . . .	12,371 14*d*	-	12,371 14*d*	6,750 00	2,736 76	1,806 40	-
33	Hartford & Worcester, . . .	-	-	-	-	-	-	-
34	Haverhill & Amesbury, . . .	35,441 32	-	35,441 32	26,500 00	9,094 59	2,021 76	-
35	Haverhill, Danvers & Ipswich, .	-	-	-	-	-	-	-
36	Haverhill, Georgetown & Danvers,	7,028 77	-	7,028 77	1,750 00	1,554 55	1,891 93	-
37	{Haverhill & Plaistow, . . .	-	2,700 00	2,700 00	1,500 00	-	-	-
	{Haverhill & Plaistow (lessee), .	1,620 36	-	1,620 36	-	-	320 22	2,700 00
38	Haverhill & Southern New Hamp.,	1,788 00	-	1,788 00	2,333 33	1,704 10	917 77	-
39	Holyoke, ...	107,395 65	10,308 06	117,703 71	30,000 00	6,840 19	26,629 65	6,000 00
40	Hoosac Valley, ...	42,024 99	2,891 09	44,916 08	5,000 00	4,396 20	7,042 66	-
41	Horse Neck Beach, ...	-	-	-	-	-	-	-
42	Interstate Consolidated, . . .	27,055 71	-	27,055 71	-	-	8,216 92	-
43	Lawrence & Methuen, ...	467 44	-	467 44	3,645 84	2,735 25	1,426 08	-
44	Leominster, Shirley & Ayer, . .	2,584 67	-	2,584 67	-	-	-	-
45	Lexington & Boston, ...	37,244 21	-	37,244 21	15,750 00	22,077 06	9,170 82	-

d Deficit.

Tabulated Statements from Reports of Street Railway Companies — Continued.

	RAILWAY COMPANIES.	EXHIBIT FOR THE YEAR ENDING SEPTEMBER 30, 1904—Continued.						
		50. — Net Earnings from Operation.	**51.** — All other Income.	**52.** — Total Income above Operating Expenses.	**53.** — Interest on Funded Debt.	**54.** — Interest and Discount on Unfunded Debt.	**55.** — Taxes.	**56.** — Rentals of Leased Railways.
46	Linwood,	$1,783 42	-	$1,783 42	-	-	$477 04	-
47	Lowell, Acton & Maynard,	520 08*d*	-	520 08*d*	-	-	-	-
48	Lowell & Boston,	11,637 48*d*	-	11,637 48*d*	$2,025 00	$5,482 49	989 87	-
	Lowell & Boston (receivers),	3,379 29*d*	-	3,379 29*d*	2,030 06	-	62 36	-
49	Lowell & Fitchburg,	-	-	-	-	-	-	-
50	Lowell & Pelham,	1,887 49	-	1,887 49	1,166 66	710 65	578 60	-
51	Marlborough & Framingham,	546 64*d*	-	546 64*d*	-	-	76 34	-
52	Marlborough & Westborough,	8,781 78	$1,000 00	9,781 78	8,000 00	2,860 00	1,779 33	-
53	Martha's Vineyard,	-	-	-	-	-	-	-
54	Medfield & Medway,	3,945 80	-	3,945 80	5,000 00	1,833 45	611 17	-
55	Middleboro', Wareham & Buz. Bay,	946 42*d*	155 09	791 33*d*	-	-	-	-
	Middleboro', Wareham & Buzzard's Bay (receivers),	11,083 65	-	11,083 65	3,858 23	-	455 07	-
56	Milford, Attleboro' & Woonsocket,	20,968 87	-	20,968 87	12,500 00	911 69	3,300 89	-
57	Milford & Uxbridge,	34,734 12	-	34,734 12	20,750 00	3,034 05	8,920 72	-
58	Mount Tom,	-	6,035 05	6,035 05	-	-	-	-
59	Natick & Cochituate,	12,416 12	-	12,416 12	-	6,343 26	4,726 91	-
60	Natick & Needham,	-	48 21	48 21	2,500 00	-	-	-
61	New Bedford & Onset,	27,319 13	-	27,319 13	14,000 00	3,525 46	6,435 10	-
62	Newton,	77,567 09	-	77,567 09	18,437 50	31,586 05	16,809 39	-
63	Newton & Boston,	2,399 52	-	2,399 52	10,000 00	16,700 50	3,640 02	-
64	Newtonville & Watertown,	-	8,136 50	8,136 50	-	2,960 97	1,057 50	-
65	Norfolk & Bristol,	4,903 84*d*	-	4,903 84*d*	-	10,529 56	1,692 56	-

No.	Name							
66	Norfolk Western,	345 23	-	345 23	1,471 10	1,190 87	139 20	-
	Norfolk Western (receiver),	400 18d	-	400 18d	10,783 33	499 29	712 20	-
67	Northampton,	39,265 60	-	39,265 60	10,250 00	9,079 85	11,014 69	-
68	Northampton & Amherst,	8,006 88	-	8,006 88	9,000 00	857 47	2,086 51	-
69	North End,	-	8,000 00	8,000 00	3,750 00	-	-	-
70	Norton & Taunton,	862 35d	-	862 35d	14,800 00	975 81	584 74	-
71	Norwood, Canton & Sharon,	1,716 64d	-	1,716 64d	-	9,776 58	592 45	-
72	Old Colony,	687,527 00	97,833 15	785,360 15	244,057 14	82,201 08	143,541 66	$72,419 72
73	Pittsfield Electric,	44,279 52	100 00	44,379 52	8,150 00	1,684 03	7,496 78	-
74	Plymouth, Carver & Wareham,	-	-	-	-	-	-	-
75	Plymouth & Sandwich,	2,280 71	-	2,280 71	-	750 60	573 03	-
76	Providence & Fall River,	10,231 64	-	10,231 64	8,250 00	3,326 50	2,422 90	-
77	Shelburne Falls & Colrain,	5,813 75	-	5,813 75	3,000 00	312 42	234 01	-
78	Somerville,	-	9,180 00	9,180 00	-	-	-	-
79	Southbridge & Sturbridge,	9,711 30	58 80	9,770 10	3,000 00	1,270 51	3,373 68	-
80	South Middlesex,	11,016 86	-	11,016 86	5,000 00	356 41	2,191 36	-
81	Springfield,	268,713 66	-	268,713 66	55,000 00	14,829 96	68,727 12	-
82	Springfield & Eastern,	32,248 07	823 55	33,071 62	16,500 00	2,690 90	7,098 00	-
83	Templeton,	8,755 89	-	8,755 89	-	20,833 74	402 17	-
84	Union,	126,959 04	-	126,959 04	20,000 00	5,213 94	23,774 99	-
85	Uxbridge & Blackstone,	10,434 46	-	10,434 46	4,000 00	1,725 00	1,418 83	-
86	Waltham,	13,512 91d	-	13,512 91d	-	10,051 30	36 02	-
87	Warren, Brookfield & Spencer,	22,076 20	-	22,076 20	6,250 00	3,517 29	2,434 74	-
88	Webster & Dudley,	-	19,779 86	19,779 86	1,500 00	-	1,071 71	14,491 51
	Webster & Dudley and Worcester & Webster (lessee),	23,892 57	2,179 16	26,071 73	-	-	-	19,779 86
89	Wellesley & Boston,	2,595 47	-	2,595 47	-	459 25	986 64	-
90	Westborough & Hopkinton,	956 97	-	956 97	2,000 00	297 50	463 49	-

d Deficit.

Tabulated Statements from Reports of Street Railway Companies — Continued.

	RAILWAY COMPANIES.	EXHIBIT FOR THE YEAR ENDING SEPTEMBER 30, 1904 — Continued.						
		50. — Net Earnings from Operation.	**51.** — All other Income.	**52.** — Total Income above Operating Expenses.	**53.** — Interest on Funded Debt.	**54.** — Interest and Discount on Unfunded Debt.	**55.** — Taxes.	**56.** — Rentals of Leased Railways.
91	West End, ...	–	$1,192,553 99	$1,192,553 99	–	–	–	–
92	Winnisimmet, ...	–	3,000 00	3,000 00	–	–	–	–
93	Woonsocket (of Rhode Island), .	$17,273 55	–	17,273 55	$8,500 00	$5,926 31	$7,875 75	–
94	Worcester & Blackstone Valley, .	24,565 25	–	24,565 25	–	20,402 07	3,521 34	–
95	Worcester Consolidated, . . .	523,285 98	–	523,285 98	49,950 00	99,607 92	103,028 96	$12,750 00
96	Worcester & Holden, ...	11,871 71	–	11,871 71	5,000 00	398 00	427 78	–
97	Worcester, Roch. & Charl. Depot,	–	900 00	900 00	900 00	–	–	–
98	Worcester & Shrewsbury R.R., .	–	3,750 00	3,750 00	1,100 00	–	–	–
99	Worcester & Shrewsbury St. R'y,	–	1,000 00	1,000 00	–	–	–	–
100	Worcester & Southbridge, . . .	30,689 00	18,610 96	49,299 96	20,739 80	16,112 89	5,878 90	7,884 16
101	Worcester & Webster, . . .	–	14,491 51	14,491 51	7,500 00	–	3,043 26	–
102	Woronoco, ...	21,444 47	1,250 00	22,694 47	3,750 00	1,948 17	4,150 19	–
	Totals, ...	$7,809,955 21	$1,552,088 27	$9,362,043 48	$1,985,224 47	$685,764 55	$1,761,082 65	$1,486,385 11

Tabulated Statements from Reports of Street Railway Companies — Continued.

	RAILWAY COMPANIES.	EXHIBIT FOR THE YEAR ENDING SEPTEMBER 30, 1904 — Continued.						
		57. — Payments to Sinking Funds, etc.	**58.** — Other Deductions from Income.	**59.** — Total Charges on Income.	**60.** — Net Divisible Income.	**61.** — Dividends Declared.	**62.** — Percentage of Dividend Declared.	**63.** — Surplus for the Year.
1	Amesbury & Hampton,	–	–	$5,000 00	$4,000 00	–	–	$4,000 00
	Amesbury & Hampton (lessee),	–	–	9,564 87	11,113 27*d*	–	–	–
2	Amherst & Sunderland,	–	–	6,737 34	3,554 54*d*	–	–	–
3	Athol & Orange,	–	–	5,666 66	8,539 24	$5,960 00	8	2,579 24
4	Berkshire,	–	$5,636 05	67,865 16	26,508 19	–	–	26,508 19
5	Blue Hill,	–	–	19,584 64	6,358 78*d*	–	–	–
6	Boston & Chelsea,	–	–	–	7,260 00	7,260 00	6	–
7	Boston Elevated,	–	197,206 26	2,975,268 00	829,772 71	798,000 00	6	31,772 71
8	Boston & Northern,	–	25,329 56	935,953 42	188,880 47	241,500 00	2.5	–
9	Boston & Revere Electric,	–	–	–	2,500 00	2,500 00	5	–
10	Boston & Worcester,	–	–	84,510 61	91,369 53	46,944 00	3 [1]	44,425 53
11	Bristol County,	–	–	12,561 75	32,742 71*d*	–	–	–
	Bristol County (receivers),	–	–	5,604 62	2,277 24	–	–	2,277 24
12	Bristol & Norfolk,	–	11 98	5,046 12	4,612 80*d*	–	–	–
13	Brockton & Plymouth,	–	7,387 71	35,511 97	7,955 15	–	–	7,955 15
14	Citizens' Electric,	–	1,287 50	20,553 91	17,464 09	13,200 00	5.5	4,264 09
15	Commonwealth Avenue,	–	–	5,114 17	7,714 61*d*	–	–	–

[1] On $1,564,800 of capital stock. *d* Deficit.

Tabulated Statements from Reports of Street Railway Companies — Continued.

	RAILWAY COMPANIES.	Exhibit for the Year ending September 30, 1904 — Continued.						
		57. — Payments to Sinking Funds, etc.	**58.** — Other Deductions from Income.	**59.** — Total Charges on Income.	**60.** — Net Divisible Income.	**61.** — Dividends Declared.	**62.** — Percentage of Dividend Declared.	**63.** — Surplus for the Year.
16	Concord & Boston,	–	$247 72	$2,551 05	$710 51*d*	–	–	–
17	Concord, Maynard & Hudson,	–	–	17,763 28	7,280 30*d*	–	–	–
18	Conway Electric,	–	–	3,729 09	146 56	–	–	$146 56
19	Cottage City & Edgartown Traction,	–	–	357 78	346 43	–	–	346 43
20	Dartmouth & Westport,	$1,500 00	2,114 91	15,206 58	38,399 06	$12,000 00	8	26,399 06
21	East Middlesex,	–	–	–	30,033 25	29,770 00	10	263 25
22	East Taunton,	–	4,612 66	9,029 81	3,406 61	5,500 00	5	–
23	Essex County,	–	–	–	–	–	–	–
24	Fitchburg & Leominster,	–	24,039 69	66,755 47	27,492 26	21,000 00	6	6,492 26
25	Fram., Southboro' & Marlboro',	–	–	1,844 32	636 31*d*	–	–	–
26	Framingham Union,	–	–	1,761 06	1,186 63	–	–	1,186 63
27	Gardner, Westminster & Fitchburg,	–	1,243 03	15,061 01	7,455 32	–	–	7,455 32
28	Georgetown, Rowley & Ipswich,	–	–	13,443 43	9,842 52*d*	–	–	–
29	Greenfield, Deerfield & Northamp.,	–	19,264 78	28,081 71	8,130 48*d*	–	–	–
30	Greenfield & Turner's Falls,	–	2,783 38	12,416 38	6,848 70	6,500 00	5	348 70
31	Hampshire,	–	2,544 00	3,125 89	3,461 87	–	–	3,461 87
32	Hampshire & Worcester,	–	2,026 51	13,319 67	25,690 81*d*	–	–	–
33	Hartford & Worcester,	–	–	–	–	–	–	–
34	Haverhill & Amesbury,	–	–	37,616 35	2,175 03*d*	–	–	–
35	Haverhill, Danvers & Ipswich,	–	–	–	–	–	–	–

36	Haverhill, Georgetown & Danvers,	-	-	5,196 48	1,832 29	-	-	1,832 29
37	Haverhill & Plaistow,	-	-	1,500 00	1,200 00	-	-	1,200 00
	Haverhill & Plaistow (lessee),	-	-	3,020 22	1,399 86*d*	-	-	-
38	Haverhill & Southern New Hamp.,	-	-	4,955 20	3,167 20*d*	-	-	-
39	Holyoke,	-	587 76	70,057 60	47,646 11	56,000 00	8	-
40	Hoosac Valley,	-	5,157 65	21,596 51	23,319 57	24,000 00	6	-
41	Horse Neck Beach,	-	-	-	-	-	-	-
42	Interstate Consolidated,	-	-	8,216 92	18,838 79	30,250 00	11	-
43	Lawrence & Methuen,	-	-	7,807 17	7,339 73*d*	-	-	-
44	Leominster, Shirley & Ayer,	-	-	-	2,584 67	-	-	2,584 67
45	Lexington & Boston,	-	-	46,997 88	9,753 67*d*	5,250 00	1	-
46	Linwood,	-	-	477 04	1,306 38	720 00	6	586 38
47	Lowell, Acton & Maynard,	-	-	-	520 08*d*	-	-	-
48	Lowell & Boston,	-	-	8,497 36	20,134 84*d*	-	-	-
	Lowell & Boston (receivers),	-	-	2,092 42	5,471 71*d*	-	-	-
49	Lowell & Fitchburg,	-	-	-	-	-	-	-
50	Lowell & Pelham,	-	-	2,455 91	568 42*d*	-	-	-
51	Marlborough & Framingham,	-	-	76 34	622 98*d*	-	-	-
52	Marlborough & Westborough,	-	2,058 88	14,698 21	4,916 43*d*	-	-	-
53	Martha's Vineyard,	-	-	-	-	-	-	-
54	Medfield & Medway,	-	-	7,444 62	3,498 82*d*	-	-	-
55	Middleboro', Wareham & Buz. Bay,	-	-	-	791 33*d*	-	-	-
	Middleboro', Wareham & Buz. Bay (receivers),	-	-	4,313 30	6,770 35	-	-	6,770 35
56	Milford, Attleboro' & Woonsocket,	-	-	16,712 58	4,256 29	-	-	4,256 29
57	Milford & Uxbridge,	-	1,900 63	34,605 40	128 72	6,600 00	1.5	-
58	Mount Tom,	-	-	-	6,035 05	6,000 00	6	35 05
59	Natick & Cochituate,	-	-	11,070 17	1,345 95	2,000 00	2	-
60	Natick & Needham,	-	-	2,500 00	2,451 79*d*	-	-	-

d Deficit.

Tabulated Statements from Reports of Street Railway Companies — Continued.

	RAILWAY COMPANIES.	EXHIBIT FOR THE YEAR ENDING SEPTEMBER 30, 1904 — Continued.						
		57. — Payments to Sinking Funds, etc.	**58.** — Other Deductions from Income.	**59.** — Total Charges on Income.	**60.** — Net Divisible Income.	**61.** — Dividends Declared.	**62.** — Percentage of Dividend Declared.	**63.** — Surplus for the Year.
61	New Bedford & Onset,	–	–	$23,960 56	$3,358 57	–	–	$3,358 57
62	Newton,	–	–	66,832 94	10,734 15	$20,740 00	4 [1]	–
63	Newton & Boston,	–	–	30,340 52	27,941 00*d*	–	–	–
64	Newtonville & Watertown,	–	$450 00	4,468 47	3,668 03	3,600 00	7.2	68 03
65	Norfolk & Bristol,	–	–	12,222 12	17,125 96*d*	–	–	–
66	Norfolk Western,	–	–	2,801 17	2,455 94*d*	–	–	–
	Norfolk Western (receiver),	–	–	11,994 82	12,395 00*d*	–	–	–
67	Northampton,	–	–	30,344 54	8,921 06	18,000 00	6	–
68	Northampton & Amherst,	–	–	11,943 98	3,937 10*d*	–	–	–
69	North End,	–	62 00	3,812 00	4,188 00	4,125 00	3.75	63 00
70	Norton & Taunton,	–	–	16,360 55	17,222 90*d*	–	–	–
71	Norwood, Canton & Sharon,	–	–	10,369 03	12,085 67*d*	–	–	–
72	Old Colony,	–	22,098 50	564,318 10	221,042 05	204,378 00	3	16,664 05
73	Pittsfield Electric,	$7,697 90	4,399 66	29,428 37	14,951 15	12,000 00	6	2,951 15
74	Plymouth, Carver & Wareham,	–	–	–	–	–	–	–
75	Plymouth & Sandwich,	–	–	1,323 63	957 08	–	–	957 08
76	Providence & Fall River,	–	–	13,999 40	3,767 76*d*	–	–	–
77	Shelburne Falls & Colrain,	–	–	3,546 43	2,267 32	500 00	1	1,767 32
78	Somerville,	–	–	–	9,180 00	9,180 00	6	–
79	Southbridge & Sturbridge,	–	–	7,644 19	2,125 91	–	–	2,125 91
80	South Middlesex,	–	–	7,547 77	3,469 09	–	–	3,469 09

81	Springfield,	–	–	138,557 08	130,156 58	156,672 00	8	–
82	Springfield & Eastern,	–	3,097 56	29,386 46	3,685 16	–	–	3,685 16
83	Templeton,	–	–	21,235 91	12,480 02*d*	–	–	–
84	Union,	–	–	48,988 93	77,970 11	72,000 00	8	5,970 11
85	Uxbridge & Blackstone,	–	–	7,143 83	3,290 63	3,200 00	4	90 63
86	Waltham,	–	–	10,087 32	23,600 23*d*	–	–	–
87	Warren, Brookfield & Spencer,	–	2,757 19	14,959 22	7,116 98	–	–	7,116 98
88	Webster & Dudley,	–	216 64	17,279 86	2,500 00	2,500 00	5	–
	Webster & Dudley and Worcester & Webster (lessee),	–	–	19,779 86	6,291 87	–	–	6,291 87
89	Wellesley & Boston,	–	–	1,445 89	1,149 58	–	–	1,149 58
90	Westborough & Hopkinton,	–	3 89	2,764 88	1,807 91*d*	–	–	–
91	West End,	–	7,137 89	7,137 89	1,185,416 10	1,184,997 50	7 and 8 [2]	418 60
92	Winnisimmet,	–	–	–	3,000 00	3,000 00	6	–
93	Woonsocket (of Rhode Island),	–	–	22,302 06	5,028 51*d*	–	–	–
94	Worcester & Blackstone Valley,	–	–	23,923 41	641 84	–	–	641 84
95	Worcester Consolidated,	–	79,477 16	344,814 04	178,471 94	177,500 00	5	971 94
96	Worcester & Holden,	–	4,307 61	10,133 39	1,738 32	–	–	1,738 32
97	Worcester, Roch. & Charl. Depot,	–	–	900 00	–	–	–	–
98	Worcester & Shrewsbury R.R.,	–	–	1,100 00	2,650 00	2,649 74	7.22	26
99	Worcester & Shrewsbury St. R'y,	–	–	–	1,000 00	1,000 00	5	–
100	Worcester & Southbridge,	–	1,053 37	51,669 12	2,369 16*d*	–	–	–
101	Worcester & Webster,	3,000 00	948 25	14,491 51	–	–	–	–
102	Woronoco,	–	1,824 86	11,673 22	11,021 25	17,500 00	7	–
	Totals,	$12,197 90	$433,275 24	$6,363,929 92	$2,998,113 56	$3,214,496 24	4.69	$246,646 75

[1] Two per cent on $315,000 and two per cent on $722,000 of capital stock. [2] Eight per cent on preferred and seven per cent on common stock. *d* Deficit.

Tabulated Statements from Reports of Street Railway Companies — Continued.

	RAILWAY COMPANIES.	EXHIBIT FOR THE YEAR ENDING SEPTEMBER 30, 1904 — Continued.						
		64. — Deficit for the Year.	**65.** — Surplus Sept. 30, 1903.	**66.** — Deficit Sept. 30, 1903.	**67.** — Credits during Year.	**68.** — Debits during Year.	**69.** — Surplus Sept. 30, 1904.	**70.** — Deficit Sept. 30, 1904.
1	Amesbury & Hampton,	–	$10,034 95	–	–	–	$14,034 95	–
	Amesbury & Hampton (lessee),	$11,113 27	–	–	$11,113 27	–	–	–
2	Amherst & Sunderland,	3,554 54	–	$4,160 24	–	$96 00	–	$7,810 78
3	Athol & Orange,	–	20,245 07	–	–	–	22,824 31	–
4	Berkshire,	–	45,939 52	–	–	–	72,447 71	–
5	Blue Hill,	6,358 78	–	22,744 05	–	–	–	29,102 83
6	Boston & Chelsea,	–	–	–	–	–	–	–
7	Boston Elevated,	–	2,327,687 94	–	–	–	2,359,460 65	–
8	Boston & Northern,	52,619 53	453,422 03	–	–	345,089 53	55,712 97	–
9	Boston & Revere Electric,	–	–	11,363 18	–	–	–	11,363 18
10	Boston & Worcester,	–	42,580 77	–	23,461 10[1]	53,201 07[2]	57,266 33	–
11	Bristol County,	32,742 71	2,812 48	–	–	50,476 86	–	80,407 09
	Bristol County (receivers),	–	–	–	–	–	2,277 24	–
12	Bristol & Norfolk,	4,612 80	–	835 61	–	–	–	5,448 41
13	Brockton & Plymouth,	–	–	2,066 76	–	–	5,888 39	–
14	Citizens' Electric,	–	31,978 27	–	–	12,077 03	24,165 33	–
15	Commonwealth Avenue,	7,714 61	–	5,715 46	13,430 07	–	–	–
16	Concord & Boston,	710 51	–	2,824 25	–	6,260 45	–	9,795 21
17	Concord, Maynard & Hudson,	7,280 30	9,705 52	–	–	–	2,425 22	–
18	Conway Electric,	–	–	9,165 31	8,000 00	–	–	1,018 75
19	Cottage City & Edgartown Traction,	–	–	404 60	–	–	–	58 17
20	Dartmouth & Westport,	–	24,397 24	–	–	816 66	49,979 64	–

21	East Middlesex,	-	-	11,001 68	-	-	-	10,738 43
22	East Taunton,	2,093 39	18,049 68	-	-	-	15,956 29	-
23	Essex County,	-	-	-	-	-	-	-
24	Fitchburg & Leominster,	-	21,996 54	-	-	13,457 94	15,030 86	-
25	Fram., Southboro' & Marlboro',	636 31	8,548 99	-	-	7,912 68	-	-
26	Framingham Union,	-	32,740 78	-	-	33,927 41	-	-
27	Gardner, Westminster & Fitchburg,	-	-	10,702 88	-	2,564 23	-	5,811 79
28	Georgetown, Rowley & Ipswich,	9,842 52	5,705 70	-	-	-	-	4,136 82
29	Greenfield, Deerfield & Northamp.,	8,130 48	6,395 88	-	-	-	-	1,734 60
30	Greenfield & Turner's Falls,	-	9,831 02	-	5,000 00	1,326 72	13,853 00	-
31	Hampshire,	-	1,875 54	-	-	-	5,337 41	-
32	Hampshire & Worcester,	25,690 81	2,474 53	-	-	-	-	23,216 28
33	Hartford & Worcester,	-	-	-	-	-	-	-
34[1]	Haverhill & Amesbury,	2,175 03	-	22,563 58	-	8,416 78	-	33,155 39
35	Haverhill, Danvers & Ipswich,	-	-	-	-	-	-	-
36	Haverhill, Georgetown & Danvers,	-	11,713 61	-	-	-	13,545 90	-
37	Haverhill & Plaistow,	-	1,950 00	-	-	-	3,150 00	-
	Haverhill & Plaistow (lessee),	1,399 86	-	-	1,399 86	-	-	-
38	Haverhill & Southern New Hamp.,	3,167 20	-	4,600 78	-	-	-	7,767 98
39	Holyoke,	8,353 89	73,321 24	-	-	-	64,967 35	-
40	Hoosac Valley,	680 43	47,789 94	-	-	3,333 34	43,776 17	-
41	Horse Neck Beach,	-	-	-	-	-	-	-
42	Interstate Consolidated,	11,411 21	44,120 13	-	-	-	32,708 92	-
43	Lawrence & Methuen,	7,339 73	1,780 41	-	-	-	-	5,559 32
44	Leominster, Shirley & Ayer,	-	-	-	-	-	2,584 67	-
45	Lexington & Boston,	15,003 67	17,108 45	-	-	-	2,104 78	-

[1] Contribution from stockholders.

[2] Paid on account of accidents.

Tabulated Statements from Reports of Street Railway Companies — Continued.

	RAILWAY COMPANIES.	EXHIBIT FOR THE YEAR ENDING SEPTEMBER 30, 1904 — Continued.						
		64. — Deficit for the Year.	**65.** — Surplus Sept. 30, 1903.	**66.** — Deficit Sept. 30, 1903.	**67.** — Credits during Year.	**68.** — Debits during Year.	**69.** — Surplus Sept. 30, 1904.	**70.** — Deficit Sept. 30, 1904.
46	Linwood,	-	$1,892 86	-	-	-	$2,479 24	-
47	Lowell, Acton & Maynard,	$520 08	-	-	-	-	-	$520 08
48	Lowell & Boston,	20,134 84	-	$31,358 69	-	-	-	51,493 53
48	Lowell & Boston (receivers),	5,471 71	-	-	-	-	-	5,471 71
49	Lowell & Fitchburg,	-	-	-	-	-	-	-
50	Lowell & Pelham,	568 42	-	1,668 47	-	-	-	2,236 89
51	Marlborough & Framingham,	622 98	414 53	-	$2,192 03	$1,983 58	-	-
52	Marlborough & Westborough,	4,916 43	2,016 90	-	-	-	-	2,899 53
53	Martha's Vineyard,	-	532 03	-	-	-	532 03	-
54	Medfield & Medway,	3,498 82	-	3,706 53	-	-	-	7,205 35
55	Middleboro', Wareham & Buz. Bay,	791 33	7,356 58	-	-	10,506 70	-	3,941 45
55	Middleboro', Wareham & Buz. Bay (receivers),	-	-	-	-	-	6,770 35	-
56	Milford, Attleboro' & Woonsocket,	-	12,939 90	-	-	-	17,196 19	-
57	Milford & Uxbridge,	6,471 28	1,126 89	-	95 22	-	-	5,249 17
58	Mount Tom,	-	700 93	-	-	-	735 98	-
59	Natick & Cochituate,	654 05	13,967 90	-	157 32	-	13,471 17	-
60	Natick & Needham,	2,451 79	500 00	-	-	500 00	-	2,451 79
61	New Bedford & Onset,	-	23,500 72	-	-	10 00	26,849 29	-
62	Newton,	10,005 85	30,922 38	-	37 227 42	13,430 07	44,713 88	-
63	Newton & Boston,	27,941 00	-	135,286 53	-	-	-	163,227 53
64	Newtonville & Watertown,	-	1,531 60	-	-	-	1 599 63	-
65	Norfolk & Bristol,	17,125 96	-	13,036 42	-	-	-	30,162 38

66	Norfolk Western,	2,455 94	–	30,470 81	–	–	–	32,926 75
	Norfolk Western (receiver),	12,395 00	–	–	–	–	–	12,395 00
67	Northampton,	9,078 94	27,564 45	–	–	–	18,485 51	–
68	Northampton & Amherst,	3,937 10	584 53	–	–	–	–	3,352 57
69	North End,	–	–	19,024 42	–	–	–	18,961 42
70	Norton & Taunton,	17,222 90	–	27,334 51	1,556 72	–	–	43,000 69
71	Norwood, Canton & Sharon,	12,085 67	–	30,668 37	–	–	–	42,754 04
72	Old Colony,	–	239,308 30	–	–	246,835 82	9,136 53	–
73	Pittsfield Electric,	–	38,060 24	–	300 00	–	41,311 39	–
74	Plymouth, Carver & Wareham,	–	–	–	–	–	–	–
75	Plymouth & Sandwich,	–	3,010 79	–	–	–	3,967 87	–
76	Providence & Fall River,	3,767 76	–	2,531 31	–	4,176 51	–	10,475 58
77	Shelburne Falls & Colrain,	–	4,270 65	–	–	–	6,037 97	–
78	Somerville,	–	–	–	–	–	–	–
79	Southbridge & Sturbridge,	–	16,385 90	–	–	1,921 71	16,590 10	–
80	South Middlesex,	–	–	10,151 74	–	10,269 18	–	16,951 83
81	Springfield,	26,515 42	197,476 51	–	–	24,750 00	146,211 09	–
82	Springfield & Eastern,	–	13,088 04	–	–	8 49	16,764 71	–
83	Templeton,	12,480 02	–	30,292 00	–	–	–	42,772 02
84	Union,	–	175,706 59	–	592 29	1,200 00	181,068 99	–
85	Uxbridge & Blackstone,	–	7,819 20	–	–	–	7,909 83	–
86	Waltham,	23,600 23	–	8,019 71	–	–	–	31,619 94
87	Warren, Brookfield & Spencer,	–	20,973 10	–	–	2,000 00	26,090 08	–
88	Webster & Dudley,	–	–	22,051 28	–	–	–	22,051 28
	Webster & Dudley and Worcester & Webster (lessee),	–	–	–	–	6,291 87	–	–
89	Wellesley & Boston,	–	5,840 71	–	–	6,990 29	–	–
90	Westborough & Hopkinton,	1,807 91	–	734 64	–	–	–	2,542 55

Tabulated Statements from Reports of Street Railway Companies — Continued.

	RAILWAY COMPANIES.	EXHIBIT FOR THE YEAR ENDING SEPTEMBER 30, 1904 — Concluded.						
		64. — Deficit for the Year.	**65.** — Surplus Sept. 30, 1903.	**66.** — Deficit Sept. 30, 1903.	**67.** — Credits during Year.	**68.** — Debits during Year.	**69.** — Surplus Sept. 30, 1904.	**70.** — Deficit Sept. 30, 1904.
91	West End, ...	-	$654,609 98	-	$193,722 61	-	$848,751 19	-
92	Winnisimmet, ...	-	123 35	-	1 50	-	124 85	-
93	Woonsocket (of Rhode Island), .	$5,028 51	-	$32,778 71	-	-	-	$37,807 22
94	Worcester & Blackstone Valley, .	-	20,753 58	-	-	-	21,395 42	-
95	Worcester Consolidated, . . .	-	346,457 21	-	-	$10,414 13	337,015 02	-
96	Worcester & Holden, ...	-	6,710 20	-	-	-	8,448 52	-
97	Worcester, Roch. & Charl. Depot,	-	-	-	-	56,082 78	-	56,082 78
98	Worcester & Shrewsbury R.R., .	-	64,692 25	-	-	-	64,692 51	-
99	Worcester & Shrewsbury St. R'y, .	-	22 05	-	-	-	22 05	-
100	Worcester & Southbridge, . .	2,369 16	-	-	-	643,204 82	-	645,573 98
101	Worcester & Webster, ...	-	-	69,017 64	-	619 89	-	69,637 53
102	Woronoco, ...	6,478 75	12,367 02	-	-	-	5,888 27	-
	Totals, ...	$463,029 43	$5,227,434 10	$576,280 16	$298,249 41	$1,580,152 54	$4,753,757 75	$1,600,889 62

Tabulated Statements from Reports of Street Railway Companies — Continued.

	RAILWAY COMPANIES.	**71.** — Railway Line Owned.	**72.** — Second Main Track Owned.	**73.** — Total Main Track Owned.	**74.** — Sidings, Switches, etc., Owned.	**75.** — Total Track Owned.	**76.** — Leased Track and Trackage Rights.	**77.** — Total Main Track Operated.
		Description of Railway (Length in Miles).						
1	Amesbury & Hampton,	8.342	-	8.342	.409	8.751	-	-
	Amesbury & Hampton (lessee),	-	-	-	-	-	8.342	8.342
2	Amherst & Sunderland,	15.711	-	15.711	.863	16.574	-	15.711
3	Athol & Orange,	6.880	-	6.880	.440	7.320	-	6.880
4	Berkshire,	40.813	-	40.813	1.421	42.234	-	40.813
5	Blue Hill,	13.770	2.630	16.400	1.110	17.510	.180	16.580
6	Boston & Chelsea,	4.116	-	4.116	.038	4.154	-	-
7	Boston Elevated,	9.054	8.501	17.555	6.586	24.141	378.981	393.360
8	Boston & Northern,	351.293	67.420	418.713	16.973	435.686	52.754	471.467
9	Boston & Revere Electric,	1.856	1.856	3.712	.100	3.812	-	-
10	Boston & Worcester,	47.406	25.690	73.096	2.143	75.239	.524	73.620
11	Bristol County,	15.988	.470	16.458	1.439	17.897	.688	17.146
	Bristol County (receivers),							
12	Bristol & Norfolk,	10.150	-	10.150	.038	10.188	.378	5.948
13	Brockton & Plymouth,	22.091	-	22.091	1.706	23.797	-	22.091
14	Citizens' Electric,	21.862	-	21.862	1.216	23.078	.569	22.431
15	Commonwealth Avenue,*	6.946	5.553	12.499	.992	13.491	.550	13.049
16	Concord & Boston,	2.449	-	2.449	.169	2.618	-	-
17	Concord, Maynard & Hudson,	12.470	-	12.470	.600	13.070	.350	12.820
18	Conway Electric,	5.910	-	5.910	.520	6.430	-	5.910
19	Cottage City & Edgartown Traction,	5.350	-	5.350	.500	5.850	1.100	6.450
20	Dartmouth & Westport,	9.250	-	9.250	.486	9.736	11.793	21.043

Tabulated Statements from Reports of Street Railway Companies — Continued.

	RAILWAY COMPANIES.	Description of Railway (Length in Miles) — Continued.						
		71. — Railway Line Owned.	**72.** — Second Main Track Owned.	**73.** — Total Main Track Owned.	**74.** — Sidings, Switches, etc., Owned.	**75.** — Total Track Owned.	**76.** — Leased Track and Trackage Rights.	**77.** — Total Main Track Operated.
21	East Middlesex, ...	16.009	2.582	18.591	.803	19.394	–	–
22	East Taunton, ...	10.524	–	10.524	.176	10.700	.724	11.248
23	Essex County, ...	–	–	–	–	–	–	–
24	Fitchburg & Leominster, . . .	25.100	5.345	30 445	1.669	32.114	–	30.445
25	Fram., Southboro' & Marlboro',* .	14.775	–	14.775	.850	15.625	.084	14.859
26	Framingham Union,*	6.358	–	6.358	.478	6.836	.143	6.501
27	Gardner, Westminster & Fitchburg,	15.680	–	15.680	.370	16.050	–	15.680
28	Georgetown, Rowley & Ipswich, .	17.923	–	17.923	.260	18.183	.605	18.528
29	Greenfield, Deerfield & Northamp.,	14.085	–	14.085	.625	14.710	8.077	22.162
30	Greenfield & Turner's Falls, . .	17.180	–	17.180	.501	17.681	–	17.180
31	Hampshire, ...	4.340	–	4.340	.230	4.570	–	4.340
32	Hampshire & Worcester, . . .	11.710	–	11.710	.410	12.120	–	11.710
33	Hartford & Worcester, . . .	–	–	–	–	–	–	–
34	Haverhill & Amesbury, . . .	26.606	–	26.606	1.855	28.461	1.053	27.659
35	Haverhill, Danvers & Ipswich, .	–	–	–	–	–	–	–
36	Haverhill, Georgetown & Danvers,	5.871	–	5.871	.149	6.020	.487	6.358
37	Haverhill & Plaistow, . . .	2.682	–	2.682	.076	2.758	–	–
	Haverhill & Plaistow (lessee), .	–	–	–	–	–	2.682	2.682
38	Haverhill & Southern New Hamp.,	7.892	–	7.892	.296	8.188	.050	7.942
39	Holyoke, ...	35.650	7.210	42.860	3.160	46.020	.900	43.760
40	Hoosac Valley, ...	26.227	–	26.227	.921	27.148	–	26.227

41	Horse Neck Beach,	6.000	–	6.000	–	6.000	–	–
42	Interstate Consolidated,	20.554	–	20.554	1.100	21.654	–	20.554
43	Lawrence & Methuen,	12.518	–	12.518	.437	12.955	.225	12.743
44	Leominster, Shirley & Ayer,	8.567	–	8.567	–	8.567	–	8.567
45	Lexington & Boston,	27.205	2.460	29.665	2.691	32 356	3.106	32.771
46	Linwood,	1.741	–	1.741	.160	1.901 [1]	–	1.741
47	Lowell, Acton & Maynard,	2.000	–	2.000	–	2.000	–	1.963
48	Lowell & Boston, Lowell & Boston (receivers),	9.125	.126	9.251	.498	9.749	.142	9.393
49	Lowell & Fitchburg,	–	–	–	–	–	–	–
50	Lowell & Pelham,	3.167	–	3.167	.151	3.318	–	3.167
51	Marlborough & Framingham,*	7.312	–	7.312	.489	7.801	.084	7.396
52	Marlborough & Westborough,	13.510	–	13.510	.350	13.860	–	13.510
53	Martha's Vineyard,	1.100	–	1.100	–	1.100	–	–
54	Medfield & Medway,	11.009	–	11.009	.241	11.250	–	11.009
55	Middleboro', Wareham & Buz. Bay, Middleboro', Wareham & Buz. Bay (receivers),	21.451	–	21.451	.813	22.264	7.289	28.740
56	Milford, Attleboro' & Woonsocket,	30.000	–	30.000	.520	30.520	–	30.000
57	Milford & Uxbridge,	33.689	.991	34.680	1.226	35.906	.025	34.705
58	Mount Tom,	.900	–	.900	.100	1.000	–	–
59	Natick & Cochituate,	17.204	.846	18.050	.750	18.800	.284	18.334
60	Natick & Needham,	5.774	–	5.774	.048	5.822	–	–
61	New Bedford & Onset,	16.136	3.654	19.790	2.067	21.857	–	19.790
62	Newton,	26.246	8.320	34.566	2.201	36.767	.871	35.437
63	Newton & Boston,	9.031	–	9.031	.755	9.786	3.964	12.995
64	Newtonville & Watertown,	4.308	–	4.308	.357	4.665	–	–
65	Norfolk & Bristol,	20.567	–	20.567	.478	21.045	.293	20.860

[1] Owned by private parties.

Tabulated Statements from Reports of Street Railway Companies — Continued.

	RAILWAY COMPANIES.	DESCRIPTION OF RAILWAY (LENGTH IN MILES) — Concluded.						
		71. — Railway Line Owned.	**72.** — Second Main Track Owned.	**73.** — Total Main Track Owned.	**74.** — Sidings, Switches, etc., Owned.	**75.** — Total Track Owned.	**76.** — Leased Track and Trackage Rights.	**77.** — Total Main Track Operated.
66	{Norfolk Western, ... / Norfolk Western (receiver), . . }	9.079	-	9.079	.371	9.450	-	9.079
67	Northampton, ...	24.369	-	24.369	1.893	26.262	-	24.369
68	Northampton & Amherst, . .	14.147	-	14.147	.766	14.913	-	14.147
69	North End, ...	4.995	-	4.995	.135	5.130	-	-
70	Norton & Taunton, ...	29.000	-	29.000	.830	29.830	.407	29.407
71	Norwood, Canton & Sharon, . .	6.042	-	6.042	.190	6.232	-	6.042
72	Old Colony, ...	313.536	34.358	347.894	16.291	364.185	18.926	349.536
73	Pittsfield Electric, ...	24.296	.749	25.045	.738	25.783	-	25.045
74	Plymouth, Carver & Wareham, .	-	-	-	-	-	-	-
75	Plymouth & Sandwich, . . .	6.146	-	6.146	.213	6.359	-	6.146
76	Providence & Fall River, . . .	11.983	-	11.983	.546	12.529	-	11.983
77	Shelburne Falls & Colrain, . .	6.530	-	6.530	.480	7.010	-	6.530
78	Somerville, ...	6.356	1.424	7.780	.253	8.033	-	-
79	Southbridge & Sturbridge, . .	7.590	-	7.590	.400	7.990	-	7.590
80	South Middlesex, ...	12.932	-	12.932	.896	13.828	-	12.932
81	Springfield, ...	64.914	22.103	87.017	6.729	93.746	-	87.017
82	Springfield & Eastern, . . .	28.374	-	28.374	2.178	30.552	-	28.374
83	Templeton, ...	17.873	-	17.873	-	17.873	-	17.873
84	Union, ...	24.499	4.349	28.848	1.619	30.467	.167	29.015
85	Uxbridge & Blackstone, . . .	7.330	-	7.330	.290	7.620	-	7.330

86	Waltham,	6.418	–	6.418	.052	6.470	1.595	7.131
87	Warren, Brookfield & Spencer,	19.607	–	19.607	.491	20.098	–	19.607
88	Webster & Dudley,	5.650	–	5.650	.187	5.837	–	–
	Webster & Dudley and Worcester & Webster (lessee),	–	–	–	–	–	22.394	22.394
89	Wellesley & Boston,*	4.690	–	4.690	.210	4.900	4.954	9.644
90	Westborough & Hopkinton,	6.360	–	6.360	.079	6.439	–	6.360
91	West End,	181.977	157.939	339.916	40.658	380.574	–	–
92	Winnisimmet,	1.043	1.016	2.059	.128	2.187	–	–
93	Woonsocket (of Rhode Island),	21.961	–	21.961	.863	22.824	–	21.961
94	Worcester & Blackstone Valley,	15.740	–	15.740	.620	16.360	1.500	17.240
95	Worcester Consolidated,	109.406	20.699	130.105	3.372	133.477	8.610	138.715
96	Worcester & Holden,	7.449	–	7.449	.580	8.029	2.130	9.579
97	Worcester, Roch. & Charl. Depot,	1.500	1.500	3.000	–	3.000	–	–
98	Worcester & Shrewsbury R.R.,	2.700	–	2.700	.550	3.250	–	–
99	Worcester & Shrewsbury St. R'y,	.425	–	.425	.034	.459	–	–
100	Worcester & Southbridge,	16.870	.260	17.130	2.590	19.720	3.000	20.130
101	Worcester & Webster,	14.880	–	14.880	.644	15.524	–	–
102	Woronoco,	15.793	.342	16.135	.793	16.928	–	16.135
	Totals,[1]	2,191.812	382.840	2,574.652	149.660	2,724.312	545.165	2,654.479

[1] Not including the companies marked *, these companies having been consolidated during the year.

Tabulated Statements from Reports of Street Railway Companies — Continued.

	RAILWAY COMPANIES.	Description of Equipment.						
		78. — Box Passenger Cars.	**79.** — Open Passenger Cars.	**80.** — Total Passenger Cars.	**81.** — Other Service Cars.	**82.** — Snow Plows.	**83.** — Other Vehicles.	**84.** — Electric Motors.
1	{Amesbury & Hampton,	–	–	–	–	–	–	–
	{Amesbury & Hampton (lessee),	2	9	11	–	1	–	22
2	Amherst & Sunderland,	5	8	13	6	1	–	36
3	Athol & Orange,	8	5	13	–	1	1	28
4	Berkshire,	19	14	33	1	4	5	126
5	Blue Hill,	12	16	28	11	2	1	80
6	Boston & Chelsea,	–	–	–	–	–	–	–
7	Boston Elevated,	1,818	1,547	3,365	50	305	1,103	4,765
8	Boston & Northern,	466	652	1,118	54	138	186	2,371
9	Boston & Revere Electric,	–	–	–	–	–	–	–
10	Boston & Worcester,	42	25	67	5	13	9	209
11	{Bristol County, {Bristol County (receivers),	9	11	20	2	2	–	72
12	Bristol & Norfolk,	4	2	6	–	1	1	12
13	Brockton & Plymouth,	10	16	26	2	3	3	69
14	Citizens' Electric,	14	25	39	2	3	5	58
15	Commonwealth Avenue,*	30	35	65	1	3	5	140
16	Concord & Boston,	–	–	–	–	–	–	–
17	Concord, Maynard & Hudson,	9	7	16	1	2	–	56
18	Conway Electric,	3	2	5	10	1	–	10
19	Cottage City & Edgartown Traction,	2	4	6	2	–	–	8
20	Dartmouth & Westport,	11	12	23	8	2	1	98

21	East Middlesex, ...	–	–	–	–	–	–	–
22	East Taunton, ...	2	4	6	–	–	1	14
23	Essex County, ...	–	–	–	–	–	–	–
24	Fitchburg & Leominster, . . .	24	32	56	5	5	23	120
25	Fram., Southboro' & Marlboro',* .	11	15	26	1	4	3	69
26	Framingham Union,*	7	8	15	1	2	2	27
27	Gardner, Westminster & Fitch., .	9	12	21	3	2	1	42
28	Georgetown, Rowley & Ipswich, .	8	9	17	–	2	2	34
29	Greenfield, Deerfield & Northamp.,	5	6	11	2	1	–	22
30	Greenfield & Turner's Falls, . .	12	8	20	2	1	3	39
31	Hampshire, ...	–	–	–	–	–	–	–
32	Hampshire & Worcester, . . .	4	8	12	–	1	3	28
33	Hartford & Worcester, . . .	–	–	–	–	–	–	–
34	Haverhill & Amesbury, . . .	20	40	60	4	8	10	64
35	Haverhill, Danvers & Ipswich, .	–	–	–	–	–	–	–
36	Haverhill, Georgetown & Danvers,	3	3	6	–	1	–	14
37	Haverhill & Plaistow, ...	–	–	–	–	–	–	–
	Haverhill & Plaistow (lessee), .	–	–	–	–	–	–	–
38	Haverhill & Southern New Hamp.,	5	6	11	–	1	–	44
39	Holyoke, ...	39	67	106	6	9	17	220
40	Hoosac Valley, ...	15	20	35	7	3	3	98
41	Horse Neck Beach, ...	–	–	–	–	–	–	–
42	Interstate Consolidated, . . .	–	–	–	–	–	–	–
43	Lawrence & Methuen, ...	5	7	12	–	2	–	48
44	Leominster, Shirley & Ayer, . .	–	–	–	–	–	–	4
45	Lexington & Boston, ...	30	40	70	2	6	9	204

Tabulated Statements from Reports of Street Railway Companies — Continued.

	RAILWAY COMPANIES.	DESCRIPTION OF EQUIPMENT — Continued.						
		78. — Box Passenger Cars.	**79.** — Open Passenger Cars.	**80.** — Total Passenger Cars.	**81.** — Other Service Cars.	**82.** — Snow Plows.	**83.** — Other Vehicles.	**84.** — Electric Motors.
46	Linwood, ...	4	–	4	–	–	–	12
47	Lowell, Acton & Maynard, . .	–	–	–	–	–	–	–
48	{Lowell & Boston, ... / Lowell & Boston (receivers), . . }	5	8	13	1	2	–	28
49	Lowell & Fitchburg, ...	–	–	–	–	–	–	–
50	Lowell & Pelham, ...	4	5	9	–	1	–	36
51	Marlborough & Framingham,* .	5	7	12	1	2	3	29
52	Marlborough & Westborough, . .	6	6	12	1	2	–	30
53	Martha's Vineyard, ...	–	–	–	–	–	–	–
54	Medfield & Medway, ...	5	3	8	–	2	–	10
55	{Middleboro', Wareham & Buz. Bay, / Middleboro', Wareham & Buz. Bay (receivers), ... }	8	17	25	4	4	1	60
56	Milford, Attleboro' & Woonsocket,	10	16	26	–	3	1	89
57	Milford & Uxbridge, ...	21	20	41	2	8	3	104
58	Mount Tom, ...	–	–	–	–	–	–	–
59	Natick & Cochituate, ...	12	16	28	2	3	4	60
60	Natick & Needham, ...	–	–	–	–	–	–	–
61	New Bedford & Onset, ...	6	12	18	2	2	1	80
62	Newton, ...	66	81	147	2	10	19	296
63	Newton & Boston, ...	6	10	16	1	3	7	40
64	Newtonville & Watertown, . .	–	–	–	–	–	–	–
65	Norfolk & Bristol, ...	5	14	19	2	–	1	44

No.	Railway							
66	Norfolk Western, ... Norfolk Western (receiver), . .	10	3	13	1	2	2	12
67	Northampton, ...	21	23	44	9	3	9	106
68	Northampton & Amherst, . . .	7	8	15	3	2	3	30
69	North End, ...	–	–	–	–	–	–	–
70	Norton & Taunton, ...	10	8	18	3	–	–	42
71	Norwood, Canton & Sharon, . .	4	–	4	–	–	–	8
72	Old Colony, ...	306	411	717	64	78	66	1,395
73	Pittsfield Electric, ...	16	18	34	1	3	4	100
74	Plymouth, Carver & Wareham, .	–	–	–	–	–	–	–
75	Plymouth & Sandwich, ...	2	2	4	–	–	–	8
76	Providence & Fall River, . . .	8	10	18	1	3	1	60
77	Shelburne Falls & Colrain, . .	3	2	5	8	1	–	6
78	Somerville, ...	–	–	–	–	–	–	–
79	Southbridge & Sturbridge, . .	6	5	11	1	1	–	20
80	South Middlesex, ...	13	8	21	1	2	3	38
81	Springfield, ...	109	116	225	18	24	11	626
82	Springfield & Eastern, ...	13	21	34	2	6	2	120
83	Templeton, ...	7	6	13	2	3	–	26
84	Union, ...	48	67	115	8	7	14	185
85	Uxbridge & Blackstone, . . .	3	6	9	1	1	–	14
86	Waltham, ...	–	6	6	–	–	–	–
87	Warren, Brookfield & Spencer, .	7	10	17	2	2	1	32
88	Webster & Dudley, ...	–	–	–	–	–	–	–
	Webster & Dudley and Worcester & Webster (lessee), ...	9	14	23	2	3	2	78
89	Wellesley & Boston,*	5	13	18	–	2	–	43
90	Westborough & Hopkinton, . .	2	–	2	–	–	–	4

Tabulated Statements from Reports of Street Railway Companies — Continued.

	RAILWAY COMPANIES.	DESCRIPTION OF EQUIPMENT — Concluded.						
		78. — Box Passenger Cars.	**79.** — Open Passenger Cars.	**80.** — Total Passenger Cars.	**81.** — Other Service Cars.	**82.** — Snow Plows.	**83.** — Other Vehicles.	**84.** — Electric Motors.
91	West End, ...	–	–	–	–	–	–	–
92	Winnisimmet, ...	–	–	–	–	–	–	–
93	Woonsocket (of Rhode Island), .	16	21	37	2	3	10	70
94	Worcester & Blackstone Valley, .	8	10	18	2	3	1	61
95	Worcester Consolidated, . . .	155	162	317	15	36	44	739
96	Worcester & Holden, ...	3	4	7	4	–	–	28
97	Worcester, Roch. & Charl. Depot,	–	–	–	–	–	–	–
98	Worcester & Shrewsbury R.R., .	–	–	–	–	–	–	–
99	Worcester & Shrewsbury St. R'y, .	–	–	–	–	–	–	–
100	Worcester & Southbridge, . .	9	20	29	22	4	–	98
101	Worcester & Webster, ...	–	–	–	–	–	–	–
102	Woronoco, ...	12	17	29	4	2	3	60
	Totals,[1]	3,580	3,803	7,383	378	750	1,600	13,870

[1] Not including the companies marked *, these companies having been consolidated during the year.

Tabulated Statements from Reports of Street Railway Companies — Continued.

	RAILWAY COMPANIES.	VOLUME OF TRAFFIC.				STOCKHOLDERS.		91. — Stock held in Massachusetts.
		85. — Total Passengers Carried.	86. — Average Number per Mile of Main Track Operated.	87. — Car Miles Run.	88. — Number of Employees.	89. — Total Number.	90. — In Massachusetts.	
1	Amesbury & Hampton,	–	–	–	–	6	5	$500 00
	Amesbury & Hampton (lessee),	531,827	63,753	159,748	16	–	–	–
2	Amherst & Sunderland,	574,124	36,543	269,557	20	123	122	119,900 00
3	Athol & Orange,	817,396	118,808	143,984	16	10	9	73,500 00
4	Berkshire,	3,878,770	95,038	917,391	116	141	127	906,000 00
5	Blue Hill,	1,453,169	87,646	356,472	60	60	57	292,500 00
6	Boston & Chelsea,	–	–	–	–	[illegible]0	76	97,550 00
7	Boston Elevated,	241,681,945	614,404	48,317,981	7,447	2,922	2,510	10,945,300 00
8	Boston & Northern,	75,647,925	160,452	14,800,129	2,677	26	25	9,186,300 00
9	Boston & Revere Electric,	–	–	–	–	17	13	35,100 00
10	Boston & Worcester,	7,668,686	104,166	1,659,089	230	16	15	1,564,800 00
11	Bristol County,	448,224	–	172,738	–	27	22	173,200 00
	Bristol County (receivers),	440,304	–	164,979	47	–	–	–
12	Bristol & Norfolk,	166,241	27,949	71,302	8	15	15	100,000 00
13	Brockton & Plymouth,	1,955,124	88,503	429,753	58	64	60	289,000 00
14	Citizens' Electric,	2,067,102	92,154	384,436	70	30	29	233,900 00
15	Commonwealth Avenue,*	323,072	–	106,943	57	8	8	292,000 00
16	Concord & Boston,	–	–	–	–	10	10	50,000 00
17	Concord, Maynard & Hudson,	1,042,968	81,355	316,869	32	94	94	175,000 00
18	Conway Electric,	58,349	9,873	30,488	5	81	77	30,850 00
19	Cottage City & Edgartown Traction,	105,446	16,348	16,495	10	10	10	60,000 00
20	Dartmouth & Westport,	2,652,093	126,032	387,485	50	74	65	77,700 00

Tabulated Statements from Reports of Street Railway Companies — Continued.

	RAILWAY COMPANIES.	VOLUME OF TRAFFIC — Continued.				STOCKHOLDERS — Continued.		91. — Stock held in Massachusetts.
		85. — Total Passengers Carried.	86. — Average Number per Mile of Main Track Operated.	87. — Car Miles Run.	88. — Number of Employees.	89. — Total Number.	90. — In Massachusetts.	
21	East Middlesex,	-	-	-	-	117	103	$263,300 00
22	East Taunton,	697,128	61,979	153,177	14	72	72	110,000 00
23	Essex County,	-	-	-	-	20	19	12,000 00
24	Fitchburg & Leominster,	4,096,715	134,561	851,202	100	106	102	344,600 00
25	Fram., Southboro' & Marlboro',*	160,318	-	62,192	55	6	6	185,000 00
26	Framingham Union,*	169,937	-	34,006	14	9	9	30,000 00
27	Gardner, Westminster & Fitchburg,	1,198,423	76,430	254,926	50	74	72	183,400 00
28	Georgetown, Rowley & Ipswich,	751,099	40,539	257,962	29	6	6	180,000 00
29	Greenfield, Deerfield & Northamp.,	1,021,967	46,113	271,490	20	71	66	151,800 00
30	Greenfield & Turner's Falls,	1,475,295	85,873	400,866	45	120	112	122,000 00
31	Hampshire,	168,262	38,770	68,402	6	37	37	60,000 00
32	Hampshire & Worcester,	546,204	46,644	186,628	30	99	94	97,800 00
33	Hartford & Worcester,	-	-	-	-	25	24	23,000 00
34	Haverhill & Amesbury,	2,223,133	80,376	490,884	60	18	17	145,000 00
35	Haverhill, Danvers & Ipswich,	-	-	-	-	16	15	4,480 00
36	Haverhill, Georgetown & Danvers,	602,931	94,830	148,866	11	6	6	60,000 00
37	Haverhill & Plaistow,	-	-	-	-	6	5	500 00
	Haverhill & Plaistow (lessee),	309,757	115,495	76,822	6	-	-	-
38	Haverhill & Southern New Hamp.,	876,748	110,394	246,963	17	6	5	500 00
39	Holyoke,	7,378,696	168,617	1,602,293	238	212	183	636,300 00
40	Hoosac Valley,	3,021,606	115,210	791,890	80	32	30	320,000 00

41	Horse Neck Beach, ...	–	–	–	–	55	52	21,510 00
42	Interstate Consolidated, . . .	2,993,682	145,650	637,596	128	5	1	55,000 00
43	Lawrence & Methuen, . . .	1,088,544	85,423	342,082	28	6	5	500 00
44	Leominster, Shirley & Ayer, . .	77,676	9,067	11,957	4	31	31	56,247 00
45	Lexington & Boston, ...	3,173,702	96,845	780,037	99	8	8	525,000 00
46	Linwood, ...	278,862	160,173	46,032	6	17	16	11,700 00
47	Lowell, Acton & Maynard, . .	100,539	51,217	43,394	4	–	–	–
48	{Lowell & Boston, ...	–	–	–	–	17	17	90,000 00
	{Lowell & Boston (receivers), . .	74,266	–	3,985	19	–	–	–
49	Lowell & Fitchburg, ...	–	–	–	–	15	15	24,000 00
50	Lowell & Pelham, ...	413,167	130,460	75,487	8	7	6	600 00
51	Marlborough & Framingham,* .	169,157	–	37,876	40	8	8	105,000 00
52	Marlborough & Westborough, . .	715,450	52,957	172,361	23	36	35	157,500 00
53	Martha's Vineyard, ...	–	–	–	–	10	10	9,167 50
54	Medfield & Medway, ...	392,704	35,671	116,684	18	13	13	100,000 00
55	{Middleboro', Wareham & Buz. Bay,	–	–	–	–	93	93	150,000 00
	{Middleboro', Wareham & Buzzard's Bay (receivers), ...	528,782	–	117,500	26	–	–	–
56	Milford, Attleboro' & Woonsocket,	1,558,528	51,951	553,100	45	65	65	315,000 00
57	Milford & Uxbridge, ...	2,749,065	79,212	676,136	100	123	19	86,700 00
58	Mount Tom, ...	–	–	–	–	98	86	87,800 00
59	Natick & Cochituate, ...	1,742,254	95,029	527,618	61	16	16	100,000 00
60	Natick & Needham, ...	–	–	–	–	11	11	50,000 00
61	New Bedford & Onset, . . .	1,074,981	54,319	223,891	47	182	180	494,000 00
62	Newton, ...	5,895,495	166,366	1,218,003	185	8	8	722,000 00
63	Newton & Boston, ...	1,404,020	108,043	372,495	57	8	8	200,000 00
64	Newtonville & Watertown, . .	–	–	–	–	19	19	50,000 00
65	Norfolk & Bristol, ...	1,002,613	48,064	320,925	47	16	15	194,000 00

Tabulated Statements from Reports of Street Railway Companies — Continued.

	RAILWAY COMPANIES.	VOLUME OF TRAFFIC — Concluded.				STOCKHOLDERS — Concluded.		91. — Stock held in Massachusetts.
		85. — Total Passengers Carried.	86. — Average Number per Mile of Main Track Operated.	87. — Car Miles Run.	88. — Number of Employees.	89. — Total Number.	90. — In Massachusetts.	
66	Norfolk Western,	114,780	-	35,685	-	37	37	$100,000 00
	Norfolk Western (receiver),	292,977	-	68,600	16	-	-	-
67	Northampton,	2,968,042	121,796	790,154	95	196	161	248,900 00
68	Northampton & Amherst,	1,195,558	84,509	324,684	38	73	69	88,900 00
69	North End,	-	-	-	-	26	26	110,000 00
70	Norton & Taunton,	1,007,962	34,276	373,781	40	72	71	257,000 00
71	Norwood, Canton & Sharon,	159,546	26,406	58,287	10	11	11	62,500 00
72	Old Colony,	47,518,472	135,947	8,737,971	1,744	37	36	6,470,100 00
73	Pittsfield Electric,	3,112,160	124,263	651,689	76	48	45	199,300 00
74	Plymouth, Carver & Wareham,	-	-	-	-	80	80	21,388 00
75	Plymouth & Sandwich,	78,296	12,739	38,284	4	31	28	28,700 00
76	Providence & Fall River,	1,108,980	92,546	259,003	30	34	32	155,000 00
77	Shelburne Falls & Colrain,	183,434	28,091	54,398	11	108	102	42,250 00
78	Somerville,	-	-	-	-	5	5	153,000 00
79	Southbridge & Sturbridge,	736,474	97,032	175,754	15	7	1	100 00
80	South Middlesex,	1,397,548	108,069	364,813	41	40	38	99,400 00
81	Springfield,	18,930,360	217,548	4,639,621	500	500	415	1,783,200 00
82	Springfield & Eastern,	2,204,837	77,706	523,101	59	112	96	209,600 00
83	Templeton,	781,599	43,731	236,792	30	80	80	75,000 00
84	Union,	6,943,443	239,305	1,489,848	240	174	160	510,600 00
85	Uxbridge & Blackstone,	482,004	65,758	136,500	11	35	34	79,500 00

86	Waltham, ...	258,408	36,237	116,359	1	12	11	99,200 00
87	Warren, Brookfield & Spencer, .	1,311,568	66,893	371,511	36	19	17	145,300 00
88	Webster & Dudley, ...	-	-	-	-	15	7	3,900 00
	Webster & Dudley and Worcester & Webster (lessee), . . .	1,748,801	78,092	446,929	70	-	-	-
89	Wellesley & Boston,*	293,036	-	63,192	46	8	8	115,000 00
90	Westborough & Hopkinton, . .	269,733	42,411	76,701	5	8	8	40,000 00
91	West End, ...	-	-	-	-	8,214	7,162	14,434,750 00
92	Winnisimmet, ...	-	-	-	-	37	35	49,800 00
93	Woonsocket (of Rhode Island), .	2,378,815	108,320	382,540	80	19	13	281,700 00
94	Worcester & Blackstone Valley, .	1,546,611	89,711	334,946	36	7	1	100 00
95	Worcester Consolidated, . . .	27,098,275	195,352	5,103,614	718	28	27	3,549,000 00
96	Worcester & Holden, ...	723,298	75,509	224,994	16	31	31	125,000 00
97	Worcester, Roch. & Charl. Depot,	-	-	-	-	5	1	100 00
98	Worcester & Shrewsbury R.R., .	-	-	-	-	6	6	36,700 00
99	Worcester & Shrewsbury St. R'y, .	-	-	-	-	6	6	20,000 00
100	Worcester & Southbridge, . .	1,935,494	96,150	445,181	70	9	1	100 00
101	Worcester & Webster, ...	-	-	-	-	9	5	500 00
102	Woronoco, ...	1,631,529	101,117	490,957	54	70	65	247,100 00
	Totals,[1]	520,056,511	195,917	107,897,456	16,519	15,929	13,961	$60,354,192 50

[1] Not including in columns 88, 89, 90 and 91 the companies marked *, these companies having been consolidated during the year.

Tabulated Statements from Reports of Street Railway Companies — Continued.

	RAILWAY COMPANIES.	Accidents during the Year ending September 30, 1904.						
		92. — To Passengers.	**93.** — To Employees.	**94.** — To Other Persons.	**95.** — Fatal.	**96.** — Not Fatal.	**97.** — Total.	**98.** — Total during Preceding Year.
1	Amesbury & Hampton,	–	–	–	–	–	–	–
	Amesbury & Hampton (lessee),	–	–	1	–	1	1	–
2	Amherst & Sunderland,	3	–	1	–	4	4	8
3	Athol & Orange,	–	–	–	–	–	–	–
4	Berkshire,	1	–	6	2	5	7	11
5	Blue Hill,	15	1	1	1	16	17	16
6	Boston & Chelsea,	–	–	–	–	–	–	–
7	Boston Elevated,	1,794	45	1,080	26	2,893	2,919	2,274
8	Boston & Northern,	596	41	138	21	754	775	402
9	Boston & Revere Electric,	–	–	–	–	–	–	–
10	Boston & Worcester,	62	5	12	5	74	79	110
11	Bristol County,	–	–	–	–	–	–	–
	Bristol County (receivers),	–	–	1	–	1	1	4
12	Bristol & Norfolk,	–	–	–	–	–	–	–
13	Brockton & Plymouth,	5	3	5	2	11	13	16
14	Citizens' Electric,	4	–	2	1	5	6	17
15	Commonwealth Avenue,	–	–	–	–	–	–	8
16	Concord & Boston,	–	–	–	–	–	–	–
17	Concord, Maynard & Hudson,	4	–	–	–	4	4	–
18	Conway Electric,	–	–	–	–	–	–	–
19	Cottage City & Edgartown Traction,	–	–	–	–	–	–	–
20	Dartmouth & Westport,	6	–	4	–	10	10	9

No.	Company							
21	East Middlesex, ...	–	–	–	–	–	–	–
22	East Taunton, ...	–	–	–	–	–	–	3
23	Essex County, ...	–	–	–	–	–	–	–
24	Fitchburg & Leominster, . . .	24	1	8	–	33	33	21
25	Fram., Southboro' & Marlboro', .	1	–	–	–	1	1	5
26	Framingham Union, ...	–	–	1	–	1	1	5
27	Gardner, Westminster & Fitchburg,	3	1	–	–	4	4	13
28	Georgetown, Rowley & Ipswich, .	1	–	1	–	2	2	2
29	Greenfield, Deerfield & Northamp.,	3	–	1	–	4	4	1
30	Greenfield & Turner's Falls, . .	5	1	3	1	8	9	5
31	Hampshire, ...	–	–	–	–	–	–	1
32	Hampshire & Worcester, . . .	–	–	–	–	–	–	12
33	Hartford & Worcester, . . .	–	–	–	–	–	–	–
34	Haverhill & Amesbury, . . .	7	2	2	1	10	11	8
35	Haverhill, Danvers & Ipswich, .	–	–	–	–	–	–	–
36	Haverhill, Georgetown & Danvers,	4	–	–	–	4	4	–
37	Haverhill & Plaistow, . . .	–	–	–	–	–	–	–
	Haverhill & Plaistow (lessee), .	1	–	3	–	4	4	1
38	Haverhill & Southern New Hamp.,	4	–	–	–	4	4	3
39	Holyoke, ...	29	2	1	1	31	32	76
40	Hoosac Valley, ...	17	–	2	1	18	19	21
41	Horse Neck Beach, ...	–	–	–	–	–	–	–
42	Interstate Consolidated, . . .	27	2	8	–	37	37	24
43	Lawrence & Methuen, . . .	6	–	6	–	12	12	17
44	Leominster, Shirley & Ayer, . .	–	–	–	–	–	–	–
45	Lexington & Boston, ...	9	–	14	–	23	23	19

Tabulated Statements from Reports of Street Railway Companies — Continued.

	RAILWAY COMPANIES.	ACCIDENTS DURING THE YEAR ENDING SEPTEMBER 30, 1904 — Continued.						
		92. — To Passengers.	**93.** — To Employees.	**94.** — To Other Persons.	**95.** — Fatal.	**96.** — Not Fatal.	**97.** — Total.	**98.** — Total during Preceding Year.
46	Linwood,	–	–	–	–	–	–	–
47	Lowell, Acton & Maynard,	–	–	–	–	–	–	–
48	Lowell & Boston,	–	–	–	–	–	–	–
	Lowell & Boston (receivers),	–	–	–	–	–	–	2
49	Lowell & Fitchburg,	–	–	–	–	–	–	–
50	Lowell & Pelham,	1	–	–	–	1	1	4
51	Marlborough & Framingham,	1	–	1	–	2	2	4
52	Marlborough & Westborough,	2	–	1	–	3	3	8
53	Martha's Vineyard,	–	–	–	–	–	–	–
54	Medfield & Medway,	2	–	2	1	3	4	4
55	Middleboro', Wareham & Buz. Bay,	–	–	1	–	1	1	1
	Middleboro', Wareham & Buz. Bay (receivers),	–	–	–	–	–	–	
56	Milford, Attleboro' & Woonsocket,	7	–	3	3	7	10	16
57	Milford & Uxbridge,	5	–	6	2	9	11	14
58	Mount Tom,	–	–	–	–	–	–	–
59	Natick & Cochituate,	2	–	1	–	3	3	9
60	Natick & Needham,	–	–	–	–	–	–	–
61	New Bedford & Onset,	3	–	2	–	5	5	6
62	Newton,	19	3	2	–	24	24	19
63	Newton & Boston,	3	2	1	–	6	6	18
64	Newtonville & Watertown,	–	–	–	–	–	–	–
65	Norfolk & Bristol,	4	1	–	–	5	5	23

66	Norfolk Western,	–	–	–	–	–	–	4
	Norfolk Western (receiver),	1	–	1	–	2	2	
67	Northampton,	8	2	–	–	10	10	12
68	Northampton & Amherst,	2	1	2	1	4	5	3
69	North End,	–	–	–	–	–	–	–
70	Norton & Taunton,	–	–	2	–	2	2	4
71	Norwood, Canton & Sharon,	–	–	–	–	–	–	1
72	Old Colony,	296	21	59	5	371	376	213
73	Pittsfield Electric,	8	–	–	–	8	8	10
74	Plymouth, Carver & Wareham,	–	–	–	–	–	–	–
75	Plymouth & Sandwich,	–	–	–	–	–	–	–
76	Providence & Fall River,	2	–	1	–	3	3	4
77	Shelburne Falls & Colrain,	–	–	–	–	–	–	–
78	Somerville,	–	–	–	–	–	–	–
79	Southbridge & Sturbridge,	3	–	1	–	4	4	–
80	South Middlesex,	9	–	2	–	11	11	3
81	Springfield,	89	15	52	3	153	156	170
82	Springfield & Eastern,	8	–	6	1	13	14	11
83	Templeton,	–	–	–	–	–	–	–
84	Union,	21	–	10	–	31	31	32
85	Uxbridge & Blackstone,	–	–	–	–	–	–	–
86	Waltham,	1	1	1	–	3	3	4
87	Warren, Brookfield & Spencer,	18	–	2	2	18	20	15
88	Webster & Dudley,	–	–	–	–	–	–	–
	Webster & Dudley and Worcester & Webster (lessee),	7	–	–	–	7	7	16
89	Wellesley & Boston,	–	–	–	–	–	–	9
90	Westborough & Hopkinton,	–	–	1	–	1	1	3

Tabulated Statements from Reports of Street Railway Companies — Concluded.

	RAILWAY COMPANIES.	ACCIDENTS DURING THE YEAR ENDING SEPTEMBER 30, 1904 — Concluded.						
		92. — To Passengers.	**93.** — To Employees.	**94.** — To Other Persons.	**95.** — Fatal.	**96.** — Not Fatal.	**97.** — Total.	**98.** — Total during Preceding Year.
91	West End,	–	–	–	–	–	–	–
92	Winnisimmet,	–	–	–	–	–	–	–
93	Woonsocket (of Rhode Island),	15	–	7	2	20	22	11
94	Worcester & Blackstone Valley,	12	1	1	1	13	14	12
95	Worcester Consolidated,	178	7	71	5	251	256	182
96	Worcester & Holden,	–	–	–	–	–	–	–
97	Worcester, Roch. & Charl. Depot,	–	–	–	–	–	–	–
98	Worcester & Shrewsbury R.R.,	–	–	–	–	–	–	–
99	Worcester & Shrewsbury St. R'y,	–	–	–	–	–	–	–
100	Worcester & Southbridge,	9	2	5	3	13	16	13
101	Worcester & Webster,	–	–	–	–	–	–	–
102	Woronoco,	5	1	–	1	5	6	2
	Totals,	3,372	161	1,545	92	4,986	5,078	3,974

PART II.

RAILROAD AND STREET RAILWAY RETURNS.

[AS CORRECTED BY THE BOARD.]

RETURN

OF THE

ATTLEBOROUGH BRANCH RAILROAD COMPANY

FOR THE YEAR ENDING JUNE 30, 1904.

[Operated by electricity.]

GENERAL EXHIBIT FOR THE YEAR.	
Gross earnings from operation,	$10,694 40
Operating expenses,	8,722 52
NET EARNINGS FROM OPERATION,	$1,971 88
Miscellaneous income, less expense of collecting: interest on bank balances,	410 08
GROSS INCOME ABOVE OPERATING EXPENSES,	$2,381 96
Charges upon income accrued during the year: taxes,	2,183 00
NET DIVISIBLE INCOME,	$198 96
Dividends declared during the year payable on April 1, 1904, 12 per cent on $131,700,	15,804 00
Deficit for the year ending June 30, 1904,	$15,605 04
Amount of surplus June 30, 1903,	8,097 49
Debits to profit and loss account during the year: settlement of claim due prior to June 30, 1903,	250 00
TOTAL DEFICIT JUNE 30, 1904,	$7,757 55

EARNINGS FROM OPERATION.	
Passenger service: gross receipts from passengers,	$7,651 40
Freight service: gross receipts from freight,	3,043 00
GROSS EARNINGS FROM OPERATION,	$10,694 40

EXPENSES OF OPERATION.	
General expenses:	
Salaries of general officers,	$343 01
Salaries of clerks and attendants,	343 00
General office expenses and supplies,	19 28
Insurance,	36 58
TOTAL,	$741 87

Maintenance of way and structures:	
Repairs of roadway and renewals of rails and ties,	$686 25
Repairs and renewals of buildings and fixtures,	2 00
Other expenses of maintaining way and structures: repair of electric lines,	1 30
TOTAL,	$689 55
Conducting transportation:	
Superintendence,	$343 02
Train service,	2,912 23
Train supplies and expenses,	128 18
Car mileage — balance,	682 69
Hire of equipment,	1,020 47
Injuries to persons,	88 23
Other expenses of conducting transportation:	
Removing snow and ice,	230 45
Electric power purchased,	1,885 83
TOTAL,	$7,291 10
Recapitulation:	
General expenses,	$741 87
Maintenance of way and structures,	689 55
Conducting transportation,	7,291 10
TOTAL OPERATING EXPENSES,	$8,722 52
Percentage of operating expenses to gross earnings,	81.56

GENERAL BALANCE SHEET JUNE 30, 1904.

ASSETS. DR.	
Cost of road,	$121,779 19
Due from solvent companies and individuals,	2,163 26
Profit and loss balance (deficit),	7,757 55
TOTAL,	$131,700 00

LIABILITIES. CR.	
Capital stock,	$131,700 00
TOTAL,	$131,700 00

CAPITAL STOCK.

Capital stock authorized by law,	$131,700 00	
Capital stock authorized by votes of company,	131,700 00	
Capital stock issued and outstanding,		$131,700 00
Number of shares issued and outstanding,	1,317	
Number of stockholders,	6	
Number of stockholders in Massachusetts,	1	
Amount of stock held in Massachusetts,	$100 00	

Volume of Traffic, etc.

Passenger traffic:	
Number of passengers carried paying revenue,	154,833
Number of passengers carried one mile,	464,967
Number of passengers carried one mile per mile of road operated,	130,271
Average length of journey per passenger,	3 003 miles.
Average amount received per passenger per mile carried,	1.645 cents.
Passenger earnings (gross) per mile of road operated,	$2,143 25
Passenger earnings (gross) per passenger-train mile run,	16.860 cents.
Freight traffic:	
Number of tons of freight hauled earning revenue,	16,798
Number of tons of freight hauled one mile,	51,242
Number of tons of freight hauled one mile per mile of road operated,	14,354
Average length of haul per ton,	3.051 miles.
Average amount received per ton per mile hauled,	5.938 cents.
Freight earnings (gross) per mile of road operated,	$852 38
Freight earnings (gross) per freight-train mile run,	2 37
Operating expenses:	
Operating expenses per mile of road operated,	2,443 28
Operating expenses per revenue-train mile run,	18.690 cents.
Train mileage:	
Miles run by passenger trains,	45,389
Miles run by freight trains,	1,281
Total mileage of trains earning revenue,	46,670
Employees:	
Average number of persons employed,	12

Description of Railroad Owned and Operated.

(See also tabulated description in preceding appendix to report.)

Railroad Owned and Operated.	Total.	In Massachusetts.
	Miles.	Miles.
Length of main line,	3.570	3.570
Length of side track, etc.,	1.570	1.570
Total Length of Track Owned,	5.140	5.140
Equipped for Electric Power.		
Length of main line,	3.570	3.570
Length of side track, etc,	1.570	1.570
Total Length of Electric Track,	5.140	5.140

Railroad Crossings in Massachusetts.

Crossings with Highways.	
Number of crossings of railroad with highways at grade,	14
Number of highway grade crossings protected by gates,	3
Number of highway grade crossings unprotected,	11
Number of highway bridges 18 feet (or more) above track,	1
Height of lowest highway bridge above track,	18 ft., 3 in.

CORPORATE NAME AND ADDRESS OF THE COMPANY.

ATTLEBOROUGH BRANCH RAILROAD COMPANY,

PROVIDENCE, R. I.

NAMES AND BUSINESS ADDRESS OF PRINCIPAL OFFICERS.

Marsden J. Perry, *President*, Providence, R. I. C. A. Babcock, *Treasurer*, Providence, R. I. Cornelius S. Sweetland, *Clerk of Corporation*, Providence, R. I.

NAMES AND RESIDENCE OF BOARD OF DIRECTORS.

Marsden J. Perry, Providence, R. I. Benjamin A. Jackson, Providence, R. I. Albert T. Potter, Providence, R. I. Clarence L. Watson, Attleborough, Mass. Cornelius S. Sweetland, Providence, R. I.

We hereby certify that the statements contained in the foregoing return are full, just and true.

MARSDEN J. PERRY,
CORNELIUS S. SWEETLAND,
ALBERT T. POTTER,
Directors.
C. A. BABCOCK,
Treasurer.

STATE OF RHODE ISLAND AND PROVIDENCE PLANTATIONS.

PROVIDENCE, ss. PROVIDENCE, Sept. 6' 1904. Then personally appeared the above-named Marsden J. Perry, Cornelius S. Sweetland, Albert T. Potter and C. A. Babcock, and severally made oath that the foregoing certificate by them subscribed is, to the best of their knowledge and belief, true.

Before me, HENRY V. A. JOSLIN,
Justice of the Peace.

RETURN

OF THE

BERKSHIRE RAILROAD COMPANY

For the Year ending June 30, 1904.

[Leased to and operated by the New York, New Haven & Hartford.]

General Exhibit for the Year.	
Rental received from lease of road,	$36,250 00
Dividends received on stocks owned: 66 shares Berkshire Railroad Company,	396 00
Gross Income,	$36,646 00
Expenses and charges upon income accrued during the year: salaries and maintenance of organization,	413 75
Net Divisible Income,	$36,232 25
Dividends declared (6 per cent),	36,000 00
Surplus for the year ending June 30, 1904,	$232 25
Amount of surplus June 30, 1903,	15,286 67
Total Surplus June 30, 1904,	$15,518 92

General Balance Sheet June 30, 1904.	
Assets. Dr.	
Cost of road,	$600,000 00
Stock of Berkshire Railroad Company (66 shares),	3,970 00
Total Permanent Investments,	$603,970 00
Cash,	11,640 42
Total,	$615,610 42
Liabilities. Cr.	
Capital stock,	$600,000 00
Current liabilities: dividends not called for,	91 50
Profit and loss balance (surplus),	15,518 92
Total,	$615,610 42

Capital Stock.

Capital stock authorized by law, ...	$800,000 00	
Capital stock authorized by votes of company,	600,000 00	
Capital stock issued and outstanding, ...		$600,000 00
Number of shares issued and outstanding, .	6,000	
Number of stockholders, ...	233	
Number of stockholders in Massachusetts, .	132	
Amount of stock held in Massachusetts, . .	$400,600 00	

Description of Railroad Owned.

(See also tabulated description in preceding appendix to report.)

Railroad Owned.	Total.	In Massachusetts.
	Miles.	Miles.
Length of main line, ...	20.530	20.530
Length of side track, etc., ...	6.390	6.390
Total Length of Track Owned, ...	26.920	26.920

Corporate Name and Address of the Company.

BERKSHIRE RAILROAD COMPANY,

Stockbridge, Mass.

Names and Business Address of Principal Officers.

Henry T. Robbins, *President*, Great Barrington, Mass. Daniel A. Kimball, *Treasurer and Clerk of Corporation*, Housatonic National Bank, Stockbridge, Mass.

Names and Residence of Board of Directors.

Henry T. Robbins, Great Barrington, Mass. George W. Mellen, Great Barrington, Mass. John H. C. Church, Great Barrington, Mass. Eugene H. Robbins, Pittsfield, Mass. Daniel A. Kimball, Stockbridge, Mass.

We hereby certify that the statements contained in the foregoing return are full, just and true.

HENRY T. ROBBINS,
DANIEL A. KIMBALL,
EUGENE H. ROBBINS,
Directors.
DANIEL A. KIMBALL,
Treasurer.

COMMONWEALTH OF MASSACHUSETTS.

BERKSHIRE, ss. STOCKBRIDGE, Aug. 18, 1904. Then personally appeared the above-named Henry T. Robbins and Daniel A. Kimball, and severally made oath that the foregoing certificate by them subscribed is, to the best of their knowledge and belief, true.

Before me, CHAS. E. EVANS,
Justice of the Peace.

COMMONWEALTH OF MASSACHUSETTS.

BERKSHIRE, ss. PITTSFIELD, Aug. 24, 1904. Then personally appeared the above-named Eugene H. Robbins, and made oath that the foregoing certificate by him subscribed is, to the best of his knowledge and belief, true.

Before me, GEO. H. TUCKER,
Justice of the Peace.

RETURN

OF THE

BOSTON & ALBANY RAILROAD COMPANY

FOR THE YEAR ENDING JUNE 30, 1904.

[Leased to and operated by the New York Central & Hudson River.]

GENERAL EXHIBIT FOR THE YEAR.

Rental received from lease of road,			$2,403,110 00
Interest received on bonds owned: $5,500,000 New York Central & Hudson River R.R. Co., 3½ per cent debenture bonds,			192,500 00
Income from other sources:			
Interest on loans,			1,234 03
GROSS INCOME,			$2,596,844 03
Expenses and charges upon income accrued during the year:			
Salaries and maintenance of organization,		$9,978 68	
Interest on funded debt,		315,110 00	
Rentals paid:			
Ware River R.R. Co.,	$52,500 00		
Pittsfield & North Adams R.R. Co.,	22,500 00		
North Brookfield R.R. Co.,	3,000 00		
		78,000 00	
Other expenses and charges upon income:			
Interest upon New York Central & Hudson River R.R. Co., 3½ per cent bonds,		6,234 03	
Organization expenses,		21 32	
TOTAL EXPENSES AND CHARGES UPON INCOME,			409,344 03
NET DIVISIBLE INCOME,			$2,187,500 00
Dividends declared (8¾ per cent),			$2,187,500 00
Amount of surplus June 30, 1903,			$1,543,867 70
TOTAL SURPLUS JUNE 30, 1904,			$1,543,867 70

GENERAL BALANCE SHEET JUNE 30, 1904.

ASSETS.	DR.
Cost of road,	$28,015,484 61
Cost of equipment,	3,572,400 00
TOTAL PERMANENT INVESTMENTS,	$31,587,884 61

Cash,	$82,942 54	
Bills receivable,	15,000 00	
Due from solvent companies and individuals (New York Central & Hudson River R R. Co.),	2,457,734 63	
Sinking and other special funds (trustees Ware River R.R. sinking fund),	200,721 31	
Other cash assets (New York Central & Hudson River R.R. Co. 3½ per cent debenture bonds),	5,500,000 00	
TOTAL CASH AND CURRENT ASSETS,		$8,256,398 48
Other assets and property:		
Improvements at East Boston,	$700,000 00	
Cunard dock and wharf property,	300,000 00	
TOTAL MISCELLANEOUS ASSETS:		1,000,000 00
TOTAL,		$40,844,283 09

LIABILITIES.	CR.	
Capital stock,		$25,000,000 00
Funded debt,		8,485,000 00
Current liabilities:		
Dividends not called for,	$11,286 00	
Matured interest coupons unpaid (including coupons due July 1),	22,390 00	
Rentals due and unpaid (including rentals due July 1),	37,500 00	
TOTAL CURRENT LIABILITIES,		71,176 00
Sinking and other special funds:		
Real estate,	$16,751 54	
Dividend fund,	5,500,000 00	
Ware River R R. sinking fund,	200,721 31	
Interest upon New York Central & Hudson River R.R. Co. 3½ per cent debenture bonds,	22,840 83	
Organization expenses,	3,925 71	
TOTAL SINKING AND OTHER SPECIAL FUNDS,		5,744,239 39
Profit and loss balance (surplus),		1,543,867 70
TOTAL,		$40,844,283 09

CAPITAL STOCK.

Capital stock authorized by law,	$30,000,000 00	
Capital stock authorized by votes of company,	25,000,000 00	
Capital stock issued and outstanding,		$25,000,000 00
Number of shares issued and outstanding,	250,000	
Number of stockholders,	8,421	
Number of stockholders in Massachusetts,	7,636	
Amount of stock held in Massachusetts,	$21,425,500 00	

Funded Debt.

Description of Bonds.	Rate of Interest.	Date of Maturity.	Amount Outstanding.	Interest Paid during the Year.
	Per Cent.			
Boston & Albany R.R. Co. bonds, .	4	Oct. 1, 1913,	$3,627,000 00	$145,080 00
Boston & Albany R.R. Co. refunding bonds, ...	3½	April 1, 1952,	3,858,000 00	135,030 00
Boston & Albany R.R. Co. terminal bonds, ...	3½	Jan. 1, 1951,	1,000,000 00	35,000 00
Totals, ...	. .	. . . .	$8,485,000 00	$315,110 00

Sinking Funds.

Amount June 30, 1903, of Ware River R.R. sinking fund, .	$192,085 88
Additions during the year to Ware River R.R. sinking fund, .	8,635 43
Total Sinking Funds June 30, 1904, ...	$200,721 31

Description of Railroad Owned.

(See also tabulated description in preceding appendix to report)

Railroad Owned.	Total.	In Massachusetts.
	Miles.	Miles.
Length of main line, ...	199.91	161.35
Length of branch line, ...	104.18	86.85
Total Length of Line Owned, ...	304.09	248.20
Length of second track, ...	215 91	176.35
Length of third track, ...	16.83	16.83
Length of fourth track, ...	16.81	16.81
Length of side track, etc., ...	279 56	239.62
Total Length of Track Owned, ...	833.20	697.81

Corporate Name and Address of the Company.

BOSTON & ALBANY RAILROAD COMPANY,

South Terminal Station, Boston, Mass.

Names and Business Address of Principal Officers.

William Bliss, *President*, Boston, Mass. Edward D. Hayden, *Vice-President and Clerk of Corporation*, Boston, Mass. Frank H. Ratcliffe, *Treasurer*, Boston, Mass.

Names and Residence of Board of Directors.

Walter H. Barnes, Boston, Mass. William Bliss, Boston, Mass. Augustus G. Bullock, Worcester, Mass. Zenas Crane, Dalton, Mass. Edward L. Davis, Worcester, Mass. Eben S. Draper, Hopedale, Mass. Reginald Foster, Manchester, Mass. Edward D. Hayden, Woburn, Mass. Albert C. Houghton, North Adams, Mass. James A. Rumrill, Springfield, Mass. Stephen Salisbury, Worcester, Mass. Charles S. Sargent, Brookline, Mass.

We hereby certify that the statements contained in the foregoing return are full, just and true.

WILLIAM BLISS,
J. A. RUMRILL,
STEPHEN SALISBURY,
REGINALD FOSTER,
EDWARD D. HAYDEN,
EDWARD L. DAVIS,
WALTER H. BARNES,
ZENAS CRANE,
A. G. BULLOCK,
EBEN S. DRAPER,
Directors.
F. H. RATCLIFFE,
Treasurer.

Commonwealth of Massachusetts.

SUFFOLK ss. BOSTON, Sept. 28, 1904. Then personally appeared the above-named William Bliss, J. A. Rumrill, Stephen Salisbury, Reginald Foster, Edward D. Hayden, Edward L. Davis, Walter H. Barnes, Zenas Crane, A. G. Bullock, Eben S. Draper and Frank H. Ratcliffe, and severally made oath that the foregoing certificate by them subscribed is, to the best of their knowledge and belief, true.

Before me, WOODWARD HUDSON,
Justice of the Peace.

RETURN

OF THE

BOSTON & ALBANY RAILROAD

(NEW YORK CENTRAL & HUDSON RIVER RAILROAD COMPANY, LESSEE)

FOR THE YEAR ENDING JUNE 30, 1904.

General Exhibit for the Year.			
Gross earnings from operation,			$10,254,492 49
Operating expenses,			7,139,476 07
Net Earnings from Operation,			$3,115,016 42
Charges upon income accrued during the year:			
Taxes,		$944,214 21	
Rentals of leased roads:			
Boston & Albany R.R.,	$2,325,110 00		
Pittsfield & North Adams R R.,	22,500 00		
Ware River R.R.,	52,500 00		
North Brookfield R.R.,	3,000 00		
Chester & Becket R.R.,	662 67		
Providence, Webster & Springfield R.R.,	6,850 44		
		2,410,623 11	
Total Charges and Deductions from Income,			3,354,837 32
Total Deficit from Operation June 30, 1904,			$239,820 90

EARNINGS FROM OPERATION.

Department of Service.	Gross Receipts.	Deductions.	Earnings.
Passenger service:			
Gross receipts from passengers,	$4,208,229 47		
Deductions:			
Tickets redeemed,	. . . .	$15,656 66	
Excess fares refunded,	. . . .	23,180 70	
Total deductions,	. . . .	$38,837 36	
Net Revenue from Passengers (*carried forward*),		. . . .	$4,169,392 11

EARNINGS FROM OPERATION — Concluded.

Department of Service.	Gross Receipts.	Deductions.	Earnings.
Amount brought forward,	. . . .	. . . .	$4,169,392 11
From mails,	$369,374 58		
From express,	345,831 33		
From extra baggage and storage,	43,201 20		
Other earnings, passenger service:			
Newspapers,	31,143 98		
Parcels,	4,282 75		
Milk,	269 03		794,102 87
TOTAL EARNINGS, PASSENGER SERVICE,	. . . .	. . . .	$4,963,494 98
Freight service:			
Gross receipts from freight,	$5,081,417 33		
Deductions:			
Overcharge to shippers,	. . . .	$124,913 20	
NET REVENUE FROM FREIGHT,	. . . .	. . . .	$4,956,504 13
Other earnings, freight service,	. . . .	. . . .	12,597 60
TOTAL EARNINGS, FREIGHT SERVICE,	. . . .	. . . .	$4,969,101 73
TOTAL PASSENGER AND FREIGHT EARNINGS,	. . . .	. . . .	$9,932,596 71
Other earnings from operation:			
Rentals from tracks, yards and terminals,	$15,000 00		
Rentals from buildings and other property,	195,150 45		
From other sources,	111,745 33		
TOTAL OTHER EARNINGS,	. . . .	. . . .	321,895 78
GROSS EARNINGS FROM OPERATION,	. . . .	. . . .	$10,254,492 49

EXPENSES OF OPERATION.

General expenses:	
Salaries of general officers,	$43,791 66
Salaries of clerks and attendants,	102,607 55
General office expenses and supplies,	5,985 22
Insurance,	43,517 66
Law expenses,	8,794 96
Stationery and printing (general offices),	4,154 97
Other general expenses,	20,686 11
Real estate expenses and repairs (credit),	13 25
TOTAL,	$229,524 88
Maintenance of way and structures:	
Repairs of roadway,	$595,899 93
Renewals of rails,	17,063 28
Renewals of ties,	113,667 99
Repairs and renewals of bridges and culverts,	79,347 89
Repairs and renewals of fences, road crossings, signs and cattle guards,	21,637 80
Repairs and renewals of buildings and fixtures,	92,337 65
Repairs and renewals of docks and wharves,	346 48
Repairs and renewals of telegraph,	3,987 13
Stationery and printing,	2,878 56
Other expenses of maintaining way and structures,	2,640 14
TOTAL,	$929,806 85

Maintenance of equipment:	
Superintendence,	$46,105 03
Repairs and renewals of locomotives,	553,681 49
Repairs and renewals of passenger cars,	234,457 59
Repairs and renewals of freight cars,	226,706 04
Repairs and renewals of work cars,	105,372 08
Repairs and renewals of shop machinery and tools,	40,323 92
Stationery and printing,	2,507 71
Other expenses of maintaining equipment,	92,448 14
TOTAL,	$1,301,602 00
Conducting transportation:	
Superintendence,	$109,729 07
Engine and roundhouse men,	787,492 83
Fuel for locomotives,	1,109,393 41
Water supply for locomotives,	58,281 67
Oil, tallow and waste for locomotives,	36,798 68
Other supplies for locomotives,	14,010 70
Train service,	531,866 38
Train supplies and expenses,	162,136 79
Switchmen, flagmen and watchmen,	374,000 70
Telegraph expenses,	47,633 85
Station service,	548,672 38
Station supplies,	99,139 17
Switching charges — balance,	13,515 97
Car mileage — balance,	183,766 20
Hire of equipment (credit),	1,918 41
Loss and damage,	87,974 42
Injuries to persons,	54,584 23
Clearing wrecks,	6,934 68
Operating marine equipment,	86,274 36
Advertising,	23,378 91
Outside agencies,	104,097 74
Stock yards and elevators,	12,734 12
Rentals for tracks, yards and terminals,	173,480 02
Rentals of buildings and other property,	16,356 41
Stationery and printing,	36,757 76
Other expenses of conducting transportation,	1,450 30
TOTAL,	$4,678,542 34
Recapitulation:	
General expenses,	$229,524 88
Maintenance of way and structures,	929,806 85
Maintenance of equipment,	1,301,602 00
Conducting transportation,	4,678,542 34
TOTAL OPERATING EXPENSES,	$7,139,476 07
Percentage of operating expenses to gross earnings,	69.62

VOLUME OF TRAFFIC, ETC.

Passenger traffic:	
Number of passengers carried paying revenue,	10,350,181
Number of passengers carried one mile,	247,709,954
Number of passengers carried one mile per mile of road operated,	655,716
Average length of journey per passenger,	23.930 miles.
Average amount received per passenger per mile carried,	1.683 cents.

Passenger traffic — *Concluded.*	
Passenger earnings (gross) per mile of road operated (377.77 miles),	$13,138 93.000
Passenger earnings (gross) per passenger-train mile run,	1 39.424
Freight traffic:	
Number of tons of freight hauled earning revenue,	4,699,465
Number of tons of freight hauled one mile,	502,207,880
Number of tons of freight hauled one mile per mile of road operated,	1,279,543
Average length of haul per ton,	106.860 miles.
Average amount received per ton per mile hauled,	9.870 cents.
Freight earnings (gross) per mile of road operated (392.49),	$12,660 45.000
Freight earnings (gross) per freight-train mile run,	2 08.937
Operating expenses:	
Operating expenses per mile of road operated,	18,190 21.000
Operating expenses per revenue-train mile run,	1 20.780
Train mileage:	
Miles run by passenger trains,	3,532,848
Miles run by freight trains,	2,351,121
Miles run by mixed trains,	27,158
Total mileage of trains earning revenue,	5,911,127
Miles run by switching trains,	1,512,294
Miles run by construction and other trains,	96,337
Total train mileage,	7,519,758
Fares and freights:	
Average rate of fare per mile received for local and trip tickets,	1.537 cents.
Average rate of fare per mile received for mileage tickets,	2.000 "
Average rate of fare per mile received for time and commutation tickets,	.888 "
Average rate of fare per mile received for interline tickets,	2.017 "
Average rate received per ton mile for local freight,	2.362 "
Average rate received per ton mile for interline freight,	.763 "
Passengers to and from Boston:	
Number of passengers to Boston,	3,630,691
Number of passengers from Boston,	3,648,589
Employees:	
Average number of persons employed,	5,439

Description of Railroad Operated.

(See also tabulated description in preceding appendix to report.)

Railroad Operated.	Total.	In Massachusetts.
	Miles.	Miles.
Length of main line,	199.910	161.350
Length of branch line,	192.580	175.250
Total Length of Line Operated,	392.490	336.600
Length of second track,	215.910	176.350
Length of third track,	16.830	16.830
Length of fourth track,	16.810	16.810
Length of side track, etc.,	301.390	261.450
Total Length of Track Operated,	943.430	808.040
Equipped for Electric Power.		
Length of branch line,	1.090	1.090
Total Length of Electric Line,	1.090	1.090

Description of Equipment.

Rolling Stock.	Number Leased.	Equipped with Power Driving-Wheel Brakes.	Maximum Weight.	Average Weight.
Locomotives.			Lbs.	Lbs.
Inspection,	1	1	147,000	147,000
Passenger,	106	106	320,900	199.500
Freight,	139	139	301,080	213,300
Switching, etc.,	33	33	176,200	136,950
Total,	279	279	-	-

Description of Equipment — Concluded.

Rolling Stock.	Number Leased.	Equipped with Power Train Brakes.	Equipped with Automatic Couplers.	Name of Coupler Used.
Cars — Passenger Service.				
Passenger cars,	252	252	252	56 National, 142 Gould, 54 Trojan.
Combination cars,	50	50	50	28 National, 12 Gould, 10 Trojan.
Dining cars,	3	3	3	3 Gould.
Milk cars,	11	11	11	3 Gould, 8 Trojan.
Baggage, express and mail cars,	80	80	80	32 Gould, 27 National, 21 Trojan.
Other cars in passenger service (electric car),	1	1	1	1 Gould.
Total,	*397	*397	*397	
Cars — Freight Service.				
Box cars,	2,093	2,088	2,093	1,197 Trojan, 601 Gould, 185 Thurmond, 110 Dowling.
Flat cars,	429	399	429	16 Gould, 5 Thurmond, 408 Trojan.
Stock cars,	20	20	20	10 Trojan, 4 Thurmond, 6 Dowling.
Coal cars,	1,057	990	1,057	310 Gould, 20 Thurmond, 717 Trojan, 10 Dowling.
Other cars in freight service,	2	2	2	2 Trojan.
Total,	3,601	3,499	3,601	
Cars — Company's Service.				
Officers' and pay cars,	5	5	5	4 National, 1 Gould.
Gravel cars,	97	30	63	24 Empire, 2 Park, 37 Trojan.
Derrick cars,	18	14	17	17 Trojan.
Caboose cars,	91	91	91	11 Gould, 80 Trojan.
Ballast cars,	100	100	100	100 Tower.
Other cars in company's service,	155	60	72	72 Trojan.
Total,	466	300	348	

Number of 8-wheel cars in passenger service with brakes for *all* wheels, 374
Number of 12-wheel cars in passenger service with brakes for *all* wheels, 23*

* Also 19.39 per cent of four buffet cars, in Boston & Chicago Line.

RAILROAD CROSSINGS IN MASSACHUSETTS.

Crossings with Highways.	
Number of crossings of railroad with highways at grade, .	203
Number of highway grade crossings protected by gates, .	44
Number of highway grade crossings protected by flagmen, .	21
Number of highway grade crossings unprotected, . . .	138
Number of highway grade crossings now in process of abolition, ...	15
Number of highway grade crossings for abolition of which petition is pending, ...	14
Number of highway bridges 18 feet (or more) above track, .	52
Number of highway bridges less than 18 feet above track, .	100
Height of lowest highway bridge above track, . . .	14 ft., 4½ in.
Crossings with Other Railroads.	
Crossings of railroad with other railroads at grade (16 in number), viz.:	
New York, New Haven & Hartford Railroad, Taunton Division, South Framingham. New York, New Haven & Hartford Railroad, Providence Division, Worcester. New York, New Haven & Hartford Railroad, Norwich Division, Worcester. New York, New Haven & Hartford Railroad, Norwich Division, South Worcester. Worcester Viaduct Company, Worcester. Central Vermont Railway, Southern Division, Palmer Central Vermont Railway, Southern Division, Barrett's Junction. New York, New Haven & Hartford Railroad, Boston & Maine transfer tracks, Springfield. New York, New Haven & Hartford Railroad, Northampton Division, Westfield. Boston & Maine Railroad, Fitchburg Division, Baldwinville. Boston & Maine Railroad, Fitchburg Division, Somervi le. Boston & Maine Railroad, Eastern Division, Charlestown. Boston & Maine Railroad, Western Division, Charlestown. Boston & Maine Railroad, Mystic Branch, Charlestown. Boston & Maine Railroad, East Boston Branch, East Boston. Boston & Maine Railroad, Fitchburg Division, Cheshire Branch, Winchendon.	
Number of above crossings at which interlocking signals are established, ...	14

ACCIDENTS TO PERSONS.

(A detailed statement of each accident is on file in the office of the Board.)

KILLED AND INJURED.	IN MASSACHUSETTS.						TOTAL ON ALL LINES OPERATED.	
	FROM CAUSES BEYOND THEIR OWN CONTROL.		FROM THEIR OWN MISCONDUCT OR CARELESSNESS.		TOTAL.			
	Killed.	Injured.	Killed.	Injured.	Killed.	Injured.	Killed.	Injured.
Passengers, .	-	4	2	17	2	21	2	23
Employees, .	5	64	13	141	18	205	20	239
Other persons,	-	2	39	31	39	33	40	37
TOTALS, .	5	70	54	189	59	259	62	299

CORPORATE NAME AND ADDRESS OF THE COMPANY.

BOSTON & ALBANY RAILROAD
(NEW YORK CENTRAL & HUDSON RIVER RAILROAD COMPANY, LESSEE),

BOSTON, MASS.

NAMES AND BUSINESS ADDRESS OF PRINCIPAL OFFICERS FOR LESSEE COMPANY.

Edgar Van Etten, *Second Vice-President of Lessee Company, in charge*, Boston, Mass. Edward L. Rossiter, *Treasurer*, Grand Central Station, New York, N. Y. Woodward Hudson, *Attorney*, Boston, Mass. Marshal L. Bacon, *General Auditor*, Grand Central Station, New York, N. Y. Henry B. Chapin, *Traffic Manager*, Boston, Mass. Arthur S. Hanson, *General Passenger Agent*, Boston, Mass. Joseph B. Stewart, *Superintendent*, Boston, Mass.

We hereby certify that the statements contained in the foregoing return are full, just and true.

EDWARD L. ROSSITER,
Treasurer of the Lessee Company.
MARSHAL L. BACON,
Auditor of the Lessee Company.

STATE OF NEW YORK.

COUNTY OF NEW YORK, ss. AUGUST 30, 1904. Then personally appeared the above-named Edward L. Rossiter, treasurer, and Marshal L. Bacon, auditor, and severally made oath that the foregoing certificate by them subscribed is, to the best of their knowledge and belief, true.

Before me, LOUIS BENDER,
Notary Public, New York County, N. Y.

RETURN

OF THE

BOSTON & LOWELL RAILROAD CORPORATION

For the Year ending June 30, 1904.

[Leased to and operated by the Boston & Maine.]

General Exhibit for the Year.

Rental received from lease of road,		$877,656 68
Expenses and charges upon income accrued during the year:		
Salaries and maintenance of organization,	$7,000 00	
Interest on funded debt,	330,800 00	
Interest and discount on unfunded debts and loans,	11,904 68	
Total Expenses and Charges upon Income,		349,704 68
Net Divisible Income,		$527,952 00
Dividends declared (8 per cent),		$527,952 00
Amount of surplus June 30, 1903,		$1,436,063 91
Total Surplus June 30, 1904,		$1,436,063 91

General Balance Sheet June 30, 1904.

Assets.		Dr.
Cost of road,		$12,320,779 85
Cost of equipment,		833,583 94
Stock of St. Johnsbury & Lake Champlain R.R. Co.,	$360,470 50	
Stock of Peterborough R.R. Co.,	19,860 00	
Stock of Essex Marine Ry. Co.,	3,775 00	
		384,105 50
Bonds of Central Massachusetts R.R. Co.,	$2,000,000 00	
Bonds of St. Johnsbury & Lake Champlain R.R. Co.,	895,000 00	
		2,895,000 00
Total Permanent Investments,		$16,433,469 29
Cash,	$16,361 94	
Due from solvent companies and individuals,	683,807 19	
Total Cash and Current Assets,		700,169 13
Total,		$17,133,638 42

LIABILITIES.	CR.	
Capital stock,		$6,599,400 00
Funded debt,		8,528,000 00
Current liabilities:		
Dividends not called for,	$263,996 00	
Matured interest coupons unpaid (including coupons due July 1),	37,932 50	
TOTAL CURRENT LIABILITIES,		301,928 50
Accrued liabilities: interest accrued and not yet due,		59,098 35
Sinking and other special funds:		
Premium on capital stock,	$97,824 19	
Premium and discount on bonds,	99,617 78	
Miscellaneous account,	11,705 69	
TOTAL SINKING AND OTHER SPECIAL FUNDS,		209,147 66
Profit and loss balance (surplus),		1,436,063 91
TOTAL,		$17,133,638 42

PROPERTY ACCOUNTS.		
Additions to construction account:		
Roadbed and track,	$200 00	
Bridges and culverts,	22,602 92	
Land damages,	17,777 38	
Other additions to construction account: wharves and wharf property,	39,146 58	
TOTAL ADDITIONS TO CONSTRUCTION ACCOUNT,		$79,726 88
Deductions from property accounts (property sold or reduced in valuation and credited to property accounts): construction account, — land damages,		290 00
NET ADDITION TO PROPERTY ACCOUNTS FOR THE YEAR,		$79,436 88

CAPITAL STOCK.		
Capital stock authorized by law,	$7,379,400 00	
Capital stock authorized by votes of company,	6,599,400 00	
Capital stock issued and outstanding,		$6,599,400 00
Number of shares issued and outstanding,	65,994	
Number of stockholders,	2,179	
Number of stockholders in Massachusetts,	1,855	
Amount of stock held in Massachusetts,	$5,698,700 00	

FUNDED DEBT.

Description of Bonds.	Rate of Interest.	Date of Maturity.	Amount Outstanding.	Interest Paid during the Year.
Debentures: —	Per Cent.			
Bonds dated September 1, 1885, . .	4	Sept. 1, 1905,	$500,000 00	$20,000 00
Bonds dated November 1, 1886, . .	4	Nov. 1, 1906,	500,000 00	20,000 00
Bonds dated June 1, 1887, . . .	4	June 1, 1907,	2,000,000 00	80,000 00
Bonds dated July 1, 1887, . . .	4	July 1, 1907,	325,000 00	13,000 00
Bonds dated April 1, 1889, . . .	4	April 1, 1909,	350,000 00	14,000 00
Bonds dated April 1, 1892, . . .	4	April 1, 1932,	1,000,000 00	40,000 00
Bonds dated February 1, 1893, . .	4	Feb. 1, 1913,	1,000,000 00	40,000 00
Bonds dated March 1, 1895, . .	4	March 1, 1915,	500,000 00	20,000 00
Bonds dated July 1, 1896, . . .	4	July 1, 1916,	750,000 00	30,000 00
Bonds dated October 1, 1897, . .	4	Oct. 1, 1917,	200,000 00	8,000 00
Bonds dated October 1, 1898, . .	4	Oct. 1, 1918,	214,000 00	8,560 00
Bonds dated July 1, 1899, . . .	3½	July 1, 1919,	620,000 00	21,700 00
Bonds dated July 1, 1901, . . .	3½	July 1, 1921,	319,000 00	11,165 00
Bonds dated May 1, 1903, . . .	3½	May 1, 1923,	250,000 00	4,375 00*
Totals, ...	. .	. . .	$8,528,000 00	$330,800 00

DESCRIPTION OF RAILROAD OWNED.

(See also tabulated description in preceding appendix to report.)

Railroad Owned.	Total.	In Massachusetts.
	Miles.	Miles.
Length of main line, ...	26.750	26.750
Length of branch line,†	85.000	70.200
Total Length of Line Owned, ...	111.750	96.950
Length of second track, ...	41.910	41.910
Length of side track, etc., ...	127.220	120.550
Total Length of Track Owned,†	280.880	259.410

CORPORATE NAME AND ADDRESS OF THE COMPANY.

BOSTON & LOWELL RAILROAD CORPORATION,
BOSTON, MASS.

NAMES AND BUSINESS ADDRESS OF PRINCIPAL OFFICERS.

Walter C. Baylies, *President*, Boston, Mass. Charles E. Cotting, *Vice-President*, Boston, Mass. Henry B. Cabot, *Treasurer and Clerk of Corporation*, Brookline, Mass.

* Six months interest, bonds sold and issued in November, 1903.

† Includes one-half of the mileage of the Manchester & Keene Railroad.

NAMES AND RESIDENCE OF BOARD OF DIRECTORS.

Walter C. Baylies, Boston, Mass. T. Jefferson Coolidge, Manchester, Mass. Francis L. Higginson, Boston, Mass. Edwin Morey, Boston, Mass. Charles E. Cotting, Boston, Mass. George A. Gardner, Boston, Mass. Henry B. Cabot, Brookline, Mass.

We hereby certify that the statements contained in the foregoing return are full, just and true.

WALTER C. BAYLIES,
T. JEFFERSON COOLIDGE,
GEO. A. GARDNER,
F. L. HIGGINSON,
CHAS. E. COTTING,
HENRY B. CABOT,
Directors.
HENRY B. CABOT,
Treasurer.

COMMONWEALTH OF MASSACHUSETTS.

SUFFOLK SS. AUG. 1, 1904. Then personally appeared the above-named Henry B. Cabot (July 26), Walter C. Baylies (July 28), Charles E. Cotting and Francis L. Higginson (July 29), and T. Jefferson Coolidge and Geo. A. Gardner (August 1), and severally made oath that the foregoing certificate by them subscribed is, to the best of their knowledge and belief, true.

Before me, GEO. W. BRAINARD,
Notary Public.

RETURN

OF THE

BOSTON & MAINE RAILROAD

For the Year ending June 30, 1904.

General Exhibit for the Year.			
Gross earnings from operation,			$34,894,608 19
Operating expenses,			25,271,907 63
Net Earnings from Operation,			$9,622,700 56
Dividends received on stocks owned:			
Maine Central R.R. (25,160 shares, 7 per cent),	$176,120 00		
Portland & Ogdensburg R.R. (3,952 4/10 shares, 2 per cent),	7,904 80		
St. John Bridge & R'y Ex'tn Co. (240 shares, par $50, 15 per cent),	1,800 00		
York Harbor & Beach R R. (5,071 shares, par $50, 2 per cent),	5,071 00		
Suncook Valley R R. (owned by C. & M. R.R., 630 3/5 shares, 6 per cent),	3,783 60		
Pemigewasset Valley R.R. (owned by C. & M. R.R., 381 shares, 6 per cent),	2,286 00		
New Boston R R. (owned by C. & M. R.R., 100 shares, 4 per cent),	400 00		
Mt. Washington R'y (owned by C. & M. R.R., 1,099 shares, 4 per cent),	4,396 00		
Mt. Washington R'y (owned by C. & P. R. R R., 194 shares, 4 per cent),	776 00		
Vermont Valley R.R (owned by Conn. River R.R, 9,734 shares, par $50, 7 per cent),	34,069 00		
Peterborough R.R. (owned by B. & L. R.R., 331 shares, 4 per cent),	1,324 00		
		$237,930 40	
Interest received on bonds owned:			
Woodsville Aqueduct Co. (owned by B. & M. R.R., $5,450, 1 year, 4 per cent),	$218 00		
Woodsville Aqueduct Co., (owned by C. & M. R.R., $10,000, 1 year, 4 per cent),	400 00		
		618 00	

Miscellaneous income, less expense of collecting:				
Rents of tenements, lands, etc.,	$321,848 44			
Less expense, .	46,971 10			
		$274,877 34		
Bridge tolls, .	$10,308 99			
Less expense, .	1,449 80			
		8,859 19		
Interest received, ...		36,019 53		
Sundry items, ...		18,579 71		
			$338,335 77	
TOTAL INCOME FROM SOURCES OTHER THAN OPERATION,				$576,884 17
GROSS INCOME ABOVE OPERATING EXPENSES, . . .				$10,199,584 73
Charges upon income accrued during the year:				
Interest on funded debt, ...			$1,383,479 96	
Interest and discount on unfunded debts and loans (real estate mortgages, etc.), .			98,815 68	
Taxes, ...			1,633,269 90	
Rentals of leased roads:				
Fitchburg R.R., ...		$1,823,797 07		
Boston & Lowell R.R., .		775,920 56		
Concord & Montreal R.R., .		804,616 33		
Connecticut River R.R., .		349,065 00		
Worc., Nash. & Roch. R.R.,		250,000 00		
Vermont & Mass. R.R., .		221,600 00		
Conn. & Pass. Rivers R.R.,		213,000 00		
Northern R.R., ...		216,104 00		
Nashua & Lowell R.R., .		73,000 00		
Lowell & Andover R.R., .		52,500 00		
Manchester & Law. R.R., .		112,960 00		
Stony Brook R.R., . . .		21,500 00		
Wilton R.R., ...		20,400 00		
Peterborough R.R., . . .		15,700 00		
Concord & Portsm'th R.R.,		25,000 00		
Pemigewasset Valley R.R.,		32,790 00		
Suncook Valley R.R., .		14,700 00		
Massawippi Valley R.R., .		40,000 00		
Kenneb'k & K'b'kport R.R.,		2,925 00		
New Boston R.R., . .		2,800 00		
Troy & Bennington R.R., .		15,400 00		
Newport & Richford R.R.,	$17,500 00			
Sub-let to C. P. R'y for .	18,000 00			
Credit, ...		500 00		
			5,083,277 96	
Payments to sinking and other special funds:				
Sinking fund, Eastern R.R.,		$100,000 00		
Sinking fund, Boston & Maine R.R., . . .		51,285 00		
			151,285 00	
TOTAL CHARGES AND DEDUCTIONS FROM INCOME, .				8,350,128 50
NET DIVISIBLE INCOME, ...				$1,849,456 23

Dividends declared during the year payable on —		
October 1, 1903, 1¾ per cent on $22,707,700, common,	$397,384 75	
January 1, 1904, 1¾ per cent on $22,707,700, common,	397,384 75	
April 1, 1904, 1¾ per cent on $22,709,200, common,	397,411 00	
July 1, 1904, 1¾ per cent on $22,709,200, common,	397,411 00	
September 1, 1903, 3 per cent on $3,149,800, preferred,	94,494 00	
March 1, 1904, 3 per cent on $3,149,800, preferred,	94,494 00	
Amount paid in lieu of dividends on common stock issued in exchange for stocks of roads purchased,	420 00	
Total Dividends Declared,		$1,778,999 50
Surplus for the year ending June 30, 1904,		$70,456 73
Amount of surplus June 30, 1903,		1,565,165 45
Debits to profit and loss account during the year:		
Discount on bonds,	$27,090 50	
Amount transferred to contingent fund,	70,456 73	
Total Debits,		97,547 23
Total Surplus June 30, 1904,		$1,538,074 95

Earnings from Operation.

Department of Service.	Gross Receipts.	Deductions.	Earnings.
Passenger service:			
Gross receipts from passengers,	$12,466,301 09		
Deductions:			
Tickets redeemed,	. . .	$23,525 83	
Excess fares refunded,	. . .	104,593 73	
Total deductions,	. . .	$128,119 56	
Net Revenue from Passengers,*	. . .	. . .	$12,338,181 53
From mails,	$457,551 45		
From express,	1,027,086 51		
From extra baggage and storage,	148,453 73		1,633,091 69
Total Earnings, Passenger Service,†	. . .	. . .	$13,971,273 22
Freight service:			
Gross receipts from freight,	$20,516,898 36		
Deductions:			
Overcharge to shippers,	. . .	$153,292 98	
Net Revenue from Freight,	. . .	. . .	$20,363,605 38
From stock yards,	$2,127 57		
From elevators,	52,694 55		
Other earnings, freight service: storage and miscellaneous,	239,841 36		294,663 48
Total Earnings, Freight Service,	. . .	. . .	$20,658,268 86
Total Passenger and Freight Earnings	*(carried for*	*ward)*,	$34,629,542 08

* On steam roads, $12,168,345.83; on electric street railways, $169,835.70.

† $13,800,938.78, steam roads; $170,334.44, electric street railways.

EARNINGS FROM OPERATION — Concluded.

DEPARTMENT OF SERVICE.	Gross Receipts.	Deductions.	Earnings.
Amount brought forward,	. . .	. . .	$34,629,542 08
Other earnings from operation:			
Switching charges — balance,	$130,510 44		
Telegraph companies,	18,892 45		
Rentals from tracks, yards and terminals,	60,047 62		
From other sources:			
Hire of equipment — balance,	32,946 26		
Steamer "Mt. Washington,"	19,272 87		
Steamer "Lady of the Lake,"	3,396 47		
TOTAL OTHER EARNINGS,	. . .	. . .	265,066 11
GROSS EARNINGS FROM OPERATION,	. . .	. . .	$34,894,608 19

EXPENSES OF OPERATION.

General expenses:	
Salaries of general officers,	$117,214 95
Salaries of clerks and attendants,	228,739 60
General office expenses and supplies,	29,126 34
Insurance,	216,666 33
Law expenses,	185,935 11
Stationery and printing (general offices),	16,853 12
Other general expenses: miscellaneous expense,	26,283 69
TOTAL,	$820,819 14
Maintenance of way and structures:	
Repairs of roadway,	$2,300,368 06
Renewals of rails,	104,769 96
Renewals of ties,	517,934 39
Repairs and renewals of bridges and culverts,	268,292 21
Repairs and renewals of fences, road crossings, signs and cattle guards,	130,810 24
Repairs and renewals of buildings and fixtures,	448,261 53
Repairs and renewals of docks and wharves,	25,231 33
Repairs and renewals of telegraph,	12,287 44
Stationery and printing,	4,089 80
Other expenses of maintaining way and structures:	
Repairs of electric line,	4,552 00
Tools and machinery,	9,659 70
Miscellaneous expense,	2,445 83
TOTAL,	$3,828,702 49
Maintenance of equipment:	
Superintendence,	$123,260 60
Repairs and renewals of locomotives (includes $158,350 new locomotives),	1,379,593 11
Repairs and renewals of passenger cars (includes $87,420.44 new passenger cars),	789,659 39
Repairs and renewals of freight cars (includes $101,732.27 new freight cars),	1,080,844 04
Repairs and renewals of work cars (includes $3,485 47 new work cars),	27,977 03

Maintenance of equipment — *Concluded.*	
Repairs and renewals of marine equipment,	$4,745 06
Repairs and renewals of shop machinery and tools,	53,857 03
Stationery and printing,	7,835 60
Other expenses of maintaining equipment: miscellaneous expenses (watching, etc.),	179,048 65
TOTAL,	$3,646,820 51
Conducting transportation:	
Superintendence,	$322,152 86
Engine and roundhouse men,	2,432,949 77
Fuel for locomotives,	4,443,986 19
Water supply for locomotives,	167,612 62
Oil, tallow and waste for locomotives,	89,248 22
Other supplies for locomotives,	23,683 13
Train service,	2,028,960 02
Train supplies and expenses,	430,763 02
Switchmen, flagmen and watchmen,	1,976,214 84
Telegraph expenses,	338,897 77
Station service,	2,546,136 58
Station supplies,	355,095 13
Car service — balance,	704,149 13
Loss and damage,	207,217 24
Injuries to persons,	318,154 40
Clearing wrecks,	41,907 43
Operating marine equipment,	16,876 03
Advertising,	84,903 60
Outside agencies,	89,233 67
Stock yards and elevators,	36,240 40
Rentals for tracks, yards and terminals,	27,622 29
Rentals of buildings and other property,	42,286 17
Stationery and printing,	172,708 66
Other expenses of conducting transportation:	
Electric motive power,	56,730 72
Miscellaneous expenses,	21,835 60
TOTAL,	$16,975,565 49
Recapitulation:	
General expenses,	$820,819 14
Maintenance of way and structures,	3,828,702 49
Maintenance of equipment,	3,646,820 51
Conducting transportation,	16,975,565 49
TOTAL OPERATING EXPENSES,*	$25,271,907 63
Percentage of operating expenses to gross earnings,	72.420

GENERAL BALANCE SHEET JUNE 30, 1904.

ASSETS.	DR.	
Cost of road,		$42,979,441 32
Cost of equipment,		7,223,320 26
Real estate, Nashua, N. H.,	$215,197 55	
Real estate, Fabyan, N. H.,	1,631 98	
Land at Somerville, Mass.,	440,368 47	
Land at Medford, Mass.,	38,192 64	
Land at Malden, Mass.,	28,383 40	

* Steam roads, $25,092,545.27; electric street railways, $179,362.36.

Land at Melrose and Melrose Highlands, Mass.,	$21,958 51	
Land at Wakefield, Mass.,	3,300 00	
Land at Boxford, Mass.,	519 10	
Land at Georgetown, Mass.,	825 00	
Land at Dover, N. H.,	20,234 69	
Land at Rollinsford, N. H.,	1,051 00	
Land at Saco and Biddeford, Me.,	23,701 65	
Land at Kennebunk, Me.,	501 75	
Land at Old Orchard, Me.,	7,648 52	
Land at Portland, Me.,	27,349 29	
Land at Bar Harbor, Me.,	45,104 37	
Land at Boston, Mass.,	190,894 99	
Land at Everett, Mass.,	30,239 40	
Land at Chelsea, Mass.,	21,836 30	
Land at Revere, Mass.,	19,517 92	
Land at Cliftondale, Mass.,	4,565 00	
Land at Saugus, Mass.,	525 00	
Land at Lynn, Mass.,	72,574 81	
Land at Salem, Mass.,	1,000 00	
Land at Peabody, Mass.,	435 10	
Land at Danvers, Mass.,	1,000 00	
Land at Beverly, Mass.,	9,274 25	
Land at Hamilton, Mass.,	5,000 00	
Land at Manchester, Mass.,	1,000 00	
Land at Rockport, Mass.,	1,911 46	
Land at Newbury, Mass.,	300 00	
Land at Newburyport, Mass.,	4,400 00	
Land at Hampton, N. H.,	150 70	
Land at Portsmouth, N. H.,	4,690 70	
Land at Wells, Me.,	64 12	
Land at Rochester, N. H.,	2,200 00	
Land at East Cambridge, Mass.,	44,509 52	
Land at Clematis Brook, Mass.,	501 67	
Land at Arlington, Mass.,	2,500 00	
Land at Wilmington, Mass.,	561 50	
Land at Chelmsford, Mass.,	1,500 00	
Land at Lowell, Mass.,	4,613 80	
Land at Harrisville, N. H.,	150 00	
Land at Marlborough, N. H.,	65 00	
Land at Tremont, N. H.,	400 00	
Land at Windham, N. H.,	81 70	
Land on line of N. A. & B. Branch,	334 00	
Land at Kingston, N. H.,	142 10	
Land at Andover, Mass.,	206 57	
Land at Ayer, Mass.,	30 87	
Land at Peabody, Mass.,	560 06	
Land at Haverhill, Mass.,	151 15	
Land at Manchester, N. H.,	480 66	
Land at Northfield, N. H.,	326 27	
Land at North Hampton, N. H.,	1,013 70	
TOTAL,		$1,305,676 24
Stock of Fitchburg R.R., common, 54,547 shares,	$5,454,549 75	
Stock of Maine Central R.R., 25,160 shares,	2,516,000 00	
Stock of Boston & Maine R.R., common, 11,282 shares,	1,293,559 95	
Stock of York Harbor & Beach R.R., 5,071 shares, par $50,	250,050 00	
Stock of Portland & Ogdensburg R.R., 3,952 4/10 shares,	146,238 80	

Stock of Portland Union Railway Station Co., 250 shares,	$25,000 00	
Stock of Portland, Mt. Desert & Machias Steamboat Co., 300 shares, par $50,	15,000 00	
Stock of St. Johnsbury & Lake Champlain R.R , 809 shares, par $50,	4,303 56	
Stock of Newburyport R.R., 1,481 shares,	4,443 00	
Stock of Danvers R.R., 493 shares,	2,411 00	
Stock of Portsmouth Bridge, 400 shares,	4,000 00	
Stock of St. John Bridge & Railway Extension Co., 240 shares, par $50,	684 00	
Stock of Montreal & Atlantic Ry. Co., 373 shares,	3,000 00	
Stock of Concord & Claremont (N. H.) R.R., 32 shares,	640 00	
Stock of Proprietors Wells River Bridge, 11 shares,	1,090 00	
TOTAL,		$9,720,970 06
Bonds of Newburyport R.R. Co. ($300,000),	$298,464 95	
Bonds of Danvers R.R. Co. ($125,000),	125,000 00	
Bonds of Fitchburg R.R. Co. ($63,000),	63,000 00	
Bonds of St. Johnsbury & Lake Champlain R.R. Co. ($432,000),	432,000 00	
Bonds of Woodsville Aqueduct Co. ($5,450),	5,618 50	
TOTAL,		924,083 45
Other permanent property:		
Steamer "Mt. Washington" and wharves,	$69,260 24	
Richford, Vt., elevator,	52,261 43	
TOTAL,		121,521 67
TOTAL PERMANENT INVESTMENTS,		$62,275,013 00
Cash,	$2,483,452 52	
Bills receivable,	962,729 51	
Due from agents,	1,706,537 88	
Traffic balances due from other companies,	372,083 87	
Due from solvent companies and individuals,	2,755,085 00	
Sinking and other special funds,	1,339,337 14	
TOTAL CASH AND CURRENT ASSETS,		9,619,225 92
Materials and supplies,	$3,393,064 60	
Other assets and property:		
Prepaid insurance premiums, etc.,	170,423 76	
Elimination of grade crossings in process,	150,135 85	
TOTAL MISCELLANEOUS ASSETS,		3,713,624 21
TOTAL,		$75,607,863 13

LIABILITIES.		CR.	
Capital stock, common:			
Boston & Maine,	$23,837,500 00		
Boston & Maine, scrip,	570 70		
		$23,838,070 70	
Capital stock, preferred,		3,149,800 00	
TOTAL CAPITAL STOCK,			$26,987,870 70

Premium on Boston & Maine R.R. common stock sold,		$2,272,218 90
Funded debt,		31,405,008 41
Real estate mortgages,		594,800 00
Current liabilities:		
Loans and notes payable,	$1,700,000 00	
Audited vouchers and accounts,	1,536,383 50	
Salaries and wages,	709,931 68	
Traffic balances due to other companies,	1,129,949 05	
Dividends not called for,	4,880 25	
Matured interest coupons unpaid (including coupons due July 1),	285,825 79	
Rentals due and unpaid (including rentals due July 1),	1,182,286 36	
Miscellaneous current liabilities: dividend on common stock due July 1,	397,411 00	
TOTAL CURRENT LIABILITIES,		6,946,667 63
Accrued liabilities:		
Interest accrued and not yet due,	$292,738 50	
Taxes accrued and not yet due,	577,979 74	
Rentals accrued and not yet due,	427,262 65	
TOTAL ACCRUED LIABILITIES,		1,297,980 89
Amounts due leased roads at termination of leases,		1,823,079 10
Sinking and other special funds:		
Sinking funds for redemption of Boston & Maine R.R. bonds,	$1,337,865 60	
Sinking funds for redemption of Eastern R.R. bonds,	360,321 52	
Injury fund,	150,000 00	
Contingent fund,	65,010 22	
Suspense account,	828,965 21	
TOTAL SINKING AND OTHER SPECIAL FUNDS,		2,742,162 55
Profit and loss balance (surplus),		1,538,074 95
TOTAL,		$75,607,863 13

PROPERTY ACCOUNTS.

Additions to construction account:		
Grading and masonry,	$2,291 52	
Bridging (credit),	4,258 78	
Superstructure, including rails,	75,601 17	
Lands, land damages and fences (credit),	535 06	
Passenger and freight stations, coal sheds and water stations,	10,703 64	
Engineering and other expenses incident to construction (credit),	459 75	
Elimination of grade crossings,	269,577 33	
Other additions to construction account:		
Portsmouth Electric R'y construction,	3,352 77	
Central Massachusetts purchase,	2,528 00	
TOTAL ADDITIONS TO CONSTRUCTION ACCOUNT,		$358,800 84
Additions to equipment account:		
Locomotives (23 in number),	$307,950 00	
Cars for freight service (206 in number),	137,748 42	
TOTAL ADDITIONS TO EQUIPMENT ACCOUNT,		445,698 42

Other expenditures charged to property accounts:		
111 shares stock of Newburyport Railroad,	$333 00	
22 shares stock of Danvers Railroad,	66 00	
Land at Somerville, Mass.,	12,613 03	
Land at Medford, Mass.,	6,502 51	
Land at Malden, Mass.,	886 77	
Land at Boxford, Mass.,	559 10	
Land at Saco and Biddeford, Me.,	351 65	
Land at Kennebunk, Me.,	501 75	
Land at Portland, Me.,	261 25	
Land at Revere, Mass.,	517 92	
Land at Peabody, Mass.,	132 50	
Land at Andover, Mass.,	101 67	
Land at Northfield, N. H.,	326 27	
Land at Haverhill, Mass.,	151 15	
Land at Manchester, N. H.,	480 66	
Land at Kingston, N. H.,	142 10	
TOTAL,		$23,927 33
TOTAL ADDITIONS TO PROPERTY ACCOUNTS,		$828,426 59
Deductions from property accounts (property sold or reduced in valuation and credited to property accounts):		
Fitchburg Railroad Co. bonds sold,	$114,000 00	
Land at Boxford, Mass., sold,	141 25	
Land at Peabody, Mass., sold,	1,566 19	
Land at Valley Falls, N. Y., transferred to improvement account, Fitchburg R.R.,	1,402 50	
Land at Exeter, N. H., transferred to construction,	300 00	
TOTAL DEDUCTIONS FROM PROPERTY ACCOUNTS,		117,409 94
NET ADDITION TO PROPERTY ACCOUNTS FOR THE YEAR,		$711,016 65

CAPITAL STOCK.

Capital stock authorized by law, common,	$24,996,725 30	
Capital stock authorized by law, preferred,	3,149,800 00	
Total capital stock authorized by law,	$28,146,525 30	
Capital stock authorized by votes of company, common,	$24,653,125 30	
Capital stock authorized by votes of company, preferred,	3,149,800 00	
Total capital stock authorized by vote,	$27,802,925 30	
Capital stock issued and outstanding, common,		$23,837,500 00
Capital stock issued and outstanding, preferred,		3,149,800 00
Total capital stock outstanding,		$26,987,300 00
Scrip convertible into stock,		570 70
TOTAL CAPITAL STOCK LIABILITY,		$26,987,870 70

Number of shares issued and outstanding, common, ...	238,375	
Number of shares issued and outstanding, preferred, . .	31,498	
Total number of shares outstanding,		269,873
Number of stockholders, common, .	6,818	
Number of stockholders, preferred, .	725	
Total number of stockholders, . .		7,543
Number of stockholders in Massachusetts, common, . . .	4,283	
Number of stockholders in Massachusetts, preferred, . .	572	
Total stockholders in Massachusetts,		4,855
Amount of stock held in Massachusetts, common, ...		$13,685,700 00
Amount of stock held in Massachusetts, preferred, ...		2,549,800 00
Total stock held in Massachusetts, . . .		$16,235,500 00

REAL ESTATE MORTGAGES.

DESCRIPTION OF MORTGAGED PROPERTY.	Rate of Interest.	Mortgage when Due.	Amount.	Interest Paid during the Year.
	Per Cent.			
Land in Charlestown, Mass., . .	4	Sept. 1, 1906,	$594,800 00	$23,792 00

FUNDED DEBT.

DESCRIPTION OF BONDS.	Rate of Interest.	Date of Maturity.	Amount Outstanding.	Interest Paid during the Year.
	Per Cent.			
Boston & Maine R.R. bonds, . .	4½	Jan. 1, 1944,	$6,000,000 00	$269,842 50
Boston & Maine R.R. bonds, . .	4	Aug. 1, 1942,	2,500,000 00	100,040 00
Boston & Maine R.R. bonds, . .	3	July 1, 1950,	5,454,000 00	163,770 00
Boston & Maine R.R. bonds, . .	3½	Nov. 1, 1921,	1,000,000 00	34,527 50
Boston & Maine R.R. bonds, . .	3½	Jan. 1, 1923,	2,000,000 00	34,842 50
Boston & Maine R.R. improvement bonds.	4	Feb. 2, 1905,	1,000,000 00	40,000 00
Boston & Maine R.R. improvement bonds.	4	Feb. 1, 1907,	500,000 00	20,000 00
Boston & Maine R.R. improvement bonds.	4	Feb. 1, 1937,	1,919,000 00	76,760 00
Eastern R.R. certificates of indebtedness, United States gold.	6	Sept. 1, 1906,	6,406,000 21	387,015 00
Eastern R.R. certificates of indebtedness, £ sterling.	6	Sept. 1, 1906,	1,512,508 20	90,808 90
Amounts carried forward, . .	. .	. . . .	$28,291,508 41	$1,217,606 40

FUNDED DEBT — Concluded.

DESCRIPTION OF BONDS.	Rate of Interest.	Date of Maturity.	Amount Outstanding	Interest Paid during the Year.
Amounts brought forward, . .	. .	. . . .	$28,291,508 41	$1,217,606 40
Portsmouth, Great Falls & Conway R.R. bonds.	4½	June 1, 1937,	998,000 00	45,697 50
Portsmouth, Great Falls & Conway R.R. bonds (7 per cent).	4½	Dec. 1, 1892,*	2,000 00	-
Portland & Rochester R.R. terminal bonds.	4	Oct. 1, 1907,	113,500 00	4,490 00
Central Massachusetts R.R. bonds, .	5	Oct. 1, 1906,	2,000,000 00	100,000 00
TOTALS, ...	. .	. . . .	$31,405,008 41	$1,367,793 90

SINKING AND OTHER SPECIAL FUNDS.

Sinking Funds.		
Amount June 30, 1903, for redemption of Boston & Maine R.R. improvement bonds sinking fund, ...		$1,238,338 67
Amount June 30, 1903, of Eastern R.R. bonds sinking fund, .		265,693 05
TOTAL SINKING FUNDS JUNE 30, 1903, ...		$1,504,031 72
Additions during the year to Boston & Maine R.R. improvement bonds sinking fund, .	$99,526 93	
Additions during the year to Eastern R.R., sinking fund, ...	100,042 01	
		199,568 94
TOTAL, INCLUDING ADDITIONS, ...		$1,703,600 66
Deductions during the year from Eastern R.R. sinking fund,		5,413 54
TOTAL SINKING FUNDS JUNE 30, 1904, ...		$1,698,187 12
Injury Fund.		
Amount of injury fund June 30, 1903, ...		$150,000 00
Additions during the year, ...		318,154 40
TOTAL, INCLUDING ADDITIONS, ...		$468,154 40
Deductions during the year, ...		318,154 40
TOTAL INJURY FUND JUNE 30, 1904, ...		$150,000 00
Contingent Fund.		
Amount of contingent fund June 30, 1903, ...		$94,553 49
Additions during the year, ...		70,456 73
TOTAL, INCLUDING ADDITIONS, ...		$165,010 22
Deductions during the year:		
Cost of 4 locomotives, ...	$5,175 00	
Cost of 4 baggage and 3 combination cars, .	34,545 19	
Cost of 173 freight cars and 4 snow ploughs,	60,279 81	
		100,000 00
TOTAL CONTINGENT FUND JUNE 30, 1904, ...		$65,010 22

* The $2,000 of old bonds of Portsmouth, Great Falls & Conway Railroad have not yet been presented for exchange for the new bonds due June 1, 1937.

VOLUME OF TRAFFIC, ETC.

Passenger traffic:	
Number of passengers carried paying revenue (on steam roads, 37,689,433; on electric street roads, 2,567,868) .	40,257,301
Number of passengers carried one mile,*	681,938,257
Number of passengers carried one mile per mile of road operated (average miles of road operated: steam, 2,244.080; electric, 41.380),*	303,883
Average length of journey per passenger,*	18.090 miles.
Average amount received per passenger per mile carried,* .	1.784 cents.
Passenger earnings (gross) per average mile of road operated, including electric street roads, ...	$6,113 11.000
Passenger earnings (gross) per passenger-train mile run,*	1 21.409
Freight traffic:	
Number of tons of freight hauled earning revenue, . .	19,395,452
Number of tons of freight hauled one mile, . . .	1,728,422,684
Number of tons of freight hauled one mile per mile of road operated,*	770,214
Average length of haul per ton, ...	89.110 miles.
Average amount received per ton per mile hauled, . .	1.178 cents.
Freight earnings (gross) per mile of road operated,* . .	$9,205 67.000
Freight earnings (gross) per freight-train mile run, . .	2 42.563
Operating expenses:	
Operating expenses per mile of road operated,* . . .	11,181 66.000
Operating expenses per revenue-train mile run,* . . .	1 27.342
Train mileage:	
Miles run by passenger trains, ...	11,188,201
Miles run by freight trains, ...	8,337,524
Miles run by mixed trains, ...	179,142
Total mileage of trains earning revenue, ...	19,704,867
Miles run by switching trains, ...	7,444,385
Miles run by construction and other trains, ...	1,627,485
Total train mileage, ...	28,776,737
Fares and freights:	
Average rate of fare per mile received for local and trip tickets,*	1.763 cents.
Average rate of fare per mile received for mileage tickets: 500 miles, 2¼ cents; 1,000 miles, 2 cents.	
Average rate of fare per mile received for time and commutation tickets: within suburban circuit, 1 to 2 cents; outside suburban circuit, 2 to 2¼ cents.	
Average rate of fare per mile received for interline tickets,	1.905 "
Average rate received per ton mile for local freight, . .	2.124 "
Average rate received per ton mile for interline freight, .	.771 "
Passengers to and from Boston:	
Number of passengers to Boston, ...	9,922,117
Number of passengers from Boston, ...	10,245,650
Employees:	
Average number of persons employed, ...	22,999

* Does not include electric street railroads.

Description of Railroad Owned and Operated.

(See also tabulated description in preceding appendix to report).

Railroad Owned.	Total.	In Massachusetts.
	Miles.	Miles.
Length of main line,	446.520	173.700
Length of branch line,	169.480	89.770
Total Length of Line Owned,	616.000	263.470
Length of second track,	167.800	107.220
Length of third track,	2.260	2.260
Length of side track, etc.,	338.820	207.050
Total Length of Track Owned,	1,124.880	580.000
Railroad Operated.		
Length of main line,	1,353.900	459.440
Length of branch line,	936.400	330.060
Total Length of Line Operated,*	2,290.300	789.500
Length of second track,	512.960	376.200
Length of third track,	8.310	6.960
Length of fourth track,	2.020	2.020
Length of side track, etc.,	1,216.800	640.420
Total Length of Track Operated,	4,030.390	1,815.100
Equipped for Electric Power.		
Length of main line,	46.220	-
Length of side track, etc.,	3.400	-
Total Length of Electric Track,	49.620	-

Description of Equipment.

Rolling Stock.	Number Owned.	Number Owned by Leased Roads.	Total Owned and Leased.	Equipped with Power Driving-Wheel Brakes.	Maximum Weight.	Average Weight.
Locomotives.					Lbs.	Lbs.
Passenger,	182	212	394	393	156,000	99,100
Freight,	182	210	392	392	175,000	123,450
Switching, etc.,	96	129	225	224	114,000	81,580
Total,	460	551	1,011	1,009	-	-

* Average length of line operated during the year, 2,285.460 miles.

DESCRIPTION OF EQUIPMENT — Concluded.

ROLLING STOCK.	Number Owned.	Number Owned by Leased Roads.	Total Owned and Leased.	Equipped with Power Train Brakes.	Equipped with Automatic Couplers.	Name of Coupler Used.
CARS — PASSENGER SERVICE.						
Passenger cars,	552	436	988	965	925	439 Gould, 4 Miller, 472 National, 10 Tower.
Combination cars,	102	138	240	240	240	52 Gould, 188 National.
Parlor cars,	1	8	9	9	9	6 Gould, 3 National.
Baggage, express and mail cars,	143	159	302	302	302	68 Gould, 198 National, 32 Trojan, 4 Tower.
Other cars in passenger service,	40	26	66	66	66	16 Gould, 49 National, 1 Trojan.
TOTAL,	838	767	1,605	1,582	1,542	
CARS — FREIGHT SERVICE.						
Box cars,	2,864	5,607	8,471	7,680	8,471	1 Burns, 8,062 Gould, 2 Janney, 406 Trojan.
Flat cars,	1,000	2,073	3,073	2,445	3,073	3 Burns, 2,831 Gould, 1 National, 234 Trojan, 1 Standard, 3 Janney.
Stock cars,	108	52	160	150	160	2 Trojan, 158 Gould.
Coke cars,	165	–	165	165	165	165 Gould.
Coal cars,	2,306	2,540	4,846	3,168	4,158	3,844 Gould, 1 Norton, 40 Tower, 273 Trojan.
Logging trucks,	–	61	61	–	–	–
Refrigerator cars,	137	–	137	137	137	133 Gould, 4 Trojan.
TOTAL,	6,580	10,333	16,913	13,745	16,164	
CARS — COMPANY'S SERVICE.						
Officers' and pay cars,	4	3	7	7	7	2 Gould, 5 National.
Air-brake instruction cars,	1	1	2	2	2	1 Gould, 1 National.
Derrick cars,	33	25	58	35	53	50 Gould, 3 Trojan.
Caboose cars,	186	183	369	310	369	4 Diamond, 361 Gould, 2 National, 1 Trojan, 1 Tower.
Other cars in company's service (including two electric cars).	207	97	304	191	299	282 Gould, 1 Janney, 3 National, 13 Trojan.
TOTAL,	431	309	740	545	730	
Snow ploughs,	45	49	94	66	15	13 Gould, 2 Trojan.
Electric snow ploughs,	1	3	4	4*	–	–

Number of 8-wheel cars in passenger service with brakes for *all* wheels, 1,559
Number of 12-wheel cars in passenger service with brakes for *all* wheels, 20

* Hand brake.

Railroad Crossings in Massachusetts.

Crossings with Highways.	
Number of crossings of railroad with highways at grade,	768
Number of highway grade crossings protected by gates,	281
Number of highway grade crossings protected by flagmen,	206
Number of highway grade crossings protected by electric signals only,	33
Number of highway grade crossings unprotected,	248
Number of highway grade crossings finally abolished during the year,	6
Number of highway grade crossings now in process of abolition,	5
Number of highway grade crossings for abolition of which petition is pending,	56
Number of highway bridges 18 feet (or more) above track,	62
Number of highway bridges less than 18 feet above track,	193
Height of lowest highway bridge above track,	14 ft. 5 in.
Crossings with Other Railroads.	
Crossings of railroad with other railroads at grade (11 in number), viz.:	
Boston, with Boston & Albany Railroad. Boston, Charlestown Branch with Boston & Albany Railroad. Boston, Mystic Branch with Boston & Albany Railroad. East Boston, East Boston Branch with Boston & Albany Railroad. South Sudbury, Southern Division with New York, New Haven & Hartford Railroad. Somerville, Fitchburg Division with Boston & Albany Railroad. Concord Junction, Fitchburg Division with New York, New Haven & Hartford Railroad. Fitchburg, Fitchburg Division with New York, New Haven & Hartford Railroad. Baldwinville, Fitchburg Division with Boston & Albany Railroad. Winchendon, Cheshire Branch with Boston & Albany Railroad. Clinton, Worcester, Nashua & Portland Division with New York, New Haven & Hartford Railroad.	
Number of above crossings at which interlocking signals are established,	9

Accidents to Persons

(A detailed statement of each accident is on file in the office of the Board.)

KILLED AND INJURED.	In Massachusetts.						Total on All Lines Operated.	
	From causes beyond their own control.		From their own misconduct or carelessness.		Total.			
	Killed.	Injured.	Killed.	Injured.	Killed.	Injured.	Killed.	Injured.
Passengers,	-	-	-	1	-	1	1	10
Employees,	-	-	38	41	38	41	62	68
Other persons,	-	-	78	1	78	1	112	14
Totals,	-	-	116	43	116	43	175	92

CORPORATE NAME AND ADDRESS OF THE COMPANY.

BOSTON & MAINE RAILROAD,

BOSTON, MASS.

NAMES AND BUSINESS ADDRESS OF PRINCIPAL OFFICERS.

Lucius Tuttle, *President*, Boston, Mass. William F. Berry, *Second Vice-President and General Traffic Manager*, Boston, Mass. Frank Barr, *Third Vice-President and General Manager*, Boston, Mass. William J. Hobbs, *Fourth Vice-President and General Auditor*, Boston, Mass. Stuart H. McIntosh, *Assistant General Auditor*, Boston, Mass. Herbert E. Fisher, *Treasurer*, Boston, Mass. John F. Webster, *Assistant Treasurer*, Concord, N. H. William B. Lawrence, *Clerk of Corporation*, Boston, Mass. Richard Olney, *General Counsel*, Boston, Mass Edgar J. Rich, *General Solicitor*, Boston, Mass. Charles E. Lee, *Assistant General Manager*, Boston, Mass. Daniel W. Sanborn, *General Superintendent*, Boston, Mass. Dana J. Flanders, *General Passenger and Ticket Agent*, Boston, Mass. Michael T. Donovan, *Freight Traffic Manager*, Boston, Mass. Amos S. Crane, *Export Freight Traffic Manager*, Boston, Mass.

NAMES AND RESIDENCE OF BOARD OF DIRECTORS.

Lucius Tuttle, Boston, Mass. Samuel C. Lawrence, Medford, Mass. Richard Olney, Boston, Mass. Alvah W. Sulloway, Franklin, N. H. Joseph H. White, Brookline, Mass. Walter Hunnewell, Wellesley, Mass. Henry R. Reed, Boston, Mass. Lewis Cass Ledyard, New York, N. Y. Henry M. Whitney, Brookline, Mass. Henry F. Dimock, New York, N. Y. William Whiting, Holyoke, Mass. Charles M. Pratt, New York, N. Y. Alexander Cochrane, Boston, Mass.

We hereby certify that the statements contained in the foregoing return are full, just and true.

LUCIUS TUTTLE,
SAMUEL C. LAWRENCE,
RICHARD OLNEY,
HENRY R. REED,
HENRY M. WHITNEY,
H. F. DIMOCK,
A. W. SULLOWAY,
WILLIAM WHITING,
JOSEPH H. WHITE,
LEWIS CASS LEDYARD,
Directors.
HERBERT E. FISHER,
Treasurer.
WM. J. HOBBS,
Fourth Vice-President and General Auditor.
(*Chief Accounting Officer.*)

COMMONWEALTH OF MASSACHUSETTS.

SUFFOLK, ss. BOSTON, Sept. 8, 1904. Then personally appeared the above-named Lucius Tuttle, Samuel C. Lawrence, Richard Olney, Henry R. Reed, Henry M. Whitney, H. F. Dimock, A. W. Sulloway, William Whiting, Joseph H. White and Lewis Cass Ledyard, directors of the Boston & Maine R.R., and Herbert E. Fisher, its treasurer and W. J. Hobbs, its chief accounting officer, and severally made oath that the foregoing certificate by them subscribed is, to the best of their knowledge and belief, true.

Before me, WILLIAM B. LAWRENCE,
Justice of the Peace.

Approved: GEO. H. POOR,
Commissioner for Massachusetts.

REPORT OF THE CONDITION OF THE SINKING FUND OF THE EASTERN RAILROAD COMPANY ON THE THIRTIETH DAY OF JUNE, 1904.

CR.			
Amount on hand as per report of June 30, 1903,		$1,543 45	
Amount of payment to sinking fund by the Boston & Maine Railroad Company for the year ending Sept. 1, 1903, . . .		100,000 00	
Amount received from the Boston & Maine Railroad Company, being excess of cost of certificates of indebtedness over the fair value fixed by the trustees, Oct. 17, 1903, ...		72 00	
Amount received from the Boston & Maine Railroad Company, being amount allowed R. L. D. & Co., for clerical error in their bid, Oct. 22, 1903, ...		174 22	
Interest on deposits at National Shawmut Bank, June 30, 1904, ...		314 48	$102,104 15
DR.			
Paid Putnam & Putnam, legal services, July 8, 1903, ...		$272 47	
Cost of certificates of indebtedness purchased Oct. 22, 1903 (£400 and $93,000),	$99,553 09		
Accrued interest paid on same,	807 05	$100,360 14	
		$100,632 61	
Balance on hand, June 30, 1904, deposited at National Shawmut Bank, . . .		1,471 54	$102,104 15

CHARLES R. CODMAN,
JOSHUA CRANE,
CHAS. E. COTTING,
Trustees Eastern Railroad.

BOSTON, June 30, 1904.

To the Railroad Commissioners of Massachusetts.

We hereby certify that the mortgage certificates of indebtedness of the Eastern Railroad Company issued by us and outstanding on the thirtieth day of June, 1904, were as follows: —

Certificates payable in sterling money of Great Britain,	£310,800
Certificates payable in gold dollars of the United States of America, ...	$6,406,000
Scrip certificates, ...	21 cents.

The above shows a decrease from amount last reported of £400 and $93,000, being certificates purchased under provisions of chapter 373 of the Acts of 1888, by written request of the Boston & Maine Railroad Corporation.

CHARLES R. CODMAN,
JOSHUA CRANE,
CHAS. E. COTTING,
Trustees Eastern Railroad.

BOSTON, June 30, 1904.

RETURN

OF THE

BOSTON & PROVIDENCE RAILROAD CORPORATION

FOR THE YEAR ENDING JUNE 30, 1904.

[Leased to and operated by the New York, New Haven & Hartford.]

General Exhibit for the Year.		
Rental received from lease of road,		$495,533 86
Dividends received on stocks owned,		400 00
Gross Income,		$495,933 86
Expenses and charges upon income accrued during the year:		
Salaries and maintenance of organization,	$6,561 62	
Interest on funded debt,	86,800 00	
Total Expenses and Charges upon Income,		93,361 62
Net Divisible Income,		$402,572 24
Dividends declared (10 per cent),		400,000 00
Surplus for the year ending June 30, 1904,		$2,572 24
Amount of surplus June 30, 1903,		80,712 58
Total Surplus June 30, 1904,		$83,284 82

General Balance Sheet June 30, 1904. Assets.		Dr.
Cost of road,		$5,046,088 30
Cost of equipment,		871,234 35
Lands in Massachusetts,		82,183 94
Stock of Providence, Warren & Bristol Railroad Company,	$158,505 00	
Stock of Union Freight Railroad Company,	79,014 42	
Stock of Boston Terminal Company,	100,000 00	
		337,519 42
Total Permanent Investments,		$6,337,026 01
Cash (book balance in bank),	$146,807 19	
Second National Bank back dividends,	3,592 50	
Sinking and other special funds,	10,090 00	
Other cash assets (New York, New Haven & Hartford),	3,561 62	
Total Cash and Current Assets,		164,051 31
Total,		$6,501,077 32

LIABILITIES.	CR.	
Capital stock,		$4,000,000 00
Funded debt,		2,170,000 00
Current liabilities:		
Dividend due July 1, 1904,	$100,000 00	
Dividends not called for,	3,592 50	
Matured interest coupons unpaid (including coupons due July 1),	44,200 00	
Miscellaneous current liabilities: New York New Haven & Hartford Railroad Co.,	100,000 00	
TOTAL CURRENT LIABILITIES,		247,792 50
Profit and loss balance (surplus),		83,284 82
TOTAL,		$6,501,077 32

CAPITAL STOCK.		
Capital stock authorized by law,	$4,000,000 00	
Capital stock authorized by votes of company,	4,000,000 00	
Capital stock issued and outstanding,		$4,000,000 00
Number of shares issued and outstanding,	40,000	
Number of stockholders,	1,611	
Number of stockholders in Massachusetts,	1,310	
Amount of stock held in Massachusetts,	$3,385,600 00	

FUNDED DEBT.

DESCRIPTION OF BONDS.	Rate of Interest.	Date of Maturity.	Amount Outstanding.	Interest Paid during the Year.
	Per Cent.			
Plain bonds,	4	July 1, 1918,	$2,170,000 00	$88,580 00

DESCRIPTION OF RAILROAD OWNED.

(See also tabulated description in preceding appendix to report.)

RAILROAD OWNED.	Total.	In Massachusetts.
	Miles.	Miles.
Length of main line,	41.890	38.700
Length of branch line,	21.140	16.580
TOTAL LENGTH OF LINE OWNED,*	63.030	55.280
Length of second track,	54.980	51.790
Length of third track,	12.880	10.730
Length of fourth track,	12.880	10.730
Length of side track,	94.870	69.910
TOTAL LENGTH OF TRACK OWNED,*	238.640	198.440

* Including only one-half the length of joint tracks between Providence station and Boston switch, so called, all in Rhode Island, viz.: 5.000 miles of first or single track; 5.000 miles of second track; 4.300 miles of third track; 4.300 miles of fourth track; and 10.120 miles of sidings; these distances being the total length.

Corporate Name and Address of the Company.

BOSTON & PROVIDENCE RAILROAD CORPORATION,

526 South Station, Boston, Mass.

Name and Business Address of Principal Officers.

Royal C. Taft, *President*, Providence, R. I. Benjamin B. Torrey, *Treasurer and Clerk of Corporation*, 526 South Station, Boston, Mass.

Names and Residence of Board of Directors.

Royal C. Taft, Providence, R. I. Robert H. Stevenson, 28 State Street, Boston, Mass. Charles P. Bowditch, 28 State Street, Boston, Mass. Robert I. Gammell, Providence, R. I. Geo. A. Gardner, 22 Congress Street, Boston, Mass. John C. Gray, 60 State Street, Boston, Mass. Philip Dexter, 40 State Street, Boston, Mass.

We hereby certify that the statements contained in the foregoing return are full, just and true.

ROYAL C. TAFT,
JOHN C. GRAY,
PHILIP DEXTER,
CHARLES P. BOWDITCH,
Directors.
B. B. TORREY,
Treasurer.

Commonwealth of Massachusetts.

Suffolk, ss. Boston, Oct. 12, 1904. Then personally appeared the above-named Royal C. Taft, John C. Gray, Philip Dexter, directors, and B. B. Torrey, treasurer, and severally made oath that the foregoing certificate by them subscribed is, to the best of their knowledge and belief, true.

Before me, ALFRED H. LITCHFIELD,
Justice of the Peace.

Commonwealth of Massachusetts.

Suffolk, ss. Boston, Oct. 14, 1904. Then personally appeared the above-named Charles P. Bowditch, and made oath that the foregoing certificate by him subscribed, was, to the best of his knowledge and belief, true.

Before me, GEORGE B. PHIPPEN,
Justice of the Peace.

RETURN

OF THE

BOSTON, REVERE BEACH & LYNN RAILROAD COMPANY

FOR THE YEAR ENDING JUNE 30, 1903.

[A narrow-gauge road.]

GENERAL EXHIBIT FOR THE YEAR.		
Gross earnings from operation,		$589,743 25
Operating expenses,		525,224 92
NET EARNING FROM OPERATION,		$64,518 33
Miscellaneous income, less expense of collecting: sale of old materials, rents, etc.,		16,613 81
GROSS INCOME ABOVE OPERATING EXPENSES,		$81,132 14
Charges upon income accrued during the year:		
Interest on funded debt,	$39,695 00	
Interest and discount on unfunded debts and loans,	13,275 06	
Taxes,	10,713 46	
TOTAL CHARGES AND DEDUCTIONS FROM INCOME,		63,683 52
NET DIVISIBLE INCOME,		$17,448 62
Dividends declared during the year payable on:—		
Jannary 1, 1904, 1 per cent on $850,000,	$8,500 00	
July 1, 1904, 1 per cent on $850,000,	8,500 00	
TOTAL DIVIDENDS DECLARED,		17,000 00
Surplus for the year ending June 30, 1904,		$448 62
Amount of surplus June 30, 1903,		58,983 77
TOTAL SURPLUS JUNE 30, 1904,		$59,432 39

EARNINGS FROM OPERATION.

DEPARTMENT OF SERVICE.	Gross Receipts.	Deductions.	Earnings.
Passenger service:			
Gross receipts from passengers,	$621,728 65		
Deductions:			
Excess fares refunded,	. . .	$31,985 40	
NET REVENUE FROM PASSENGERS,	. . .	. . .	$589,743 25
GROSS EARNINGS FROM OPERATION,	. . .	. . .	$589,743 25

EXPENSES OF OPERATION.

General expenses:	
Salaries of general officers,	$9,520 00
Salaries of clerks and attendants,	5,961 11
General office expenses and supplies,	1,741 45
Insurance,	17,202 68
Law expenses,	2,686 15
Stationery and printing (general offices),	1,971 67
TOTAL,	$39,083 06
Maintenance of way and structures:	
Repairs of roadway,	$60,505 55
Renewals of rails,	9,500 00
Renewals of ties,	2,298 00
Repairs and renewals of bridges and culverts,	2,031 49
Repairs and renewals of fences, road crossings, signs and cattle guards,	330 60
Repairs and renewals of buildings and fixtures,	18,899 04
TOTAL,	$93,564 68
Maintenance of equipment:	
Repairs and renewals of locomotives,	$14,788 65
Repairs and renewals of passenger cars,	33,757 23
Repairs and renewals of marine equipment,	7,545 38
TOTAL,	$56,091 26
Conducting transportation:	
Engine and roundhouse men,	$44,509 50
Fuel for locomotives,	51,132 70
Water supply for locomotives,	7,233 39
Oil, tallow, waste and other supplies for locomotives,	2,540 44
Train service,	78,090 80
Train supplies and expenses,	8,002 61
Switchmen, flagmen and watchmen,	29,837 50
Telegraph expenses,	2,179 10
Station service,	39,705 05
Station supplies,	16,308 35
Loss and damage,	199 83
Injuries to persons,	7,672 00
Operating marine equipment,	42,590 60
Advertising,	3,984 05
Stationery and printing,	2,500 00
TOTAL,	$336,485 92
Recapitulation:	
General expenses,	$39,083 06
Maintenance of way and structures,	93,564 68
Maintenance of equipment,	56,091 26
Conducting transportation,	336,485 92
TOTAL OPERATING EXPENSES,	$525,224 92
Percentage of operating expenses to gross earnings,	89.05

General Balance Sheet, June 30, 1904.

Assets.	Dr.	
Cost of road,		$1,445,927 38
Cost of equipment,		258,434 89
Lands,		85,087 00
Other permanent property: 3 ferry boats,		131,000 00
Total Permanent Investments,		$1,920,449 27
Cash,	$28,769 42	
Due from solvent companies and individuals,	1,008 99	
Other cash assets,	205,794 81	
Total Cash and Current Assets,		235,573 22
Materials and supplies,		21,641 64
Total,		$2,177,664 13

Liabilities.	Cr.	
Capital stock,		$850,000 00
Funded debt,		850,000 00
Current liabilities:		
Loans and notes payable,	$305,000 00	
Audited vouchers and accounts,	18,641 81	
Dividends not called for,	40 00	
Miscellaneous current liabilities,	51,049 93	
Total Current Liabilities,		374,731 74
Accrued liabilities: dividend due July 1, 1904,		8,500 00
Sinking and other special funds: injury fund,		35,000 00
Profit and loss balance (surplus),		59,432 39
Total,		$2,177,664 13

Capital Stock.

Capital stock authorized by law,	$1,125,000 00	
Capital stock authorized by votes of company,	1,125,000 00	
Capital stock issued and outstanding,		$850,000 00
Number of shares issued and outstanding,	8,500	
Number of stockholders,	246	
Number of stockholders in Massachusetts,	221	
Amount of stock held in Massachusetts,	$824,700 00	

Funded Debt.

Description of Bonds.	Rate of Interest.	Date of Maturity.	Amount Outstanding.	Interest Paid during the Year.
	Per Cent.			
Mortgage bonds,	4½	July 15, 1927,	$561,000 00	$25,245 00
Mortgage bonds, Winthrop Branch,	5	Sept. 1, 1906,	289,000 00	14,450 00
Totals,			$850,000 00	$39,695 00

Sinking and Other Special Funds.

Injury Fund.	
Amount of injury fund, June 30, 1903,	$25,000 00
Additions during the year,	10,000 00
Total Injury Fund, June 30, 1904,	$35,000 00

Volume of Traffic, etc.

Passenger traffic:	
Number of passengers carried paying revenue,	9,743,855
Number of passengers carried one mile,	57,158,595
Number of passengers carried one mile per mile of road operated,	4,330,196
Average length of journey per passenger,	5.866 miles.
Average amount received per passenger per mile carried,	1.030 cents.
Passenger earnings (gross) per mile of road operated,	$44,677 51
Passenger earnings (gross) per passenger-train mile run,	85.118 cents.
Operating expenses:	
Operating expenses per mile of road operated,	$39,789 76
Operating expenses per revenue-train mile run,	75.835 cents.
Train mileage:	
Miles run by passenger trains,	692,849
Miles run by construction and other trains,	4,611
Total train mileage,	697,460
Fares and freights:	
Average rate of fare per mile received for local and trip tickets,	1.030 cents.
Passengers to and from Boston:	
Number of passengers to Boston (estimated),	4,009,940
Number of passengers from Boston (estimated),	4,009,940
Employees:	
Average number of persons employed,	413

Description of Railroad Owned and Operated.

(See also tabulated description in preceding appendix to report.)

Railroad Owned and Operated.	Total.	In Massachusetts.
	Miles.	Miles.
Length of main line,	8.800	8.800
Length of branch line,	4.400	4.400
Total Length of Line Owned,	13.200	13.200
Length of second track,	13.200	13.200
Length of side track, etc.,	4.100	4.100
Total Length of Track Owned,	30.500	30.500

Description of Equipment.

Rolling Stock.	Number Owned.	Equipped with Power Driving-wheel Brakes.	Equipped with Power Train Brakes.	Equipped with Automatic Couplers.	Maximum Weight.	Average Weight.	Name of Coupler Used.
Locomotives.					Lbs.	Lbs.	
Passenger,	15	15	-	-	76,000	76,000	-
Cars — Passenger Service.							
Passenger cars,	66	-	66	66	-	-	Miller.
Combination cars,	13	-	13	13	-	-	-
Total,	79	-	79	79	-	-	-
Cars — Company's Service.							
Gravel cars,	12	-	-	-	-	-	-
Other cars in company's service,	6	-	2	2	-	-	Miller.
Total,	18	-	2	2	-	-	-

Number of 8-wheel cars in passenger service with brakes for *all* wheels, . 78

Railroad Crossings in Massachusetts.

Crossings with Highways.	
Number of crossings of railroad with highways at grade,	11
Number of highway grade crossings protected by gates,	6
Number of highway grade crossings protected by flagmen,	5
Height of lowest highway bridge above track,	12 ft. 6 in.

Accidents to Persons.

(A detailed statement of each accident is on file in the office of the Board.)

Killed and Injured.	In Massachusetts.						Total on All Lines Operated.	
	From causes beyond their own control.		From their own misconduct or carelessness.		Total.			
	Killed.	Injured.	Killed.	Injured.	Killed.	Injured.	Killed.	Injured.
Passengers,	-	4	-	22	-	26	-	26
Employees,	-	1	-	9	-	10	-	10
Other persons,	-	-	1	8	1	8	1	8
Totals,	-	5	1	39	1	44	1	44

Corporate Name and Address of the Company.

BOSTON, REVERE BEACH & LYNN RAILROAD COMPANY,

Boston, Mass.

NAMES AND BUSINESS ADDRESS OF PRINCIPAL OFFICERS.

Melvin O. Adams, *President*, Boston, Mass. Henry R. Reed, *Vice-President*, Boston, Mass. John A. Fenno, *Treasurer and Superintendent*, Boston, Mass. Henry L. Hoyt, *General Passenger Agent*, Boston, Mass.

NAMES AND RESIDENCE OF BOARD OF DIRECTORS.

Melvin O. Adams, Boston, Mass. Henry R. Reed, Boston, Mass. Henry F. Hurlburt, Boston, Mass. William S. Spaulding, Beverly Mass. John A. Fenno, Newton, Mass.

We hereby certify that the statements contained in the foregoing return are full, just and true.

MELVIN O. ADAMS,
HENRY R. REED,
WILLIAM S. SPAULDING,
JOHN A. FENNO,
Directors.
JOHN A. FENNO,
Treasurer.

COMMONWEALTH OF MASSACHUSETTS.

SUFFOLK SS. BOSTON, Aug. 29, 1904. Then personally appeared the above named John A. Fenno, and made oath that the foregoing certificate by him subscribed is, to the best of his knowledge and belief, true.

Before me, MELVIN O. ADAMS,
Justice of the Peace.

COMMONWEALTH OF MASSACHUSETTS.

SUFFOLK SS. BOSTON, Aug. 29, 1904. Then personally appeared the above-named Melvin O. Adams, Henry R. Reed and William S. Spaulding, and severally made oath that the foregoing certificate by them subscribed is, to the best of their knowledge and belief, true.

Before me, JOHN A. FENNO,
Justice of the Peace.

RETURN

OF THE

CAPE ANN GRANITE RAILROAD COMPANY

FOR THE YEAR ENDING JUNE 30, 1904.

GENERAL EXHIBIT FOR THE YEAR.	
Gross earnings from operation,	$4,788 21
Operating expenses,	4,714 38
NET EARNINGS FROM OPERATION,	$73 83
Charges upon income accrued during the year: taxes,	37 35
Surplus for the year ending June 30, 1904,	$36 48
Amount of deficit June 30, 1903,	329 84
TOTAL DEFICIT JUNE 30, 1904,	$293 36
EARNINGS FROM OPERATION.	
Freight service: gross receipts from freight,	$4,788 21
GROSS EARNINGS FROM OPERATION,	$4,788 21
EXPENSES OF OPERATION.	
General expenses: insurance,	$75 00
Maintenance of way and structures: renewals of ties,	$295 20
Maintenance of equipment: repairs and renewals of locomotives,	$400 00
Conducting transportation:	
Engine and roundhouse men,	$904 80
Fuel for locomotives,	1,532 25
Oil, tallow and waste for locomotives,	190 10
Train service,	624 00
Switchmen, flagmen and watchmen,	312 00
Other expenses of conducting transportation: wharfage,	381 03
TOTAL,	$3,944 18
Recapitulation:	
General expenses,	$75 00
Maintenance of way and structures,	295 20
Maintenance of equipment,	400 00
Conducting transportation,	3,944 18
TOTAL OPERATING EXPENSES,	$4,714 38

General Balance Sheet June 30, 1904.

Assets.	Dr.	
Cost of road,		$22,381 63
Cost of equipment,		10,500 00
Total Permanent Investments,		$32,881 63
Profit and loss balance (deficit),		293 36
Total,		$33,174 99

Liabilities.	Cr.	
Capital stock,		$20,000 00
Current liabilities:		
Loans and notes payable,	$12,881 63	
Audited vouchers and accounts,	293 36	
Total Current Liabilities,		13,174 99
Total,		$33,174 99

Capital Stock.

Capital stock authorized by law,	$20,000 00	
Capital stock authorized by votes of company,	20,000 00	
Capital stock issued and outstanding,		$20,000 00
Number of shares issued and outstanding,	200	
Number of stockholders,	6	
Number of stockholders in Massachusetts,	6	
Amount of stock held in Massachusetts,	$20,000 00	

Volume of Traffic, etc.

Freight traffic:	
Number of tons of freight hauled earning revenue,	22,801
Number of tons of freight hauled one mile,	32,742
Train mileage:	
Miles run by freight trains,	1,782
Total mileage of trains earning revenue,	1,782
Employees:	
Average number of persons employed,	4

Description of Railroad Owned and Operated.

(See also tabulated description in preceding appendix to report.)

Railroad Owned and Operated.	Total.	In Massachusetts.
	Miles.	Miles.
Length of main line,	1.436	1.436
Length of side track, etc.,	.781	.781
Total Length of Track Owned and Operated,	2.217	2.217

Description of Equipment.

Rolling Stock.	Number Owned.	Equipped with Power Driving-Wheel Brakes.	Maximum Weight.	Average Weight.
Locomotives.			Lbs.	Lbs.
Freight,	1	1	60,000	60,000
Cars — Freight Service.				
Flat cars,	15	-	-	-

Railroad Crossings in Massachusetts.

Crossings with Highways.	
Number of crossings of railroad with highways at grade,	2
Number of highway grade crossings protected by gates,	1
Number of highway grade crossings protected by flagmen,	1

Corporate Name and Address of the Company.

CAPE ANN GRANITE RAILROAD COMPANY,

50 Congress Street, Boston, Mass.

Names and Business Address of Principal Officers.

Henry M. Whitney, *President*, Brookline, Mass. Grenville D. Braman, *Treasurer*, Cohasset, Mass. Marquis F. Dickinson, *Clerk of Corporation*, Brookline, Mass.

Names and Residence of Board of Directors.

Henry M. Whitney, Brookline, Mass. Grenville D. Braman, Cohasset, Mass. Marquis F. Dickinson, Brookline, Mass.

We hereby certify that the statements contained in the foregoing return are full, just and true.

HENRY M. WHITNEY,
President.
HENRY M. WHITNEY,
GRENVILLE D. BRAMAN,
MARQUIS F. DICKINSON,
Directors.
GRENVILLE D. BRAMAN,
Treasurer.

Commonwealth of Massachusetts.

Suffolk, ss. Sept. 22, 1904. Then personally appeared the above-named Henry M. Whitney, Grenville D. Braman and Marquis F. Dickinson, and severally made oath that the foregoing certificate by them subscribed is, to the best of their knowledge and belief, true.

Before me, CHARLES F. KELLOGG,
Justice of the Peace.

RETURN

OF THE

CHATHAM RAILROAD COMPANY

FOR THE YEAR ENDING JUNE 30, 1904.

[Leased to and operated by the New York, New Haven & Hartford.]

GENERAL EXHIBIT FOR THE YEAR.		
Rental received from lease of road,		$4,161 93
Interest received on bonds owned:		
Greenfield, Deerfield & Northampton Street Railway Company,	$25 00	
Chatham Railroad Company,	30 00	
		55 00
Income from other sources:		
Store rental,	$100 00	
Interest on deposit,	3 50	
		103 50
GROSS INCOME,		$4,320 43
Expenses and charges upon income accrued during the year:		
Salaries and maintenance of organization,	$119 48	
Interest on funded debt,	1,050 00	
Interest and discount on unfunded debts and loans,	21 00	
Taxes,	140 77	
Other expenses and charges upon income:		
Insurance,	6 57	
Repairs on store,	71 57	
Premium on bond bought,	45 00	
TOTAL EXPENSES AND CHARGES UPON INCOME,		1,454 39
Surplus for the year ending June 30, 1904,		$2,866 04
Amount of surplus June 30, 1903,		14,455 51
Credits to profit and loss account during the year: reduction of accrued interest,		10 00
TOTAL SURPLUS JUNE 30, 1904,		$17,331 55

GENERAL BALANCE SHEET JUNE 30, 1904.	
ASSETS. DR.	
Cost of road,	$98,435 58
Bonds of Greenfield, Deerfield & Northampton Street Railway Company,	1,000 00
Other permanent property: one store,	1,055 55
TOTAL PERMANENT INVESTMENTS,	$100,491 13

Cash,	$1,310 33	
Bills receivable,	900 09	
Total Cash and Current Assets,		$2,210 42
Total,		$102,701 55

Liabilities.	Cr.
Capital stock,	$68,200 00
Funded debt,	17,000 00
Accrued liabilities: interest accrued and not yet due,	170 00
Profit and loss balance (surplus),	17,331 55
Total,	$102,701 55

Capital Stock.

Capital stock authorized by law,	$70,000 00	
Capital stock authorized by votes of company,	85,000 00	
Capital stock issued and outstanding,		$68,200 00
Number of shares issued and outstanding,	682	
Number of stockholders,	131	
Number of stockholders in Massachusetts,	119	
Amount of stock held in Massachusetts,	$63,200 00	

Funded Debt.

Description of Bonds.	Rate of Interest.	Date of Maturity.	Amount Outstanding.	Interest Paid during the Year.
	Per Cent.			
First mortgage,	6	Nov. 1, 1907,	$17,000 00	$1,050 00

Description of Railroad Owned.

(See also tabulated description in preceding appendix to report.)

Railroad Owned.	Total.	In Massachusetts.
	Miles.	Miles.
Length of main line,	7.070	7.070
Length of side track, etc.,	.770	.770
Total Length of Track Owned,	7.840	7.840

Corporate Name and Address of the Company.

CHATHAM RAILROAD COMPANY,

Chatham, Mass.

Names and Business Address of Principal Officers.

Osborn Nickerson, *President*, Chathamport, Mass. Charles Bassett, *Treasurer and Clerk of Corporation*, South Chatham, Mass.

Names and Residence of Board of Directors.

Osborn Nickerson, Chathamport, Mass. Oliver E. Eldredge, Chatham, Mass. Daniel W. Nickerson, Chatham, Mass. Cyrus S. Kent, Chatham, Mass. Marcus W. Howard, Chatham, Mass. Alvin Z. Atkins, North Chatham, Mass. Clarendon A. Freeman, North Chatham, Mass. Meriton E. Nickerson, South Chatham, Mass. Charles Bassett, South Chatham, Mass.

We hereby certify that the statements contained in the foregoing return are full, just and true.

OSBORN NICKERSON,
OLIVER E. ELDREDGE,
ALVIN Z. ATKINS,
DANIEL W. NICKERSON,
MERITON E. NICKERSON,
C. A. FREEMAN,
Directors.
CHARLES BASSETT,
Treasurer.

Commonwealth of Massachusetts.

Barnstable, ss. Chatham, Aug. 20, 1904. Then personally appeared the above-named Osborn Nickerson, Oliver E. Eldredge, Alvin Z. Atkins, Daniel W. Nickerson, Meriton E. Nickerson, C. A. Freeman and Charles Bassett, and severally made oath that the foregoing certificate by them subscribed is, to the best of their knowledge and belief, true.

Before me, ERASTUS T. BEARSE,
Notary Public.

RETURN

OF THE

CHESTER & BECKET RAILROAD COMPANY

FOR THE YEAR ENDING JUNE 30, 1904.

[Leased to and operated by the Boston & Albany (New York Central & Hudson River, lessee).]

General Exhibit for the Year.		
Rental received from lease of road,		$662 67
Expenses and charges upon income accrued during the year:		
Salaries and maintenance of organization,	$8 00	
Interest on funded debt,	2,500 00	
Interest and discount on unfunded debts and loans,	1,812 58	
Total Expenses and Charges upon Income,		4,320 58
Deficit for the year ending June 30, 1904,		$3,657 91
Amount of deficit June 30, 1903,		21,699 30
Total Deficit June 30, 1904,		$25,357 21

General Balance Sheet June 30, 1904.		
Assets.	Dr.	
Cost of road,		$136,893 98
Cash,	$22 33	
Due from solvent companies and individuals,	82 78	
Total Cash and Current Assets,		105 11
Profit and loss balance (deficit),		25,357 21
Total,		$162,356 30
Liabilities.	Cr.	
Capital stock,		$50,000 00
Funded debt,		50,000 00
Current liabilities:		
Loans and notes payable,	$35,845 43	
Matured interest coupons unpaid (including coupons due July 1),	15,000 00	
Miscellaneous current liabilities: interest on notes payable,	11,510 87	
Total Current Liabilities,		62,356 30
Total,		$162,356 30

Capital Stock.

Capital stock authorized by law,	$50,000 00	
Capital stock authorized by votes of company,	50,000 00	
Capital stock issued and outstanding,		$50,000 00
Number of shares issued and outstanding,	500	
Number of stockholders,	16	
Number of stockholders in Massachusetts,	4	
Amount of stock held in Massachusetts,	$13,400 00	

Funded Debt.

Description of Bonds.	Rate of Interest.	Date of Maturity.	Amount Outstanding.	Interest Paid during the Year.
	Per Cent.			
Mortgage bonds,	5	July 1, 1917,	$50,000 00	-

Description of Railroad Owned.

(See also tabulated description in preceding appendix to report.)

Railroad Owned.	Total.	In Massachusetts.
	Miles.	Miles.
Length of main line,	5.270	5.270
Length of side track, etc.,	2.110	2.110
Total Length of Track Owned,	7.380	7.380

Corporate Name and Address of the Company.

CHESTER & BECKET RAILROAD COMPANY,

South Station, Boston, Mass.

Names and Business Address of Principal Officers.

James A. Rumrill, *President*, Springfield, Mass. Frank H. Ratcliffe, *Treasurer and Clerk of Corporation*, Boston, Mass.

Names and Residence of Board of Directors.

Chester W. Bliss, Springfield, Mass. Frederick J. Collier, Hudson, N. Y. Zenas Crane, Dalton, Mass. Edward D. Hayden, Woburn, Mass. William J. Harder, Jr., Hudson, N. Y. James A. Rumrill, Springfield, Mass. Stephen Salisbury, Worcester, Mass. Smith Thompson, Hudson, N. Y.

We hereby certify that the statements contained in the foregoing return are full, just and true.

J. A. RUMRILL,
ZENAS CRANE,
STEPHEN SALISBURY,
EDWARD D. HAYDEN,
Directors.
F H. RATCLIFFE,
Treasurer.

COMMONWEALTH OF MASSACHUSETTS.

SUFFOLK SS. BOSTON, Sept. 28, 1904. Then personally appeared the above-named J. A. Rumrill, Zenas Crane, Edward D. Hayden and F. H. Ratcliffe, and severally made oath that the foregoing certificate by them subscribed is, to the best of their knowledge and belief, true.

Before me, WOODWARD HUDSON,
Justice of the Peace.

RETURN

OF THE

CONNECTICUT RIVER RAILROAD COMPANY

For the Year ending June 30, 1904.

[Leased to and operated by the Boston & Maine.]

General Exhibit for the Year.		
Rental received from lease of road,		$349,065 00
Expenses and charges upon income accrued during the year:		
Salaries and maintenance of organization,	$2,000 00	
Interest on funded debt,	84,065 00	
Total Expenses and Charges upon Income,		86,065 00
Net Divisible Income,		$263,000 00
Dividends declared (10 per cent),		$263,000 00
Amount of deficit June 30, 1903,		$193,884 84
Total Deficit June 30, 1904,		$193,884 84

General Balance Sheet June 30, 1904. Assets.	Dr.	
Cost of road,		$3,597,366 50
Cost of equipment,		455,977 66
Lands in Chicopee and Brightwood,	$39,175 00	
Lands in Greenfield, Mass.,	75 00	
		39,250 00
Stock of Vermont Valley R.R. Co. of 1871,	$579,220 00	
Stock of Hampden Park,	23,987 50	
		603,207 50
Total Permanent Investments,		$4,695,801 66
Cash,	$28,237 31	
Due from solvent companies and individuals,	159,552 89	
Total Cash and Current Assets,		187,790 20
Profit and loss balance (deficit),		193,884 84
Total,		$5,077,476 70

LIABILITIES.	CR.	
Capital stock,		$2,630,000 00
Funded debt,		2,263,150 00
Current liabilities:		
Dividends not called for,	$430 00	
Matured interest coupons unpaid (including coupons due July 1),	23,098 50	
Miscellaneous current liabilities: Boston & Maine R.R.,	146,906 05	
TOTAL CURRENT LIABILITIES,		170,434 55
Accrued liabilities: interest accrued and not yet due,		13,333 34
Sinking and other special funds: fund for corporation expenses,		558 81
TOTAL,		$5,077,476 70

PROPERTY ACCOUNTS.	
Additions to construction account: permanent additions and improvements by Boston & Maine R.R.,	$33,626 72
Other expenditures charged to property accounts: land in Greenfield, Mass.,	75 00
TOTAL ADDITIONS TO PROPERTY ACCOUNTS,	$33,701 72

CAPITAL STOCK.		
Capital stock authorized by law,	$2,670,000 00	
Capital stock authorized by votes of company,	2,630,000 00	
Capital stock issued and outstanding,		$2,630,000 00
Number of shares issued and outstanding,	26,300	
Number of stockholders,	954	
Number of stockholders in Massachusetts,	724	
Amount of stock held in Massachusetts,	$1,888,600 00	

FUNDED DEBT.

DESCRIPTION OF BONDS.	Rate of Interest.	Date of Maturity.	Amount Outstanding.	Interest Paid during the Year.
	Per Cent.			
Scrip 10-year bonds,	4	Jan. 1, 1903,	$4,150 00	$121 00
Gold 50-year bonds,	4	Sept. 1, 1943,	1,000,000 00	40,040 00
Gold 20-year bonds,	3½	Jan. 1, 1921,	290,000 00	10,150 00
Gold 20-year bonds,	3½	Jan. 1, 1923,	969,000 00	33,915 00
TOTALS,	. .	. . .	$2,263,150 00	$84,226 00

Description of Railroad Owned.

(See also tabulated description in preceding appendix to report.)

Railroad Owned.	Total.	In Massachusetts.
	Miles.	Miles.
Length of main line,	74.000	50.080
Length of branch line,	5.850	5.850
Total Length of Line Owned,	79.850	55.930
Length of second track,	36.000	36.000
Length of third track,	.800	.800
Length of side track, etc.,	64.740	57.630
Total Length of Track Owned,	181.390	150.360

Corporate Name and Address of the Company.

CONNECTICUT RIVER RAILROAD COMPANY,

Springfield, Mass.

Names and Business Address of Principal Officers.

William Whiting, *President*, Holyoke, Mass. George R. Yerrall, *Treasurer and Clerk of Corporation*, Springfield, Mass.

Names and Residence of Board of Directors.

William Whiting, Holyoke, Mass. Oscar Edwards, Northampton, Mass. James H. Williams, Bellows Falls, Vt. John H. Albin, Concord, N. H. Edmund P. Kendrick, Springfield, Mass. Seth M. Richards, Newport, N. H. Joseph W. Stevens, Greenfield, Mass. Lucius Tuttle, Boston, Mass. William W. McClench, Springfield, Mass. George H. Ball (deceased).

We hereby certify that the statements contained in the foregoing return are full, just and true.

WILLIAM WHITING,
OSCAR EDWARDS,
EDMUND P. KENDRICK,
JOSEPH W. STEVENS,
WILLIAM W. McCLENCH,
Directors.
GEORGE R. YERRALL,
Treasurer.

Commonwealth of Massachusetts.

Hampden, ss. Sept. 3, 1904. Then personally appeared the above-named William Whiting, Oscar Edwards, Edmund P. Kendrick, Joseph W. Stevens, William W. McClench and George R. Yerrall, and severally made oath that the foregoing certificate by them subscribed is, to the best of their knowledge and belief, true.

Before me, STUART M. ROBSON,
Justice of the Peace.

RETURN

OF THE

DANVERS RAILROAD COMPANY

FOR THE YEAR ENDING JUNE 30, 1904.

[Leased to and operated by the Boston & Maine. Its operations are included in the return of that road, being so intimately connected that separate accounts are not kept.]

GENERAL BALANCE SHEET JUNE 30, 1904.

ASSETS. DR.	
Cost of road,	$239,678 15
TOTAL,	$239,678 15

LIABILITIES. CR.	
Capital stock,	$67,500 00
Funded debt,	125,000 00
Current liabilities: due Boston & Maine Railroad,	25,000 00
Profit and loss balance (surplus),	22,178 15
TOTAL,	$239,678 15

CAPITAL STOCK.

Capital stock authorized by law,	$100,000 00	
Capital stock authorized by votes of company,	100,000 00	
Capital stock issued and outstanding,		$58,300 00
Amount paid in on shares not yet issued,		9,200 00
TOTAL CAPITAL STOCK LIABILITY,		$67,500 00
Number of shares issued and outstanding,	583	
Number of stockholders,	44	
Number of stockholders in Massachusetts,	44	
Amount of stock held in Massachusetts,	$67,500 00	

FUNDED DEBT.

DESCRIPTION OF BONDS.	Rate of Interest.	Date of Maturity.	Amount Outstanding.	Interest Paid during the Year.
	Per Cent.			
Coupon bonds,	6	March 1, 1875,	$125,000 00	-

Description of Railroad Owned.

(See also tabulated description in preceding appendix to report.)

Railroad Owned.	Total.	In Massachusetts.
	Miles.	Miles.
Length of main line,	9.260	9.260
Length of side track, etc.,	2.280	2.280
Total Length of Track Owned,	11.540	11.540

Corporate Name and Address of the Company.

DANVERS RAILROAD COMPANY,

Boston, Mass.

Names and Business Address of Principal Officers.

Lucius Tuttle, *President*, Boston, Mass. Herbert E. Fisher, *Treasurer*, Boston, Mass. William B. Lawrence, *Clerk of Corporation*, Boston, Mass. William J. Hobbs, *Auditor*, Boston, Mass.

Names and Residence of Board of Directors.

Lucius Tuttle, Boston, Mass. Samuel C. Lawrence, Medford, Mass. Walter Hunnewell, Wellesley, Mass. Henry M. Whitney, Brookline, Mass. Henry R. Reed, Boston, Mass. Joseph H. White, Brookline, Mass. William J. Hobbs, Malden, Mass.

We hereby certify that the statements contained in the foregoing return are full, just and true.

LUCIUS TUTTLE,
SAMUEL C. LAWRENCE,
HENRY R. REED,
HENRY M. WHITNEY,
WALTER HUNNEWELL,
JOSEPH H. WHITE,
WM. J. HOBBS,
Directors.
HERBERT E. FISHER,
Treasurer.
WM. J. HOBBS,
Chief Accounting Officer.

Commonwealth of Massachusetts.

Suffolk, ss. Boston, Sept. 8, 1904. Then personally appeared the above-named Lucius Tuttle, Samuel C. Lawrence, Henry R. Reed, Henry M. Whitney, Walter Hunnewell, Joseph H. White and William J. Hobbs, directors, Herbert E. Fisher, treasurer, and William J. Hobbs, chief accounting officer, and severally made oath that the foregoing certificate by them subscribed is, to the best of their knowledge and belief, true.

Before me, WILLIAM B. LAWRENCE,
Justice of the Peace.

RETURN

OF THE

FITCHBURG RAILROAD COMPANY

FOR THE YEAR ENDING JUNE 30, 1904.

[Leased to and operated by the Boston & Maine.]

GENERAL EXHIBIT FOR THE YEAR.			
Rental received from lease of road,			$1,852,496 54
Income from other sources:			
Interest on bank deposit,		$1,695 72	
Boston & Maine Railroad,		23,878 35	
			25,574 07
GROSS INCOME,			$1,878,070 61
Expenses and charges upon income accrued during the year:			
Salaries and maintenance of organization,		$8,744 11	
Interest on funded debt,		833,161 67	
Interest and discount on unfunded debts and loans,		144,334 87	
Other expenses and charges upon income:			
Commission placing notes,	$22,938 47		
Contingent fund,	891 49		
		23,829 96	
TOTAL EXPENSES AND CHARGES UPON INCOME,			1,010,070 61
NET DIVISIBLE INCOME,			$868,000 00
Dividends declared (5 per cent on preferred stock),			$868,000 00
Amount of surplus June 30, 1903,			$742,463 47
Debits to profit and loss account during the year: net disbursement account business prior to July 1, 1900,			11,307 98
TOTAL SURPLUS JUNE 30, 1904,			$731,155 49

GENERAL BALANCE SHEET JUNE 30, 1904.	
ASSETS. DR.	
Cost of road,	$40,131,779 09
Cost of equipment,	3,828,354 47
Bonds of Vermont & Massachusetts Railroad,	772,000 00
Other permanent property: improvements,	2,250,040 36
TOTAL PERMANENT INVESTMENTS,	$46,982,173 92

Cash,	$8,654 24	
Due from solvent companies and individuals,	60,805 00	
Other cash assets,	323,422 70	
TOTAL CASH AND CURRENT ASSETS,		$392,881 94
Other assets and property:		
Rental accrued not due,	$238,934 39	
Boston & Maine Railroad, lessee,	936,034 06	
TOTAL MISCELLANEOUS ASSETS,		1,174,968 45
TOTAL,		$48,550,024 31

LIABILITIES.	CR.	
Capital stock, common,	$7,000,000 00	
Capital stock, preferred,	17,360,000 00	
TOTAL CAPITAL STOCK,		$24,360,000 00
Funded debt,		19,010,000 00
Current liabilities:		
Loans and notes payable,	$3,932,000 00	
Audited vouchers and accounts,	56,484 32	
Dividends not called for,	1,391 50	
Matured interest coupons unpaid (including coupons due July 1),	64,145 00	
Miscellaneous current liabilities: Boston & Maine Railroad lease improvements,	155,783 61	
TOTAL CURRENT LIABILITIES,		4,209,804 43
Accrued liabilities:		
Interest accrued and not yet due,	$238,934 39	
Miscellaneous accrued liabilities: Boston, Barre & Gardner Railroad stockholders,	130 00	
TOTAL ACCRUED LIABILITIES,		239,064 39
Profit and loss balance (surplus),		731,155 49
TOTAL,		$48,550,024 31

PROPERTY ACCOUNTS.

Additions to construction account:		
Bridging,	$2,845 63	
Superstructure, including rails,	4,104 31	
Passenger and freight stations, coal sheds and water stations, and engine-houses, car houses and turn-tables,	1,412 52	
Elimination of grade crossings,	206 75	
Other additions to construction account:		
Cheshire Railroad consolidation,	93 54	
Sidings and yard extensions,	1,430 03	
Improvements in process — incomplete,	43,384 38	
TOTAL ADDITIONS TO CONSTRUCTION ACCOUNT,		$53,477 16

Other expenditures charged to property accounts: land, land damages and fences and release of crossing, Hoosick, N. Y.,		$250 00
Total Additions to Property Accounts,		$53,727 16
Deductions from property accounts (property sold or reduced in valuation and credited to property accounts):		
Land, land damages and fences:		
Award, land taken by town of Winchendon, Mass.,	$100 00	
Award, land taken by village of Saratoga Springs, N. Y.,	400 00	
Total Deductions from Property Accounts,		500 00
Net Addition to Property Accounts for the Year,		$53,227 16

Capital Stock.

Capital stock authorized by law, common,		$7,000,000 00	
Capital stock authorized by law, preferred,		17,360,000 00	
Total capital stock authorized by law,		$24,360,000 00	
Capital stock authorized by votes of company, common,		$7,000,000 00	
Capital stock authorized by votes of company, preferred,		17,360,000 00	
Total capital stock authorized by vote,		$24,360,000 00	
Capital stock issued and outstanding, common,			$7,000,000 00
Capital stock issued and outstanding, preferred,			17,360,000 00
Total capital stock outstanding,			$24,360,000 00
Number of shares issued and outstanding, common,	70,000		
Number of shares issued and outstanding, preferred,	173,600		
Total number of shares outstanding,		243,600	
Number of stockholders, common,	2		
Number of stockholders, preferred,	6,103		
Total number of stockholders,		6,105	
Number of stockholders in Massachusetts, common,	2		
Number of stockholders in Massachusetts, preferred,	4,921		
Total stockholders in Massachusetts,		4,923	
Amount of stock held in Massachusetts, common,		$7,000,000 00	
Amount of stock held in Massachusetts, preferred,		15,127,000 00	
Total stock held in Massachusetts,		$22,127,000 00	

Funded Debt.

Description of Bonds.	Rate of Interest.	Date of Maturity.	Amount Outstanding.	Interest Paid during the Year.
	Per Cent.			
Fitchburg Railroad plain bonds, .	5	Oct. 1, 1901,	$1,000 00	-
Fitchburg Railroad plain bonds, .	4	March 1, 1904,	1,000 00	$19,980 00
Fitchburg Railroad plain bonds, .	4	June 1, 1905,	500,000 00	19,880 00
Fitchburg Railroad plain bonds, .	4	Feb. 1, 1907,	5,000,000 00	200,000 00
Fitchburg Railroad plain bonds, .	4	April 1, 1907,	1,500,000 00	59,720 00
Fitchburg Railroad plain bonds, .	5	May 1, 1908,	2,000,000 00	100,225 00
Fitchburg Railroad plain bonds, .	4	June 1, 1920,	500,000 00	20,240 00
Fitchburg Railroad plain bonds, .	4	March 1, 1903,	-*	60 00
Fitchburg Railroad plain bonds, .	5	Sept. 1, 1903,	-*	9,450 00
Fitchburg Railroad plain bonds, .	5	Nov. 1, 1903,	1,000 00	26,150 00
Fitchburg Railroad plain bonds, .	5	Dec. 1, 1903,	-*	13,400 00
Fitchburg Railroad plain bonds, .	4½	May 1, 1914,	500,000 00	22,522 50
Fitchburg Railroad plain bonds, .	4	March 1, 1915,	1,359,000 00	54,480 00
Fitchburg Railroad plain bonds, .	4	July 1, 1916,	500,000 00	19,620 00
Fitchburg Railroad plain bonds, .	4	March 1, 1927,	2,750,000 00	109,880 00
Fitchburg Railroad plain bonds, .	4	Jan. 1, 1928,	1,450,000 00	57,780 00
Fitchburg Railroad plain bonds, .	3½	Oct. 1, 1920,	500,000 00	17,500 00
Fitchburg Railroad plain bonds, .	3½	Oct. 1, 1921,	1,775,000 00	62,387 50
Troy & Boston first mortgage bonds,	7	July 1, 1924,	573,000 00	40,110 00
Brookline & Pepperell Railroad plain bonds.	5	Dec. 1, 1911,	100,000 00	5,225 00
Totals, ...	. .	. . . .	$19,010,000 00	$858,610 00

Description of Railroad Owned.

(See also tabulated description in preceding appendix to report.)

Railroad Owned.	Total.	In Massachusetts.
	Miles.	Miles.
Length of main line, ...	249.050	104.420
Length of branch line, ...	145.090	83.840
Total Length of Line Owned, ...	394.140	188.260
Length of second track, ...	127.220	100.630
Length of third track, ...	3.900	3.900
Length of fourth track, ...	2.020	2.020
Length of side track, etc., ...	251.340	151.140
Total Length of Track Owned, ...	778.620	445.950

* Matured.

Corporate Name and Address of the Company.

FITCHBURG RAILROAD COMPANY,

Boston, Mass.

Names and Business Address of Principal Officers.

Moses Williams, *President*, Boston, Mass. Daniel A. Gleason, *Treasurer*, Boston, Mass. Paul Crocker, *Clerk of Corporation*, Boston, Mass.

Names and Residence of Board of Directors.

Gordon Abbott, Boston, Mass. Brigham N. Bullock, Fitchburg, Mass. Charles T. Crocker, Fitchburg, Mass. William H. Hollister, New York, N. Y. Charles Lowell, Boston, Mass. William E. Rice, Worcester, Mass. Joseph B. Russell, Belmont, Mass. Francis Smith, Rockland, Me. Frederic J. Stimson, Dedham, Mass. George R. Wallace, Fitchburg, Mass. Charles E. Ware, Fitchburg, Mass. Moses Williams, Brookline, Mass. Robert Winsor, Boston, Mass.

We hereby certify that the statements contained in the foregoing return are full, just and true.

MOSES WILLIAMS,
JOSEPH B. RUSSELL,
ROBERT WINSOR,
CHAS. E. WARE,
B. N. BULLOCK,
GEORGE R. WALLACE,
C. T. CROCKER,
GORDON ABBOTT,
Directors.
DAN. A. GLEASON,
Treasurer and Chief Accounting Officer.

Commonwealth of Massachusetts.

Suffolk ss. Sept. 7, 1904. Then personally appeared the above-named directors of the Fitchburg Railroad Company, namely: Moses Williams, J. B. Russell, Robert Winsor, Charles E. Ware, B. N. Bullock, George R. Wallace, Charles T. Crocker and Gordon Abbott, and severally made oath that the foregoing certificate by them subscribed is, to the best of their knowledge and belief, true.

Before me, REGINALD CARY HEATH,
Justice of the Peace.

RETURN

OF THE

GRAFTON & UPTON RAILROAD COMPANY

FOR THE YEAR ENDING JUNE 30, 1904.

GENERAL EXHIBIT FOR THE YEAR.		
Gross earnings from operation,		$75,037 36
Operating expenses,		60,891 30
NET EARNINGS FROM OPERATION,		$14,146 06
Miscellaneous income, less expense of collecting: interest on deposits,		53 96
GROSS INCOME ABOVE OPERATING EXPENSES,		$14,200 02
Charges upon income accrued during the year:		
Interest on funded debt,	$10,900 00	
Interest and discount on unfunded debts and loans,	3,248 56	
Taxes,	459 76	
TOTAL CHARGES AND DEDUCTIONS FROM INCOME,		$14,608 32
Deficit for the year ending June 30, 1904,		$408 30
Amount of surplus June 30, 1903,		7,328 45
Credits to profit and loss account during the year: for rearrangement of tracks,	$5,000 00	
Debits to profit and loss account during the year: reduction in equipment account,	$5,000 00	
TOTAL SURPLUS JUNE 30, 1904,		$6,920 15

EARNINGS FROM OPERATION.

DEPARTMENT OF SERVICE.	Gross Receipts.	Deductions.	Earnings.
Passenger service:			
Gross receipts from passengers,			$28,081 61
From mails,			1,133 51
From express,			3,604 80
TOTAL EARNINGS, PASSENGER SERVICE,			$32,819 92
Freight service:			
Gross receipts from freight,	$42,708 32		
Deductions:			
Overcharge to shippers,		$490 88	
TOTAL EARNINGS, FREIGHT SERVICE,			42,217 44
GROSS EARNINGS FROM OPERATION,			$75,037 36

EXPENSES OF OPERATION.

General expenses:	
Salaries of general officers,	$2,500 00
General office expenses and supplies,	110 75
Insurance,	150 25
Law expenses,	25 00
Stationery and printing (general offices),	51 10
TOTAL,	$2,837 10
Maintenance of way and structures:	
Repairs of roadway,	$5,789 98
Renewals of ties,	2,143 90
Repairs and renewals of bridges and culverts,	306 15
Repairs and renewals of fences, road crossings, signs and cattle guards,	144 16
Repairs and renewals of buildings and fixtures,	1,125 51
Other expenses of maintaining way and structures: spikes, bolts, track tools, etc.,	575 69
TOTAL,	$10,085 39
Maintenance of equipment:	
Repairs and renewals of locomotives,	$3,419 90
Repairs and renewals of freight cars,	346 59
TOTAL,	$3,766 49
Conducting transportation:	
Superintendence,	$1,200 00
Engine and roundhouse men,	3,936 50
Fuel for locomotives,	4,953 49
Water supply for locomotives,	385 71
Oil, tallow and waste for locomotives,	463 42
Other supplies for locomotives,	103 00
Train service,	3,398 25
Train supplies and expenses,	170 50
Switchmen, flagmen and watchmen,	954 00
Telegraph expenses,	55 66
Station service,	4,138 39
Station supplies,	278 47
Car mileage — balance,	4,742 84
Loss and damage,	452 85
Rentals for tracks, yards and terminals,	1,225 00
Stationery and printing,	153 35
Other expenses of conducting transportation:	
Petty expenses of superintendent, travelling, etc.,	61 23
Paid by contract for operation of passenger cars by electricity,	17,529 66
TOTAL,	$44,202 32
Recapitulation:	
General expenses,	$2,837 10
Maintenance of way and structures,	10,085 39
Maintenance of equipment,	3,766 49
Conducting transportation,	44,202 32
TOTAL OPERATING EXPENSES,	$60,891 30
Percentage of operating expenses to gross earnings,	81⅛

General Balance Sheet June 30, 1904.

Assets. Dr.	
Cost of road,	$523,917 68
Cost of equipment,	68,082 32
Total Permanent Investments,	$592,000 00
Cash,	6,920 15
Total,	$598,920 15

Liabilities. Cr.	
Capital stock,	$250,000 00
Funded debt,	268,000 00
Current liabilities: loans and notes payable,	74,000 00
Profit and loss balance (surplus),	6,920 15
Total,	$598,920 15

Property Accounts.

Additions to equipment account: locomotives (one in number),	$12,000 00
Deductions from property accounts (property sold or reduced in valuation and credited to property accounts): reduction in equipment account,	5,000 00
Net Addition to Property Accounts for the Year,	$7,000 00

Capital Stock.

Capital stock authorized by law,	$250,000 00	
Capital stock authorized by votes of company,	250,000 00	
Capital stock issued and outstanding,		$250,000 00
Number of shares issued and outstanding,	2,500	
Number of stockholders,	17	
Number of stockholders in Massachusetts,	15	
Amount of stock held in Massachusetts,	$239,200 00	

Funded Debt.

Description of Bonds.	Rate of Interest.	Date of Maturity.	Amount Outstanding.	Interest Paid during the Year.
	Per Cent.			
First mortgage bonds,	4	Nov. 1, 1912,	$250,000 00	$10,000 00
Second mortgage bonds,	5	July 1, 1913,	18,000 00	900 00
Totals,	. .	. . . .	$268,000 00	$10,900 00

Volume of Traffic, etc.

Passenger traffic:	
Number of passengers carried paying revenue,	305,193
Number of passengers carried one mile,	2,441,544

Passenger traffic — *Concluded.*	
Number of passengers carried one mile per mile of road operated,	180,855
Average length of journey per passenger,	8 miles.
Average amount received per passenger per mile carried,	.91 cent.
Passenger earnings (gross) per mile of road operated,	$2,431 03
Passenger earnings (gross) per passenger-train mile run,	15.575 cents.
Freight traffic:	
Number of tons of freight hauled earning revenue,	80,809
Number of tons of freight hauled one mile,	727,281
Number of tons of freight hauled one mile per mile of road operated,	45,455
Average length of haul per ton,	9 miles.
Average amount received per ton per mile hauled,	5.800 cents.
Freight earnings (gross) per mile of road operated,	$2,638 55
Freight earnings (gross) per freight-train mile run,	2.387
Operating expenses:	
Operating expenses per mile of road operated,	$3,690 36
Operating expenses per revenue-train mile run,	22.320 cents.
Train mileage:	
Miles run by passenger trains (electric),	210,719
Miles run by freight trains (steam),	17,640
Total mileage of trains earning revenue,	228,359
Miles run by switching trains (steam),	10,908
Miles run by construction and other trains (steam),	275
Total train mileage (steam and electric),	239,542
Fares and freights:	
Average rate of fare per mile received for local and trip tickets,	.900 cent.
Average rate received per ton mile for local freight,	3.640 cents.
Average rate received per ton mile for interline freight,	2.910 cents.
Employees:	
Average number of persons employed,	30

Description of Railroad Owned and Operated.

(See also tabulated description in preceding appendix to report).

Railroad Owned and Operated.	Total.	In Massachusetts.
	Miles	Miles.
Length of main line,	16.500	16.500
Length of electric loop,	2.620	2.620
Total Length of Line Owned,	19.120	19.120
Length of side track, etc.,	3.790	3.790
Total Length of Track Owned,	22.910	22.910
Equipped for Electric Power.		
Length of main line,	13.500	13.500
Length of branch line,	2.620	2.620
Total Length of Electric Line,	16.120	16.120
Length of side track, etc.,	.200	.200
Total Length of Electric Track,	16.320	16.320

Description of Equipment.

Rolling Stock.	Number Owned.	Equipped with Power Driving-wheel Brakes.	Equipped with Automatic Couplers.	Maximum Weight.	Average Weight.	Name of Coupler Used.
Locomotives.						
Freight,	4	4	-	Lbs. 103,000	Lbs. 82,000	-
Cars — Passenger Service.*						
Cars — Freight Service.						
Flat cars,	1	-	-	-	-	-
Cars — Company's Service.						
Caboose cars,	2	-	2	-	-	Miller.

Railroad Crossings in Massachusetts.

Crossings with Highways.	
Number of crossings of railroad with highways at grade,	29
Number of highway grade crossings protected by flagmen,	4
Number of highway grade crossings unprotected,	25
Number of highway bridges 18 feet (or more) above track,	1
Height of lowest highway bridge above track,	18 ft.

Corporate Name and Address of the Company.

GRAFTON & UPTON RAILROAD COMPANY,

Grafton, Mass.

Names and Business Address of Principal Officers.

Edward P. Usher, *President, Treasurer, Clerk of Corporation and General Manager*, Grafton, Mass. Geo. A. Draper, *Vice-President*, Hopedale, Mass. Levi W. Moore, *Superintendent*, Milford, Mass.

Names and Residence of Board of Directors.

George A. Draper, Hopedale, Mass. Eben D. Bancroft, Hopedale, Mass. Frank J. Dutcher, Hopedale, Mass. George W. Knowlton, West Upton, Mass. Edward P. Usher, Grafton, Mass.

* Grafton & Upton passenger service performed with electric cars furnished by the Milford & Uxbridge Street Railway Company.

We hereby certify that the statements contained in the foregoing return are full, just and true.

EDWARD P. USHER,
EBEN D. BANCROFT,
GEO. A. DRAPER,
Directors.
EDWARD P. USHER,
Treasurer.
EDWARD P. USHER,
Chief Accounting Officer.

COMMONWEALTH OF MASSACHUSETTS.

WORCESTER, SS. HOPEDALE, Aug. 15, 1904. Then personally appeared the above-named Eben D. Bancroft and George A. Draper, and severally made oath that the foregoing certificate by them subscribed is, to the best of their knowledge and belief, true.

Before me, EDWARD P. USHER,
Justice of the Peace.

COMMONWEALTH OF MASSACHUSETTS.

WORCESTER, SS. GRAFTON, Aug. 23, 1904. Then personally appeared the above-named Edward P. Usher, and made oath that the foregoing certificate by him subscribed is, to the best of his knowledge and belief, true.

Before me, EDWIN A. HOWE,
Justice of the Peace.

RETURN

OF THE

HOLYOKE & WESTFIELD RAILROAD COMPANY

For the Year ending June 30, 1904.

[Leased to and operated by the New York, New Haven & Hartford.]

General Exhibit for the Year.		
Rental received from lease of road,		$40,879 07
Income from other sources: interest on cash balances,		482 87
Gross Income,		$41,361 94
Expenses and charges upon income accrued during the year:		
Salaries and maintenance of organization,	$522 55	
Interest on funded debt,	8,000 00	
Taxes,	2,906 85	
Total Expenses and Charges upon Income,		11,429 40
Net Divisible Income,		$29,932 54
Dividends declared (12 per cent),		31,200 00
Deficit for the year ending June 30, 1904,		$1,267 46
Amount of surplus June 30, 1903,		30,184 14
Total Surplus June 30, 1904,		$28,916 68

General Balance Sheet June 30, 1904.		
Assets.	Dr.	
Cost of road,		$460,000 00
Cash,	$20,047 88	
Traffic balances due from other companies,	8,868 80	
Total Cash and Current Assets,		28,916 68
Total,		$488,916 68
Liabilities.	Cr.	
Capital stock,		$260,000 00
Funded debt,		200,000 00
Profit and loss balance (surplus),		28,916 68
Total,		$488,916 68

Capital Stock.

Capital stock authorized by law,	$350,000 00	
Capital stock authorized by votes of company,	260,000 00	
Capital stock issued and outstanding,		$260,000 00
Number of shares issued and outstanding,	2,600	
Number of stockholders,	14	
Number of stockholders in Massachusetts,	12	
Amount of stock held in Massachusetts,	$238,000 00	

Funded Debt.

Description of Bonds.	Rate of Interest.	Date of Maturity.	Amount Outstanding.	Interest Paid during the Year.
First mortgage bonds,	Per Cent. 4	April 1, 1911,	$200,000 00	$8,000 00

Description of Railroad Owned.

(See also tabulated description in preceding appendix to report.)

Railroad Owned.	Total.	In Massachusetts.
	Miles.	Miles.
Length of main line,	10.320	10.320
Length of side track, etc.,	14.280	14.280
Total Length of Track Owned,	24.600	24.600

Corporate Name and Address of the Company.

HOLYOKE & WESTFIELD RAILROAD COMPANY,

Holyoke, Mass.

Names and Business Address of Principal Officers.

Edward W. Chapin, *President*, Holyoke, Mass. Charles B. Prescott, *Vice-President*, Holyoke, Mass. Fred F. Partridge, *Treasurer*, Holyoke, Mass. James Kirkpatrick, *Clerk of Corporation*, Holyoke, Mass.

Names and Residence of Board of Directors.

Edward W. Chapin, Holyoke, Mass. Charles B. Prescott, Holyoke, Mass. James H. Newton, Holyoke, Mass. Joseph Metcalf, Holyoke, Mass. Henry H. Alderman, Holyoke, Mass. Joseph Markham, Holyoke, Mass. John O'Neil, Holyoke, Mass. August W. Boy, Holyoke, Mass. N. J. Blanchard, Holyoke, Mass.

We hereby certify that the statements contained in the foregoing return are full, just and true.

EDWARD W. CHAPIN,
CHARLES B. PRESCOTT,
HENRY H. ALDERMAN,
JOSEPH METCALF,
JAMES H. NEWTON,
Directors.
FRED F. PARTRIDGE,
Treasurer.

COMMONWEALTH OF MASSACHUSETTS.

HAMPDEN, ss. HOLYOKE, Sept. 6, 1904. Then personally appeared the above-named Edward W. Chapin, Charles B. Prescott, Henry H. Alderman, Joseph Metcalf, James H. Newton and Fred F. Partridge, and severally made oath that the foregoing certificate by them subscribed is, to the best of their knowledge and belief, true.

Before me, FRANK J. PHELPS,
Justice of the Peace.

RETURN

OF THE

HOOSAC TUNNEL & WILMINGTON RAILROAD COMPANY

For the Year ending June 30, 1904.

[A narrow-gauge road.]

General Exhibit for the Year.		
Gross earnings from operation,		$67,421 90
Operating expenses,		50,870 48
Net Earnings from Operation,		$16,551 42
Miscellaneous income, less expense of collecting: miscellaneous account,		756 72
Gross Income above Operating Expenses,		$17,308 14
Charges upon income accrued during the year:		
Interest on funded debt,	$12,500 00	
Interest and discount on unfunded debts and loans,	1,001 91	
Taxes,	1,585 80	
Total Charges and Deductions from Income,		15,087 71
Net Divisible Income,		$2,220 43
Dividends declared during the year payable on December 31, 1903, 2 per cent on $250,000,		5,000 00
Deficit for the year ending June 30, 1904,		$2,779 57
Amount of surplus June 30, 1903,		8,040 97
Debits to profit and loss account during the year: suspense account,		4,036 66
Total Surplus June 30, 1904,		$1,224 74

Earnings from Operation.	
Passenger service:	
Gross receipts from passengers,	$14,807 01
From mails,	1,115 26
From express,	1,886 92
Total Earnings, Passenger Service,	$17,809 19
Freight service: gross receipts from freight,	49,612 71
Gross Earnings from Operation,	$67,421 90

Expenses of Operation.

General expenses:	
Salaries of general officers,	$1,050 00
Salaries of clerks and attendants,	1,011 15
General office expenses and supplies,	340 00
Insurance,	1,304 00
Law expenses,	203 84
Stationery and printing (general offices),	200 00
Other general expenses,	564 00
Total,	$4,672 99
Maintenance of way and structures:	
Repairs of roadway,	$7,063 54
Renewals of ties,	5,774 89
Repairs and renewals of buildings and fixtures,	3,725 49
Repairs and renewals of telegraph,	257 19
Total,	$16,821 11
Maintenance of equipment:	
Repairs and renewals of locomotives,	$3,954 05
Repairs and renewals of passenger cars,	786 20
Repairs and renewals of freight cars,	2,869 50
Repairs and renewals of shop machinery and tools,	1,749 22
Total,	$9,358 97
Conducting transportation:	
Engine and roundhouse men,	$3,155 82
Fuel for locomotives,	6,223 01
Water supply for locomotives,	30 00
Oil, tallow and waste for locomotives,	15 00
Other supplies for locomotives,	12 36
Train service,	2,580 38
Switchmen, flagmen and watchmen,	990 36
Station service,	1,800 00
Station supplies,	14 00
Advertising,	12 00
Other expenses of conducting transportation: transferring,	5,184 48
Total,	$20,017 41
Recapitulation:	
General expenses,	$4.672 99
Maintenance of way and structures,	16,821 11
Maintenance of equipment,	9,358 97
Conducting transportation,	20,017 41
Total Operating Expenses,	$50,870 48

General Balance Sheet June 30, 1904.

Assets.	Dr.
Cost of road,	$436,566 29
Cost of equipment,	77,853 74
Total Permanent Investments,	$514,420 03

Cash,	$429 08	
Bills receivable,	10,000 00	
Due from agents,	4,759 69	
Traffic balances due from other companies,	327 33	
Due from solvent companies and individuals,	7,925 09	
TOTAL CASH AND CURRENT ASSETS,		$23,441 19
Materials and supplies,		9,886 93
TOTAL,		$547,748 15

LIABILITIES.		CR.
Capital stock,		$250,000 00
Funded debt,		250,000 00
Current liabilities:		
Loans and notes payable,	$36,240 65	
Audited vouchers and accounts,	4,219 44	
Salaries and wages,	1,896 65	
TOTAL CURRENT LIABILITIES,		42,356 74
Accrued liabilities: interest accrued and not yet due,		4,166 67
Profit and loss balance (surplus),		1,224 74
TOTAL,		$547,748 15

PROPERTY ACCOUNTS.

Additions to construction account: real estate,		$4,055 00
Additions to equipment account:		
Cars for freight service (10 in number),	$2,000 00	
Other additions to equipment account: air brakes,	3,477 44	
TOTAL ADDITIONS TO EQUIPMENT ACCOUNT,		5,477 44
TOTAL ADDITIONS TO PROPERTY ACCOUNTS,		$9,532 44

CAPITAL STOCK.

Capital stock authorized by law,	$250,000 00	
Capital stock authorized by votes of company,	250,000 00	
Capital stock issued and outstanding,		$250,000 00
Number of shares issued and outstanding,	2,500	
Number of stockholders,	44	
Number of stockholders in Massachusetts,	16	
Amount of stock held in Massachusetts,	$168,600 00	

FUNDED DEBT.

DESCRIPTION OF BONDS.	Rate of Interest.	Date of Maturity.	Amount Outstanding.	Interest Paid during the Year.
First mortgage bonds,	Per Cent. 5	Sept. 1, 1922,	$250,000 00	$12,500 00

Volume of Traffic, etc.

Passenger traffic:	
Number of passengers carried paying revenue,	32,524
Number of passengers carried one mile,	383,436
Number of passengers carried one mile per mile of road operated,	15,337
Average length of journey per passenger,	11 790 miles.
Average amount received per passenger per mile carried,	45.526 cents.
Passenger earnings (gross) per mile of road operated,	$712 36.760
Passenger earnings (gross) per passenger-train mile run,	46.371
Freight traffic:	
Number of tons of freight hauled earning revenue,	50,215
Number of tons of freight hauled one mile,	786,663
Number of tons of freight hauled one mile per mile of road operated,	31,467
Average length of haul per ton,	15.670 miles.
Average amount received per ton hauled,	98.801 cents.
Freight earnings (gross) per mile of road operated,	$1,984 50.840
Freight earnings (gross) per freight-train mile run,	3 38.283
Operating expenses:	
Operating expenses per mile of road operated,	2,034 81.920
Operating expenses per revenue-train mile run,	1 10.049
Train mileage:	
Miles run by passenger trains,	31,560
Miles run by freight trains,	7,820
Miles run by mixed trains,	6,846
Total mileage of trains earning revenue,	46,226
Miles run by construction and other trains,	679
Total train mileage,	46,905
Fares and freights:	
Average rate of fare per mile received for local and trip tickets,	4.000 cents.
Average rate of fare per mile received for mileage tickets,	3.000 "
Average rate of fare per mile received for interline tickets,	2.200 "
Average rate received per ton mile for local freight,	6.307 "
Employees:	
Average number of persons employed,	58

Description of Railroad Owned and Operated.

(See also tabulated description in preceding appendix to report.)

Railroad Owned and Operated.	Total.	In Massachusetts.
	Miles.	Miles.
Length of main line,	24.250	8.220
Length of branch line, Hartwellville Branch and Mountain Mills Branch,	.750	-
Total Length of Line Owned and Operated,	25.000	8.220
Length of side track, etc.,	3.000	1.000
Total Length of Track Owned and Operated,	28.000	9.220

DESCRIPTION OF EQUIPMENT.

ROLLING STOCK.	Number Owned.	Equipped with Power Driving-wheel Brakes.	Equipped with Power Train Brakes.	Equipped with Automatic Couplers.	Name of Coupler Used.
LOCOMOTIVES.					
Passenger,	4	4*	-	-	-
Freight,	2	2†	-	-	-
TOTAL,	6	6	-	-	-
CARS — PASSENGER SERVICE.					
Passenger cars,	3	-	3‡	3	Trojan.
Combination cars,	1	-	1‡	1	Trojan.
Other cars in passenger service (excursion),	2	-	1‡	1	Trojan.
TOTAL,	6	-	5	5	-
CARS — FREIGHT SERVICE.					
Box cars,	52	-	33§	52	Trojan.
Flat cars,	45	-	45§	45	Trojan.
Coal cars,	17	-	-	13	Trojan.
Refrigerator cars,	1	-	1§	1	Trojan.
TOTAL,	115	-	79	111	-
CARS — COMPANY'S SERVICE.					
Caboose cars,	1	-	-	1	Trojan.
Other cars in company's service,	5	-	-	-	-
TOTAL,	6	-	-	1	-

CORPORATE NAME AND ADDRESS OF THE COMPANY.

HOOSAC TUNNEL & WILMINGTON RAILROAD COMPANY,

CORPORATION OFFICE, HOLYOKE, MASS.; GENERAL OFFICE, WILMINGTON, VT.

NAMES AND BUSINESS ADDRESS OF PRINCIPAL OFFICERS.

Daniel H. Newton, *President*, Holyoke, Mass. Martin A. Brown, *Treasurer, General Passenger Agent, General Freight Agent and Superintendent*, Wilmington, Vt. Edward T. Newton, *Clerk of Corporation*, Holyoke, Mass. Moses Newton, *General Manager*, Holyoke, Mass.

NAMES AND RESIDENCE OF BOARD OF DIRECTORS.

Daniel H. Newton, Holyoke, Mass. James H. Newton, Holyoke, Mass. Moses Newton, Holyoke, Mass. J. S. Pishon, Boston, Mass. Martin A. Brown, Wilmington, Vt.

* One New York air brake and automatic couplers; three Eames Vacuum.
† One Eames vacuum; one New York air brake and automatic couplers.
‡ Eames Vacuum. § New York air brakes.

We hereby certify that the statements contained in the foregoing return are full, just and true

DANIEL H. NEWTON,
MOSES NEWTON,
MARTIN A. BROWN,
Directors.
MARTIN A. BROWN,
Treasurer.

STATE OF VERMONT.

WINDHAM COUNTY, ss. WILMINGTON, Sept. 19, 1904. Subscribed and sworn to before me this day by Martin A. Brown, and Moses Newton.

LEONARD A. BROWN,
Notary Public.

COMMONWEALTH OF MASSACHUSETTS.

HAMPDEN, ss. HOLYOKE, Oct. 7, 1904. Then personally appeared the above-named Daniel H. Newton, and made oath that the foregoing certificate by him subscribed is, to the best of his knowledge and belief, true.

Before me, FRED F. PARTRIDGE,
Notary Public.

RETURN

OF THE

HORN POND BRANCH RAILROAD COMPANY

For the Year ending June 30, 1904.

[This road is merely the spur of an ice company, used for the transportation of its ice.]

General Balance Sheet June 30, 1904.

Assets. Dr.	
Cost of road,	$15,238 46
Total,	$15,238 46

Liabilities. Cr.	
Capital stock,	$2,000 00
Profit and loss balance (surplus),	13,238 46
Total,	$15,238 46

Capital Stock.

Capital stock authorized by law,	$40,000 00	
Capital stock authorized by votes of company,	2,000 00	
Capital stock issued and outstanding,		$2,000 00
Number of shares issued and outstanding,	100	
Number of stockholders,	5	
Number of stockholders in Massachusetts,	5	
Amount of stock held in Massachusetts,	$2,000 00	

Description of Railroad Owned.

(See also tabulated description in preceding appendix to report.)

Railroad Owned.	Total.	In Massachusetts.
	Miles.	Miles.
Length of main line,	.663	.663
Length of side track, etc.,	.076	.076
Total Length of Track Owned,	.739	.739

Corporate Name and Address of the Company.

HORN POND BRANCH RAILROAD COMPANY,

110 State Street, Boston, Mass.

Names and Business Address of Principal Officers.

R. W. Hopkins, *President*, 110 State Street, Boston, Mass. Frank J. Bartlett, *Treasurer and Clerk of Corporation*, 110 State Street, Boston, Mass.

Names and Residence of Board of Directors.

Reuben W. Hopkins, Boston, Mass. Frank J. Bartlett, Malden, Mass. Charles Russell, Watertown, Mass. Jeremiah Flanders, Melrose, Mass.

We hereby certify that the statements contained in the foregoing return are full, just and true.

REUBEN W. HOPKINS,
FRANK J. BARTLETT,
CHARLES RUSSELL,
JEREMIAH FLANDERS,
Directors.
FRANK J. BARTLETT,
Treasurer.

Commonwealth of Massachusetts.

Suffolk, ss. Sept. 17, 1904. Then personally appeared the above-named Reuben W. Hopkins, Frank J. Bartlett, Charles Russell and Jeremiah Flanders, and severally made oath that the foregoing certificate by them subscribed is, to the best of their knowledge and belief, true.

Before me, ALBERT F. ORNE,
Justice of the Peace.

RETURN

OF THE

LOWELL & ANDOVER RAILROAD COMPANY

FOR THE YEAR ENDING JUNE 30, 1904.

[Leased to and operated by the Boston & Maine.]

GENERAL EXHIBIT FOR THE YEAR.		
Rental received from lease of road,		$52,500 00
Income from other sources: interest on bank deposits,		38 88
GROSS INCOME,		$52,538 88
Expenses and charges upon income accrued during the year:		
Salaries and maintenance of organization,	$192 50	
Taxes,	16 34	
TOTAL EXPENSES AND CHARGES UPON INCOME,		208 84
NET DIVISIBLE INCOME,		$52,330 04
Dividends declared (9 per cent),		56,250 00
Deficit for the year ending June 30, 1904,		$3,919 96
Amount of surplus June 30, 1903,		147,862 36
TOTAL SURPLUS JUNE 30, 1904,		$143,942 40

GENERAL BALANCE SHEET JUNE 30, 1904.	
ASSETS. DR.	
Cost of road,	$767,050 24
Cash,	1,892 16
TOTAL,	$768,942 40
LIABILITIES. CR.	
Capital stock,	$625,000 00
Profit and loss balance (surplus),	143,942 40
TOTAL,	$768,942 40

CAPITAL STOCK.		
Capital stock authorized by law,	Unlimited.	
Capital stock authorized by votes of company,	$625,000 00	
Capital stock issued and outstanding,		$625,000 00
Number of shares issued and outstanding,	6,250	
Number of stockholders,	191	
Number of stockholders in Massachusetts,	164	
Amount of stock held in Massachusetts,	$569,900 00	

Description of Railroad Owned.

(See also tabulated description in preceding appendix to report.)

Railroad Owned.	Total.	In Massachusetts.
	Miles.	Miles.
Length of main line,	8.850	8.850
Length of second track,	7.280	7.280
Length of side track, etc.,	6.230	6.230
Total Length of Track Owned,	22.360	22.360

Corporate Name and Address of the Company.

LOWELL & ANDOVER RAILROAD COMPANY,

Lowell, Mass.

Names and Business Address of Principal Officers.

Frederick Ayer, *President*, Lowell, Mass. Austin K. Chadwick, *Treasurer*, Lowell, Mass. Grenville Hovey, *Clerk of Corporation*, Lowell, Mass.

Names and Residence of Board of Directors.

Frederick Ayer, Lowell, Mass. Frederick F. Ayer, New York, N. Y. George Ripley, Andover, Mass. Oliver H. Moulton, Lowell, Mass. Prescott C. Gates, Lowell, Mass. Jacob Rogers, Lowell, Mass.

We hereby certify that the statements contained in the foregoing return are full, just and true.

JACOB ROGERS,
OLIVER H. MOULTON,
PRESCOTT C. GATES,
FREDERICK AYER,
Directors.
AUSTIN K. CHADWICK,
Treasurer.

Commonwealth of Massachusetts.

Middlesex, ss. Aug. 31, 1904. Then personally appeared the above-named Jacob Rogers, Oliver H. Moulton, Prescott C. Gates, Frederick Ayer and Austin K. Chadwick, and severally made oath that the foregoing certificate by them subscribed is, to the best of their knowledge and belief, true.

Before me, CHARLES A. RICHARDSON,
Justice of the Peace.

RETURN

OF THE

MILFORD, FRANKLIN & PROVIDENCE RAILROAD COMPANY

FOR THE YEAR ENDING JUNE 30, 1904.

[Leased to and operated by the New York, New Haven & Hartford.]

GENERAL EXHIBIT FOR THE YEAR.		
Rental received from lease of road,		$2,300 00
Expenses and charges upon income accrued during the year:		
Interest on funded debt,	$600 00	
Other expenses and charges upon income: envelopes, stamps, etc.,	2 50	
TOTAL EXPENSES AND CHARGES UPON INCOME,		602 50
NET DIVISIBLE INCOME,		$1,697 50
Dividends declared (1½ per cent),		1,500 00
Surplus for the year ending June 30, 1904,		$197 50
Amount of deficit June 30, 1903,		6,538 49
TOTAL DEFICIT JUNE 30, 1904,		$6,340 99

GENERAL BALANCE SHEET JUNE 30, 1904.	
ASSETS. DR.	
Cost of road,	$101,308 23
Cash,	2,350 78
Profit and loss balance (deficit),	6,340 99
TOTAL,	$110,000 00
LIABILITIES. CR.	
Capital stock,	$100,000 00
Funded debt,	10,000 00
TOTAL,	$110,000 00

Capital Stock.

Capital stock authorized by law, . . .	$100,000 00	
Capital stock authorized by votes of company,	100,000 00	
Capital stock issued and outstanding, ...		$100,000 00
Number of shares issued and outstanding, .	1,000	
Number of stockholders, ...	20	
Number of stockholders in Massachusetts, .	19	
Amount of stock held in Massachusetts, . .	$99,000 00	

Funded Debt.

Description of Bonds.	Rate of Interest.	Date of Maturity.	Amount Outstanding.	Interest Paid during the Year.
	Per Cent.			
First mortgage bonds, . . .	6	Jan. 1, 1909, .	$10,000 00	$600 00

Description of Railroad Owned.

(See also tabulated description in preceding appendix to report.)

Railroad Owned.	Total.	In Massachusetts.
	Miles.	Miles.
Length of main line, ...	4.650	4.650
Length of side track, etc., ...	.440	.440
Total Length of Track Owned, ...	5.090	5.090

Corporate Name and Address of the Company.

MILFORD, FRANKLIN & PROVIDENCE RAILROAD COMPANY,

Franklin, Mass.

Names and Business Address of Principal Officers.

Edgar K. Ray, *President*, Franklin, Mass. William F. Draper, *Vice-President*, Hopedale, Mass. Adelbert D. Thayer, *Treasurer*, Franklin, Mass. George W. Wiggin, *Clerk of Corporation*, Franklin, Mass.

Names and Residence of Board of Directors.

Edgar K. Ray, Franklin, Mass. Adelbert D. Thayer, Franklin, Mass. William F. Draper, Hopedale, Mass. Eben S. Draper, Hopedale, Mass. George W. Wiggin, Franklin, Mass. J. B. Bancroft, Hopedale, Mass. George A. Draper, Hopedale, Mass. James F. Ray, Franklin, Mass. William A. Wyckoff, Franklin, Mass.

We hereby certify that the statements contained in the foregoing return are full, just and true.

EDGAR K. RAY,
ADELBERT D. THAYER,
JAMES F. RAY,
GEORGE W. WIGGIN,
Directors.
ADELBERT D. THAYER,
Treasurer.

COMMONWEALTH OF MASSACHUSETTS.

NORFOLK, SS. FRANKLIN, Sept. 15, 1904. Then personally appeared the above-named Edgar K. Ray, Adelbert D. Thayer, James F. Ray and George W. Wiggin, and severally made oath that the foregoing certificate by them subscribed, is, to the best of his knowledge and belief, true.

Before me, WILLIAM A. WYCKOFF,
Justice of the Peace.

RETURN

OF THE

MILFORD & WOONSOCKET RAILROAD COMPANY

For the Year ending June 30, 1904.

[Leased to and operated by the New York, New Haven & Hartford.]

General Exhibit for the Year.		
Rental received from lease of road,		$4,700 00
Expenses and charges upon income accrued during the year:		
Salaries and maintenance of organization,	$179 25	
Interest on funded debt,	3,000 00	
Total Expenses and Charges upon Income,		3,179 25
Net Divisible Income,		$1,520 75
Dividends declared (1 per cent),		1,486 00
Surplus for the year ending June 30, 1904,		$34 75
Amount of deficit June 30, 1903,		35,176 63
Total Deficit June 30, 1904,		$35,141 88

General Balance Sheet June 30, 1904.	
Assets. Dr.	
Cost of road,	$173,381 13
Cash,	76 99
Profit and loss balance (deficit),	35,141 88
Total,	$208,600 00
Liabilities. Cr.	
Capital stock,	$148,600 00
Funded debt,	60,000 00
Total,	$208,600 00

Capital Stock.		
Capital stock authorized by law,	$200,000 00	
Capital stock authorized by votes of company,	148,600 00	
Capital stock issued and outstanding,		$148,600 00
Number of shares issued and outstanding,	1,486	
Number of stockholders,	33	
Number of stockholders in Massachusetts,	29	
Amount of stock held in Massachusetts,	$146,500 00	

FUNDED DEBT.

DESCRIPTION OF BONDS.	Rate of Interest.	Date of Maturity.	Amount Outstanding.	Interest Paid during the Year.
First mortgage bonds, ...	Per Cent. 5	Dec. 1, 1908, .	$60,000 00	$3,000 00

DESCRIPTION OF RAILROAD OWNED.

(See also tabulated description in preceding appendix to report)

RAILROAD OWNED.	Total.	In Massachusetts.
	Miles.	Miles.
Length of main line, ...	15.130	15.130
Length of side track, etc., ...	3.820	3.820
TOTAL LENGTH OF TRACK OWNED, ...	18.950	18.950

CORPORATE NAME AND ADDRESS OF THE COMPANY.

MILFORD & WOONSOCKET RAILROAD COMPANY,

MILFORD, MASS.

NAMES AND BUSINESS ADDRESS OF PRINCIPAL OFFICERS.

William F. Draper, *President*, Hopedale, Mass. James E. Walker, *Treasurer and Clerk of Corporation*, Milford, Mass.

NAMES AND RESIDENCE OF BOARD OF DIRECTORS.

William F. Draper, Hopedale, Mass. Charles F. Claflin, Milford, Mass. John P. Daniels, Milford, Mass. Eben S. Draper, Hopedale, Mass. George A. Draper, Hopedale, Mass. Edgar K. Ray, Franklin, Mass.

We hereby certify that the statements contained in the foregoing return are full, just and true.

C. F. CLAFLIN,
JOHN P. DANIELS,
GEO. A. DRAPER,
EBEN S. DRAPER,
Directors.
JAMES E. WALKER,
Treasurer.

COMMONWEALTH OF MASSACHUSETTS.

WORCESTER, SS. JULY 30, 1904. Then personally appeared the above-named C. F. Claflin, John P. Daniels, Geo. A. Draper, Eben S. Draper and James E. Walker, and severally made oath that the foregoing certificate by them subscribed is, to the best of their knowledge and belief, true.

Before me, JESSE A. TAFT,
Justice of the Peace.

RETURN

OF THE

NANTUCKET CENTRAL RAILROAD COMPANY

For the Year ending June 30, 1904.

[A narrow-gauge railroad.]

General Exhibit for the Year.		
Gross earnings from operation,		$4,766 66
Operating expenses,		4,725 89
Net Earnings from Operation,		$40 77
Charges upon income accrued during the year:		
Interest on funded debt,	$1,020 00	
Taxes,	40 77	
Total Charges and Deductions from Income,		1,060 77
Deficit for the year ending June 30, 1904,		$1,020 00
Amount of deficit June 30, 1903,		1,600 00
Total Deficit June 30, 1904,		$2,620 00
Earnings from Operation.		
Passenger service:		
Gross receipts from passengers,		$3,880 30
From mails,		99 23
From express,		554 46
From extra baggage and storage,		232 67
Gross Earnings from Operation,		$4,766 66
Expenses of Operation.		
General expenses:		
Salaries of general officers,		$99 23
Salaries of clerks and attendants,		319 50
Stationery and printing (general offices),		142 75
Total,		$561 48
Maintenance of way and structures: repairs of roadway,		$1,985 86

Maintenance of equipment:	
Repairs and renewals of locomotives,	$106 89
Repairs and renewals of passenger cars,	193 75
TOTAL,	$300 64
Conducting transportation:	
Engine and roundhouse men,	$626 33
Fuel for locomotives,	754 15
Water supply for locomotives,	35 00
Oil, tallow and waste for locomotives,	58 13
Train service,	227 00
Switchmen, flagmen and watchmen,	177 30
TOTAL,	$1,877 91
Recapitulation:	
General expenses,	$561 48
Maintenance of way and structures,	1,985 86
Maintenance of equipment,	300 64
Conducting transportation,	1,877 91
TOTAL OPERATING EXPENSES,	$4,725 89

GENERAL BALANCE SHEET, JUNE 30, 1904.

ASSETS. DR.	
Cost of road and equipment,	$35,000 00
Profit and loss balance (deficit),	2,620 00
TOTAL,	$37,620 00

LIABILITIES. CR.	
Capital stock,	$18,000 00
Funded debt,	17,000 00
Current liabilities: matured interest coupons unpaid (including coupons due July 1),	2,620 00
TOTAL,	$37,620 00

CAPITAL STOCK.

Capital stock authorized by law,	$18,000 00	
Capital stock authorized by votes of company,	18,000 00	
Capital stock issued and outstanding,		$18,000 00
Number of shares issued and outstanding,	180	
Number of stockholders,	5	
Number of stockholders in Massachusetts,	5	
Amount of stock held in Massachusetts,	$18,000 00	

FUNDED DEBT.

DESCRIPTION OF BONDS.	Rate of Interest.	Date of Maturity.	Amount Outstanding.	Interest Paid during the Year.
Mortgage bonds,	Per Cent. 6	Feb. 1, 1906,	$17,000 00	-

Volume of Traffic, etc.

Passenger traffic:	
Number of passengers carried paying revenue, ...	13,335
Number of passengers carried one mile, ...	113,347
Number of passengers carried one mile per mile of road operated, ...	13,335
Average length of journey per passenger, ...	8.500 miles.
Average amount received per passenger per mile carried, .	3.423 cents.
Passenger earnings (gross) per mile of road operated, .	$456 55.000
Train mileage:	
Miles run by passenger trains, ...	7,000
Total train mileage, ...	7,000
Fares and freights:	
Average rate of fare per mile received for local and trip tickets, ...	3.423 cents.
Employees:	
Average number of persons employed, ...	16

Description of Railroad Owned and Operated.

(See also tabulated description in preceding appendix to report.)

Railroad Owned and Operated.	Total.	In Massachusetts.
	Miles.	Miles.
Length of main line, ...	8.500	8.500
Length of side track, etc., ...	.200	.200
Total Length of Track Owned and Operated, . . .	8.700	8.700

Description of Equipment.

Rolling Stock.	Number Owned.	Average Weight.	Equipped with Automatic Couplers.	Name of Coupler Used.
Locomotives.		Lbs.		
Passenger, ...	1	40,000	-	-
Cars — Passenger Service.				
Passenger cars, ...	3	-	3	Miller.
Baggage, express and mail cars, ...	1	-	-	-
Total, ...	4	-	3	-
Cars — Freight Service.				
Flat cars, ...	3	-	-	-
Cars — Company's Service.				
Gravel cars, ...	1	-	-	-

RAILROAD CROSSINGS IN MASSACHUSETTS.

Crossings with Highways.	
Number of crossings of railroad with highways at grade, .	5
Number of highway grade crossings protected by flagmen, .	5

CORPORATE NAME AND ADDRESS OF THE COMPANY.

NANTUCKET CENTRAL RAILROAD COMPANY,

WALTHAM, MASS.

NAME AND BUSINESS ADDRESS OF PRINCIPAL OFFICERS.

Henry S. Milton, *President*, 10 Tremont Street, Boston, Mass. Delmont L. Weeks, *Treasurer, Clerk of Corporation and General Manager*, Waltham, Mass.

NAMES AND RESIDENCE OF BOARD OF DIRECTORS.

Henry S. Milton, Waltham, Mass. Byron B. Johnson, Waltham, Mass. George R. Taber, Waltham, Mass. Delmont L. Weeks, Waltham, Mass. Fred C. Hinds, Newtonville, Mass.

We hereby certify that the statements contained in the foregoing return are full, just and true.

DELMONT L. WEEKS,
FRED C. HINDS,
HENRY S. MILTON,
Directors.
DELMONT L. WEEKS,
Treasurer.

COMMONWEALTH OF MASSACHUSETTS.

SUFFOLK, SS. BOSTON, October, 1904. Then personally appeared the above-named Delmont L. Weeks, Fred C. Hinds, and Henry S. Milton, and severally made oath that the foregoing certificate by them subscribed is, to the best of their knowledge and belief, true.

Before me, CHARLES E. ROWE,
Notary Public.

RETURN

OF THE

NASHUA, ACTON & BOSTON RAILROAD COMPANY

For the Year ending June 30, 1904.

[Leased to and operated by the Boston & Maine.]

General Balance Sheet June 30, 1904.

Assets.	Dr.	
Cost of road and equipment,		$1,057,031 20
Due from solvent companies and individuals,		6,257 41
Profit and loss balance (deficit),		646,694 29
Total,		$1,709,982 90

Liabilities.	Cr.	
Capital stock,		$500,000 00
Funded debt,		500,000 00
Current liabilities:		
Loans and notes payable,	$105,509 90	
Matured interest coupons unpaid (including coupons due October 1, 1894),	604,473 00	
Total Current Liabilities,		709,982 90
Total,		$1,709,982 90

Capital Stock.

Capital stock authorized by law,	$600,000 00	
Capital stock authorized by votes of company,	500,000 00	
Capital stock issued and outstanding,		$500,000 00
Number of shares issued and outstanding,	5,000	
Number of stockholders,	138	
Number of stockholders in Massachusetts,	79	
Amount of stock held in Massachusetts,	$55,100 00	

Funded Debt.

Description of Bonds.	Rate of Interest.	Date of Maturity.	Amount Outstanding.	Interest Paid during the Year.
	Per Cent.			
First mortgage bonds,	6	Oct. 1, 1894,	$500,000 00	–

Description of Railroad Owned.

(See also tabulated description in preceding appendix to report.)

Railroad Owned.	Total.	In Massachusetts.
	Miles.	Miles.
Length of main line,	20.120	15.140
Length of side track, etc.,	5.300	2.910
Total Length of Track Owned,	25.420	18.050

Corporate Name and Address of the Company.

NASHUA, ACTON & BOSTON RAILROAD COMPANY,

Concord, N. H.

Names and Business Address of Principal Officers.

Benjamin A. Kimball, *President*, Concord, N. H. John F. Webster, *Treasurer and Clerk of Corporation*, Concord, N. H.

Names and Residence of Board of Directors.

Benjamin A. Kimball, Concord, N. H. John F. Webster, Concord, N. H. Fred S. Heath, Concord, N. H. Frank A. Merrill, Concord, N. H. William C. Wendt, Concord, N. H. Harry H. Dudley, Concord, N. H. Herman F. Straw, Manchester, N. H.

We hereby certify that the statements contained in the foregoing return are full, just and true.

BENJAMIN A. KIMBALL,
JOHN F. WEBSTER,
HARRY H. DUDLEY,
FRANK A. MERRILL,
Directors.
JOHN F. WEBSTER,
Treasurer.

State of New Hampshire.

Merrimack, ss. Concord, Sept. 6, 1904. Then personally appeared the above-named Benjamin A. Kimball, John F. Webster, Harry H. Dudley and Frank A. Merrill, all of Concord, N. H., and severally made oath that the foregoing certificate by them subscribed is, to the best of their knowledge and belief, true.

Before me, GEORGE E. SHEPARD,
Notary Public.

RETURN

OF THE

NASHUA & LOWELL RAILROAD CORPORATION

FOR THE YEAR ENDING JUNE 30, 1904.

[Leased to and operated by the Boston & Maine.]

GENERAL EXHIBIT FOR THE YEAR.

Rental received from lease of road,	$73,000 00
Dividends received on stocks owned: Boston & Maine R.R.,	1,572 00
Income from other sources: office rent, $60; interest, $687.10,	747 10
GROSS INCOME,	$75,319 10
Expenses and charges upon income accrued during the year: salaries and maintenance of organization,	941 90
NET DIVISIBLE INCOME,	$74,377 20
Dividends declared (9 per cent),	72,000 00
Surplus for the year ending June 30, 1904,	$2,377 20
Amount of surplus June 30, 1903,	163,849 39
TOTAL SURPLUS JUNE 30, 1904,	$166,226 59

GENERAL BALANCE SHEET JUNE 30, 1904.

ASSETS.	DR.	
Cost of road,		$684,242 07
Cost of equipment,		218,242 95
TOTAL PERMANENT INVESTMENTS,		$902,485 02
Cash,	$4,645 82	
Bills receivable and stock,	60,306 25	
TOTAL CASH AND CURRENT ASSETS,		64,952 07
TOTAL,		$967,437 09
LIABILITIES.	**CR.**	
Capital stock,		$800,000 00
Current liabilities:		
Dividends not called for,	$1,198 50	
Matured interest coupons unpaid,	12 00	
TOTAL CURRENT LIABILITIES,		1,210 50
Profit and loss balance (surplus),		166,226 59
TOTAL,		$967,437 09

CAPITAL STOCK.

Capital stock authorized by law, ...	$800,000 00	
Capital stock authorized by votes of company,	800,000 00	
Capital stock issued and outstanding, ...		$800,000 00
Number of shares issued and outstanding, .	8,000	
Number of stockholders, ...	412	
Number of stockholders in Massachusetts, .	236	
Amount of stock held in Massachusetts, . .	$529,500 00	

DESCRIPTION OF RAILROAD OWNED.

(See also tabulated description in preceding appendix to report.)

RAILROAD OWNED.	Total.	In Massachusetts.
	Miles.	Miles.
Length of main line, ...	14.500	9.250
Length of second track, ...	14.500	9.250
Length of side track, etc., ...	13.040	8.140
TOTAL LENGTH OF TRACK OWNED, ...	42.040	26.640

CORPORATE NAME AND ADDRESS OF THE COMPANY.

NASHUA & LOWELL RAILROAD CORPORATION,

50 STATE STREET, BOSTON, MASS.

NAMES AND BUSINESS ADDRESS OF PRINCIPAL OFFICERS.

David P. Kimball, *President*, 40 Water Street, Boston, Mass. John Brooks, *Treasurer*, 50 State Street, Boston, Mass. Walter A. Lovering, *Clerk of Corporation*, Nashua, N. H.

NAMES AND RESIDENCE OF BOARD OF DIRECTORS.

David P. Kimball, Boston, Mass. Alfred S. Hall, Winchester, Mass. Edward A. Newell, Wilton, N. H. Frederick Brooks, Boston, Mass. John Brooks, Cambridge, Mass.

We hereby certify that the statements contained in the foregoing return are full, just and true.

FRED. BROOKS,
ALFRED S. HALL,
JOHN BROOKS,
Directors.
JOHN BROOKS,
Treasurer.

COMMONWEALTH OF MASSACHUSETTS.

SUFFOLK SS. SEPT. 29, 1904. Then personally appeared the above-named Fred. Brooks, Alfred S. Hall and John Brooks, a majority of the directors, and John Brooks, the treasurer, of the Nashua & Lowell Railroad Corporation, and severally made oath that the foregoing certificate by them subscribed is, to the best of their knowledge and belief, true.

Before me, S. K. HAMILTON,
Justice of the Peace.

RETURN

OF THE

NEWBURYPORT RAILROAD COMPANY

FOR THE YEAR ENDING JUNE 30, 1904.

[Leased to and operated by the Boston & Maine. Its operations are included in the return of that road, being so intimately connected that separate accounts are not kept.]

GENERAL BALANCE SHEET JUNE 30, 1904.

ASSETS.	DR.	
Cost of road,		$597,386 32
TOTAL,		$597,386 32

LIABILITIES.	CR.	
Capital stock,		$220,340 02
Funded debt,		300,000 00
Profit and loss balance (surplus),		77,046 30
TOTAL,		$597,386 32

CAPITAL STOCK.

Capital stock authorized by law,	$430,000 00	
Capital stock authorized by votes of company,	202,100 00	
Capital stock issued and outstanding,		$200,900 00
Amount paid in on shares not yet issued,		19,440 02
TOTAL CAPITAL STOCK LIABILITY,		$220,340 02
Number of shares issued and outstanding,	2,009	
Number of stockholders,	252	
Number of stockholders in Massachusetts,	251	
Amount of stock held in Massachusetts,	$200,800 00	

FUNDED DEBT.

DESCRIPTION OF BONDS.	Rate of Interest.	Date of Maturity.	Amount Outstanding.	Interest Paid during the Year.
	Per Cent.			
Mortgage bonds,	6	Nov. 15, 1852,	$3,900 00	-
Mortgage bonds,	6	Oct. 16, 1854,	30,200 00	-
Mortgage bonds,	6	Dec. 15, 1857,	113,100 00	-
Mortgage bonds,	6	March 1, 1870,	298,600 00	-
TOTALS,	. .	. . .	$445,800 00*	-

* All of which are owned by the Boston & Maine Railroad and for which the liability of the Newburyport Railroad Company at the termination of the lease is $300,000.

Description of Railroad Owned.

(See also tabulated description in preceding appendix to report.)

Railroad Owned.	Total.	In Massachusetts.
	Miles.	Miles.
Length of main line,	26.980	26.980
Length of side track, etc.,	4.920	4.920
Total Length of Track Owned,	31.900	31.900

Corporate Name and Address of the Company.

NEWBURYPORT RAILROAD COMPANY,

Boston, Mass.

Names and Business Address of Principal Officers.

Lucius Tuttle, *President*, Boston, Mass. Herbert E. Fisher, *Treasurer*, Boston, Mass. William B. Lawrence, *Clerk of Corporation*, Boston, Mass. William J. Hobbs, *Auditor*, Boston, Mass.

Names and Residence of Board of Directors.

Lucius Tuttle, Boston, Mass. Samuel C. Lawrence, Medford, Mass. Walter Hunnewell, Wellesley, Mass. Henry M. Whitney, Brookline, Mass. Henry R. Reed, Boston, Mass. Joseph H. White, Brookline, Mass. William J. Hobbs, Malden, Mass.

We hereby certify that the statements contained in the foregoing return are full, just and true.

LUCIUS TUTTLE,
SAMUEL C. LAWRENCE,
HENRY R. REED,
HENRY M. WHITNEY,
WALTER HUNNEWELL,
JOSEPH H. WHITE,
WM. J. HOBBS,
Directors.
HERBERT E. FISHER,
Treasurer.
WM. J. HOBBS,
Chief Accounting Officer.

Commonwealth of Massachusetts.

Suffolk, ss. Boston, Sept. 8, 1904. Then personally appeared the above-named Lucius Tuttle, Samuel C. Lawrence, Henry R. Reed, Henry M. Whitney, Walter Hunnewell, Joseph H. White and William J. Hobbs, directors of the Newburyport Railroad Company, and Herbert E. Fisher its treasurer, and William J. Hobbs its chief accounting officer, and severally made oath that the foregoing certificate by them subscribed is, to the best of their knowledge and belief, true.

Before me, WILLIAM B. LAWRENCE,
Justice of the Peace.

RETURN

OF THE

NEW ENGLAND RAILROAD COMPANY

FOR THE YEAR ENDING JUNE 30, 1904.

[Leased to and operated by the New York, New Haven & Hartford.]

GENERAL EXHIBIT FOR THE YEAR.		
Rental received from lease of road,		$1,120,241 00
Expenses and charges upon income accrued during the year:		
Salaries and maintenance of organization,	$241 00	
Interest on funded debt,	970,000 00	
TOTAL EXPENSES AND CHARGES UPON INCOME,		970,241 00
NET DIVISIBLE INCOME,		$150,000 00
Dividends declared (3 per cent on preferred stock),		$150,000 00
Amount of deficit June 30, 1903,		$351,550 99
TOTAL DEFICIT JUNE 30, 1904,		$351,550 99

GENERAL BALANCE SHEET JUNE 30, 1904.		
ASSETS.	DR.	
Cost of road,		$27,898,211 79
Cost of equipment (appraised value),		2,416,608 87
Underlying liens, being mortgages of the New York & New England Railroad Company,		11,500,000 00
TOTAL PERMANENT INVESTMENTS,		$41,814,820 66
Sinking and other special funds,	$130 00	
Other cash assets,	886,214 08	
TOTAL CASH AND CURRENT ASSETS,		886,344 08
Profit and loss balance (deficit),		351,550 99
TOTAL,		$43,052,715 73
LIABILITIES.	CR.	
Capital stock, common,	$20,000,000 00	
Capital stock, preferred,	5,000,000 00	
TOTAL CAPITAL STOCK,		$25,000,000 00

Funded debt,		$6,500,000 00
Mortgage debt of the New York & New England R.R. Co.,		11,500,000 00
Current liabilities:		
Traffic balances due to other companies,	$16,628 51	
Matured interest coupons unpaid (including coupons due July 1),	130 00	
Miscellaneous current liabilities: from Norwich & New York Transportation Co.,	35,957 22	
TOTAL CURRENT LIABILITIES,		52,715 73
TOTAL,		$43,052,715 73

PROPERTY ACCOUNTS.

Additions to construction account:		
Grading and masonry,	$19,417 33	
Bridging, etc.,	210,681 03	
Superstructure, including rails,	15,055 83	
Lands, land damages and fences,	177,907 75	
Passenger and freight stations, coal sheds and water stations,	206,542 16	
Elimination of grade crossings, etc.,	887,024 41	
TOTAL ADDITIONS TO CONSTRUCTION ACCOUNT,		$1,516,628 51

CAPITAL STOCK.

Capital stock authorized by law, common,		$20,000,000 00	
Capital stock authorized by law, preferred,		5,000,000 00	
Total capital stock authorized by law,		$25,000,000 00	
Capital stock authorized by votes of company, common,		$20,000,000 00	
Capital stock authorized by votes of company, preferred,		5,000,000 00	
Total capital stock authorized by vote,		$25,000,000 00	
Capital stock issued and outstanding, common,			$20,000,000 00
Capital stock issued and outstanding, preferred,			5,000,000 00
Total capital stock outstanding,			$25,000,000 00
Number of shares issued and outstanding, common,	200,000		
Number of shares issued and outstanding, preferred,	50,000		
Total number of shares outstanding,		250,000	
Number of stockholders, common,	20		
Number of stockholders, preferred,	18		
Total number of stockholders,		38	
Number of stockholders in Massachusetts, common,	7		
Number of stockholders in Massachusetts, preferred,	8		
Total stockholders in Massachusetts,		15	

Amount of stock held in Massachusetts, common, ...	$27,200 00
Amount of stock held in Massachusetts, preferred, ...	16,800 00
Total stock held in Massachusetts, ...	$44,000 00

Funded Debt.

Description of Bonds.	Rate of Interest.	Date of Maturity.	Amount Outstanding.	Interest Paid during the Year.
Consolidated mortgage bonds, . .	Per Cent. 5	July 1, 1945, .	$6,500,000 00	$250,000 00

Mortgage Debt of the New York & New England Railroad Company.

First mortgage bonds, . . .	7	Jan. 1, 1905,	$6,000,000 00	$420,000 00
First mortgage bonds, . . .	6	Jan. 1, 1905,	4,000,000 00	240,000 00
Boston terminal first mortgage bonds,	4	April 1, 1939,	1,500,000 00	60,000 00
Totals, ...	. .	. . . .	$11,500,000 00	$720,000 00

Description of Railroad Owned.

(See also tabulated description in preceding appendix to report.)

Railroad Owned.	Total.	In Massachusetts.
	Miles.	Miles.
Length of main line, ...	215.270	50.630
Length of branch line, ...	143.890	52.320
Total Length of Line Owned, ...	359.160	102.950
Length of second track, ...	117.670	51.670
Length of side track, etc., ...	203.810	80.640
Total Length of Track Owned, ...	680.640	235.260

Corporate Name and Address of the Company.

NEW ENGLAND RAILROAD COMPANY,

Boston, Mass.

Names and Business Address of Principal Officers.

Charles S. Mellen, *President*, New Haven, Conn. Fayette S. Curtis, *Vice-President*, Boston, Mass. George B. Phippen, *Treasurer*, Boston, Mass. James W. Perkins, *Secretary*, Boston, Mass.

Names and Residence of Board of Directors.

Charles S. Mellen, New Haven, Conn. John M. Hall, New Haven, Conn. Frank W. Cheney, South Manchester, Conn. J. Pierpont Morgan, New York, N. Y. Fayette S. Curtis, Boston, Mass. Edward G. Buckland, New Haven, Conn. Charles F. Brooker, Torrington, Conn. Nathaniel Thayer, Boston, Mass. George J. Brush, New Haven, Conn. D. Newton Barney, Hartford, Conn. Robert W. Taft, Providence, R. I.

We hereby certify that the statements contained in the foregoing return are full, just and true.

C. S. MELLEN,
JOHN M. HALL,
N. THAYER,
FAYETTE S. CURTIS,
EDWARD G. BUCKLAND,
GEO. J. BRUSH,
Directors.
GEO. B. PHIPPEN,
Treasurer.

State of New York.

City and County of New York, ss. Sept. 17, 1904. Then personally appeared the above-named C. S. Mellen, John M. Hall, N. Thayer, Fayette S. Curtis, Edward G. Buckland and Geo. J. Brush, and severally made oath that the foregoing certificate by them subscribed is, to the best of their knowledge and belief, true.

Before me, FRANK E. HALL,
Notary Public, New York County.

Commonwealth of Massachusetts.

Suffolk, ss. Boston, Sept. 20, 1904. Then personally appeared the above-named George B. Phippen, treasurer, and made oath that the foregoing certificate by him subscribed is, to the best of his knowledge and belief true.

Before me, ARTHUR P. RUSSELL,
Justice of the Peace.

RETURN

OF THE

NEW HAVEN & NORTHAMPTON COMPANY

For the Year ending June 30, 1904.

[Leased to and operated by the New York, New Haven & Hartford.]

General Exhibit for the Year.

Rental received from lease of road,		$296,317 28
Dividends received on stocks owned,		2,888 67
Gross Income,		$299,205 95
Expenses and charges upon income accrued during the year:		
Salaries and maintenance of organization,	$152 50	
Interest on funded debt,	142,000 00	
Rentals paid: Holyoke & Westfield Railroad,	40,917 28	
Other expenses and charges upon income: payments to sinking fund,	15,000 00	
Total Expenses and Charges upon Income,		198,069 78
Net Divisible Income,		$101,136 17
Dividends declared (4 per cent),		98,400 00
Surplus for the year ending June 30, 1904,		$2,736 17
Amount of surplus June 30, 1903,		1,552,582 78
Total Surplus June 30, 1904,		$1,555,318 95

General Balance Sheet June 30, 1904.

Assets.	Dr.	
Cost of road,		$5,731,586 62
Cost of equipment,		850,430 62
Stock of Holyoke & Westfield R.R., 200 shares,	$20,000 00	
Stock of New York, New Haven & Hartford R.R., 58 shares,	12,081 50	
Stock of Southington Water Co., 10 shares,	1,000 00	
		33,081 50
Total Permanent Investments,		$6,615,098 74
Cash,	$220 21	
Sinking and other special funds,	375,000 00	
Total Cash and Current Assets,		375,220 21
Total,		$6,990,318 95

LIABILITIES. CR.	
Capital stock,	$2,460,000 00
Funded debt,	2,600,000 00
Sinking and other special funds: consolidated 6 per cent bonds,	375,000 00
Profit and loss balance (surplus),	1,555,318 95
TOTAL,	$6,990,318 95

CAPITAL STOCK.

Capital stock authorized by law,	$5,000,000 00	
Capital stock authorized by votes of company,	2,460,000 00	
Capital stock issued and outstanding,		$2,460,000 00
Number of shares issued and outstanding,	24,600	
Number of stockholders,	1*	

FUNDED DEBT.

DESCRIPTION OF BONDS.	Rate of Interest.	Date of Maturity.	Amount Outstanding.	Interest Paid during the Year.
	Per Cent.			
Mortgage and sinking fund bonds,	6	April 1, 1909,	$1,200,000 00	$72,000 00
Northern extension bonds,	5	April 1, 1911,	700,000 00	35,000 00
Convertible (no mortgage) bonds,	5	July 1, 1904,	700,000 00	35,000 00
TOTALS,	. .	. . .	$2,600,000 00	$142,000 00

SINKING FUNDS.

Amount June 30, 1903, of consolidated 6 per cent bonds sinking fund,	$360,000 00
Additions during the year to consolidated 6 per cent bonds sinking fund,	15,000 00
TOTAL SINKING FUNDS JUNE 30, 1904,	$375,000 00

DESCRIPTION OF RAILROAD OWNED.

(See also tabulated description in preceding appendix to report.)

RAILROAD OWNED.	Total.	In Massachusetts.
	Miles.	Miles.
Length of main line,	94.640	43.380
Length of branch line,	31.670	17.580
TOTAL LENGTH OF LINE OWNED,	126.310	60.960
Length of side track, etc.,	55.840	28.780
TOTAL LENGTH OF TRACK OWNED,	182.150	89.740

* The New York, New Haven & Hartford Railroad Company.

CORPORATE NAME AND ADDRESS OF THE COMPANY.

NEW HAVEN & NORTHAMPTON COMPANY,

NEW HAVEN, CONN.

NAMES AND BUSINESS ADDRESS OF PRINCIPAL OFFICERS.

Charles S. Mellen, *President*, New Haven, Conn. Hiram M. Kochersperger, *Vice-President*, New Haven, Conn. Edward A. Ray, *Treasurer and Secretary*, New Haven, Conn.

NAMES AND RESIDENCE OF BOARD OF DIRECTORS.

George J. Brush, New Haven, Conn. A. Heaton Robertson, New Haven, Conn. John M. Hall, New Haven, Conn. Samuel E. Merwin, New Haven, Conn. Fayette S. Curtis, Southern Terminal Station, Boston, Mass. Arthur D. Osborne, New Haven, Conn. Charles S. Mellen, New Haven, Conn. Hiram M. Kochersperger, New Haven, Conn. William Skinner, Holyoke, Mass.

We hereby certify that the statements contained in the foregoing return are full, just and true.

A. HEATON ROBERTSON,
JOHN M. HALL,
FAYETTE S. CURTIS,
C. S. MELLEN,
H. M. KOCHERSPERGER,
Directors.
EDWARD A. RAY,
Treasurer and Chief Accounting Officer.

STATE OF CONNECTICUT.

NEW HAVEN COUNTY, ss. NEW HAVEN, Sept. 6, 1904. Then personally appeared the above-named A. Heaton Robertson, John M. Hall, C. S. Mellen, H. M. Kochersperger and Edward A. Ray, and severally made oath that the foregoing certificate by them subscribed is, to the best of their knowledge and belief, true.

Before me, AVERY CLARK,
Notary Public.

COMMONWEALTH OF MASSACHUSETTS.

SUFFOLK, ss. BOSTON, Sept. 7, 1904. Then personally appeared the above-named Fayette S. Curtis, and made oath that the foregoing certificate by him subscribed is, to the best of his knowledge and belief, true.

Before me, FRANK A. FARNHAM,
Justice of the Peace.

RETURN

OF THE

NEW LONDON NORTHERN RAILROAD COMPANY

FOR THE YEAR ENDING JUNE 30, 1904.

[Leased to and operated by the Central Vermont.]

GENERAL EXHIBIT FOR THE YEAR (LESSEE'S ACCOUNT.)		
Gross earnings from operation,		$1,010,531 39
Operating expenses,		863,078 73
NET EARNINGS FROM OPERATION,		$147,452 66
Miscellaneous income: rents, etc.,		25,096 71
GROSS INCOME ABOVE OPERATING EXPENSES,		$172,549 37
Charges upon income accrued during the year:		
Taxes,	$47,778 97	
Rental of New London Northern Railroad,	203,952 50	
TOTAL CHARGES AND DEDUCTIONS FROM INCOME,		251,731 47
DEFICIT JUNE 30, 1904,		$79,182 10

GENERAL EXHIBIT FOR THE YEAR (LESSOR'S ACCOUNT),		
Income from lease of road,		$213,552 50
Salaries and expenses of organization,		4,874 66
NET EARNINGS,		$208,677 84
Charges upon income accrued during the year:		
Interest on funded debt,	$68,120 00	
Interest and discount on unfunded debts and loans,	402 20	
TOTAL CHARGES AND DEDUCTIONS FROM INCOME,		68,522 20
NET DIVISIBLE INCOME,		$140,155 64
Dividends declared during the year payable on —		
July, 1903, 2¼ per cent on $1,500,000,	$33,750 00	
October, 1903, 2¼ per cent on $1,500,000,	33,750 00	

Dividends declared, etc. — *Concluded.*		
January, 1904, 2¼ per cent on $1,500,000,	$33,750 00	
April, 1904, 2¼ per cent on $1,500,000,	33,750 00	
TOTAL DIVIDENDS DECLARED,		$135,000 00
Surplus for the year ending June 30, 1904,		$5,155 64
Amount of surplus June 30, 1903,		516,184 98
Credits to profit and loss account during the year: interest,		963 70
TOTAL SURPLUS JUNE 30, 1904,		$522,304 32

EARNINGS FROM OPERATION (LESSEE'S ACCOUNT).

DEPARTMENT OF SERVICE.	Gross Receipts.	Deductions.	Earnings.
Passenger service:			
Gross receipts from passengers,	$198,738 88		
Deductions:			
Tickets redeemed,		$331 07	
Excess fares refunded,		2,394 65	
Total deductions,		$2,725 72	
NET REVENUE FROM PASSENGERS,			$196,013 16
From mails,	$17,929 32		
From express,	19,419 91		
From extra baggage and storage,	2,239 19		39,588 42
TOTAL EARNINGS, PASSENGER SERVICE,			$235,601 58
Freight service:			
Gross receipts from freight,	$792,042 29		
Deduction:			
Overcharge to shippers,		$17,112 48	
TOTAL EARNINGS, FREIGHT SERVICE,			774,929 81
GROSS EARNINGS FROM OPERATION,			$1,010,531 39

EXPENSES OF OPERATION (LESSEE'S ACCOUNT).

General expenses:	
Salaries of general officers,	$5,266 44
Salaries of clerks and attendants,	12,127 32
General office expenses and supplies,	1,907 76
Insurance,	3,430 40
Law expenses,	4,146 06
Stationery and printing (general offices),	1,143 19
Other general expenses,	188 96
TOTAL,	$28,210 13
Maintenance of way and structures:	
Repairs of roadway,	$59,208 29
Renewals of rails,	8,075 24
Renewals of ties,	13,737 17
Repairs and renewals of bridges and culverts,	2,994 00

Maintenance of way and structures — *Concluded.*	
Repairs and renewals of fences, road crossings, signs and cattle guards,	$6,358 86
Repairs and renewals of buildings and fixtures,	11,935 95
Repairs and renewals of docks and wharves,	3,744 95
Repairs and renewals of telegraph,	683 40
Stationery and printing,	106 23
TOTAL,	$106,844 09
Maintenance of equipment:	
Superintendence,	$5,588 00
Repairs and renewals of locomotives,	7,863 27
Repairs and renewals of passenger cars,	4,811 02
Repairs and renewals of freight cars,	9,712 04
Repairs and renewals of work cars,	424 87
Repairs and renewals of shop machinery and tools,	724 22
Stationery and printing,	261 37
Other expenses of maintaining equipment,	3,297 16
TOTAL,	$32,681 95
Conducting transportation:	
Superintendence,	$13,730 58
Engine and roundhouse men,	52,125 42
Fuel for locomotives,	171,846 91
Water supply for locomotives,	4,206 98
Oil, tallow and waste for locomotives,	2,270 34
Other supplies for locomotives,	1,213 62
Train service,	44,841 85
Train supplies and expenses,	7,835 96
Switchmen, flagmen and watchmen,	18,065 57
Telegraph expenses,	13,443 28
Station service,	198,347 37
Station supplies,	9,004 17
Car mileage — balance,	44,705 31
Hire of equipment,	33,032 21
Loss and damage,	20,533 99
Injuries to persons,	16,295 56
Clearing wrecks,	1,063 79
Advertising,	1,546 10
Outside agencies,	15,343 24
Commissions,	707 49
Rentals for tracks, yards and terminals,	7 80
Rentals of buildings and other property,	18,952 49
Stationery and printing,	6,076 22
Other expenses of conducting transportation,	146 31
TOTAL,	$695,342 56
Recapitulation:	
General expenses,	$28,210 13
Maintenance of way and structures,	106,844 09
Maintenance of equipment,	32,681 95
Conducting transportation,	695,342 56
TOTAL OPERATING EXPENSES,	$863,078 73
Percentage of operating expenses to gross earnings,	85.00

GENERAL BALANCE SHEET JUNE 30, 1904 (LESSOR'S ACCOUNT).

ASSETS.	DR.	
Cost of road,		$3,064,629 47
Cost of equipment,		248,420 44
Bonds of Brattleboro & Whitehall Railroad,		150,000 00
Other permanent property: steamboat property,		5,000 00
TOTAL PERMANENT INVESTMENTS,		$3,468,049 91
Cash,	$66,531 55	
Due from solvent companies and individuals,	1,000 00	
TOTAL CASH AND CURRENT ASSETS,		67,531 55
TOTAL,		$3,535,581 46

LIABILITIES.	CR.	
Capital stock,		$1,500,000 00
Funded debt,		1,500,000 00
Current liabilities:		
Loans and notes payable,	$10,000 00	
Dividends not called for,	2,877 80	
Matured interest coupons unpaid,	399 34	
TOTAL CURRENT LIABILITIES,		13,277 14
Profit and loss balance (surplus),		522,304 32
TOTAL,		$3,535,581 46

CAPITAL STOCK (LESSOR'S ACCOUNT.)

Capital stock authorized by law,	$2,000,000 00	
Capital stock authorized by votes of company,	1,500,000 00	
Capital stock issued and outstanding,		$1,500,000 00
Number of shares issued and outstanding,	15,000	
Number of stockholders,	383	
Number of stockholders in Massachusetts,	186	
Amount of stock held in Massachusetts,	$768,600 00	

FUNDED DEBT (LESSOR'S ACCOUNT).

DESCRIPTION OF BONDS.	Rate of Interest.	Date of Maturity.	Amount Outstanding.	Interest Paid during the Year.
	Per Cent.			
Consolidated bonds,	5	June 1, 1910,	$812,000 00	$40,600 00
Consolidated bonds,	4	June 1, 1910,	688,000 00	27,520 00
TOTALS,	. .	. . .	$1,500,000 00	$68,120 00

VOLUME OF TRAFFIC, ETC. (LESSEE'S ACCOUNT).

Passenger traffic:	
Number of passengers carried paying revenue,	495,984
Number of passengers carried one mile,	8,076,799
Number of passengers carried one mile per mile of road operated,	66,750

Passenger traffic — *Concluded.*	
Average length of journey per passenger,	16.280 miles.
Average amount received per passenger per mile carried,	2.427 cents.
Passenger earnings (gross) per mile of road operated,	$1,907 70.000
Passenger earnings (gross) per passenger-train mile run,	76.777
Freight traffic:	
Number of tons of freight hauled earning revenue,	1,627,018
Number of tons of freight hauled one mile,	51,066,363
Number of tons of freight hauled one mile per mile of road operated,	413,493
Average length of haul per ton,	31.390 miles.
Average amount received per ton per mile hauled,	1.517 cents.
Freight earnings (gross) per mile of road operated,	$6,274 73.000
Freight earnings (gross) per freight-train mile run,	1 86.738
Operating expenses:	
Operating expenses per mile of road operated,	6,988 49.000
Operating expenses per revenue-train mile run,	1 19.561
Train mileage:	
Miles run by passenger trains,	306,890
Miles run by freight trains,	414,982
Total mileage of trains earning revenue,	721,872
Miles run by switching trains,	196,591
Total train mileage,	918,463
Fares and freights:	
Average rate of fare per mile received for local and trip tickets,	2.920 cents.
Average rate of fare per mile received for mileage tickets,	2.000 "
Average rate of fare per mile received for time and commutation tickets,	1.200 "
Average rate of fare per mile received for interline tickets,	2.070 "
Employees:	
Average number of persons employed,	768

Description of Railroad Owned and Operated.

(See also tabulated description in preceding appendix to report.)

Railroad Owned (Lessor's Account).	Total.	In Massachusetts.
	Miles.	Miles.
Length of main line,	121.000	54.900
Length of side track, etc.,	38.700	13.500
Total Length of Track Owned,	159.700	68.400
Railroad Operated (Lessee's Account).		
Length of main line,	121.000	54.900
Length of side track, etc.,	38.700	13.500
Total Length of Track Operated,	159.700	68.400

Description of Equipment (Lessee's Account).

Rolling Stock.	Total Owned and Leased.	Equipped with Power Driving-Wheel Brakes.	Maximum Weight.	Average Weight.	Equipped with Power Train Brakes.	Equipped with Automatic Couplers.	Name of Coupler Used.
Locomotives.			Lbs.	Lbs.			
Passenger,	4	4	140,000	134,000	-	-	-
Freight,	9	9	184,000	170,000	-	-	-
Switching, etc.,	1	1	118,000	118,000	-	-	-
Total,	14	14	-	-	-	-	-
Cars — Passenger Service.							
Passenger cars,	5	-	-	-	5	5	Tower.
Combination cars,	8	-	-	-	8	6 2	Tower. Miller.
Baggage, express and mail cars,	2	-	-	-	2	2	Tower.
Other cars in passenger service,	6	-	-	-	6	4 2	Tower. Miller.
Total,	21	-	-	-	21	21	-
Cars — Freight Service.							
Box cars,	39	-	-	-	-	18 21	Trojan. Detroit.
Flat cars,	8	-	-	-	1	5 3	Detroit. Trojan.
Coal cars,	115	-	-	-	8	57 58	Trojan. Detroit.
Total,	162	-	-	-	9	162	-
Cars — Company's Service.							
Derrick cars,	1	-	-	-	-	1	Detroit.
Caboose cars,	9	-	-	-	-	9	Detroit.
Other cars in company's service,	32	-	-	-	-	9	Detroit.
Total,	42	-	-	-	-	19	-

Railroad Crossings in Massachusetts (Lessee's Account).

Crossings with Highways.	
Number of crossings of railroad with highways at grade,	44
Number of highway grade crossings protected by flagmen,	3
Number of highway grade crossings protected by electric signals only,	1
Number of highway grade crossings unprotected,	40
Number of highway grade crossings finally abolished during the year,	1
Number of highway bridges 18 feet (or more) above track,	5
Number of highway bridges less than 18 feet above track,	2
Height of lowest highway bridge above track,	17 ft., 3 in.
Crossings with Other Railroads.	
Crossings of railroad with other railroads at grade (3 in number), viz.: Boston & Albany, Palmer. Boston & Albany, Barrett's Junction. Boston & Maine, South Vernon.	
Number of above crossings at which interlocking signals are established, Palmer,	-

Accidents to Persons (Lessee's Account).

(A detailed statement of each accident is on file in the office of the Board.)

KILLED AND INJURED.	In Massachusetts.						Total on All Lines Operated.	
	From causes beyond their own control.		From their own misconduct or carelessness.		Total.			
	Killed.	Injured.	Killed.	Injured.	Killed.	Injured.	Killed.	Injured.
Passengers, .	-	1	-	1	-	2	-	2
Employees, .	-	7	-	1	-	8	-	8
Other persons,	-	-	1	3	1	3	1	3
Totals, .	-	8	1	5	1	13	1	13

Corporate Name and Address of the Company.

NEW LONDON NORTHERN RAILROAD COMPANY,

New London, Conn.

Names and Business Address of Principal Officers.

Walter C. Noyes, *President*, New London, Conn. John C. Averill, *Treasurer*, New London, Conn. Justus A. Southard, *Clerk of Corporation*, New London, Conn. Augustus Brandegee, *General Counsel*, New London, Conn. W. G. Crabbe, *General Auditor*, St. Albans, Vt. E. H. Fitzhugh, *General Manager*, St. Albans, Vt. John E. Bentley, *General Passenger Agent*, St. Albans, Vt. J. E. Dalrymple, *General Freight Agent*, St. Albans, Vt.

Names and Residence of Board of Directors.

Augustus Brandegee, New London, Conn. Charles H. Osgood, Norwich, Conn. James A. Rumrill, Springfield, Mass. Thomas B. Eaton, Worcester, Mass. Edward C. Smith, St. Albans, Vt. John C. Averill, Norwich, Conn. Guilford Smith, South Windham, Conn. Walter C. Noyes, New London, Conn.

We hereby certify that the statements contained in the foregoing return are full, just and true.

AUGUSTUS BRANDEGEE,
WALTER C. NOYES,
CHARLES H. OSGOOD,
J. A. RUMRILL,
JOHN C. AVERILL,
Directors.
JOHN C. AVERILL,
Treasurer.

State of Connecticut.

New London County, ss. Sept. 12, 1904. Then personally appeared the above-named Augustus Brandegee, Walter C. Noyes, Charles H. Osgood, J. A. Rumrill, and John C. Averill, and severally made oath that the foregoing certificate by them subscribed is, to the best of their knowledge and belief, true.

Before me, JUSTUS A. SOUTHARD,
Notary Public.

RETURN

OF THE

NEW YORK, NEW HAVEN & HARTFORD RAILROAD COMPANY

FOR THE YEAR ENDING JUNE 30, 1904.

GENERAL EXHIBIT FOR THE YEAR.

Gross earnings from operation,			$48,282,909 20
Operating expenses,			35,159,210 70
NET EARNINGS FROM OPERATION,			$13,123,698 50
Dividends received on stocks owned:			
Providence & Springfield R.R. Co.,	$18,241 00		
New London Steamboat Co.,	13,452 00		
Old Colony R.R. Co.,	9,226 00		
Danbury & Norwalk R.R. Co.,	3,376 25		
Boston & New York Air Line R.R. Co.,	2,890 00		
Naugatuck R.R. Co.,	2,585 00		
New Haven & Derby R.R. Co.,	1,876 00		
Rhode Island & Massachusetts R.R. Co., R. I. Division,	1,584 88		
Boston & Providence R.R. Co.,	1,517 50		
Stockbridge & Pittsfield R.R. Co.,	1,291 50		
Berkshire R.R. Co.,	516 00		
Narragansett Pier R.R. Co.,	374 00		
New York Transfer Co.,	100 00		
New England R.R. Co.,	90 00		
Iron Works Aqueduct Co.,	6 00		
		$57,126 13	
Interest received on bonds owned:			
Providence & Springfield R.R. Co.,	$37,500 00		
New Haven & Northampton R.R. Co.,	17,500 00		
Pawtuxet Valley R.R. Co.,	6,400 00		
Nantasket Beach R.R. Co.,	6,124 99		
New Haven Steamboat Co.,	6,250 00		
New London Steamboat Co.,	1,350 00		
Meriden Horse R.R. Co.,	5,050 00		
		80,174 99	

Miscellaneous income, less expense of collecting:			
Dividends on stocks leased:			
Old Colony Steamboat Co.,	$300,000 00		
Providence, Warren & Bristol R R. Co., . . .	20,226 00		
Union Freight R.R. Co., .	20,090 00		
New Bedford, Martha's Vineyard & Nantucket Steamboat Co., . . .	2,000 00		
Interest on deposits, advances, etc., ...	426,818 72		
		$769,134 72	
TOTAL INCOME FROM SOURCES OTHER THAN OPERATION,			$906,435 84
GROSS INCOME ABOVE OPERATING EXPENSES, . .			$14,030,134 34
Charges upon income accrued during the year:			
Interest on funded debt, ...		$779,667 87	
Interest and discount on unfunded debts and loans, ...		53,764 86	
Interest on instalments new capital stock, .		226,228 62	
Taxes, ...		2,455,434 27	
Rentals of leased roads,*		4,420,282 74	
TOTAL CHARGES AND DEDUCTIONS FROM INCOME, .			7,935,378 36
NET DIVISIBLE INCOME, ...			$6,094,755 98

* RENTALS OF LEASED ROADS.

NAME OF ROAD.	Total.	Less Dividends Received on Stocks Exchanged for N. Y., N. H. & H. R.R. Stock.	Net Amount.
Old Colony Railroad, ...	$1,890,621 47	$389,795 00	$1,500,826 47
New England Railroad, ...	1,120,241 00	148,138 00	972,103 00
Boston & Providence Railroad, ...	498,361 62	-	498,361 62
Providence & Worcester Railroad, . . .	416,000 00	-	416,000 00
Norwich & Worcester Railroad, . . .	290,060 75	-	290,060 75
New Haven & Northampton Railroad, . .	157,000 00	-	157,000 00
Naugatuck Railroad, ...	221,869 98	98,740 00	123,129 98
Boston & New York Air Line Railroad, . .	144,940 00	68,085 00	76,855 00
Harlem River & Port Chester Railroad, . .	72,500 00	-	72,500 00
Providence & Springfield Railroad, . . .	58,198 00	-	58,198 00
Danbury & Norwalk Railroad, ...	63,500 00	22,435 00	41,065 00
Holyoke & Westfield Railroad, ...	40,917 28	-	40,917 28
Berkshire Railroad, ...	36,250 00	-	36,250 00
New Haven & Derby Railroad, ...	46,630 00	15,990 00	30,640 00
Providence, Warren & Bristol Railroad, . .	27,788 71	-	27,788 71
Stockbridge & Pittsfield Railroad, . . .	27,172 00	-	27,172 00
Pawtuxet Valley Railroad, ...	13,463 00	-	13,463 00
Plymouth & Middleborough Railroad, . .	11,350 00	-	11,350 00
Nantasket Beach Railroad, ...	6,250 00	-	6,250 00
Woonsocket & Pascoag Railroad, . . .	5,000 00	-	5,000 00
Milford & Woonsocket Railroad, . . .	4,700 00	-	4,700 00
Chatham Railroad, ...	4,161 93	-	4,161 93
Rockville Railroad, ...	2,440 00	-	2,440 00
Milford, Franklin & Providence Railroad, .	2,300 00	-	2,300 00
Colchester Railroad, ...	1,750 00	-	1,750 00
	$5,163,465 74	$743,183 00	$4,420,282 74

Dividends declared during the year payable on—		
September 30, 1903, 2 per cent on $69,988,500,	$1,399,770 00	
December 31, 1903, 2 per cent on $70,333,900,	1,406,678 00	
March 31, 1904, 2 per cent on $80,000,000, .	1,600,000 00	
June 30, 1904, 2 per cent on $80,000,000, .	1,600,000 00	
TOTAL DIVIDENDS DECLARED, ...		$6,006,448 00
Surplus for the year ending June 30, 1904, ...		$88,307 98
Amount of surplus June 30, 1903, ...		13,819,565 66
Credits to profit and loss account during the year:		
Premium on sale of capital stock and bonds,	$7,397,531 03	
Adjustments with leased lines, account of advances, ...	1,642,325 73	
TOTAL CREDITS, ...	$9,039,856 76	

Debits to profit and loss account during the year:			
Expenditures for new equipment during the year, .	$7,326,781 10		
Expenditures for improvements at Bridgeport, .	970,241 27		
Settlement of old claims against leased lines prior to leases, and worthless accounts charged off, .	1,671 36		
TOTAL DEBITS, ...		8,298,693 73	
NET AMOUNT CREDITED TO PROFIT AND LOSS, . . .			741,163 03
TOTAL SURPLUS JUNE 30, 1904, ...			$14,649,036 67

EARNINGS FROM OPERATION.

DEPARTMENT OF SERVICE.	Gross Receipts.	Deductions.	Earnings.
Passenger service:			
Gross receipts from passengers, ...	$19,813,567 81		
Deductions:			
Tickets redeemed, ...	. . . .	$146,123 01	
Excess fares refunded, ...	. . . .	70,434 80	
Total deductions, ...	. . . .	$216,557 81	
NET REVENUE FROM PASSENGERS, . .	. . . .	. . . .	$19,597,010 00
From mails, ...	$665,182 66		
From express, ...	1,549,731 25		
From extra baggage and storage, ...	188,498 24		
Other earnings, passenger service:			
Parlor, sleeping, dining and buffet cars, . .	1,204,140 05		
Special trains, etc., ...	220,610 77		
			3,828,162 97
TOTAL EARNINGS, PASSENGER SERVICE, .	. . . .	. . . .	$23,425,172 97
Freight service:			
Gross receipts from freight, ...	$23,877,339 74		
Deductions:			
Overcharge to shippers, ...	. . . .	$148,363 81	
Other repayments, ...	. . . .	91,152 72	
Total deductions, ...	. . . .	$239,516 53	
NET REVENUE FROM FREIGHT, . . .	(*carried for*	*ward*), .	$23,637,823 21

EARNINGS FROM OPERATION — Concluded.

DEPARTMENT OF SERVICE.	Gross Receipts.	Deductions.	Earnings.
Amount brought forward,	. . . .	. . . .	$23,637,823 21
From elevators,	$29,658 67		
Other earnings, freight service:			
Hoisting,	382,148 84		
Switching,	116,579 02		
Trackage,	146,899 36		
Wharfage,	31,906 91		
Weighing,	34,890 00		
Miscellaneous,	33,639 97		
			775,717 77
TOTAL EARNINGS, FREIGHT SERVICE,	. . . .	. . . .	$24,413,540 98
TOTAL PASSENGER AND FREIGHT EARNINGS,	. . . .	. . . .	$47,838,713 95
Other earnings from operation:			
Telegraph receipts,	$50,768 73		
Rentals from buildings and other property,	393,426 52		
TOTAL OTHER EARNINGS,	. . . .	. . . .	444,195 25
GROSS EARNINGS FROM OPERATION,	. . . .	. . . .	$48,282,909 20

EXPENSES OF OPERATION.

General expenses:	
Salaries of general officers,	$177,926 52
Salaries of clerks and attendants,	323,482 43
General office expenses and supplies,	53,615 40
Insurance,	152,254 74
Law expenses,	198,712 44
Stationery and printing (general offices),	38,059 29
Other general expenses:	
Real estate,	50,150 55
All other expenses,	82,588 68
TOTAL,	$1,076,790 05
Maintenance of way and structures:	
Repairs of roadway,	$2,603,663 73
Renewals of rails,	343,143 84
Renewals of ties,	593,542 61
Repairs and renewals of bridges and culverts,	750,208 36
Repairs and renewals of fences, road crossings, signs and cattle guards,	127,804 79
Repairs and renewals of buildings and fixtures,	952,887 59
Repairs and renewals of docks and wharves,	61,654 93
Repairs and renewals of telegraph,	13,578 20
Stationery and printing,	2,222 79
Other expenses of maintaining way and structures:	
Incidentals,	310 24
Current conductors "electric,"	18,183 94
TOTAL,	$5,467,201 02
Maintenance of equipment:	
Superintendence,	$139,328 12
Repairs and renewals of locomotives,	1,862,081 19
Repairs and renewals of passenger cars,	819,996 08

Maintenance of equipment — *Concluded.*	
Repairs and renewals of freight cars,	$905,608 76
Repairs and renewals of work cars,	23,398 99
Repairs and renewals of marine equipment,	176,550 50
Repairs and renewals of shop machinery and tools,	239,364 61
Stationery and printing,	7,012 96
Other expenses of maintaining equipment:	
Electric equipment,	37,495 55
Shop expenses, heat, light, water and fuel,	493,036 02
TOTAL,	$4,703,872 78
Conducting transportation:	
Superintendence,	$383,850 72
Engine and roundhouse men,	3,126,670 04
Fuel for locomotives,	5,066,558 57
Water supply for locomotives,	292,118 55
Oil, tallow and waste for locomotives,	142,995 82
Other supplies for locomotives,	70,072 34
Train service,	2,849,842 01
Train supplies and expenses,	638,730 72
Switchmen, flagmen and watchmen,	2,115,764 02
Telegraph and telephone expenses,	411,514 48
Station service,	4,714,185 26
Station supplies,	384,512 32
Car mileage — balance,	1,094,539 72
Loss and damage,	174,594 65
Injuries to persons,	425,000 16
Clearing wrecks,	39,954 51
Operating marine equipment,	756,278 79
Advertising,	71,123 53
Outside agencies,	42,191 33
Stock yards and elevators,	16,576 76
Rentals for tracks, yards and terminals,	387,062 26
Rentals of buildings and other property,	46,258 85
Stationery and printing,	245,824 26
Other expenses of conducting transportation:	
Electric department,	92,104 09
All other expenses,	323,023 09
TOTAL,	$23,911,346 85
Recapitulation:	
General expenses,	$1,076,790 05
Maintenance of way and structures,	5,467,201 02
Maintenance of equipment,	4,703,872 78
Conducting transportation,	23,911,346 85
TOTAL OPERATING EXPENSES,	$35,159,210 70
Percentage of operating expenses to gross earnings,	72.82

GENERAL BALANCE SHEET JUNE 30, 1904.

ASSETS.	DR.	
Cost of road,		$45,982,160 71
Cost of equipment,		15,380,976 22
Stocks owned:		
Old Colony R.R. Co.,	$1,439,801 75	
Providence & Springfield R.R. Co.,	508,303 72	

Stocks owned — *Concluded*		
Danbury & Norwalk R.R. Co.,	$207,481 98	
Boston & Providence R.R. Corporation,	192,967 80	
Rhode Island & Massachusetts R.R. Co., Massachusetts Division,	191,700 00	
Rhode Island & Massachusetts R.R. Co, Rhode Island Division,	189,299 50	
Woonsocket & Pascoag R.R. Co.,	100,000 00	
Middletown, Meriden & Waterbury R.R. Co.,	100,000 00	
Naugatuck R.R. Co.,	61,835 63	
New York Connecting R.R. Co.,	50,000 00	
Rockville R.R. Co, common stock,	7,502 86	
Rockville R.R. Co., preferred stock,	44,459 64	
Boston & New York Air Line R.R. Co., common stock,	37,430 00	
Boston & New York Air Line R.R. Co, preferred stock,	30,288 47	
Stockbridge & Pittsfield R.R. Co.,	37,227 14	
Berkshire R.R. Co.,	22,722 02	
Wood River Branch R.R. Co.,	21,467 50	
Narragansett Pier R.R. Co.,	18,700 00	
New England R.R. Co., common stock,	2,550 00	
New England R.R. Co., preferred stock,	7,070 00	
Hartford & Connecticut Western R.R. Co.,	2,312 50	
New Haven & Derby R.R. Co.,	1,340 00	
Lowell & Framingham R.R. Co.,	28 00	
Boston Terminal Co.,	200,000 00	
Consolidated Railway Co.,	9,898,087 50	
Providence & Stonington Steamship Co.,	2,528,189 39	
New Haven Steamboat Co.,	700,000 00	
Bridgeport Steamboat Co.,	287,950 00	
New London Steamboat Co., common stock,	250,000 00	
New London Steamboat Co., preferred stock,	89,280 00	
New York, Providence & Boston and Old Colony Terminal Co.,	37,500 00	
New York Transfer Co.,	1,600 00	
Derby Paper Mills,	895 00	
		$17,267,990 40
Stocks and bonds of leased lines (not merged) received in exchange for stock of New York, New Haven & Hartford R.R., June 30, 1904:		
Old Colony R.R., 56,190 shares,	$5,057,100 00	
New England R.R., 49,440 shares (preferred),	2,547,991 50	
New England R.R., 199,575 shares (common),	3,991,500 00	
Naugatuck R.R., 10,026 shares,	1,002,600 00	
Harlem River & Port Chester R.R., 10,000 shares,	1,000,000 00	
New Haven & Northampton R.R., 24,600 shares,	984,000 00	
Boston & New York Air Line R.R., 17,380 shares (preferred),	695,200 00	
Danbury & Norwalk R.R., 9,020 shares,	225,500 00	
New Haven & Derby R.R., 4,459 shares,	137,200 00	
West Stockbridge R.R., 396 shares,	39,600 00	
Stockbridge & Pittsfield R.R., 110 shares,	6,600 00	
Berkshire R.R., 30 shares,	1,800 00	
	$15,689,091 50	
New Haven & Derby R.R., 7,050 bonds,	705,000 00	
		16,394,091 50

Bonds owned:			
Central New England R.R. Co.,		$5,000,000 00	
New England R.R. Co.,		1,500,000 00	
Providence & Springfield R.R. Co.,		750,000 00	
New Haven & Northampton Co.,		348,612 50	
Pawtuxet Valley R R. Co.,		160,000 00	
Nantasket Beach R.R. Co.,		150,000 00	
New Haven Steamboat Co.,		175,000 00	
New London Steamboat Co.,		23,610 00	
Meriden Horse R.R. Co.,		90,900 00	
Stamford Street R R. Co.,		76,881 53	
			$8,275,004 03
TOTAL PERMANENT INVESTMENTS,			$103,300,222 86
Cash,		$4,094,557 73	
Bills receivable,		3,106,941 65	
Due from agents,		2,220,142 44	
Due from solvent companies and individuals,		4,199,131 07	
Sinking and other special funds (trustees insurance fund),		272,000 00	
Other cash assets (prepaid insurance, taxes, etc.),		93,106 78	
TOTAL CASH AND CURRENT ASSETS,			13,985,879 67
Materials and supplies,		$3,166,355 49	
Other assets and property (contingent assets):			
Harlem River & Port Chester R.R. Co.,	$6,913,333 69		
Park Square property, Boston,	5,120,000 00		
Property South Street, New York City,	90,000 00		
New York, Providence & Boston and Old Colony R.R. Terminal Co.,	1,535,130 42		
Terminal lands at Providence,	756,117 00		
Advances for betterments on leased lines,	1,432,708 76		
Dedham and Hyde Park improvements,	137,145 94		
		15,984,435 81	
TOTAL MISCELLANEOUS ASSETS,			19,150,791 30
TOTAL,			$136,436,893 83
LIABILITIES.		CR.	
Capital stock,			$80,000,000 00
Funded debt,			34,491,000 00
Current liabilities:			
Loans and notes payable,		$1,500,000 00	
Audited vouchers and accounts,		3,517,483 70	
Salaries and wages,		442,565 55	
Traffic balances due to other companies,		960,950 82	
Dividends not called for,		2,058 00	
Matured interest coupons unpaid (including coupons due July 1),		1,260 00	
Rentals due and unpaid (including rentals due July 1),		2,477 09	
TOTAL CURRENT LIABILITIES,			6,426,795 16

Accrued liabilities:		
Interest accrued and not yet due, . . .	$394,316 53	
Rentals accrued and not yet due, . . .	203,745 47	
TOTAL ACCRUED LIABILITIES, ...		$598,062 00
Sinking and other special funds: insurance fund, . . .		272,000 00
Profit and loss balance (surplus), ...		14,649,036 67
TOTAL, ...		$136,436,893 83

PROPERTY ACCOUNTS.

Additions to construction account:		
Lands, land damages and fences, . . .	$896,117 65	
Other additions to construction account: crossings, cattle guards and signs, .	32,678 91	
TOTAL ADDITIONS TO CONSTRUCTION ACCOUNT, . . .		$928,796 56
Additions to equipment account: adjustment of book value of equipment to actual inventory value transferred from construction account (see deduction below), . . .		7,938,229 52
TOTAL ADDITIONS TO PROPERTY ACCOUNTS, ...		$8,867,026 08
Deductions from property accounts:		
Equipment transferred to Harlem River & Port Chester R.R., ...	$147,640 09	
Betterments on leased roads, ...	1,227,890 73	
Adjustment of book value of equipment to actual inventory value transferred to equipment account (see addition above),	7,938,229 52	
TOTAL DEDUCTIONS FROM PROPERTY ACCOUNTS, . .		9,313,760 34
NET DEDUCTION FROM PROPERTY ACCOUNTS FOR THE YEAR, ...		$446,734 26

CAPITAL STOCK.

Capital stock authorized by law, . .	$100,000,000 00	
Capital stock authorized by votes of company,*	80,000,000 00	
Capital stock issued and outstanding, ...		$80,000,000 00
Number of shares issued and outstanding, .	800,000	
Number of stockholders, ...	11,622	
Number of stockholders in Massachusetts, .	5,381	
Amount of stock held in Massachusetts, . .	$26,038,500 00	

FUNDED DEBT.

DESCRIPTION OF BONDS.	Rate of Interest.	Date of Maturity.	Amount Outstanding.	Interest Accrued during the Year.
	Per Cent.			
New York, New Haven & Hartford R.R. Co. bonds secured by mortgage on Harlem River & Port Chester R.R. Co., ...	4	May 1, 1954,	$5,500,000 00	$34,388 90
General mortgage bonds, New York, New Haven & Hartford R.R. Co., .	4	April 1, 1942,	1,000,000 00	40,000 00
First mortgage bonds, Shore Line R'y Co., ...	4½	March 1, 1910,	200,000 00	9,000 00
Amounts carried forward, . .	. .	. . . .	$6,700,000 00	$83,388 90

* Subject to further increase by authorized exchanges for leased lines stock.

FUNDED DEBT — Concluded.

DESCRIPTION OF BONDS.	Rate of Interest.	Date of Maturity.	Amount Outstanding.	Interest Accrued during the Year.
Amounts brought forward, . .	. .	. . . .	$6,700,000 00	$83,388 90
First mortgage bonds, Housatonic R. R. Co., ...	4	April 1, 1910,	100,000 00	4,000 00
Consolidated mortgage bonds, Housatonic R.R. Co., ...	5	Nov. 1, 1937,	2,839,000 00	141,950 00
Convertible debenture certificates, .	4	Apr. 1, 1903-8,	185,300 00	7,412 00
Non-convertible debentures, . .	4	March 1, 1947,	5,000,000 00	200,000 00
Non-convertible debentures, . .	3½	March 1, 1947,	5,000,000 00	175,000 00
Non-convertible debentures, . .	4	Feb. 1, 1914,	5,000,000 00	83,333 34
Non-convertible debentures, . .	3½	April 1, 1954,	9,666,700 00	84,583 63
TOTALS, ...	. .	. . . .	$34,491,000 00	$779,667 87

VOLUME OF TRAFFIC, ETC.

Passenger traffic:	
Number of passengers carried paying revenue, ...	63,130,459
Number of passengers carried one mile, ...	1,135,702,328
Average length of journey per passenger, ...	17.990 miles.
Average amount received per passenger per mile carried, .	1.725 cents.
Passenger earnings (gross) per mile of road operated, .	$11,530 52.000
Passenger earnings (gross) per passenger-train mile run, .	1 47.287
Freight traffic:	
Number of tons of freight hauled earning revenue, . .	17,560,485
Number of tons of freight hauled one mile, . . .	1,661,382,186
Average length of haul per ton, ...	94.610 miles.
Average amount received per ton per mile hauled, . .	1.423 cents.
Freight earnings (gross) per mile of road operated, . .	$12,017 02.000
Freight earnings (gross) per freight-train mile run, . .	3 06.509
Operating expenses:	
Operating expenses per mile of road operated, . . .	17,306 34.000
Operating expenses per revenue-train mile run, . . .	1 48.096
Train mileage:	
Miles run by passenger trains, ...	15,775,762
Miles run by freight trains, ...	7,836,361
Miles run by mixed trains, ...	128,668
Total mileage of trains earning revenue, ...	23,740,791
Miles run by switching trains, ...	6,535,110
Miles run by construction and other trains, ...	446,309
Total train mileage, ...	30,722,210
Fares and freights:	
Average rate of fare per mile received for local and trip tickets, ...	1.9186 cents.
Average rate of fare per mile received for mileage tickets,	2.0000 "
Average rate of fare per mile received for time and commutation tickets, ...	.5837 "
Average rate of fare per mile received for interline tickets,	1.9943 "
Average rate received per ton mile for local freight, . .	2.7828 "
Average rate received per ton mile for interline freight, .	1.0221 "
Passengers to and from Boston:	
Number of passengers to Boston, ...	10,482,238
Number of passengers from Boston, ...	10,466,087
Employees:	
Average number of persons employed, ...	30,375

Description of Railroad Owned and Operated.

(See also tabulated description in preceding appendix to report).

Railroad Owned.	Total.	In Massachusetts.
	Miles.	Miles.
Length of main line,	233.940	5.950
Length of branch line,	204.360	-
Total Length of Line Owned,	438.300	5.950
Length of second track,	238.780	5.950
Length of third track,	55.320	-
Length of fourth track,	55.320	-
Length of side-track, etc.,	293.850	8.490
Total Length of Track Owned,	1,081.570	20.390
Railroad Operated.		
Length of main line,	1,487.720	665.550
Length of branch line,	570.240	227.500
Total Length of Line Operated,	2,057.960	893.050
Length of second track,	685.200	313.520
Length of third track,	90.610	17.710
Length of fourth track,	89.660	16.760
Length of side track, etc.,	1,231.030	509.770
Total Length of Track Operated,	4,154.460	1,750.810
Equipped for Electric Power.		
Length of main line,	29.850	12.010
Length of branch line,	39.930	12.770
Total Length of Electric Line,	69.780	24.780
Length of second, third and fourth track,	26.490	15.540
Length of side track, etc.,	8.910	5.250
Total Length of Electric Track,	105.180	45.570

Description of Equipment.

Rolling Stock.	Number Owned.	Number Leased.	Total Owned and Leased.	Equipped with Power Driving-Wheel Brakes.	Maximum Weight.	Average Weight.
Locomotives.					Lbs.	Lbs.
Passenger,	331	218	549	549	137,000	98,000
Freight,	222	121	343	343	157,000	132,000
Switching, etc.,	103	60	163	163	132,000	90,000
Total,	656	399	1,055	1,055	-	-

DESCRIPTION OF EQUIPMENT — Concluded.

ROLLING STOCK.	Number Owned.	Number Leased.	Total Owned and Leased.	Equipped with Power Train Brakes.	Equipped with Automatic Couplers.	Name of Coupler Used.
CARS — PASSENGER SERVICE.						
Passenger cars,	846	509	1,355	1,355	1,334	1,258 National Hinson, 16 Tower, 38 Van Dorn, 18 Miller, 4 Janney-Miller.
Combination cars,	84	179	263	263	257	248 National Hinson, 9 Van Dorn.
Dining cars,	10	2	12	12	12	5 National Hinson, 7 Gould.
Parlor cars,	111	7	118	118	118	113 National Hinson, 5 Gould.
Sleeping cars,	33	-	33	33	33	National Hinson.
Baggage, express and mail cars,	188	81	269	269	268	National Hinson.
TOTAL,	1,272	778	2,050	2,050	2,022	
CARS — FREIGHT SERVICE.						
Box cars,	6,389	2,437	8,826	8,744	8,826	-
Flat cars,	1,668	500	2,168	2,126	2,168	- -
Stock cars,	4	1	5	5	5	4 Janney, 1 Tower.
Coal cars,	4,365	1,762	6,127	6,024	6,127	- -
Tank cars,	-	1	1	1	1	Tower.
Refrigerator cars,	1	-	1	1	1	Tower.
TOTAL,	12,427	4,701	17,128	16,901	17,128	
CARS — COMPANY'S SERVICE.						
Officers' and pay cars,	7	6	13	13	13	National Hinson.
Derrick cars,	24	21	45	35	45	5 Janney, 4 Trojan, 34 Tower, 1 American, 1 Buckeye.
Caboose cars,	216	76	292	238	292	103 Janney, 1 Trojan, 139 Tower, 11 Chicago, 1 Gould, 30 Major, 4 Janney-Tower, 3 Tower-Chicago.
Other cars in company's service,	189	73	262	205	247	42 Janney, 1 Trojan, 173 Tower, 2 Chicago, 1 National, 4 American, 4 Gould, 1 Major, 17 National Hinson, 1 Janney-Standard, 1 Major-Monarch.
TOTAL,	436	176	612	491	597	

Number of 8-wheel cars in passenger service with brakes for *all* wheels, ... 1,967

Number of 12-wheel cars in passenger service with brakes for *all* wheels, ... 83

Railroad Crossings in Massachusetts.

Crossings with Highways.	
Number of crossings of railroad with highways at grade, .	846
Number of highway grade crossings protected by gates, .	191
Number of highway grade crossings protected by flagmen, .	201
Number of highway grade crossings protected by electric signals only, ...	102
Number of highway grade crossings unprotected, . . .	352
Number of highway grade crossings finally abolished during the year, ...	10
Number of highway grade crossings now in process of abolition, ...	13
Number of highway grade crossings for abolition of which petition is pending, ...	76
Number of highway bridges 18 feet (or more) above track, .	114
Number of highway bridges less than 18 feet above track, .	143
Height of lowest highway bridge above track, . . .	14 ft. 2 in.
Crossings with Other Railroads.	
Crossings of railroad with other railroads at grade (10 in number), viz.: With Boston & Albany at Westfield. With Boston & Albany at Worcester. With Boston & Albany (freight tracks) at Worcester. With Boston & Albany at South Framingham. With Boston & Albany (freight tracks) at South Worcester. With Fitchburg at Concord Junction. With Fitchburg at Fitchburg. With Boston & Maine at Clinton. With Boston & Maine at South Sudbury. With Worcester Viaduct Company at Worcester.	
Number of above crossings at which interlocking signals are established, ...	8

Accidents to Persons.

(A detailed statement of each accident is on file in the office of the Board.)

KILLED AND INJURED.	In Massachusetts.						Total on All Lines Operated.	
	From causes beyond their own control.		From their own misconduct or carelessness.		Total.			
	Killed.	Injured.	Killed.	Injured.	Killed.	Injured.	Killed.	Injured.
Passengers, .	-	21	-	15	-	36	3	122
Employees, .	-	29	27	137	27	166	84	747
Other persons,	-	1	56	60	56	61	209	184
Totals, .	-	51	83	212	83	263	296	1,053

Corporate Name and Address of the Company.

NEW YORK, NEW HAVEN & HARTFORD RAILROAD COMPANY,

New Haven, Conn.

NAMES AND BUSINESS ADDRESS OF PRINCIPAL OFFICERS.

Charles S. Mellen, *President*, New Haven, Conn. Charles F. Brooker, *Vice-President of the Board*, Ansonia, Conn. Percy R. Todd, *First Vice-President*, New Haven, Conn. F. S Curtis, *Second Vice-President*, Boston, Mass. H. M. Kochersperger, *Third Vice-President*, New Haven, Conn. E. H. McHenry, *Fourth Vice-President*, New Haven, Conn. John G. Parker, *Secretary*, New Haven, Conn. A. S. May, *Treasurer*, New Haven, Conn. E. G. Buckland, *Attorney*, New Haven, Conn. F. A. Farnham, *Attorney*, Boston, Mass. S. Higgins, *General Manager*, New Haven, Conn. O. M. Shepard, *General Superintendent*, New Haven, Conn. J. W. Miller, *General Manager, Marine District*, New York, N. Y. G. L. Connor, *Passenger Traffic Manager*, New Haven, Conn. C. T. Hempstead, *General Passenger Agent, Rail Lines West of New London and Willimantic*, New Haven, Conn. A. C. Kendall, *General Passenger Agent, Rail Lines East of New London and Willimantic*, Boston, Mass. O. H. Taylor, *General Passenger Agent, Marine District*, New York, N. Y. E. L. Somers, *Freight Traffic Manager*, Boston, Mass. F. S. Holbrook, *General Freight Agent*, New Haven, Conn.

NAMES AND RESIDENCE OF BOARD OF DIRECTORS.

William D. Bishop,* Bridgeport, Conn. Chauncey M. Depew,† New York, N. Y. William Rockefeller, New York, N. Y. J. Pierpont Morgan, New York, N. Y. George Macculloch Miller, New York, N. Y. John M. Hall, New Haven, Conn. Charles F. Choate, Boston, Mass. Nathaniel Thayer, Boston, Mass. Royal C. Taft,‡ Providence, R. I. Charles F. Brooker, Ansonia, Conn. George J. Brush, New Haven, Conn. I. DeVer Warner, Bridgeport, Conn. Arthur D. Osborne, New Haven, Conn. Frank W. Cheney, South Manchester, Conn. Edwin Milner, Moosup, Conn. D. Newton Barney, Hartford, Conn. William Skinner, Holyoke, Mass. Richard A. McCurdy, New York, N. Y. Charles S. Mellen, New Haven, Conn. H. McK. Twombly, New York, N. Y. William D. Bishop, Bridgeport, Conn. Robert W. Taft, Providence, R. I.

We hereby certify that the statements contained in the foregoing return are full, just and true.

C. S. MELLEN,
GEO. MACCULLOCH MILLER,
WM. D. BISHOP,
I. DE VER WARNER,
N. THAYER,
EDWIN MILNER,
ARTHUR D. OSBORNE,
CHARLES F. CHOATE,
GEORGE J. BRUSH,
JOHN M. HALL,
Directors.
A. S. MAY,
Treasurer.
H. M. KOCHERSPERGER,
Third Vice-President.

* William D. Bishop died Feb. 4, 1904, and his son William D. Bishop was elected in his place.
† Chauncey M. Depew resigned Nov. 14, 1903, and Richard A. McCurdy was elected in his place.
‡ Royal C. Taft resigned May 14, 1904, and his son Robert W. Taft was elected in his place.

STATE OF NEW YORK.

CITY AND COUNTY OF NEW YORK, ss. SEPT. 17, 1904. Then personally appeared the above-named C. S. Mellen, Geo. Macculloch Miller, Wm. D. Bishop, I. De Ver Warner, N. Thayer, Edwin Milner, Arthur D. Osborne, Charles F. Choate, George J. Brush, and John M. Hall, and severally made oath that the foregoing certificate by them subscribed is, to the best of their knowledge and belief, true.

Before me, FRANK E. HALL,
Notary Public, New York County.

STATE OF CONNECTICUT.

CITY AND COUNTY OF NEW HAVEN, ss. SEPT. 17, 1904. Then personally appeared the above-named A. S. May and H. M. Kochersperger, and made oath that the foregoing certificate by them subscribed is, to the best of their knowledge and belief, true.

Before me, ARTHUR E. CLARK,
Notary Public.

RETURN

OF THE

NORTH BROOKFIELD RAILROAD COMPANY

FOR THE YEAR ENDING JUNE 30, 1904.

[Leased to and operated by the Boston & Albany (New York Central & Hudson River, lessee).]

GENERAL EXHIBIT FOR THE YEAR.		
Rental received from lease of road,		$3,000 00
Income from other sources: interest on deposit,		13 10
GROSS INCOME,		$3,013 10
Expenses and charges upon income accrued during the year:		
Taxes,	$500 73	
Other expenses and charges upon income: printing and postage,	3 75	
TOTAL EXPENSES AND CHARGES UPON INCOME,		504 48
NET DIVISIBLE INCOME,		$2,508 62
Dividends declared (2½ per cent),		2,500 00
Surplus for the year ending June 30, 1904,		$8 62
Amount of surplus June 30, 1903,		546 49
TOTAL SURPLUS JUNE 30, 1904,		$555 11

GENERAL BALANCE SHEET JUNE 30, 1904.	
ASSETS. DR.	
Cost of road,	$100,000 00
Cash,	555 11
TOTAL,	$100,555 11
LIABILITIES. CR.	
Capital stock,	$100,000 00
Profit and loss balance (surplus),	555 11
TOTAL,	$100,555 11

CAPITAL STOCK.		
Capital stock authorized by law,	$100,000 00	
Capital stock authorized by votes of company,	100,000 00	
Capital stock issued and outstanding,		$100,000 00
Number of shares issued and outstanding,	1,000	
Number of stockholders,	41	
Number of stockholders in Massachusetts,	40	
Amount of stock held in Massachusetts,	$99,900 00	

Description of Railroad Owned.

(See also tabulated description in preceding appendix to report.)

Railroad Owned.	Total.	In Massachusetts.
	Miles.	Miles.
Length of main line,	4.000	4.000
Length of side track, etc.,	1.310	1.310
Total Length of Track Owned,	5.310	5.310

Corporate Name and Address of the Company.

NORTH BROOKFIELD RAILROAD COMPANY,

North Brookfield, Mass.

Names and Business Address of Principal Officers.

Sumner Holmes, *President*, North Brookfield, Mass. Samuel A. Clark, *Vice-President*, North Brookfield, Mass. Charles E. Batcheller, *Treasurer*, North Brookfield, Mass. George R. Hamant, *Clerk of Corporation*, North Brookfield, Mass.

Names and Residence of Board of Directors.

George R. Hamant, North Brookfield, Mass. Edward A. Batcheller, North Brookfield, Mass. Freeman R. Doane, North Brookfield, Mass. Samuel A. Clark, North Brookfield, Mass. Sumner Holmes, North Brookfield, Mass. Charles E. Batcheller, North Brookfield, Mass. Alfred W. Burrill, North Brookfield, Mass.

We hereby certify that the statements contained in the foregoing return are full, just and true.

GEO. R. HAMANT,
SAMUEL A. CLARK,
SUMNER HOLMES,
ALFRED W. BURRILL,
Directors.
CHARLES E. BATCHELLER,
Treasurer.

Commonwealth of Massachusetts.

Worcester, ss. Sept. 8, 1904. Then personally appeared the above-named George R. Hamant, Samuel A. Clark and Alfred W. Burrill, and severally made oath that the foregoing certificate by them subscribed is, to the best of their knowledge and belief, true.

Before me, CLARENCE E. BROWN,
Justice of the Peace.

RETURN

OF THE

NORWICH & WORCESTER RAILROAD COMPANY

For the Year ending June 30, 1904.

[Leased to and operated by the New York, New Haven & Hartford].

General Exhibit for the Year.		
Rentals received from lease of road,		$290,060 75
Income from other sources: interest received,		745 30
Gross Income,		$290,806 05
Expenses and charges upon income accrued during the year:		
Salaries and maintenance of organization,	$2,580 40	
Interest on funded debt,	48,000 00	
Total Expenses and Charges upon Income,		50,580 40
Net Divisible Income,		$240,225 65
Dividends declared (8 per cent),		240,000 00
Surplus for the year ending June 30, 1904,		$225 65
Amount of surplus June 30, 1903,		1,232,150 87
Total Surplus June 30, 1904,		$1,232,376 52

General Balance Sheet June 30, 1904.		
Assets.	Dr.	
Cost of road,		$3,983,816 51
Cost of equipment,		179,750 67
Lands in Massachusetts,		3,107 08
Stock of Norwich & New York Transportation Company,		500,000 00
Total Permanent Investments,		$4,666,674 26
Cash,	$87,768 61	
Bills receivable,	285,000 00	
Other cash assets,	28,512 00	
Total Cash and Current Assets,		401,280 61
Materials and supplies,		450,869 65
Total,		$5,518,824 52
Liabilities.	Cr.	
Capital stock, common,	$6,600 00	
Capital stock, preferred,	3,000,000 00	
Total Capital Stock,		$3,006,600 00

Funded debt,		$1,200,000 00
Current liabilities:		
Audited vouchers and accounts,	$203 00	
Dividends not called for,	3,023 00	
Matured interest coupons unpaid (including coupons due July 1),	180 00	
Rentals due and unpaid (including rentals due July 1),	60,442 00	
TOTAL CURRENT LIABILITIES,		63,848 00
Accrued liabilities: interest accrued and not yet due,		16,000 00
Profit and loss balance (surplus),		1,232,376 52
TOTAL,		$5,518,824 52

CAPITAL STOCK.

Capital stock authorized by law,		$3,825,000 00	
Capital stock authorized by votes of company,		3,000,000 00	
Capital stock issued and outstanding, common,			$6,600 00
Capital stock issued and outstanding, preferred,			3,000,000 00
Total capital stock outstanding,			$3,006,600 00
Number of shares issued and outstanding, common,	66		
Number of shares issued and outstanding, preferred,	30,000		
Total number of shares outstanding,		30,066	
Number of stockholders, preferred,		956	
Number of stockholders in Massachusetts, preferred,		787	
Amount of stock held in Massachusetts, preferred,		$2,502,900 00	

FUNDED DEBT.

DESCRIPTION OF BONDS.	Rate of Interest.	Date of Maturity.	Amount Outstanding.	Interest Paid during the Year.
Debenture bonds,	Per Cent. 4	March 1, 1927,	$1,200,000 00	$48,000 00

DESCRIPTION OF RAILROAD OWNED.

(See also tabulated description in preceding appendix to report)

RAILROAD OWNED.	Total.	In Massachusetts.
	Miles.	Miles.
Length of main line,	70.970	17.830
Length of branch line,	.630	-
TOTAL LENGTH OF LINE OWNED,	71.600	17.830
Length of side track, etc.,	36.720	11.530
TOTAL LENGTH OF TRACK OWNED,	108.320	29.360

CORPORATE NAME AND ADDRESS OF THE COMPANY.

NORWICH & WORCESTER RAILROAD COMPANY,

NEW HAVEN, CONN.

NAMES AND BUSINESS ADDRESS OF PRINCIPAL OFFICERS.

A. George Bullock, *President*, Worcester, Mass. Massena M. Whittemore, *Treasurer and Clerk of Corporation*, New Haven, Conn.

NAMES AND RESIDENCE OF BOARD OF DIRECTORS.

Edward L. Davis, Worcester, Mass.
Josiah H. Clarke (died May 30, 1904).
A. George Bullock, Worcester, Mass.
Stephen Salisbury, Worcester, Mass.
Thomas B. Eaton, Worcester, Mass.
Francis H. Dewey, Worcester, Mass.
Charles P. Cogswell, Norwich, Conn.

We hereby certify that the statements contained in the foregoing return are full, just and true.

THOMAS B. EATON,
FRANCIS H. DEWEY,
A. G. BULLOCK,
CHARLES P. COGSWELL,
STEPHEN SALISBURY,
Directors.
M. M. WHITTEMORE,
Treasurer.

COMMONWEALTH OF MASSACHUSETTS.

WORCESTER, SS. SEPT. 14, 1904. Then personally appeared the above-named Thomas B. Eaton, Charles P. Cogswell, Stephen Salisbury, M. M. Whittemore, and on Sept. 30, 1904, the above-named Francis H. Dewey and A. G. Bullock, and severally made oath that the foregoing certificate by them subscribed is, to the best of their knowledge and belief, true.

Before me, GEO. W. MACKINTIRE,
Justice of the Peace.

RETURN

OF THE

OLD COLONY RAILROAD COMPANY

For the Year ending June 30, 1904.

[Leased to and operated by the New York, New Haven & Hartford.]

General Exhibit for the Year.		
Rental received from lease of road,		$1,890,621 47
Expenses and charges upon income accrued during the year:		
Salaries and maintenance of organization,	$6,860 98	
Interest on funded debt,	667,454 16	
Interest and discount on unfunded debts and loans,	9,933 33	
Total Expenses and Charges upon Income,		684,248 47
Net Divisible Income,		$1,206,373 00
Dividends declared (7 per cent),		$1,206,373 00
Amount of surplus June 30, 1903,		$767,206 72
Credits to profit and loss account during the year: interest received on proceeds of bonds issued for purchase of lands in South Boston,		120 47
Total Surplus June 30, 1904,		$767,327 19

General Balance Sheet June 30, 1904.

Assets.	Dr.	
Cost of road,		$29,956,723 97
Cost of equipment,		3,161,518 83
Stock of Old Colony Steamboat Co.,	$1,277,500 00	
Stock of New York, Providence & Boston and Old Colony R.R. Terminal Co.,	52,850 00	
Stock of the Boston Terminal Co.,	100,000 00	
Stock of New Bedford, Martha's Vineyard & Nantucket Steamboat Co.,	15,340 83	
Stock of Union Freight Railroad Co.,	79,014 42	
Stock of Lowell & Framingham R.R. Co.,	10,529 69	
Stock of Fall River R.R. Co.,	245 00	
Stock of Providence, Warren & Bristol R.R. Co.,	1,600 00	
Stock of Oak Bluffs Land & Wharf Co.,	70 00	
		1,537,149 94
Other permanent property: Providence terminal improvement,		74,016 78
Total Permanent Investments,		$34,729,409 52

Cash,	$437,420 62	
Bills receivable,	26,338 73	
Due from solvent companies and individuals,	55,515 25	
Total Cash and Current Assets,		$519,274 60
Other assets and property: Boston & Providence Railroad Company improvement account,		3,268,072 18
Total,		$38,516,756 30

Liabilities.	Cr.	
Capital stock,		$17,871,400 00
Stock liability,		8,725 00
Funded debt,		15,519,200 00
Current liabilities:		
Loans and notes payable,	$12,000 00	
Audited vouchers and accounts,	684,687 51	
Dividends not called for,	320,664 06	
Matured interest coupons unpaid (including coupons due July 1),	167,473 50	
Total Current Liabilities,		1,184,825 07
Accrued liabilities: interest accrued and not yet due,		68,660 00
Premium received on sale of stock and bonds,		3,096,619 04
Profit and loss balance (surplus),		767,327 19
Total,		$38,516,756 30

Property Accounts.

Additions to construction account:		
Grading and masonry,	$94,366 96	
Superstructure, including rails,	110,195 09	
Lands, land damages and fences,	68,383 72	
Passenger and freight stations, coal sheds and water stations,	50,747 23	
Engine-houses, car-houses and turn-tables,	105,020 44	
Engineering and other expenses incident to construction,	5,087 83	
Elimination of grade crossings,	414,174 06	
Total Additions to Construction Account,		$847,975 33
Other expenditures charged to property accounts: Boston & Providence Railroad Company improvement account,		569 50
Total Additions to Property Accounts,		$848,544 83

Capital Stock.

Capital stock authorized by law,	$20,020,000 00	
Capital stock authorized by votes of company,	20,020,000 00	
Capital stock issued and outstanding,		$17,871,400 00
Scrip convertible into stock,		107 37
Other paid stock liability,		8,617 63
Total Capital Stock Liability,		$17,880,125 00
Number of shares issued and outstanding,	178,714	
Number of stockholders,	5,371	
Number of stockholders in Massachusetts,*	4,958	
Amount of stock held in Massachusetts,*	$16,339,900 00	

* Including the New York, New Haven & Hartford Railroad Company as a stockholder and the shares held by it.

Real Estate Mortgages.

Description of Mortgaged Property.	Rate of Interest.	Mortgage when Due.	Amount.	Interest Paid during the Year.
	Per Cent.			
Mortgage note of $175,000 paid June 26, 1904.	. .	. . . .	. . .	$9,333 33

Funded Debt.

Description of Bonds.	Rate of Interest.	Date of Maturity.	Amount Outstanding.	Interest Paid during the Year.
	Per Cent.			
New Bedford R.R. bonds (matured),	. .	July 1, 1894,	$1,000 00	-
Fitchburg & Worcester R.R. bonds (matured),	. .	Oct. 1, 1881,	200 00	-
Old Colony R.R. bonds (matured), .	. .	April 1, 1904,	3,000 00	-
Interest on same,	4½	. . .	-	$22,590 00
Old Colony R.R. bonds (matured), .	. .	July 1, 1904,	5,000 00	-
Interest on same,	4	. . .	-	30,000 00
Boston, Clinton, Fitchburg & New Bedford R.R. bonds, first mortgage, coupon,	5	Jan. 1, 1910,	1,912,000 00	47,825 00
Old Colony R.R. plain bonds, gold, .	4	Feb. 1, 1924,	3,000,000 00	118,280 00
Old Colony R.R. plain bonds, .	4	Jan. 1, 1938,	4,000,000 00	160,000 00
Old Colony R.R. plain bonds, .	4	Dec. 1, 1925,	5,598,000 00	209,786 66
Old Colony R.R. plain bonds, .	3½	July 1, 1932,	1,000,000 00	35,000 00
Totals,	. .	. . .	$15,519,200 00	$623,481 66

Description of Railroad Owned.

(See also tabulated description in preceding appendix to report.)

Railroad Owned.	Total.	In Massachusetts.
	Miles.	Miles.
Length of main line,	368.700	352.510
Length of branch line,	142.650	140.520
Total Length of Line Owned,	511.350	493.030
Length of second track,	159.740	159.740
Length of third track,	6.560	6.560
Length of fourth track,	5.610	5.610
Length of side track, etc.,	246.700	239.040
Total Length of Track Owned,	929.960	903.980

Corporate Name and Address of the Company.

OLD COLONY RAILROAD COMPANY,

Room 526, South Terminal Station, Boston, Mass.

NAMES AND BUSINESS ADDRESS OF PRINCIPAL OFFICERS.

Charles F. Choate, *President*, Boston, Mass. Charles L. Lovering, *Vice-President*, Boston, Mass. Benjamin B. Torrey, *Treasurer*, Boston, Mass. Alfred H. Litchfield, *Clerk of Corporation*, Boston, Mass.

NAMES AND RESIDENCE OF BOARD OF DIRECTORS.

Charles F. Choate, Southborough, Mass. Oliver Ames, Boston, Mass. John S. Brayton, Fall River, Mass. Fayette S. Curtis, Boston, Mass. Thomas Dunn, Newport, R. I. George A. Gardner, Boston, Mass. Charles L. Lovering, Taunton, Mass. Joshua M. Sears, Boston, Mass. Nathaniel Thayer, Lancaster, Mass.

We hereby certify that the statements contained in the foregoing return are full, just and true.

CHARLES F. CHOATE,
OLIVER AMES,
JOSHUA M. SEARS,
CHARLES L. LOVERING,
THOS. DUNN,
FAYETTE S. CURTIS,
Directors.
B. B. TORREY,
Treasurer.

COMMONWEALTH OF MASSACHUSETTS.

SUFFOLK, ss. BOSTON, Sept. 8, 1904. Then personally appeared the above-named Charles F. Choate, Oliver Ames, Joshua M. Sears, Charles L. Lovering, Thomas Dunn and Fayette S. Curtis, and severally made oath that the foregoing certificate by them subscribed is, to the best of their knowledge and belief, true.

Before me, ALFRED H. LITCHFIELD,
Justice of the Peace.

COMMONWEALTH OF MASSACHUSETTS.

SUFFOLK, ss. BOSTON, Sept. 14, 1904. Then personally appeared B. B. Torrey, and made oath that the foregoing certificate by him subscribed is, to the best of his knowledge and belief, true,

Before me, ALFRED H. LITCHFIELD,
Justice of the Peace.

RETURN

OF THE

PITTSFIELD & NORTH ADAMS RAILROAD COMPANY

FOR THE YEAR ENDING JUNE 30, 1904.

[Leased to and operated by the Boston & Albany (New York Central & Hudson River, lessee).]

General Exhibit for the Year.

Rental received from lease of road,	$22,500 00
Dividends declared (5 per cent),	22,500 00

General Balance Sheet June 30, 1904.

Assets. Dr.	
Cost of road,	$438,752 57
Cost of equipment,	11,247 43
Total,	$450,000 00
Liabilities. Cr.	
Capital stock,	$450,000 00
Total,	$450,000 00

Capital Stock.

Capital stock authorized by law,	$500,000 00	
Capital stock authorized by votes of company,	450,000 00	
Capital stock issued and outstanding,		$450,000 00
Number of shares issued and outstanding,	4,500	
Number of stockholders,	110	
Number of stockholders in Massachusetts,	104	
Amount of stock held in Massachusetts,	$371,900 00	

Description of Railroad Owned.

(See also tabulated description in preceding appendix to report.)

Railroad Owned.	Total.	In Massachusetts.
	Miles.	Miles.
Length of main line,	18.550	18.550
Length of side track, etc.,	7.770	7.770
Total Length of Track Owned,	26.320	26.320

CORPORATE NAME AND ADDRESS OF THE COMPANY.

PITTSFIELD & NORTH ADAMS RAILROAD COMPANY,

SOUTH STATION, BOSTON, MASS.

NAMES AND BUSINESS ADDRESS OF PRINCIPAL OFFICERS.

James A. Rumrill, *President*, Springfield, Mass. Frank H. Ratcliffe, *Treasurer and Clerk of Corporation*, Boston, Mass.

NAMES AND RESIDENCE OF BOARD OF DIRECTORS.

Francis H. Appleton, Peabody, Mass. Zenas Crane, Dalton, Mass. Albert C. Houghton, North Adams, Mass. Edward Jackson, Boston, Mass. James A. Rumrill, Springfield, Mass.

We hereby certify that the statements contained in the foregoing return are full, just and true.

J. A. RUMRILL,
ZENAS CRANE,
EDWARD JACKSON,
FRANCIS H. APPLETON,
Directors.
F. H. RATCLIFFE,
Treasurer.

COMMONWEALTH OF MASSACHUSETTS.

SUFFOLK, ss. BOSTON, Sept. 28, 1904. Then personally appeared the above-named J. A. Rumrill, Zenas Crane, Edward Jackson, Francis H. Appleton and F. H. Ratcliffe, and severally made oath that the foregoing certificate by them subscribed is, to the best of their knowledge and belief, true.

Before me, WOODWARD HUDSON,
Justice of the Peace.

RETURN

OF THE

PLYMOUTH & MIDDLEBOROUGH RAILROAD COMPANY

FOR THE YEAR ENDING JUNE 30, 1904.

[Leased to and operated by the New York, New Haven & Hartford.]

GENERAL BALANCE SHEET JUNE 30, 1904.

ASSETS. DR.	
Cost of road,	$305,000 00
TOTAL,	$305,000 00

LIABILITIES. CR.	
Capital stock,	$80,000 00
Funded debt,	225,000 00
TOTAL,	$305,000 00

CAPITAL STOCK.

Capital stock authorized by law,	$240,000 00	
Capital stock authorized by votes of company,	80,000 00	
Capital stock issued and outstanding,		$80,000 00
Number of shares issued and outstanding,	800	
Number of stockholders,	24	
Number of stockholders in Massachusetts,	24	
Amount of stock held in Massachusetts,	$80,000 00	

FUNDED DEBT.

DESCRIPTION OF BONDS.	Rate of Interest.	Date of Maturity.	Amount Outstanding.	Interest Paid during the Year.
	Per Cent.			
First mortgage bonds,	5	Jan. 1, 1912,	$225,000 00	$11,250 00

DESCRIPTION OF RAILROAD OWNED.

(See also tabulated description in preceding appendix to report.)

RAILROAD OWNED.	Total.	In Massachusetts.
	Miles.	Miles.
Length of main line,	15.030	15.030
Length of side track, etc.,	1.020	1.020
TOTAL LENGTH OF TRACK OWNED,	16.050	16.050

CORPORATE NAME AND ADDRESS OF THE COMPANY.

PLYMOUTH & MIDDLEBOROUGH RAILROAD COMPANY,
PLYMOUTH, MASS.

NAMES AND BUSINESS ADDRESS OF PRINCIPAL OFFICERS.

Thomas D. Shumway, *President and Treasurer*, Plymouth, Mass. Leavitt T. Robbins, *Vice-President*, Plymouth, Mass. Benjamin A. Hathaway, *Clerk of Corporation*, Plymouth, Mass.

NAMES AND RESIDENCE OF BOARD OF DIRECTORS.

Thomas D. Shumway, Plymouth, Mass. Horace M. Saunders, Plymouth, Mass. Leavitt T. Robbins, Plymouth, Mass. William S. Kyle, Plymouth, Mass. Jason W. Mixter, Plymouth, Mass. Joseph E. Beals, Middleborough, Mass. John C. Sullivan, Middleborough, Mass. Edwin F. Witham, Middleborough, Mass. George F. Morse, North Carver, Mass.

We hereby certify that the statements contained in the foregoing return are full, just and true.

T. D. SHUMWAY,
JOHN C. SULLIVAN,
GEORGE F. MORSE,
L. T. ROBBINS,
JASON W. MIXTER,
WM. S. KYLE,
HORACE M. SAUNDERS,
Directors.
T. D. SHUMWAY,
Treasurer.

COMMONWEALTH OF MASSACHUSETTS.

PLYMOUTH, SS. SEPT. 26, 1904. Then personally appeared the above-named Thos. D. Shumway, John C. Sullivan, Geo. F. Morse, Leavitt T. Robbins, Jason W. Mixter, Wm. S. Kyle and Horace M. Saunders, and severally made oath that the foregoing certificate by them subscribed is, to the best of their knowledge and belief, true.

Before me, B. A. HATHAWAY,
Justice of the Peace.

RETURN

OF THE

PROVIDENCE & SPRINGFIELD RAILROAD COMPANY

For the Year ending June 30, 1904.

[Leased to and operated by the New York, New Haven & Hartford.]

General Exhibit for the Year.	
Rental received from lease of road,	$58,198 00
Income from other sources: interest on deposits,	5 23
Gross Income,	$58,203 23
Expenses and charges upon income accrued during the year: interest on funded debt,	37,500 00
Net Divisible Income,	$20,703 23
Dividends declared (4 per cent),	20,698 00
Surplus for the year ending June 30, 1904,	$5 23
Amount of surplus June 30, 1903,	272 91
	$278 14
Debits to profit and loss account during the year: reconveyance of land,	250 00
Total Surplus June 30, 1904,	$28 14

General Balance Sheet June 30, 1904.	
Assets. Dr.	
Cost of road,	$1,267,450 00
Cash,	28 14
Total,	$1,267,478 14
Liabilities. Cr.	
Capital stock,	$517,450 00
Funded debt,	750,000 00
Profit and loss balance (surplus),	28 14
Total,	$1,267,478 14

Capital Stock.

Capital stock authorized by law,	$1,000,000 00	
Capital stock authorized by votes of company,	517,450 00	
Capital stock issued and outstanding,		$517,450 00
Number of shares issued and outstanding,	5,174½	
Number of stockholders,	31	
Number of stockholders in Massachusetts,	None.	
Amount of stock held in Massachusetts,	None.	

Funded Debt.

Description of Bonds.	Rate of Interest.	Date of Maturity.	Amount Outstanding.	Interest Paid during the Year.
	Per Cent.			
First mortgage bonds,	5	July 1, 1922,	$750,000 00	$37,500 00

Description of Railroad Owned.

(See also tabulated description in preceding appendix to report.)

Railroad Owned.	Total.	In Massachusetts.
	Miles.	Miles.
Length of main line,	27.730	1.630
Length of side track, etc.,	5.650	.700
Total Length of Track Owned,	33.380	2.330

Corporate Name and Address of the Company.

PROVIDENCE & SPRINGFIELD RAILROAD COMPANY,

Providence, R. I.

Names and Business Address of Principal Officers.

William Tinkham, *President*, Providence, R. I. Edward G. Buckland, *Treasurer and Clerk of Corporation*, Providence, R. I.

Names and Residence of Board of Directors.

William Tinkham, Providence, R. I. Royal C. Taft, Providence, R. I. William W. Douglas, Providence, R. I. Fenner H. Peckham, Jr., Providence, R. I. William H. Pope, Providence, R. I. Arthur D. Osborne, New Haven, Conn. Edwin Milner, Moosup, Conn. Charles S. Mellen, New Haven, Conn. Edward G. Buckland, Providence, R. I.

We hereby certify that the statements contained in the foregoing return are full, just and true.

WM. TINKHAM,
C. S. MELLEN,
WM. W. DOUGLAS,
WILLIAM H. POPE,
EDWIN MILNER,
EDWARD G. BUCKLAND,
Directors.
EDWARD G. BUCKLAND,
Treasurer.

STATE OF RHODE ISLAND.

PROVIDENCE, S.C. AUG. 12, 1904. Then personally appeared the above-named William Tinkham, William W. Douglas, William H. Pope, Edwin Milner, Edward G. Buckland and Charles S. Mellen, and severally made oath that the foregoing certificate by them subscribed is, to the best of their knowledge and belief, true.

Before me, SAMUEL P. CORBETT,
Notary Public.

RETURN

OF THE

PROVIDENCE, WEBSTER & SPRINGFIELD RAILROAD COMPANY

FOR THE YEAR ENDING JUNE 30, 1904.

[Leased to and operated by the Boston & Albany (New York Central & Hudson River, lessee).]

GENERAL EXHIBIT FOR THE YEAR.		
Rental received from lease of road,		$6,802 42
Income from other sources: interest on cash in bank,		35 13
GROSS INCOME,		$6,837 55
Expenses and charges upon income accrued during the year:		
Salaries and maintenance of organization,	$3 45	
Interest and discount on unfunded debts and loans,	3,102 89	
Taxes,	399 86	
Other expenses and charges upon income:		
Repairs on buildings,	41 28	
Repairs on fences,	11 56	
TOTAL EXPENSES AND CHARGES UPON INCOME,		3,559 04
Surplus for the year ending June 30, 1904,		$3,278 51
Amount of surplus June 30, 1903,		18,865 86
TOTAL SURPLUS JUNE 30, 1904,		$22,144 37

GENERAL BALANCE SHEET JUNE 30, 1904. ASSETS. DR.	
Cost of road,	$243,361 12
Traffic balances due from other companies,	1,770 24
TOTAL,	$245,131 36

Liabilities.	Cr.	
Capital stock,		$160,000 00
Current liabilities:		
Loans and notes payable,	$60,901 50	
Audited vouchers and accounts,	2,085 49	
Total Current Liabilities,		62,986 99
Profit and loss balance (surplus),		22,144 37
Total,		$245,131 36

Capital Stock.		
Capital stock authorized by law,	$160,000 00	
Capital stock authorized by votes of company,	160,000 00	
Capital stock issued and outstanding,		$160,000 00
Number of shares issued and outstanding,	1,600	
Number of stockholders,	7	
Number of stockholders in Massachusetts,	7	
Amount of stock held in Massachusetts,	$160,000 00	

Description of Railroad Owned.

(See also tabulated description in preceding appendix to report.)

Railroad Owned.	Total.	In Massachusetts.
	Miles.	Miles.
Length of main line,	11.230	11.230
Length of side track, etc.,	3.240	3.240
Total Length of Track Owned,	14.470	14.470

Corporate Name and Address of the Company.

PROVIDENCE, WEBSTER & SPRINGFIELD RAILROAD COMPANY,

Webster, Mass.

Names and Business Address of Principal Officers.

Charles G. Washburn, *President*, 314 Main Street, Worcester, Mass. Amos Bartlett, *Vice-President*, Webster, Mass. Frank B. Smith, *Treasurer*, 314 Main Street, Worcester, Mass. Charles Gerber, *Clerk of Corporation*, Webster, Mass.

Names and Residence of Board of Directors.

Charles G. Washburn, 314 Main Street, Worcester, Mass. Frank B. Smith, 314 Main Street, Worcester, Mass. Amos Bartlett, Webster, Mass. Elias P. Morton, Webster, Mass. Charles Gerber, Webster, Mass. Edwin Bartlett, North Oxford, Mass. Samuel Slater, Boston, Mass.

We hereby certify that the statements contained in the foregoing return are full, just and true.

C. G. WASHBURN,
AMOS BARTLETT,
CHARLES GERBER,
FRANK BULKELEY SMITH,
Directors.
FRANK BULKELEY SMITH,
Treasurer.
CHARLES GERBER,
Chief Accounting Officer.

COMMONWEALTH OF MASSACHUSETTS.

WORCESTER, ss. SEPT. 13, 1904. Then personally appeared the above-named C. G. Washburn and Frank Bulkeley Smith, and severally made oath that the foregoing certificate by them subscribed is, to the best of their knowledge and belief, true.

Before me, EARLE BROWN,
Justice of the Peace.

RETURN

OF THE

PROVIDENCE & WORCESTER RAILROAD COMPANY

For the Year ending June 30, 1904.

[Leased to and operated by the New York, New Haven & Hartford.]

General Exhibit for the Year.		
Rental received from lease of road,		$416,000 00
Income from other sources: interest on balances,		1,583 84
Gross Income,		$417,583 84
Expenses and charges upon income accrued during the year:		
Salaries and maintenance of organization,	$6,071 79	
Interest on funded debt,	60,000 00	
Total Expenses and Charges upon Income,		66,071 79
Net Divisible Income,		$351,512 05
Dividends declared (10 per cent),		350,000 00
Surplus for the year ending June 30, 1904,		$1,512 05
Amount of surplus June 30, 1903,		225,916 70
Total Surplus June 30, 1904,		$227,428 75

General Balance Sheet June 30, 1904.		
Assets.	Dr.	
Cost of road,		$4,276,250 00
Cost of equipment,		828,887 40
Total Permanent Investments,		$5,105,137 40
Cash,	$41,543 38	
Due from solvent companies and individuals,	80,747 97	
Total Cash and Current Assets,		122,291 35
Total,		$5,227,428 75
Liabilities.	Cr.	
Capital stock,		$3,500,000 00
Funded debt,		1,500,000 00
Profit and loss balance (surplus),		227,428 75
Total,		$5,227,428 75

Capital Stock.

Capital stock authorized by law, ...	$3,500,000 00	
Capital stock authorized by votes of company,	3,500,000 00	
Capital stock issued and outstanding, ...		$3,500,000 00
Number of shares issued and outstanding, .	35,000	
Number of stockholders, ...	899	
Number of stockholders in Massachusetts, .	489	
Amount of stock held in Massachusetts, . .	$1,916,700 00	

Funded Debt.

Description of Bonds.	Rate of Interest.	Date of Maturity.	Amount Outstanding.	Interest Paid during the Year.
	Per Cent.			
First mortgage, currency, coupon, .	4	Oct. 1, 1947, .	$1,500,000 00	$60,000 00

Description of Railroad Owned.

(See also tabulated description in preceding appendix to report)

Railroad Owned.	Total.	In Massachusetts.
	Miles.	Miles.
Length of main line, ...	40.900	25.500
Length of branch line, ...	7.000	.500
Total Length of Line Owned, ...	47.900	26.000
Length of second track, ...	46.480	24.980
Length of third track, ...	2.150	-
Length of fourth track, ...	2.150	-
Length of side track, etc., ...	71.690	23.330
Total Length of Track Owned,*	170.370	74.310

Corporate Name and Address of the Company.

PROVIDENCE & WORCESTER RAILROAD COMPANY,

Providence, R. I.

Names and Business Address of Principal Officers.

Moses B. I. Goddard, *President*, Providence, R. I. William A. Leete, *Treasurer and Clerk of Corporation*, Providence, R. I.

* Includes only one-half of five (5) miles of main line and second track, the third and fourth tracks and 10.120 miles of sidings owned jointly with the Boston & Providence Railroad Corporation, all in Rhode Island.

NAMES AND RESIDENCE OF BOARD OF DIRECTORS.

Moses B. I. Goddard, Warwick, R. I. Joseph E. Davis, Boston, Mass. John W. Danielson, Providence, R. I. G. Marston Whitin, Whitinsville, Mass. A. George Bullock, Worcester, Mass. Waldo Lincoln, Worcester, Mass. Walter F. Angell, Providence, R. I.

We hereby certify that the statements contained in the foregoing return are full, just and true.

MOSES B. I. GODDARD,
G. MARSTON WHITIN,
WALDO LINCOLN,
WALTER F. ANGELL,
Directors.
WM. A. LEETE,
Treasurer.

STATE OF RHODE ISLAND.

PROVIDENCE, ss. AUG. 26, 1904. Then personally appeared the above-named Moses B. I. Goddard, G. Marston Whitin, Waldo Lincoln and Walter F. Angell, directors, and Wm. A. Leete, treasurer, and severally made oath that the foregoing certificate by them subscribed is, to the best of their knowledge and belief, true.

Before me, EDWARD P. JASTRAM,
Notary Public for State of Rhode Island.

RETURN

OF THE

RHODE ISLAND & MASSACHUSETTS RAILROAD COMPANY

FOR THE YEAR ENDING JUNE 30, 1904.

[Leased to and operated by the New York, New Haven & Hartford.]

GENERAL BALANCE SHEET JUNE 30, 1904.

Assets. Dr.	
Cost of road,	$112,321 13
Due from solvent companies and individuals,	2,500 00
TOTAL,	$114,821 13

Liabilities. Cr.	
Capital stock,	$100,000 00
Profit and loss balance (surplus),	14,821 13
TOTAL,	$114,821 13

CAPITAL STOCK.

Capital stock authorized by law,	$100,000 00	
Capital stock authorized by votes of company,	100,000 00	
Capital stock issued and outstanding,		$100,000 00
Number of shares issued and outstanding,	1,000	
Number of stockholders,	2	

DESCRIPTION OF RAILROAD OWNED.

(See also tabulated description in preceding appendix to report.)

RAILROAD OWNED AND OPERATED.	Total.	In Massachusetts.
	Miles.	Miles.
Length of main line,	6.520	6.520
Length of side track, etc.,	.860	.860
TOTAL LENGTH OF TRACK OWNED,	7.380	7.380

Corporate Name and Address of the Company.

RHODE ISLAND & MASSACHUSETTS RAILROAD COMPANY (MASSACHUSETTS DIVISION),

PROVIDENCE, R. I.

Names and Business Address of Principal Officers.

John M. Hall, *President*, New Haven, Conn. Edward G. Buckland, *Treasurer and Clerk of Corporation*, Providence, R. I.

Names and Residence of Board of Directors.

John M. Hall, New Haven, Conn. Fayette S. Curtis, Boston, Mass. Lawson B. Bidwell, Boston, Mass. James W. Perkins, Salem, Mass. Edward G. Buckland, Providence, R. I.

We hereby certify that the statements contained in the foregoing return are full, just and true.

JOHN M. HALL,
EDWARD G. BUCKLAND,
LAWSON B. BIDWELL,
FAYETTE S. CURTIS,
JAMES W. PERKINS,
Directors.
EDWARD G. BUCKLAND,
Treasurer.

State of Connecticut.

NEW HAVEN COUNTY, ss. NEW HAVEN, Aug. 12, 1904. Then personally appeared the above-named John M. Hall and Edward G. Buckland, and severally made oath that the foregoing certificate by them subscribed is, to the best of their knowledge and belief, true.

Before me, AVERY CLARK,
Notary Public.

Commonwealth of Massachusetts.

SUFFOLK, SS. BOSTON, Sept. 1, 1904. Then personally appeared the above named Lawson B. Bidwell, Fayette S. Curtis and James W. Perkins, and severally made oath that the foregoing certificate by them subscribed is, to the best of their knowledge and belief, true.

Before me, ARTHUR P. RUSSELL,
Justice of the Peace.

RETURN

OF THE

STOCKBRIDGE & PITTSFIELD RAILROAD COMPANY

For the Year Ending June 30, 1904.

[Leased to and operated by the New York, New Haven & Hartford.]

General Exhibit for the Year.	
Rental received from lease of road,	$27,172 00
Dividends received on stocks owned: 34 shares Stockbridge & Pittsfield Railroad Company,	204 00
Gross Income,	$27,376 00
Expenses and charges upon income accrued during the year: salaries and maintenance of organization,	352 60
Net Divisible Income,	$27,023 40
Dividends declared (6 per cent),	26,922 00
Surplus for the year ending June 30, 1904,	$101 40
Amount of surplus June 30, 1903,	10,330 85
Total Surplus June 30, 1904,	$10,432 25

General Balance Sheet June 30, 1904.	
Assets. Dr.	
Cost of road,	$448,700 00
Stock of Stockbridge & Pittsfield Railroad Company, 34 shares,	2,550 00
Total Permanent Investments,	$451,250 00
Cash,	8,398 25
Total,	$459,648 25
Liabilities. Cr.	
Capital stock,	$448,700 00
Current liabilities: dividends not called for,	516 00
Profit and loss balance (surplus),	10,432 25
Total,	$459,648 25

Capital Stock.		
Capital stock authorized by law,	$550,000 00	
Capital stock authorized by votes of company,	448,700 00	
Capital stock issued and outstanding,		$448,700 00
Number of shares issued and outstanding,	4,487	
Number of stockholders,	215	
Number of stockholders in Massachusetts,	153	
Amount of stock held in Massachusetts,	$298,000 00	

DESCRIPTION OF RAILROAD OWNED.

(See also tabulated description in preceding appendix to report.)

RAILROAD OWNED.	Total.	In Massachusetts.
	Miles.	Miles.
Length of main line,	22.020	22.020
Length of side track, etc.,	14.340	14.340
TOTAL LENGTH OF TRACK OWNED,	36.360	36.360

CORPORATE NAME AND ADDRESS OF THE COMPANY.

STOCKBRIDGE & PITTSFIELD RAILROAD COMPANY,

STOCKBRIDGE, MASS.

NAMES AND BUSINESS ADDRESS OF PRINCIPAL OFFICERS.

Henry W. Taft, *President*, Third National Bank, Pittsfield, Mass. Daniel A. Kimball, *Treasurer and Clerk of Corporation*, Housatonic National Bank, Stockbridge, Mass.

NAMES AND RESIDENCE OF BOARD OF DIRECTORS.

Henry W. Taft, Pittsfield, Mass. Ferdinand Hoffmann, Stockbridge, Mass. John B. Hull, Stockbridge, Mass. William A. Seymour, Stockbridge, Mass. George H. Tucker, Pittsfield, Mass. Frank H. Wright, Great Barrington, Mass. Daniel A. Kimball, Stockbridge, Mass.

We hereby certify that the statements contained in the foregoing return are full, just and true.

GEO. H. TUCKER,
FRANK H. WRIGHT,
WILLIAM A. SEYMOUR,
DANIEL A. KIMBALL,
Directors.
DANIEL A. KIMBALL,
Treasurer.

COMMONWEALTH OF MASSACHUSETTS.

BERKSHIRE, SS. STOCKBRIDGE, July 27, 1904. Then personally appeared the above-named George H. Tucker, Frank H. Wright, William A. Seymour and Daniel A. Kimball, and severally made oath that the foregoing certificate by them subscribed is, to the best of their knowledge and belief, true.

Before me, CHAS. E. EVANS,
Justice of the Peace.

RETURN

OF THE

STONY BROOK RAILROAD CORPORATION

FOR THE YEAR ENDING JUNE 30, 1904.

[Leased to and operated by the Boston & Maine.]

GENERAL EXHIBIT FOR THE YEAR.		
Rental received from lease of road,		$21,500 00
Expenses and charges upon income accrued during the year: salaries and maintenance of organization,		379 91
NET DIVISIBLE INCOME,		$21,120 09
Dividends declared:		
7 per cent on common stock,	$21,000 00	
1 per cent on common stock, extra,	3,000 00	
		24,000 00
Deficit for the year ending June 30, 1904,		$2,879 91
Amount of surplus June 30, 1903,		1,054 36
Credits to profit and loss account during the year: interest on funds in savings banks,		567 93
TOTAL DEFICIT JUNE 30, 1904,		$1,257 62

GENERAL BALANCE SHEET JUNE 30, 1904.	
ASSETS. DR.	
Cost of road,	$276,601 19
Cost of equipment,	21,492 38
TOTAL PERMANENT INVESTMENTS,	$298,093 57
Cash,	648 81
Profit and loss balance (deficit),	1,257 62
TOTAL,	$300,000 00
LIABILITIES. CR.	
Capital stock,	$300,000 00
TOTAL,	$300,000 00

CAPITAL STOCK.		
Capital stock authorized by law,	$300,000 00	
Capital stock authorized by votes of company,	300,000 00	
Capital stock issued and outstanding,		$300,000 00
Number of shares issued and outstanding,	3,000	
Number of stockholders,	236	
Number of stockholders in Massachusetts,	212	
Amount of stock held in Massachusetts,	$279,900 00	

Description of Railroad Owned.

(See also tabulated description in preceding appendix to report.)

Railroad Owned.	Total.	In Massachusetts.
	Miles.	Miles.
Length of main line,	13.160	13.160
Length of side track, etc.,	6.060	6.060
Total Length of Track Owned,	19.220	19.220

Corporate Name and Address of the Company.

STONY BROOK RAILROAD CORPORATION,

61 Merrimack Street, Lowell, Mass.

Names and Business Address of Principal Officers.

George F. Richardson, *President*, Lowell, Mass. Frank E. Dunbar, *Treasurer*, Lowell, Mass.

Names and Residence of Board of Directors.

George F. Richardson, Lowell, Mass. Jacob Rogers, Lowell, Mass. George S. Motley, Lowell, Mass. Alexander G. Cumnock, Lowell, Mass. Alphonso S. Covel, Boston, Mass. Edward N. Burke, Lowell, Mass. Charles L. Hildreth, Lowell, Mass.

We hereby certify that the statements contained in the foregoing return are full, just and true.

LUCIUS TUTTLE,
RICHARD OLNEY,
SAMUEL C. LAWRENCE,
HENRY R. REED,
HENRY M. WHITNEY,
H. F. DIMOCK,
A. W. SULLOWAY,
WILLIAM WHITING,
WALTER HUNNEWELL,
JOSEPH H. WHITE,
LEWIS CASS LEDYARD,
Directors of the Boston & Maine Railroad.
HERBERT E. FISHER,
Treasurer of the Boston & Maine Railroad.
WM. J. HOBBS,
Chief Accounting Officer of the Boston & Maine Railroad.

Commonwealth of Massachusetts.

Suffolk, ss. Boston, Sept. 8, 1904. Then personally appeared the above-named Lucius Tuttle, Richard Olney, Samuel C. Lawrence, Henry R. Reed, Henry M. Whitney, H. E. Dimock, A. W. Sulloway, William Whiting, Walter Hunnewell, Joseph H. White and Lewis Cass Ledyard, directors of the Boston & Maine Railroad, Herbert E. Fisher, its treasurer, and Wm. J. Hobbs, its chief accounting officer, and severally made oath that the foregoing certificate by them subscribed is, to the best of their knowledge and belief, true.

Before me, WILLIAM B. LAWRENCE,
Justice of the Peace.

RETURN

OF THE

UNION FREIGHT RAILROAD COMPANY

For the Year ending June 30, 1904.

General Exhibit for the Year.		
Gross earnings from operation,		$85,354 95
Operating expenses,		56,461 98
Net Earnings from Operation,		$28,892 97
Dividends received on stocks owned: Union Freight R.R. Co.,		910 00
Gross Income above Operating Expenses,		$29,802 97
Charges upon income accrued during the year:		
Interest and discount on unfunded debts and loans,	$2,493 01	
Taxes,	2,672 97	
Other deductions from income: reserve for settlement of unadjusted claims,	5,000 00	
Total Charges and Deductions from Income,		$10,165 98
Net Divisible Income,		$19,636 99
Dividends declared during the year (March, 1904, 7 per cent on $300,000),		21,000 00
Deficit for the year ending June 30, 1904,		$1,363 01
Amount of surplus June 30, 1903,		50,409 69
Credits to profit and loss account during the year: amount transferred from "reserve for settlement of unadjusted claims,"		2,137 50
Total Surplus June 30, 1904,		$51,184 18

Earnings from Operation.

Department of Service.	Gross Receipts.	Deductions.	Earnings.
Freight service:			
Gross receipts from freight,	$85,719 39		
Deductions:			
Other repayments,	. . . .	$412 45	
Net Revenue from Freight,	. . . .	. . . .	$85,306 94
Other earnings from operation:			
Car mileage — balance,	. . . .	. . . .	48 01
Gross Earnings from Operation,	. . . .	. . . .	$85,354 95

Expenses of Operation.

General expenses:	
Salaries of general officers,	$6,641 87
Salaries of clerks and attendants,	671 00
General office expenses and supplies,	46 25
Law expenses,	1,934 25
Total,	$9,293 37
Maintenance of way and structures:	
Repairs of roadway,	$9,955 35
Repairs and renewals of buildings and fixtures,	31 11
Total,	$9,986 46
Maintenance of equipment: repairs and renewals of locomotives,	$5,022 66
Conducting transportation:	
Engine and roundhouse men,	$7,652 80
Fuel for locomotives,	5,661 65
Water supply for locomotives,	256 20
Oil, tallow and waste for locomotives,	327 13
Train service,	11,285 45
Train supplies and expenses,	40 25
Switchmen, flagmen and watchmen,	1,224 30
Telegraph expenses,	156 50
Station service,	2,522 05
Station supplies,	113 56
Loss and damage,	527 05
Injuries to persons,	2,287 50
Stationery and printing,	105 05
Total,	$32,159 49
Recapitulation:	
General expenses,	$9,293 37
Maintenance of way and structures,	9,986 46
Maintenance of equipment,	5,022 66
Conducting transportation,	32,159 49
Total Operating Expenses,	$56,461 98
Percentage of operating expenses to gross earnings,	66.15

General Balance Sheet June 30, 1904.

Assets.	Dr.	
Cost of road,		$401,069 67
Cost of equipment,		12,000 00
Stock of Union Freight Railroad Company,		13,000 00
Total Permanent Investments,		$426,069 67
Cash,	$23,993 24	
Due from agents,	1,765 56	
Total Cash and Current Assets,		25,758 80
Materials and supplies,		1,402 85
Total,		$453,231 32

Liabilities.	Cr.	
Capital stock,		$300,000 00
Real estate mortgages,		88,500 00
Current liabilities:		
Audited vouchers and accounts,	$5,162 14	
Salaries and wages,	522 50	
Total Current Liabilities,		5,684 64
Sinking and other special funds: reserve for unadjusted claims,		7,862 50
Profit and loss balance (surplus),		51,184 18
Total,		$453,231 32

Capital Stock.		
Capital stock authorized by law,	$500,000 00	
Capital stock authorized by votes of company,	300,000 00	
Capital stock issued and outstanding,		$300,000 00
Number of shares issued and outstanding,	3,000	
Number of stockholders,	3	
Number of stockholders in Massachusetts,	3	
Amount of stock held in Massachusetts,	$300,000 00	

Real Estate Mortgages.

Description of Mortgaged Property.	Rate of Interest.	Mortgage when Due.	Amount.	Interest Paid during the Year.
	Per Cent.			
Real estate in Boston,	3½	June 16, 1908,	$88,500 00	$3,097 50

Volume of Traffic, etc.

Freight traffic:	
Number of tons of freight hauled earning revenue,	291,269
Number of tons of freight hauled one mile,	400,494
Number of tons of freight hauled one mile per mile of road operated,	164,814
Average length of haul per ton,	1.375 miles.
Average amount received per ton per mile hauled,	21.300 cents.
Freight earnings (gross) per mile of road operated,	$35,105 74
Freight earnings (gross) per freight-train mile run,	3 37
Operating expenses:	
Operating expenses per mile of road operated,	$23,235 35
Operating expenses per revenue-train mile run,	2 23
Train mileage:	
Miles run by freight trains,	25,331
Total train mileage,	25,331
Fares and freights:	
Average rate received per ton mile for local freight,	21.353 cents.
Employees:	
Average number of persons employed,	42

Description of Railroad Owned and Operated.

(See also tabulated description in preceding appendix to report).

Railroad Owned and Operated.	Total.	In Massachusetts.
	Miles.	Miles.
Length of main line,	2.431	2.431
Length of second track,	.937	.937
Length of side track, etc.,	1.280	1.280
Total Length of Track Owned,	4.648	4.648

Description of Equipment.

Rolling Stock.	Number Owned.	Equipped with Power Driving-Wheel Brakes.	Maximum Weight.	Average Weight.
Locomotives.			Lbs.	Lbs.
Freight,	4	4	62,000	62,000

Accidents to Persons.

(A detailed statement of each accident is on file in the office of the Board.)

Killed and Injured.	In Massachusetts.						Total on All Lines Operated.	
	From causes beyond their own control.		From their own misconduct or carelessness.		Total.			
	Killed.	Injured.	Killed.	Injured.	Killed.	Injured.	Killed.	Injured.
Passengers,	-	-	-	-	-	-	-	-
Employees,	1	1	-	-	-	-	1	1
Other persons,	-	-	1	1	-	-	1	1
Totals,	1	1	1	1	-	-	2	2

Corporate Name and Address of the Company.

UNION FREIGHT RAILROAD COMPANY,

South Terminal Station, Boston, Mass.

Names and Business Address of Principal Officers.

Fayette S. Curtis, *President*, Boston, Mass. Austin W. Adams, *Treasurer and Clerk of Corporation*, Boston, Mass. Frank A. Farnham, *Counsel*, Boston, Mass. George L. Winlock, *General Freight Agent*, Boston, Mass. Amasa H. Grovenor, *Superintendent*, Boston, Mass.

NAMES AND RESIDENCE OF BOARD OF DIRECTORS.

Fayette S. Curtis, Boston, Mass. Charles F. Choate, Southborough, Mass.
George A. Gardner, Boston, Mass. Charles S. Mellen, New Haven, Conn.
Joshua M. Sears, Boston, Mass. Nathaniel Thayer, Lancaster, Mass.

We hereby certify that the statements contained in the foregoing return are full, just and true.

CHARLES F. CHOATE,
JOSHUA M. SEARS,
FAYETTE S. CURTIS,
C. S. MELLEN,
Directors.
AUSTIN W. ADAMS,
Treasurer.

COMMONWEALTH OF MASSACHUSETTS.

SUFFOLK, SS. BOSTON, Sept. 8, 1904. Then personally appeared the above-named Charles F. Choate, Joshua M. Sears, Fayette S. Curtis and Austin W. Adams, and severally made oath that the foregoing certificate by them subscribed is, to the best of their knowledge and belief, true.

Before me, ALFRED H. LITCHFIELD,
Justice of the Peace.

STATE OF CONNECTICUT.

COUNTY OF NEW HAVEN, SS. SEPT. 9, 1904. Then personally appeared the above-named Charles S. Mellen, and made oath that the foregoing certificate by him subscribed is, to the best of his knowledge and belief, true.

Before me, ALBERT H. POWELL,
Notary Public.

RETURN

OF THE

VERMONT & MASSACHUSETTS RAILROAD COMPANY

FOR THE YEAR ENDING JUNE 30, 1904.

[Leased to and operated by the Boston & Maine.]

General Exhibit for the Year.		
Rental received from lease of road,		$194,580 00
Expenses and charges upon income accrued during the year: salaries and maintenance of organization,		3,000 00
Net Divisible Income,		$191,580 00
Dividends declared (6 per cent),		191,580 00
Amount of surplus June 30, 1903,		2,268,054 64
Credits to profit and loss account during the year:		
Payment of bonds by Fitchburg Railroad Company,	$36,000 00	
Cash City Institution for Savings, Lowell,	5 86	
Total Credits,	$36,005 86	
Debits to profit and loss account during the year: auditing corporation accounts,	100 79	
Net Amount Credited to Profit and Loss,		35,905 07
Total Surplus June 30, 1904,		$2,303,959 71

General Balance Sheet June 30, 1904.	
Assets. Dr.	
Cost of road,	$3,334,940 82
Cost of equipment,	261,233 64
Lands in Massachusetts,	2,107 65
Turner's Falls Branch,	145,300 63
Betterments to road made since January 1, 1874, as reported by Fitchburg Railroad Company,	2,525,376 97
Total Permanent Investments,	$6,268,959 71
Cash,	12,687 50
Total,	$6,281,647 21

LIABILITIES. Cr.	
Capital stock,	$3,193,000 00
Funded debt,	772,000 00
Current liabilities: dividends not called for,	12,687 50
Profit and loss balance (surplus),	2,303,959 71
TOTAL,	$6,281,647 21

CAPITAL STOCK.		
Capital stock authorized by law,	$4,700,000 00	
Capital stock authorized by votes of company,	3,193,000 00	
Capital stock issued and outstanding,		$3,193,000 00
Number of shares issued and outstanding,	31,930	
Number of stockholders,	1,313	
Number of stockholders in Massachusetts,	1,124	
Amount of stock held in Massachusetts,	2,937,500 00	

FUNDED DEBT.

DESCRIPTION OF BONDS.	Rate of Interest.	Date of Maturity.	Amount Outstanding.	Interest Paid during the Year.
Plain bonds,	Per Cent. 3½	May 1, 1923,	$772,000 00	$27,020 00

DESCRIPTION OF RAILROAD OWNED.

(See also tabulated description in preceding appendix to report.)

RAILROAD OWNED.	Total.	In Massachusetts.
	Miles.	Miles.
Length of main line,	55.780	55.780
Length of branch line,	2.800	2.800
TOTAL LENGTH OF LINE OWNED,	58.580	58.580
Length of second track,	55.780	55.780
Length of side track, etc.,	41.920	41.920
TOTAL LENGTH OF TRACK OWNED,	156.280	156.280

CORPORATE NAME AND ADDRESS OF THE COMPANY.

VERMONT & MASSACHUSETTS RAILROAD COMPANY,

TREASURER'S OFFICE, 53 DEVONSHIRE STREET, BOSTON, MASS.

NAMES AND BUSINESS ADDRESS OF PRINCIPAL OFFICERS.

Charles E. Ware, *President*, Fitchburg, Mass. F. B. Shepley, *Treasurer*, 53 Devonshire Street, Boston, Mass. Charles E. Hatfield, *Clerk of Corporation*, Barrister's Hall, Boston, Mass.

NAMES AND RESIDENCE OF BOARD OF DIRECTORS.

Francis Goodhue, Brattleboro, Vt. Edward L. Davis, Worcester, Mass. Alvah Crocker, Fitchburg, Mass. Charles A. Welch, Cohasset, Mass. George F. Richardson, Lowell, Mass. Charles E. Ware, Fitchburg, Mass. Charles T. Crocker, Fitchburg, Mass.

We hereby certify that the statements contained in the foregoing return are full, just and true.

CHAS. E. WARE,
B. N. BULLOCK,
GEORGE R. WALLACE,
C. T. CROCKER,
GORDON ABBOTT,
JOSEPH B. RUSSELL,
ROBERT WINSOR,
Directors.
DAN. A. GLEASON,
Treasurer and Chief Accounting Officer.

COMMONWEALTH OF MASSACHUSETTS.

SUFFOLK, SS. SEPT. 8, 1904. Then personally appeared the above-named Fitchburg directors, namely: Charles E. Ware, B. N. Bullock, George R. Wallace, C. T. Crocker, Gordon Abbott, J. B. Russell, Robert Winsor, and severally made oath that the foregoing certificate by them subscribed is, to the best of their knowledge and belief, true.

Before me, REGINALD CARY HEATH,
Justice of the Peace.

RETURN

OF THE

WARE RIVER RAILROAD COMPANY

FOR THE YEAR ENDING JUNE 30, 1904.

[Leased to and operated by the Boston & Albany (New York Central & Hudson River, lessee).]

GENERAL EXHIBIT FOR THE YEAR.	
Rental received from lease of road,	$52,500 00
Dividends declared (7 per cent),	$52,500 00

GENERAL BALANCE SHEET JUNE 30, 1904.	
ASSETS. DR.	
Cost of road,	$1,115,163 82
TOTAL,	$1,115,163 82
LIABILITIES. CR.	
Capital stock,	$750,000 00
Unfunded debt,	365,163 82
TOTAL,	$1,115,163 82

CAPITAL STOCK.		
Capital stock authorized by law,	$1,000,000 00	
Capital stock authorized by votes of company,	750,000 00	
Capital stock issued and outstanding,		$750,000 00
Number of shares issued and outstanding,	7,500	
Number of stockholders,	152	
Number of stockholders in Massachusetts,	142	
Amount of stock held in Massachusetts,	$605,300 00	

DESCRIPTION OF RAILROAD OWNED.

(See also tabulated description in preceding appendix to report.)

RAILROAD OWNED.	Total.	In Massachusetts.
	Miles.	Miles.
Length of main line,	49.350	49.350
Length of side track, etc.,	7.400	7.400
TOTAL LENGTH OF TRACK OWNED,	56.750	56.750

Corporate Name and Address of the Company.

WARE RIVER RAILROAD COMPANY,

Boston, Mass.

Names and Business Address of Principal Officers.

James A. Rumrill, *President*, Springfield, Mass. Frank H. Ratcliffe, *Treasurer*, Boston, Mass. Edgar W. Long, *Clerk of Corporation*, Boston, Mass.

Names and Residence of Board of Directors.

James A. Rumrill, Springfield, Mass. Henry B. Chapin, Boston, Mass. Charles S. Sargent, Brookline, Mass. Charles E. Stevens, Ware, Mass. Frederick H. Gillett, Springfield, Mass. Chester W. Bliss, Springfield, Mass. Frank H. Ratcliffe, Newton Centre, Mass.

We hereby certify that the statements contained in the foregoing return are full, just and true.

J. A. RUMRILL,
HENRY B. CHAPIN,
Directors.
F. H. RATCLIFFE,
Treasurer.

Commonwealth of Massachusetts.

Suffolk, ss. Boston, Sept. 28, 1904. Then personally appeared the above-named J. A. Rumrill, Henry B. Chapin and F. H. Ratcliffe, and severally made oath that the foregoing certificate by them subscribed is, to the best of their knowledge and belief, true.

Before me, WOODWARD HUDSON,
Justice of the Peace.

RETURN

OF THE

WEST STOCKBRIDGE RAILROAD CORPORATION

For the Year ending June 30, 1904.

[Leased to and operated by the New York, New Haven & Hartford.]

General Exhibit for the Year.

This road being virtually owned by the New York, New Haven & Hartford, no income from the lease to that company is reported. [R.R. Com.]

Amount of surplus June 30, 1903,	$450 00
Debits to profit and loss account during the year: accounts receivable cancelled,	$450 00

General Balance Sheet June 30, 1904.

Assets. Dr.	
Cost of road,	$39,600 00
Total,	$39,600 00

Liabilities. Cr.	
Capital stock,	$39,600 00
Total,	$39,600 00

Capital Stock.

Capital stock authorized by law,	$75,000 00	
Capital stock authorized by votes of company,	39,600 00	
Capital stock issued and outstanding,		$39,600 00
Number of shares issued and outstanding,	396	
Number of stockholders,	5	

Description of Railroad Owned.

(See also tabulated description in preceding appendix to report.)

Railroad Owned.	Total.	In Massachusetts.
	Miles.	Miles.
Length of main line,	2.640	2.640
Length of side track, etc.,	.930	.930
Total Length of Track Owned,	3.570	3.570

CORPORATE NAME AND ADDRESS OF THE COMPANY.

WEST STOCKBRIDGE RAILROAD CORPORATION,

NEW HAVEN, CONN.

NAMES AND BUSINESS ADDRESS OF PRINCIPAL OFFICERS.

John M. Hall, *President*, New Haven, Conn. H. M. Kochersperger, *Treasurer and Clerk of Corporation*, New Haven, Conn.

NAMES AND RESIDENCE OF BOARD OF DIRECTORS.

John M. Hall, New Haven, Conn. Percy R. Todd, New Haven, Conn. H. M. Kochersperger, New Haven, Conn. Charles S. Mellen, New Haven, Conn.

We hereby certify that the statements contained in the foregoing return are full, just and true.

JOHN M. HALL,
PERCY R. TODD,
C. S. MELLEN,
H. M. KOCHERSPERGER,
Directors.
H. M. KOCHERSPERGER,
Treasurer.

STATE OF CONNECTICUT.

CITY AND COUNTY OF NEW HAVEN, SS., SEPT. 17, 1904. Then personally appeared the above-named H. M. Kochersperger, and made oath that the foregoing certificate by him subscribed is, to the best of his knowledge and belief, true.

Before me, ARTHUR E. CLARK,
Notary Public.

STATE OF NEW YORK.

CITY AND COUNTY OF NEW YORK, SS. SEPT. 17, 1904. Then personally appeared the above-named John M. Hall, Percy R. Todd, and C. S. Mellen, and severally made oath that the foregoing certificate by them subscribed is, to the best of their knowledge and belief, true.

Before me, FRANK E. HALL,
Notary Public, New York County.

RETURN

OF THE

WORCESTER, NASHUA & ROCHESTER RAILROAD COMPANY

For the Year ending June 30, 1904.

[Leased to and operated by the Boston & Maine.]

General Exhibit for the Year.		
Rental received from lease of road,		$250,000 00
Income from other sources: interest on bank account,		150 32
Gross Income,		$250,150 32
Expenses and charges upon income accrued during the year:		
Salaries and maintenance of organization,	$2,267 10	
Interest on funded debt,	71,040 00	
Total Expenses and Charges upon Income,		73,307 10
Net Divisible Income,		$176,843 22
Dividends declared (5¾ per cent on 30,644 shares),		176,203 00
Surplus for the year ending June 30, 1904,		$640 22
Amount of deficit June 30, 1903,		280,122 03
Total Deficit June 30, 1904,		$279,481 81

General Balance Sheet June 30, 1904.		
Assets.		Dr.
Cost of road,		$4,138,584 99
Cost of equipment,		415,336 03
Total Permanent Investments,		$4,553,921 02
Cash,	$38,857 17	
Bills receivable: Worcester, Nashua & Rochester stock,	35,400 00	
Total Cash and Current Assets,		74,257 17
Profit and loss balance (deficit),		279,481 81
Total,		$4,907,660 00

LIABILITIES. CR.	
Capital stock,	$3,099,800 00
Funded debt,	1,776,000 00
Current liabilities: matured interest coupons unpaid (including coupons due July 1),	28,060 00
Accrued liabilities: interest accrued and not yet due,	3,800 00
TOTAL,	$4,907,660 00

CAPITAL STOCK.		
Capital stock authorized by law,	$3,600,000 00	
Capital stock authorized by votes of company,	3,099,800 00	
Capital stock issued and outstanding,		$3,099,800 00
Number of shares issued and outstanding,	30,998	
Number of stockholders,	792	
Number of stockholders in Massachusetts,	542	
Amount of stock held in Massachusetts,	$942,800 00	

FUNDED DEBT.

DESCRIPTION OF BONDS.	Rate of Interest.	Date of Maturity.	Amount Outstanding.	Interest Paid during the Year.
	Per Cent.			
First mortgage bonds,	4	Jan. 1, 1906,	$150,000 00	$6,000 00
First mortgage bonds,	4	Jan. 1, 1913,	511,000 00	20,440 00
First mortgage bonds,	4	Jan. 1, 1930,	735,000 00	29,360 00
First mortgage bonds,	4	Oct. 1, 1934,	380,000 00	15,180 00
TOTALS,			$1,776,000 00	$70,980 00

DESCRIPTION OF RAILROAD OWNED.

(See also tabulated description in preceding appendix to report.)

RAILROAD OWNED.	Total.	In Massachusetts.
	Miles.	Miles.
Length of main line,	94.480	39.460
Length of second track,	18.130	18.130
Length of side track, etc.,	50.130	31.590
TOTAL LENGTH OF TRACK OWNED,	162.740	89.180

CORPORATE NAME AND ADDRESS OF THE COMPANY.

WORCESTER, NASHUA & ROCHESTER RAILROAD COMPANY,

BOSTON, MASS.

NAMES AND BUSINESS ADDRESS OF PRINCIPAL OFFICERS.

George G. Haven, *President*, 32 Nassau Street, New York, N. Y. Charles H. Bowen, *Treasurer and Clerk of Corporation*, 53 State Street, Boston, Mass.

NAMES AND RESIDENCE OF BOARD OF DIRECTORS.

George G. Haven, New York, N. Y. James N. Jarvie, New York, N. Y. Adrian Iselin, Jr., New York, N. Y. Frederic Cromwell, New York, N. Y. Richard A. McCurdy, New York, N. Y. Henry L. Higginson, Boston, Mass. Nathaniel Thayer, Lancaster, Mass. Albert Wallace, Rochester, N. H. Charles H. Bowen, Brookline, Mass.

We hereby certify that the statements contained in the foregoing return are full, just and true.

G. G. HAVEN,
ADRIAN ISELIN, JR.,
HENRY L. HIGGINSON,
ALBERT WALLACE,
C. H. BOWEN,
Directors.
C. H. BOWEN,
Treasurer.

COMMONWEALTH OF MASSACHUSETTS.

SUFFOLK, SS. JULY 29, 1904. Then personally appeared the above-named Henry L. Higginson, Albert Wallace and C. H. Bowen, and severally made oath that the foregoing certificate by them subscribed is, to the best of their knowledge and belief, true.

Before me, EUGENE W. LEIGHTON,
Notary Public.

STATE OF NEW YORK.

COUNTY OF NEW YORK, SS. NEW YORK, Aug. 2, 1904. Then personally appeared the above-named G. G. Haven and Adrian Iselin, Jr., and severally made oath that the foregoing certificate by them subscribed is, to the best of their knowledge and belief, true.

Before me, MARTIN EICHE,
Notary Public, New York County.

To the Honorable Board of Railroad Commissioners for the Commonwealth of Massachusetts.

The undersigned, commissioner of Worcester & Nashua Railroad Company for the Commonwealth of Massachusetts, having examined the report of the president and directors of said company for the year ending June 30, 1904, believes it to be correct, and hereby approves the same.

WORCESTER, Aug. 19, 1904.

The undersigned, commissioner of the Commonwealth of Massachusetts for the Worcester & Nashua Railroad Company, on the above-named date examined the aforesaid report of said company to said honorable Board of Commissioners, for the year aforesaid, so far as to determine what proportion of the receipts and expenditures of said company pertained to that part of the road lying in Massachusetts, and what proportion to the part lying in New Hampshire, with the following result: —

Total cost of road and equipment,		$4,553,921 02
Cost of road and equipment lying in Massachusetts,		$2,268,583 28
Cost of road and equipment lying in New Hampshire,		$2,285,337 74
Income of the entire road for the year,		$250,000 00
Interest on bank account,		150 32
GROSS INCOME,		$250,150 32
Expenses and charges for the year:		
Salaries and maintenance of organization,	$2,267 10	
Interest on funded debt,	71,040 00	
TOTAL,		73,307 10
NET DIVISIBLE INCOME,		$176,843 22

The road being under lease to the Boston & Maine Railroad Company, no account is taken of permanent improvements or the expenditures and receipts connected with its operation by said company.

An equal apportionment is hereby made of income and expenses to the parts of the road lying respectively in Massachusetts and New Hampshire, on the basis of the nearly equal cost of these separate sections, including equipments.

JOHN J. PUTNAM,
Commissioner.

REPORT

OF THE

AMESBURY & HAMPTON STREET RAILWAY COMPANY

FOR THE YEAR ENDING SEPTEMBER 30, 1904.

[Leased to and operated by the Exeter, Hampton & Amesbury of New Hampshire.]

GENERAL EXHIBIT FOR THE YEAR.	
Rental received from lease of railway, ...	$9,000 00
Expenses and charges upon income accrued during the year: interest on funded debt, ...	5,000 00
Surplus for the year ending September 30, 1904, ...	$4,000 00
Amount of surplus September 30, 1903, ...	10,034 95
TOTAL SURPLUS SEPTEMBER 30, 1904, ...	$14,034 95

GENERAL BALANCE SHEET SEPTEMBER 30, 1904.		
ASSETS.	DR.	
Cost of railway:		
Roadbed and tracks, ...	$117,506 31	
Electric line construction, including poles, wiring, feeder lines, etc., . . .	33,902 95	
Engineering and other expenses incident to construction, ...	5,406 47	
TOTAL COST OF RAILWAY OWNED, ...		156,815 73
Cost of equipment:		
Cars and other rolling stock and vehicles, .	$15,586 36	
Electric equipment of same, ...	15,000 00	
Other items of equipment: furniture and fixtures, ...	11 25	
TOTAL COST OF EQUIPMENT OWNED, ...		30,597 61
Cost of land and buildings and rights of way:		
Land necessary for operation of railway, .	$2,531 75	
Electric power stations, including equipment,	36,823 00	
Other buildings necessary for operation of railway, ...	13,705 37	
TOTAL COST OF LAND AND BUILDINGS OWNED, . .		53,060 12
TOTAL PERMANENT INVESTMENTS, ...		$240,473 46
Cash and current assets: bills and accounts receivable, . .		13,500 00
TOTAL, ...		$253,973 46

LIABILITIES.	CR.	
Capital stock,		$100,000 00
Funded debt,		100,000 00
Current liabilities:		
Loans and notes payable,	$37,438 51	
Matured interest coupons unpaid (including coupons due October 1),	2,500 00	
TOTAL CURRENT LIABILITIES,		39,938 51
Profit and loss balance (surplus),		14,034 95
TOTAL,		$253,973 46

PROPERTY ACCOUNTS.		
Additions to railway:		
Extension of tracks,	$2,675 97	
New electric line construction,	4,406 90	
Other additions to railway: engineering and expense,	127 65	
TOTAL ADDITIONS TO RAILWAY,		$7,210 52
Additions to equipment: furniture and fixtures,		11 25
Additions to land and buildings:		
Rights of way,	$6 75	
New buildings necessary for operation of railway,	2,205 59	
TOTAL ADDITIONS TO LAND AND BUILDINGS,		2,212 34
TOTAL ADDITIONS TO PROPERTY ACCOUNTS,		$9,434 11

CAPITAL STOCK.		
Capital stock authorized by law,	$100,000 00	
Capital stock authorized by votes of company,	100,000 00	
Capital stock issued and outstanding,		$100,000 00
Number of shares issued and outstanding,	1,000	
Number of stockholders,	6	
Number of stockholders in Massachusetts,	5	
Amount of stock held in Massachusetts,	$500 00	

FUNDED DEBT.

DESCRIPTION OF BONDS.	Rate of Interest.	Date of Maturity.	Amount Outstanding.	Interest Paid during the Year.
	Per Cent.			
First mortgage gold bonds,	5	Oct. 1, 1919,	$100,000 00	$2,500 00

RAILWAY OWNED.

Length of railway line,	8.342 miles.
Length of sidings, switches, etc.,	.409 "
Total, computed as single track,	8.751 "

RAILWAY OWNED AND LOCATED OUTSIDE OF PUBLIC WAYS.

Length of railway line, ...	.207 mile.

Names of the several cities and towns in which the railway owned by the company is located: Sàlisbury and Amesbury.

CORPORATE NAME AND ADDRESS OF THE COMPANY.

AMESBURY & HAMPTON STREET RAILWAY COMPANY,
50 MERRIMAC STREET, HAVERHILL, MASS.

NAMES AND BUSINESS ADDRESS OF PRINCIPAL OFFICERS.

David A. Belden, *President*, 50 Merrimac Street, Haverhill, Mass. Frederick P. Royce, *Vice-President*, 84 State Street, Boston, Mass. Samuel P. Russell, *Treasurer and Auditor*, 50 Merrimac Street, Haverhill, Mass. Reginald H. Johnson, *Clerk of Corporation*, 53 State Street, Boston, Mass. Franklin Woodman, *General Manager*, 50 Merrimac Street, Haverhill, Mass. Clarence P. Hayden, *Superintendent*, Hampton, N. H.

NAMES AND RESIDENCE OF BOARD OF DIRECTORS.

David A. Belden, Haverhill, Mass. Reginald H. Johnson, Braintree, Mass. Frederick P. Royce, Dedham, Mass. Frank W. Stearns, Newton, Mass. John Dearborn, Boston, Mass.

We hereby certify that the statements contained in the foregoing report are full, just and true.

DAVID A. BELDEN,
F. P. ROYCE,
REGINALD H. JOHNSON,
Directors.
SAM'L P. RUSSELL,
Treasurer.
FRANKLIN WOODMAN,
General Manager.

COMMONWEALTH OF MASSACHUSETTS.

ESSEX, ss. Nov. 17, 1904. Then personally appeared the above-named David A. Belden, Samuel P. Russell and Franklin Woodman, and severally made oath that the foregoing certificate by them subscribed is, to the best of their knowledge and belief, true.

Before me, EDMUND B. FULLER,
Justice of the Peace.

COMMONWEALTH OF MASSACHUSETTS.

SUFFOLK, ss. Nov. 29, 1904. Then personally appeared the above-named F. P. Royce and Reginald H. Johnson, and severally made oath that the foregoing certificate by them subscribed is, to the best of their knowledge and belief, true.

Before me, HAROLD WILLIAMS, JR.,
Justice of the Peace.

REPORT

OF THE

AMESBURY & HAMPTON STREET RAILWAY

(EXETER, HAMPTON & AMESBURY STREET RAILWAY COMPANY, LESSEE)

FOR THE YEAR ENDING SEPTEMBER 30, 1904.

GENERAL EXHIBIT FOR THE YEAR.		
Gross earnings from operation,		$25,485 06
Operating expenses,		27,033 46
GROSS LOSS ABOVE OPERATING EXPENSES,		$1,548 40
Charges upon income accrued during the year:		
Taxes, State and local,	$564 87	
Rentals of leased railways,	9,000 00	
TOTAL CHARGES AND DEDUCTIONS FROM INCOME,		9,564 87
Deficit for the year ending September 30, 1904,		$11,113 27
Amount of deficit September 30, 1903,		13,485 39
TOTAL DEFICIT SEPTEMBER 30, 1904,		$24,598 66

EARNINGS FROM OPERATION.	
Receipts from passengers carried,	$24,729 62
Receipts from carriage of mails,	672 73
Receipts from advertising in cars,	82 71
GROSS EARNINGS FROM OPERATION,	$25,485 06

EXPENSES OF OPERATION.	
General expenses:	
Salaries of general officers and clerks,	$1,008 49
General office expenses and supplies,	240 32
Insurance,	488 02
Other general expenses: store room, $75.08; miscellaneous general expenses, $203.95,	279 03

Maintenance of roadway and buildings:	
Repair of roadbed and track,	$1,794 83
Repair of electric line construction,	615 17
Repair of buildings,	195 70
Maintenance of equipment:	
Repair of cars and other vehicles,	1,665 63
Repair of electric equipment of cars,	1,596 49
Transportation expenses:	
Cost of electric motive power,	7,467 43
Wages and compensation of persons employed in conducting transportation,	6,772 42
Removal of snow and ice,	1,257 70
Damages for injuries to persons and property,	1,107 71
Tolls for trackage over other railways,	696 66
Rentals of buildings and other property,	41 84
Other transportation expenses: advertising, $399.80; car barn and machine shop expense, $1.406.22,	1,806 02
Total Operating Expenses,	$27,033 46

Volume of Traffic, etc.

Number of passengers paying revenue carried during the year,	531,827
Number carried per mile of main railway track operated,	63,753
Number of car miles run,	159,748
Average number of persons employed,	16

Description of Equipment.

Description of Equipment.	Equipped for Electric Power.	Equipped with Fenders.	Equipped with Electric Heaters.	Number of Motors.
Cars — Passenger Service.				
Box passenger cars,	2	2	2	4
Open passenger cars,	9	9	-	18
Total,	11	11	2	22
Snow ploughs,	1	-	-	-

Railway Leased and Operated (by Electric Power).

Length of railway line,	8.342 miles.
Length of sidings, switches, etc.,	.409 "
Total, computed as single track,	8.751 "

RAILWAY LOCATED OUTSIDE OF PUBLIC WAYS.

Length of railway line, ...	.207 mile.

Names of the several cities and towns in which the railways operated by the company are located: Salisbury and Amesbury.

ACCIDENTS TO PERSONS.

(A detailed statement of each accident is on file in the office of the Board.)

KILLED AND INJURED.	FROM CAUSES BEYOND THEIR OWN CONTROL.		FROM THEIR OWN MISCONDUCT OR CARELESSNESS.		TOTAL.	
	Killed.	Injured.	Killed.	Injured.	Killed.	Injured.
Passengers, ...	-	-	-	-	-	-
Employees, ...	-	-	-	-	-	-
Other persons, ...	-	-	-	1	-	1
TOTALS, ...	-	-	-	1	-	1

CORPORATE NAME AND ADDRESS OF THE COMPANY

AMESBURY & HAMPTON STREET RAILWAY COMPANY,

50 MERRIMAC STREET, HAVERHILL, MASS.

NAMES AND BUSINESS ADDRESS OF PRINCIPAL OFFICERS.

David A. Belden, *President*, 50 Merrimac Street, Haverhill, Mass. Frederick P. Royce, *Vice-President*, 84 State Street, Boston, Mass. Samuel P. Russell, *Treasurer and Auditor*, 50 Merrimac Street, Haverhill, Mass. Reginald H. Johnson, *Clerk of Corporation*, 53 State Street, Boston, Mass. Franklin Woodman, *General Manager*, 50 Merrimac Street, Haverhill, Mass. Clarence P. Hayden, *Superintendent*, Hampton, N. H.

NAMES AND RESIDENCE OF BOARD OF DIRECTORS.

David A. Belden, Haverhill, Mass. Reginald H. Johnson, Braintree, Mass. Frederick P. Royce, Dedham, Mass. Frank W. Stearns, Newton, Mass. John Dearborn, Boston, Mass.

We hereby certify that the statements contained in the foregoing report are full, just and true.

DAVID A. BELDEN,
F. P. ROYCE,
REGINALD H. JOHNSON,
Directors.
SAM'L P. RUSSELL,
Treasurer.
FRANKLIN WOODMAN,
General Manager.

COMMONWEALTH OF MASSACHUSETTS.

ESSEX, ss. Nov. 17, 1904. Then personally appeared the above-named David A. Belden, Samuel P. Russell and Franklin Woodman, and severally made oath that the foregoing certificate by them subscribed is, to the best of their knowledge and belief, true.

Before me, EDMUND B. FULLER,
Justice of the Peace.

COMMONWEALTH OF MASSACHUSETTS.

SUFFOLK, ss. Nov. 29, 1904. Then personally appeared the above-named F. P. Royce and Reginald H. Johnson, and severally made oath that the foregoing certificate by them subscribed is, to the best of their knowledge and belief, true.

Before me, HAROLD WILLIAMS, JR.,
Justice of the Peace.

REPORT

OF THE

AMHERST & SUNDERLAND STREET RAILWAY COMPANY

For the Year ending September 30, 1904.

General Exhibit for the Year.		
Gross earnings from operation,		$31,633 81
Operating expenses,		28,451 01
Gross Income above Operating Expenses,		$3,182 80
Charges upon income accrued during the year:		
Interest and discount on unfunded debts and loans,	$4,756 50	
Taxes, State and local,	1,980 84	
Total Charges and Deductions from Income,		6,737 34
Deficit for the year ending September 30, 1904,		$3,554 54
Amount of deficit September 30, 1903,		4,160 24
Debits to profit and loss account during the year:		
Accounts receivable lost,		96 00
Total Deficit September 30, 1904,		$7,810 78

Earnings from Operation.	
Receipts from passengers carried,	$28,375 01
Receipts from carriage of mails,	200 00
Receipts from carriage of freight,	2,815 12
Receipts from advertising in cars,	150 00
Other earnings from operation:	
Hay sold,	15 00
Rent of station,	78 68
Gross Earnings from Operation,	$31,633 81

Expenses of Operation.	
General expenses:	
Salaries of general officers and clerks,	$1,917 18
General office expenses and supplies,	162 50
Legal expenses,	73 10
Insurance,	411 86
Maintenance of roadway and buildings:	
Repair of roadbed and track,	1,720 83
Repair of electric line construction,	6 80
Repair of buildings,	157 42

Maintenance of equipment:	
Repair of cars and other vehicles,	$1,583 52
Repair of electric equipment of cars,	2,303 61
Transportation expenses:	
Cost of electric motive power, $10,439.97; less power sold, $591.60; net,	9,848 37
Wages and compensation of persons employed in conducting transportation,	7,784 15
Removal of snow and ice,	784 97
Damages for injuries to persons and property,	175 00
Tolls for trackage over other railways,	181 30
Other transportation expenses: oil, waste, etc., for cars, track grease, labor, etc.,	1,340 40
TOTAL OPERATING EXPENSES,	$28,451 01

PROPERTY ACCOUNTS.

Additions to railway:		
Extension of tracks (length, 426 feet),	$1,264 04	
New electric line construction (feed wire, etc.),	107 93	
Other additions to railway: engineering, $481 70; interest accrued during construction of railway, $1,361,	1,842 70	
TOTAL ADDITIONS TO RAILWAY,		$3,214 67
Additions to equipment:		
Additional cars (3 in number),	$710 40	
Electric equipment of same,	61 69	
Other additions to equipment: sundry equipment,	76 80	
TOTAL ADDITIONS TO EQUIPMENT,		848 89
Additions to land and buildings:		
Additional land necessary for operation of railway,	$405 63	
Additional equipment of power stations,	2,423 67	
New buildings necessary for operation of railway,	1,304 50	
TOTAL ADDITIONS TO LAND AND BUILDINGS,		4,133 80
TOTAL ADDITIONS TO PROPERTY ACCOUNTS,		$8,197 36

GENERAL BALANCE SHEET SEPTEMBER 30, 1904.

ASSETS.	DR.	
Cost of railway:		
Roadbed and tracks,	$116,407 22	
Electric line construction, including poles, wiring, feeder lines, etc.,	19,172 64	
Interest accrued during construction of railway,	2,822 94	
Engineering and other expenses incident to construction,	5,955 10	
TOTAL COST OF RAILWAY OWNED,		$144,357 90

Cost of equipment:		
Cars and other rolling stock and vehicles,	$26,257 42	
Electric equipment of same,	21,298 19	
Other items of equipment: sundry equipment,	577 75	
TOTAL COST OF EQUIPMENT OWNED,		$48,133 36
Cost of land and buildings:		
Land necessary for operation of railway,	$2,294 32	
Electric power stations, including equipment,	28,930 69	
Other buildings necessary for operation of railway,	7,864 20	
TOTAL COST OF LAND AND BUILDINGS OWNED,		39,089 21
TOTAL PERMANENT INVESTMENTS,		$231,580 47
Cash and current assets:		
Cash,	$1,016 28	
Bills and accounts receivable,	2,508 49	
TOTAL CASH AND CURRENT ASSETS,		3,524 77
Miscellaneous assets: materials and supplies,		3,462 83
Profit and loss balance (deficit),		7,810 78
TOTAL,		$246,378 85

LIABILITIES.		CR.
Capital stock,		$120,000 00
Current liabilities:		
Loans and notes payable,	$119,500 00	
Audited vouchers and accounts,	4,968 21	
TOTAL CURRENT LIABILITIES,		124,468 21
Accrued liabilities:		
Interest accrued and not yet due,	$1,462 50	
Taxes accrued and not yet due,	448 14	
TOTAL ACCRUED LIABILITIES,		1,910 64
TOTAL,		$246,378 85

CAPITAL STOCK.

Capital stock authorized by law,	$120,000 00	
Capital stock authorized by votes of company,	120,000 00	
Capital stock issued and outstanding,		$120,000 00
Number of shares issued and outstanding,	1,200	
Number of stockholders,	123	
Number of stockholders in Massachusetts,	122	
Amount of stock held in Massachusetts,	$119,900 00	

FUNDED DEBT.

DESCRIPTION OF BONDS.	Rate of Interest.	Date of Maturity.	Amount Outstanding.	Interest Paid during the Year.
	Per Cent.			
Gold bonds used as collateral for an equal amount,	5	Feb. 1, 1924,	$117,000 00	-

Volume of Traffic, etc.

Number of passengers paying revenue carried during the year,	574,124
Number carried per mile of main railway track operated, .	36,543
Number of car miles run, ...	269,557
Average number of persons employed, ...	20

Description of Equipment.

Description of Equipment.	Equipped for Electric Power.	Not Equipped.	Equipped with Fenders.	Equipped with Electric Heaters.	Number of Motors.
Cars — Passenger Service.					
Box passenger cars, ...	5	-	5	5	10
Open passenger cars, ...	8	-	8	-	22
Total, ...	13	-	13	5	32
Cars — Other Service,					
Box freight cars, ...	1	-	-	-	4
Platform freight cars, ...	-	2	-	-	-
Work cars, ...	1	2	-	-	-
Total, ...	2	4	-	-	4
Snow ploughs, ...	1	-	-	-	-

Railway Owned and Operated (by Electric Power).

Length of railway line, ...	15.711 miles.
Length of sidings, switches, etc., ...	.863 "
Total, computed as single track, ...	16.574 "

Railway Located Outside of Public Ways.

Length of railway line, ...	1.873 miles.

Names of the several cities and towns in which the railways operated by the company are located: Amherst, Sunderland and Pelham.

Grade Crossings with Railroads.

Grade Crossings with Railroads.	Number of Tracks at Crossing.	
	Railroad.	Railway.
Crossings of railways with railroads at grade (1 in number), viz.:		
With New London Northern Railroad, on Main Street, Amherst, .	1	1

Number of above crossings at which *frogs* are inserted in the tracks, . 1

ACCIDENTS TO PERSONS.

(A detailed statement of each accident is on file in the office of the Board.)

KILLED AND INJURED.	FROM CAUSES BEYOND THEIR OWN CONTROL.		FROM THEIR OWN MISCONDUCT OR CARELESSNESS.		TOTAL.	
	Killed.	Injured.	Killed.	Injured.	Killed.	Injured.
Passengers,	-	2	-	1	-	3
Employees,	-	-	-	-	-	-
Other persons,	-	-	-	1	-	1
TOTALS,	-	2	-	2	-	4

CORPORATE NAME AND ADDRESS OF THE COMPANY.

AMHERST & SUNDERLAND STREET RAILWAY COMPANY,
AMHERST, MASS.

NAMES AND BUSINESS ADDRESS OF PRINCIPAL OFFICERS.

Walter D. Cowls, *President*, North Amherst, Mass. Mason A. Dickinson, *Vice-President* and *Treasurer*, Amherst, Mass. Charles H. Edwards, *Clerk of Corporation*, Amherst, Mass. Heman M. Aldrich, *Superintendent*, Amherst, Mass.

NAMES AND RESIDENCE OF BOARD OF DIRECTORS.

Walter D. Cowls, North Amherst, Mass. Mason A. Dickinson, Amherst, Mass. Theodore L. Paige, Amherst, Mass. Charles Fred Deuel, Amherst, Mass. Edward D. Marsh, Amherst, Mass. Henry B. Edwards, Amherst, Mass. Frederick L. Whitmore, Sunderland, Mass.

We hereby certify that the statements contained in the foregoing report are full, just and true.

WALTER D. COWLS,
MASON A. DICKINSON,
C. FRED DEUEL,
E. D. MARSH,
H. B. EDWARDS,
Directors.
MASON A. DICKINSON,
Treasurer.
H. M. ALDRICH,
Superintendent.

COMMONWEALTH OF MASSACHUSETTS.

HAMPSHIRE, ss. OCT. 28, 1904. Then personally appeared the above-named Mason A. Dickinson, C. Fred Deuel, E. D. Marsh, H. B. Edwards and Walter D. Cowls, and severally made oath that the foregoing certificate by them subscribed is, to the best of their knowledge and belief, true.

Before me, E. D. BANGS,
Justice of the Peace.

REPORT

OF THE

ATHOL & ORANGE STREET RAILWAY COMPANY

FOR THE YEAR ENDING SEPTEMBER 30, 1904.

GENERAL EXHIBIT FOR THE YEAR.		
Gross earnings from operation,		$39,513 80
Operating expenses,		25,307 90
GROSS INCOME ABOVE OPERATING EXPENSES,		$14,205 90
Charges upon income accrued during the year:		
Interest on funded debt,	$3,000 00	
Interest and discount on unfunded debts and loans,	23 06	
Taxes, State and local,	2,643 60	
TOTAL CHARGES AND DEDUCTIONS FROM INCOME,		5,666 66
NET DIVISIBLE INCOME,		$8,539 24
Dividends declared (8 per cent),		5,960 00
Surplus for the year ending September 30, 1904,		$2,579 24
Amount of surplus September 30, 1903,		20,245 07
TOTAL SURPLUS SEPTEMBER 30, 1904,		$22,824 31
EARNINGS FROM OPERATION.		
Receipts from passengers carried,		$39,388 80
Receipts from advertising in cars,		125 00
GROSS EARNINGS FROM OPERATION,		$39,513 80
EXPENSES OF OPERATION.		
General expenses:		
Salaries of general officers and clerks,		$1,596 00
General office expenses and supplies,		185 04
Insurance,		2,057 65
Other general expenses: amusements, etc.,		2,837 41
Maintenance of roadway and buildings:		
Repair of roadbed and track,		1,231 66
Repair of electric line construction,		429 46

Maintenance of equipment:		
Repair of cars and other vehicles,		$829 20
Repair of electric equipment of cars,		1,429 48
Transportation expenses:		
Cost of electric motive power,		6,074 84
Wages and compensation of persons employed in conducting transportation,		7,481 39
Removal of snow and ice,		479 00
Other transportation expenses: grease, oil and truckage freight,		676 77
TOTAL OPERATING EXPENSES,		$25,307 90

PROPERTY ACCOUNTS.

Additions to equipment:		
Additional cars (3 in number),	$6,065 80	
Electric equipment of same,	3,803 80	
TOTAL ADDITIONS TO EQUIPMENT,		$9,869 60

GENERAL BALANCE SHEET SEPTEMBER 30, 1904.

ASSETS.	DR.	
Cost railway:		
Roadbed and tracks,	$70,000 00	
Electric line construction, including poles, wiring, feeder lines, etc.,	17,893 46	
Engineering and other expenses incident to construction,	6,020 57	
TOTAL COST OF RAILWAY OWNED,		$93,914 03
Cost of equipment:		
Cars and other rolling stock and vehicles,	$16,877 04	
Electric equipment of same,	15,803 80	
Other items of equipment: generator, etc.,	4,641 74	
TOTAL COST OF EQUIPMENT OWNED,		37,322 58
Cost of land and buildings: land necessary for operation of railway,		8,000 00
Other permanent property: park, buildings, etc.,		17,000 00
TOTAL PERMANENT INVESTMENTS,		$156,236 61
Cash and current assets: cash,		1,087 70
Miscellaneous assets: materials and supplies,		750 00
TOTAL,		$158,074 31

LIABILITIES.	CR.
Capital stock,	$74,500 00
Funded debt,	60,000 00
Accrued liabilities: interest accrued and not yet due,	750 00
Profit and loss balance (surplus),	22,824 31
TOTAL,	$158,074 31

Capital Stock.

Capital stock authorized by law,	$74,500 00	
Capital stock authorized by votes of company,	74,500 00	
Capital stock issued and outstanding,		$74,500 00
Number of shares issued and outstanding,	745	
Number of stockholders,	10	
Number of stockholders in Massachusetts,	9	
Amount of stock held in Massachusetts,	$73,500 00	

Funded Debt.

Description of Bonds.	Rate of Interest.	Date of Maturity.	Amount Outstanding.	Interest Paid during the Year.
	Per Cent.			
First mortgage bonds,	5	Jan. 1, 1915,	$60,000 00	$3,000 00

Volume of Traffic, etc.

Number of passengers paying revenue carried during the year,	817,396
Number carried per mile of main railway track operated,	118,808
Number of car miles run,	143,984
Average number of persons employed,	16

Description of Equipment.

Description of Equipment.	Equipped for Electric Power.	Equipped with Electric Heaters.	Number of Motors.
Cars — Passenger Service.			
Box passenger cars,	8	8	16
Open passenger cars,	5	-	10
Totals,	13	8	26
Snow ploughs,	1	-	2

Miscellaneous Equipment.

Highway vehicles: trolley or tower wagon,	1

Railway Owned and Operated (by Electric Power).

Length of railway line,	6.880 miles.
Length of sidings, switches, etc.,	.440 "
Total, computed as single track,	7.320 "

CORPORATE NAME AND ADDRESS OF THE COMPANY.

ATHOL & ORANGE STREET RAILWAY COMPANY,

ATHOL, MASS.

NAMES AND BUSINESS ADDRESS OF PRINCIPAL OFFICERS.

George D. Bates, *President*, Athol, Mass. Albert N. Ellis, *Treasurer and Clerk of Corporation*, Athol, Mass. Arthur F. Tyler, *Auditor*, Athol, Mass. Wilson D. Smith, *General Manager and Superintendent*, Athol, Mass.

NAMES AND RESIDENCE OF BOARD OF DIRECTORS.

George D. Bates, Athol, Mass. Hollis M. Slate, Athol, Mass. Arthur F. Tyler, Athol, Mass. Wilson D. Smith, Athol, Mass. William D. Luey, Worcester, Mass. John W. Wheeler, Orange, Mass. Warren M. King, Northampton, Mass.

We hereby certify that the statements contained in the foregoing report are full, just and true.

GEORGE D. BATES,
HOLLIS M. SLATE,
ARTHUR F. TYLER,
WILSON D. SMITH,
WILLIAM D. LUEY,
Directors.
ALBERT N. ELLIS,
Treasurer.
WILSON D. SMITH,
Superintendent.

COMMONWEALTH OF MASSACHUSETTS.

WORCESTER, SS. ATHOL, Oct. 3, 1904. Then personally appeared the above-named George D. Bates, Hollis M. Slate, Arthur F. Tyler, Wilson D. Smith, and Albert N. Ellis, and severally made oath that the foregoing certificate by them subscribed is, to the best of their knowledge and belief, true.

Before me, PARKE B. SWIFT,
Justice of the Peace.

COMMONWEALTH OF MASSACHUSETTS.

WORCESTER, SS. OCT. 6, 1904. Then personally appeared the above-named Wm. D. Luey, and made oath that the foregoing certificate subscribed by him is, to the best of his knowledge and belief, true.

Before me, HENRY A. MARSH,
Justice of the Peace.

REPORT

OF THE

BERKSHIRE STREET RAILWAY COMPANY

For the Year ending September 30, 1904.

General Exhibit for the Year.

Gross earnings from operation,		$193,557 16
Operating expenses,		105,921 58
Net Earnings from Operation,		$87,635 58
Miscellaneous income: parks, athletic field and miscellaneous receipts,		6,737 77
Gross Income above Operating Expenses,		$94,373 35
Charges upon income accrued during the year:		
Interest on funded debt,	$40,000 00	
Interest and discount on unfunded debts and loans,	12,500 00	
Taxes, State and local, . . . $7,088 40		
Taxes, commutation, . . . 2,640 71	9,729 11	
Other deductions from income: park expenses,	5,636 05	
Total Charges and Deductions from Income,		67,865 16
Surplus for the year ending September 30, 1904,		$26,508 19
Amount of surplus September 30, 1903,		45,939 52
Total Surplus September 30, 1904,		$72,447 71

Earnings from Operation.

Receipts from passengers carried,	$192,539 85
Receipts from carriage of newspapers,	588 45
Receipts from rentals of buildings and other property,	428 86
Gross Earnings from Operation,	$193,557 16

Expenses of Operation.

General expenses:	
Salaries of general officers and clerks,	$5,489 28
General office expenses and supplies,	847 25
Legal expenses,	751 12
Insurance,	3,330 00
Other general expenses: sundry operating expenses,	1,638 60

Maintenance of roadway and buildings:		
Repair of roadbed and track,		$2,213 03
Repair of electric line construction,		954 64
Repair of buildings and fences,		203 83
Maintenance of equipment:		
Repair of cars and other vehicles,		2,852 96
Repair of electric equipment of cars,		5,413 45
Renewal of horses, harnesses, shoeing, etc.,		29 48
Provender and stabling for horses,		681 60
Transportation expenses:		
Cost of electric motive power,		33,855 97
Wages and compensation of persons employed in conducting transportation,		39,730 08
Removal of snow and ice,		1,949 47
Damages for injuries to persons and property,		2,734 45
Other transportation expenses: sundry expenses of transportation,		3,246 37
TOTAL OPERATING EXPENSES,		$105,921 58
PROPERTY ACCOUNTS.		
Additions to railway:		
Completion of tracks, roadway,	$22,832 70	
Completion of new electric line construction,	11,107 59	
TOTAL ADDITIONS TO RAILWAY,		$33,940 29
Additions to equipment:		
Additional equipment of cars,	$12,481 39	
Electric equipment of same,	10,162 23	
Other additions to equipment:		
Office furniture,	41 85	
Stable equipment,	51 00	
TOTAL ADDITIONS TO EQUIPMENT,		22,736 47
Additions to land and buildings:		
Additional land necessary for operation of railway,	$275 18	
New electric power stations, including machinery, etc.,	41,255 98	
Other new buildings necessary for operation of railway,	19,449 21	
TOTAL ADDITIONS TO LAND AND BUILDINGS,		60,980 37
Additions to other permanent property: parks and athletic field,		9,587 81
TOTAL ADDITIONS TO PROPERTY ACCOUNTS,		$127,244 94
GENERAL BALANCE SHEET SEPTEMBER 30, 1904.		
ASSETS.	DR.	
Cost of railway:		
Roadbed and tracks,	$1,011,704 36	
Electric line construction, including poles, wiring, feeder lines, etc.,	171,033 08	
Interest accrued during construction of railway,	48,245 95	
Engineering and other expenses incident to construction,	95,764 13	
TOTAL COST OF RAILWAY OWNED,		$1,326,747 52

Cost of equipment:		
Cars and other rolling stock and vehicles,	$148,034 19	
Electric equipment of same,	135,435 61	
Horses and stable equipment,	158 44	
Other items of equipment: office furniture,	1,913 47	
TOTAL COST OF EQUIPMENT OWNED,*		$285,541 71
Cost of land and buildings:		
Land necessary for operation of railway,	$52,317 58	
Electric power stations, including equipment,	347,205 98	
Other buildings necessary for operation of railway,	70,518 29	
TOTAL COST OF LAND AND BUILDINGS OWNED,*		470,041 85
Other permanent property: parks,		34,912 35
TOTAL PERMANENT INVESTMENTS,		$2,117,243 43
Cash and current assets:		
Cash,	$33,753 55	
Bills and accounts receivable,	17,412 72	
Other cash and current assets: prepaid taxes, insurance and interest,	7,211 35	
TOTAL CASH AND CURRENT ASSETS,		58,377 62
Miscellaneous assets: materials and supplies,		27,560 03
TOTAL,		$2,203,181 08

LIABILITIES.		CR.
Capital stock,		$976,600 00
Funded debt,		800,000 00
Current liabilities:		
Loans and notes payable,	$314,269 99	
Audited vouchers and accounts,	23,579 09	
Miscellaneous current liabilities: outstanding tickets,	260 52	
TOTAL CURRENT LIABILITIES,		338,109 60
Accrued liabilities:		
Interest accrued and not yet due,	$13,333 33	
Taxes accrued and not yet due,	2,690 44	
TOTAL ACCRUED LIABILITIES,		16,023 77
Profit and loss balance (surplus),		72,447 71
TOTAL,		$2,203,181 08

CAPITAL STOCK.

Capital stock authorized by law,	$1,000,000 00	
Capital stock authorized by votes of company,	1,000,000 00	
Capital stock issued and outstanding,		$976,600 00
Number of shares issued and outstanding,	9,766	
Number of stockholders,	141	
Number of stockholders in Massachusetts,	127	
Amount of stock held in Massachusetts,	$906,000 00	

* Two hundred dollars for tower wagon transferred from stable equipment account to cars and other vehicles account. Three thousand one hundred dollars for land at Berkshire Park transferred from land account to Berkshire Park account.

Funded Debt.

Description of Bonds.	Rate of Interest.	Date of Maturity.	Amount Outstanding.	Interest Paid during the Year.
	Per Cent.			
First mortgage gold bonds,	5	June 2, 1922,	$800,000 00	$40,000 00

Volume of Traffic, etc.

Number of passengers paying revenue carried during the year,	3,878,770
Number carried per mile of main railway track operated,	95,038
Number of car miles run,	917,391
Average number of persons employed,	116

Description of Equipment.

Description of Equipment.	Equipped for Electric Power.	Not Equipped.	Equipped with Fenders.	Equipped with Electric Heaters.	Equipped with Stoves.	Number of Motors.
Cars — Passenger Service.						
Box passenger cars,	19	-	19	19	-	68
Open passenger cars,	14	-	14	-	-	52
Total,	33	-	33	19	-	120
Cars — Other Service.						
Platform freight cars,	-	1	-	-	-	-
Snow ploughs,	4	-	-	-	4	6

Miscellaneous Equipment.

Other railway rolling stock: 1 hand car, 1 velocipede car,	2
Highway vehicles: 2 wagons for line work, 1 tower wagon,	3

Railway Owned and Operated (by Electric Power).

Length of railway line,	40.813 miles.
Length of sidings, switches, etc.,	1 421 "
Total, computed as single track,	42.234 "

Railway Located Outside of Public Ways.

Length of railway line, ...	12.726 miles.

Names of several cities and towns in which the railways operated by the company are located: Cheshire, Lanesboro, Pittsfield, Lenox, Lee, Stockbridge, Great Barrington.

Grade Crossings with Railroads.

Grade Crossings with Railroads.	Number of Tracks at Crossing.	
	Railroad.	Railway.
Crossings of railways with railroads at grade (2 in number), viz.:		
With Boston & Albany Railroad at Dalton Road, Pittsfield, . .	1	1
With New York, New Haven & Hartford Railroad at Pleasant Street, Lee, ...	1	1
Total Number of Tracks at Crossings, ...	2	2

Accidents to Persons.

(A detailed statement of each accident is on file in the office of the Board.)

Killed and Injured.	From Causes beyond their own Control.		From their own Misconduct or Carelessness.		Total.	
	Killed.	Injured.	Killed.	Injured.	Killed.	Injured.
Passengers, ...	-	-	-	1	-	1
Employees, ...	-	-	-	-	-	-
Other persons, ...	-	-	2	4	2	4
Totals, ...	-	-	2	5	2	5

Corporate Name and Address of the Company.

BERKSHIRE STREET RAILWAY COMPANY,

Pittsfield, Mass.

Names and Business Address of Principal Officers.

Ralph D. Gillett, *President*, Westfield, Mass. Arthur W. Eaton, *Treasurer*, Pittsfield, Mass. Franklin Weston, *Clerk of Corporation*, Dalton, Mass. Charles E. Hibbard, *General Counsel*, Pittsfield, Mass. Henry C. Page, *General Manager*, Pittsfield, Mass.

Names and Residence of Board of Directors.

Ralph D. Gillett, Westfield, Mass. Arthur W. Eaton, Pittsfield, Mass. Franklin Weston, Dalton, Mass. Thomas Post, Lenox, Mass. Thomas D. Peck, Pittsfield, Mass. John P. Pomeroy, Great Barrington, Mass.

We hereby certify that the statements contained in the foregoing report are full, just and true.

RALPH D. GILLETT,
A. W. EATON,
JOHN P. POMEROY,
THOMAS POST,
FRANKLIN WESTON,
THOMAS D. PECK,
Directors.
A. W. EATON,
Treasurer.
H. C. PAGE,
General Manager.

COMMONWEALTH OF MASSACHUSETTS.

BERKSHIRE, ss. Nov. 2, 1904. Then personally appeared the above-named Ralph D. Gillett, A. W. Eaton, John P. Pomeroy, Thomas Post, Franklin Weston, Thomas D. Peck and H. C. Page, and severally made oath that the foregoing certificate by them subscribed, is, to the best of their knowledge and belief, true.

Before me, A. D. ROBINSON,
Notary Public.

REPORT

OF THE

BLUE HILL STREET RAILWAY COMPANY

For the Year ending September 30, 1904.

General Exhibit for the Year.			
Gross earnings from operation,			$72,864 10
Operating expenses,			59,638 24
Gross Income above Operating Expenses,			$13,225 86
Charges upon income accrued during the year:			
Interest on funded debt,		$7,864 58	
Interest and discount on unfunded debts and loans,		8,469 42	
Taxes, State and local,	$2,522 03		
Taxes, commutation,	728 61		
		3,250 64	
Total Charges and Deductions from Income,			19,584 64
Deficit for the year ending September 30, 1904,			$6,358 78
Amount of deficit September 30, 1903,			22,744 05
Total Deficit September 30, 1904,			$29,102 83

Earnings from Operation.	
Receipts from passengers carried,	$72,450 30
Receipts from carriage of mails,	200 00
Receipts from advertising in cars,	210 82
Receipts from interest on deposits,	2 98
Gross Earnings from Operation,	$72,864 10

Expenses of Operation.	
General expenses:	
Salaries of general officers and clerks,	$2,991 00
General office expenses and supplies,	415 64
Legal expenses,	23 45
Insurance,	1,644 06
Other general expenses: advertising and general expenses,	1,560 59
Maintenance of roadway and buildings:	
Repair of roadbed and track,	1,167 00
Repair of electric line construction,	532 39
Repair of buildings,	180 67

Maintenance of equipment:		
Repair of cars and other vehicles,		$2,099 05
Repair of electric equipment of cars,		4,457 29
Transportation expenses:		
Cost of electric motive power, $19,793.01; less power sold, $2,907.36; net,		16,885 65
Wages and compensation of persons employed in conducting transportation,		22,704 27
Removal of snow and ice,		1,571 97
Damages for injuries to persons and property,		1,800 00
Tolls for trackage over other railways,		546 56
Rentals of buildings and other property,		203 66
Other transportation expenses: sanding and oiling tracks, etc.,		854 99
TOTAL OPERATING EXPENSES,		$59,638 24

PROPERTY ACCOUNTS.

Additions to railway:		
Extension of tracks (length, 10,143 feet),	$62,845 64	
New electric line construction (length, 10,143 feet),	12,232 33	
Other additions to railway:		
Organization,	4,398 99	
Right of way,	14,571 78	
Interest during construction,	13,750 00	
TOTAL ADDITIONS TO RAILWAY,		$107,798 74
Additions to equipment:		
Additional cars (12 in number),	$32,618 26	
Electric equipment of same,	20,895 24	
Other additional rolling stock and vehicles,	1,854 77	
Other additions to equipment:		
Tools and instruments,	267 69	
Office furniture and fixtures,	103 34	
TOTAL ADDITIONS TO EQUIPMENT,		55,739 30
Additions to land and buildings:		
New electric power stations, including machinery, etc.,	$546 59	
Other new buildings necessary for operation of railway,	5,560 84	
TOTAL ADDITIONS TO LAND AND BUILDINGS,		6,107 43
TOTAL ADDITIONS TO PROPERTY ACCOUNTS,		$169,645 47
Deductions from property accounts (property sold or reduced in valuation and credited to property accounts): cars sold (4),		6,130 00
NET ADDITION TO PROPERTY ACCOUNTS FOR THE YEAR,		$163,515 47

GENERAL BALANCE SHEET SEPTEMBER 30, 1904.

ASSETS.	DR.	
Cost of railway:		
Roadbed and tracks,	$269,866 71	
Electric line construction, including poles, wiring, feeder lines, etc.,	58,839 47	

Cost of railway — *Concluded.*		
Interest accrued during construction of railway,	$13,750 00	
Other items of railway cost: organization and right of way,	38,969 61	
TOTAL COST OF RAILWAY OWNED,		$381,425 79
Cost of equipment:		
Cars and other rolling stock and vehicles,	$72,094 31	
Electric equipment of same,	57,934 81	
Office furniture and fixtures,	535 28	
Other items of equipment: shop tools and machinery,	521 08	
TOTAL COST OF EQUIPMENT OWNED,		131,085 48
Cost of land and buildings:		
Land necessary for operation of railway,	$2,000 00	
Electric power stations, including equipment,	88,427 28	
Other buildings necessary for operation of railway,	20,906 31	
TOTAL COST OF LAND AND BUILDINGS OWNED,		111,333 59
TOTAL PERMANENT INVESTMENTS,		$623,844 86
Cash and current assets:		
Cash,	$27,070 76	
Bills and accounts receivable,	1,039 65	
Other cash and current assets:		
Unexpired insurance,	552 88	
Interest paid in advance,	1,881 32	
TOTAL CASH AND CURRENT ASSETS,		30,544 61
Miscellaneous assets: materials and supplies,		9,103 80
Profit and loss balance (deficit),		29,102 83
TOTAL,		$692,596 10

LIABILITIES.	CR.	
Capital stock,		$300,000 00
Funded debt,		250,000 00
Current liabilities:		
Loans and notes payable,	$135,000 00	
Audited vouchers and accounts,	6,255 77	
Salaries and wages,	922 07	
TOTAL CURRENT LIABILITIES,		142,177 84
Sinking and other special funds: injury fund,		418 26
TOTAL,		$692,596 10

CAPITAL STOCK.

Capital stock authorized by law,	$300,000 00	
Capital stock authorized by votes of company,	300,000 00	
Capital stock issued and outstanding,		$300,000 00
Number of shares issued and outstanding,	3,000	
Number of stockholders,	60	
Number of stockholders in Massachusetts,	57	
Amount of stock held in Massachusetts,	$292,500 00	

Funded Debt.

Description of Bonds.	Rate of Interest.	Date of Maturity.	Amount Outstanding.	Interest Paid during the Year.
First mortgage 20-year gold bonds,	Per Cent. 5	Oct. 1, 1923,	$250,000 00	$7,864 58

Volume of Traffic, etc.

Number of passengers paying revenue carried during the year,	1,453,169
Number carried per mile of main railway track operated,	87,646
Number of car miles run,	356,472
Average number of persons employed,	60

Description of Equipment.

Description of Equipment.	Equipped for Electric Power.	Not Equipped.	Equipped with Fenders.	Equipped with Electric Heaters.	Number of Motors.
Cars — Passenger Service.					
Box passenger cars,	12	-	12	12	44
Open passenger cars,	16	-	16	-	36
Total,	28	-	28	12	80
Cars — Other Service.					
Platform freight cars,	-	1	-	-	-
Work cars,	-	10	-	-	-
Total,	-	11	-	-	-
Snow ploughs,	2	-	-	-	-

Miscellaneous Equipment.

Highway vehicles: trolley wagon,	1

Railway Owned, Leased and Operated (by Electric Power).

Railway Owned, etc.	Owned.	Trackage over Other Railways.	Total Operated.
	Miles.	Miles.	Miles.
Length of railway line,	13.770	.090	13.860
Length of second main track,	2.630	.090	2.720
Total Length of Main Track,	16.400	.180	16.580
Length of sidings, switches, etc.,	1.110	-	1.110
Total, computed as Single Track,	17.510	.180	17.690

Railway Located Outside of Public Ways.

Length of railway line,	.640 miles.
Length of second main track,	.278 "
Total length of main track,	.918 "

Names of the several cities and towns in which the railways operated by the company are located: Stoughton, Canton and Milton; .409 mile of track in town of Hyde Park not operated.

Grade Crossings with Railroads.

Grade Crossings with Railroads.	Number of Tracks at Crossing.	
	Railroad.	Railway.
Crossings of railways with railroads at grade (1 in number), viz.:—		
With New York, New Haven & Hartford Railroad, on Washington Street, Canton,	2	1
With Kinsley Iron & Machine Company's private crossing, operated by oxen, on Washington Street, Canton,	2	1
Total Number of Tracks at Crossings,	4	2

Number of above crossings at which *frogs* are inserted in the tracks, . 3

Accidents to Persons.

(A detailed statement of each accident is on file in the office of the Board.)

Killed and Injured.	From Causes Beyond their own Control.		From their own Misconduct or Carelessness.		Total.	
	Killed.	Injured.	Killed.	Injured.	Killed.	Injured.
Passengers,	-	13	-	2	-	15
Employees,	-	-	-	1	-	1
Other persons,	-	-	1	-	1	-
Totals,	-	13	1	3	1	16

Corporate Name and Address of the Company.

BLUE HILL STREET RAILWAY COMPANY,

84 State Street, Boston, Mass.

Names and Business Address of Principal Officers.

Charles H. French, *President*, Canton, Mass. Frederick S. Pratt, *Vice-President*, 84 State Street, Boston, Mass. Edmund J. B. Huntoon, *Second Vice-President*, Canton Junction, Mass. A. Stuart Pratt, *Treasurer*, 84 State Street, Boston, Mass. Henry R. Hayes, *Clerk of Corporation*, 84 State Street, Boston, Mass. Stone & Webster, *General Managers*, 84 State Street, Boston, Mass. Preston Player, *Local Manager*, Canton Junction, Mass. Albert H. Walcott, *Superintendent*, Canton, Mass.

NAMES AND RESIDENCE OF BOARD OF DIRECTORS.

Henry G. Bradley, 84 State Street, Boston, Mass. Allan Forbes, Milton, Mass. Chas. H. French, Canton, Mass. Edmund J. B. Huntoon, Canton Junction, Mass. Frederick S. Pratt, Newton, Mass. Charles A. Stone, Newton, Mass. Arthur Wainwright, Milton, Mass. Charles F. Wallace, Wellesley Hills, Mass. Edwin S. Webster, Newton, Mass.

We hereby certify that the statements contained in the foregoing report are full, just and true.

CHARLES H. FRENCH,
CHARLES F. WALLACE,
EDMUND J. B. HUNTOON,
FRED'K S. PRATT,
CHARLES A. STONE,
ALLAN FORBES,
Directors.
A. STUART PRATT,
Treasurer.
ALBERT H. WALCOTT,
Superintendent.

COMMONWEALTH OF MASSACHUSETTS.

SUFFOLK, SS. Nov. 2, 1904. Then personally appeared the above-named Charles H. French, Charles F. Wallace, Edmund J. B. Huntoon, Fred'k S. Pratt, Charles A. Stone, Allan Forbes, A. Stuart Pratt and Albert H. Walcott, and severally made oath that the foregoing certificate by them subscribed is, to the best of their knowledge and belief, true.

Before me, JOHN W. HALLOWELL,
Justice of the Peace.

REPORT

OF THE

BOSTON & CHELSEA RAILROAD COMPANY

FOR THE YEAR ENDING SEPTEMBER 30, 1904.

[Leased to the Boston Elevated and operated by the Boston & Northern.]

GENERAL EXHIBIT FOR THE YEAR.

Rental received from lease of railway,	$7,260 00
Dividends declared (6 per cent),	$7,260 00

GENERAL BALANCE SHEET SEPTEMBER 30, 1904.

ASSETS. DR.	
Cost of railway,	$121,000 00
TOTAL,	$121,000 00
LIABILITIES. CR.	
Capital stock,	$121,000 00
TOTAL,	$121,000 00

CAPITAL STOCK.

Capital stock authorized by law,	$300,000 00	
Capital stock authorized by votes of company,	121,000 00	
Capital stock issued and outstanding,		$121,000 00
Number of shares issued and outstanding,	2,420	
Number of stockholders,	100	
Number of stockholders in Massachusetts,	76	
Amount of stock held in Massachusetts,	$97,550 00	

RAILWAY OWNED.

Length of railway line,	4 116 miles.
Length of sidings, switches, etc.,	.038 "
Total, computed as single track,	4.154 "

Names of the several cities and towns in which the railway owned by the company is located: Chelsea and (Charlestown District) Boston.

Corporate Name and Address of the Company.

BOSTON & CHELSEA RAILROAD COMPANY,

Sullivan Square Terminal, Boston, Mass.

Names and Business Address of Principal Officers.

William G. Wheildon, *President*, Boston, Mass. John H. Studley, *Treasurer and Clerk of Corporation*, Sullivan Square Terminal, Charlestown, Mass.

Names and Residence of Board of Directors.

William G. Wheildon, Boston, Mass. Charles E. Fuller, Boston, Mass. David H. Coolidge, Boston, Mass. T. Quincy Browne, Concord, Mass. John H. Studley, Malden, Mass.

We hereby certify that the statements contained in the foregoing report are full, just and true.

WILLIAM G. WHEILDON,
DAVID H. COOLIDGE,
JOHN H. STUDLEY,
Directors.
JOHN H. STUDLEY,
Treasurer.

Commonwealth of Massachusetts.

Suffolk, ss. Boston, Nov. 4, 1904. Then personally appeared the above-named William G. Wheildon, David H. Coolidge and John H. Studley, and severally made oath that the foregoing certificate by them subscribed is, to the best of their knowledge and belief, true,

Before me, GUSTAF A. DANIELSON,
Justice of the Peace.

REPORT

OF THE

BOSTON ELEVATED RAILWAY COMPANY

For the Year ending September 30, 1904.

General Exhibit for the Year.

Gross earnings from operation,			$12,391,353 07
Operating expenses,			8,631,553 08
Net Earnings from Operation,			$3,759,799 99
Miscellaneous income: interest from special deposits,			45,240 72
Gross Income above Operating Expenses,			$3,805,040 71
Charges upon income accrued during the year:			
Interest on funded debt of West End Street Railway Company,		$629,599 90	
Taxes, State and local,	$818,531 39		
Taxes, commutation,	106,887 28		
		925,418 67	
Rentals of leased railways:			
West End Street Railway Company,	$1,180,751 60		
Old Colony Street Railway Company,	33,111 57		
Somerville Horse Railroad Company,	9,180 00		
		1,223,043 17	
Other deductions from income: rent of subway,	$216,948 55		
Less amount collected of Boston & Northern Street Railway,	19,742 29		
		197,206 26	
Total Charges and Deductions from Income,			2,975,268 00
Net Divisible Income,			$829,772 71
Dividends declared (6 per cent),			798,000 00
Surplus for the year ending September 30, 1904,			$31,772 71
Amount of surplus September 30, 1903,			2,327,687 94
Total Surplus September 30, 1904,			$2,359,460 65

Earnings from Operation.

Receipts from passengers carried,	$12,078,800 39
Receipts from carriage of mails,	24,015 04
Receipts from tolls for use of tracks by other companies,	47,990 04
Receipts from rentals of buildings and other property,	116,655 56
Receipts from advertising in cars and stations,	90,705 41
Receipts from interest on deposits,	29,204 07
Other earnings from operation: miscellaneous,	3,982 56
Gross Earnings from Operation,	$12,391,353 07

Expenses of Operation.

General expenses:	
Salaries of general officers and clerks,	$208,591 81
General office expenses and supplies,	95,462 69
Legal expenses,	254,833 66
Insurance,	108,479 29
Other general expenses:	
Telephone expenses, $24,994 31; subscriptions and gratuities, $81,566.78,	106,561 09
Advertising, $10,218.17; West End Street Railway Company organization, $9,300; miscellaneous, $94,409.90,	113,928 07
Maintenance of roadway and buildings:	
Repair of roadbed and track,	546,129 25
Repair of electric line construction,	170,640 42
Repair of buildings,	112,721 57
Maintenance of equipment:	
Repair of cars and other vehicles,	489,217 83
Repair of electric equipment of cars,	325,094 53
Renewal of horses, harnesses, shoeing, etc.,	7,964 29
Provender and stabling for horses,	24,265 17
Transportation expenses:	
Cost of electric motive power, $984,454.29; less power sold, $41,716.45; net,	942,737 84
Wages and compensation of persons employed in conducting transportation,	3,912,151 17
Removal of snow and ice,	284,476 26
Damages for injuries to persons and property,	563,013 82
Tolls for trackage over other railways,	8,882 92
Rentals of buildings and other property,	49,164 97
Other transportation expenses: car service supplies, $40,948.91; miscellaneous car service expenses, $175,706.99; station and signal system expenses, $73,619.02; cleaning tracks, $16,961.51,	307,236 43
Total Operating Expenses,	$8,631,553 08

Property Accounts.

Additions to railway:		
Extension of tracks, including foundations, structure, etc.,	$2,154,877 79	
New electric line construction,	10 58	
Other additions to railway: engineering and other expenses incident to construction,	24,851 04	
Total Additions to Railway,		$2,179,739 41

Additions to equipment:		
Additional cars (24 in number),	$142,850 18	
Electric equipment of same,	78,738 15	
Other additions to equipment: machinery, tools, etc.,	9,578 86	
TOTAL ADDITIONS TO EQUIPMENT,		$231,167 19
Additions to land and buildings:		
Additional land necessary for operation of railway,	$179,087 33	
Additional construction and equipment of power stations,	44,557 08	
Other new buildings necessary for operation of railway,	8,601 97	
TOTAL ADDITIONS TO LAND AND BUILDINGS,		232,246 38
Additions to other permanent property: subway and tunnel construction and equipment,		159,234 41
TOTAL ADDITIONS TO PROPERTY ACCOUNTS,		$2,802,387 39

GENERAL BALANCE SHEET SEPTEMBER 30, 1904.

ASSETS.	DR.	
Cost of railway:		
Roadbed and tracks, including foundations, structure, etc.,	$6,396,234 52	
Electric line construction, including poles, wiring, feeder lines, etc.,	194,807 35	
Engineering and other expenses incident to construction,	722,056 89	
TOTAL COST OF RAILWAY OWNED,		$7,313,098 76
Cost of equipment:		
Cars and other rolling stock and vehicles,	$835,054 00	
Electric equipment of same,	911,485 36	
Other items of equipment: machinery, tools, etc.,	98,960 73	
TOTAL COST OF EQUIPMENT OWNED,		1,845,500 09
Cost of land and buildings:		
Land necessary for operation of railway,	$2,371,831 95	
Electric power stations, including equipment,	1,515,953 16	
Other buildings necessary for operation of railway,	1,449,359 79	
TOTAL COST OF LAND AND BUILDINGS OWNED,		5,337,144 90
Other permanent property: subway and tunnel construction and equipment,		319,577 79
TOTAL PERMANENT INVESTMENTS,		$14,815,321 54
Cash and current assets:		
Cash,	$2,059,456 56	
Bills and accounts receivable,	796,723 54	
Other cash and current assets:		
Stocks and bonds,	208,010 72	
Bonds deposited with State Treasurer,	500,000 00	
TOTAL CASH AND CURRENT ASSETS,		3,564,190 82

Miscellaneous assets:		
Materials and supplies,	$662,147 56	
Other assets and property:		
Somerville Horse Railroad account,	102,851 11	
Old Colony Street Railway Company property account,	300,508 87	
West End Street Railway Company property account, $218,573.13; open account, $760,266.34,	978,839 47	
Total Miscellaneous Assets,		$2,044,347 01
Total,		$20,423,859 37

Liabilities.	Cr.	
Capital stock,		$13,300,000 00
Current liabilities:		
Audited vouchers and accounts,	$288,529 84	
Salaries and wages,	131,329 47	
Dividends not called for,	12,834 75	
Matured interest coupons unpaid (including coupons due October 1),	20,017 50	
Rentals due and unpaid (including rentals due October 1),	333,873 75	
Miscellaneous current liabilities: outstanding tickets and checks,	25,037 33	
Total Current Liabilities,		811,622 64
Accrued liabilities:		
Interest accrued and not yet due,	$114,513 33	
Taxes accrued and not yet due,	908,455 60	
Rentals accrued and not yet due,	142,849 25	
Miscellaneous accrued liabilities: West End Street Railway Company lease account,	1,207,201 98	
Total Accrued Liabilities,		2,373,020 16
Sinking and other special funds:		
Damage fund,	$598,015 93	
Insurance fund,	381,739 99	
Depreciation fund,	600,000 00	
Total Sinking and Other Special Funds,		1,579,755 92
Profit and loss balance (surplus),		2,359,460 65
Total,		$20,423,859 37

Capital Stock.		
Capital stock authorized by law,	$20,000,000 00	
Capital stock authorized by votes of company,	15,000,000 00	
Capital stock issued and outstanding,		$13,300,000 00
Number of shares issued and outstanding,	133,000	
Number of stockholders,	2,922	
Number of stockholders in Massachusetts,	2,510	
Amount of stock held in Massachusetts,	$10,945,300 00	

Sinking and Other Special Funds.

Amount September 30, 1903, of damage fund,	$598,015 93
Amount September 30, 1903, of insurance fund,	360,000 00
Amount September 30, 1903, of depreciation fund,	600,000 00
Total, September 30, 1903,	$1,558,015 93
Additions during the year to insurance fund,	21,739 99
Total Sinking and Other Special Funds, September 30, 1904,	$1,579,755 92

Volume of Traffic, etc.

Number of passengers paying revenue carried during the year,	241,681,945
Number carried per mile of main railway track operated,	614,404
Number of car miles run,	48,317,981
Average number of persons employed,	7,447

Description of Equipment Owned and Leased.

Description of Equipment.	Equipped for Electric Power.	Not Equipped.	Total Passenger Cars.	Equipped with Fenders.	Equipped with Electric Heaters.	Number of Motors.
Cars — Passenger Service.						
Box passenger cars,*	1,798	20	1,818	1,624	1,798	-
Open passenger cars,	1,542	5	1,547	1,542	-	-
Total,	3,340	25	3,365	3,166	1,798	4,715
Cars — Other Service.						
Mail cars,	12	-	-	12	12	24
Work cars,	10	24	-	34	-	24
Other cars,	-	4	-	-	-	-
Total,	22	28	-	46	12	48
Snow ploughs,	230	75	-	-	-	2

Miscellaneous Equipment.

Barges and omnibuses,	9
Carts and snow sleds,	827
Other railway rolling stock:	
Levellers, 61; road machines, 15; scrapers, 4,	80
Sweepers,	10

* Including 174 cars for elevated lines.

MISCELLANEOUS EQUIPMENT — Concluded.

Other highway vehicles:	
Buggies, 51; caravans and jiggers, 45,	96
Ambulance, 1; sleighs and pungs, 80,	81
Horses,	278
Other items of equipment: machinery, tools, etc.	

RAILWAY OWNED, LEASED AND OPERATED (BY ELECTRIC POWER).

RAILWAY OWNED, ETC.	Owned.	Held under Lease or Contract.	Trackage over Other Railways.	Total Owned, Leased, etc.	Total Operated.
ELEVATED.	Miles.	Miles.	Miles.	Miles.	Miles.
Length of railway line,	6.644	-	-	6.644	6.644
Length of second main track,	6.468	-	-	6.468	6.468
TOTAL LENGTH OF MAIN TRACK,	13.112	-	-	13.112	13.112
Length of sidings, switches, etc.,	2.903	-	-	2.903	2.903
TOTAL, COMPUTED AS SINGLE TRACK,	16.015	-	-	16.015	16.015
SURFACE.					
Length of railway line,	2.410	205.266	2.237	209.913	208.273
Length of second main track,	2.033	170.432	1.046	173.511	171.975
TOTAL LENGTH OF MAIN TRACK,	4.443	375.698	3.283	383.424	380.248
Length of sidings, switches, etc.,	3.683	41.704	-	45.387	42.963
TOTAL, COMPUTED AS SINGLE TRACK,	8.126	417.402	3.283	428.811	423.211

RAILWAY LOCATED OUTSIDE OF PUBLIC WAYS.

	Owned.	Operated.
	Miles.	Miles.
Length of railway line for elevated cars,	.461	.461
Length of railway line for surface cars,	.863	.863
Length of railway line for subway and tunnel cars,	1.411	2.523
Length of second main track for elevated cars,	.489	.489
Length of second main track for surface cars,	.862	.862
Length of second main track for subway and tunnel cars,	1.378	2.413
TOTAL LENGTH OF MAIN TRACK,	5.464	7.611

Names of the several cities and towns in which the railways operated by the company are located: Boston, Cambridge, Chelsea, Everett, Malden, Medford, Newton, Somerville, Arlington, Belmont, Brookline and Watertown.

Grade Crossings with Railroads.

Grade Crossings with Railroads.	Number of Tracks at Crossing.	
	Railroad.	Railway.
Crossings of railway with railroads at grade (59 in number), viz.: —		
With Boston & Albany Railroad:		
At Main Street, Cambridge,*	2	2
At Broadway, Cambridge,*	4	2
At Cambridge Street, Cambridge,*	2	2
At Massachusetts Avenue, Cambridge,*	3	2
At North Beacon Street, Brighton,*	1	1
At Saratoga Street, East Boston,*	2	1
At Sumner Street, East Boston,*	2	1
With Boston & Maine Railroad:		
At Saratoga Street, East Boston, Eastern Division,*	2	1
At Sumner Street, East Boston, Eastern Division,*	5	1
At Main Street, Charlestown, Southern Division,*	2	2
At Main Street, Malden, Eastern Division,	2	2
At Pleasant Street, Malden, Western Division,	2	2
At Holland Street, Somerville, Southern Division,	2	2
At Massachusetts Avenue, Cambridge, Southern Division,	2	2
At Massachusetts Avenue, Arlington, Southern Division,	2	2
At Beverly Street, Boston & Maine Yard,*†	1	2
At Newton Street, Somerville, Fitchburg Division,	2	1
At Webster Avenue, Somerville, Fitchburg Division,	2	1
At Warren Avenue, Charlestown, Fitchburg Division,*	2	2
At Somerville Avenue, Somerville, Fitchburg Division,*‡	5	1
At Somerville Avenue, Somerville, Fitchburg Division,	2	1
At Somerville Avenue, Somerville,*	1	1
At Mt. Auburn Street, Watertown,	2	1
At Arsenal Street to Watertown Arsenal,*	2	2
With New York, New Haven & Hartford Railroad:		
At Dudley Street, Midland Division,	2	2
At Neponset Avenue,	1	2
Dorchester Avenue, at Shawmut Branch,	1	2
With Union Freight Railroad:		
Atlantic Avenue, at Summer Street,*	1	6
Atlantic Avenue, at High Street,*	1	2
Atlantic Avenue, at Broad Street,*	1	2
Atlantic Avenue, at Commercial Wharf,*	2	1
Atlantic Avenue, at Lewis Wharf,*	2	1
Atlantic Avenue, at Fleet Street,*	2	1
Atlantic Avenue, at Kneeland Street,*	1	2
Atlantic Avenue, at Beach Street,*	1	4
Atlantic Avenue, at Clinton Market,*	2	1
Atlantic Avenue, at Union Freight Railroad Yard,*	3	1
Commercial Street, at Eastern Avenue,*	1	1
Commercial Street, at Sargent's Wharf,*	1	1
Commercial Street, at Union Wharf,*	1	1
Commercial Street, at Slate Wharf,*	1	1
Commercial Street, at Battery Street,*	2	5
Commercial Street, at Constitution Wharf,*	1	1
Commercial Street, at Harris Wharf,*	1	1
Commercial Street, at Hanover Street,*	2	2
Commercial Street, at gas house,*	1	1
Commercial Street, at Battery Wharf,*	1	1
Causeway Street, at Charlestown Street,*	1	5
Causeway Street, at Boston & Maine Railroad Yard, Fitchburg Division,*	1	2
Causeway Street, at Canal Street,*	1	4
Causeway Street, west of Charlestown Street,*	1	1
Causeway Street, at Medford Street,*	1	1
Causeway Street, at Haverhill Street,*	1	1
Causeway Street, at Portland Street,*	1	4
Causeway Street, at Merrimac Street,*	1	2
Causeway Street, at Staniford Street,*	1	1
Lowell Street, at Causeway Street,*	1	1
Lowell Street, at Brighton Street,*	1	1
Causeway Street, at subway entrance,*	1	4
Total Number of Tracks at Crossings,	98	106

* Used for freight only.

† Private track branching from Fitchburg Division of Boston & Maine.

‡ One of these is a private track branching from Fitchburg Division of Boston & Maine.

ACCIDENTS TO PERSONS.

(A detailed statement of each accident is on file in the office of the Board.)

Killed and Injured.	From Causes beyond their own Control.		From their own Misconduct or Carelessness.		Total.	
	Killed.	Injured.	Killed.	Injured.	Killed.	Injured.
Passengers,	-	398	4	1,392	4	1,790
Employees,	-	8	1	36	1	44
Other persons,	-	7	21	1,052	21	1,059
Totals,	-	413	26	2,480	26	2,893

CORPORATE NAME AND ADDRESS OF THE COMPANY.

BOSTON ELEVATED RAILWAY COMPANY,

101 MILK STREET, BOSTON, MASS.

NAMES AND BUSINESS ADDRESS OF PRINCIPAL OFFICERS.

William A. Bancroft, *President*, 101 Milk Street, Boston, Mass. Charles S. Sergeant, *Vice-President*, 101 Milk Street, Boston, Mass. William Hooper, *Treasurer*, 101 Milk Street, Boston, Mass. John T. Burnett, *Clerk of Corporation*, 101 Milk Street, Boston, Mass. J. Otis Wardwell, *General Counsel*, 85 State Street, Boston, Mass. Henry L. Wilson, *Auditor*, 101 Milk Street, Boston, Mass.

NAMES AND RESIDENCE OF BOARD OF DIRECTORS.

Frederick Ayer, Lowell, Mass. William A. Bancroft, Cambridge, Mass. John J. Bright, Cambridge, Mass. Samuel Carr, Boston, Mass. T. Jefferson Coolidge, Jr., Manchester, Mass. James Phillips, Jr., Boston, Mass. James M. Prendergast, Boston, Mass. N. W. Rice, Boston, Mass. Quincy A. Shaw, Jr., Boston, Mass. William S. Spaulding, Beverly, Mass. Walter S. Swan, Cambridge, Mass. Francis H. Peabody, Boston, Mass. Robert Winsor, Weston, Mass.

We hereby certify that the statements contained in the foregoing report are full, just and true.

WILLIAM A. BANCROFT,
ROBERT WINSOR,
JAS. M. PRENDERGAST,
SAMUEL CARR,
N. W. RICE,
JOHN J. BRIGHT,
FRANCIS H. PEABODY,
WILLIAM S. SPAULDING,
WALTER S. SWAN,
FREDERICK AYER,
Directors.

WILLIAM HOOPER,
Treasurer.

COMMONWEALTH OF MASSACHUSETTS.

SUFFOLK, ss. Nov. 28, 1904. Then personally appeared the above-named Robert Winsor, James M. Prendergast, Samuel Carr, N. W. Rice, John J. Bright, Francis H. Peabody, William S. Spaulding, Walter S. Swan, Frederick Ayer and William Hooper, and severally made oath that the foregoing certificate by them subscribed is, to the best of their knowledge and belief, true.

Before me, J. T. BURNETT,
Justice of the Peace.

REPORT

OF THE

BOSTON & NORTHERN STREET RAILWAY COMPANY

For the Year ending September 30, 1904.

General Exhibit for the Year.

Gross earnings from operation,			$3,750,968 48
Operating expenses,			2,641,579 53
Net Earnings from Operation,			$1,109,388 95
Miscellaneous income: receipts from parks,			15,444 94
Gross Income above Operating Expenses,			$1,124,833 89
Charges upon income accrued during the year:			
Interest on funded debt,		$436,191 76	
Interest and discount on unfunded debts and loans,		133,073 26	
Taxes, State and local,	$140,943 08		
Taxes, commutation,	82,099 07		
		223,042 15	
Rentals of leased railways:			
East Middlesex,	$40,600 00		
Winnisimmet,	3,400 00		
Boston & Chelsea,	7,560 00		
Boston & Revere,	3,908 34		
Nashua,	24,500 00		
Boston Elevated,	38,348 35		
		118,316 69	
Other deductions from income: park expense,		25,329 56	
Total Charges and Deductions from Income,			935,953 42
Net Divisible Income,			$188,880 47
Dividends declared (2½ per cent),			241,500 00
Deficit for the year ending September 30, 1904,			$52,619 53
Amount of surplus, September 30, 1903,			453,422 03
Debits to profit and loss account during the year:			
Discount on bonds,		$60,690 00	
Injury and damage claims prior to insurance,		4,872 22	
Reconstruction,		150,669 49	
Adjustment of accounts,		128,857 82	
Total Debits,			345,089 53
Total Surplus September 30, 1904,			$55,712 97

Earnings from Operation.

Receipts from passengers carried,	$3,717,364 36
Receipts from carriage of mails,	1,094 12
Receipts from tolls for use of tracks by other companies,	10,313 78
Receipts from rentals of buildings and other property,	5,784 80
Receipts from advertising in cars,	11,025 03
Receipts from interest on deposits,	4,395 79
Other earnings from operation: miscellaneous,	990 60
Gross Earnings from Operation,	$3,750,968 48

Expenses of Operation.

General expenses:	
Salaries of general officers and clerks,	$83,731 59
General office expenses and supplies,	20,013 55
Legal expenses,	22,229 53
Insurance,	234,581 33
Other general expenses: storeroom, $7,398.30; advertising, $5,448.19; miscellaneous general, $42,786.90,	55,633 39
Maintenance of roadway and buildings:	
Repair of roadbed and track,	91,909 75
Repair of electric line construction,	40,601 14
Repair of buildings,	20,306 62
Maintenance of equipment:	
Repair of cars and other vehicles,	141,202 70
Repair of electric equipment of cars,	169,160 50
Renewal of horses, harnesses, shoeing, etc.,	1,172 42
Provender and stabling for horses,	8,907 17
Transportation expenses:	
Cost of electric motive power, $444,472.56; less power sold, $25.084.46; net,	419,388 10
Wages and compensation of persons employed in conducting transportation,	1,025,214 62
Removal of snow and ice,	137,055 52
Damages for injuries to persons and property,	16,055 42
Tolls for trackage over other railways,	49,034 72
Rentals of buildings and other property,	18,672 39
Other transportation expenses: car service supplies, $10,665.54; miscellaneous car service expenses, $55,236.31; cleaning, oiling and sanding track, $20,807.22,	86,709 07
Total Operating Expenses,	$2,641,579 53

Property Accounts.

Additions to railway:		
Extension of tracks,	$121,077 22	
Betterment in reconstruction transferred to track,	302,189 88	
New electric line construction,	19,294 09	
Betterment in reconstruction transferred to line,	5,625 00	
Other additions to railway:		
Interest, $9,450.21; engineering, $20,986.33,	30,436 54	
Reconstruction,	353,093 92	
Total Additions to Railway,		$831,716 65

Additions to equipment:		
Additional cars,	$51,640 13	
Betterment in reconstructed cars, transferred to cars,	132,635 29	
Electric equipment of same,	65,441 18	
Betterment in reconstructed cars, transferred to electric equipment,	13,106 20	
Other additions to equipment:		
Reconstructed cars,	12,758 23	
Sundry equipment,	12,849 34	
TOTAL ADDITIONS TO EQUIPMENT,		$288,430 37
Additions to land and buildings:		
Additional land necessary for operation of railway,	$720 04	
New electric power stations, including machinery, etc.,	86,896 72	
Other new buildings necessary for operation of railway,	13,250 34	
TOTAL ADDITIONS TO LAND AND BUILDINGS,		100,867 10
TOTAL ADDITIONS TO PROPERTY ACCOUNTS,		$1,221,014 12
Deductions from property accounts (property sold or reduced in valuation and credited to property accounts):		
Roadbed and track,	$870 24	
Electric line,	178 50	
Betterment in reconstruction allowed upon appraisal by Railroad Commissioners, transferred to track and line,	307,814 88	
Cars and other rolling stock,	1,500 74	
Electric equipment,	810 46	
Betterment in reconstructed cars allowed upon appraisal by Railroad Commissioners, transferred to cars and electric equipment,	145,741 49	
Power station and machinery,	35,000 00	
Park property,	89 06	
Land,	4,036 75	
Reconstruction,	150,669 49	
TOTAL DEDUCTIONS FROM PROPERTY ACCOUNTS,		646,711 61
NET ADDITION TO PROPERTY ACCOUNTS FOR THE YEAR,		$574,302 51

GENERAL BALANCE SHEET SEPTEMBER 30, 1904.

ASSETS.	DR.	
Cost of railway:		
Roadbed and tracks,	$9,716,878 80	
Electric line construction, including poles, wiring, feeder lines, etc.,	1,591,742 61	
Interest accrued during construction of railway,	203,640 80	
Engineering and other expenses incident to construction,	492,177 13	
Other items of railway cost: reconstruction,	366,321 39	
TOTAL COST OF RAILWAY OWNED,		$12,370,760 73

Cost of equipment:		
Cars and other rolling stock and vehicles,	$2,248,083 46	
Reconstructed cars,	10,273 99	
Electric equipment of same,	2,212,793 65	
Horses,	7,283 26	
Other items of equipment: sundry equipment,	248,328 27	
TOTAL COST OF EQUIPMENT OWNED,		$4,726,762 63
Cost of land and buildings:		
Land and buildings necessary for operation of railway,	$1,136,496 24	
Electric power stations, including equipment,	2,632,339 90	
TOTAL COST OF LAND AND BUILDINGS OWNED,		3,768,836 14
Other permanent property:		
Park property,	$104,222 59	
Tenements,	2,162 00	
Discontinued car houses and stables,	77,188 93	
TOTAL COST OF OTHER PERMANENT PROPERTY OWNED,		183,573 52
TOTAL PERMANENT INVESTMENTS,		$21,049,933 02
Cash and current assets:		
Cash,	$439,521 78	
Bills and accounts receivable,	64,492 24	
Boston & Revere Electric St. R'y Co. bonds,	23,000 00	
Other cash and current assets: coupon deposits, $37,737.50; prepaid taxes, $35,493.73; prepaid fire insurance, $2,486.90; deposit redemption of bonds, $18,630.,	94,348 13	
TOTAL CASH AND CURRENT ASSETS,		621,362 15
Miscellaneous assets:		
Materials and supplies,	$393,933 61	
Other assets and property:		
Nashua Street Railway property account,	23,660 93	
Nashua Street Railway lease account,	10,625 26	
TOTAL MISCELLANEOUS ASSETS,		428,219 80
TOTAL,		$22,099,514 97

LIABILITIES.	CR.	
Capital stock,		$9,660,000 00
Funded debt,		9,005,000 00
Coupon notes,		427,500 00
Current liabilities:		
Loans and notes payable,	$2,290,000 00	
Audited vouchers and accounts,	334,235 78	
Salaries and wages,	24,845 77	
Matured interest coupons unpaid (including coupons due October 1),	37,737 50	
Miscellaneous current liabilities:		
Employees' deposits,	19,058 60	
Tickets outstanding,	10,491 62	
TOTAL CURRENT LIABILITIES,		2,716,369 27

Accrued liabilities:		
Interest accrued and not yet due,	$130,751 84	
Taxes accrued and not yet due,	82,979 68	
Rentals accrued and not yet due,	20,608 33	
Miscellaneous accrued liabilities: miscellaneous,	592 88	
TOTAL ACCRUED LIABILITIES,		$234,932 73
Profit and loss balance (surplus),		55,712 97
TOTAL,		$22,099,514 97

CAPITAL STOCK.

Capital stock authorized by law,	$9,660,000 00	
Capital stock authorized by votes of company,	9,660,000 00	
Capital stock issued and outstanding,		$9,660,000 00
Number of shares issued and outstanding,	96,600	
Number of stockholders,	26	
Number of stockholders in Massachusetts,	25	
Amount of stock held in Massachusetts,	$9,186,300 00	

FUNDED DEBT.

DESCRIPTION OF BONDS.	Rate of Interest.	Date of Maturity.	Amount Outstanding.	Interest Paid during the Year.
	Per Cent.			
Lynn & Boston Railroad debenture bonds,	5	April 1, 1907,	$100,000 00	$5,000 00
Lynn & Boston Railroad debenture bonds,	5	March 1, 1912,	186,000 00	9,300 00
Lynn & Boston Railroad first mortgage gold bonds,	5	Dec. 1, 1924,	5,218,000 00	186,150 00
Lynn & Boston Railroad coupon notes,	6	April 1, 1917,	405,000 00	24,300 00
Rockport Street Railway coupon notes,	6	Oct. 15, 1916,	12,500 00	750 00
Lynn Belt Line Street Railway first mortgage bonds,	5	May 1, 1910,	100,000 00	5,000 00
Essex Electric Street Railway first mortgage bonds,	6	Jan. 1, 1911,	100,000 00	6,000 00
Naumkeag Street Railway first mortgage bonds,	5	June 1, 1906,	215,000 00	10,750 00
Naumkeag Street Railway debenture bonds,	5	April 1, 1907,	49,000 00	2,450 00
Naumkeag Street Railway first consolidated mortgage bonds,	5	July 1, 1910,	711,000 00	35,550 00
Naumkeag Street Railway debenture bonds,	6	Sept. 1, 1910,	24,000 00	1,440 00
Naumkeag Street Railway debenture bonds,	6	July 1, 1911,	10,000 00	600 00
Gloucester Street Railway first mortgage gold bonds,	5	April 1, 1907,	60,000 00	3,000 00
Gloucester, Essex & Beverly Street Railway first mortgage gold bonds,	5	Dec. 1, 1916,	125,000 00	6,250 00
Mystic Valley Street Railway first mortgage bonds,	5	Jan. 1, 1919,	60,000 00	3,000 00
Wakefield & Stoneham Street Railway first mortgage gold bonds,	5	March 1, 1915,	150,000 00	7,500 00
Merrimack Valley Street Railway first mortgage bonds,	5	April 1, 1911,	342,000 00	17,100 00
People's Street Railway first mortgage bonds,	5	Jan. 1, 1928,	64,000 00	3,200 00
Amounts carried forward,			$7,931,500 00	$327,340 00

FUNDED DEBT — Concluded.

DESCRIPTION OF BONDS.	Rate of Interest.	Date of Maturity.	Amount Outstanding.	Interest Paid during the Year.
Amounts brought forward, . .	. .	. . . .	$7,931,500 00	$327,340 00
Lowell, Lawrence & Haverhill Street Railway first mortgage bonds, .	5	June 1, 1923,	986,000 00	49,025 00
Lowell & Suburban Street Railway first mortgage gold bonds, . . .	5	Dec. 1, 1911,	1,000,000 00	50,000 00
Gloucester & Rockport Street Railway coupon notes, ...	6	Feb. 1, 1915,	10,000 00	600 00
Boston & Northern Street Railway refunding gold bonds, . . .	4	July 1, 1954,	1,000,000 00	9,226 76
			$10,927,500 00	-
Less Lynn & Boston Railroad first mortgage bonds held in trust to redeem other issues, ...	. .	. . . .	1,495,000 00	-
TOTALS, ...	. .	. . . .	$9,432,500 00	$436,191 76

VOLUME OF TRAFFIC, ETC.

Number of passengers paying revenue carried during the year,	75,647,925
Number carried per mile of main railway track operated, .	160,452
Number of car miles run, ...	14,800,129
Average number of persons employed, ...	2,677

DESCRIPTION OF EQUIPMENT.

DESCRIPTION OF EQUIPMENT.	Equipped for Electric Power.	Not Equipped.	Total Passenger Cars.	Equipped with Fenders.	Equipped with Electric Heaters.	Number of Motors.
CARS — PASSENGER SERVICE.						
Box passenger cars, ...	464	2	466	457	457	-
Open passenger cars, ...	631	21	652	631	-	-
TOTAL, ...	1,095	23	1,118	1,088	457	2,211
CARS — OTHER SERVICE.						
Box freight cars, ...	2	-	-	-	-	-
Platform freight cars, ...	7	11	-	-	-	-
Work cars, ...	5	-	-	-	-	-
Other cars, ...	29	-	-	-	-	-
TOTAL, ...	43	11	-	-	-	76
Snow ploughs, ...	115	23	-	-	-	84

Miscellaneous Equipment.

Carts and snow sleds,	46
Other highway vehicles: 28 levellers, 4 road machines, 4 scrapers, 1 sweeper, 1 oil wagon, 9 buggies, 3 caravans, 11 tower wagons, 1 watering cart, 5 emergency wagons, 37 sleighs and pungs, 31 express wagons, 1 surrey, 2 walkaways, 2 line wagons,	140
Horses,	37

Railway Owned, Leased and Operated (by Electric Power).

Railway Owned, etc.	Owned.	Held under Lease or Contract.	Trackage over Other Railways.	Total Owned, Leased, etc.	Total Operated.
	Miles	Miles.	Miles.	Miles.	Miles.
Length of railway line,	351.293	35.253	5.700	392.246	392.246
Length of second main track,	67.420	8.360	3.441	79.221	79.221
Total Length of Main Track,	418.713	43 613	9.141	471.467	471.467
Length of sidings, switches, etc.,	16.973	1.679.	.061	18.713	18.713
Total Computed as Single Track,	435.686	45.292	9.202	490.180	490.180

Railway Located Outside of Massachusetts.

Length of railway line,	14.169 miles.
Length of second main track,	.730 "
Total length of main track,	14.899 "
Length of sidings, switches, etc.,	.621 "
Total, computed as single track,	15.520 "

Railway Located Outside of Public Ways.

	Owned.	Operated.
	Miles.	Miles.
Length of railway line,	11.399	13.453
Length of sidings,	2.018	2.063
Length of second main track,	.475	1.158
Total Length of Main Track,	13.892	16.674

Names of the several cities and towns in which the railways operated by the company are located: Andover, Arlington, Beverly, Billerica, Boston, Chelmsford, Chelsea, Danvers, Dracut, Essex, Everett, Gloucester, Groveland, Hamilton, Haverhill, Ipswich, Lawrence, Lowell, Lynn, Lynnfield, Malden, Marblehead, Medford, Melrose, Methuen, Middleton, Newburyport, North Andover, North Reading, Peabody, Reading, Revere, Rockport, Salem, Saugus, Stoneham, Swampscott, Tewksbury, Tyngsborough, Wakefield, Wenham, West Newbury, Wilmington, Winchester and Woburn, Mass.; Nashua and Hudson, N. H.

GRADE CROSSINGS WITH RAILROADS.

GRADE CROSSINGS WITH RAILROADS.	NUMBER OF TRACKS AT CROSSING.	
	Railroad.	Railway.
Crossings of railways with railroads at grade (88 in number), viz.:		
With Union Freight Railroad, Causeway Street, Boston, ...	1	4
With Fitchburg Division, Boston & Maine Railroad, Warren Avenue, Boston,*	2	2
With Boston & Maine Railroad and Boston & Albany Railroad, Everett Avenue, Chelsea, ...	4	2
With Cape Ann Granite Company, Granite Street, Rockport,* .	1	1
With Rockport Granite Company, Granite Street, Rockport,* . .	1	1
With Lanesville Granite Company, Langsford Street, Gloucester,* .	1	1
With Rockport Granite Company, Washington Street, Gloucester,*	2	1
With New York, New Haven & Hartford Railroad, Chelmsford Centre, ...	1	1
With Revere Beach & Lynn Railroad, Winthrop Avenue, Revere, .	2	1
With Boston & Maine Railroad as follows:		
Cabot Street, Beverly, ...	2	1
Cabot Street, Beverly, ...	2	1
Cabot Street, Beverly,*	1	2
Elliot Street, Beverly, ...	4	1
Elliot Street, Beverly,*	1	1
Enon Street, Beverly,*	3	1
Essex Street, Beverly, ...	2	1
Main Street, Billerica, ...	2	1
Tyngsborough Line, Chelmsford, ...	2	2
Elm Street, Danvers, ...	2	1
Holten Street, Danvers, ...	1	1
Maple Street, Danvers, ...	1	1
Water Street, Danvers,*	2	1
Washington Street, Gloucester, ...	1	1
Essex Street, Hamilton, ...	1	1
Willow Street, Hamilton, ...	1	1
Essex Street, Haverhill, ...	4	1
Washington Street, Haverhill, ...	4	2
Andover Street, Lawrence, ...	5	1
South Broadway, Lawrence, ...	5	1
South Broadway, Lawrence, ...	2	1
Union Street, Lawrence (2 places),*	2	1
Water Street, Lawrence, ...	6	1
Bridge Street, Lowell,*	2	2
Broadway, Lowell,*	1	1
Central Street, Lowell,*	1	2
Dutton and Merrimack streets, Lowell,*	1	3
Dutton and Fletcher streets, Lowell, ...	2	2
Gorham Street, Lowell, ...	1	2
East Merrimack Street, Lowell,*	1	2
Middlesex Street, Lowell (2 places), ...	5	1
Lawrence Street, Lowell, ...	2	1
Lawrence Street, Lowell, ...	1	1
Blossom Street, Lynn, ...	2	1
Boston Street, Lynn, ...	2	1
Central Square, Lynn, ...	2	4
Chatham Street, Lynn, ...	2	1
Commercial Street, Lynn, ...	3	1
Market Street, Lynn, ...	2	2
Summer Street, Lynn, ...	2	1
Summer Street, Lynn, ...	2	1
Western Avenue, Lynn, ...	3	2
Beach Street, Malden, ...	2	1
Ferry Street, Malden, ...	2	2
Pleasant Street, Marblehead, ...	1	1
Franklin Street, Melrose, ...	2	1
Main Street, North Andover, ...	2	1
Sutton Street, North Andover, ...	2	1
Main Street, North Reading, ...	1	1
Central Street, Peabody (2 places), ...	3	2
Lowell Street, Peabody, ...	1	1
High Street, near Reading Station, Reading, ...	2	1
Salem Street, Revere, ...	2	1
Derby Street, Salem, ...	6	1
Fort Avenue, Salem, ...	3	1
Lafayette Street, Salem, ...	1	1
Loring Avenue, Salem, ...	1	1

* Used exclusively for carrying freight to corporations.

GRADE CROSSINGS WITH RAILROADS — Concluded.

GRADE CROSSINGS WITH RAILROADS.	NUMBER OF TRACKS AT CROSSING.	
	Railroad.	Railway.
Crossings of railways with railroads at grade — *Concluded.*		
With Boston & Maine Railroad — *Concluded.*		
North Street, Salem,	3	2
Central Avenue, Saugus,	2	1
Main Street, Stoneham,	2	1
MontVale Avenue, Stoneham,	1	1
Orient Street, Swampscott,	1	1
Albion Street, Wakefield,	2	1
Main Street, Wakefield,	2	1
Railroad Street, Wakefield,*	1	1
Railroad Street, Wakefield,*	3	1
Water Street, Wakefield,	2	1
Main Street, Wilmington,	3	1
Pleasant Street, Winchester,	3	1
Main Street, Woburn,	2	1
Main Street, Woburn,	2	1
Acton Branch, East Hollis Street, Nashua, N. H.,	2	1
Freight, East Hollis Street, Nashua, N. H.,	1	1
Southern Division, East Hollis Street, Nashua, N. H.,	6	1
Acton Branch, Main Street, Nashua, N. H.,	1	1
Keene Division, Main Street, Nashua, N. H.,	2	1
Worcester, Nashua & Rochester Div., Main Street, Nashua, N. H.,	2	1
Acton Branch and Worcester, Nashua & Rochester Division, Temple Street, Nashua, N. H.,	2	1
Keene Division, Temple Street, Nashua, N. H.,	2	1
TOTAL NUMBER OF TRACKS AT CROSSINGS,	186	111

ACCIDENTS TO PERSONS.

(A detailed statement of each accident is on file in the office of the Board.)

KILLED AND INJURED.	FROM CAUSES BEYOND THEIR OWN CONTROL.		FROM THEIR OWN MISCONDUCT OR CARELESSNESS.		TOTAL.	
	Killed.	Injured.	Killed.	Injured.	Killed.	Injured.
Passengers,	9	261	3	323	12	584
Employees,	-	-	-	41	-	41
Other persons,	-	2	9	127	9	129
TOTALS,	9	263	12	491	21	754

CORPORATE NAME AND ADDRESS OF THE COMPANY.

BOSTON & NORTHERN STREET RAILWAY COMPANY,

84 STATE STREET, BOSTON, MASS.

NAMES AND BUSINESS ADDRESS OF PRINCIPAL OFFICERS.

Patrick F. Sullivan, *President*, Boston, Mass. Robert S. Goff, *Vice-President and General Manager*, Boston, Mass. Joseph H. Goodspeed, *Treasurer*, Boston, Mass. Charles Williams, *Clerk of Corporation*, Lynn, Mass. Warren & Garfield, *General Counsel*, Boston, Mass. D. Dana Bartlett, *General Auditor*, Boston, Mass. Frank C. Wilkinson, *Superintendent*, Division 1, Lynn, Mass. Thos. Lees, *Superintendent*, Division 2, Lowell, Mass.

* Used exclusively for carrying freight to corporations.

NAMES AND RESIDENCE OF BOARD OF DIRECTORS.

Patrick F. Sullivan, Lowell, Mass. Robert S. Goff, Fall River, Mass. Joseph H. Goodspeed, Boston, Mass. Henry P. Moulton, Salem, Mass. John S. Bartlett, Lynn, Mass. Chas. H. Newhall, Lynn, Mass. John H. Cunningham, Chelsea, Mass. Alexander B. Bruce, Lawrence, Mass. Percy Parker, Lowell, Mass.

We hereby certify that the statements contained in the foregoing report are full, just and true.

P. F. SULLIVAN,
PERCY PARKER,
ROBERT S. GOFF,
J. H. CUNNINGHAM,
JOSEPH H. GOODSPEED,
J. S. BARTLETT,
ALEX. B. BRUCE,
Directors.
JOSEPH H. GOODSPEED,
Treasurer.
ROBERT S. GOFF,
Superintendent.

COMMONWEALTH OF MASSACHUSETTS.

SUFFOLK, SS. BOSTON, Nov. 16, 1904. Then personally appeared the above-named P. F. Sullivan, Percy Parker, Robert S. Goff, J. H. Cunningham, Joseph H. Goodspeed, J. S. Bartlett and Alex. B. Bruce, and severally made oath that the foregoing certificate by them subscribed is, to the best of their knowledge and belief, true.

Before me, D. DANA BARTLETT,
Justice of the Peace.

COMMONWEALTH OF MASSACHUSETTS.

SUFFOLK, SS. BOSTON, Nov. 24, 1904. Then personally appeared the above-named Robert S. Goff and made oath that the foregoing certificate by him subscribed is, to the best of his knowledge and belief, true.

Before me, D. DANA BARTLETT,
Justice of the Peace.

REPORT

OF THE

BOSTON & REVERE ELECTRIC STREET RAILWAY COMPANY

For the Year ending September 30, 1904.

[Leased to and operated by the Boston & Northern.]

General Exhibit for the Year.	
Rental received from lease of railway,	$2,50 00
Dividends declared (5 per cent),	$2,500 00
Amount of deficit September 30, 1903,	$11,363 18
Total Deficit September 30, 1904,	$11,363 18

General Balance Sheet September 30, 1904.	
Assets. Dr.	
Cost of railway,	$73,815 23
Cost of equipment,	9,919 79
Cost of land and buildings,	4,901 80
Total Permanent Investments,	$88,636 82
Profit and loss balance (deficit),	11,363 18
Total,	$100,000 00
Liabilities. Cr.	
Capital stock,	$50,000 00
Funded debt,	27,000 00
Current liabilities: Boston & Northern Street Railway Company, lessee (bonds retired),	23,000 00
Total,	$100,000 00

Capital Stock.		
Capital stock authorized by law,	$50,000 00	
Capital stock authorized by votes of company,	50,000 00	
Capital stock issued and outstanding,		$50,000 00
Number of shares issued and outstanding,	500	
Number of stockholders,	17	
Number of stockholders in Massachusetts,	13	
Amount of stock held in Massachusetts,	$35,100 00	

Funded Debt.

Description of Bonds.	Rate of Interest.	Date of Maturity.	Amount Outstanding.	Interest Paid during the Year.
	Per Cent.			
First mortgage bonds, ...	5	Feb. 1, 1910, .	$27,000 00	–*

Railway Owned.

Length of railway line, ...	1.856 miles.
Length of second main track, ...	1.856 "
Total length of main track, ...	3.712 "
Length of sidings, switches, etc., ...	.100 "
Total, computed as single track, ...	3.812 "

Railway Owned and Located Outside of Public Ways.

Length of railway line, ...	.684 miles.
Length of second main track, ...	.683 "
Total length of main track, ...	1.367 "

Names of the several cities and towns in which the railway owned by the company is located: Boston (East Boston) and Revere.

Corporate Name and Address of the Company.

BOSTON & REVERE ELECTRIC STREET RAILWAY COMPANY,

84 State Street, Boston, Mass.

Names and Business Address of Principal Officers.

Patrick F. Sullivan, *President*, Boston, Mass. Robert S. Goff, *Vice-President*, Boston, Mass. Joseph H. Goodspeed, *Treasurer*, Boston, Mass. Charles Williams, *Clerk of Corporation*, Lynn, Mass.

Names and Residence of Board of Directors.

Patrick F. Sullivan, Lowell, Mass. Joseph H. Goodspeed, Boston, Mass. Bentley W. Warren, Boston, Mass. Charles Williams, Wakefield, Mass. Robert S. Goff, Fall River, Mass.

* Paid by lessee.

We hereby certify that the statements contained in the foregoing report are full, just and true.

P. F. SULLIVAN,
ROBERT S. GOFF,
J. H. GOODSPEED,
BENTLEY W. WARREN,
Directors.
J. H. GOODSPEED,
Treasurer.

COMMONWEALTH OF MASSACHUSETTS.

SUFFOLK, ss. BOSTON, Oct. 13, 1904. Then personally appeared the above-named P. F. Sullivan, Robert S. Goff, J. H. Goodspeed and Bentley W. Warren, and severally made oath that the foregoing certificate by them subscribed is, to the best of their knowledge and belief, true,

Before me, D. DANA BARTLETT,
Justice of the Peace.

REPORT

OF THE

BOSTON AND WORCESTER STREET RAILWAY COMPANY

For the Year ending September 30, 1904.

General Exhibit for the Year.

Gross earnings from operation,			$370,883 51
Operating expenses,			195,003 37
Gross Income above Operating Expenses,			$175,880 14
Charges upon income accrued during the year:			
Interest on funded debt,		$48,452 44	
Interest and discount on unfunded debts and loans,		11,447 96	
Taxes, State and local,	$17,245 00		
Taxes, commutation,	7,365 21		
		24,610 21	
Total Charges and Deductions from Income,			84,510 61
Net Divisible Income,			$91,369 53
Dividends declared (3 per cent. on $1,564,800),			46,944 00
Surplus for the year ending September 30, 1904,			$44,425 53
Amount of surplus September 30, 1903,			42,580 77
Credits to profit and loss account during the year: contribution of stockholders for settlement of damage claims,		$23,461 10	
Debits to profit and loss account during the year:			
Settlement of damage claims,	$53,089 00		
Settlement of old accounts,	112 07		
Total Debits,		53,201 07	
Net Amount Debited to Profit and Loss,			29,739 97
Total Surplus September 30, 1904,			$57,266 33

Earnings from Operation.

Receipts from passengers carried,	$368,758 38
Receipts from carriage of mails,	187 50
Receipts from carriage of freight,	100 00
Receipts from tolls for use of tracks by other companies,	195 63
Receipts from rentals of buildings and other property,	752 04
Receipts from advertising in cars,	889 96
Gross Earnings from Operation,	$370,883 51

Expenses of Operation.

General expenses:	
Salaries of general officers and clerks,	$11,292 00
General office expenses and supplies,	2,256 70
Insurance,	6,000 00
Other general expenses: miscellaneous,	5,566 83
Maintenance of roadway and buildings:	
Repair of roadbed and track,	10,898 01
Repair of electric line construction,	3,959 22
Repair of buildings,	115 47
Maintenance of equipment:	
Repair of cars and other vehicles,	18,920 71
Repair of electric equipment of cars,	16,467 46
Transportation expenses:	
Cost of electric motive power, $61,475.19; less power sold, $3,140.12; net,	58,335 07
Wages and compensation of persons employed in conducting transportation,	58,182 80
Removal of snow and ice,	2,074 83
Damages for injuries to persons and property,*	934 27
Total Operating Expenses,	$195,003 37

Property Accounts.

Additions to railway:		
Extension of tracks (length, 29,040 feet),	$185,338 97	
New electric line construction (length, 29,040 feet),	16,970 34	
Other additions to railway: property of the Framingham Union and Framingham, Southborough & Marlborough Street Railways,	297,811 80	
Total Additions to Railway,		$500,121 11
Additions to equipment:		
Additional cars (10 in number),	$54,492 26	
Electric equipment of same,	39,940 19	
Other additions to equipment:		
Ploughs, machine shop tools, etc.,	20,969 60	
Property of the Framingham Union and Framingham, Southborough & Marlborough Street Railways,	102,800 00	
Total Additions to Equipment,		218,202 05
Additions to land and buildings:		
Additional land necessary for operation of railway,	$2,445 00	
Additional equipment of power stations,	102,303 23	
New buildings necessary for operation of railway,	3,823 97	
Property of Framingham Union and Framingham, Southborough & Marlborough Street Railways,	33,738 75	
Total Additions to Land and Buildings,		142,310 95
Total Additions to Property Accounts,		$860,634 11

* In addition to this amount $53,201.07 was paid on account of accidents and was charged against surplus account, to which account $23,461.10 was credited as a contribution from stockholders. Taking the similar action of 1903, $79,739.97 has been charged against surplus account for injuries to persons, and $50,000 credited to surplus account as a contribution from stockholders.

GENERAL BALANCE SHEET SEPTEMBER 30, 1904.

ASSETS.	DR.	
Cost of railway:		
Roadbed and tracks,	$1,714,977 92	
Electric line construction, including poles, wiring, feeder lines, etc.,	286,270 80	
Interest accrued during construction of railway,	62,076 90	
Engineering and other expenses incident to construction,	231,573 00	
TOTAL COST OF RAILWAY OWNED,		$2,294,898 62
Cost of equipment:		
Cars and other rolling stock and vehicles,	$211,270 56	
Electric equipment of same,	212,076 59	
Other items of equipment: snow ploughs, air brakes, heaters, registers, fenders, headlights, etc.,	73,638 10	
TOTAL COST OF EQUIPMENT OWNED,		496,985 25
Cost of land and buildings:		
Land necessary for operation of railway,	$72,910 40	
Electric power stations, including equipment,	486,729 61	
Other buildings necessary for operation of railway,	124,087 72	
TOTAL COST OF LAND AND BUILDINGS OWNED,		683,727 73
TOTAL PERMANENT INVESTMENTS,		$3,475,611 60
Cash and current assets:		
Cash,	$42,444 24	
Bills and accounts receivable,	4,090 94	
Due from bankers for mortgage bonds undelivered,	77,025 00	
Sinking and other special funds,	888 25	
Other cash and current assets:		
Prepaid insurance,	3,708 47	
Prepaid interest,	11,623 16	
Cash deposited as collateral for surety bonds,	40,000 00	
TOTAL CASH AND CURRENT ASSETS,		179,780 06
Miscellaneous assets: materials and supplies,	$13,344 07	
Other assets and property: mortgage bond discount,	36,250 00	
TOTAL MISCELLANEOUS ASSETS,		49,594 07
TOTAL,		$3,704,985 73

LIABILITIES.	CR.	
Capital stock,		$1,564,900 00
Funded debt,		1,557,000 00
Current liabilities:		
Loans and notes payable,	$415,988 63	
Audited vouchers and accounts,	71,492 43	
TOTAL CURRENT LIABILITIES,		487,481 06

Accrued liabilities:		
Interest accrued and not yet due,	$11,606 18	
Taxes accrued and not yet due,	25,843 91	
TOTAL ACCRUED LIABILITIES,		$37,450 09
Sinking and other special funds: for Framingham Union Street Railway Company first mortgage bonds,		888 25
Profit and loss balance (surplus),		57,266 33
TOTAL,		$3,704,985 73

CAPITAL STOCK.

Capital stock authorized by law,	$1,565,000 00	
Capital stock authorized by votes of company,	1,565,000 00	
Capital stock issued and outstanding,		$1,564,900 00
Number of shares issued and outstanding,	15,649	
Number of stockholders,	16	
Number of stockholders in Massachusetts,	15	
Amount of stock held in Massachusetts,	$1,564,800 00	

FUNDED DEBT.

DESCRIPTION OF BONDS.	Rate of Interest.	Date of Maturity.	Amount Outstanding.	Interest Paid during the Year.
	Per Cent.			
First mortgage gold bonds,	4½	Aug. 1, 1923,	$1,450,000 00	$44,689 93
First mortgage gold bonds of the Framingham, Southborough & Marlborough Street Railway Company, assumed by consolidation,	5	Jan. 1, 1919,	60,000 00	2,000 00
First mortgage gold bonds of the Framingham Union Street Railway Company, assumed by consolidation,	5	July 1, 1909,	47,000 00	1,762 51
TOTALS,	. .	. . .	$1,557,000 00	$48,452 44

SINKING AND OTHER SPECIAL FUNDS.

Amount September 30, 1903, of Framingham Union Street Railway Company sinking fund,	$888 25
TOTAL SINKING AND OTHER SPECIAL FUNDS, SEPTEMBER 30, 1904,	$888 25

VOLUME OF TRAFFIC, ETC.

Number of passengers paying revenue carried during the year,	7,668,686
Number carried per mile of main railway track operated,	104,166
Number of car miles run,	1,659,089
Average number of persons employed,	230

Description of Equipment.

Description of Equipment.	Equipped for Electric Power.	Not Equipped.	Equipped with Fenders.	Equipped with Electric Heaters.	Number of Motors.
Cars — Passenger Service.					
Box passenger cars,	42	-	42	42	-
Open passenger cars,	25	-	25	-	-
Total,	67	-	67	42	209
Cars — Other Service.					
Box freight cars,	2	-	-	-	-
Work cars,	1	2	-	-	-
Total,	3	2	-	-	-
Snow ploughs,	12	1	-	-	-

Miscellaneous Equipment.

Carts and snow sleds,	2
Other highway vehicles: 1 sleigh, 2 express wagons, 1 buggy, 3 tower wagons,	7
Horses,	2
Other items of equipment: single harnesses,	3

Railway Owned, Leased and Operated (by Electric Power).

Railway Owned, etc.	Owned.	Trackage over Other Railways.	Total Owned, Leased, etc.	Total Operated.
	Miles.	Miles.	Miles.	Miles.
Length of railway line,	47.406	.524	47.930	47.930
Length of second main track,	25.690	-	25.690	25.690
Total Length of Main Track,	73.096	.524	73.620	73.620
Length of sidings, switches, etc.,	2.143	-	2.143	2.143
Total, Computed as Single Track,	75.239	.524	75.763	75.763

Railway Located Outside of Public Ways.

Length of railway line,	12.845 miles.
Length of second main track,	12.584 "
Total length of main track,	25.429 "

Names of the several cities and towns in which the railways operated by the company are located: Newton, Wellesley, Natick, Framingham, Southborough, Marlborough, Hudson, Northborough, Westborough and Shrewsbury.

Grade Crossings with Railroads.

Grade Crossings with Railroads.	Number of Tracks at Crossing.	
	Railroad.	Railway.
Crossings of railways with railroads at grade (3 in number), viz.:—		
With Boston & Albany Railroad, Elm Street, Saxonville, . . .	1	1
With Boston & Albany Railroad, Elm Street, Saxonville, . . .	1	1
With New York, New Haven & Hartford Railroad, Worcester Street, Framingham, ...	3	1
Total Number of Tracks at Crossings, ...	5	3

Number of above crossings at which *frogs* are inserted in the tracks, . 3

General Remarks and Explanations.

Framingham Union Street Railway Company consolidated with this company by approval of Board of Railroad Commissioners, dated Dec. 8, 1903. Framingham, Southborough & Marlborough Street Railway Company consolidated with this company by approval of Board of Railroad Commissioners, dated Feb. 1, 1904.

Accidents to Persons.

(A detailed statement of each accident is on file in the office of the Board.)

Killed and Injured.	From Causes beyond their own Control.		From their own Misconduct or Carelessness.		Total.	
	Killed.	Injured.	Killed.	Injured.	Killed.	Injured.
Passengers, ...	1	45	-	16	1	61
Employees, ...	1	1	-	3	1	4
Other persons, ...	-	-	3	9	3	9
Totals, ...	2	46	3	28	5	74

Corporate Name and Address of the Company.

BOSTON AND WORCESTER STREET RAILWAY COMPANY,

8 Congress Street, Boston, Mass.

Names and Business Address of Principal Officers.

William M. Butler, *President*, Tremont Building, Boston, Mass. H. Fisher Eldredge, *Vice-President*, Portsmouth, N. H. George A. Butman, *Treasurer and Clerk of Corporation*, 8 Congress Street, Boston, Mass. E. P. Shaw, Jr., *Superintendent*, South Framingham, Mass.

Names and Residence of Board of Directors.

William M. Butler, Edgartown, Mass. H. Fisher Eldredge, Portsmouth, N. H. Charles W. Shippee, Milford, Mass. Albion R. Clapp, Wellesley, Mass. Alex. B. Bruce, Lawrence, Mass. Arthur E. Childs, Boston, Mass.

Phineas W. Sprague, Malden, Mass. George A. Butman, Malden, Mass. Walter H. Trumbull, Salem, Mass. John J. Whipple, Brockton, Mass. Chas. C. Peirce, Brookline, Mass. James F. Shaw, Manchester, Mass. Samuel Farquhar, Newton, Mass. Edward P. Shaw, Newburyport, Mass.

We hereby certify that the statements contained in the foregoing report are full, just and true.

WILLIAM M. BUTLER,
JAMES F. SHAW,
GEO. A. BUTMAN,
EDWARD P. SHAW,
ALEX. B. BRUCE,
ARTHUR E. CHILDS,
CHAS. W. SHIPPEE,
ALBION R. CLAPP,
Directors.
GEO. A. BUTMAN,
Treasurer.
EDWARD P. SHAW.
General Superintendent.

COMMONWEALTH OF MASSACHUSETTS.

SUFFOLK, SS. BOSTON, Nov. 15, 1904. Then personally appeared the above-named William M. Butler, Jas. F. Shaw, Geo. A. Butman, Edward P. Shaw, Alex. B. Bruce, Arthur E. Childs, Chas. W. Shippee, Albion R. Clapp and Edward P. Shaw, Jr., and severally made oath that the foregoing certificate by them subscribed is, to the best of their knowledge and belief, true.

Before me, ARTHUR W. CLAPP.
Justice of the Peace.

REPORT

OF THE

BRISTOL COUNTY STREET RAILWAY COMPANY

For the Period ending May 2, 1904.

[Railway in hands of receivers, May 3, 1904.]

General Exhibit for the Period.			
Gross earnings from operation,			$21,879 86
Operating expenses,			42,060 82
Gross Deficit above Operating Expenses,			$20,180 96
Charges upon income accrued during the year:			
Interest on funded debt,		$6,000 00	
Interest and discount on unfunded debts and loans,		3,253 57	
Taxes, State and local,	$3,089 38		
Taxes, commutation,	218 80		
		3,308 18	
Total Charges and Deductions from Income,			12,561 75
Deficit for the period ending May 2, 1904,			$32,742 71
Amount of surplus September 30, 1903,			2,812 48
Debits to profit and loss account during the year:			
Commissions,		$43,228 12	
Suspense account,		7,248 74	
Total Debits,			50,476 86
Total Deficit, May 2, 1904,			$80,407 09

Earnings from Operation.	
Receipts from passengers carried,	$21,532 91
Receipts from rentals of buildings and other property,	36 10
Receipts from advertising in cars,	125 00
Other earnings from operation: electric lighting,	185 85
Gross Earnings from Operation,	$21,879 86

Expenses of Operation.

General expenses:	
Salaries of general officers and clerks,	$309 01
General office expenses and supplies,	272 11
Legal expenses,	297 94
Insurance,	1,635 97
Other general expenses: advertising, $205.17; miscellaneous, $915.94,	1,121 11
Maintenance of roadway and buildings:	
Repair of roadbed and track,	1,535 88
Repair of electric line construction,	1,575 25
Repair of buildings,	33 87
Maintenance of equipment:	
Repair of cars and other vehicles,	4,507 31
Repair of electric equipment of cars,	5,397 78
Repair of steam and electric plant,	2,117 37
Transportation expenses:	
Cost of electric motive power,	12,687 78
Wages and compensation of persons employed in conducting transportation,	8,334 24
Removal of snow and ice,	454 92
Tolls for trackage over other railways,	703 60
Other transportation expenses: car service, $985.14; hired equipment, $87.70; fare payments, $3.84,	1,076 68
Total Operating Expenses,	$42,060 82

General Balance Sheet May 2, 1904.

Assets.	Dr.	
Cost of railway:		
Roadbed and tracks,	$218,270 72	
Electric line construction, including poles, wiring, feeder lines, etc.,	50,702 30	
Interest accrued during construction of railway,	15,370 67	
Engineering and other expenses incident to construction,	7,491 05	
Other items of railway cost,	33,272 48	
Rights of way,	309 19	
Extensions,	7,487 87	
Total Cost of Railway Owned,		$332,904 28
Cost of equipment:		
Cars and other rolling stock and vehicles,	$73,936 28	
Electric equipment of same,	48,309 87	
Other items of equipment,	479 43	
Total Cost of Equipment Owned,		122,725 58
Cost of land and buildings:		
Land necessary for operation of railway,	$11,355 00	
Electric power stations, including equipment,	92,258 70	
Total Cost of Land and Buildings Owned,		103,613 70
Total Permanent Investments,		$559,243 56

Cash and current assets:		
Cash,		$120,097 62
Bills and accounts receivable,		38,256 39
TOTAL CASH AND CURRENT ASSETS,		$158,354 01
Miscellaneous assets: materials and supplies,		9,496 17
Profit and loss balance (deficit),		80,407 09
TOTAL,		$807,500 83
LIABILITIES.	CR.	
Capital stock,		$200,000 00
Funded debt,		200,000 00
Current liabilities:		
Loans and notes payable,	$383,459 36	
Audited vouchers and accounts,	23,193 32	
Salaries and wages,	683 15	
Miscellaneous current liabilities: employees' deposits,	165 00	
TOTAL CURRENT LIABILITIES,		407,500 83
TOTAL,		$807,500 83

The foregoing balance sheet is drawn from the records of the corporation now in our hands.

Any discrepancies between the foregoing and that for the previous year are to be found in the aforesaid records.

Receivers of the Bristol County Street Railway Company.

CAPITAL STOCK.		
Capital stock authorized by law,	$200,000 00	
Capital stock authorized by votes of company,	200,000 00	
Capital stock issued and outstanding,		$200,000 00
Number of shares issued and outstanding,	2,000	
Number of stockholders,	27	
Number of stockholders in Massachusetts,	22	
Amount of stock held in Massachusetts,	$173,200 00	

FUNDED DEBT.

DESCRIPTION OF BONDS.	Rate of Interest.	Date of Maturity.	Amount Outstanding.	Interest Paid during the Year.
	Per Cent.			
First mortgage bonds,	5	Jan. 1, 1921,	$200,000 00	$6,000 00

Volume of Traffic, etc.

Number of passengers paying revenue carried during the year,	448,224
Number carried per mile of main railway track operated,	26,143
Number of car miles run,	172,738
Average number of persons employed,	47

Description of Equipment.

Description of Equipment.	Equipped for Electric Power.	Not Equipped.	Equipped with Fenders.	Equipped with Electric Heaters.	Number of Motors.
Cars — Passenger Service.					
Box passenger cars,	9	-	9	9	-
Open passenger cars,	11	-	11	-	-
Totals,	20	-	20	9	68
Cars — Other Service.					
Platform freight cars,	1	1	-	-	-
Totals,	1	1	-	-	4
Snow ploughs,	2	-	-	-	-

Railway Owned, Leased and Operated (by Electric Power).

Railway Owned, etc.	Owned.	Trackage over Other Railways.	Total Owned, Leased, etc.
	Miles.	Miles.	Miles.
Length of railway line,	15.988	.688	16.676
Length of second main track,	.470	-	.470
Total Length of Main Track,	16.458	.688	17.146
Length of sidings, switches, etc.,	1.439	-	1.439
Total Computed as Single Track,	17.897	.688	18.585

Railway Located Outside of Public Ways.

Length of railway line,	1.641 miles.

Names of the several cities and towns in which the railways operated by the company are located: Taunton, Rehoboth, Attleborough and Seekonk.

GRADE CROSSINGS WITH RAILROADS.

GRADE CROSSINGS WITH RAILROADS.	NUMBER OF TRACKS AT CROSSING.	
	Railroad.	Railway.
Crossings of railways with railroads at grade (1 in number), viz.: With New York, New Haven & Hartford Railroad at Taunton, at Oak Street Crossing, owned by Old Colony Street Railway Co.,	4	1

CORPORATE NAME AND ADDRESS OF THE COMPANY.

BRISTOL COUNTY STREET RAILWAY COMPANY,

43 MILK STREET, BOSTON, MASS.

NAMES AND BUSINESS ADDRESS OF PRINCIPAL OFFICERS.

Isaac Patch, *President*, Gloucester, Mass. Charles S. Cummings, 2d, *Treasurer*, Boston, Mass. Horace N. Pedrick, *Superintendent*, Attleborough, Mass.

NAMES AND RESIDENCE OF BOARD OF DIRECTORS.

Isaac Patch, Gloucester, Mass. George H. Swazey, Malden, Mass. Charles S. Cummings, 2d, Boston, Mass. Edward A. Mead, Dorchester, Mass. Charles B. Waterman, Brookline, Mass. S. Edgar Whittaker, Woburn, Mass.

We hereby certify that the statements contained in the foregoing report are full, just and true, according to the records of the corporation now in our hands.

JOHN T. BURNETT,
JOHN L. HALL,
Receivers.

COMMONWEALTH OF MASSACHUSETTS.

SUFFOLK, ss. OCT. 31, 1904. Then personally appeared the above-named John T. Burnett and John L. Hall, and severally made oath that the foregoing certificate by them subscribed is, to the best of their knowledge and belief, true.

Before me, JOSHUA M. SEARS, JR.,
Justice of the Peace.

REPORT

OF THE

RECEIVERS OF THE BRISTOL COUNTY STREET RAILWAY

For the Period from May 3, to September 30, 1904.

The Circuit Court of the United States for District of Massachusetts authorized the receivers of the Bristol County Street Railway Company to borrow $21,117.53 on receivers' certificates to be issued by them. Certificates to the extent of $21,117.49 have been issued.

The object of this so-called "budget" was to pay off some preferred claims, as taxes, etc., and to put the road in a condition where it might be safely operated.

It has been expended as follows: —

Material and repairs of cars, etc.,	$2,030 96
Repair of track,	600 00
Labor,	1,937 00
Insurance,	868 00
Taxes,	2,065 23
Land,	1,000 00
Office expenses, etc.,	1,055 00
Cars,	11,561 30
	$21,117 49

Receivers of the Bristol County Street Railway Company.

General Exhibit for the Period.			
Gross earnings from operation,			$25,338 54
Operating expenses,			17,456 68
Gross Income above Operating Expenses,			$7,881 86
Charges upon income accrued during the year:			
Interest on funded debt,		$5,017 61	
Taxes, State and local,	$114 84		
Taxes, commutation,	472 17		
		587 01	
Total Charges and Deductions from income,			5,604 62
Surplus for the period ending September 30, 1904,			$2,277 24
Total Surplus September 30, 1904,			$2,277 24

Earnings from Operation.

Receipts from passengers carried,	$25,257 69
Receipts from rental of buildings and other property,	20 00
Receipts from advertising in cars,	37 50
Other earnings from operation: old material,	23 35
Gross Earnings from Operation,	$25,338 54

Expenses of Operation.

General expenses: general office expenses and supplies,	$331 10
Maintenance of roadway and buildings:	
Repair of roadbed and track,	13 65
Repair of electric line construction,	5 63
Repair of buildings,	76 13
Maintenance of equipment: repair of cars and other vehicles,	1,079 72
Transportation expenses:	
Cost of electric motive power,	5,288 50
Wages and compensation of persons employed in conducting transportation,	9,945 69
Damages for injuries to persons and property,	50 00
Tolls for trackage over other railways,	641 51
Other transportation expenses: inspection,	24 75
Total Operating Expenses,	$17,456 68

General Balance Sheet September 30, 1904.

Assets.	Dr.	
Cash and current assets:		
Cash,	$5,214 18	
Bills and accounts receivable,	1,009 57	
Total Cash and Current Assets,		$6,223 75
Miscellaneous assets: expenditures, etc., as per budget account annexed,		21,117 49
Total,		$27,341 24

Liabilities.	Cr.	
Current liabilities:		
Receivers' certificates,	$21,117 49	
Audited vouchers and accounts,	3,474 34	
Total Current Liabilities,		$24,591 83
Accrued liabilities: taxes accrued and not yet due,		472 17
Profit and loss balance (surplus),		2,277 24
Total,		$27,341 24

Volume of Traffic, etc.

Number of passengers paying revenue carried during the period,	440,304
Number carried per mile of main railway track operated,	25,679
Number of car miles run,	164,979
Average number of persons employed,	47

ACCIDENTS TO PERSONS.

(A detailed statement of each accident is on file in the office of the Board.)

KILLED AND INJURED.	FROM CAUSES BEYOND THEIR OWN CONTROL.		FROM THEIR OWN MISCONDUCT OR CARELESSNESS.		TOTAL.	
	Killed.	Injured.	Killed.	Injured.	Killed.	Injured.
Passengers,	-	-	-	-	-	-
Employees,	-	-	-	-	-	-
Other persons,	-	-	-	1	-	1
TOTALS,	-	-	-	1	-	1

CORPORATE NAME AND ADDRESS OF THE COMPANY.

RECEIVERS OF THE BRISTOL COUNTY STREET RAILWAY COMPANY,

705 SEARS BUILDING, BOSTON, MASS.

NAMES AND RESIDENCE OF RECEIVERS.

John T. Burnett, Southborough, Mass. John L. Hall, Boston, Mass.

We hereby certify that the statements contained in the foregoing report are full, just and true.

JOHN T. BURNETT,
JOHN L. HALL,
Receivers.

COMMONWEALTH OF MASSACHUSETTS.

SUFFOLK, ss. OCT. 31, 1904. Then personally appeared the above-named John T. Burnett and John L. Hall, and severally made oath that the foregoing certificate by them subscribed is, to the best of their knowledge and belief, true.

Before me, JOSHUA M. SEARS, JR.,
Justice of the Peace.

REPORT

OF THE

BRISTOL & NORFOLK STREET RAILWAY COMPANY

For the Year ending September 30, 1904.

General Exhibit for the Year.

Gross earnings from operation,		$8,660 92
Operating expenses,		8,227 60
Gross Income above Operating Expenses,		$433 32
Charges upon income accrued during the year:		
Interest on funded debt,	$3,500 00	
Interest and discount on unfunded debts and loans,	1,397 56	
Taxes, commutation,	136 58	
Other deductions from income: paid carrying mail,	11 98	
Total Charges and Deductions from Income,		5,046 12
Deficit for the year ending September 30, 1904,		$4,612 80
Amount of deficit September 30, 1903,		835 61
Total Deficit September 30, 1904,		$5,448 41

Earnings from Operation.

Receipts from passengers carried,	$8,331 45
Receipts from carriage of mails,	60 00
Receipts from rentals of buildings and other property,	187 85
Receipts from advertising in cars,	75 00
Other earnings from operation: sale of old material,	6 62
Gross Earnings from Operation,	$8,660 92

Expenses of Operation.

General expenses:	
Salaries of general officers and clerks,	$1,092 00
General office expenses and supplies,	180 07
Legal expenses,	56 08
Insurance,	116 40
Other general expenses,	59 52

Maintenance of roadway and buildings:		
Repair of roadbed and track,		$124 36
Repair of electric line construction,		53 41
Maintenance of equipment:		
Repair of cars and other vehicles,		298 59
Repair of electric equipment of cars,		689 93
Transportation expenses:		
Cost of electric motive power,		2,302 98
Wages and compensation of persons employed in conducting transportation,		2,631 76
Removal of snow and ice,		156 19
Tolls for trackage over other railways,		268 22
Rentals of buildings and other property,		100 00
Other transportation expenses,		98 09
TOTAL OPERATING EXPENSES,		$8,227 60

PROPERTY ACCOUNTS.

Additions to railway: new electric line construction,	$56 52	
Other additions to railway: engineering, $80; cut out boxes, $18.43,	98 43	
TOTAL ADDITIONS TO RAILWAY,		$154 95
Additions to equipment:		
Additional cars (4 in number),	$4,318 40	
Electric equipment of same,	988 05	
Other additional rolling stock and vehicles,	482 40	
TOTAL ADDITIONS TO EQUIPMENT,		5,788 85
TOTAL ADDITIONS TO PROPERTY ACCOUNTS,		$5,943 80
Deductions from property accounts (property sold or reduced in valuation and credited to property accounts): sold three cars,		9,000 00
NET DEDUCTION FROM PROPERTY ACCOUNTS FOR THE YEAR,		$3,056 20

GENERAL BALANCE SHEET SEPTEMBER 30, 1904.

ASSETS.	DR.	
Cost of railway:		
Roadbed and tracks,	$112,552 56	
Electric line construction, including poles, wiring, feeder lines, etc.,	16,674 95	
Interest accrued during construction of railway,	5,000 00	
Engineering and other expenses incident to construction,	8,080 00	
Other items of railway cost,	8,000 00	
TOTAL COST OF RAILWAY OWNED,		$150,307 51
Cost of equipment: cars and other rolling stock and vehicles and electric equipment of same,		16,588 85

Cost of land and buildings:		
Land necessary for operation of railway,	$400 00	
Buildings necessary for operation of railway,	4,700 00	
TOTAL COST OF LAND AND BUILDINGS OWNED,		$5,100 00
TOTAL PERMANENT INVESTMENTS,		$171,996 36
Cash and current assets:		
Cash,	$973 08	
Bills and accounts receivable,	282 78	
TOTAL CASH AND CURRENT ASSETS,		1,255 86
Profit and loss balance (deficit),		5,448 41
TOTAL,		$178,700 63

LIABILITIES.	CR.	
Capital stock,		$100,000 00
Funded debt,		70,000 00
Current liabilities:		
Loans and notes payable,	$4,455 67	
Audited vouchers and accounts,	522 02	
Matured interest coupons unpaid (including coupons due October 1),	3,500 00	
TOTAL CURRENT LIABILITIES,		8,477 69
Accrued liabilities:		
Interest accrued and not yet due,	$174 80	
Taxes accrued and not yet due,	48 14	
TOTAL ACCRUED LIABILITIES,		222 94
TOTAL,		$178,700 63

CAPITAL STOCK.		
Capital stock authorized by law,	$100,000 00	
Capital stock authorized by votes of company,	100,000 00	
Capital stock issued and outstanding,		$100,000 00
Number of shares issued and outstanding,	1,000	
Number of stockholders,	15	
Number of stockholders in Massachusetts,	15	
Amount of stock held in Massachusetts,	$100,000 00	

FUNDED DEBT.

DESCRIPTION OF BONDS.	Rate of Interest.	Date of Maturity.	Amount Outstanding.	Interest Paid during the Year.
First mortgage bonds,	Per Cent. 5	June 1, 1923,	$70,000 00	-

Volume of Traffic, etc.

Number of passengers paying revenue carried during the year,	166,241
Number carried per mile of main railway track operated, .	27,949
Number of car miles run, ...	71,302
Average number of persons employed, ...	8

Description of Equipment.

Description of Equipment.	Equipped for Electric Power.	Not equipped.	Total Passenger Cars.	Equipped with Fenders.	Equipped with Electric Heaters.	Number of Motors.
Cars — Passenger Service.						
Box passenger cars, ...	3	1	4	3	3	6
Open passenger cars, ...	2	-	2	2	-	4
Total, ...	5	1	6	5	3	10
Snow ploughs, ...	1	-	-	-	-	2

Miscellaneous Equipment.

Other items of equipment: tower wagon, ...	1

Railway Owned, Leased and Operated (by Electric Power).

Railway Owned, etc.	Owned.	Trackage over Other Railways.	Total Owned, Leased, etc.	Total Operated.
	Miles.	Miles.	Miles.	Miles.
Length of railway line, ...	10.150	.378	10.528	5.948
Length of sidings, switches, etc., ...	.038	-	.038	.038
Total, Computed as Single Track, .	10.188	.378	10.566	5.986

Names of the several cities and towns in which the railways operated by the company are located: Randolph, Stoughton and Easton.

Corporate Name and Address of the Company.

BRISTOL & NORFOLK STREET RAILWAY COMPANY,

43 Tremont Street, Boston, Mass.

Names and Business Address of Principal Officers.

Henry A. Belcher, *President*, 617 Washington Street, Boston, Mass. Henry E. McElwain, *Treasurer and Clerk of Corporation*, 43 Tremont Street, Boston, Mass. George W. Anderson, *General Counsel*, 901 Carney Building, Boston, Mass. Frank J. Williams, *Superintendent*, North Stoughton, Mass.

NAMES AND RESIDENCE OF BOARD OF DIRECTORS.

Henry A. Belcher, Randolph, Mass. George W. Anderson, Boston, Mass. Weld A. Rollins, Brookline, Mass. James E. Howard, Eastondale, Mass. Henry E. McElwain, Boston, Mass.

We hereby certify that the statements contained in the foregoing report are full, just and true.

HENRY A. BELCHER,
GEORGE W. ANDERSON,
WELD A. ROLLINS,
Directors.
HENRY A. BELCHER,
Acting Treasurer.
F. J. WILLIAMS,
Superintendent.

COMMONWEALTH OF MASSACHUSETTS.

SUFFOLK, ss. Nov. 23, 1904. Then personally appeared the above-named Henry A. Belcher, George W. Anderson, and F. J. Williams, and severally made oath that the foregoing certificate by them subscribed is, to the best of their knowledge and belief, true.

Before me, ALONZO A. PULVERMAN,
Justice of the Peace.

REPORT

OF THE

BROCKTON & PLYMOUTH STREET RAILWAY COMPANY

For the Year ending September 30, 1904.

General Exhibit for the Year.		
Gross earnings from operation,		$98,752 54
Operating expenses,		60,592 15
Net Earnings from Operation,		$38,160 39
Miscellaneous income: park receipts,		5,306 73
Gross Income above Operating Expenses,		$43,467 12
Charges upon income accrued during the year:		
Interest on funded debt,	$13,159 37	
Interest and discount on unfunded debts and loans,	9,802 75	
Taxes, State and local, . . . $3,187 05		
Taxes, commutation, . . . 1,975 09		
	5,162 14	
Other deductions from income: park expenses,	7,387 71	
Total Charges and Deductions from Income,		35,511 97
Surplus for the year ending September 30, 1904,		$7,955 15
Amount of deficit September 30, 1903,		2,066 76
Total Surplus September 30, 1904,		$5,888 39
Earnings from Operation.		
Receipts from passengers carried,		$98,156 19
Receipts from carriage of mails,		371 38
Receipts from advertising in cars,		224 97
Gross Earnings from Operation,		$98,752 54
Expenses of Operation.		
General expenses:		
Salaries of general officers and clerks,		$6,305 28
General office expenses and supplies,		581 15
Legal expenses,		580 73
Insurance,		2,026 00

General expenses. — *Concluded.*		
Other general expenses:		
Advertising,		$701 16
Miscellaneous,		2,209 98
Maintenance of roadway and buildings:		
Repair of roadbed and track,		1,691 79
Repair of electric line construction,		514 62
Repair of buildings,		632 02
Maintenance of equipment:		
Repair of cars and other vehicles,		4,682 85
Repair of electric equipment of cars,		5,002 75
Renewal of horses, harnesses, shoeing, etc.,		13 25
Provender and stabling for horses,		111 00
Transportation expenses:		
Cost of electric motive power, $14,192.40; less power sold, $2,010.40; net,		12,182 00
Wages and compensation of persons employed in conducting transportation,		20,340 25
Removal of snow and ice,		896 81
Damages for injuries to persons and property,		1,134 85
Other transportation expenses: car service supplies, $460.50; telephone expenses, including maintenance of private line, $326.92; miscellaneous, $198.24,		985 66
Total Operating Expenses,		$60,592 15

Property Accounts.

Additions to railway: miscellaneous engineering charges on proposed extension,	$5,739 92
Additions to other permanent property: park, land and buildings,	26,000 00
Total Additions to Property Accounts,	$31,739 92
Deductions from property accounts (property sold or reduced in valuation and credited to property accounts): sale of wagon,	30 00
Net Addition to Property Accounts for the Year,	$31,709 92

General Balance Sheet September 30, 1904.

Assets.	Dr.	
Cost of railway:		
Roadbed and tracks,	$251,124 91	
Electric line construction, including poles, wiring, feeder lines, etc.,	103,108 05	
Engineering and other expenses incident to construction,	24,879 19	
Total Cost of Railway Owned,		$379,112 15
Cost of equipment:		
Cars and other rolling stock and vehicles,	$58,099 53	
Electric equipment of same,	42,878 01	
Shop tools and machinery,	1,001 77	
Other items of equipment: office furniture and fixtures,	310 37	
Total Cost of Equipment Owned,		102,289 68

Cost of land and buildings:		
Land necessary for operation of railway,	$8,745 00	
Electric power stations, including equipment,	202,730 00	
Other buildings necessary for operation of railway,	14,192 35	
Total Cost of Land and Buildings Owned,		$225,667 35
Other permanent property: park property,		26,000 00
Total Permanent Investments,		$733,069 18
Cash and current assets:		
Cash,	$19,057 57	
Bills and accounts receivable,	12,260 07	
Other cash and current assets:		
Unexpired insurance,	1,922 54	
Interest paid in advance, $2,408.05; suspense, $556.49,	2,964 54	
Total Cash and Current Assets,		36,204 72
Miscellaneous assets: materials and supplies,		9,662 39
Total,		$778,936 29

Liabilities.	Cr.	
Capital stock,		$295,000 00
Funded debt,		295,000 00
Current liabilities:		
Loans and notes payable,	$165,000 00	
Audited vouchers and accounts,	9,782 32	
Salaries and wages,	803 25	
Total Current Liabilities,		175,585 57
Accrued liabilities:		
Interest accrued and not yet due,	$4,452 49	
Taxes accrued and not yet due,	1,975 09	
Total Accrued Liabilities,		6,427 58
Sinking and other special funds: injury fund,		1,034 75
Profit and loss balance (surplus),		5,888 39
Total,		$778,936 29

Capital Stock.		
Capital stock authorized by law,	$295,000 00	
Capital stock authorized by votes of company,	295,000 00	
Capital stock issued and outstanding,		$295,000 00
Number of shares issued and outstanding,	2,950	
Number of stockholders,	64	
Number of stockholders in Massachusetts,	60	
Amount of stock held in Massachusetts,	$289,000 00	

Funded Debt.

Description of Bonds.	Rate of Interest.	Date of Maturity.	Amount Outstanding.	Interest Paid during the Year.
	Per Cent.			
Plymouth & Kingston Street Railway Company first mortgage bonds, .	5	Jan. 1, 1910,	$35,000 00	$1,750 00
Brockton & Plymouth Street Railway Company first mortgage bonds, .	4½	Dec. 1, 1920,	260,000 00	11,137 50
Totals, ...	. .	. . .	$295,000 00	$12,887 50

Volume of Traffic, etc.

Number of passengers paying revenue carried during the year,	1,955,124
Number carried per mile of main railway track operated, .	88,503
Number of car miles run, ...	429,753
Average number of persons employed, ...	58

Description of Equipment.

Description of Equipment.	Equipped for Electric Power.	Equipped with Fenders.	Equipped with Electric Heaters.	Number of Motors.
Cars — Passenger Service.				
Box passenger cars, ...	10	10	10	32
Open passenger cars, ...	16	16	-	32
Total, ...	26	26	10	64
Cars — Other Service.				
Work cars, ...	2	2	-	4
Snow ploughs, ...	3	-	-	1

Miscellaneous Equipment.

Carts and snow sleds, ...	2
Other railway rolling stock: tower wagon, ...	1
Horses, ...	1
Other items of equipment: repair shop equipment and machinery, sand boxes, fare registers, spare armatures and track and line tools.	

Railway Owned and Operated (by Electric Power).

Length of railway line, ...	22.091 miles.
Length of sidings, switches, etc., ...	1.706 "
Total, computed as single track, ...	23.797 "

Names of the several cities and towns in which the railways operated by the company are located: Plymouth, Kingston, Pembroke, Hanson and Whitman.

Accidents to Persons.

(A detailed statement of each accident is on file in the office of the Board.)

Killed and Injured.	From Causes beyond their own Control.		From their own Misconduct or Carelessness.		Total.	
	Killed.	Injured.	Killed.	Injured.	Killed.	Injured.
Passengers, ...	–	–	–	5	–	5
Employees, ...	–	1	1	1	1	2
Other persons, ...	–	–	1	4	1	4
Totals, ...	–	1	2	10	2	11

Corporate Name and Address of the Company.

BROCKTON & PLYMOUTH STREET RAILWAY COMPANY,

Plymouth, Mass.

Names and Business Address of Principal Officers.

James D. Thurber, *President*, Plymouth, Mass. Charles I. Litchfield, *Vice-President*, Plymouth, Mass. Frederick S. Pratt, *Second Vice-President*, 84 State Street, Boston, Mass. A. Stuart Pratt, *Treasurer*, 84 State Street, Boston, Mass. Henry R. Hayes, *Clerk of Corporation*, 84 State Street, Boston, Mass. Stone & Webster, *General Managers*, 84 State Street, Boston, Mass. Alba H. Warren, *Resident Manager*, Plymouth, Mass.

Names and Residence of Board of Directors.

Walter E. Damon, Bryantville, Mass. Charles S. Davis, Plymouth, Mass. Charles I. Litchfield, Plymouth, Mass. Frederick S. Pratt, Newton, Mass. Russell Robb, Concord, Mass. Charles A. Stone, Newton, Mass. James D. Thurber, Plymouth, Mass. Edwin S. Webster, Newton, Mass. Charles D. Wyman, Boston, Mass.

We hereby certify that the statements contained in the foregoing report are full, just and true.

JAS. D. THURBER,
CHARLES I. LITCHFIELD,
WALTER E. DAMON,
CHARLES S. DAVIS,
FRED'K S. PRATT,
CHARLES D. WYMAN,
RUSSELL ROBB,
Directors.
A. STUART PRATT,
Treasurer.
ALBA H. WARREN,
Resident Manager.

COMMONWEALTH OF MASSACHUSETTS.

PLYMOUTH, ss. Nov. 1, 1904. Then personally appeared the above-named Alba H. Warren, and made oath that the foregoing certificate by him subscribed is, to the best of his knowledge and belief, true.

Before me, EDWARD L. BURGESS,
Justice of the Peace.

COMMONWEALTH OF MASSACHUSETTS.

SUFFOLK, ss. Nov. 2, 1904. Then personally appeared the above-named Jas. D. Thurber, Charles I. Litchfield, Walter E. Damon, Charles S. Davis, Fred'k S. Pratt, Charles D. Wyman, Russell Robb and A. Stuart Pratt, and severally made oath that the foregoing certificate by them subscribed is, to the best of their knowledge and belief, true.

Before me, JOHN W. HALLOWELL,
Justice of the Peace.

REPORT

OF THE

CITIZENS' ELECTRIC STREET RAILWAY COMPANY

For the Year ending September 30, 1904.

General Exhibit for the Year.		
Gross earnings from operation, ...		$97,864 16
Operating expenses, ...		59,846 16
Gross Income above Operating Expenses, . .		$38,018 00
Charges upon income accrued during the year:		
Interest on funded debt, ...	$10,500 00	
Interest and discount on unfunded debts and loans, ...	2,999 50	
Taxes, State and local, . . . $3,840 00		
Taxes, commutation, . . . 1,926 91		
	5,766 91	
Other deductions from income: amusements,	1,287 50	
Total Charges and Deductions from Income, . .		20,553 91
Net Divisible Income, ...		$17,464 09
Dividends declared:		
3 per cent on $240,000, ...	$7,200 00	
2½ per cent on $240,000, ...	6,000 00	
Total Dividends Declared, ...		13,200 00
Surplus for the year ending September 30, 1904, ...		$4,264 09
Amount of surplus S-ptember 30, 1903, ...		31,978 27
Debits to profit and loss account during the year:		
Settlement of old damage claims, ...	$3,063 90	
Settlement of old accounts, ...	2,257 00	
Amount expended for new car house and new equipment to replace property destroyed by fire in excess of amount received for insurance, ...	6,756 13	
Total Debits, ...		12,077 03
Total Surplus September 30, 1904, ...		$24,165 33

Earnings from Operation.

Receipts from passengers carried,	$96,631 98
Receipts from carriage of mails,	141 30
Receipts from carriage of freight,	400 86
Receipts from tolls for use of tracks by other companies,	204 59
Receipts from rentals of buildings and other property,	200 43
Receipts from advertising in cars,	285 00
Gross Earnings from Operation,	$97,864 16

Expenses of Operation.

General expenses:	
Salaries of general officers and clerks,	$3,285 02
General office expenses and supplies,	290 30
Insurance,	1,440 00
Other general expenses: miscellaneous,	2,524 23
Maintenance of roadway and buildings:	
Repair of roadbed and track,	4,464 81
Repair of electric line construction,	983 25
Repair of buildings,	448 39
Maintenance of equipment:	
Repair of cars and other vehicles,	4,536 52
Repair of electric equipment of cars,	4,273 87
Transportation expenses:	
Cost of electric motive power, $19,909.78; less power sold, $4,196.26; net,	15,713 52
Wages and compensation of persons employed in conducting transportation,	18,754 94
Removal of snow and ice,	2,425 93
Damages for injuries to persons and property,	705 38
Total Operating Expenses,	$59,846 16

General Balance Sheet September 30, 1904.

Assets.	Dr.	
Cost of railway:		
Roadbed and tracks,	$241,267 82	
Electric line construction, including poles, wiring, feeder lines, etc.,	70,970 00	
Engineering and other expenses incident to construction,	10,473 58	
Total Cost of Railway Owned,		$322,711 40
Cost of equipment:		
Cars and other rolling stock and vehicles,	$45,865 15	
Electric equipment of same,	41,000 38	
Other items of equipment,	9,987 94	
Total Cost of Equipment Owned,		96,853 47
Cost of land and buildings:		
Electric power stations, including equipment,	$65,813 73	
Other buildings necessary for operation of railway, including land,	29,871 89	
Total Cost of Land and Buildings Owned,		95,685 62
Total Permanent Investments,		$515,250 49

Cash and current assets:		
Cash,	$17,983 95	
Bills and accounts receivable,	3,666 15	
Other cash and current assets:		
Prepaid insurance,	2,716 35	
Prepaid interest,	689 33	
TOTAL CASH AND CURRENT ASSETS,		$25,055 78
Miscellaneous assets: materials and supplies,		13,918 77
TOTAL,		$554,225 04

LIABILITIES.	CR.	
Capital stock,		$240,000 00
Funded debt,		210,000 00
Current liabilities:		
Loans and notes payable,	$65,732 29	
Audited vouchers and accounts,	5,000 00	
TOTAL CURRENT LIABILITIES,		70,732 29
Accrued liabilities:		
Interest accrued and not yet due,	$3,560 51	
Taxes accrued and not yet due,	5,766 91	
TOTAL ACCRUED LIABILITIES,		9,327 42
Profit and loss balance (surplus),		24,165 33
TOTAL,		$554,225 04

CAPITAL STOCK.		
Capital stock authorized by law,	$240,000 00	
Capital stock authorized by votes of company,	240,000 00	
Capital stock issued and outstanding,		$240,000 00
Number of shares issued and outstanding,	2,400	
Number of stockholders,	30	
Number of stockholders in Massachusetts,	29	
Amount of stock held in Massachusetts,	$233,900 00	

FUNDED DEBT.

DESCRIPTION OF BONDS.	Rate of Interest.	Date of Maturity.	Amount Outstanding.	Interest Paid during the Year.
First mortgage gold bonds,*	Per Cent. 5	Dec. 1, 1920,	$210,000 00	$10,500 00

* $20,000 additional bonds issued but held in treasury to provide for extension of power station in accordance with decree of the Board of Railroad Commissioners.

Volume of Traffic, etc.

Number of passengers paying revenue carried during the year,	2,067,102
Number carried per mile of main railway track operated,	92,154
Number of car miles run,	384,436
Average number of persons employed,	70

Description of Equipment.

Description of Equipment.	Equipped for Electric Power.	Not Equipped.	Total Passenger Cars.	Equipped with Fenders.	Equipped with Electric Heaters.	Number of Motors.
Cars — Passenger Service.						
Box passenger cars,	10	4	14	10	10	-
Open passenger cars,	19	6	25	17	-	-
Total,	29	10	39	27	10	58
Cars — Other Service.						
Box freight cars,	1	-	-	-	-	-
Platform freight cars,	1	-	-	-	-	-
Total,	2	-	-	-	-	-
Snow ploughs,	3	-	-	-	-	-

Miscellaneous Equipment.

Carts and snow sleds,	4
Other highway vehicles: tower wagon,	1
Horses,	2
Other items of equipment: harnesses (2 single, 1 double),	4

Railway Owned, Leased and Operated (by Electric Power).

Railway Owned, etc.	Owned.	Trackage over Other Railways.	Total Owned, Leased, etc.
	Miles.	Miles.	Miles.
Length of railway line,	21.862	.569	22.431
Length of sidings, switches, etc.,	1.216	-	1.216
Total, Computed as Single Track,	23.078	.569	23.647

Railway Located Outside of Public Ways.

Length of railway line, ...	1.672 miles.

Names of the several cities and towns in which the railways operated by the company are located: Newburyport, Newbury, Amesbury and Merrimac.

Grade Crossings with Railroads.

Grade Crossings with Railroads.	Number of Tracks at Crossing.	
	Railroad.	Railway.
Crossings of railways with railroads at grade (1 in number), viz.:— With Boston & Maine Railroad, Purchase Street, Newburyport, .	1	1

Number of above crossings at which *frogs* are inserted in the tracks, . 1

Accidents to Persons.

(A detailed statement of each accident is on file in the office of the Board.)

Killed and Injured.	From Causes beyond their own Control.		From their own Misconduct or Carelessness.		Total.	
	Killed.	Injured.	Killed.	Injured.	Killed.	Injured.
Passengers, ...	-	2	-	2	-	4
Employees, ...	-	-	-	-	-	-
Other persons, ...	-	-	1	1	1	1
Totals, ...	-	2	1	3	1	5

Corporate Name and Address of the Company.

CITIZENS' ELECTRIC STREET RAILWAY COMPANY,

Newburyport, Mass.

Names and Business Address of Principal Officers.

William M. Butler, *President*, Tremont Building, Boston, Mass. James F. Shaw, *Vice-President*, 8 Congress Street, Boston, Mass. George A. Butman, *Treasurer and Clerk of Corporation*, 8 Congress Street, Boston, Mass. Orrin F. Files, *Superintendent*, Newburyport, Mass.

Names and Residence of Board of Directors.

Edward P. Shaw, Newburyport, Mass. H. Fisher Eldredge, Portsmouth, N. H. E. P. Shaw, Jr., Newton, Mass. William M. Butler, Edgartown, Mass. Ewen R. McPherson, Cambridge, Mass. Alex. B. Bruce, Lawrence, Mass. Charles C. Peirce, Brookline, Mass. Robert Redford, Lawrence, Mass. James F. Shaw, Manchester, Mass.

We hereby certify that the statements contained in the foregoing report are full, just and true.

EDWARD P. SHAW,
JAMES F. SHAW,
ROBERT REDFORD,
CHAS. C. PEIRCE,
ALEX. B. BRUCE,
EWEN R. McPHERSON,
WM. M. BUTLER,
Directors.
GEO. A. BUTMAN,
Treasurer.
ORRIN F. FILES,
Superintendent.

COMMONWEALTH OF MASSACHUSETTS.

SUFFOLK, ss. BOSTON, Nov. 22, 1904. Then personally appeared the above-named Edward P. Shaw, Jas. F. Shaw, Robert Redford, Chas. C. Peirce, Alex. B. Bruce, Ewen R. McPherson, Wm. M. Butler, Geo. A. Butman and Orrin F. Files, and severally made oath that the foregoing certificate by them subscribed is, to the best of their knowledge and belief, true.

Before me, ARTHUR W. CLAPP,
Justice of the Peace.

REPORT

OF THE

COMMONWEALTH AVENUE STREET RAILWAY COMPANY

For the Three Months ending December 31, 1903.

(Consolidated with the Newton, December 31, 1903.)

General Exhibit for the Period.		
Gross earnings from operation,		$15,191 89
Operating expenses,		17,792 33
Gross Deficit,		$2,600 44
Charges upon income accrued during the year:		
Interest on funded debt,	$937 50	
Interest and discount on unfunded debts and loans,	2,671 46	
Taxes, State and local,	1,505 21	
Total Charges and Deductions from Income,		5,114 17
Deficit for the three months ending December 31, 1903,		$7,714 61
Amount of deficit September 30, 1903,		5,715 46
Total Deficit December 31, 1903,		$13,430 07

Earnings from Operation.	
Receipts from passengers carried,	$13,948 20
Receipts from rentals of buildings and other property,	962 14
Receipts from advertising in cars,	281 55
Gross Earnings from Operation,	$15,191 89

Expenses of Operation.	
General expenses:	
Salaries of general officers and clerks,	$1,040 50
General office expenses and supplies,	328 02
Insurance,	573 77
Maintenance of roadway and buildings:	
Repair of roadbed and track,	409 80
Repair of electric line construction,	248 42
Repair of buildings,	82 84

Maintenance of equipment:		
Repair of cars and other vehicles,		$993 56
Repair of electric equipment of cars,		1,639 45
Renewal of horses, harnesses, shoeing, etc., provender and stabling for horses,		157 72
Transportation expenses:		
Cost of electric motive power,		4,574 70
Wages and compensation of persons employed in conducting transportation,		6,670 51
Removal of snow and ice,		329 29
Damages for injuries to persons and property,		677 61
Tolls for trackage over other railways,		50
Rentals of buildings and other property,		50 04
Other transportation expenses: miscellaneous shop expense,		15 60
Total Operating Expenses,		$17,792 33

Property Accounts.

Additions to equipment:		
Additional cars and electric equipment of same,	$584 46	
Other additions to equipment:		
Shop tools and machinery,	69 84	
Sand boxes and signal lamps,	80 30	
Total Additions to Equipment,		$734 60
Additions to land and buildings:		
Additional land necessary for operation of railway,	$322 68	
Fire extinguishers,	120 75	
Total Additions to Land and Buildings,		443 43
Total Additions to Property Accounts,		$1,178 03

General Balance Sheet December 31, 1903.

Assets.	Dr.	
Cost of railway:		
Roadbed and tracks,	$154,061 80	
Electric line construction, including poles, wiring, feeder lines, etc.,	27,950 51	
Interest accrued during construction of railway,	10,097 09	
Engineering and other expenses incident to construction,	8,887 28	
Total Cost of Railway Owned,		$200,996 68
Cost of equipment:		
Cars and other rolling stock and vehicles,	$148,783 30	
Electric equipment of same,	81,874 27	
Horses,	125 00	
Other items of equipment: harness, $102.39; shop tools and machinery, $1,534.36; furniture and fixtures, $1,024.07,	2,660 82	
Total Cost of Equipment Owned,		233,443 39

Cost of land and buildings:		
Land necessary for operation of railway,	$38,312 41	
Other buildings necessary for operation of railway,	66,968 09	
TOTAL COST OF LAND AND BUILDINGS OWNED,		$105,280 50
TOTAL PERMANENT INVESTMENTS,		$539,720 57
Cash and current assets:		
Bills and accounts receivable,		5,724 26
Profit and loss balance (deficit),		13,430 07
TOTAL,		$558,874 90

LIABILITIES.	CR.	
Capital stock,		$292,000 00
Funded debt,		75,000 00
Real estate mortgages,		2,500 00
Current liabilities:		
Loans and notes payable,	$75,000 00	
Audited vouchers and accounts,	111,001 37	
Matured interest coupons unpaid (including coupons due October 1),	1,562 50	
TOTAL CURRENT LIABILITIES,		187,563 87
Accrued liabilities:		
Interest accrued and not yet due,	$305 82	
Taxes accrued and not yet due,	1,505 21	
TOTAL ACCRUED LIABILITIES,		1,811 03
TOTAL,		$558,874 90

CAPITAL STOCK.

Capital stock authorized by law,	$292,000 00	
Capital stock authorized by votes of company,	292,000 00	
Capital stock issued and outstanding,		$292,000 00
Number of shares issued and outstanding,	2,920	
Number of stockholders,	8	
Number of stockholders in Massachusetts,	8	
Amount of stock held in Massachusetts,	$292,000 00	

REAL ESTATE MORTGAGES.

DESCRIPTION OF MORTGAGED PROPERTY.	Rate of Interest.	Mortgage when Due.	Amount.	Interest Paid during the Period.
On real estate,	Per Cent. 4	Dec. 4, 1902,	$2,500 00	$50 00

FUNDED DEBT.

DESCRIPTION OF BONDS.	Rate of Interest.	Date of Maturity.	Amount Outstanding.	Interest Paid during the Period.
First mortgage gold bonds,	Per Cent. 5	Feb. 1, 1916,	$75,000 00	$937 50

Volume of Traffic, etc.

Number of passengers paying revenue carried during the period,	323,072
Number carried per mile of main railway track operated,	24,758
Number of car miles run,	106,943
Average number of persons employed,	57

Description of Equipment.

Description of Equipment.	Equipped for Electric Power.	Equipped with Fenders.	Equipped with Electric Heaters.	Number of Motors.
Cars — Passenger Service.				
Box passenger cars,	30	30	30	-
Open passenger cars,	35	35	-	-
Total,	65	65	30	140
Cars — Other Service.				
Service car,	1	-	-	-
Snow ploughs,	3	-	-	-

Miscellaneous Equipment.

Carts and snow sleds,	2
Other railway rolling stock: platform trailer,	1
Other highway vehicles: democrat and concord wagons,	2
Horses,	1
Other items of equipment: harnesses (single),	2

Railway Owned, Leased and Operated (by Electric Power).

Railway Owned, etc.	Owned.	Trackage over Other Railways.	Total Owned, Leased, etc.
	Miles.	Miles.	Miles.
Length of railway line,	6.946	.550	7.496
Length of second main track,	5.553	-	5.553
Total Length of Main Track,	12.499	.550	13.049
Length of sidings, switches, etc.,	.992	-	.992
Total, Computed as Single Track,	13.491	.550	14.041

Names of the several cities and towns in which the railways operated by the company are located: Newton.

Corporate Name and Address of the Company.

COMMONWEALTH AVENUE STREET RAILWAY COMPANY,

Newtonville, Mass.

Names and Business Address of Principal Officers.

Adams D. Claflin, *President*, Newtonville, Mass. Charles W. Smith, *Treasurer*, Newtonville, Mass. Frank W. Remick, *Clerk of Corporation*, Boston, Mass. Coolidge & Hight, *General Counsel*, Boston, Mass. Matthew C. Brush, *General Manager*, Newtonville, Mass.

Names and Residence of Board of Directors.

Adams D. Claflin, Newton Centre, Mass. William F. Hammett, Newton, Mass. Sydney Harwood, Newton, Mass. Frederic H. Lewis, Swampscott, Mass. Frank W. Remick, West Newton, Mass. James L. Richards, Newtonville, Mass. Alden E. Viles, Boston, Mass.

We hereby certify that the statements contained in the foregoing report are full, just and true.

ADAMS D. CLAFLIN,
WILLIAM F. HAMMETT,
JAMES L. RICHARDS,
FREDERIC H. LEWIS,
ALDEN E. VILES,
SYDNEY HARWOOD,
Directors.
CHAS. W. SMITH,
Treasurer.
MATTHEW C. BRUSH,
Superintendent.

Commonwealth of Massachusetts.

Suffolk, ss. Oct. 29, 1904. Then personally appeared the above-named Adams D. Claflin, William F. Hammett, James L. Richards, Frederic H. Lewis, Alden E. Viles, Sydney Harwood, Charles W. Smith and Matthew C. Brush, and severally made oath that the foregoing certificate by them subscribed is, to the best of their knowledge and belief, true.

Before me, GEO. M. COX,
Notary Public.

REPORT

OF THE

RECEIVERS OF THE CONCORD & BOSTON STREET RAILWAY

For the Year ending September 30, 1904.

[Operated by the Lexington & Boston under a contract approved Oct. 10, 1901.]

General Exhibit for the Year.

Rental received from lease of railway,		$1,742 54
Income from other sources: rental of poles,		98 00
Gross Income,		$1,840 54
Expenses and charges upon income accrued during the year:		
Interest and discount on unfunded debts and loans,	$1,879 95	
Taxes,	423 38	
Other expenses and charges upon income: insurance, $37.50; office expenses, $210.22,	247 72	
Total Expenses and Charges upon Income,		2,551 05
Deficit for the year ending September 30, 1904,		$710 51
Amount of deficit September 30, 1903,		2,824 25
Debits to profit and loss account during the year: commissions,		6,260 45
Total Deficit September 30, 1904,		$9,795 21

General Balance Sheet September 30, 1904.

Assets.	Dr.	
Cost of railway:		
Roadbed and tracks,	$61,523 96	
Electric line construction, including poles, wiring, feeder lines, etc.,	6,592 60	
Interest accrued during construction of railway,	3,463 05	
Engineering and other expenses incident to construction,	10,705 31	
Other items of railway cost,	5,340 14	
Total Cost of Railway Owned,		$87,625 06
Cost of land and buildings: land necessary for operation of railway,		306 00
Total Permanent Investments,		$87,931 06

Cash and current assets:		
Cash,	$4 35	
Bills and accounts receivable,	39,329 38	
Total Cash and Current Assets,		$39,333 73
Profit and loss balance (deficit),		9,795 21
Total,		$137,060 00

Liabilities.	Cr.	
Capital stock,		$50,000 00
Current liabilities:		
Loans and notes payable,	$87,000 00	
Audited vouchers and accounts,	60 00	
Total Current Liabilities,		87,060 00
Total,		$137,060 00

Capital Stock.

Capital stock authorized by law,	$50,000 00	
Capital stock authorized by votes of company,	50,000 00	
Capital stock issued and outstanding,		$50,000 00
Number of shares issued and outstanding,	500	
Number of stockholders,	10	
Number of stockholders in Massachusetts,	10	
Amount of stock held in Massachusetts,	$50,000 00	

Railway Owned.

Length of railway line,	2.449 miles.
Length of sidings, switches, etc.,	.169 "
Total, computed as single track,	2.618 "

Names of the several cities and towns in which the railway owned by the company is located: Waltham.

Corporate Name and Address of the Receivers.

RECEIVERS OF THE CONCORD & BOSTON STREET RAILWAY COMPANY,

705 Sears Building, Boston, Mass.

Names and Business Address of Principal Officers.

Erastus H. Smith, *President*, Concord, Mass. Edward A. Mead, *Treasurer*, Boston, Mass.

Names and Residence of Receivers.

John T. Burnett, Southborough, Mass. John L. Hall, Boston, Mass. George H. Newhall, Providence, R. I.

NAMES AND RESIDENCE OF BOARD OF DIRECTORS.

Erastus H. Smith, Concord, Mass. Edward A. Mead, Dorchester, Mass. Charles S. Cummings, 2d, Boston, Mass. S. Edgar Whitaker, Woburn, Mass. Jasper H. Yetten, Waltham, Mass.

We hereby certify that the statements contained in the foregoing report are full, just and true, according to the records of the corporation now in our hands.

JOHN L. HALL,
JOHN T. BURNETT,
Receivers.

COMMONWEALTH OF MASSACHUSETTS.

SUFFOLK, ss. Nov. 3, 1904. Then personally appeared the above-named John L. Hall and John T. Burnett, and severally made oath that the foregoing certificate by them subscribed is, to the best of their knowledge and belief, true.

Before me, JOSHUA M. SEARS, JR.,
Justice of the Peace.

REPORT

OF THE

CONCORD, MAYNARD & HUDSON STREET RAILWAY COMPANY

For the Year ending September 30, 1904.

General Exhibit for the Year.

Gross earnings from operation,			$53,945 68
Operating expenses,			43,462 70
Gross Income above Operating Expenses,			$10,482 98
Charges upon income accrued during the year:			
Interest on funded debt,		$8,250 00	
Interest and discount on unfunded debts and loans,		6,323 25	
Taxes, State and local,	$2,644 59		
Taxes, commutation,	545 44		
		3,190 03	
Total Charges and Deductions from Income,			17,763 28
Deficit for the year ending September 30, 1904,			$7,280 30
Amount of surplus September 30, 1903,			9,705 52
Total Surplus September 30, 1904,			$2,425 22

Earnings from Operation.

Receipts from passengers carried,	$52,081 53
Receipts from carriage of mails,	471 14
Receipts from tolls for use of tracks by other companies,	300 00
Receipts from rentals of buildings and other property,	893 09
Receipts from advertising in cars,	199 92
Gross Earnings from Operation,	$53,945 68

Expenses of Operation.

General expenses:	
Salaries of general officers and clerks,	$2,819 60
General office expenses and supplies,	1,319 47
Legal expenses,	400 00
Insurance,	3,100 62
Other general expenses,	1,308 50

Maintenance of roadway and buildings:	
Repair of roadbed and track,	$1,313 59
Repair of electric line construction,	300 53
Repair of buildings,	88 71
Maintenance of equipment:—	
Repair of cars and other vehicles,	1,843 62
Repair of electric equipment of cars,	2,948 30
Transportation expenses:	
Cost of electric motive power, $12,857.53; less power sold, $1,963.69; net,	10,893 84
Wages and compensation of persons employed in conducting transportation,	12,778 38
Removal of snow and ice,	1,393 24
Damages for injuries to persons and property,	85 50
Tolls for trackage over other railways,	750 00
Other transportation expenses:	
Car house labor, $740; advertising, $76,	816 00
Amusements, $50; transportation expenses, $1,252.80,	1,302 80
TOTAL OPERATING EXPENSES,	$43,462 70

PROPERTY ACCOUNTS.

Additions to railway:		
Change in tracks due to State highway,	$1,835 50	
Change in line construction due to State highway,	186 90	
Legal and engineering expenses,	2,023 30	
TOTAL ADDITIONS TO RAILWAY,		$4,045 70
Additions to equipment:		
Additional rolling stock and vehicles,	$737 58	
Other additions to equipment: sundry equipment,	128 52	
TOTAL ADDITIONS TO EQUIPMENT,		866 10
TOTAL ADDITIONS TO PROPERTY ACCOUNTS,		$4,911 80

GENERAL BALANCE SHEET SEPTEMBER 30, 1904.

ASSETS.	DR.	
Cost of railway:		
Roadbed and tracks,	$168,388 74	
Electric line construction, including poles, wiring, feeder lines, etc.,	31,933 54	
Interest accrued during construction of railway,	11,315 72	
Engineering and other expenses incident to construction,	8,519 63	
TOTAL COST OF RAILWAY OWNED,		$220,157 63
Cost of equipment:		
Cars and other rolling stock and vehicles,	$41,729 29	
Electric equipment of same,	38,589 15	
Other items of equipment: sundry equipment,	1,748 33	
TOTAL COST OF EQUIPMENT OWNED,		82,066 77

Cost of land and buildings:		
Land necessary for operation of railway, .	$15,498 46	
Electric power stations, including equipment,	74,274 27	
Other buildings necessary for operation of railway, ...	18,573 16	
TOTAL COST OF LAND AND BUILDINGS OWNED, . . .		$108,345 89
TOTAL PERMANENT INVESTMENTS, ...		$410,570 29
Cash and current assets:		
Cash, ...	$1,594 77	
Bills and accounts receivable, ...	6,759 34	
TOTAL CASH AND CURRENT ASSETS, ...		8,354 11
Miscellaneous assets: materials and supplies, .	$19,280 81	
Other assets and property:		
Prepaid insurance, ...	685 19	
Prepaid interest, ...	1,423 60	
TOTAL MISCELLANEOUS ASSETS, ...		21,389 60
TOTAL, ...		$440,314 00

LIABILITIES.	CR.	
Capital stock, ...		$175,000 00
Funded debt, ...		165,000 00
Current liabilities:		
Loans and notes payable, ...	$91,843 88	
Audited vouchers and accounts, ...	3,982 40	
TOTAL CURRENT LIABILITIES, ...		95,826 28
Accrued liabilities: interest accrued and not yet due, . .		2,062 50
Profit and loss balance (surplus), ...		2,425 22
TOTAL, ...		$440,314 00

CAPITAL STOCK.		
Capital stock authorized by law, ...	$175,000 00	
Capital stock authorized by votes of company,	175,000 00	
Capital stock issued and outstanding, ...		$175,000 00
Number of shares issued and outstanding, .	1,750	
Number of stockholders, ...	94	
Number of stockholders in Massachusetts, .	94	
Amount of stock held in Massachusetts, . .	$175,000 00	

FUNDED DEBT.

DESCRIPTION OF BONDS.	Rate of Interest.	Date of Maturity.	Amount Outstanding.	Interest Paid during the Year.
First mortgage gold bonds, . . .	Per Cent. 5	July 1, 1922,	$165,000 00	$8,250 00

VOLUME OF TRAFFIC, ETC.

Number of passengers paying revenue carried during the year,	1,042,968
Number carried per mile of main railway track operated,	71,633
Number of car miles run,	316,869
Average number of persons employed,	32

DESCRIPTION OF EQUIPMENT.

DESCRIPTION OF EQUIPMENT.	Equipped for Electric Power.	Equipped with Fenders.	Equipped with Electric Heaters.	Number of Motors.
CARS — PASSENGER SERVICE.				
Box passenger cars,	9	9	9	36
Open passenger cars,	7	7	-	14
TOTAL,	16	16	9	50
CARS — OTHER SERVICE.				
Work cars,	1	1	-	2
Snow ploughs,	2	-	-	4

RAILWAY OWNED, LEASED AND OPERATED (BY ELECTRIC POWER).

RAILWAY OWNED, ETC.	Owned.	Held under Lease or Contract	Total Owned, Leased, etc.
	Miles.	Miles.	Miles.
Length of railway line,	12.470	.350	12.820
Length of sidings, switches, etc.,	.600	-	.600
TOTAL, COMPUTED AS SINGLE TRACK,	13.070	.350	13.420

RAILWAY LOCATED OUTSIDE OF PUBLIC WAYS.

Length of railway line,	1.740 miles.

Names of the several cities and towns in which the railways operated by the company are located: Concord, Acton, Maynard, Stowe and Hudson.

GRADE CROSSINGS WITH RAILROADS.

GRADE CROSSINGS WITH RAILROADS.	NUMBER OF TRACKS AT CROSSING.	
	Railroad.	Railway.
Crossings of railways with railroads at grade (2 in number), viz.: —		
With Fitchburg Railroad, at Maynard,	1	1
With New York, New Haven & Hartford Railroad, at Concord Junction,	1	1
TOTAL NUMBER OF TRACKS AT CROSSINGS,	2	2

Accidents to Persons.

(A detailed statement of each accident is on file in the office of the Board.)

Killed and Injured.	From Causes beyond their own Control.		From their own Misconduct or Carelessness.		Total.	
	Killed.	Injured.	Killed.	Injured.	Killed.	Injured.
Passengers,	-	-	-	4	-	4
Employees,	-	-	-	-	-	-
Other persons,	-	-	-	-	-	-
Totals,	-	-	-	4	-	4

Corporate Name and Address of the Company.

CONCORD, MAYNARD & HUDSON STREET RAILWAY COMPANY,

Room 316, 53 State Street, Boston, Mass.

Names and Business Address of Principal Officers.

Walter R. Dame, *President and General Counsel*, Clinton, Mass. Charles H. Persons, *Vice-President*, Maynard, Mass. William S. Reed, *Treasurer*, 53 State Street, Boston, Mass. Harry G. Lowe, *Clerk of Corporation*, 53 State Street, Boston, Mass. John W. Ogden, *Superintendent*, Maynard, Mass.

Names and Residence of Board of Directors.

Walter R. Dame, Clinton, Mass. Wm. S. Reed, Leominster, Mass. Chas. W. Shippee, Milford, Mass. Chas. H. Persons, Maynard, Mass. Julius Loewe, Maynard, Mass. Jerome Marble, Worcester, Mass. Henry Tower, Hudson, Mass. E. A. Onthank, Fitchburg, Mass. Harry G. Lowe, Waltham, Mass.

We hereby certify that the statements contained in the foregoing report are full, just and true.

WALTER R. DAME,
CHARLES H. PERSONS,
HENRY TOWER,
JULIUS LOEWE,
CHAS. W. SHIPPEE,
WILLIAM S. REED,
Directors.
WILLIAM S. REED,
Treasurer.
JOHN W. OGDEN,
Superintendent.

COMMONWEALTH OF MASSACHUSETTS.

SUFFOLK, ss. BOSTON, Nov. 1, 1904. Then personally appeared the above-named Chas. H. Persons, Henry Tower, Julius Loewe, Chas. W. Shippee and W. R. Dame, and severally made oath that the foregoing certificate by them subscribed is, to the best of their knowledge and belief, true.

Before me, JOHN W. OGDEN,
Justice of the Peace.

COMMONWEALTH OF MASSACHUSETTS.

SUFFOLK, ss. BOSTON, Nov. 1, 1904. Then personally appeared the above-named John W. Ogden and William S. Reed and severally made oath that the foregoing certificate by them subscribed is, to the best of their knowledge and belief, true.

Before me, JAMES A. TIRRELL,
Notary Public.

REPORT

OF THE

CONWAY ELECTRIC STREET RAILWAY COMPANY

For the Year ending September 30, 1904.

General Exhibit for the Year.		
Gross earnings from operation,		$9,694 38
Operating expenses,		5,818 73
Gross Income above Operating Expenses,		$3,875 65
Charges upon income accrued during the year:		
Interest and discount on unfunded debts and loans,	$3,550 39	
Taxes, State and local,	178 70	
Total Charges and Deductions from Income,		3,729 09
Surplus for the year ending September 30, 1904,		$146 56
Amount of deficit September 30, 1903,		9,165 31
		$9,018 75
Credits to profit and loss account during the year:		
Carried to real estate,	$2,000 00	
Carried to legal expenses,	6,000 00	
Total Credits,		8,000 00
Total Deficit September 30, 1904,		$1,018 75

Earnings from Operation.	
Receipts from passengers carried,	$2,917 46
Receipts from carriage of mails,	373 72
Receipts from carriage of express and parcels,	687 25
Receipts from carriage of freight,	5,715 95
Gross Earnings from Operation,	$9,694 38

Expenses of Operation.	
General expenses:	
Salaries of general officers and clerks,	$426 93
General office expenses and supplies,	381 60
Maintenance of roadway and buildings:	
Repair of roadbed and track,	378 95
Repair of buildings,	11 50

Maintenance of equipment:		
Repair of cars and other vehicles,		$220 59
Repair of electric equipment of cars,		205 46
Transportation expenses:		
Cost of electric motive power,		1,660 65
Wages and compensation of persons employed in conducting transportation,		2,408 05
Rentals of buildings and other property,		125 00
TOTAL OPERATING EXPENSES,		$5,818 73

PROPERTY ACCOUNTS.

Additions to railway: legal expenses during construction,		$6,358 50
Additions to equipment: rolling stock and vehicles,		275 00
Additions to other permanent property: land,		2,000 00
TOTAL ADDITIONS TO PROPERTY ACCOUNTS,		$8,633 50

GENERAL BALANCE SHEET SEPTEMBER 30, 1904.

ASSETS.	DR.	
Cost of railway:		
Roadbed and tracks,	$56,154 83	
Electric line construction, including poles, wiring, feeder lines, etc.,	6,809 76	
Interest accrued during construction of railway,	521 51	
Engineering and other expenses incident to construction,	9,737 24	
TOTAL COST OF RAILWAY OWNED,		$73,223 34
Cost of equipment:		
Cars and other rolling stock and vehicles,	$6,203 84	
Electric equipment of same,	4,792 95	
TOTAL COST OF EQUIPMENT OWNED,		10,996 79
Cost of land and buildings:		
Electric power stations, including equipment,	$8,853 04	
Other buildings necessary for operation of railway,	604 17	
TOTAL COST OF LAND AND BUILDINGS OWNED,		9,457 21
Other permanent property,		2,200 00
TOTAL PERMANENT INVESTMENTS,		$95,877 34
Cash and current assets:		
Cash,	$624 96	
Bills and accounts receivable,	3,327 35	
Other cash and current assets: repairs in process, money advanced,	400 00	
TOTAL CASH AND CURRENT ASSETS,		4,352 31
Miscellaneous assets: materials and supplies, coal on hand,		110 00
Profit and loss balance (deficit),		1,018 75
TOTAL,		$101,358 40

LIABILITIES.	CR.	
Capital stock,		$35,950 00
Current liabilities:		
Loans and notes payable,	$63,200 00	
Audited vouchers and accounts,	1,436 85	
TOTAL CURRENT LIABILITIES,		64,636 85
Accrued liabilities: interest accrued and not yet due,		771 55
TOTAL,		$101,358 40

CAPITAL STOCK.		
Capital stock authorized by law,	$100,000 00	
Capital stock authorized by votes of company,	42,000 00	
Capital stock issued and outstanding,		$35,900 00
Amount paid in on one share not yet issued,		50 00
TOTAL CAPITAL STOCK LIABILITY,		$35,950 00
Number of shares issued and outstanding,	359	
Number of stockholders,	81	
Number of stockholders in Massachusetts,	77	
Amount of stock held in Massachusetts,	$30,850 00	

FUNDED DEBT.

$35,000 six per cent mortgage bonds issued and used as collateral for the notes of the company.

VOLUME OF TRAFFIC, ETC.

Number of passengers paying revenue carried during the year,	58,349
Number carried per mile of main railway track operated,	9,873
Number of car miles run,	30,488
Average number of persons employed,	5

DESCRIPTION OF EQUIPMENT.

DESCRIPTION OF EQUIPMENT.	Equipped for Electric Power.	Not Equipped.	Total Passenger Cars.	Equipped with Electric Heaters.	Number of Motors.
CARS — PASSENGER SERVICE.					
Box passenger cars,	3	-	3	3	6
Open passenger cars,	1	1	2	-	2
TOTAL,	4	1	5	3	8
CARS — OTHER SERVICE.					
Box freight cars,	-	4	-	-	-
Platform freight cars,	-	5	-	-	-
Work cars,	-	1	-	-	-
TOTAL,	-	10	-	-	-
Snow ploughs,	1	-	-	-	2

Railway Owned and Operated (by Electric Power).

Length of railway line,	5.910 miles.
Length of sidings, switches, etc.,	.520 "
Total, computed as single track,	6.430 "

Names of the several cities and towns in which the railways owned by the company are located: Conway and Deerfield.

Corporate Name and Address of the Company.

CONWAY ELECTRIC STREET RAILWAY COMPANY,

Conway, Mass.

Names and Business Address of Principal Officers.

John B. Packard, *President*, Conway, Mass. Arthur C. Guilford, *Treasurer*, Conway, Mass. John B. Laidley, *Clerk of Corporation and General Manager*, Conway, Mass. Arthur P. Delabarre, *Auditor*, Conway, Mass.

Names and Residence of Board of Directors.

John B. Packard, Conway, Mass. Emery Brown, Conway, Mass. Charles Parsons, Conway, Mass. Arthur P. Delabarre, Conway, Mass. Fred A. Delabarre, Conway, Mass.

We hereby certify that the statements contained in the foregoing report are full, just and true.

FRED A. DELABARRE,
EMERY BROWN,
JOHN B. PACKARD,
CHARLES PARSONS,
Directors.
ARTHUR C. GUILFORD,
Treasurer.
JOHN B. LAIDLEY,
Superintendent.

Commonwealth of Massachusetts.

Franklin, ss. Nov. 2, 1904. Then personally appeared the above-named John B. Laidley, Fred A. Delabarre, John B. Packard, Emery Brown, Charles Parsons and Arthur C. Guilford, and severally made oath that the foregoing certificate by them subscribed is, to the best of their knowledge and belief, true.

Before me, HENRY W. BILLINGS,
Justice of the Peace.

REPORT

OF THE

COTTAGE CITY & EDGARTOWN TRACTION COMPANY

For the Year ending September 30, 1904.

General Exhibit for the Year.		
Gross earnings from operation,		$5,272 30
Operating expenses,		4,568 09
Gross Income above Operating Expenses,		$704 21
Charges upon income accrued during the year:		
Interest and discount on unfunded debts and loans,	$169 50	
Taxes, State and local,	188 28	
Total Charges and Deductions from Income,		357 78
Surplus for the year ending September 30, 1904,		$346 43
Amount of deficit September 30, 1903,		404 60
Total Deficit September 30, 1904,		$58 17

Earnings from Operation.	
Receipts from passengers carried,	$5,272 30
Gross Earnings from Operation,	$5,272 30

Expenses of Operation.	
General expenses:	
General office expenses and supplies,	$455 49
Insurance,	68 40
Maintenance of roadway and buildings:	
Repair of roadbed and track,	659 82
Repair of electric line construction,	79 85
Repair of buildings,	59 00
Maintenance of equipment:	
Repair of cars and other vehicles,	79 91
Repair of electric equipment of cars,	745 79
Transportation expenses:	
Cost of electric motive power,	1,170 29
Wages and compensation of persons employed in conducting transportation,	1,249 54
Total Operating Expenses,	$4,568 09

General Balance Sheet September 30, 1904.

Assets.	Dr.	
Cost of railway:		
Roadbed and tracks,	$40,424 13	
Electric line construction, including poles, wiring, feeder lines, etc.,	6,000 00	
Total Cost of Railway Owned,		$46,424 13
Cost of equipment:		
Cars and other rolling stock and vehicles,	$6,500 00	
Electric equipment of same,	3,517 48	
Other items of equipment,	733 61	
Total Cost of Equipment Owned,		10,751 09
Cost of land and buildings:		
Land necessary for operation of railway,	$2,500 00	
Electric power stations, including equipment,	1,083 85	
Other buildings necessary for operation of railway,	1,161 75	
Total Cost of Land and Buildings Owned,		4,745 60
Total Permanent Investments,		$61,920 82
Cash and current assets:		
Cash,		298 00
Bills and accounts receivable,		1,500 00
Total Cash and Current Assets,		$1,798 00
Miscellaneous assets: materials and supplies,		423 01
Profit and loss balance (deficit),		58 17
Total,		$64,200 00

Liabilities.	Cr.	
Capital stock,		$60,000 00
Current liabilities:		
Loans and notes payable,	$2,500 00	
Audited vouchers and accounts,	1,700 00	
Total Current Liabilities,		4,200 00
Total,		$64,200 00

Capital Stock.

Capital stock authorized by law,	$60,000 00	
Capital stock authorized by votes of company,	60,000 00	
Capital stock issued and outstanding,		$60,000 00
Number of shares issued and outstanding,	600	
Number of stockholders,	10	
Number of stockholders in Massachusetts,	10	
Amount of stock held in Massachusetts,	$60,000 00	

Volume of Traffic, etc.

Number of passengers paying revenue carried during the year,	105,446
Number carried per mile of main railway track operated,	16,348
Number of car miles run,	16,495
Average number of persons employed,	10

Description of Equipment.

Description of Equipment.	Equipped for Electric Power.	Not Equipped.	Number of Motors.
Cars — Passenger Service.			
Box passenger cars,	2	-	-
Open passenger cars,	4	-	-
Total,	6	-	8
Cars — Other Service.			
Work cars,	-	1	-
Other cars,	-	1	-
Total,	-	2	-

Railway Owned, Leased and Operated (by Electric Power).

Railway Owned, etc.	Owned.	Held under Lease or Contract.	Total Operated.
	Miles.	Miles.	Miles.
Length of railway line,	5 350	1.100	6.450
Length of sidings, switches, etc.,	.500	-	.500
Total Computed as Single Track,	5.850	1.100	6.950

Names of the several cities and towns in which the railways operated by the company are located: Cottage City and Tisbury.

Corporate Name and Address of the Company.

COTTAGE CITY & EDGARTOWN TRACTION COMPANY,

Cottage City, Mass.

Names and Business Address of Principal Officers.

Andrew A. Highlands, *President and General Counsel*, 708 Barristers Hall, Boston, Mass. Charles Jackson, *Vice-President*, 19 Congress Street, Boston, Mass. Allen A. Brown, *Treasurer and Clerk of Corporation*, 30 Kilby Street, Boston, Mass. Edwin R. Frasier, *General Manager and Superintendent*, Cottage City, Mass.

Names and Residence of Board of Directors.

Andrew A. Highlands, Brookline, Mass. Allen A. Brown, Boston, Mass. Charles Jackson, Boston, Mass.

We hereby certify that the statements contained in the foregoing report are full, just and true.

ANDREW A. HIGHLANDS,
ALLEN A. BROWN,
Directors.
ALLEN A. BROWN,
Treasurer.
EDWIN R. FRASIER,
Superintendent.

Commonwealth of Massachusetts.

Suffolk, ss. Boston, Nov. 4, 1904. Then personally appeared the above-named Andrew A. Highlands, Allen A. Brown and Edwin R. Frasier, and severally made oath that the foregoing certificate by them subscribed is, to the best of their knowledge and belief, true.

Before me, CHARLES WHITNEY WARD,
Justice of the Peace.

REPORT

OF THE

DARTMOUTH & WESTPORT STREET RAILWAY COMPANY

For the Year ending September 30, 1904.

General Exhibit for the Year.			
Gross earnings from operation,			$147,962 56
Operating expenses,			94,356 92
Gross Income above Operating Expenses,			$53,605 64
Charges upon income accrued during the year:			
Interest on funded debt,		$4,500 00	
Interest and discount on unfunded debts and loans,		643 47	
Taxes, State and local,	$3,882 47		
Taxes, commutation,	2,565 73		
		6,448 20	
Payments to sinking and other special funds: reserve for depreciation,		1,500 00	
Other deductions from income: Lincoln park expense,		2,114 91	
Total Charges and Deductions from Income,			15,206 58
Net Divisible Income,			$38,399 06
Dividends declared (8 per cent),			12,000 00
Surplus for the year ending September 30, 1904,			$26,399 06
Amount of surplus September 30, 1903,			24,397 24
			$50,796 30
Debits to profit and loss account during the year:			
Car account,		$300 00	
Electrical equipment of cars,		516 66	
Total Debits,			816 66
Total Surplus September 30, 1904,			$49,979 64

Earnings from Operation.	
Receipts from passengers carried,	$133,679 65
Receipts from carriage of mails,	784 80
Receipts from carriage of freight,	12,135 08
Receipts from rentals of buildings and other property,	1,053 03
Receipts from advertising in cars,	310 00
Gross Earnings from Operation,	$147,962 56

Expenses of Operation.

General expenses:	
Salaries of general officers and clerks,	$3,970 38
General office expenses and supplies,	307 80
Legal expenses,	229 10
Insurance,	1,322 94
Other general expenses,	510 67
Maintenance of roadway and buildings:	
Repair of roadbed and track,	2,120 79
Repair of electric line construction,	4,402 69
Maintenance of equipment:	
Repair of cars and other vehicles,	4,383 76
Repair of electric equipment of cars,	1,319 29
Transportation expenses:	
Wages and compensation of persons employed in conducting transportation,	20,703 29
Removal of snow and ice,	276 60
Damages for injuries to persons and property,	1,246 35
Tolls for trackage over other railways,	42,397 77
Rentals of buildings and other property,	331 21
Other transportation expenses,	10,834 28
Total Operating Expenses,	$94,356 92

Property Accounts.

Additions to railway:		
Extension of tracks,	$220 69	
New electric line construction (length 37,600 feet),	5,937 19	
Total Additions to Railway,		$6,157 88
Additions to equipment:		
Additional cars (6 in number),	$14,684 56	
Electric equipment of same,	12,221 43	
Total Additions to Equipment,		26,905 99
Additions to other permanent property: Lincoln Park,		458 52
Total Additions to Property Accounts,		$33,522 39
Deductions from property accounts (property sold or reduced in valuation and credited to property accounts):		
Car account,	$1,551 58	
Electrical equipment of cars,	2,076 58	
Construction,	10 00	
Buildings,	266 96	
Total Deductions from Property Accounts,		3,905 12
Net Addition to Property Accounts for the Year,		$29,617 27

General Balance Sheet September 30, 1904.

Assets.	Dr.	
Cost of railway:		
Roadbed and tracks,	$102,181 63	
Electric line construction, including poles, wiring, feeder lines, etc.,	76,427 73	
Total Cost of Railway Owned,		$178,609 36

Cost of equipment:		
Cars and other rolling stock and vehicles, .	$62,814 19	
Electric equipment of same, ...	47,269 65	
Other items of equipment: registers, . .	475 00	
TOTAL COST OF EQUIPMENT OWNED, ...		$110,558 84
Cost of land and buildings: buildings necessary for operation of railway, ...		583 83
Other permanent property: Lincoln park, ...		12,374 50
TOTAL PERMANENT INVESTMENTS, ...		$302,126 53
Cash and current assets:		
Cash, ...	$4,148 45	
Bills and accounts receivable, ...	4,786 29	
Other cash and current assets: prepaid insurance, ...	398 56	
TOTAL CASH AND CURRENT ASSETS, ...		9,333 30
Miscellaneous assets: materials and supplies, ...		2,356 59
TOTAL, ...		$313,816 42

LIABILITIES.	CR.	
Capital stock, ...		$150,000 00
Funded debt, ...		90,000 00
Current liabilities:		
Audited vouchers and accounts, . . .	$3,766 79	
Miscellaneous current liabilities: outstanding tickets, ...	216 17	
TOTAL CURRENT LIABILITIES, ...		3,982 96
Accrued liabilities: taxes accrued and not yet due, . .		6,653 82
Sinking and other special funds: reserve for depreciation, .		13,200 00
Profit and loss balance (surplus), ...		49,979 64
TOTAL, ...		$313,816 42

CAPITAL STOCK.

Capital stock authorized by law, ...	$150,000 00	
Capital stock authorized by votes of company,	150,000 00	
Capital stock issued and outstanding, ...		$150,000 00
Number of shares issued and outstanding, .	1,500	
Number of stockholders, ...	74	
Number of stockholders in Massachusetts, .	65	
Amount of stock held in Massachusetts, . .	$77,700 00	

FUNDED DEBT.

DESCRIPTION OF BONDS.	Rate of Interest.	Date of Maturity.	Amount Outstanding.	Interest Paid during the Year.
	Per Cent.			
First mortgage coupon (may be registered) gold bonds, . . .	5	April 1, 1915,	$90,000 00	$4,500 00

Sinking and Other Special Funds.

Amount September 30, 1903, of reserve for depreciation fund,	$11,700 00
Additions during the year to reserve for depreciation fund, .	1,500 00
Total Sinking and Other Special Funds September 30, 1904, ...	$13,200 00

Volume of Traffic, etc.

Number of passengers paying revenue carried during the year,	2,652,093
Number carried per mile of main railway track operated, .	126,032
Number of car miles run, ...	387,485
Average number of persons employed, ...	50

Description of Equipment.

Description of Equipment.	Equipped for Electric Power.	Not Equipped.	Equipped with Fenders.	Equipped with Electric Heaters.	Number of Motors.
Cars — Passenger Service.					
Box passenger cars, ...	11	-	11	11	-
Open passenger cars, ...	12	-	12	-	-
Total, ...	23	-	23	11	98
Cars — Other Service.					
Box freight cars, ...	2	-	-	-	-
Work cars, ...	1	5	-	-	-
Total, ...	3	5	-	-	-
Snow ploughs, ...	2	-	-	-	-

Miscellaneous Equipment.

Other railway rolling stock: track velocipede, ...	1
Other items of equipment: track and station tools.	

Railway Owned, Leased and Operated (by Electric Power).

Railway Owned, etc.	Owned.	Trackage over Other Railways.	Total Operated.
	Miles.	Miles.	Miles.
Length of railway line, ...	9.250	7.283	16.533
Length of second main track, ...	-	4.510	4.510
Total Length of Main Track, ...	9.250	11.793	21.043
Length of sidings, switches, etc., ...	.486	.483	.979
Total, Computed as Single Track, ...	9.736	12.276	22.022

RAILWAY LOCATED OUTSIDE OF PUBLIC WAYS.

Length of railway line, ...	.212 mile.

Names of the several cities and towns in which the railways operated by the company are located: Fall River, Westport, Dartmouth and New Bedford.

GRADE CROSSINGS WITH RAILROADS.

GRADE CROSSINGS WITH RAILROADS.	NUMBER OF TRACKS AT CROSSING.	
	Railroad.	Railway.
Crossings of railways with railroads at grade (1 in number), viz.: — With New York, New Haven & Hartford Railroad Company, Eastern District, Taunton Division, at North Westport, . . .	1	1

Number of above crossings at which *frogs* are inserted in the tracks, . 1

ACCIDENTS TO PERSONS.
(A detailed statement of each accident is on file in the office of the Board.)

KILLED AND INJURED.	FROM CAUSES BEYOND THEIR OWN CONTROL.		FROM THEIR OWN MISCONDUCT OR CARELESSNESS.		TOTAL.	
	Killed.	Injured.	Killed.	Injured.	Killed.	Injured.
Passengers, ...	-	2	-	4	-	6
Employees, ...	-	-	-	-	-	-
Other persons, ...	-	1	-	3	-	4
TOTALS, ...	-	3	-	7	-	10

CORPORATE NAME AND ADDRESS OF THE COMPANY.

DARTMOUTH & WESTPORT STREET RAILWAY COMPANY,

7 PURCHASE STREET, NEW BEDFORD, MASS.

NAMES AND BUSINESS ADDRESS OF PRINCIPAL OFFICERS.

Henry H. Crapo, *President*, New Bedford, Mass. Thomas B. Tripp, *Vice-President*, New Bedford, Mass. Elton S. Wilde, *Treasurer*, New Bedford, Mass. Robert S. Goff, *Clerk of Corporation*, Boston, Mass. John F. Swift, *Auditor*, New Bedford, Mass. Edward E. Potter, *Superintendent*, New Bedford, Mass.

NAMES AND RESIDENCE OF BOARD OF DIRECTORS.

Henry H. Crapo, New Bedford, Mass. Thomas B. Tripp, New Bedford, Mass. Edward S. Brown, New Bedford, Mass. Clarence A. Cook, New Bedford, Mass. Antone L. Sylvia, New Bedford, Mass. Robert S. Goff, Fall River, Mass. Bradford D. Davol, Fall River, Mass. Walter P. Winsor, Fairhaven, Mass. Oliver Prescott, Jr., Dartmouth, Mass.

We hereby certify that the statements contained in the foregoing report are full, just and true

HENRY H. CRAPO,
THOMAS B. TRIPP,
W. P. WINSOR,
E. S. BROWN,
BRADFORD D. DAVOL,
A. L. SYLVIA,
Directors.
ELTON S. WILDE,
Treasurer.
EDWARD E. POTTER,
Superintendent.

COMMONWEALTH OF MASSACHUSETTS.

BRISTOL, ss. Nov. 3, 1904. Then personally appeared the above-named Henry H. Crapo, Thomas B. Tripp, W. P. Winsor, E. S. Brown, Bradford D. Davol, A. L. Sylvia, Elton S. Wilde and Edward E. Potter, and severally made oath that the foregoing certificate by them subscribed is, to the best of their knowledge and belief, true.

Before me, ISAAC W. PHELPS,
Justice of the Peace.

REPORT

OF THE

EAST MIDDLESEX STREET RAILWAY COMPANY

FOR THE YEAR ENDING SEPTEMBER 30, 1904.

[Leased to and operated by the Boston & Northern.]

GENERAL EXHIBIT FOR THE YEAR.	
Rental received from lease of railway,	$30,000 00
Income from other sources: interest,	33 25
NET DIVISIBLE INCOME,	$30,033 25
Dividends declared (10 per cent),	29,770 00
Surplus for the year ending September 30, 1904,	$263 25
Amount of deficit September 30, 1903,	11,001 68
TOTAL DEFICIT SEPTEMBER 30, 1904,	$10,738 43

GENERAL BALANCE SHEET SEPTEMBER 30, 1904.	
ASSETS. DR.	
Cost of railway,	$344,518 03
Cost of equipment,	102,105 79
Cost of land and buildings,	58,662 11
TOTAL PERMANENT INVESTMENTS,	$505,285 93
Cash and current assets: cash,	1,473 64
Miscellaneous assets: office furniture,	222 00
Profit and loss balance (deficit),	10,738 43
TOTAL,	$517,720 00
LIABILITIES. CR.	
Capital stock,	$297,700 00
Funded debt,	220,000 00
Current liabilities: dividends not called for,	20 00
TOTAL,	$517,720 00

CAPITAL STOCK.		
Capital stock authorized by law,	$300,000 00	
Capital stock authorized by votes of company,	300,000 00	
Capital stock issued and outstanding,		$297,700 00
Number of shares issued and outstanding,	2,977	
Number of stockholders,	117	
Number of stockholders in Massachusetts,	103	
Amount of stock held in Massachusetts,	$263,300 00	

FUNDED DEBT.

DESCRIPTION OF BONDS.	Rate of Interest.	Date of Maturity.	Amount Outstanding.	Interest Paid during the Year.
	Per Cent.			
Plain bonds, ...	5	Sept. 1, 1918,	$120,000 00	$6,000 00*
Plain bonds, ...	4	Jan. 1, 1922,	100,000 00	4,000 00*
TOTALS, ...	. .	. . . .	$220,000 00	$10,000 00

RAILWAY OWNED.

Length of railway line, ...	16.009 miles.
Length of second main track, ...	2.582 "
Total length of main track, ...	18.591 "
Length of sidings, switches, etc., ...	.803 "
Total, computed as single track, ...	19.394 "

Names of the several cities and towns in which the railway owned by the company is located: Stoneham, Melrose, Malden, Revere and Saugus.

CORPORATE NAME AND ADDRESS OF THE COMPANY.

EAST MIDDLESEX STREET RAILWAY COMPANY,

ROOM 803, 60 STATE STREET, BOSTON, MASS.

NAMES AND BUSINESS ADDRESS OF PRINCIPAL OFFICERS.

John S. Bartlett, *President*, 53 State Street, Boston, Mass. Charles H. Newhall, *Vice-President*, Lynn, Mass. E. Francis Oliver, *Treasurer and Clerk of Corporation*, 60 State Street, Boston, Mass.

NAMES AND RESIDENCE OF BOARD OF DIRECTORS.

John S. Bartlett, Lynn, Mass. Charles H. Newhall, Lynn, Mass. Amos F. Breed, Lynn, Mass. Elwin C. Foster, New Orleans, La. Frank H. Monks, Brookline, Mass. Bentley W. Warren, Williamstown, Mass.

We hereby certify that the statements contained in the foregoing report are full, just and true.

JOHN S. BARTLETT,
FRANK H. MONKS,
AMOS F. BREED,
BENTLEY W. WARREN,
Directors.
E. FRANCIS OLIVER,
Treasurer.

* Paid by lessee.

COMMONWEALTH OF MASSACHUSETTS.

SUFFOLK, ss. OCT. 17, 1904. Then personally appeared the above-named John S. Bartlett, Frank H. Monks, Amos F. Breed and E. Francis Oliver, and severally made oath that the foregoing certificate by them subscribed is, to the best of their knowledge and belief, true,

Before me, CHARLES A. STONE,
Justice of the Peace.

COMMONWEALTH OF MASSACHUSETTS.

SUFFOLK, ss. OCT. 19, 1904. Then personally appeared the above-named Bentley W. Warren, and made oath that the foregoing certificate by him subscribed is, to the best of his knowledge and belief, true.

Before me, IRVIN McDOWELL GARFIELD,
Justice of the Peace.

REPORT

OF THE

EAST TAUNTON STREET RAILWAY COMPANY

For the Year ending September 30, 1904.

General Exhibit for the Year.

Gross earnings from operation,		$34,644 27
Operating expenses,		22,207 85
Gross Income above Operating Expenses,		$12,436 42
Charges upon income accrued during the year:		
Interest on funded debt,	$2,250 00	
Taxes, state and local,	2,167 15	
Other deductions from income: abolition of grade crossing,	4,612 66	
Total Charges and Deductions from Income,		9,029 81
Net Divisible Income,		$3,406 61
Dividends declared (5 per cent),		5,500 00
Deficit for the year ending September 30, 1904,		$2,093 39
Amount of surplus September 30, 1903,		18,049 68
Total Surplus September 30, 1904,		$15,956 29

Earnings from Operation.

Receipts from passengers carried,	$34,115 26
Receipts from tolls for use of tracks by other companies,	148 00
Receipts from advertising in cars,	83 33
Receipts from interest on deposits,	297 68
Gross Earnings from Operation,	$34,644 27

Expenses of Operation.

General expenses:	
Salaries of general officers and clerks,	$700 00
General office expenses and supplies,	30 08
Legal expenses,	15 00
Insurance,	216 30
Other general expenses: miscellaneous expenses,	274 68
Maintenance of roadway and buildings:	
Repair of roadbed and track,	2,146 92
Repair of electric line construction,	117 02
Repair of buildings,	39 79

Maintenance of equipment:		
Repair of cars and other vehicles,		$799 45
Repair of electric equipment of cars,		633 40
Transportation expenses:		
Cost of electric motive power,		5,994 19
Wages and compensation of persons employed in conducting transportation,		7,900 15
Removal of snow and ice,		305 94
Damages for injuries to persons and property,		85 41
Tolls for trackage over other railways,		423 80
Rentals of buildings and other property,		1,723 73
Other transportation expenses: flagman, oil, fuel and miscellaneous car expenses,		801 99
Total Operating Expenses,		$22,207 85

Property Accounts.

Additions to land and buildings:		
Additional land necessary for operation of railway,	$1,000 00	
New buildings necessary for operation of railway,	5,000 00	
Total Additions to Property Accounts,		$6,000 00
Deductions from property accounts (property sold or reduced in valuation and credited to property accounts): sold electric equipment,		20 00
Net Addition to Property Accounts for the Year,		$5,980 00

General Balance Sheet September 30, 1904.

Assets.	Dr.	
Cost of railway:		
Roadbed and tracks,	$93,539 16	
Electric line construction, including poles, wiring, feeder lines, etc.,	47,341 04	
Interest accrued during construction of railway,	1,027 82	
Engineering and other expenses incident to construction,	6,391 55	
Total Cost of Railway Owned,		$148,299 57
Cost of equipment:		
Cars and other rolling stock and vehicles,	$10,108 60	
Electric equipment of same,	6,927 86	
Other items of equipment: sundry equipment,	993 40	
Total Cost of Equipment Owned,		18,029 86
Cost of land and buildings:		
Land necessary for operation of railway,	$1,154 30	
Buildings necessary for operation of railway,	5,096 72	
Total Cost of Land and Buildings Owned,		6,251 02
Total Permanent Investments,		$172,580 45

Cash and current assets:		
Cash,	$1,817 79	
Bills and accounts receivable,	94 33	
TOTAL CASH AND CURRENT ASSETS,		$1,912 12
TOTAL,		$174,492 57

LIABILITIES.		CR.
Capital stock,		$110,000 00
Funded debt,		45,000 00
Current liabilities:		
Audited vouchers and accounts,	$1,162 63	
Miscellaneous current liabilities: conductors' deposits,	19 00	
TOTAL CURRENT LIABILITIES,		1,181 63
Accrued liabilities:		
Interest accrued and not yet due,	$187 50	
Taxes accrued and not yet due,	2,167 15	
TOTAL ACCRUED LIABILITIES,		2,354 65
Profit and loss balance (surplus),		15,956 29
TOTAL,		$174,492 57

CAPITAL STOCK.

Capital stock authorized by law,	$110,000 00	
Capital stock authorized by votes of company,	110,000 00	
Capital stock issued and outstanding,		$110,000 00
Number of shares issued and outstanding,	1,100	
Number of stockholders,	72	
Number of stockholders in Massachusetts,	72	
Amount of stock held in Massachusetts,	$110,000 00	

FUNDED DEBT.

DESCRIPTION OF BONDS.	Rate of Interest.	Date of Maturity.	Amount Outstanding.	Interest Paid during the Year.
	Per Cent.			
First mortgage gold bonds,	5	March 1, 1920,	$45,000 00	$2,250 00

VOLUME OF TRAFFIC, ETC.

Number of passengers paying revenue carried during the year,	697,128
Number carried per mile of main railway track operated,	61,979
Number of car miles run,	153,177
Average number of persons employed,	14

Description of Equipment.

Description of Equipment.	Equipped for Electric Power.	Equipped with Fenders.	Equipped with Electric Heaters.	Number of Motors.
Cars — Passenger Service.				
Box passenger cars,	2	2	2	-
Open passenger cars,	4	4	-	-
Total,	6	6	2	14

Miscellaneous Equipment.

Other railway rolling stock: trolley wagon,	1

Railway Owned, Leased and Operated (by Electric Power).

Railway Owned, etc.	Owned.	Trackage over Other Railways.	Total Owned, Leased, etc.
	Miles.	Miles.	Miles.
Length of railway line,	10.524	.724	11.248
Length of sidings, switches, etc.,	.176	-	.176
Total, Computed as Single Track,	10.700	.724	11.424

Names of the several cities and towns in which the railways operated by the company are located: Taunton, Lakeville and Middleborough.

Grade Crossings with Railroads.

Grade Crossings with Railroads.	Number of Tracks at Crossing.	
	Railroad.	Railway.
Crossings of railways with railroads at grade (1 in number), viz.: — With New York, New Haven & Hartford Railroad at Middleborough Avenue, East Taunton, Mass.,	1	1

Number of above crossings at which *frogs* are inserted in the tracks, . 1

Corporate Name and Address of the Company.

EAST TAUNTON STREET RAILWAY COMPANY,

23 Summer Street, Taunton, Mass.

NAMES AND BUSINESS ADDRESS OF PRINCIPAL OFFICERS.

Michael A. Cavanaugh, *President*, 105 Beverly Street, Boston, Mass. Thomas F. Cavanaugh, *Vice-President*, 26 Court Street, Taunton, Mass. Joseph B. Murphy, *Treasurer*, 23 Summer Street, Taunton, Mass. James P. Dunn, *Clerk of Corporation, General Manager and Superintendent*, 172 Cohannet Street, Taunton, Mass. Arthur M. Alger, *General Counsel*, 9 Court Street, Taunton, Mass.

NAMES AND RESIDENCE OF BOARD OF DIRECTORS.

Michael A. Cavanaugh, Boston, Mass. Thomas F. Cavanaugh, Taunton, Mass. Joseph B. Murphy, Taunton, Mass. James P. Dunn, Taunton, Mass. Stephen F. O'Hara, Middleborough, Mass. Chester R. Barstow, Taunton, Mass. Charles R. Richmond, East Taunton, Mass.

We hereby certify that the statements contained in the foregoing report are full, just and true.

MICHAEL A. CAVANAUGH,
THOS. F. CAVANAUGH,
JOSEPH B. MURPHY,
JAMES P. DUNN,
STEPHEN F. O'HARA,
CHESTER R. BARSTOW,
CHARLES R. RICHMOND,
Directors.
JOSEPH B. MURPHY,
Treasurer.
JAMES P. DUNN,
Superintendent.

COMMONWEALTH OF MASSACHUSETTS.

BRISTOL, SS. TAUNTON, Nov. 1, 1904. Then personally appeared the above-named Michael A. Cavanaugh, Thomas F. Cavanaugh, Joseph B. Murphy, James P. Dunn, Stephen F. O'Hara, Chester R. Barstow and Charles R. Richmond, and severally made oath that the foregoing certificate by them subscribed is, to the best of their knowledge and belief, true.

Before me, RICHARD P. COUGHLIN,
Justice of the Peace.

REPORT

OF THE

ESSEX COUNTY STREET RAILWAY COMPANY

For the Year ending September 30, 1904.

[Obtained a certificate of incorporation but has not commenced the construction of its railway.]

General Balance Sheet September 30, 1904.

Assets.	Dr.	
Cost of railway:		
Roadbed and tracks,	$9,019 97	
Engineering and other expenses incident to construction,	3,541 98	
Other items of railway cost: services J. N. Greene,	2,313 49	
Total Cost of Railway Owned,		$14,875 44

Liabilities.	Cr.
Capital stock, amount paid in (first and second assessments),	$12,500 00
Miscellaneous current liabilities: estate J. N. Greene for services and sundry payments,	2,375 44
Total,	$14,875 44

Property Accounts.

Additions to railway:		
Miscellaneous expenses,	$133 82	
Services J. N. Greene,	2,313 49	
Total Additions to Property Accounts,		$2,446 31

Capital Stock.

Capital stock authorized by law,	$25,000 00	
Amount paid in on 250 shares not yet issued,		$12,500 00
Number of stockholders,	20	
Number of stockholders in Massachusetts,	19	
Amount of stock held in Massachusetts,	$12,000 00	

Names of the several cities and towns in which the railway owned by the company is located: Danvers, Topsfield, Boxford and Georgetown.

GENERAL REMARKS AND EXPLANATIONS.

Length of railway as published in the articles of association, 10 miles.

CORPORATE NAME AND ADDRESS OF THE COMPANY.

ESSEX COUNTY STREET RAILWAY COMPANY,

15 SCHOOL STREET, ROOM 64, BOSTON, MASS.

NAMES AND BUSINESS ADDRESS OF PRINCIPAL OFFICERS.

Lewis D. Greene, *President*, 15 School Street, Room 64, Boston, Mass. William R. Arey, *Treasurer*, National Bank of the Republic, Boston, Mass. Edward D. Hewins, *Clerk of Corporation*, 15 School Street, Room 64, Boston, Mass.

NAMES AND RESIDENCE OF BOARD OF DIRECTORS.

Lewis D. Greene, Chicago, Ill. Edmund B. Fuller, Haverhill, Mass. Alphonso T. Merrill, Topsfield, Mass. William R. Arey, Salem, Mass. Edward D. Hewins, Boston, Mass.

We hereby certify that the statements contained in the foregoing report are full, just and true.

LEWIS D. GREENE,
WILLIAM R. AREY,
EDWARD D. HEWINS,
Directors.
WILLIAM R. AREY,
Treasurer.

COMMONWEALTH OF MASSACHUSETTS.

SUFFOLK, ss. OCT. 26, 1904. Then personally appeared the above-named William R. Arey, and made oath that the foregoing certificate by him subscribed is, to the best of his knowledge and belief, true.

Before me, EDWARD D. HEWINS,
Justice of the Peace.

STATE OF ILLINOIS.

COUNTY OF COOK, ss. OCT. 29, 1904. Personally appeared the above-named Lewis D. Greene, and made oath that the foregoing certificate by him subscribed is, to the best of his knowledge and belief, true.

Before me, P. S. ELWELL,
Notary Public, Cook County, Ill.

COMMONWEALTH OF MASSACHUSETTS.

SUFFOLK, ss. OCT. 31, 1904. Then personally appeared the above-named Edward D. Hewins, and made oath that the foregoing certificate by him subscribed is, to the best of his knowledge and belief, true.

Before me, FRANKLIN MEAD,
Justice of the Peace.

REPORT

OF THE

FITCHBURG & LEOMINSTER STREET RAILWAY COMPANY

For the Year ending September 30, 1904.

General Exhibit for the Year.

Gross earnings from operation,		$202,790 02
Operating expenses,		132,155 27
Net Earnings from Operation,		$70,634 75
Miscellaneous income: Whalom Park receipts,		23,612 98
Gross Income above Operating Expenses,		$94,247 73
Charges upon income accrued during the year:		
Interest on funded debt,	$14,250 00	
Interest and discount on unfunded debts and loans,	16,490 24	
Taxes, State and local, . . . $8,418 20		
Taxes, commutation, . . . 3,557 34	11,975 54	
Other deductions from income: Whalom Park expense,	24,039 69	
Total Charges and Deductions from Income,		66,755 47
Net Divisible Income,		$27,492 26
Dividends declared (6 per cent),		21,000 00
Surplus for the year ending September 30, 1904,		$6,492 26
Amount of surplus September 30, 1903,		21,996 54
Debits to profit and loss account during the year: paid on account of accidents occurring previous to September 30, 1903,		13,457 94
Total Surplus September 30, 1904,		$15,030 86

Earnings from Operation.

Receipts from passengers carried,	$202,176 70
Receipts from advertising in cars,	613 32
Gross Earnings from Operation,	$202,790 02

Expenses of Operation.

General expenses:	
Salaries of general officers and clerks,	$8,032 93
General office expenses and supplies,	2,519 63
Legal expenses,	30 47
Insurance,	1,968 71
Other general expenses: miscellaneous entertainments,	30 25

Maintenance of roadway and buildings:		
Repair of roadbed and track,		$5,431 50
Repair of electric line construction,		1,338 60
Repair of buildings,		440 31
Maintenance of equipment:		
Repair of cars and other vehicles,		9,154 55
Repair of electric equipment of cars,		6,108 96
Renewal of horses, harnesses, shoeing, etc., and provender and stabling for horses,		1,295 17
Transportation expenses:		
Cost of electric motive power, $26,495.82; less power sold, $755.80; net,		25,740 02
Wages and compensation of persons employed in conducting transportation,		47,922 31
Removal of snow and ice,		3,101 56
Damages for injuries to persons and property,		6,549 40
Rentals of buildings and other property,		1,074 70
Other transportation expenses:		
Miscellaneous car house expenses,		5,337 85
Printing tickets and transfers; lamps, oil and lubricants for cars, tracks, etc.; cleaning track; sand, etc.,		6,078 35
TOTAL OPERATING EXPENSES,		$132,155 27

PROPERTY ACCOUNTS.

Additions to railway: new electric line construction, signals and Whalom lighting,	$1,890 24	
Other additions to railway: cross-over and paving,	1,520 31	
TOTAL ADDITIONS TO RAILWAY,		$3,410 55
Additions to equipment: additional cars and electric equipment of same,	$6,844 26	
Other additions to equipment:		
Miscellaneous,	625 81	
Horses,	270 00	
TOTAL ADDITIONS TO EQUIPMENT,		7,740 07
Additions to land and buildings: additional equipment of power stations,		5,588 55
Additions to other permanent property: Whalom Park property,		1,806 92
TOTAL ADDITIONS TO PROPERTY ACCOUNTS,		$18,546 09
Deductions from property accounts (property sold or reduced in valuation and credited to property accounts): horses sold,		200 00
NET ADDITION TO PROPERTY ACCOUNTS FOR THE YEAR,		$18,346 09

GENERAL BALANCE SHEET SEPTEMBER 30, 1904.

ASSETS.	DR.	
Cost of railway:		
Roadbed and tracks,	$504,340 45	
Electric line construction, including poles, wiring, feeder lines, etc.,	72,880 77	
TOTAL COST OF RAILWAY OWNED,		$577,221 22

Cost of equipment:		
Cars and other rolling stock and vehicles and electric equipment of same,	$166,304 89	
Horses,	855 00	
Other items of equipment,	10,195 39	
TOTAL COST OF EQUIPMENT OWNED,		$177,355 28
Cost of land and buildings:		
Land necessary for operation of railway,	$11,793 96	
Electric power stations, including equipment,	85,114 04	
Other buildings necessary for operation of railway,	24,259 21	
TOTAL COST OF LAND AND BUILDINGS OWNED,		121,167 21
Other permanent property:		
Fitchburg Park Company stock,	$125 00	
Whalom Park property,	81,560 33	
TOTAL COST OF OTHER PERMANENT PROPERTY OWNED,		81,685 33
TOTAL PERMANENT INVESTMENTS,		$957,429 04
Cash and current assets:		
Cash,	$6,777 86	
Bills and accounts receivable,	9,849 82	
TOTAL CASH AND CURRENT ASSETS,		16,627 68
Miscellaneous assets: materials and supplies,		37,906 74
TOTAL,		$1,011,963 46

LIABILITIES.	CR.	
Capital stock,		$350,000 00
Funded debt,		300,000 00
Current liabilities:		
Loans and notes payable,	$340,000 00	
Audited vouchers and accounts,	1,966 88	
Salaries and wages,	862 84	
Miscellaneous current liabilities: tickets issued but not redeemed,	774 55	
TOTAL CURRENT LIABILITIES,		343,604 27
Accrued liabilities:		
Interest accrued and not yet due,	$2,753 81	
Taxes accrued and not yet due,	574 52	
TOTAL ACCRUED LIABILITIES,		3,328 33
Profit and loss balance (surplus),		15,030 86
TOTAL,		$1,011,963 46

CAPITAL STOCK.

Capital stock authorized by law,	$350,000 00	
Capital stock authorized by votes of company,	350,000 00	
Capital stock issued and outstanding,		$350,000 00
Number of shares issued and outstanding,	3,500	
Number of stockholders,	106	
Number of stockholders in Massachusetts,	102	
Amount of stock held in Massachusetts,	$344,600 00	

Funded Debt.

Description of Bonds.	Rate of Interest.	Date of Maturity.	Amount Outstanding.	Interest Paid during the Year.
	Per Cent.			
First mortgage bonds,	5	April 1, 1917,	$150,000 00	$7,500 00
Consolidated mortgage bonds,	4½	Feb. 1, 1921,	150,000 00	6,750 00
Totals,	. .	. . .	$300,000 00	$14,250 00

Volume of Traffic, etc.

Number of passengers paying revenue carried during the year,	4,096,715
Number carried per mile of main railway track operated,	134,561
Number of car miles run,	851,202
Average number of persons employed,	100

Description of Equipment.

Description of Equipment.	Equipped for Electric Power.	Not Equipped.	Equipped with Fenders.	Equipped with Electric Heaters.	Number of Motors.
Cars — Passenger Service.					
Box passenger cars,	24	-	24	24	-
Open passenger cars,	32	-	32	-	-
Total,	56	-	56	24	120
Cars — Other Service.					
Work cars,	4	1	-	-	-
Snow ploughs,	5	-	-	-	-

Miscellaneous Equipment.

Carts and snow sleds,	20
Other highway vehicles: 2 carriages, 1 sleigh,	3
Horses,	6
Other items of equipment: office furniture, punches, telephones, etc.	

Railway Owned and Operated (by Electric Power).

Length of railway line,	25.100 miles.
Length of second main track,	5.345 "
Total length of main track,	30.445 "
Length of sidings, switches, etc.,	1.669 "
Total, computed as single track,	32.114 "

Railway Located Outside of Public Ways.

Length of railway line,	1.935 miles.
Length of second main track,	.875 "
Total length of main track,	2.810 "

Names of the several cities and towns in which the railways operated by the company are located: Fitchburg, Leominster and Lunenburg.

Grade Crossings with Railroads.

Grade Crossings with Railroads.	Number of Tracks at Crossing.	
	Railroad.	Railway.
Crossings of railways with railroads at grade (6 in number), viz.: —		
With Boston & Maine Railroad, River Street, Fitchburg (mill siding),	1	2
With Boston & Maine Railroad, River Street, Fitchburg (mill siding),	1	2
With Boston & Maine Railroad, River Street, Fitchburg (mill siding),	1	2
With Boston & Maine Railroad, River Street, Fitchburg (mill siding),	1	2
With New York, New Haven & Hartford Railroad, Main Street, Fitchburg (mill siding),	1	2
With New York, New Haven & Hartford Railroad, Main Street, Leominster,	2	1
Total Number of Tracks at Crossings,	7	11

Number of above crossings at which *frogs* are inserted in the tracks, . 6

Accidents to Persons.

(A detailed statement of each accident is on file in the office of the Board.)

Killed and Injured.	From Causes beyond their own Control.		From their own Misconduct or Carelessness.		Total.	
	Killed.	Injured.	Killed.	Injured.	Killed.	Injured.
Passengers,	-	1	-	23	-	24
Employees,	-	-	-	1	-	1
Other persons,	-	1	-	7	-	8
Totals,	-	2	-	31	-	33

Corporate Name and Address of the Company.

FITCHBURG & LEOMINSTER STREET RAILWAY COMPANY,

Fitchburg, Mass.

Names and Business Address of Principal Officers.

Henry A. Willis, *President*, Fitchburg, Mass. Herbert I. Wallace, *Vice-President*, Fitchburg, Mass. Robert N. Wallis, *Treasurer*, Fitchburg, Mass. Charles F. Baker, *Clerk of Corporation*, Fitchburg, Mass. Wesley W. Sargent, *Superintendent*, Fitchburg, Mass.

NAMES AND RESIDENCE OF BOARD OF DIRECTORS.

Henry A. Willis, Fitchburg, Mass. Herbert I. Wallace, Fitchburg, Mass. Charles F. Baker, Fitchburg, Mass. Wesley W. Sargent, Fitchburg, Mass. George E. Clifford, Fitchburg, Mass. George N. Proctor, Fitchburg, Mass. Manson D. Haws, North Leominster, Mass.

We hereby certify that the statements contained in the foregoing report are full, just and true.

HENRY A. WILLIS,
HERBERT I. WALLACE,
CHARLES F. BAKER,
WESLEY W. SARGENT,
MANSON D. HAWS,
Directors.
ROBERT N. WALLIS,
Treasurer.
WESLEY W. SARGENT,
Superintendent.

COMMONWEALTH OF MASSACHUSETTS.

WORCESTER, SS. NOV. 2, 1904. Then personally appeared the above-named Henry A. Willis, Herbert I. Wallace, Charles F. Baker, Wesley W. Sargent, Manson D. Haws and Robert N. Wallis, and severally made oath that the foregoing certificate by them subscribed is, to the best of their knowledge and belief, true.

Before me, WILBUR B. TENNEY,
Justice of the Peace.

REPORT

OF THE

FRAMINGHAM, SOUTHBOROUGH & MARLBOROUGH STREET RAILWAY COMPANY

For the Period ending January 31, 1904.

[Consolidated with the Boston & Worcester, February 1, 1904.]

General Exhibit for the Period.		
Gross earnings from operation,		$9,187 66
Operating expenses,		7,979 65
Gross Income above Operating Expenses,		$1,208 01
Charges upon income accrued during the period:		
Interest on funded debt,	$1,000 00	
Interest and discount on unfunded debts and loans,	755 33	
Taxes, commutation,	88 99	
Total Charges and Deductions from income,		1,844 32
Deficit January 31, 1904,		$636 31
Amount of surplus September 30, 1903,		8,548 99
Debits to profit and loss account during the year:		
Settlement of old damage claims,	$500 00	
Adjustment of unsettled accounts,	1,169 44	
Dividend of 6 per cent paid November 30, 1903, from surplus earnings for year ending September 30, 1903,	4,800 00	
Total Debits,		6,469 44
Total Surplus January 31, 1904,		$1,443 24

Earnings from Operation.	
Receipts from passengers carried,	$9,015 49
Receipts from tolls for use of tracks by other companies,	32 92
Receipts from rentals of buildings and other property,	76 75
Receipts from advertising in cars,	62 50
Gross Earnings from Operation,	$9,187 66

Expenses of Operation.

General expenses:	
Salaries of general officers and clerks,	$741 71
General office expenses and supplies,	13 60
Insurance,	418 00
Other general expenses,	106 82
Maintenance of roadway and buildings:	
Repair of roadbed and track,	45 46
Repair of electric line construction,	16 66
Maintenance of equipment:	
Repair of cars and other vehicles,	150 02
Repair of electric equipment of cars,	3 12
Transportation expenses:	
Cost of electric motive power,	2,966 11
Wages and compensation of persons employed in conducting transportation,	3,157 23
Removal of snow and ice,	278 64
Damages for injuries to persons and property,	63 80
Other transportation expenses,	18 48
Total Operating Expenses,	$7,979 65

Property Accounts.

Additions to railway: Marlborough & Framingham Street Railway Company property purchase, approved by Board of Railroad Commissioners, December 8, 1903,	$105,728 91
Total Additions to Property Accounts,	$105,728 91

General Balance Sheet January 31, 1904.

Assets.	Dr.	
Cost of railway:		
Roadbed and tracks,	$112,702 14	
Electric line construction, including poles, wiring, feeder lines, etc.,	33,500 00	
Engineering and other expenses incident to construction,	760 54	
Other items of railway cost: Marlborough & Framingham Street Railway Company property purchase, approved by Board of Railroad Commissioners, December 8, 1903,	105,728 91	
Total Cost of Railway Owned,		$252,691 59
Cost of equipment: cars and other rolling stock and vehicles, and electric equipment of same,		45,124 84
Cost of land and buildings: buildings necessary for operation of railway, including land,		437 84
Total Permanent Investments,		$298,254 27
Cash and current assets:		
Cash,	$301 70	
Bills and accounts receivable,	685 03	

Cash and current assets — *Concluded.*		
Other cash and current assets:		
Prepaid insurance,	$238 50	
Prepaid interest,	101 30	
TOTAL CASH AND CURRENT ASSETS,		$1,326 53
Miscellaneous assets: materials and supplies,		258 69
TOTAL,		$299,839 49

LIABILITIES.	CR.	
Capital stock,		$185,000 00
Funded debt,		60,000 00
Current liabilities:		
Loans and notes payable,	$51,159 04	
Audited vouchers and accounts,	1,715 02	
TOTAL CURRENT LIABILITIES,		52,874 06
Accrued liabilities:		
Interest accrued and not yet due,	$433 20	
Taxes accrued and not yet due,	88 99	
TOTAL ACCRUED LIABILITIES,		522 19
Profit and loss balance (surplus),		1,443 24
TOTAL,		$299,839 49

CAPITAL STOCK.

Capital stock authorized by law,	$185,000 00	
Capital stock authorized by votes of company,	185,000 00	
Capital stock issued and outstanding,		$185,000 00
Number of shares issued and outstanding,	1,850	
Number of stockholders,	6	
Number of stockholders in Massachusetts,	6	
Amount of stock held in Massachusetts,	$185,000 00	

FUNDED DEBT.

DESCRIPTION OF BONDS.	Rate of Interest.	Date of Maturity.	Amount Outstanding.	Interest Paid during the Period.
	Per Cent.			
First mortgage gold bonds,	5	Jan. 1, 1919,	$60,000 00	$1,000 00

VOLUME OF TRAFFIC, ETC.

Number of passengers paying revenue carried during the period,	160,318
Number carried per mile of main railway track operated,	10,789
Number of car miles run,	62,192
Average number of persons employed,	55

Description of Equipment.

Description of Equipment.	Equipped for Electric Power.	Not equipped.	Equipped with Fenders.	Equipped with Electric Heaters.	Number of Motors.
Cars — Passenger Service.					
Box passenger cars,	11	-	11	11	-
Open passenger cars,	15	-	15	-	-
Total,	26	-	26	11	69
Cars — Other Service.					
Work cars,	-	1	-	-	-
Snow ploughs,	4	-	-	-	-

Miscellaneous Equipment.

Carts and snow sleds,	1
Other highway vehicles:	
Tower wagon,	1
Lumber wagon,	1
Horses,	1

Railway Owned, Leased and Operated (by Electric Power).

Railway Owned, etc.	Owned.	Trackage over Other Railways.	Total Owned, Leased, etc.
	Miles.	Miles.	Miles.
Length of railway line,	14.775	.084	14.859
Length of sidings, switches, etc.,	.850	-	.850
Total, Computed as Single Track,	15.625	.084	15.709

Railway Located Outside of Public Ways.

Length of railway line,	1.830 miles.

Names of the several cities and towns in which the railways operated by the company are located: Hudson, Marlborough, Framingham, and Southborough.

Grade Crossings with Railroads.

Grade Crossings with Railroads.	Number of Tracks at Crossing.	
	Railroad.	Railway.
Crossings of railways with railroads at grade (1 in number), viz.:— With New York, New Haven & Hartford Railroad Company at Worcester Street, Framingham,	3	1

Number of above crossings at which *frogs* are inserted in the tracks, 1

ACCIDENTS TO PERSONS.

(A detailed statement of each accident is on file in the office of the Board.)

KILLED AND INJURED.	FROM CAUSES BEYOND THEIR OWN CONTROL.		FROM THEIR OWN MISCONDUCT OR CARELESSNESS.		TOTAL.	
	Killed.	Injured.	Killed.	Injured	Killed.	Injured.
Passengers,	-	-	-	1	-	1
Employees,	-	-	-	-	-	-
Other persons,	-	-	-	-	-	-
TOTALS,	-	-	-	1	-	1

CORPORATE NAME AND ADDRESS OF THE COMPANY.

FRAMINGHAM, SOUTHBOROUGH & MARLBOROUGH STREET RAILWAY COMPANY,

SOUTH FRAMINGHAM, MASS.

NAMES AND BUSINESS ADDRESS OF PRINCIPAL OFFICERS.

William M. Butler, *President*, Tremont Building, Boston, Mass. Arthur E. Childs, *Vice-President*, Board of Trade Building, Boston, Mass. George A. Butman, *Treasurer and Clerk of Corporation*, 8 Congress Street, Boston, Mass.

NAMES AND RESIDENCE OF BOARD OF DIRECTORS.

William M. Butler, Boston, Mass. George A. Butman, Malden, Mass. Arthur E. Childs, Boston, Mass. Edward P. Shaw, Newburyport, Mass. James F. Shaw, Manchester, Mass.

We hereby certify that the statements contained in the foregoing report are full, just and true.

GEO. A. BUTMAN,
EDWARD P. SHAW,
JAMES F. SHAW,
Directors.
GEO. A. BUTMAN,
Treasurer.

COMMONWEALTH OF MASSACHUSETTS.

SUFFOLK, SS. BOSTON, Nov. 7, 1904. Then personally appeared the above-named Geo. A. Butman, Edward P. Shaw and Jas. F. Shaw, and severally made oath that the foregoing certificate by them subscribed is, to the best of their knowledge and belief, true.

Before me, ARTHUR W. CLAPP,
Justice of the Peace.

REPORT

OF THE

FRAMINGHAM UNION STREET RAILWAY COMPANY

For the Period ending December 21, 1903.

[Consolidated with the Boston & Worcester December 21, 1903.]

General Exhibit for the Period.			
Gross earnings from operation,			$7,786 80
Operating expenses,			4,839 11
Gross Income above Operating Expenses,			$2,947 69
Charges upon income accrued during the period:			
Interest on funded debt,		$587 49	
Interest and discount on unfunded debts and loans,		873 17	
Taxes, State and local,	$150 00		
Taxes, commutation,	150 40		
		300 40	
Total Charges and Deductions from Income,			1,761 06
Surplus December 21, 1903,			$1,186 63
Amount of surplus September 30, 1903,			32,740 78
Debits to profit and loss account during the year:			
Adjustment of unsettled accounts,		$828 81	
Dividend of 8 per cent paid November 30, 1903, from surplus earnings for year ending September 30, 1903,		2,400 00	
Total Debits,			3,228 81
Total Surplus December 21, 1903,			$30,698 60

Earnings from Operation.	
Receipts from passengers carried,	$7,286 65
Receipts from carriage of mails,	62 50
Receipts from carriage of freight,	100 00
Receipts from rentals of buildings and other property,	262 65
Receipts from advertising in cars,	75 00
Gross Earnings from Operation,	$7,786 80

Expenses of Operation.

General expenses:	
Salaries of general officers and clerks,	$592 76
General office expenses and supplies,	11 75
Insurance,	111 00
Other general expenses,	133 55
Maintenance of roadway and buildings:	
Repair of roadbed and track,	34 51
Repair of electric line construction,	28 74
Repair of buildings,	2 01
Maintenance of equipment:	
Repair of cars and other vehicles,	96 50
Repair of electric equipment of cars,	177 61
Transportation expenses:	
Cost of electric motive power,	1,360 25
Wages and compensation of persons employed in conducting transportation,	2,286 69
Removal of snow and ice,	3 74
Total Operating Expenses,	$4,839 11

General Balance Sheet December 21, 1903.

Assets.	Dr.	
Cost of railway:		
Roadbed and tracks and electric line construction, including poles, wiring, feeder lines, etc.,	$114,174 83	
Engineering and other expenses incident to construction,	538 59	
Total Cost of Railway Owned,		$114,713 42
Cost of equipment: cars and other rolling stock and vehicles and electric equipment of same,	$40,129 02	
Other items of equipment: snow ploughs, heaters, etc.,	2,023 17	
Total Cost of Equipment Owned,		42,152 19
Cost of land and buildings: buildings necessary for operation of railway, including land,		8,831 02
Total Permanent Investments,		$165,696 63
Cash and current assets:		
Cash,	$723 72	
Bills and accounts receivable,	2 60	
Sinking and other special funds,	888 25	
Other cash and current assets:		
Prepaid interest,	385 41	
Prepaid insurance,	298 80	
Total Cash and Current Assets,		2,298 78
Miscellaneous assets: materials and supplies,		324 10
Total,		$168,319 51

Liabilities.

	Cr.	
Capital stock,		$30,000 00
Funded debt,		47,000 00
Current liabilities:		
Loans and notes payable,	$59,100 00	
Audited vouchers and accounts,	210 90	
Total Current Liabilities,		59,310 90
Accrued liabilities:		
Interest accrued and not yet due,	$121 36	
Taxes accrued and not yet due,	300 40	
Total Accrued Liabilities,		421 76
Sinking and other special funds,		888 25
Profit and loss balance (surplus),		30,698 60
Total,		$168,319 51

Capital Stock.

Capital stock authorized by law,	$60,000 00	
Capital stock authorized by votes of company,	60,000 00	
Capital stock issued and outstanding,		$30,000 00
Number of shares issued and outstanding,	300	
Number of stockholders,	9	
Number of stockholders in Massachusetts,	9	
Amount of stock held in Massachusetts,	$30,000 00	

Funded Debt.

Description of Bonds.	Rate of Interest.	Date of Maturity.	Amount Outstanding.	Interest Paid during the Period.
	Per Cent.			
First mortgage gold bonds,	5	July 1, 1909,	$47,000 00	$587 49

Sinking and Other Special Funds.

Amount September 30, 1903, of sinking fund,	$888 25
Total Sinking and Other Special Funds, December 21, 1903,	$888 25

Volume of Traffic, etc.

Number of passengers paying revenue carried during the period,	169,937
Number carried per mile of main railway track operated,	26,140
Number of car miles run,	34,006
Average number of persons employed,	14

Description of Equipment.

Description of Equipment.	Equipped for Electric Power.	Not equipped.	Equipped with Fenders.	Equipped with Electric Heaters.	Number of Motors.
Cars — Passenger Service.					
Box passenger cars,	7	-	7	7	-
Open passenger cars,	8	-	8	-	-
Total,	15	-	15	7	27
Cars — Other Service.					
Work cars,	-	1	-	-	-
Snow ploughs,	1	1	-	-	-

Miscellaneous Equipment.

Highway vehicles:	
Tower wagon,	1
Cart,	1

Railway Owned, Leased and Operated (by Electric Power).

Railway Owned, etc.	Owned.	Trackage over Other Railways.	Total Owned, Leased, etc.
	Miles.	Miles.	Miles.
Length of railway line,	6.358	.143	6.501
Length of sidings, switches, etc.,	.478	-	.478
Total, Computed as Single Track,	6.836	.143	6.979

Names of the several cities and towns in which the railways operated by the company are located: Framingham.

Grade Crossings with Railroads.

Grade Crossings with Railroads.	Number of Tracks at Crossing.	
	Railroad.	Railway.
Crossings of railways with railroads at grade (2 in number), viz.:		
With Boston & Albany Railroad, Elm Street, Saxonville,	1	1
With Boston & Albany Railroad, Elm Street, Saxonville,	1	1
Total Number of Tracks at Crossings,	2	2

Number of above crossings at which *frogs* are inserted in the tracks, . 2

General Remarks and Explanations.

Consolidated with the Boston & Worcester Street Railway Company by approval of Board of Railroad Commissioners dated December 8, 1903.

Accidents to Persons.

(A detailed statement of each accident is on file in the office of the Board.)

Killed and Injured.	From Causes beyond their own Control.		From their own Misconduct or Carelessness.		Total.	
	Killed.	Injured.	Killed.	Injured.	Killed.	Injured.
Passengers,	-	-	-	-	-	-
Employees,	-	-	-	-	-	-
Other persons,	-	1	-	-	-	1
Totals,	-	1	-	-	-	1

Corporate Name and Address of the Company.

FRAMINGHAM UNION STREET RAILWAY COMPANY,

South Framingham, Mass.

Names and Business Address of Principal Officers.

William M. Butler, *President*, Tremont Building, Boston, Mass. George A. Butman, *Treasurer and Clerk of Corporation*, 8 Congress Street, Boston, Mass.

Names and Residence of Board of Directors.

William M. Butler, Boston, Mass. James F. Shaw, Manchester, Mass. Arthur E. Childs, Boston, Mass. Edward P. Shaw, Newburyport, Mass. George A. Butman, Malden, Mass.

We hereby certify that the statements contained in the foregoing report are full, just and true.

GEO. A. BUTMAN,
EDWARD P. SHAW,
JAMES F. SHAW,
Directors.
GEO. A. BUTMAN,
Treasurer.

Commonwealth of Massachusetts.

Suffolk, ss. Boston, Nov. 7, 1904. Then personally appeared the above-named Geo. A. Butman, Edw. P. Shaw and Jas. F. Shaw, and severally made oath that the foregoing certificate by them subscribed is, to the best of their knowledge and belief, true.

Before me, ARTHUR W. CLAPP,
Justice of the Peace.

REPORT

OF THE

GARDNER, WESTMINSTER & FITCHBURG STREET RAILWAY COMPANY

For the Year ending September 30, 1904.

General Exhibit for the Year.			
Gross earnings from operation,			$61,177 63
Operating expenses,			38,987 66
Net Earnings from Operation,			$22,189 97
Miscellaneous income: use of park,			326 36
Gross Income above Operating Expenses,			$22,516 33
Charges upon income accrued during the year:			
Interest on funded debt,		$7,500 00	
Interest and discount on unfunded debts and loans,		4,162 59	
Taxes, State and local,	$1,569 73		
Taxes, commutation,	585 66		
		2,155 39	
Other deductions from income: maintenance of pleasure grounds,		1,243 03	
Total Charges and Deductions from Income,			15,061 01
Surplus for the year ending September 30, 1904,			$7,455 32
Amount of deficit September 30, 1903,			10,702 88
Debits to profit and loss account during the year: paid damages, accident, 1901,			2,564 23
Total Deficit September 30, 1904,			$5,811 79

Earnings from Operation.	
Receipts from passengers carried,	$59,542 99
Receipts from carriage of mails,	23 67
Receipts from tolls for use of tracks by other companies,	1,310 97
Receipts from advertising in cars,	300 00
Gross Earnings from Operation,	$61,177 63

Expenses of Operation.

General expenses:	
Salaries of general officers and clerks,	$1,898 00
General office expenses and supplies,	1,206 67
Legal expenses,	446 32
Insurance,	1,551 90
Other general expenses: general expense,	462 02
Maintenance of roadway and buildings:	
Repair of roadbed and track,	1,932 38
Repair of electric line construction,	555 25
Repair of buildings,	84 17
Maintenance of equipment:	
Repair of cars and other vehicles,	1,790 97
Repair of electric equipment of cars,	1,654 49
Transportation expenses:	
Cost of electric motive power,	9,495 37
Wages and compensation of persons employed in conducting transportation,	13,450 72
Removal of snow and ice,	666 76
Damages for injuries to persons and property,	2,900 37
Other transportation expenses,	892 27
Total Operating Expenses,	$38,987 66

Property Accounts.

Additions to railway: change in tracks due to State highway,	$3,126 45
Net Additions to Property Accounts for the Year,	$3,126 45

General Balance Sheet September 30, 1904.

Assets.	Dr.	
Cost of railway:		
Roadbed and tracks,	$164,540 71	
Electric line construction, including poles, wiring, feeder lines, etc.,	44,391 56	
Interest accrued during construction of railway,	1,267 74	
Engineering and other expenses incident to construction,	10,000 00	
Other items of railway cost,	13,700 00	
Telephone line,	3,000 00	
Total Cost of Railway Owned,		$236,900 01
Cost of equipment:		
Cars and other rolling stock and vehicles,	$32,625 05	
Electric equipment of same,	27,204 96	
Total Cost of Equipment Owned,		59,830 01
Cost of land and buildings:		
Land necessary for operation of railway,	$3,902 93	
Electric power stations, including equipment,	59,328 56	
Other buildings necessary for operation of railway,	10,832 53	
Total Cost of Land and Buildings Owned,		74,064 02
Other permanent property: pleasure grounds,		22,662 94
Total Permanent Investments,		$393,456 98

Cash and current assets:		
Cash,	$6,653 96	
Other cash and current assets: prepaid insurance,	471 51	
TOTAL CASH AND CURRENT ASSETS,		$7,125 47
Miscellaneous assets: materials and supplies,		7,163 41
Profit and loss balance (deficit),		5,811 79
TOTAL,		$413,557 65

LIABILITIES.	CR.	
Capital stock,		$185,000 00
Funded debt,		150,000 00
Current liabilities:		
Loans and notes payable,	$78,000 00	
Audited vouchers and accounts,	557 65	
TOTAL CURRENT LIABILITIES,		78,557 65
TOTAL,		$413,557 65

CAPITAL STOCK.

Capital stock authorized by law,	$185,000 00	
Capital stock authorized by votes of company,	185,000 00	
Capital stock issued and outstanding,		$185,000 00
Number of shares issued and outstanding,	1,850	
Number of stockholders,	74	
Number of stockholders in Massachusetts,	72	
Amount of stock held in Massachusetts,	$183,400 00	

FUNDED DEBT.

DESCRIPTION OF BONDS.	Rate of Interest.	Date of Maturity.	Amount Outstanding.	Interest Paid during the Year.
First mortgage gold bonds,	Per Cent. 5	Feb. 1, 1920,	$150,000 00	$7,500 00

VOLUME OF TRAFFIC, ETC.

Number of passengers paying revenue carried during the year,	1,198,423
Number carried per mile of main railway track operated,	76,430
Number of car miles run,	254,926
Average number of persons employed,	50

Description of Equipment.

Description of Equipment.	Equipped for Electric Power.	Equipped with Fenders.	Equipped with Electric Heaters.	Number of Motors.
Cars — Passenger Service.				
Box passenger cars,	9	9	9	18
Open passenger cars,	12	12	-	24
Total,	21	21	9	42
Cars — Other Service.				
Box freight cars (coal),	2	-	-	-
Platform freight cars (construction),	1	-	-	-
Total,	3	-	-	-
Snow ploughs,	2	-	-	-

Miscellaneous Equipment.

Highway vehicles: tower wagon,	1

Railway Owned and Operated (by Electric Power).

Length of railway line,	15.680 miles.
Length of sidings, switches, etc.,	.370 "
Total, computed as single track,	16.050 "

Names of the several cities and towns in which the railways operated by the company are located: Gardner, Westminster and Fitchburg.

Grade Crossings with Railroads.

Grade Crossings with Railroads.	Number of Tracks at Crossing.	
	Railroad.	Railway.
Crossings of railways with railroads at grade (5 in number), viz.: —		
With Worcester Division of Fitchburg Division, Boston & Maine Railroad, at Park Street, Gardner (1 main, 2 side),	3	1
With freight side track, North Main Street, Gardner,	1	1
With Worcester Division of Fitchburg Division, Boston & Maine Railroad, at North Main Street, Gardner (1 main, 2 side),	3	1
With Worcester Division of Fitchburg Division, Boston & Maine Railroad, at South Main Street, Gardner (known as Kendall's Crossing),	1	1
With Worcester Division of Fitchburg Division, Boston & Maine Railroad, at South Main Street, Gardner (known as Sawins Crossing),	1	1
Total Number of Tracks at Crossings,	9	5

Number of above crossings at which *frogs* are inserted in the tracks, . 5

Accidents to Persons.

(A detailed statement of each accident is on file in the office of the Board.)

Killed and Injured.	From Causes beyond their own Control		From their own Misconduct or Carelessness.		Total.	
	Killed.	Injured.	Killed.	Injured.	Killed.	Injured.
Passengers,	-	-	-	3	-	3
Employees,	-	1	-	-	-	1
Other persons,	-	-	-	-	-	-
Totals,	-	1	-	3	-	4

Corporate Name and Address of the Company.

GARDNER, WESTMINSTER & FITCHBURG STREET RAILWAY CO.,

Gardner, Mass.

Names and Business Address of Principal Officers.

Frederick S. Coolidge, *President*, Fitchburg, Mass. Edward F. Blodgett, *Vice-President*, Leominster, Mass. James A. Stiles, *Treasurer*, *Clerk of Corporation and General Counsel*, Gardner, Mass. Charles A. Jefts, *Superintendent*, Gardner, Mass.

Names and Residence of Board of Directors.

Frederick S. Coolidge, Fitchburg, Mass. Edward F. Blodgett, Leominster, Mass. James A. Stiles, Gardner, Mass. George R. Damon, Leominster, Mass. William S. Reed, Leominster, Mass. Albert N. Wood, Leominster, Mass. Walter R. Dame, Clinton, Mass.

We hereby certify that the statements contained in the foregoing report are full, just and true.

ALBERT N. WOOD,
JAMES A. STILES,
GEO. R. DAMON,
WALTER R. DAME,
Directors.
JAMES A. STILES,
Treasurer.
CHARLES A. JEFTS,
Superintendent.

Commonwealth of Massachusetts.

Worcester, ss. Oct. 11, 1904. Then personally appeared the above-named Albert N. Wood, James A. Stiles, Geo. R. Damon, Walter R. Dame and Charles A. Jefts, and severally made oath that the foregoing certificate by them subscribed is, to the best of their knowledge and belief, true.

Before me, HARRY G. TOWNEND,
Notary Public.

REPORT

OF THE

GEORGETOWN, ROWLEY & IPSWICH STREET RAILWAY COMPANY

For the Year ending September 30, 1904.

General Exhibit for the Year.		
Gross earnings from operation,		$36,460 91
Operating expenses,		32,860 00
Gross Income above Operating Expenses,		$3,600 91
Charges upon income accrued during the year:		
Interest on funded debt,	$9,000 00	
Interest and discount on unfunded debts and loans,	3,448 36	
Taxes, State and local,	995 07	
Total Charges and Deductions from Income,		13,443 43
Deficit for the year ending September 30, 1904,		$9,842 52
Amount of surplus S-ptember 30, 1903,		5,705 70
Total Deficit September 30, 1904,		$4,136 82

Earnings from Operation.	
Receipts from passengers carried,	$35,866 83
Receipts from carriage of mails,	200 00
Receipts from advertising in cars,	167 31
Receipts from interest on deposits,	50 72
Other earnings from operation: receipts not included in other accounts,	176 05
Gross Earnings from Operation,	$36,460 91

Expenses of Operation.	
General expenses:	
Salaries of general officers and clerks,	$1,373 40
General office expenses and supplies,	603 27
Legal expenses,	300 00

General expenses — *Concluded.*	
Insurance,	$1,500 10
Other general expenses,	694 51
Maintenance of roadway and buildings:	
Repair of roadbed and track,	2,843 92
Repair of electric line construction,	184 54
Repair of buildings,	22 60
Maintenance of equipment:	
Repair of cars and other vehicles,	5,696 56
Repair of electric equipment of cars,	14 55
Transportation expenses:	
Cost of electric motive power, $9,031.80; less power sold, $6,434.62; net,	2,597 18
Wages and compensation of persons employed in conducting transportation,	11,562 71
Removal of snow and ice,	3,459 10
Damages for injuries to persons and property,	1,789 44
Tolls for trackage over other railways,	218 12
TOTAL OPERATING EXPENSES,	$32,860 00

PROPERTY ACCOUNTS.

Additions to railway: engineering, etc.,	$10 00
Additions to equipment: electric equipment of cars,	172 00
TOTAL ADDITIONS TO PROPERTY ACCOUNTS,	$182 00

GENERAL BALANCE SHEET SEPTEMBER 30, 1904.

ASSETS.	DR.	
Cost of railway:		
Roadbed and tracks,	$193,427 27	
Electric line construction, including poles, wiring, feeder lines, etc.,	62,231 07	
Engineering and other expenses incident to construction,	7,510 00	
TOTAL COST OF RAILWAY OWNED,		$263,168 34
Cost of equipment:		
Cars and other rolling stock and vehicles,	$34,799 45	
Electric equipment of same,	20,626 88	
Horses,	98 00	
Other items of equipment: sundry equipment of rolling stock,	9,360 31	
TOTAL COST OF EQUIPMENT OWNED,		64,884 64
Cost of land and buildings:		
Land necessary for operation of railway,	$1,450 00	
Electric power stations, including equipment,	65,533 00	
Other buildings necessary for operation of railway,	17,074 11	
TOTAL COST OF LAND AND BUILDINGS OWNED,		84,057 11
TOTAL PERMANENT INVESTMENTS,		$412,110 09

Cash and current assets:		
Cash,	$963 88	
Bills and accounts receivable,	38 69	
Other cash and current assets: unsettled fire loss,	4,943 85	
Total Cash and Current Assets,		$5,946 42
Miscellaneous assets: materials and supplies,		1,320 08
Profit and loss balance (deficit),		4,136 82
Total,		$423,513 41

Liabilities.	Cr.	
Capital stock,		$180,000 00
Funded debt,		180,000 00
Current liabilities:		
Loans and notes payable,	$59,500 00	
Audited vouchers and accounts,	484 07	
Total Current Liabilities,		59,984 07
Accrued liabilities:		
Interest accrued and not yet due,	$3,000 00	
Taxes accrued and not yet due,	529 34	
Total Accrued Liabilities,		3,529 34
Total,		$423,513 41

Capital Stock.

Capital stock authorized by law,	$180,000 00	
Capital stock authorized by votes of company,	180,000 00	
Capital stock issued and outstanding,		$180,000 00
Number of shares issued and outstanding,	1,800	
Number of stockholders,	6	
Number of stockholders in Massachusetts,	6	
Amount of stock held in Massachusetts,	$180,000 00	

Funded Debt.

Description of Bonds.	Rate of Interest.	Date of Maturity.	Amount Outstanding.	Interest Paid during the Year.
First mortgage bonds,	Per Cent. 5	June 1, 1920,	$180,000 00	$9,000 00

Volume of Traffic, etc.

Number of passengers paying revenue carried during the year,	751,099
Number carried per mile of main railway track operated,	40,539
Number of car miles run,	257,962
Average number of persons employed,	29

Description of Equipment.

Description of Equipment.	Equipped for Electric Power.	Equipped with Fenders.	Equipped with Electric Heaters.	Number of Motors.
Cars — Passenger Service.				
Box passenger cars,	8	8	8	16
Open passenger cars,	9	9	-	18
Total,	17	17	8	34
Snow ploughs,	2	-	-	-

Miscellaneous Equipment.

Highway vehicles:	
Tip cart,	1
Trolley wagon,	1
Horses,	1
Other items of equipment: single harness,	1

Railway Owned, Leased and Operated (by Electric Power).

Railway Owned, etc.	Owned.	Trackage over Other Railways.	Total Owned, Leased, etc.
	Miles.	Miles.	Miles.
Length of railway line,	17.923	.605	18.528
Length of sidings, switches, etc.,	.260	-	.260
Total, Computed as Single Track,	18.183	.605	18.788

Names of the several cities and towns in which the railways operated by the company are located: Georgetown, Ipswich, Newbury, Newburyport and Rowley.

Grade Crossings with Railroads.

Grade Crossings with Railroads.	Number of Tracks at Crossing.	
	Railroad.	Railway.
Crossings of railways with railroads at grade (1 in number), viz.:— With Boston & Maine Railroad, State Street, Newburyport,	2	1

ACCIDENTS TO PERSONS.

(A detailed statement of each accident is on file in the office of the Board.)

KILLED AND INJURED.	FROM CAUSES BEYOND THEIR OWN CONTROL.		FROM THEIR OWN MISCONDUCT OR CARELESSNESS.		TOTAL.	
	Killed.	Injured.	Killed.	Injured.	Killed.	Injured.
Passengers,	-	-	-	1	-	1
Employees,	-	-	-	-	-	-
Other persons,	-	-	-	1	-	1
TOTALS,	-	-	-	2	-	2

CORPORATE NAME AND ADDRESS OF THE COMPANY.

GEORGETOWN, ROWLEY & IPSWICH STREET RAILWAY COMPANY,

222 BOYLSTON STREET, BOSTON, MASS.

NAMES AND BUSINESS ADDRESS OF PRINCIPAL OFFICERS.

Alfred Rodman, *President*, 222 Boylston Street, Boston, Mass. Thomas K. Cummins, *Treasurer and Clerk of Corporation*; 222 Boylston Street, Boston, Mass. George W. Pratt, *Superintendent*, Byfield, Mass.

NAMES AND RESIDENCE OF BOARD OF DIRECTORS.

Alfred Rodman, Dedham, Mass. A. LeBaron Russell, Boston, Mass. Thomas K. Cummins, Milton, Mass. William Atherton, Boston, Mass. James A. Roberts, Milton, Mass.

We hereby certify that the statements contained in the foregoing report are full, just and true.

ALFRED RODMAN,
THOMAS K. CUMMINS,
JAMES A. ROBERTS,
A. LEBARON RUSSELL,
Directors.
THOMAS K. CUMMINS,
Treasurer.
GEO. W. PRATT,
Superintendent.

COMMONWEALTH OF MASSACHUSETTS.

SUFFOLK, SS. BOSTON, Oct. 27, 1904. Then personally appeared the above-named Alfred Rodman, Thomas K. Cummins, James A. Roberts, A. LeBaron Russell and George W. Pratt, and severally made oath that the foregoing certificate by them subscribed is, to the best of their knowledge and belief, true.

Before me, WILLIAM ATHERTON,
Justice of the Peace.

REPORT

OF THE

GREENFIELD, DEERFIELD & NORTHAMPTON STREET RAILWAY COMPANY

For the Year ending September 30, 1904.

General Exhibit for the Year.

Gross earnings from operation,			$50,752 98
Operating expenses,			30,801 75
Gross Income above Operating Expenses,			$19,951 23
Charges upon income accrued during the year:			
Interest on funded debt,		$4,520 83	
Interest and discount on unfunded debts and loans,		2,059 57	
Taxes, State and local, and commutation,		2,236 53	
Other deductions from income:			
Credits to Northampton & Amherst Street Railway Company, account trackage contract,	$14,889 80		
Credits to Greenfield & Turner's Falls Street Railway Company, account trackage contract,	4,374 98		
		19,264 78	
Total Charges and Deductions from Income,			28,081 71
Deficit for the year ending September 30, 1904,			$8,130 48
Amount of surplus September 30, 1903,			6,395 88
Total Deficit September 30, 1904,			$1,734 60

Earnings from Operation.

Receipts from passengers carried,	$49,126 73
Receipts from carriage of mails,	127 01
Receipts from advertising,	523 85
Receipts from interest on deposits,	870 77
Other earnings from operation: amusements,	104 62
Gross Earnings from Operation,	$50,752 98

Expenses of Operation.

General expenses:	
Salaries of officers,	$3,499 79
General office expenses and supplies,	987 66
Advertising,	540 75
Insurance,	1,536 74
General expenses,	164 57
Fuel,	42 53
Maintenance of roadway and buildings:	
Repair of roadbed and track,	1,299 43
Repair of buildings,	31 15
Maintenance of equipment:	
Repair of cars and other vehicles,	828 70
Repair of electric equipment of cars,	619 16
Transportation expenses:	
Cost of electric motive power,	6,704 65
Wages and compensation of persons employed in conducting transportation,	11,045 07
Removal of snow and ice,	2,098 16
Damages for injuries to persons and property,	24 75
Oil and waste,	173 63
Transportation expenses,	404 39
Car house labor,	699 13
Amusements,	101 49
Total Operating Expenses,	$30,801 75

Property Accounts.

Additions to railway:		
Extension of tracks (length, 600 feet), 4 new turnouts,	$1,148 30	
New electric line construction,	161 27	
Other additions to railway:		
Legal and engineering expenses incident to construction,	858 63	
Telephone line charged to overhead line,	717 89	
Total Additions to Railway,		$2,886 09
Additions to equipment:		
One snow plough,	$529 95	
Electric equipment of same,	3,676 02	
Other additions to equipment: headlights, etc.,	342 01	
Total Additions to Equipment,		4,547 98
Additions to land and buildings: new buildings necessary for operation of railway,		1,033 83
Total Additions to Property Accounts,		$8,467 90
Deductions from property accounts (property sold or reduced in valuation and credited to property accounts): telephone line charged to overhead line,		717 89
Net Addition to Property Accounts for the Year,		$7,750 01

General Balance Sheet September 30, 1904.

Assets.	Dr.	
Cost of railway:		
Roadbed and tracks,	$237,866 01	
Electric line construction, including poles, wiring, feeder lines, etc.,	30,099 56	
Interest accrued during construction of railway,	5,675 36	
Engineering and other expenses incident to construction,	9,988 89	
Total Cost of Railway Owned,		$283,629 82
Cost of equipment:		
Cars and other rolling stock and vehicles,	$37,693 98	
Electric equipment of same,	17,698 42	
Other items of equipment: sundry equipment and tools,	450 76	
Total Cost of Equipment Owned,		55,843 16
Cost of land and buildings: land necessary for operation of railway,		19,236 49
Total Permanent Investments,		$358,709 47
Cash and current assets:		
Cash,	$300 74	
Bills and accounts receivable,	583 41	
Total Cash and Current Assets,		884 15
Miscellaneous assets: materials and supplies,	$979 10	
Other assets and property: office fixtures,	466 79	
Total Miscellaneous Assets,		1,445 89
Profit and loss balance (deficit),		1,734 60
Total,		$362,774 11

Liabilities.	Cr.	
Capital stock,		$180,000 00
Funded debt,		150,000 00
Current liabilities:		
Loans and notes payable,	$25,399 46	
Audited vouchers and accounts,	5,281 72	
Miscellaneous current liabilities: unredeemed tickets,	197 83	
Total Current Liabilities,		30,879 01
Sinking and other special funds: reserve for abolition of Sprout's Crossing,		1,895 10
Total,		$362,774 11

Capital Stock.

Capital stock authorized by law,	$180,000 00	
Capital stock authorized by votes of company,	180,000 00	
Capital stock issued and outstanding,		$180,000 00
Number of shares issued and outstanding,	1,800	
Number of stockholders,	71	
Number of stockholders in Massachusetts,	66	
Amount of stock held in Massachusetts,	$151,800 00	

FUNDED DEBT.

DESCRIPTION OF BONDS.	Rate of Interest.	Date of Maturity.	Amount Outstanding.	Interest Paid during the Year.
First mortgage gold bonds,	Per Cent. 5	July 1, 1923,	$150,000 00	$4,520 83

VOLUME OF TRAFFIC, ETC.

Number of passengers paying revenue carried during the year,	1,021,967
Number carried per mile of main railway track operated,	46,113
Number of car miles run,	271,490
Average number of persons employed,	20

DESCRIPTION OF EQUIPMENT.

DESCRIPTION OF EQUIPMENT.	Equipped for Electric Power.	Not Equipped.	Total Passenger Cars.	Equipped with Fenders.	Equipped with Electric Heaters.	Number of Motors.
CARS — PASSENGER SERVICE.						
Box passenger cars,	5	-	5	5	5	-
Open passenger cars,	4	2	6	6	-	-
TOTAL,	9	2	11	11	5	22
CARS — OTHER SERVICE.						
Work cars,	-	2	-	-	-	-
Snow ploughs,	-	1	-	-	-	-

RAILWAY OWNED, LEASED AND OPERATED (BY ELECTRIC POWER).

RAILWAY OWNED, ETC.	Owned.	Trackage over Other Railways.	Total Operated.
	Miles.	Miles.	Miles.
Length of railway line,	14.085	8.077	22.162
Length of sidings, switches, etc.,	.625	-	.625
TOTAL, COMPUTED AS SINGLE TRACK,	14.710	8.077	22.787

RAILWAY LOCATED OUTSIDE OF PUBLIC WAYS.

Length of railway line,	1.915 miles.

Names of the several cities and towns in which the railways operated by the company are located: Greenfield, Deerfield, Whately, Hatfield and Northampton.

Accidents to Persons.

(A detailed statement of each accident is on file in the office of the Board.)

Killed and Injured.	From Causes beyond their own Control.		From their own Misconduct or Carelessness.		Total.	
	Killed.	Injured.	Killed.	Injured.	Killed.	Injured.
Passengers,	-	1	-	2	-	3
Employees,	-	-	-	-	-	-
Other persons,	-	-	-	1	-	1
Totals,	-	1	-	3	-	4

Corporate Name and Address of the Company.

GREENFIELD, DEERFIELD & NORTHAMPTON STREET RAILWAY COMPANY,

Greenfield, Mass.

Names and Business Address of Principal Officers.

Fred. E. Pierce, *President*, Greenfield, Mass. Daniel P. Abercrombie, Jr., *Treasurer and Clerk of Corporation*, Greenfield, Mass. Irwin & Hardy, *General Counsel*, Northampton, Mass. John A. Taggart, *Superintendent*, Greenfield, Mass.

Names and Residence of Board of Directors.

John A. Taggart, Miller's Falls, Mass. Fred. E. Pierce, Greenfield, Mass. Edward C. Crosby, Brattleboro, Vt. Marcus A. Coolidge, Fitchburg, Mass. Benjamin E. Cook, Northampton, Mass. Charles W. Clapp, Greenfield, Mass. Daniel P. Abercrombie, Jr., Turner's Falls, Mass.

We hereby certify that the statements contained in the foregoing report are full, just and true.

FRED. E. PIERCE,
EDWARD C. CROSBY,
MARCUS A. COOLIDGE,
BENJAMIN E. COOK,
C. W. CLAPP,
JOHN A. TAGGART,
DANIEL P. ABERCROMBIE, Jr.,
Directors.
DANIEL P. ABERCROMBIE, Jr.,
Treasurer.
JOHN A. TAGGART,
Superintendent.

COMMONWEALTH OF MASSACHUSETTS.

FRANKLIN, ss. Nov. 2, 1904. Then personally appeared the above-named Fred. E. Pierce, C. W. Clapp, John A. Taggart and Daniel P. Abercrombie, Jr., and severally made oath that the foregoing certificate by them subscribed is, to the best of their knowledge and belief, true.

Before me, WM. A. DAVENPORT,
Justice of the Peace.

COMMONWEALTH OF MASSACHUSETTS.

HAMPSHIRE, ss. Nov. 4, 1904. Personally appeared the above-named Benjamin E. Cook, and made oath that the foregoing certificate by him subscribed is, to the best of his knowledge and belief, true.

Before me, JAMES W. O'BRIEN,
Justice of the Peace.

STATE OF VERMONT.

WINDHAM COUNTY, ss. At Brattleboro, in said county, this 7th day of November, 1904, personally appeared the above-named Edward C. Crosby, and made oath that the foregoing certificate by him subscribed is, to the best of his knowledge and belief, true.

Before me, ARTHUR C. SPENCER,
Notary Public.

COMMONWEALTH OF MASSACHUSETTS.

WORCESTER, ss. Nov. 8, 1904. Then personally appeared the above-named Marcus A. Coolidge, and made oath that the foregoing certificate by him subscribed is, to the best of his knowledge and belief, true.

Before me, CLARENCE E. TUPPER,
Justice of the Peace.

REPORT

OF THE

GREENFIELD & TURNER'S FALLS STREET RAILWAY COMPANY

For the Year ending September 30, 1904.

General Exhibit for the Year.		
Gross earnings from operation,		$65,703 12
Operating expenses,		46,438 04
Gross Income above Operating Expenses,		$19,265 08
Charges upon income accrued during the year:		
Interest on funded debt,	$6,445 00	
Interest and discount on unfunded debts and loans,	1,101 20	
Taxes, State, local and commutation,	2,086 80	
Other deductions from income: amusements,	2,783 38	
Total Charges and Deductions from Income,		12,416 38
Net Divisible Income,		$6,848 70
Dividends declared (5 per cent),		6,500 00
Surplus for the year ending September 30, 1904,		$348 70
Amount of surplus September 30, 1903,		9,831 02
Credits to profit and loss account during the year: reserve for depreciation,	$5,000 00	
Debits to profit and loss account during the year: telephone line,	1,326 72	
Net Amount Credited to Profit and Loss,		3,673 28
Total Surplus September 30, 1904,		$13,853 00

Earnings from Operation.	
Receipts from passengers carried,	$58,908 19
Receipts from carriage of mails,	422 60
Receipts from carriage of express and parcels,	1,693 30
Receipts from advertising in cars,	200 00
Receipts from interest on deposits,	121 07
Other earnings from operation: Greenfield, Deerfield and Northampton cars,	4,357 96
Gross Earnings from Operation,	$65,703 12

EXPENSES OF OPERATION.		
General expenses:		
Salaries of general officers and clerks,		$3,292 26
General office expenses and supplies,		1,046 99
Legal expenses and engineering expenses,		322 76
Insurance,		897 37
Other general expenses:		
General expense,		89 99
Advertising,		202 65
Maintenance of roadway and buildings:		
Repair of roadbed and track,		3,192 15
Repair of electric line construction,		416 84
Repair of buildings,		33 44
Maintenance of equipment:		
Repair of cars and other vehicles,		2,495 28
Repair of electric equipment of cars,		2,590 15
Transportation expenses:		
Cost of electric motive power, $10,005.46; less power sold, $2,764 55; net,		7,240 91
Wages and compensation of persons employed in conducting transportation,		17,004 07
Removal of snow and ice,		3,298 86
Damages for injuries to persons and property,		658 84
Other transportation expenses: Transportation expenses, $403.96; car house labor, $2,690.11; oil and waste, $257.61; Fuel, $185.25; repairs of telephone line, $118.55,		3,655 48
TOTAL OPERATING EXPENSES,		$46,438 04

PROPERTY ACCOUNTS.		
Additions to railway: completion of Conway Street extension,		$12,068 29
Additions to equipment:		
Additional cars (2 in number),	$2,546 00	
Electric equipment of same,	1,000 00	
TOTAL ADDITIONS TO EQUIPMENT,		$3,546 00
Additions to land and buildings:		
Additional equipment of power stations,	$3,483 41	
Additional equipment of storage battery,	962 60	
TOTAL ADDITIONS TO LAND AND BUILDINGS,		4,446 01
TOTAL ADDITIONS TO PROPERTY ACCOUNTS,		$20,060 30
Deductions from property accounts (property sold or reduced in valuation and credited to property accounts): telephone line,		1,326 72
NET ADDITION TO PROPERTY ACCOUNTS FOR THE YEAR,		$18,733 58

GENERAL BALANCE SHEET SEPTEMBER 30, 1904.

ASSETS.	DR.	
Cost of railway:		
Roadbed and tracks,	$199,866 29	
Electric line construction, including poles, wiring, feeder lines, etc.,	27,036 00	
TOTAL COST OF RAILWAY OWNED,		$226,902 29

Cost of equipment:		
Cars and other rolling stock and vehicles,	$17,774 20	
Electric equipment of same,	16,000 00	
TOTAL COST OF EQUIPMENT OWNED,		$33,774 20
Cost of land and buildings:		
Land necessary for operation of railway,	$10,750 00	
Electric power stations, including equipment,	18,483 41	
Other buildings necessary for operation of railway, storage battery,	9,637 61	
TOTAL COST OF LAND AND BUILDINGS OWNED,		38,871 02
TOTAL PERMANENT INVESTMENTS,		$299,547 51
Cash and current assets:		
Cash,	$725 76	
Bills and accounts receivable,	1,477 36	
Other cash and current assets: cash reserve,	5,180 36	
TOTAL CASH AND CURRENT ASSETS,	$7,383 48	
TOTAL,		$306,930 99

LIABILITIES.	CR.	
Capital stock,		$130,000 00
Funded debt,		130,000 00
Current liabilities:		
Loans and notes payable,	$29,500 00	
Audited vouchers and accounts,	3,577 99	
TOTAL CURRENT LIABILITIES,		33,077 99
Profit and loss balance (surplus),		13,853 00
TOTAL,		$306,930 99

CAPITAL STOCK.

Capital stock authorized by law,	$130,000 00	
Capital stock authorized by votes of company,	130,000 00	
Capital stock issued and outstanding,		$130,000 00
Number of shares issued and outstanding,	1,300	
Number of stockholders,	120	
Number of stockholders in Massachusetts,	112	
Amount of stock held in Massachusetts,	122,000 00	

FUNDED DEBT.

DESCRIPTION OF BONDS.	Rate of Interest.	Date of Maturity.	Amount Outstanding.	Interest Paid during the Year.
	Per Cent.			
First mortgage gold bonds,	5	June 1, 1916,	$82,000 00	$4,100 00
First consolidated gold bonds,	5	June 1, 1923,	48,000 00	2,345 00
TOTALS,	. .	. . .	$130,000 00	$6,445 00

Sinking and Other Special Funds.

Amount September 30, 1903, of cash reserve fund,	$3,513 23
Additions during the year to cash reserve fund,	2,521 07
Total, Including Additions,	$6,034 30
Deductions during the year from cash reserve fund,	853 94
Total Sinking and Other Special Funds, September 30, 1904,	$5,180 36

Volume of Traffic, etc.

Number of passengers paying revenue carried during the year,	1,475,295
Number carried per mile of main railway track operated,	85,873
Number of car miles run,	400,866
Average number of persons employed,	45

Description of Equipment.

Description of Equipment.	Equipped for Electric Power.	Not Equipped.	Equipped with Fenders.	Equipped with Electric Heaters.	Number of Motors.
Cars — Passenger Service.					
Box passenger cars,	12	-	12	12	-
Open passenger cars,	8	-	8	-	-
Total,	20	-	20	12	39
Cars — Other Service.					
Platform freight cars,	-	1	-	-	-
Work cars,	1	-	1	-	-
Snow ploughs,	-	1	-	-	-

Miscellaneous Equipment.

Carts and snow sleds,	1
Other highway vehicles:	
Wagon,	1
Tower wagon,	1

Railway Owned and Operated (by Electric Power).

Length of railway line,	17.180 miles.
Length of sidings, switches, etc.,	.501 "
Total, computed as single track,	17.681 "

Railway Located Outside of Public Ways.

Length of railway line, ...	3.660 miles.

Names of the several cities and towns in which the railways operated by the company are located: Greenfield and Montague.

Grade Crossings with Railroads.

Grade Crossings with Railroads.	Number of Tracks at Crossing.	
	Railroad.	Railway.
Crossings of railways with railroads at grade (1 in number), viz :— With Boston & Maine Railroad (Fitchburg Division), . . .	1	1

Number of above crossings at which *frogs* are inserted in the tracks, . 1

Accidents to Persons.

(A detailed statement of each accident is on file in the office of the Board.)

Killed and Injured.	From Causes beyond their own Control.		From their own Misconduct or Carelessness.		Total.	
	Killed.	Injured.	Killed.	Injured.	Killed.	Injured.
Passengers, ...	-	1	-	4	-	5
Employees, ...	-	1	-	-	-	1
Other persons, ...	-	-	1	2	1	2
Totals, ...	-	2	1	6	1	8

Corporate Name and Address of the Company.

GREENFIELD & TURNER'S FALLS STREET RAILWAY COMPANY,

Greenfield, Mass.

Names and Business Address of Principal Officers.

F. E. Pierce, *President*, Greenfield, Mass. Daniel P. Abercrombie, Jr., *Treasurer and Clerk of Corporation*, Greenfield, Mass. John E. Donovan, *Auditor*, Greenfield, Mass. John A. Taggart, *Superintendent*, Greenfield, Mass.

Names and Residence of Board of Directors.

John A. Taggart, Miller's Falls, Mass. Joseph W. Stevens, Greenfield, Mass. Fred. E. Pierce, Greenfield, Mass. Albert T. Hall, Greenfield, Mass. Nahum S. Cutler, Greenfield, Mass. Charles W. Clapp, Greenfield, Mass. Isaac Chenery, Montague, Mass. Daniel P. Abercrombie, Sr., Turner's Falls, Mass. Daniel P. Abercrombie, Jr., Turner's Falls, Mass.

We hereby certify that the statements contained in the foregoing report are full, just and true.

FRED. E. PIERCE,
ISAAC CHENERY,
D. P. ABERCROMBIE,
ALBERT T. HALL,
JOSEPH W. STEVENS,
N. S. CUTLER,
JOHN A. TAGGART,
C. W. CLAPP,
DANIEL P. ABERCROMBIE, JR.,
Directors.
DANIEL P. ABERCROMBIE, JR.,
Treasurer.
JOHN A. TAGGART,
Superintendent.

COMMONWEALTH OF MASSACHUSETTS.

FRANKLIN, SS. OCT. 26, 1904. Then personally appeared the above-named Fred. E. Pierce, Albert T. Hall, Joseph W. Stevens, N. S. Cutler, John A. Taggart, C. W. Clapp and D. P. Abercrombie, Jr., and severally made oath that the foregoing certificate by them subscribed is, to the best of their knowledge and belief, true.

Before me, JOHN E. DONOVAN,
Justice of the Peace.

COMMONWEALTH OF MASSACHUSETTS.

FRANKLIN, SS. OCT. 27, 1904. Then personally appeared the above-named Isaac Chenery and D. P. Abercrombie, and severally made oath that the foregoing certificate by them subscribed is, to the best of their knowledge and belief, true.

Before me, W. C. D. THOMAS,
Justice of the Peace.

REPORT

OF THE

HAMPSHIRE STREET RAILWAY COMPANY

For the Year ending September 30, 1904.

General Exhibit for the Year.			
Gross earnings from operation,			$10,702 92
Operating expenses,			4,115 16
Gross Income above Operating Expenses,			$6,587 76
Charges upon income accrued during the year:			
Taxes, State and local,	$497 76		
Taxes, commutation,	84 13		
		$581 89	
Other deductions from income: interest paid to subscribers of capital stock previous to issue,		2,544 00	
Total Charges and Deductions from Income,			3,125 89
Surplus for the year ending September 30, 1904,			$3,461 87
Amount of surplus September 30, 1903,			1,875 54
Total Surplus September 30, 1904,			$5,337 41

Earnings from Operation.	
Receipts from passengers carried,	$8,413 12
Receipts from carriage of freight (hauling stone for State highway),	2,115 40
Receipts from interest on deposits,	174 40
Gross Earnings from Operation,	$10,702 92

Expenses of Operation.	
General expenses:	
General office expenses and supplies,	$22 80
Other general expenses: printing,	8 69
Maintenance of roadway and buildings: repair of roadbed and track,	629 97
Transportation expenses:	
Cost of electric motive power,	649 87
Wages and compensation of persons employed in conducting transportation,	2,048 96
Removal of snow and ice,	265 62
Other transportation expenses: rental of car,	489 25
Total Operating Expenses,	$4,115 16

Property Accounts.

Additions to railway: engineering, turnout and land damages,	$543 64
Total Additions to Property Accounts,	$543 64

General Balance Sheet September 30, 1904.

Assets.	Dr.	
Cost of railway:		
Roadbed and tracks,	$54,249 01	
Electric line construction, including poles, wiring, feeder lines, etc.,	3,574 01	
Engineering and other expenses incident to construction,	2,235 36	
Total Cost of Railway Owned,		$60,058 38
Cash and current assets: cash,		6,010 92
Total,		$66,069 30

Liabilities.	Cr.
Capital stock,	$60,000 00
Current liabilities: audited vouchers and accounts,	150 00
Accrued liabilities: taxes accrued and not yet due,	581 89
Profit and loss balance (surplus),	5,337 41
Total,	$66,069 30

Capital Stock.

Capital stock authorized by law,	$60,000 00	
Capital stock authorized by votes of company,	60,000 00	
Capital stock issued and outstanding,		$60,000 00
Number of shares issued and outstanding,	600	
Number of stockholders,	37	
Number of stockholders in Massachusetts,	37	
Amount of stock held in Massachusetts,	$60,000 00	

Volume of Traffic, etc.

Number of passengers paying revenue carried during the year,	168,262
Number carried per mile of main railway track operated,	38,770
Number of car miles run,	68,402
Average number of persons employed,	6

Railway Owned and Operated (by Electric Power).

Length of railway line,	4.340 miles.
Length of sidings, switches, etc.,	.230 "
Total, computed as single track,	4.570 "

RAILWAY LOCATED OUTSIDE OF PUBLIC WAYS.

Length of railway line, ...	2.390 miles.

Names of the several cities and towns in which the railways operated by the company are located: South Hadley and Granby.

CORPORATE NAME AND ADDRESS OF THE COMPANY.

HAMPSHIRE STREET RAILWAY COMPANY,

25 CANAL STREET, HOLYOKE, MASS.

NAMES AND BUSINESS ADDRESS OF PRINCIPAL OFFICERS.

Walter D. Cowls, *President*, Amherst, Mass. William S. Loomis, *Treasurer and General Manager*, Holyoke, Mass. Louis D. Pellissier, *Clerk of Corporation*, Holyoke, Mass. Brooks & Hamilton, *General Counsel*, Holyoke, Mass. John G. Mackintosh, *Auditor*, Holyoke, Mass.

NAMES AND RESIDENCE OF BOARD OF DIRECTORS.

Walter D. Cowls, Amherst, Mass. William S. Loomis, Holyoke, Mass. Frederick Harris, Springfield, Mass. Ellis J. Aldrich, Hadley, Mass. Alvin L. Wright, Granby, Mass. Louis D. Pellissier, Holyoke, Mass.

We hereby certify that the statements contained in the foregoing report are full, just and true.

WM. S. LOOMIS,
J. G. MACKINTOSH,
FREDERICK HARRIS,
LOUIS D. PELLISSIER,
Directors.
WM. S. LOOMIS,
Treasurer.
GEO. H. HUNTER,
Superintendent.

COMMONWEALTH OF MASSACHUSETTS.

HAMPDEN SS. OCT. 24, 1904. Then personally appeared the above-named Wm. S. Loomis, J. G. Mackintosh, Frederick Harris and Louis D Pellissier, and severally made oath that the foregoing certificate by them subscribed is, to the best of their knowledge and belief, true.

Before me, THOMAS W. SPENCER,
Notary Public.

REPORT

OF THE

HAMPSHIRE & WORCESTER STREET RAILWAY COMPANY

For the Year ending September 30, 1904.

General Exhibit for the Year.		
Gross earnings from operation,		$27,282 98
Operating expenses,		39,654 12
Gross Deficit above Operating Expenses,		$12,371 14
Charges upon income accrued during the year:		
Interest on funded debt,	$6,750 00	
Interest and discount on unfunded debts and loans,	2,736 76	
Taxes, State and local,	1,806 40	
Other deductions from income: park expenses,	2,026 51	
Total Charges and Deductions from Income,		13,319 67
Deficit for the year ending September 30, 1904,		$25,690 81
Amount of surplus September 30, 1903,		2,474 53
Total Deficit September 30, 1904,		$23,216 28

Earnings from Operation.	
Receipts from passengers carried,	$27,199 68
Receipts from advertising in cars,	83 30
Gross Earnings from Operation,	$27,282 98

Expenses of Operation.	
General expenses:	
Salaries of general officers and clerks,	$1,500 00
General office expenses and supplies,	858 72
Insurance,	404 50
Other general expenses: sundry expenses,	1,850 97
Maintenance of roadway and buildings: repair of roadbed and track,	1,579 54
Maintenance of equipment:	
Repair of cars and other vehicles,	3,497 67
Repair of electric equipment of cars,	1,847 34

Transportation expenses:		
Cost of electric motive power,		$16,466 25
Wages and compensation of persons employed in conducting transportation,		8,914 17
Removal of snow and ice,		575 61
Damages for injuries to persons and property,		1,468 66
Other transportation expenses: sundry transportation, printing, lubricants, etc.,		690 69
TOTAL OPERATING EXPENSES,		$39,654 12

PROPERTY ACCOUNTS.

Additions to railway,		$10,144 30
Additions to land and buildings:		
New electric power stations, including machinery, etc.,	$554 04	
Other new buildings necessary for operation of railway,	36 81	
TOTAL ADDITIONS TO LAND AND BUILDINGS,		590 85
TOTAL ADDITIONS TO PROPERTY ACCOUNTS,		$10,735 15

GENERAL BALANCE SHEET SEPTEMBER 30, 1904.

ASSETS.	DR.	
Cost of railway:		
Roadbed and tracks,	$169,601 38	
Electric line construction, including poles, wiring, feeder lines, etc.,	28,895 43	
Interest accrued during construction of railway,	2,327 66	
Engineering and other expenses incident to construction,	10,343 70	
TOTAL COST OF RAILWAY OWNED,		$211,168 17
Cost of equipment:		
Cars and other rolling stock and vehicles,	$22,963 29	
Electric equipment of same,	18,096 40	
Horses and wagon,	225 00	
TOTAL COST OF EQUIPMENT OWNED,		41,284 69
Cost of land and buildings:		
Land necessary for operation of railway,	$2,624 30	
Electric power stations, including equipment,	56,001 78	
Other buildings necessary for operation of railway,	7,948 80	
TOTAL COST OF LAND AND BUILDINGS OWNED,		66,574 88
TOTAL PERMANENT INVESTMENTS,		$319,027 74
Cash and current assets:		
Cash,	$36 63	
Bills and accounts receivable,	1,678 93	
Other cash and current assets: bonds Massachusetts Park and Street Railway Association,	450 00	
TOTAL CASH AND CURRENT ASSETS,		2,165 56

Miscellaneous assets:		
Materials and supplies, ...	$8,846 40	
Other assets and property: tools and office furniture, ...	3,234 63	
TOTAL MISCELLANEOUS ASSETS, ...		$12,081 03
Profit and loss balance (deficit), ...		23,216 28
TOTAL, ...		$356,490 61
LIABILITIES.	CR.	
Capital stock, ...		$155,000 00
Funded debt, ...		135,000 00
Current liabilities:		
Loans and notes payable, ...	$51,703 48	
Audited vouchers and accounts, . . .	12,537 13	
Matured interest coupons unpaid (including coupons due October 1), ...	2,250 00	
TOTAL CURRENT LIABILITIES, ...		66,490 61
TOTAL, ...		$356,490 61

CAPITAL STOCK.

Capital stock authorized by law, ...	$155,000 00	
Capital stock authorized by votes of company,	155,000 00	
Capital stock issued and outstanding, ...		$155,000 00
Number of shares issued and outstanding, .	1,550	
Number of stockholders, ...	99	
Number of stockholders in Massachusetts, .	94	
Amount of stock held in Massachusetts, . .	$97,800	

FUNDED DEBT.

DESCRIPTION OF BONDS.	Rate of Interest.	Date of Maturity.	Amount Outstanding.	Interest Paid during the Year.
First mortgage gold bonds, . .	Per Cent. 5	Dec. 1, 1921,	$135,000 00	$6,750 00

VOLUME OF TRAFFIC, ETC.

Number of passengers paying revenue carried during the year,	546,204
Number carried per mile of main railway track operated, .	46,644
Number of car miles run, ...	186,628
Average number of persons employed, ...	30

Description of Equipment.

Description of Equipment.	Equipped for Electric Power.	Equipped with Fenders.	Equipped with Electric Heaters.	Number of Motors.
Cars — Passenger Service.				
Box passenger cars,	4	4	4	8
Open passenger cars,	8	-	-	20
Total,	12	4	4	28
Snow ploughs,	1	-	-	-

Miscellaneous Equipment.

Highway vehicles:	
Express wagon,	1
Overhead construction towers,	2
Horses,	1
Other items of equipment: single harness,	1

Railway Owned and Operated (by Electric Power).

Length of railway line,	11.710 miles.
Length of sidings, switches, etc.,	.410 "
Total, computed as single track,	12.120 "

Railway Located Outside of Public Ways.

Length of railway line,	2,597 feet.

Names of the several cities and towns in which the railways operated by the company are located: Ware, West Brookfield, New Braintree and Hardwick.

Grade Crossings with Railroads.

Grade Crossings with Railroads.	Number of Tracks at Crossing.	
	Railroad.	Railway.
Crossings of railways with railroads at grade (1 in number), viz.: — With Boston & Maine (Central Massachusetts Division), siding at Otis Company's mills, used for freight only,	1	1

Number of above crossings at which *frogs* are inserted in the tracks, . 1

Corporate Name and Address of the Company.

HAMPSHIRE & WORCESTER STREET RAILWAY COMPANY,

Ware, Mass.

Names and Business Address of Principal Officers.

Hubert M. Coney, *President*, Ware, Mass. Frank H. Bates, *Treasurer and Clerk of Corporation*, Hyde Park, Mass. Charles F. Jenney, *General Counsel*, Boston, Mass. David E. Pepin, *Superintendent*, Ware, Mass.

Names and Residence of Board of Directors.

Hubert M. Coney, Ware, Mass. John M. Whiting, East Bridgewater, Mass. James F. Hill, Warren, Mass. Frank H. Bates, Hyde Park, Mass.

We hereby certify that the statements contained in the foregoing report are full, just and true.

FRANK H. BATES,
JOHN M. WHITING,
HUBERT M. CONEY,
JAMES F. HILL,
Directors.
FRANK H. BATES,
Treasurer.
DAVID E. PEPIN,
Superintendent.

Commonwealth of Massachusetts.

Suffolk, ss. Boston, Jan. 13, 1905. Then personally appeared the above-named Frank H. Bates and John M. Whiting, and severally made oath that the foregoing certificate by them subscribed is, to the best of their knowledge and belief, true.

Before me, FREDERICK H. POLLARD,
Justice of the Peace.

Commonwealth of Massachusetts.

Hampshire, ss. Ware, Jan. 14, 1905. Then personally appeared the above-named Hubert M. Coney, James F. Hill and David E. Pepin, and made oath that the foregoing certificate by them subscribed is, to the best of their knowledge and belief, true.

Before me, J. H. SCHOONMAKER,
Justice of the Peace.

REPORT

OF THE

HARTFORD & WORCESTER STREET RAILWAY COMPANY

For the Year ending September 30, 1904.

[Obtained a certificate of incorporation, but has not commenced the construction of its railway.]

General Balance Sheet September 30, 1904.

Assets.	Dr.
Cash and current assets: cash,	$30,000 00
Total,	$30,000 00

Liabilities.	Cr.
Capital stock (amount paid in),	$30,000 00
Total,	$30,000 00

Capital Stock.

Capital stock authorized by law,	$300,000 00	
Capital stock authorized by agreement of association of company,	300,000 00	
Amount paid in on 3,000 shares not yet issued,		$30,000 00
Number of subscribers,	25	
Number of subscribers in Massachusetts,	24	
Amount of subscriptions held in Massachusetts,	$23,000 00	

Names of the several cities and towns in which the railway owned by the company is located: Leicester, Oxford, Charlton, Sturbridge, Brimfield, Holland and Wales.

Corporate Name and Address of the Company.

HARTFORD & WORCESTER STREET RAILWAY COMPANY,

323 Exchange Building, Boston, Mass.

Names and Business Address of Principal Officers.

Fred C. Hinds, *President*, 323 Exchange Building, Boston, Mass. Thos. C. Perkins, *Vice-President*, Hartford, Conn. Charles H. Wilson, *Treasurer and Clerk of Corporation*, 323 Exchange Building, Boston, Mass. George S. Taft, *General Counsel*, 314 Main Street, Worcester, Mass.

NAMES AND RESIDENCE OF BOARD OF DIRECTORS.

Fred C. Hinds, Newton, Mass. Thos. C. Perkins, Hartford, Conn. Edward Akers, Charlton City, Mass. John F. Hebard, Fiskdale, Mass. Charles S. Tarbell, Brimfield, Mass. Herbert E. Shaw, Wales, Mass. Charles H. Wilson, Brookline, Mass.

We hereby certify that the statements contained in the foregoing report are full, just and true.

EDWARD AKERS,
CHARLES H. WILSON,
JOHN F. HEBARD,
THOMAS C. PERKINS,
FRED C. HINDS,
Directors.
CHARLES H. WILSON,
Treasurer.

COMMONWEALTH OF MASSACHUSETTS.

WORCESTER, ss. OCT. 28, 1904. Then personally appeared the above-named Edward Akers, Charles H. Wilson and John F. Hebard, and severally made oath that the foregoing certificate by them subscribed is, to the best of their knowledge and belief, true.

Before me, LEON M. LAMB,
Notary Public.

COMMONWEALTH OF MASSACHUSETTS.

SUFFOLK, ss. OCT. 29, 1904. Then personally appeared the above-named Fred C. Hinds and Thomas C. Perkins, and severally made oath that the foregoing certificate by them subscribed is, to the best of their knowledge and belief, true.

Before me, DELMONT L. WEEKS,
Notary Public.

REPORT

OF THE

HAVERHILL & AMESBURY STREET RAILWAY COMPANY

FOR THE YEAR ENDING SEPTEMBER 30, 1904.

GENERAL EXHIBIT FOR THE YEAR.

Gross earnings from operation,			$109,013 48
Operating expenses,			73,572 16
GROSS INCOME ABOVE OPERATING EXPENSES,			$35,441 32
Charges upon income accrued during the year:			
Interest on funded debt,		$26,500 00	
Interest and discount on unfunded debts and loans,		9,094 59	
Taxes, State and local,	$960 00		
Taxes, commutation,	1,061 76		
		2,021 76	
TOTAL CHARGES AND DEDUCTIONS FROM INCOME,			37,616 35
Deficit for the year ending September 30, 1904,			$2,175 03
Amount of deficit September 30, 1903,			22,563 58
Debits to profit and loss account during the year:			
Settlement of old damage claims,		$6,900 00	
Settlement of old accounts,		1,516 78	
TOTAL DEBITS,			8,416 78
TOTAL DEFICIT SEPTEMBER 30, 1904,			$33,155 39

EARNINGS FROM OPERATION.

Receipts from passengers carried,	$106,208 24
Receipts from carriage of mails,	486 40
Receipts from rentals of buildings and other property,	1,968 84
Receipts from advertising in cars,	350 00
GROSS EARNINGS FROM OPERATION,	$109,013 48

EXPENSES OF OPERATION.

General expenses:	
Salaries of general officers and clerks,	$2,323 44
General office expenses and supplies,	135 82
Insurance,	1,620 00
Other general expenses: miscellaneous,	1,622 70

Maintenance of roadway and buildings:		
Repair of roadbed and track,		$3,152 24
Repair of electric line construction,		595 68
Repair of buildings,		369 87
Maintenance of equipment:		
Repair of cars and other vehicles,		5,301 21
Repair of electric equipment of cars,		7,435 78
Transportation expenses:		
Cost of electric motive power, $25,087 90; less power sold, $711.63; net,		24,376 27
Wages and compensation of persons employed in conducting transportation,		23,112 87
Removal of snow and ice,		3,250 46
Damages for injuries to persons and property,		123 73
Tolls for trackage over other railways,		152 09
TOTAL OPERATING EXPENSES,		$73,572 16

PROPERTY ACCOUNTS.

Additions to railway:		
Extension of tracks (length, 1,300 feet) and reconstruction on account of State highway,	$11,978 28	
New electric line construction (length, 1,300 feet),	1,048 37	
TOTAL ADDITIONS TO RAILWAY,		$13,026 65
Additions to equipment:		
Additional cars (2 in number),	$1,000 00	
Electric equipment of same,	112 68	
Other additions to equipment: miscellaneous,	260 25	
TOTAL ADDITIONS TO EQUIPMENT,		1,372 93
Additions to land and buildings: new buildings necessary for operation of railway,		735 61
TOTAL ADDITIONS TO PROPERTY ACCOUNTS,		$15,135 19
Deductions from property accounts (property sold or reduced in valuation and credited to property accounts): sold 1 pair horses,		262 50
NET ADDITION TO PROPERTY ACCOUNTS FOR THE YEAR,		$14,872 69

GENERAL BALANCE SHEET SEPTEMBER 30, 1904.

ASSETS.	DR.	
Cost of railway:		
Roadbed and tracks,	$273,851 66	
Electric line construction, including poles, wiring, feeder lines, etc.,	60,865 94	
Interest accrued during construction of railway,	9,506 88	
Engineering and other expenses incident to construction,	5,939 83	
Other items of railway cost: Black Rocks and Salisbury Beach Street Railway property,	308,526 81	
TOTAL COST OF RAILWAY OWNED,		$658,691 12

Cost of equipment:		
Cars and other rolling stock and vehicles,	$41,061 47	
Electric equipment of same,	78,789 04	
Other items of equipment,	21,389 41	
TOTAL COST OF EQUIPMENT OWNED,		$141,239 92
Cost of land and buildings:		
Laud necessary for operation of railway,	$2,658 39	
Electric power stations, including equipment,	44,108 60	
Other buildings necessary for operation of railway,	9,780 17	
TOTAL COST OF LAND AND BUILDINGS OWNED,		56,547 16
TOTAL PERMANENT INVESTMENTS,		$856,478 20
Cash and current assets:		
Cash,	$161 65	
Bills and accounts receivable,	9,817 04	
Other cash and current assets:		
Prepaid insurance,	2,195 84	
Prepaid interest,	1,588 17	
TOTAL CASH AND CURRENT ASSETS,		13,762 70
Miscellaneous assets: materials and supplies, including coal supply,		7,016 81
Profit and loss balance (deficit),		33,155 39
TOTAL,		$910,413 10

LIABILITIES.	CR.	
Capital stock,		$150,000 00
Funded debt,		490,000 00
Current liabilities:		
Loans and notes payable,	$258,604 47	
Audited vouchers and accounts,	1,776 04	
TOTAL CURRENT LIABILITIES,		260,380 51
Accrued liabilities:		
Interest accrued and not yet due,	$8,010 83	
Taxes accrued and not yet due,	2,021 76	
TOTAL ACCRUED LIABILITIES,		10,032 59
TOTAL,		$910,413 10

CAPITAL STOCK.

Capital stock authorized by law,	$150,000 00	
Capital stock authorized by votes of company,	150,000 00	
Capital stock issued and outstanding,		$150,000 00
Number of shares issued and outstanding,	1,500	
Number of stockholders,	18	
Number of stockholders in Massachusetts,	17	
Amount of stock held in Massachusetts,	$145,000 00	

FUNDED DEBT.

DESCRIPTION OF BONDS.	Rate of Interest.	Date of Maturity.	Amount Outstanding.	Interest Paid during the Year.
	Per Cent.			
$290,000 first mortgage gold bonds, .	5	July 1, 1912,	$196,000 00	$9,800 00
$94,000 first mortgage gold bonds of the Black Rocks & Salisbury Beach Street Railway Company are outstanding for which $94,000 Haverhill & Amesbury Street Railway Company bonds are held in trust to retire or exchange for same, .	5	Jan. 1, 1911,	94,000 00	4,700 00
Coupon notes, ...	6	Dec. 1, 1911,	200,000 00	12,000 00
TOTALS, ...	. .	. . .	$490,000 00	$26,500 00

VOLUME OF TRAFFIC, ETC.

Number of passengers paying revenue carried during the year,	2,223,133
Number carried per mile of main railway track operated, .	80,376
Number of car miles run, ...	490,884
Average number of persons employed, ...	60

DESCRIPTION OF EQUIPMENT.

DESCRIPTION OF EQUIPMENT.	Equipped for Electric Power.	Not Equipped.	Total Passenger Cars.	Equipped with Fenders.	Equipped with Electric Heaters.	Number of Motors.
CARS — PASSENGER SERVICE.						
Box passenger cars, ...	17	3	20	18	17	-
Open passenger cars, ...	32	8	40	33	-	-
TOTAL, ...	49	11	60	51	17	64
CARS — OTHER SERVICE.						
Work cars, ...	1	3	-	-	-	-
Snow ploughs, ...	5	3	-	-	-	-

MISCELLANEOUS EQUIPMENT.

Carts and snow sleds, ...	7
Other highway vehicles: 1 tower wagon, 1 concord buggy, 1 express wagon, ...	3
Horses, ...	3
Other items of equipment:	
Double harnesses, ...	3
Single harnesses, ...	3

Railway Owned, Leased and Operated (by Electric Power).

Railway Owned, etc.	Owned.	Trackage over Other Railways.	Total Owned, Leased, etc.
	Miles.	Miles.	Miles.
Length of railway line,	26.606	1.053	27.659
Length of sidings, switches, etc.,	1.855	-	1.855
Total, Computed as Single Track,	28.461	1.053	29.514

Railway Located Outside of Public Ways.

Length of railway line,	4.500 miles.

Names of the several cities and towns in which the railways operated by the company are located: Haverhill, Merrimac, Amesbury, Salisbury and Newburyport.

Grade Crossings with Railroads.

Grade Crossings with Railroads.	Number of Tracks at Crossing.	
	Railroad.	Railway.
Crossings of railways with railroads at grade (1 in number), viz.: — With Boston & Maine Railroad, Elm Street, Amesbury,	1	1

Number of above crossings at which *frogs* are inserted in the tracks, . 1

Accidents to Persons.

(A detailed statement of each accident is on file in the office of the Board.)

Killed and Injured.	From Causes Beyond their own Control.		From their own Misconduct or Carelessness.		Total.	
	Killed.	Injured.	Killed.	Injured.	Killed.	Injured.
Passengers,	-	1	-	6	-	7
Employees,	-	-	-	2	-	2
Other persons,	-	1	1	-	1	1
Totals,	-	2	1	8	1	10

Corporate Name and Address of the Company.

HAVERHILL & AMESBURY STREET RAILWAY COMPANY,

Merrimac, Mass.

Names and Business Address of Principal Officers.

Edward P. Shaw, *President*, Newburyport, Mass. George A. Butman, *Treasurer and Clerk of Corporation*, 8 Congress Street, Boston, Mass. E. P. Shaw, Jr., *General Manager*, South Framingham, Mass. Leander E. Lynde, *Superintendent*, Merrimac, Mass.

Names and Residence of Board of Directors.

Edward P. Shaw, Newburyport, Mass. Leander E. Lynde, Merrimac, Mass. Edward P. Shaw, Jr., Newton, Mass. Albert E. Pond, Brookline, Mass. George A. Butman, Malden, Mass.

We hereby certify that the statements contained in the foregoing report are full, just and true.

EDWARD P. SHAW,
GEO. A. BUTMAN,
LEANDER E. LYNDE,
Directors.
GEO. A. BUTMAN,
Treasurer.
LEANDER E. LYNDE,
Superintendent.

Commonwealth of Massachusetts.

Suffolk, ss. Nov. 29, 1904. Then personally appeared the above-named Edward P. Shaw, Geo. A. Butman and Leander E. Lynde, and severally made oath that the foregoing certificate by them subscribed is, to the best of their knowledge and belief, true.

Before me, ARTHUR W. CLAPP,
Justice of the Peace.

REPORT

OF THE

HAVERHILL, DANVERS & IPSWICH STREET RAILWAY COMPANY

FOR THE YEAR ENDING SEPTEMBER 30, 1904.

[Obtained a certificate of incorporation but has not commenced the construction of its railway.]

GENERAL BALANCE SHEET SEPTEMBER 30, 1904.		
ASSETS.	DR.	
Cost of railway:		
Engineering and other expenses incident to construction,	$4,776 26	
Other items of railway cost: services, J. N. Greene,	602 60	
TOTAL COST OF RAILWAY OWNED,		$5,378 86
TOTAL,		$5,378 86
LIABILITIES.	CR.	
Capital stock, amount paid in (first assessment),		$5,000 00
Current liabilities: estate J. N. Greene, services,		378 86
TOTAL,		$5,378 86

PROPERTY ACCOUNTS.		
Additions to railway:		
Miscellaneous expenses,	$303 10	
Services, J. N. Greene,	602 60	
TOTAL ADDITIONS TO RAILWAY,		$905 70
TOTAL ADDITIONS TO PROPERTY ACCOUNTS,		$905 70

CAPITAL STOCK.		
Capital stock authorized by law,	$50,000 00	
Capital stock authorized by votes of company,	50,000 00	
Amount paid in on 500 shares not yet issued,		$5,000 00
Number of subscribers,	16	
Number of subscribers in Massachusetts,	15	
Amount of payments on stock held in Massachusetts,	$4,480 00	

Names of the several cities and towns in which the railway owned by the company is located: Topsfield, Boxford, Georgetown, Groveland, Rowley and Ipswich.

General Remarks and Explanations.

Length of railway located as published in the articles of association, 20 miles.

Corporate Name and Address of the Company.

HAVERHILL, DANVERS & IPSWICH STREET RAILWAY COMPANY,

Room 64, 15 School Street, Boston, Mass.

Names and Business Address of Principal Officers.

Lewis D. Greene, *President*, Room 64, 15 School Street, Boston, Mass.
William R. Arey, *Treasurer*, National Bank of the Republic, Boston, Mass.
Edward D. Hewins, *Clerk of Corporation*, Room 64, 15 School Street, Boston, Mass.

Names and Residence of Board of Directors.

Lewis D. Greene, Chicago, Ill. Charles M. Perley, Ipswich, Mass. Alphonso T. Merrill, Topsfield, Mass. William R. Arey, Salem, Mass. Edward D. Hewins, Boston, Mass.

We hereby certify that the statements contained in the foregoing report are full, just and true.

LEWIS D. GREENE,
WILLIAM R. AREY,
EDWARD D. HEWINS,
Directors.
WILLIAM R. AREY,
Treasurer.

Commonwealth of Massachusetts.

Suffolk, ss. Oct. 26, 1904. Then personally appeared the above-named William R. Arey, and made oath that the foregoing certificate by him subscribed is, to the best of his knowledge and belief, true.

Before me, EDWARD D. HEWINS,
Justice of the Peace.

State of Illinois.

County of Cook, ss. Oct. 29, 1904. Personally appeared the above-named Lewis D. Greene, and made oath that the foregoing certificate by him subscribed is, to the best of his knowledge and belief, true.

Before me, P. S. ELWELL,
Notary Public, Cook County, Illinois.

Commonwealth of Massachusetts.

Suffolk, ss. Oct. 31, 1904. Then personally appeared the above-named Edward D. Hewins, and made oath that the foregoing certificate by him subscribed is, to the best of his knowledge and belief, true.

Before me, FRANKLIN MEAD,
Justice of the Peace.

REPORT

OF THE

HAVERHILL, GEORGETOWN & DANVERS STREET RAILWAY COMPANY

FOR THE YEAR ENDING SEPTEMBER 30, 1904.

GENERAL EXHIBIT FOR THE YEAR.		
Gross earnings from operation,		$29,410 16
Operating expenses,		22,381 39
GROSS INCOME ABOVE OPERATING EXPENSES,		$7,028 77
Charges upon income accrued during the year:		
Interest on funded debt,	$1,750 00	
Interest and discount on unfunded debts and loans,	1,554 55	
Taxes, state and local,	1,891 93	
TOTAL CHARGES AND DEDUCTIONS FROM INCOME,		5,196 48
Surplus for the year ending September 30, 1904,		$1,832 29
Amount of surplus September 30, 1903,		11,713 61
TOTAL SURPLUS SEPTEMBER 30, 1904,		$13,545 90

EARNINGS FROM OPERATION.	
Receipts from passengers carried,	$29,150 57
Receipts from advertising in cars,	80 19
Receipts from interest on deposits,	60 20
Other earnings from operation: receipts not included in other accounts,	119 20
GROSS EARNINGS FROM OPERATION,	$29,410 16

EXPENSES OF OPERATION.	
General expenses:	
Salaries of general officers and clerks,	$590 60
General office expenses and supplies,	68 21
Legal expenses,	300 00
Insurance,	359 60
Other general expenses,	441 63

Maintenance of roadway and buildings:	
Repair of roadbed and track,	$1,363 40
Repair of electric line construction,	374 14
Repair of buildings,	1 44
Maintenance of equipment:	
Repair of cars and other vehicles,	357 75
Repair of electric equipment of cars,	5 40
Transportation expenses:	
Cost of electric motive power,	7,110 93
Wages and compensation of persons employed in conducting transportation,	6,870 14
Removal of snow and ice,	1,163 27
Damages for injuries to persons and property,	2,889 07
Tolls for trackage over other railways,	485 81
TOTAL OPERATING EXPENSES,	$22,381 39

GENERAL BALANCE SHEET SEPTEMBER 30, 1904.

ASSETS.	DR.	
Cost of railway:		
Roadbed and tracks,	$74,963 18	
Electric line construction, including poles, wiring, feeder lines, etc.,	18,756 75	
Engineering and other expenses incident to construction,	6,709 20	
TOTAL COST OF RAILWAY OWNED,		$100,429 13
Cost of equipment:		
Cars and other rolling stock and vehicles,	$12,315 86	
Electric equipment of same,	5,885 66	
Other items of equipment: sundry equipment of rolling stock,	2,874 72	
TOTAL COST OF EQUIPMENT OWNED,		21,076 24
Cost of land and buildings:		
Land necessary for operation of railway,	$625 00	
Buildings necessary for operation of railway,	4,900 00	
TOTAL COST OF LAND AND BUILDINGS OWNED,		5,525 00
TOTAL PERMANENT INVESTMENTS,		$127,030 37
Cash and current assets:		
Cash,	$1,874 26	
Bills and accounts receivable,	801 00	
Other cash and current assets: unsettled fire loss,	1,615 01	
TOTAL CASH AND CURRENT ASSETS,		$4,290 27
Miscellaneous assets:		
Materials and supplies,	$1,338 71	
Other assets and property:		
Accounts payable,	92 73	
Special account,	2,665 25	
TOTAL MISCELLANEOUS ASSETS,		4,096 69
TOTAL,		$135,417 33

Liabilities.	Cr.	
Capital stock,		$60,000 00
Funded debt,		35,000 00
Current liabilities: loans and notes payable,		25,000 00
Accrued liabilities:		
Interest accrued and not yet due,	$145 83	
Taxes accrued and not yet due,	1,725 60	
Total Accrued Liabilities,		1,871 43
Profit and loss balance (surplus),		13,545 90
Total,		$135,417 33

Capital Stock.		
Capital stock authorized by law,	$60,000 00	
Capital stock authorized by votes of company,	60,000 00	
Capital stock issued and outstanding,		$60,000 00
Number of shares issued and outstanding,	600	
Number of stockholders,	6	
Number of stockholders in Massachusetts,	6	
Amount of stock held in Massachusetts,	$60,000 00	

Funded Debt.

Description of Bonds.	Rate of Interest.	Date of Maturity.	Amount Outstanding.	Interest Paid during the Year.
	Per Cent.			
First mortgage bonds,	5	March 1, 1919,	$35,000 00	$1,750 00

Volume of Traffic, etc.

Number of passengers paying revenue carried during the year,	602,931
Number carried per mile of main railway track operated,	94,830
Number of car miles run,	148,866
Average number of persons employed,	11

Description of Equipment.

Description of Equipment.	Equipped for Electric Power.	Equipped with Fenders.	Equipped with Electric Heaters.	Number of Motors.
Cars — Passenger Service.				
Box passenger cars,	3	3	3	6
Open passenger cars,	3	3	-	6
Total,	6	6	3	12
Snow ploughs,	1	-	-	2

Railway Owned, Leased and Operated (by Electric Power).

Railway Owned, etc.	Owned.	Trackage over Other Railways.	Total Owned, Leased, etc.
	Miles.	Miles.	Miles.
Length of railway line,	5.871	.487	6.358
Length of sidings, switches, etc.,	.149	.029	.178
Total, Computed as Single Track,	6.020	.516	6.536

Names of the several cities and towns in which the railways operated by the company are located: Haverhill, Groveland and Georgetown.

Grade Crossings with Railroads.

Grade Crossings with Railroads.	Number of Tracks at Crossing.	
	Railroad.	Railway.
Crossings of railways with railroads at grade (2 in number), viz.:—		
With Boston & Maine Railroad, Georgetown,	2	1
With Boston & Maine Railroad, Georgetown,	3	1
Total Number of Tracks at Crossings,	5	2

Number of above crossings at which *frogs* are inserted in the tracks, . 1

Accidents to Persons.

(A detailed statement of each accident is on file in the office of the Board.)

Killed and Injured.	From Causes beyond their own Control.		From their own Misconduct or Carelessness.		Total.	
	Killed.	Injured.	Killed.	Injured.	Killed.	Injured.
Passengers,	-	1	-	3	-	4
Employees,	-	-	-	-	-	-
Other persons,	-	-	-	-	-	-
Totals,	-	1	-	3	-	4

Corporate Name and Address of the Company.

HAVERHILL, GEORGETOWN & DANVERS STREET RAILWAY COMPANY,

222 Boylston Street, Boston, Mass.

Names and Business Address of Principal Officers.

Alfred Rodman, *President*, 222 Boylston Street, Boston, Mass. Thomas K. Cummins, *Treasurer and Clerk of Corporation*, 222 Boylston Street, Boston, Mass. George W. Pratt, *Superintendent*, Byfield, Mass.

NAMES AND RESIDENCE OF BOARD OF DIRECTORS.

Alfred Rodman, Dedham, Mass. A. LeBaron Russell, Boston, Mass. Thomas K. Cummins, Milton, Mass. William Atherton, Boston, Mass. James A. Roberts, Milton, Mass.

We hereby certify that the statements contained in the foregoing report are full, just and true.

ALFRED RODMAN,
THOMAS K. CUMMINS,
JAMES A. ROBERTS,
A. LEBARON RUSSELL,
Directors.
THOMAS K. CUMMINS,
Treasurer.
GEO. W. PRATT,
Superintendent.

COMMONWEALTH OF MASSACHUSETTS.

SUFFOLK, ss. BOSTON, Oct. 27, 1904. Then personally appeared the above-named Alfred Rodman, Thomas K. Cummins, James A. Roberts, A. LeBaron Russell and George W. Pratt, and severally made oath that the foregoing certificate by them subscribed is, to the best of their knowledge and belief, true.

Before me, WILLIAM ATHERTON,
Justice of the Peace.

REPORT

OF THE

HAVERHILL & PLAISTOW STREET RAILWAY COMPANY

FOR THE YEAR ENDING SEPTEMBER 30, 1904.

[Leased to and operated by the Exeter, Hampton & Amesbury of New Hampshire.]

GENERAL EXHIBIT FOR THE YEAR.	
Rental received from lease of railway,	$2,700 00
Expenses and charges upon income accrued during the year: interest on funded debt,	1,500 00
Surplus for the year ending September 30, 1904,	$1,200 00
Amount of surplus September 30, 1903,	1,950 00
TOTAL SURPLUS SEPTEMBER 30, 1904,	$3,150 00

GENERAL BALANCE SHEET SEPTEMBER 30, 1904.

ASSETS.	DR.	
Cost of railway:		
Roadbed and tracks,	$45,643 76	
Electric line construction, including poles, wiring, feeder lines, etc.,	7,920 25	
Engineering and other expenses incident to construction,	7,857 40	
TOTAL COST OF RAILWAY OWNED,		$61,421 41
Cost of equipment: furniture and fixtures,		8 65
Cost of land and buildings:		
Rights of way,	$6,478 00	
Buildings necessary for operation of railway,	11 66	
TOTAL COST OF LAND AND BUILDINGS OWNED,		6,489 66
TOTAL PERMANENT INVESTMENTS,		$67,919 72
Cash and current assets: bills and accounts receivable,		5,025 00
TOTAL,		$72,944 72

LIABILITIES.	CR.
Capital stock,	$30,000 00
Funded debt,	30,000 00

Current liabilities:		
Loans and notes payable,	$7,919 72	
Matured interest coupons unpaid (including coupons due July 1),	1,500 00	
Accrued interest coupons,	375 00	
TOTAL CURRENT LIABILITIES,		$9,794 72
Profit and loss balance (surplus),		3,150 00
TOTAL,		$72,944 72

PROPERTY ACCOUNTS.

Additions to railway:		
Extension of tracks,	$3,658 65	
New electric line construction,	119 25	
Other additions to railway: engineering and expense,	2,507 40	
TOTAL ADDITIONS TO RAILWAY,		$6,285 30
Additions to equipment: furniture and fixtures,		8 65
Additions to land and buildings:		
Rights of way,	$478 00	
New buildings necessary for operation of railway,	11 66	
TOTAL ADDITIONS TO LAND AND BUILDINGS,		489 66
TOTAL ADDITIONS TO PROPERTY ACCOUNTS,		$6,783 61

CAPITAL STOCK.

Capital stock authorized by law,	$30,000 00	
Capital stock authorized by votes of company,	30,000 00	
Capital stock issued and outstanding,		$30,000 00
Number of shares issued and outstanding,	300	
Number of stockholders,	6	
Number of stockholders in Massachusetts,	5	
Amount of stock held in Massachusetts,	$500 00	

FUNDED DEBT.

DESCRIPTION OF BONDS.	Rate of Interest.	Date of Maturity.	Amount Outstanding.	Interest Paid during the Year.
First mortgage gold bonds,	Per Cent. 5	July 1, 1921,	$30,000 00	-

RAILWAY OWNED.

Length of railway line,	2.682 miles.
Length of sidings, switches, etc.,	.076 "
Total, computed as single track,	2.758 "

RAILWAY OWNED AND LOCATED OUTSIDE OF PUBLIC WAYS.

Length of railway line, ...	.619 mile.

Names of the several cities and towns in which the railway owned by the company is located: Haverhill.

CORPORATE NAME AND ADDRESS OF THE COMPANY.

HAVERHILL & PLAISTOW STREET RAILWAY COMPANY,

50 MERRIMAC STREET, HAVERHILL, MASS.

NAMES AND BUSINESS ADDRESS OF PRINCIPAL OFFICERS.

David A. Belden, *President*, 50 Merrimac Street, Haverhill, Mass. Frederick P. Royce, *Vice-President*, 84 State Street, Boston, Mass. Samuel P. Russell, *Treasurer and Auditor*, 50 Merrimac Street, Haverhill, Mass. Reginald H. Johnson, *Clerk of Corporation*, 53 State Street, Boston, Mass. Franklin Woodman, *General Manager*, 50 Merrimac Street, Haverhill, Mass. Clarence P. Hayden, *Superintendent*, Hampton, N. H.

NAMES AND RESIDENCE OF BOARD OF DIRECTORS.

David A. Belden, Haverhill, Mass. Reginald H. Johnson, Braintree, Mass. Frederick P. Royce, Dedham, Mass. Frank W. Stearns, Newton, Mass. John Dearborn, Boston, Mass.

We hereby certify that the statements contained in the foregoing report are full, just and true.

DAVID A. BELDEN,
F. P. ROYCE,
REGINALD H. JOHNSON,
Directors.
SAMUEL P. RUSSELL,
Treasurer.
FRANKLIN WOODMAN,
General Manager.

COMMONWEALTH OF MASSACHUSETTS.

ESSEX, ss. Nov. 17, 1904. Then personally appeared the above-named David A. Belden, Samuel P. Russell, and Franklin Woodman, and severally made oath that the foregoing certificate by them subscribed is, to the best of their knowledge and belief, true.

Before me, EDMUND B. FULLER,
Justice of the Peace.

COMMONWEALTH OF MASSACHUSETTS.

SUFFOLK, ss. Nov. 29, 1904. Then personally appeared the above-named F. P. Royce and Reginald H. Johnson, and severally made oath that the foregoing certificate by them subscribed is, to the best of their knowledge and belief, true.

Before me, HAROLD WILLIAMS, JR.,
Justice of the Peace.

REPORT

OF THE

HAVERHILL & PLAISTOW STREET RAILWAY

(EXETER, HAMPTON & AMESBURY STREET RAILWAY COMPANY, LESSEE)

For the Year ending September 30, 1904.

General Exhibit for the Year.		
Gross earnings from operation,		$15,117 49
Operating expenses,		13,497 13
Gross Income above Operating Expenses,		$1,620 36
Charges upon income accrued during the year:		
Taxes, State and local,	$320 22	
Rentals of leased railways,	2,700 00	
Total Charges and Deductions from Income,		3,020 22
Deficit for the year ending September 30, 1904,		$1,399 86
Amount of surplus September 30, 1903,		132 64
Total Deficit September 30, 1904,		$1,267 22

Earnings from Operation.	
Receipts from passengers carried,	$15,061 54
Receipts from advertising in cars,	41 92
Other earnings from operation: sale of old material,	14 03
Gross Earnings from Operation,	$15,117 49

Expenses of Operation.	
General expenses:	
Salaries of general officers and clerks,	$508 23
General office expenses and supplies,	122 53
Insurance,	241 84
Other general expenses: store room, $38.53; miscellaneous general expense, $108.14,	146 67
Maintenance of roadway and buildings:	
Repair of roadbed and track,	894 51
Repair of electric line construction,	307 98
Repair of buildings,	95 74
Maintenance of equipment:	
Repair of cars and other vehicles,	827 26
Repair of electric equipment of cars,	803 52

Transportation expenses:	
Cost of electric motive power,	$3,793 47
Wages and compensation of persons employed in conducting transportation,	3,421 13
Removal of snow and ice,	628 85
Damages for injuries to persons and property,	598 51
Tolls for trackage over other railways,	5 83
Rentals of buildings and other property,	21 37
Other transportation expenses: advertising, $182.34; car barn and machine shop expenses, $897.35,	1,079 69
TOTAL OPERATING EXPENSES,	$13,497 13

VOLUME OF TRAFFIC, ETC.

Number of passengers paying revenue carried during the year,	309,757
Number carried per mile of main railway track operated,	115,495
Number of car miles run,	76,822
Average number of persons employed,	6

RAILWAY LEASED AND OPERATED (BY ELECTRIC POWER).

Length of railway line,	2.682 miles.
Length of sidings, switches, etc.,	.076 "
Total, computed as single track,	2.758 "

RAILWAY LOCATED OUTSIDE OF PUBLIC WAYS.

Length of railway line,	.619 mile.

Names of the several cities and towns in which the railways operated by the company are located: Haverhill.

ACCIDENTS TO PERSONS.

(A detailed statement of each accident is on file in the office of the Board.)

KILLED AND INJURED.	FROM CAUSES BEYOND THEIR OWN CONTROL.		FROM THEIR OWN MISCONDUCT OR CARELESSNESS.		TOTAL.	
	Killed.	Injured.	Killed.	Injured.	Killed.	Injured.
Passengers,	-	-	-	1	-	1
Employees,	-	-	-	-	-	-
Other persons,	-	-	-	3	-	3
TOTALS,	-	-	-	4	-	4

Corporate Name and Address of the Company.

HAVERHILL & PLAISTOW STREET RAILWAY COMPANY,

50 Merrimac Street, Haverhill, Mass.

Names and Business Address of Principal Officers.

David A. Belden, *President*, 50 Merrimac Street, Haverhill, Mass. Frederick P. Royce, *Vice-President*, 84 State Street, Boston, Mass. Samuel P. Russell, *Treasurer and Auditor*, 50 Merrimac Street, Haverhill, Mass. Reginald H. Johnson, *Clerk of Corporation*, 53 State Street, Boston, Mass. Franklin Woodman, *General Manager*, 50 Merrimac Street, Haverhill, Mass. Clarence P. Hayden, *Superintendent*, Hampton, N. H.

Names and Residence of Board of Directors.

David A. Belden, Haverhill, Mass. Reginald H. Johnson, Braintree, Mass. Frederick P. Royce, Dedham, Mass. Frank W. Stearns, Newton, Mass. John Dearborn, Boston, Mass.

We hereby certify that the statements contained in the foregoing report are full, just and true.

DAVID A. BELDEN,
F. P. ROYCE,
REGINALD H. JOHNSON,
Directors.
SAMUEL P. RUSSELL,
Treasurer.
FRANKLIN WOODMAN,
General Manager.

Commonwealth of Massachusetts.

Essex, ss. Nov. 17, 1904. Then personally appeared the above-named David A. Belden, Samuel P. Russell and Franklin Woodman, and severally made oath that the foregoing certificate by them subscribed is, to the best of their knowledge and belief, true.

Before me, EDMUND B. FULLER,
Justice of the Peace.

Commonwealth of Massachusetts.

Suffolk, ss. Nov. 29, 1904. Then personally appeared the above-named F. P. Royce and Reginald H. Johnson, and severally made oath that the foregoing certificate by them subscribed is, to the best of their knowledge and belief, true.

Before me, HAROLD WILLIAMS, Jr.,
Justice of the Peace.

REPORT

OF THE

HAVERHILL & SOUTHERN NEW HAMPSHIRE STREET RAILWAY COMPANY

FOR THE YEAR ENDING SEPTEMBER 30, 1904.

General Exhibit for the Year.		
Gross earnings from operation,		$39,977 97
Operating expenses,		38,189 97
Gross Income above Operating Expenses,		$1,788 00
Charges upon income accrued during the year:		
Interest on funded debt,	$2,333 33	
Interest and discount on unfunded debts and loans,	1,704 10	
Taxes, State and local,	917 77	
Total Charges and Deductions from Income,		4,955 20
Deficit for the year ending September 30, 1904,		$3,167 20
Amount of deficit September 30, 1903,		4,600 78
Total Deficit September 30, 1904,		$7,767 98

Earnings from Operation.	
Receipts from passengers carried,	$39,837 17
Receipts from advertising in cars,	140 80
Gross Earnings from Operation,	$39,977 97

Expenses of Operation.	
General expenses:	
Salaries of general officers and clerks,	$1,616 50
General office expenses and supplies,	413 78
Legal expenses,	37 28
Insurance,	439 00
Other general expenses: store room, $122.56; miscellaneous general expense, $332.38,	454 94
Maintenance of roadway and buildings:	
Repair of roadbed and track,	2,132 03
Repair of electric line construction,	625 18
Repair of buildings,	124 08

Maintenance of equipment:		
Repair of cars and other vehicles,		$3,455 37
Repair of electric equipment of cars,		2,502 92
Transportation expenses:		
Cost of electric motive power,		11,413 21
Wages and compensation of persons employed in conducting transportation,		9,953 88
Removal of snow and ice,		762 69
Damages for injuries to persons and property,		1,645 85
Tolls for trackage over other railways,		67 61
Rentals of buildings and other property,		71 24
Other transportation expenses:		
Advertising,	$592 36	
Car barn and machine shop expenses,	1,882 05	
		2,474 41
TOTAL OPERATING EXPENSES,		$38,189 97

PROPERTY ACCOUNTS.

Additions to railway:		
Extension of tracks,	$1,838 20	
New electric line construction,	28 99	
Other additions to railway: engineering and expense,	205 07	
TOTAL ADDITIONS TO RAILWAY,		$2,072 26
Additions to equipment: additional cars,		759 97
TOTAL ADDITIONS TO PROPERTY ACCOUNTS,		$2,832 23

GENERAL BALANCE SHEET SEPTEMBER 30, 1904.

ASSETS.	DR.	
Cost of railway:		
Roadbed and tracks,	$110,577 59	
Electric line construction, including poles, wiring, feeder lines, etc.,	23,784 58	
Interest accrued during construction of railway,	1,959 51	
Engineering and other expenses incident to construction,	24,107 93	
TOTAL COST OF RAILWAY OWNED,		$160,429 61
Cost of equipment:		
Tools,	$29 65	
Cars and other rolling stock and vehicles,	28,130 97	
Electric equipment of same,	26,411 30	
Furniture and fixtures,	297 92	
Other items of equipment: snow ploughs,	1,788 99	
TOTAL COST OF EQUIPMENT OWNED,		56,658 83
Cost of land and buildings: Land necessary for operation of railway and rights of way,		3,830 67
TOTAL PERMANENT INVESTMENTS,		$220,919 11
Profit and loss balance (deficit),		7,767 98
TOTAL,		$228,687 09

LIABILITIES.	CR.	
Capital stock,		$80,000 00
Funded debt,		80,000 00
Current liabilities:		
Loans and notes payable,	$66,353 76	
Matured interest coupons unpaid (including coupons due July 1),	1,333 33	
Accrued interest coupons,	1,000 00	
TOTAL CURRENT LIABILITIES,		68,687 09
TOTAL,		$228,687 09

CAPITAL STOCK.		
Capital stock authorized by law,	$80,000 00	
Capital stock authorized by votes of company,	80,000 00	
Capital stock issued and outstanding,		$80,000 00
Number of shares issued and outstanding,	800	
Number of stockholders,	6	
Number of stockholders in Massachusetts,	5	
Amount of stock held in Massachusetts,	500 00	

FUNDED DEBT.

DESCRIPTION OF BONDS.	Rate of Interest.	Date of Maturity.	Amount Outstanding.	Interest Paid during the Year.
	Per Cent.			
First mortgage gold bonds,	5	Jan. 1, 1923,	$80,000 00	-

VOLUME OF TRAFFIC, ETC.

Number of passengers paying revenue carried during the year,	876,748
Number carried per mile of main railway track operated,	110,394
Number of car miles run,	246,963
Average number of persons employed,	17

DESCRIPTION OF EQUIPMENT.

DESCRIPTION OF EQUIPMENT.	Equipped for Electric Power.	Equipped with Fenders.	Equipped with Electric Heaters.	Number of Motors.
CARS — PASSENGER SERVICE.				
Box passenger cars,	5	5	5	20
Open passenger cars,	6	6	-	24
TOTAL,	11	11	5	44
Snow ploughs,	1	-	-	-

RAILWAY OWNED, LEASED AND OPERATED (BY ELECTRIC POWER).

RAILWAY OWNED, ETC.	Owned.	Trackage over Other Railways.	Total Operated.
	Miles.	Miles.	Miles.
Length of railway line,	7.892	.050	7.942
Length of sidings, switches, etc.,	.296	–	.296
TOTAL, COMPUTED AS SINGLE TRACK,	8.188	.050	8.238

RAILWAY LOCATED OUTSIDE OF PUBLIC WAYS.

Length of railway line,	1.625 miles.

Names of the several cities and towns in which the railways operated by the company are located: Methuen, Haverhill and Ayer's Village.

ACCIDENTS TO PERSONS.

(A detailed statement of each accident is on file in the office of the Board.)

KILLED AND INJURED.	FROM CAUSES BEYOND THEIR OWN CONTROL.		FROM THEIR OWN MISCONDUCT OR CARELESSNESS.		TOTAL.	
	Killed.	Injured.	Killed.	Injured.	Killed.	Injured.
Passengers,	–	–	–	4	–	4
Employees,	–	–	–	–	–	–
Other persons,	–	–	–	–	–	–
TOTALS,	–	–	–	4	–	4

CORPORATE NAME AND ADDRESS OF THE COMPANY.

HAVERHILL & SOUTHERN NEW HAMPSHIRE STREET RAILWAY COMPANY,

50 MERRIMAC STREET, HAVERHILL, MASS.

NAMES AND BUSINESS ADDRESS OF PRINCIPAL OFFICERS.

David A. Belden, *President*, 50 Merrimac Street, Haverhill, Mass. Frederick P. Royce, *Vice-President*, 84 State Street, Boston, Mass. Samuel P. Russell, *Treasurer and Auditor*, 50 Merrimac Street, Haverhill, Mass. Reginald H. Johnson, *Clerk of Corporation*, 53 State Street, Boston, Mass. Franklin Woodman, *General Manager*, 50 Merrimac Street, Haverhill, Mass. Robert H. Dunbar, *Superintendent*, Salem, N. H.

NAMES AND RESIDENCE OF BOARD OF DIRECTORS.

David A. Belden, Haverhill, Mass. Reginald H. Johnson, Braintree, Mass. Frederick P. Royce, Dedham, Mass. Frank W. Stearns, Newton, Mass. John Dearborn, Boston, Mass.

We hereby certify that the statements contained in the foregoing report are full, just and true.

DAVID A. BELDEN,
F. P. ROYCE,
REGINALD H. JOHNSON,
Directors.
SAM'L P. RUSSELL,
Treasurer.
FRANKLIN WOODMAN,
General Manager.

COMMONWEALTH OF MASSACHUSETTS.

ESSEX, ss. Nov. 17, 1904. Then personally appeared the above-named David A. Belden, Samuel P. Russell and Franklin Woodman, and severally made oath that the foregoing certificate by them subscribed is, to the best of their knowledge and belief, true.

Before me, EDMUND B. FULLER,
Justice of the Peace.

COMMONWEALTH OF MASSACHUSETTS.

SUFFOLK, SS. Nov. 29, 1904. Then personally appeared the above-named F. P. Royce and Reginald H. Johnson, and severally made oath that the foregoing certificate by them subscribed is, to the best of their knowledge and belief, true.

Before me, HAROLD WILLIAMS, JR.,
Justice of the Peace.

REPORT

OF THE

HOLYOKE STREET RAILWAY COMPANY

For the Year ending September 30, 1904.

General Exhibit for the Year.

Gross earnings from operation,			$373,103 39
Operating expenses,			265,707 74
Net Earnings from Operation,			$107,395 65
Miscellaneous income: from use of Mt. Tom pavilion, grounds, entertainments, etc.,			10,308 06
Gross Income above Operating Expenses,			$117,703 71
Charges upon income accrued during the year:			
Interest on funded debt,		$30,000 00	
Interest and discount on unfunded debts and loans,		6,840 19	
Taxes, State and local,	$18,367 49		
Taxes, commutation,	8,262 16		
		26,629 65	
Rentals of leased railways: Mt. Tom railroad,		6,000 00	
Other deductions from income: Mountain Park expense,		587 76	
Total Charges and Deductions from Income,			70,057 60
Net Divisible Income,			$47,646 11
Dividends declared (8 per cent),			56,000 00
Deficit for the year ending September 30, 1904,			$8,353 89
Amount of surplus September 30, 1903,			73,321 24
Total Surplus September 30, 1904,			$64,967 35

Earnings from Operation.

Receipts from passengers carried,	$367,207 29
Receipts from carriage of mails,	1,589 48
Receipts from carriage of freight (hauling stone for State highway),	964 10
Receipts from tolls for use of tracks by other companies (American Car Sprinkler Company),	505 27
Receipts from rentals of buildings and other property,	245 50
Receipts from advertising in cars,	1,503 03

Receipts from interest on deposits,	$599 47
Other earnings from operation: rental of car to the Hampshire Street Railway Company,	489 25
GROSS EARNINGS FROM OPERATION,	$373,103 39

EXPENSES OF OPERATION.

General expenses:	
Salaries of general officers and clerks,	$8,354 51
General office expenses and supplies,	716 96
Insurance,	3,876 15
Other general expenses: telephones, $185.55; directors, $280; auditor, $70; printing, $71.28; donations, $264; travelling expenses, $271.90; Massachusetts Street Railway Association, $200; periodicals, $58.36; sundries, $144.94,	1,546 03
Maintenance of roadway and buildings:	
Repair of roadbed and track,	42,694 67
Repair of electric line construction,	3,338 78
Repair of buildings,	1,392 07
Maintenance of equipment:	
Repair of cars and other vehicles,	20,403 88
Repair of electric equipment of cars,	17,207 75
Transportation expenses:	
Cost of electric motive power, $42,728.37; less power sold, $649.87; net,	42,078 50
Wages and compensation of persons employed in conducting transportation,	94,579 29
Removal of snow and ice,	4,059 46
Damages for injuries to persons and property,	24,331 64
Other transportation expenses: coal, $276.88; oil, $129.07; printing, $416.97; detective service, 90.47; water rent, $149.70; sundries, $64.96,	1,128 05
TOTAL OPERATING EXPENSES,	$265,707 74

PROPERTY ACCOUNTS.

Additions to railway: feed wire, block signals, improvement of roadbed,		$7,852 47
Additions to equipment:		
Additional cars (2 in number),	$3,460 00	
Electric equipment of same,	1,100 00	
Other additional rolling stock and vehicles,	300 00	
Other additions to equipment: air brakes,	574 21	
TOTAL ADDITIONS TO EQUIPMENT,		5,434 21
Additions to land and buildings:		
Additional equipment of power stations,	$351 10	
Other new buildings necessary for operation of railway,	1,549 36	
TOTAL ADDITIONS TO LAND AND BUILDINGS,		1,900 46
TOTAL ADDITIONS TO PROPERTY ACCOUNTS,		$15,187 14
Deductions from property accounts (property sold or reduced in valuation and credited to property accounts): five single-truck car bodies and trucks,		3,400 00
NET ADDITION TO PROPERTY ACCOUNTS FOR THE YEAR,		$11,787 14

General Balance Sheet September 30, 1904.

Assets.	Dr.	
Cost of railway:		
Roadbed and tracks,	$659,827 04	
Electric line construction, including poles, wiring, feeder lines, etc.,	113,994 62	
Total Cost of Railway Owned,		$773,821 66
Cost of equipment:		
Cars and other rolling stock and vehicles,	$313,442 94	
Horses,	1,000 00	
Total Cost of Equipment Owned,		314,442 94
Cost of land and buildings:		
Land necessary for operation of railway,	$53,610 00	
Electric power stations, including equipment,	272,071 00	
Other buildings necessary for operation of railway,	51,123 20	
Total Cost of Land and Buildings Owned,		376,804 20
Other permanent property:		
Grover Street block,	$5,000 00	
Mountain Park investment,	29,000 00	
Total Cost of Other Permanent Property Owned,		34,000 00
Total Permanent Investments,		$1,499,068 80
Cash and current assets:		
Cash,	$28,524 66	
Bills and accounts receivable,	3,799 94	
Total Cash and Current Assets,		32,324 60
Miscellaneous assets: materials and supplies,		37,222 92
Total,		$1,568,616 32
Liabilities.	**Cr.**	
Capital stock,		$700,000 00
Funded debt,		600,000 00
Current liabilities:		
Loans and notes payable,	$155,735 98	
Audited vouchers and accounts,	16,365 89	
Total Current Liabilities,		172,101 87
Accrued liabilities:		
Interest accrued and not yet due,	$450 00	
Taxes accrued and not yet due,	25,097 10	
Rentals accrued and not yet due,	6,000 00	
Total Accrued Liabilities,		31,547 10
Profit and loss balance (surplus),		64,967 35
Total,		$1,568,616 32

Capital Stock.

Capital stock authorized by law, ...	$700,000 00	
Capital stock authorized by votes of company,	700,000 00	
Capital stock issued and outstanding, ...		$700,000 00
Number of shares issued and outstanding, .	7,000	
Number of stockholders, ...	212	
Number of stockholders in Massachusetts, .	183	
Amount of stock held in Massachusetts, . .	$636,300 00	

Funded Debt.

Description of Bonds.	Rate of Interest.	Date of Maturity.	Amount Outstanding.	Interest Paid during the Year.
	Per Cent.			
Two hundred bonds of one thousand dollars each, ...	5	April 1, 1915,	$200,000 00	$10,000 00
One hundred bonds of five hundred dollars each, ...	5	April 1, 1915,	50,000 00	2,500 00
One hundred thirty-five bonds of five hundred dollars each, ...	5	Oct. 1, 1920,	67,500 00	3,375 00
One hundred seventy-five bonds of one hundred dollars each, . . .	5	Oct. 1, 1920,	17,500 00	875 00
Two hundred ten bonds of one thousand dollars each, ...	5	April 1, 1923,	210,000 00	10,500 00
Seventy bonds of five hundred dollars each, ...	5	April 1, 1923,	35,000 00	1,750 00
Two hundred bonds of one hundred dollars each, ...	5	April 1, 1923,	20,000 00	1,000 00
Totals, ...	. .	. . . .	$600,000 00	$30,000 00

Volume of Traffic, etc.

Number of passengers paying revenue carried during the year,	7,378,696
Number carried per mile of main railway track operated, .	168,617
Number of car miles run, ...	1,602,293
Average number of persons employed, ...	238

Description of Equipment.

Description of Equipment.	Equipped for Electric Power.	Equipped with Fenders.	Number of Motors.
Cars — Passenger Service.			
Box passenger cars, ...	39	39	-
Open passenger cars (Mt. Tom, 2), ...	67	65	-
Total, ...	106	104	220
Cars — Other Service.			
Mail cars, ...	½	-	-
Work cars, ...	3	3	-
Other cars, ...	3	-	-
Total, ...	6½	3	-
Snow ploughs, ...	9	-	-

Miscellaneous Equipment.

Carts and snow sleds (1 cart, 1 sled),	2
Other railway rolling stock: 1 sweeper, 6 dump cars, 4 flat cars,	11
Other highway vehicles: 1 tower wagon, 2 other wagons, 1 sleigh,	4
Horses,	4
Other items of equipment: 2 double and 2 single harnesses,	

Railway Owned, Leased and Operated (by Electric Power).

Railway Owned, etc.	Owned.	Held under Lease or Contract	Total Owned, Leased, etc.
	Miles.	Miles.	Miles.
Length of railway line,	35.650	.900	36.550
Length of second main track,	7.210	-	7.210
Total Length of Main Track,	42.860	.900	43.760
Length of sidings, switches, etc.,	3.160	.100	3.260
Total, Computed as Single Track,	46.020	1.000	47.020

Railway Located Outside of Public Ways.

	Owned.	Operated.
	Miles.	Miles.
Length of railway line,	8.205	9.105
Length of second main track,	1.957	1.957
Total Length of Main Track,	10.162	11.062

Names of the several cities and towns in which the railways operated by the company are located: Holyoke, Chicopee, Northampton and South Hadley.

Grade Crossings with Railroads.

Grade Crossings with Railroads.	Number of Tracks at Crossing.	
	Railroad.	Railway.
Crossings of railways with railroads at grade (4 in number), viz.:		
With New York, New Haven & Hartford Railroad, at Dwight and Front streets,	2	2
With Boston & Maine Railroad, Main Street, near Cross Street,	1	2
With Boston & Maine Railroad, Cabot Street, near third-level canal,	3	1
With Boston & Maine Railroad, Cabot Street, near Race Street,	1	1
Total Number of Tracks at Crossings,	7	6

ACCIDENTS TO PERSONS.

(A detailed statement of each accident is on file in the office of the Board.)

KILLED AND INJURED.	FROM CAUSES BEYOND THEIR OWN CONTROL.		FROM THEIR OWN MISCONDUCT OR CARELESSNESS.		TOTAL.	
	Killed.	Injured.	Killed.	Injured.	Killed.	Injured.
Passengers,	-	16	-	13	-	29
Employees,	-	-	-	2	-	2
Other persons,	-	-	1	-	1	-
TOTALS,	-	16	1	15	1	31

CORPORATE NAME AND ADDRESS OF THE COMPANY.

HOLYOKE STREET RAILWAY COMPANY,

25 CANAL STREET, HOLYOKE, MASS.

NAMES AND BUSINESS ADDRESS OF PRINCIPAL OFFICERS.

William S. Loomis, *President and General Manager*, 25 Canal Street, Holyoke, Mass. Louis D. Pellissier, *Treasurer and Clerk of Corporation*, 25 Canal Street, Holyoke, Mass. Brooks & Hamilton, *General Counsel*, Holyoke, Mass. George H. Hunter, *Superintendent*, 25 Canal Street, Holyoke, Mass.

NAMES AND RESIDENCE OF BOARD OF DIRECTORS.

William S. Loomis, Holyoke, Mass. John G. Mackintosh, Holyoke, Mass. Frederick Harris, Springfield, Mass. John Olmsted, Springfield, Mass. Newrie D. Winter, Springfield, Mass. Jeremiah F. Sullivan, Holyoke, Mass. Louis D. Pellissier, Holyoke, Mass.

We hereby certify that the statements contained in the foregoing report are full, just and true.

WM. S. LOOMIS,
JOHN OLMSTED,
FREDERICK HARRIS,
J. G. MACKINTOSH,
J. F. SULLIVAN,
NEWRIE D. WINTER,
LOUIS D. PELLISSIER,
Directors.
LOUIS D. PELLISSIER,
Treasurer.
GEO. H. HUNTER,
Superintendent.

COMMONWEALTH OF MASSACHUSETTS.

HAMPDEN, SS. OCT. 24, 1904. Then personally appeared the above-named Wm. S. Loomis, John Olmsted, Frederick Harris, J. G. Mackintosh, J. F. Sullivan, Newrie D. Winter and Louis D. Pellissier, and severally made oath that the foregoing certificate by them subscribed is, to the best of their knowledge and belief, true.

Before me, THOMAS W. SPENCER,
Notary Public.

REPORT

OF THE

HOOSAC VALLEY STREET RAILWAY COMPANY

FOR THE YEAR ENDING SEPTEMBER 30, 1904.

General Exhibit for the Year.			
Gross earnings from operation,			$152,638 94
Operating expenses,			110,613 95
Net Earnings from Operation,			$42,024 99
Miscellaneous income:			
Hay sold,		$18 83	
Park receipts,		2,471 95	
Scrap sold,		400 31	
Total Miscellaneous Income,			2,891 09
Gross Income above Operating Expenses,			$44,916 08
Charges upon income accrued during the year:			
Interest on funded debt,		$5,000 00	
Interest and discount on unfunded debts and loans,		4,396 20	
Taxes, State and local,	$4,170 45		
Taxes, commutation,	2,872 21		
		7,042 66	
Other deductions from income: park expenses,		5,157 65	
Total Charges and Deductions from Income,			21,596 51
Net Divisible Income,			$23,319 57
Dividends declared (6 per cent),			24,000 00
Deficit for the year ending September 30, 1904,			$680 43
Amount of surplus September 30, 1903,			47,789 94
Debits to profit and loss account during the year: discount on sale of 250 $1,000 bonds,			3,333 34
Total Surplus September 30, 1904,			$43,776 17

Earnings from Operation.	
Receipts from passengers carried,	$151,080 30
Receipts from carriage of express and parcels,	700 60

Receipts from rentals of buildings and other property,		$299 69
Other earnings from operation: special cars,		558 35
Gross Earnings from Operation,		$152,638 94

Expenses of Operation.

General expenses:		
Salaries of general officers and clerks,		$2,925 92
General office expenses and supplies,		1,718 05
Legal expenses,		237 12
Insurance,		2,433 32
Maintenance of roadway and buildings:		
Repair of roadbed and track,		5,951 12
Repair of electric line construction,		1,468 65
Repair of buildings,		67 96
Maintenance of equipment:		
Repair of cars and other vehicles,		7,962 58
Repair of electric equipment of cars,		6,067 43
Transportation expenses:		
Cost of electric motive power,		40,461 68
Wages and compensation of persons employed in conducting transportation,		33,345 02
Removal of snow and ice,		1,708 81
Damages for injuries to persons and property,		1,894 27
Other transportation expenses,		2,317 28
Repair of power plant machinery,		2,054 74
Total Operating Expenses,		$110,613 95

Property Accounts.

Additions to railway:		
Extension of tracks (length, 46,834 feet),	$76,771 82	
New electric line construction (length, 8,026 feet),	7,322 39	
Other additions to railway: interest during construction,	7,030 30	
Total Additions to Railway,		$91,124 51
Additions to equipment:		
Additional cars (4 in number),	$15,691 25	
Electric equipment of same,	9,705 93	
Other additions to equipment: tools and appliances,	481 82	
Total Additions to Equipment,		25,879 00
Additions to land and buildings:		
New electric power stations, including machinery, etc.,	$3,044 37	
Additional equipment of power stations,	1,510 56	
Other new buildings necessary for operation of railway,	21,502 28	
Total Additions to Land and Buildings,		26,057 21
Additions to other permanent property: additions to park,		5,811 26
Total Additions to Property Accounts,		$148,871 98

GENERAL BALANCE SHEET SEPTEMBER 30, 1904.

ASSETS.	DR.	
Cost of railway:		
Roadbed and tracks,	$502,825 20	
Electric line construction, including poles, wiring, feeder lines, etc.,	66,318 48	
Interest accrued during construction of railway,	12,408 96	
TOTAL COST OF RAILWAY OWNED,		$581,552 64
Cost of equipment:		
Cars and other rolling stock and vehicles,	$81,013 74	
Electric equipment of same,	58,256 03	
Other items of equipment: tools and appliances,	9,279 19	
TOTAL COST OF EQUIPMENT OWNED,		148,548 96
Cost of land and buildings:		
Land necessary for operation of railway,	$24,775 33	
Electric power stations, including equipment,	73,160 71	
Other buildings necessary for operation of railway,	41,837 14	
TOTAL COST OF LAND AND BUILDINGS OWNED,		139,773 18
Other permanent property:		
Park,	$14,658 40	
Morey farm,	7,500 00	
TOTAL COST OF OTHER PERMANENT PROPERTY OWNED,		22,158 40
TOTAL PERMANENT INVESTMENTS,		$892,033 18
Cash and current assets: cash,		1,780 12
Miscellaneous assets: materials and supplies,		398 93
TOTAL,		$894,212 23

LIABILITIES.	CR.	
Capital stock,		$400,000 00
Funded debt,		350,000 00
Current liabilities:		
Loans and notes payable,	$100,000 00	
Audited vouchers and accounts,	436 06	
TOTAL CURRENT LIABILITIES,		100,436 06
Profit and loss balance (surplus),		43,776 17
TOTAL,		$894,212 23

CAPITAL STOCK.

Capital stock authorized by law,	$500,000 00	
Capital stock authorized by votes of company,	500,000 00	
Capital stock issued and outstanding,		$400,000 00
Number of shares issued and outstanding,	4,000	
Number of stockholders,	32	
Number of stockholders in Massachusetts,	30	
Amount of stock held in Massachusetts,	$320,000 00	

Funded Debt.

Description of Bonds.	Rate of Interest.	Date of Maturity.	Amount Outstanding.	Interest Paid during the Year.
	Per Cent.			
First mortgage bonds,	5	July 1, 1917,	$100,000 00	$5,000 00
Refunding mortgage bonds,	4	Sept. 1, 1924,	250,000 00	-
Totals,			$350,000 00	$5,000 00

Volume of Traffic, etc.

Number of passengers paying revenue carried during the year,	3,021,606
Number carried per mile of main railway track operated,	115,210
Number of car miles run,	791,890
Average number of persons employed,	80

Description of Equipment.

Description of Equipment.	Equipped for Electric Power.	Not Equipped.	Equipped with Fenders.	Equipped with Electric Heaters.	Number of Motors.
Cars — Passenger Service.					
Box passenger cars,	15	-	15	15	48
Open passenger cars,	20	-	20	-	46
Total,	35	-	35	15	94
Cars — Other Service.					
Other cars,	2	5	-	-	4
Snow ploughs,	3	-	-	-	-

Miscellaneous Equipment.

Carts and snow sleds,	3
Horses,	1

Railway Owned and Operated (by Electric Power).

Length of railway line,	26.227 miles.
Length of sidings, switches, etc.,	.921 "
Total, computed as single track,	27.148 "

Railway Located Outside of Public Ways.

Length of railway line,	4.920 miles.
Length of second main track,	.185 "
Total length of main track,	5.105 "

Names of the several cities and towns in which the railways operated by the company are located: North Adams, Williamstown, Adams, Clarksburg and Cheshire.

Grade Crossings with Railroads.

Grade Crossings with Railroads.	Number of Tracks at Crossing.	
	Railroad.	Railway.
Crossings of railways with railroads at grade (6 in number), viz.: —		
With Boston & Maine Railroad, West Main Street, North Adams,	2	1
With Boston & Maine Railroad, Cole Avenue, Williamstown,	2	1
With Boston & Maine Railroad, State Street, North Adams,	2	1
With Boston & Albany Railroad, Park Street, Adams,	1	1
With Boston & Albany Railroad, Commercial Street, Adams,	1	1
With Boston & Albany Railroad, Columbia Street, Adams,	1	1
Total Number of Tracks at Crossings,	9	6

Number of above crossings at which *frogs* are inserted in the tracks, . 6

Accidents to Persons.

(A detailed statement of each accident is on file in the office of the Board.)

Killed and Injured.	From Causes beyond their own Control.		From their own Misconduct or Carelessness.		Total.	
	Killed.	Injured.	Killed.	Injured.	Killed.	Injured.
Passengers,	-	3	-	14	-	17
Employees,	-	-	-	-	-	-
Other persons,	-	1	1	-	1	1
Totals,	-	4	1	14	1	18

Corporate Name and Address of the Company.

HOOSAC VALLEY STREET RAILWAY COMPANY,

North Adams, Mass.

Names and Business Address of Principal Officers.

Arthur H. Rice, *President*, Pittsfield, Mass. Ezra D. Whitaker, *Vice-President*, North Adams, Mass. William L. Adam, *Treasurer*, Pittsfield, Mass. S. Proctor Thayer, *Clerk of Corporation and General Counsel*, North Adams, Mass. Peter C. and Patrick H. Dolan, *General Managers*, Pittsfield, Mass. William T. Nary, *Superintendent*, North Adams, Mass.

Names and Residence of Board of Directors.

Arthur H. Rice, Pittsfield, Mass. Ezra D. Whitaker, North Adams, Mass. William L. Adam, Pittsfield, Mass. S. Proctor Thayer, North Adams, Mass. Patrick H. Dolan, Pittsfield, Mass. William B. Plunkett, Adams, Mass.

We hereby certify that the statements contained in the foregoing report are full, just and true.

A. H. RICE,
WILLIAM L. ADAM,
W. B. PLUNKETT,
S. PROCTOR THAYER,
EZRA D. WHITAKER,
Directors.
WILLIAM L. ADAM,
Treasurer.
WILLIAM T. NARY,
Superintendent.

Commonwealth of Massachusetts.

Berkshire, ss. Oct. 28, 1904. Then personally appeared the above-named A. H. Rice, William L. Adam, W. B. Plunkett, S. Proctor Thayer and Ezra D. Whitaker, and severally made oath that the foregoing certificate by them subscribed is, to the best of their knowledge and belief, true.

Before me, HUGH P. DRYSDALE,
Justice of the Peace.

REPORT

OF THE

HORSE NECK BEACH STREET RAILWAY COMPANY

FOR THE YEAR ENDING SEPTEMBER 30, 1904.

[Railway in process of construction.]

GENERAL BALANCE SHEET SEPTEMBER 30, 1904.

ASSETS.	DR.	
Cost of railway:		
Roadbed and tracks,	$23,602 82	
Engineering and other expenses incident to construction,	7,453 85	
Other items of railway cost,	54 61	
TOTAL COST OF RAILWAY OWNED,		$31,111 28
Cost of equipment: office furniture,		287 65
Cost of land and buildings: land necessary for operation of railway,		1,200 00
Other permanent property: land,		100 00
TOTAL PERMANENT INVESTMENTS,		$32,698 93
Cash and current assets:		
Cash,	$15 53	
Bills and accounts receivable,	200 00	
Other cash and current assets: unexpired insurance,	6 50	
TOTAL CASH AND CURRENT ASSETS,		222 03
TOTAL,		$32,920 96

LIABILITIES.	CR.	
Capital stock, amount paid in,		$22,710 00
Current liabilities:		
Loans and notes payable,	$304 00	
Audited vouchers and accounts,	9,184 73	
Salaries and wages,	722 23	
TOTAL CURRENT LIABILITIES,		10,210 96
TOTAL,		$32,920 96

Capital Stock.

Capital stock authorized by law, ...	$200,000 00	
Capital stock authorized by votes of company,	200,000 00	
Amount paid in on 228 shares not yet issued, .	. . . .	$22,710 00
Number of subscribers, ...	55	
Number of subscribers in Massachusetts, .	52	
Amount of subscriptions held in Massachusetts,	$21,510 00	

Railway Owned.

Length of railway line (in process of construction and partially completed), ...	6.000 miles.

Corporate Name and Address of the Company.

HORSE NECK BEACH STREET RAILWAY COMPANY,

262 Washington Street, Boston, Mass.

Names and Business Address of Principal Officers.

N. Lewis Sheldon, *Vice-President and General Counsel*, 27 School Street, Boston, Mass. Benjamin W. Carlow, *Treasurer*, 262 Washington Street, Boston, Mass. Frank H. Walker, *Clerk of Corporation and Auditor*, 262 Washington Street, Boston, Mass. Charles F. Parker, *General Manager*, Woonsocket, R. I.

Names and Residence of Board of Directors.

N. Lewis Sheldon, Boston, Mass. Benjamin W. Carlow, Worcester, Mass. Charles F. Parker, Woonsocket, R. I. Clarence M. Wing, Palmer, Mass. Frank H. Walker, Newton, Mass.

We hereby certify that the statements contained in the foregoing report are full, just and true.

FRANK H. WALKER,
CHARLES F. PARKER,
BENJ. W. CARLOW,
N. LEWIS SHELDON,
CLARENCE M. WING,
Directors.
BENJ. W. CARLOW,
Treasurer.

Commonwealth of Massachusetts.

Suffolk, ss. Nov. 2, 1904. Then personally appeared the above-named Frank H. Walker, Charles F. Parker, Benjamin W. Carlow, N. Lewis Sheldon and Clarence M. Wing, and severally made oath that the foregoing certificate by them subscribed is, to the best of their knowledge and belief, true.

Before me, GUY E. CLIFFORD,
Justice of the Peace.

REPORT

OF THE

INTERSTATE CONSOLIDATED STREET RAILWAY COMPANY

For the Year ending September 30, 1904.

General Exhibit for the Year.	
Gross earnings from operation,	$150,664 67
Operating expenses,	123,608 96
Gross Income above Operating Expenses,	$27,055 71
Charges upon income accrued during the year: taxes, State and local,	8,216 92
Net Divisible Income,	$18,838 79
Dividends declared (11 per cent),	30,250 00
Deficit for the year ending September 30, 1904,	$11,411 21
Amount of surplus September 30, 1903,	44,120 13
Total Surplus September 30, 1904,	$32,708 92

Earnings from Operation.	
Receipts from passengers carried,	$150,664 67
Gross Earnings from Operation,	$150,664 67

Expenses of Operation.	
General expenses:	
Salaries of general officers and clerks,	$2,925 00
General office expenses and supplies,	100 00
Maintenance of roadway and buildings,	23,000 00
Transportation expenses:	
Cost of electric motive power,	36,024 18
Wages and compensation of persons employed in conducting transportation,	44,567 96
Damages for injuries to persons and property,	9,021 87
Rentals of buildings and other property,	7,969 95
Total Operating Expenses,	$123,608 96

General Balance Sheet September 30, 1904.

Assets.	Dr.	
Cost of railway:		
Roadbed and tracks,	$171,857 21	
Electric line construction, including poles, wiring, feeder lines, etc.,	74,923 87	
Total Cost of Railway Owned,		$246,781 08
Cost of equipment,		1,218 92
Cost of land and buildings:		
Land necessary for operation of railway,	$2,000 00	
Buildings necessary for operation of railway,	25,000 00	
Total Cost of Land and Buildings Owned,		27,000 00
Total Permanent Investments,		$275,000 00
Cash and current assets:		
Bills and accounts receivable,		32,708 92
Total,		$307,708 92

Liabilities.	Cr.
Capital stock,	$275,000 00
Profit and loss balance (surplus),	32,708 92
Total,	$307,708 92

Capital Stock.

Capital stock authorized by law,	$275,000 00	
Capital stock authorized by votes of company,	275,000 00	
Capital stock issued and outstanding,		$275,000 00
Number of shares issued and outstanding,	2,750	
Number of stockholders,	5	
Number of stockholders in Massachusetts,	1	
Amount of stock held in Massachusetts,	$55,000 00	

Volume of Traffic, etc.

Number of passengers paying revenue carried during the year,	2,993,682
Number carried per mile of main railway track operated,	145,650
Number of car miles run,	637,596
Average number of persons employed,	128

Railway Owned and Operated (by Electric Power).

Length of railway line,	20.554 miles.
Length of sidings, switches, etc.,	1.100 "
Total, computed as single track,	21.654 "

Names of the several cities and towns in which the railways operated by the company are located: Attleborough, North Attleborough, Seekonk and Wrentham.

Grade Crossings with Railroads.

Grade Crossings with Railroads.	Number of Tracks at Crossing.	
	Railroad.	Railway.
Crossings of railways with railroads at grade (2 in number), viz.: —		
With New York, New Haven & Hartford Railroad, at North Main Street, Attleborough, Mass.,	1	1
With New York, New Haven & Hartford Railroad, at Commonwealth Avenue, North Attleborough, Mass.,	3	1
Total Number of Tracks at Crossings,	4	2

Number of above crossings at which *frogs* are inserted in the tracks, . 1

Accidents to Persons.

(A detailed statement of each accident is on file in the office of the Board.)

Killed and Injured.	From Causes beyond their own Control.		From their own Misconduct or Carelessness.		Total.	
	Killed.	Injured.	Killed.	Injured.	Killed.	Injured.
Passengers,	-	17	-	10	-	27
Employees,	-	2	-	-	-	2
Other persons,	-	8	-	-	-	8
Totals,	-	27	-	10	-	37

Corporate Name and Address of the Company.

INTERSTATE CONSOLIDATED STREET RAILWAY COMPANY,

Providence, R. I.

Names and Business Address of Principal Officers.

Marsden J. Perry, *President,* Providence, R. I. Cyril A. Babcock, *Treasurer,* Providence, R. I. Cornelius S. Sweetland, *Clerk of Corporation,* Providence, R. I. Albert T. Potter, *General Manager,* Providence, R. I.

Names and Residence of Board of Directors.

Marsden J. Perry, Providence, R. I. Clarence L. Watson, Attleborough, Mass. Benjamin A. Jackson, Providence, R. I. Albert T. Potter, Providence, R. I. Cornelius S. Sweetland, Providence, R. I.

We hereby certify that the statements contained in the foregoing report are full, just and true.

MARSDEN J. PERRY,
BENJ. A. JACKSON,
CORNELIUS S. SWEETLAND,
CLARENCE L. WATSON,
ALBERT T. POTTER,
Directors.
C. A. BABCOCK,
Treasurer.

STATE OF RHODE ISLAND AND PROVIDENCE PLANTATIONS.

PROVIDENCE, SS. CITY OF PROVIDENCE, Oct. 29, 1904. Then personally appeared the above-named Marsden J. Perry, Benjamin A. Jackson, Cornelius S. Sweetland, Clarence L. Watson, Albert T. Potter and C. A. Babcock, and severally made oath that the foregoing certificate by them subscribed is, to the best of their knowledge and belief, true.

Before me, HENRY V. A. JOSLIN,
Justice of the Peace

REPORT

OF THE

LAWRENCE & METHUEN STREET RAILWAY COMPANY

For the Year ending September 30, 1904.

General Exhibit for the Year.		
Gross earnings from operation,		$55,335 44
Operating expenses,		54,868 00
Gross Income above Operating Expenses,		$467 44
Charges upon income accrued during the year:		
Interest on funded debt,	$3,645 84	
Interest and discount on unfunded debts and loans,	2,735 25	
Taxes, State and local,	1,426 08	
Total Charges and Deductions from Income,		7,807 17
Deficit for the year ending September 30, 1904,		$7,339 73
Amount of surplus September 30, 1903,		1,780 41
Total Deficit September 30, 1904,		$5,559 32

Earnings from Operation.	
Receipts from passengers carried,	$55,155 13
Receipts from advertising in cars,	180 31
Gross Earnings from Operation,	$55,335 44

Expenses of Operation.		
General expenses:		
Salaries of general officers and clerks,		$2,300 22
General office expenses and supplies,		578 52
Legal expenses,		78 73
Insurance,		616 55
Other general expenses:		
Store room,	$175 17	
Miscellaneous general expenses,	407 42	
		582 59

Maintenance of roadway and buildings:		
Repair of roadbed and track,		$2,947 01
Repair of electric line construction,		868 50
Repair of buildings,		167 57
Maintenance of equipment:		
Repair of cars and other vehicles,		4,996 87
Repair of electric equipment of cars,		3,678 81
Transportation expenses:		
Cost of electric motive power,		16,170 21
Wages and compensation of persons employed in conducting transportation,		13,874 76
Removal of snow and ice,		1,363 53
Damages for injuries to persons and property,		2,365 98
Tolls for trackage over other railways,		629 44
Rentals of buildings and other property,		101 65
Other transportation expenses:		
Advertising,	$799 21	
Car barn and machine shop expenses,	2,747 85	
		3,547 06
TOTAL OPERATING EXPENSES,		$54,868 00

PROPERTY ACCOUNTS.

Additions to railway:		
Extension of tracks,	$1,841 02	
Other additions to railway: engineering and expense,	380 38	
TOTAL ADDITIONS TO RAILWAY,		$2,221 40
Additions to equipment: additional cars,		774 93
Additions to land and buildings: rights of way,		45 00
TOTAL ADDITIONS TO PROPERTY ACCOUNTS,		$3,041 33
Deductions from property accounts (property sold or reduced in valuation and credited to property accounts): electric line construction,		188 80
NET ADDITION TO PROPERTY ACCOUNTS FOR THE YEAR,		$2,852 53

GENERAL BALANCE SHEET SEPTEMBER 30, 1904.

ASSETS.	DR.	
Cost of railway:		
Roadbed and tracks and bridges,	$198,625 77	
Electric line construction, including poles, wiring, feeder lines, etc.,	45,895 25	
Interest accrued during construction of railway,	1,056 72	
Engineering and other expenses incident to construction,	25,678 48	
TOTAL COST OF RAILWAY OWNED,		$271,256 22
Cost of equipment:		
Cars and other rolling stock and vehicles,	$31,595 07	
Electric equipment of same,	28,863 00	

Cost of equipment — *Concluded.*		
Furniture and fixtures,	$231 55	
Other items of equipment: snow ploughs,	3,577 98	
TOTAL COST OF EQUIPMENT OWNED,		$64,267 60
Cost of land and buildings: land necessary for operation of railway and rights of way,		16,790 29
TOTAL PERMANENT INVESTMENTS,		$352,314 11
Profit and loss balance (deficit),		5,559 32
TOTAL,		$357,873 43

LIABILITIES.	CR.	
Capital stock,		$150,000 00
Funded debt,		125,000 00
Current liabilities:		
Loans and notes payable,	$79,227 59	
Matured interest coupons unpaid (including coupons due July 1),	2,083 34	
Accrued interest coupons,	1,562 50	
TOTAL CURRENT LIABILITIES,		82,873 43
TOTAL,		$357,873 43

CAPITAL STOCK.

Capital stock authorized by law,	$150,000 00	
Capital stock authorized by votes of company,	150,000 00	
Capital stock issued and outstanding,		$150,000 00
Number of shares issued and outstanding,	1,500	
Number of stockholders,	6	
Number of stockholders in Massachusetts,	5	
Amount of stock held in Massachusetts,	$500 00	

FUNDED DEBT.

DESCRIPTION OF BONDS.	Rate of Interest.	Date of Maturity.	Amount Outstanding.	Interest Paid during the Year.
	Per Cent.			
First mortgage gold bonds,	5	Jan. 1, 1923,	$125,000 00	-

VOLUME OF TRAFFIC, ETC.

Number of passengers paying revenue carried during the year,	1,088,544
Number carried per mile of main railway track operated,	85,423
Number of car miles run,	342,082
Average number of persons employed,	28

Description of Equipment.

Description of Equipment.	Equipped for Electric Power.	Equipped with Fenders.	Equipped with Electric Heaters.	Number of Motors.
Cars — Passenger Service.				
Box passenger cars,	5	5	5	20
Open passenger cars,	7	7	-	28
Total,	12	12	5	48
Snow ploughs,	2	-	-	-

Railway Owned and Operated (by Electric Power).

Railway Owned, etc.	Owned.	Trackage over Other Railways.	Total Owned, etc.
	Miles.	Miles.	Miles.
Length of railway line,	12.518	.225	12.743
Length of sidings, switches, etc.,	.437	-	.437
Total, Computed as Single Track,	12.955	.225	13.180

Railway Located Outside of Public Ways.

Length of railway line,	2.700 miles.

Names of the several cities and towns in which the railways operated by the company are located: Lawrence and Methuen.

Accidents to Persons.

(A detailed statement of each accident is on file in the office of the Board.)

Killed and Injured.	From Causes beyond their own Control.		From their own Misconduct or Carelessness.		Total.	
	Killed.	Injured.	Killed.	Injured.	Killed.	Injured.
Passengers,	-	4	-	2	-	6
Employees,	-	-	-	-	-	-
Other persons,	-	1	-	5	-	6
Totals,	-	5	-	7	-	12

CORPORATE NAME AND ADDRESS OF THE COMPANY.

LAWRENCE & METHUEN STREET RAILWAY COMPANY,

50 MERRIMAC STREET, HAVERHILL, MASS.

NAMES AND BUSINESS ADDRESS OF PRINCIPAL OFFICERS.

David A. Belden, *President,* 50 Merrimac Street, Haverhill, Mass. Frederick P. Royce, *Vice-President,* 84 State Street, Boston, Mass. Samuel P. Russell, *Treasurer and Auditor,* 50 Merrimac Street, Haverhill, Mass. Reginald H. Johnson, *Clerk of Corporation,* 53 State Street, Boston, Mass. Franklin Woodman, *General Manager,* 50 Merrimac Street, Haverhill, Mass. Robert H. Dunbar, *Superintendent,* Salem, N. H.

NAMES AND RESIDENCE OF BOARD OF DIRECTORS.

David A. Belden, Haverhill, Mass. Reginald H. Johnson, Braintree, Mass. Frederick P. Royce, Dedham, Mass. Frank W. Stearns, Newton, Mass. John Dearborn, Boston, Mass.

We hereby certify that the statements contained in the foregoing report are full, just and true.

DAVID A. BELDEN,
F. P. ROYCE,
REGINALD H. JOHNSON,
Directors.
SAMUEL P. RUSSELL,
Treasurer.
FRANKLIN WOODMAN,
General Manager.

COMMONWEALTH OF MASSACHUSETTS.

ESSEX, SS. Nov. 17, 1904. Then personally appeared the above-named David A. Belden, Samuel P. Russell and Franklin Woodman, and severally made oath that the foregoing certificate by them subscribed is, to the best of their knowledge and belief, true.

Before me, EDMUND B. FULLER,
Justice of the Peace.

COMMONWEALTH OF MASSACHUSETTS.

SUFFOLK, SS. Nov. 29, 1904. Then personally appeared the above-named F. P. Royce and Reginald H. Johnson, and severally made oath that the foregoing certificate by them subscribed is, to the best of their knowledge and belief, true.

Before me, HAROLD WILLIAMS, JR.,
Justice of the Peace.

REPORT

OF THE

LEOMINSTER, SHIRLEY & AYER STREET RAILWAY COMPANY

For the Year ending September 30, 1904.

[Commenced operation July 30, 1904.]

General Exhibit for the Year.

Gross earnings from operation,	$3,918 80
Operating expenses,	1,334 13
Gross Income above Operating Expenses,	$2,584 67
Surplus for the year ending September 30, 1904,	$2,584 67
Total Surplus September 30, 1904,	$2,584 67

Earnings from Operation.

Receipts from passengers carried,	$3,918 80
Gross Earnings from Operation,	$3,918 80

Expenses of Operation.

General expenses:	
Salaries of general officers and clerks,	$72 07
General office expenses and supplies,	22 59
Maintenance of roadway and buildings: repair of buildings,	3 94
Maintenance of equipment: provender and stabling for horses,	13 73
Transportation expenses:	
Cost of electric motive power,	478 30
Wages and compensation of persons employed in conducting transportation,	308 75
Rentals of property,	358 70
Other transportation expenses: printing tickets, etc.,	76 05
Total Operating Expenses,	$1,334 13

Property Accounts.

Additions to railway:		
Extension of tracks (length, 45,234 feet),	$163,114 11	
New electric line construction (length, 45,234 feet),	22,912 20	

Additions to railway — *Concluded.*		
Other additions to railway:		
Salaries, engineering and other incidental expenses,	$11,645 73	
Interest accrued during construction,	2,165 62	
TOTAL ADDITIONS TO RAILWAY,		$199,837 66
Additions to equipment: electric equipment of cars,		4,308 74
Additions to land and buildings:		
Additional land necessary for operation of railway,	$6,619 41	
New electric power stations, including machinery, etc.,	7,176 41	
TOTAL ADDITIONS TO LAND AND BUILDINGS,		13,795 82
TOTAL ADDITIONS TO PROPERTY ACCOUNTS,		$217,942 22

GENERAL BALANCE SHEET SEPTEMBER 30, 1904.

ASSETS.	DR.	
Cost of railway:		
Roadbed and tracks,	$165,159 61	
Electric line construction, including poles, wiring, feeder lines, etc.,	22,912 20	
Interest accrued during construction of railway,	2,165 62	
Engineering and other expenses incident to construction,	15,411 41	
TOTAL COST OF RAILWAY OWNED,		$205,648 84
Cost of equipment: electric equipment of cars,		4,308 74
Cost of land and buildings:		
Land necessary for operation of railway,	$6,619 41	
Electric power stations, including equipment,	7,176 41	
TOTAL COST OF LAND AND BUILDINGS OWNED,		13,795 82
TOTAL PERMANENT INVESTMENTS,		$223,753 40
Cash and current assets: cash,		5,340 35
Miscellaneous assets: materials and supplies,		2,441 68
TOTAL,		$231,535 43

LIABILITIES.	CR.	
Capital stock,		$56,247 00
Current liabilities:		
Loans and notes payable,	$150,000 00	
Audited vouchers and accounts,	19,097 79	
Salaries and wages,	2,602 85	
TOTAL CURRENT LIABILITIES,		171,700 64
Accrued liabilities: interest accrued and not yet due,		1,003 12
Profit and loss balance (surplus),		2,584 67
TOTAL,		$231,535 43

Capital Stock.

Capital stock authorized by law, ...	$100,000 00	
Capital stock authorized by votes of company,	100,000 00	
Amount paid in on 1,000 shares not yet issued,	. . . .	$56,247 00
Number of subscribers, ...	31	
Number of subscribers in Massachusetts, .	31	
Amount of subscriptions held in Massachusetts,	$56,247 00	

Volume of Traffic, etc.

Number of passengers paying revenue carried during the year,	77,676
Number carried per mile of main railway track operated, .	9,067
Number of car miles run, ...	11,957
Average number of persons employed, ...	4
Company commenced operation July 30, 1904.	

Description of Equipment.

Passenger service: number of motors, ...	4

Railway Owned and Operated (by Electric Power).

Length of railway line, ...	8.567 miles.

Railway Located Outside of Public Ways.

Length of railway line, ...	5.940 miles.

Names of the several cities and towns in which the railways operated by the company are located: Leominster, Lunenburg, Shirley, Ayer and Harvard.

Corporate Name and Address of the Company.

LEOMINSTER, SHIRLEY & AYER STREET RAILWAY COMPANY,

Fitchburg, Mass.

Names and Business Address of Principal Officers.

George E. Clifford, *President*, Fitchburg, Mass. Wesley W. Sargent, *Vice-President, General Manager and Superintendent*, Fitchburg, Mass. Robert N. Wallis, *Treasurer*, Fitchburg, Mass. Charles F. Baker, *Clerk of Corporation*, Fitchburg, Mass. Baker & Hall, *General Counsel*, Fitchburg, Mass.

NAMES AND RESIDENCE OF BOARD OF DIRECTORS.

George E. Clifford, Fitchburg, Mass. Wesley W. Sargent, Fitchburg, Mass. Charles F. Baker, Fitchburg, Mass. George N. Proctor, Fitchburg, Mass. Thomas H. Shea, Fitchburg, Mass. Manson D. Haws, Leominster, Mass. Thomas L. Hazen, Shirley, Mass.

We hereby certify that the statements contained in the foregoing report are full, just and true.

THOMAS H. SHEA,
CHARLES F. BAKER,
WESLEY W. SARGENT,
MANSON D. HAWS,
Directors
ROBERT N. WALLIS,
Treasurer.
WESLEY W. SARGENT,
Superintendent.

COMMONWEALTH OF MASSACHUSETTS.

WORCESTER, ss. Nov. 2, 1904. Then personally appeared the above-named Thomas H. Shea, Charles F. Baker, Wesley W. Sargent, Manson D. Haws and Robert N. Wallis, and severally made oath that the foregoing certificate by them subscribed is, to the best of their knowledge and belief, true.

Before me, WILBUR B. TENNEY,
Justice of the Peace.

REPORT

OF THE

LEXINGTON & BOSTON STREET RAILWAY COMPANY

FOR THE YEAR ENDING SEPTEMBER 30, 1904.

GENERAL EXHIBIT FOR THE YEAR.

Gross earnings from operation,		$161,995 88
Operating expenses,		124,751 67
GROSS INCOME ABOVE OPERATING EXPENSES,		$37,244 21
Charges upon income accrued during the year:		
Interest on funded debt,	$15,750 00	
Interest and discount on unfunded debts and loans,	22,077 06	
Taxes, State and local,	9,170 82	
TOTAL CHARGES AND DEDUCTIONS FROM INCOME,		46,997 88
NET DEFICIT,		$9,753 67
Dividends declared (1 per cent),		5,250 00
Deficit for the year ending September 30, 1904,		15,003 67
Amount of surplus September 30, 1903,		17,108 45
TOTAL SURPLUS SEPTEMBER 30, 1904,		$2,104 78

EARNINGS FROM OPERATION.

Receipts from passengers carried,	$152,818 17
Receipts from tolls for use of tracks by other companies,	312 73
Receipts from rentals of buildings and other property,	7,345 65
Receipts from advertising in cars,	1,165 00
Receipts from interest on deposits,	23 22
Other earnings from operation:	
Discount,	34 66
Other sources,	296 45
GROSS EARNINGS FROM OPERATION,	$161,995 88

EXPENSES OF OPERATION.

General expenses:	
Salaries of general officers and clerks,	$8,073 09
General office expenses and supplies,	4,430 65
Legal expenses,	2,750 50
Insurance,	4,274 35
Other general expenses: storeroom expense,	301 98

Maintenance of roadway and buildings:		
Repair of roadbed and track,		$4,865 13
Repair of electric line construction,		2,783 91
Repair of buildings,		563 57
Maintenance of equipment:		
Repair of cars and other vehicles,		7,561 17
Repair of electric equipment of cars,		5,496 02
Renewal of horses, harnesses, shoeing, etc., and provender and stabling for horses,		835 71
Transportation expenses:		
Cost of electric motive power, $24,600.86; less power sold, $593.90; net,		24,006 96
Wages and compensation of persons employed in conducting transportation,		42,499 85
Removal of snow and ice,		4,937 13
Damages for injuries to persons and property,		7,650 71
Tolls for trackage over other railways,		2,875 50
Rentals of buildings and other property,		738 99
Other transportation expenses: miscellaneous shop expense,		106 45
TOTAL OPERATING EXPENSES,		$124,751 67

PROPERTY ACCOUNTS.

Additions to railway:		
Extension of tracks (length, 140 feet),	$99 57	
New electric line construction (length, 140 feet),	148 31	
Other additions to railway:		
Engineering,	1,322 86	
Improvement of double track,	1,945 94	
TOTAL ADDITIONS TO RAILWAY,		$3,516 68
Additions to equipment:		
Additional cars (1 in number) second-hand,	$477 67	
Electric equipment of same,	150 00	
Other additions to equipment:		
Automobile,	1,206 50	
Shop tools and machinery,	29 00	
TOTAL ADDITIONS TO EQUIPMENT,		1,863 17
Additions to land and buildings:		
Additional equipment of power stations,	$772 59	
Buildings necessary for operation of railway,	1,650 46	
TOTAL ADDITIONS TO LAND AND BUILDINGS,		2,423 05
TOTAL ADDITIONS TO PROPERTY ACCOUNTS,		$7,802 90
Deductions from property accounts (property sold or reduced in valuation and credited to property accounts):		
Rail and paving blocks,	$8,050 51	
Trolley wire,	308 76	
Automobile,	400 00	
Five cars,	11,434 33	
TOTAL DEDUCTIONS FROM PROPERTY ACCOUNTS,		20,193 60
NET DEDUCTIONS FROM PROPERTY ACCOUNTS FOR THE YEAR,		$12,390 70

General Balance Sheet September 30, 1904.

Assets.		Dr.	
Cost of railway:			
Roadbed and tracks,		$443,767 88	
Electric line construction, including poles, wiring, feeder lines, etc.,		124,529 20	
Interest accrued during construction of railway,		25,587 22	
Engineering and other expenses incident to construction,		37,654 01	
Other items of railway cost,		27,134 78	
Total Cost of Railway Owned,			$658,673 09
Cost of equipment:			
Cars and other rolling stock and vehicles,		$168,731 64	
Electric equipment of same,		138,306 23	
Horses,		210 00	
Other items of equipment:			
Auto,	$1,304 50		
Storage battery,	38,604 17		
Shop tools and machinery,	150 67		
		40,059 34	
Total Cost of Equipment Owned,			347,307 21
Cost of land and buildings:			
Land and buildings necessary for operation of railway,*		$90,794 80	
Electric power stations, including equipment,*		141,023 56	
Total Cost of Land and Buildings Owned,			231,818 36
Total Permanent Investments,			$1,237,798 66
Cash and current assets:			
Cash,		$50 00	
Bills and accounts receivable,		20,888 50	
Total Cash and Current Assets,			20,938 50
Miscellaneous assets: materials and supplies,		$4,421 04	
Other assets and property: unexpired insurance,		70 25	
Total Miscellaneous Assets,			4,491 29
Total,			$1,263,228 45

Liabilities.	Cr.	
Capital stock,		$525,000 00
Funded debt,		350,000 00
Current liabilities:		
Loans and notes payable,	$379,000 00	
Audited vouchers and accounts,	5,789 77	
Salaries and wages,	1,143 23	
Total Current Liabilities,		385,933 00
Accrued liabilities: interest accrued and not yet due,		190 67
Profit and loss balance (surplus),		2,104 78
Total,		$1,263,228 45

* Booster at $2,700 transferred from one account to the other.

Capital Stock.

Capital stock authorized by law,	$525,000 00	
Capital stock authorized by votes of company,	525,000 00	
Capital stock issued and outstanding,	. . . .	$525,000 00
Number of shares issued and outstanding,	5,250	
Number of stockholders,	8	
Number of stockholders in Massachusetts,	8	
Amount of stock held in Massachusetts,	$525,000 00	

Funded Debt.

Description of Bonds.	Rate of Interest.	Date of Maturity.	Amount Outstanding.	Interest Paid during the Year.
	Per Cent.			
First mortgage gold bonds,	4½	July 1, 1920,	$350,000 00	$15,750 00

Volume of Traffic, etc.

Number of passengers paying revenue carried during the year,	3,173,702
Number carried per mile of main railway track operated,	96,845
Number of car miles run,	780,037
Average number of persons employed,	99

Description of Equipment.

Description of Equipment.	Equipped for Electric Power.	Equipped with Fenders.	Equipped with Electric Heaters.	Number of Motors.
Cars — Passenger Service.				
Box passenger cars,	30	30	30	-
Open passenger cars,	40	40	-	-
Total,	70	70	30	204
Cars — Other Service.				
Work cars (sand car),	1	-	-	-
Other cars (service car),	1	1	-	-
Total,	2	1	-	-
Snow ploughs,	6	-	-	-

Miscellaneous Equipment.

Carts and snow sleds: 1 cart,	1
Other highway vehicles: 1 snow leveller, 1 sleigh, 1 pung, 1 trolley wagon, 1 dinkey, 1 automobile, 1 concord and 1 express wagon,	8
Horses,	2
Other items of equipment: harnesses,	2

Railway Owned, Leased and Operated (by Electric Power).

Railway Owned, etc.	Owned.	Held under Lease or Contract.	Trackage over Other Railways.	Total Owned, Leased, etc.
	Miles.	Miles.	Miles.	Miles.
Length of railway line,	27.205	2.662	.444	30.311
Length of second main track,	2.460	-	-	2.460
Total Length of Main Track,	29.665	2.662	.444	32.771
Length of sidings, switches, etc.,	2.691	-	-	2.691
Total, Computed as Single Track,	32.356	2.662	.444	35.462

Names of the several cities and towns in which the railways operated by the company are located: Arlington, Belmont, Bedford, Billerica, Concord, Lexington, Waltham and Woburn.

Grade Crossings with Railroads.

Grade Crossings with Railroads.	Number of Tracks at Crossing.	
	Railroad.	Railway.
Crossings of railways with railroads at grade (2 in number), viz.:—		
With Boston & Maine Railroad, at Lexington Street, Waltham,	1	1
With Boston & Maine Railroad, at Loomis Street, Bedford,	2	1
Total Number of Tracks at Crossings,	3	2

Accidents to Persons.

(A detailed statement of each accident is on file in the office of the Board.)

Killed and Injured.	From Causes Beyond their own Control.		From their own Misconduct or Carelessness.		Total.	
	Killed.	Injured.	Killed.	Injured.	Killed.	Injured.
Passengers,	-	6	-	3	-	9
Employees,	-	-	-	-	-	-
Other persons,	-	10	-	4	-	14
Totals,	-	16	-	7	-	23

Corporate Name and Address of the Company.

LEXINGTON & BOSTON STREET RAILWAY COMPANY,

Newtonville, Mass.

Names and Business Address of Principal Officers.

Adams D. Claflin, *President*, Newtonville, Mass. Sydney Harwood, *Vice-President*, Newton, Mass. Charles W. Smith, *Treasurer*, Newtonville, Mass. Frank W. Remick, *Clerk of Corporation*, Boston, Mass. Coolidge & Hight, *General Counsel*, Boston Mass. Matthew C. Brush, *General Manager*, Newtonville, Mass.

NAMES AND RESIDENCE OF BOARD OF DIRECTORS.

Adams D. Claflin, Newton Centre, Mass. William F. Hammett, Newton, Mass. Sydney Harwood, Newton, Mass. Frederic H. Lewis, Swampscott, Mass. Frank W. Remick, West Newton, Mass. James L. Richards, Newtonville, Mass. Alden E. Viles, Boston, Mass.

We hereby certify that the statements contained in the foregoing report are full, just and true.

ADAMS D. CLAFLIN,
WILLIAM F. HAMMETT,
SYDNEY HARWOOD,
JAMES L. RICHARDS,
FREDERIC H. LEWIS,
ALDEN E. VILES,
Directors.
CHAS. W. SMITH,
Treasurer.
MATTHEW C. BRUSH,
General Manager.

COMMONWEALTH OF MASSACHUSETTS.

SUFFOLK, SS. OCT. 29, 1904. Then personally appeared the above-named Adams D. Claflin, William F. Hammett, Sydney Harwood, James L. Richards, Frederic H. Lewis, Alden E. Viles, Chas. W. Smith and Matthew C. Brush, and severally made oath that the foregoing certificate by them subscribed is, to the best of their knowledge and belief, true.

Before me, GEO. M. COX,
Notary Public.

REPORT

OF THE

LINWOOD STREET RAILWAY COMPANY

For the Year ending September 30, 1904.

General Exhibit for the Year.		
Gross earnings from operation,		$12,348 45
Operating expenses,		10,565 03
Gross Income above Operating Expenses,		$1,783 42
Charges upon income accrued during the year:		
Taxes, State and local,	$199 20	
Taxes, commutation,	277 84	
Total Charges and Deductions from Income,		477 04
Net Divisible Income,		$1,306 38
Dividends declared (6 per cent),		720 00
Surplus for the year ending September 30, 1904,		$586 38
Amount of surplus September 30, 1903,		1,892 86
Total Surplus September 30, 1904,		$2,479 24

Earnings from Operation.	
Receipts from passengers carried,	$12,348 45
Gross Earnings from Operation,	$12,348 45

Expenses of Operation.	
General expenses:	
Salaries of general officers and clerks,	$1,443 75
General office expenses and supplies,	515 48
Maintenance of roadway and buildings: repair of roadbed and track,	83 24
Maintenance of equipment: repair of cars and other vehicles,	626 41
Transportation expenses:	
Cost of electric motive power,	1,841 28
Wages and compensation of persons employed in conducting transportation,	3,724 91
Tolls for trackage over other railways,	1,380 96

Transportation expenses — *Concluded.*		
Rentals of buildings and other property,		$400 00
Other transportation expenses: lighting,		549 00
TOTAL OPERATING EXPENSES,		$10,565 03

PROPERTY ACCOUNTS.

Additions to equipment:		
Additional cars,	$2,565 81	
Electric equipment of same,	1,235 29	
TOTAL ADDITIONS TO EQUIPMENT,		$3,801 10
TOTAL ADDITIONS TO PROPERTY ACCOUNTS,		$3,801 10

GENERAL BALANCE SHEET SEPTEMBER 30, 1904.

ASSETS.	DR.	
Cost of railway:		
Roadbed and tracks,	$5,425 90	
Electric line construction, including poles, wiring, feeder lines, etc.,	587 20	
TOTAL COST OF RAILWAY OWNED,		$6,013 10
Cost of equipment:		
Cars and other rolling stock and vehicles,	$6,091 51	
Electric equipment of same,	5,596 20	
Other items of equipment: trucks and fenders,	1,274 00	
TOTAL COST OF EQUIPMENT OWNED,		12,961 71
TOTAL PERMANENT INVESTMENTS,		$18,974 81
Cash and current assets: cash,		391 42
Miscellaneous assets: materials and supplies,		269 17
TOTAL,		$19,635 40

LIABILITIES.	CR.
Capital stock,	$12,000 00
Current liabilities: audited vouchers and accounts,	5,156 16
Profit and loss balance (surplus),	2,479 24
TOTAL,	$19,635 40

CAPITAL STOCK.

Capital stock authorized by law,	$12,000 00	
Capital stock authorized by votes of company,	12,000 00	
Capital stock issued and outstanding,		$12,000 00
Number of shares issued and outstanding,	120	
Number of stockholders,	17	
Number of stockholders in Massachusetts,	16	
Amount of stock held in Massachusetts,	$11,700 00	

Volume of Traffic, etc.

Number of passengers paying revenue carried during the year,	278,862
Number carried per mile of main railway track operated, .	160,173
Number of car miles run, ...	46,032
Average number of persons employed, ...	6

Description of Equipment.

Description of Equipment.	Equipped for Electric Power.	Equipped with Fenders.	Equipped with Electric Heaters.	Number of Motors.
Cars — Passenger Service.				
Box passenger cars, ...	4	4	4	12

Railway Operated (by Electric Power).*

Length of railway line, ...	1.741 miles.
Length of sidings, switches, etc., ...	.160 "
Total, computed as single track (trackage rights), . .	1.901 "

Railway Located Outside of Public Ways.

Length of railway line, ...	.662 mile.

Names of the several cities and towns in which the railways operated by the company are located: Northbridge.

Corporate Name and Address of the Company.

LINWOOD STREET RAILWAY COMPANY,

Whitinsville, Mass.

Names and Business Address of Principal Officers.

Cyrus A. Taft, *President*, Whitinsville, Mass. G. M. Whitin, *Vice-President*, Whitinsville, Mass. J. M. Lasell, *Treasurer and Clerk of Corporation*, Whitinsville, Mass. Warren & Garfield, *General Counsel*, Boston, Mass. George Wilmot, *Superintendent*, Linwood, Mass.

Names and Residence of Board of Directors.

Cyrus A. Taft, Whitinsville, Mass. William L. Taft, Whitinsville, Mass. George M. Whitin, Whitinsville, Mass. Chester W. Lasell, Whitinsville, Mass. Josiah M. Lasell, Whitinsville, Mass.

* Owned by private parties.

We hereby certify that the statements contained in the foregoing report are full, just and true.

J. M. LASELL,
GEORGE M. WHITIN,
CYRUS A. TAFT,
Directors.
J. M. LASELL,
Treasurer.
GEO. WILMOT,
Superintendent.

COMMONWEALTH OF MASSACHUSETTS.

WORCESTER, SS. OCT. 28, 1904. Then personally appeared the above-named J. M. Lasell, George M. Whitin and Cyrus A. Taft, and severally made oath that the foregoing certificate by them subscribed is, to the best of their knowledge and belief, true.

Before me, ROBERT K. BROWN,
Justice of the Peace.

REPORT

OF THE

LOWELL, ACTON & MAYNARD STREET RAILWAY COMPANY

For the Year ending September 30, 1904.

General Exhibit for the Year.	
Gross earnings from operation,	$5,001 73
Operating expenses,	5,521 81
Gross Deficit above Operating Expenses,	$520 08
Total Deficit September 30, 1904,	$520 08
Earnings from Operation.	
Receipts from passengers carried,	$5,001 73
Gross Earnings from Operation,	$5,001 73
Expenses of Operation.	
Transportation expenses:	
Cost of electric motive power,	$2,002 39
Wages and compensation of persons employed in conducting transportation,	2,829 10
Removal of snow and ice,	25 63
Rentals of buildings and other property,	654 99
Other transportation expenses:	
Oil for track,	7 25
Sand pails,	2 45
Total Operating Expenses,	$5,521 81

General Balance Sheet September 30, 1904.

Assets.	Dr.	
Cost of railway:		
Roadbed and tracks,	$30,487 23	
Electric line construction, including poles, wiring, feeder lines, etc.,	1,546 36	
Interest accrued during construction of railway,	2,283 11	
Engineering and other expenses incident to construction,	11,092 93	
Total Cost of Railway Owned,		$45,409 63

Cash and current assets:		
Cash,	$53 03	
Bills and accounts receivable,	120 36	
TOTAL CASH AND CURRENT ASSETS,		$173 39
Miscellaneous assets: materials and supplies,		5,000 00
Profit and loss balance (deficit),		520 08
TOTAL,		$51,103 10

LIABILITIES.	CR	
Capital stock (amount paid in),		$20,000 00
Current liabilities:		
Loans and notes payable,	$25,400 00	
Audited vouchers and accounts,	5,703 10	
TOTAL CURRENT LIABILITIES,		31,103 10
TOTAL,		$51,103 10

CAPITAL STOCK.

Capital stock authorized by law,	$20,000 00	
Capital stock authorized by votes of company,	20,000 00	
Amount paid in on 200 shares not yet issued,		$20,000 00

VOLUME OF TRAFFIC, ETC.

Number of passengers paying revenue carried during the [illegible] year,	100,539
Number carried per mile of main railway track operated,	51,217
Number of car miles run,	43,394
Average number of persons employed,	4

RAILWAY OWNED AND OPERATED (BY ELECTRIC POWER).

RAILWAY OWNED, ETC.	Owned.	Total Operated.
	Miles.	Miles.
Length of main line,	2.000	1.963
TOTAL,	2.000	1.963

RAILWAY LOCATED OUTSIDE OF PUBLIC WAYS.

Length of railway line,	1,320 feet.

Names of the several cities and towns in which the railways operated by the company are located: Maynard and Acton.

CORPORATE NAME AND ADDRESS OF THE COMPANY.

LOWELL, ACTON & MAYNARD STREET RAILWAY COMPANY,

MAYNARD, MASS.

NAMES AND BUSINESS ADDRESS OF PRINCIPAL OFFICERS.

Walter R. Dame, *President and General Counsel*, Clinton, Mass. Charles H. Persons, *Vice-President*, Maynard, Mass. John W. Ogden, *Treasurer and Superintendent*, Maynard, Mass. Edmund B. Fuller, *Clerk of Corporation*, Haverhill, Mass. H. G. Lowe, *Auditor*, Waltham, Mass.

NAMES AND RESIDENCE OF BOARD OF DIRECTORS.

Walter R. Dame, Clinton, Mass. Chas. H. Persons, Maynard, Mass. Chas. W. Shippee, Milford, Mass. William S. Reed, Leominster, Mass. Henry Tower, Hudson, Mass. Chas. B. Stone, West Acton, Mass. Julius Loewe, Maynard, Mass. E. B. Fuller, Haverhill, Mass. F. P. Bond, Stow, Mass.

We hereby certify that the statements contained in the foregoing report are full, just and true.

WALTER R. DAME,
CHAS. W. SHIPPEE,
HENRY TOWER,
JULIUS LOEWE,
CHARLES H. PERSONS.
Directors.
JOHN W. OGDEN,
Treasurer.
JOHN W. OGDEN,
Superintendent.

COMMONWEALTH OF MASSACHUSETTS.

SUFFOLK, SS. BOSTON, Nov. 22, 1904. Then personally appeared the above-named Walter R. Dame, Chas. W. Shippee, Henry Tower, Julius Loewe, Charles H. Persons and John W. Ogden, and severally made oath that the foregoing certificate by them subscribed is, to the best of their knowledge and belief, true.

Before me, JAMES A. TIRRELL,
Notary Public.

REPORT

OF THE

LOWELL & BOSTON STREET RAILWAY COMPANY

For the Period ending May 9, 1904.

[Railway placed in hands of receivers May 10, 1904.]

General Exhibit for the Period.		
Gross earnings from operation,		$3,829 81
Operating expenses,		15,467 29
Gross Deficit above Operating Expenses,		$11,637 48
Charges upon income accrued during the period:		
Interest on funded debt,	$2,025 00	
Interest and discount on unfunded debts and loans,	5,482 49	
Taxes, State and local,	989 87	
Total Charges and Deductions from Income,		8,497 36
Deficit for the period ending May 9, 1904,		$20,134 84
Amount of deficit September 30, 1903,		31,358 69
Total Deficit May 9, 1904,		$51,493 53

Earnings from Operation.	
Receipts from passengers carried,	$3,218 55
Receipts from tolls for use of tracks by other companies,	34 13
Receipts from rentals of buildings and other property,	50 00
Receipts from advertising in cars,	77 50
Other earnings from operation: car rentals,	449 63
Gross Earnings from Operation,	$3,829 81

Expenses of Operation.	
General expenses:	
Salaries of general officers and clerks,	$280 00
General office expenses and supplies,	71 50
Legal expenses,	180 57
Insurance,	530 36
Other general expenses,	179 96

Maintenance of roadway and buildings:	
Repair of roadbed and track,	$469 17
Repair of electric line construction,	233 58
Repair of buildings,	6 73
Maintenance of equipment:	
Repair of cars and other vehicles,	1,339 03
Repair of electric equipment of cars,	2,357 77
Transportation expenses:	
Cost of electric motive power,	4,985 52
Wages and compensation of persons employed in conducting transportation,	2,964 49
Removal of snow and ice,	1,376 40
Damages for injuries to persons and property,	175 20
Other transportation expenses: car service and shop expense,	317 01
TOTAL OPERATING EXPENSES,	$15,467 29

GENERAL BALANCE SHEET MAY 9, 1904.

ASSETS.	DR.	
Cost of railway:		
Roadbed and tracks,	$144,538 30	
Electric line construction, including poles, wiring, feeder lines, etc.,	48,093 46	
Interest accrued during construction of railway,	9,264 23	
Engineering and other expenses incident to construction,	32,784 05	
Other items of railway cost: extensions,	7,770 48	
TOTAL COST OF RAILWAY OWNED,		$242,450 52
Cost of equipment:		
Cars and other rolling stock and vehicles,	$36,290 00	
Electric equipment of same,	30,097 59	
Other items of equipment,	620 67	
TOTAL COST OF EQUIPMENT OWNED,		67,008 26
Cost of land and buildings:		
Land necessary for operation of railway,	$8,357 84	
Real estate,	25,322 50	
Buildings necessary for operation of railway,	1,406 67	
TOTAL COST OF LAND AND BUILDINGS OWNED,		35,087 01
TOTAL PERMANENT INVESTMENTS,		$344,545 79
Cash and current assets:		
Cash,	$61,668 40	
Bills and accounts receivable,	4,889 67	
Sinking and other special funds,	46,735 50	
TOTAL CASH AND CURRENT ASSETS,		113,293 57
Miscellaneous assets: materials and supplies,		1,985 37
Profit and loss balance (deficit),		51,493 53
TOTAL,		$511,318 26

LIABILITIES.		CR.
Capital stock,		$90,000 00
Funded debt,		90,000 00
Current liabilities:		
Loans and notes payable,	$325,834 67	
Audited vouchers and accounts,	3,380 64	
Salaries and wages,	2,102 95	
TOTAL CURRENT LIABILITIES,		331,318 26
TOTAL,		$511,318 26

The foregoing balance sheet is drawn from the records of the corporation now in our hands.

Any discrepancies between the foregoing and that for the previous year are to be found in the aforesaid records.

Receivers of the Lowell & Boston Street Railway Company.

CAPITAL STOCK.		
Capital stock authorized by law,	$90,000 00	
Capital stock authorized by votes of company,	90,000 00	
Capital stock issued and outstanding,		$90,000 00
Number of shares issued and outstanding,	900	
Number of stockholders,	17	
Number of stockholders in Massachusetts,	17	
Amount of stock held in Massachusetts,	$90,000 00	

FUNDED DEBT.

DESCRIPTION OF BONDS.	Rate of Interest.	Date of Maturity.	Amount Outstanding.	Interest Paid during the Period.
	Per Cent.			
First mortgage bonds,	4½	Nov. 1921,	$90,000 00	$2,025 00

DESCRIPTION OF EQUIPMENT.

DESCRIPTION OF EQUIPMENT.	Equipped for Electric Power.	Equipped with Fenders.	Equipped with Electric Heaters.	Number of Motors.
CARS — PASSENGER SERVICE.				
Box passenger cars,	5	5	5	-
Open passenger cars,	8	8	-	-
TOTAL,	13	13	5	28
CARS — OTHER SERVICE.				
Platform freight cars,	1	-	-	-
Snow ploughs,	2	-	-	-

RAILWAY OWNED AND OPERATED (BY ELECTRIC POWER).

RAILWAY OWNED, ETC.	Owned.	Trackage over Other Railways.	Total Owned, etc.
	Miles.	Miles.	Miles.
Length of railway line,	9.125	.142	9.267
Length of second main track,	.126	-	.126
TOTAL LENGTH OF MAIN TRACK,	9.251	.142	9.393
Length of sidings, switches, etc.,	.498	-	.498
TOTAL, COMPUTED AS SINGLE TRACK,	9.749	.142	9.891

RAILWAY LOCATED OUTSIDE OF PUBLIC WAYS.

Length of railway line,	.514 miles.
Length of second main track,	.140 "
Total length of main track,	.654 "

Names of the several cities and towns in which the railways operated by the company are located: Woburn, Burlington and Billerica.

CORPORATE NAME AND ADDRESS OF THE COMPANY.

LOWELL & BOSTON STREET RAILWAY COMPANY,

43 MILK STREET, BOSTON, MASS.

NAMES AND BUSINESS ADDRESS OF PRINCIPAL OFFICERS.

Thomas I. Reed, *President*, Burlington, Mass. Frank E. Cotton, *Vice-President*, Woburn, Mass. Edward A. Mead, *Treasurer*, Boston, Mass. C. W. E. Harrison, *Superintendent*, Woburn, Mass.

NAMES AND RESIDENCE OF BOARD OF DIRECTORS.

Thomas I. Reed, Burlington, Mass. Frank E. Cotton, Woburn, Mass. Edward A. Mead, Boston, Mass. Frank A. Partridge, Woburn, Mass. Richard Faulkner, Billerica, Mass.

We hereby certify that the statements contained in the foregoing report are full, just and true, according to the records of the corporation now in our hands.

JOHN T. BURNETT,
JOHN L. HALL,
Receivers.

COMMONWEALTH OF MASSACHUSETTS.

SUFFOLK, SS. OCT. 31, 1904. Then personally appeared the above-named John T. Burnett and John L. Hall, and severally made oath that the foregoing certificate by them subscribed is, to the best of their knowledge and belief, true.

Before me, JOSHUA M. SEARS, JR.,
Justice of the Peace.

REPORT

OF THE

RECEIVERS OF THE LOWELL & BOSTON STREET RAILWAY

For the Period from May 10 to September 30, 1904.

General Exhibit for the Period.			
Gross earnings from operation,			$3,872 69
Operating expenses,			7,251 98
Gross Deficit above Operating Expenses,			$3,379 29
Charges upon income accrued during the period:			
Interest on funded debt,		$2,030 06	
Taxes, State and local,	$22 82		
Taxes, commutation,	39 54		
		62 36	
Total Charges and Deductions from Income,			2,092 42
Deficit for the period ending September 30, 1904,			$5,471 71
Total Deficit September 30, 1904,			$5,471 71

Earnings from Operation.	
Receipts from passengers carried,	$3,802 80
Receipts from tolls for use of tracks by other companies,	8 66
Receipts from advertising in cars,	31 23
Other earnings from operation: sale of hay,	30 00
Gross Earnings from Operation,	$3,872 69

Expenses of Operation.	
General expenses:	
Salaries of general officers and clerks,	$348 54
General office expenses and supplies,	50 00
Legal expenses,	5 00
Insurance,	679 80
Maintenance of roadway and buildings: repair of roadbed and track,	2 31
Maintenance of equipment: repair of cars and other vehicles,	432 52

Transportation expenses:		
Cost of electric motive power,		$2,642 14
Wages and compensation of persons employed in conducting transportation,		3,061 17
Tolls for trackage over other railways,		2 50
Other transportation expenses: sundries,		28 00
TOTAL OPERATING EXPENSES,		$7,251 98

GENERAL BALANCE SHEET SEPTEMBER 30, 1904.

ASSETS.	DR.	
Cash and current assets:		
Cash,	$3,811 25	
Bills and accounts receivable,	32 83	
TOTAL CASH AND CURRENT ASSETS,		$3,844 08
Miscellaneous assets: operating expenses from budget,		3,603 98
Profit and loss balance (deficit),		5,471 71
TOTAL,		$12,919 77

LIABILITIES.	CR.	
Current liabilities:		
Receivers' certificates,	$10,000 00	
Audited vouchers and accounts,	2,919 77	
TOTAL CURRENT LIABILITIES,		$12,919 77
TOTAL,		$12,919 77

VOLUME OF TRAFFIC, ETC.

Number of passengers paying revenue carried during the year,	74,266
Number carried per mile of main railway track operated,	424
Number of car miles run,	3,985
Average number of persons employed,	19
The receivers commenced operation of cars, June 14, 1904.	

NAME AND ADDRESS OF THE RECEIVERS.

RECEIVERS OF THE LOWELL & BOSTON STREET RAILWAY COMPANY,

705 SEARS BUILDING, BOSTON, MASS.

NAMES AND BUSINESS ADDRESS OF RECEIVERS.

John T. Burnett, Southborough, Mass., John L. Hall, Boston, Mass., George H. Newhall, Providence, R. I., *Receivers.*

We hereby certify that the statements contained in the foregoing report are full, just and true.

JOHN L. HALL,
JOHN T. BURNETT,
Receivers.

COMMONWEALTH OF MASSACHUSETTS.

SUFFOLK, SS. DEC. 9, 1904. Then personally appeared the above-named John T. Burnett and John L. Hall, and severally made oath that the foregoing certificate by them subscribed is, to the best of their knowledge and belief, true.

Before me, JOSHUA M. SEARS, JR.,
Justice of the Peace.

REPORT

OF THE

LOWELL & FITCHBURG STREET RAILWAY COMPANY

FOR THE YEAR ENDING SEPTEMBER 30, 1904.

[Obtained a certificate of incorporation, but has not commenced the construction of its railway.]

GENERAL BALANCE SHEET SEPTEMBER 30, 1904.

ASSETS. DR.	
Cost of railway: engineering and other expenses incident to construction,	$22,998 30
Cost of land and buildings: land necessary for operation of railway,	1,001 70
TOTAL PERMANENT INVESTMENTS,	$24,000 00
TOTAL,	$24,000 00

LIABILITIES. CR.	
Capital stock (amount paid in),	$24,000 00
TOTAL,	$24,000 00

CAPITAL STOCK.

Capital stock authorized by law,	$240,000 00	
Capital stock authorized by votes of company,	240,000 00	
Capital stock issued and outstanding,	240,000 00	
Amount paid in on 2,400 shares not yet issued,		$24,000 00
Number of subscribers,	15	
Number of subscribers in Massachusetts,	15	
Amount of subscriptions to stock held in Massachusetts,	$24,000 00	

GENERAL REMARKS AND EXPLANATIONS.

Franchise granted and approved by Railroad Commissioners in towns of Ayer, Groton, Westford and Chelmsford. Surveys completed in above-mentioned towns, but construction not yet started.

CORPORATE NAME AND ADDRESS OF THE COMPANY.

LOWELL & FITCHBURG STREET RAILWAY COMPANY,

ROOM 305, 53 STATE STREET, BOSTON, MASS.

NAMES AND BUSINESS ADDRESS OF PRINCIPAL OFFICERS.

Loring N. Farnum, *President*, Boston, Mass. Howard O. Weaver, *Treasurer*, Boston, Mass. William Odlin, *Clerk of Corporation and General Counsel*, Boston, Mass.

NAMES AND RESIDENCE OF BOARD OF DIRECTORS.

Loring N. Farnum, North Andover, Mass. William S. Murray, Boston, Mass. Howard O. Weaver, Boston, Mass. Arthur H. Sheldon, North Chelmsford, Mass. George T. Day, Westford, Mass.

We hereby certify that the statements contained in the foregoing report are full, just and true.

LORING N. FARNUM,
WM. S. MURRAY,
HOWARD O. WEAVER,
GEORGE T. DAY,
ARTHUR H. SHELDON,
Directors.
HOWARD O. WEAVER,
Treasurer.

COMMONWEALTH OF MASSACHUSETTS.

SUFFOLK, ss. BOSTON, Nov. 30, 1904. Then personally appeared the above-named Loring N. Farnum, Wm. S. Murray, Howard O. Weaver, George T. Day and Arthur H. Sheldon, and severally made oath that the foregoing certificate by them subscribed is, to the best of their knowledge and belief, true.

Before me, H. RUFUS STANLEY,
Justice of the Peace.

REPORT

OF THE

LOWELL & PELHAM STREET RAILWAY COMPANY

For the Year ending September 30, 1904.

General Exhibit for the Year.		
Gross earnings from operation,		$16,192 25
Operating expenses,		14,304 76
Gross Income above Operating Expenses,		$1,887 49
Charges upon income accrued during the year:		
Interest on funded debt,	$1,166 66	
Interest and discount on unfunded debts and loans,	710 65	
Taxes, State and local,	578 60	
Total Charges and Deductions from Income,		2,455 91
Deficit for the year ending September 30, 1904,		$568 42
Amount of deficit September 30, 1903,		1,668 47
Total Deficit September 30, 1904,		$2,236 89

Earnings from Operation.	
Receipts from passengers carried,	$16,153 92
Receipts from advertising in cars,	38 33
Gross Earnings from Operation,	$16,192 25

Expenses of Operation.	
General expenses:	
Salaries of general officers and clerks,	$469 23
General office expenses and supplies,	119 44
Legal expenses,	32 63
Insurance,	137 67
Other general expenses: store room, $35.61; miscellaneous general expenses, $105.01,	140 62
Maintenance of roadway and buildings:	
Repair of roadbed and track,	668 80
Repair of electric line construction,	195 03
Repair of buildings,	39 17

Maintenance of equipment:	
Repair of cars and other vehicles,	$1,004 98
Repair of electric equipment of cars,	718 21
Transportation expenses:	
Cost of electric motive power,	3,418 70
Wages and compensation of persons employed in conducting transportation,	3,093 27
Removal of snow and ice,	163 34
Damages for injuries to persons and property,	638 39
Tolls for trackage over other railways,	2,685 77
Rentals of buildings and other property,	19 75
Other transportation expenses: advertising, $213.39; car barn and machine shop expense, $546.37,	759 76
TOTAL OPERATING EXPENSES,	$14,304 76

PROPERTY ACCOUNTS.

Additions to railway:		
Extension of tracks,	$92 89	
New electric line construction,	140 00	
Other additions to railway,	85 24	
TOTAL ADDITIONS TO RAILWAY,		$318 13
Additions to equipment: additional cars,		464 96
Additions to land and buildings: rights of way,		50 64
TOTAL ADDITIONS TO PROPERTY ACCOUNTS,		$833 73

GENERAL BALANCE SHEET SEPTEMBER 30, 1904.

ASSETS.	DR.	
Cost of railway:		
Roadbed and tracks,	$34,401 04	
Electric line construction, including poles, wiring, feeder lines, etc.,	13,045 90	
Engineering and other expenses incident to construction,	7,702 16	
TOTAL COST OF RAILWAY OWNED,		$55,149 10
Cost of equipment:		
Cars and other rolling stock and vehicles,	$23,205 06	
Electric equipment of same,	16,807 00	
Furniture and fixtures,	152 92	
Other items of equipment: snow ploughs,	1,788 99	
TOTAL COST OF EQUIPMENT OWNED,		41,953 97
Cost of land and buildings: rights of way,		133 64
TOTAL PERMANENT INVESTMENTS,		$97,236 71
Profit and loss balance (deficit),		2,236 89
TOTAL,		$99,473 60

Liabilities.	Cr.	
Capital stock,		$40,000 00
Funded debt,		40,000 00
Current liabilities:		
Loans and notes payable,	$18,306 94	
Matured interest coupons unpaid (including coupons due July 1),	666 66	
Accrued interest coupons,	500 00	
Total Current Liabilities,		19,473 60
Total,		$99,473 60

Capital Stock.		
Capital stock authorized by law,	$40,000 00	
Capital stock authorized by votes of company,	40,000 00	
Capital stock issued and outstanding,		$40,000 00
Number of shares issued and outstanding,	400	
Number of stockholders,	7	
Number of stockholders in Massachusetts,	6	
Amount of stock held in Massachusetts,	$600,00	

Funded Debt.

Description of Bonds.	Rate of Interest.	Date of Maturity.	Amount Outstanding.	Interest Paid during the Year.
	Per Cent.			
First mortgage gold bonds,	5	Jan. 1, 1923,	$40,000 00	-

Volume of Traffic, etc.

Number of passengers paying revenue carried during the year,	413,167
Number carried per mile of main railway track operated,	130,460
Number of car miles run,	75,487
Average number of persons employed,	8

Description of Equipment.

Description of Equipment.	Equipped for Electric Power.	Equipped with Fenders.	Equipped with Electric Heaters.	Number of Motors.
Cars — Passenger Service.				
Box passenger cars,	4	4	4	16
Open passenger cars,	5	5	-	20
Total,	9	9	4	36
Snow ploughs,	1	-	-	-

Railway Owned and Operated (by Electric Power).

Length of railway line,	3.167 miles.
Length of sidings, switches, etc.,	.151 "
Total, computed as single track,	3.318 "

Railway Located Outside of Public Ways.

Length of railway line,	.607 mile.

Names of the several cities and towns in which the railways operated by the company are located: Dracut.

Accidents to Persons.

(A detailed statement of each accident is on file in the office of the Board.)

Killed and Injured.	From Causes beyond their own Control.		From their own Misconduct or Carelessness		Total.	
	Killed.	Injured.	Killed.	Injured.	Killed.	Injured.
Passengers,	-	-	-	1	-	1
Employees,	-	-	-	-	-	-
Other persons,	-	-	-	-	-	-
Totals,	-	-	-	1	-	1

Corporate Name and Address of the Company.

LOWELL & PELHAM STREET RAILWAY COMPANY,

50 Merrimac Street, Haverhill, Mass.

Names and Business Address of Principal Officers.

David A. Belden, *President*, 50 Merrimac Street, Haverhill, Mass. Frederick P. Royce, *Vice-President*, 84 State Street, Boston, Mass. Samuel P. Russell, *Treasurer and Auditor*, 50 Merrimac Street, Haverhill, Mass. Reginald H. Johnson, *Clerk of Corporation*, 53 State Street, Boston, Mass. Franklin Woodman, *General Manager*, 50 Merrimac Street, Haverhill, Mass. Robert H. Dunbar, *Superintendent*, Salem, N. H.

Names and Residence of Board of Directors.

David A. Belden, Haverhill, Mass. Reginald H. Johnson, Braintree, Mass. Frederick P. Royce, Dedham, Mass. Frank W. Stearns, Newton, Mass. John Dearborn, Boston, Mass.

We hereby certify that the statements contained in the foregoing report are full, just and true.

DAVID A. BELDEN,
F. P. ROYCE,
REGINALD H. JOHNSON,
Directors.
SAM'L P. RUSSELL,
Treasurer.
FRANKLIN WOODMAN,
General Manager.

COMMONWEALTH OF MASSACHUSETTS.

ESSEX, SS. Nov. 17, 1904. Then personally appeared the above-named David A. Belden, Samuel P. Russell and Franklin Woodman, and severally made oath that the foregoing certificate by them subscribed is, to the best of their knowledge and belief, true.

Before me, EDMUND B. FULLER,
Justice of the Peace.

COMMONWEALTH OF MASSACHUSETTS.

SUFFOLK, SS. Nov. 29, 1904. Then personally appeared the above-named F. P. Royce and Reginald H. Johnson, and severally made oath that the foregoing certificate by them subscribed is, to the best of their knowledge and belief, true.

Before me, HAROLD WILLIAMS, JR.,
Justice of the Peace.

REPORT

OF THE

MARLBOROUGH & FRAMINGHAM STREET RAILWAY COMPANY

For the Period ending December 21, 1903.

[Consolidated with the Framingham, Southborough & Marlborough, December 21, 1903.]

General Exhibit for the Period.	
Gross earnings from operation,	$7,782 02
Operating expenses,	8,328 66
Gross Deficit above Operating Expenses,	$546 64
Charges upon income accrued during the year: taxes, state and local,	76 34
Deficit for the period ending December 21, 1903,	$622 98
Amount of surplus September 30, 1903,	414 53
Debits to profit and loss account during the period: amount expended for reconstruction of track and line,	1,983 58
Total Deficit December 21, 1903,	$2,192 03

Earnings from Operation.	
Receipts from passengers carried,	$7,634 40
Receipts from tolls for use of tracks by other companies,	81 62
Receipts from rentals of buildings and other property,	28 50
Receipts from advertising in cars,	37 50
Gross Earnings from Operation,	$7,782 02

Expenses of Operation.	
General expenses:	
Salaries of general officers and clerks,	$676 94
Insurance,	110 11
Other general expenses,	107 01
Maintenance of roadway and buildings:	
Repair of roadbed and track,	202 13
Repair of electric line construction,	16 43
Repair of buildings,	1 60
Maintenance of equipment:	
Repair of cars and other vehicles,	158 47
Repair of electric equipment of cars,	116 64

Transportation expenses:		
Cost of electric motive power,		$2,833 08
Wages and compensation of persons employed in conducting transportation,		3,412 26
Removal of snow and ice,		10 64
Damages for injuries to persons and property,		1 00
Rentals of buildings and other property,		503 65
Other transportation expenses: oil, grease, cotton waste, etc.,		178 70
TOTAL OPERATING EXPENSES,		$8,328 66

GENERAL BALANCE SHEET DECEMBER 21, 1903.

ASSETS.	DR.	
Cost of railway:		
Roadbed and tracks,	$64,575 00	
Electric line construction, including poles, wiring, feeder lines, etc.,	8,000 00	
TOTAL COST OF RAILWAY OWNED,		$72,575 00
Cost of equipment: cars and other rolling stock and vehicles, and electric equipment of same,		15,000 00
Cost of land and buildings:		
Land necessary for operation of railway, including buildings,	$10,000 00	
Electric power stations, including equipment,	5,000 00	
TOTAL COST OF LAND AND BUILDINGS OWNED,		15,000 00
TOTAL PERMANENT INVESTMENTS,		$102,575 00
Cash and current assets:		
Cash,	$100 71	
Bills and accounts receivable,	117 47	
Other cash and current assets: prepaid insurance,	935 00	
TOTAL CASH AND CURRENT ASSETS,		1,153 18
Profit and loss balance (deficit),		2,192 03
TOTAL,		$105,920 21

LIABILITIES.	CR.
Capital stock,	$105,000 00
Current liabilities: audited vouchers and accounts,	843 87
Accrued liabilities: taxes accrued and not yet due,	76 34
TOTAL,	$105,920 21

CAPITAL STOCK.

Capital stock authorized by law,	$105,000 00	
Capital stock authorized by votes of company,	105,000 00	
Capital stock issued and outstanding,		$105,000 00
Number of shares issued and outstanding,	1,050	
Number of stockholders,	8	
Number of stockholders in Massachusetts,	8	
Amount of stock held in Massachusetts,	$105,000 00	

Volume of Traffic, etc.

Number of passengers paying revenue carried during the period,	169,157
Number carried per mile of main railway track operated,	22,871
Number of car miles run,	37,876
Average number of persons employed,	40

Description of Equipment.

Description of Equipment.	Equipped for Electric Power.	Not equipped.	Equipped with Fenders.	Equipped with Electric Heaters	Number of Motors.
Cars — Passenger Service.					
Box passenger cars,	5	-	5	5	-
Open passenger cars,	7	-	7	-	-
Total,	12	-	12	5	29
Cars — Other Service.					
Work cars,	-	1	-	-	-
Snow ploughs,	2	-	-	-	-

Miscellaneous Equipment.

Carts and snow sleds,	1
Other highway vehicles: 1 tower wagon, 1 lumber wagon,	2
Horses,	1

Railway Owned and Operated (by Electric Power).

Railway Owned, etc.	Owned.	Trackage over Other Railways.	Total Owned, etc.
	Miles.	Miles.	Miles.
Length of railway line,	7.312	.084	7.396
Length of sidings, switches, etc.,	.489	-	.489
Total, Computed as Single Track,	7.801	.084	7.885

Railway Located Outside of Public Ways.

Length of railway line,	1.755 miles.

Names of the several cities and towns in which the railways operated by the company are located: Hudson and Marlborough.

ACCIDENTS TO PERSONS.

(A detailed statement of each accident is on file in the office of the Board.)

KILLED AND INJURED.	FROM CAUSES BEYOND THEIR OWN CONTROL.		FROM THEIR OWN MISCONDUCT OR CARELESSNESS.		TOTAL.	
	Killed.	Injured.	Killed.	Injured.	Killed.	Injured.
Passengers,	-	1	-	-	-	1
Employees,	-	-	-	-	-	-
Other persons,	-	-	-	1	-	1
TOTALS,	-	1	-	1	-	2

CORPORATE NAME AND ADDRESS OF THE COMPANY.

MARLBOROUGH & FRAMINGHAM STREET RAILWAY COMPANY,

SOUTH FRAMINGHAM, MASS.

NAMES AND BUSINESS ADDRESS OF PRINCIPAL OFFICERS.

William M. Butler, *President*, Tremont Building, Boston, Mass. Arthur E. Childs, *Vice-President*, Board of Trade Building, Boston, Mass. George A. Butman, *Treasurer and Clerk of Corporation*, 8 Congress Street, Boston, Mass.

NAMES AND RESIDENCE OF BOARD OF DIRECTORS.

William M. Butler, Boston, Mass. George A. Butman, Malden, Mass. Samuel Farquhar, Newton, Mass. Arthur E. Childs, Boston, Mass. Charles C. Peirce, Brookline, Mass. Thomas Lahey, Haverhill, Mass. John J. Whipple, Brockton, Mass.

We hereby certify that the statements contained in the foregoing report are full, just and true.

GEO. A. BUTMAN,
CHARLES C. PEIRCE,
ARTHUR E. CHILDS,
JOHN J. WHIPPLE,
Directors.
GEO. A. BUTMAN,
Treasurer.

COMMONWEALTH OF MASSACHUSETTS.

SUFFOLK, ss. BOSTON, Nov. 7, 1904. Then personally appeared the above-named George A. Butman, Chas. C. Peirce, Arthur E. Childs and John J. Whipple, and severally made oath that the foregoing certificate by them subscribed is, to the best of their knowledge and belief, true.

Before me, ARTHUR W. CLAPP,
Justice of the Peace.

REPORT

OF THE

MARLBOROUGH & WESTBOROUGH STREET RAILWAY COMPANY

For the Year ending September 30, 1904.

General Exhibit for the Year.			
Gross earnings from operation,			*$32,703 08
Operating expenses,			23,921 30
Net Earnings from Operation,			$8,781 78
Miscellaneous income: use of park,			1,000 00
Gross Income above Operating Expenses,			$9,781 78
Charges upon income accrued during the year:			
Interest on funded debt,		$8,000 00	
Interest and discount on unfunded debts and loans,		2,860 00	
Taxes, State and local,	$1,426 96		
Taxes, commutation,	352 37		
		1,779 33	
Other deductions from income:			
Paid town of Southborough for use of highway under franchise requirements,	$365 00		
Maintenance of pleasure grounds,	1,693 88		
		2,058 88	
Total Charges and Deductions from Income,			14,698 21
Deficit for the year ending September 30, 1904,			$4,916 43
Amount of surplus September 30, 1903,			2,016 90
Total Deficit September 30, 1904,			$2,899 53

Earnings from Operation.	
Receipts from passengers carried,	$31,976 77
Receipts from advertising in cars,	150 00
Other earnings from operation: cars used by other roads,	576 31
Gross Earnings from Operation,	$32,703 08

Expenses of Operation.	
General expenses:	
Salaries of general officers and clerks,	$1,581 46
General office expenses and supplies,	341 54

General expenses — *Concluded.*	
Legal expenses,	$85 35
Insurance,	1,228 79
Other general expenses: general expenses,	821 97
Maintenance of roadway and buildings:	
Repair of roadbed and track,	745 82
Repair of electric line construction,	114 03
Repair of buildings,	162 54
Maintenance of equipment:	
Repair of cars and other vehicles,	927 40
Repair of electric equipment of cars,	2,677 96
Transportation expenses:	
Cost of electric motive power, $10,456.65; less power sold, $5,683.19; net,	4,773 46
Wages and compensation of persons employed in conducting transportation,	8,109 78
Removal of snow and ice,	511 45
Damages for injuries to persons and property,	676 50
Other transportation expenses,	1,163 25
TOTAL OPERATING EXPENSES,	$23,921 30

PROPERTY ACCOUNTS.

Additions to railway: changes caused by State road,	$1,042 09
Additions to other permanent property: additions to pleasure grounds, boat house,	200 00
TOTAL ADDITIONS TO PROPERTY ACCOUNTS,	$1,242 09

GENERAL BALANCE SHEET SEPTEMBER 30, 1904.

ASSETS.	DR.	
Cost of railway:		
Roadbed and tracks,	$163,784 56	
Electric line construction, including poles, wiring, feeder lines, etc.,	38,246 19	
Interest accrued during construction of railway,	4,223 62	
Engineering and other expenses incident to construction,	8,440 60	
TOTAL COST OF RAILWAY OWNED,		$214,694 97
Cost of equipment:		
Cars and other rolling stock and vehicles,	$35,695 40	
Electric equipment of same,	22,851 83	
Other items of equipment,	1,999 27	
TOTAL COST OF EQUIPMENT OWNED,		60,546 50
Cost of land and buildings:		
Land necessary for operation of railway,	$4,816 68	
Electric power stations, including equipment,	70,370 04	
Other buildings necessary for operation of railway,	9,373 95	
TOTAL COST OF LAND AND BUILDINGS OWNED,		84,560 67
Other permanent property: pleasure grounds,		15,648 71
TOTAL PERMANENT INVESTMENTS,		$375,450 85

Cash and current assets:		
Cash,	$451 67	
Bills and accounts receivable,	360 23	
TOTAL CASH AND CURRENT ASSETS,		$811 90
Miscellaneous assets: materials and supplies,	$2,367 77	
Other assets and property: prepaid insurance,	670 79	
TOTAL MISCELLANEOUS ASSETS,		3,038 56
Profit and loss balance (deficit),		2,899 53
TOTAL,		$382,200 84

LIABILITIES.	CR.	
Capital stock,		$160,000 00
Funded debt,		160,000 00
Current liabilities:		
Loans and notes payable,	$58,625 00	
Audited vouchers and accounts,	1,201 61	
TOTAL CURRENT LIABILITIES,		59,826 61
Accrued liabilities: interest accrued and not yet due,		2,374 23
TOTAL,		$382,200 84

CAPITAL STOCK.

Capital stock authorized by law,	$160,000 00	
Capital stock authorized by votes of company,	160,000 00	
Capital stock issued and outstanding,		$160,000 00
Number of shares issued and outstanding,	1,600	
Number of stockholders,	36	
Number of stockholders in Massachusetts,	35	
Amount of stock held in Massachusetts,	$157,500 00	

FUNDED DEBT.

DESCRIPTION OF BONDS.	Rate of Interest.	Date of Maturity.	Amount Outstanding.	Interest Paid during the Year.
First mortgage bonds,	Per Cent. 5	July 1, 1921,	$160,000 00	$8,000 00

VOLUME OF TRAFFIC, ETC.

Number of passengers paying revenue carried during the year,	715,450
Number carried per mile of main railway track operated,	52,957
Number of car miles run,	172,361
Average number of persons employed,	23

Description of Equipment.

Description of Equipment.	Equipped for Electric Power.	Equipped with Fenders.	Equipped with Electric Heaters	Number of Motors.
Cars — Passenger Service.				
Box passenger cars,	6	6	6	12
Open passenger cars,	6	6	-	12
Total,	12	12	6	24
Cars — Other Service.				
Work cars,	1	1	-	2
Snow ploughs,	2	-	-	4

Railway Owned and Operated (by Electric Power).

Length of railway line,	13.510 miles.
Length of sidings, switches, etc.,	.350 "
Total, computed as single track,	13.860 "

Railway Located Outside of Public Ways.

Length of railway line,	2.089 miles.

Names of the several cities and towns in which the railways operated by the company are located: Marlborough, Southborough, Westborough and Grafton.

Grade Crossings with Railroads.

Grade Crossings with Railroads.	Number of Tracks at Crossing.	
	Railroad.	Railway.
Crossings of railways with railroads at grade (3 in number), viz: —		
With Grafton & Upton Railroad, at Westborough Street, Grafton,	1	1
With Grafton & Upton Railroad, at junction of Shrewsbury and Oak Streets, Grafton,	1	1
With New York, New Haven & Hartford Railroad, at Florence Street, Marlborough,	1	1
Total Number of Tracks at Crossings,	3	3

Number of above crossings at which *frogs* are inserted in the tracks, . 3

ACCIDENTS TO PERSONS.

(A detailed statement of each accident is on file in the office of the Board.)

KILLED AND INJURED.	FROM CAUSES BEYOND THEIR OWN CONTROL.		FROM THEIR OWN MISCONDUCT OR CARELESSNESS.		TOTAL.	
	Killed.	Injured.	Killed.	Injured.	Killed.	Injured.
Passengers,	-	2	-	-	-	2
Employees,	-	-	-	-	-	-
Other persons,	-	-	-	1	-	1
TOTALS,	-	2	-	1	-	3

CORPORATE NAME AND ADDRESS OF THE COMPANY.

MARLBOROUGH & WESTBOROUGH STREET RAILWAY COMPANY,

WESTBOROUGH, MASS.

NAMES AND BUSINESS ADDRESS OF PRINCIPAL OFFICERS.

William N. Davenport, *President*, Marlborough, Mass. Edward F. Blodgett, *Vice-President*, Leominster, Mass. Walter R. Dame, *Treasurer and Clerk of Corporation*, Clinton, Mass. Dame & Saunders, *General Counsel*, Clinton, Mass. Harry C. Garfield, *Superintendent*, Westborough, Mass.

NAMES AND RESIDENCE OF BOARD OF DIRECTORS.

William N. Davenport, Marlborough, Mass. Edward F. Blodgett, Leominster, Mass. George R. Damon, Leominster, Mass. Adams Franklin Brown, Westborough, Mass. Jerome Marble, Worcester, Mass. M. P. Clough, Lynn, Mass. Walter R. Dame, Clinton, Mass.

We hereby certify that the statements contained in the foregoing report are full, just and true.

WILLIAM N. DAVENPORT,
EDW. F. BLODGETT,
ADAMS F. BROWN,
GEO. R. DAMON,
WALTER R. DAME,
Directors.
WALTER R. DAME,
Treasurer.
HARRY C. GARFIELD,
Superintendent.

COMMONWEALTH OF MASSACHUSETTS.

SUFFOLK, ss. OCT. 26, 1904. Then personally appeared the above-named William N. Davenport, Edward F. Blodgett, George R. Damon, Walter R. Dame and Harry C. Garfield, and severally made oath that the foregoing certificate by them subscribed is, to the best of their knowledge and belief, true.

Before me, ADAMS F. BROWN,
Justice of the Peace.

COMMONWEALTH OF MASSACHUSETTS.

SUFFOLK, ss. BOSTON, Oct. 26, 1904. Then personally appeared the above-named Adams F. Brown, and made oath that the foregoing certificate by him subscribed is, to the best of his knowledge and belief, true.

Before me, W. N. DAVENPORT,
Justice of the Peace.

REPORT

OF THE

MARTHA'S VINEYARD STREET RAILWAY COMPANY

For the Year Ending September 30, 1904.

[Operated by the Cottage City & Edgartown Traction Company. No income reported.]

General Balance Sheet September 30, 1904.

Assets.	Dr.	
Cost of railway:		
Roadbed and tracks,	$4,636 48	
Electric line construction, including poles, wiring, feeder lines, etc.,	957 47	
Engineering and other expenses incident to construction,	820 34	
Total Cost of Railway Owned,		$6,414 29
Cost of equipment:		
Cars and other rolling stock and vehicles,	$800 00	
Electric equipment of same,	566 45	
Total Cost of Equipment Owned,		1,366 45
Cost of land and buildings: land necessary for operation of railway,		2,500 00
Total Permanent Investments,		$10,280 74
Cash and current assets: cash,		71 14
Total,		$10,351 88

Liabilities.	Cr.
Capital stock,	$9,167 50
Current liabilities: audited vouchers and accounts,	652 35
Profit and loss balance (surplus),	532 03
Total,	$10,351 88

Capital Stock.

Capital stock authorized by law,	$150,000 00	
Capital stock authorized by votes of company,	12,000 00	
Amount paid in on 120 shares not yet issued,		$9,167 50
Number of subscribers,	10	
Number of subscribers in Massachusetts,	10	
Amount of subscriptions held in Massachusetts,	$9,167 50	

RAILWAY OWNED.

Length of railway line, ...	1.100 miles.

CORPORATE NAME AND ADDRESS OF THE COMPANY.

MARTHA'S VINEYARD STREET RAILWAY COMPANY,

246 WASHINGTON STREET, BOSTON, MASS.

NAMES AND BUSINESS ADDRESS OF PRINCIPAL OFFICERS.

Albert E. Pond, *President*, 19 Congress Street, Boston, Mass. Harlan P. Leighton, *Treasurer*, 246 Washington Street, Boston, Mass. Winthrop Pattee, *Clerk of Corporation*, 7 Pemberton Square, Boston, Mass.

NAMES AND RESIDENCE OF BOARD OF DIRECTORS.

Albert E. Pond, Boston, Mass. Herbert W. Pattee, Reading, Mass. Harlan P. Leighton, Medford, Mass. Winthrop Pattee, Arlington, Mass. John F. Merrill, Quincy, Mass. M. H. Curley, Boston, Mass.

We hereby certify that the statements contained in the foregoing report are full, just and true.

ALBERT E. POND,
HARLAN P. LEIGHTON,
HERBERT W. PATTEE,
WINTHROP PATTEE,
Directors.
HARLAN P. LEIGHTON,
Treasurer.

COMMONWEALTH OF MASSACHUSETTS.

SUFFOLK, ss. DEC. 27, 1904. Then personally appeared the above-named Albert E. Pond and Harlan P. Leighton, and severally made oath that the foregoing certificate by them subscribed is, to the best of their knowledge and belief, true.

Before me, JOHN J. BOYLE, JR.
Justice of the Peace.

REPORT

OF THE

MEDFIELD & MEDWAY STREET RAILWAY COMPANY

For the Year ending September 30, 1904.

General Exhibit for the Year.		
Gross earnings from operation,		$19,552 98
Operating expenses,		15,607 18
Gross Income above Operating Expenses,		$3,945 80
Charges upon income accrued during the year:		
Interest on funded debt,	$5,000 00	
Interest and discount on unfunded debts and loans,	1,833 45	
Taxes, State and local, . . . $378 85		
Taxes, commutation, . . . 232 32	611 17	
Total Charges and Deductions from Income,		7,444 62
Deficit for the year ending September 30, 1904,		$3,498 82
Amount of deficit September 30, 1903,		3,706 53
Total Deficit September 30, 1904,		$7,205 35

Earnings from Operation.	
Receipts from passengers carried,	$19,400 00
Receipts from advertising in cars,	114 88
Other earnings from operation: chartered cars,	38 10
Gross Earnings from Operation,	$19,552 98

Expenses of Operation.	
General expenses:	
Salaries of general officers and clerks,	$681 57
General office expenses and supplies,	38 04
Legal expenses,	97 80
Other general expenses:	
Advertising,	10 20
Miscellaneous general expenses,	246 06

Maintenance of roadway and buildings:		
Repair of roadbed and track,		$212 37
Repair of electric line construction,		1,052 96
Maintenance of equipment:		
Repair of cars and other vehicles,		361 66
Repair of electric equipment of cars,		172 00
Transportation expenses:		
Cost of electric motive power,		4,826 03
Wages and compensation of persons employed in conducting transportation,		6,480 07
Removal of snow and ice,		449 14
Damages for injuries to persons and property,		38 00
Rentals of buildings and other property,		453 67
Other transportation expenses:		
Cleaning, oiling and sanding tracks,		469 04
Miscellaneous car service supplies and expenses,		18 57
TOTAL OPERATING EXPENSES,		$15,607 18

GENERAL BALANCE SHEET SEPTEMBER 30, 1904.

ASSETS.	DR.	
Cost of railway:		
Roadbed and tracks,	$151,226 77	
Electric line construction, including poles, wiring, feeder lines, etc.,	50,607 12	
Interest accrued during construction of railway,	1,086 41	
Engineering and other expenses incident to construction,	11,868 37	
TOTAL COST OF RAILWAY OWNED,		$214,788 67
Cost of equipment:		
Cars and other rolling stock and vehicles,	$15,415 28	
Electric equipment of same,	5,861 87	
Other items of equipment,	42 88	
TOTAL COST OF EQUIPMENT OWNED,		21,320 03
Cost of land and buildings: land necessary for operation of railway,		1,352 39
TOTAL PERMANENT INVESTMENTS,		$237,461 09
Cash and current assets:		
Cash,	$317 90	
Bills and accounts receivable,	900 00	
TOTAL CASH AND CURRENT ASSETS,		1,217 90
Profit and loss balance (deficit),		7,205 35
TOTAL,		$245,884 34

LIABILITIES.	CR.
Capital stock,	$100,000 00
Funded debt,	100,000 00

Current liabilities:		
Loans and notes payable,	$29,264 58	
Audited vouchers and accounts,	14,059 85	
Miscellaneous current liabilities: outstanding tickets,	17 36	
TOTAL CURRENT LIABILITIES,		$43,341 79
Accrued liabilities: interest accrued and not yet due,		2,542 55
TOTAL,		$245,884 34

CAPITAL STOCK.

Capital stock authorized by law,	$100,000 00	
Capital stock authorized by votes of company,	100,000 00	
Capital stock issued and outstanding,		$100,000 00
Number of shares issued and outstanding,	1,000	
Number of stockholders,	13	
Number of stockholders in Massachusetts,	13	
Amount of stock held in Massachusetts,	$100,000 00	

FUNDED DEBT.

DESCRIPTION OF BONDS.	Rate of Interest.	Date of Maturity.	Amount Outstanding.	Interest Paid during the Year.
First mortgage gold bonds,	Per Cent. 5	July 1, 1920,	$100,000 00	$5,000 00

VOLUME OF TRAFFIC, ETC.

Number of passengers paying revenue carried during the year,	392,704
Number carried per mile of main railway track operated,	35,671
Number of car miles run,	116,684
Average number of persons employed,	18

DESCRIPTION OF EQUIPMENT.

DESCRIPTION OF EQUIPMENT.	Equipped for Electric Power.	Not Equipped.	Total Passenger Cars.	Equipped with Fenders.	Equipped with Electric Heaters.	Number of Motors.
CARS — PASSENGER SERVICE.						
Box passenger cars,	2	3	5	2	2	-
Open passenger cars,	3	-	3	3	-	-
TOTAL,	5	3	8	5	2	10
Snow ploughs,	2	-	-	-	-	-

RAILWAY OWNED AND OPERATED (BY ELECTRIC POWER).

Length of railway line,	11.009 miles.
Length of sidings, switches, etc.,	.241 "
Total, computed as single track,	11.250 "

Names of the several cities and towns in which the railways operated by the company are located: Medfield, Millis, Medway and Franklin.

GRADE CROSSINGS WITH RAILROADS.

GRADE CROSSINGS WITH RAILROADS.	NUMBER OF TRACKS AT CROSSING.	
	Railroad.	Railway.
Crossings of railways with railroads at grade (1 in number), viz.:— With New York, New Haven & Hartford Railroad, Main Street, Medfield,	2	1

Number of above crossings at which *frogs* are inserted in the tracks, . 1

ACCIDENTS TO PERSONS.

(A detailed statement of each accident is on file in the office of the Board.)

KILLED AND INJURED.	FROM CAUSES BEYOND THEIR OWN CONTROL.		FROM THEIR OWN MISCONDUCT OR CARELESSNESS.		TOTAL.	
	Killed.	Injured.	Killed.	Injured.	Killed.	Injured.
Passengers,	-	-	-	2	-	2
Employees,	-	-	-	-	-	-
Other persons,	-	-	1	1	1	1
TOTALS,	-	-	1	3	1	3

CORPORATE NAME AND ADDRESS OF THE COMPANY.

MEDFIELD & MEDWAY STREET RAILWAY COMPANY,

WESTWOOD, MASS.

NAMES AND BUSINESS ADDRESS OF PRINCIPAL OFFICERS.

Fred S. Gore, *President and General Manager*, 54 Kilby Street, Boston, Mass. Charles N. Chase, *Treasurer*, 28 State Street, Boston, Mass. James A. Fitton, *Clerk of Corporation*, 85 Water Street, Boston, Mass. Ezra E. Savage, *Superintendent*, Westwood, Mass.

NAMES AND RESIDENCE OF BOARD OF DIRECTORS.

Fred S. Gore, Dorchester, Mass. John F. Merrill, Quincy, Mass. James A. Fitton, Dorchester, Mass. Edward E. Blodgett, Brookline, Mass. John R. Graham, Quincy, Mass. Charles N. Chase, Stoughton, Mass. Hiram M. Burton, Winchester, Mass.

We hereby certify that the statements contained in the foregoing report are full, just and true.

FRED S. GORE,
JOHN F. MERRILL,
CHARLES N. CHASE,
JAMES A. FITTON,
Directors.
CHARLES N. CHASE,
Treasurer.
EZRA E. SAVAGE,
Superintendent.

COMMONWEALTH OF MASSACHUSETTS.

SUFFOLK, ss. BOSTON, Oct. 15, 1904. Then personally appeared the above-named Fred S. Gore, John F. Merrill, Charles N. Chase, James A. Fitton and Ezra E. Savage, and severally made oath that the foregoing certificate by them subscribed is, to the best of their knowledge and belief, true.

Before me, ROBERT E. GOODWIN,
Justice of the Peace.

REPORT

OF THE

MIDDLEBOROUGH, WAREHAM & BUZZARDS BAY STREET RAILWAY COMPANY

For the Period ending February 29, 1904.

[Railway in hands of receivers, March 1, 1904.]

General Exhibit for the Period.		
Gross earnings from operation,		$12,354 45
Operating expenses,		13,300 87
Net Deficit from Operation,		$946 42
Miscellaneous income: sales — old material, $95.09; horse, $60,		155 09
Gross Deficit above Operating Expenses,		$791 33
Deficit for the period ending February 29, 1904,		$791 33
Amount of surplus September 30, 1903,		7,356 58
Debits to profit and loss account during the year:		
Error in 1903 in report of salary,	$1,800 00	
Error in 1903 in report of bills payable,	8,706 70	
Total Debits,		10,506 70
Total Deficit February 29, 1904,		$3,941 45

Earnings from Operation.	
Receipts from passengers carried,	$12,019 20
Receipts from carriage of express and parcels,	195 25
Receipts from advertising in cars,	140 00
Gross Earnings from Operation,	$12,354 45

Expenses of Operation.	
General expenses:	
Salaries of general officers and clerks,	$860 00
General office expenses and supplies,	145 70
Insurance,	932 50
Other general expenses: general expenses, $73.01; advertising, $62.71; amusements, $90; February cash not posted, $377.20,	602 92

Maintenance of roadway and buildings:	
Repair of roadbed and track,	$51 65
Repair of electric line construction,	51 39
Repair of buildings,	1 40
Maintenance of equipment:	
Repair of cars and other vehicles,	219 27
Repair of electric equipment of cars,	433 28
Provender and stabling for horses,	69 47
Transportation expenses:	
Cost of electric motive power,	4,205 71
Wages and compensation of persons employed in conducting transportation,	4,877 48
Removal of snow and ice,	492 26
Rentals of buildings and other property,	1 00
Other transportation expenses,	356 81
TOTAL OPERATING EXPENSES,	$13,300 87

GENERAL BALANCE SHEET FEBRUARY 29, 1904.

ASSETS.	DR.	
Cost of railway:		
Roadbed and tracks,	$298,601 22	
Electric line construction, including poles, wiring, feeder lines, etc.,	106,713 76	
Interest accrued during construction of railway,	17,030 47	
Engineering and other expenses incident to construction,	18,958 04	
Other items of railway cost: bridges and culverts,	32,826 08	
TOTAL COST OF RAILWAY OWNED,		$474,129 57
Cost of equipment:		
Cars and other rolling stock and vehicles,	$75,189 37	
Electric equipment of same,	42,552 17	
Other items of equipment: tools,	2,644 81	
TOTAL COST OF EQUIPMENT OWNED,		120,386 35
Cost of land and buildings:		
Land necessary for operation of railway,	$3,000 00	
Buildings necessary for operation of railway,	13,346 12	
TOTAL COST OF LAND AND BUILDINGS OWNED,		16,346 12
TOTAL PERMANENT INVESTMENTS,		$610,862 04
Cash and current assets:		
Cash,	$13 65	
Bills and accounts receivable,	2,527 76	
Other cash and current assets: balance of cash used by contractor to date, sundry debits and credits in general cash book,	4,639 41	
TOTAL CASH AND CURRENT ASSETS,		7,180 82
Profit and loss balance (deficit),		3,941 45
TOTAL,		$621,984 31

LIABILITIES. CR.	
Capital stock,	$150,000 00
Funded debt,	150,000 00
Current liabilities: loans and notes payable, vouchers and accounts,	321,984 31
TOTAL,	$621,984 31

The foregoing balance sheet is drawn from the records of the corporation now in our hands.

Any discrepancies between the foregoing and that for the previous year are to be found in the aforesaid records.

Receivers of the Middleborough, Wareham & Buzzards Bay Street Railway Company.

CAPITAL STOCK.		
Capital stock authorized by law,	$150,000 00	
Capital stock authorized by votes of company,	150,000 00	
Capital stock issued and outstanding,		$150,000 00
Number of shares issued and outstanding,	1,500	
Number of stockholders,	93	
Number of stockholders in Massachusetts,	93	
Amount of stock held in Massachusetts,	$150,000 00	

FUNDED DEBT.

DESCRIPTION OF BONDS.	Rate of Interest.	Date of Maturity.	Amount Outstanding.	Interest Paid during the Year.
First mortgage gold bonds,	Per Cent. 5	1921,	$150,000 00	-

DESCRIPTION OF EQUIPMENT.

DESCRIPTION OF EQUIPMENT.	Equipped for Electric Power.	Not equipped.	Total Passenger Cars.	Equipped with Fenders.	Equipped with Electric Heaters.	Number of Motors.
CARS — PASSENGER SERVICE.						
Box passenger cars,	8	-	8	8	8	20
Open passenger cars,	15	2	17	17	-	36
TOTAL,	23	2	25	25	8	56
CARS — OTHER SERVICE.						
Box freight cars,	1	-	-	-	-	4
Platform freight cars,	-	2	-	-	-	-
Other cars,	-	1	-	-	-	-
TOTAL,	1	3	-	-	-	4
Snow ploughs,	-	4	-	-	-	-

MISCELLANEOUS EQUIPMENT.

Highway vehicles: express wagon, ...	1

RAILWAY OWNED AND OPERATED (BY ELECTRIC POWER).

RAILWAY OWNED, ETC.	Owned.	Trackage over Other Railways.	Total Owned, etc.
	Miles.	Miles.	Miles.
Length of railway line, ...	21.451	4.012	25.463
Length of second main track, ...	-	3.277	3.277
TOTAL LENGTH OF MAIN TRACK, ...	21.451	7.289	28.740
Length of sidings, switches, etc., ...	.813	.188	1.001
TOTAL, COMPUTED AS SINGLE TRACK, ...	22.264	7.477	29.741

RAILWAY LOCATED OUTSIDE OF PUBLIC WAYS.

Length of railway line, ...	5 382 miles.
Length of second main track, ...	1.856 "
Total length of main track, ...	7.238 "

Names of the several cities and towns in which the railways operated by the company are located: Middleborough, Rochester, Wareham and Bourne.

GRADE CROSSINGS WITH RAILROADS.

GRADE CROSSINGS WITH RAILROADS.	NUMBER OF TRACKS AT CROSSING.	
	Railroad.	Railway.
Crossings of railways with railroads at grade (2 in number), viz.:—		
With New York, New Haven & Hartford Railroad, spur track just east of Wareham Narrows Bridge, Wareham, Mass, . .	1	1
With New York, New Haven & Hartford Railroad, at Bourne Station, Mass., ...	1	1
TOTAL NUMBER OF TRACKS AT CROSSINGS, ...	2	2

ACCIDENTS TO PERSONS.

(A detailed statement of each accident is on file in the office of the Board.)

KILLED AND INJURED.	FROM CAUSES BEYOND THEIR OWN CONTROL.		FROM THEIR OWN MISCONDUCT OR CARELESSNESS.		TOTAL.	
	Killed.	Injured.	Killed.	Injured.	Killed.	Injured.
Passengers, ...	-	-	-	-	-	-
Employees, ...	-	-	-	-	-	-
Other persons, ...	-	-	-	1	-	1
TOTALS, ...	-	-	-	1	-	1

Corporate Name and Address of the Company.

MIDDLEBOROUGH, WAREHAM & BUZZARDS BAY STREET RAILWAY COMPANY,

Middleborough, Mass.

Names and Business Address of Principal Officers.

A. M. Bearse, *President*, Middleborough, Mass. Edwin F. Witham, *Vice-President*, Middleborough, Mass. Thomas F. Carey, *Treasurer and Clerk of Corporation*, Boston, Mass. Nathan Washburn, *General Counsel*, Middleborough, Mass. Horace B. Parker, *General Manager*, Boston, Mass. Charles H. Cox, *Superintendent*, Middleborough, Mass.

Names and Residence of Board of Directors.

A. M. Bearse, Middleborough, Mass. Edwin F. Witham, Middleborough, Mass. Nathan Washburn, Middleborough, Mass. Thomas F. Carey, Boston, Mass. C. S. Gleason, Wareham, Mass. B. F. Bourne, Bourne, Mass. C. S. Cummings, 2d, Boston, Mass. S. E. Whitaker, Boston, Mass.

We hereby certify that the statements contained in the foregoing report are full, just and true, according to the records of the corporation now in our hands.

J. T. BURNETT,
JOHN L. HALL,
Receivers.

Commonwealth of Massachusetts.

Suffolk, ss. Oct. 26, 1904. Then personally appeared the above-named John T. Burnett and John L. Hall, and severally made oath that the foregoing certificate by them subscribed is, to the best of their knowledge and belief, true.

Before me, JOSHUA M. SEARS, Jr.,
Justice of the Peace.

REPORT

OF THE

RECEIVERS OF THE MIDDLEBOROUGH, WAREHAM & BUZZARDS BAY STREET RAILWAY

FOR THE PERIOD FROM MARCH 1 TO SEPTEMBER 30, 1904.

The Circuit Court of the United States for District of Massachusetts authorized the receivers of the Middleborough, Wareham & Buzzards Bay Street Railway Company to borrow $20,110.57 on receivers' certificates to be issued by them. Of this amount $15,000 has been borrowed.

The object of this so-called "budget" was to pay off some preferred claims — as taxes, etc., and to put the road in a condition where it might be safely operated.

It has been expended as follows: —

Materials and repairs of equipment of track,	$2,165 49
Labor and power,	2,650 44
Taxes,	2,176 20
Insurance, interest on mortgage, current expenses, etc.,	5,532 32
Cash on hand,	2,515 55
	$15,000 00

Receivers of the Middleborough, Wareham & Buzzards Bay Street Railway Company.

GENERAL EXHIBIT FOR THE PERIOD.			
Gross earnings from operation,			$26,938 14
Operating expenses,			15,854 49
GROSS INCOME ABOVE OPERATING EXPENSES,			$11,083 65
Charges upon income accrued during the period:			
Interest on funded debt,		$3,858 23	
Taxes, State and local,	$185 69		
Taxes, commutation,	269 38		
		455 07	
TOTAL CHARGES AND DEDUCTIONS FROM INCOME,			4,313 30
TOTAL SURPLUS SEPTEMBER 30, 1904,			$6,770 35

Earnings from Operation.

Receipts from passengers carried,	$26,339 60
Receipts from carriage of freight,	571 87
Receipts from advertising in cars,	23 33
Receipts from interest on deposits,	3 34
Gross Earnings from Operation,	$26,938 14

Expenses of Operation.

General expenses:	
Salaries and general office expenses and supplies,	$305 92
Legal expenses,	22 60
Insurance,	1,085 01
Maintenance of roadway and buildings: repair of roadbed and track,	291 76
Maintenance of equipment: repair of cars and other vehicles, and repair of electric equipment of cars,	848 54
Transportation expenses:	
Cost of electric motive power,	6,008 55
Wages and compensation of persons employed in conducting transportation,	4,924 72
Tolls for trackage over other railways,	961 69
Rentals of buildings and other property,	1,060 81
Other transportation expenses: advertising, $32.86; transportation sundries, $312 03,	344 89
Total Operating Expenses,	$15,854 49

General Balance Sheet September 30, 1904.

Assets. Dr.		
Cash and current assets: cash,		$8,666 06
Miscellaneous assets: expenditures, cash, etc., as per budget account,		15,000 00
Total,		$23,666 06

Liabilities. Cr.		
Current liabilities:		
Receivers' certificates,	$15,000 00	
Audited vouchers and accounts,	1,623 48	
Total Current Liabilities,		$16,623 48
Accrued liabilities: taxes accrued and not yet due,		272 23
Profit and loss balance (surplus),		6,770 35
Total,		$23,666 06

Volume of Traffic, etc.

Number of passengers paying revenue carried during the period,	528,782
Number carried per mile of main railway track operated,	183,988
Number of car miles run,	117,500
Average number of persons employed,	26
Receivers commenced operation March 1, 1904.	

CORPORATE NAME AND ADDRESS OF THE COMPANY.

RECEIVERS OF THE MIDDLEBOROUGH, WAREHAM & BUZZARDS BAY STREET RAILWAY COMPANY,

705 SEARS BUILDING, BOSTON, MASS.

NAMES AND RESIDENCE OF THE RECEIVERS.

John T. Burnett, Southborough, Mass., John L. Hall, Boston, Mass.

We hereby certify that the statements contained in the foregoing report are full, just and true.

JOHN T. BURNETT,
JOHN L. HALL,
Receivers.

COMMONWEALTH OF MASSACHUSETTS.

SUFFOLK, ss. OCT. 31, 1904. Then personally appeared the above-named John T. Burnett and John L. Hall, and severally made oath that the foregoing certificate by them subscribed is, to the best of their knowledge and belief, true.

Before me, JOSHUA M. SEARS, JR.,
Justice of the Peace.

REPORT

OF THE

MILFORD, ATTLEBOROUGH & WOONSOCKET STREET RAILWAY COMPANY

For the Year ending September 30, 1904.

General Exhibit for the Year.

Gross earnings from operation,		$78,874 76
Operating expenses,		57,905 89
Gross Income above Operating Expenses,		$20,968 87
Charges upon income accrued during the year:		
Interest on funded debt,	$12,500 00	
Interest and discount on unfunded debts and loans,	911 69	
Taxes, State and local,	3,300 89	
Total Charges and Deductions from Income,		16,712 58
Surplus for the year ending September 30, 1904,		$4,256 29
Amount of surplus September 30, 1903,		12,939 90
Total Surplus September 30, 1904,		$17,196 19

Earnings from Operation.

Receipts from passengers carried,	$77,702 61
Receipts from rentals of buildings and other property,	902 15
Receipts from advertising in cars,	270 00
Gross Earnings from Operation,	$78,874 76

Expenses of Operation.

General expenses:	
Salaries of general officers and clerks,	$1,248 00
General office expenses and supplies,	278 00
Legal expenses,	86 00
Insurance,	1,837 45
Other general expenses: oils, salt, etc.,	1,061 74
Maintenance of roadway and buildings:	
Repair of roadbed and track,	3,935 19
Repair of electric line construction,	331 00
Repair of buildings,	116 00
Maintenance of equipment:	
Repair of cars and other vehicles,	4,913 71
Repair of electric equipment of cars,	3,548 30

Transportation expenses:		
Cost of electric motive power, $17,048.11; less power sold, $3,314; net,		$13,734 11
Wages and compensation of persons employed in conducting transportation,		23,349 99
Removal of snow and ice,		819 55
Damages for injuries to persons and property,		1,826 47
Tolls for trackage over other railways,		366 46
Rentals of buildings and other property,		267 92
Other transportation expenses: advertising, time tables, etc.,		186 00
TOTAL OPERATING EXPENSES,		$57,905 89

PROPERTY ACCOUNTS.

Additions to land and buildings: additional equipment of power stations,		$518 68
Additions to other permanent property:		
Building at Hoag Lake,	$259 02	
Interest on disputed construction bill,	73 30	
TOTAL ADDITIONS TO OTHER PERMANENT PROPERTY,		332 32
TOTAL ADDITIONS TO PROPERTY ACCOUNTS,		$851 00

GENERAL BALANCE SHEET SEPTEMBER 30, 1904.

ASSETS.	DR.	
Cost of railway:		
Roadbed and tracks,	$287,799 63	
Electric line construction, including poles, wiring, feeder lines, etc.,	71,904 70	
Interest accrued during construction of railway,	17,396 83	
Engineering and other expenses incident to construction,	10,558 59	
TOTAL COST OF RAILWAY OWNED,		$387,659 75
Cost of equipment: cars and other rolling stock and vehicles, and electric equipment of same,		82,493 47
Cost of land and buildings:		
Land necessary for operation of railway,	$6,405 02	
Electric power stations, including equipment,	80,932 79	
TOTAL COST OF LAND AND BUILDINGS OWNED,		87,337 81
Other permanent property: tenements and buildings at Hoag Lake,		31,414 86
TOTAL PERMANENT INVESTMENTS,		$588,905 89
Cash and current assets:		
Cash,	$2,138 98	
Bills and accounts receivable,	24,458 56	
Other cash and current assets: prepaid insurance,	965 12	
TOTAL CASH AND CURRENT ASSETS,		27,562 66
TOTAL,		$616,468 55

LIABILITIES.	CR.	
Capital stock,		$315,000 00
Funded debt,		250,000 00
Current liabilities:		
Loans and notes payable,	$26,000 00	
Audited vouchers and accounts,	8,272 36	
TOTAL CURRENT LIABILITIES,		34,272 36
Profit and loss balance (surplus),		17,196 19
TOTAL,		$616,468 55

CAPITAL STOCK.

Capital stock authorized by law,	$315,000 00	
Capital stock authorized by votes of company,	315,000 00	
Capital stock issued and outstanding,		$315,000 00
Number of shares issued and outstanding,	3,150	
Number of stockholders,	65	
Number of stockholders in Massachusetts,	65	
Amount of stock held in Massachusetts,	$315,000 00	

FUNDED DEBT.

DESCRIPTION OF BONDS.	Rate of Interest.	Date of Maturity.	Amount Outstanding.	Interest Paid during the Year.
First mortgage bonds,	Per Cent. 5	Oct. 1, 1919,	$250,000 00	$12,500 00

VOLUME OF TRAFFIC, ETC.

Number of passengers paying revenue carried during the year,	$1,558,528
Number carried per mile of main railway track operated,	51,951
Number of car miles run,	553,100
Average number of persons employed,	45

DESCRIPTION OF EQUIPMENT.

DESCRIPTION OF EQUIPMENT.	Equipped for Electric Power.	Equipped with Fenders.	Equipped with Electric Heaters.	Number of Motors.
CARS — PASSENGER SERVICE.				
Box passenger cars,	10	4	10	-
Open passenger cars,	16	6	-	-
TOTAL,	26	10	10	86
Snow ploughs,	3	-	-	3

Miscellaneous Equipment.

Highway vehicles: tower wagon, ...	1

Railway Owned and Operated (by Electric Power).

Length of railway line, ...	30.000 miles.
Length of sidings, switches, etc., ...	.520 "
Total, computed as single track, ...	30.520 "

Railway Located Outside of Public Ways.

Length of railway line, ...	5.725 miles.

Names of the several cities and towns in which the railways operated by the company are located: Milford, Mendon, Bellingham, Hopedale, Franklin and Wrentham.

Grade Crossings with Railroads.

Grade Crossings with Railroads.	Number of Tracks at Crossing.	
	Railroad.	Railway.
Crossings of railways with railroads at grade (1 in number), viz.: — With Grafton & Upton Railroad, at South Main Street, Milford, .	1	1

Number of above crossings at which *frogs* are inserted in the tracks, . 1

Accidents to Persons.

(A detailed statement of each accident is on file in the office of the Board.)

Killed and Injured.	From Causes beyond their own Control.		From their own Misconduct or Carelessness.		Total.	
	Killed.	Injured.	Killed.	Injured.	Killed.	Injured.
Passengers, ...	-	4	-	3	-	7
Employees, ...	-	-	-	-	-	-
Other persons, ...	-	-	3	-	3	-
Totals, ...	-	4	3	3	3	7

Corporate Name and Address of the Company.

MILFORD, ATTLEBOROUGH & WOONSOCKET STREET RAILWAY COMPANY,

Franklin, Mass.

NAMES AND BUSINESS ADDRESS OF PRINCIPAL OFFICERS.

George W. Wiggin, *President and General Counsel*, Franklin, Mass. Edgar K. Ray, *Treasurer and General Manager*, Woonsocket, R. I. Wm. H. Tyler, *Clerk of Corporation*, Worcester, Mass. Herbert M. Young, *Superintendent*, Woonsocket, R. I.

NAMES AND RESIDENCE OF BOARD OF DIRECTORS.

Edgar K. Ray, Franklin, Mass. George W. Wiggin, Franklin, Mass. James F. Ray, Franklin, Mass. Wm. S. Reed, Leominster, Mass. Wm. H. Tyler, Worcester, Mass. Chas. Shippee, Milford, Mass. Adelbert D. Thayer, Franklin, Mass. Harry G. Lowe, Waltham, Mass. John W. Knibs, Worcester, Mass.

We hereby certify that the statements contained in the foregoing report are full, just and true.

EDGAR K. RAY,
GEORGE W. WIGGIN,
WILLIAM S. REED,
CHAS. M. SHIPPEE,
JAMES F. RAY,
JOHN W. KNIBS,
Directors.
EDGAR K. RAY,
Treasurer.
HERBERT M. YOUNG,
Superintendent.

STATE OF RHODE ISLAND.

WOONSOCKET, R. I. OCT. 11, 1904. Then personally appeared the above-named Edgar K. Ray, treasurer, and Herbert M. Young, superintendent, and severally made oath that the foregoing certificate by them subscribed is, to the best of their knowledge and belief, true.

Before me, WINTHROP B. NYE,
Notary Public.

COMMONWEALTH OF MASSACHUSETTS.

NORFOLK, SS. FRANKLIN, Oct. 12, 1904. Then personally appeared the above-named George W. Wiggin, William S. Reed, Chas. W. Shippee, James F. Ray and John W. Knibs, and severally made oath that the foregoing certificate by them subscribed is, to the best of their knowledge and belief, true.

Before me, WILLIAM A. WYCKOFF,
Justice of the Peace.

REPORT

OF THE

MILFORD & UXBRIDGE STREET RAILWAY COMPANY

FOR THE YEAR ENDING SEPTEMBER 30, 1904.

GENERAL EXHIBIT FOR THE YEAR.			
Gross earnings from operation,			$142,744 68
Operating expenses,			108,010 56
GROSS INCOME ABOVE OPERATING EXPENSES,			$34,734 12
Charges upon income accrued during the year:			
Interest on funded debt,		$20,750 00	
Interest and discount on unfunded debts and loans,		3,034 05	
Taxes, State and local,	$7,393 76		
Taxes, commutation,	1,526 96		
		8,920 72	
Other deductions from income: amusements,		1,900 63	
TOTAL CHARGES AND DEDUCTIONS FROM INCOME,			34,605 40
NET DIVISIBLE INCOME,			$128 72
Dividends declared (1½ per cent),			6,600 00
Deficit for the year ending September 30, 1904,			$6,471 28
Amount of surplus September 30, 1903,			1,126 89
Credits to profit and loss account during the year: excise tax,			95 22
TOTAL DEFICIT SEPTEMBER 30, 1904,			$5,249 17

EARNINGS FROM OPERATION.	
Receipts from passengers carried,	$141,804 05
Receipts from carriage of mails,	364 26
Receipts from rentals of buildings and other property,	8 00
Receipts from advertising in cars,	416 64
Other earnings from operation: transportation of papers,	151 73
GROSS EARNINGS FROM OPERATION,	$142,744 68

EXPENSES OF OPERATION.	
General expenses:	
Salaries of general officers and clerks,	$4,956 55
General office expenses and supplies,	217 12
Legal expenses,	126 45
Insurance,	2,760 00
Other general expenses: printing, advertising, etc.,	1,709 28

Maintenance of roadway and buildings:		
Repair of roadbed and track,		$7,128 10
Repair of electric line construction,		1,997 85
Repair of buildings,		1,455 54
Maintenance of equipment:		
Repair of cars and other vehicles,		4,112 57
Repair of electric equipment of cars,		3,707 78
Transportation expenses:		
Cost of electric motive power, $35,389.14; less power sold, $13,627.80; net,		21,761 34
Wages and compensation of persons employed in conducting transportation,		39,766 60
Removal of snow and ice,		2,704 47
Damages for injuries to persons and property,		13,594 29
Other transportation expenses: oils, waste, etc.,		2,012 62
TOTAL OPERATING EXPENSES,		$108,010 56

PROPERTY ACCOUNTS.

Additions to railway: new electric line construction (length, 2,640 feet),		$620 50
Additions to equipment:		
Additional cars (1 in number),	$3,400 00	
Electric equipment of same,	2,675 50	
Other additional rolling stock and vehicles,	3,859 78	
Other additions to equipment: new motors,	9,893 66	
TOTAL ADDITIONS TO EQUIPMENT,		19,828 94
Additions to land and buildings:		
Additional land necessary for operation of railway,	$999 60	
Additional equipment of power stations,	212 80	
New buildings necessary for operation of railway,	99 09	
TOTAL ADDITIONS TO LAND AND BUILDINGS,		1,311 49
TOTAL ADDITIONS TO PROPERTY ACCOUNTS,		$21,760 93

GENERAL BALANCE SHEET SEPTEMBER 30, 1904.

ASSETS.	DR.	
Cost of railway:		
Roadbed and tracks,	$374,943 16	
Electric line construction, including poles, wiring, feeder lines, etc.,	104,330 51	
Engineering and other expenses incident to construction,	10,290 63	
TOTAL COST OF RAILWAY OWNED,		$489,564 30
Cost of equipment:		
Cars and other rolling stock and vehicles,	$71,041 55	
Electric equipment of same,	75,509 58	
Other items of equipment: heaters, registers, etc.,	36,525 95	
TOTAL COST OF EQUIPMENT OWNED,		183,077 08

Cost of land and buildings:		
Land necessary for operation of railway,	$7,546 30	
Electric power stations, including equipment,	152,069 55	
Other buildings necessary for operation of railway,	59,798 41	
TOTAL COST OF LAND AND BUILDINGS OWNED,		$219,414 26
Other permanent property: Nipmuc park property,		28,355 24
TOTAL PERMANENT INVESTMENTS,		$920,410 88
Cash and current assets:		
Cash,	$1,726 68	
Bills and accounts receivable,	2,198 90	
Other cash and current assets:		
Prepaid interest,	1,657 52	
Prepaid insurance,	2,524 70	
TOTAL CASH AND CURRENT ASSETS,		8,107 80
Miscellaneous assets:		
Materials and supplies,	$12,188 14	
Other assets and property: fuel on hand,	2,914 27	
TOTAL MISCELLANEOUS ASSETS,		15,102 41
Profit and loss balance (deficit),		5,249 17
TOTAL,		$948,870 26

LIABILITIES.	CR.	
Capital stock,		$440,000 00
Funded debt,		415,000 00
Current liabilities:		
Loans and notes payable,	$62,047 00	
Audited vouchers and accounts,	26,654 44	
TOTAL CURRENT LIABILITIES,		88,701 44
Accrued liabilities:		
Interest accrued and not yet due,	$3,641 86	
Taxes accrued and not yet due,	1,526 96	
TOTAL ACCRUED LIABILITIES,		5,168 82
TOTAL,		$948,870 26

CAPITAL STOCK.

Capital stock authorized by law,	$441,500 00	
Capital stock authorized by votes of company,	441,500 00	
Capital stock issued and outstanding,		$440,000 00
Number of shares issued and outstanding,	4,400	
Number of stockholders,	123	
Number of stockholders in Massachusetts,	19	
Amount of stock held in Massachusetts,	$86,700 00	

FUNDED DEBT.

Description of Bonds.	Rate of Interest.	Date of Maturity.	Amount Outstanding.	Interest Paid during the Year.
	Per Cent.			
First mortgage gold bonds,* . . .	5	Jan. 1, 1918, .	$165,000 00	$8,250 00
First mortgage gold bonds, . .	5	Jan. 1, 1918, .	50,000 00	2,500 00
First mortgage gold bonds, . .	5	Jan. 1, 1918, .	200,000 00	10,000 00
Totals, ...	. .	. . . .	$415,000 00	$20,750 00

VOLUME OF TRAFFIC, ETC.

Number of passengers paying revenue carried during the year, ...	2,749,065
Number carried per mile of main railway track operated, .	79,212
Number of car miles run, ...	676,136
Average number of persons employed, ...	100

DESCRIPTION OF EQUIPMENT.

Description of Equipment.	Equipped for Electric Power.	Equipped with Fenders.	Equipped with Electric Heaters.	Number of Motors.
Cars — Passenger Service.				
Box passenger cars, ...	21	21	21	-
Open passenger cars, ...	20	20	-	-
Total, ...	41	41	21	104
Cars — Other Service.				
Platform freight cars, ...	2	-	-	-
Snow ploughs, ...	8	-	-	-

MISCELLANEOUS EQUIPMENT.

Railway rolling stock:	
Snow leveller, ...	1
Walkaways, ...	2

* Milford, Holliston & Framingham Street Railway Company, now consolidated with Milford & Uxbridge Street Railway Company.

Railway Owned and Operated (by Electric Power).

Railway Owned, etc.	Owned.	Trackage over Other Railways.	Total Owned, etc.
	Miles.	Miles.	Miles.
Length of railway line,	33.689	.025	33.714
Length of second main track,	.991	-	.991
Total Length of Main Track,	34.680	.025	34.705
Length of sidings, switches, etc.,	1.226	-	1.226
Total, Computed as Single Track,	35.906	.025	35.931

Railway Located Outside of Public Ways.

Length of railway line,	5.025 miles.

Names of the several cities and towns in which the railways operated by the company are located: South Framingham, Ashland, Holliston, Milford, Hopedale, Mendon, Uxbridge, Medway, Bellingham and Hopkinton.

Grade Crossings with Railroads.

Grade Crossings with Railroads.	Number of Tracks at Crossing.	
	Railroad.	Railway.
Crossings of railways with railroads at grade (3 in number), viz.: —		
With Grafton & Upton Railroad, at Hopedale,	2	1
With New York, New Haven & Hartford Railroad, at Milford,	1	1
With Boston & Albany Railroad, at Hollis Street, South Framingham,	1	1
Total Number of Tracks at Crossings,	4	3

Number of above crossings at which *frogs* are inserted in the tracks, . 4

Accidents to Persons.

(A detailed statement of each accident is on file in the office of the Board.)

Killed and Injured.	From Causes beyond their own Control.		From their own Misconduct or Carelessness.		Total.	
	Killed.	Injured.	Killed.	Injured	Killed.	n ured.
Passengers,	-	3	1	1	1	4
Employees,	-	-	-	-	-	-
Other persons,	-	-	1	5	1	5
Totals,	-	3	2	6	2	9

Corporate Name and Address of the Company.

MILFORD & UXBRIDGE STREET RAILWAY COMPANY,

Milford, Mass.

Names and Business Address of Principal Officers.

John T. Manson, *President*, New Haven, Conn. Sydney Harwood, *Vice-President*, 53 State Street, Boston, Mass. James E. Walker, *Treasurer*, Milford, Mass. Wendell Williams, *Clerk of Corporation, General Counsel and Auditor*, Milford, Mass. Walter L. Adams, *Superintendent*, Milford, Mass.

Names and Residence of Board of Directors.

John T. Manson, New Haven, Conn. Sydney Harwood, Newton, Mass. Chas. E. Graham, New Haven, Conn. Herbert C. Fuller, New Haven, Conn. Geo. A. Draper, Hopedale, Mass. James E. Walker, Milford, Mass. J. Willis Downs, New Haven, Conn.

We hereby certify that the statements contained in the foregoing report are full, just and true.

J. WILLIS DOWNS,
CHAS. E. GRAHAM,
GEO. A. DRAPER,
JOHN T. MANSON,
J. E. WALKER,
Directors.
J. E. WALKER,
Treasurer.
W. L. ADAMS,
Superintendent.

Commonwealth of Massachusetts.

Worcester, ss. Oct. 25, 1904. Then personally appeared the above-named J. Willis Downs, Chas. E. Graham, George A. Draper, John T. Manson, J. E. Walker and W. L. Adams, and severally made oath that the foregoing certificate by them subscribed is, to the best of their knowledge and belief, true.

Before me, WENDELL WILLIAMS,
Justice of the Peace.

REPORT

OF THE

MOUNT TOM RAILROAD COMPANY

FOR THE YEAR ENDING SEPTEMBER 30, 1904.

[Leased to and operated by the Holyoke.]

GENERAL EXHIBIT FOR THE YEAR.	
Rental received from lease of railway,	$6,000 00
Income from other sources: interest on loan,	35 05
GROSS INCOME,	$6,035 05
Dividends declared (6 per cent),	6,000 00
Surplus for the year ending September 30, 1904,	$35 05
Amount of surplus September 30, 1903,	700 93
TOTAL SURPLUS SEPTEMBER 30, 1904,	$735 98

GENERAL BALANCE SHEET SEPTEMBER 30, 1904.	
ASSETS. DR.	
Cost of railway,	$58,216 46
Cost of equipment,	4,900 00
Cost of land and buildings,	36,883 54
TOTAL PERMANENT INVESTMENTS,	$100,000 00
Cash and current assets: bills and accounts receivable,	735 98
TOTAL,	$100,735 98
LIABILITIES. CR.	
Capital stock,	$100,000 00
Profit and loss balance (surplus),	735 98
TOTAL,	$100,735 98

CAPITAL STOCK.		
Capital stock authorized by law,	$100,000 00	
Capital stock authorized by votes of company,	100,000 00	
Capital stock issued and outstanding,		$100,000 00
Number of shares issued and outstanding,	1,000	
Number of stockholders,	98	
Number of stockholders in Massachusetts,	86	
Amount of stock held in Massachusetts,	$87,800 00	

RAILWAY OWNED.

Length of railway line, ...	.900 mile.
Length of sidings, switches, etc., ...	.100 "
Total, computed as single track, ...	1.000 "

RAILWAY LOCATED OUTSIDE OF PUBLIC WAYS.

Length of railway line, ...	.900 mile.

Names of the several cities and towns in which the railway owned by the company is located: Northampton.

CORPORATE NAME AND ADDRESS OF THE COMPANY.

MOUNT TOM RAILROAD COMPANY,

25 CANAL STREET, HOLYOKE, MASS.

NAMES AND BUSINESS ADDRESS OF PRINCIPAL OFFICERS.

William S. Loomis, *President, General Manager and Superintendent,* 25 Canal Street, Holyoke, Mass. Henry O. Hastings, *Treasurer,* 199 High Street, Holyoke, Mass. Louis D. Pellissier, *Clerk of Corporation,* 25 Canal Street, Holyoke, Mass. Brooks & Hamilton, *General Counsel,* Holyoke, Mass.

NAMES AND RESIDENCE OF BOARD OF DIRECTORS.

William S. Loomis, Holyoke, Mass. Frederick Harris, Springfield, Mass. Henry O. Hastings, Holyoke, Mass. N. Saxton Cooley, Windsor Locks, Conn. L. Clark Seelye, Northampton, Mass.

We hereby certify that the statements contained in the foregoing report are full, just and true.

WM. S. LOOMIS,
H. O. HASTINGS,
FREDERICK HARRIS,
Directors.
H. O. HASTINGS,
Treasurer.
WM. S. LOOMIS,
Superintendent.

COMMONWEALTH OF MASSACHUSETTS.

HAMPDEN, SS. OCT. 24, 1904. Then personally appeared the above-named Wm. S. Loomis, H. O. Hastings, and Frederick Harris, and severally made oath that the foregoing certificate by them subscribed is, to the best of their knowledge and belief, true,

Before me, THOMAS W. SPENCER,
Notary Public.

REPORT

OF THE

NATICK & COCHITUATE STREET RAILWAY COMPANY

FOR THE YEAR ENDING SEPTEMBER 30, 1904.

GENERAL EXHIBIT FOR THE YEAR.		
Gross earnings from operation,		$89,438 32
Operating expenses,		77,022 20
GROSS INCOME ABOVE OPERATING EXPENSES,		$12,416 12
Charges upon income accrued during the year:		
Interest and discount on unfunded debts and loans,	$6,343 26	
Taxes, State and local,	4,726 91	
TOTAL CHARGES AND DEDUCTIONS FROM INCOME,		11,070 17
NET DIVISIBLE INCOME,		$1,345 95
Dividends declared (2 per cent),		2,000 00
Deficit for the year ending September 30, 1904,		$654 05
Amount of surplus September 30, 1903,		13,967 90
Credits to profit and loss account during the year: unredeemed tickets,		157 32
TOTAL SURPLUS SEPTEMBER 30, 1904,		$13,471 17

EARNINGS FROM OPERATION.	
Receipts from passengers carried,	$86,156 73
Receipts from carriage of mails,	249 99
Receipts from carriage of express and parcels,	22 80
Receipts from rental of buildings and other property,	2,523 95
Receipts from advertising in cars,	390 00
Other earnings from operation:	
Discount,	23 25
Other sources,	71 60
GROSS EARNINGS FROM OPERATION,	$89,438 32

EXPENSES OF OPERATION.	
General expenses:	
Salaries of general officers and clerks,	$6,832 61
General office expenses and supplies,	1,741 71
Legal expenses,	647 50
Insurance,	843 87
Other general expenses: storeroom expense,	241 75

Maintenance of roadway and buildings:	
Repair of roadbed and track,	$5,785 08
Repair of electric line construction,	46 37
Repair of buildings,	80 01
Maintenance of equipment:	
Repair of cars and other vehicles,	3,765 89
Repair of electric equipment of cars,	4,803 65
Renewal of horses, harnesses, shoeing, etc., and provender and stabling for horses,	296 63
Transportation expenses:	
Cost of electric motive power,	18,709 30
Wages and compensation of persons employed in conducting transportation,	26,627 87
Removal of snow and ice,	1,739 81
Damages for injuries to persons and property,	4,307 82
Rentals of buildings and other property,	431 73
Other transportation expenses: miscellaneous shop expense,	120 60
TOTAL OPERATING EXPENSES,	$77,022 20

PROPERTY ACCOUNTS.

Additions to railway: new feeders and signal system,		$10,525 77
Additions to equipment:		
Additional cars (1 in number),	$2,300 00	
Electric equipment of same,	1,200 00	
Other additions to equipment:		
Registers and air brakes,	1,304 00	
Shop tools and machinery, $385.93; furniture and fixtures, $125.11,	511 04	
TOTAL ADDITIONS TO EQUIPMENT,		5,315 04
Additions to land and buildings:		
Additional land necessary for operation of railway,	$10,457 50	
Buildings necessary for operation of railway,	11,016 15	
TOTAL ADDITIONS TO LAND AND BUILDINGS,		21,473 65
TOTAL ADDITIONS TO PROPERTY ACCOUNTS,		$37,314 46
Deductions from property accounts (property sold or reduced in valuation and credited to property accounts): two car bodies and motors,		207 50
NET ADDITION TO PROPERTY ACCOUNTS FOR THE YEAR,		$37,106 96

GENERAL BALANCE SHEET SEPTEMBER 30, 1904.

ASSETS.	DR.	
Cost of railway:		
Roadbed and tracks,	$116,302 19	
Electric line construction, including poles, wiring, feeder lines, etc.,	41,018 09	
Engineering and other expenses incident to construction,	1,019 57	
TOTAL COST OF RAILWAY OWNED,		$158,339 85

Cost of equipment:		
Cars and other rolling stock and vehicles,	$32,513 49	
Electric equipment of same,	23,379 11	
Horses,	30 46	
Other items of equipment:		
Furniture and fixtures,	138 61	
Shop tools and machinery,	430 29	
TOTAL COST OF EQUIPMENT OWNED,		$56,491 96
Cost of land and buildings:		
Land necessary for operation of railway,	$13,427 50	
Buildings necessary for operation of railway,	17,998 76	
TOTAL COST OF LAND AND BUILDINGS OWNED,		31,426 26
TOTAL PERMANENT INVESTMENTS,		$246,258 07
Cash and current assets:		
Cash,	$1,912 24	
Bills and accounts receivable,	32,528 24	
TOTAL CASH AND CURRENT ASSETS,		34,440 48
Miscellaneous assets: unexpired insurance,		27 77
TOTAL,		$280,726 32

LIABILITIES.	CR.	
Capital stock,		$100,000 00
Current liabilities:		
Loans and notes payable,	$160,000 00	
Audited vouchers and accounts,	6,428 84	
Salaries and wages,	763 81	
TOTAL CURRENT LIABILITIES,		167,192 65
Accrued liabilities: interest accrued and not yet due,		62 50
Profit and loss balance (surplus),		13,471 17
TOTAL,		$280,726 32

CAPITAL STOCK.

Capital stock authorized by law,	$100,000 00	
Capital stock authorized by votes of company,	100,000 00	
Capital stock issued and outstanding,		$100,000 00
Number of shares issued and outstanding,	1,000	
Number of stockholders,	16	
Number of stockholders in Massachusetts,	16	
Amount of stock held in Massachusetts,	$100,000 00	

VOLUME OF TRAFFIC, ETC.

Number of passengers paying revenue carried during the year,	1,742,254
Number carried per mile of main railway track operated,	95,029
Number of car miles run,	527,618
Average number of persons employed,	61

Description of Equipment.

Description of Equipment.	Equipped for Electric Power.	Equipped with Fenders.	Equipped with Electric Heaters.	Number of Motors.
Cars — Passenger Service.				
Box passenger cars,	12	12	12	-
Open passenger cars,	16	16	-	-
Total,	28	28	12	60
Cars — Other Service.				
Platform freight cars,	1	-	-	-
Other cars,	1	-	-	-
Total,	2	-	-	-
Snow ploughs,	3	-	-	-

Miscellaneous Equipment.

Carts and snow sleds,	1
Other highway vehicles: tower wagon, express wagon, pung,	3
Horses,	1
Other items of equipment: harnesses,	2

Railway Owned and Operated (by Electric Power).

Railway Owned, etc.	Owned.	Trackage over Other Railways.	Total Owned, etc.
	Miles.	Miles.	Miles.
Length of railway line,	17.204	.284	17.488
Length of second main track,	.846	-	.846
Total Length of Main Track,	18.050	.284	18.334
Length of sidings, switches, etc.,	.750	-	.750
Total, Computed as Single Track,	18.800	.284	19.084

Names of the several cities and towns in which the railways operated by the company are located: Framingham, Natick, Needham, Wayland and Wellesley.

Grade Crossings with Railroads.

Grade Crossings with Railroads.	Number of Tracks at Crossing.	
	Railroad.	Railway.
Crossings of railways with railroads at grade (2 in number), viz.:—		
With Boston & Albany Railroad at Central Street, Wellesley (side track),	1	1
With Boston & Albany Railroad, at Washington Street, Wellesley (side track),	1	1
Total Number of Tracks at Crossings,	2	2

Accidents to Persons.

(A detailed statement of each accident is on file in the office of the Board.)

Killed and Injured.	From Causes beyond their own Control.		From their own Misconduct or Carelessness.		Total.	
	Killed.	Injured.	Killed.	Injured.	Killed.	Injured.
Passengers,	-	-	-	2	-	2
Employees,	-	-	-	-	-	-
Other persons,	-	-	-	1	-	1
Totals,	-	-	-	3	-	3

Corporate Name and Address of the Company.

NATICK & COCHITUATE STREET RAILWAY COMPANY,

Newtonville, Mass.

Names and Business Address of Principal Officers.

Harrison Harwood, *President*, Natick, Mass. Charles W. Smith, *Treasurer*, Newtonville, Mass. Frank W. Remick, *Clerk of Corporation*, Boston, Mass. Coolidge & Hight, *General Counsel*, Boston, Mass. Adams D. Claflin, *General Manager*, Newtonville, Mass.

Names and Residence of Board of Directors.

Harrison Harwood, Natick, Mass. Robert W. Harwood, Natick, Mass. Sydney Harwood, Newton, Mass. Frederic H. Lewis, Swampscott, Mass. Alden E. Viles, Boston, Mass. James L. Richards, Newtonville, Mass. Frank W. Remick, West Newton, Mass. William F. Hammett, Newton, Mass. Adams D. Claflin, Newton Centre, Mass.

We hereby certify that the statements contained in the foregoing report are full, just and true.

ADAMS D. CLAFLIN,
WILLIAM F. HAMMETT,
SYDNEY HARWOOD,
JAMES L. RICHARDS,
FREDERIC H. LEWIS,
HARRISON HARWOOD,
ALDEN E. VILES,
Directors.
CHAS. W. SMITH,
Treasurer.
ADAMS D. CLAFLIN,
General Manager.

Commonwealth of Massachusetts.

Suffolk, ss. Oct. 29, 1904. Then personally appeared the above-named Adams D. Claflin, William F. Hammett, Sydney Harwood, James L. Richards, Frederic H. Lewis, Harrison Harwood, Chas. W. Smith and Alden E. Viles, and severally made oath that the foregoing certificate by them subscribed is, to the best of their knowledge and belief, true.

Before me, GEO. M. COX,
Notary Public.

REPORT

OF THE

NATICK & NEEDHAM STREET RAILWAY COMPANY

For the Year ending September 30, 1904.

[Railway in hands of a receiver and not in operation.]

General Exhibit for the Year.		
Sale of old material,		$48 21
Expenses and charges upon income accrued during the year: interest on funded debt,		2,500 00
Deficit for the year ending September 30, 1904,		$2,451 79
Amount of surplus September 30, 1903,		500 00
Debits to profit and loss account during the year: accrued rental not received,		500 00
Total Deficit September 30, 1904,		$2,451 79

General Balance Sheet September 30, 1904.		
Assets.	Dr.	
Cost of railway:		
Roadbed and tracks,	$54,409 25	
Electric line construction, including poles, wiring, feeder lines, etc,	8,201 91	
Interest accrued during construction of railway,	3,760 28	
Total Cost of Railway Owned,		$66,371 44
Cost of equipment:		
Cars and other rolling stock and vehicles,	$9,400 00	
Electric equipment of same,	12,400 00	
Other items of equipment: air brakes, snow plough, etc.,	2,950 00	
Total Cost of Equipment Owned,		24,750 00
Cost of land and buildings: land necessary for operation of railway,		1,050 00
Total Permanent Investments,		$92,171 44
Cash and current assets: cash,		260 77
Profit and loss balance (deficit),		2,451 79
Total,		$94,884 00

Liabilities. Cr.	
Capital stock,	$50,000 00
Funded debt,	42,384 00
Current liabilities: matured interest coupons unpaid (including coupons due October 1),	2,500 00
Total,	$94,884 00

Capital Stock.		
Capital stock authorized by law,	$50,000 00	
Capital stock authorized by votes of company,	50,000 00	
Capital stock issued and outstanding,		$50,000 00
Number of shares issued and outstanding,	500	
Number of stockholders,	11	
Number of stockholders in Massachusetts,	11	
Amount of stock held in Massachusetts,	$50,000 00	

Funded Debt.

Description of Bonds.	Rate of Interest.	Date of Maturity.	Amount Outstanding.	Interest Paid during the Year.
	Per Cent.			
First mortgage bonds,	5	Feb. 1, 1921,	$50,000 00	-
Less paid by sale of wire,	. .	. . .	7,616 00	-
Totals,	. .	. . .	$42,384 00	-

Railway Owned.

Length of railway line,	5.774 miles.
Length of sidings, switches, etc.,	.048 "
Total, computed as single track,	5.822 "

Railway Owned and Located Outside of Public Ways.

Length of railway line,	.185 mile.

Names of the several cities and towns in which the railway owned by the company is located: Natick, Needham and Dover.

General Remarks and Explanations.

The property of this company is in the custody of N. Sumner Myrick, receiver, and the report is that of the corporation and of the receiver.

The receiver, under authority of the court, ceased operating the railway in Jannary, 1904.

CORPORATE NAME AND ADDRESS OF THE COMPANY.

NATICK & NEEDHAM STREET RAILWAY COMPANY,

SOUTH FRAMINGHAM, MASS.

NAMES AND BUSINESS ADDRESS OF PRINCIPAL OFFICERS.

N. Sumner Myrick, *President and Receiver*, 601 Barristers' Hall, Boston, Mass. Andrew F. Mars, *Treasurer and Clerk of Corporation*, South Framingham, Mass.

NAMES AND RESIDENCE OF BOARD OF DIRECTORS.

N. Sumner Myrick, Wellesley, Mass. Harvey H. Whitney, Natick, Mass. Chandler Hovey, Chestnut Hill, Mass. Reginald Bradlee, Medford, Mass. Daniel W. Weeks, Medford, Mass. Sidney Gleason, Medford, Mass. Frank S. Jones, Boston, Mass.

I hereby certify that the statements contained in the foregoing report are full, just and true.

N. SUMNER MYRICK,
Receiver.

COMMONWEALTH OF MASSACHUSETTS.

SUFFOLK, ss. Nov. 30, 1904. Then personally appeared the above-named N. Sumner Myrick, receiver, and made oath that the foregoing certificate by him subscribed is, to the best of his knowledge and belief, true.

Before me, CHARLES N. HARRIS,
Justice of the Peace.

REPORT

OF THE

NEW BEDFORD & ONSET STREET RAILWAY COMPANY

For the Year ending September 30, 1904.

General Exhibit for the Year.

Gross earnings from operation,			$65,279 08
Operating expenses,			37,959 95
Gross Income above Operating Expenses,			$27,319 13
Charges upon income accrued during the year:			
Interest on funded debt,		$14,000 00	
Interest and discount on unfunded debts and loans,		3,525 46	
Taxes, State and local,	$5,865 05		
Taxes, commutation,	570 05		
		6,435 10	
Total Charges and Deductions from Income,			23,960 56
Surplus for the year ending September 30, 1904,			$3,358 57
Amount of surplus September 30, 1903,			23,500 72
Debits to profit and loss account during the year: adjustment of account,			10 00
Total Surplus September 30, 1904,			$26,849 29

Earnings from Operation.

Receipts from passengers carried,	$50,911 07
Receipts from carriage of freight,	5,730 38
Receipts from tolls for use of tracks by other companies,	1,276 16
Receipts from rentals of buildings and other property,	6,998 13
Receipts from advertising in cars,	363 34
Gross Earnings from Operation,	$65,279 08

Expenses of Operation.

General expenses:	
Salaries of general officers and clerks,	$1,323 46
General office expenses and supplies,	106 98
Legal expenses,	10 00
Insurance,	1,127 50
Other general expenses,	234 58

Maintenance of roadway and buildings:		
Repair of roadbed and track,		$676 47
Repair of electric line construction,		778 09
Repair of buildings,		206 22
Maintenance of equipment:		
Repair of cars and other vehicles,		3,969 03
Repair of electric equipment of cars,		1,306 92
Transportation expenses:		
Cost of electric motive power, $21,373.68; less power sold, $10,150.85; net,		11,222 83
Wages and compensation of persons employed in conducting transportation,		10,553 70
Removal of snow and ice,		755 10
Damages for injuries to persons and property,		830 53
Rentals of buildings and other property,		51 00
Other transportation expenses,		4,807 54
TOTAL OPERATING EXPENSES,		$37,959 95

PROPERTY ACCOUNTS.

Additions to railway:		
Extension of tracks,	$744 15	
New electric line construction,	83 90	
Other additions to railway: land and right of way,	110 09	
TOTAL ADDITIONS TO RAILWAY,		$938 14
Additions to equipment:		
Additional cars (1 in number),	$570 38	
Electrical equipment of same,	1,323 67	
Other additions to equipment: tools,	100 00	
TOTAL ADDITIONS TO EQUIPMENT,		1,994 05
Additions to land and buildings: new electric power stations, including machinery, etc.,		1,551 70
TOTAL ADDITIONS TO PROPERTY ACCOUNTS,		$4,483 89
Deductions from property accounts (property sold or reduced in valuation and credited to property accounts):		
Construction,	$83 13	
Electric line construction,	135 68	
Car account,	399 89	
Horse account,	50 00	
TOTAL DEDUCTIONS FROM PROPERTY ACCOUNTS,		668 70
NET ADDITION TO PROPERTY ACCOUNTS FOR THE YEAR,		$3,815 19

GENERAL BALANCE SHEET SEPTEMBER 30, 1904.

ASSETS.	DR.	
Cost of railway:		
Roadbed and tracks,	$412,273 06	
Electric line construction, including poles, wiring, feeder lines, etc.,	114,821 51	

Cost of railway — *Concluded.*		
Interest accrued during construction of railway,	$10,877 32	
Engineering and other expenses incident to construction,	21,820 83	
Other items of railway cost: legal and miscellaneous expenses,	10,689 70	
TOTAL COST OF RAILWAY OWNED,		$570,482 42
Cost of equipment:		
Cars and other rolling stock and vehicles,	$52,561 40	
Electric equipment of same,	43,069 01	
Other items of equipment: tools, etc.,	361 46	
TOTAL COST OF EQUIPMENT OWNED,		95,991 87
Cost of land and buildings:		
Land necessary for operation of railway,	$9,802 00	
Electric power stations, including equipment,	135,840 92	
Other buildings necessary for operation of railway,	50,257 34	
TOTAL COST OF LAND AND BUILDINGS OWNED,		195,900 26
TOTAL PERMANENT INVESTMENTS,		$862,374 55
Cash and current assets:		
Cash,	$5,310 24	
Bills and accounts receivable,	1,729 70	
Other cash and current assets: prepaid insurance and interest,	882 47	
TOTAL CASH AND CURRENT ASSETS,		7,922 41
Miscellaneous assets: materials and supplies,		3,643 50
TOTAL,		$873,940 46

LIABILITIES.		CR.
Capital stock,		$500,000 00
Funded debt,		280,000 00
Current liabilities:		
Loans and notes payable,	$56,500 00	
Audited vouchers and accounts,	663 86	
Miscellaneous current liabilities: outstanding tickets,	54 97	
TOTAL CURRENT LIABILITIES,		57,218 83
Accrued liabilities:		
Interest accrued and not yet due,	$3,500 00	
Taxes accrued and not yet due,	6,372 34	
TOTAL ACCRUED LIABILITIES,		9,872 34
Profit and loss balance (surplus),		26,849 29
TOTAL,		$873,940 46

Capital Stock.

Capital stock authorized by law,	$500,000 00	
Capital stock authorized by votes of company,	500,000 00	
Capital stock issued and outstanding,		$500,000 00
Number of shares issued and outstanding,	5,000	
Number of stockholders,	182	
Number of stockholders in Massachusetts,	180	
Amount of stock held in Massachusetts,	$494,000 00	

Funded Debt.

Description of Bonds.	Rate of Interest.	Date of Maturity.	Amount Outstanding.	Interest Paid during the Year.
	Per Cent.			
First mortgage gold bonds,	5	Jan. 1, 1922,	$280,000 00	$14,000 00

Volume of Traffic, etc.

Number of passengers paying revenue carried during the year,	1,074,981
Number carried per mile of main railway track operated,	54,319
Number of car miles run,	223,891
Average number of persons employed,	47

Description of Equipment.

Description of Equipment.	Equipped for Electric Power.	Equipped with Fenders.	Equipped with Electric Heaters.	Number of Motors.
Cars — Passenger Service.				
Box passenger cars,	6	6	6	-
Open passenger cars,	12	12	-	-
Total,	18	18	6	80
Cars — Other Service.				
Box freight cars,	1	-	-	-
Work cars,	1	-	-	-
Total,	2	-	-	-
Snow ploughs,	2	-	-	-

Miscellaneous Equipment.

Other railway rolling stock: flat car,	1

RAILWAY OWNED AND OPERATED (BY ELECTRIC POWER).

Length of railway line,	16.136 miles.
Length of second main track,	3.654 "
Total length of main track,	19.790 "
Length of sidings, switches, etc.,	2.067 "
Total computed as single track,	21.857 "

RAILWAY LOCATED OUTSIDE OF PUBLIC WAYS.

Length of railway line,	3.051 miles.
Length of second main track and sidings,	3.050 "
Total length of main track,	6.101 "

Names of the several cities and towns in which the railways operated by the company are located: Mattapoisett, Marion and Wareham.

GRADE CROSSINGS WITH RAILROADS.

GRADE CROSSINGS WITH RAILROADS.	NUMBER OF TRACKS AT CROSSING.	
	Railroad.	Railway.
Crossings of railways with railroads at grade (1 in number), viz.: — With spur track of the New York, New Haven & Hartford Railroad in the town of Wareham, at the "Narrows,"	2	1

Number of above crossings at which *frogs* are inserted in the tracks, . 1

ACCIDENTS TO PERSONS.

(A detailed statement of each accident is on file in the office of the Board.)

KILLED AND INJURED.	FROM CAUSES BEYOND THEIR OWN CONTROL.		FROM THEIR OWN MISCONDUCT OR CARELESSNESS.		TOTAL.	
	Killed.	Injured.	Killed.	Injured.	Killed.	Injured.
Passengers,	-	2	-	1	-	3
Employees,	-	-	-	-	-	-
Other persons,	-	-	-	2	-	2
TOTALS,	-	2	-	3	-	5

CORPORATE NAME AND ADDRESS OF THE COMPANY.

NEW BEDFORD & ONSET STREET RAILWAY COMPANY,

NO. 7 PURCHASE STREET, NEW BEDFORD, MASS.

NAMES AND BUSINESS ADDRESS OF PRINCIPAL OFFICERS.

Henry H. Crapo, *President*, New Bedford, Mass. Thomas B. Tripp, *Vice-President*, New Bedford, Mass. Elton S. Wilde, *Treasurer*, New Bedford, Mass. Clarence A. Cook, *Clerk of Corporation*, New Bedford, Mass. Oliver Prescott, Jr., *General Counsel*, New Bedford, Mass. John F. Swift, *Auditor*, New Bedford, Mass. Edward E. Potter, *Superintendent*, New Bedford, Mass.

NAMES AND RESIDENCE OF BOARD OF DIRECTORS.

Henry H. Crapo, New Bedford, Mass. Thomas B. Tripp, New Bedford, Mass. Clarence A. Cook, New Bedford, Mass. Edward S. Brown, New Bedford, Mass. Thomas S. Hathaway, New Bedford, Mass. Charles H. Lawton (deceased). Walter P. Winsor, Fairhaven, Mass. Joseph K. Nye, Fairhaven, Mass. Oliver Prescott, Jr., Dartmouth, Mass.

We hereby certify that the statements contained in the foregoing report are full, just and true.

HENRY H. CRAPO,
THOMAS B. TRIPP,
OLIVER PRESCOTT, JR.,
E. S. BROWN,
JOS. K. NYE,
Directors.
ELTON S. WILDE,
Treasurer.
E. E. POTTER,
Superintendent.

COMMONWEALTH OF MASSACHUSETTS.

BRISTOL, SS. OCT. 20, 1904. Then personally appeared the above-named Henry H. Crapo, Thomas B. Tripp, Oliver Prescott, Jr., E. S. Brown, Joseph K. Nye, Elton S. Wilde and E. E. Potter, and severally made oath that the foregoing certificate by them subscribed is, to the best of their knowledge and belief, true.

Before me, ISAAC W. PHELPS,
Justice of the Peace.

REPORT

OF THE

NEWTON STREET RAILWAY COMPANY

For the Year ending September 30, 1904.

General Exhibit for the Year.		
Gross earnings from operation,		$283,542 24
Operating expenses,		205,975 15
Gross Income above Operating Expenses,		$77,567 09
Charges upon income accrued during the year:		
Interest on funded debt,	$18,437 50	
Interest and discount on unfunded debts and loans,	31,586 05	
Taxes, State and local,	16,809 29	
Total Charges and Deductions from Income,		66,832 94
Net Divisible Income,		$10,734 15
Dividends declared:		
2 per cent on $315,000,	$6,300 00	
2 per cent on $722,000,	14,440 00	
Total Dividends Declared,		20,740 00
Deficit for the year ending September 30, 1904,		$10,005 85
Amount of surplus September 30, 1903,		30,922 38
Credits to profit and loss account during the year:		
Surplus of Wellesley & Boston Street Railway Company,	$6,990 29	
Premiums on bonds, $7,121.36; profit on sale of real estate and machinery, $23,115.77,	30,237 13	
Total Credits,	$37,227 42	
Debits to profit and loss account during the year:		
Deficit of Commonwealth Avenue Street Railway Company,	13,430 07	
Net Amount Credited to Profit and Loss,		23,797 35
Total Surplus September 30, 1904,		$44,713 88

Earnings from Operation.	
Receipts from passengers carried,	$272,344 26
Receipts from tolls for use of tracks by other companies,	3,218 39
Receipts from rentals of buildings and other property,	5,735 81

Receipts from advertising in cars,		$1,999 91
Receipts from interest on deposits,		88 88
Other earnings from operation:		
Discount,		68 12
Other sources,		86 87
GROSS EARNINGS FROM OPERATION,		$283,542 24

EXPENSES OF OPERATION.

General expenses:		
Salaries of general officers and clerks,		$9,338 51
General office expenses and supplies,		6,908 19
Legal expenses,		950 00
Insurance,		4,948 47
Other general expenses: storeroom expense,		558 23
Maintenance of roadway and buildings:		
Repair of roadbed and track,		5,279 63
Repair of electric line construction,		5,234 77
Repair of buildings,		1,040 65
Maintenance of equipment:		
Repair of cars and other vehicles,		7,191 73
Repair of electric equipment of cars,		8,914 80
Renewal of horses, harnesses, shoeing, etc., provender and stabling for horses,		1,117 92
Transportation expenses:		
Cost of electric motive power,		47,696 05
Wages and compensation of persons employed in conducting transportation,		85,262 92
Removal of snow and ice,		6,403 33
Damages for injuries to persons and property,		13,606 95
Tolls for trackage over other railways,		453 84
Rentals of buildings and other property,		875 36
Other transportation expenses: miscellaneous shop expense,		193 80
TOTAL OPERATING EXPENSES,		$205,975 15

PROPERTY ACCOUNTS.

Additions to railway:		
Improvement of track,	$3,443 91	
Property of Commonwealth Avenue Street Railway Company, $200,996.68; Wellesley & Boston Street Railway Company, $100,816.96,	301,813 64	
TOTAL ADDITIONS TO RAILWAY,		$305,257 55
Additions to equipment:		
Other additional rolling stock and vehicles: 2 pungs and automobile,	$973 60	
Other additions to equipment:		
Air brakes and sand boxes,	4,215 06	
Furniture and fixtures, $1,463.89; shop tools and machinery, $76.62,	1,540 51	
Property of Commonwealth Avenue Street Railway Company, $233,443.39; Wellesley & Boston Street Railway Company, $53,896.60,	287,339 99	
TOTAL ADDITIONS TO EQUIPMENT,		294,069 16

Additions to land and buildings:		
Additional land necessary for operation of railway,	$20,673 79	
Addition to car barns,	8,238 01	
Property of Commonwealth Avenue Street Railway Company, $105,280.50; Wellesley & Boston Street Railway Company, $5,240,	110,520 50	
TOTAL ADDITIONS TO LAND AND BUILDINGS,		$139,432 30
TOTAL ADDITIONS TO PROPERTY ACCOUNTS,		$738,759 01
Deductions from property accounts (property sold or reduced in valuation and credited to property accounts):		
Power plant machinery,	$26,207 79	
Land,	20,673 79	
Building,	5,240 00	
Twelve cars, complete,	15,275 92	
Miscellaneous material and equipment,	14,328 37	
Rebate city of Waltham, account of paving,	282 10	
TOTAL DEDUCTIONS FROM PROPERTY ACCOUNTS,		82,007 97
NET ADDITION TO PROPERTY ACCOUNTS FOR THE YEAR,		$656,751 04

GENERAL BALANCE SHEET SEPTEMBER 30, 1904.

ASSETS.	DR.	
Cost of railway:		
Roadbed and tracks,	$672,393 26	
Electric line construction, including poles, wiring, feeder lines, etc.,	112,866 65	
Interest accrued during construction of railway,	29,806 49	
Engineering and other expenses incident to construction,	38,706 52	
Other items of railway cost: purchase of Waltham & Newton Street Railway Company, $45,582.56; city of Newton for street widening, $22,846.47; city of Waltham, paving, etc., $23,286.65,	91,715 68	
TOTAL COST OF RAILWAY OWNED,		$945,488 60
Cost of equipment:		
Cars and other rolling stock and vehicles,	$330,486 96	
Electric equipment of same,	188,904 21	
Horses,	325 00	
Other items of equipment: harness, $102.39; furniture and fixtures, $6,836.62; shop tools and machinery, $2,850.81,	9,789 82	
TOTAL COST OF EQUIPMENT OWNED,		529,505 99*
Cost of land and buildings:		
Land and building necessary for operation of railway,	$81,941 79	
Other buildings necessary for operation of railway,	171,682 28	
TOTAL COST OF LAND AND BUILDINGS OWNED,		253,624 07*
TOTAL PERMANENT INVESTMENTS,		$1,728,618 66

* Safe transferred from land and buildings to furniture and fixtures, $93.10.

Cash and current assets :		
Cash, ...	$10,853 40	
Bills and accounts receivable, . . .	61,808 57	
TOTAL CASH AND CURRENT ASSETS, ...		$72,661 97
Miscellaneous assets :		
Materials and supplies, ...	$26,252 54	
Other assets and property : unexpired insurance,	3,891 23	
TOTAL MISCELLANEOUS ASSETS :		30,143 77
TOTAL, ...		$1,831,424 40

LIABILITIES.		CR.
Capital stock, ...		$722,000 00
Funded debt, ...		575,000 00
Real estate mortgages, ...		2,500 00
Current liabilities :		
Loans and notes payable, ...	$402,000 00	
Audited vouchers and accounts, . . .	70,654 26	
Salaries and wages, ...	2,049 05	
Matured interest coupons unpaid (including coupons due October 1), ...	3,750 00	
TOTAL CURRENT LIABILITIES, ...		478,453 31
Accrued liabilities : interest accrued and not yet due, . .		1,257 21
Sinking and other special funds : insurance fund, . . .		7,500 00
Profit and loss balance (surplus), ...		44,713 88
TOTAL, ...		$1,831,424 40

CAPITAL STOCK.		
Capital stock authorized by law, ...	$907,000 00	
Capital stock authorized by votes of company,	907,000 00	
Capital stock issued and outstanding, ...		$722,000 00
Number of shares issued and outstanding, .	7,220	
Number of stockholders, ...	8	
Number of stockholders in Massachusetts, .	8	
Amount of stock held in Massachusetts, . .	$722,000 00	

REAL ESTATE MORTGAGES.

DESCRIPTION OF MORTGAGED PROPERTY.	Rate of Interest.	Mortgage when Due.	Amount.	Interest Paid during the Year.
	Per Cent.			
On real estate, ...	4	Dec. 4, 1902,	$2,500 00	$50 00

FUNDED DEBT.

DESCRIPTION OF BONDS.	Rate of Interest.	Date of Maturity.	Amount Outstanding.	Interest Paid during the Year.
	Per Cent.			
First mortgage bonds, ...	5	July 20, 1912,	$500,000 00	$15,625 00
First mortgage bonds, ...	5	Feb. 1, 1916,	75,000 00	2,812 50
TOTALS, ...	. . .	. . . .	$575,000 00	$18,437 50

Sinking and Other Special Funds.

Amount January 1, 1904, of insurance fund, ...	$7,500 00
Total Sinking and Other Special Funds, September 30, 1904, ...	$7,500 00

Volume of Traffic, etc.

Number of passengers paying revenue carried during the year,	5,895,495
Number carried per mile of main railway track operated, .	166,366
Number of car miles run, ...	1,218,003
Average number of persons employed, ...	185

Description of Equipment.

Description of Equipment.	Equipped for Electric Power.	Not Equipped.	Total Passenger Cars.	Equipped with Fenders.	Equipped with Electric Heaters.	Number of Motors.
Cars — Passenger Service.						
Box passenger cars, ...	65	1	66	65	65	-
Open passenger cars, ...	81	-	81	81	-	-
Total, ...	146	1	147	146	65	296
Cars — Other Service.						
Other cars, ...	2	-	-	-	-	-
Snow ploughs, ...	10	-	-	-	-	-

Miscellaneous Equipment.

Carts and snow sleds, ...	3
Other railway rolling stock: 1 platform trailer, ...	1
Other highway vehicles: 1 democrat wagon, 1 concord wagon, 1 heavy express wagon, 4 express wagons, 3 pungs, 3 snow levellers, 1 tower wagon and 1 automobile, . .	15
Horses, ...	4
Other items of equipment: harnesses (double, 1; single, 5), .	6

Railway Owned and Operated (by Electric Power).

Railway Owned, etc.	Owned.	Trackage over Other Railways.	Total Owned, etc.
	Miles.	Miles.	Miles.
Length of railway line, ...	26.246	.871	27.117
Length of second main track, ...	8.320	-	8.320
Total Length of Main Track, ...	34.566	.871	35.437
Length of sidings, switches, etc., ...	2.201	-	2.201
Total, Computed as Single Track, ...	36.767	.871	37.638

Names of the several cities and towns in which the railways operated by the company are located: Newton, Waltham and Watertown.

GRADE CROSSINGS WITH RAILROADS.

GRADE CROSSINGS WITH RAILROADS.	NUMBER OF TRACKS AT CROSSING.	
	Railroad.	Railway.
Crossings of railways with railroads at grade (3 in number), viz.: —		
With Boston & Maine Railroad (Fitchburg Division), Main Street, Waltham,	2	1
With Boston & Maine Railroad (Fitchburg Division), Moody Street, Waltham,	3	1
With Boston & Maine Railroad (Fitchburg Division), River Street, Waltham,	2	1
TOTAL NUMBER OF TRACKS AT CROSSINGS,	7	3

Number of above crossings at which *frogs* are inserted in the tracks, . 7

ACCIDENTS TO PERSONS.

(A detailed statement of each accident is on file in the office of the Board.)

KILLED AND INJURED.	FROM CAUSES BEYOND THEIR OWN CONTROL.		FROM THEIR OWN MISCONDUCT OR CARELESSNESS.		TOTAL.	
	Killed.	Injured.	Killed.	Injured.	Killed.	Injured.
Passengers,	-	14	-	5	-	19
Employees,	-	-	-	3	-	3
Other persons,	-	-	-	2	-	2
TOTALS,	-	14	-	10	-	24

CORPORATE NAME AND ADDRESS OF THE COMPANY.

NEWTON STREET RAILWAY COMPANY,

NEWTONVILLE, MASS.

NAMES AND BUSINESS ADDRESS OF PRINCIPAL OFFICERS.

Adams D. Claflin, *President*, Newtonville, Mass. Alden E. Viles, *Vice-President*, Boston, Mass. Charles W. Smith, *Treasurer*, Newtonville, Mass. Frank W. Remick, *Clerk of Corporation*, Boston, Mass. Coolidge & Hight, *General Counsel*, Boston, Mass. Matthew C. Brush, *General Manager*, Newtonville, Mass.

NAMES AND RESIDENCE OF BOARD OF DIRECTORS.

Adams D. Claflin, Newton Centre, Mass. William F. Hammett, Newton, Mass. Sydney Harwood, Newton, Mass. Frederic H. Lewis, Swampscott, Mass. Frank W. Remick, West Newton, Mass. James L. Richards, Newtonville, Mass. Alden E. Viles, Boston, Mass.

We hereby certify that the statements contained in the foregoing report are full, just and true.

ADAMS D. CLAFLIN,
WILLIAM F. HAMMETT,
SYDNEY HARWOOD,
JAMES L. RICHARDS,
FREDÉRIC H. LEWIS,
ALDEN E. VILES,
Directors.
CHAS. W. SMITH,
Treasurer.
MATTHEW C. BRUSH,
General Manager.

COMMONWEALTH OF MASSACHUSETTS.

SUFFOLK SS. OCT. 29, 1904. Then personally appeared the above-named Adams D. Claflin, William F. Hammett, Sydney Harwood, James L. Richards, Frederic H. Lewis, Alden E. Viles, Chas. W. Smith and Matthew C. Brush, and severally made oath that the foregoing certificate by them subscribed is, to the best of their knowledge and belief, true.

Before me, GEO. M. COX,
Notary Public.

REPORT

OF THE

NEWTON & BOSTON STREET RAILWAY COMPANY

FOR THE YEAR ENDING SEPTEMBER 30, 1904.

GENERAL EXHIBIT FOR THE YEAR.		
Gross earnings from operation,		$62,074 80
Operating expenses,		59,675 28
GROSS INCOME ABOVE OPERATING EXPENSES,		$2,399 52
Charges upon income accrued during the year:		
Interest on funded debt,	$10,000 00	
Interest and discount on unfunded debts and loans,	16,700 50	
Taxes, State and local,	3,640 02	
TOTAL CHARGES AND DEDUCTIONS FROM INCOME,		30,340 52
Deficit for the year ending September 30, 1904,		$27,941 00
Amount of deficit September 30, 1903,		135,286 53
TOTAL DEFICIT SEPTEMBER 30, 1904,		$163,227 53

EARNINGS FROM OPERATION.	
Receipts from passengers carried,	$60,083 09
Receipts from tolls for use of tracks by other companies,	455 82
Receipts from rentals of buildings and other property,	668 64
Receipts from advertising in cars,	505 00
Receipts from interest on deposits,	20 76
Other earnings from operation:	
Discount,	26 29
Other sources,	315 20
GROSS EARNINGS FROM OPERATION,	$62,074 80

EXPENSES OF OPERATION.	
General expenses:	
Salaries of general officers and clerks,	$2,207 52
General office expenses and supplies,	1,579 06
Legal expenses,	2,650 00
Insurance,	2,370 46
Other general expenses: storeroom expense,	125 60
Maintenance of roadway and buildings:	
Repair of roadbed and track,	3,420 76
Repair of electric line construction,	2,253 93
Repair of buildings,	815 75

Maintenance of equipment:		
Repair of cars and other vehicles,		$5,130 04
Repair of electric equipment of cars,		4,007 46
Renewal of horses, harnesses, shoeing, etc., and provender and stabling for horses,		552 27
Transportation expenses:		
Cost of electric motive power, $50,725.91; less power sold, $49,073.33; net,		1,652 58
Wages and compensation of persons employed in conducting transportation,		23,288 08
Removal of snow and ice,		2,623 62
Damages for injuries to persons and property,		3,004 10
Tolls for trackage over other railways,		3,330 27
Rentals of buildings and other property,		595 82
Other transportation expenses: miscellaneous shop expense,		67 96
TOTAL OPERATING EXPENSES,		$59,675 28

PROPERTY ACCOUNTS.

Additions to railway:		
Improvement of tracks,	$367 50	
New feeder,	4,589 30	
TOTAL ADDITIONS TO RAILWAY,		$4,956 80
Additions to equipment:		
Additional cars (1 in number),	$4,606 12	
Electric equipment of same,	2,194 95	
Other additions to equipment: shop tools and machinery,	2 00	
TOTAL ADDITIONS TO EQUIPMENT,		6,803 07
Additions to land and buildings:		
Additional equipment of power stations,	$2,073 58	
New buildings necessary for operation of railway,	6,244 66	
TOTAL ADDITIONS TO LAND AND BUILDINGS,		8,318 24
TOTAL ADDITIONS TO PROPERTY ACCOUNTS,		$20,078 11
Deductions from property accounts (property sold or reduced in valuation and credited to property accounts): sixteen cars and equipment,		20,728 46
NET DEDUCTION FROM PROPERTY ACCOUNTS FOR THE YEAR,		$650 35

GENERAL BALANCE SHEET SEPTEMBER 30, 1904.

ASSETS.	DR.	
Cost of railway:		
Roadbed and tracks,	$156,516 97	
Electric line construction, including poles, wiring, feeder lines, etc.,	48,150 25	
Engineering and other expenses incident to construction,	687 46	
TOTAL COST OF RAILWAY OWNED,		$205,354 68

Cost of equipment:			
Cars and other rolling stock and vehicles,		$56,369 02	
Electric equipment of same,		66,762 73	
Horses,		403 00	
Other items of equipment:			
Furniture and fixtures,	$527 05		
Shop tools and machinery,	395 65		
		922 70	
TOTAL COST OF EQUIPMENT OWNED,			$124,457 45
Cost of land and buildings:			
Land necessary for operation of railway,		$7,500 00	
Electric power stations, including equipment,		152,238 40	
Other buildings necessary for operation of railway,		34,226 50	
TOTAL COST OF LAND AND BUILDINGS OWNED,			193,964 90
TOTAL PERMANENT INVESTMENTS,			$523,777 03
Cash and current assets:			
Cash,		$30 00	
Bills and accounts receivable,		13,663 25	
TOTAL CASH AND CURRENT ASSETS,			13,693 25
Miscellaneous assets: materials and supplies,			1,698 75
Profit and loss balance (deficit),			163,227 53
TOTAL,			$702,396 56

LIABILITIES.	CR.	
Capital stock,		$200,000 00
Funded debt,		200,000 00
Current liabilities:		
Loans and notes payable,	$291,500 00	
Audited vouchers and accounts,	10,340 75	
Salaries and wages,	555 81	
TOTAL CURRENT LIABILITIES,		302,396 56
TOTAL,		$702,396 56

CAPITAL STOCK.

Capital stock authorized by law,	$250,000 00	
Capital stock authorized by votes of company,	200,000 00	
Capital stock issued and outstanding,		$200,000 00
Number of shares issued and outstanding,	2,000	
Number of stockholders,	8	
Number of stockholders in Massachusetts,	8	
Amount of stock held in Massachusetts,	$200,000 00	

FUNDED DEBT.

DESCRIPTION OF BONDS.	Rate of Interest.	Date of Maturity.	Amount Outstanding.	Interest Paid during the Year.
First mortgage bonds,	Per Cent. 5	July 1, 1912,	$200,000 00	$10,000 00

Volume of Traffic, etc.

Number of passengers paying revenue carried during the year,	1,404,020
Number carried per mile of main railway track operated, .	108,043
Number of car miles run, ...	372,495
Average number of persons employed, ...	57

Description of Equipment.

Description of Equipment.	Equipped for Electric Power.	Equipped with Fenders.	Equipped with Electric Heaters.	Number of Motors.
Cars — Passenger Service.				
Box passenger cars, ...	6	6	6	-
Open passenger cars, ...	10	10	-	-
Total, ...	16	16	6	40
Cars — Other Service.				
Other cars, ...	1	-	-	-
Snow ploughs, ...	3	-	-	-

Miscellaneous Equipment.

Carts and snow sleds, ...	1
Other highway vehicles: 1 concord wagon, 1 pung, 1 sleigh, 1 tower wagon and 2 snow levellers, ...	6
Horses, ...	3
Other items of equipment: single harnesses, ...	4

Railway Owned and Operated (by Electric Power).

Railway Owned, etc.	Owned.	Trackage over Other Railways.	Total Owned, etc.
	Miles.	Miles.	Miles.
Length of railway line, ...	9.031	3.964	12.995
Length of sidings, switches, etc., ...	.755	.096	.851
Total Computed as Single Track, ...	9.786	4.060	13.846

Names of the several cities and towns in which the railways operated by the company are located: Needham, Newton and Watertown.

ACCIDENTS TO PERSONS.

(A detailed statement of each accident is on file in the office of the Board.)

KILLED AND INJURED.	FROM CAUSES BEYOND THEIR OWN CONTROL.		FROM THEIR OWN MISCONDUCT OR CARELESSNESS.		TOTAL.	
	Killed.	Injured.	Killed.	Injured.	Killed.	Injured.
Passengers,	-	-	-	3	-	3
Employees,	-	1	-	1	-	2
Other persons,	-	-	-	1	-	1
TOTALS,	-	1	-	5	-	6

CORPORATE NAME AND ADDRESS OF THE COMPANY.

NEWTON & BOSTON STREET RAILWAY COMPANY,

NEWTONVILLE, MASS.

NAMES AND BUSINESS ADDRESS OF PRINCIPAL OFFICERS.

Adams D. Claflin, *President,* Newtonville, Mass. William F. Hammett, *Vice-President,* Newton, Mass. Charles W. Smith, *Treasurer,* Newtonville, Mass. Frank W. Remick, *Clerk of Corporation,* Boston, Mass. Coolidge & Hight, *General Counsel,* Boston Mass. Matthew C. Brush, *General Manager,* Newtonville, Mass.

NAMES AND RESIDENCE OF BOARD OF DIRECTORS.

Adams D. Claflin, Newton Centre, Mass. William F. Hammett, Newton, Mass. Sydney Harwood, Newton, Mass. Frederic H. Lewis, Swampscott, Mass. Frank W. Remick, West Newton, Mass. James L. Richards, Newtonville, Mass. Alden E. Viles, Boston, Mass.

We hereby certify that the statements contained in the foregoing report are full, just and true.

ADAMS D. CLAFLIN,
WILLIAM F. HAMMETT,
SYDNEY HARWOOD,
JAMES L. RICHARDS,
FREDERIC H. LEWIS,
ALDEN E. VILES,
Directors.
CHAS. W. SMITH,
Treasurer.
MATTHEW C. BRUSH,
General Manager.

COMMONWEALTH OF MASSACHUSETTS.

SUFFOLK, ss. OCT. 29, 1904. Then personally appeared the above-named Adams D. Claflin, William F. Hammett, Sydney Harwood, James L. Richards, Frederic H. Lewis, Alden E. Viles, Chas. W. Smith and Matthew C. Brush, and severally made oath that the foregoing certificate by them subscribed is, to the best of their knowledge and belief, true.

Before me, GEO. M. COX,
Notary Public.

REPORT

OF THE

NEWTONVILLE & WATERTOWN STREET RAILWAY COMPANY

For the Year ending September 30, 1904.

[Tracks used by the Newton & Boston.]

General Exhibit for the Year.		
Rental received from lease of railway,		$8,136 50
Expenses and charges upon income accrued during the year:		
Salaries and maintenance of organization,	$450 00	
Interest and discount on unfunded debts and loans,	2,960 97	
Taxes,	1,057 50	
Total Expenses and Charges upon Income,		4,468 47
Net Divisible Income,		$3,668 03
Dividends declared (7⁹⁄₁₀ per cent),		3,600 00
Surplus for the year ending September 30, 1904,		$68 03
Amount of surplus September 30, 1903,		1,531 60
Total Surplus September 30, 1904,		$1,599 63

General Balance Sheet September 30, 1904.

Assets.	Dr.	
Cost of railway:		
Roadbed and tracks,	$89,208 05	
Electric line construction, including poles, wiring, feeder lines, etc.,	18,200 54	
Interest accrued during construction of railway,	51 25	
Engineering and other expenses incident to construction,	1,105 10	
Total Cost of Railway Owned,		$108,564 94

Cash and current assets:		
Cash,	$1,640 81	
Bills and accounts receivable,	1,043 88	
TOTAL CASH AND CURRENT ASSETS,		$2,684 69
TOTAL,		$111,249 63

LIABILITIES.	CR.
Capital stock,	$50,000 00
Current liabilities: loans and notes payable,	59,650 00
Profit and loss balance (surplus),	1,599 63
TOTAL,	$111,249 63

CAPITAL STOCK.

Capital stock authorized by law,	$100,000 00	
Capital stock authorized by votes of company,	100,000 00	
Capital stock issued and outstanding,		$50,000 00
Number of shares issued and outstanding,	500	
Number of stockholders,	19	
Number of stockholders in Massachusetts,	19	
Amount of stock held in Massachusetts,	$50,000 00	

RAILWAY OWNED.

Length of railway line,	4.308 miles.
Length of sidings, switches, etc.,	.357 "
Total, computed as single track,	4.665 "

Names of the several cities and towns in which the railway owned by the company is located: Newton, Boston and Watertown.

CORPORATE NAME AND ADDRESS OF THE COMPANY.

NEWTONVILLE & WATERTOWN STREET RAILWAY COMPANY,

115 DEVONSHIRE STREET, BOSTON, MASS.

NAMES AND BUSINESS ADDRESS OF PRINCIPAL OFFICERS.

James L. Richards, *President*, 24 West Street, Boston, Mass. Joseph Remick, *Treasurer and Clerk of Corporation*, 115 Devonshire Street, Boston, Mass.

NAMES AND RESIDENCE OF BOARD OF DIRECTORS.

James L. Richards, Newton, Mass. William Endicott, Jr., Boston, Mass. R. Elmer Townsend, Boston, Mass. Horace B. Parker, Newton, Mass. William H. Allen, Newton, Mass. Joseph Remick, Melrose, Mass.

We hereby certify that the statements contained in the foregoing report are full, just and true.

JOSEPH REMICK,
JAMES L. RICHARDS,
R. ELMER TOWNSEND,
W. H. ALLEN,
WILLIAM ENDICOTT, Jr.,
Directors.
JOSEPH REMICK,
Treasurer.

COMMONWEALTH OF MASSACHUSETTS.

SUFFOLK, ss. BOSTON, Nov. 14, 1904. Then personally appeared the above-named Joseph Remick, James L. Richards, R. Elmer Townsend, W. H. Allen and William Endicott, Jr., and severally made oath that the foregoing certificate by them subscribed is, to the best of their knowledge and belief, true.

Before me, GEO. E. PERRIN,
Notary Public.

REPORT

OF THE

NORFOLK & BRISTOL STREET RAILWAY COMPANY

FOR THE YEAR ENDING SEPTEMBER 30, 1904.

GENERAL EXHIBIT FOR THE YEAR.			
Gross earnings from operation,			$50,011 33
Operating expenses,			54,915 17
GROSS DEFICIT ABOVE OPERATING EXPENSES,			$4,903 84
Charges upon income accrued during the year:			
Interest and discount on unfunded debts and loans,		$10,529 56	
Taxes, State and local,	$1,192 45		
Taxes commutation,	500 11		
		1,692 56	
TOTAL CHARGES AND DEDUCTIONS FROM INCOME,			12,222 12
Deficit for the year ending September 30, 1904,			$17,125 96
Amount of deficit September 30, 1903,			13,036 42
TOTAL DEFICIT SEPTEMBER 30, 1904,			$30,162 38

EARNINGS FROM OPERATION.	
Receipts from passengers carried,	$47,981 21
Receipts from carriage of mails,	188 15
Receipts from rentals of buildings and other property,	90 37
Receipts from advertising in cars,	221 00
Other earnings from operation:	
Ticket sales,	1,308 60
Special cars,	222 00
GROSS EARNINGS FROM OPERATION,	$50,011 33

EXPENSES OF OPERATION.	
General expenses:	
Salaries of general officers and clerks,	$5,239 18
General office expenses and supplies,	150 05
Legal expenses,	1,611 59
Insurance,	1,280 24
Other general expenses: contingent expenses,	459 56

Maintenance of roadway and buildings:	
Repair of roadbed and track,	$1,299 66
Repair of electric line construction,	959 91
Repair of buildings,	56 08
Maintenance of equipment:	
Repair of cars and other vehicles,	2,535 11
Repair of electric equipment of cars,	6,317 89
Transportation expenses:	
Cost of electric motive power, $17,972.09; less power sold, $1,929.79; net,	16,042 30
Wages and compensation of persons employed in conducting transportation,	16,453 03
Removal of snow and ice,	1,639 64
Damages for injuries to persons and property,	771 46
Tolls for trackage over other railways,	57 92
Rentals of buildings and other property,	41 55
TOTAL OPERATING EXPENSES,	$54,915 17

PROPERTY ACCOUNTS.

Deductions from property accounts (property sold or reduced in valuation and credited to property accounts):		
Cars and rolling stock,	$9,523 79	
Electric equipment of cars,	2,531 69	
Real estate and buildings,	2,391 50	
Electric power station,	540 50	
TOTAL DEDUCTIONS FROM PROPERTY ACCOUNTS,		$14,987 48

GENERAL BALANCE SHEET SEPTEMBER 30, 1904.

ASSETS.	DR.	
Cost of railway:		
Roadbed and tracks,	$222,503 09	
Electric line construction, including poles, wiring, feeder lines, etc.,	43,061 47	
Other items of railway cost: organization,	181 48	
TOTAL COST OF RAILWAY OWNED,		$265,746 04
Cost of equipment:		
Cars and other rolling stock and vehicles,	$17,335 63	
Electric equipment of same,	22,003 02	
TOTAL COST OF EQUIPMENT OWNED,		39,338 65
Cost of land and buildings:		
Land necessary for operation of railway,	$39,510 04	
Electric power stations, including equipment,	39,658 65	
TOTAL COST OF LAND AND BUILDINGS OWNED,		79,168 69
TOTAL PERMANENT INVESTMENTS,		$384,253 38
Cash and current assets:		
Cash,	$3,382 02	
Bills and accounts receivable,	1,304 58	
Other cash and current assets: fire loss,	15,053 68	
TOTAL CASH AND CURRENT ASSETS,		19,740 28

Miscellaneous assets: materials and supplies,	$7,956 85	
Other assets and property:		
Unexpired insurance,	607 20	
Rent paid in advance,	29 40	
TOTAL MISCELLANEOUS ASSETS,		$8,593 45
Profit and loss balance (deficit),		30,162 38
TOTAL,		$442,749 49
LIABILITIES.	CR.	
Capital stock,		$200,000 00
Current liabilities:		
Loans and notes payable,	$211,500 00	
Audited vouchers and accounts,	2,454 85	
Salaries and wages,	724 16	
TOTAL CURRENT LIABILITIES,		214,679 01
Accrued liabilities:		
Interest accrued and not yet due,	$27,660 53	
Taxes accrued and not yet due,	409 95	
TOTAL ACCRUED LIABILITIES,		28,070 48
TOTAL,		$442,749 49

CAPITAL STOCK.

Capital stock authorized by law,	$200,000 00	
Capital stock authorized by votes of company,	200,000 00	
Capital stock issued and outstanding,		$200,000 00
Number of shares issued and outstanding,	2,000	
Number of stockholders,	16	
Number of stockholders in Massachusetts,	15	
Amount of stock held in Massachusetts,	$194,000 00	

VOLUME OF TRAFFIC, ETC.

Number of passengers paying revenue carried during the year,	1,002,613
Number carried per mile of main railway track operated,	48,064
Number of car miles run,	320,925
Average number of persons employed,	47

DESCRIPTION OF EQUIPMENT.

DESCRIPTION OF EQUIPMENT.	Equipped for Electric Power.	Not Equipped.	Total Passenger Cars.	Equipped with Fenders.	Equipped with Electric Heaters.	Number of Motors.
CARS — PASSENGER SERVICE.						
Box passenger cars,	5	-	5	4	5	22
Open passenger cars,	12	2	14	12	-	22
TOTAL,	17	2	19	16	5	44
CARS — OTHER SERVICE.						
Work cars,	-	2	-	-	-	-

MISCELLANEOUS EQUIPMENT.

Highway vehicles: trolley wagon, ...	1

RAILWAY OWNED AND OPERATED (BY ELECTRIC POWER).

RAILWAY OWNED, ETC.	Owned.	Trackage over Other Railways.	Total Owned, etc.
	Miles.	Miles.	Miles.
Length of railway line, ...	20.567	.293	20.860
Length of sidings, switches, etc., ...	.478	-	.478
TOTAL, COMPUTED AS SINGLE TRACK, . . .	21.045	.293	21.338

Names of the several cities and towns in which the railways operated by the company are located: Mansfield, Foxborough, Wrentham, Walpole and Norwood.

ACCIDENTS TO PERSONS.

(A detailed statement of each accident is on file in the office of the Board.)

KILLED AND INJURED.	FROM CAUSES BEYOND THEIR OWN CONTROL.		FROM THEIR OWN MISCONDUCT OR CARELESSNESS.		TOTAL.	
	Killed.	Injured.	Killed.	Injured.	Killed.	Injured.
Passengers, ...	-	1	-	3	-	4
Employees, ...	-	-	-	1	-	1
Other persons, ...	-	-	-	-	-	-
TOTALS, ...	-	1	-	4	-	5

CORPORATE NAME AND ADDRESS OF THE COMPANY.

NORFOLK & BRISTOL STREET RAILWAY COMPANY,

84 STATE STREET, BOSTON, MASS.

NAMES AND BUSINESS ADDRESS OF PRINCIPAL OFFICERS.

Edmund D. Codman, *President*, Boston, Mass. Henry F. Smith, *Treasurer*, Boston, Mass. Norman I. Adams, *Clerk of Corporation*, Boston, Mass. Gaston, Snow & Saltonstall, *General Counsel*, Boston, Mass. Stone & Webster, *General Managers*, Boston, Mass. Edmund J. B. Huntoon, *Manager*, Boston, Mass.

NAMES AND RESIDENCE OF BOARD OF DIRECTORS.*

Edmund D. Codman, Boston, Mass. Henry F. Smith, Boston, Mass. Micajah P. Clough, Lynn, Mass. Norman I. Adams, Winthrop, Mass. Frank A. Newell, Medford, Mass.

* Directors at date of this report.

We hereby certify that the statements contained in the foregoing report are full, just and true.

MICAJAH P. CLOUGH,
HENRY F. SMITH,
NORMAN I. ADAMS,
FRANK A. NEWELL,
C. H. BOWEN,
*Directors.**
HENRY F. SMITH,
Treasurer.
E. J. B. HUNTOON,
Superintendent.

COMMONWEALTH OF MASSACHUSETTS.

SUFFOLK, SS. BOSTON, Nov. 8, 1904. Then personally appeared the above-named Micajah P. Clough, Henry F. Smith, Norman I. Adams, Frank A. Newell and C. H. Bowen, and severally made oath that the foregoing certificate by them subscribed is, to the best of their knowledge and belief, true.

Before me, FRANCIS B. SEARS,
Justice of the Peace.

---

* Directors chosen at annual meeting held November 1, 1904.

REPORT

OF THE

NORFOLK WESTERN STREET RAILWAY COMPANY

For the Period ending January 20, 1904.

[Railway in hands of receivers, January 20, 1904.]

General Exhibit for the Period.			
Gross earnings from operation,			$5,604 14
Operating expenses,			5,258 91
Gross Income above Operating Expenses,			$345 23
Charges upon income accrued during the period:			
Interest on funded debt,		$1,471 10	
Interest and discount on unfunded debts and loans,		1,190 87	
Taxes, State and local,	$58 92		
Taxes, commutation,	80 28		
		139 20	
Total Charges and Deductions from Income,			2,801 17
Deficit for the period ending January 20, 1904,			$2,455 94
Amount of deficit September 30, 1903,			30,470 81
Total Deficit January 20, 1904,			$32,926 75

Earnings from Operation.	
Receipts from passengers carried,	$5,581 29
Other earnings from operation: chartered cars,	22 85
Gross Earnings from Operation,	$5,604 14

Expenses of Operation.	
General expenses:	
Salaries of general officers and clerks,	$982 00
General office expenses and supplies,	4 42
Legal expenses,	150 00
Insurance,	134 36
Other general expenses:	
Advertising,	17 65
Miscellaneous general expenses,	70 58
Maintenance of roadway and buildings:	
Repair of roadbed and track,	42 80
Repair of electric line construction,	47 50

Maintenance of equipment:	
Repair of cars and other vehicles,	$170 79
Repair of electric equipment of cars,	139 82
Renewals tools and machinery,	5 35
Transportation expenses:	
Cost of electric motive power,	1,346 83
Wages and compensation of persons employed in conducting transportation,	1,623 97
Removal of snow and ice,	171 96
Damages for injuries to persons and property,	77 50
Other transportation expenses: car service supplies, $34.57; miscellaneous car service expenses, $22.72; cleaning, oiling and sanding tracks, $216.09,	273 38
TOTAL OPERATING EXPENSES,	$5,258 91

GENERAL BALANCE SHEET JANUARY 20, 1904.

ASSETS.	DR.	
Cost of railway:		
Roadbed and tracks,	$125,737 12	
Electric line construction, including poles, wiring, feeder lines, etc.,	29,305 65	
Interest accrued during construction of railway,	4,906 70	
Engineering and other expenses incident to construction,	16,032 12	
TOTAL COST OF RAILWAY OWNED,		$175,981 59
Cost of equipment:		
Cars and other rolling stock and vehicles,	$18,032 16	
Electric equipment of same,	9,500 59	
Horses,	612 35	
Other items of equipment: office furniture, $492.98; sundry equipment, $257.55,	750 53	
TOTAL COST OF EQUIPMENT OWNED,		28,895 63
Cost of land and buildings:		
Land necessary for operation of railway,	$1,075 00	
Electric power stations, including equipment,	18,600 00	
Other buildings necessary for operation of railway,	29,587 31	
TOTAL COST OF LAND AND BUILDINGS OWNED,		49,262 31
TOTAL PERMANENT INVESTMENTS,		$254,139 53
Cash and current assets:		
Cash,	$45 69	
Bills and accounts receivable,	773 84	
Other cash and current assets: prepaid interest, insurance and taxes,	503 80	
TOTAL CASH AND CURRENT ASSETS,		1,323 33
Miscellaneous assets: materials and supplies,		1,639 27
Profit and loss balance (deficit),		32,926 75
TOTAL,		$290,028 88

Liabilities.	Cr.	
Capital stock,		$100,000 00
Funded debt,		100,000 00
Current liabilities:		
Loans and notes payable,	$64,603 17	
Audited vouchers and accounts,	20,831 26	
Miscellaneous current liabilities: outstanding tickets,	45 35	
Total Current Liabilities,		85,479 78
Accrued liabilities: interest accrued and not yet due,		4,549 10
Total,		$290,028 88

Capital Stock.		
Capital stock authorized by law,	$100,000 00	
Capital stock authorized by votes of company,	100,000 00	
Capital stock issued and outstanding,		$100,000 00
Number of shares issued and outstanding,	1,000	
Number of stockholders,	37	
Number of stockholders in Massachusetts,	37	
Amount of stock held in Massachusetts,	$100,000 00	

Funded Debt.

Description of Bonds.	Rate of Interest.	Date of Maturity.	Amount Outstanding.	Interest Paid during the Year.
	Per Cent.			
First mortgage gold bonds,	5	Aug. 1, 1919,	$100,000 00	-

Volume of Traffic, etc.

Number of passengers paying revenue carried during the period,	114,780
Number carried per mile of main railway track operated,	12,642
Number of car miles run,	35,685
Average number of persons employed,	16

Description of Equipment.

Description of Equipment.	Equipped for Electric Power.	Not Equipped.	Total Passenger Cars.	Equipped with Fenders.	Equipped with Electric Heaters.	Number of Motors.
Cars — Passenger Service.						
Box passenger cars,	5	5	10	5	5	-
Open passenger cars,	3	-	3	3	-	-
Total,	8	5	13	8	5	12
Cars — Other Service.						
Water car,	1	-	-	-	-	-
Snow ploughs,	2	-	-	-	-	-

MISCELLANEOUS EQUIPMENT.

Highway vehicles:	
Tower wagon,	1
Tip cart,	1
Other items of equipment: double harness,	1

RAILWAY OWNED AND OPERATED (BY ELECTRIC POWER).

Length of railway line,	9.079 miles.
Length of sidings, switches, etc.,	.371 "
Total, computed as single track,	9.450 "

Names of the several cities and towns in which the railways operated by the company are located: Dedham, Westwood, Walpole, Dover and Medfield.

CORPORATE NAME AND ADDRESS OF THE COMPANY.

NORFOLK WESTERN STREET RAILWAY COMPANY,

WESTWOOD, MASS.

NAMES AND BUSINESS ADDRESS OF PRINCIPAL OFFICERS.

John F. Merrill, *President*, Quincy, Mass. Fred S. Gore, *Treasurer*, 54 Kilby Street, Boston, Mass. James A. Fitton, *Clerk of Corporation*, 85 Water Street, Boston, Mass. Ezra E. Savage, *Superintendent*, Westwood, Mass.

NAMES AND RESIDENCE OF BOARD OF DIRECTORS.

James A. Fitton, Dorchester, Mass. John F. Merrill, Quincy, Mass. Fred S. Gore, Dorchester, Mass. Walter H. Grose, South Boston, Mass. Joseph Maloney, Boston, Mass. Alfred D. Gore, Dorchester, Mass. John E. Smith, Norwood, Mass.

We hereby certify that the statements contained in the foregoing report are full, just and true.

WALTER H. GROSE,
FRED S. GORE,
JOHN F. MERRILL,
JAMES A. FITTON,
Directors.
FRED S. GORE,
Treasurer.
EZRA E. SAVAGE,
Superintendent.

COMMONWEALTH OF MASSACHUSETTS.

SUFFOLK, SS. BOSTON, Oct. 15, 1904. Then personally appeared the above-named Walter H. Grose, Fred S. Gore, John F. Merrill, James A. Fitton and Ezra E. Savage, and severally made oath that the foregoing certificate by them subscribed is, to the best of their knowledge and belief, true.

Before me, ROBERT E. GOODWIN,
Justice of the Peace.

REPORT

OF THE

RECEIVERS OF THE NORFOLK WESTERN STREET RAILWAY

For the Period from January 20 to September 30, 1904.

General Exhibit for the Period.			
Gross earnings from operation,			$14,671 74
Operating expenses,			15,071 92
Gross Deficit above Operating Expenses,			$400 18
Charges upon income accrued during the period:			
Interest on funded debt,		$10,783 33	
Interest and discount on unfunded debts and loans,		499 29	
Taxes, State and local,	$276 71		
Taxes, commutation,	435 49		
		712 20	
Total Charges and Deductions from Income,			11,994 82
Total Deficit September 30, 1904,			$12,395 00

Earnings from Operation.	
Receipts from passengers carried,	$14,436 50
Receipts from rentals of buildings and other property,	166 67
Receipts from advertising in cars,	27 32
Other earnings from operation: chartered cars,	41 25
Gross Earnings from Operation,	$14,671 74

Expenses of Operation.	
General expenses:	
Salaries of general officers and clerks,	$492 95
General office expenses and supplies,	62 61
Legal expenses,	26 33
Insurance,	220 62
Other general expenses:	
Advertising,	235 15
Miscellaneous general expenses,	764 97

Maintenance of roadway and buildings:	
Repair of roadbed and track,	$1,174 15
Repair of electric line construction,	2,476 12
Repair of buildings,	126 16
Maintenance of equipment:	
Repair of cars and other vehicles,	1,027 83
Repair of electric equipment of cars,	889 52
Renewals tools and machinery,	63 52
Transportation expenses:	
Cost of electric motive power,	2,610 79
Wages and compensation of persons employed in conducting transportation,	3,558 72
Removal of snow and ice,	426 70
Other transportation expenses:	
Car service expenses and supplies,	528 39
Cleaning, oiling and sanding tracks,	387 39
TOTAL OPERATING EXPENSES,	$15,071 92

GENERAL BALANCE SHEET SEPTEMBER 30, 1904.

ASSETS.	DR.	
Cash and current assets:		
Cash,	$6,407 72	
Bills and accounts receivable,	24 60	
Other cash and current assets: accrued insurance,	152 43	
TOTAL CASH AND CURRENT ASSETS,		$6,584 75
Miscellaneous assets: materials and supplies,		160 36
Profit and loss balance (deficit),		12,395 00
TOTAL,		$19,140 11

LIABILITIES.	CR.	
Current liabilities:		
Receivers' certificates,	$14,413 25	
Audited vouchers and accounts,	833 41	
Miscellaneous current liabilities: outstanding tickets,	85 35	
TOTAL CURRENT LIABILITIES,		$15,332 01
Accrued liabilities: interest accrued and not yet due,		3,808 10
TOTAL,		$19,140 11

VOLUME OF TRAFFIC, ETC.

Number of passengers paying revenue carried during the period,	292,977
Number carried per mile of main railway track operated,	32,270
Number of car miles run,	68,600
Average number of persons employed,	16

ACCIDENTS TO PERSONS.

(A detailed statement of each accident is on file in the office of the Board.)

KILLED AND INJURED.	FROM CAUSES BEYOND THEIR OWN CONTROL.		FROM THEIR OWN MISCONDUCT OR CARELESSNESS.		TOTAL.	
	Killed.	Injured.	Killed.	Injured.	Killed.	Injured.
Passengers,	-	-	-	1	-	1
Employees,	-	-	-	-	-	-
Other persons,	-	-	-	1	-	1
TOTALS,	-	-	-	2	-	2

NAMES AND BUSINESS ADDRESS OF PRINCIPAL OFFICERS.

Geo. H. Poor, 54 Devonshire Street, Boston, Mass.; Albert F. Hayden, 84 State Street, Boston, Mass., *Receivers.* Ezra E. Savage, *Superintendent,* Westwood, Mass.

We hereby certify that the statements contained in the foregoing report are full, just and true.

GEO. H. POOR,
ALBERT F. HAYDEN,
Receivers.
EZRA E. SAVAGE,
Superintendent.

COMMONWEALTH OF MASSACHUSETTS.

SUFFOLK, SS. BOSTON, Oct. 15, 1904. Then personally appeared the above-named George H. Poor, Albert F. Hayden and Ezra E. Savage, and severally made oath that the foregoing certificate by them subscribed is, to the best of their knowledge and belief, true.

Before me, ALBERT F. CONVERSE,
Justice of the Peace.

REPORT

OF THE

NORTHAMPTON STREET RAILWAY COMPANY

For the Year ending September 30, 1904.

General Exhibit for the Year.			
Gross earnings from operation,			$149,386 74
Operating expenses,			110,121 14
Gross Income above Operating Expenses,			$39,265 60
Charges upon income accrued during the year:			
Interest on funded debt,		$10,250 00	
Interest and discount on unfunded debts and loans,		9,079 85	
Taxes, State and local,	$7,647 36		
Taxes, commutation,	3,367 33		
		11,014 69	
Total Charges and Deductions from Income,			30,344 .54
Net Divisible Income,			$8,921 06
Dividends declared (6 per cent),			18,000 00
Deficit for the year ending September 30, 1904,			$9,078 94
Amount of surplus September 30, 1903,			27,564 45
Total Surplus September 30, 1904,			$18,485 51

Earnings from Operation.	
Receipts from passengers carried,	$145,198 52
Receipts from carriage of mails,	2,099 75
Receipts from rentals of buildings and other property,	1,001 75
Receipts from advertising in cars,	898 00
Receipts from interest on deposits,	188 72
Gross Earnings from Operation,	$149,386 74

Expenses of Operation.	
General expenses:	
Salaries of general officers and clerks,	$5,400 00
General office expenses and supplies,	1,841 83
Legal expenses,	564 11

General expenses — *Concluded.*		
Insurance,		$2,083 77
Other general expenses: water rent,		177 91
Maintenance of roadway and buildings:		
Repair of roadbed and track,		9,765 91
Repair of electric line construction,		3,510 63
Repair of buildings,		637 06
Maintenance of equipment:		
Repair of cars and other vehicles,		7,249 27
Repair of electric equipment of cars,		10,016 24
Provender and stabling for horses,		458 51
Transportation expenses:		
Cost of electric motive power,		19,413 26
Wages and compensation of persons employed in conducting transportation,		39,478 44
Removal of snow and ice,		4,394 20
Damages for injuries to persons and property,		3,375 17
Other transportation expenses: sundry transportation expenses,		1,754 83
Total Operating Expenses,		$110,121 14

Property Accounts.

Additions to railway: two blocks U. S. signals,		$243 12
Additions to equipment:		
Sundry equipment,	$1,395 63	
One car truck,	275 00	
Total Additions to Equipment,		1,670 63
Total Additions to Property Accounts,		$1,913 75
Deductions from property accounts (property sold or reduced in valuation and credited to property accounts): two snow ploughs sold,		900 00
Net Addition to Property Accounts for the Year,		$1,013 75

General Balance Sheet September 30, 1904.

Assets.	Dr.	
Cost of railway:		
Roadbed and tracks,	$315,433 83	
Electric line construction, including poles, wiring, feeder lines, etc.,	59,937 95	
Engineering and other expenses incident to construction,	11,183 17	
Total Cost of Railway Owned,		$386,554 95
Cost of equipment:		
Cars and other rolling stock and vehicles,	$80,206 77	
Electric equipment of same,	71,507 22	
Horses,	280 00	
Other items of equipment: sundry equipment,	14,818 04	
Total Cost of Equipment Owned,		166,812 03

Cost of land and buildings:		
Land necessary for operation of railway, .	$20,630 21	
Electric power stations, including equipment,	103,196 99	
Other buildings necessary for operation of railway, ...	34,492 35	
TOTAL COST OF LAND AND BUILDINGS OWNED, . .		$158,319 55
Other permanent property: Meadow park, ...		2,010 76
TOTAL PERMANENT INVESTMENTS, ...		$713,697 29
Cash and current assets: cash, ...		13,565 58
Miscellaneous assets: materials and supplies, ...		9,222 64
TOTAL, ...		$736,485 51

LIABILITIES. CR.	
Capital stock, ...	$300,000 00
Funded debt, ...	225,000 00
Current liabilities: loans and notes payable, ...	193,000 00
Profit and loss balance (surplus), ...	18,485 51
TOTAL, ...	$736,485 51

CAPITAL STOCK.

Capital stock authorized by law, ...	$300,000 00	
Capital stock authorized by votes of company,	300,000 00	
Capital stock issued and outstanding, ...		$300,000 00
Number of shares issued and outstanding, .	3,000	
Number of stockholders, ...	196	
Number of stockholders in Massachusetts, .	161	
Amount of stock held in Massachusetts, . .	$248,900	

FUNDED DEBT.

DESCRIPTION OF BONDS.	Rate of Interest.	Date of Maturity.	Amount Outstanding.	Interest Paid during the Year.
	Per Cent.			
Fifty coupon bonds $500 each, trustee, Springfield Safe Deposit and Trust Company, Springfield, Mass.,	5	April 1, 1909,	$25,000 00	$1,250 00
Twenty bonds $10,000 each, Ralph B. Bardwell & Erwin H. Kennedy of Pittsfield, Mass., trustees, . .	4½	June 1, 1910,	200,000 00	9,000 00
TOTALS, ...	. .	. . .	$225,000 00	$10,250 00

VOLUME OF TRAFFIC, ETC.

Number of passengers paying revenue carried during the year,	2,968,042
Number carried per mile of main railway track operated, .	121,796
Number of car miles run, ...	790,154
Average number of persons employed, ...	95

Description of Equipment.

Description of Equipment.	Equipped for Electric Power.	Not Equipped.	Equipped with Fenders.	Equipped with Electric Heaters.	Number of Motors.
Cars — Passenger Service.					
Box passenger cars,	21	-	21	21	56
Open passenger cars,	23	-	23	-	38
Total,	44	-	44	21	94
Cars — Other Service.					
Mail cars,	1	-	1	1	4
Work cars,	1	4	-	-	2
Other cars,	3	-	3	-	6
Total,	5	4	4	1	12
Snow ploughs,	3	-	-	-	-

Miscellaneous Equipment.

Carts and snow sleds,	5
Other highway vehicles: 1 buggy, 1 sleigh, 1 wagon,	3
Horses,	3
Other items of equipment: tower wagon,	1

Railway Owned and Operated (by Electric Power).

Length of railway line,	24.369 miles.
Length of sidings, switches, etc.,	1.893 "
Total, computed as single track,	26.262 "

Railway Located Outside of Public Ways.

Length of railway line,	4.079 miles.

Names of the several cities and towns in which the railways operated by the company are located: Northampton, Easthampton and Williamsburg.

Grade Crossings with Railroads.

Grade Crossings with Railroads.	Number of Tracks at Crossing.	
	Railroad.	Railway.
Crossings of railways with railroads at grade (2 in number), viz.: —		
With New York, New Haven & Hartford Railroad, at brass shop, Haydenville, Mass.,*	1	1
With Boston & Maine Railroad, at Mt. Tom, Mass.,*	1	1
Total Number of Tracks at Crossings,	2	2

* Both of above are switch tracks and are used for freight purposes only.

ACCIDENTS TO PERSONS.

(A detailed statement of each accident is on file in the office of the Board.)

KILLED AND INJURED.	FROM CAUSES BEYOND THEIR OWN CONTROL.		FROM THEIR OWN MISCONDUCT OR CARELESSNESS.		TOTAL.	
	Killed.	Injured.	Killed.	Injured.	Killed.	Injured.
Passengers,	-	6	-	2	-	8
Employees,	-	-	-	2	-	2
Other persons,	-	-	-	-	-	-
TOTALS,	-	6	-	4	-	10

CORPORATE NAME AND ADDRESS OF THE COMPANY.

NORTHAMPTON STREET RAILWAY COMPANY,

NORTHAMPTON, MASS.

NAMES AND BUSINESS ADDRESS OF PRINCIPAL OFFICERS.

John Olmsted, *President*, Springfield, Mass. Newrie D. Winter, *Vice-President and Treasurer*, Springfield, Mass. Henry P. Field, *Clerk of Corporation*, Northampton, Mass. John C. Hammond, *General Counsel*, Northampton, Mass. Edwin C. Clark, *Superintendent*, Northampton, Mass.

NAMES AND RESIDENCE OF BOARD OF DIRECTORS.

John C. Hammond, Northampton, Mass. John A. Sullivan, Northampton, Mass. Henry M. Tyler, Northampton, Mass. John Olmsted, Springfield, Mass. Newrie D. Winter, Springfield, Mass. Frank H. Goldthwait, Springfield, Mass. George W. Cook, Springfield, Mass.

We hereby certify that the statements contained in the foregoing report are full, just and true.

JOHN OLMSTED,
JOHN C. HAMMOND,
J. A. SULLIVAN,
F. H. GOLDTHWAIT,
HENRY M. TYLER,
GEO. W. COOK,
NEWRIE D. WINTER,
Directors.
NEWRIE D. WINTER,
Treasurer.
EDWIN C. CLARK,
Superintendent.

COMMONWEALTH OF MASSACHUSETTS.

HAMPSHIRE, SS. OCT. 11, 1904. Then personally appeared the above-named John Olmsted, John C. Hammond, J. A. Sullivan, F. H. Goldthwait, Henry M. Tyler, Geo. W. Cook, Newrie D. Winter and Edwin C. Clark, and severally made oath that the foregoing certificate by them subscribed is, to the best of their knowledge and belief, true.

Before me, HENRY P. FIELD,
Justice of the Peace.

REPORT

OF THE

NORTHAMPTON & AMHERST STREET RAILWAY COMPANY

For the Year ending September 30, 1904.

General Exhibit for the Year.			
Gross earnings from operation,			$57,666 76
Operating expenses,			49,659 88
Gross Income above Operating Expenses,			$8,006 88
Charges upon income accrued during the year:			
Interest on funded debt,		$9,000 00	
Interest and discount on unfunded debts and loans,		857 47	
Taxes, State and local,	$1,566 93		
Taxes, commutation,	519 58		
		2,086 51	
Total Charges and Deductions from Income,			11,943 98
Deficit for the year ending September 30, 1904,			$3,937 10
Amount of surplus September 30, 1903,			584 53
Total Deficit September 30, 1904,			$3,352 57

Earnings from Operation.	
Receipts from passengers carried,	$56,361 63
Receipts from carriage of mails,	539 42
Receipts from carriage of express and parcels,	565 71
Receipts from advertising in cars,	200 00
Gross Earnings from Operation,	$57,666 76

Expenses of Operation.	
General expenses:	
Salaries of general officers and clerks,	$2,129 92
General office expenses and supplies,	202 71
Legal expenses,	200 00
Insurance,	877 60
Other general expenses:	
Maintenance of horse and wagon, advertising, printing, telephone,	1,084 37
Park account,	36 75

Maintenance of roadway and buildings:	
Repair of roadbed and track,	$2,748 43
Repair of electric line construction,	933 08
Repair of buildings,	209 48
Maintenance of equipment:	
Repair of cars and other vehicles,	2,099 72
Repair of electric equipment of cars,	4,699 05
Transportation expenses:	
Cost of electric motive power, $22,785.07; less power sold, $4,606.77; net,	18,178 30
Wages and compensation of persons employed in conducting transportation,	9,323 22
Removal of snow and ice,	1,602 25
Damages for injuries to persons and property,	497 25
Rentals of overhead system,	75 00
Other transportation expenses:	
Greasing, sanding track, etc.,	565 80
Car house labor,	4,196 95
TOTAL OPERATING EXPENSES,	$49,659 88

PROPERTY ACCOUNTS.

Additions to railway:	
Track construction work,	$1,976 41
New feed wire work,	606 20
TOTAL ADDITIONS TO RAILWAY,	$2,582 61
Additions to land and buildings: additional equipment of power stations,	1,378 16
TOTAL ADDITIONS TO PROPERTY ACCOUNTS,	$3,960 77

GENERAL BALANCE SHEET SEPTEMBER 30, 1904.

ASSETS.	DR.	
Cost of railway:		
Roadbed and tracks,	$233,019 50	
Electric line construction, including poles, wiring, feeder lines, etc.,	36,528 46	
Engineering and other expenses incident to construction,	15,000 00	
TOTAL COST OF RAILWAY OWNED,		$284,547 96
Cost of equipment:		
Cars and other rolling stock and vehicles and electric equipment of same,	$57,887 56	
Horses,	320 00	
TOTAL COST OF EQUIPMENT OWNED,		58,207 56
Cost of land and buildings:		
Land necessary for operation of railway,	$5,776 25	
Electric power stations, including equipment,	39,236 40	
Other buildings necessary for operation of railway,	4,245 35	
TOTAL COST OF LAND AND BUILDINGS OWNED,		49,258 00
TOTAL PERMANENT INVESTMENTS,		$392,013 52

Cash and current assets:		
Cash,	$2,406 85	
Bills and accounts receivable,	1,206 35	
TOTAL CASH AND CURRENT ASSETS,		$3,613 20
Miscellaneous assets:		
Materials and supplies,	$3,202 15	
Other assets and property: office fixtures,	250 00	
TOTAL MISCELLANEOUS ASSETS,		3,452 15
Profit and loss balance (deficit),		3,352 57
TOTAL,		$402,431 44

LIABILITIES.	CR.	
Capital stock,		$180,000 00
Funded debt,		180,000 00
Current liabilities:		
Loans and notes payable,	$35,777 36	
Audited vouchers and accounts,	6,654 08	
TOTAL CURRENT LIABILITIES,		42,431 44
TOTAL,		$402,431 44

CAPITAL STOCK.

Capital stock authorized by law,	$180,000 00	
Capital stock authorized by votes of company,	180,000 00	
Capital stock issued and outstanding,		$180,000 00
Number of shares issued and outstanding,	1,800	
Number of stockholders,	73	
Number of stockholders in Massachusetts,	69	
Amount of stock held in Massachusetts,	$88,900 00	

FUNDED DEBT.

DESCRIPTION OF BONDS.	Rate of Interest.	Date of Maturity.	Amount Outstanding.	Interest Paid during the Year.
First mortgage gold bonds, subject to call after 10 years at 105,	Per Cent. 5	Sept. 1, 1920,	$180,000 00	$9,000 00

VOLUME OF TRAFFIC, ETC.

Number of passengers paying revenue carried during the year,	1,195,558
Number carried per mile of main railway track operated,	84,509
Number of car miles run,	324,684
Average number of persons employed,	38

Description of Equipment.

Description of Equipment.	Equipped for Electric Power.	Not Equipped.	Total Passenger Cars.	Equipped with Fenders.	Equipped with Electric Heaters.	Number of Motors.
Cars — Passenger Service.						
Box passenger cars,	5	2	7	7	7	16
Open passenger cars,	5	3	8	8	-	12
Total,	10	5	15	15	7	28
Cars — Other Service.						
Work cars,	1	-	-	-	-	2
Other cars,	-	2	-	-	-	-
Snow ploughs,	-	2	-	-	-	-

Miscellaneous Equipment.

Barges and omnibuses,	1
Other highway vehicles: 1 buggy, 1 express wagon,	2
Horses,	1
Other items of equipment: harnesses, blankets, etc.	

Railway Owned and Operated (by Electric Power).

Length of railway line,	14.147 miles.
Length of sidings, switches, etc.,	.766 "
Total, computed as single track,	14.913 "

Railway Located Outside of Public Ways.

Length of railway line,	.341 mile.
Length of second main track, sidings and switches,	.104 "
Total length of main track,	.445 "

Names of the several cities and towns in which the railways operated by the company are located: Hatfield, Hadley, Amherst and Northampton.

Accidents to Persons.

(A detailed statement of each accident is on file in the office of the board.)

Killed and Injured.	From Causes beyond their own Control.		From their own Misconduct or Carelessness.		Total.	
	Killed.	Injured.	Killed.	Injured.	Killed.	Injured.
Passengers,	-	1	1	-	1	1
Employees,	-	-	-	1	-	1
Other persons,	-	-	-	2	-	2
Totals,	-	1	1	3	1	4

Corporate Name and Address of the Company.

NORTHAMPTON & AMHERST STREET RAILWAY COMPANY,

102 Main Street, Northampton, Mass.

Names and Business Address of Principal Officers.

Frederic S. Coolidge, *President*, Fitchburg, Mass. Benjamin E. Cook, *Vice-President*, Northampton, Mass. Philip Witherell, *Treasurer and Clerk of Corporation*, Northampton, Mass. Irwin & Hardy, *General Counsel*, Northampton, Mass. Crosby & Coolidge, *General Managers*, Northampton, Mass. Wm. F. Carty, *Assistant Superintendent*, Northampton, Mass.

Names and Residence of Board of Directors.

Frederic S. Coolidge, Fitchburg, Mass. Marcus A. Coolidge, Fitchburg, Mass. Edward C. Crosby, Brattleboro, Vt. Cyrus W. Wyman, deceased during the year. Clarence K. Graves, Northampton, Mass. Henry L. Williams, Northampton, Mass. Benjamin E. Cook, Northampton, Mass.

We hereby certify that the statements contained in the foregoing report are full, just and true.

FREDERIC S. COOLIDGE,
BENJAMIN E. COOK,
CLARENCE K. GRAVES,
EDWARD C. CROSBY,
HENRY L. WILLIAMS,
MARCUS A. COOLIDGE,
Directors.
PHILIP WITHERELL,
Treasurer.
WILLIAM F. CARTY,
Assistant Superintendent.

COMMONWEALTH OF MASSACHUSETTS.

HAMPSHIRE, SS. NORTHAMPTON, Oct. 11, 1904. Then personally appeared the above-named Benjamin E. Cook, Clarence K. Graves and Edward C. Crosby, directors, and Philip Witherell, treasurer, and severally made oath that the foregoing certificate by them subscribed is, to the best of their knowledge and belief, true.

Before me, ERNEST W. HARDY,
Justice of the Peace.

COMMONWEALTH OF MASSACHUSETTS.

HAMPSHIRE, SS. NORTHAMPTON, Oct. 15, 1904. Then personally appeared the within named Henry L. Williams and Marcus A. Coolidge, directors, and William F. Carty, assistant superintendent, and severally made oath that the within certificate by them subscribed is, to the best of their knowledge and belief, true.

Before me, ERNEST W. HARDY,
Justice of the Peace.

COMMONWEALTH OF MASSACHUSETTS.

WORCESTER, SS. FITCHBURG, MASS., Oct. 17, 1904. Then personally appeared Frederic S. Coolidge, and made oath that the foregoing statement by him subscribed is, to the best of his knowledge and belief, true.

Before me, FREDERICK A. CURRIER,
Notary Public.

REPORT

OF THE

NORTH END STREET RAILWAY COMPANY

FOR THE YEAR ENDING SEPTEMBER 30, 1904.

[Leased to and operated by the Worcester Consolidated.]

GENERAL EXHIBIT FOR THE YEAR.

Rental received from lease of railway,		$8,000 00
Expenses and charges upon income accrued during the year:		
Salaries and maintenance of organization,	$50 00	
Interest on funded debt,	3,750 00	
Other expenses and charges upon income:		
Treasurer's bond,	10 00	
Postage,	2 00	
TOTAL EXPENSES AND CHARGES UPON INCOME,		3,812 00
NET DIVISIBLE INCOME,		$4,188 00
Dividends declared (3¾ per cent),		4,125 00
Surplus for the year ending September 30, 1904,		$63 00
Amount of deficit September 30, 1903,		19,024 42
TOTAL DEFICIT SEPTEMBER 30, 1904,		$18,961 42

GENERAL BALANCE SHEET SEPTEMBER 30, 1904.

ASSETS.	DR.	
Cost of railway:		
Roadbed and tracks,	$86,552 86	
Electric line construction, including poles, wiring, feeder lines, etc.,	13,927 42	
TOTAL COST OF RAILWAY OWNED,		$100,480 28
Cost of equipment:		
Cars and other rolling stock and vehicles,	$12,700 00	
Electric equipment of same,	20,750 00	
Other items of equipment,	17,905 04	
TOTAL COST OF EQUIPMENT OWNED,		51,355 04

Cost of land and buildings:		
Land necessary for operation of railway, .	$6,194 70	
Buildings necessary for operation of railway, ...	7,480 06	
TOTAL COST OF LAND AND BUILDINGS OWNED, . .		$13,674 76
*TOTAL PERMANENT INVESTMENTS, ...		$165,510 08
Cash and current assets: cash, ...		528 50
Profit and loss balance (deficit), ...		18,961 42
TOTAL, ...		$185,000 00

LIABILITIES. CR.

Capital stock, ...	$110,000 00
Funded debt, ...	75,000 00
TOTAL, ...	$185,000 00

CAPITAL STOCK.

Capital stock authorized by law, ...	$110,000 00	
Capital stock authorized by votes of company,	110,000 00	
Capital stock issued and outstanding, ...		$110,000 00
Number of shares issued and outstanding, .	1,100	
Number of stockholders, ...	26	
Number of stockholders in Massachusetts, .	26	
Amount of stock held in Massachusetts, . .	$110,000 00	

FUNDED DEBT.

DESCRIPTION OF BONDS.	Rate of Interest.	Date of Maturity.	Amount Outstanding.	Interest Paid during the Year.
Coupon bonds, ...	Per Cent. 5	Feb. 1, 1915, .	$75,000 00	$3,750 00

RAILWAY OWNED.

Length of railway line, ...	4.995 miles.
Length of sidings, switches, etc., ...	.135 "
Total, computed as single track, ...	5.130 "

Names of the several cities and towns in which the railway owned by the company is located: Worcester.

CORPORATE NAME AND ADDRESS OF THE COMPANY.

NORTH END STREET RAILWAY COMPANY,

WORCESTER, MASS.

NAMES AND BUSINESS ADDRESS OF PRINCIPAL OFFICERS.

Charles A. Chase, *President*, Worcester, Mass. Thomas G. Kent, *Vice-President*, Worcester, Mass. George A. Smith, *Treasurer and Clerk of Corporation*, Worcester, Mass.

NAMES AND RESIDENCE OF BOARD OF DIRECTORS.

Charles A. Chase, Worcester, Mass. Stephen Salisbury, Worcester, Mass. Thomas G. Kent, Worcester, Mass. Thomas H. Gage, Worcester, Mass. Albert Wood, Worcester, Mass. Hosea M. Quinby, Worcester, Mass. Waldo Lincoln, Worcester, Mass. Edwin P. Curtis, Worcester, Mass. Henry S. Pratt, Worcester, Mass.

We hereby certify that the statements contained in the foregoing report are full, just and true.

CHARLES A. CHASE,
HENRY S. PRATT,
Directors.
GEO. A. SMITH,
Treasurer.

COMMONWEALTH OF MASSACHUSETTS.

WORCESTER, SS. OCT. 1, 1904. Then personally appeared the above-named Charles A. Chase, Henry S. Pratt and Geo. A. Smith, and severally made oath or affirmation that the foregoing certificate by them subscribed is, to the best of their knowledge and belief, true.

Before me, WILLIAM D. LUEY,
Justice of the Peace.

REPORT

OF THE

NORTON & TAUNTON STREET RAILWAY COMPANY

For the Year ending September 30, 1904.

General Exhibit for the Year.

Gross earnings from operation,		$48,864 08
Operating expenses,		49,726 43
Gross Deficit above Operating Expenses,		$862 35
Charges upon income accrued during the year:		
Interest on funded debt,	$14,800 00	
Interest and discount on unfunded debts and loans,	975 81	
Taxes, State and local,	584 74	
Total Charges and Deductions from Income,		16,360 55
Deficit for the year ending September 30, 1904,		$17,222 90
Amount of deficit September 30, 1903,		27,334 51
Credits to profit and loss account during the year: tools, fixtures,		1,556 72
Total Deficit September 30, 1904,		$43,000 69

Earnings from Operation.

Receipts from passengers carried,	$47,222 91
Receipts from carriage of mails,	761 53
Receipts from carriage of express and parcels,	255 25
Receipts from rentals of buildings and other property,	268 50
Receipts from advertising in cars,	250 00
Other earnings from operation: sale of old iron,	105 89
Gross Earnings from Operation,	$48,864 08

Expenses of Operation.

General expenses:	
Salaries of general officers and clerks,	$1,807 00
General office expenses and supplies,	174 75
Insurance,	1,125 00

Maintenance of roadway and buildings:	
Repair of roadbed and track,	$2,721 09
Repair of electric line construction,	754 55
Repair of buildings,	12 54
Maintenance of equipment:	
Repair of cars and other vehicles,	3,060 24
Repair of electric equipment of cars,	3,670 96
Transportation expenses:	
Cost of electric motive power,	10,941 53
Wages and compensation of persons employed in conducting transportation,	15,076 35
Removal of snow and ice,	5,079 10
Damages for injuries to persons and property,	268 93
Tolls for trackage over other railways,	864 12
Rentals of buildings and other property,	440 00
Other transportation expenses: track greasing, advertising, sanding, miscellaneous supplies,	3,730 27
TOTAL OPERATING EXPENSES,	$49,726 43

PROPERTY ACCOUNTS.

Additions to railway: light, arresters installed, span work, new,		$1,155 38
Additions to equipment:		
Additional cars (1 in number),	$450 00	
Other additions to equipment: additional motors, armatures and truck parts,	3,514 83	
TOTAL ADDITIONS TO EQUIPMENT,		3,964 83
Additions to land and buildings: additional equipment of power stations,		1,521 87
TOTAL ADDITIONS TO PROPERTY ACCOUNTS,		$6,642 08

GENERAL BALANCE SHEET SEPTEMBER 30, 1904.

ASSETS.	DR.	
Cost of railway:		
Roadbed and tracks,	$368,501 15	
Electric line construction, including poles, wiring, feeder lines, etc.,	85,102 78	
Interest accrued during construction of railway,	3,122 26	
Engineering and other expenses incident to construction,	18,700 74	
Other items of railway cost: telephone line,	856 53	
TOTAL COST OF RAILWAY OWNED,		$476,283 46
Cost of equipment:		
Cars and other rolling stock and vehicles,	$37,649 34	
Electric equipment of same,	25,104 65	
Other items of equipment: wheels and ploughs,	5,924 47	
TOTAL COST OF EQUIPMENT OWNED,		68,678 46

Cost of land and buildings:		
Land necessary for operation of railway, .	$1,502 50	
Electric power stations, including equipment,	61,206 80	
Other buildings necessary for operation of railway, ...	14,991 81	
TOTAL COST OF LAND AND BUILDINGS OWNED, . .		$77,701 11
TOTAL PERMANENT INVESTMENTS, ...		$622,663 03
Cash and current assets:		
Cash, ...	$213 38	
Bills and accounts receivable, . . .	1,482 41	
TOTAL CASH AND CURRENT ASSETS, ...		1,695 79
Miscellaneous assets: materials and supplies, . . .		5,177 54
Profit and loss balance (deficit), ...		43,000 69
TOTAL, ...		$672,537 05

LIABILITIES.	CR.	
Capital stock, ...		$297,000 00
Funded debt, ...		296,000 00
Current liabilities:		
Loans and notes payable, ...	$43,321 85	
Audited vouchers and accounts, . . .	14,248 53	
Matured interest coupons unpaid, . .	21,966 67	
TOTAL CURRENT LIABILITIES, ...		79,537 05
TOTAL, ...		$672,537 05

CAPITAL STOCK.

Capital stock authorized by law, . . .	$297,000 00	
Capital stock authorized by votes of company,	297,000 00	
Capital stock issued and outstanding, ...		$297,000 00
Number of shares issued and outstanding, .	2,970	
Number of stockholders, ...	72	
Number of stockholders in Massachusetts, .	71	
Amount of stock held in Massachusetts, . .	$257,000 00	

FUNDED DEBT.

DESCRIPTION OF BONDS.	Rate of Interest.	Date of Maturity.	Amount Outstanding.	Interest Paid during the Year.
First mortgage gold bonds, . .	Per Cent. 5	May 1, 1920, .	$296,000 00	-

VOLUME OF TRAFFIC, ETC.

Number of passengers paying revenue carried during the year, ...	1,007,962
Number carried per mile of main railway track operated, .	34,276
Number of car miles run, ...	373,781
Average number of persons employed, ...	40

Description of Equipment.

Description of Equipment.	Equipped for Electric Power.	Not Equipped.	Equipped with Fenders.	Equipped with Electric Heaters.	Number of Motors.
Cars — Passenger Service.					
Box passenger cars,	10	-	10	10	22
Open passenger cars,	8	-	8	-	16
Total,	18	-	18	10	38
Cars — Other Service.					
Box freight cars,	1	-	1	-	2
Work cars,	1	-	1	-	2
Other cars,	-	1	1	-	-
Total,	2	1	3	-	4

Railway Owned and Operated (by Electric Power).

Railway Owned, etc.	Owned.	Trackage over Other Railways.	Total Owned, etc
	Miles.	Miles.	Miles.
Length of railway line,	29.000	.407	29.407
Length of sidings, switches, etc.,	.830	-	.830
Total, Computed as Single Track,	29.830	.407	30.237

Names of the several cities and towns in which the railways operated by the company are located: Norton, Attleborough, Mansfield, Easton and Taunton.

Grade Crossings with Railroads.

Grade Crossings with Railroads.	Number of Tracks at Crossing.	
	Railroad.	Railway.
Crossings of railways with railroads at grade (1 in number), viz.: — With New York, New Haven & Hartford Railroad, Oak Street, Taunton,	4	1

Number of above crossings at which *frogs* are inserted in the tracks, 1

ACCIDENTS TO PERSONS.

(A detailed statement of each accident is on file in the office of the Board.)

KILLED AND INJURED.	FROM CAUSES BEYOND THEIR OWN CONTROL.		FROM THEIR OWN MISCONDUCT OR CARELESSNESS.		TOTAL.	
	Killed.	Injured.	Killed.	Injured.	Killed.	Injured.
Passengers,	-	-	-	-	-	-
Employees,	-	-	-	-	-	-
Other persons,	-	-	-	2	-	2
TOTALS,	-	-	-	2	-	2

CORPORATE NAME AND ADDRESS OF THE COMPANY.

NORTON & TAUNTON STREET RAILWAY COMPANY,

NORTON, MASS.

NAMES AND BUSINESS ADDRESS OF PRINCIPAL OFFICERS.

Daniel Coolidge, *President*, Philadelphia, Pa. George L. Wetherell, *Vice-President*, Chartley, Mass. Andrew H. Sweet, *Treasurer*, Norton, Mass. Robert W. Hewins, *Clerk of Corporation and Superintendent*, Norton, Mass. James A. Stiles, *General Counsel*, Gardner, Mass. Frank B. Barney, *Auditor*, Chartley, Mass.

NAMES AND RESIDENCE OF BOARD OF DIRECTORS.

Daniel Coolidge, Philadelphia, Pa. James A. Stiles, Gardner, Mass. Geo. L. Wetherell, Chartley, Mass. Frank P. Barney, Chartley, Mass. Andrew H. Sweet, Norton, Mass. Lemuel K. Wilbur, Easton, Mass. David E. Harding, Mansfield, Mass.

We hereby certify that the statements contained in the foregoing report are full, just and true.

ANDREW H. SWEET,
GEO. L. WETHERELL,
FRANK P. BARNEY,
DAVID E. HARDING,
Directors.
ANDREW H. SWEET,
Treasurer.
ROBERT W. HEWINS,
Superintendent.

COMMONWEALTH OF MASSACHUSETTS.

BRISTOL, ss. NOV. 22, 1904. Then personally appeared the above-named Andrew H. Sweet, George L. Wetherell, Frank P. Barney, David E. Harding and Robert W. Hewins, and severally made oath that the foregoing certificate by them subscribed is, to the best of their knowledge and belief, true.

Before me, JACOB A. LEONARD,
Justice of the Peace.

REPORT

OF THE

NORWOOD, CANTON & SHARON STREET RAILWAY COMPANY

For the Year ending September 30, 1904.

General Exhibit for the Year.			
Gross earnings from operation,			$8,262 24
Operating expenses,			9,978 88
Gross Deficit above Operating Expenses,			$1,716 64
Charges upon income accrued during the year:			
Interest and discount on unfunded debts and loans,		$9,776 58	
Taxes, State and local,	$514 40		
Taxes, commutation,	78 05		
		592 45	
Total Charges and Deductions from Income,			10,369 03
Deficit for the year ending September 30, 1904,			$12,085 67
Amount of deficit September 30, 1903,			30,668 37
Total Deficit September 30, 1904,			$42,754 04

Earnings from Operation.	
Receipts from passengers carried,	$7,837 15
Receipts from rentals of buildings and other property,	318 86
Receipts from advertising in cars,	106 23
Gross Earnings from Operation,	$8,262 24

Expenses of Operation.	
General expenses:	
Salaries of general officers and clerks,	$1,000 00
General office expenses and supplies,	67 27
Other general expenses: printing, advertising, travelling expenses, etc.,	171 36

Maintenance of roadway and buildings:		
Repair of roadbed and track,		$77 12
Repair of electric line construction,		85 74
Repair of buildings,		147 36
Maintenance of equipment:		
Repair of cars and other vehicles,		264 12
Repair of electric equipment of cars,		1,047 90
Transportation expenses:		
Cost of electric motive power,		2,382 36
Wages and compensation of persons employed in conducting transportation,		3,935 52
Removal of snow and ice,		346 50
Damages for injuries to persons and property,		40
Rentals of buildings and other property,		199 90
Other transportation expenses: storage grease and waste,		253 33
TOTAL OPERATING EXPENSES,		$9,978 88

PROPERTY ACCOUNTS.

Additions to railway: telephone box,		$26 62
Additions to equipment: new armature,		150 00
Additions to land and buildings: new buildings necessary for operation of railway,		17 75
TOTAL ADDITIONS TO PROPERTY ACCOUNTS,		$194 37

GENERAL BALANCE SHEET SEPTEMBER 30, 1904.

ASSETS.	DR.	
Cost of railway:		
Roadbed and tracks,	$109,408 86	
Electric line construction, including poles, wiring, feeder lines, etc.,	13,730 15	
Interest accrued during construction of railway,	2,855 87	
Engineering and other expenses incident to construction,	2,746 28	
TOTAL COST OF RAILWAY OWNED,		$128,741 16
Cost of equipment:		
Cars and other rolling stock and vehicles,	$7,100 00	
Electric equipment of same,	5,756 61	
TOTAL COST OF EQUIPMENT OWNED,		12,856 61
Cost of land and buildings: land necessary for operation of railway,		7,815 37
TOTAL PERMANENT INVESTMENTS,		$149,413 14
Cash and current assets:		
Cash,	$95 01	
Bills and accounts receivable,	3,052 33	
Other cash and current assets: interest prepaid,	316 05	
TOTAL CASH AND CURRENT ASSETS,		3,463 39

Miscellaneous assets:		
Materials and supplies,	$1,791 15	
Other assets and property: tools and office furniture,	644 40	
Total Miscellaneous Assets,		$2,435 55
Profit and loss balance (deficit),		42,754 04
Total,		$198,066 12

Liabilities.	Cr.	
Capital stock,		$62,500 00
Current liabilities:		
Loans and notes payable,	$118,755 00	
Audited vouchers and accounts,	15,435 00	
Total Current Liabilities,		134,190 00
Accrued liabilities:		
Interest accrued and not yet due,	$540 60	
Taxes accrued and not yet due,	835 52	
Total Accrued Liabilities,		1,376 12
Total,		$198,066 12

Capital Stock.

Capital stock authorized by law,	$125,000 00	
Capital stock authorized by votes of company,	125,000 00	
Amount paid in on 1,250 shares not yet issued,		$62,500 00
Number of stockholders,	11	
Number of stockholders in Massachusetts,	11	
Amount of receipts for stock held in Massachusetts,	$62,500 00	

Volume of Traffic, etc.

Number of passengers paying revenue carried during the year,	159,546
Number carried per mile of main railway track operated,	26,406
Number of car miles run,	58,287
Average number of persons employed,	10

Description of Equipment.

Description of Equipment.	Equipped for Electric Power.	Equipped with Fenders.	Equipped with Electric Heaters.	Number of Motors.
Cars — Passenger Service.				
Box passenger cars,	4	4	4	8

Railway Owned and Operated (by Electric Power).

Length of railway line, ...	6.042 miles.
Length of sidings, switches, etc., ...	.190 "
Total, computed as single track, ...	6.232 "

Names of the several cities and towns in which the railways operated by the company are located: Norwood and Sharon.

Corporate Name and Address of the Company.

NORWOOD, CANTON & SHARON STREET RAILWAY COMPANY,

8 Beacon Street, Boston, Mass.

Names and Business Address of Principal Officers.

William O. Faxon, *President*, Stoughton, Mass. John F. Perry, *Treasurer and Clerk of Corporation*, 8 Beacon Street, Boston, Mass. Tower, Talbot & Hiler, *General Counsel*, 27 State Street, Boston, Mass. Dennis G. Trayers, *Superintendent*, Sharon, Mass.

Names and Residence of Board of Directors.

William O. Faxon, Stoughton, Mass. John F. Perry, Brookline, Mass. Albert B. Stearns, Boston, Mass. Cyrus A. Noyes, Sharon, Mass. Dennis G. Trayers, Canton, Mass. George T. Bosson, Melrose Highlands, Mass. Wendell P. Battles, Weymouth, Mass.

We hereby certify that the statements contained in the foregoing report are full, just and true.

WILLIAM O. FAXON,
JOHN F. PERRY,
WENDELL P. BATTLES,
CYRUS A. NOYES,
DENNIS G. TRAYERS,
Directors.
JOHN F. PERRY,
Treasurer.
DENNIS G. TRAYERS,
Superintendent.

Commonwealth of Massachusetts.

Suffolk, ss. Nov. 25, 1904. Then personally appeared the above-named William O. Faxon, John F. Perry, Wendell P. Battles, Cyrus A. Noyes and Dennis G. Trayers, and severally made oath that the foregoing certificate by them subscribed is, to the best of their knowledge and belief, true.

Before me, EDMUND H. TALBOT,
Justice of the Peace.

REPORT

OF THE

OLD COLONY STREET RAILWAY COMPANY

For the Year ending September 30, 1904.

General Exhibit for the Year.			
Gross earnings from operation,			$2,319,996 43
Operating expenses,			1,632,469 43
Net Earnings from Operation,			$687,527 00
Miscellaneous income:			
Income from lease of road,		$27,736 67	
Park receipts,		10,725 75	
Illuminating department,		59,370 73	
Total Miscellaneous Income,			97,833 15
Gross Income above Operating Expenses,			$785,360 15
Charges upon income accrued during the year:			
Interest on funded debt,		$244,057 14	
Interest and discount on unfunded debts and loans,		82,201 08	
Taxes, State and local,	$99,342 25		
Taxes, commutation,	44,199 41		
		143,541 66	
Rentals of leased railways: Newport & Fall River Street Railway,		72,419 72	
Other deductions from income: park expenses,		22,098 50	
Total Charges and Deductions from Income,			564,318 10
Net Divisible Income,			$221,042 05
Dividends declared (8 per cent),			204,378 00
Surplus for the year ending September 30, 1904,			$16,664 05
Amount of surplus September 30, 1903,			239,308 30
Debits to profit and loss account during the year:			
Discount on bonds,		$67,087 50	
Injuries and damages prior to suspense,		975 10	
Reconstruction,		97,470 84	
Adjustment of accounts,		81,302 38	
Total Debits,			246,835 82
Total Surplus September 30, 1904,			$9,136 53

Earnings from Operation.

Receipts from passengers carried,	$2,269,710 29
Receipts from carriage of mails,	4,494 40
Receipts from tolls for use of tracks by other companies,	24,750 06
Receipts from rentals of buildings and other property,	7,442 38
Receipts from advertising in cars,	7,249 91
Receipts from interest on deposits,	4,817 34
Other earnings from operation: miscellaneous,	1,532 05
Gross Earnings from Operation,	$2,319,996 43

Expenses of Operation.

General expenses:	
Salaries of general officers and clerks,	$45,805 02
General office expenses and supplies,	13,919 93
Legal expenses,	12,059 65
Insurance,	144,880 52
Other general expenses: store room, $4,747.66; advertising, $2,082.45; miscellaneous general expenses, $32,740.19,	39,570 30
Maintenance of roadway and buildings:	
Repair of roadbed and track,	56,945 48
Repair of electric line construction,	38,037 65
Repair of buildings,	5,450 79
Maintenance of equipment:	
Repair of cars and other vehicles,	75,890 06
Repair of electric equipment of cars,	85,629 37
Renewal of horses, harnesses, shoeing, etc.,	391 61
Provender and stabling for horses,	3,389 13
Transportation expenses:	
Cost of electric motive power, $396,678.84; less power sold, $12,575.18; net,	384,103 66
Wages and compensation of persons employed in conducting transportation,	608,418 15
Removal of snow and ice,	36,029 29
Damages for injuries to persons and property,	8,942 52
Tolls for trackage over other railways,	905 32
Rentals of buildings and other property,	11,612 95
Other transportation expenses: car service supplies, $6,055.20; miscellaneous car service expenses, $36,768.26; cleaning, oiling and sanding track, $17,664.57,	60,488 03
Total Operating Expenses,	$1,632,469 43

Property Accounts.

Additions to railway:		
Extension of tracks,	$41,739 50	
Betterment in reconstruction, transferred track,	125,045 00	
New electric line construction,	173,665 85	
Other additions to railway:		
Reconstruction,	165,771 18	
Engineering,	48,903 77	
Interest during construction,	28,572 79	
Total Additions to Railway,		$583,698 09

Additions to equipment:		
Additional cars,	$6,589 78	
Betterment in reconstructed cars transferred to cars,	79,930 55	
Electric equipment of same,	1,205 97	
Betterment in reconstructed cars transferred to electric equipment,	17,307 84	
Other additions to equipment:		
Reconstructed cars,	5,862 59	
Sundry equipment,	5,259 14	
TOTAL ADDITIONS TO EQUIPMENT,		$116,155 87
Additions to land and buildings:		
Additional land necessary for operation of railway,	$16,693 19	
New electric power stations, including machinery, etc.,	731,432 06	
Other new buildings necessary for operation of railway,	5,586 67	
TOTAL ADDITIONS TO LAND AND BUILDINGS,		753,711 92
TOTAL ADDITIONS TO PROPERTY ACCOUNTS,		$1,453,565 88
Deductions from property accounts (property sold or reduced in valuation and credited to property accounts):		
Betterment in reconstruction allowed upon appraisal by Railroad Commissioners transferred to track,	$125,045 00	
Reconstruction,	99,037 49	
Cars and other vehicles,	75 00	
Betterment in reconstructed cars allowed upon appraisal by Railroad Commissioners transferred to cars and electric equipment,	97,238 39	
Land and buildings,	300 00	
Power stations,	26,246 01	
TOTAL DEDUCTIONS FROM PROPERTY ACCOUNTS,		347,941 89
NET ADDITION TO PROPERTY ACCOUNTS FOR THE YEAR,		$1,105,623 99

GENERAL BALANCE SHEET SEPTEMBER 30, 1904.

ASSETS.	DR.	
Cost of railway:		
Roadbed and tracks,	$6,389,665 94	
Electric line construction, including poles, wiring, feeder lines, etc.,	1,530,692 80	
Interest accrued during construction of railway,	179,621 10	
Engineering and other expenses incident to construction,	253,785 69	
Other items of railway cost:		
Reconstruction,	198,320 89	
Water works,	3,500 00	
TOTAL COST OF RAILWAY OWNED,		$8,555,586 42

Cost of equipment:		
Cars and other rolling stock and vehicles,	$1,689,819 38	
Reconstructed cars,	8,944 13	
Electric equipment of same,	687,626 83	
Horses,	1,675 00	
Other items of equipment: sundry equipment,	87,765 42	
TOTAL COST OF EQUIPMENT OWNED,		$2,475,830 76
Cost of land and buildings:		
Land and buildings necessary for operation of railway,	$768,804 17	
Electric power stations, including equipment,	2,074,395 60	
TOTAL COST OF LAND AND BUILDINGS OWNED,		2,843,199 77
Other permanent property: park property,		230,981 59
TOTAL PERMANENT INVESTMENTS,		$14,105,598 54
Cash and current assets:		
Cash,	$304,623 99	
Bills and accounts receivable,	100,821 53	
Sinking and other special funds,	51,809 54	
Other cash and current assets:		
Bonds in treasury,	6,000 00	
Prepaid rental, $1,333.33; prepaid fire insurance, $1,478.22; prepaid taxes, $23,683.98; prepaid interest, $2,114.62; coupon deposits, $46,090,	74,700 15	
TOTAL CASH AND CURRENT ASSETS,		537,955 21
Miscellaneous assets: materials and supplies,	$299,832 44	
Other assets and property: Newport & Fall River Street Railway lease account,	110,103 47	
TOTAL MISCELLANEOUS ASSETS,		409,935 91
TOTAL,		$15,053,489 66

LIABILITIES.		CR.
Capital stock,		$6,812,600 00
Funded debt,		5,667,000 00
Current liabilities:		
Loans and notes payable,	$1,965,500 00	
Audited vouchers and accounts,	380,220 83	
Salaries and wages,	15,946 59	
Dividends not called for,	34,108 00	
Matured interest coupons unpaid (including coupons due October 1),	46,090 00	
Miscellaneous current liabilities:		
Tickets outstanding,	10,742 78	
Employees' deposits,	5,219 93	
Meter deposits,	597 50	
TOTAL CURRENT LIABILITIES,		2,458,425 63
Accrued liabilities:		
Interest accrued and not yet due,	$43,533 31	
Taxes accrued and not yet due,	43,991 01	

Accrued liabilities — *Concluded.*		
Rentals accrued and not yet due, . . .	$18,788 34	
Miscellaneous accrued liabilities: miscellaneous, ...	14 84	
TOTAL ACCRUED LIABILITIES, ...		$106,327 50
Profit and loss balance (surplus), ...		9,136 53
TOTAL, ...		$15,053,489 66

CAPITAL STOCK.

Capital stock authorized by law, . . .	$6,816,500 00	
Capital stock authorized by votes of company,	6,816,500 00	
Capital stock issued and outstanding, ...		$6,812,600 00
Number of shares issued and outstanding, .	68,126	
Number of stockholders, ...	37	
Number of stockholders in Massachusetts, .	36	
Amount of stock held in Massachusetts, . .	$6,470,100 00	

FUNDED DEBT.

DESCRIPTION OF BONDS.	Rate of Interest.	Date of Maturity.	Amount Outstanding.	Interest Paid during the Year.
	Per Cent.			
Brockton Street Railway Company first mortgage bonds, . . .	5	Oct. 1, 1924,	$686,000 00	$33,950 00
Brockton Street Railway Company debenture bonds, ...	4½	April 1, 1905,	9,000 00	405 00
Brockton Street Railway Company debenture bonds, ...	4½	April 1, 1906,	6,000 00	585 00
Brockton Street Railway Company debenture bonds, ...	4½	April 1, 1910,	33,000 00	1,485 00
Brockton Street Railway Company debenture bonds, ...	5	Jan. 1, 1912,	16,000 00	800 00
Braintree Street Railway Company first mortgage bonds, . . .	6	July 25, 1914,	35,000 00	2,100 00
Boston, Milton & Brockton Street Railway Company first mortgage bonds, ...	5	July 1, 1919,	100,000 00	5,000 00
Brockton, Bridgewater & Taunton Street Railway Company first mortgage bonds, ...	5	Aug. 1, 1917,	200,000 00	10,000 00
Brockton & East Bridgewater Street Railway Company first mortgage bonds, ...	5	Feb. 1, 1918,	30,000 00	1,500 00
Dighton, Somerset & Swansea Street Railway Company first mortgage bonds, ...	5	Dec. 1, 1915,	125,000 00	6,250 00
Globe Street Railway Company first mortgage bonds, ...	5	April 1, 1912,	750,000 00	37,500 00
Globe Street Railway Company debenture bonds, ...	5	July 1, 1912,	550,000 00	27,500 00
Globe Street Railway Company debenture bonds, ...	5	March 1, 1910,	125,000 00	6,250 00
Norfolk Central Street Railway Company first mortgage bonds, . .	5	July 1, 1918,	60,000 00	3,000 00
Norfolk Suburban Street Railway Company first mortgage bonds, .	5	July 1, 1914,	67,000 00	3,350 00
New Bedford, Middleborough & Brockton Street Railway Company first mortgage bonds, ...	5	Jan. 1, 1920,	325,000 00	16,250 00
Providence & Taunton Street Railway Company first mortgage bonds, .	5	Sept. 1, 1918,	150,000 00	7,500 00
Amounts carried forward, . .	. .	. . . .	$3,267,000 00	$163,425 00

FUNDED DEBT — Concluded.

DESCRIPTION OF BONDS.	Rate of Interest.	Date of Maturity.	Amount Outstanding.	Interest Paid during the Year.
Amounts brought forward, . .	. .	. . . .	$3,267,000 00	$163,425 00
	Per Cent.			
South Shore & Boston Street Railway Company first mortgage bonds, .	5	Aug. 1, 1919,	335,000 00	16,750 00
Rockland & Abington Street Railway Company first mortgage bonds, .	6	May 1, 1915,	100,000 00	6,000 00
Braintree & Weymouth Street Railway Company first mortgage bonds,	5	March 1, 1917,	80,000 00	4,000 00
Bridgewater, Whitman & Rockland Street Railway Company first mortgage bonds, ...	5	Nov. 1, 1917,	85,000 00	4,250 00
Taunton Street Railway Company first mortgage bonds, . . .	5	Jan. 1, 1914,	350,000 00	17,500 00
Taunton Street Railway Company debenture bonds, ...	5	March 1, 1914,	200,000 00	10,000 00
Taunton & Brockton Street Railway Company first mortgage bonds, .	5	Aug. 1, 1917,	100,000 00	5,000 00
West Roxbury & Roslindale Street Railway Company first mortgage bonds, ...	5	Sept. 1, 1916,	150,000 00	7,500 00
Old Colony Street Railway Company first mortgage refunding bonds, .	4	July 1, 1954,	1,000,000 00	9,632 14
TOTALS, ...	. .	. . . .	$5,667,000 00	$244,057 14

VOLUME OF TRAFFIC, ETC.

Number of passengers paying revenue carried during the year,	47,518,472
Number carried per mile of main railway track operated, .	135,947
Number of car miles run, ...	8,737,971
Average number of persons employed, ...	1,744

DESCRIPTION OF EQUIPMENT.

DESCRIPTION OF EQUIPMENT.	Equipped for Electric Power.	Not Equipped.	Total Passenger Cars.	Equipped with Fenders.	Equipped with Electric Heaters.	Number of Motors.
CARS — PASSENGER SERVICE.						
Box passenger cars, ...	303	3	306	303	303	-
Open passenger cars, ...	396	15	411	398	-	-
TOTAL, ...	699	18	717	701	303	1,309
CARS — OTHER SERVICE.						
Box freight cars, ...	5	3	-	-	-	-
Platform freight cars, ...	4	14	-	-	-	-
Work cars, ...	11	-	-	-	-	-
Other cars, ...	27	-	-	-	-	-
TOTAL, ...	47	17	-	-	-	76
Snow ploughs, ...	78	-	-	-	-	10

Miscellaneous Equipment.

Carts and snow sleds, ...	21
Other highway vehicles: 9 tower wagons, 1 roller, 1 road scraper, 2 pole wagons, 3 buggies, 1 caravan, 2 democrats, 10 express wagons, 12 levellers, 1 trolley wagon, 3 walkaways, ...	45
Horses, ...	15

Railway Owned, Leased and Operated (by Electric Power).

Railway Owned, etc.	Owned.	Held under Lease or Contract.	Total Owned, Leased, etc.	Total Operated.
	Miles.	Miles.	Miles.	Miles.
Length of railway line, ...	313.536	18.492	332.028	317.553
Length of second main track, ...	34.358	.434	34.792	31.983
Total Length of Main Track, . .	347.894	18.926	366.820	349.536
Length of sidings, switches, etc., . . .	16.291	1.253	17.544	17.339
Total, Computed as Single Track, .	364.185	20.179	384.364	366.875

Railway Located Outside of Massachusetts.

Length of railway line, ...	18.492 miles.
Length of second main track, ...	.434 "
Total length of main track, ...	18.926 "
Length of sidings, switches, etc., ...	1.253 "
Total, computed as single track, ...	20.179 "

Railway Located Outside of Public Ways.

	Owned.	Operated.
	Miles.	Miles.
Length of railway line, ...	4.328	4.328
Length of second main track, ...	2.938	3.243
Total Length of Main Track, ...	7.266	7.571

Names of the several cities and towns in which the railways operated by the company are located: Abington, Avon, Boston, Braintree, Bridgewater, Brockton, Dedham, Dighton, Easton, East Bridgewater, Fall River, Freetown, Hanover, Hingham, Holbrook, Hull, Hyde Park, Lakeville, Milton, Middleborough, Needham, New Bedford, Norwell, Norwood, Quincy, Randolph, Raynham, Rehoboth, Rockland, Seekonk, Somerset, Stoughton, Taunton, Walpole, West Bridgewater, Westwood, Weymouth and Whitman, Mass., and Newport, Portsmouth, Tiverton and Middletown, R. I.

Grade Crossings with Railroads.

Grade Crossings with Railroads.	Number of Tracks at Crossing.	
	Railroad.	Railway.
Crossings of railways with railroads at grade (21 in number), viz.: —		
With Fore River Ship & Engine Company, as follows:		
At Adams Street, Braintree,	1	1
At Quincy Avenue, Quincy,	1	1
With New York, New Haven & Hartford Railroad, as follows:		
At Wales Street, Abington,	4	1
At Commercial Street, Braintree,	3	1
At Main Street, Dighton,	2	1
At Central Street, East Bridgewater,	2	1
At Freetown, siding to pumping station,	1	1
At Main Street, Hingham,	2	1
At Rockland Street, Hingham,	2	1
At Nantasket Avenue, Hull,	2	1
At Water Street, Quincy,	3	1
At Union Street Rockland,	1	1
At Pleasant Street, Somerset,	2	1
At Park Street, Stoughton,	2	1
At South Avenue, Whitman,	5	1
At Dean Street, Taunton,	2	1
At Oak Street, Taunton,	4	1
At Warren Street, Taunton,	2	1
At Weir Street, Taunton (2 crossings),	4	1
At Whittenton Street, Taunton,	2	1
At Winthrop Street, Taunton,	2	1
Total Number of Tracks at Crossings,	49	21

Accidents to Persons.

(A detailed statement of each accident is on file in the office of the Board.)

Killed and Injured.	From Causes beyond their own Control.		From their own Misconduct or Carelessness.		Total.	
	Killed.	Injured.	Killed.	Injured.	Killed.	Injured.
Passengers,	-	107	-	189	-	296
Employees,	-	-	1	20	1	20
Other persons,	-	-	4	55	4	55
Totals,	-	107	5	264	5	371

Corporate Name and Address of the Company.

OLD COLONY STREET RAILWAY COMPANY,

84 State Street, Boston, Mass.

Names and Business Address of Principal Officers.

Patrick F. Sullivan, *President*, Boston, Mass. Robert S. Goff, *Vice-President and General Manager*, Boston, Mass. Joseph H. Goodspeed, *Treasurer*, Boston, Mass. Charles Williams, *Clerk of Corporation*, Lynn, Mass. Warren & Garfield, *General Counsel*, Boston, Mass. D. Dana Bartlett, *General Auditor*, Boston, Mass. George F. Seibel, *General Superintendent*, Taunton, Mass.

NAMES AND RESIDENCE OF BOARD OF DIRECTORS.

Patrick F. Sullivan, Lowell, Mass. Robert S. Goff, Fall River, Mass. Joseph H. Goodspeed, Boston, Mass. Bradford D. Davol, Fall River, Mass. Frederick S. Hall, Taunton, Mass. John P. Morse, Brockton, Mass. Edward B. Nevin, South Weymouth, Mass.

We hereby certify that the statements contained in the foregoing report are full, just and true.

P. F. SULLIVAN,
ROBERT S. GOFF,
JOHN P. MORSE,
JOSEPH H. GOODSPEED,
BRADFORD D. DAVOL,
Directors.
JOSEPH H. GOODSPEED,
Treasurer.
ROBERT S. GOFF,
General Manager.

COMMONWEALTH OF MASSACHUSETTS.

SUFFOLK, ss. BOSTON, Nov. 16, 1904. Then personally appeared the above-named P. F. Sullivan, John P. Morse, Joseph H. Goodspeed and Bradford D. Davol, and severally made oath that the foregoing certificate by them subscribed is, to the best of their knowledge and belief, true.

Before me, D. DANA BARTLETT,
Justice of the Peace.

COMMONWEALTH OF MASSACHUSETTS.

SUFFOLK, ss. BOSTON, Nov. 24, 1904. Then personally appeared the above-named Robert S. Goff, and made oath that the foregoing certificate by him subscribed is, to the best of his knowledge and belief, true.

Before me, D. DANA BARTLETT,
Justice of the Peace.

REPORT

OF THE

PITTSFIELD ELECTRIC STREET RAILWAY COMPANY

For the Year ending September 30, 1904.

General Exhibit for the Year.		
Gross earnings from operation,		$154,067 91
Operating expenses,		109,788 39
Net Earnings from Operation,		$44,279 52
Miscellaneous income: income from park,		100 00
Gross Income above Operating Expenses,		$44,379 52
Charges upon income accrued during the year:		
Interest on funded debt,	$8,150 00	
Interest and discount on unfunded debts and loans,	1,684 03	
Taxes, State and local,	7,496 78	
Payments to sinking and other special funds: insurance fund,	7,697 90	
Other deductions from income: maintenance of park,	4,399 66	
Total Charges and Deductions from Income,		29,428 37
Net Divisible Income,		$14,951 15
Dividends declared (6 per cent),		12,000 00
Surplus for the year ending September 30, 1904,		$2,951 15
Amount of surplus September 30, 1903,		38,060 24
Credits to profit and loss account during the year: premium on bonds,		300 00
Total Surplus September 30, 1904,		$41,311 39

Earnings from Operation.	
Receipts from passengers carried,	$153,957 91
Receipts from rentals of buildings and other property,	110 00
Gross Earnings from Operation,	$154,067 91

Expenses of Operation.	
General expenses:	
Salaries of general officers and clerks,	$3,800 00
General office expenses and supplies,	573 72

General expenses — *Concluded.*		
Legal expenses,		$3,268 40
Insurance,		998 70
Other general expenses,		646 67
Maintenance of roadway and buildings:		
Repair of roadbed and track,		8,882 42
Repair of electric line construction,		1,691 28
Repair of buildings,		278 45
Maintenance of equipment:		
Repair of cars and other vehicles,		6,267 55
Repair of electric equipment of cars,		12,215 03
Renewal of horses, harnesses, shoeing, etc.,		60 93
Provender and stabling for horses,		545 48
Transportation expenses:		
Cost of electric motive power,		32,944 60
Wages and compensation of persons employed in conducting transportation,		32,773 11
Removal of snow and ice,		2,689 02
Other transportation expenses,		2,153 03
TOTAL OPERATING EXPENSES,		$109,788 39

PROPERTY ACCOUNTS.

Additions to railway:		
Extension of tracks (length, 2,000 feet),	$7,588 63	
New electric line construction (length, 2,000 feet),	939 73	
Other additions to railway: paving and rights of way,	18,563 90	
TOTAL ADDITIONS TO RAILWAY,		$27,092 26
Additions to equipment:		
Additional cars (2 in number),	$7,340 00	
Electric equipment of same,	4,400 00	
TOTAL ADDITIONS TO EQUIPMENT,		11,740 00
TOTAL ADDITIONS TO PROPERTY ACCOUNTS,		$38,832 26

GENERAL BALANCE SHEET SEPTEMBER 30, 1904.

ASSETS.	DR.	
Cost of railway:		
Roadbed and tracks,	$290,077 74	
Electric line construction, including poles, wiring, feeder lines, etc.,	44,601 01	
TOTAL COST OF RAILWAY OWNED,		$334,678 75
Cost of equipment:		
Cars and other rolling stock and vehicles,	$61,257 02	
Electric equipment of same,	40,230 04	
Horses,	147 50	
TOTAL COST OF EQUIPMENT OWNED,		101,634 56

Cost of land and buildings:		
Land necessary for operation of railway, .	$10,258 41	
Electric power stations, including equipment,	22,608 07	
Other buildings necessary for operation of railway, ...	26,039 19	
Total Cost of Land and Buildings Owned, . .		$58,905 67
Total Permanent Investments, ...		$495,218 98
Cash and current assets: cash, ...		2,008 94
Total, ...		$497,227 92

Liabilities.	Cr.	
Capital stock, ...		$200,000 00
Funded debt, ...		200,000 00
Current liabilities: loans and notes payable, ...		50,000 00
Sinking and other special funds:		
Reserve for taxes, ...	$3,079 15	
Insurance fund, ...	2,837 38	
Total Sinking and Other Special Funds, . . .		5,916 53
Profit and loss balance (surplus), ...		41,311 39
Total, ...		$497,227 92

Capital Stock.		
Capital stock authorized by law, ...	$300,000 00	
Capital stock authorized by votes of company,	300,000 00	
Capital stock issued and outstanding, ...		$200,000 00
Number of shares issued and outstanding, .	2,000	
Number of stockholders, ...	48	
Number of stockholders in Massachusetts, .	45	
Amount of stock held in Massachusetts, . .	$199,300 00	

Funded Debt.

Description of Bonds.	Rate of Interest.	Date of Maturity.	Amount Outstanding.	Interest Paid during the Year.
First mortgage bonds, ...	Per Cent. 4	July 1, 1923, .	$200,000 00	$8,150 00

Volume of Traffic, etc.

Number of passengers paying revenue carried during the year, ...	3,112,160
Number carried per mile of main railway track operated, .	124,263
Number of car miles run, ...	651,689
Average number of persons employed, ...	76

Description of Equipment.

Description of Equipment.	Equipped for Electric Power.	Equipped with Fenders.	Equipped with Electric Heaters.	Number of Motors.
Cars — Passenger Service.				
Box passenger cars,	16	16	16	46
Open passenger cars,	18	18	-	44
Total,	34	34	16	90
Cars — Other Service.				
Work cars,	1	1	-	2
Snow ploughs,	3	-	-	8

Miscellaneous Equipment.

Carts and snow sleds,	1
Other highway vehicles: carriage, gravel wagon and trolley wagon,	3
Horses,	3

Railway Owned and Operated (by Electric Power).

Length of railway line,	24 296 miles.
Length of second main track,	.749 "
Total length of main track,	25.045 "
Length of sidings, switches, etc.,	.738 "
Total, computed as single track,	25.783 "

Railway Located Outside of Public Ways.

Length of railway line,	1.558 miles.

Names of the several cities and towns in which the railways operated by the company are located: Pittsfield, Lanesborough, Cheshire, Dalton and Hinsdale.

Accidents to Persons.

(A detailed statement of each accident is on file in the office of the Board.)

Killed and Injured.	From Causes beyond their own Control.		From their own Misconduct or Carelessness.		Total.	
	Killed.	Injured.	Killed.	Injured.	Killed.	Injured.
Passengers,	-	-	-	8	-	8
Employees,	-	-	-	-	-	-
Other persons,	-	-	-	-	-	-
Totals,	-	-	-	8	-	8

Corporate Name and Address of the Company.

PITTSFIELD ELECTRIC STREET RAILWAY COMPANY,

Pittsfield, Mass.

Names and Business Address of Principal Officers.

Joseph Tucker, *President*, Pittsfield, Mass. Charles E. Merrill, *Treasurer*, Pittsfield, Mass. John M. Stevenson, *Clerk of Corporation*, Pittsfield, Mass. Peter C. Dolan, *General Manager*, Pittsfield, Mass. Patrick H. Dolan, *Superintendent*, Pittsfield, Mass.

Names and Residence of Board of Directors.

Joseph Tucker, Pittsfield, Mass. Peter C. Dolan, Pittsfield, Mass. James W. Hull, Pittsfield, Mass. Alexander Kennedy, Pittsfield, Mass. James L. Bacon, Pittsfield, Mass. John M. Stevenson, Pittsfield, Mass. Charles E. Merrill, Pittsfield, Mass.

We hereby certify that the statements contained in the foregoing report are full, just and true.

JOSEPH TUCKER,
P. C. DOLAN,
ALEXANDER KENNEDY,
J. M. STEVENSON,
C. E. MERRILL,
JAS. W. HULL,
J. L. BACON,
Directors.
CHARLES E. MERRILL,
Treasurer.
PATRICK H. DOLAN,
Superintendent.

Commonwealth of Massachusetts.

Berkshire, ss. Pittsfield, Mass., Oct. 19, 1904. Then personally appeared the above-named Joseph Tucker, P. C. Dolan, Alexander Kennedy, J. M. Stevenson, C. E. Merrill and P. H. Dolan, and severally made oath that the foregoing certificate by them subscribed is, to the best of their knowledge and belief, true.

Before me, WILLIAM L. ADAM,
Justice of the Peace.

REPORT

OF THE

PLYMOUTH, CARVER & WAREHAM STREET RAILWAY COMPANY

FOR THE YEAR ENDING SEPTEMBER 30, 1904.

[Obtained a certificate of incorporation, but has not commenced the construction of its railway.]

GENERAL BALANCE SHEET SEPTEMBER 30, 1904.

ASSETS. DR.	
Cost of railway: engineering and other expenses incident to construction,	$1,111 59
Cash and current assets: cash,	20,276 41
TOTAL,	$21,388 00
LIABILITIES. CR.	
Capital stock (amount paid in),	$21,388 00
TOTAL,	$21,388 00

CAPITAL STOCK.

Capital stock authorized by law,	$45,000 00	
Capital stock authorized by votes of company,	45,000 00	
Amount paid in on shares not yet issued,		$21,388 00
Number of subscribers,	80	
Number of subscribers in Massachusetts,	80	
Amount of subscriptions held in Massachusetts,	$21,388 00	

Names of the several cities and towns in which the railway owned by the company is located: Plymouth, Carver and Wareham.

CORPORATE NAME AND ADDRESS OF THE COMPANY.

PLYMOUTH, CARVER & WAREHAM STREET RAILWAY COMPANY,

PLYMOUTH, MASS.

NAMES AND BUSINESS ADDRESS OF PRINCIPAL OFFICERS.

Henry S. Griffith, *President*, South Carver, Mass. William S. Kyle, *Vice-President*, Plymouth, Mass. James B. Collingwood, *Treasurer and Clerk of Corporation*, Plymouth, Mass. Nathan Washburn, *General Counsel*, Middleborough, Mass.

NAMES AND RESIDENCE OF BOARD OF DIRECTORS.

Henry S. Griffith, South Carver, Mass. William S. Kyle, Plymouth, Mass. John T. Pierce, Wareham, Mass. Horace M. Saunders, Plymouth, Mass. Eugene E. Shaw, Carver, Mass. Theodore T. Vaughan, Carver, Mass. James B. Collingwood, Plymouth, Mass.

We hereby certify that the statements contained in the foregoing report are full, just and true.

HENRY S. GRIFFITH,
JOHN T. PIERCE,
WM. S. KYLE,
THEODORE T. VAUGHAN,
EUGENE E. SHAW,
HORACE M. SAUNDERS,
JAS. B. COLLINGWOOD,
Directors.
JAS. B. COLLINGWOOD,
Treasurer.

COMMONWEALTH OF MASSACHUSETTS.

PLYMOUTH, ss. Nov. 12, 1904. Then personally appeared the above-named Henry S. Griffith, John T. Pierce, Wm. S. Kyle, Theodore T. Vaughan, Eugene E. Shaw, Horace M. Saunders and James B. Collingwood, and severally made oath that the foregoing certificate by them subscribed is, to the best of their knowledge and belief, true.

Before me, EDWARD L. BURGESS,
Justice of the Peace.

REPORT

OF THE

PLYMOUTH & SANDWICH STREET RAILWAY COMPANY

For the Year ending September 30, 1904.

General Exhibit for the Year.		
Gross earnings from operation,		$7,254 45
Operating expenses,		4,973 74
Gross Income above Operating Expenses,		$2,280 71
Charges upon income accrued during the year:		
Interest and discount on unfunded debts and loans,	$750 60	
Taxes, State and local,	573 03	
Total Charges and Deductions from Income,		1,323 63
Surplus for the year ending September 30, 1904,		$957 08
Amount of surplus September 30, 1903,		3,010 79
Total Surplus September 30, 1904,		$3,967 87

Earnings from Operation.	
Receipts from passengers carried,	$7,229 45
Receipts from advertising in cars,	25 00
Gross Earnings from Operation,	$7,254 45

Expenses of Operation.	
General expenses:	
Salaries of general officers and clerks,	$383 84
General office expenses and supplies,	112 65
Maintenance of roadway and buildings:	
Repair of roadbed and track,	101 50
Repair of electric line construction,	7 80
Maintenance of equipment: repair of cars and other vehicles,	167 43
Transportation expenses:	
Cost of electric motive power,	1,920 33
Wages and compensation of persons employed in conducting transportation,	2,036 00
Removal of snow and ice,	244 19
Total Operating Expenses,	$4,973 74

Property Accounts.

Additions to railway: engineering and other expenses,		$150 00
Total Additions to Property Accounts,		$150 00

General Balance Sheet September 30, 1904.

Assets.	Dr.	
Cost of railway:		
Roadbed and tracks,	$46,303 05	
Electric line construction, including poles, wiring, feeder lines, etc.,	3,290 83	
Engineering and other expenses incident to construction,	2,395 94	
Total Cost of Railway Owned,		$51,989 82
Cost of equipment:		
Cars and other rolling stock and vehicles,	$4,976 06	
Electric equipment of same,	4,251 11	
Total Cost of Equipment Owned,		9,227 17
Cost of land and buildings:		
Land necessary for operation of railway,	$238 50	
Buildings necessary for operation of railway,	3,136 14	
Total Cost of Land and Buildings Owned,		3,374 64
Total Permanent Investments,		$64,591 63
Cash and current assets: cash,		1,520 16
Total,		$66,111 79

Liabilities.	Cr.
Capital stock,	$36,800 00
Current liabilities: loans and notes payable,	25,343 92
Profit and loss balance (surplus),	3,967 87
Total,	$66,111 79

Capital Stock.

Capital stock authorized by law,	$60,000 00	
Capital stock authorized by votes of company,	45,000 00	
Capital stock issued and outstanding,		$36,800 00
Number of shares issued and outstanding,	368	
Number of stockholders,	31	
Number of stockholders in Massachusetts,	28	
Amount of stock held in Massachusetts,	$28,700 00	

Volume of Traffic, etc.

Number of passengers paying revenue carried during the year,	78,296
Number carried per mile of main railway track operated,	12,739
Number of car miles run,	38,284
Average number of persons employed,	4

Description of Equipment.

Description of Equipment.	Equipped for Electric Power.	Equipped with Fenders.	Equipped with Electric Heaters.	Number of Motors.
Cars — Passenger Service.				
Box passenger cars,	2	2	2	4
Open passenger cars,	2	2	-	4
Total,	4	4	2	8

Railway Owned and Operated (by Electric Power).

Length of railway line,	6.146 miles.
Length of sidings, switches, etc.,	.213 "
Total, computed as single track,	6.359 "

Railway Located Outside of Public Ways.

Length of railway line,	.161 mile.

Names of the several cities and towns in which the railways operated by the company are located: Plymouth.

Corporate Name and Address of the Company.

PLYMOUTH & SANDWICH STREET RAILWAY COMPANY,

Plymouth, Mass.

Names and Business Address of Principal Officers.

Horace B. Taylor, *President*, 235 Franklin Street, Boston, Mass. Thomas E. Cornish, *Vice-President*, Plymouth, Mass. Walter L. Boyden, *Treasurer and Clerk of Corporation*, Plymouth, Mass. N. H. Dunbar, *Superintendent*, Manomet, Mass.

Names and Residence of Board of Directors.

Horace B. Taylor, Boston, Mass. Eben Kimball, Boston, Mass. Thomas E. Cornish, Plymouth, Mass. Walter L. Boyden, Plymouth, Mass. Thomas Arnold, North Abington, Mass. William Arnold, North Abington, Mass. John H. Marshall, Manomet, Mass.

We hereby certify that the statements contained in the foregoing report are full, just and true.

J. H. MARSHALL,
WALTER L. BOYDEN,
WILLIAM B. ARNOLD,
THOMAS ARNOLD,
Directors.
W. L. BOYDEN,
Treasurer.
N. H. DUNBAR,
Superintendent.

COMMONWEALTH OF MASSACHUSETTS.

PLYMOUTH, SS. Nov. 16, 1904. Then personally appeared the above-named J. H. Marshall, Walter L. Boyden, N. H. Dunbar, William B. Arnold and Thomas Arnold, and severally made oath that the foregoing certificate by them subscribed is, to the best of their knowledge and belief, true.

Before me, CHARLES B. STODDARD,
Justice of the Peace.

For Wm. B. and Thos. Arnold,

CHAS. O. TYLER,
Notary Public.

REPORT

OF THE

PROVIDENCE & FALL RIVER STREET RAILWAY COMPANY

For the Year ending September 30, 1904.

General Exhibit for the Year.

Gross earnings from operation,			$46,937 80
Operating expenses,			36,706 16
Gross Income above Operating Expenses,			$10,231 64
Charges upon income accrued during the year:			
Interest on funded debt,		$8,250 00	
Interest and discount on unfunded debts and loans,		3,326 50	
Taxes, State and local,	$1,980 00		
Taxes, commutation,	442 90		
		2,422 90	
Total Charges and Deductions from Income,			13,999 40
Deficit for the year ending September 30, 1904,			$3,767 76
Amount of deficit September 30, 1903,			2,531 31
Debits to profit and loss account during the year: settlement of old damage claims and accounts,			4,176 51
Total Deficit September 30, 1904,			$10,475 58

Earnings from Operation.

Receipts from passengers carried,	$44,572 57
Receipts from carriage of mails,	528 26
Receipts from rentals of buildings and other property,	1,626 97
Receipts from advertising in cars,	210 00
Gross Earnings from Operation,	$46,937 80

Expenses of Operation.

General expenses:	
Salaries of general officers and clerks,	$2,226 94
General office expenses and supplies,	112 31
Insurance,	1,392 00
Other general expenses: miscellaneous,	657 89

Maintenance of roadway and buildings:	
Repair of roadbed and track,	$1,947 39
Repair of electric line construction,	390 11
Repair of buildings,	105 56
Maintenance of equipment:	
Repair of cars and other vehicles,	4,817 81
Repair of electric equipment of cars,	4,812 24
Transportation expenses:	
Cost of electric motive power,	11,012 18
Wages and compensation of persons employed in conducting transportation,	8,329 49
Removal of snow and ice,	232 18
Damages for injuries to persons and property,	670 06
TOTAL OPERATING EXPENSES,	$36,706 16

PROPERTY ACCOUNTS.

Additions to railway:		
Extension of tracks (straightening curves),	$1,092 70	
New electric line construction,	70 30	
Other additions to railway: miscellaneous,	84 90	
TOTAL ADDITIONS TO RAILWAY,		$1,247 90
Additions to equipment:		
Additional cars (1 in number),	$1,352 17	
Electric equipment of same,	2,488 30	
Other additions to equipment: miscellaneous,	179 83	
TOTAL ADDITIONS TO EQUIPMENT,		4,020 30
TOTAL ADDITIONS TO PROPERTY ACCOUNTS,		$5,268 20

GENERAL BALANCE SHEET SEPTEMBER 30, 1904.

ASSETS.	DR.	
Cost of railway:		
Roadbed and tracks,	$169,979 94	
Electric line construction, including poles, wiring, feeder lines, etc.,	73,601 69	
Engineering and other expenses incident to construction,	6,255 97	
TOTAL COST OF RAILWAY OWNED,		$249,837 60
Cost of equipment:		
Cars and other rolling stock and vehicles,	$43,142 22	
Electric equipment of same,	45,193 36	
Other items of equipment,	5,634 67	
TOTAL COST OF EQUIPMENT OWNED,		93,970 25
Cost of land and buildings:		
Land necessary for operation of railway,	$8,096 75	
Buildings necessary for operation of railway,	23,090 83	
TOTAL COST OF LAND AND BUILDINGS OWNED,		31,187 58
TOTAL PERMANENT INVESTMENTS,		$374,995 43

Cash and current assets:		
Cash,	$3,795 02	
Bills and accounts receivable,	1,068 94	
Other cash and current assets:		
Prepaid insurance,	1,066 69	
Prepaid interest,	817 05	
TOTAL CASH AND CURRENT ASSETS,		$6,747 70
Miscellaneous assets: materials and supplies,		4,714 72
Profit and loss balance (deficit),		10,475 58
TOTAL,		$396,933 43

LIABILITIES.	CR.	
Capital stock,		$165,000 00
Funded debt,		165,000 00
Current liabilities:		
Loans and notes payable,	$62,500 00	
Audited vouchers and accounts,	91 69	
TOTAL CURRENT LIABILITIES,		62,591 69
Accrued liabilities:		
Interest accrued and not yet due,	$2,266 64	
Taxes accrued and not yet due,	2,075 10	
TOTAL ACCRUED LIABILITIES,		4,341 74
TOTAL,		$396,933 43

CAPITAL STOCK.

Capital stock authorized by law,	$165,000 00	
Capital stock authorized by votes of company,	165,000 00	
Capital stock issued and outstanding,		$165,000 00
Number of shares issued and outstanding,	1,650	
Number of stockholders,	34	
Number of stockholders in Massachusetts,	32	
Amount of stock held in Massachusetts,	$155,000 00	

FUNDED DEBT.

DESCRIPTION OF BONDS.	Rate of Interest.	Date of Maturity.	Amount Outstanding.	Interest Paid during the Year.
	Per Cent.			
First mortgage gold bonds,	5	July 1, 1921,	$165,000 00	$8,250 00

VOLUME OF TRAFFIC, ETC.

Number of passengers paying revenue carried during the year,	1,108,980
Number carried per mile of main railway track operated,	92,546
Number of car miles run,	259,003
Average number of persons employed,	30

Description of Equipment.

Description of Equipment.	Equipped for Electric Power.	Equipped with Fenders.	Equipped with Electric Heaters.	Number of Motors.
Cars — Passenger Service.				
Box passenger cars,	8	8	8	-
Open passenger cars,	10	10	-	-
Total,	18	18	8	60
Cars — Other Service.				
Box freight cars,	1	-	-	-
Snow ploughs,	3	-	-	-

Miscellaneous Equipment.

Carts and snow sleds,	1

Railway Owned and Operated (by Electric Power).

Length of railway line,	11.983 miles.
Length of sidings, switches, etc.,	.546 "
Total, computed as single track,	12.529 "

Railway Located Outside of Public Ways.

Length of railway line,	3.489 miles.

Names of the several cities and towns in which the railways operated by the company are located: Swansea, Rehoboth and Seekonk.

Accidents to Persons.

(A detailed statement of each accident is on file in the office of the Board.)

Killed and Injured.	From Causes beyond their own Control.		From their own Misconduct or Carelessness.		Total.	
	Killed.	Injured.	Killed.	Injured.	Killed.	Injured.
Passengers,	-	2	-	-	-	2
Employees,	-	-	-	-	-	-
Other persons,	-	-	-	1	-	1
Totals,	-	2	-	1	-	3

CORPORATE NAME AND ADDRESS OF THE COMPANY.

PROVIDENCE & FALL RIVER STREET RAILWAY COMPANY,

SWANSEA CENTRE, MASS.

NAMES AND BUSINESS ADDRESS OF PRINCIPAL OFFICERS.

John J. Whipple, *President*, 52 Boylston Street, Boston, Mass. Walter H. Trumbull, *Vice-President*, 25 Congress Street, Boston, Mass. George A. Butman, *Treasurer and Clerk of Corporation*, 8 Congress Street, Boston, Mass. George P. Dole, *Superintendent*, Swansea Centre, Mass.

NAMES AND RESIDENCE OF BOARD OF DIRECTORS.

John J. Whipple, Brockton, Mass. Walter H. Trumbull, Salem, Mass. Fred C. Hinds, Newton, Mass. Alex. B. Bruce, Lawrence, Mass. Robert Redford, Lawrence, Mass. Thomas Lahey, Haverhill, Mass. Lorenzo P. Sturtevant, Swansea, Mass. Algernon H. Barney, Swansea, Mass. George A. Butman, Malden, Mass.

We hereby certify that the statements contained in the foregoing report are full, just and true.

JOHN J. WHIPPLE,
ALEX. B. BRUCE,
ROBERT REDFORD,
FRED C. HINDS,
W. H. TRUMBULL,
THOMAS LAHEY,
GEO. A. BUTMAN,
Directors.
GEO. A. BUTMAN,
Treasurer.
GEO P. DOLE,
Superintendent.

COMMONWEALTH OF MASSACHUSETTS.

SUFFOLK, SS. BOSTON, Nov. 22, 1904. Then personally appeared the above-named John J. Whipple, Alex. B. Bruce, Robt. Redford, Fred C. Hinds, W. H. Trumbull, Thos. Lahey, Geo. A. Butman and Geo. P. Dole, and severally made oath that the foregoing certificate by them subscribed is, to the best of their knowledge and belief, true.

Before me, ARTHUR W. CLAPP,
Justice of the Peace.

REPORT

OF THE

SHELBURNE FALLS & COLRAIN STREET RAILWAY COMPANY

FOR THE YEAR ENDING SEPTEMBER 30, 1904.

GENERAL EXHIBIT FOR THE YEAR.

Gross earnings from operation,		$16,132 13
Operating expenses,		10,318 38
GROSS INCOME ABOVE OPERATING EXPENSES,		$5,813 75
Charges upon income accrued during the year:		
Interest on funded debt,	$3,000 00	
Interest and discount on unfunded debts and loans,	312 42	
Taxes, State and local,	234 01	
TOTAL CHARGES AND DEDUCTIONS FROM INCOME,		3,546 43
NET DIVISIBLE INCOME,		$2,267 32
Dividends declared (1 per cent),		500 00
Surplus for the year ending September 30, 1904,		$1,767 32
Amount of surplus September 30, 1903,		4,270 65
TOTAL SURPLUS SEPTEMBER 30, 1904,		$6,037 97

EARNINGS FROM OPERATION.

Receipts from passengers carried,	$8,264 59
Receipts from carriage of mails,	305 36
Receipts from carriage of freight,	6,542 38
Receipts from advertising in cars,	30 00
Other earnings from operation: rental of power,	989 80
GROSS EARNINGS FROM OPERATION,	$16,132 13

EXPENSES OF OPERATION.

General expenses:	
Salaries of general officers and clerks,	$880 97
General office expenses and supplies,	79 34
Insurance,	514 99
Maintenance of roadway and buildings:	
Repair of roadbed and track,	1,832 58
Repair of electric line construction,	131 82
Repair of buildings,	67 18

Maintenance of equipment:		
Repair of cars and other vehicles,		$384 01
Repair of electric equipment of cars,		406 93
Transportation expenses:		
Cost of electric motive power,		1,353 74
Wages and compensation of persons employed in conducting transportation,		2,416 24
Removal of snow and ice,		238 45
Rentals of buildings and other property,		50 00
Other transportation expenses: transferring freight, $1,952.90; sundries, $9.23,		1,962 13
TOTAL OPERATING EXPENSES,		$10,318 38

GENERAL BALANCE SHEET SEPTEMBER 30, 1904.

ASSETS.	DR.	
Cost of railway:		
Roadbed and tracks,	$51,344 86	
Electric line construction, including poles, wiring, feeder lines, etc.,	13,995 23	
Engineering and other expenses incident to construction,	5,414 79	
TOTAL COST OF RAILWAY OWNED,		$70,754 88
Cost of equipment:		
Cars and other rolling stock and vehicles,	$7,187 72	
Electric equipment of same,	3,498 92	
TOTAL COST OF EQUIPMENT OWNED,		10,686 64
Cost of land and buildings:		
Land necessary for operation of railway,	$2,030 67	
Electric power stations, including equipment,	21,517 37	
Other buildings necessary for operation of railway,	2,465 64	
TOTAL COST OF LAND AND BUILDINGS OWNED,		26,013 68
Other permanent property: equipment for renting power,		868 06
TOTAL PERMANENT INVESTMENTS,		$108,323 26
Cash and current assets:		
Cash,	$1,809 36	
Bills and accounts receivable,	303 21	
TOTAL CASH AND CURRENT ASSETS,		2,112 57
Miscellaneous assets: materials and supplies,		1,047 62
TOTAL,		$111,483 45

LIABILITIES.	CR.	
Capital stock,		$50,000 00
Funded debt,		50,000 00
Current liabilities:		
Loans and notes payable,	$4,592 70	
Matured interest coupons unpaid (including coupons due October 1),	465 00	
TOTAL CURRENT LIABILITIES,		5,057 70
Accrued liabilities: interest accrued and not yet due,		387 78
Profit and loss balance (surplus),		6,037 97
TOTAL,		$111,483 45

Capital Stock.

Capital stock authorized by law,	$50,000 00	
Capital stock authorized by votes of company,	50,000 00	
Capital stock issued and outstanding,		$50,000 00
Number of shares issued and outstanding,	500	
Number of stockholders,	108	
Number of stockholders in Massachusetts,	102	
Amount of stock held in Massachusetts,	$42,250 00	

Funded Debt.

Description of Bonds.	Rate of Interest.	Date of Maturity.	Amount Outstanding.	Interest Paid during the Year.
First mortgage bonds,	Per Cent. 6	Sept. 1, 1916,	$50,000 00	$3,000 00

Volume of Traffic, etc.

Number of passengers paying revenue carried during the year,	183,434
Number carried per mile of main railway track operated,	28,091
Number of car miles run,	54,398
Average number of persons employed,	11

Description of Equipment.

Description of Equipment.	Equipped for Electric Power.	Not Equipped.	Total Passenger Cars.	Equipped with Electric Heaters.	Number of Motors.
Cars — Passenger Service.					
Box passenger cars,	2	1	3	2	4
Open passenger cars,	1	1	2	-	2
Total,	3	2	5	2	6
Cars — Other Service.					
Box freight cars,	-	4	-	-	-
Platform freight cars,	-	4	-	-	-
Total,	-	8	-	-	-
Snow ploughs,	1	-	-	-	-

Railway Owned and Operated (by Electric Power).

Length of railway line,	6 530 miles.
Length of sidings, switches, etc.,	.480 "
Total, computed as single track,	7.010 "

RAILWAY LOCATED OUTSIDE OF PUBLIC WAYS.

Length of railway line, ...	2.550 miles.

Names of the several cities and towns in which the railways operated by the company are located: Shelburne and Colrain.

CORPORATE NAME AND ADDRESS OF THE COMPANY.

SHELBURNE FALLS & COLRAIN STREET RAILWAY COMPANY,

SHELBURNE FALLS, MASS.

NAMES AND BUSINESS ADDRESS OF PRINCIPAL OFFICERS.

Charles A. Marcy, *President*, Colrain, Mass. Francis J. Canedy, *Vice-President*, Shelburne Falls, Mass. Wilfred S. Ball, *Treasurer and Clerk of Corporation*, Shelburne Falls, Mass. Dana Malone, *General Counsel*, Greenfield, Mass. H. Burt Upton, *Superintendent*, Shelburne Falls, Mass.

NAMES AND RESIDENCE OF BOARD OF DIRECTORS.

Charles A. Marcy, Colrain, Mass. Lorenzo Griswold, Griswoldville, Mass. Edwin Baker, Shelburne Falls, Mass. Herbert Newell, Shelburne Falls, Mass. Francis J. Canedy, Shelburne Falls, Mass. Freeman L. Davenport, Shelburne Falls, Mass. Juan C. Wood, Shelburne Falls, Mass.

We hereby certify that the statements contained in the foregoing report are full, just and true.

F. J. CANEDY,
EDWIN BAKER,
H. NEWELL,
LORENZO GRISWOLD,
J. C. WOOD,
F. L. DAVENPORT,
CHARLES A. MARCY,
Directors.
W. S. BALL,
Treasurer.
H. B. UPTON,
Superintendent.

COMMONWEALTH OF MASSACHUSETTS.

FRANKLIN, SS. OCT. 18, 1904. Then personally appeared the above-named F. J. Canedy, Edwin Baker, H. Newell, Lorenzo Griswold, J. C. Wood, F. L. Davenport, Charles A. Marcy, W. S. Ball and H. B. Upton, and severally made oath that the foregoing certificate by them subscribed is, to the best of their knowledge and belief, true.

Before me, GEO. W. JENKS,
Justice of the Peace.

REPORT

OF THE

SOMERVILLE HORSE RAILROAD COMPANY

FOR THE YEAR ENDING SEPTEMBER 30, 1904.

[Leased to and operated by the Boston Elevated.]

GENERAL EXHIBIT FOR THE YEAR.

Rental received from lease of railway,	$9,180 00
Dividends declared (6 per cent),	$9,180 00

GENERAL BALANCE SHEET SEPTEMBER 30, 1904.

ASSETS. DR.	
Cost of railway,	$153,000 00
TOTAL,	$153,000 00

LIABILITIES. CR.	
Capital stock,	$153,000 00
TOTAL,	$153,000 00

CAPITAL STOCK.

Capital stock authorized by law,	$153,000 00	
Capital stock authorized by votes of company,	153,000 00	
Capital stock issued and outstanding,		$153,000 00
Number of shares issued and outstanding,	3,060	
Number of stockholders,	5	
Number of stockholders in Massachusetts,	5	
Amount of stock held in Massachusetts,	$153,000 00	

RAILWAY OWNED.

Length of railway line,	6.356 miles.
Length of second main track,	1.424 "
Total length of main track,	7.780 "
Length of sidings, switches, etc.,	.253 "
Total, computed as single track,	8.033 "

CORPORATE NAME AND ADDRESS OF THE COMPANY.

SOMERVILLE HORSE RAILROAD COMPANY,

SULLIVAN SQUARE TERMINAL, CHARLESTOWN, MASS.

NAMES AND BUSINESS ADDRESS OF PRINCIPAL OFFICERS.

William Hooper, *President*, Boston, Mass. John H. Studley, *Treasurer and Clerk of Corporation*, Boston, Mass.

NAMES AND RESIDENCE OF BOARD OF DIRECTORS.

William Hooper, Manchester, Mass. David L. Prendergast, Boston, Mass. Albert J. Holley, Everett, Mass. Geo. C. Travis, Newton, Mass. John H. Studley, Malden, Mass.

We hereby certify that the statements contained in the foregoing report are full, just and true.

WILLIAM HOOPER,
ALBERT J. HOLLEY,
DAVID L. PRENDERGAST,
JOHN H. STUDLEY,
GEORGE C. TRAVIS,
Directors.
JOHN H. STUDLEY,
Treasurer.

COMMONWEALTH OF MASSACHUSETTS.

SUFFOLK, SS. BOSTON, Nov. 2, 1904. Then personally appeared the above-named William Hooper, Albert J. Holley, Daniel L. Prendergast, John H. Studley and George C. Travis, and severally made oath that the foregoing certificate by them subscribed is, to the best of their knowledge and belief, true,

Before me, GUSTAF A. DANIELSON,
Justice of the Peace.

REPORT

OF THE

SOUTHBRIDGE & STURBRIDGE STREET RAILWAY COMPANY

For the Year ending September 30, 1904.

General Exhibit for the Year.		
Gross earnings from operation,		$34,522 81
Operating expenses,		24,811 51
Net Earnings from Operation,		$9,711 30
Miscellaneous income: from sale of old material,		58 80
Gross Income above Operating Expenses,		$9,770 10
Charges upon income accrued during the year:		
Interest on funded debt,	$3,000 00	
Interest and discount on unfunded debts and loans,	1,270 51	
Taxes, State and local,	3,373 68	
Total Charges and Deductions from Income,		7,644 19
Surplus for the year ending September 30, 1904,		$2,125 91
Amount of surplus September 30, 1903,		16,385 90
Debits to profit and loss account during the year: adjustment,		1,921 71
Total Surplus September 30, 1904,		$16,590 10

Earnings from Operation	
Receipts from passengers carried,	$33,141 45
Receipts from carriage of mails,	435 08
Receipts from carriage of express and parcels,	308 80
Receipts from tolls for use of tracks by other companies,	358 98
Receipts from rentals of buildings and other property,	218 00
Receipts from advertising in cars,	12 50
Other earnings from operation: chartered cars,	48 00
Gross Earnings from Operation,	$34,522 81

Expenses of Operation.	
General expenses:	
Salaries of general officers and clerks,	$609 99
General office expenses and supplies,	99 01
Legal expenses,	53 00
Other general expenses: miscellaneous,	683 61

Maintenance of roadway and buildings:		
Repair of roadbed and track,		$1,179 59
Repair of electric line construction,		63 69
Repair of buildings,		11 90
Maintenance of equipment:		
Repair of cars and other vehicles,		2,326 33
Repair of electric equipment of cars,		1,093 97
Transportation expenses:		
Cost of electric motive power,		7,622 49
Wages and compensation of persons employed in conducting transportation,		10,633 48
Removal of snow and ice,		110 35
Damages for injuries to persons and property,		125 00
Other transportation expenses: miscellaneous,		199 10
TOTAL OPERATING EXPENSES,		$24,811 51

PROPERTY ACCOUNTS.

Additions to railway: new electric line construction,		$800 08
TOTAL ADDITIONS TO PROPERTY ACCOUNTS,		$800 08

GENERAL BALANCE SHEET SEPTEMBER 30, 1904.

ASSETS.	DR.	
Cost of railway:		
Roadbed and tracks,	$92,650 88	
Electric line construction, including poles, wiring, feeder lines, etc.,	24,981 58	
Engineering and other expenses incident to construction,	3,000 00	
TOTAL COST OF RAILWAY OWNED,		$120,632 46
Cost of equipment: cars and other rolling stock and vehicles,		22,544 41
Cost of land and buildings:		
Land necessary for operation of railway,	$610 00	
Electric power stations, including equipment,	4,232 88	
Other buildings necessary for operation of railway,	5,001 08	
TOTAL COST OF LAND AND BUILDINGS OWNED,		9,843 96
Other permanent property:		
Pleasure resorts,	$5,312 06	
Tenement property,	3,000 00	
TOTAL COST OF OTHER PERMANENT PROPERTY OWNED,		8,312 06
TOTAL PERMANENT INVESTMENTS,		$161,332 89
Cash and current assets:		
Cash,	$5,446 99	
Bills and accounts receivable,	286 13	
Other cash and current assets: bank deposits on account coupons,	1,500 00	
TOTAL CASH AND CURRENT ASSETS,		7,233 12
TOTAL,		$168,566 01

Liabilities.	Cr.	
Capital stock,		$60,000 00
Funded debt,		60,000 00
Current liabilities:		
Loans and notes payable,	$26,000 00	
Audited vouchers and accounts,	1,618 90	
Matured interest coupons unpaid (including coupons due October 1),	1,500 00	
Total Current Liabilities,		29,118 90
Accrued liabilities:		
Interest accrued and not yet due,	$1,129 16	
Taxes accrued and not yet due,	1,727 85	
Total Accrued Liabilities,		2,857 01
Profit and loss balance (surplus),		16,590 10
Total,		$168,566 01

Capital Stock.		
Capital stock authorized by law,	$60,000 00	
Capital stock authorized by votes of company,	60,000 00	
Capital stock issued and outstanding,		$60,000 00
Number of shares issued and outstanding,	600	
Number of stockholders,	7	
Number of stockholders in Massachusetts,	1	
Amount of stock held in Massachusetts,	$100 00	

Funded Debt.

Description of Bonds.	Rate of Interest.	Date of Maturity.	Amount Outstanding.	Interest Paid during the Year.
First mortgage gold bonds,	Per Cent. 5	Jan. 1, 1917,	$60,000 00	$3,000 00

Volume of Traffic, etc.

Number of passengers paying revenue carried during the year (estimated),	736,474
Number carried per mile of main railway track operated,	97,032
Number of car miles run,	175,754
Average number of persons employed,	15

Description of Equipment.

Description of Equipment.	Equipped for Electric Power.	Not Equipped.	Total Passenger Cars.	Equipped with Fenders.	Equipped with Electric Heaters.	Number of Motors.
Cars — Passenger Service.						
Box passenger cars,	5	1	6	6	6	10
Open passenger cars,	5	-	5	5	-	10
Total,	10	1	11	11	6	20
Cars — Other Service.						
Work cars,	-	1	-	-	-	-
Snow ploughs,	-	1	-	-	-	-

Railway Owned and Operated (by Electric Power).

Length of railway line,	7.590 miles.
Length of sidings, switches, etc.,	.400 "
Total, computed as single track,	7.990 "

Names of the several cities and towns in which the railways operated by the company are located: Southbridge and Sturbridge.

Accidents to Persons.

(A detailed statement of each accident is on file in the office of the Board.)

Killed and Injured.	From Causes beyond their own Control.		From their own Misconduct or Carelessness.		Total.	
	Killed.	Injured.	Killed.	Injured.	Killed.	Injured.
Passengers,	-	1	-	2	-	3
Employees,	-	-	-	-	-	-
Other persons,	-	1	-	-	-	1
Totals,	-	2	-	2	-	4

Corporate Name and Address of the Company.

SOUTHBRIDGE & STURBRIDGE STREET RAILWAY COMPANY,

New Haven, Conn.

Names and Business Address of Principal Officers.

F. S. Curtis, *President*, Boston, Mass. A. S. May, *Treasurer*, New Haven, Conn. John G. Parker, *Clerk of Corporation*, New Haven, Conn. Samuel Anderson, *General Manager*, Putnam, Conn. Leavenworth Wheeler, *Superintendent*, Charlton City, Mass.

NAMES AND RESIDENCE OF BOARD OF DIRECTORS.

F. S. Curtis, Boston, Mass. C. S. Mellen, New Haven, Conn. Geo. J. Brush, New Haven, Conn. Edwin Milner, Moosup, Conn. Charles F. Brooker, Ansonia, Conn. E. H. McHenry, New Haven, Conn. F. W. Cheney, South Manchester, Conn.

We hereby certify that the statements contained in the foregoing report are full, just and true.

F. S. CURTIS,
C. S. MELLEN,
CHAS. F. BROOKER,
F. W. CHENEY,
EDWIN MILNER,
Directors.
A. S. MAY,
Treasurer.
LEAVENWORTH WHEELER,
Superintendent.

COMMONWEALTH OF MASSACHUSETTS.

WORCESTER, ss. Nov. 16, 1904. Personally appeared the above-named Leavenworth Wheeler, and made oath that the foregoing certificate by him subscribed is, to the best of his knowledge and belief, true.

Before me, JOHN A. HALL,
Justice of the Peace.

COMMONWEALTH OF MASSACHUSETTS.

SUFFOLK, ss. BOSTON, Nov. 18, 1904. Personally appeared the above-named F. S. Curtis and made oath that the foregoing certificate by him subscribed is, to the best of his knowledge and belief, true.

Before me, ERIC H. HAGBERG,
Justice of the Peace.

STATE OF CONNECTICUT.

COUNTY OF NEW HAVEN, ss. Nov. 12, 1904. Then personally appeared the above-named C. S. Mellen, Chas. F. Brooker, F. W. Cheney, Edwin Milner and A. S. May, and severally made oath that the foregoing certificate by them subscribed is, to the best of their knowledge and belief, true.

Before me, ALBERT H. POWELL,
Notary Public.

REPORT

OF THE

SOUTH MIDDLESEX STREET RAILWAY COMPANY

FOR THE YEAR ENDING SEPTEMBER 30, 1904.

[Railway in hands of a receiver.]

General Exhibit for the Year.			
Gross earnings from operation,			$69,591 26
Operating expenses,			58,574 40
Gross Income above Operating Expenses,			$11,016 86
Charges upon income accrued during the year:			
Interest on funded debt,		$5,000 00	
Interest and discount on unfunded debts and loans,		356 41	
Taxes, State and local,	$1,500 00		
Taxes, commutation,	691 36		
		2,191 36	
Total Charges and Deductions from Income,			7,547 77
Surplus for the year ending September 30, 1904,			$3,469 09
Amount of deficit September 30, 1903,			10,151 74
Debits to profit and loss account during the year: Natick & Needham Street Railway lease annulled and charged off,			10,269 18
Total Deficit September 30, 1904,			$16,951 83
Earnings from Operation.			
Receipts from passengers carried,			$69,137 30
Receipts from carriage of mails,			200 00
Receipts from advertising in cars,			249 96
Other earnings from operation: carrying papers,			4 00
Gross Earnings from Operation,			$69,591 26
Expenses of Operation.			
General expenses:			
Salaries of general officers and clerks,			$2,338 85
General office expenses and supplies,			1,743 82
Insurance,			1,728 00
Maintenance of roadway and buildings:			
Repair of roadbed and track,			1,473 13
Repair of electric line construction,			1,039 86
Repair of buildings,			494 54

Maintenance of equipment:	
Repair of cars and other vehicles,	$2,882 80
Repair of electric equipment of cars,	3,907 95
Transportation expenses:	
Cost of electric motive power, $20,685.18; less power sold, $2,749.52; net,	17,935 66
Wages and compensation of persons employed in conducting transportation,	19,026 62
Removal of snow and ice,	839 52
Damages for injuries to persons and property,	1,598 50
Rentals of buildings and other property,	3,565 15
TOTAL OPERATING EXPENSES,	$58,574 40

PROPERTY ACCOUNTS.

Additions to railway: new construction under contract not possible to divide until completed,		$50,000 00
Additions to land and buildings:		
Additional equipment of power stations,	$43,058 45	
Buildings necessary for operation of railway,	15,000 00	
TOTAL ADDITIONS TO LAND AND BUILDINGS,		58,058 45
TOTAL ADDITIONS TO PROPERTY ACCOUNTS,		$108,058 45
Deductions from property accounts (property sold or reduced in valuation and credited to property accounts): sale of cars and electric equipment,		1,358 69
NET ADDITION TO PROPERTY ACCOUNTS FOR THE YEAR,		$106,699 76

GENERAL BALANCE SHEET SEPTEMBER 30, 1904.

ASSETS.	DR.	
Cost of railway:		
Roadbed and tracks,	$151,723 18	
Electric line construction, including poles, wiring, feeder lines, etc.,	46,803 52	
Engineering and other expenses incident to construction,	3,591 68	
TOTAL COST OF RAILWAY OWNED,		$202,118 38
Cost of equipment:		
Cars and other rolling stock and vehicles and electric equipment of same,	$79,731 60	
Other items of equipment: office furniture and fixtures,	509 43	
TOTAL COST OF EQUIPMENT OWNED,		80,241 03
Cost of land and buildings:		
Land necessary for operation of railway,	$5,882 00	
Electric power stations, including equipment,	93,807 55	
Other buildings necessary for operation of railway,	33,350 32	
TOTAL COST OF LAND AND BUILDINGS OWNED,		133,039 87
Other permanent property: West Natick pavilion,		500 00
TOTAL PERMANENT INVESTMENTS,		$415,899 28

Cash and current assets:		
Cash,	$13,900 57	
Bills and accounts receivable,	1,585 01	
Sinking and other special funds,	8,351 50	
Other cash and current assets: unexpired insurance,	2,855 75	
TOTAL CASH AND CURRENT ASSETS,		$26,692 83
Miscellaneous assets: materials and supplies,		2,412 29
Profit and loss balance (deficit),		16,951 83
TOTAL,		$461,956 23

LIABILITIES.	CR.	
Capital stock,		$100,000 00
Funded debt,		100,000 00
Current liabilities:		
Loans and notes payable,	$182,672 20	
Audited vouchers and accounts,	65,037 16	
Matured interest coupons unpaid (including coupons due October 1),	3,333 33	
TOTAL CURRENT LIABILITIES,		251,042 69
Accrued liabilities:		
Interest accrued and not yet due,	$1,645 37	
Rentals accrued and not yet due,	916 67	
TOTAL ACCRUED LIABILITIES,		2,562 04
Sinking funds,		8,351 50
TOTAL,		$461,956 23

CAPITAL STOCK.

Capital stock authorized by law,	$100,000 00	
Capital stock authorized by votes of company,	100,000 00	
Capital stock issued and outstanding,		$100,000 00
Number of shares issued and outstanding,	1,000	
Number of stockholders,	40	
Number of stockholders in Massachusetts,	38	
Amount of stock held in Massachusetts,	$99,400 00	

FUNDED DEBT.

DESCRIPTION OF BONDS.	Rate of Interest.	Date of Maturity.	Amount Outstanding.	Interest Paid during the Year.
First mortgage bonds,	Per Cent. 5	Feb. 1, 1915,	$100,000 00	$2,500 00

Sinking and Other Special Funds.

Amount September 30, 1903, of sinking fund, ...	$8,351 50
Total Sinking and Other Special Funds September 30, 1904, ...	$8,351 50

Volume of Traffic, etc.

Number of passengers paying revenue carried during the year,	1,397,548
Number carried per mile of main railway track operated, .	108,069
Number of car miles run, ...	364,813
Average number of persons employed, ...	41

Description of Equipment.

Description of Equipment.	Equipped for Electric Power.	Equipped with Fenders.	Equipped with Electric Heaters.	Number of Motors.
Cars — Passenger Service.				
Box passenger cars, ...	13	13	13	26
Open passenger cars, ...	8	8	-	12
Total, ...	21	21	13	38
Cars — Other Service.				
Platform freight cars, ...	1	-	-	-
Snow ploughs, ...	2	-	-	-

Miscellaneous Equipment.

Railway rolling stock: snow levellers, ...	2
Highway vehicles: tower wagon, ...	1

Railway Owned and Operated (by Electric Power).

Length of railway line, ...	12.932 miles.
Length of sidings, switches, etc., ...	.896 "
Total, computed as single track, ...	13.828 "

Names of the several cities and towns in which the railways operated by the company are located: Natick, Sherborn, Framingham, Ashland and Hopkinton.

Grade Crossings with Railroads.

Grade Crossings with Railroads.	Number of Tracks at Crossing.	
	Railroad.	Railway.
Crossings of railways with railroads at grade (5 in number), viz.:—		
With New York, New Haven & Hartford Railroad, Waverly Street, Framingham,	2	1
With Boston & Albany Railroad, Waverly Street, Framingham,	1	1
With Boston & Albany Railroad, Waverly Street, Framingham,	1	1
With Boston & Albany Railroad, Waverly Street, Framingham,	1	1
With New York, New Haven & Hartford Railroad, Ashland,	1	1
Total Number of Tracks at Crossings,	6	5

Number of above crossings at which *frogs* are inserted in the tracks, . 5

General Remarks and Explanations.

The property of the company is in the custody of N. Sumner Myrick, receiver, who has operated the railway during the year covered by the report, the latter being that of both the corporation and the receiver.

Accidents to Persons.

(A detailed statement of each accident is on file in the office of the Board.)

Killed and Injured.	From Causes beyond their own Control.		From their own Misconduct or Carelessness.		Total.	
	Killed.	Injured.	Killed.	Injured.	Killed.	Injured.
Passengers,	-	4	-	5	-	9
Employees,	-	-	-	-	-	-
Other persons,	-	-	-	2	-	2
Totals,	-	4	-	7	-	11

Corporate Name and Address of the Company.

SOUTH MIDDLESEX STREET RAILWAY COMPANY,

South Framingham, Mass.

Names and Business Address of Principal Officers.

N. Sumner Myrick, *President, General Counsel and Receiver*, 601 Barristers' Hall, Boston, Mass. Andrew F. Mars, *Treasurer, Clerk of Corporation and Superintendent*, South Framingham, Mass.

Names and Residence of Board of Directors.

Clifford M. Brewer, Medford, Mass. Francis Bigelow, Natick, Mass. H. H. Whitney, Natick, Mass. John M. Fiske, Natick, Mass. Warren A. Bird, Natick, Mass. Roscoe R. Stever, Boston, Mass. Reginald Bradlee, Medford, Mass. Daniel W. Weeks, Medford, Mass. N. Sumner Myrick, Wellesley, Mass.

I hereby certify that the statements contained in the foregoing report are full, just and true.

N. SUMNER MYRICK,
Receiver.

COMMONWEALTH OF MASSACHUSETTS.

SUFFOLK, ss. Nov. 30, 1904. Then personally appeared the above-named N. Sumner Myrick, receiver, and made oath that the foregoing certificate by him subscribed is, to the best of his knowledge and belief, true.

Before me, CHARLES N. HARRIS,
Justice of the Peace.

REPORT

OF THE

SPRINGFIELD STREET RAILWAY COMPANY

For the Year ending September 30, 1904.

General Exhibit for the Year.

Gross earnings from operation,			$947,862 91
Operating expenses,			679,149 25
Gross Income above Operating Expenses,			$268,713 66
Charges upon income accrued during the year:			
Interest on funded debt,	$58,500 00		
Less interest on reserve fund,	3,500 00		
		$55,000 00	
Interest and discount on unfunded debts and loans,		14,829 96	
Taxes, State and local,	$47,545 94		
Taxes, commutation,	21,181 18		
		68,727 12	
Total Charges and Deductions from Income,			138,557 08
Net Divisible Income,			$130,156 58
Dividends declared: 8 per cent,			156,672 00
Deficit for the year ending September 30, 1904,			26,515 42
Amount of surplus September 30, 1903,			197,476 51
Debits to profit and loss account during the year:			
Discount on sale of 900 $1,000 bonds,			24,750 00
Total Surplus September 30, 1904,			$146,211 09

Earnings from Operation.

Receipts from passengers carried,	$939,881 85
Receipts from carriage of mails,	1,504 09
Receipts from rentals of buildings and other property,	3,176 97
Receipts from advertising in cars,	3,300 00
Gross Earnings from Operation,	$947,862 91

Expenses of Operation.

General expenses:	
Salaries of general officers and clerks,	$25,500 00
General office expenses and supplies,	1,384 96
Legal expenses,	4,811 77

General expenses — *Concluded.*		
Insurance,		$10,771 76
Other general expenses:		
Incidental expense,	$3,036 56	
Street sprinkling,	2,090 26	
		5,126 82
Maintenance of roadway and buildings:		
Repair of roadbed and track,		42,368 20
Repair of electric line construction,		14,195 20
Repair of buildings,		4,877 49
Maintenance of equipment:		
Repair of cars and other vehicles,		46,749 48
Repair of electric equipment of cars,		43,812 93
Renewal of horses, harnesses, shoeing, etc.,		1,439 76
Transportation expenses:		
Cost of electric motive power,		153,001 20
Wages and compensation of persons employed in conducting transportation,		278,995 93
Removal of snow and ice,		15,023 50
Damages for injuries to persons and property,		31,090 25
TOTAL OPERATING EXPENSES,		$679,149 25

PROPERTY ACCOUNTS.

Additions to railway:		
Extension of tracks,	$9,586 91	
New electric line construction,	1,622 82	
Other additions to railway:		
Block signals,	5,501 64	
Underground conduits and wires,	16,667 18	
TOTAL ADDITIONS TO RAILWAY,		$33,378 55
Additions to equipment:		
Additional cars and electrical equipment of same,	$595 15	
Other additions to equipment:		
Snow ploughs,	1,736 00	
Sundry equipment,	300 00	
TOTAL ADDITIONS TO EQUIPMENT,		2,631 15
Additions to land and buildings:		
Additional land and buildings necessary for operation of railway,	$4,426 06	
Additional equipment of power stations,	99,620 52	
TOTAL ADDITIONS TO LAND AND BUILDINGS,		104,046 58
TOTAL ADDITIONS TO PROPERTY ACCOUNTS,		$140,056 28

GENERAL BALANCE SHEET SEPTEMBER 30, 1904.

ASSETS.	DR.	
Cost of railway:		
Roadbed and tracks,	$1,465,863 39	
Electric line construction, including poles, wiring, feeder lines, etc.,	228,200 95	
Block signals,	17,165 15	
Other items of railway cost: underground conduits and wires,	262,524 88	
TOTAL COST OF RAILWAY OWNED,		$1,973,754 37

Cost of equipment:		
Cars and other rolling stock and vehicles and electric equipment of same,	$645,464 29	
Horses,	1,750 00	
Other items of equipment: sundry,	15,049 90	
TOTAL COST OF EQUIPMENT OWNED,		$662,264 19
Cost of land and buildings:		
Land and buildings necessary for operation of railway,	$389,484 30	
Electric power stations, including equipment,	737,769 41	
TOTAL COST OF LAND AND BUILDINGS OWNED,		1,127,253 71
TOTAL PERMANENT INVESTMENTS,		$3,763,272 27
Cash and current assets:		
Cash,	$17,331 18	
Sinking and other special funds,	100,000 00	
TOTAL CASH AND CURRENT ASSETS,		117,331 18
Miscellaneous assets: materials and supplies,		46,994 18
TOTAL,		$3,927,597 63

LIABILITIES.	CR.	
Capital stock,		$1,958,400 00
Funded debt,		1,500,000 00
Current liabilities:		
Loans and notes payable,	$296,000 00	
Audited vouchers and accounts,	361 70	
Salaries and wages,	4,810 74	
TOTAL CURRENT LIABILITIES,		301,172 44
Accrued liabilities:		
Interest accrued and not yet due,	$632 92	
Taxes accrued and not yet due,	21,181 18	
TOTAL ACCRUED LIABILITIES,		21,814 10
Profit and loss balance (surplus),		146,211 09
TOTAL,		$3,927,597 63

CAPITAL STOCK.

Capital stock authorized by law,	$1,958,400 00	
Capital stock authorized by votes of company,	1,958,400 00	
Capital stock issued and outstanding,		$1,958,400 00
Number of shares issued and outstanding,	19,584	
Number of stockholders,	500	
Number of stockholders in Massachusetts,	415	
Amount of stock held in Massachusetts,	$1,783,200 00	

Funded Debt.

Description of Bonds.	Rate of Interest.	Date of Maturity.	Amount Outstanding.	Interest Paid during the Year.
	Per Cent.			
Four 15-year bonds of $25,000 each, redeemable in five years from April 1, 1900, at the option of the company, dated April 1, 1895, . .	4	April 1, 1910,	$100,000 00	$4,000 00
First mortgage bonds, . . .	4	April 1, 1923,	1,400,000 00	54,500 00
Totals, ...	. .	. . .	$1,500,000 00	$58,500 00

Sinking and Other Special Funds.

Amount September 30, 1903, of reserve fund, ...	$100,000 00
Total Sinking and Other Special Funds, September 30, 1904, ...	$100,000 00

Volume of Traffic, etc.

Number of passengers paying revenue carried during the year,	18,930,360
Number carried per mile of main railway track operated, .	217,548
Number of car miles run, ...	4,639,621
Average number of persons employed, ...	500

Description of Equipment.

Description of Equipment.	Equipped for Electric Power.	Not Equipped.	Equipped with Fenders.	Equipped with Electric Heaters.	Number of Motors.
Cars — Passenger Service.					
Box passenger cars, ...	109	-	109	109	-
Open passenger cars, ...	116	-	116	-	-
Total, ...	225	-	225	109	626
Cars — Other Service.					
Box freight cars, ...	9	-	-	-	-
Platform freight cars, ...	4	5	-	-	-
Total, ...	13	5	-	-	-
Snow ploughs, ...	1	23	-	-	-

Miscellaneous Equipment.

Highway vehicles: 2 buggies, 4 sleighs, 5 wagons, . .	11
Horses, ...	10
Other items of equipment: 2 lathes, 1 wheel press, 2 upright drills, 2 field spool winders, 1 retaping machine, 1 10-horse-power stationary motor, shafting, pulleys, belts, etc.	

Railway Owned and Operated (by Electric Power).

Length of railway line, ...	64.914 miles.
Length of second main track, ...	22.103 "
Total length of main track, ...	87.017 "
Length of sidings, switches, etc., ...	6.729 "
Total, computed as single track, ...	93.746 "

Railway Located Outside of Public Ways.

Length of railway line, ...	3.237 miles.

Names of the several cities and towns in which the railways operated by the company are located: Springfield, West Springfield, Chicopee, Longmeadow, East Longmeadow and Agawam.

Grade Crossings with Railroads.

Grade Crossings with Railroads.	Number of Tracks at Crossing.	
	Railroad.	Railway.
Crossings of railways with railroads at grade (3 in number), viz.: —		
With New York, New Haven & Hartford Railroad at Boston Road,	1	1
With New York, New Haven & Hartford Railroad at Wilbraham Road, ...	1	1
With spur track, Chapman Valve Manufacturing Company at Indian Orchard, used once a day for freight only, ...	1	2
Total Number of Tracks at Crossings, ...	3	4

Accidents to Persons.

(A detailed statement of each accident is on file in the office of the Board.)

Killed and Injured.	From Causes beyond their own Control.		From their own Misconduct or Carelessness.		Total.	
	Killed.	Injured.	Killed.	Injured.	Killed.	Injured.
Passengers, ...	-	34	-	55	-	89
Employees, ...	-	9	-	6	-	15
Other persons, ...	-	19	3	30	3	49
Totals, ...	-	62	3	91	3	153

CORPORATE NAME AND ADDRESS OF THE COMPANY.

SPRINGFIELD STREET RAILWAY COMPANY,

SPRINGFIELD, MASS.

NAMES AND BUSINESS ADDRESS OF PRINCIPAL OFFICERS.

John Olmsted, *President*, Springfield, Mass. Frederick Harris, *Treasurer*, Springfield, Mass. Jonathan Barnes, *Clerk of Corporation*, Springfield, Mass. Lucius E. Ladd, *Auditor*, Springfield, Mass. Geo. W. Cook, *Superintendent*, Springfield, Mass.

NAMES AND RESIDENCE OF BOARD OF DIRECTORS.

John Olmsted, Springfield, Mass. Frederick Harris, Springfield, Mass. Alonzo Willard Damon, Springfield, Mass. George W. Cook, Springfield, Mass.

We hereby certify that the statements contained in the foregoing report are full, just and true.

JOHN OLMSTED,
FREDERICK HARRIS,
ALONZO W. DAMON,
GEO. W. COOK,
Directors.
FREDERICK HARRIS,
Treasurer.
GEO. W. COOK,
Superintendent.

COMMONWEALTH OF MASSACHUSETTS.

HAMPDEN, SS. OCT. 25, 1904. Then personally appeared the above-named John Olmsted, Frederick Harris, Alonzo W. Damon and George W. Cook, and severally made oath that the foregoing certificate by them subscribed is, to the best of their knowledge and belief, true.

Before me, JONATHAN BARNES,
Justice of the Peace.

REPORT

OF THE

SPRINGFIELD & EASTERN STREET RAILWAY COMPANY

For the Year ending September 30, 1904.

General Exhibit for the Year.		
Gross earnings from operation,		$109,626 31
Operating expenses,		77,378 24
Net Earnings from Operation,		$32,248 07
Miscellaneous income:		
Forest Lake Park,	$736 50	
Weighing and gum machines,	87 05	
Total Miscellaneous Income,		823 55
Gross Income above Operating Expenses,		$33,071 62
Charges upon income accrued during the year:		
Interest on funded debt,	$16,500 00	
Interest and discount on unfunded debts and loans,	2,690 90	
Taxes, State and local,	7,098 00	
Other deductions from income: Forest Lake Park,	3,097 56	
Total Charges and Deductions from Income,		29,386 46
Surplus for the year ending September 30, 1904,		$3,685 16
Amount of surplus September 30, 1903,		13,088 04
Debits to profit and loss account during the year: donated account,		8 49
Total Surplus September 30, 1904,		$16,764 71

Earnings from Operation.	
Receipts from passengers carried,	$108,949 41
Receipts from carriage of mails,	501 90
Receipts from advertising in cars,	175 00
Gross Earnings from Operation,	$109,626 31

Expenses of Operation.	
General expenses:	
Salaries of general officers and clerks,	$3,249 76
General office expenses and supplies,	2,366 28

General expenses — *Concluded.*		
Legal expenses,		$532 50
Insurance,		3,674 70
Other general expenses: advertising and attractions,		419 00
Maintenance of roadway and buildings:		
Repair of roadbed and track,		5,539 47
Repair of electric line construction,		1,665 63
Repair of buildings,		462 31
Maintenance of equipment:		
Repair of cars and other vehicles,		3,026 94
Repair of electric equipment of cars,		2,911 38
Transportation expenses:		
Cost of electric motive power,		25,164 99
Wages and compensation of persons employed in conducting transportation,		24,087 13
Removal of snow and ice,		2,528 50
Damages for injuries to persons and property,		449 44
Rentals of buildings and other property,		334 00
Other transportation expenses:		
Car service supplies,		607 28
Miscellaneous car service expenses,		358 93
TOTAL OPERATING EXPENSES,		$77,378 24

PROPERTY ACCOUNTS.

Additions to railway: new signals and drains,		$576 27
Additions to equipment:		
Electric equipment of cars,	$70 00	
Other additions to equipment of cars,	60 65	
TOTAL ADDITIONS TO EQUIPMENT,		130 65
Additions to land and buildings:		
New electric power stations, including machinery, etc.,	$322 12	
Additional equipment of power stations,	177 11	
Other new buildings necessary for operation of railway,	46 54	
TOTAL ADDITIONS TO LAND AND BUILDINGS,		545 77
Additions to other permanent property: Forest Lake Park property,		114 47
TOTAL ADDITIONS TO PROPERTY ACCOUNTS,		$1,367 16

GENERAL BALANCE SHEET SEPTEMBER 30, 1904.

ASSETS.	DR.	
Cost of railway:		
Roadbed and tracks,	$368,785 55	
Electric line construction, including poles, wiring, feeder lines, etc.,	129,432 39	
Engineering and other expenses incident to construction,	3,145 60	
Other items of railway cost: right of way,	6,138 87	
TOTAL COST OF RAILWAY OWNED,		$507,502 41

Cost of equipment:		
Cars and other rolling stock and vehicles,	$89,565 37	
Electric equipment of same,	20,643 82	
Other items of equipment: ploughs,	8,696 14	
TOTAL COST OF EQUIPMENT OWNED,		$118,905 33
Cost of land and buildings:		
Land necessary for operation of railway,	$1,216 24	
Electric power stations, including equipment,	81,396 19	
Other buildings necessary for operation of railway,	8,661 75	
TOTAL COST OF LAND AND BUILDINGS OWNED,		91,274 18
Other permanent property: Forest Lake Park property,		27,697 76
TOTAL PERMANENT INVESTMENTS,		$745,379 68
Cash and current assets:		
Cash,	$15,939 09	
Bills and accounts receivable,	5,735 33	
Other cash and current assets: personal property,	1,289 17	
TOTAL CASH AND CURRENT ASSETS,		22,963 59
Miscellaneous assets:		
Materials and supplies,	$2,738 76	
Other assets and property: unexpired insurance,	2,677 55	
TOTAL MISCELLANEOUS ASSETS,		5,416 31
TOTAL,		$773,759 58

LIABILITIES.	CR.	
Capital stock,		$370,000 00
Funded debt,		330,000 00
Current liabilities:		
Loans and notes payable,	$39,000 00	
Audited vouchers and accounts,	9,439 01	
Matured interest coupons unpaid (including coupons due October 1),	4,125 00	
TOTAL CURRENT LIABILITIES,		52,564 01
Accrued liabilities: taxes accrued and not yet due,		4,430 86
Profit and loss balance (surplus),		16,764 71
TOTAL,		$773,759 58

CAPITAL STOCK.		
Capital stock authorized by law,	$370,000 00	
Capital stock authorized by votes of company,	370,000 00	
Capital stock issued and outstanding,		$370,000 00
Number of shares issued and outstanding,	3,700	
Number of stockholders,	112	
Number of stockholders in Massachusetts,	96	
Amount of stock held in Massachusetts,	$209,600 00	

Funded Debt.

Description of Bonds.	Rate of Interest.	Date of Maturity.	Amount Outstanding.	Interest Paid during the Year.
First mortgage gold bonds,	Per Cent. 5	Jan. 1, 1922,	$330,000 00	$16,500 00

Volume of Traffic, etc.

Number of passengers paying revenue carried during the year,	2,204,837
Number carried per mile of main railway track operated,	77,706
Number of car miles run,	523,101
Average number of persons employed,	59

Description of Equipment.

Description of Equipment.	Equipped for Electric Power.	Not Equipped.	Equipped with Fenders.	Equipped with Electric Heaters.	Number of Motors.
Cars — Passenger Service.					
Box passenger cars,	13	-	13	13	-
Open passenger cars,	21	-	19	-	-
Total,	34	-	32	13	102
Cars — Other Service.					
Work cars,	-	1	-	-	-
Other cars,	1	-	-	-	2
Snow ploughs,	6	-	-	-	16

Miscellaneous Equipment.

Railway rolling stock: walkaway plow,	1
Highway vehicles: tip cart,	1

Railway Owned and Operated (by Electric Power).

Length of railway line,	28.374 miles.
Length of sidings, switches, etc.,	2.178 "
Total, computed as single track,	30.552 "

Railway Located Outside of Public Ways.

Length of railway line, ...	6.100 miles.

Names of the several cities and towns in which the railways operated by the company are located: Palmer, Monson, Ware and Wilbraham.

Grade Crossings with Railroads.

Grade Crossings with Railroads.	Number of Tracks at Crossing.	
	Railroad.	Railway.
Crossings of railways with railroads at grade (1 in number), viz.: — With Ware River Branch, Boston & Albany Railroad, near Town House, ...	1	1

Accidents to Persons.

(A detailed statement of each accident is on file in the office of the Board.)

Killed and Injured.	From Causes beyond their own Control.		From their own Misconduct or Carelessness.		Total.	
	Killed.	Injured.	Killed.	Injured.	Killed.	Injured.
Passengers, ...	-	1	-	7	-	8
Employees, ...	-	-	-	-	-	-
Other persons, ...	-	-	1	5	1	5
Totals, ...	-	1	1	12	1	13

Corporate Name and Address of the Company.

SPRINGFIELD & EASTERN STREET RAILWAY COMPANY,

Palmer, Mass.

Names and Business Address of Principal Officers.

Charles F. Grosvenor, *President*, Palmer, Mass. Elbridge G. Hastings, *Vice-President*, Palmer, Mass. Arthur J. Purington, *Treasurer, Clerk of Corporation and General Manager*, Palmer, Mass. Thomas W. Kenefick, *General Counsel*, Palmer, Mass. Henry L. Merry, *Auditor*, New York, N. Y. Frank S. Hunnewell, *Superintendent*, Palmer, Mass.

Names and Residence of Board of Directors.

Charles F. Grosvenor, Palmer, Mass. Elbridge G. Hastings, Palmer, Mass. Hiram E. W. Clark, Thorndike, Mass. Elmer G. Childs, Bondsville, Mass. George C. Flynt, Monson, Mass. Henry M. Clark, Springfield, Mass. Fred T. Ley, Springfield, Mass. Allan W. Paige, Bridgeport, Conn. Arthur J. Purinton, Palmer, Mass.

We hereby certify that the statements contained in the foregoing report are full, just and true.

CHAS. F. GROSVENOR,
A. W. PAIGE,
ELBRIDGE G. HASTINGS,
FRED T. LEY,
HENRY M. CLARK,
A. J. PURINTON,
GEORGE C. FLYNT,
H. E. W. CLARK,
ELMER G. CHILDS,
Directors.
ARTHUR J. PURINTON,
Treasurer.
ARTHUR J. PURINTON,
General Manager.

COMMONWEALTH OF MASSACHUSETTS.

HAMPDEN, ss. OCT. 28, 1904. Then personally appeared the above-named Fred T. Ley, Henry M. Clark and H. E. W. Clark, and severally made oath that the foregoing certificate by them subscribed is, to the best of their knowledge and belief, true.

Before me, THOMAS W. KENEFICK,
Justice of the Peace.

COMMONWEALTH OF MASSACHUSETTS.

HAMPDEN, ss. OCT. 29, 1904. Then personally appeared the above-named Chas. F. Grosvenor, Elbridge G. Hastings, Arthur J. Purinton, George C. Flynt and Elmer G. Childs, and severally made oath that the foregoing certificate by them subscribed is, to the best of their knowledge and belief, true.

Before me, ERNEST E. HOBSON,
Justice of the Peace.

STATE OF CONNECTICUT.

COUNTY OF FAIRFIELD, ss. BRIDGEPORT, Oct. 27, 1904. Then personally appeared A. W. Paige, and made oath that the foregoing certificate by him subscribed is, to the best of his knowledge and belief, true.

Before me, CARRIE B. WILSON,
Notary Public.

STATE OF CONNECTICUT.

COUNTY OF FAIRFIELD, COUNTY CLERK'S OFFICE. I, William R. Shelton, clerk of said county, and of the Superior Court, in and for said county, the same being a court of record, hereby certify, that Carrie B. Wilson, whose name is subscribed to the certificate of proof, or acknowledgment of the annexed instrument, and thereon written, was at the time of taking such proof or acknowledgment, a notary public, within and for said county, residing in said county, duly appointed, commissioned and sworn, and authorized by the laws of said State, to administer oaths, and take the acknowledgment of deeds and other instruments, to be recorded therein, and to certify the same; that I am well acquainted with her handwriting, and verily believe that the signature to the instrument hereto annexed is genuine; and that said instrument is executed and acknowledged in conformity with the laws of this State.

In testimony whereof, I have hereunto set my hand and affixed the seal of said court, at Bridgeport, in said county and State, on the twenty-seventh day of October, 1904.

WM. R. SHELTON,
Clerk.

REPORT

OF THE

TEMPLETON STREET RAILWAY COMPANY

For the Year ending September 30, 1904.

General Exhibit for the Year.		
Gross earnings from operation,		$42,372 93
Operating expenses,		33,617 04
Gross Income above Operating Expenses,		$8,755 89
Charges upon income accrued during the year:		
Interest and discount on unfunded debts and loans,	$20,833 74	
Taxes, State and local,	402 17	
Total Charges and Deductions from Income,		21,235 91
Deficit for the year ending September 30, 1904,		$12,480 02
Amount of deficit September 30, 1903,		30,292 00
Total Deficit September 30, 1904,		$42,772 02

Earnings from Operation.	
Receipts from passengers carried,	$39,803 48
Receipts from carriage of mails,	248 00
Receipts from carriage of express and parcels,	918 25
Receipts from carriage of freight,	915 81
Receipts from advertising in cars,	181 12
Other earnings from operation,	306 27
Gross Earnings from Operation,	$42,372 93

Expenses of Operation.	
General expenses:	
Salaries of general officers and clerks,	$675 00
General office expenses and supplies,	143 81
Legal expenses,	473 36
Insurance,	78 93
Other general expenses,	227 79
Maintenance of roadway and buildings:	
Repair of roadbed and track,	2,218 75
Repair of electric line construction,	190 60
Maintenance of equipment:	
Repair of cars and other vehicles,	2,188 29
Repair of electric equipment of cars,	2,241 92

Transportation expenses:	
Cost of electric motive power,	$10,669 07
Wages and compensation of persons employed in conducting transportation,	12,980 73
Removal of snow and ice,	1,028 62
Damages for injuries to persons and property,	289 45
Other transportation expenses: freight, $208.72; express, $2,	210 72
TOTAL OPERATING EXPENSES,	$33,617 04

PROPERTY ACCOUNTS.

Deductions from property accounts (property sold or reduced in valuation and credited to property accounts): depreciation on box car,	$17 27

GENERAL BALANCE SHEET SEPTEMBER 30, 1904.

ASSETS. DR.	
Cost of railway,*	$391,768 98
Cash and current assets: cash,	4,522 69
Profit and loss balance (deficit),	42,772 02
TOTAL,	$439,063 69

LIABILITIES. CR.	
Capital stock,	$75,000 00
Current liabilities: loans and notes payable,	364,063 69
TOTAL,	$439,063 69

CAPITAL STOCK.

Capital stock authorized by law,	$75,000 00	
Capital stock authorized by votes of company,	75,000 00	
Capital stock issued and outstanding,		$75,000 00
Number of shares issued and outstanding,	750	
Number of stockholders,	80	
Number of stockholders in Massachusetts,	80	
Amount of stock held in Massachusetts,	$75,000 00	

VOLUME OF TRAFFIC, ETC.

Number of passengers paying revenue carried during the year,	781,599
Number carried per mile of main railway track operated,	43,731
Number of car miles run,	236,792
Average number of persons employed,	30

* No way of ascertaining items of cost of construction and equipment.

Description of Equipment.

Description of Equipment.	Equipped for Electric Power.	Not Equipped.	Equipped with Fenders.	Equipped with Electric Heaters.	Number of Motors.
Cars — Passenger Service.					
Box passenger cars,	7	-	7	7	-
Open passenger cars,	6	-	6	-	-
Total,	13	-	13	7	26
Cars — Other Service.					
Box freight cars,	1	-	1	-	-
Platform freight cars,	-	1	-	-	-
Snow ploughs,	2	-	1	-	-

Railway Owned and Operated (by Electric Power).

Length of railway line,	17.873 miles.

Grade Crossings with Railroads.

Grade Crossings with Railroads.	Number of Tracks at Crossing.	
	Railroad.	Railway.
Crossings of railways with railroads at grade (1 in number), viz.:— With Boston & Albany Railroad, at Templeton,	1	1

Corporate Name and Address of the Company.

TEMPLETON STREET RAILWAY COMPANY,

309 Washington Street, Boston, Mass.

Names and Business Address of Principal Officers.

Charles H. Adams, *President,* 311 Washington Street, Boston, Mass. Margaret A. McElroy, *Treasurer and Clerk of Corporation,* 309 Washington Street, Boston, Mass.

Names and Residence of Board of Directors.

Charles H. Adams, Melrose, Mass. George F. McEnaney, Newton, Mass. Frederick G. Roberts, Boston, Mass. Percival Blodgett, Templeton, Mass. Frederick Greenwood, Templeton, Mass.

We hereby certify that the statements contained in the foregoing report are full, just and true.

GEORGE McENANEY,
CHAS. H. ADAMS,
FRED'K G. ROBERTS,
Directors.

COMMONWEALTH OF MASSACHUSETTS.

SUFFOLK, ss. Nov. 2, 1904. Then personally appeared the above-named George F. McEnaney, Chas. H. Adams and Fred'k G. Roberts, and severally made oath that the foregoing certificate by them subscribed is, to the best of their knowledge and belief, true.

Before me, EDWARD L. COLLINS,
Justice of the Peace.

REPORT

OF THE

UNION STREET RAILWAY COMPANY

For the Year ending September 30, 1904.

General Exhibit for the Year.			
Gross earnings from operation,			$365,409 80
Operating expenses,			238,450 76
Gross Income above Operating Expenses,			$126,959 04
Charges upon income accrued during the year:			
Interest on funded debt,		$20,000 00	
Interest and discount on unfunded debts and loans,		5,213 94	
Taxes, State and local,	$16,149 71		
Taxes, commutation,	7,625 28		
		23,774 99	
Total Charges and Deductions from Income,			48,988 93
Net Divisible Income,			$77,970 11
Dividends declared (8 per cent),			72,000 00
Surplus for the year ending September 30, 1904,			$5,970 11
Amount of surplus September 30, 1903,			175,706 59
Credits to profit and loss account during the year: adjustment of supply account,		$592 29	
Debits to profit and loss account during the year: loss by fire,		1,200 00	
Net Amount Debited to Profit and Loss,			607 71
Total Surplus September 30, 1904,			$181,068 99

Earnings from Operation.	
Receipts from passengers carried,	$337,286 96
Receipts from carriage of mails,	250 00
Receipts from tolls for use of tracks by other companies,	22,486 99
Receipts from rentals of buildings and other property,	1,477 53
Receipts from advertising in cars,	1,240 00
Receipts from interest on deposits,	209 53
Other earnings from operation:	
Special receipts,	124 40
Miscellaneous receipts,	2,334 39
Gross Earnings from Operation,	$365,409 80

Expenses of Operation.		
General expenses:		
Salaries of general officers and clerks,		$8,772 96
General office expenses and supplies,		461 99
Legal expenses,		356 60
Insurance,		4,339 58
Other general expenses,		1,471 84
Engineering,		19 30
Maintenance of roadway and buildings:		
Repair of roadbed and track,		7,242 82
Repair of electric line construction,		2,580 82
Repair of buildings,		2,686 97
Maintenance of equipment:		
Repair of cars and other vehicles,		12,336 53
Repair of electric equipment of cars,		7,676 63
Renewal of horses, harnesses, shoeing, etc.,		163 84
Provender and stabling for horses,		339 09
Repair shop tools and machinery,		697 45
Transportation expenses:		
Cost of electric motive power, $46,548.73; less power sold, $1,789.13; net,		44,759 60
Wages and compensation of persons employed in conducting transportation,		111,120 50
Removal of snow and ice,		3,218 78
Damages for injuries to persons and property,		16,136 24
Rentals of buildings and other property,		8,629 38
Other transportation expenses,		5,439 84
Total Operating Expenses,		$238,450 76

Property Accounts.		
Additions to railway: extension of tracks,		$3,854 36
Additions to equipment:		
Additional cars (1 in number),	$600 00	
Electric equipment of same,	516 67	
Other additional rolling stock and vehicles,	1,433 47	
Other additions to equipment:		
Horse account,	40 00	
Tools and machinery,	1,766 16	
Total Additions to Equipment,		4,356 30
Additions to land and buildings:		
New electric power stations, including machinery, etc.,	$17,716 19	
Other new buildings necessary for operation of railway,	558 08	
Total Additions to Land and Buildings,		18,274 27
Total Additions to Property Accounts,		$26,484 93
Deductions from property accounts (property sold or reduced in valuation and credited to property accounts):		
Electric line construction,	$2,488 26	
Buildings,	1,572 50	
Car account,	75 00	
Electric equipment of cars,	375 00	
Power station equipment,	1,272 70	
Total Deductions from Property Accounts,		5,783 46
Net Addition to Property Accounts for the Year,		$20,701 47

General Balance Sheet September 30, 1904.

Assets.	Dr.	
Cost of railway:		
Roadbed and tracks,	$650,835 23	
Electric line construction, including poles, wiring, feeder lines, etc.,	138,643 47	
Total Cost of Railway Owned,		$789,478 70
Cost of equipment:		
Cars and other rolling stock and vehicles,	$165,966 70	
Electric equipment of same,	82,379 56	
Horses,	740 00	
Other items of equipment: tools and machinery, $16,327.39; registers, $1,740.00,	18,067 39	
Total Cost of Equipment Owned,		267,153 65
Cost of land and buildings:		
Land necessary for operation of railway,	$107,960 95	
Electric power stations, including equipment,	259,757 55	
Other buildings necessary for operation of railway,	109,556 33	
Total Cost of Land and Buildings Owned,		477,274 83
Total Permanent Investments,		$1,533,907 18
Cash and current assets:		
Cash,	$18,802 39	
Bills and accounts receivable,	2,153 21	
Sinking and other special funds,	5,173 77	
Other cash and current assets,	3,630 87	
Total Cash and Current Assets,		29,760 24
Miscellaneous assets: materials and supplies,		51,139 23
Total,		$1,614,806 65

Liabilities.	Cr.	
Capital stock,		$900,000 00
Funded debt,		400,000 00
Current liabilities:		
Loans and notes payable,	$119,191 02	
Audited vouchers and accounts,	5,558 60	
Miscellaneous current liabilities: outstanding tickets,	1,362 76	
Total Current Liabilities,		126,112 38
Accrued liabilities: taxes accrued and not yet due,		7,625 28
Profit and loss balance (surplus),		181,068 99
Total,		$1,614,806 65

Capital Stock.

Capital stock authorized by law,	$900,000 00	
Capital stock authorized by votes of company,	900,000 00	
Capital stock issued and outstanding,		$900,000 00
Number of shares issued and outstanding,	9,000	
Number of stockholders,	174	
Number of stockholders in Massachusetts,	160	
Amount of stock held in Massachusetts,	$510,600 00	

Funded Debt.

Description of Bonds.	Rate of Interest.	Date of Maturity.	Amount Outstanding.	Interest Paid during the Year.
	Per Cent.			
Consolidated mortgage gold bonds (may be registered), . . .	5	Jan. 2, 1914, .	$400,000 00	$20,000 00

Sinking and Other Special Funds.

Amount September 30, 1903, of supply adjustment fund, .	$351 81
Deductions during the year from supply adjustment fund, .	$351 81

Volume of Traffic, etc.

Number of passengers paying revenue carried during the year,	6,943,443
Number carried per mile of main railway track operated, .	239,305
Number of car miles run, ...	1,489,848
Average number of persons employed, ...	240

Description of Equipment.

Description of Equipment.	Equipped for Electric Power.	Not Equipped.	Total Passenger Cars.	Equipped with Fenders.	Equipped with Electric Heaters.	Number of Motors.
Cars — Passenger Service.						
Box passenger cars, ...	48	-	48	48	48	-
Open passenger cars, ...	65	2	67	65	-	-
Total, ...	113	2	115	113	48	185
Cars — Other Service.						
Platform freight cars, ...	-	1	-	-	-	-
Work cars, ...	4	-	-	-	-	-
Other cars, ...	3	-	-	-	-	-
Total, ...	7	-	-	-	-	-
Snow ploughs, ...	7	-	-	-	-	-

Miscellaneous Equipment.

Railway rolling stock: 1 sweeper, ...	1
Highway vehicles: 1 low gear, 2 road machines, 1 democrat wagon, 1 sleigh, 1 express wagon, 3 tower wagons, 1 buggy, 3 tip carts, ...	13
Horses, ...	6

Railway Owned and Operated (by Electric Power).

Railway Owned, etc.	Owned.	Trackage over Other Railways.	Total Owned, etc.
	Miles.	Miles.	Miles.
Length of railway line,	24.499	.167	24.666
Length of second main track,	4.349	-	4.349
Total Length of Main Track,	28.848	.167	29.015
Length of sidings, switches, etc.,	1.619	.026	1.645
Total, Computed as Single Track,	30.467	.193	30.660

Names of the several cities and towns in which the railways operated by the company are located: New Bedford, Fairhaven and Dartmouth.

Grade Crossings with Railroads.

Grade Crossings with Railroads.	Number of Tracks at Crossing.	
	Railroad.	Railway.
Crossings of railways with railroads at grade (2 in number), viz.:—		
With New York, New Haven & Hartford Railroad, Eastern District, as follows:—		
At Weld Street, New Bedford, Taunton Division,	3	1
At Main Street, Fairhaven, Cape Cod Division,	2	1
Total Number of Tracks at Crossings,	5	2

Number of above crossings at which *frogs* are inserted in the tracks, . 2

Accidents to Persons.

(A detailed statement of each accident is on file in the office of the Board.)

Killed and Injured.	From Causes beyond their own Control.		From their own Misconduct or Carelessness.		Total.	
	Killed.	Injured.	Killed.	Injured.	Killed.	Injured.
Passengers,	-	2	-	19	-	21
Employees,	-	-	-	-	-	-
Other persons,	-	7	-	3	-	10
Totals,	-	9	-	22	-	31

Corporate Name and Address of the Company.

UNION STREET RAILWAY COMPANY,

7 Purchase Street, New Bedford, Mass.

NAMES AND BUSINESS ADDRESS OF PRINCIPAL OFFICERS.

Henry H. Crapo, *President*, New Bedford, Mass. Thomas B. Tripp, *Vice-President*, New Bedford, Mass. Elton S. Wilde, *Treasurer*, New Bedford, Mass. Clarence A. Cook, *Clerk of Corporation*, New Bedford, Mass. Walter Clifford, *General Counsel*, New Bedford, Mass. John F. Swift, *Auditor*, New Bedford, Mass. Edward E. Potter, *Superintendent*, New Bedford, Mass.

NAMES AND RESIDENCE OF BOARD OF DIRECTORS.

Henry H. Crapo, New Bedford, Mass. Thomas B. Tripp, New Bedford, Mass. Clarence A. Cook. New Bedford, Mass. Edward S. Brown, New Bedford, Mass. Lot B. Bates, New Bedford, Mass. Thomas S. Hathaway, New Bedford, Mass. Charles H. Lawton (deceased). Walter P. Winsor, Fairhaven, Mass. Oliver Prescott, Jr., Dartmouth, Mass.

We hereby certify that the statements contained in the foregoing report are full, just and true.

HENRY H. CRAPO,
THOMAS B. TRIPP,
W. P. WINSOR,
E. S. BROWN,
LOT B. BATES,
Directors.
ELTON S. WILDE,
Treasurer.
EDWARD E. POTTER,
Superintendent.

COMMONWEALTH OF MASSACHUSETTS.

BRISTOL, SS. NOV. 3, 1904. Then personally appeared the above-named Henry H. Crapo, Thomas B. Tripp, W. P. Winsor, E. S. Brown, Lot B. Bates, Elton S. Wilde and Edward E. Potter, and severally made oath that the foregoing certificate by them subscribed is, to the best of their knowledge and belief, true.

Before me, ISAAC W. PHELPS,
Justice of the Peace.

REPORT

OF THE

UXBRIDGE & BLACKSTONE STREET RAILWAY COMPANY

For the Year ending September 30, 1904.

General Exhibit for the Year.

Gross earnings from operation,		$23,781 45
Operating expenses,		13,346 99
Gross Income above Operating Expenses,		$10,434 46
Charges upon income accrued during the year:		
Interest on funded debt,	$4,000 00	
Interest and discount on unfunded debts and loans,	1,725 00	
Taxes, State and local,	1,418 83	
Total Charges and Deductions from Income,		7,143 83
Net Divisible Income,		$3,290 63
Dividends declared (4 per cent),		3,200 00
Surplus for the year ending September 30, 1904,		$90 63
Amount of surplus September 30, 1903,		7,819 20
Total Surplus September 30, 1904,		$7,909 83

Earnings from Operation.

Receipts from passengers carried,	$23,750 20
Receipts from advertising in cars,	31 25
Gross Earnings from Operation,	$23,781 45

Expenses of Operation.

General expenses:	
Salaries of general officers and clerks,	$1,033 26
General office expenses and supplies,	172 66
Legal expenses,	30 50
Insurance,	332 25
Maintenance of roadway and buildings:	
Repair of roadbed and track,	228 84
Repair of buildings,	11 00
Maintenance of equipment:	
Repair of cars and other vehicles,	506 91
Repair of electric equipment of cars,	315 90

Transportation expenses:		
Cost of electric motive power,		$4,292 96
Wages and compensation of persons employed in conducting transportation,		5,880 41
Removal of snow and ice,		77 48
Other transportation expenses:		
Rental of waiting station, $60; tickets, signs, etc., $183.33		243 33
Car service supplies, — oil, waste, parts, etc.,		221 49
TOTAL OPERATING EXPENSES,		$13,346 99

PROPERTY ACCOUNTS.

Additions to railway:		
Extension of tracks (length, 264 feet),	$2,637 14	
Other additions to railway:		
Engineering and legal,	332 35	
Telephone system,	269 44	
TOTAL ADDITIONS TO RAILWAY,		$3,238 93
Additions to equipment:		
Electric equipment of cars,	$329 07	
Additional rolling stock and vehicles,	249 28	
Other additions to equipment: office furniture and fixtures,	85 25	
TOTAL ADDITIONS TO EQUIPMENT,		663 60
Additions to land and buildings:		
Additional land necessary for operation of railway,	$65 00	
New buildings necessary for operation of railway,	141 66	
TOTAL ADDITIONS TO LAND AND BUILDINGS,		206 66
TOTAL ADDITIONS TO PROPERTY ACCOUNTS,		$4,109 19

GENERAL BALANCE SHEET SEPTEMBER 30, 1904.

ASSETS.	DR.	
Cost of railway:		
Roadbed and tracks,	$120,172 15	
Electric line construction, including poles, wiring, feeder lines, etc.,	20,509 72	
Interest accrued during construction of railway,	3,845 61	
Engineering and other expenses incident to construction,	14,014 55	
Other items of railway cost: telephone system,	269 44	
TOTAL COST OF RAILWAY OWNED,		$158,811 47
Cost of equipment:		
Cars and other rolling stock and vehicles,	$13,887 48	
Electric equipment of same,	13,374 57	
Other items of equipment: office furniture and fixtures,	183 50	
TOTAL COST OF EQUIPMENT OWNED,		27,445 55

Cost of land and buildings:		
Land necessary for operation of railway,	$5,586 00	
Buildings necessary for operation of railway,	6,642 76	
TOTAL COST OF LAND AND BUILDINGS OWNED,		$12,228 76
TOTAL PERMANENT INVESTMENTS,		$198,485 78
Cash and current assets:		
Cash,	$442 28	
Bills and accounts receivable,	97 86	
TOTAL CASH AND CURRENT ASSETS,		540 14
Miscellaneous assets: prepaid taxes,		251 21
TOTAL,		$199,277 13

LIABILITIES.	CR.	
Capital stock,		$80,000 00
Funded debt,		80,000 00
Current liabilities:		
Loans and notes payable,	$30,100 00	
Audited vouchers and accounts,	325 71	
TOTAL CURRENT LIABILITIES,		30,425 71
Accrued liabilities: interest accrued and not yet due,		941 59
Profit and loss balance (surplus),		7,909 83
TOTAL,		$199,277 13

CAPITAL STOCK.

Capital stock authorized by law,	$80,000 00	
Capital stock authorized by votes of company,	80,000 00	
Capital stock issued and outstanding,		$80,000 00
Number of shares issued and outstanding,	800	
Number of stockholders,	35	
Number of stockholders in Massachusetts,	34	
Amount of stock held in Massachusetts,	$79,500 00	

FUNDED DEBT.

DESCRIPTION OF BONDS.	Rate of Interest.	Date of Maturity.	Amount Outstanding.	Interest Paid during the Year.
First mortgage bonds,	Per Cent. 5	Feb. 2, 1923,	$80,000 00	$2,000 00

VOLUME OF TRAFFIC, ETC.

Number of passengers paying revenue carried during the year,	482,004
Number carried per mile of main railway track operated,	65,758
Number of car miles run,	136,500
Average number of persons employed,	11

Description of Equipment.

Description of Equipment.	Equipped for Electric Power.	Not Equipped.	Total Passenger Cars.	Equipped with Fenders.	Equipped with Electric Heaters.	Number of Motors.
Cars — Passenger Service.						
Box passenger cars,	-	3	3	3	3	-
Open passenger cars,	6	-	6	6	-	12
Total,	6	3	9	9	3	12
Cars — Other Service.						
Work car,	-	1	-	-	-	-
Snow ploughs,	1	-	-	-	-	2

Railway Owned and Operated (by Electric Power).

Length of railway line,	7.330 miles.
Length of sidings, switches, etc.,	.290 "
Total, computed as single track,	7.620 "

Railway Located Outside of Public Ways.

Length of railway line,	3.590 miles.

Names of the several cities and towns in which the railways operated by the company are located: Uxbridge, Blackstone and Millville.

Grade Crossings with Railroads.

Grade Crossings with Railroads.	Number of Tracks at Crossing.	
	Railroad.	Railway.
Crossings of railways with railroads at grade (1 in number), viz.:— With New York, New Haven & Hartford Railroad (Providence division), siding used by Blanchard Bros., Main Street, Uxbridge,*	1	1

Number of above crossings at which *frogs* are inserted in the tracks, . 1

Corporate Name and Address of the Company.

UXBRIDGE & BLACKSTONE STREET RAILWAY COMPANY,

831 State Mutual Building, Worcester, Mass.

* The siding above named is operated only by horse-power, and is seldom used.

NAMES AND BUSINESS ADDRESS OF PRINCIPAL OFFICERS.

Theodore S. Johnson, *President*, Worcester, Mass. John E. Sayles, *Vice-President*, Uxbridge, Mass. Frank H. Viele, *Treasurer and Clerk of Corporation*, Worcester, Mass. Charles L. Rogers, *Superintendent*, Uxbridge, Mass.

NAMES AND RESIDENCE OF BOARD OF DIRECTORS.

Theodore S. Johnson, Worcester, Mass. Otis E. Putnam, Worcester, Mass. William H. Tyler, Worcester, Mass. Horace Wyman, Worcester, Mass. A. B. R. Sprague, Worcester, Mass. Frank H. Viele, Worcester, Mass. John E. Sayles, Uxbridge, Mass.

We hereby certify that the statements contained in the foregoing report are full, just and true.

THEODORE S. JOHNSON,
WILLIAM H. TYLER,
FRANK H. VIELE,
OTIS E. PUTNAM,
Directors.
FRANK H. VIELE,
Treasurer.
C. L. ROGERS,
Superintendent.

COMMONWEALTH OF MASSACHUSETTS.

WORCESTER, SS. OCT. 24, 1904. Then personally appeared the above-named Theodore S. Johnson, William H. Tyler, Frank H. Viele, Otis E. Putnam and Chas. L. Rogers, and severally made oath that the foregoing certificate by them subscribed is, to the best of their knowledge and belief, true.

Before me, W. P. MCPHERSON,
Justice of the Peace.

REPORT

OF THE

WALTHAM STREET RAILWAY COMPANY

FOR THE YEAR ENDING SEPTEMBER 30, 1904.

[Operated by the Newton.]

GENERAL EXHIBIT FOR THE YEAR.		
Gross earnings from operation,		$11,811 13
Operating expenses,		25,324 04
GROSS DEFICIT FROM OPERATION,		$13,512 91
Charges upon income accrued during the year:		
Interest and discount on unfunded debts and loans,	$10,051 30	
Taxes, commutation,	36 02	
TOTAL CHARGES AND DEDUCTIONS FROM INCOME,		10,087 32
Deficit for the year ending September 30, 1904,		$23,600 23
Amount of deficit September 30, 1903,		8,019 71
TOTAL DEFICIT SEPTEMBER 20, 1904,		$31,619 94

EARNINGS FROM OPERATION.	
Receipts from passengers carried,	$11,802 66
Receipts from tolls for use of tracks by other companies,	8 47
GROSS EARNINGS FROM OPERATION,	$11,811 13

EXPENSES OF OPERATION.	
General expenses:	
Salaries of general officers and clerks,	$1,801 00
General office expenses and supplies,	428 13
Legal expenses,	80 00
Insurance,	156 27
Maintenance of roadway and buildings: repair of roadbed and track,	631 93

Transportation expenses:		
Removal of snow and ice,		$467 78
Tolls for trackage over other railways,		337 67
Rentals of buildings and other property,		878 75
Other transportation expenses: paid to Newton Street Railway Company for operation of road per agreement,		20,542 51
TOTAL OPERATING EXPENSES,		$25,324 04

PROPERTY ACCOUNTS.

Additions to railway:		
Extension of tracks (length, 3,693 feet),	$6,452 28	
New electric line construction (length, 3,693 feet),	945 50	
Other additions to railway:		
New paving,	30 55	
New fencing, 450 feet, $68.07; land damages, $925,	993 07	
Legal and engineering expenses,	3,075 00	
TOTAL ADDITIONS TO RAILWAY,		$11,496 40
Deductions from property accounts (property sold or reduced in valuation and credited to property accounts):		
Sold interest in poles,	$195 50	
Sale of sundry equipment,	50 00	
Sale of trucks and air brake equipment,	7,350 00	
Sale of switchboard,	200 00	
TOTAL DEDUCTIONS FROM PROPERTY ACCOUNTS,		7,795 50
NET ADDITION TO PROPERTY ACCOUNTS FOR THE YEAR,		$3,700 90

GENERAL BALANCE SHEET SEPTEMBER 30, 1904.

ASSETS.	DR.	
Cost of railway:		
Roadbed and tracks,	$189,035 49	
Electric line construction, including poles, wiring, feeder lines, etc.,	16,431 85	
Interest accrued during construction of railway,	23,225 79	
Engineering and other expenses incident to construction,	29,800 90	
Other items of railway cost: general expenses during construction,	4,965 35	
TOTAL COST OF RAILWAY OWNED,		$263,459 38
Cost of equipment:		
Cars and other rolling stock and vehicles,	$14,419 95	
Other items of equipment: sundry equipment,	128 74	
TOTAL COST OF EQUIPMENT OWNED,		14,548 69
Cost of land and buildings: land necessary for operation of railway,		2,608 26
TOTAL PERMANENT INVESTMENTS,		$280,616 33

Cash and current assets:		
Cash,	$40,403 35	
Bills and accounts receivable,	8,021 30	
Total Cash and Current Assets,		$48,424 65
Miscellaneous assets: materials and supplies,		16,578 39
Profit and loss balance (deficit),		31,619 94
Total,		$377,239 31

Liabilities.	Cr.	
Capital stock,		$100,000 00
Current liabilities:		
Loans and notes payable,	$207,500 00	
Audited vouchers and accounts,	69,739 31	
Total Current Liabilities,		277,239 31
Total,		$377,239 31

Capital Stock.

Capital stock authorized by law,	$100,000 00	
Capital stock authorized by votes of company,	100,000 00	
Capital stock issued and outstanding,		$100,000 00
Number of shares issued and outstanding,	1,000	
Number of stockholders,	12	
Number of stockholders in Massachusetts,	11	
Amount of stock held in Massachusetts,	$99,200 00	

Volume of Traffic, etc.

Number of passengers paying revenue carried during the year,	258,408
Number carried per mile of main railway track operated,	36,237
Number of car miles run,	116,359
Average number of persons employed,	1

Description of Equipment.

Open passenger cars (not equipped),	6

Railway Owned and Operated (by Electric Power).

Railway Owned, etc.	Owned.	Trackage over Other Railways.	Total Owned, etc.	Total Operated.
	Miles.	Miles.	Miles.	Miles.
Length of railway line,	6.418	1.595	8.013	7.131
Length of sidings, switches, etc.,	.052	-	.052	.052
Total Computed as Single Track,	6.470	1.595	8.065	7.183

Names of the several cities and towns in which the railways operated by the company are located: Waltham and Belmont.

GENERAL REMARKS AND EXPLANATIONS.

This railway is operated by the Newton Street Railway Company under an agreement.

ACCIDENTS TO PERSONS.

(A detailed statement of each accident is on file in the office of the Board.)

KILLED AND INJURED.	FROM CAUSES BEYOND THEIR OWN CONTROL.		FROM THEIR OWN MISCONDUCT OR CARELESSNESS.		TOTAL.	
	Killed.	Injured.	Killed.	Injured.	Killed.	Injured.
Passengers,	-	1	-	-	-	1
Employees,	-	1	-	-	-	1
Other persons,	-	-	-	1	-	1
TOTALS,	-	2	-	1	-	3

CORPORATE NAME AND ADDRESS OF THE COMPANY.

WALTHAM STREET RAILWAY COMPANY,

53 STATE STREET, BOSTON, MASS.

NAMES AND BUSINESS ADDRESS OF PRINCIPAL OFFICERS.

Eugene H. Mather, *President*, Portland, Me. Harry G. Lowe, *Treasurer, Clerk of Corporation and Superintendent*, 53 State Street, Boston, Mass.

NAMES AND RESIDENCE OF BOARD OF DIRECTORS.

Eugene H. Mather, Portland, Me. Oliver E. Williams, Boston, Mass. Willis P. Howard, Boston, Mass. Louis deP. Cole, Boston, Mass. Bradshaw S. Tolman, Waltham, Mass.

We hereby certify that the statements contained in the foregoing report are full, just and true.

EUGENE H. MATHER,
O. E. WILLIAMS,
WILLIS P. HOWARD,
LOUIS DEP. COLE,
Directors.
HARRY G. LOWE,
Treasurer.
HARRY G. LOWE,
Superintendent.

COMMONWEALTH OF MASSACHUSETTS.

SUFFOLK, SS. BOSTON, Nov. 4, 1904. Then personally appeared the above-named Eugene H. Mather, O. E. Williams, Willis P. Howard, Louis deP. Cole and Harry G. Lowe, and severally made oath that the foregoing certificate by them subscribed is, to the best of their knowledge and belief, true.

Before me, GEORGE A. FERNALD,
Notary Public.

REPORT

OF THE

WARREN, BROOKFIELD & SPENCER STREET RAILWAY COMPANY

FOR THE YEAR ENDING SEPTEMBER 30, 1904.

GENERAL EXHIBIT FOR THE YEAR.			
Gross earnings from operation,			$63,512 11
Operating expenses,			41,435 91
GROSS INCOME ABOVE OPERATING EXPENSES,			$22,076 20
Charges upon income accrued during the year:			
Interest on funded debt,		$6,250 00	
Interest and discount on unfunded debts and loans,		3,517 29	
Taxes, State and local,	$1,800 00		
Taxes, commutation,	634 74		
		2,434 74	
Other deductions from income: park expenses,		2,757 19	
TOTAL CHARGES AND DEDUCTIONS FROM INCOME,			14,959 22
Surplus for the year ending September 30, 1904,			$7,116 98
Amount of surplus September 30, 1903,			20,973 10
Debits to profit and loss account during the year: carried to reserve for depreciation,			2,000 00
TOTAL SURPLUS SEPTEMBER 30, 1904,			$26,090 08

EARNINGS FROM OPERATION.	
Receipts from passengers carried,	$63,202 15
Receipts from advertising in cars,	210 00
Other earnings from operation: carrying papers,	99 96
GROSS EARNINGS FROM OPERATION,	$63,512 11

EXPENSES OF OPERATION.	
General expenses:	
Salaries of general officers and clerks,	$2,624 29
General office expenses and supplies,	1,066 87
Insurance,	1,209 75

Maintenance of roadway and buildings:	
Repair of roadbed and track,	$2,698 48
Repair of electric line construction,	766 76
Repair of buildings,	1,120 54
Maintenance of equipment:	
Repair of cars and other vehicles,	1,582 70
Repair of electric equipment of cars,	1,928 18
Transportation expenses:	
Cost of electric motive power,	10,302 55
Wages and compensation of persons employed in conducting transportation,	15,772 68
Removal of snow and ice,	1,300 41
Damages for injuries to persons and property,	796 13
Other transportation expenses: oil, waste, etc.,	266 57
TOTAL OPERATING EXPENSES,	$41,435 91

PROPERTY ACCOUNTS.

Additions to railway: expenses of State highway construction,	$718 29
TOTAL ADDITIONS TO PROPERTY ACCOUNTS,	$718 29

GENERAL BALANCE SHEET SEPTEMBER 30, 1904.

ASSETS.	DR.	
Cost of railway:		
Roadbed and tracks,	$201,212 07	
Electric line construction, including poles, wiring, feeder lines, etc.,	46,735 88	
Engineering and other expenses incident to construction,	6,039 94	
TOTAL COST OF RAILWAY OWNED,		$253,987 89
Cost of equipment:		
Cars and other rolling stock and vehicles,	$21,028 29	
Electric equipment of same,	14,795 20	
Other items of equipment: snow ploughs, heaters, registers, etc.,	4,902 83	
TOTAL COST OF EQUIPMENT OWNED,		40,726 32
Cost of land and buildings:		
Land necessary for operation of railway,	$2,729 55	
Electric power stations, including equipment,	51,035 76	
Other buildings necessary for operation of railway,	12,323 91	
TOTAL COST OF LAND AND BUILDINGS OWNED,		66,089 22
TOTAL PERMANENT INVESTMENTS,		$360,803 43
Cash and current assets:		
Cash,	$115 68	
Bills and accounts receivable,	988 50	
Sinking and other special funds,	8,426 11	

Cash and current assets — *Concluded.*		
Other cash and current assets:		
Prepaid interest,	$337 50	
Unexpired insurance,	836 87	
TOTAL CASH AND CURRENT ASSETS,		$10,704 66
Miscellaneous assets: materials and supplies,		1,753 63
TOTAL,		$373,261 72

LIABILITIES.	CR.	
Capital stock,		$150,000 00
Funded debt,		125,000 00
Current liabilities:		
Loans and notes payable,	$55,910 43	
Audited vouchers and accounts,	734 65	
TOTAL CURRENT LIABILITIES,		56,645 08
Accrued liabilities:		
Interest accrued and not yet due,	$2,760 49	
Taxes accrued and not yet due,	2,339 96	
TOTAL ACCRUED LIABILITIES,		5,100 45
Special and other sinking funds: reserve for depreciation,		10,426 11
Profit and loss balance (surplus),		26,090 08
TOTAL,		$373,261 72

CAPITAL STOCK.

Capital stock authorized by law,	$220,000 00	
Capital stock authorized by votes of company,	220,000 00	
Capital stock issued and outstanding,		$150,000 00
Number of shares issued and outstanding,	1,500	
Number of stockholders,	19	
Number of stockholders in Massachusetts,	17	
Amount of stock held in Massachusetts,	$145,300 00	

FUNDED DEBT.

DESCRIPTION OF BONDS.	Rate of Interest.	Date of Maturity.	Amount Outstanding.	Interest Paid during the Year.
First mortgage gold bonds,	Per Cent. 5	Nov. 1, 1916,	$125,000 00	$6,250 00

SINKING AND OTHER SPECIAL FUNDS.

Amount September 30, 1903, of sinking fund,	$8,426 11
Additions during the year to sinking fund,	2,000 00
TOTAL SINKING AND OTHER SPECIAL FUNDS, SEPTEMBER 30, 1904,	$10,426 11

Volume of Traffic, etc.

Number of passengers paying revenue carried during the year,	1,311,568
Number carried per mile of main railway track operated,	66,893
Number of car miles run,	371,511
Average number of persons employed,	36

Description of Equipment.

Description of Equipment.	Equipped for Electric Power.	Not Equipped.	Equipped with Fenders.	Equipped with Electric Heaters.	Number of Motors.
Cars — Passenger Service.					
Box passenger cars,	7	-	7	7	-
Open passenger cars,	10	-	10	-	-
Total,	17	-	17	7	32
Cars — Other Service.					
Work cars,	1	1	-	-	-
Snow ploughs,	2	-	-	-	-

Miscellaneous Equipment.

Highway vehicles: tower wagon,	1

Railway Owned and Operated (by Electric Power).

Length of railway line,	19.607 miles.
Length of sidings, switches, etc.,	.491 "
Total, computed as single track,	20.098 "

Railway Located Outside of Public Ways.

Length of railway line,	.075 mile.

Names of the several cities and towns in which the railways operated by the company are located: Warren, West Warren, Brookfield, West Brookfield, North Brookfield and Spencer.

Grade Crossings with Railroads.

Grade Crossings with Railroads.	Number of Tracks at Crossing.	
	Railroad.	Railway.
Crossings of railways with railroads at grade (1 in number), viz.:— With Boston & Albany Railroad, Main Street, East Brookfield, .	1	1

Number of above crossings at which *frogs* are inserted in the tracks, . 1

Accidents to Persons.

(A detailed statement of each accident is on file in the office of the board.)

Killed and Injured.	From Causes beyond their own Control.		From their own Misconduct or Carelessness.		Total.	
	Killed.	Injured.	Killed.	Injured.	Killed.	Injured.
Passengers, ...	-	14	-	4	-	18
Employees, ...	-	-	-	-	-	-
Other persons, ...	-	-	2	-	2	-
Totals, ...	-	14	2	4	2	18

Corporate Name and Address of the Company.

WARREN, BROOKFIELD & SPENCER STREET RAILWAY COMPANY,

Brookfield, Mass.

Names and Business Address of Principal Officers.

Alex. B. Bruce, *President*, Lawrence, Mass. Ewen R. McPherson, *Vice-President*, Boston, Mass. Augustus Nickerson, *Treasurer and Clerk of Corporation*, Boston, Mass. Henry Clark, *Superintendent*, Brookfield, Mass.

Names and Residence of Board of Directors.

Alex. B. Bruce, Lawrence, Mass. Ewen R. McPherson, Cambridge, Mass. Robert Redford, Lawrence, Mass. N. Sumner Myrick, Canton, Mass. Alonzo G. Van Nostrand, Boston, Mass. Josiah Q. Bennett, Cambridge, Mass.

We hereby certify that the statements contained in the foregoing report are full, just and true.

ALEX. B. BRUCE,
EWEN R. McPHERSON,
ROBERT REDFORD,
N. SUMNER MYRICK,
Directors.
AUGUSTUS NICKERSON,
Treasurer.
HENRY CLARK,
Superintendent.

COMMONWEALTH OF MASSACHUSETTS.

SUFFOLK, ss. OCT. 28, 1904. Then personally appeared the above-named Alexander B. Bruce, Ewen R. McPherson, Robert Redford and N. Sumner Myrick, a majority of the board of directors, and Augustus Nickerson, treasurer, and severally made oath that the foregoing certificate by them subscribed is, to the best of their knowledge and belief, true.

Before me, E. BERTRAM NEWTON,
Justice of the Peace.

COMMONWEALTH OF MASSACHUSETTS.

WORCESTER, ss. BROOKFIELD, Oct. 25, 1904. Then personally appeared Henry Clark, and made oath that the foregoing certificate by him subscribed is, to the best of his knowledge and belief, true.

Before me, GEORGE H. CHAPIN,
Justice of the Peace.

REPORT

OF THE

WEBSTER & DUDLEY STREET RAILWAY COMPANY

FOR THE YEAR ENDING SEPTEMBER 30, 1904.

[Leased to and operated by the Consolidated Railway Company of Connecticut.]

GENERAL EXHIBIT FOR THE YEAR.		
Rental received from lease of railway,		$19,779 86
Expenses and charges upon income accrued during the year:		
Interest on funded debt,	$1,500 00	
Taxes,	1,071 71	
Other expenses and charges upon income:		
Insurance premiums,	216 64	
Rental of Worcester & Webster Street Railway,	14,491 51	
TOTAL EXPENSES AND CHARGES UPON INCOME,		17,279 86
NET DIVISIBLE INCOME,		$2,500 00
Dividends declared (5 per cent),		$2,500 00
Amount of deficit September 30, 1903,		$22,051 28
TOTAL DEFICIT SEPTEMBER 30, 1904,		$22,051 28

GENERAL BALANCE SHEET SEPTEMBER 30, 1904.		
ASSETS.	DR.	
Cost of railway:		
Roadbed and tracks,	$63,153 44	
Other items of railway cost:		
Transmission line and sub-station,	50,000 00	
Telephone and block signal system,	403 62	
Grading, etc., Beacon Park,	1,033 78	
TOTAL COST OF RAILWAY OWNED,		$114,590 84
Cost of equipment: cars and other rolling stock and vehicles, and electric equipment of same,		12,968 91

Cost of land and buildings:		
Land necessary for operation of railway,	$1,047 00	
Electric power stations, including equipment,	3,388 92	
Other buildings necessary for operation of railway,	3,329 84	
TOTAL COST OF LAND AND BUILDINGS OWNED,		$7,765 76
TOTAL PERMANENT INVESTMENTS,		$135,325 51
Profit and loss balance (deficit),		22,051 28
TOTAL,		$157,376 79

LIABILITIES. CR.

Capital stock,	$50,000 00
Funded debt,	30,000 00
Contingent liabilities: The Consolidated Railway Company, for payment of floating debt,	77,376 79
TOTAL,	$157,376 79

CAPITAL STOCK.

Capital stock authorized by law,	$50,000 00	
Capital stock authorized by votes of company,	50,000 00	
Capital stock issued and outstanding,		$50,000 00
Number of shares issued and outstanding,	500	
Number of stockholders,	15	
Number of stockholders in Massachusetts,	7	
Amount of stock held in Massachusetts,	$3,900 00	

FUNDED DEBT.

DESCRIPTION OF BONDS.	Rate of Interest.	Date of Maturity.	Amount Outstanding.	Interest Paid during the Year.
First mortgage gold bonds,	Per Cent. 5	Nov. 1, 1919,	$30,000 00	$1,500 00

RAILWAY OWNED.

Length of railway line,	5.650 miles.
Length of sidings, switches, etc.,	.187 "
Total, computed as single track,	5.837 "

RAILWAY OWNED AND LOCATED OUTSIDE OF PUBLIC WAYS.

Length of railway line,	.870 mile.

Names of the several cities and towns in which the railway owned by the company is located: Webster.

CORPORATE NAME AND ADDRESS OF THE COMPANY.

WEBSTER & DUDLEY STREET RAILWAY COMPANY,

WEBSTER, MASS.

NAMES AND BUSINESS ADDRESS OF PRINCIPAL OFFICERS.

Lyman R. Eddy, *President*, Webster, Mass. Elisha N. Bigelow, *Vice-President*, Webster, Mass. John Flint, *Treasurer*, Webster, Mass. Charles Haggerty, *Clerk of Corporation*, Webster, Mass.

NAMES AND RESIDENCE OF BOARD OF DIRECTORS.

Lyman R. Eddy, Webster, Mass. Elisha N. Bigelow, Webster, Mass. John Flint, Webster, Mass. Charles Haggerty, Webster, Mass. Oscar Shumway, Webster, Mass. Warren D. Chase, Hartford, Conn. Charles L. Campbell, New Haven, Conn. J. B. Potter, Webster, Mass. Harry E. Back, Danielson, Conn.

We hereby certify that the statements contained in the foregoing report are full, just and true.

LYMAN R. EDDY,
ELISHA N. BIGELOW,
JOHN FLINT,
CHARLES HAGGERTY,
OSCAR SHUMWAY,
J. B. POTTER,
Directors.
JOHN FLINT,
Treasurer.

COMMONWEALTH OF MASSACHUSETTS.

WORCESTER, ss. WEBSTER, Oct. 12, 1904. Then personally appeared the above-named Lyman R. Eddy, Elisha N. Bigelow, John Flint, Charles Haggerty, Oscar Shumway and J. B. Potter, and severally made oath that the foregoing certificate by them subscribed is, to the best of their knowledge and belief, true.

Before me, WILLIAM F. GALE,
Justice of the Peace.

REPORT

OF THE

WEBSTER & DUDLEY AND WORCESTER & WEBSTER STREET RAILWAYS

(CONSOLIDATED RAILWAY COMPANY, LESSEE)

FOR THE YEAR ENDING SEPTEMBER 30, 1904.

GENERAL EXHIBIT FOR THE YEAR.	
Gross earnings from operation,	$80,067 90
Operating expenses,	56,175 33
NET EARNINGS FROM OPERATION,	$23,892 57
Miscellaneous income: park earnings,	2,179 16
GROSS INCOME ABOVE OPERATING EXPENSES,	$26,071 73
Charges upon income accrued during the year: rentals of leased railways: Worcester & Webster and Webster & Dudley,	19,779 86
NET PROFIT FROM OPERATION,	$6,291 87

EARNINGS FROM OPERATION.	
Receipts from passengers carried,	$78,696 05
Receipts from carriage of mails,	228 97
Receipts from carriage of express and parcels,	88 32
Receipts from rentals of buildings and other property,	33 69
Receipts from advertising in cars,	281 12
Other earnings from operation: chartered cars,	739 75
GROSS EARNINGS FROM OPERATION,	$80,067 90

EXPENSES OF OPERATION.	
General expenses:	
Salaries of general officers and clerks,	$2,612 44
General office expenses and supplies,	1,295 82
Legal expenses,	522 25
Insurance,	355 50
Other general expenses,	4,453 56

Maintenance of roadway and buildings:	
Repair of roadbed and track,	$4,301 64
Repair of electric line construction,	1,372 77
Repair of buildings,	184 62
Maintenance of equipment:	
Repair of cars and other vehicles,	4,434 65
Repair of electric equipment of cars,	3,238 75
Transportation expenses:	
Cost of electric motive power, $13,945.25; less power sold, $189.60; net,	13,755 65
Wages and compensation of persons employed in conducting transportation,	15,325 97
Removal of snow and ice,	618 81
Damages for injuries to persons and property,	2,206 50
Rentals of buildings and other property,	126 21
Other transportation expenses,	1,370 19
TOTAL OPERATING EXPENSES,	$56,175 33

VOLUME OF TRAFFIC, ETC.

Number of passengers paying revenue carried during the year,	1,748,801
Number carried per mile of main railway track operated,	78,092
Number of car miles run,	446,929
Average number of persons employed,	70

DESCRIPTION OF EQUIPMENT.

DESCRIPTION OF EQUIPMENT.	Equipped for Electric Power.	Not Equipped.	Equipped with Fenders.	Equipped with Electric Heaters.	Number of Motors.
CARS — PASSENGER SERVICE.					
Box passenger cars,	9	-	9	9	32
Open passenger cars,	14	-	14	-	40
TOTAL,	23	-	23	9	72
CARS — OTHER SERVICE.					
Work cars,	1	1	-	-	2
Snow ploughs,	3	-	-	-	4

MISCELLANEOUS EQUIPMENT.

Highway vehicles:	
Tower wagon,	1
Road machine,	1

Railway Leased and Operated (by Electric Power).

Railway Owned, etc.	Held under Lease or Contract.	Trackage over Other Railways.	Total Owned, Leased, etc.
	Miles.	Miles.	Miles.
Length of railway line,	20.794	1.600	22.394
Length of sidings, switches, etc.,	.831	-	.831
Total, Computed as Single Track,	21.625	1.600	23.225

Railway Located Outside of Public Ways.

Length of railway line,	1.193 miles.

Names of the several cities and towns in which the railways operated by the company are located: Worcester, Auburn, Oxford and Webster.

General Remarks and Explanations.

This report is of the Worcester & Webster Street Railway and of the Webster & Dudley Street Railway, both of which are leased and operated by the Consolidated Railway Company.

Accidents to Persons.

(A detailed statement of each accident is on file in the office of the Board.)

Killed and Injured.	From Causes beyond their own Control.		From their own Misconduct or Carelessness.		Total.	
	Killed.	Injured.	Killed.	Injured.	Killed.	Injured.
Passengers,	-	2	-	5	-	7
Employees,	-	-	-	-	-	-
Other persons,	-	-	-	-	-	-
Totals,	-	2	-	5	-	7

Corporate Name and Address of the Lessee Company.

THE CONSOLIDATED RAILWAY COMPANY,

New Haven, Conn.

Names and Business Address of Principal Officers.

C. S. Mellen, *President*, New Haven, Conn. E. H. McHenry, *First Vice-President*, New Haven, Conn. H. M. Kochersperger, *Second Vice-President*, New Haven, Conn. A. S. May, *Treasurer*, New Haven, Conn. J. G. Parker, *Clerk of Corporation*, New Haven, Conn. Edward G. Buckland, *General Counsel*, New Haven, Conn. C. L. Campbell, *Auditor*, New Haven, Conn. Samuel Anderson, *General Manager*, Putnam, Conn. J. B. Potter, *Superintendent*, Webster, Mass.

NAMES AND RESIDENCE OF BOARD OF DIRECTORS.

George J. Brush, New Haven, Conn. Edwin Milner, Moosup, Conn. F. S. Curtis, Boston, Mass. Charles F. Brooker, Ansonia, Conn. C. S. Mellen, New Haven, Conn. H. M. Kochersperger, New Haven, Conn. J. S. Hemingway, New Haven, Conn. E. D. Robbins, Hartford, Conn. A. D. Osborne, New Haven, Conn. F. W. Cheney, South Manchester, Conn. I. D. Warner, Bridgeport, Conn. D. N. Barney, Farmington, Conn. E. H. McHenry, New Haven, Conn. John M. Hall, New Haven, Conn. Percy R. Todd, New Haven, Conn.

We hereby certify that the statements contained in the foregoing report are full, just and true.

C. S. MELLEN,
PERCY R. TODD,
CHAS. F. BROOKER,
ARTHUR D. OSBORNE,
H. M. KOCHERSPERGER,
JAMES S. HEMINGWAY,
JOHN M. HALL,
GEO. J. BRUSH,
Directors.
A. S. MAY,
Treasurer.

STATE OF CONNECTICUT.

COUNTY OF NEW HAVEN, ss. DEC. 5, 1904. Then personally appeared the above-named C. S. Mellen, Percy R. Todd, Chas. F. Brooker, Arthur D. Osborne, H. M. Kochersperger, James S. Hemingway, John M. Hall and Geo. J. Brush, and severally made oath that the foregoing certificate by them subscribed is, to the best of their knowledge and belief, true.

Before me, ALBERT H. POWELL,
Notary Public.

REPORT

OF THE

WELLESLEY & BOSTON STREET RAILWAY COMPANY

FOR THE PERIOD ENDING DECEMBER 31, 1903.

[Consolidated with the Newton, December 31, 1903.]

GENERAL EXHIBIT FOR THE PERIOD.		
Gross earnings from operation,		$12,829 92
Operating expenses,		10,234 45
GROSS INCOME ABOVE OPERATING EXPENSES,		$2,595 47
Charges upon income accrued during the year:		
Interest and discount on unfunded debts and loans,	$459 25	
Taxes, State and local,	986 64	
TOTAL CHARGES AND DEDUCTIONS FROM INCOME,		1,445 89
Surplus for the period ending December 31, 1903,		$1,149 58
Amount of surplus September 30, 1903,		5,840 71
TOTAL SURPLUS DECEMBER 31, 1903,		$6,990 29

EARNINGS FROM OPERATION.	
Receipts from passengers carried,	$12,055 20
Receipts from tolls for use of tracks by other companies,	109 81
Receipts from rentals of buildings and other property,	616 37
Receipts from advertising in cars,	48 54
GROSS EARNINGS FROM OPERATION,	$12,829 92

EXPENSES OF OPERATION.	
General expenses:	
Salaries of general officers and clerks,	$1,848 11
General office expenses and supplies,	163 49
Insurance,	127 52
Maintenance of roadway and buildings:	
Repair of roadbed and track,	335 45
Repair of electric line construction,	288 09
Maintenance of equipment:	
Repair of cars and other vehicles and electric equipment of cars,	149 62
Renewal of horses, harnesses, shoeing, etc., and provender and stabling for horses,	119 88

Transportation expenses:		
Cost of electric motive power,		$2,697 73
Wages and compensation of persons employed in conducting transportation,		3,707 91
Removal of snow and ice,		105 90
Damages for injuries to persons and property,		602 76
Rentals of buildings and other property,		83 35
Other transportation expenses: miscellaneous shop expense,		4 64
TOTAL OPERATING EXPENSES,		$10,234 45

PROPERTY ACCOUNTS.

Additions to equipment: 4 sets Peckham double trucks,	$2,200 00
Deductions from property accounts (property sold or reduced in valuation and credited to property accounts): two K No. 10 controllers,	100 00
NET ADDITION TO PROPERTY ACCOUNTS FOR THE PERIOD,	$2,100 00

GENERAL BALANCE SHEET DECEMBER 31, 1903.

ASSETS.	DR.	
Cost of railway:		
Roadbed and tracks,	$80,762 42	
Electric line construction, including poles, wiring, feeder lines, etc.,	16,000 11	
Interest accrued during construction of railway,	600 00	
Engineering and other expenses incident to construction,	3,454 43	
TOTAL COST OF RAILWAY OWNED,		$100;816 96
Cost of equipment:		
Cars and other rolling stock and vehicles,	$28,453 81	
Electric equipment of same,	25,442 79	
TOTAL COST OF EQUIPMENT OWNED,		53,896 60
Cost of land and buildings,		5,240 00
TOTAL PERMANENT INVESTMENTS,		$159,953 56
Cash and current assets: bills and accounts receivable,		3,673 32
TOTAL,		$163,626 88

LIABILITIES.	CR.	
Capital stock,		$115,000 00
Current liabilities:		
Loans and notes payable,	$15,000 00	
Audited vouchers and accounts,	19,136 59	
TOTAL CURRENT LIABILITIES,		34,136 59
Sinking and other special funds: insurance fund,		7,500 00
Profit and loss balance (surplus),		6,990 29
TOTAL,		$163,626 88

Capital Stock.

Capital stock authorized by law,	$115,000 00	
Capital stock authorized by votes of company,	115,000 00	
Capital stock issued and outstanding,		$115,000 00
Number of shares issued and outstanding,	1,150	
Number of stockholders,	8	
Number of stockholders in Massachusetts,	8	
Amount of stock held in Massachusetts,	$115,000 00	

Sinking and Other Special Funds.

Amount September 30, 1903, of insurance fund,	$7,500 00
Total Sinking and Other Special Funds, December 31, 1903,	$7,500 00

Volume of Traffic, etc.

Number of passengers paying revenue carried during the period,	293,036
Number carried per mile of main railway track operated,	30,385
Number of car miles run,	63,192
Average number of persons employed,	46

Description of Equipment.

Description of Equipment.	Equipped for Electric Power.	Equipped with Fenders.	Equipped with Electric Heaters.	Number of Motors.
Cars — Passenger Service.				
Box passenger cars,	5	5	5	-
Open passenger cars,	13	13	-	-
Total,	18	18	5	43
Snow ploughs,	2	-	-	-

Railway Owned and Operated (by Electric Power).

Railway Owned, etc.	Owned.	Trackage over Other Railways.	Total Owned, etc.
	Miles.	Miles.	Miles.
Length of railway line,	4.690	4.954	9.644
Length of sidings, switches, etc.,	.210	-	.210
Total, Computed as Single Track,	4.900	4.954	9.854

Names of the several cities and towns in which the railways operated by the company are located: Newton.

CORPORATE NAME AND ADDRESS OF THE COMPANY.

WELLESLEY & BOSTON STREET RAILWAY COMPANY,

NEWTONVILLE, MASS.

NAMES AND BUSINESS ADDRESS OF PRINCIPAL OFFICERS.

Adams D. Claflin, *President*, Newtonville, Mass. James L. Richards, *Vice-President*, Boston, Mass. Charles W. Smith, *Treasurer*, Newtonville, Mass. Frank W. Remick, *Clerk of Corporation*, Boston, Mass. Coolidge & Hight, *General Counsel*, Boston, Mass. Matthew C. Brush, *General Manager*, Newtonville, Mass.

NAMES AND RESIDENCE OF BOARD OF DIRECTORS.

Adams D. Claflin, Newton Centre, Mass. William F. Hammett, Newton, Mass. Sydney Harwood, Newton, Mass. Frederic H. Lewis, Swampscott, Mass. Frank W. Remick, West Newton, Mass. James L. Richards, Newtonville, Mass. Alden E. Viles, Boston, Mass.

We hereby certify that the statements contained in the foregoing report are full, just and true.

ADAMS D. CLAFLIN,
WILLIAM F. HAMMETT,
SYDNEY HARWOOD,
JAMES L. RICHARDS,
FREDERIC H. LEWIS,
ALDEN E. VILES,
Directors.
CHARLES W. SMITH,
Treasurer.
MATTHEW C. BRUSH,
General Manager.

COMMONWEALTH OF MASSACHUSETTS.

SUFFOLK, SS. OCT. 29, 1904. Then personally appeared the above-named Adams D. Claflin, William F. Hammett, Sydney Harwood, James L. Richards, Frederic H. Lewis, Alden E. Viles, Chas. W. Smith and Matthew C. Brush, and severally made oath that the foregoing certificate by them subscribed is, to the best of their knowledge and belief, true.

Before me, GEO. M. COX,
Notary Public.

REPORT

OF THE

WESTBOROUGH & HOPKINTON STREET RAILWAY COMPANY

For the Year ending September 30, 1904.

General Exhibit for the Year.			
Gross earnings from operation,			$13,605 79
Operating expenses,			12,648 82
Gross Income above Operating Expenses,			$956 97
Charges upon income accrued during the year:			
Interest on funded debt,		$2,000 00	
Interest and discount on unfunded debts and loans,		297 50	
Taxes, State and local,	$332 41		
Taxes, commutation,	131 08		
		463 49	
Other deductions from income: amusements,		3 89	
Total Charges and Deductions from Income,			2,764 88
Deficit for the year ending September 30, 1904,			$1,807 91
Amount of deficit September 30, 1903,			734 64
Total Deficit September 30, 1904,			$2,542 55

Earnings from Operation.	
Receipts from passengers carried,	$13,108 91
Receipts from carriage of mails,	496 88
Gross Earnings from Operation,	$13,605 79

Expenses of Operation.	
General expenses:	
Salaries of general officers and clerks,	$1,293 00
General office expenses and supplies,	541 48
Legal expenses,	269 62
Insurance,	139 10
Maintenance of roadway and buildings:	
Repair of roadbed and track,	284 42
Repair of electric line construction,	40 54

Maintenance of equipment:		
Repair of cars and other vehicles,		$845 32
Repair of electric equipment of cars,		176 55
Transportation expenses:		
Cost of electric motive power,		5,110 52
Wages and compensation of persons employed in conducting transportation,		2,761 00
Removal of snow and ice,		350 58
Damages for injuries to persons and property,		150 00
Other transportation expenses: use of cars,		686 69
TOTAL OPERATING EXPENSES,		$12,648 82

PROPERTY ACCOUNTS.

Additions to railway:		
Extension of tracks (length, 120 feet), siding,	$108 65	
New électric line construction (length, 120 feet), siding,	23 00	
TOTAL ADDITIONS TO RAILWAY,		$131 65
Additions to equipment: additional cars (2 in number),		5,200 00
TOTAL ADDITIONS TO PROPERTY ACCOUNTS,		$5,331 65

GENERAL BALANCE SHEET SEPTEMBER 30, 1904.

ASSETS.	DR.	
Cost of railway:		
Roadbed and tracks,	$66,240 84	
Electric line construction, including poles, wiring, feeder lines, etc.,	14,167 46	
Interest accrued during construction of railway,	639 12	
Engineering and other expenses incident to construction,	3,868 03	
TOTAL COST OF RAILWAY OWNED,		$84,915 45
Cost of equipment: cars and other rolling stock and vehicles,		5,200 00
Cost of land and buildings: land necessary for operation of railway,		200 00
TOTAL PERMANENT INVESTMENTS,		$90,315 45
Cash and current assets:		
Cash,	$483 13	
Bills and accounts receivable,	158 54	
TOTAL CASH AND CURRENT ASSETS,		641 67
Miscellaneous assets: materials and supplies,		317 78
Profit and loss balance (deficit),		2,542 55
TOTAL,		$93,817 45

LIABILITIES.	CR.	
Capital stock,		$40,000 00
Funded debt,		40,000 00

Current liabilities:		
Loans and notes payable,	$7,224 36	
Audited vouchers and accounts,	5,300 00	
TOTAL CURRENT LIABILITIES,		$12,524 36
Accrued liabilities:		
Interest accrued and not yet due,	$833 33	
Taxes accrued and not yet due,	459 76	
TOTAL ACCRUED LIABILITIES,		1,293 09
TOTAL,		$93,817 45

CAPITAL STOCK.

Capital stock authorized by law,	$40,000 00	
Capital stock authorized by votes of company,	40,000 00	
Capital stock issued and outstanding,		$40,000 00
Number of shares issued and outstanding,	400	
Number of stockholders,	8	
Number of stockholders in Massachusetts,	8	
Amount of stock held in Massachusetts,	$40,000 00	

FUNDED DEBT.

DESCRIPTION OF BONDS.	Rate of Interest.	Date of Maturity.	Amount Outstanding.	Interest Paid during the Year.
	Per Cent.			
First mortgage bonds,	5	Nov. 1, 1922,	$40,000 00	$2,000 00

VOLUME OF TRAFFIC, ETC.

Number of passengers paying revenue carried during the year,	269,733
Number carried per mile of main railway track operated,	42,411
Number of car miles run,	76,701
Average number of persons employed,	5

DESCRIPTION OF EQUIPMENT.

DESCRIPTION OF EQUIPMENT.	Equipped for Electric Power.	Equipped with Fenders.	Equipped with Electric Heaters.	Number of Motors.
CARS — PASSENGER SERVICE.				
Box passenger cars,	2	2	2	4

Railway Owned and Operated (by Electric Power).

Length of railway line, ...	6.360 miles.
Length of sidings, switches, etc., ...	.079 "
Total, computed as single track, ...	6.439 "

Railway Located Outside of Public Ways.

Length of railway line, ...	.103 mile.
Length of switch, ...	.056 "
Total length of main track, ...	.159 "

Names of the several cities and towns in which the railways operated by the company are located: Westborough and Hopkinton.

Grade Crossings with Railroads.

Grade Crossings with Railroads.	Number of Tracks at Crossing.	
	Railroad.	Railway.
Crossings of railways with railroads at grade (1 in number), viz.: — With Milford & Woonsocket Railroad, leased to New York, New Haven & Hartford Railroad, ...	2	1

Number of above crossings at which *frogs* are inserted in the tracks, . 2

Accidents to Persons.

(A detailed statement of each accident is on file in the office of the Board.)

Killed and Injured.	From Causes beyond their own Control.		From their own Misconduct or Carelessness.		Total.	
	Killed.	Injured.	Killed.	Injured.	Killed.	Injured.
Passengers, ...	-	-	-	-	-	-
Employees, ...	-	-	-	-	-	-
Other persons, ...	-	-	-	1	-	1
Totals, ...	-	-	-	1	-	1

Corporate Name and Address of the Company.

WESTBOROUGH & HOPKINTON STREET RAILWAY COMPANY,

Hopkinton, Mass.

Names and Business Address of Principal Officers.

Adams D. Claflin, *President*, Newtonville, Mass. James L. Richards, *Vice-President*, Newtonville, Mass. George L. Hemenway, *Treasurer and Clerk of Corporation*, Hopkinton, Mass. Matthew C. Brush, *General Manager*, Newtonville, Mass. Harry C. Garfield, *Superintendent*, Westborough, Mass.

NAMES AND RESIDENCE OF BOARD OF DIRECTORS.

Adams D. Claflin, Newtonville, Mass. James L. Richards, Newtonville, Mass. William F. Hammett, Newton, Mass. Sydney Harwood, Newton, Mass. Frank W. Remick, Newton, Mass. Alden E. Viles, Boston, Mass. George L. Hemenway, Hopkinton, Mass.

We hereby certify that the statements contained in the foregoing report are full, just and true.

ADAMS D. CLAFLIN,
WILLIAM F. HAMMETT,
ALDEN E. VILES,
JAMES L. RICHARDS,
SYDNEY HARWOOD,
Directors.
GEORGE L. HEMENWAY,
Treasurer.
HARRY C. GARFIELD,
Superintendent.
MATTHEW C. BRUSH,
General Manager.

COMMONWEALTH OF MASSACHUSETTS.

MIDDLESEX, ss. OCT. 28, 1904. Then personally appeared the above-named Harry C. Garfield, and made oath that the foregoing statement by him subscribed is, to the best of his knowledge and belief, true.

Before me, GEORGE L. HEMENWAY,
Justice of the Peace.

COMMONWEALTH OF MASSACHUSETTS.

SUFFOLK, ss. OCT. 29, 1904. Then personally appeared the above-named Adams D. Claflin, William F. Hammett, Alden E. Viles, James L. Richards, Sydney Harwood, George L. Hemenway and Matthew C. Brush, and severally made oath that the foregoing certificate by them subscribed is, to the best of their knowledge and belief, true.

Before me, GEO. M. COX,
Notary Public.

REPORT

OF THE

WEST END STREET RAILWAY COMPANY

For the Year ending September 30, 1904.

[Leased to and operated by the Boston Elevated.]

General Exhibit for the Year.		
Rental received from lease of railway for expenses of organization,		$7,500 00
Income from other sources:		
Amount of dividends paid under the lease directly to stockholders of this company by the Boston Elevated Railway Company,	$1,184,997 50	
Interest on bank deposit,	56 49	
		1,185,053 99
Gross Income,		$1,192,553 99
Expenses and charges upon income accrued during the year: salaries and maintenance of organization,		7,137 89
Net Divisible Income,		$1,185,416 10
Dividends:		
3½ per cent on $9,539,250 common, } 3½ per cent on $9,689,250 common, }	$672,997 50	
8 per cent on $6,400,000, preferred,	512,000 00	
Total Dividends,		1,184,997 50
Surplus for the year ending September 30, 1904,		$418 60
Amount of surplus September 30, 1903,		654,609 98
Credits to profit and loss account during the year:		
Premium on 3,000 shares common stock sold,	$119,970 83	
Premium on $148,000, par value 4 per cent bonds, 1915, sold,	2,273 28	
Premium on $1,450,000, par value 4 per cent bonds, 1932, sold,	71,478 50	
Total Credits,		193,722 61
Total Surplus September 30, 1904,		$848,751 19

GENERAL BALANCE SHEET SEPTEMBER 30, 1904.

ASSETS.	DR.	
Cost of railway:		
Roadbed and tracks,	$8,282,760 77	
Electric line construction, including poles, wiring, feeder lines, etc.,	2,926,143 31	
Engineering and other expenses incident to construction,	175,712 54	
TOTAL COST OF RAILWAY OWNED,		$11,384,616 62
Cost of equipment:		
Cars and other rolling stock and vehicles,	$4,516,887 14	
Electric equipment of same,	3,683,868 91	
Other items of equipment: horses, tools, furniture, etc.,	361,678 88	
TOTAL COST OF EQUIPMENT OWNED,		8,562,434 93
Cost of land and buildings:		
Land necessary for operation of railway,	$2,910,597 37	
Electric power stations, including equipment,	4,745,731 03	
Other buildings necessary for operation of railway,	3,773,143 17	
TOTAL COST OF LAND AND BUILDINGS OWNED,		11,429,471 57
Other permanent property: subway equipment,		276,764 30
TOTAL PERMANENT INVESTMENTS,		$31,653,287 42
Cash and current assets:		
Cash,	$4,925 27	
Bills and accounts receivable,	43,815 69	
Other cash and current assets: amount deposited with American Loan and Trust Company for payment of matured bonds,	14,000 00	
TOTAL CASH AND CURRENT ASSETS,		62,740 96
Miscellaneous assets: Boston Elevated Railway Company lease account,		1,207,201 98
TOTAL,		$32,923,230 36

LIABILITIES.	CR.
Capital stock, common,	$9,689,250 00
Capital stock, preferred,	6,400,000 00
TOTAL CAPITAL STOCK,	$16,089,250 00
Funded debt,	15,981,000 00
Current liabilities: accrued dividend on 3,000 shares common stock to be paid Boston Elevated Railway Company when authorized so to do by the Board of Railroad Commissioners,	4,229 17
Profit and loss balance (surplus),	848,751 19
TOTAL,	$32,923,230 36

Property Accounts.

Additions to railway:		
Extension of tracks (length, 34,760 feet), .	$158,411 98	
New electric line construction, . . .	372,714 35	
Other additions to railway: track betterment,	8,774 54	
Total Additions to Railway, ...		$539,900 87
Additions to equipment:		
Additional cars (55 in number), . . .	$129,834 64	
Electric equipment of same, ...	64,406 97	
Other additional rolling stock and vehicles, .	30,876 64	
Other additions to equipment:		
Sand boxes and vestibuling cars, . .	80,553 69	
Additional horses, tools, furniture, machinery, etc., ...	19,792 80	
Total Additions to Equipment, ...		325,464 74
Additions to land and buildings:		
Additional land necessary for operation of railway, ...	$30,284 36	
Additions to electric power stations, including machinery, etc., ...	191,992 68	
Additional equipment of power stations, .	58,631 17	
Other new buildings necessary for operation of railway, ...	7,090 44	
Total Additions to Land and Buildings, . .		287,998 65
Additions to other permanent property: subway equipment, .		3,358 84
Total Additions to Property Accounts, . . .		$1,156,723 10
Deductions from property accounts (property sold or reduced in valuation and credited to property accounts):		
6,614 feet (1.2527 miles) track taken up, .	$26,403 05	
Cars, trucks and motors sold, destroyed or transferred, ...	19,339 53	
Machinery, tools, etc., sold, destroyed or transferred, ...	77 40	
Equipment of power stations sold, destroyed or transferred, ...	27,589 97	
Subway equipment removed, includes 68 feet track, ...	2,334 03	
Total Deductions from Property Accounts, . .		75,743 98
Net Addition to Property Accounts for the Year,		$1,080,979 12

Capital Stock.

Capital stock authorized by law, common, .	$9,689,250 00	
Capital stock authorized by law, preferred, .	6,400,000 00	
Total capital stock authorized by law, . .	$16,089,250 00	
Capital stock authorized by votes of company, common, ...	$9,689,250 00	
Capital stock authorized by votes of company, preferred, ...	6,400,000 00	
Total capital stock authorized by vote, . .	$16,089,250 00	
Capital stock issued and outstanding, common, . . .		$9,689,250 00
Capital stock issued and outstanding, preferred, . . .		6,400,000 00
Total capital stock outstanding, ...		$16,089,250 00

Number of shares issued and outstanding, common,	193,785	
Number of shares issued and outstanding, preferred,	128,000	
Total number of shares outstanding,		321,785
Number of stockholders, common,	4,457	
Number of stockholders, preferred,	3,757	
Total number of stockholders,		8,214
Number of stockholders in Massachusetts, common,	3,908	
Number of stockholders in Massachusetts, preferred,	3,254	
Total stockholders in Massachusetts,		7,162
Amount of stock held in Massachusetts, common,		$8,652,050 00
Amount of stock held in Massachusetts, preferred,		5,782,700 00
Total stock held in Massachusetts,		$14,434,750 00

Funded Debt.

Description of Bonds.	Rate of Interest.	Date of Maturity.	Amount Outstanding.	Interest Paid during the Year.
	Per Cent.			
West End Street Railway Co., matured,	4	Nov. 1, 1902,	$2,000 00	-
Metropolitan Railroad Co., matured,	5	Dec. 15, 1903,	2,000 00	-
Middlesex Railroad, matured,	5	July 1, 1904,	3,000 00	-
Charles River Street Railway Co., matured,	5	April 1, 1904,	7,000 00	-
South Boston Horse Railway Co.,	5	May 1, 1905,	200,000 00	-
Boston Consolidated Street Railway Co.,	5	Jan. 1, 1907,	500,000 00	-
West End Street Railway Co.,	4½	March 1, 1914,	2,000,000 00	-
West End Street Railway Co.,	4	Aug. 1, 1915,	4,743,000 00	-
West End Street Railway Co.,	4	May 1, 1916,	815,000 00	-
West End Street Railway Co.,	4	Feb. 1, 1917,	2,700,000 00	-
West End Street Railway Co.,	4	Aug. 1, 1932,	5,009,000 00	-
Totals,			$15,981,000 00	-*

Railway Owned.

Length of railway line,	181.977 miles.
Length of second main track,	157.939 "
Total length of main track,	339.916 "
Length of sidings, switches, etc.,	40.658 "
Total, computed as single track,	380.574 "

Railway Owned and Located Outside of Public Ways.

Length of railway line, ... 3.861 miles.

Names of the several cities and towns in which the railway owned by the company is located: Boston, Cambridge, Chelsea, Everett, Malden, Medford, Newton, Somerville, Arlington, Belmont, Brookline and Watertown.

* Interest paid by the Boston Elevated Railway Company.

GENERAL REMARKS AND EXPLANATIONS.

Certain expenditures upon the property have been made by the lessee during the six months from April 1, 1904, to October 1, 1904, for permanent additions, alterations and improvements, which if allowed by us would increase the mileage and would change the figures in this report; but as these expenditures have not yet been audited and allowed by this company they are not included in this report.

CORPORATE NAME AND ADDRESS OF THE COMPANY.

WEST END STREET RAILWAY COMPANY,

101 MILK STREET, BOSTON, MASS.

NAMES AND BUSINESS ADDRESS OF PRINCIPAL OFFICERS.

Joseph B. Russell, *President*, 114 State Street, Boston, Mass. John Parkinson, *Vice-President*, 53 State Street, Boston, Mass. Parkman Dexter, *Treasurer and Clerk of Corporation*, 101 Milk Street, Boston, Mass.

NAMES AND RESIDENCE OF BOARD OF DIRECTORS.

Edwin F. Atkins, Belmont, Mass. Charles M. Baker, Longwood, Mass. Parkman Dexter, Boston, Mass. John Parkinson, Bourne, Mass. Samuel Spencer, New York, N. Y. Joseph B. Russell, Belmont, Mass. C. Minot Weld, Milton, Mass. Stephen M. Weld, Dedham, Mass. Charles A. Williams, Brookline, Mass. Moses Williams, Brookline, Mass. Alfred Winsor, Brookline, Mass.

We hereby certify that the statements contained in the foregoing report are full, just and true.

JOSEPH B. RUSSELL,
E. F. ATKINS,
JOHN PARKINSON,
MOSES WILLIAMS,
CHARLES A. WILLIAMS,
CHARLES M. BAKER,
ALFRED WINSOR,
PARKMAN DEXTER,
Directors.
PARKMAN DEXTER,
Treasurer.

COMMONWEALTH OF MASSACHUSETTS.

SUFFOLK, ss. OCT. 19, 1904. Then personally appeared the above-named Joseph B. Russell, E. F. Atkins, John Parkinson, Moses Williams, Charles A. Williams, Charles M. Baker, Alfred Winsor and Parkman Dexter, directors, and Parkman Dexter, treasurer, and severally made oath that the foregoing certificate by them subscribed is, to the best of their knowledge and belief, true.

Before me, CHARLES B. GLEASON,
Justice of the Peace.

REPORT

OF THE

WINNISIMMET RAILROAD COMPANY

FOR THE YEAR ENDING SEPTEMBER 30, 1904.

[Leased to and operated by the Boston & Northern.]

GENERAL EXHIBIT FOR THE YEAR.		
Rental received from lease of railway,		$3,000 00
Dividends declared (6 per cent),		$3,000 00
Amount of surplus September 30, 1903,		$123 35
Credits to profit and loss account during the year: unclaimed dividend charged off,		1 50
TOTAL SURPLUS SEPTEMBER 30, 1904,		$124 85
GENERAL BALANCE SHEET SEPTEMBER 30, 1904.		
ASSETS.	DR.	
Cost of railway,		$50,000 00
Cash and current assets: cash,		74 85
Miscellaneous assets: office furniture,		50 00
TOTAL,		$50,124 85
LIABILITIES.	CR.	
Capital stock,		$50,000 00
Profit and loss balance (surplus),		124 85
TOTAL,		$50,124 85
CAPITAL STOCK.		
Capital stock authorized by law,	$75,000 00	
Capital stock authorized by votes of company,	50,000 00	
Capital stock issued and outstanding,		$50,000 00
Number of shares issued and outstanding,	1,000	
Number of stockholders,	37	
Number of stockholders in Massachusetts,	35	
Amount of stock held in Massachusetts,	$49,800 00	

RAILWAY OWNED.

Length of railway line,	1.043 miles.
Length of second main track,	1.016 "
Total length of main track,	2.059 "
Length of sidings, switches, etc.,	.128 "
Total, computed as single track,	2.187 "

Names of the several cities and towns in which the railway owned by the company is located: Chelsea.

CORPORATE NAME AND ADDRESS OF THE COMPANY.

WINNISIMMET RAILROAD COMPANY,

60 STATE STREET, ROOM 803, BOSTON, MASS.

NAMES AND BUSINESS ADDRESS OF PRINCIPAL OFFICERS.

Bentley W. Warren, *President*, 60 State Street, Boston, Mass. E. Francis Oliver, *Treasurer and Clerk of Corporation*, 60 State Street, Boston, Mass.

NAMES AND RESIDENCE OF BOARD OF DIRECTORS.

Bentley W. Warren, Williamstown, Mass. David H. Coolidge, Boston, Mass. E. Francis Oliver, Boston, Mass. Edward Russell, Brookline, Mass. Edward R. Cogswell, Cambridge, Mass.

We hereby certify that the statements contained in the foregoing report are full, just and true.

BENTLEY W. WARREN,
DAVID H. COOLIDGE,
EDWARD R. COGSWELL,
E. FRANCIS OLIVER,
Directors.
E. FRANCIS OLIVER,
Treasurer.

COMMONWEALTH OF MASSACHUSETTS.

SUFFOLK, SS. OCT. 13, 1904. Then personally appeared the above-named Bentley W. Warren, David H. Coolidge and E. Francis Oliver, and severally made oath that the foregoing certificate by them subscribed is, to the best of their knowledge and belief, true.

Before me, IRVIN McDOWELL GARFIELD,
Justice of the Peace.

COMMONWEALTH OF MASSACHUSETTS.

SUFFOLK, SS. OCT. 18, 1904. Then personally appeared the above-named Edward R. Cogswell, and made oath that the foregoing certificate by him subscribed is, to the best of his knowledge and belief, true.

Before me, IRVIN McDOWELL GARFIELD,
Justice of the Peace.

REPORT

OF THE

WOONSOCKET STREET RAILWAY COMPANY

For the Year ending September 30, 1904.

General Exhibit for the Year.		
Gross earnings from operation,		$119,388 43
Operating expenses,		102,114 88
Gross Income above Operating Expenses,		$17,273 55
Charges upon income accrued during the year:		
Interest on funded debt,	$8,500 00	
Interest and discount on unfunded debts and loans,	5,926 31	
Taxes, State and local,	7,875 75	
Total Charges and Deductions from Income,		22,302 06
Deficit for the year ending September 30, 1904,		$5,028 51
Amount of deficit September 30, 1903,		32,778 71
Total Deficit September 30, 1904,		$37,807 22

Earnings from Operation.	
Receipts from passengers carried,	$118,910 60
Receipts from carriage of mails,	267 83
Receipts from advertising in cars,	210 00
Gross Earnings from Operation,	$119,388 43

Expenses of Operation.	
General expenses:	
Salaries of general officers and clerks,	$1,560 00
Legal expenses,	600 00
Insurance,	1,646 57
Other general expenses: oils, fuel, salt, etc.,	7,695 73
Maintenance of roadway and buildings:	
Repair of roadbed and track,	14,273 78
Repair of electric line construction,	920 43
Repair of buildings,	728 27

Maintenance of equipment:		
Repair of cars and other vehicles,		$7,024 77
Repair of electric equipment of cars,		4,872 02
Renewal of horses, harnesses, shoeing, etc.,		54 10
Provender and stabling for horses,		608 62
Transportation expenses:		
Cost of electric motive power,		21,204 05
Wages and compensation of persons employed in conducting transportation,		34,251 45
Removal of snow and ice,		2,017 25
Damages for injuries to persons and property,		3,749 93
Rentals of buildings and other property,		372 50
Other transportation expenses: advertising, time tables,		535 41
TOTAL OPERATING EXPENSES,		$102,114 88

PROPERTY ACCOUNTS.

Additions to railway:		
Extension of tracks (length, 5,185 feet),	$4,847 38	
New electric line construction (length, 5,185 feet),	3,667 11	
TOTAL ADDITIONS TO RAILWAY,		$8,514 49
TOTAL ADDITIONS TO PROPERTY ACCOUNTS,		$8,514 49

GENERAL BALANCE SHEET SEPTEMBER 30, 1904.

ASSETS.	DR.	
Cost of railway:		
Roadbed and tracks,	$344,079 76	
Electric line construction, including poles, wiring, feeder lines, etc.,	59,310 54	
Other items of railway cost: tools and construction supplies,	6,281 80	
TOTAL COST OF RAILWAY OWNED,		$409,672 10
Cost of equipment:		
Cars and other rolling stock and vehicles,	$128,395 08	
Horses,	2,021 68	
Other items of equipment: punches, registers, clocks, etc.,	2,041 76	
TOTAL COST OF EQUIPMENT OWNED,		132,458 52
Cost of land and buildings: buildings necessary for operation of railway,		15,596 95
TOTAL PERMANENT INVESTMENTS,		$557,727 57
Cash and current assets:		
Cash,	$5,646 99	
Bills and accounts receivable,	4,861 47	
Other cash and current assets: prepaid insurance,	171 62	
TOTAL CASH AND CURRENT ASSETS,		10,680 08
Profit and loss balance (deficit),		37,807 22
TOTAL,		$606,214 87

Liabilities.	Cr.	
Capital stock,		$300,000 00
Current liabilities:		
Loans and notes payable,	$90,316 28	
Audited vouchers and accounts,	43,038 35	
Total Current Liabilities,		133,354 63
Accrued liabilities:		
Interest accrued and not yet due,	$2,062 50	
Taxes accrued and not yet due,	797 74	
Total Accrued Liabilities,		2,860 24
Total,		$606,214 87

Capital Stock.		
Capital stock authorized by law,	$400,000 00	
Capital stock authorized by votes of company,	300,000 00	
Capital stock issued and outstanding,		$300,000 00
Number of shares issued and outstanding,	3,000	
Number of stockholders,	19	
Number of stockholders in Massachusetts,	13	
Amount of stock held in Massachusetts,	$281,700 00	

Funded Debt.

Description of Bonds.	Rate of Interest.	Date of Maturity.	Amount Outstanding.	Interest Paid during the Year.
	Per Cent.			
First mortgage bonds,	5	July 1, 1913,	$170,000 00	$8,500 00

Volume of Traffic, etc.

Number of passengers paying revenue carried during the year,	2,378,815
Number carried per mile of main railway track operated,	108,320
Number of car miles run,	382,540
Average number of persons employed,	80

Description of Equipment.

Description of Equipment.	Equipped for Electric Power.	Total Passenger Cars.	Equipped with Fenders.	Equipped with Electric Heaters.	Number of Motors.
Cars — Passenger Service.					
Box passenger cars,	16	-	2	16	-
Open passenger cars,	21	-	-	-	-
Total,	37	37	2	16	70
Cars — Other Service.					
Platform freight cars,	2	-	-	-	-
Snow ploughs,	3	-	-	-	-

Miscellaneous Equipment.

Highway vehicles: 2 carts, 1 sled, 2 tower wagons, water cart, lumber wagon, platform wagon, express wagon, reach,	10
Horses,	4
Other items of equipment: 4 sets harnesses.	

Railway Owned and Operated (by Electric Power).

Length of railway line,	21.961 miles.
Length of sidings, switches, etc.,	.863 "
Total, computed as single track,	22.824 "

Railway Located Outside of Massachusetts.

Length of railway line,	18.766 miles.
Length of sidings, switches, etc.,	.760 "
Total, computed as single track,	19.526 "

Names of the several cities and towns in which the railways operated by the company are located: Woonsocket, R. I., Cumberland, R. I., North Smithfield, R. I., Blackstone, Mass.

Accidents to Persons.

(A detailed statement of each accident is on file in the office of the Board.)

Killed and Injured.	From Causes beyond their own Control.		From their own Misconduct or Carelessness.		Total.	
	Killed.	Injured.	Killed.	Injured.	Killed.	Injured.
Passengers,	-	8	-	7	-	15
Employees,	-	-	-	-	-	-
Other persons,	-	2	2	3	2	5
Totals,	-	10	2	10	2	20

Corporate Name and Address of the Company.

WOONSOCKET STREET RAILWAY COMPANY,

6 South Main Street, Woonsocket, R. I.

Names and Business Address of Principal Officers.

Edgar K. Ray, *President and General Manager*, Woonsocket, R. I. Walter Whittlesey, *Treasurer*, Chelsea, Mass. Willard Kent, *Clerk of Corporation*, Woonsocket, R. I. John J. Heffernan, *General Counsel*, Woonsocket, R. I. Herbert M. Young, *Superintendent*, Woonsocket, R. I.

NAMES AND RESIDENCE OF BOARD OF DIRECTORS.

Thomas Martin, Chelsea, Mass. Walter Whittlesey, Chelsea, Mass. Edgar K. Ray, Franklin, Mass. Edward H. Rathbun, Woonsocket, R. I. Willard Kent, Woonsocket, R. I. Henry L. Whittlesey, Newton, Mass. Jas. F. Ray, Franklin, Mass.

We hereby certify that the statements contained in the foregoing report are full, just and true.

EDGAR K. RAY,
EDWARD H. RATHBUN,
WILLARD KENT,
WALTER WHITTLESEY,
HENRY L. WHITTLESEY,
Directors.
WALTER WHITTLESEY,
Treasurer.
HERBERT M. YOUNG,
Superintendent.

COMMONWEALTH OF MASSACHUSETTS.

SUFFOLK, SS. NOV. 1, 1904. Then personally appeared the above-named Henry L. Whittlesey, and made oath that the foregoing certificate by him subscribed is, to the best of his knowledge and belief, true.

Before me, ALLEN D. BOSSON,
Justice of the Peace.

COMMONWEALTH OF MASSACHUSETTS.

SUFFOLK, SS. NOV. 1, 1904. Then personally appeared the above-named Walter Whittlesey, director and treasurer, and made solemn oath that the foregoing certificate by him subscribed is, to the best of his knowledge and belief, true.

Before me, HENRY L. WHITTLESEY,
Notary Public.

STATE OF RHODE ISLAND.

PROVIDENCE, SS. OCT. 29, 1904. Then personally appeared the above-named Edgar K. Ray, Willard Kent and Edward H. Rathbun, directors, and Herbert M. Young, superintendent, and made solemn oath that the foregoing certificate by them subscribed is, to the best of their knowledge and belief, true.

Before me, WINTHROP B. NYE,
Notary Public.

REPORT

OF THE

WORCESTER & BLACKSTONE VALLEY STREET RAILWAY COMPANY

For the Year ending September 30, 1904.

General Exhibit for the Year.		
Gross earnings from operation,		$67,685 26
Operating expenses,		43,120 01
Gross Income above Operating Expenses,		$24,565 25
Charges upon income accrued during the year:		
Interest and discount on unfunded debts and loans,	$20,402 07	
Taxes, State and local,	3,521 34	
Total Charges and Deductions from Income,		23,923 41
Surplus for the year ending September 30, 1904,		$641 84
Amount of surplus September 30, 1903,		20,753 58
Total Surplus September 30, 1904,		$21,395 42

Earnings from Operation.	
Receipts from passengers carried,	$66,727 73
Receipts from rentals of buildings and other property,	266 61
Receipts from advertising in cars,	280 00
Receipts from interest on deposits,	95 87
Other earnings from operation: chartered cars,	315 05
Gross Earnings from Operation,	$67,685 26

Expenses of Operation.	
General expenses:	
Salaries of general officers and clerks,	$2,422 00
General office expenses and supplies,	372 48

General expenses — *Concluded.*		
Insurance,		$1,528 30
Other general expenses,		431 17
Maintenance of roadway and buildings:		
Repair of roadbed and track,		3,220 53
Repair of electric line construction,		314 05
Repair of buildings,		261 36
Maintenance of equipment:		
Repair of cars and other vehicles,		2,967 82
Repair of electric equipment of cars,		2,958 77
Transportation expenses:		
Cost of electric motive power,		11,859 30
Wages and compensation of persons employed in conducting transportation,		12,009 32
Removal of snow and ice,		538 12
Damages for injuries to persons and property,		3,682 64
Tolls for trackage over other railways,		554 15
TOTAL OPERATING EXPENSES,		$43,120 01

PROPERTY ACCOUNTS.

Additions to railway: interest and legal expenses,		$15,878 97
Additions to equipment:		
Electric equipment of cars,	$1,040 90	
Other additions to equipment: tools,	75 00	
TOTAL ADDITIONS TO EQUIPMENT,		1,115 90
Additions to land and buildings:		
Additional equipment of power stations,	$2,886 06	
New buildings necessary for operation of railway,	228 01	
TOTAL ADDITIONS TO LAND AND BUILDINGS,		3,114 07
TOTAL ADDITIONS TO PROPERTY ACCOUNTS,		$20,108 94

GENERAL BALANCE SHEET SEPTEMBER 30, 1904.

ASSETS.	DR.	
Cost of railway:		
Roadbed and tracks,	$187,524 41	
Electric line construction, including poles, wiring, feeder lines, etc.,	43,094 55	
Interest accrued during construction of railway,	24,117 56	
Engineering and other expenses incident to construction,	13,696 50	
TOTAL COST OF RAILWAY OWNED,		$268,433 02
Cost of equipment:		
Cars and other rolling stock and vehicles,	$38,426 77	
Electric equipment of same,	29,117 19	
Other items of equipment: tools,	474 73	
TOTAL COST OF EQUIPMENT OWNED,		68,018 69

Cost of land and buildings:		
Land necessary for operation of railway,	$3,454 37	
Electric power stations, including equipment,	119,647 58	
Other buildings necessary for operation of railway,	6,975 83	
TOTAL COST OF LAND AND BUILDINGS OWNED,		$130,077 78
Other permanent property:		
Tenement property,	$8,578 24	
Office fixtures,	50 00	
TOTAL COST OF OTHER PERMANENT PROPERTY OWNED,		8,628 24
TOTAL PERMANENT INVESTMENTS,		$475,157 73
Cash and current assets:		
Cash,	$1,349 19	
Bills and accounts receivable,	322 00	
TOTAL CASH AND CURRENT ASSETS,		1,671 19
TOTAL,		$476,828 92

LIABILITIES.		CR.
Capital stock,		$60,000 00
Current liabilities:		
Loans and notes payable,	$393,037 23	
Audited vouchers and accounts,	508 26	
Dividends not called for,	36 00	
Miscellaneous current liabilities: property found,	16 00	
TOTAL CURRENT LIABILITIES,		393,597 49
Accrued liabilities: interest accrued and not yet due,		1,836 01
Profit and loss balance (surplus),		21,395 42
TOTAL,		$476,828 92

CAPITAL STOCK.

Capital stock authorized by law,	$60,000 00	
Capital stock authorized by votes of company,	60,000 00	
Capital stock issued and outstanding,		$60,000 00
Number of shares issued and outstanding,	600	
Number of stockholders,	7	
Number of stockholders in Massachusetts,	1	
Amount of stock held in Massachusetts,	$100 00	

VOLUME OF TRAFFIC, ETC.

Number of passengers paying revenue carried during the year,	1,546,611
Number carried per mile of main railway track operated,	89,711
Number of car miles run,	334,946
Average number of persons employed,	36

Description of Equipment.

Description of Equipment.	Equipped for Electric Power.	Not Equipped.	Equipped with Fenders.	Equipped with Electric Heaters.	Number of Motors.
Cars — Passenger Service.					
Box passenger cars,	8	-	8	8	24
Open passenger cars,	10	-	10	-	32
Total,	18	-	18	8	56
Cars — Other Service.					
Platform freight cars,	-	1	-	-	-
Work cars,	1	-	1	-	2
Total,	1	1	1	-	2
Snow ploughs,	1	2	-	-	3

Miscellaneous Equipment.

Highway vehicles: tower wagon,	1

Railway Owned and Operated (by Electric Power).

Railway Owned, etc.	Owned.	Trackage over Other Railways.	Total Owned, etc.
	Miles.	Miles.	Miles.
Length of railway line,	15.740	1.500	17.240
Length of sidings, switches, etc.,	.620	-	.620
Total, Computed as Single Track,	16.360	1.500	17.860

Railway Located Outside of Public Ways.

Length of railway line,	.840 mile.

Names of the several cities and towns in which the railways operated by the company are located: Worcester, Millbury, Sutton, Grafton and Northbridge.

Grade Crossings with Railroads.

Grade Crossings with Railroads.	Number of Tracks at Crossing.	
	Railroad.	Railway.
Crossings of railways with railroads at grade (1 in number), viz.: — With New York, New Haven & Hartford Railroad, private track to Fisher's Manufacturing Company mill, and is always attended by a watchman when in use,	1	1

ACCIDENTS TO PERSONS.

(A detailed statement of each accident is on file in the office of the Board.)

KILLED AND INJURED.	FROM CAUSES BEYOND THEIR OWN CONTROL.		FROM THEIR OWN MISCONDUCT OR CARELESSNESS.		TOTAL.	
	Killed.	Injured.	Killed.	Injured.	Killed.	Injured.
Passengers,	-	10	-	2	-	12
Employees,	-	-	-	1	-	1
Other persons,	-	-	1	-	1	-
TOTALS,	-	10	1	3	1	13

CORPORATE NAME AND ADDRESS OF THE COMPANY.

WORCESTER & BLACKSTONE VALLEY STREET RAILWAY COMPANY,

NEW HAVEN, CONN.

NAMES AND BUSINESS ADDRESS OF PRINCIPAL OFFICERS.

F. S. Curtis, *President*, Boston, Mass. E. H. McHenry, *Vice-President*, New Haven, Conn. A. S. May, *Treasurer*, New Haven, Conn. J. G. Parker, *Clerk of Corporation*, New Haven, Conn. James W. Anderson, *Superintendent*, Millbury, Mass.

NAMES AND RESIDENCE OF BOARD OF DIRECTORS.

Edwin Milner, Moosup, Conn. Fayette S. Curtis, Boston, Mass. Robert W. Taft, Providence, R. I. H. M. Kochersperger, New Haven, Conn. Edward G. Buckland, New Haven, Conn. C. S. Mellen, New Haven, Conn. E. H. McHenry, New Haven, Conn.

We hereby certify that the statements contained in the foregoing report are full, just and true.

F. S. CURTIS,
C. S. MELLEN,
EDWARD G. BUCKLAND,
H. M. KOCHERSPERGER,
Directors.
A. S. MAY,
Treasurer.
JAMES W. ANDERSON,
Superintendent.

COMMONWEALTH OF MASSACHUSETTS.

WORCESTER, SS. WORCESTER, Nov. 18, 1904. Then personally appeared James W. Anderson, and made oath that the foregoing certificate by him subscribed is, to the best of his knowledge and belief, true.

Before me, JOHN R. THAYER,
Justice of the Peace and Notary Public.

COMMONWEALTH OF MASSACHUSETTS.

SUFFOLK, ss. BOSTON, Nov. 21, 1904. Then personally appeared F. S. Curtis, and made oath that the foregoing certificate by him subscribed, is, to the best of his knowledge and belief, true.

Before me, DANIEL M. GOODRIDGE,
Notary Public.

STATE OF CONNECTICUT.

COUNTY OF NEW HAVEN, ss. Nov. 17, 1904. Then personally appeared the above-named C. S. Mellen, E. G. Buckland, H. M. Kochersperger and A. S. May, and severally made oath that the foregoing certificate by them subscribed is, to the best of their knowledge and belief, true.

Before me, ALBERT H. POWELL,
Notary Public.

REPORT

OF THE

WORCESTER CONSOLIDATED STREET RAILWAY COMPANY

For the Year ending September 30, 1904.

General Exhibit for the Year.			
Gross earnings from operation,			$1,336,440 86
Operating expenses,			813,154 88
Gross Income above Operating Expenses,			$523,285 98
Charges upon income accrued during the year:			
Interest on funded debt,		$49,950 00	
Interest and discount on unfunded debts and loans,		99,607 92	
Taxes, State and local,	$73,316 32		
Taxes, commutation,	29,712 64		
		103,028 96	
Rentals of leased railways:			
North End Street Railway,	$8,000 00		
Worcester & Shrewsbury Street Railway,	1,000 00		
Worcester & Shrewsbury Railroad,	3,750 00		
		12,750 00	
Other deductions from income:			
Rent and expenses of Lincoln park,	$29,477 16		
Rent of power house,	50,000 00		
		79,477 16	
Total Charges and Deductions from Income,			344,814 04
Net Divisible Income,			$178,471 94
Dividends declared (5 per cent),			177,500 00
Surplus for the year ending September 30, 1904,			$971 94
Amount of surplus September 30, 1903,			346,457 21
Debits to profit and loss account during the year:			
Premium on Leominster & Clinton Street Railway Company bonds,		$7,150 00	
Settlement of Worcester & Southbridge Street Railway Company account,		21 40	
Adjustment of U. S. mail contract, account of reduction of mileage,		3,242 73	
Total Debits,			10,414 13
Total Surplus September 30, 1904,			$337,015 02

Earnings from Operation.

Receipts from passengers carried,	$1,320,561 83
Receipts from carriage of mails,	2,002 28
Receipts from tolls for use of tracks by other companies,	2,539 99
Receipts from rentals of buildings and other property,	2,484 60
Receipts from advertising in cars,	3,500 00
Receipts from interest on deposits,	1,285 44
Other earnings from operation:	
Chartered cars,	2,566 72
Transportation of mail carriers,	1,500 00
Gross Earnings from Operation,	$1,336,440 86

Expenses of Operation.

General expenses:	
Salaries of general officers and clerks,	$41,253 43
General office expenses and supplies,	7,290 11
Legal expenses,	5,691 80
Insurance,	21,101 45
Other general expenses: miscellaneous general expense,	9,991 60
Maintenance of roadway and buildings:	
Repair of roadbed and track,	14,095 65
Repair of electric line construction,	14,446 40
Repair of buildings,	6,318 10
Maintenance of equipment:	
Repair of cars and other vehicles,	49,145 65
Repair of electric equipment of cars,	48,821 67
Renewal of horses, harnesses, shoeing, etc.,	615 78
Provender and stabling for horses,	4,546 30
Transportation expenses:	
Cost of electric motive power, $207,728.88; less power sold, $6,143.51; net,	201,585 37
Wages and compensation of persons employed in conducting transportation,	288,523 88
Removal of snow and ice,	13,198 67
Damages for injuries to persons and property,	53,327 00
Tolls for trackage over other railways,	433 40
Rentals of buildings and other property,	181 50
Other transportation expenses:	
Repairs of tools and machinery,	3,477 54
Miscellaneous car service expense and supplies, $18,092.74; cleaning, oiling and sanding track, $8,223.51; hired equipment, $2,793.33,	29,109 58
Total Operating Expenses,	$813,154 88

Property Accounts.

Additions to railway:		
Extension of tracks,	$234 11	
New electric line construction,	683 12	
Other additions to railway: State highway,	3,717 53	
Total Additions to Railway,		$4,634 76
Additions to equipment,		3,840 49

Additions to land and buildings:		
Additional land necessary for operation of railway,	$8,793 50	
New electric power stations, including machinery, etc.,	3,568 54	
Other new buildings necessary for operation of railway,	51,020 64	
TOTAL ADDITIONS TO LAND AND BUILDINGS,		$63,382 68
TOTAL ADDITIONS TO PROPERTY ACCOUNTS,		$71,857 93
Deductions from property accounts (property sold or reduced in valuation and credited to property accounts):		
Cars sold,	$8,819 64	
Electric equipment sold,	1,102 95	
Park buildings,	75 00	
TOTAL DEDUCTIONS FROM PROPERTY ACCOUNTS,		9,997 59
NET ADDITION TO PROPERTY ACCOUNTS FOR THE YEAR,		$61,860 34

GENERAL BALANCE SHEET SEPTEMBER 30, 1904.

ASSETS.	DR.	
Cost of railway:		
Roadbed and tracks,	$2,738,578 83	
Electric line construction, including poles, wiring, feeder lines, etc.,	498,604 60	
Engineering and other expenses incident to construction,	79,438 16	
Other items of railway cost: State highway,	83,932 67	
TOTAL COST OF RAILWAY OWNED,		$3,400,554 26
Cost of equipment:		
Cars and other rolling stock and vehicles,	$620,424 78	
Electric equipment of same,	618,674 40	
Other items of equipment,	148,008 13	
TOTAL COST OF EQUIPMENT OWNED,		1,387,107 31
Cost of land and buildings:		
Land necessary for operation of railway,	$266,507 98	
Electric power stations, including equipment,	428,078 02	
Other buildings necessary for operation of railway,	555,843 46	
TOTAL COST OF LAND AND BUILDINGS OWNED,		1,250,429 46
Other permanent property: parks and park buildings,		44,052 89
TOTAL PERMANENT INVESTMENTS,		$6,082,143 92
Cash and current assets:		
Cash,	$59,827 82	
Bills and accounts receivable,	57,872 97	
Sinking and other special funds,	1,000 00	
Other cash and current assets: reconstruction of track,	160,899 70	
TOTAL CASH AND CURRENT ASSETS,		279,600 49

Miscellaneous assets:		
Materials and supplies,	$120,473 26	
Other assets and property:		
Prepaid interest,	1,643 36	
Prepaid fire insurance,	15,079 46	
TOTAL MISCELLANEOUS ASSETS,		$137,196 08
TOTAL,		$6,498,940 49

LIABILITIES.	CR.	
Capital stock,		$3,550,000 00
Funded debt,		1,060,000 00
Real estate mortgages,		59,500 00
Current liabilities:		
Loans and notes payable,	$1,294,500 00	
Audited vouchers and accounts,	134,593 35	
Matured interest coupons unpaid (including coupons due October 1),	12,062 50	
Rentals due and unpaid (including rentals due October 1),	27,540 83	
TOTAL CURRENT LIABILITIES,		1,468,696 68
Accrued liabilities: interest accrued and not yet due,		23,728 79
Profit and loss balance (surplus),		337,015 02
TOTAL,		$6,498,940 49

CAPITAL STOCK.		
Capital stock authorized by law,	$4,345,000 00	
Capital stock authorized by votes of company,	3,550,000 00	
Capital stock issued and outstanding,		$3,550,000 00
Number of shares issued and outstanding,	35,500	
Number of stockholders,	28	
Number of stockholders in Massachusetts,	27	
Amount of stock held in Massachusetts,	$3,549,000 00	

REAL ESTATE MORTGAGES.

DESCRIPTION OF MORTGAGED PROPERTY.	Rate of Interest.	Mortgage when Due.	Amount.	Interest Paid during the Year.
	Per Cent.			
Land on Shrewsbury Street, Worcester.	5	Demand,	$4,500 00	$225 00
Land corner of Main and Market streets, Worcester.	4	July 1, 1905,	30,000 00	1,200 00
Land in Fitchburg,	4½	July 1, 1905,	10,000 00	450 00
Land on Union Street, Worcester,	4½	July 1, 1905,	15,000 00	675 00
TOTALS,	. .	. . .	$59,500 00	$2,550 00

Funded Debt.

Description of Bonds.	Rate of Interest.	Date of Maturity.	Amount Outstanding.	Interest Paid during the Year.
	Per Cent.			
Worcester Consolidated Street Railway debentures,	4½	March, 1920,	$700,000 00	$31,500 00
Worcester & Marlborough Street Railway first mortgage.	5	Oct. 1, 1917,	200,000 00	10,000 00
Worcester & Clinton Street Railway first mortgage.	5	Jan. 1, 1919,	115,000 00	5,750 00
Leominster & Clinton Street Railway coupon notes.	6	April 1, 1912,	45,000 00	2,700 00
Totals,	. .	. . .	$1,060,000 00	$49,950 00

Sinking and Other Special Funds.

Amount September 30, 1903, of sinking fund,	$1,000 00
Total Sinking and Other Special Funds, September 30, 1904,	$1,000 00

Volume of Traffic, etc.

Number of passengers paying revenue carried during the year,	27,098,275
Number carried per mile of main railway track operated,	195,352
Number of car miles run,	5,103,614
Average number of persons employed,	718

Description of Equipment.

Description of Equipment.	Equipped for Electric Power.	Equipped with Fenders.	Equipped with Electric Heaters.	Number of Motors.
Cars — Passenger Service.				
Box passenger cars,	155	155	151	739
Open passenger cars,	162	162	-	-
Total,	317	317	151	739
Cars — Other Service.				
Platform freight cars,	5	5	-	-
Work cars,	3	3	-	-
Other cars,	7	7	-	-
Total,	15	15	-	-
Snow ploughs,	36	-	-	-

Miscellaneous Equipment.

Carts and snow sleds,	10
Other railway highway stock: 7 tower wagons; 8 express wagons; 12 road machines; 7 buggies,	34
Horses,	16
Other items of equipment: harnesses,	16

Railway Owned, Leased and Operated (by Electric Power).

Railway Owned, etc.	Owned.	Held under Lease or Contract.	Trackage over Other Railways.	Total Owned, Leased, etc.
	Miles.	Miles.	Miles.	Miles.
Length of railway line,	109.406	8.120	.490	118.016
Length of second main track,	20.699	-	-	20.699
Total Length of Main Track,	130.105	8.120	.490	138.715
Length of sidings, switches, etc.,	3.372	.719	-	4.091
Total, Computed as Single Track,	133.477	8.839	.490	142.806

Railway Located Outside of Public Ways.

Length of railway line,	8.080 miles.

Names of the several cities and towns in which the railways operated by the company are located: Fitchburg, Leominster, Lancaster, Clinton, Berlin, Hudson, Boylston, Shrewsbury, Northborough, Westborough, Marlborough, Worcester, Grafton, Millbury, Leicester and Spencer.

Grade Crossings with Railroads.

Grade Crossings with Railroads.	Number of Tracks at Crossing.	
	Railroad.	Railway.
Crossings of railways with railroads at grade (14 in number), viz.: —		
With New York, New Haven & Hartford Railroad, West Berlin,	3	1
With New York, New Haven & Hartford Railroad, Water Street, Leominster,	2	1
With New York, New Haven & Hartford Railroad, Northborough,	1	1
With New York, New Haven & Hartford Railroad, Lancaster Street, Leominster,	1	1
With New York, New Haven & Hartford Railroad and Boston & Albany Railroad, Green Street, Worcester,	6	1
With Boston & Albany Railroad and New York, New Haven & Hartford Railroad, Grafton Street, Worcester,	10	1
With Boston & Maine Railroad, Shrewsbury Street, Worcester,	3	1
With Boston & Maine Railroad, Summer Street, Worcester,	3	2
With Boston & Maine Railroad, Thomas Street, Worcester,	2	1
With Boston & Maine Railroad, Lincoln Street, Worcester,	3	2
With Boston & Maine Railroad, Barber's Crossing, Worcester,	3	1
With New York, New Haven & Hartford Railroad, Millbury Street, Worcester,	2	1
Total Number of Tracks at Crossings,	39	14

Number of above crossings at which *frogs* are inserted in the tracks, . 3

Accidents to Persons.

(A detailed statement of each accident is on file in the office of the Board.)

Killed and Injured.	From Causes beyond their own Control.		From their own Misconduct or Carelessness.		Total.	
	Killed.	Injured.	Killed.	Injured.	Killed.	Injured.
Passengers,	-	51	1	126	1	177
Employees,	-	2	-	5	-	7
Other persons,	-	6	4	61	4	67
Totals,	-	59	5	192	5	251

Corporate Name and Address of the Company.

WORCESTER CONSOLIDATED STREET RAILWAY COMPANY,

Worcester, Mass.

Names and Business Address of Principal Officers.

Francis H. Dewey, *President and General Counsel*, Worcester, Mass. A. George Bullock, *Vice-President*, Worcester, Mass. Justin W. Lester, *Treasurer and Clerk of Corporation*, Worcester, Mass. Frederick A. Huntress, *General Manager*, Worcester, Mass. John B. Gorman, Thomas A. Leach, George H. Burgess, *Superintendents*, Worcester, Mass.

Names and Residence of Board of Directors.

A. George Bullock, Worcester, Mass. Francis H. Dewey, Worcester, Mass. Alfred D. Foster, Boston, Mass. Francis R. Hart, Boston, Mass. Pierre Jay, Boston, Mass. Frederick W. Kendrick, Boston, Mass. Lincoln N. Kinnicutt, Worcester, Mass. Stephen Salisbury, Worcester, Mass. Samuel E. Winslow, Worcester, Mass.

We hereby certify that the statements contained in the foregoing report are full, just and true.

F. H. DEWEY,
A. G. BULLOCK,
STEPHEN SALISBURY,
LINCOLN N. KINNICUTT,
SAMUEL E. WINSLOW,
ALFRED D. FOSTER,
F. W. KENDRICK,
Directors.
JUSTIN W. LESTER,
Treasurer.
FREDERICK A. HUNTRESS,
General Manager.

COMMONWEALTH OF MASSACHUSETTS.

WORCESTER, SS. OCT. 31, 1904. Then personally appeared the above-named F. H. Dewey, A. G. Bullock, Samuel E. Winslow, Stephen Salisbury, Lincoln N. Kinnicutt, Justin W. Lester, Frederick A. Huntress, Alfred D. Foster* and Frederick W. Kendrick,* and severally made oath that the foregoing certificate by them subscribed is, to the best of their knowledge and belief, true.

Before me, CHANDLER BULLOCK,
Justice of the Peace.
*JUSTIN W. LESTER,
Notary Public.

REPORT

OF THE

WORCESTER & HOLDEN STREET RAILWAY COMPANY

For the Year ending September 30, 1904.

General Exhibit for the Year.			
Gross earnings from operation,			$36,244 20
Operating expenses,			24,372 49
Gross Income above Operating Expenses,			$11,871 71
Charges upon income accrued during the year:			
Interest on funded debt,		$5,000 00	
Interest and discount on unfunded debts and loans,		398 00	
Taxes, State and local,	$371 72		
Taxes, commutation,	56 06		
		427 78	
Other deductions from income: Worcester Consolidated Street Railway Company,		4,307 61	
Total Charges and Deductions from Income,			10,133 39
Surplus for the year ending September 30, 1904,			$1,738 32
Amount of surplus September 30, 1903,			6,710 20
Total Surplus September 30, 1904,			$8,448 52

Earnings from Operation.	
Receipts from passengers carried,	$36,087 22
Receipts from carriage of mails,	47 77
Receipts from advertising in cars,	72 82
Receipts from interest on deposits,	36 39
Gross Earnings from Operation,	$36,244 20

Expenses of Operation.	
General expenses:	
Salaries of general officers and clerks,	$2,808 36
General office expenses and supplies,	580 96
Legal expenses,	79 85
Insurance,	145 40
Maintenance of roadway and buildings:	
Repair of roadbed and track,	419 69
Repair of electric line construction,	299 50
Repair of buildings,	79 43

Maintenance of equipment:		
Repair of cars and other vehicles,		$741 85
Repair of electric equipment of cars,		18 86
Transportation expenses:		
Cost of electric motive power,		9,886 25
Wages and compensation of persons employed in conducting transportation,		8,052 96
Removal of snow and ice,		326 47
Tolls for trackage over other railways,		179 44
Other transportation expenses: oils, waste, tickets, etc.,		753 47
TOTAL OPERATING EXPENSES,		$24,372 49

PROPERTY ACCOUNTS.

Additions to railway:		
Completion of tracks,	$14,908 19	
Electric line construction,	11,789 80	
Other additions to railway: engineering, interest, insurance, commission,	10,926 40	
TOTAL ADDITIONS TO RAILWAY,		$37,624 39
Additions to equipment:		
Additional cars,	$7,030 76	
Electric equipment of same,	11,173 08	
Other additions to equipment: tools,	303 02	
TOTAL ADDITIONS TO EQUIPMENT,		18,506 86
Additions to land and buildings:		
Additional land necessary for operation of railway,	$2,484 00	
Additional equipment of power stations,	9,322 83	
New buildings necessary for operation of railway,	4,983 87	
TOTAL ADDITIONS TO LAND AND BUILDINGS,		16,790 70
TOTAL ADDITIONS TO PROPERTY ACCOUNTS,		$72,921 95

GENERAL BALANCE SHEET SEPTEMBER 30, 1904.

ASSETS.	DR.	
Cost of railway:		
Roadbed and tracks,	$157,990 71	
Electric line construction, including poles, wiring, feeder lines, etc.,	38,899 62	
Interest accrued during construction of railway,	8,698 34	
Engineering and other expenses incident to construction,	16,236 33	
TOTAL COST OF RAILWAY OWNED,		$221,825 00
Cost of equipment:		
Cars and other rolling stock and vehicles,	$21,320 47	
Electric equipment of same,	23,264 99	
Other items of equipment,	3,376 68	
TOTAL COST OF EQUIPMENT OWNED,		47,962 14

Cost of land and buildings:		
Land necessary for operation of railway,	$8,964 31	
Electric power stations, including equipment,	37,968 66	
Other buildings necessary for operation of railway,	11,533 47	
TOTAL COST OF LAND AND BUILDINGS OWNED,		$58,466 44
TOTAL PERMANENT INVESTMENTS,		$328,253 58
Cash and current assets: cash,		4,636 39
Miscellaneous assets: materials and supplies,		5,615 23
TOTAL,		$338,505 20

LIABILITIES.	CR.	
Capital stock,		$125,000 00
Funded debt,		125,000 00
Current liabilities:		
Loans and notes payable,	$74,453 21	
Audited vouchers and accounts,	5,262 53	
Miscellaneous current liabilities: construction bill,	340 94	
TOTAL CURRENT LIABILITIES,		80,056 68
Profit and loss balance (surplus),		8,448 52
TOTAL,		$338,505 20

CAPITAL STOCK.		
Capital stock authorized by law,	$125,000 00	
Capital stock authorized by votes of company,	125,000 00	
Capital stock issued and outstanding,		$125,000 00
Number of shares issued and outstanding,	1,250	
Number of stockholders,	31	
Number of stockholders in Massachusetts,	31	
Amount of stock held in Massachusetts,	$125,000 00	

FUNDED DEBT.

DESCRIPTION OF BONDS.	Rate of Interest.	Date of Maturity.	Amount Outstanding.	Interest Paid during the Year.
First mortgage bonds,	Per Cent. 5	Oct. 1, 1923,	$125,000 00	$5,000 00

VOLUME OF TRAFFIC, ETC.

Number of passengers paying revenue carried during the year,	723,298
Number carried per mile of main railway track operated,	75,509
Number of car miles run,	224,994
Average number of persons employed,	16

Description of Equipment.

Description of Equipment.	Equipped for Electric Power.	Not Equipped.	Equipped with Fenders.	Equipped with Electric Heaters.	Number of Motors.
Cars — Passenger Service.					
Box passenger cars,	3	-	3	3	12
Open passenger cars,	4	-	4	-	16
Total,	7	-	7	3	28
Cars — Other Service.					
Platform freight cars,	-	1	-	-	-
Work cars,	-	3	-	-	-
Total,	-	4	-	-	-

Railway Owned and Operated (by Electric Power).

Railway Owned, etc.	Owned.	Trackage over Other Railways.	Total Owned, etc.
	Miles.	Miles.	Miles.
Length of railway line,	7.449	2.130	9.579
Length of sidings, switches, etc.,	.580	-	.580
Total, Computed as Single Track,	8.029	2.130	10.159

Names of the several cities and towns in which the railways operated by the company are located: Worcester and Holden.

Corporate Name and Address of the Company.

WORCESTER & HOLDEN STREET RAILWAY COMPANY,

Holden, Mass.

Names and Business Address of Principal Officers.

Henry W. Warren, *President*, Holden, Mass. Otis E. Putnam, *Vice-President*, Main Street, Worcester, Mass. Edgar S. Douglass, *Treasurer*, *Clerk of Corporation and Superintendent*, Holden, Mass. Charles C. Milton, *General Counsel*, 340 Main Street, Worcester, Mass. Lewis C. Muzzy, *Auditor*, Elm Street, Worcester, Mass.

Names and Residence of Board of Directors.

Henry W. Warren, Holden, Mass. Otis E. Putnam, Worcester, Mass. Stephen Salisbury, Worcester, Mass. Francis Murdock, Newton, Mass. James E. Fuller, Worcester, Mass. Charles C. Milton, Worcester, Mass. Albion R. Clapp, Wellesley Hills, Mass.

We hereby certify that the statements contained in the foregoing report are full, just and true.

HENRY W. WARREN,
STEPHEN SALISBURY,
CHARLES C. MILTON,
OTIS E. PUTNAM,
Directors.
E. S. DOUGLASS,
Treasurer.
E. S. DOUGLASS,
Superintendent.

COMMONWEALTH OF MASSACHUSETTS.

WORCESTER, ss. Nov. 16, 1904. Then personally appeared the above-named Henry W. Warren, Stephen Salisbury, Charles C. Milton, Otis E. Putnam and E. S. Douglass, and severally made oath that the foregoing certificate by them subscribed is, to the best of their knowledge and belief, true.

Before me, GEORGE A. GASKILL,
Justice of the Peace.

REPORT

OF THE

WORCESTER, ROCHDALE & CHARLTON DEPOT STREET RAILWAY COMPANY

For the Year ending September 30, 1904.

[Operated by the Worcester & Southbridge.]

General Exhibit for the Year.

Rental received from lease of railway,	$900 00
Expenses and charges upon income accrued during the year: interest on funded debt,	$900 00
Debits to profit and loss account during the year: adjustment,	$56,082 78
Total Deficit September 30, 1904,	$56,082 78

General Balance Sheet September 30, 1904.

Assets.	Dr.
Cost of railway,	$109,917 22
Profit and loss balance (deficit),	56,082 78
Total,	$166,000 00

Liabilities.	Cr.
Capital stock,	$40,000 00
Funded debt,	40,000 00
Current liabilities: loans and notes payable,	86,000 00
Total,	$166,000 00

Capital Stock.

Capital stock authorized by law,	$40,000 00	
Capital stock authorized by votes of company,	40,000 00	
Capital stock issued and outstanding,		$40,000 00
Number of shares issued and outstanding,	400	
Number of stockholders,	5	
Number of stockholders in Massachusetts,	1	
Amount of stock held in Massachusetts,	$100 00	

FUNDED DEBT.

DESCRIPTION OF BONDS.	Rate of Interest.	Date of Maturity.	Amount Outstanding.	Interest Paid during the Year.
First mortgage bonds, ...	Per Cent. 4½	July 1, 1923, .	$40,000 00	$900 00

RAILWAY OWNED.

Length of railway line, ...	1.500 miles.
Length of second main track, ...	1.500 "
Total length of main track, ...	3.000 "

Names of the several cities and towns in which the railway owned by the company is located: Worcester.

CORPORATE NAME AND ADDRESS OF THE COMPANY.

WORCESTER, ROCHDALE & CHARLTON DEPOT STREET RAILWAY COMPANY,

NEW HAVEN, CONN.

NAMES AND BUSINESS ADDRESS OF PRINCIPAL OFFICERS.

F. S. Curtis, *President*, Boston, Mass. Edwin Milner, *Vice-President*, Moosup, Conn. A. S. May, *Treasurer*, New Haven, Conn. John G. Parker, *Clerk of Corporation*, New Haven, Conn. H. M. Kochersperger, *Auditor*, New Haven, Conn.

NAMES AND RESIDENCE OF BOARD OF DIRECTORS.

F. S. Curtis, Boston, Mass. C. S. Mellen, New Haven, Conn. Edwin Milner, Moosup, Conn. E. H. McHenry, New Haven, Conn. Charles F. Brooker, Ansonia, Conn.

We hereby certify that the statements contained in the foregoing report are full, just and true.

F. S. CURTIS,
C. S. MELLEN,
CHAS. F. BROOKER,
Directors.
A. S. MAY,
Treasurer.

COMMONWEALTH OF MASSACHUSETTS.

SUFFOLK, SS. BOSTON, Nov. 29, 1904. Then personally appeared the above-named F. S. Curtis, and made oath that the foregoing certificate by him subscribed is, to the best of his knowledge and belief, true.

Before me, DANIEL M. GOODRIDGE,
Notary Public.

STATE OF CONNECTICUT.

COUNTY OF NEW HAVEN, SS. NOV. 28, 1904. Then personally appeared the above-named C. S. Mellen, Chas. F. Brooker and A. S. May, and severally made oath that the foregoing certificate by them subscribed is, to the best of their knowledge and belief, true.

Before me, ALBERT H. POWELL,
Notary Public.

THE CONSOLIDATED RAILWAY COMPANY,
OFFICE OF THE AUDITOR,
NEW HAVEN, CONN., Dec. 10, 1904.

Honorable Board of Railroad Commissioners, Boston, Mass.

GENTLEMEN: — Referring to the report of the Worcester, Rochdale & Charlton Depot Street Railway Company, for the year ending Sept. 30, 1904, which was filed with you, I wish to state that when the present management took charge of that company we found that there were no books of account. After spending some time in making a search for the books and for information with which to open the books, we finally concluded that the original books could not be found, and on May 22, 1904, we opened the present books with the best information available. We made an appraisal of the property, and set that up on our books as the cost, and on the other side we set up the liabilities as they appeared May 22, 1904.

We regret very much that we cannot furnish a more complete report than the one sent you, but we have done the very best we could, and have sent you all the information we have been able to obtain from the records of the company.

Yours truly, C. L. CAMPBELL,
Auditor.

REPORT

OF THE

WORCESTER & SHREWSBURY RAILROAD COMPANY

For the Year ending September 30, 1904.

[Leased to and operated by the Worcester Consolidated.]

General Exhibit for the Year.	
Rental received from lease of railway,	$2,650 00
Income from other sources: interest on $22,000 bonds at 5 per cent.,	1,100 00
Gross Income,	$3,750 00
Expenses and charges upon income accrued during the year: interest on funded debt,	1,100 00
Net Divisible Income,	$2,650 00
Dividends declared (7 22/100 per cent on $36,700),	2,649 74
Surplus for the year ending September 30, 1904,	$0 26
Amount of surplus September 30, 1903,	64,692 25
Total Surplus September 30, 1904,	$64,692 51

General Balance Sheet September 30, 1904.	
Assets. Dr.	
Cost of railway,	$70,803 58
Cost of equipment,	52,710 86
Total Permanent Investments,	$123,514 44
Cash and current assets: cash,	3 07
Total,	$123,517 51
Liabilities. Cr.	
Capital stock,	$36,825 00
Funded debt,	22,000 00
Profit and loss balance (surplus),	64,692 51
Total,	$123,517 51

Capital Stock.

Capital stock authorized by law,	$40,000 00	
Capital stock authorized by votes of company,	36,700 00	
Capital stock issued and outstanding,		$36,700 00
Amount paid in on shares not yet issued,		125 00
Total Capital Stock Liability,		$36,825 00
Number of shares issued and outstanding,	367	
Number of stockholders,	6	
Number of stockholders in Massachusetts,	6	
Amount of stock held in Massachusetts,	$36,700 00	

Funded Debt.

Description of Bonds.	Rate of Interest.	Date of Maturity.	Amount Outstanding.	Interest Paid during the Year.
First mortgage bonds,	Per Cent. 5	Jan. 1, 1905,	$22,000 00	$1,100 00

Railway Owned.

Length of railway line,	2.700 miles.
Length of sidings, switches, etc.,	.550 "
Total, computed as single track,	3.250 "

Names of the several cities and towns in which the railway owned by the company is located: Worcester.

Corporate Name and Address of the Company.

WORCESTER & SHREWSBURY RAILROAD COMPANY,

Room 6, 11 Foster Street, Worcester, Mass.

Names and Business Address of Principal Officers.

Horace H. Bigelow, *President*, 11 Foster Street, Worcester, Mass. Irving E. Bigelow, *Treasurer and Clerk of Corporation*, 11 Foster Street, Worcester, Mass.

Names and Residence of Board of Directors.

Horace H. Bigelow, Worcester, Mass. James M. Drennan, Worcester, Mass. George A. Stevens, Worcester, Mass. Francis H. Bigelow, Worcester, Mass. Irving E. Bigelow, Shrewsbury, Mass.

We hereby certify that the statements contained in the foregoing report are full, just and true.

HORACE H. BIGELOW,
GEO. A. STEVENS,
FRANCIS H. BIGELOW,
IRVING E. BIGELOW,
Directors.
IRVING E. BIGELOW,
Treasurer.

COMMONWEALTH OF MASSACHUSETTS.

WORCESTER, ss. WORCESTER, Nov. 25, 1904. Then personally appeared the above-named Horace H. Bigelow, George A. Stevens, Francis H. Bigelow and Irving E. Bigelow, and severally made oath that the foregoing certificate by them subscribed is, to the best of their knowledge and belief, true.

Before me, HOLLIS W. COBB,
Justice of the Peace.

REPORT

OF THE

WORCESTER & SHREWSBURY STREET RAILWAY COMPANY

FOR THE YEAR ENDING SEPTEMBER 30, 1904.

[Leased to and operated by the Worcester Consolidated.]

GENERAL EXHIBIT FOR THE YEAR.		
Rental received from lease of railway,		$1,000 00
Dividends declared (5 per cent),		$1,000 00
Amount of surplus September 30, 1903,		$22 05
TOTAL SURPLUS SEPTEMBER 30, 1904,		$22 05
GENERAL BALANCE SHEET SEPTEMBER 30, 1904.		
ASSETS.	DR.	
Cost of railway:		
Roadbed and tracks,	$9,263 00	
Electric line construction, including poles, wiring, feeder lines, etc.,	2,137 00	
Interest accrued during construction of railway,	300 00	
TOTAL COST OF RAILWAY OWNED,		$11,700 00
Cost of equipment:		
Cars and other rolling stock and vehicles,	$2,800 00	
Electric equipment of same,	3,500 00	
Other items of equipment,	2,000 00	
TOTAL COST OF EQUIPMENT OWNED,		8,300 00
TOTAL PERMANENT INVESTMENTS,		$20,000 00
Cash and current assets: cash,		22 05
TOTAL,		$20,022 05
LIABILITIES.	CR.	
Capital stock,		$20,000 00
Profit and loss balance (surplus),		22 05
TOTAL,		$20,022 05

Capital Stock.

Capital stock authorized by law,	$20,000 00	
Capital stock authorized by votes of company,	20,000 00	
Capital stock issued and outstanding,		$20,000 00
Number of shares issued and outstanding,	200	
Number of stockholders,	6	
Number of stockholders in Massachusetts,	6	
Amount of stock held in Massachusetts,	$20,000 00	

Railway Owned.

Length of railway line,	.425 miles.
Length of sidings, switches, etc.,	.034 "
Total, computed as single track,	.459 "

Names of the several cities and towns in which the railway owned by the company is located: Worcester.

Corporate Name and Address of the Company

WORCESTER & SHREWSBURY STREET RAILWAY COMPANY,

Room 6, 11 Foster Street, Worcester, Mass.

Names and Business Address of Principal Officers.

Horace H. Bigelow, *President and Treasurer*, 11 Foster Street, Worcester, Mass. Irving E. Bigelow, *Clerk of Corporation*, 11 Foster Street, Worcester, Mass.

Names and Residence of Board of Directors.

Horace H. Bigelow, Worcester, Mass. James M. Drennan, Worcester, Mass. Julian F. Bigelow, Worcester, Mass. Francis H. Bigelow, Worcester, Mass. Irving E. Bigelow, Shrewsbury, Mass.

We hereby certify that the statements contained in the foregoing report are full, just and true.

HORACE H. BIGELOW,
FRANCIS H. BIGELOW,
IRVING E. BIGELOW,
Directors.

Commonwealth of Massachusetts.

Worcester, ss. Worcester, Nov. 25, 1904. Then personally appeared the above-named Horace H. Bigelow, Francis H. Bigelow and Irving E. Bigelow, and severally made oath that the foregoing certificate by them subscribed is, to the best of their knowledge and belief, true.

Before me, HOLLIS W. COBB,
Justice of the Peace.

REPORT

OF THE

WORCESTER & SOUTHBRIDGE STREET RAILWAY COMPANY

For the Year ending September 30, 1904.

General Exhibit for the Year.		
Gross earnings from operation,		$91,145 16
Operating expenses,		60,456 16
Net Earnings from Operation,		$30,689 00
Miscellaneous income: from sale of material and supplies,		18,610 96
Gross Income above Operating Expenses,		$49,299 96
Charges upon income accrued during the year:		
Interest on funded debt,	$20,739 80	
Interest and discount on unfunded debts and loans,	16,112 89	
Taxes, State and local,	5,878 90	
Rentals of leased railways: Worcester, Rochdale & Charlton Depot Street Railway,	7,884 16	
Other deductions from income: operation of park,	1,053 37	
Total Charges and Deductions from Income,		51,669 12
Deficit for the year ending September 30, 1904,		$2,369 16
Debits to profit and loss account during the year: adjustment,		643,204 82
Total Deficit September 30, 1904,		$645,573 98

Earnings from Operation.	
Receipts from passengers carried,	$87,097 23
Receipts from carriage of mails,	1,280 44
Receipts from carriage of express and parcels,	82 60
Receipts from carriage of freight,	652 90
Receipts from rentals of buildings and other property,	541 43
Receipts from advertising in cars,	468 00
Receipts from sale of old material,	150 71
Other earnings from operation: from chartered cars,	871 85
Gross Earnings from Operation,	$91,145 16

Expenses of Operation.

General expenses:		
Salaries of general officers and clerks,		$3,346 75
General office expenses and supplies,		1,000 91
Legal expenses,		282 10
Insurance,		3,644 04
Other general expenses: miscellaneous,		4,154 97
Maintenance of roadway and buildings:		
Repair of roadbed and track,		3,002 38
Repair of electric line construction,		1,568 23
Repair of buildings,		334 30
Maintenance of equipment:		
Repair of cars and other vehicles,		5,699 47
Repair of electric equipment of cars,		6,203 29
Transportation expenses:		
Cost of electric motive power, $23,805.10; less power sold, $11,744.32; net,		12,060 78
Wages and compensation of persons employed in conducting transportation,		16,958 00
Removal of snow and ice,		599 76
Damages for injuries to persons and property,		739 12
Tolls for trackage over other railways,		640 96
Rentals of buildings and other property,		221 10
Total Operating Expenses,		$60,456 16

General Balance Sheet September 30, 1904.

Assets.	Dr.	
Cost of railway,		$640,792 18
Cost of equipment,		164,700 00
Cost of land and buildings,		330,417 00
Total Permanent Investments,*		$1,135,909 18
Cash and current assets:		
Cash,	$11,611 12	
Bills and accounts receivable,	3,068 20	
Other cash and current assets: bank deposits on account coupons,	12,150 00	
Total Cash and Current Assets,		26,829 32
Miscellaneous assets: materials and supplies,		522 75
Profit and loss balance (deficit),		645,573 98
Total,		$1,808,835 23

Liabilities.	Cr.	
Capital stock,		$500,000 00
Funded debt,		500,000 00
Current liabilities:		
Loans and notes payable,	$775,000 00	
Audited vouchers and accounts,	2,006 40	
Matured interest coupons unpaid (including coupons due October 1),	12,150 00	
Total Current Liabilities,		789,156 40

* Detailed cost of construction not available; also see letter at end of report.

Accrued liabilities:		
Interest accrued and not yet due,	$13,177 06	
Taxes accrued and not yet due,	4,797 61	
Rentals accrued and not yet due,	1,704 16	
TOTAL ACCRUED LIABILITIES,		$19,678 83
TOTAL,		$1,808,835 23

CAPITAL STOCK.

Capital stock authorized by law,	$500,000 00	
Capital stock authorized by votes of company,	500,000 00	
Capital stock issued and outstanding,		$500,000 00
Number of shares issued and outstanding,	5,000	
Number of stockholders,	9	
Number of stockholders in Massachusetts,	1	
Amount of stock held in Massachusetts,	$100 00	

FUNDED DEBT.

DESCRIPTION OF BONDS.	Rate of Interest.	Date of Maturity.	Amount Outstanding.	Interest Paid during the Year.
First mortgage bonds,	Per Cent. 4½	Sept. 1, 1922,	$500,000 00	$20,739 80

VOLUME OF TRAFFIC, ETC.

Number of passengers paying revenue carried during the year (estimated),	1,935,494
Number carried per mile of main railway track operated,	96,150
Number of car miles run,	445,181
Average number of persons employed,	70

DESCRIPTION OF EQUIPMENT.

DESCRIPTION OF EQUIPMENT.	Equipped for Electric Power.	Not Equipped.	Total Passenger Cars.	Equipped with Fenders.	Equipped with Electric Heaters.	Number of Motors.
CARS — PASSENGER SERVICE.						
Box passenger cars (including 1 parlor car),	9	-	9	9	9	36
Open passenger cars,	12	8	20	12	-	48
TOTAL,	21	8	29	21	9	84
CARS — OTHER SERVICE.						
Box freight cars,	-	3	-	-	-	-
Platform freight cars,	-	6	-	-	-	-
Mail cars,	3	1	-	-	-	12
Work cars,	1	8	-	-	-	2
TOTAL,	4	18	-	-	-	14
Snow ploughs,	2	2	-	-	-	-

Railway Owned and Operated (by Electric Power).

Railway Owned, etc.	Owned.	Trackage over Other Railways.	Total Owned, etc.
	Miles.	Miles.	Miles.
Length of railway line,	16.870	1.500	18.370
Length of second main track,	.260	1.500	1.760
Total Length of Main Track,	17.130	3.000	20.130
Length of sidings, switches, etc.,	2.590	-	2.590
Total, Computed as Single Track,	19.720	3.000	22.720

Railway Located Outside of Public Ways.

Length of railway line,	11.530 miles.

Names of the several cities and towns in which the railways operated by the company are located: Auburn, Oxford, Charlton and Southbridge.

Accidents to Persons.

(A detailed statement of each accident is on file in the office of the Board.)

Killed and Injured.	From Causes beyond their own Control.		From their own Misconduct or Carelessness.		Total.	
	Killed.	Injured.	Killed.	Injured.	Killed.	Injured.
Passengers,	-	5	1	3	1	8
Employees,	-	1	-	1	-	2
Other persons,	-	1	2	2	2	3
Totals,	-	7	3	6	3	13

Corporate Name and Address of the Company.

WORCESTER & SOUTHBRIDGE STREET RAILWAY COMPANY,

New Haven, Conn.

Names and Business Address of Principal Officers.

F. S. Curtis, *President*, Boston, Mass. Edwin Milner, *Vice-President*, Moosup, Conn. A. S. May, *Treasurer*, New Haven, Conn. John G. Parker, *Clerk of Corporation*, New Haven, Conn. H. M. Kochersperger, *Auditor*, New Haven, Conn. Leavenworth Wheeler, *Superintendent*, Charlton City, Mass.

Names and Residence of Board of Directors.

F. S. Curtis, Boston, Mass. C. S. Mellen, New Haven, Conn. George J. Brush, New Haven, Conn. Charles F. Brooker, Ansonia, Conn. Edwin Milner, Moosup, Conn. F. W. Cheney, South Manchester, Conn. Robert W. Taft, Providence, R. I. H. M. Kochersperger, New Haven, Conn. E. H. McHenry, New Haven, Conn.

We hereby certify that the statements contained in the foregoing report are full, just and true.

F. S. CURTIS,
C. S. MELLEN,
CHAS. F. BROOKER,
GEO. J. BRUSH,
H. M. KOCHERSPERGER,
Directors.
A. S. MAY,
Treasurer.

COMMONWEALTH OF MASSACHUSETTS

SUFFOLK, ss. BOSTON, Nov. 29, 1904. Then personally appeared the above-named F. S. Curtis, and made oath that the foregoing certificate by him subscribed is, to the best of his knowledge and belief, true.

Before me, DANIEL M. GOODRIDGE,
Notary Public.

STATE OF CONNECTICUT.

COUNTY OF NEW HAVEN, ss. Nov. 28, 1904. Then personally appeared the above-named C. S. Mellen, Chas. F. Brooker, Geo. J. Brush, H. M. Kochersperger and A. S. May, and severally made oath that the foregoing certificate by them subscribed is, to the best of their knowledge and belief, true.

Before me, ALBERT H. POWELL,
Notary Public.

THE CONSOLIDATED RAILWAY COMPANY,
OFFICE OF THE AUDITOR,
NEW HAVEN, CONN., Dec. 9, 1904.

Honorable Board of Railroad Commissioners, Boston, Mass.

GENTLEMEN:—Referring to the report of the Worcester & Southbridge Street Railway Company, for the year ending Sept. 30, 1904, which has been filed with you, I wish to state that when the present management took charge of that company, we found that there were no books of account, excepting a cash book. After spending some time in making a search for the books and for information with which to open the books, we finally concluded that the original books could not be found, and on May 22, 1904, we opened the present books with the best information available. We made an appraisal of the property, and set that up on our books as the cost, and on the other side we set up the liabilities as they appeared May 22, 1904.

The figures in the general exhibit on pages 3 and 4 were taken from the cash book, and are as nearly correct as we can obtain them; but they are not intended to agree in any particular with the figures in the balance sheet, as the latter figures were taken from the ledger.

We regret very much that we cannot furnish a more complete report than the one sent you, but we have done the very best we could, and have sent you all the information which we have been able to obtain from the records of the company.

Yours respectfully, C. L. CAMPBELL,
Auditor.

REPORT

OF THE

WORCESTER & WEBSTER STREET RAILWAY COMPANY

For the Year ending September 30, 1904.

[Leased to and operated by the Consolidated Railway Company of Connecticut.]

General Exhibit for the Year.		
Rental received from lease of railway,		$14,491 51
Expenses and charges upon income accrued during the year:		
Interest on funded debt,	$7,500 00	
Taxes,	3,043 26	
Other expenses and charges upon income:		
Insurance premiums,	948 25	
Payment to sinking fund,	3,000 00	
Total Expenses and Charges upon Income,		$14,491 51
Amount of deficit September 30, 1903,		$69,017 64
Debits to profit and loss account during the year: sundry old accounts paid,		619 89
Total Deficit September 30, 1904,		$69,637 53

General Balance Sheet September 30, 1904.		
Assets.	Dr.	
Cost of railway:		
Roadbed and tracks,	$190,996 64	
Electric line construction, including poles, wiring, feeder lines, etc.,	49,540 78	
Engineering and other expenses incident to construction,	5,058 45	
Total Cost of Railway Owned,		$245,595 87
Cost of equipment:		
Cars and other rolling stock and vehicles,	$32,521 73	
Electric equipment of same,	56,029 90	
Other items of equipment,	475 00	
Total Cost of Equipment Owned,		89,026 63
Cost of land and buildings:		
Land necessary for operation of railway,	$9,644 68	
Electric power stations, including equipment,	85,893 32	
Other buildings necessary for operation of railway,	49,353 77	
Total Cost of Land and Buildings Owned,		144,891 77
Total Permanent Investments,		$479,514 27

Cash and current assets: sinking and other special funds,	$12,000 00
Profit and loss balance (deficit),	69,637 53
Total,	$561,151 80

Liabilities. Cr.	
Capital stock,	$150,000 00
Funded debt,	150,000 00
Contingent liabilities: the Consolidated Railway Company for payment of floating debt,	249,151 80
Sinking fund for 5 per cent. bonds,	12,000 00
Total,	$561,151 80

Capital Stock.

Capital stock authorized by law,	$150,000 00	
Capital stock authorized by votes of company,	150,000 00	
Capital stock issued and outstanding,		$150,000 00
Number of shares issued and outstanding,	1,500	
Number of stockholders,	9	
Number of stockholders in Massachusetts,	5	
Amount of stock held in Massachusetts,	$500 00	

Funded Debt.

Description of Bonds.	Rate of Interest.	Date of Maturity.	Amount Outstanding.	Interest Paid during the Year.
First mortgage gold bonds,	Per Cent. 5	Dec. 1, 1919,	$150,000 00	$7,500 00

Sinking and Other Special Funds.

Amount September 30, 1903, of sinking fund,	$9,000 00
Additions during the year to sinking fund,	3,000 00
Total Sinking and Other Special Funds September 30, 1904,	$12,000 00

Railway Owned.

Length of railway line,	14.880 miles.
Length of sidings, switches, etc.,	.644 "
Total, computed as single track,	15.524 "

Railway Owned and Located Outside of Public Ways.

Length of railway line,	.363 mile.

Names of the several cities and towns in which the railway owned by the company is located: Worcester, Auburn, Oxford and Webster.

Corporate Name and Address of the Company.

WORCESTER & WEBSTER STREET RAILWAY COMPANY,

Webster, Mass.

Names and Business Address of Principal Officers.

Edgar S. Hill, *President*, Webster, Mass. J. Boise Potter, *Treasurer*, Webster, Mass. Harry E. Back, *Clerk of Corporation*, Danielson, Conn.

Names and Residence of Board of Directors.

Edgar S. Hill, Webster, Mass. Geo. A. Carmichael, Worcester, Mass. William F. Little, Worcester, Mass. Samuel Anderson, Arlington, Mass. J. Boise Potter, Webster, Mass. Edwin N. Sanderson, New York, N. Y. Harry E. Back, Danielson, Conn.

We hereby certify that the statements contained in the foregoing report are full, just and true.

J. B. POTTER,
EDGAR S. HILL,
SAMUEL ANDERSON,
HARRY E. BACK,
Directors.
J. B. POTTER,
Treasurer.

Commonwealth of Massachusetts.

Worcester, ss. Oct. 20, 1904. Then personally appeared the above-named J. B. Potter, Edgar S. Hill, Samuel Anderson and Harry E. Back, and severally made oath that the foregoing certificate by them subscribed is, to the best of their knowledge and belief, true.

Before me, PATRICK PROUT,
Justice of the Peace.

REPORT

OF THE

WORONOCO STREET RAILWAY COMPANY

For the Year ending September 30, 1904.

General Exhibit for the Year.		
Gross earnings from operation,		$81,475 45
Operating expenses,		60,030 98
Net Earnings from Operation,		$21,444 47
Miscellaneous income: park,		1,250 00
Gross Income above Operating Expenses,		$22,694 47
Charges upon income accrued during the year:		
Interest on funded debt,	$3,750 00	
Interest and discount on unfunded debts and loans,	1,948 17	
Taxes, State and local, $2,626 26		
Taxes, commutation, 1,523 93		
	4,150 19	
Other deductions from income: park,	1,824 86	
Total Charges and Deductions from Income,		11,673 22
Net Divisible Income,		$11,021 25
Dividends declared (7 per cent),		17,500 00
Deficit for the year ending September 30, 1904,		$6,478 75
Amount of surplus September 30, 1903,		12,367 02
Total Surplus September 30, 1904,		$5,888 27

Earnings from Operation.	
Receipts from passengers carried,	$81,175 45
Receipts from advertising in cars,	300 00
Gross Earnings from Operation,	$81,475 45

Expenses of Operation.	
General expenses:	
Salaries of general officers and clerks,	$4,579 00
General office expenses and supplies,	564 79
Legal expenses,	756 00
Insurance,	1,457 83
Other general expenses,	314 24

Maintenance of roadway and buildings:		
Repair of roadbed and track,		$2,059 83
Repair of electric line construction,		1,142 24
Repair of buildings,		216 94
Maintenance of equipment:		
Repair of cars and other vehicles,		6,840 38
Repair of electric equipment of cars,		2,424 93
Renewal of horses, harnesses, shoeing, etc.,		246 85
Transportation expenses:		
Cost of electric motive power,		15,205 08
Wages and compensation of persons employed in conducting transportation,		21,233 21
Removal of snow and ice,		1,962 19
Damages for injuries to persons and property,		293 75
Rentals of buildings and other property,		485 43
Other transportation expenses,		248 29
TOTAL OPERATING EXPENSES,		$60,030 98

PROPERTY ACCOUNTS.

Additions to railway:		
Extension of tracks,	$680 52	
New electric line construction (block signals),	1,125 51	
Other additions to railway: engineering agencies and other expenses incident to construction,	1,362 98	
TOTAL ADDITIONS TO RAILWAY,		$3,169 01
Additions to equipment: two 4-motor equipments,		4,282 41
Additions to land and buildings:		
Additional equipment of power stations,	$18,874 40	
New buildings necessary for operation of railway,	162 10	
TOTAL ADDITIONS TO LAND AND BUILDINGS,		19,036 50
Additions to other permanent property: Pequot park,		5,199 70
TOTAL ADDITIONS TO PROPERTY ACCOUNTS,		$31,687 62
Deductions from property accounts (property sold or reduced in valuation and credited to property accounts): car account, buggy sold,		35 00
NET ADDITION TO PROPERTY ACCOUNTS FOR THE YEAR,		$31,652 62

GENERAL BALANCE SHEET SEPTEMBER 30, 1904.

ASSETS.	DR.	
Cost of railway:		
Roadbed and tracks,	$156,834 40	
Electric line construction, including poles, wiring, feeder lines, etc.,	39,206 46	
Engineering and other expenses incident to construction,	13,164 55	
TOTAL COST OF RAILWAY OWNED,		$209,205 41

Cost of equipment:		
Cars and other rolling stock and vehicles, .	$42,369 14	
Electric equipment of same, ...	31,934 94	
Horses, ...	154 50	
Other items of equipment: tools, . . .	880 25	
TOTAL COST OF EQUIPMENT OWNED, ...		$75,338 83
Cost of land and buildings:		
Land necessary for operation of railway, .	$5,241 61	
Electric power stations, including equipment, ...	50,382 90	
Other buildings necessary for operation of railway, ...	16,995 66	
TOTAL COST OF LAND AND BUILDINGS OWNED, . .		72,620 17
Other permanent property:		
Office furniture and fixtures, ...	$352 38	
Pequot park, ...	15,112 49	
TOTAL COST OF OTHER PERMANENT PROPERTY OWNED, .		15,464 87
TOTAL PERMANENT INVESTMENTS, ...		$372,629 28
Cash and current assets:		
Cash, ...	$4,012 83	
Bills and accounts receivable, . . .	240 37	
TOTAL CASH AND CURRENT ASSETS, ...		4,253 20
Miscellaneous assets: materials and supplies, . . .		4,005 79
TOTAL, ...		$380,888 27

LIABILITIES. CR.	
Capital stock, ...	$250,000 00
Funded debt, ...	75,000 00
Current liabilities:	
Loans and notes payable, ...	50,000 00
Profit and loss balance (surplus), ...	5,888 27
TOTAL, ...	$380,888 27

CAPITAL STOCK.

Capital stock authorized by law, ...	$250,000 00	
Capital stock authorized by votes of company,	250,000 00	
Capital stock issued and outstanding, ...		$250,000 00
Number of shares issued and outstanding, .	2,500	
Number of stockholders, ...	70	
Number of stockholders in Massachusetts, .	65	
Amount of stock held in Massachusetts, . .	$247,100 00	

Funded Debt.

Description of Bonds.	Rate of Interest.	Date of Maturity.	Amount Outstanding.	Interest Paid during the Year.
	Per Cent.			
First mortgage bonds, ...	5	Jan. 1, 1920, .	$75,000 00	$3,750 00

Volume of Traffic, etc.

Number of passengers paying revenue carried during the year, ...	1,631,529
Number carried per mile of main railway track operated, .	101,117
Number of car miles run, ...	490,957
Average number of persons employed, ...	54

Description of Equipment.

Description of Equipment.	Equipped for Electric Power.	Not Equipped.	Equipped with Fenders.	Equipped with Electric Heaters.	Number of Motors.
Cars — Passenger Service.					
Box passenger cars, ...	12	-	12	12	24
Open passenger cars, ...	17	-	17	-	36
Total, ...	29	-	29	12	60
Cars — Other Service.					
Work cars, ...	-	2	-	-	-
Other cars, ...	-	2	-	-	-
Total, ...	-	4	-	-	-
Snow ploughs, ...	2	-	-	-	-

Miscellaneous Equipment.

Highway vehicles:	
Tower wagons, ...	2
Express wagon, ...	1
Horses, ...	1

RAILWAY OWNED AND OPERATED (BY ELECTRIC POWER).

Length of railway line, ...	15.793 miles.
Length of second main track, ...	.342 "
Total length of main track, ...	16.135 "
Length of sidings, switches, etc., ...	.793 "
Total, computed as single track, ...	16.928 "

RAILWAY LOCATED OUTSIDE OF PUBLIC WAYS.

Length of railway line, ...	2.967 miles.

Names of the several cities and towns in which the railways operated by the company are located: Westfield and West Springfield.

ACCIDENTS TO PERSONS.

(A detailed statement of each accident is on file in the office of the Board.)

KILLED AND INJURED.	FROM CAUSES BEYOND THEIR OWN CONTROL.		FROM THEIR OWN MISCONDUCT OR CARELESSNESS.		TOTAL.	
	Killed.	Injured.	Killed.	Injured.	Killed.	Injured.
Passengers, ...	-	2	-	3	-	5
Employees, ...	-	-	1	-	1	-
Other persons, ...	-	-	-	-	-	-
TOTALS, ...	-	2	1	3	1	5

CORPORATE NAME AND ADDRESS OF THE COMPANY.

WORONOCO STREET RAILWAY COMPANY,

WESTFIELD, MASS.

NAMES AND BUSINESS ADDRESS OF PRINCIPAL OFFICERS.

James H. Bryan, *President and General Manager*, Westfield, Mass. Robert B. Crane, *Vice-President*, Westfield, Mass. Charles J. Little, *Treasurer and Clerk of Corporation*, Westfield, Mass. Henry W. Ely, *General Counsel*, Westfield, Mass. John H. Ashley, *Auditor*, Westfield, Mass. William H. Savery, *Superintendent*, Westfield, Mass.

NAMES AND RESIDENCE OF BOARD OF DIRECTORS.

James H. Bryan, Westfield, Mass. Robert B. Crane, Westfield, Mass. James A. Crane, Westfield, Mass. Ralph D. Gillett, Westfield, Mass. Henry

M. Van Deusen, Westfield, Mass. Henry W. Ely, Westfield, Mass. Luke S. Stowe, Springfield, Mass. Henry C. Page, Pittsfield, Mass. John P. Pomeroy, Great Barrington, Mass. Charles J. Little, Westfield, Mass.

We hereby certify that the statements contained in the foregoing report are full, just and true.

JAS. H. BRYAN,
ROBERT B. CRANE,
JAMES A. CRANE,
LUKE S. STOWE,
HENRY W. ELY,
CHARLES J. LITTLE,
RALPH D. GILLETT,
Directors.
CHARLES J. LITTLE,
Treasurer.
W. H. SAVERY,
Superintendent.

COMMONWEALTH OF MASSACHUSETTS.

HAMPDEN, ss. Nov. 1, 1904. Then personally appeared the above-named James H. Bryan, Robert B. Crane, James A. Crane, Luke S. Stowe, Henry W. Ely, Charles J. Little, Ralph D. Gillett and W. H. Savery, and severally made oath that the foregoing certificate by them subscribed is, to the best of their knowledge and belief, true.

Before me, CHARLES F. ELY,
Justice of the Peace.

LEASES.

LEASES.

LEASE TO THE HUDSON, PELHAM & SALEM ELECTRIC RAILWAY COMPANY OF THE HAVERHILL & SOUTHERN NEW HAMPSHIRE STREET RAILWAY.

THIS INDENTURE, made this first day of January, in the year 1904, by and between the HAVERHILL & SOUTHERN NEW HAMPSHIRE STREET RAILWAY COMPANY, incorporated by and under the laws of the State of Massachusetts (hereinafter called the Lessor), of the one part, and the HUDSON, PELHAM & SALEM ELECTRIC RAILWAY COMPANY, incorporated by and under the laws of the State of New Hampshire (hereinafter called the Lessee), of the other part,

WITNESSETH, that the Lessor doth hereby lease unto the Lessee all and singular its railways, lands, franchises and other property of every description now owned, or hereafter to be acquired, together with all the rights, privileges, easements and appurtenances thereunto belonging, including the right to demand and receive to the Lessee's own use all tolls, rents, revenues, income and profits of the demised premises, excepting from the said premises all cash, cheques, bills, notes and moneys now due to the Lessor, and its common seal and books of record and account,

TO HAVE AND TO HOLD the same unto the Lessee, its successors and assigns, for the term of twenty-five years from the day of the date hereof. Subject however to the mortgage hereinafter described.

1. The Lessor covenants that during the continuance of this lease it will maintain its corporate organization in due form of law, and for that purpose will hold all necessary meetings, elect all necessary officers and make and keep all necessary records, reports and returns required by law at an expense not to exceed $100 per annum, which the Lessee covenants to pay to it on or before the date of the annual meeting of the stockholders of the Lessor in each year.

2. The Lessee may use the name of the Lessor in bringing or defending any suits or proceedings in law or equity which may be necessary for the due protection, preservation and full enjoyment by the Lessee of all the property, rights and privileges hereby leased, but the Lessee shall save and hold the Lessor harmless and indemnified rom and against all loss, cost, damage and expense arising therefrom.

3. The Lessor covenants that in case the Lessee deems any part of the rea. estate or personal property hereby demised unnecessary for the purposes of the said railway and desires to sell the same, and the directors of the Lessor approve such sale, the Lessor will concur with the Lessee in such sale and in executing and delivering such instruments as may be necessary to transfer its titles therein to the vendee, and will cause such votes to be passed by its shareholders and directors as may be necessary; provided that the proceeds of any such sale, subject to the provisions of the mortgage hereinafter mentioned, shall be applied to the substitution of property of equal value to that sold, or shall be expended to increase the value of other property hereby demised, as the directors of the Lessor shall approve, and the Lessee agrees so to apply or expend the proceeds. And the Lessee may with the approval of the directors of the Lessor, subject to the said mortgage, pull down, alter and repair buildings and structures, and change the location or position of the lines of rails, but shall replace any buildings or structures pulled down in whole or in part with permanent improvements of as great value. And the Lessee shall be at liberty, without any such approval or concurrence as aforesaid,

subject to the mortgage, to use and consume fuel and supplies, and to replace any of the rails, rolling stock, equipment, machinery and tools comprised in this lease with others, and to sell such of them as shall have been replaced or worn out as it may think fit, and without any obligation on the part of any purchaser to ascertain the occurrence of the event in which any such last-mentioned sale is authorized.

4. In consideration of the premises the Lessee covenants with the Lessor, for the benefit of the shareholders for the time being of the Lessor, to pay to the said shareholders respectively, as and for rent hereunder, a semi-annual dividend of two per cent. on the shares of the capital stock of the Lessor lawfully issued and from time to time outstanding to the aggregate principal amount of $80,000, and a like dividend upon any shares of the capital stock of the Lessor lawfully issued in excess of the said principal amount of $80,000, for the purposes and in the manner hereinafter provided, the said dividends to be paid on the first days of January and July in each year during the term of this lease to the persons registered as holders of the said shares on the tenth day next preceding each day for the payment of such dividend, the first payment to be made on the first day of July, 1904; and in case this lease is terminated at any time prior to the first day of Jannary in the year 1929 a proportionate part of such semi-annual dividend to be paid for the portion unelapsed of the half year to the then registered holders of the said shares. And such payments of dividends shall be free and clear of all other charges, expenses and payments to be made or incurred under the provisions hereof. And an agreement for the payment of the said dividends by the Lessee shall be indorsed upon the certificates of the capital stock of the Lessor under the common seal of the Lessee, signed by its duly authorized officer, and shall be substantially in the following form:

"The Hudson, Pelham & Salem Electric Railway Company having taken a lease of the railways, properties and franchises of the Haverhill & Southern New Hampshire Street Railway Company for twenty-five years from the first of January, 1904, upon the terms (among others) of paying a semi-annual dividend of two per cent. on the shares of the last-mentioned company on the first of January and July in every year during the continuance of the said lease to the persons registered as holders of the said shares on the tenth day preceding each such dividend day, and of entering into this agreement in consideration thereof agrees with the said registered holder of the within-mentioned shares to pay the said dividends accordingly and to enter into a like agreement with every holder of the said shares to whom a new certificate shall be issued, and to indorse such agreement upon every such certificate. Witness the common seal of the Hudson, Pelham & Salem Electric Railway Company and the signature of its duly authorized officer the day of . 19 ."

5. The Lessee covenants and agrees to pay as and for further rent hereunder all interest that may be due or that may become due during the term of this lease upon such of the floating debt of the Lessor existing at the date of the execution of this lease (the particulars of which are contained in a schedule of even date herewith and signed by the respective presidents of the Lessor and Lessee), and upon such of the floating debt of the Lessor that may hereafter exist for or on account of any past acts or transactions of the Lessor, as shall not be capitalized by the issue of stock or funded by the issue of bonds of the Lessor during the term of this lease in the manner hereinafter provided.

6. The Lessee covenants to perform and observe all the covenants and agreements of the Lessor contained in its mortgage to the New York Security and Trust Company, dated the first day of January, 1903, for purpose of reference in the bonds thereby secured, and also as and for further rent hereunder the Lessee agrees to assume and pay the interest and to guarantee the payment of the principal of the bonds to the aggregate principal amount of $80,000 secured by the said mortgage, and also to assume and agree to pay the interest payable during the said term of all bonds issued or to be issued in pursuance hereof and to guarantee the payment of the principal of all such bonds payable during the said term. And an agreement by the Lessee for such payment shall be indorsed upon the said bonds under the common seal of the Lessee, signed by its duly authorized officer. And in case the said agreement relates to the payment of

interest and the guaranty of the principal of the said bonds it shall be substantially in the following form:

"The Hudson, Pelham & Salem Electric Railway Company having taken a lease dated the first day of January, 1904, of the railways, properties and franchises of the maker of this bond upon the terms (among others) of paying the interest and of guaranteeing the payment of the principal thereof, and of entering into this agreement in consideration thereof, agrees with the bearer, or, if registered, with the registered owner for the time being of this bond (such holder waiving none of the obligations of the maker), to pay the interest and to guarantee the payment of the principal thereof as the same become payable respectively. Witness the common seal of the said Hudson, Pelham & Salem Electric Railway Company and the signature of its duly authorized officer the of , 19 ."

But in case the said agreement relates merely to the payment of interest up to the end of the term of this lease it shall be in the following form:

"The Hudson, Pelham & Salem Electric Railway Company having taken a lease dated the first day of January, 1904, of the railways, properties and franchises of the maker of this bond upon the terms (among others) of paying the interest thereof payable during the term of the said lease and of entering into this agreement in consideration thereof, agrees with the bearer, or, if registered, with the registered owner for the time being of this bond (such holder waiving none of the obligations of the maker), to pay the interest thereof accruing during the term of the said lease as the same becomes payable respectively. Witness the common seal of the said Hudson, Pelham & Salem Electric Railway Company and the signature of its duly authorized officer the of , 19 ."

And the Lessee covenants to cancel and destroy all coupons for the said interest upon any of the said bonds as and when the said coupons are paid by the Lessee.

7. The Lessee covenants to pay all franchise and other taxes, charges and assessments whatsoever lawfully assessed upon or in respect of the leased premises or any part thereof during the term of this lease, including those assessed during the year 1904.

8. The Lessee covenants to insure and keep insured such parts of the premises as are of an insurable nature for such sums and in such manner as shall reasonably protect the same against loss or damage by fire and to exhibit to the Lessor or its agents the policies whenever reasonably requested, and all sums received by virtue of any such insurance shall be applied to making good the loss and damage, and so that all such insurance shall be in accordance with such or the like provisions as are contained in the said mortgage during the continuance of such mortgage or of any such future mortgage of the premises as is hereinafter mentioned.

9. The Lessee covenants to keep the said railway and other leased property in as good repair, order and condition as at the inception of this lease, and to replace all such rails, rolling stock, equipment, machinery and tools as may be worn out, and to mark with the name of the Lessor in the manner hereinafter provided all rolling stock used to replace any comprised in this lease. And at the termination of the lease to surrender the leased premises and all property added thereto or substituted therefor in like good repair, order and condition.

10. The Lessee covenants to save the Lessor harmless from all actions, suits, proceedings, claims, damages and expense on account of anything that has already happened, or by reason of any acts or omissions of the Lessee in the management or use of the leased premises during the continuance of this lease, and at its own expense to defend all actions, suits and proceedings already or to be hereafter brought against the Lessor or the leased property on account of any such matter, and to pay all sums recovered as damages or costs in any such action, suit or proceeding.

11. The Lessee covenants at its own cost and expense to maintain, work and use the leased railway and property in accordance with the laws of the Commonwealth of Massachusetts, and all lawful orders of State and local boards or other officials charged with the protection of public interest; to make all returns and perform all obligations lawfully required of any person or company operating a street railway in the Commonwealth of Massachusetts; to furnish all information necessary to enable the Lessor to

make all returns and perform all obligations required of it under the laws of the said Commonwealth; and generally to perform the public service in as satisfactory a manner as could be required or secured were the railway maintained and operated by the Lessor. And the Lessee further covenants to furnish all cars, equipment and apparatus of every description required for the due use and working of said railway in addition to the property hereby demised.

12. The Lessor covenants that it will issue, subject to the approval of the Board of Railroad Commissioners as required by law or in accordance with existing laws and at the expense of the Lessee, additional shares or bonds, or both, for the purpose of raising money to pay the principal of the existing floating debt of the Lessor (the particulars of which are contained in the said schedule of even date herewith), as well as the principal of such floating debt of the Lessor as may hereafter exist on account of its past transactions, and also to pay for permanent improvements and permanent additions to the leased premises, and to an amount or amounts sufficient for any and all of these purposes, whenever requested by vote of the board of directors of the Lessee, provided that such purposes shall be approved by the directors of the Lessor, and will deliver such shares and bonds to the Lessee to be used for the said purposes, and will also issue bonds whenever so requested for the purpose of renewing or refunding its existing bonds, or any bonds hereafter issued under these presents. And none of the said shares or bonds shall be sold for less than par. All such bonds shall be secured by mortgage of all the property of the Railway Company on terms similar to those contained in the mortgage hereinbefore mentioned, except so far as they may be varied with the approval of the directors of both of the said companies, and the Lessee shall concur in any such mortgage to the extent of its estate hereby acquired. And any benefits from reduced rates of interest during the continuance of this lease, consequent upon such renewal or refunding, shall enure to the benefit of the Lessee, and any premium obtained from the sale of bonds of the Lessor so issued to renew or refund its bonds shall be used to provide permanent improvements and permanent additions to the leased premises, except such as are herein required to be provided by the Lessee. And the Lessor agrees that its directors and stockholders shall pass all votes and make all applications to the Board of Railroad Commissioners or other authority, and take any other steps that may be necessary in order to issue stock or bonds as herein provided. And the Lessor covenants that it will not issue any stock or bonds without the express request of the board of directors of the Lessee.

13. The Lessor and Lessee mutually covenant that there shall forthwith be made a full and complete inventory and appraisal of the land, buildings, tracks, overhead construction, rolling stock, equipment and all other property of every nature and description demised by this lease, a copy of which inventory shall be furnished to the Lessor and also to the Lessee, and the same shall be conclusive evidence in any and all cases in which the question of the condition and value of the said property at the time of making this lease shall arise between them. The said inventory and appraisal shall be made at the expense of the Lessee by two disinterested persons, one selected by the Lessor and one by the Lessee, who in case of any disagreement may choose a third, and the decision of a majority shall be final. And all the rolling stock of the Lessor shall at the like expense be marked with its name, so that the same can be identified, but this provision shall not prevent the Lessee from marking the same with its own name. On the termination of this lease, whether by lapse of time or otherwise, a like inventory and appraisal shall be made of all the property then surrendered by the Lessee to the Lessor, and if the property surrendered is thus found to be of greater value than the appraised value at the commencement of the lease, with the addition of a sum equal to all amounts of money received by the Lessee from the issue of shares of stock and bonds of the Lessor (excepting the principal of bonds issued to retire the said floating debt and of renewal and refunding bonds and excepting the principal of any bonds of the Lessor that shall be paid off by the Lessee), the difference shall be paid by the Lessor to the Lessee in money within one year from the termination of this lease with interest at the rate of 5 per cent. per annum from such termination until the time of payment. And, if the property surrendered is of less value than the appraised value at the commencement of

this lease and the said sum received from stock and bonds as aforesaid, the difference shall be paid by the Lessee to the Lessor in money within the same time and with the like interest. And the Lessor and its agents shall be at liberty at reasonable times to enter upon the leased premises and inspect the same, and the Lessee shall afford all proper facilities therefor.

14. This lease is upon condition that if the Lessee, its successors or assigns shall fail to make any semi-annual payment of rent as hereinbefore stipulated or any part thereof or shall fail to pay the interest of the said bonds in accordance with its agreement, or to perform and observe any of its other covenants or agreements herein contained, and such default continues for one month after written notice thereof from the Lessor to the Lessee, or if the estate hereby granted or possession of the premises or any part thereof shall be taken from the Lessee by legal proceedings or the appointment of a receiver, or if the Lessee or its successors or assigns shall assign or underlet the said premises or any part thereof without the assent of the Lessor on each occasion in writing, and notwithstanding any assent or waiver on any prior occasion, then and in any of the said cases, and without any other notice or demand, the Lessor may thereupon re-enter upon the demised premises or any part thereof in the name of the whole, and the same have and possess as of its former estate without prejudice to its right of action for arrears of rent or breach of covenant, and upon such entry the said term shall end.

15. The notes printed in the margin of these presents are not a part thereof and shall not be regarded in determining any questions relating to the construction or interpretation of any of the provisions thereof.

In witness whereof, the said parties have caused these presents to be executed in duplicate by their respective officers, thereunto duly authorized and their respective corporate seals to be hereto affixed the day and year first above written.

HAVERHILL & SOUTHERN NEW HAMPSHIRE STREET RAILWAY COMPANY, Lessor,

By *President.*
Treasurer.

HUDSON, PELHAM & SALEM ELECTRIC RAILWAY COMPANY, Lessee,

By *President.*
Treasurer.

[Terms of lease approved by the Board February 25, 1904.]

LEASE TO THE HUDSON, PELHAM & SALEM ELECTRIC RAILWAY COMPANY OF THE LAWRENCE & METHUEN STREET RAILWAY.

This Indenture, made this first day of January, in the year 1904, by and between the Lawrence & Methuen Street Railway Company, incorporated by and under the laws of the State of Massachusetts (hereinafter called the Lessor), of the one part, and the Hudson, Pelham & Salem Electric Railway Company, incorporated by and under the laws of the State of New Hampshire (hereinafter called the Lessee), of the other part,

Witnesseth, that the Lessor doth hereby lease unto the Lessee all and singular its railways, lands, franchises and other property of every description now owned, or hereafter to be acquired, together with all the rights, privileges, easements and appurtenances thereunto belonging, including the right to demand and receive to the Lessee's own use all tolls, rents, revenues, income and profits of the demised premises, excepting from the said premises all cash, cheques, bills, notes and moneys now due to the Lessor, and its common seal and books of record and account,

To have and to hold the same unto the Lessee, its successors and assigns, for the term of twenty-five years from the day of the date hereof. Subject however to the mortgage hereinafter described.

1. The Lessor covenants that during the continuance of this lease it will maintain its corporate organization in due form of law, and for that purpose will hold all necessary meetings, elect all necessary officers and make and keep all necessary records, reports and returns required by law at an expense not to exceed $100 per annum, which the Lessee covenants to pay to it on or before the date of the annual meeting of the stockholders of the Lessor in each year.

2. The Lessee may use the name of the Lessor in bringing or defending any suits or proceedings in law or equity which may be necessary for the due protection, preservation and full enjoyment by the Lessee of all the property, rights and privileges hereby leased, but the Lessee shall save and hold the Lessor harmless and indemnified from and against all loss, cost, damage and expense arising therefrom.

3. The Lessor covenants that in case the Lessee deems any part of the real estate or personal property hereby demised unnecessary for the purposes of the said railway and desires to sell the same, and the directors of the Lessor approve such sale, the Lessor will concur with the Lessee in such sale and in executing and delivering such instruments as may be necessary to transfer its titles therein to the vendee, and will cause such votes to be passed by its shareholders and directors as may be necessary; provided that the proceeds of any such sale, subject to the provisions of the mortgage hereinafter mentioned, shall be applied to the substitution of property of equal value to that sold, or shall be expended to increase the value of other property hereby demised, as the directors of the Lessor shall approve, and the Lessee agrees so to apply or expend the proceeds. And the Lessee may with the approval of the directors of the Lessor, subject to the said mortgage, pull down, alter and repair buildings and structures, and change the location or position of the lines of rails, but shall replace any buildings or structures pulled down in whole or in part with permanent improvements of as great value. And the Lessee shall be at liberty, without any such approval or concurrence as aforesaid, subject to the mortgage, to use and consume fuel and supplies, and to replace any of the rails, rolling stock, equipment, machinery and tools comprised in this lease with others, and to sell such of them as shall have been replaced or worn out as it may think fit, and without any obligation on the part of any purchaser to ascertain the occurrence of the event in which any such last-mentioned sale is authorized.

4. In consideration of the premises the Lessee covenants with the Lessor, for the benefit of the shareholders for the time being of the Lessor, to pay to the said shareholders respectively, as and for rent hereunder, a semi-annual dividend of two per cent. on the shares of the capital stock of the Lessor lawfully issued and from time to time outstanding to the aggregate principal amount of $150,000, and a like dividend upon any shares of the capital stock of the Lessor lawfully issued in excess of the said principal amount of $150,000, for the purposes and in the manner hereinafter provided, the said dividends to be paid on the first days of January and July in each year during the term of this lease to the persons registered as holders of the said shares on the tenth day next preceding each day for the payment of such dividend, the first payment to be made on the first day of July, 1904; and in case this lease is terminated at any time prior to the first day of January in the year 1929 a proportionate part of such semi-annual dividend to be paid for the portion unelapsed of the half year to the then registered holders of the said shares. And such payments of dividends shall be free and clear of all other charges, expenses and payments to be made or incurred under the provisions hereof. And an agreement for the payment of the said dividends by the Lessee shall be indorsed upon the certificates of the capital stock of the Lessor under the common seal of the Lessee, signed by its duly authorized officer, and shall be substantially in the following form:

"The Hudson, Pelham & Salem Electric Railway Company having taken a lease of the railways, properties and franchises of the Lawrence & Methuen Street Railway Company for twenty-five years from the first of January, 1904, upon the terms (among others) of paying a semi-annual dividend of two per cent. on the shares of the last-mentioned company on the first of January and July in every year during the continuance of the said lease to the persons registered as holders of the said shares on the tenth day preceding each such dividend day, and of entering into this agreement in consideration thereof agrees with the said registered holder of the within-mentioned shares to pay the said dividends accordingly and to enter into a like agreement with every holder of the said shares to whom a new certificate shall be issued, and to indorse such agreement upon every such certificate. Witness the common seal of the Hudson, Pelham & Salem Electric Railway Company and the signature of its duly authorized officer the day of 19 ."

5. The Lessee covenants and agrees to pay as and for further rent hereunder all interest that may be due or that may become due during the term of this lease upon such of the floating debt of the Lessor existing at the date of the execution of this lease (the particulars of which are contained in a schedule of even date herewith and signed by the respective presidents of the Lessor and Lessee), and upon such of the floating debt of the Lessor that may hereafter exist for or on account of any past acts or transactions of the Lessor, as shall not be capitalized by the issue of stock or funded by the issue of bonds of the Lessor during the term of this lease in the manner hereinafter provided.

6. The Lessee covenants to perform and observe all the covenants and agreements of the Lessor contained in its mortgage to the New York Security and Trust Company, dated the first day of January, 1903, for purpose of reference in the bonds thereby secured, and also as and for further rent hereunder the Lessee agrees to assume and pay the interest and to guarantee the payment of the principal of the bonds to the aggregate principal amount of $125,000 secured by the said mortgage, and also to assume and agree to pay the interest payable during the said term of all bonds issued or to be issued in pursuance hereof and to guarantee the payment of the principal of all such bonds payable during the said term. And an agreement by the Lessee for such payment shall be indorsed upon the said bonds under the common seal of the Lessee, signed by its duly authorized officer. And in case the said agreement relates to the payment of interest and the guaranty of the principal of the said bonds it shall be substantially in the following form:

"The Hudson, Pelham & Salem Electric Railway Company having taken a lease dated the first day of January, 1904, of the railways, properties and franchises of the maker of this bond upon the terms (among others) of paying the interest and of guaranteeing the payment of the principal thereof, and of entering into this agreement in consideration thereof, agrees with the bearer, or, if registered, with the registered owner for the time being of this bond (such holder waiving none of the obligations of the maker), to pay the interest and to guarantee the payment of the principal thereof as the same become payable respectively. Witness the common seal of the said Hudson, Pelham & Salem Electric Railway Company and the signature of its duly authorized officer the of , 19 ."

But in case the said agreement relates merely to the payment of interest up to the end of the term of this lease it shall be in the following form:

"The Hudson, Pelham & Salem Electric Railway Company having taken a lease dated the first day of January, 1904, of the railways, properties and franchises of the maker of this bond upon the terms (among others) of paying the interest thereof payable during the term of the said lease and of entering into this agreement in consideration thereof, agrees with the bearer, or, if registered, with the registered owner for the time being of this bond (such holder waiving none of the obligations of the maker), to pay the interest thereof accruing during the term of the said lease as the same becomes payable respectively. Witness the common seal of the said Hudson, Pelham & Salem Electric Railway Company and the signature of its duly authorized officer the of , 19 ."

And the Lessee covenants to cancel and destroy all coupons for the said interest upon any of the said bonds as and when the said coupons are paid by the Lessee.

7. The Lessee covenants to pay all franchise and other taxes, charges and assessments whatsoever lawfully assessed upon or in respect of the leased premises or any part thereof during the term of this lease, including those assessed during the year 1904.

8. The Lessee covenants to insure and keep insured such parts of the premises as are of an insurable nature for such sums and in such manner as shall reasonably protect the same against loss or damage by fire and to exhibit to the Lessor or its agents the policies whenever reasonably requested, and all sums received by virtue of any

such insurance shall be applied to making good the loss and damage, and so that all such insurance shall be in accordance with such or the like provisions as are contained in the said mortgage during the continuance of such mortgage or of any such future mortgage of the premises as is hereinafter mentioned.

9. The Lessee covenants to keep the said railway and other leased property in as good repair, order and condition as at the inception of this lease, and to replace all such rails, rolling stock, equipment, machinery and tools as may be worn out, and to mark with the name of the Lessor in the manner hereinafter provided all rolling stock used to replace any comprised in this lease. And at the termination of the lease to surrender the leased premises and all property added thereto or substituted therefor in like good repair, order and condition.

10. The Lessee covenants to save the Lessor harmless from all actions, suits, proceedings, claims, damages and expense on account of anything that has already happened, or by reason of any acts or omissions of the Lessee in the management or use of the leased premises during the continuance of this lease, and at its own expense to defend all actions, suits and proceedings already or to be hereafter brought against the Lessor or the leased property on account of any such matter, and to pay all sums recovered as damages or costs in any such action, suit or proceeding.

11. The Lessee covenants at its own cost and expense to maintain, work and use the leased railway and property in accordance with the laws of the Commonwealth of Massachusetts, and all lawful orders of State and local boards or other officials charged with the protection of public interest; to make all returns and perform all obligations lawfully required of any person or company operating a street railway in the Commonwealth of Massachusetts; to furnish all information necessary to enable the Lessor to make all returns and perform all obligations required of it under the laws of the said Commonwealth; and generally to perform the public service in as satisfactory a manner as could be required or secured were the railway maintained and operated by the Lessor. And the Lessee further covenants to furnish all cars, equipment and apparatus of every description required for the due use and working of said railway in addition to the property hereby demised.

12. The Lessor covenants that it will issue, subject to the approval of the Board of Railroad Commissioners as required by law or in accordance with existing laws and at the expense of the Lessee, additional shares or bonds, or both, for the purpose of raising money to pay the principal of the existing floating debt of the Lessor (the particulars of which are contained in the said schedule of even date herewith), as well as the principal of such floating debt of the Lessor as may hereafter exist on account of its past transactions, and also to pay for permanent improvements and permanent additions to the leased premises, and to an amount or amounts sufficient for any and all of these purposes, whenever requested by vote of the board of directors of the Lessee, provided that such purposes shall be approved by the directors of the Lessor, and will deliver such shares and bonds to the Lessee to be used for the said purposes, and will also issue bonds whenever so requested for the purpose of renewing or refunding its existing bonds, or any bonds hereafter issued under these presents. And none of the said shares or bonds shall be sold for less than par. All such bonds shall be secured by mortgage of all the property of the railway company on terms similar to those contained in the mortgage hereinbefore mentioned, except so far as they may be varied with the approval of the directors of both of the said companies, and the Lessee shall concur in any such mortgage to the extent of its estate hereby acquired. And any benefits from reduced rates of interest during the continuance of this lease, consequent upon such renewal or refunding, shall enure to the benefit of the Lessee, and any premium obtained from the sale of bonds of the Lessor so issued to renew or refund its bonds shall be used to provide permanent improvements and permanent additions to the leased premises, except such as are herein required to be provided by the Lessee. And the Lessor agrees that its directors and stockholders shall pass all votes and make all applications to the Board of Railroad Commissioners or other authority, and take any other steps that may be necessary in order to issue stock or bonds as herein provided. And the Lessor covenants that it will not issue any stock or bonds without the express request of the board of directors of the Lessee.

13. The Lessor and Lessee mutually covenant that there shall forthwith be made a full and complete inventory and appraisal of the land, buildings, tracks, overhead construction, rolling stock, equipment and all other property of every nature and description demised by this lease, a copy of which inventory shall be furnished to the Lessor and also to the Lessee, and the same shall be conclusive evidence in any and all cases in which the question of the condition and value of the said property at the time of making this lease shall arise between them. The said inventory and appraisal shall be made at the expense of the Lessee by two disinterested persons, one selected by the Lessor and one by the Lessee, who in case of any disagreement may choose a third, and the decision of a majority shall be final. And all the rolling stock of the Lessor shall at the like expense be marked with its name, so that the same can be identified, but this provision shall not prevent the Lessee from marking the same with its own name. On the termination of this lease, whether by lapse of time or otherwise, a like inventory and appraisal shall be made of all the property then surrendered by the Lessee to the Lessor, and if the property surrendered is thus found to be of greater value than the appraised value at the commencement of the lease, with the addition of a sum equal to all amounts of money received by the Lessee from the issue of shares of stock and bonds of the Lessor (excepting the principal of bonds issued to retire the said floating debt and of renewal and refunding bonds and excepting the principal of any bonds of the Lessor that shall be paid off by the Lessee), the difference shall be paid by the Lessor to the Lessee in money within one year from the termination of this lease with interest at the rate of 5 per cent. per annum from such termination until the time of payment. And, if the property surrendered is of less value than the appraised value at the commencement of this lease and the said sum received from stock and bonds as aforesaid, the difference shall be paid by the Lessee to the Lessor in money within the same time and with the like interest. And the Lessor and its agents shall be at liberty at reasonable times to enter upon the leased premises and inspect the same, and the Lessee shall afford all proper facilities therefor.

14. This lease is upon condition that if the Lessee, its successors or assigns shall fail to make any semi-annual payment of rent as hereinbefore stipulated or any part thereof or shall fail to pay the interest of the said bonds in accordance with its agreement, or to perform and observe any of its other covenants or agreements herein contained, and such default continues for one month after written notice thereof from the Lessor to the Lessee, or if the estate hereby granted or possession of the premises or any part thereof shall be taken from the Lessee by legal proceedings or the appointment of a receiver, or if the Lessee or its successors or assigns shall assign or underlet the said premises or any part thereof without the assent of the Lessor on each occasion in writing, and notwithstanding any assent or waiver on any prior occasion, then and in any of the said cases, and without any other notice or demand, the Lessor may thereupon re-enter upon the demised premises or any part thereof in the name of the whole, and the same have and possess as of its former estate without prejudice to its right of action for arrears of rent or breach of covenant, and upon such entry the said term shall end.

15. The notes printed in the margin of these presents are not a part thereof and shall not be regarded in determining any questions relating to the construction or interpretation of any of the provisions thereof.

IN WITNESS WHEREOF, the said parties have caused these presents to be executed in duplicate by their respective officers, thereunto duly authorized and their respective corporate seals to be hereto affixed the day and year first above written.

LAWRENCE & METHUEN STREET RAILWAY COMPANY, Lessor,
By *President.*
Treasurer.

HUDSON, PELHAM & SALEM ELECTRIC RAILWAY COMPANY, Lessee,
By *President.*
Treasurer.

[Terms of lease approved by the Board February 25, 1904.]

LEASE TO THE HUDSON, PELHAM & SALEM ELECTRIC RAILWAY COMPANY OF THE LOWELL & PELHAM STREET RAILWAY.

THIS INDENTURE, made this first day of January, in the year 1904, by and between the LOWELL & PELHAM STREET RAILWAY COMPANY, incorporated by and under the laws of the State of Massachusetts (hereinafter called the Lessor), of the one part, and the HUDSON, PELHAM & SALEM ELECTRIC RAILWAY COMPANY, incorporated by and under the laws of the State of New Hampshire (hereinafter called the Lessee), of the other part,

WITNESSETH, that the Lessor doth hereby lease unto the Lessee all and singular its railways, lands, franchises and other property of every description now owned, or hereafter to be acquired, together with all the rights, privileges, easements and appurtenances thereunto belonging, including the right to demand and receive to the Lessee's own use all tolls, rents, revenues, income and profits of the demised premises, excepting from the said premises all cash, cheques, bills, notes and moneys now due to the Lessor, and its common seal and books of record and account,

TO HAVE AND TO HOLD the same unto the Lessee, its successors and assigns, for the term of twenty-five years from the day of the date hereof. Subject however to the mortgage hereinafter described.

1. The Lessor covenants that during the continuance of this lease it will maintain its corporate organization in due form of law, and for that purpose will hold all necessary meetings, elect all necessary officers and make and keep all necessary records, reports and returns required by law at an expense not to exceed $100 per annum, which the Lessee covenants to pay to it on or before the date of the annual meeting of the stockholders of the Lessor in each year.

2. The Lessee may use the name of the Lessor in bringing or defending any suits or proceedings in law or equity which may be necessary for the due protection, preservation and full enjoyment by the Lessee of all the property, rights and privileges hereby leased, but the Lessee shall save and hold the Lessor harmless and indemnified from and against all loss, cost, damage and expense arising therefrom.

3. The Lessor covenants that in case the Lessee deems any part of the real estate or personal property hereby demised unnecessary for the purposes of the said railway and desires to sell the same, and the directors of the Lessor approve such sale, the Lessor will concur with the Lessee in such sale and in executing and delivering such instruments as may be necessary to transfer its titles therein to the vendee, and will cause such votes to be passed by its shareholders and directors as may be necessary; provided that the proceeds of any such sale, subject to the provisions of the mortgage hereinafter mentioned, shall be applied to the substitution of property of equal value to that sold, or shall be expended to increase the value of other property hereby demised, as the directors of the Lessor shall approve, and the Lessee agrees so to apply or expend the proceeds. And the Lessee may with the approval of the directors of the Lessor, subject to the said mortgage, pull down, alter and repair buildings and structures, and change the location or position of the lines of rails, but shall replace any buildings or structures pulled down in whole or in part with permanent improvements of as great value. And the Lessee shall be at liberty, without any such approval or concurrence as aforesaid, subject to the mortgage, to use and consume fuel and supplies, and to replace any of the rails, rolling stock, equipment, machinery and tools comprised in this lease with others, and to sell such of them as shall have been replaced or worn out as it may think fit, and without any obligation on the part of any purchaser to ascertain the occurrence of the event in which any such last-mentioned sale is authorized.

4. In consideration of the premises the Lessee covenants with the Lessor, for the benefit of the shareholders for the time being of the Lessor, to pay to the said shareholders respectively, as and for rent hereunder, a semi-annual dividend of two per cent. on the shares of the capital stock of the Lessor lawfully issued and from time to time outstanding to the aggregate principal amount of $40,000, and a like dividend upon

any shares of the capital stock of the Lessor lawfully issued in excess of the said principal amount of $40,000, for the purposes and in the manner hereinafter provided, the said dividends to be paid on the first days of January and July in each year during the term of this lease to the persons registered as holders of the said shares on the tenth day next preceding each day for the payment of such dividend, the first payment to be made on the first day of July, 1904; and in case this lease is terminated at any time prior to the first day of January in the year 1929 a proportionate part of such semi-annual dividend to be paid for the portion unelapsed of the half year to the then registered holders of the said shares. And such payments of dividends shall be free and clear of all other charges, expenses and payments to be made or incurred under the provisions hereof. And an agreement for the payment of the said dividends by the Lessee shall be indorsed upon the certificates of the capital stock of the Lessor under the common seal of the Lessee, signed by its duly authorized officer, and shall be substantially in the following form:

"The Hudson, Pelham & Salem Electric Railway Company having taken a lease of the railways, properties and franchises of the Lowell & Pelham Street Railway Company for twenty-five years from the first of January, 1904, upon the terms (among others) of paying a semi-annual dividend of two per cent. on the shares of the last-mentioned company on the first of Jannary and July in every year during the continuance of the said lease to the persons registered as holders of the said shares on the tenth day preceding each such dividend day, and of entering into this agreement in consideration thereof agrees with the said registered holder of the within-mentioned shares to pay the said dividends accordingly and to enter into a like agreement with every holder of the said shares to whom a new certificate shall be issued, and to indorse such agreement upon every such certificate. Witness the common seal of the Hudson, Pelham & Salem Electric Railway Company and the signature of its duly authorized officer the day of 19 ."

5. The Lessee covenants and agrees to pay as and for further rent hereunder all interest that may be due or that may become due during the term of this lease upon such of the floating debt of the Lessor existing at the date of the execution of this lease (the particulars of which are contained in a schedule of even date herewith and signed by the respective Presidents of the Lessor and Lessee), and upon such of the floating debt of the Lessor that may hereafter exist for or on account of any past acts or transactions of the Lessor, as shall not be capitalized by the issue of stock or funded by the issue of bonds of the Lessor during the term of this lease in the manner hereinafter provided.

6. The Lessee covenants to perform and observe all the covenants and agreements of the Lessor contained in its mortgage to the New York Security and Trust Company, dated the first day of January, 1903, for purpose of reference in the bonds thereby secured, and also as and for further rent hereunder the Lessee agrees to assume and pay the interest and to guarantee the payment of the principal of the bonds to the aggregate principal amount of $40,000 secured by the said mortgage, and also to assume and agree to pay the interest payable during the said term of all bonds issued or to be issued in pursuance hereof and to guarantee the payment of the principal of all such bonds payable during the said term. And an agreement by the Lessee for such payment shall be indorsed upon the said bonds under the common seal of the Lessee, signed by its duly authorized officer. And in case the said agreement relates to the payment of interest and the guaranty of the principal of the said bonds it shall be substantially in the following form:

"The Hudson, Pelham & Salem Electric Railway Company having taken a lease dated the first day of January, 1904, of the railways, properties and franchises of the maker of this bond upon the terms (among others) of paying the interest and of guaranteeing the payment of the principal thereof, and of entering into this agreement in consideration thereof, agrees with the bearer, or, if registered, with the registered owner for the time being of this bond (such holder waiving none of the obligations of the maker), to pay the interest and to guarantee the payment of the principal thereof as the same become payable respectively. Witness the common seal of the said Hudson,

Pelham & Salem Electric Railway Company and the signature of its duly authorized officer the of , 19 ."

But in case the said agreement relates merely to the payment of interest up to the end of the term of this lease it shall be in the following form:

"The Hudson, Pelham & Salem Electric Railway Company having taken a lease dated the first day of January, 1904, of the railways, properties and franchises of the maker of this bond upon the terms (among others) of paying the interest thereof payable during the term of the said lease and of entering into this agreement in consideration thereof, agrees with the bearer, or, if registered, with the registered owner for the time being of this bond (such holder waiving none of the obligations of the maker), to pay the interest thereof accruing during the term of the said lease as the same becomes payable respectively. Witness the common seal of the said Hudson, Pelham & Salem Electric Railway Company and the signature of its duly authorized officer the of , 19 ."

And the Lessee covenants to cancel and destroy all coupons for the said interest upon any of the said bonds as and when the said coupons are paid by the Lessee.

7. The Lessee covenants to pay all franchise and other taxes, charges and assessments whatsoever lawfully assessed upon or in respect of the leased premises or any part thereof during the term of this lease, including those assessed during the year 1904.

8. The Lessee covenants to insure and keep insured such parts of the premises as are of an insurable nature for such sums and in such manner as shall reasonably protect the same against loss or damage by fire and to exhibit to the Lessor or its agents the policies whenever reasonably requested, and all sums received by virtue of any such insurance shall be applied to making good the loss and damage, and so that all such insurance shall be in accordance with such or the like provisions as are contained in the said mortgage during the continuance of such mortgage or of any such future mortgage of the premises as is hereinafter mentioned.

9. The Lessee covenants to keep the said railway and other leased property in as good repair, order and condition as at the inception of this lease, and to replace all such rails, rolling stock, equipment, machinery and tools as may be worn out, and to mark with the name of the Lessor in the manner hereinafter provided all rolling stock used to replace any comprised in this lease. And at the termination of the lease to surrender the leased premises and all property added thereto or substituted therefor in like good repair, order and condition.

10. The Lessee covenants to save the Lessor harmless from all actions, suits, proceedings, claims, damages and expense on account of anything that has already happened, or by reason of any acts or omissions of the Lessee in the management or use of the leased premises during the continuance of this lease, and at its own expense to defend all actions, suits and proceedings already or to be hereafter brought against the Lessor or the leased property on account of any such matter, and to pay all sums recovered as damages or costs in any such action, suit or proceeding.

11. The Lessee covenants at its own cost and expense to maintain, work and use the leased railway and property in accordance with the laws of the Commonwealth of Massachusetts, and all lawful orders of State and local boards or other officials charged with the protection of public interest; to make all returns and perform all obligations lawfully required of any person or company operating a street railway in the Commonwealth of Massachusetts; to furnish all information necessary to enable the Lessor to make all returns and perform all obligations required of it under the laws of the said Commonwealth; and generally to perform the public service in as satisfactory a manner as could be required or secured were the railway maintained and operated by the Lessor. And the Lessee further covenants to furnish all cars, equipment and apparatus of every description required for the due use and working of said railway in addition to the property hereby demised.

12. The Lessor covenants that it will issue, subject to the approval of the Board of Railroad Commissioners as required by law or in accordance with existing laws and at the expense of the Lessee, additional shares or bonds, or both, for the purpose of raising money to pay the principal of the existing floating debt of the Lessor (the particu-

lars of which are contained in the said schedule of even date herewith), as well as the principal of such floating debt of the Lessor as may hereafter exist on account of its past transactions, and also to pay for permanent improvements and permanent additions to the leased premises, and to an amount or amounts sufficient for any and all of these purposes, whenever requested by vote of the board of directors of the Lessee, provided that such purposes shall be approved by the directors of the Lessor, and will deliver such shares and bonds to the Lessee to be used for the said purposes, and will also issue bonds whenever so requested for the purpose of renewing or refunding its existing bonds, or any bonds hereafter issued under these presents. And none of the said shares or bonds shall be sold for less than par. All such bonds shall be secured by mortgage of all the property of the railway company on terms similar to those contained in the mortgage hereinbefore mentioned, except so far as they may be varied with the approval of the directors of both of the said companies, and the Lessee shall concur in any such mortgage to the extent of its estate hereby acquired. And any benefits from reduced rates of interest during the continuance of this lease, consequent upon such renewal or refunding, shall enure to the benefit of the Lessee, and any premium obtained from the sale of bonds of the Lessor so issued to renew or refund its bonds shall be used to provide permanent improvements and permanent additions to the leased premises, except such as are herein required to be provided by the Lessee. And the Lessor agrees that its directors and stockholders shall pass all votes and make all applications to the Board of Railroad Commissioners or other authority, and take any other steps that may be necessary in order to issue stock or bonds as herein provided. And the Lessor covenants that it will not issue any stock or bonds without the express request of the board of directors of the Lessee.

13. The Lessor and Lessee mutually covenant that there shall forthwith be made a full and complete inventory and appraisal of the land, buildings, tracks, overhead construction, rolling stock, equipment and all other property of every nature and description demised by this lease, a copy of which inventory shall be furnished to the Lessor and also to the Lessee, and the same shall be conclusive evidence in any and all cases in which the question of the condition and value of the said property at the time of making this lease shall arise between them. The said inventory and appraisal shall be made at the expense of the Lessee by two disinterested persons, one selected by the Lessor and one by the Lessee, who in case of any disagreement may choose a third, and the decision of a majority shall be final. And all the rolling stock of the Lessor shall at the like expense be marked with its name, so that the same can be identified, but this provision shall not prevent the Lessee from marking the same with its own name. On the termination of this lease, whether by lapse of time or otherwise, a like inventory and appraisal shall be made of all the property then surrendered by the Lessee to the Lessor, and if the property surrendered is thus found to be of greater value than the appraised value at the commencement of the lease, with the addition of a sum equal to all amounts of money received by the Lessee from the issue of shares of stock and bonds of the Lessor (excepting the principal of bonds issued to retire the said floating debt and of renewal and refunding bonds and excepting the principal of any bonds of the Lessor that shall be paid off by the Lessee), the difference shall be paid by the Lessor to the Lessee in money within one year from the termination of this lease with interest at the rate of 5 per cent. per annum from such termination until the time of payment. And, if the property surrendered is of less value than the appraised value at the commencement of this lease and the said sum received from stock and bonds as aforesaid, the difference shall be paid by the Lessee to the Lessor in money within the same time and with the like interest. And the Lessor and its agents shall be at liberty at reasonable times to enter upon the leased premises and inspect the same, and the Lessee shall afford all proper facilities therefor.

14. This lease is upon condition that if the Lessee, its successors or assigns shall fail to make any semi-annual payment of rent as hereinbefore stipulated or any part thereof or shall fail to pay the interest of the said bonds in accordance with its agreement, or to perform and observe any of its other covenants or agreements herein contained, and such default continues for one month after written notice thereof from the Lessor

to the Lessee, or if the estate hereby granted or possession of the premises or any part hereof shall be taken from the Lessee by legal proceedings or the appointment of a treceiver, or if the Lessee or its successors or assigns shall assign or underlet the said premises or any part thereof without the assent of the Lessor on each occasion in writing, and notwithstanding any assent or waiver on any prior occasion, then and in any of the said cases, and without any other notice or demand, the Lessor may thereupon re-enter upon the demised premises or any part thereof in the name of the whole, and the same have and possess as of its former estate without prejudice to its right of action for arrears of rent or breach of covenant, and upon such entry the said term shall end.

15. The notes printed in the margin of these presents are not a part thereof and shall not be regarded in determining any questions relating to the construction or interpretation of any of the provisions thereof.

In witness whereof, the said parties have caused these presents to be executed in duplicate by their respective officers, thereunto duly authorized and their respective corporate seals to be hereto affixed the day and year first above written.

LOWELL & PELHAM STREET RAILWAY COMPANY, Lessor,
By *President.*
Treasurer.

HUDSON, PELHAM & SALEM ELECTRIC RAILWAY COMPANY, Lessee,
By *President.*
Treasurer.

[Terms of lease approved by the Board February 25, 1904.]

INDEX.

INDEX.

RAILROAD RETURNS.

STREET RAILWAY REPORTS.

LEASES.

Lightning Source UK Ltd.
Milton Keynes UK
UKHW022225081218
333475UK00009B/1190/P